GNU Compiler Collection Internals

For GCC version 8.0.1 (pre-release)

(GCC)

Richard M. Stallman and the GCC Developer Community

Copyright © 1988-2018 Free Software Foundation, Inc.

Permission is granted to copy, distribute and/or modify this document under the terms of the GNU Free Documentation License, Version 1.3 or any later version published by the Free Software Foundation; with the Invariant Sections being "Funding Free Software", the Front-Cover Texts being (a) (see below), and with the Back-Cover Texts being (b) (see below). A copy of the license is included in the section entitled "GNU Free Documentation License".

(a) The FSF's Front-Cover Text is:

A GNU Manual

(b) The FSF's Back-Cover Text is:

You have freedom to copy and modify this GNU Manual, like GNU software. Copies published by the Free Software Foundation raise funds for GNU development.

Short Contents

Introduction		1
1	Contributing to GCC Development	3
2	GCC and Portability	5
3	Interfacing to GCC Output	7
4	The GCC low-level runtime library	9
5	Language Front Ends in GCC	59
6	Source Tree Structure and Build System	61
7	Testsuites	79
8	Option specification files	115
9	Passes and Files of the Compiler	123
10	Sizes and offsets as runtime invariants	139
11	GENERIC	153
12	GIMPLE	199
13	Analysis and Optimization of GIMPLE tuples	237
14	RTL Representation	249
15	Control Flow Graph	307
16	Analysis and Representation of Loops	317
17	Machine Descriptions	327
18	Target Description Macros and Functions	461
19	Host Configuration	643
20	Makefile Fragments	647
21	collect2	651
22	Standard Header File Directories	653
23	Memory Management and Type Information	655
24	Plugins	665
25	Link Time Optimization	673
26	Match and Simplify	681
Funding Free Software		687
The GNU Project and GNU/Linux		689
GNU General Public License		691
GNU Free Documentation License		703
Contributors to GCC		711
Option Index		729
Concept Index		731

Table of Contents

Introduction 1

1 Contributing to GCC Development 3

2 GCC and Portability 5

3 Interfacing to GCC Output 7

4 The GCC low-level runtime library 9
    4.1 Routines for integer arithmetic 9
        4.1.1 Arithmetic functions 9
        4.1.2 Comparison functions 10
        4.1.3 Trapping arithmetic functions 11
        4.1.4 Bit operations 11
    4.2 Routines for floating point emulation 12
        4.2.1 Arithmetic functions 12
        4.2.2 Conversion functions 13
        4.2.3 Comparison functions 15
        4.2.4 Other floating-point functions 16
    4.3 Routines for decimal floating point emulation 16
        4.3.1 Arithmetic functions 17
        4.3.2 Conversion functions 17
        4.3.3 Comparison functions 20
    4.4 Routines for fixed-point fractional emulation 22
        4.4.1 Arithmetic functions 22
        4.4.2 Comparison functions 30
        4.4.3 Conversion functions 30
    4.5 Language-independent routines for exception handling 56
    4.6 Miscellaneous runtime library routines 57
        4.6.1 Cache control functions 57
        4.6.2 Split stack functions and variables 57

5 Language Front Ends in GCC 59

6 Source Tree Structure and Build System 61
    6.1 Configure Terms and History 61
    6.2 Top Level Source Directory 61
    6.3 The 'gcc' Subdirectory 63
        6.3.1 Subdirectories of 'gcc' 63
        6.3.2 Configuration in the 'gcc' Directory 64
            6.3.2.1 Scripts Used by `configure` 64

6.3.2.2 The 'config.build'; 'config.host'; and 'config.gcc' Files 64
6.3.2.3 Files Created by configure 65
6.3.3 Build System in the 'gcc' Directory 66
6.3.4 Makefile Targets 66
6.3.5 Library Source Files and Headers under the 'gcc' Directory 68
6.3.6 Headers Installed by GCC 68
6.3.7 Building Documentation 69
    6.3.7.1 Texinfo Manuals 69
    6.3.7.2 Man Page Generation 70
    6.3.7.3 Miscellaneous Documentation 71
6.3.8 Anatomy of a Language Front End 71
    6.3.8.1 The Front End 'language' Directory 72
    6.3.8.2 The Front End 'config-lang.in' File 73
    6.3.8.3 The Front End 'Make-lang.in' File 74
6.3.9 Anatomy of a Target Back End 75

7 Testsuites 79

7.1 Idioms Used in Testsuite Code 79
7.2 Directives used within DejaGnu tests 80
  7.2.1 Syntax and Descriptions of test directives 80
    7.2.1.1 Specify how to build the test 80
    7.2.1.2 Specify additional compiler options 81
    7.2.1.3 Modify the test timeout value 81
    7.2.1.4 Skip a test for some targets 81
    7.2.1.5 Expect a test to fail for some targets 82
    7.2.1.6 Expect the test executable to fail 82
    7.2.1.7 Verify compiler messages 82
    7.2.1.8 Verify output of the test executable 83
    7.2.1.9 Specify additional files for a test 83
    7.2.1.10 Add checks at the end of a test 84
  7.2.2 Selecting targets to which a test applies 84
  7.2.3 Keywords describing target attributes 84
    7.2.3.1 Data type sizes 84
    7.2.3.2 Fortran-specific attributes 85
    7.2.3.3 Vector-specific attributes 86
    7.2.3.4 Thread Local Storage attributes 89
    7.2.3.5 Decimal floating point attributes 90
    7.2.3.6 ARM-specific attributes 90
    7.2.3.7 AArch64-specific attributes 93
    7.2.3.8 MIPS-specific attributes 94
    7.2.3.9 PowerPC-specific attributes 94
    7.2.3.10 Other hardware attributes 95
    7.2.3.11 Environment attributes 96
    7.2.3.12 Other attributes 98
    7.2.3.13 Local to tests in gcc.target/i386 100
    7.2.3.14 Local to tests in gcc.target/spu/ea 100

		7.2.3.15 Local to tests in gcc.test-framework............. 100
	7.2.4	Features for dg-add-options........................... 100
	7.2.5	Variants of dg-require-*support*....................... 102
	7.2.6	Commands for use in dg-final 103
		7.2.6.1 Scan a particular file 103
		7.2.6.2 Scan the assembly output 103
		7.2.6.3 Scan optimization dump files 104
		7.2.6.4 Verify that an output files exists or not 104
		7.2.6.5 Check for LTO tests.............................. 104
		7.2.6.6 Checks for gcov tests............................. 104
		7.2.6.7 Clean up generated test files..................... 105
7.3	Ada Language Testsuites................................... 106	
7.4	C Language Testsuites 106	
7.5	Support for testing link-time optimizations 108	
7.6	Support for testing gcov 108	
7.7	Support for testing profile-directed optimizations 109	
7.8	Support for testing binary compatibility...................... 110	
7.9	Support for torture testing using multiple options 111	
7.10	Support for testing GIMPLE passes......................... 112	
7.11	Support for testing RTL passes 113	

8 Option specification files...................... 115

8.1	Option file format.. 115
8.2	Option properties 117

9 Passes and Files of the Compiler 123

9.1	Parsing pass 123	
9.2	Gimplification pass... 124	
9.3	Pass manager 124	
9.4	Tree SSA passes 125	
9.5	RTL passes 131	
9.6	Optimization info 135	
	9.6.1	Dump setup 135
	9.6.2	Optimization groups 135
	9.6.3	Dump files and streams 136
	9.6.4	Dump output verbosity 136
	9.6.5	Dump types.. 137
	9.6.6	Dump examples...................................... 137

10 Sizes and offsets as runtime invariants 139

- 10.1 Overview of `poly_int` 139
- 10.2 Consequences of using `poly_int` 140
- 10.3 Comparisons involving `poly_int` 141
  - 10.3.1 Comparison functions for `poly_int` 141
  - 10.3.2 Properties of the `poly_int` comparisons 142
  - 10.3.3 Comparing potentially-unordered `poly_ints` 142
  - 10.3.4 Comparing ordered `poly_ints` 143
  - 10.3.5 Checking for a `poly_int` marker value 143
  - 10.3.6 Range checks on `poly_ints` 144
  - 10.3.7 Sorting `poly_ints` 145
- 10.4 Arithmetic on `poly_ints` 145
  - 10.4.1 Using `poly_int` with C++ arithmetic operators 145
  - 10.4.2 `wi` arithmetic on `poly_ints` 146
  - 10.4.3 Division of `poly_ints` 146
  - 10.4.4 Other `poly_int` arithmetic 147
- 10.5 Alignment of `poly_ints` 147
- 10.6 Computing bounds on `poly_ints` 149
- 10.7 Converting `poly_ints` 149
- 10.8 Miscellaneous `poly_int` routines 150
- 10.9 Guidelines for using `poly_int` 151

11 GENERIC 153

- 11.1 Deficiencies 153
- 11.2 Overview 153
  - 11.2.1 Trees 154
  - 11.2.2 Identifiers 155
  - 11.2.3 Containers 155
- 11.3 Types 155
- 11.4 Declarations 160
  - 11.4.1 Working with declarations 160
  - 11.4.2 Internal structure 162
    - 11.4.2.1 Current structure hierarchy 162
    - 11.4.2.2 Adding new DECL node types 163
- 11.5 Attributes in trees 164
- 11.6 Expressions 165
  - 11.6.1 Constant expressions 165
  - 11.6.2 References to storage 167
  - 11.6.3 Unary and Binary Expressions 169
  - 11.6.4 Vectors 176
- 11.7 Statements 178
  - 11.7.1 Basic Statements 178
  - 11.7.2 Blocks 180
  - 11.7.3 Statement Sequences 180
  - 11.7.4 Empty Statements 180
  - 11.7.5 Jumps 180
  - 11.7.6 Cleanups 181
  - 11.7.7 OpenMP 181

		11.7.8	OpenACC	183

- 11.8 Functions... 184
    - 11.8.1 Function Basics... 184
    - 11.8.2 Function Properties...................................... 186
- 11.9 Language-dependent trees................................... 187
- 11.10 C and C++ Trees.. 187
    - 11.10.1 Types for C++ 187
    - 11.10.2 Namespaces 189
    - 11.10.3 Classes 191
    - 11.10.4 Functions for C++ 192
    - 11.10.5 Statements for C++ 195
        - 11.10.5.1 Statements................................... 195
    - 11.10.6 C++ Expressions 198
- 11.11 Java Trees... 198

12 GIMPLE 199

- 12.1 Tuple representation 200
    - 12.1.1 `gimple (gsbase)`.. 200
    - 12.1.2 `gimple_statement_with_ops`.................... 201
    - 12.1.3 `gimple_statement_with_memory_ops`..... 201
- 12.2 Class hierarchy of GIMPLE statements.................. 202
- 12.3 GIMPLE instruction set 205
- 12.4 Exception Handling... 205
- 12.5 Temporaries 206
- 12.6 Operands... 206
    - 12.6.1 Compound Expressions 207
    - 12.6.2 Compound Lvalues..................................... 207
    - 12.6.3 Conditional Expressions............................. 207
    - 12.6.4 Logical Operators....................................... 207
    - 12.6.5 Manipulating operands 207
    - 12.6.6 Operand vector allocation......................... 208
    - 12.6.7 Operand validation 209
    - 12.6.8 Statement validation.................................. 209
- 12.7 Manipulating GIMPLE statements......................... 210
    - 12.7.1 Common accessors 210
- 12.8 Tuple specific accessors 213
    - 12.8.1 `GIMPLE_ASM`.. 213
    - 12.8.2 `GIMPLE_ASSIGN` 214
    - 12.8.3 `GIMPLE_BIND` 215
    - 12.8.4 `GIMPLE_CALL` 216
    - 12.8.5 `GIMPLE_CATCH` 217
    - 12.8.6 `GIMPLE_COND` 218
    - 12.8.7 `GIMPLE_DEBUG` 219
    - 12.8.8 `GIMPLE_EH_FILTER`.................................... 220
    - 12.8.9 `GIMPLE_LABEL` 221
    - 12.8.10 `GIMPLE_GOTO` 221
    - 12.8.11 `GIMPLE_NOP`.. 221
    - 12.8.12 `GIMPLE_OMP_ATOMIC_LOAD` 221

- 12.8.13 GIMPLE_OMP_ATOMIC_STORE 222
- 12.8.14 GIMPLE_OMP_CONTINUE 222
- 12.8.15 GIMPLE_OMP_CRITICAL 223
- 12.8.16 GIMPLE_OMP_FOR 223
- 12.8.17 GIMPLE_OMP_MASTER 224
- 12.8.18 GIMPLE_OMP_ORDERED 225
- 12.8.19 GIMPLE_OMP_PARALLEL 225
- 12.8.20 GIMPLE_OMP_RETURN 226
- 12.8.21 GIMPLE_OMP_SECTION 226
- 12.8.22 GIMPLE_OMP_SECTIONS 226
- 12.8.23 GIMPLE_OMP_SINGLE 227
- 12.8.24 GIMPLE_PHI 227
- 12.8.25 GIMPLE_RESX 228
- 12.8.26 GIMPLE_RETURN 228
- 12.8.27 GIMPLE_SWITCH 228
- 12.8.28 GIMPLE_TRY 229
- 12.8.29 GIMPLE_WITH_CLEANUP_EXPR 230
- 12.9 GIMPLE sequences 230
- 12.10 Sequence iterators 231
- 12.11 Adding a new GIMPLE statement code 234
- 12.12 Statement and operand traversals 235

13 Analysis and Optimization of GIMPLE tuples 237

- 13.1 Annotations 237
- 13.2 SSA Operands 237
  - 13.2.1 Operand Iterators And Access Routines 239
  - 13.2.2 Immediate Uses 241
- 13.3 Static Single Assignment 242
  - 13.3.1 Preserving the SSA form 243
  - 13.3.2 Examining SSA_NAME nodes 245
  - 13.3.3 Walking the dominator tree 245
- 13.4 Alias analysis 246
- 13.5 Memory model 247

14 RTL Representation 249

- 14.1 RTL Object Types 249
- 14.2 RTL Classes and Formats 250
- 14.3 Access to Operands 252
- 14.4 Access to Special Operands 253
- 14.5 Flags in an RTL Expression 256
- 14.6 Machine Modes 261
- 14.7 Constant Expression Types 268
- 14.8 Registers and Memory 272
- 14.9 RTL Expressions for Arithmetic 278
- 14.10 Comparison Operations 282
- 14.11 Bit-Fields 284

14.12	Vector Operations	284
14.13	Conversions	285
14.14	Declarations	287
14.15	Side Effect Expressions	287
14.16	Embedded Side-Effects on Addresses	292
14.17	Assembler Instructions as Expressions	293
14.18	Variable Location Debug Information in RTL	294
14.19	Insns	294
14.20	RTL Representation of Function-Call Insns	303
14.21	Structure Sharing Assumptions	304
14.22	Reading RTL	305

15 Control Flow Graph 307

15.1	Basic Blocks	307
15.2	Edges	309
15.3	Profile information	312
15.4	Maintaining the CFG	313
15.5	Liveness information	315

16 Analysis and Representation of Loops 317

16.1	Loop representation	317
16.2	Loop querying	319
16.3	Loop manipulation	320
16.4	Loop-closed SSA form	320
16.5	Scalar evolutions	321
16.6	IV analysis on RTL	322
16.7	Number of iterations analysis	322
16.8	Data Dependency Analysis	324

17 Machine Descriptions 327

17.1	Overview of How the Machine Description is Used	327
17.2	Everything about Instruction Patterns	327
17.3	Example of `define_insn`	329
17.4	RTL Template	329
17.5	Output Templates and Operand Substitution	333
17.6	C Statements for Assembler Output	334
17.7	Predicates	336
	17.7.1 Machine-Independent Predicates	336
	17.7.2 Defining Machine-Specific Predicates	338
17.8	Operand Constraints	340
	17.8.1 Simple Constraints	340
	17.8.2 Multiple Alternative Constraints	345
	17.8.3 Register Class Preferences	346
	17.8.4 Constraint Modifier Characters	346
	17.8.5 Constraints for Particular Machines	347
	17.8.6 Disable insn alternatives using the `enabled` attribute	377
	17.8.7 Defining Machine-Specific Constraints	378

- 17.8.8 Testing constraints from C 381
- 17.9 Standard Pattern Names For Generation 382
- 17.10 When the Order of Patterns Matters 419
- 17.11 Interdependence of Patterns 419
- 17.12 Defining Jump Instruction Patterns 419
- 17.13 Defining Looping Instruction Patterns 420
- 17.14 Canonicalization of Instructions 422
- 17.15 Defining RTL Sequences for Code Generation 423
- 17.16 Defining How to Split Instructions 426
- 17.17 Including Patterns in Machine Descriptions 429
  - 17.17.1 RTL Generation Tool Options for Directory Search 430
- 17.18 Machine-Specific Peephole Optimizers 430
  - 17.18.1 RTL to Text Peephole Optimizers 431
  - 17.18.2 RTL to RTL Peephole Optimizers 433
- 17.19 Instruction Attributes 434
  - 17.19.1 Defining Attributes and their Values 434
  - 17.19.2 Attribute Expressions 436
  - 17.19.3 Assigning Attribute Values to Insns 438
  - 17.19.4 Example of Attribute Specifications 440
  - 17.19.5 Computing the Length of an Insn 441
  - 17.19.6 Constant Attributes 442
  - 17.19.7 Mnemonic Attribute 442
  - 17.19.8 Delay Slot Scheduling 443
  - 17.19.9 Specifying processor pipeline description 444
- 17.20 Conditional Execution 450
- 17.21 RTL Templates Transformations 451
  - 17.21.1 `define_subst` Example 451
  - 17.21.2 Pattern Matching in `define_subst` 453
  - 17.21.3 Generation of output template in `define_subst` 453
- 17.22 Constant Definitions 453
- 17.23 Iterators 455
  - 17.23.1 Mode Iterators 456
    - 17.23.1.1 Defining Mode Iterators 456
    - 17.23.1.2 Substitution in Mode Iterators 456
    - 17.23.1.3 Mode Iterator Examples 457
  - 17.23.2 Code Iterators 458
  - 17.23.3 Int Iterators 459
  - 17.23.4 Subst Iterators 460

18 Target Description Macros and Functions
  461

- 18.1 The Global `targetm` Variable 461
- 18.2 Controlling the Compilation Driver, 'gcc' 462
- 18.3 Run-time Target Specification 468
- 18.4 Defining data structures for per-function information. 471
- 18.5 Storage Layout 472
- 18.6 Layout of Source Language Data Types 482
- 18.7 Register Usage 487

18.7.1	Basic Characteristics of Registers	487
18.7.2	Order of Allocation of Registers	489
18.7.3	How Values Fit in Registers	490
18.7.4	Handling Leaf Functions	492
18.7.5	Registers That Form a Stack	493
18.8	Register Classes	493
18.9	Stack Layout and Calling Conventions	504
18.9.1	Basic Stack Layout	504
18.9.2	Exception Handling Support	508
18.9.3	Specifying How Stack Checking is Done	510
18.9.4	Registers That Address the Stack Frame	512
18.9.5	Eliminating Frame Pointer and Arg Pointer	514
18.9.6	Passing Function Arguments on the Stack	516
18.9.7	Passing Arguments in Registers	518
18.9.8	How Scalar Function Values Are Returned	525
18.9.9	How Large Values Are Returned	527
18.9.10	Caller-Saves Register Allocation	529
18.9.11	Function Entry and Exit	529
18.9.12	Generating Code for Profiling	532
18.9.13	Permitting tail calls	533
18.9.14	Shrink-wrapping separate components	534
18.9.15	Stack smashing protection	535
18.9.16	Miscellaneous register hooks	535
18.10	Implementing the Varargs Macros	535
18.11	Trampolines for Nested Functions	539
18.12	Implicit Calls to Library Routines	541
18.13	Addressing Modes	542
18.14	Anchored Addresses	551
18.15	Condition Code Status	552
18.15.1	Representation of condition codes using (cc0)	552
18.15.2	Representation of condition codes using registers	553
18.16	Describing Relative Costs of Operations	556
18.17	Adjusting the Instruction Scheduler	562
18.18	Dividing the Output into Sections (Texts, Data, ...)	570
18.19	Position Independent Code	575
18.20	Defining the Output Assembler Language	576
18.20.1	The Overall Framework of an Assembler File	576
18.20.2	Output of Data	579
18.20.3	Output of Uninitialized Variables	582
18.20.4	Output and Generation of Labels	583
18.20.5	How Initialization Functions Are Handled	591
18.20.6	Macros Controlling Initialization Routines	593
18.20.7	Output of Assembler Instructions	595
18.20.8	Output of Dispatch Tables	599
18.20.9	Assembler Commands for Exception Regions	600
18.20.10	Assembler Commands for Alignment	602
18.21	Controlling Debugging Information Format	604
18.21.1	Macros Affecting All Debugging Formats	604

- 18.21.2 Specific Options for DBX Output 605
- 18.21.3 Open-Ended Hooks for DBX Format 607
- 18.21.4 File Names in DBX Format 607
- 18.21.5 Macros for DWARF Output 608
- 18.21.6 Macros for VMS Debug Format 610
- 18.22 Cross Compilation and Floating Point..................... 611
- 18.23 Mode Switching Instructions.............................. 612
- 18.24 Defining target-specific uses of __attribute__ 613
- 18.25 Emulating TLS... 616
- 18.26 Defining coprocessor specifics for MIPS targets............ 617
- 18.27 Parameters for Precompiled Header Validity Checking...... 617
- 18.28 C++ ABI parameters..................................... 618
- 18.29 Adding support for named address spaces 619
- 18.30 Miscellaneous Parameters................................. 621

19 Host Configuration 643
- 19.1 Host Common 643
- 19.2 Host Filesystem.. 644
- 19.3 Host Misc 645

20 Makefile Fragments 647
- 20.1 Target Makefile Fragments................................ 647
- 20.2 Host Makefile Fragments.................................. 650

21 collect2 651

22 Standard Header File Directories........... 653

23 Memory Management and Type Information 655
- 23.1 The Inside of a GTY(()) 656
- 23.2 Support for inheritance 660
- 23.3 Support for user-provided GC marking routines 660
  - 23.3.1 User-provided marking routines for template types....... 661
- 23.4 Marking Roots for the Garbage Collector................... 662
- 23.5 Source Files Containing Type Information.................. 662
- 23.6 How to invoke the garbage collector 663
- 23.7 Troubleshooting the garbage collector 664

24 Plugins... 665
- 24.1 Loading Plugins 665
- 24.2 Plugin API 665
  - 24.2.1 Plugin license check................................... 665
  - 24.2.2 Plugin initialization 666
  - 24.2.3 Plugin callbacks....................................... 667
- 24.3 Interacting with the pass manager........................... 668
- 24.4 Interacting with the GCC Garbage Collector 669
- 24.5 Giving information about a plugin 669
- 24.6 Registering custom attributes or pragmas 669
- 24.7 Recording information about pass execution................. 670
- 24.8 Controlling which passes are being run 671
- 24.9 Keeping track of available passes........................... 671
- 24.10 Building GCC plugins 671

25 Link Time Optimization..................... 673
- 25.1 Design Overview... 673
  - 25.1.1 LTO modes of operation 674
- 25.2 LTO file sections.. 674
- 25.3 Using summary information in IPA passes................... 676
  - 25.3.1 Virtual clones... 677
  - 25.3.2 IPA references 678
  - 25.3.3 Jump functions 678
- 25.4 Whole program assumptions, linker plugin and symbol visibilities 678
- 25.5 Internal flags controlling `lto1`............................. 680

26 Match and Simplify......................... 681
- 26.1 GIMPLE API 681
- 26.2 The Language 682

Funding Free Software........................... 687

The GNU Project and GNU/Linux 689

GNU General Public License 691

GNU Free Documentation License 703
- ADDENDUM: How to use this License for your documents 710

Contributors to GCC............................. 711

Option Index..................................... 729

Concept Index.................................... 731

Introduction

This manual documents the internals of the GNU compilers, including how to port them to new targets and some information about how to write front ends for new languages. It corresponds to the compilers (GCC) version 8.0.1. The use of the GNU compilers is documented in a separate manual. See Section "Introduction" in *Using the GNU Compiler Collection (GCC)*.

This manual is mainly a reference manual rather than a tutorial. It discusses how to contribute to GCC (see Chapter 1 [Contributing], page 3), the characteristics of the machines supported by GCC as hosts and targets (see Chapter 2 [Portability], page 5), how GCC relates to the ABIs on such systems (see Chapter 3 [Interface], page 7), and the characteristics of the languages for which GCC front ends are written (see Chapter 5 [Languages], page 59). It then describes the GCC source tree structure and build system, some of the interfaces to GCC front ends, and how support for a target system is implemented in GCC.

Additional tutorial information is linked to from http://gcc.gnu.org/readings.html.

1 Contributing to GCC Development

If you would like to help pretest GCC releases to assure they work well, current development sources are available by SVN (see `http://gcc.gnu.org/svn.html`). Source and binary snapshots are also available for FTP; see `http://gcc.gnu.org/snapshots.html`.

If you would like to work on improvements to GCC, please read the advice at these URLs:

> `http://gcc.gnu.org/contribute.html`
> `http://gcc.gnu.org/contributewhy.html`

for information on how to make useful contributions and avoid duplication of effort. Suggested projects are listed at `http://gcc.gnu.org/projects/`.

2 GCC and Portability

GCC itself aims to be portable to any machine where `int` is at least a 32-bit type. It aims to target machines with a flat (non-segmented) byte addressed data address space (the code address space can be separate). Target ABIs may have 8, 16, 32 or 64-bit `int` type. `char` can be wider than 8 bits.

GCC gets most of the information about the target machine from a machine description which gives an algebraic formula for each of the machine's instructions. This is a very clean way to describe the target. But when the compiler needs information that is difficult to express in this fashion, ad-hoc parameters have been defined for machine descriptions. The purpose of portability is to reduce the total work needed on the compiler; it was not of interest for its own sake.

GCC does not contain machine dependent code, but it does contain code that depends on machine parameters such as endianness (whether the most significant byte has the highest or lowest address of the bytes in a word) and the availability of autoincrement addressing. In the RTL-generation pass, it is often necessary to have multiple strategies for generating code for a particular kind of syntax tree, strategies that are usable for different combinations of parameters. Often, not all possible cases have been addressed, but only the common ones or only the ones that have been encountered. As a result, a new target may require additional strategies. You will know if this happens because the compiler will call `abort`. Fortunately, the new strategies can be added in a machine-independent fashion, and will affect only the target machines that need them.

3 Interfacing to GCC Output

GCC is normally configured to use the same function calling convention normally in use on the target system. This is done with the machine-description macros described (see Chapter 18 [Target Macros], page 461).

However, returning of structure and union values is done differently on some target machines. As a result, functions compiled with PCC returning such types cannot be called from code compiled with GCC, and vice versa. This does not cause trouble often because few Unix library routines return structures or unions.

GCC code returns structures and unions that are 1, 2, 4 or 8 bytes long in the same registers used for `int` or `double` return values. (GCC typically allocates variables of such types in registers also.) Structures and unions of other sizes are returned by storing them into an address passed by the caller (usually in a register). The target hook `TARGET_STRUCT_VALUE_RTX` tells GCC where to pass this address.

By contrast, PCC on most target machines returns structures and unions of any size by copying the data into an area of static storage, and then returning the address of that storage as if it were a pointer value. The caller must copy the data from that memory area to the place where the value is wanted. This is slower than the method used by GCC, and fails to be reentrant.

On some target machines, such as RISC machines and the 80386, the standard system convention is to pass to the subroutine the address of where to return the value. On these machines, GCC has been configured to be compatible with the standard compiler, when this method is used. It may not be compatible for structures of 1, 2, 4 or 8 bytes.

GCC uses the system's standard convention for passing arguments. On some machines, the first few arguments are passed in registers; in others, all are passed on the stack. It would be possible to use registers for argument passing on any machine, and this would probably result in a significant speedup. But the result would be complete incompatibility with code that follows the standard convention. So this change is practical only if you are switching to GCC as the sole C compiler for the system. We may implement register argument passing on certain machines once we have a complete GNU system so that we can compile the libraries with GCC.

On some machines (particularly the SPARC), certain types of arguments are passed "by invisible reference". This means that the value is stored in memory, and the address of the memory location is passed to the subroutine.

If you use `longjmp`, beware of automatic variables. ISO C says that automatic variables that are not declared `volatile` have undefined values after a `longjmp`. And this is all GCC promises to do, because it is very difficult to restore register variables correctly, and one of GCC's features is that it can put variables in registers without your asking it to.

4 The GCC low-level runtime library

GCC provides a low-level runtime library, 'libgcc.a' or 'libgcc_s.so.1' on some platforms. GCC generates calls to routines in this library automatically, whenever it needs to perform some operation that is too complicated to emit inline code for.

Most of the routines in libgcc handle arithmetic operations that the target processor cannot perform directly. This includes integer multiply and divide on some machines, and all floating-point and fixed-point operations on other machines. libgcc also includes routines for exception handling, and a handful of miscellaneous operations.

Some of these routines can be defined in mostly machine-independent C. Others must be hand-written in assembly language for each processor that needs them.

GCC will also generate calls to C library routines, such as memcpy and memset, in some cases. The set of routines that GCC may possibly use is documented in Section "Other Builtins" in *Using the GNU Compiler Collection (GCC)*.

These routines take arguments and return values of a specific machine mode, not a specific C type. See Section 14.6 [Machine Modes], page 261, for an explanation of this concept. For illustrative purposes, in this chapter the floating point type float is assumed to correspond to SFmode; double to DFmode; and long double to both TFmode and XFmode. Similarly, the integer types int and unsigned int correspond to SImode; long and unsigned long to DImode; and long long and unsigned long long to TImode.

4.1 Routines for integer arithmetic

The integer arithmetic routines are used on platforms that don't provide hardware support for arithmetic operations on some modes.

4.1.1 Arithmetic functions

int __ashlsi3 (*int* a, *int* b) [Runtime Function]
long __ashldi3 (*long* a, *int* b) [Runtime Function]
long long __ashlti3 (*long long* a, *int* b) [Runtime Function]
    These functions return the result of shifting *a* left by *b* bits.

int __ashrsi3 (*int* a, *int* b) [Runtime Function]
long __ashrdi3 (*long* a, *int* b) [Runtime Function]
long long __ashrti3 (*long long* a, *int* b) [Runtime Function]
    These functions return the result of arithmetically shifting *a* right by *b* bits.

int __divsi3 (*int* a, *int* b) [Runtime Function]
long __divdi3 (*long* a, *long* b) [Runtime Function]
long long __divti3 (*long long* a, *long long* b) [Runtime Function]
    These functions return the quotient of the signed division of *a* and *b*.

int __lshrsi3 (*int* a, *int* b) [Runtime Function]
long __lshrdi3 (*long* a, *int* b) [Runtime Function]
long long __lshrti3 (*long long* a, *int* b) [Runtime Function]
    These functions return the result of logically shifting *a* right by *b* bits.

`int __modsi3 (int a, int b)` [Runtime Function]
`long __moddi3 (long a, long b)` [Runtime Function]
`long long __modti3 (long long a, long long b)` [Runtime Function]
   These functions return the remainder of the signed division of a and b.

`int __mulsi3 (int a, int b)` [Runtime Function]
`long __muldi3 (long a, long b)` [Runtime Function]
`long long __multi3 (long long a, long long b)` [Runtime Function]
   These functions return the product of a and b.

`long __negdi2 (long a)` [Runtime Function]
`long long __negti2 (long long a)` [Runtime Function]
   These functions return the negation of a.

`unsigned int __udivsi3 (unsigned int a, unsigned int b)` [Runtime Function]
`unsigned long __udivdi3 (unsigned long a, unsigned long b)` [Runtime Function]
`unsigned long long __udivti3 (unsigned long long a,` [Runtime Function]
      `unsigned long long b)`
   These functions return the quotient of the unsigned division of a and b.

`unsigned long __udivmoddi4 (unsigned long a, unsigned long` [Runtime Function]
      `b, unsigned long *c)`
`unsigned long long __udivmodti4 (unsigned long long a,` [Runtime Function]
      `unsigned long long b, unsigned long long *c)`
   These functions calculate both the quotient and remainder of the unsigned division of a and b. The return value is the quotient, and the remainder is placed in variable pointed to by c.

`unsigned int __umodsi3 (unsigned int a, unsigned int b)` [Runtime Function]
`unsigned long __umoddi3 (unsigned long a, unsigned long b)` [Runtime Function]
`unsigned long long __umodti3 (unsigned long long a,` [Runtime Function]
      `unsigned long long b)`
   These functions return the remainder of the unsigned division of a and b.

4.1.2 Comparison functions

The following functions implement integral comparisons. These functions implement a low-level compare, upon which the higher level comparison operators (such as less than and greater than or equal to) can be constructed. The returned values lie in the range zero to two, to allow the high-level operators to be implemented by testing the returned result using either signed or unsigned comparison.

`int __cmpdi2 (long a, long b)` [Runtime Function]
`int __cmpti2 (long long a, long long b)` [Runtime Function]
   These functions perform a signed comparison of a and b. If a is less than b, they return 0; if a is greater than b, they return 2; and if a and b are equal they return 1.

`int __ucmpdi2 (unsigned long a, unsigned long b)` [Runtime Function]
`int __ucmpti2 (unsigned long long a, unsigned long long b)` [Runtime Function]
   These functions perform an unsigned comparison of a and b. If a is less than b, they return 0; if a is greater than b, they return 2; and if a and b are equal they return 1.

Chapter 4: The GCC low-level runtime library

4.1.3 Trapping arithmetic functions

The following functions implement trapping arithmetic. These functions call the libc function `abort` upon signed arithmetic overflow.

`int __absvsi2` (*int a*) [Runtime Function]
`long __absvdi2` (*long a*) [Runtime Function]
    These functions return the absolute value of *a*.

`int __addvsi3` (*int a, int b*) [Runtime Function]
`long __addvdi3` (*long a, long b*) [Runtime Function]
    These functions return the sum of *a* and *b*; that is `a + b`.

`int __mulvsi3` (*int a, int b*) [Runtime Function]
`long __mulvdi3` (*long a, long b*) [Runtime Function]
    The functions return the product of *a* and *b*; that is `a * b`.

`int __negvsi2` (*int a*) [Runtime Function]
`long __negvdi2` (*long a*) [Runtime Function]
    These functions return the negation of *a*; that is `-a`.

`int __subvsi3` (*int a, int b*) [Runtime Function]
`long __subvdi3` (*long a, long b*) [Runtime Function]
    These functions return the difference between *b* and *a*; that is `a - b`.

4.1.4 Bit operations

`int __clzsi2` (*unsigned int a*) [Runtime Function]
`int __clzdi2` (*unsigned long a*) [Runtime Function]
`int __clzti2` (*unsigned long long a*) [Runtime Function]
    These functions return the number of leading 0-bits in *a*, starting at the most significant bit position. If *a* is zero, the result is undefined.

`int __ctzsi2` (*unsigned int a*) [Runtime Function]
`int __ctzdi2` (*unsigned long a*) [Runtime Function]
`int __ctzti2` (*unsigned long long a*) [Runtime Function]
    These functions return the number of trailing 0-bits in *a*, starting at the least significant bit position. If *a* is zero, the result is undefined.

`int __ffsdi2` (*unsigned long a*) [Runtime Function]
`int __ffsti2` (*unsigned long long a*) [Runtime Function]
    These functions return the index of the least significant 1-bit in *a*, or the value zero if *a* is zero. The least significant bit is index one.

`int __paritysi2` (*unsigned int a*) [Runtime Function]
`int __paritydi2` (*unsigned long a*) [Runtime Function]
`int __parityti2` (*unsigned long long a*) [Runtime Function]
    These functions return the value zero if the number of bits set in *a* is even, and the value one otherwise.

`int __popcountsi2 (`*unsigned int* `a)` [Runtime Function]
`int __popcountdi2 (`*unsigned long* `a)` [Runtime Function]
`int __popcountti2 (`*unsigned long long* `a)` [Runtime Function]
> These functions return the number of bits set in *a*.

`int32_t __bswapsi2 (`*int32_t* `a)` [Runtime Function]
`int64_t __bswapdi2 (`*int64_t* `a)` [Runtime Function]
> These functions return the *a* byteswapped.

4.2 Routines for floating point emulation

The software floating point library is used on machines which do not have hardware support for floating point. It is also used whenever '`-msoft-float`' is used to disable generation of floating point instructions. (Not all targets support this switch.)

For compatibility with other compilers, the floating point emulation routines can be renamed with the `DECLARE_LIBRARY_RENAMES` macro (see Section 18.12 [Library Calls], page 541). In this section, the default names are used.

Presently the library does not support `XFmode`, which is used for `long double` on some architectures.

4.2.1 Arithmetic functions

`float __addsf3 (`*float* `a,` *float* `b)` [Runtime Function]
`double __adddf3 (`*double* `a,` *double* `b)` [Runtime Function]
`long double __addtf3 (`*long double* `a,` *long double* `b)` [Runtime Function]
`long double __addxf3 (`*long double* `a,` *long double* `b)` [Runtime Function]
> These functions return the sum of *a* and *b*.

`float __subsf3 (`*float* `a,` *float* `b)` [Runtime Function]
`double __subdf3 (`*double* `a,` *double* `b)` [Runtime Function]
`long double __subtf3 (`*long double* `a,` *long double* `b)` [Runtime Function]
`long double __subxf3 (`*long double* `a,` *long double* `b)` [Runtime Function]
> These functions return the difference between *b* and *a*; that is, $a - b$.

`float __mulsf3 (`*float* `a,` *float* `b)` [Runtime Function]
`double __muldf3 (`*double* `a,` *double* `b)` [Runtime Function]
`long double __multf3 (`*long double* `a,` *long double* `b)` [Runtime Function]
`long double __mulxf3 (`*long double* `a,` *long double* `b)` [Runtime Function]
> These functions return the product of *a* and *b*.

`float __divsf3 (`*float* `a,` *float* `b)` [Runtime Function]
`double __divdf3 (`*double* `a,` *double* `b)` [Runtime Function]
`long double __divtf3 (`*long double* `a,` *long double* `b)` [Runtime Function]
`long double __divxf3 (`*long double* `a,` *long double* `b)` [Runtime Function]
> These functions return the quotient of *a* and *b*; that is, a/b.

`float __negsf2 (`*float* `a)` [Runtime Function]
`double __negdf2 (`*double* `a)` [Runtime Function]
`long double __negtf2 (`*long double* `a)` [Runtime Function]

`long double __negxf2` (*long double* a) [Runtime Function]

These functions return the negation of a. They simply flip the sign bit, so they can produce negative zero and negative NaN.

4.2.2 Conversion functions

`double __extendsfdf2` (*float* a) [Runtime Function]
`long double __extendsftf2` (*float* a) [Runtime Function]
`long double __extendsfxf2` (*float* a) [Runtime Function]
`long double __extenddftf2` (*double* a) [Runtime Function]
`long double __extenddfxf2` (*double* a) [Runtime Function]

These functions extend a to the wider mode of their return type.

`double __truncxfdf2` (*long double* a) [Runtime Function]
`double __trunctfdf2` (*long double* a) [Runtime Function]
`float __truncxfsf2` (*long double* a) [Runtime Function]
`float __trunctfsf2` (*long double* a) [Runtime Function]
`float __truncdfsf2` (*double* a) [Runtime Function]

These functions truncate a to the narrower mode of their return type, rounding toward zero.

`int __fixsfsi` (*float* a) [Runtime Function]
`int __fixdfsi` (*double* a) [Runtime Function]
`int __fixtfsi` (*long double* a) [Runtime Function]
`int __fixxfsi` (*long double* a) [Runtime Function]

These functions convert a to a signed integer, rounding toward zero.

`long __fixsfdi` (*float* a) [Runtime Function]
`long __fixdfdi` (*double* a) [Runtime Function]
`long __fixtfdi` (*long double* a) [Runtime Function]
`long __fixxfdi` (*long double* a) [Runtime Function]

These functions convert a to a signed long, rounding toward zero.

`long long __fixsfti` (*float* a) [Runtime Function]
`long long __fixdfti` (*double* a) [Runtime Function]
`long long __fixtfti` (*long double* a) [Runtime Function]
`long long __fixxfti` (*long double* a) [Runtime Function]

These functions convert a to a signed long long, rounding toward zero.

`unsigned int __fixunssfsi` (*float* a) [Runtime Function]
`unsigned int __fixunsdfsi` (*double* a) [Runtime Function]
`unsigned int __fixunstfsi` (*long double* a) [Runtime Function]
`unsigned int __fixunsxfsi` (*long double* a) [Runtime Function]

These functions convert a to an unsigned integer, rounding toward zero. Negative values all become zero.

`unsigned long __fixunssfdi` (*float* a) [Runtime Function]
`unsigned long __fixunsdfdi` (*double* a) [Runtime Function]
`unsigned long __fixunstfdi` (*long double* a) [Runtime Function]

`unsigned long __fixunsxfdi` (*long double* a)	[Runtime Function]

    These functions convert *a* to an unsigned long, rounding toward zero. Negative values all become zero.

`unsigned long long __fixunssfti` (*float* a)	[Runtime Function]
`unsigned long long __fixunsdfti` (*double* a)	[Runtime Function]
`unsigned long long __fixunstfti` (*long double* a)	[Runtime Function]
`unsigned long long __fixunsxfti` (*long double* a)	[Runtime Function]

    These functions convert *a* to an unsigned long long, rounding toward zero. Negative values all become zero.

`float __floatsisf` (*int* i)	[Runtime Function]
`double __floatsidf` (*int* i)	[Runtime Function]
`long double __floatsitf` (*int* i)	[Runtime Function]
`long double __floatsixf` (*int* i)	[Runtime Function]

    These functions convert *i*, a signed integer, to floating point.

`float __floatdisf` (*long* i)	[Runtime Function]
`double __floatdidf` (*long* i)	[Runtime Function]
`long double __floatditf` (*long* i)	[Runtime Function]
`long double __floatdixf` (*long* i)	[Runtime Function]

    These functions convert *i*, a signed long, to floating point.

`float __floattisf` (*long long* i)	[Runtime Function]
`double __floattidf` (*long long* i)	[Runtime Function]
`long double __floattitf` (*long long* i)	[Runtime Function]
`long double __floattixf` (*long long* i)	[Runtime Function]

    These functions convert *i*, a signed long long, to floating point.

`float __floatunsisf` (*unsigned int* i)	[Runtime Function]
`double __floatunsidf` (*unsigned int* i)	[Runtime Function]
`long double __floatunsitf` (*unsigned int* i)	[Runtime Function]
`long double __floatunsixf` (*unsigned int* i)	[Runtime Function]

    These functions convert *i*, an unsigned integer, to floating point.

`float __floatundisf` (*unsigned long* i)	[Runtime Function]
`double __floatundidf` (*unsigned long* i)	[Runtime Function]
`long double __floatunditf` (*unsigned long* i)	[Runtime Function]
`long double __floatundixf` (*unsigned long* i)	[Runtime Function]

    These functions convert *i*, an unsigned long, to floating point.

`float __floatuntisf` (*unsigned long long* i)	[Runtime Function]
`double __floatuntidf` (*unsigned long long* i)	[Runtime Function]
`long double __floatuntitf` (*unsigned long long* i)	[Runtime Function]
`long double __floatuntixf` (*unsigned long long* i)	[Runtime Function]

    These functions convert *i*, an unsigned long long, to floating point.

Chapter 4: The GCC low-level runtime library

4.2.3 Comparison functions

There are two sets of basic comparison functions.

int __cmpsf2 (*float* a, *float* b) [Runtime Function]
int __cmpdf2 (*double* a, *double* b) [Runtime Function]
int __cmptf2 (*long double* a, *long double* b) [Runtime Function]

> These functions calculate $a <=> b$. That is, if a is less than b, they return -1; if a is greater than b, they return 1; and if a and b are equal they return 0. If either argument is NaN they return 1, but you should not rely on this; if NaN is a possibility, use one of the higher-level comparison functions.

int __unordsf2 (*float* a, *float* b) [Runtime Function]
int __unorddf2 (*double* a, *double* b) [Runtime Function]
int __unordtf2 (*long double* a, *long double* b) [Runtime Function]

> These functions return a nonzero value if either argument is NaN, otherwise 0.

There is also a complete group of higher level functions which correspond directly to comparison operators. They implement the ISO C semantics for floating-point comparisons, taking NaN into account. Pay careful attention to the return values defined for each set. Under the hood, all of these routines are implemented as

```
if (__unordXf2 (a, b))
   return E;
return __cmpXf2 (a, b);
```

where E is a constant chosen to give the proper behavior for NaN. Thus, the meaning of the return value is different for each set. Do not rely on this implementation; only the semantics documented below are guaranteed.

int __eqsf2 (*float* a, *float* b) [Runtime Function]
int __eqdf2 (*double* a, *double* b) [Runtime Function]
int __eqtf2 (*long double* a, *long double* b) [Runtime Function]

> These functions return zero if neither argument is NaN, and a and b are equal.

int __nesf2 (*float* a, *float* b) [Runtime Function]
int __nedf2 (*double* a, *double* b) [Runtime Function]
int __netf2 (*long double* a, *long double* b) [Runtime Function]

> These functions return a nonzero value if either argument is NaN, or if a and b are unequal.

int __gesf2 (*float* a, *float* b) [Runtime Function]
int __gedf2 (*double* a, *double* b) [Runtime Function]
int __getf2 (*long double* a, *long double* b) [Runtime Function]

> These functions return a value greater than or equal to zero if neither argument is NaN, and a is greater than or equal to b.

int __ltsf2 (*float* a, *float* b) [Runtime Function]
int __ltdf2 (*double* a, *double* b) [Runtime Function]
int __lttf2 (*long double* a, *long double* b) [Runtime Function]

> These functions return a value less than zero if neither argument is NaN, and a is strictly less than b.

int __lesf2 (*float a, float b*)	[Runtime Function]
int __ledf2 (*double a, double b*)	[Runtime Function]
int __letf2 (*long double a, long double b*)	[Runtime Function]

These functions return a value less than or equal to zero if neither argument is NaN, and *a* is less than or equal to *b*.

int __gtsf2 (*float a, float b*)	[Runtime Function]
int __gtdf2 (*double a, double b*)	[Runtime Function]
int __gttf2 (*long double a, long double b*)	[Runtime Function]

These functions return a value greater than zero if neither argument is NaN, and *a* is strictly greater than *b*.

4.2.4 Other floating-point functions

float __powisf2 (*float a, int b*)	[Runtime Function]
double __powidf2 (*double a, int b*)	[Runtime Function]
long double __powitf2 (*long double a, int b*)	[Runtime Function]
long double __powixf2 (*long double a, int b*)	[Runtime Function]

These functions convert raise *a* to the power *b*.

complex float __mulsc3 (*float a, float b, float c, float d*)	[Runtime Function]
complex double __muldc3 (*double a, double b, double c, double d*)	[Runtime Function]
complex long double __multc3 (*long double a, long double b, long double c, long double d*)	[Runtime Function]
complex long double __mulxc3 (*long double a, long double b, long double c, long double d*)	[Runtime Function]

These functions return the product of $a + ib$ and $c + id$, following the rules of C99 Annex G.

complex float __divsc3 (*float a, float b, float c, float d*)	[Runtime Function]
complex double __divdc3 (*double a, double b, double c, double d*)	[Runtime Function]
complex long double __divtc3 (*long double a, long double b, long double c, long double d*)	[Runtime Function]
complex long double __divxc3 (*long double a, long double b, long double c, long double d*)	[Runtime Function]

These functions return the quotient of $a + ib$ and $c + id$ (i.e., $(a + ib)/(c + id)$), following the rules of C99 Annex G.

4.3 Routines for decimal floating point emulation

The software decimal floating point library implements IEEE 754-2008 decimal floating point arithmetic and is only activated on selected targets.

The software decimal floating point library supports either DPD (Densely Packed Decimal) or BID (Binary Integer Decimal) encoding as selected at configure time.

Chapter 4: The GCC low-level runtime library

4.3.1 Arithmetic functions

`_Decimal32 __dpd_addsd3 (`_Decimal32_ `a,` _Decimal32_ `b)`	[Runtime Function]
`_Decimal32 __bid_addsd3 (`_Decimal32_ `a,` _Decimal32_ `b)`	[Runtime Function]
`_Decimal64 __dpd_adddd3 (`_Decimal64_ `a,` _Decimal64_ `b)`	[Runtime Function]
`_Decimal64 __bid_adddd3 (`_Decimal64_ `a,` _Decimal64_ `b)`	[Runtime Function]
`_Decimal128 __dpd_addtd3 (`_Decimal128_ `a,` _Decimal128_ `b)`	[Runtime Function]
`_Decimal128 __bid_addtd3 (`_Decimal128_ `a,` _Decimal128_ `b)`	[Runtime Function]

These functions return the sum of a and b.

`_Decimal32 __dpd_subsd3 (`_Decimal32_ `a,` _Decimal32_ `b)`	[Runtime Function]
`_Decimal32 __bid_subsd3 (`_Decimal32_ `a,` _Decimal32_ `b)`	[Runtime Function]
`_Decimal64 __dpd_subdd3 (`_Decimal64_ `a,` _Decimal64_ `b)`	[Runtime Function]
`_Decimal64 __bid_subdd3 (`_Decimal64_ `a,` _Decimal64_ `b)`	[Runtime Function]
`_Decimal128 __dpd_subtd3 (`_Decimal128_ `a,` _Decimal128_ `b)`	[Runtime Function]
`_Decimal128 __bid_subtd3 (`_Decimal128_ `a,` _Decimal128_ `b)`	[Runtime Function]

These functions return the difference between b and a; that is, $a - b$.

`_Decimal32 __dpd_mulsd3 (`_Decimal32_ `a,` _Decimal32_ `b)`	[Runtime Function]
`_Decimal32 __bid_mulsd3 (`_Decimal32_ `a,` _Decimal32_ `b)`	[Runtime Function]
`_Decimal64 __dpd_muldd3 (`_Decimal64_ `a,` _Decimal64_ `b)`	[Runtime Function]
`_Decimal64 __bid_muldd3 (`_Decimal64_ `a,` _Decimal64_ `b)`	[Runtime Function]
`_Decimal128 __dpd_multd3 (`_Decimal128_ `a,` _Decimal128_ `b)`	[Runtime Function]
`_Decimal128 __bid_multd3 (`_Decimal128_ `a,` _Decimal128_ `b)`	[Runtime Function]

These functions return the product of a and b.

`_Decimal32 __dpd_divsd3 (`_Decimal32_ `a,` _Decimal32_ `b)`	[Runtime Function]
`_Decimal32 __bid_divsd3 (`_Decimal32_ `a,` _Decimal32_ `b)`	[Runtime Function]
`_Decimal64 __dpd_divdd3 (`_Decimal64_ `a,` _Decimal64_ `b)`	[Runtime Function]
`_Decimal64 __bid_divdd3 (`_Decimal64_ `a,` _Decimal64_ `b)`	[Runtime Function]
`_Decimal128 __dpd_divtd3 (`_Decimal128_ `a,` _Decimal128_ `b)`	[Runtime Function]
`_Decimal128 __bid_divtd3 (`_Decimal128_ `a,` _Decimal128_ `b)`	[Runtime Function]

These functions return the quotient of a and b; that is, a/b.

`_Decimal32 __dpd_negsd2 (`_Decimal32_ `a)`	[Runtime Function]
`_Decimal32 __bid_negsd2 (`_Decimal32_ `a)`	[Runtime Function]
`_Decimal64 __dpd_negdd2 (`_Decimal64_ `a)`	[Runtime Function]
`_Decimal64 __bid_negdd2 (`_Decimal64_ `a)`	[Runtime Function]
`_Decimal128 __dpd_negtd2 (`_Decimal128_ `a)`	[Runtime Function]
`_Decimal128 __bid_negtd2 (`_Decimal128_ `a)`	[Runtime Function]

These functions return the negation of a. They simply flip the sign bit, so they can produce negative zero and negative NaN.

4.3.2 Conversion functions

`_Decimal64 __dpd_extendsddd2 (`_Decimal32_ `a)`	[Runtime Function]
`_Decimal64 __bid_extendsddd2 (`_Decimal32_ `a)`	[Runtime Function]
`_Decimal128 __dpd_extendsdtd2 (`_Decimal32_ `a)`	[Runtime Function]
`_Decimal128 __bid_extendsdtd2 (`_Decimal32_ `a)`	[Runtime Function]

_Decimal128 __dpd_extendddtd2 (_Decimal64 a) [Runtime Function]
_Decimal128 __bid_extendddtd2 (_Decimal64 a) [Runtime Function]
_Decimal32 __dpd_truncddsd2 (_Decimal64 a) [Runtime Function]
_Decimal32 __bid_truncddsd2 (_Decimal64 a) [Runtime Function]
_Decimal32 __dpd_trunctdsd2 (_Decimal128 a) [Runtime Function]
_Decimal32 __bid_trunctdsd2 (_Decimal128 a) [Runtime Function]
_Decimal64 __dpd_trunctdd2 (_Decimal128 a) [Runtime Function]
_Decimal64 __bid_trunctdd2 (_Decimal128 a) [Runtime Function]

These functions convert the value a from one decimal floating type to another.

_Decimal64 __dpd_extendsfdd (float a) [Runtime Function]
_Decimal64 __bid_extendsfdd (float a) [Runtime Function]
_Decimal128 __dpd_extendsftd (float a) [Runtime Function]
_Decimal128 __bid_extendsftd (float a) [Runtime Function]
_Decimal128 __dpd_extenddftd (double a) [Runtime Function]
_Decimal128 __bid_extenddftd (double a) [Runtime Function]
_Decimal128 __dpd_extendxftd (long double a) [Runtime Function]
_Decimal128 __bid_extendxftd (long double a) [Runtime Function]
_Decimal32 __dpd_truncdfsd (double a) [Runtime Function]
_Decimal32 __bid_truncdfsd (double a) [Runtime Function]
_Decimal32 __dpd_truncxfsd (long double a) [Runtime Function]
_Decimal32 __bid_truncxfsd (long double a) [Runtime Function]
_Decimal32 __dpd_trunctfsd (long double a) [Runtime Function]
_Decimal32 __bid_trunctfsd (long double a) [Runtime Function]
_Decimal64 __dpd_truncxfdd (long double a) [Runtime Function]
_Decimal64 __bid_truncxfdd (long double a) [Runtime Function]
_Decimal64 __dpd_trunctfdd (long double a) [Runtime Function]
_Decimal64 __bid_trunctfdd (long double a) [Runtime Function]

These functions convert the value of a from a binary floating type to a decimal floating type of a different size.

float __dpd_truncddsf (_Decimal64 a) [Runtime Function]
float __bid_truncddsf (_Decimal64 a) [Runtime Function]
float __dpd_trunctdsf (_Decimal128 a) [Runtime Function]
float __bid_trunctdsf (_Decimal128 a) [Runtime Function]
double __dpd_extendsddf (_Decimal32 a) [Runtime Function]
double __bid_extendsddf (_Decimal32 a) [Runtime Function]
double __dpd_trunctddf (_Decimal128 a) [Runtime Function]
double __bid_trunctddf (_Decimal128 a) [Runtime Function]
long double __dpd_extendsdxf (_Decimal32 a) [Runtime Function]
long double __bid_extendsdxf (_Decimal32 a) [Runtime Function]
long double __dpd_extendddxf (_Decimal64 a) [Runtime Function]
long double __bid_extendddxf (_Decimal64 a) [Runtime Function]
long double __dpd_trunctdxf (_Decimal128 a) [Runtime Function]
long double __bid_trunctdxf (_Decimal128 a) [Runtime Function]
long double __dpd_extendsdtf (_Decimal32 a) [Runtime Function]
long double __bid_extendsdtf (_Decimal32 a) [Runtime Function]
long double __dpd_extendddtf (_Decimal64 a) [Runtime Function]

Chapter 4: The GCC low-level runtime library

long double __bid_extendddtf (_Decimal64 a) [Runtime Function]
: These functions convert the value of a from a decimal floating type to a binary floating type of a different size.

_Decimal32 __dpd_extendsfsd (float a) [Runtime Function]
_Decimal32 __bid_extendsfsd (float a) [Runtime Function]
_Decimal64 __dpd_extenddfdd (double a) [Runtime Function]
_Decimal64 __bid_extenddfdd (double a) [Runtime Function]
_Decimal128 __dpd_extendtftd (long double a) [Runtime Function]
_Decimal128 __bid_extendtftd (long double a) [Runtime Function]
float __dpd_truncsdsf (_Decimal32 a) [Runtime Function]
float __bid_truncsdsf (_Decimal32 a) [Runtime Function]
double __dpd_truncdddf (_Decimal64 a) [Runtime Function]
double __bid_truncdddf (_Decimal64 a) [Runtime Function]
long double __dpd_trunctdtf (_Decimal128 a) [Runtime Function]
long double __bid_trunctdtf (_Decimal128 a) [Runtime Function]
: These functions convert the value of a between decimal and binary floating types of the same size.

int __dpd_fixsdsi (_Decimal32 a) [Runtime Function]
int __bid_fixsdsi (_Decimal32 a) [Runtime Function]
int __dpd_fixddsi (_Decimal64 a) [Runtime Function]
int __bid_fixddsi (_Decimal64 a) [Runtime Function]
int __dpd_fixtdsi (_Decimal128 a) [Runtime Function]
int __bid_fixtdsi (_Decimal128 a) [Runtime Function]
: These functions convert a to a signed integer.

long __dpd_fixsddi (_Decimal32 a) [Runtime Function]
long __bid_fixsddi (_Decimal32 a) [Runtime Function]
long __dpd_fixdddi (_Decimal64 a) [Runtime Function]
long __bid_fixdddi (_Decimal64 a) [Runtime Function]
long __dpd_fixtddi (_Decimal128 a) [Runtime Function]
long __bid_fixtddi (_Decimal128 a) [Runtime Function]
: These functions convert a to a signed long.

unsigned int __dpd_fixunssdsi (_Decimal32 a) [Runtime Function]
unsigned int __bid_fixunssdsi (_Decimal32 a) [Runtime Function]
unsigned int __dpd_fixunsddsi (_Decimal64 a) [Runtime Function]
unsigned int __bid_fixunsddsi (_Decimal64 a) [Runtime Function]
unsigned int __dpd_fixunstdsi (_Decimal128 a) [Runtime Function]
unsigned int __bid_fixunstdsi (_Decimal128 a) [Runtime Function]
: These functions convert a to an unsigned integer. Negative values all become zero.

unsigned long __dpd_fixunssddi (_Decimal32 a) [Runtime Function]
unsigned long __bid_fixunssddi (_Decimal32 a) [Runtime Function]
unsigned long __dpd_fixunsdddi (_Decimal64 a) [Runtime Function]
unsigned long __bid_fixunsdddi (_Decimal64 a) [Runtime Function]
unsigned long __dpd_fixunstddi (_Decimal128 a) [Runtime Function]

unsigned long __bid_fixunstddi (_Decimal128 a) [Runtime Function]
> These functions convert a to an unsigned long. Negative values all become zero.

_Decimal32 __dpd_floatsisd (int i) [Runtime Function]
_Decimal32 __bid_floatsisd (int i) [Runtime Function]
_Decimal64 __dpd_floatsidd (int i) [Runtime Function]
_Decimal64 __bid_floatsidd (int i) [Runtime Function]
_Decimal128 __dpd_floatsitd (int i) [Runtime Function]
_Decimal128 __bid_floatsitd (int i) [Runtime Function]
> These functions convert i, a signed integer, to decimal floating point.

_Decimal32 __dpd_floatdisd (long i) [Runtime Function]
_Decimal32 __bid_floatdisd (long i) [Runtime Function]
_Decimal64 __dpd_floatdidd (long i) [Runtime Function]
_Decimal64 __bid_floatdidd (long i) [Runtime Function]
_Decimal128 __dpd_floatditd (long i) [Runtime Function]
_Decimal128 __bid_floatditd (long i) [Runtime Function]
> These functions convert i, a signed long, to decimal floating point.

_Decimal32 __dpd_floatunssisd (unsigned int i) [Runtime Function]
_Decimal32 __bid_floatunssisd (unsigned int i) [Runtime Function]
_Decimal64 __dpd_floatunssidd (unsigned int i) [Runtime Function]
_Decimal64 __bid_floatunssidd (unsigned int i) [Runtime Function]
_Decimal128 __dpd_floatunssitd (unsigned int i) [Runtime Function]
_Decimal128 __bid_floatunssitd (unsigned int i) [Runtime Function]
> These functions convert i, an unsigned integer, to decimal floating point.

_Decimal32 __dpd_floatunsdisd (unsigned long i) [Runtime Function]
_Decimal32 __bid_floatunsdisd (unsigned long i) [Runtime Function]
_Decimal64 __dpd_floatunsdidd (unsigned long i) [Runtime Function]
_Decimal64 __bid_floatunsdidd (unsigned long i) [Runtime Function]
_Decimal128 __dpd_floatunsditd (unsigned long i) [Runtime Function]
_Decimal128 __bid_floatunsditd (unsigned long i) [Runtime Function]
> These functions convert i, an unsigned long, to decimal floating point.

4.3.3 Comparison functions

int __dpd_unordsd2 (_Decimal32 a, _Decimal32 b) [Runtime Function]
int __bid_unordsd2 (_Decimal32 a, _Decimal32 b) [Runtime Function]
int __dpd_unorddd2 (_Decimal64 a, _Decimal64 b) [Runtime Function]
int __bid_unorddd2 (_Decimal64 a, _Decimal64 b) [Runtime Function]
int __dpd_unordtd2 (_Decimal128 a, _Decimal128 b) [Runtime Function]
int __bid_unordtd2 (_Decimal128 a, _Decimal128 b) [Runtime Function]
> These functions return a nonzero value if either argument is NaN, otherwise 0.

There is also a complete group of higher level functions which correspond directly to comparison operators. They implement the ISO C semantics for floating-point comparisons, taking NaN into account. Pay careful attention to the return values defined for each set. Under the hood, all of these routines are implemented as

Chapter 4: The GCC low-level runtime library

```
if (__bid_unordXd2 (a, b))
  return E;
return __bid_cmpXd2 (a, b);
```

where E is a constant chosen to give the proper behavior for NaN. Thus, the meaning of the return value is different for each set. Do not rely on this implementation; only the semantics documented below are guaranteed.

int __dpd_eqsd2 (*_Decimal32* a, *_Decimal32* b) [Runtime Function]
int __bid_eqsd2 (*_Decimal32* a, *_Decimal32* b) [Runtime Function]
int __dpd_eqdd2 (*_Decimal64* a, *_Decimal64* b) [Runtime Function]
int __bid_eqdd2 (*_Decimal64* a, *_Decimal64* b) [Runtime Function]
int __dpd_eqtd2 (*_Decimal128* a, *_Decimal128* b) [Runtime Function]
int __bid_eqtd2 (*_Decimal128* a, *_Decimal128* b) [Runtime Function]

These functions return zero if neither argument is NaN, and *a* and *b* are equal.

int __dpd_nesd2 (*_Decimal32* a, *_Decimal32* b) [Runtime Function]
int __bid_nesd2 (*_Decimal32* a, *_Decimal32* b) [Runtime Function]
int __dpd_nedd2 (*_Decimal64* a, *_Decimal64* b) [Runtime Function]
int __bid_nedd2 (*_Decimal64* a, *_Decimal64* b) [Runtime Function]
int __dpd_netd2 (*_Decimal128* a, *_Decimal128* b) [Runtime Function]
int __bid_netd2 (*_Decimal128* a, *_Decimal128* b) [Runtime Function]

These functions return a nonzero value if either argument is NaN, or if *a* and *b* are unequal.

int __dpd_gesd2 (*_Decimal32* a, *_Decimal32* b) [Runtime Function]
int __bid_gesd2 (*_Decimal32* a, *_Decimal32* b) [Runtime Function]
int __dpd_gedd2 (*_Decimal64* a, *_Decimal64* b) [Runtime Function]
int __bid_gedd2 (*_Decimal64* a, *_Decimal64* b) [Runtime Function]
int __dpd_getd2 (*_Decimal128* a, *_Decimal128* b) [Runtime Function]
int __bid_getd2 (*_Decimal128* a, *_Decimal128* b) [Runtime Function]

These functions return a value greater than or equal to zero if neither argument is NaN, and *a* is greater than or equal to *b*.

int __dpd_ltsd2 (*_Decimal32* a, *_Decimal32* b) [Runtime Function]
int   bid_ltsd2 (*_Decimal32* a, *_Decimal32* b) [Runtime Function]
int __dpd_ltdd2 (*_Decimal64* a, *_Decimal64* b) [Runtime Function]
int   bid_ltdd2 (*_Decimal64* a, *_Decimal64* b) [Runtime Function]
int __dpd_lttd2 (*_Decimal128* a, *_Decimal128* b) [Runtime Function]
int __bid_lttd2 (*_Decimal128* a, *_Decimal128* b) [Runtime Function]

These functions return a value less than zero if neither argument is NaN, and *a* is strictly less than *b*.

int __dpd_lesd2 (*_Decimal32* a, *_Decimal32* b) [Runtime Function]
int __bid_lesd2 (*_Decimal32* a, *_Decimal32* b) [Runtime Function]
int __dpd_ledd2 (*_Decimal64* a, *_Decimal64* b) [Runtime Function]
int __bid_ledd2 (*_Decimal64* a, *_Decimal64* b) [Runtime Function]
int __dpd_letd2 (*_Decimal128* a, *_Decimal128* b) [Runtime Function]

int __bid_letd2 (*_Decimal128* a, *_Decimal128* b) [Runtime Function]
These functions return a value less than or equal to zero if neither argument is NaN, and a is less than or equal to b.

int __dpd_gtsd2 (*_Decimal32* a, *_Decimal32* b) [Runtime Function]
int __bid_gtsd2 (*_Decimal32* a, *_Decimal32* b) [Runtime Function]
int __dpd_gtdd2 (*_Decimal64* a, *_Decimal64* b) [Runtime Function]
int __bid_gtdd2 (*_Decimal64* a, *_Decimal64* b) [Runtime Function]
int __dpd_gttd2 (*_Decimal128* a, *_Decimal128* b) [Runtime Function]
int __bid_gttd2 (*_Decimal128* a, *_Decimal128* b) [Runtime Function]
These functions return a value greater than zero if neither argument is NaN, and a is strictly greater than b.

4.4 Routines for fixed-point fractional emulation

The software fixed-point library implements fixed-point fractional arithmetic, and is only activated on selected targets.

For ease of comprehension `fract` is an alias for the `_Fract` type, `accum` an alias for `_Accum`, and `sat` an alias for `_Sat`.

For illustrative purposes, in this section the fixed-point fractional type `short fract` is assumed to correspond to machine mode `QQmode`; `unsigned short fract` to `UQQmode`; `fract` to `HQmode`; `unsigned fract` to `UHQmode`; `long fract` to `SQmode`; `unsigned long fract` to `USQmode`; `long long fract` to `DQmode`; and `unsigned long long fract` to `UDQmode`. Similarly the fixed-point accumulator type `short accum` corresponds to `HAmode`; `unsigned short accum` to `UHAmode`; `accum` to `SAmode`; `unsigned accum` to `USAmode`; `long accum` to `DAmode`; `unsigned long accum` to `UDAmode`; `long long accum` to `TAmode`; and `unsigned long long accum` to `UTAmode`.

4.4.1 Arithmetic functions

short fract __addqq3 (*short fract* a, *short fract* b) [Runtime Function]
fract __addhq3 (*fract* a, *fract* b) [Runtime Function]
long fract __addsq3 (*long fract* a, *long fract* b) [Runtime Function]
long long fract __adddq3 (*long long fract* a, *long long fract* b) [Runtime Function]
unsigned short fract __adduqq3 (*unsigned short fract* a, *unsigned short fract* b) [Runtime Function]
unsigned fract __adduhq3 (*unsigned fract* a, *unsigned fract* b) [Runtime Function]
unsigned long fract __addusq3 (*unsigned long fract* a, *unsigned long fract* b) [Runtime Function]
unsigned long long fract __addudq3 (*unsigned long long fract* a, *unsigned long long fract* b) [Runtime Function]
short accum __addha3 (*short accum* a, *short accum* b) [Runtime Function]
accum __addsa3 (*accum* a, *accum* b) [Runtime Function]
long accum __addda3 (*long accum* a, *long accum* b) [Runtime Function]
long long accum __addta3 (*long long accum* a, *long long accum* b) [Runtime Function]

Chapter 4: The GCC low-level runtime library

<code>unsigned short accum __adduha3</code> (*unsigned short accum* a, *unsigned short accum* b)   [Runtime Function]

<code>unsigned accum __addusa3</code> (*unsigned accum* a, *unsigned accum* b)   [Runtime Function]

<code>unsigned long accum __adduda3</code> (*unsigned long accum* a, *unsigned long accum* b)   [Runtime Function]

<code>unsigned long long accum __adduta3</code> (*unsigned long long accum* a, *unsigned long long accum* b)   [Runtime Function]

    These functions return the sum of *a* and *b*.

<code>short fract __ssaddqq3</code> (*short fract* a, *short fract* b)   [Runtime Function]

<code>fract __ssaddhq3</code> (*fract* a, *fract* b)   [Runtime Function]

<code>long fract __ssaddsq3</code> (*long fract* a, *long fract* b)   [Runtime Function]

<code>long long fract __ssadddq3</code> (*long long fract* a, *long long fract* b)   [Runtime Function]

<code>short accum __ssaddha3</code> (*short accum* a, *short accum* b)   [Runtime Function]

<code>accum __ssaddsa3</code> (*accum* a, *accum* b)   [Runtime Function]

<code>long accum __ssaddda3</code> (*long accum* a, *long accum* b)   [Runtime Function]

<code>long long accum __ssaddta3</code> (*long long accum* a, *long long accum* b)   [Runtime Function]

    These functions return the sum of *a* and *b* with signed saturation.

<code>unsigned short fract __usadduqq3</code> (*unsigned short fract* a, *unsigned short fract* b)   [Runtime Function]

<code>unsigned fract __usadduhq3</code> (*unsigned fract* a, *unsigned fract* b)   [Runtime Function]

<code>unsigned long fract __usaddusq3</code> (*unsigned long fract* a, *unsigned long fract* b)   [Runtime Function]

<code>unsigned long long fract __usaddudq3</code> (*unsigned long long fract* a, *unsigned long long fract* b)   [Runtime Function]

<code>unsigned short accum __usadduha3</code> (*unsigned short accum* a, *unsigned short accum* b)   [Runtime Function]

<code>unsigned accum __usaddusa3</code> (*unsigned accum* a, *unsigned accum* b)   [Runtime Function]

<code>unsigned long accum __usadduda3</code> (*unsigned long accum* a, *unsigned long accum* b)   [Runtime Function]

<code>unsigned long long accum __usadduta3</code> (*unsigned long long accum* a, *unsigned long long accum* b)   [Runtime Function]

    These functions return the sum of *a* and *b* with unsigned saturation.

<code>short fract __subqq3</code> (*short fract* a, *short fract* b)   [Runtime Function]

<code>fract __subhq3</code> (*fract* a, *fract* b)   [Runtime Function]

<code>long fract __subsq3</code> (*long fract* a, *long fract* b)   [Runtime Function]

<code>long long fract __subdq3</code> (*long long fract* a, *long long fract* b)   [Runtime Function]

<code>unsigned short fract __subuqq3</code> (*unsigned short fract* a, *unsigned short fract* b)   [Runtime Function]

unsigned fract __subuhq3 (*unsigned fract* a, *unsigned fract* b) [Runtime Function]

unsigned long fract __subusq3 (*unsigned long fract* a, *unsigned long fract* b) [Runtime Function]

unsigned long long fract __subudq3 (*unsigned long long fract* a, *unsigned long long fract* b) [Runtime Function]

short accum __subha3 (*short accum* a, *short accum* b) [Runtime Function]

accum __subsa3 (*accum* a, *accum* b) [Runtime Function]

long accum __subda3 (*long accum* a, *long accum* b) [Runtime Function]

long long accum __subta3 (*long long accum* a, *long long accum* b) [Runtime Function]

unsigned short accum __subuha3 (*unsigned short accum* a, *unsigned short accum* b) [Runtime Function]

unsigned accum __subusa3 (*unsigned accum* a, *unsigned accum* b) [Runtime Function]

unsigned long accum __subuda3 (*unsigned long accum* a, *unsigned long accum* b) [Runtime Function]

unsigned long long accum __subuta3 (*unsigned long long accum* a, *unsigned long long accum* b) [Runtime Function]

These functions return the difference of a and b; that is, a - b.

short fract __sssubqq3 (*short fract* a, *short fract* b) [Runtime Function]

fract __sssubhq3 (*fract* a, *fract* b) [Runtime Function]

long fract __sssubsq3 (*long fract* a, *long fract* b) [Runtime Function]

long long fract __sssubdq3 (*long long fract* a, *long long fract* b) [Runtime Function]

short accum __sssubha3 (*short accum* a, *short accum* b) [Runtime Function]

accum __sssubsa3 (*accum* a, *accum* b) [Runtime Function]

long accum __sssubda3 (*long accum* a, *long accum* b) [Runtime Function]

long long accum __sssubta3 (*long long accum* a, *long long accum* b) [Runtime Function]

These functions return the difference of a and b with signed saturation; that is, a - b.

unsigned short fract __ussubuqq3 (*unsigned short fract* a, *unsigned short fract* b) [Runtime Function]

unsigned fract __ussubuhq3 (*unsigned fract* a, *unsigned fract* b) [Runtime Function]

unsigned long fract __ussubusq3 (*unsigned long fract* a, *unsigned long fract* b) [Runtime Function]

unsigned long long fract __ussubudq3 (*unsigned long long fract* a, *unsigned long long fract* b) [Runtime Function]

unsigned short accum __ussubuha3 (*unsigned short accum* a, *unsigned short accum* b) [Runtime Function]

unsigned accum __ussubusa3 (*unsigned accum* a, *unsigned accum* b) [Runtime Function]

unsigned long accum __ussubuda3 (*unsigned long accum* a, *unsigned long accum* b) [Runtime Function]

Chapter 4: The GCC low-level runtime library

unsigned long long accum __ussubuta3 (*unsigned long long accum* a, *unsigned long long accum* b)   [Runtime Function]
> These functions return the difference of a and b with unsigned saturation; that is, a - b.

short fract __mulqq3 (*short fract* a, *short fract* b)   [Runtime Function]
fract __mulhq3 (*fract* a, *fract* b)   [Runtime Function]
long fract __mulsq3 (*long fract* a, *long fract* b)   [Runtime Function]
long long fract __muldq3 (*long long fract* a, *long long fract* b)   [Runtime Function]
unsigned short fract __muluqq3 (*unsigned short fract* a, *unsigned short fract* b)   [Runtime Function]
unsigned fract __muluhq3 (*unsigned fract* a, *unsigned fract* b)   [Runtime Function]
unsigned long fract __mulusq3 (*unsigned long fract* a, *unsigned long fract* b)   [Runtime Function]
unsigned long long fract __muludq3 (*unsigned long long fract* a, *unsigned long long fract* b)   [Runtime Function]
short accum __mulha3 (*short accum* a, *short accum* b)   [Runtime Function]
accum __mulsa3 (*accum* a, *accum* b)   [Runtime Function]
long accum __mulda3 (*long accum* a, *long accum* b)   [Runtime Function]
long long accum __multa3 (*long long accum* a, *long long accum* b)   [Runtime Function]
unsigned short accum __muluha3 (*unsigned short accum* a, *unsigned short accum* b)   [Runtime Function]
unsigned accum __mulusa3 (*unsigned accum* a, *unsigned accum* b)   [Runtime Function]
unsigned long accum __muluda3 (*unsigned long accum* a, *unsigned long accum* b)   [Runtime Function]
unsigned long long accum __muluta3 (*unsigned long long accum* a, *unsigned long long accum* b)   [Runtime Function]
> These functions return the product of a and b.

short fract __ssmulqq3 (*short fract* a, *short fract* b)   [Runtime Function]
fract __ssmulhq3 (*fract* a, *fract* b)   [Runtime Function]
long fract __ssmulsq3 (*long fract* a, *long fract* b)   [Runtime Function]
long long fract __ssmuldq3 (*long long fract* a, *long long fract* b)   [Runtime Function]
short accum __ssmulha3 (*short accum* a, *short accum* b)   [Runtime Function]
accum __ssmulsa3 (*accum* a, *accum* b)   [Runtime Function]
long accum __ssmulda3 (*long accum* a, *long accum* b)   [Runtime Function]
long long accum __ssmulta3 (*long long accum* a, *long long accum* b)   [Runtime Function]
> These functions return the product of a and b with signed saturation.

`unsigned short fract` **__usmuluqq3** (*unsigned short fract* a, *unsigned short fract* b) [Runtime Function]

`unsigned fract` **__usmuluhq3** (*unsigned fract* a, *unsigned fract* b) [Runtime Function]

`unsigned long fract` **__usmulusq3** (*unsigned long fract* a, *unsigned long fract* b) [Runtime Function]

`unsigned long long fract` **__usmuludq3** (*unsigned long long fract* a, *unsigned long long fract* b) [Runtime Function]

`unsigned short accum` **__usmuluha3** (*unsigned short accum* a, *unsigned short accum* b) [Runtime Function]

`unsigned accum` **__usmulusa3** (*unsigned accum* a, *unsigned accum* b) [Runtime Function]

`unsigned long accum` **__usmuluda3** (*unsigned long accum* a, *unsigned long accum* b) [Runtime Function]

`unsigned long long accum` **__usmuluta3** (*unsigned long long accum* a, *unsigned long long accum* b) [Runtime Function]

> These functions return the product of a and b with unsigned saturation.

`short fract` **__divqq3** (*short fract* a, *short fract* b) [Runtime Function]
`fract` **__divhq3** (*fract* a, *fract* b) [Runtime Function]
`long fract` **__divsq3** (*long fract* a, *long fract* b) [Runtime Function]
`long long fract` **__divdq3** (*long long fract* a, *long long fract* b) [Runtime Function]
`short accum` **__divha3** (*short accum* a, *short accum* b) [Runtime Function]
`accum` **__divsa3** (*accum* a, *accum* b) [Runtime Function]
`long accum` **__divda3** (*long accum* a, *long accum* b) [Runtime Function]
`long long accum` **__divta3** (*long long accum* a, *long long accum* b) [Runtime Function]

> These functions return the quotient of the signed division of a and b.

`unsigned short fract` **__udivuqq3** (*unsigned short fract* a, *unsigned short fract* b) [Runtime Function]

`unsigned fract` **__udivuhq3** (*unsigned fract* a, *unsigned fract* b) [Runtime Function]

`unsigned long fract` **__udivusq3** (*unsigned long fract* a, *unsigned long fract* b) [Runtime Function]

`unsigned long long fract` **__udivudq3** (*unsigned long long fract* a, *unsigned long long fract* b) [Runtime Function]

`unsigned short accum` **__udivuha3** (*unsigned short accum* a, *unsigned short accum* b) [Runtime Function]

`unsigned accum` **__udivusa3** (*unsigned accum* a, *unsigned accum* b) [Runtime Function]

`unsigned long accum` **__udivuda3** (*unsigned long accum* a, *unsigned long accum* b) [Runtime Function]

`unsigned long long accum` **__udivuta3** (*unsigned long long accum* a, *unsigned long long accum* b) [Runtime Function]

> These functions return the quotient of the unsigned division of a and b.

Chapter 4: The GCC low-level runtime library

short fract __ssdivqq3 (*short fract* a, *short fract* b) [Runtime Function]
fract __ssdivhq3 (*fract* a, *fract* b) [Runtime Function]
long fract __ssdivsq3 (*long fract* a, *long fract* b) [Runtime Function]
long long fract __ssdivdq3 (*long long fract* a, *long long fract* b) [Runtime Function]
short accum __ssdivha3 (*short accum* a, *short accum* b) [Runtime Function]
accum __ssdivsa3 (*accum* a, *accum* b) [Runtime Function]
long accum __ssdivda3 (*long accum* a, *long accum* b) [Runtime Function]
long long accum __ssdivta3 (*long long accum* a, *long long accum* b) [Runtime Function]
> These functions return the quotient of the signed division of a and b with signed saturation.

unsigned short fract __usdivuqq3 (*unsigned short fract* a, *unsigned short fract* b) [Runtime Function]
unsigned fract __usdivuhq3 (*unsigned fract* a, *unsigned fract* b) [Runtime Function]
unsigned long fract __usdivusq3 (*unsigned long fract* a, *unsigned long fract* b) [Runtime Function]
unsigned long long fract __usdivudq3 (*unsigned long long fract* a, *unsigned long long fract* b) [Runtime Function]
unsigned short accum __usdivuha3 (*unsigned short accum* a, *unsigned short accum* b) [Runtime Function]
unsigned accum __usdivusa3 (*unsigned accum* a, *unsigned accum* b) [Runtime Function]
unsigned long accum __usdivuda3 (*unsigned long accum* a, *unsigned long accum* b) [Runtime Function]
unsigned long long accum __usdivuta3 (*unsigned long long accum* a, *unsigned long long accum* b) [Runtime Function]
> These functions return the quotient of the unsigned division of a and b with unsigned saturation.

short fract __negqq2 (*short fract* a) [Runtime Function]
fract __neghq2 (*fract* a) [Runtime Function]
long fract __negsq2 (*long fract* a) [Runtime Function]
long long fract __negdq2 (*long long fract* a) [Runtime Function]
unsigned short fract __neguqq2 (*unsigned short fract* a) [Runtime Function]
unsigned fract __neguhq2 (*unsigned fract* a) [Runtime Function]
unsigned long fract __negusq2 (*unsigned long fract* a) [Runtime Function]
unsigned long long fract __negudq2 (*unsigned long long fract* a) [Runtime Function]
short accum __negha2 (*short accum* a) [Runtime Function]
accum __negsa2 (*accum* a) [Runtime Function]
long accum __negda2 (*long accum* a) [Runtime Function]
long long accum __negta2 (*long long accum* a) [Runtime Function]
unsigned short accum __neguha2 (*unsigned short accum* a) [Runtime Function]
unsigned accum __negusa2 (*unsigned accum* a) [Runtime Function]
unsigned long accum __neguda2 (*unsigned long accum* a) [Runtime Function]

unsigned long long accum __neguta2 (*unsigned long long*   [Runtime Function]
    accum a)

    These functions return the negation of *a*.

short fract __ssnegqq2 (*short fract* a)   [Runtime Function]
fract __ssneghq2 (*fract* a)   [Runtime Function]
long fract __ssnegsq2 (*long fract* a)   [Runtime Function]
long long fract __ssnegdq2 (*long long fract* a)   [Runtime Function]
short accum __ssnegha2 (*short accum* a)   [Runtime Function]
accum __ssnegsa2 (*accum* a)   [Runtime Function]
long accum __ssnegda2 (*long accum* a)   [Runtime Function]
long long accum __ssnegta2 (*long long accum* a)   [Runtime Function]

    These functions return the negation of *a* with signed saturation.

unsigned short fract __usneguqq2 (*unsigned short fract* a)   [Runtime Function]
unsigned fract __usneguhq2 (*unsigned fract* a)   [Runtime Function]
unsigned long fract __usnegusq2 (*unsigned long fract* a)   [Runtime Function]
unsigned long long fract __usnegudq2 (*unsigned*   [Runtime Function]
    long long fract a)
unsigned short accum __usneguha2 (*unsigned short accum*   [Runtime Function]
    a)
unsigned accum __usnegusa2 (*unsigned accum* a)   [Runtime Function]
unsigned long accum __usneguda2 (*unsigned long accum* a)   [Runtime Function]
unsigned long long accum __usneguta2 (*unsigned long*   [Runtime Function]
    long accum a)

    These functions return the negation of *a* with unsigned saturation.

short fract __ashlqq3 (*short fract* a, *int* b)   [Runtime Function]
fract __ashlhq3 (*fract* a, *int* b)   [Runtime Function]
long fract __ashlsq3 (*long fract* a, *int* b)   [Runtime Function]
long long fract __ashldq3 (*long long fract* a, *int* b)   [Runtime Function]
unsigned short fract __ashluqq3 (*unsigned short fract* a,   [Runtime Function]
    int b)
unsigned fract __ashluhq3 (*unsigned fract* a, *int* b)   [Runtime Function]
unsigned long fract __ashlusq3 (*unsigned long fract* a, *int*   [Runtime Function]
    b)
unsigned long long fract __ashludq3 (*unsigned long long*   [Runtime Function]
    fract a, *int* b)
short accum __ashlha3 (*short accum* a, *int* b)   [Runtime Function]
accum __ashlsa3 (*accum* a, *int* b)   [Runtime Function]
long accum __ashlda3 (*long accum* a, *int* b)   [Runtime Function]
long long accum __ashlta3 (*long long accum* a, *int* b)   [Runtime Function]
unsigned short accum __ashluha3 (*unsigned short accum* a,   [Runtime Function]
    int b)
unsigned accum __ashlusa3 (*unsigned accum* a, *int* b)   [Runtime Function]
unsigned long accum __ashluda3 (*unsigned long accum* a,   [Runtime Function]
    int b)

Chapter 4: The GCC low-level runtime library

<code>unsigned long long accum __ashluta3</code> (*unsigned long long accum* a, *int* b) [Runtime Function]

These functions return the result of shifting a left by b bits.

<code>short fract __ashrqq3</code> (*short fract* a, *int* b) [Runtime Function]
<code>fract __ashrhq3</code> (*fract* a, *int* b) [Runtime Function]
<code>long fract __ashrsq3</code> (*long fract* a, *int* b) [Runtime Function]
<code>long long fract __ashrdq3</code> (*long long fract* a, *int* b) [Runtime Function]
<code>short accum __ashrha3</code> (*short accum* a, *int* b) [Runtime Function]
<code>accum __ashrsa3</code> (*accum* a, *int* b) [Runtime Function]
<code>long accum __ashrda3</code> (*long accum* a, *int* b) [Runtime Function]
<code>long long accum __ashrta3</code> (*long long accum* a, *int* b) [Runtime Function]

These functions return the result of arithmetically shifting a right by b bits.

<code>unsigned short fract __lshruqq3</code> (*unsigned short fract* a, *int* b) [Runtime Function]
<code>unsigned fract __lshruhq3</code> (*unsigned fract* a, *int* b) [Runtime Function]
<code>unsigned long fract __lshrusq3</code> (*unsigned long fract* a, *int* b) [Runtime Function]
<code>unsigned long long fract __lshrudq3</code> (*unsigned long long fract* a, *int* b) [Runtime Function]
<code>unsigned short accum __lshruha3</code> (*unsigned short accum* a, *int* b) [Runtime Function]
<code>unsigned accum __lshrusa3</code> (*unsigned accum* a, *int* b) [Runtime Function]
<code>unsigned long accum __lshruda3</code> (*unsigned long accum* a, *int* b) [Runtime Function]
<code>unsigned long long accum __lshruta3</code> (*unsigned long long accum* a, *int* b) [Runtime Function]

These functions return the result of logically shifting a right by b bits.

<code>fract __ssashlhq3</code> (*fract* a, *int* b) [Runtime Function]
<code>long fract __ssashlsq3</code> (*long fract* a, *int* b) [Runtime Function]
<code>long long fract __ssashldq3</code> (*long long fract* a, *int* b) [Runtime Function]
<code>short accum __ssashlha3</code> (*short accum* a, *int* b) [Runtime Function]
<code>accum __ssashlsa3</code> (*accum* a, *int* b) [Runtime Function]
<code>long accum __ssashlda3</code> (*long accum* a, *int* b) [Runtime Function]
<code>long long accum __ssashlta3</code> (*long long accum* a, *int* b) [Runtime Function]

These functions return the result of shifting a left by b bits with signed saturation.

<code>unsigned short fract __usashluqq3</code> (*unsigned short fract* a, *int* b) [Runtime Function]
<code>unsigned fract __usashluhq3</code> (*unsigned fract* a, *int* b) [Runtime Function]
<code>unsigned long fract __usashlusq3</code> (*unsigned long fract* a, *int* b) [Runtime Function]
<code>unsigned long long fract __usashludq3</code> (*unsigned long long fract* a, *int* b) [Runtime Function]
<code>unsigned short accum __usashluha3</code> (*unsigned short accum* a, *int* b) [Runtime Function]

`unsigned accum __usashlusa3 (`*unsigned accum* `a,` *int* `b)`	[Runtime Function]
`unsigned long accum __usashluda3 (`*unsigned long accum* `a,` *int* `b)`	[Runtime Function]
`unsigned long long accum __usashluta3 (`*unsigned long long accum* `a,` *int* `b)`	[Runtime Function]

These functions return the result of shifting *a* left by *b* bits with unsigned saturation.

4.4.2 Comparison functions

The following functions implement fixed-point comparisons. These functions implement a low-level compare, upon which the higher level comparison operators (such as less than and greater than or equal to) can be constructed. The returned values lie in the range zero to two, to allow the high-level operators to be implemented by testing the returned result using either signed or unsigned comparison.

`int __cmpqq2 (`*short fract* `a,` *short fract* `b)`	[Runtime Function]
`int __cmphq2 (`*fract* `a,` *fract* `b)`	[Runtime Function]
`int __cmpsq2 (`*long fract* `a,` *long fract* `b)`	[Runtime Function]
`int __cmpdq2 (`*long long fract* `a,` *long long fract* `b)`	[Runtime Function]
`int __cmpuqq2 (`*unsigned short fract* `a,` *unsigned short fract* `b)`	[Runtime Function]
`int __cmpuhq2 (`*unsigned fract* `a,` *unsigned fract* `b)`	[Runtime Function]
`int __cmpusq2 (`*unsigned long fract* `a,` *unsigned long fract* `b)`	[Runtime Function]
`int __cmpudq2 (`*unsigned long long fract* `a,` *unsigned long long fract* `b)`	[Runtime Function]
`int __cmpha2 (`*short accum* `a,` *short accum* `b)`	[Runtime Function]
`int __cmpsa2 (`*accum* `a,` *accum* `b)`	[Runtime Function]
`int __cmpda2 (`*long accum* `a,` *long accum* `b)`	[Runtime Function]
`int __cmpta2 (`*long long accum* `a,` *long long accum* `b)`	[Runtime Function]
`int __cmpuha2 (`*unsigned short accum* `a,` *unsigned short accum* `b)`	[Runtime Function]
`int __cmpusa2 (`*unsigned accum* `a,` *unsigned accum* `b)`	[Runtime Function]
`int __cmpuda2 (`*unsigned long accum* `a,` *unsigned long accum* `b)`	[Runtime Function]
`int __cmputa2 (`*unsigned long long accum* `a,` *unsigned long long accum* `b)`	[Runtime Function]

These functions perform a signed or unsigned comparison of *a* and *b* (depending on the selected machine mode). If *a* is less than *b*, they return 0; if *a* is greater than *b*, they return 2; and if *a* and *b* are equal they return 1.

4.4.3 Conversion functions

`fract __fractqqhq2 (`*short fract* `a)`	[Runtime Function]
`long fract __fractqqsq2 (`*short fract* `a)`	[Runtime Function]
`long long fract __fractqqdq2 (`*short fract* `a)`	[Runtime Function]
`short accum __fractqqha (`*short fract* `a)`	[Runtime Function]
`accum __fractqqsa (`*short fract* `a)`	[Runtime Function]
`long accum __fractqqda (`*short fract* `a)`	[Runtime Function]
`long long accum __fractqqta (`*short fract* `a)`	[Runtime Function]
`unsigned short fract __fractqquqq (`*short fract* `a)`	[Runtime Function]
`unsigned fract __fractqquhq (`*short fract* `a)`	[Runtime Function]

Chapter 4: The GCC low-level runtime library

`unsigned long fract __fractqqusq` (*short fract* a)	[Runtime Function]
`unsigned long long fract __fractqqudq` (*short fract* a)	[Runtime Function]
`unsigned short accum __fractqquha` (*short fract* a)	[Runtime Function]
`unsigned accum __fractqqusa` (*short fract* a)	[Runtime Function]
`unsigned long accum __fractqquda` (*short fract* a)	[Runtime Function]
`unsigned long long accum __fractqquta` (*short fract* a)	[Runtime Function]
`signed char __fractqqqi` (*short fract* a)	[Runtime Function]
`short __fractqqhi` (*short fract* a)	[Runtime Function]
`int __fractqqsi` (*short fract* a)	[Runtime Function]
`long __fractqqdi` (*short fract* a)	[Runtime Function]
`long long __fractqqti` (*short fract* a)	[Runtime Function]
`float __fractqqsf` (*short fract* a)	[Runtime Function]
`double __fractqqdf` (*short fract* a)	[Runtime Function]
`short fract __fracthqqq2` (*fract* a)	[Runtime Function]
`long fract __fracthqsq2` (*fract* a)	[Runtime Function]
`long long fract __fracthqdq2` (*fract* a)	[Runtime Function]
`short accum __fracthqha` (*fract* a)	[Runtime Function]
`accum __fracthqsa` (*fract* a)	[Runtime Function]
`long accum __fracthqda` (*fract* a)	[Runtime Function]
`long long accum __fracthqta` (*fract* a)	[Runtime Function]
`unsigned short fract __fracthquqq` (*fract* a)	[Runtime Function]
`unsigned fract __fracthquhq` (*fract* a)	[Runtime Function]
`unsigned long fract __fracthqusq` (*fract* a)	[Runtime Function]
`unsigned long long fract __fracthqudq` (*fract* a)	[Runtime Function]
`unsigned short accum __fracthquha` (*fract* a)	[Runtime Function]
`unsigned accum __fracthqusa` (*fract* a)	[Runtime Function]
`unsigned long accum __fracthquda` (*fract* a)	[Runtime Function]
`unsigned long long accum __fracthquta` (*fract* a)	[Runtime Function]
`signed char __fracthqqi` (*fract* a)	[Runtime Function]
`short __fracthqhi` (*fract* a)	[Runtime Function]
`int __fracthqsi` (*fract* a)	[Runtime Function]
`long __fracthqdi` (*fract* a)	[Runtime Function]
`long long __fracthqti` (*fract* a)	[Runtime Function]
`float __fracthqsf` (*fract* a)	[Runtime Function]
`double __fracthqdf` (*fract* a)	[Runtime Function]
`short fract __fractsqqq2` (*long fract* a)	[Runtime Function]
`fract __fractsqhq2` (*long fract* a)	[Runtime Function]
`long long fract __fractsqdq2` (*long fract* a)	[Runtime Function]
`short accum __fractsqha` (*long fract* a)	[Runtime Function]
`accum __fractsqsa` (*long fract* a)	[Runtime Function]
`long accum __fractsqda` (*long fract* a)	[Runtime Function]
`long long accum __fractsqta` (*long fract* a)	[Runtime Function]
`unsigned short fract __fractsquqq` (*long fract* a)	[Runtime Function]
`unsigned fract __fractsquhq` (*long fract* a)	[Runtime Function]
`unsigned long fract __fractsqusq` (*long fract* a)	[Runtime Function]
`unsigned long long fract __fractsqudq` (*long fract* a)	[Runtime Function]
`unsigned short accum __fractsquha` (*long fract* a)	[Runtime Function]

unsigned accum __fractsqusa (*long fract* a)	[Runtime Function]
unsigned long accum __fractsquda (*long fract* a)	[Runtime Function]
unsigned long long accum __fractsquta (*long fract* a)	[Runtime Function]
signed char __fractsqqi (*long fract* a)	[Runtime Function]
short __fractsqhi (*long fract* a)	[Runtime Function]
int __fractsqsi (*long fract* a)	[Runtime Function]
long __fractsqdi (*long fract* a)	[Runtime Function]
long long __fractsqti (*long fract* a)	[Runtime Function]
float __fractsqsf (*long fract* a)	[Runtime Function]
double __fractsqdf (*long fract* a)	[Runtime Function]
short fract __fractdqqq2 (*long long fract* a)	[Runtime Function]
fract __fractdqhq2 (*long long fract* a)	[Runtime Function]
long fract __fractdqsq2 (*long long fract* a)	[Runtime Function]
short accum __fractdqha (*long long fract* a)	[Runtime Function]
accum __fractdqsa (*long long fract* a)	[Runtime Function]
long accum __fractdqda (*long long fract* a)	[Runtime Function]
long long accum __fractdqta (*long long fract* a)	[Runtime Function]
unsigned short fract __fractdquqq (*long long fract* a)	[Runtime Function]
unsigned fract __fractdquhq (*long long fract* a)	[Runtime Function]
unsigned long fract __fractdqusq (*long long fract* a)	[Runtime Function]
unsigned long long fract __fractdqudq (*long long fract* a)	[Runtime Function]
unsigned short accum __fractdquha (*long long fract* a)	[Runtime Function]
unsigned accum __fractdqusa (*long long fract* a)	[Runtime Function]
unsigned long accum __fractdquda (*long long fract* a)	[Runtime Function]
unsigned long long accum __fractdquta (*long long fract* a)	[Runtime Function]
signed char __fractdqqi (*long long fract* a)	[Runtime Function]
short __fractdqhi (*long long fract* a)	[Runtime Function]
int __fractdqsi (*long long fract* a)	[Runtime Function]
long __fractdqdi (*long long fract* a)	[Runtime Function]
long long __fractdqti (*long long fract* a)	[Runtime Function]
float __fractdqsf (*long long fract* a)	[Runtime Function]
double __fractdqdf (*long long fract* a)	[Runtime Function]
short fract __fracthaqq (*short accum* a)	[Runtime Function]
fract __fracthahq (*short accum* a)	[Runtime Function]
long fract __fracthasq (*short accum* a)	[Runtime Function]
long long fract __fracthadq (*short accum* a)	[Runtime Function]
accum __fracthasa2 (*short accum* a)	[Runtime Function]
long accum __fracthada2 (*short accum* a)	[Runtime Function]
long long accum __fracthata2 (*short accum* a)	[Runtime Function]
unsigned short fract __fracthauqq (*short accum* a)	[Runtime Function]
unsigned fract __fracthauhq (*short accum* a)	[Runtime Function]
unsigned long fract __fracthausq (*short accum* a)	[Runtime Function]
unsigned long long fract __fracthaudq (*short accum* a)	[Runtime Function]
unsigned short accum __fracthauha (*short accum* a)	[Runtime Function]
unsigned accum __fracthausa (*short accum* a)	[Runtime Function]

unsigned long accum __fracthauda (*short accum* a) [Runtime Function]
unsigned long long accum __fracthauta (*short accum* a) [Runtime Function]
signed char __fracthaqi (*short accum* a) [Runtime Function]
short __fracthahi (*short accum* a) [Runtime Function]
int __fracthasi (*short accum* a) [Runtime Function]
long __fracthadi (*short accum* a) [Runtime Function]
long long __fracthati (*short accum* a) [Runtime Function]
float __fracthasf (*short accum* a) [Runtime Function]
double __fracthadf (*short accum* a) [Runtime Function]
short fract __fractsaqq (*accum* a) [Runtime Function]
fract __fractsahq (*accum* a) [Runtime Function]
long fract __fractsasq (*accum* a) [Runtime Function]
long long fract __fractsadq (*accum* a) [Runtime Function]
short accum __fractsaha2 (*accum* a) [Runtime Function]
long accum __fractsada2 (*accum* a) [Runtime Function]
long long accum __fractsata2 (*accum* a) [Runtime Function]
unsigned short fract __fractsauqq (*accum* a) [Runtime Function]
unsigned fract __fractsauhq (*accum* a) [Runtime Function]
unsigned long fract __fractsausq (*accum* a) [Runtime Function]
unsigned long long fract __fractsaudq (*accum* a) [Runtime Function]
unsigned short accum __fractsauha (*accum* a) [Runtime Function]
unsigned accum __fractsausa (*accum* a) [Runtime Function]
unsigned long accum __fractsauda (*accum* a) [Runtime Function]
unsigned long long accum __fractsauta (*accum* a) [Runtime Function]
signed char __fractsaqi (*accum* a) [Runtime Function]
short __fractsahi (*accum* a) [Runtime Function]
int __fractsasi (*accum* a) [Runtime Function]
long __fractsadi (*accum* a) [Runtime Function]
long long __fractsati (*accum* a) [Runtime Function]
float __fractsasf (*accum* a) [Runtime Function]
double __fractsadf (*accum* a) [Runtime Function]
short fract __fractdaqq (*long accum* a) [Runtime Function]
fract __fractdahq (*long accum* a) [Runtime Function]
long fract __fractdasq (*long accum* a) [Runtime Function]
long long fract __fractdadq (*long accum* a) [Runtime Function]
short accum __fractdaha2 (*long accum* a) [Runtime Function]
accum __fractdasa2 (*long accum* a) [Runtime Function]
long long accum __fractdata2 (*long accum* a) [Runtime Function]
unsigned short fract __fractdauqq (*long accum* a) [Runtime Function]
unsigned fract __fractdauhq (*long accum* a) [Runtime Function]
unsigned long fract __fractdausq (*long accum* a) [Runtime Function]
unsigned long long fract __fractdaudq (*long accum* a) [Runtime Function]
unsigned short accum __fractdauha (*long accum* a) [Runtime Function]
unsigned accum __fractdausa (*long accum* a) [Runtime Function]
unsigned long accum __fractdauda (*long accum* a) [Runtime Function]
unsigned long long accum __fractdauta (*long accum* a) [Runtime Function]
signed char __fractdaqi (*long accum* a) [Runtime Function]

short `__fractdahi` (*long accum* a)	[Runtime Function]
int `__fractdasi` (*long accum* a)	[Runtime Function]
long `__fractdadi` (*long accum* a)	[Runtime Function]
long long `__fractdati` (*long accum* a)	[Runtime Function]
float `__fractdasf` (*long accum* a)	[Runtime Function]
double `__fractdadf` (*long accum* a)	[Runtime Function]
short fract `__fracttaqq` (*long long accum* a)	[Runtime Function]
fract `__fracttahq` (*long long accum* a)	[Runtime Function]
long fract `__fracttasq` (*long long accum* a)	[Runtime Function]
long long fract `__fracttadq` (*long long accum* a)	[Runtime Function]
short accum `__fracttaha2` (*long long accum* a)	[Runtime Function]
accum `__fracttasa2` (*long long accum* a)	[Runtime Function]
long accum `__fracttada2` (*long long accum* a)	[Runtime Function]
unsigned short fract `__fracttauqq` (*long long accum* a)	[Runtime Function]
unsigned fract `__fracttauhq` (*long long accum* a)	[Runtime Function]
unsigned long fract `__fracttausq` (*long long accum* a)	[Runtime Function]
unsigned long long fract `__fracttaudq` (*long long accum* a)	[Runtime Function]
unsigned short accum `__fracttauha` (*long long accum* a)	[Runtime Function]
unsigned accum `__fracttausa` (*long long accum* a)	[Runtime Function]
unsigned long accum `__fracttauda` (*long long accum* a)	[Runtime Function]
unsigned long long accum `__fracttauta` (*long long accum* a)	[Runtime Function]
signed char `__fracttaqi` (*long long accum* a)	[Runtime Function]
short `__fracttahi` (*long long accum* a)	[Runtime Function]
int `__fracttasi` (*long long accum* a)	[Runtime Function]
long `__fracttadi` (*long long accum* a)	[Runtime Function]
long long `__fracttati` (*long long accum* a)	[Runtime Function]
float `__fracttasf` (*long long accum* a)	[Runtime Function]
double `__fracttadf` (*long long accum* a)	[Runtime Function]
short fract `__fractuqqqq` (*unsigned short fract* a)	[Runtime Function]
fract `__fractuqqhq` (*unsigned short fract* a)	[Runtime Function]
long fract `__fractuqqsq` (*unsigned short fract* a)	[Runtime Function]
long long fract `__fractuqqdq` (*unsigned short fract* a)	[Runtime Function]
short accum `__fractuqqha` (*unsigned short fract* a)	[Runtime Function]
accum `__fractuqqsa` (*unsigned short fract* a)	[Runtime Function]
long accum `__fractuqqda` (*unsigned short fract* a)	[Runtime Function]
long long accum `__fractuqqta` (*unsigned short fract* a)	[Runtime Function]
unsigned fract `__fractuqquhq2` (*unsigned short fract* a)	[Runtime Function]
unsigned long fract `__fractuqqusq2` (*unsigned short fract* a)	[Runtime Function]
unsigned long long fract `__fractuqqudq2` (*unsigned short fract* a)	[Runtime Function]
unsigned short accum `__fractuqquha` (*unsigned short fract* a)	[Runtime Function]
unsigned accum `__fractuqqusa` (*unsigned short fract* a)	[Runtime Function]

`unsigned long accum __fractuqquda` (*unsigned short fract* a) [Runtime Function]
`unsigned long long accum __fractuqquta` (*unsigned short fract* a) [Runtime Function]
`signed char __fractuqqqi` (*unsigned short fract* a) [Runtime Function]
`short __fractuqqhi` (*unsigned short fract* a) [Runtime Function]
`int __fractuqqsi` (*unsigned short fract* a) [Runtime Function]
`long __fractuqqdi` (*unsigned short fract* a) [Runtime Function]
`long long __fractuqqti` (*unsigned short fract* a) [Runtime Function]
`float __fractuqqsf` (*unsigned short fract* a) [Runtime Function]
`double __fractuqqdf` (*unsigned short fract* a) [Runtime Function]
`short fract __fractuhqqq` (*unsigned fract* a) [Runtime Function]
`fract __fractuhqhq` (*unsigned fract* a) [Runtime Function]
`long fract __fractuhqsq` (*unsigned fract* a) [Runtime Function]
`long long fract __fractuhqdq` (*unsigned fract* a) [Runtime Function]
`short accum __fractuhqha` (*unsigned fract* a) [Runtime Function]
`accum __fractuhqsa` (*unsigned fract* a) [Runtime Function]
`long accum __fractuhqda` (*unsigned fract* a) [Runtime Function]
`long long accum __fractuhqta` (*unsigned fract* a) [Runtime Function]
`unsigned short fract __fractuhquqq2` (*unsigned fract* a) [Runtime Function]
`unsigned long fract __fractuhqusq2` (*unsigned fract* a) [Runtime Function]
`unsigned long long fract __fractuhqudq2` (*unsigned fract* a) [Runtime Function]
`unsigned short accum __fractuhquha` (*unsigned fract* a) [Runtime Function]
`unsigned accum __fractuhqusa` (*unsigned fract* a) [Runtime Function]
`unsigned long accum __fractuhquda` (*unsigned fract* a) [Runtime Function]
`unsigned long long accum __fractuhquta` (*unsigned fract* a) [Runtime Function]
`signed char __fractuhqqi` (*unsigned fract* a) [Runtime Function]
`short __fractuhqhi` (*unsigned fract* a) [Runtime Function]
`int __fractuhqsi` (*unsigned fract* a) [Runtime Function]
`long __fractuhqdi` (*unsigned fract* a) [Runtime Function]
`long long __fractuhqti` (*unsigned fract* a) [Runtime Function]
`float __fractuhqsf` (*unsigned fract* a) [Runtime Function]
`double __fractuhqdf` (*unsigned fract* a) [Runtime Function]
`short fract __fractusqqq` (*unsigned long fract* a) [Runtime Function]
`fract __fractusqhq` (*unsigned long fract* a) [Runtime Function]
`long fract __fractusqsq` (*unsigned long fract* a) [Runtime Function]
`long long fract __fractusqdq` (*unsigned long fract* a) [Runtime Function]
`short accum __fractusqha` (*unsigned long fract* a) [Runtime Function]
`accum __fractusqsa` (*unsigned long fract* a) [Runtime Function]
`long accum __fractusqda` (*unsigned long fract* a) [Runtime Function]
`long long accum __fractusqta` (*unsigned long fract* a) [Runtime Function]
`unsigned short fract __fractusquqq2` (*unsigned long fract* a) [Runtime Function]
`unsigned fract __fractusquhq2` (*unsigned long fract* a) [Runtime Function]

unsigned long long fract __fractusqudq2 (*unsigned long fract* a) [Runtime Function]
unsigned short accum __fractusquha (*unsigned long fract* a) [Runtime Function]
unsigned accum __fractusqusa (*unsigned long fract* a) [Runtime Function]
unsigned long accum __fractusquda (*unsigned long fract* a) [Runtime Function]
unsigned long long accum __fractusquta (*unsigned long fract* a) [Runtime Function]
signed char __fractusqqi (*unsigned long fract* a) [Runtime Function]
short __fractusqhi (*unsigned long fract* a) [Runtime Function]
int __fractusqsi (*unsigned long fract* a) [Runtime Function]
long __fractusqdi (*unsigned long fract* a) [Runtime Function]
long long __fractusqti (*unsigned long fract* a) [Runtime Function]
float __fractusqsf (*unsigned long fract* a) [Runtime Function]
double __fractusqdf (*unsigned long fract* a) [Runtime Function]
short fract __fractudqqq (*unsigned long long fract* a) [Runtime Function]
fract __fractudqhq (*unsigned long long fract* a) [Runtime Function]
long fract __fractudqsq (*unsigned long long fract* a) [Runtime Function]
long long fract __fractudqdq (*unsigned long long fract* a) [Runtime Function]
short accum __fractudqha (*unsigned long long fract* a) [Runtime Function]
accum __fractudqsa (*unsigned long long fract* a) [Runtime Function]
long accum __fractudqda (*unsigned long long fract* a) [Runtime Function]
long long accum __fractudqta (*unsigned long long fract* a) [Runtime Function]
unsigned short fract __fractudquqq2 (*unsigned long long fract* a) [Runtime Function]
unsigned fract __fractudquhq2 (*unsigned long long fract* a) [Runtime Function]
unsigned long fract __fractudqusq2 (*unsigned long long fract* a) [Runtime Function]
unsigned short accum __fractudquha (*unsigned long long fract* a) [Runtime Function]
unsigned accum __fractudqusa (*unsigned long long fract* a) [Runtime Function]
unsigned long accum __fractudquda (*unsigned long long fract* a) [Runtime Function]
unsigned long long accum __fractudquta (*unsigned long long fract* a) [Runtime Function]
signed char __fractudqqi (*unsigned long long fract* a) [Runtime Function]
short __fractudqhi (*unsigned long long fract* a) [Runtime Function]
int __fractudqsi (*unsigned long long fract* a) [Runtime Function]
long __fractudqdi (*unsigned long long fract* a) [Runtime Function]
long long __fractudqti (*unsigned long long fract* a) [Runtime Function]
float __fractudqsf (*unsigned long long fract* a) [Runtime Function]
double __fractudqdf (*unsigned long long fract* a) [Runtime Function]
short fract __fractuhaqq (*unsigned short accum* a) [Runtime Function]
fract __fractuhahq (*unsigned short accum* a) [Runtime Function]
long fract __fractuhasq (*unsigned short accum* a) [Runtime Function]
long long fract __fractuhadq (*unsigned short accum* a) [Runtime Function]
short accum __fractuhaha (*unsigned short accum* a) [Runtime Function]

`accum __fractuhasa (`*`unsigned short accum`* `a)` [Runtime Function]
`long accum __fractuhada (`*`unsigned short accum`* `a)` [Runtime Function]
`long long accum __fractuhata (`*`unsigned short accum`* `a)` [Runtime Function]
`unsigned short fract __fractuhauqq (`*`unsigned short accum`* `a)` [Runtime Function]
`unsigned fract __fractuhauhq (`*`unsigned short accum`* `a)` [Runtime Function]
`unsigned long fract __fractuhausq (`*`unsigned short accum`* `a)` [Runtime Function]
`unsigned long long fract __fractuhaudq (`*`unsigned short accum`* `a)` [Runtime Function]
`unsigned accum __fractuhausa2 (`*`unsigned short accum`* `a)` [Runtime Function]
`unsigned long accum __fractuhauda2 (`*`unsigned short accum`* `a)` [Runtime Function]
`unsigned long long accum __fractuhauta2 (`*`unsigned short accum`* `a)` [Runtime Function]
`signed char __fractuhaqi (`*`unsigned short accum`* `a)` [Runtime Function]
`short __fractuhahi (`*`unsigned short accum`* `a)` [Runtime Function]
`int __fractuhasi (`*`unsigned short accum`* `a)` [Runtime Function]
`long __fractuhadi (`*`unsigned short accum`* `a)` [Runtime Function]
`long long __fractuhati (`*`unsigned short accum`* `a)` [Runtime Function]
`float __fractuhasf (`*`unsigned short accum`* `a)` [Runtime Function]
`double __fractuhadf (`*`unsigned short accum`* `a)` [Runtime Function]
`short fract __fractusaqq (`*`unsigned accum`* `a)` [Runtime Function]
`fract __fractusahq (`*`unsigned accum`* `a)` [Runtime Function]
`long fract __fractusasq (`*`unsigned accum`* `a)` [Runtime Function]
`long long fract __fractusadq (`*`unsigned accum`* `a)` [Runtime Function]
`short accum __fractusaha (`*`unsigned accum`* `a)` [Runtime Function]
`accum __fractusasa (`*`unsigned accum`* `a)` [Runtime Function]
`long accum __fractusada (`*`unsigned accum`* `a)` [Runtime Function]
`long long accum __fractusata (`*`unsigned accum`* `a)` [Runtime Function]
`unsigned short fract __fractusauqq (`*`unsigned accum`* `a)` [Runtime Function]
`unsigned fract __fractusauhq (`*`unsigned accum`* `a)` [Runtime Function]
`unsigned long fract __fractusausq (`*`unsigned accum`* `a)` [Runtime Function]
`unsigned long long fract __fractusaudq (`*`unsigned accum`* `a)` [Runtime Function]
`unsigned short accum __fractusauha2 (`*`unsigned accum`* `a)` [Runtime Function]
`unsigned long accum __fractusauda2 (`*`unsigned accum`* `a)` [Runtime Function]
`unsigned long long accum __fractusauta2 (`*`unsigned accum`* `a)` [Runtime Function]
`signed char __fractusaqi (`*`unsigned accum`* `a)` [Runtime Function]
`short __fractusahi (`*`unsigned accum`* `a)` [Runtime Function]
`int __fractusasi (`*`unsigned accum`* `a)` [Runtime Function]
`long __fractusadi (`*`unsigned accum`* `a)` [Runtime Function]
`long long __fractusati (`*`unsigned accum`* `a)` [Runtime Function]
`float __fractusasf (`*`unsigned accum`* `a)` [Runtime Function]
`double __fractusadf (`*`unsigned accum`* `a)` [Runtime Function]
`short fract __fractudaqq (`*`unsigned long accum`* `a)` [Runtime Function]

fract __fractudahq (*unsigned long accum* a) [Runtime Function]
long fract __fractudasq (*unsigned long accum* a) [Runtime Function]
long long fract __fractudadq (*unsigned long accum* a) [Runtime Function]
short accum __fractudaha (*unsigned long accum* a) [Runtime Function]
accum __fractudasa (*unsigned long accum* a) [Runtime Function]
long accum __fractudada (*unsigned long accum* a) [Runtime Function]
long long accum __fractudata (*unsigned long accum* a) [Runtime Function]
unsigned short fract __fractudauqq (*unsigned long accum* a) [Runtime Function]
unsigned fract __fractudauhq (*unsigned long accum* a) [Runtime Function]
unsigned long fract __fractudausq (*unsigned long accum* a) [Runtime Function]
unsigned long long fract __fractudaudq (*unsigned long accum* a) [Runtime Function]
unsigned short accum __fractudauha2 (*unsigned long accum* a) [Runtime Function]
unsigned accum __fractudausa2 (*unsigned long accum* a) [Runtime Function]
unsigned long long accum __fractudauta2 (*unsigned long accum* a) [Runtime Function]
signed char __fractudaqi (*unsigned long accum* a) [Runtime Function]
short __fractudahi (*unsigned long accum* a) [Runtime Function]
int __fractudasi (*unsigned long accum* a) [Runtime Function]
long __fractudadi (*unsigned long accum* a) [Runtime Function]
long long __fractudati (*unsigned long accum* a) [Runtime Function]
float __fractudasf (*unsigned long accum* a) [Runtime Function]
double __fractudadf (*unsigned long accum* a) [Runtime Function]
short fract __fractutaqq (*unsigned long long accum* a) [Runtime Function]
fract __fractutahq (*unsigned long long accum* a) [Runtime Function]
long fract __fractutasq (*unsigned long long accum* a) [Runtime Function]
long long fract __fractutadq (*unsigned long long accum* a) [Runtime Function]
short accum __fractutaha (*unsigned long long accum* a) [Runtime Function]
accum __fractutasa (*unsigned long long accum* a) [Runtime Function]
long accum __fractutada (*unsigned long long accum* a) [Runtime Function]
long long accum __fractutata (*unsigned long long accum* a) [Runtime Function]
unsigned short fract __fractutauqq (*unsigned long long accum* a) [Runtime Function]
unsigned fract __fractutauhq (*unsigned long long accum* a) [Runtime Function]
unsigned long fract __fractutausq (*unsigned long long accum* a) [Runtime Function]
unsigned long long fract __fractutaudq (*unsigned long long accum* a) [Runtime Function]
unsigned short accum __fractutauha2 (*unsigned long long accum* a) [Runtime Function]
unsigned accum __fractutausa2 (*unsigned long long accum* a) [Runtime Function]
unsigned long accum __fractutauda2 (*unsigned long long accum* a) [Runtime Function]

`signed char __fractutaqi` (*unsigned long long accum* a)	[Runtime Function]
`short __fractutahi` (*unsigned long long accum* a)	[Runtime Function]
`int __fractutasi` (*unsigned long long accum* a)	[Runtime Function]
`long __fractutadi` (*unsigned long long accum* a)	[Runtime Function]
`long long __fractutati` (*unsigned long long accum* a)	[Runtime Function]
`float __fractutasf` (*unsigned long long accum* a)	[Runtime Function]
`double __fractutadf` (*unsigned long long accum* a)	[Runtime Function]
`short fract __fractqiqq` (*signed char* a)	[Runtime Function]
`fract __fractqihq` (*signed char* a)	[Runtime Function]
`long fract __fractqisq` (*signed char* a)	[Runtime Function]
`long long fract __fractqidq` (*signed char* a)	[Runtime Function]
`short accum __fractqiha` (*signed char* a)	[Runtime Function]
`accum __fractqisa` (*signed char* a)	[Runtime Function]
`long accum __fractqida` (*signed char* a)	[Runtime Function]
`long long accum __fractqita` (*signed char* a)	[Runtime Function]
`unsigned short fract __fractqiuqq` (*signed char* a)	[Runtime Function]
`unsigned fract __fractqiuhq` (*signed char* a)	[Runtime Function]
`unsigned long fract __fractqiusq` (*signed char* a)	[Runtime Function]
`unsigned long long fract __fractqiudq` (*signed char* a)	[Runtime Function]
`unsigned short accum __fractqiuha` (*signed char* a)	[Runtime Function]
`unsigned accum __fractqiusa` (*signed char* a)	[Runtime Function]
`unsigned long accum __fractqiuda` (*signed char* a)	[Runtime Function]
`unsigned long long accum __fractqiuta` (*signed char* a)	[Runtime Function]
`short fract __fracthiqq` (*short* a)	[Runtime Function]
`fract __fracthihq` (*short* a)	[Runtime Function]
`long fract __fracthisq` (*short* a)	[Runtime Function]
`long long fract __fracthidq` (*short* a)	[Runtime Function]
`short accum __fracthiha` (*short* a)	[Runtime Function]
`accum __fracthisa` (*short* a)	[Runtime Function]
`long accum __fracthida` (*short* a)	[Runtime Function]
`long long accum __fracthita` (*short* a)	[Runtime Function]
`unsigned short fract __fracthiuqq` (*short* a)	[Runtime Function]
`unsigned fract __fracthiuhq` (*short* a)	[Runtime Function]
`unsigned long fract __fracthiusq` (*short* a)	[Runtime Function]
`unsigned long long fract __fracthiudq` (*short* a)	[Runtime Function]
`unsigned short accum __fracthiuha` (*short* a)	[Runtime Function]
`unsigned accum __fracthiusa` (*short* a)	[Runtime Function]
`unsigned long accum __fracthiuda` (*short* a)	[Runtime Function]
`unsigned long long accum __fracthiuta` (*short* a)	[Runtime Function]
`short fract __fractsiqq` (*int* a)	[Runtime Function]
`fract __fractsihq` (*int* a)	[Runtime Function]
`long fract __fractsisq` (*int* a)	[Runtime Function]
`long long fract __fractsidq` (*int* a)	[Runtime Function]
`short accum __fractsiha` (*int* a)	[Runtime Function]
`accum __fractsisa` (*int* a)	[Runtime Function]
`long accum __fractsida` (*int* a)	[Runtime Function]
`long long accum __fractsita` (*int* a)	[Runtime Function]

unsigned short fract __fractsiuqq (*int* a)	[Runtime Function]
unsigned fract __fractsiuhq (*int* a)	[Runtime Function]
unsigned long fract __fractsiusq (*int* a)	[Runtime Function]
unsigned long long fract __fractsiudq (*int* a)	[Runtime Function]
unsigned short accum __fractsiuha (*int* a)	[Runtime Function]
unsigned accum __fractsiusa (*int* a)	[Runtime Function]
unsigned long accum __fractsiuda (*int* a)	[Runtime Function]
unsigned long long accum __fractsiuta (*int* a)	[Runtime Function]
short fract __fractdiqq (*long* a)	[Runtime Function]
fract __fractdihq (*long* a)	[Runtime Function]
long fract __fractdisq (*long* a)	[Runtime Function]
long long fract __fractdidq (*long* a)	[Runtime Function]
short accum __fractdiha (*long* a)	[Runtime Function]
accum __fractdisa (*long* a)	[Runtime Function]
long accum __fractdida (*long* a)	[Runtime Function]
long long accum __fractdita (*long* a)	[Runtime Function]
unsigned short fract __fractdiuqq (*long* a)	[Runtime Function]
unsigned fract __fractdiuhq (*long* a)	[Runtime Function]
unsigned long fract __fractdiusq (*long* a)	[Runtime Function]
unsigned long long fract __fractdiudq (*long* a)	[Runtime Function]
unsigned short accum __fractdiuha (*long* a)	[Runtime Function]
unsigned accum __fractdiusa (*long* a)	[Runtime Function]
unsigned long accum __fractdiuda (*long* a)	[Runtime Function]
unsigned long long accum __fractdiuta (*long* a)	[Runtime Function]
short fract __fracttiqq (*long long* a)	[Runtime Function]
fract __fracttihq (*long long* a)	[Runtime Function]
long fract __fracttisq (*long long* a)	[Runtime Function]
long long fract __fracttidq (*long long* a)	[Runtime Function]
short accum __fracttiha (*long long* a)	[Runtime Function]
accum __fracttisa (*long long* a)	[Runtime Function]
long accum __fracttida (*long long* a)	[Runtime Function]
long long accum __fracttita (*long long* a)	[Runtime Function]
unsigned short fract __fracttiuqq (*long long* a)	[Runtime Function]
unsigned fract __fracttiuhq (*long long* a)	[Runtime Function]
unsigned long fract __fracttiusq (*long long* a)	[Runtime Function]
unsigned long long fract __fracttiudq (*long long* a)	[Runtime Function]
unsigned short accum __fracttiuha (*long long* a)	[Runtime Function]
unsigned accum __fracttiusa (*long long* a)	[Runtime Function]
unsigned long accum __fracttiuda (*long long* a)	[Runtime Function]
unsigned long long accum __fracttiuta (*long long* a)	[Runtime Function]
short fract __fractsfqq (*float* a)	[Runtime Function]
fract __fractsfhq (*float* a)	[Runtime Function]
long fract __fractsfsq (*float* a)	[Runtime Function]
long long fract __fractsfdq (*float* a)	[Runtime Function]
short accum __fractsfha (*float* a)	[Runtime Function]
accum __fractsfsa (*float* a)	[Runtime Function]
long accum __fractsfda (*float* a)	[Runtime Function]

`long long accum __fractsfta (`*float* a`)`	[Runtime Function]
`unsigned short fract __fractsfuqq (`*float* a`)`	[Runtime Function]
`unsigned fract __fractsfuhq (`*float* a`)`	[Runtime Function]
`unsigned long fract __fractsfusq (`*float* a`)`	[Runtime Function]
`unsigned long long fract __fractsfudq (`*float* a`)`	[Runtime Function]
`unsigned short accum __fractsfuha (`*float* a`)`	[Runtime Function]
`unsigned accum __fractsfusa (`*float* a`)`	[Runtime Function]
`unsigned long accum __fractsfuda (`*float* a`)`	[Runtime Function]
`unsigned long long accum __fractsfuta (`*float* a`)`	[Runtime Function]
`short fract __fractdfqq (`*double* a`)`	[Runtime Function]
`fract __fractdfhq (`*double* a`)`	[Runtime Function]
`long fract __fractdfsq (`*double* a`)`	[Runtime Function]
`long long fract __fractdfdq (`*double* a`)`	[Runtime Function]
`short accum __fractdfha (`*double* a`)`	[Runtime Function]
`accum __fractdfsa (`*double* a`)`	[Runtime Function]
`long accum __fractdfda (`*double* a`)`	[Runtime Function]
`long long accum __fractdfta (`*double* a`)`	[Runtime Function]
`unsigned short fract __fractdfuqq (`*double* a`)`	[Runtime Function]
`unsigned fract __fractdfuhq (`*double* a`)`	[Runtime Function]
`unsigned long fract __fractdfusq (`*double* a`)`	[Runtime Function]
`unsigned long long fract __fractdfudq (`*double* a`)`	[Runtime Function]
`unsigned short accum __fractdfuha (`*double* a`)`	[Runtime Function]
`unsigned accum __fractdfusa (`*double* a`)`	[Runtime Function]
`unsigned long accum __fractdfuda (`*double* a`)`	[Runtime Function]
`unsigned long long accum __fractdfuta (`*double* a`)`	[Runtime Function]

These functions convert from fractional and signed non-fractionals to fractionals and signed non-fractionals, without saturation.

`fract __satfractqqhq2 (`*short fract* a`)`	[Runtime Function]
`long fract __satfractqqsq2 (`*short fract* a`)`	[Runtime Function]
`long long fract __satfractqqdq2 (`*short fract* a`)`	[Runtime Function]
`short accum __satfractqqha (`*short fract* a`)`	[Runtime Function]
`accum __satfractqqsa (`*short fract* a`)`	[Runtime Function]
`long accum __satfractqqda (`*short fract* a`)`	[Runtime Function]
`long long accum __satfractqqta (`*short fract* a`)`	[Runtime Function]
`unsigned short fract __satfractqquqq (`*short fract* a`)`	[Runtime Function]
`unsigned fract __satfractqquhq (`*short fract* a`)`	[Runtime Function]
`unsigned long fract __satfractqqusq (`*short fract* a`)`	[Runtime Function]
`unsigned long long fract __satfractqqudq (`*short fract* a`)`	[Runtime Function]
`unsigned short accum __satfractqquha (`*short fract* a`)`	[Runtime Function]
`unsigned accum __satfractqqusa (`*short fract* a`)`	[Runtime Function]
`unsigned long accum __satfractqquda (`*short fract* a`)`	[Runtime Function]
`unsigned long long accum __satfractqquta (`*short fract* a`)`	[Runtime Function]
`short fract __satfracthqqq2 (`*fract* a`)`	[Runtime Function]
`long fract __satfracthqsq2 (`*fract* a`)`	[Runtime Function]

long long fract `__satfracthqdq2` (*fract* a) [Runtime Function]
short accum `__satfracthqha` (*fract* a) [Runtime Function]
accum `__satfracthqsa` (*fract* a) [Runtime Function]
long accum `__satfracthqda` (*fract* a) [Runtime Function]
long long accum `__satfracthqta` (*fract* a) [Runtime Function]
unsigned short fract `__satfracthquqq` (*fract* a) [Runtime Function]
unsigned fract `__satfracthquhq` (*fract* a) [Runtime Function]
unsigned long fract `__satfracthqusq` (*fract* a) [Runtime Function]
unsigned long long fract `__satfracthqudq` (*fract* a) [Runtime Function]
unsigned short accum `__satfracthquha` (*fract* a) [Runtime Function]
unsigned accum `__satfracthqusa` (*fract* a) [Runtime Function]
unsigned long accum `__satfracthquda` (*fract* a) [Runtime Function]
unsigned long long accum `__satfracthquta` (*fract* a) [Runtime Function]
short fract `__satfractsqqq2` (*long fract* a) [Runtime Function]
fract `__satfractsqhq2` (*long fract* a) [Runtime Function]
long long fract `__satfractsqdq2` (*long fract* a) [Runtime Function]
short accum `__satfractsqha` (*long fract* a) [Runtime Function]
accum `__satfractsqsa` (*long fract* a) [Runtime Function]
long accum `__satfractsqda` (*long fract* a) [Runtime Function]
long long accum `__satfractsqta` (*long fract* a) [Runtime Function]
unsigned short fract `__satfractsquqq` (*long fract* a) [Runtime Function]
unsigned fract `__satfractsquhq` (*long fract* a) [Runtime Function]
unsigned long fract `__satfractsqusq` (*long fract* a) [Runtime Function]
unsigned long long fract `__satfractsqudq` (*long fract* a) [Runtime Function]
unsigned short accum `__satfractsquha` (*long fract* a) [Runtime Function]
unsigned accum `__satfractsqusa` (*long fract* a) [Runtime Function]
unsigned long accum `__satfractsquda` (*long fract* a) [Runtime Function]
unsigned long long accum `__satfractsquta` (*long fract* a) [Runtime Function]
short fract `__satfractdqqq2` (*long long fract* a) [Runtime Function]
fract `__satfractdqhq2` (*long long fract* a) [Runtime Function]
long fract `__satfractdqsq2` (*long long fract* a) [Runtime Function]
short accum `__satfractdqha` (*long long fract* a) [Runtime Function]
accum `__satfractdqsa` (*long long fract* a) [Runtime Function]
long accum `__satfractdqda` (*long long fract* a) [Runtime Function]
long long accum `__satfractdqta` (*long long fract* a) [Runtime Function]
unsigned short fract `__satfractdquqq` (*long long fract* a) [Runtime Function]
unsigned fract `__satfractdquhq` (*long long fract* a) [Runtime Function]
unsigned long fract `__satfractdqusq` (*long long fract* a) [Runtime Function]
unsigned long long fract `__satfractdqudq` (*long long fract* a) [Runtime Function]
unsigned short accum `__satfractdquha` (*long long fract* a) [Runtime Function]
unsigned accum `__satfractdqusa` (*long long fract* a) [Runtime Function]
unsigned long accum `__satfractdquda` (*long long fract* a) [Runtime Function]
unsigned long long accum `__satfractdquta` (*long long fract* a) [Runtime Function]
short fract `__satfracthaqq` (*short accum* a) [Runtime Function]
fract `__satfracthahq` (*short accum* a) [Runtime Function]

Chapter 4: The GCC low-level runtime library

`long fract __satfracthasq` (*short accum* a) [Runtime Function]
`long long fract __satfracthadq` (*short accum* a) [Runtime Function]
`accum __satfracthasa2` (*short accum* a) [Runtime Function]
`long accum __satfracthada2` (*short accum* a) [Runtime Function]
`long long accum __satfracthata2` (*short accum* a) [Runtime Function]
`unsigned short fract __satfracthauqq` (*short accum* a) [Runtime Function]
`unsigned fract __satfracthauhq` (*short accum* a) [Runtime Function]
`unsigned long fract __satfracthausq` (*short accum* a) [Runtime Function]
`unsigned long long fract __satfracthaudq` (*short accum* a) [Runtime Function]
`unsigned short accum __satfracthauha` (*short accum* a) [Runtime Function]
`unsigned accum __satfracthausa` (*short accum* a) [Runtime Function]
`unsigned long accum __satfracthauda` (*short accum* a) [Runtime Function]
`unsigned long long accum __satfracthauta` (*short accum* a) [Runtime Function]
`short fract __satfractsaqq` (*accum* a) [Runtime Function]
`fract __satfractsahq` (*accum* a) [Runtime Function]
`long fract __satfractsasq` (*accum* a) [Runtime Function]
`long long fract __satfractsadq` (*accum* a) [Runtime Function]
`short accum __satfractsaha2` (*accum* a) [Runtime Function]
`long accum __satfractsada2` (*accum* a) [Runtime Function]
`long long accum __satfractsata2` (*accum* a) [Runtime Function]
`unsigned short fract __satfractsauqq` (*accum* a) [Runtime Function]
`unsigned fract __satfractsauhq` (*accum* a) [Runtime Function]
`unsigned long fract __satfractsausq` (*accum* a) [Runtime Function]
`unsigned long long fract __satfractsaudq` (*accum* a) [Runtime Function]
`unsigned short accum __satfractsauha` (*accum* a) [Runtime Function]
`unsigned accum __satfractsausa` (*accum* a) [Runtime Function]
`unsigned long accum __satfractsauda` (*accum* a) [Runtime Function]
`unsigned long long accum __satfractsauta` (*accum* a) [Runtime Function]
`short fract __satfractdaqq` (*long accum* a) [Runtime Function]
`fract __satfractdahq` (*long accum* a) [Runtime Function]
`long fract __satfractdasq` (*long accum* a) [Runtime Function]
`long long fract __satfractdadq` (*long accum* a) [Runtime Function]
`short accum __satfractdaha2` (*long accum* a) [Runtime Function]
`accum __satfractdasa2` (*long accum* a) [Runtime Function]
`long long accum __satfractdata2` (*long accum* a) [Runtime Function]
`unsigned short fract __satfractdauqq` (*long accum* a) [Runtime Function]
`unsigned fract __satfractdauhq` (*long accum* a) [Runtime Function]
`unsigned long fract __satfractdausq` (*long accum* a) [Runtime Function]
`unsigned long long fract __satfractdaudq` (*long accum* a) [Runtime Function]
`unsigned short accum __satfractdauha` (*long accum* a) [Runtime Function]
`unsigned accum __satfractdausa` (*long accum* a) [Runtime Function]
`unsigned long accum __satfractdauda` (*long accum* a) [Runtime Function]
`unsigned long long accum __satfractdauta` (*long accum* a) [Runtime Function]

short fract __satfracttaqq (*long long accum* a)	[Runtime Function]
fract __satfracttahq (*long long accum* a)	[Runtime Function]
long fract __satfracttasq (*long long accum* a)	[Runtime Function]
long long fract __satfracttadq (*long long accum* a)	[Runtime Function]
short accum __satfracttaha2 (*long long accum* a)	[Runtime Function]
accum __satfracttasa2 (*long long accum* a)	[Runtime Function]
long accum __satfracttada2 (*long long accum* a)	[Runtime Function]
unsigned short fract __satfracttauqq (*long long accum* a)	[Runtime Function]
unsigned fract __satfracttauhq (*long long accum* a)	[Runtime Function]
unsigned long fract __satfracttausq (*long long accum* a)	[Runtime Function]
unsigned long long fract __satfracttaudq (*long long accum* a)	[Runtime Function]
unsigned short accum __satfracttauha (*long long accum* a)	[Runtime Function]
unsigned accum __satfracttausa (*long long accum* a)	[Runtime Function]
unsigned long accum __satfracttauda (*long long accum* a)	[Runtime Function]
unsigned long long accum __satfracttauta (*long long accum* a)	[Runtime Function]
short fract __satfractuqqqq (*unsigned short fract* a)	[Runtime Function]
fract __satfractuqqhq (*unsigned short fract* a)	[Runtime Function]
long fract __satfractuqqsq (*unsigned short fract* a)	[Runtime Function]
long long fract __satfractuqqdq (*unsigned short fract* a)	[Runtime Function]
short accum __satfractuqqha (*unsigned short fract* a)	[Runtime Function]
accum __satfractuqqsa (*unsigned short fract* a)	[Runtime Function]
long accum __satfractuqqda (*unsigned short fract* a)	[Runtime Function]
long long accum __satfractuqqta (*unsigned short fract* a)	[Runtime Function]
unsigned fract __satfractuqquhq2 (*unsigned short fract* a)	[Runtime Function]
unsigned long fract __satfractuqqusq2 (*unsigned short fract* a)	[Runtime Function]
unsigned long long fract __satfractuqqudq2 (*unsigned short fract* a)	[Runtime Function]
unsigned short accum __satfractuqquha (*unsigned short fract* a)	[Runtime Function]
unsigned accum __satfractuqqusa (*unsigned short fract* a)	[Runtime Function]
unsigned long accum __satfractuqquda (*unsigned short fract* a)	[Runtime Function]
unsigned long long accum __satfractuqquta (*unsigned short fract* a)	[Runtime Function]
short fract __satfractuhqqq (*unsigned fract* a)	[Runtime Function]
fract __satfractuhqhq (*unsigned fract* a)	[Runtime Function]
long fract __satfractuhqsq (*unsigned fract* a)	[Runtime Function]
long long fract __satfractuhqdq (*unsigned fract* a)	[Runtime Function]
short accum __satfractuhqha (*unsigned fract* a)	[Runtime Function]
accum __satfractuhqsa (*unsigned fract* a)	[Runtime Function]
long accum __satfractuhqda (*unsigned fract* a)	[Runtime Function]
long long accum __satfractuhqta (*unsigned fract* a)	[Runtime Function]

unsigned short fract __satfractuhquqq2 (*unsigned fract* a) [Runtime Function]
unsigned long fract __satfractuhqusq2 (*unsigned fract* a) [Runtime Function]
unsigned long long fract __satfractuhqudq2 (*unsigned fract* a) [Runtime Function]
unsigned short accum __satfractuhquha (*unsigned fract* a) [Runtime Function]
unsigned accum __satfractuhqusa (*unsigned fract* a) [Runtime Function]
unsigned long accum __satfractuhquda (*unsigned fract* a) [Runtime Function]
unsigned long long accum __satfractuhquta (*unsigned fract* a) [Runtime Function]
short fract __satfractusqqq (*unsigned long fract* a) [Runtime Function]
fract __satfractusqhq (*unsigned long fract* a) [Runtime Function]
long fract __satfractusqsq (*unsigned long fract* a) [Runtime Function]
long long fract __satfractusqdq (*unsigned long fract* a) [Runtime Function]
short accum __satfractusqha (*unsigned long fract* a) [Runtime Function]
accum __satfractusqsa (*unsigned long fract* a) [Runtime Function]
long accum __satfractusqda (*unsigned long fract* a) [Runtime Function]
long long accum __satfractusqta (*unsigned long fract* a) [Runtime Function]
unsigned short fract __satfractusquqq2 (*unsigned long fract* a) [Runtime Function]
unsigned fract __satfractusquhq2 (*unsigned long fract* a) [Runtime Function]
unsigned long long fract __satfractusqudq2 (*unsigned long fract* a) [Runtime Function]
unsigned short accum __satfractusquha (*unsigned long fract* a) [Runtime Function]
unsigned accum __satfractusqusa (*unsigned long fract* a) [Runtime Function]
unsigned long accum __satfractusquda (*unsigned long fract* a) [Runtime Function]
unsigned long long accum __satfractusquta (*unsigned long fract* a) [Runtime Function]
short fract __satfractudqqq (*unsigned long long fract* a) [Runtime Function]
fract __satfractudqhq (*unsigned long long fract* a) [Runtime Function]
long fract __satfractudqsq (*unsigned long long fract* a) [Runtime Function]
long long fract __satfractudqdq (*unsigned long long fract* a) [Runtime Function]
short accum __satfractudqha (*unsigned long long fract* a) [Runtime Function]
accum __satfractudqsa (*unsigned long long fract* a) [Runtime Function]
long accum __satfractudqda (*unsigned long long fract* a) [Runtime Function]
long long accum __satfractudqta (*unsigned long long fract* a) [Runtime Function]
unsigned short fract __satfractudquqq2 (*unsigned long long fract* a) [Runtime Function]
unsigned fract __satfractudquhq2 (*unsigned long long fract* a) [Runtime Function]

unsigned long fract __satfractudqusq2 (*unsigned long long fract* a) [Runtime Function]

unsigned short accum __satfractudquha (*unsigned long long fract* a) [Runtime Function]

unsigned accum __satfractudqusa (*unsigned long long fract* a) [Runtime Function]

unsigned long accum __satfractudquda (*unsigned long long fract* a) [Runtime Function]

unsigned long long accum __satfractudquta (*unsigned long long fract* a) [Runtime Function]

short fract __satfractuhaqq (*unsigned short accum* a) [Runtime Function]
fract __satfractuhahq (*unsigned short accum* a) [Runtime Function]
long fract __satfractuhasq (*unsigned short accum* a) [Runtime Function]
long long fract __satfractuhadq (*unsigned short accum* a) [Runtime Function]
short accum __satfractuhaha (*unsigned short accum* a) [Runtime Function]
accum __satfractuhasa (*unsigned short accum* a) [Runtime Function]
long accum __satfractuhada (*unsigned short accum* a) [Runtime Function]
long long accum __satfractuhata (*unsigned short accum* a) [Runtime Function]
unsigned short fract __satfractuhauqq (*unsigned short accum* a) [Runtime Function]

unsigned fract __satfractuhauhq (*unsigned short accum* a) [Runtime Function]
unsigned long fract __satfractuhausq (*unsigned short accum* a) [Runtime Function]

unsigned long long fract __satfractuhaudq (*unsigned short accum* a) [Runtime Function]

unsigned accum __satfractuhausa2 (*unsigned short accum* a) [Runtime Function]

unsigned long accum __satfractuhauda2 (*unsigned short accum* a) [Runtime Function]

unsigned long long accum __satfractuhauta2 (*unsigned short accum* a) [Runtime Function]

short fract __satfractusaqq (*unsigned accum* a) [Runtime Function]
fract __satfractusahq (*unsigned accum* a) [Runtime Function]
long fract __satfractusasq (*unsigned accum* a) [Runtime Function]
long long fract __satfractusadq (*unsigned accum* a) [Runtime Function]
short accum __satfractusaha (*unsigned accum* a) [Runtime Function]
accum __satfractusasa (*unsigned accum* a) [Runtime Function]
long accum __satfractusada (*unsigned accum* a) [Runtime Function]
long long accum __satfractusata (*unsigned accum* a) [Runtime Function]
unsigned short fract __satfractusauqq (*unsigned accum* a) [Runtime Function]

unsigned fract __satfractusauhq (*unsigned accum* a) [Runtime Function]
unsigned long fract __satfractusausq (*unsigned accum* a) [Runtime Function]

unsigned long long fract __satfractusaudq (*unsigned accum* a) [Runtime Function]

Chapter 4: The GCC low-level runtime library

unsigned short accum `__satfractusauha2` (*unsigned accum* a) [Runtime Function]

unsigned long accum `__satfractusauda2` (*unsigned accum* a) [Runtime Function]

unsigned long long accum `__satfractusauta2` (*unsigned accum* a) [Runtime Function]

short fract `__satfractudaqq` (*unsigned long accum* a) [Runtime Function]

fract `__satfractudahq` (*unsigned long accum* a) [Runtime Function]

long fract `__satfractudasq` (*unsigned long accum* a) [Runtime Function]

long long fract `__satfractudadq` (*unsigned long accum* a) [Runtime Function]

short accum `__satfractudaha` (*unsigned long accum* a) [Runtime Function]

accum `__satfractudasa` (*unsigned long accum* a) [Runtime Function]

long accum `__satfractudada` (*unsigned long accum* a) [Runtime Function]

long long accum `__satfractudata` (*unsigned long accum* a) [Runtime Function]

unsigned short fract `__satfractudauqq` (*unsigned long accum* a) [Runtime Function]

unsigned fract `__satfractudauhq` (*unsigned long accum* a) [Runtime Function]

unsigned long fract `__satfractudausq` (*unsigned long accum* a) [Runtime Function]

unsigned long long fract `__satfractudaudq` (*unsigned long accum* a) [Runtime Function]

unsigned short accum `__satfractudauha2` (*unsigned long accum* a) [Runtime Function]

unsigned accum `__satfractudausa2` (*unsigned long accum* a) [Runtime Function]

unsigned long long accum `__satfractudauta2` (*unsigned long accum* a) [Runtime Function]

short fract `__satfractutaqq` (*unsigned long long accum* a) [Runtime Function]

fract `__satfractutahq` (*unsigned long long accum* a) [Runtime Function]

long fract `__satfractutasq` (*unsigned long long accum* a) [Runtime Function]

long long fract `__satfractutadq` (*unsigned long long accum* a) [Runtime Function]

short accum `__satfractutaha` (*unsigned long long accum* a) [Runtime Function]

accum `__satfractutasa` (*unsigned long long accum* a) [Runtime Function]

long accum `__satfractutada` (*unsigned long long accum* a) [Runtime Function]

long long accum `__satfractutata` (*unsigned long long accum* a) [Runtime Function]

unsigned short fract `__satfractutauqq` (*unsigned long long accum* a) [Runtime Function]

unsigned fract `__satfractutauhq` (*unsigned long long accum* a) [Runtime Function]

unsigned long fract `__satfractutausq` (*unsigned long long accum* a) [Runtime Function]

unsigned long long fract `__satfractutaudq` (*unsigned long long accum* a) [Runtime Function]

unsigned short accum `__satfractutauha2` (*unsigned long long accum* a) [Runtime Function]

`unsigned accum __satfractutausa2` (*unsigned long long accum* a)	[Runtime Function]
`unsigned long accum __satfractutauda2` (*unsigned long long accum* a)	[Runtime Function]
`short fract __satfractqiqq` (*signed char* a)	[Runtime Function]
`fract __satfractqihq` (*signed char* a)	[Runtime Function]
`long fract __satfractqisq` (*signed char* a)	[Runtime Function]
`long long fract __satfractqidq` (*signed char* a)	[Runtime Function]
`short accum __satfractqiha` (*signed char* a)	[Runtime Function]
`accum __satfractqisa` (*signed char* a)	[Runtime Function]
`long accum __satfractqida` (*signed char* a)	[Runtime Function]
`long long accum __satfractqita` (*signed char* a)	[Runtime Function]
`unsigned short fract __satfractqiuqq` (*signed char* a)	[Runtime Function]
`unsigned fract __satfractqiuhq` (*signed char* a)	[Runtime Function]
`unsigned long fract __satfractqiusq` (*signed char* a)	[Runtime Function]
`unsigned long long fract __satfractqiudq` (*signed char* a)	[Runtime Function]
`unsigned short accum __satfractqiuha` (*signed char* a)	[Runtime Function]
`unsigned accum __satfractqiusa` (*signed char* a)	[Runtime Function]
`unsigned long accum __satfractqiuda` (*signed char* a)	[Runtime Function]
`unsigned long long accum __satfractqiuta` (*signed char* a)	[Runtime Function]
`short fract __satfracthiqq` (*short* a)	[Runtime Function]
`fract __satfracthihq` (*short* a)	[Runtime Function]
`long fract __satfracthisq` (*short* a)	[Runtime Function]
`long long fract __satfracthidq` (*short* a)	[Runtime Function]
`short accum __satfracthiha` (*short* a)	[Runtime Function]
`accum __satfracthisa` (*short* a)	[Runtime Function]
`long accum __satfracthida` (*short* a)	[Runtime Function]
`long long accum __satfracthita` (*short* a)	[Runtime Function]
`unsigned short fract __satfracthiuqq` (*short* a)	[Runtime Function]
`unsigned fract __satfracthiuhq` (*short* a)	[Runtime Function]
`unsigned long fract __satfracthiusq` (*short* a)	[Runtime Function]
`unsigned long long fract __satfracthiudq` (*short* a)	[Runtime Function]
`unsigned short accum __satfracthiuha` (*short* a)	[Runtime Function]
`unsigned accum __satfracthiusa` (*short* a)	[Runtime Function]
`unsigned long accum __satfracthiuda` (*short* a)	[Runtime Function]
`unsigned long long accum __satfracthiuta` (*short* a)	[Runtime Function]
`short fract __satfractsiqq` (*int* a)	[Runtime Function]
`fract __satfractsihq` (*int* a)	[Runtime Function]
`long fract __satfractsisq` (*int* a)	[Runtime Function]
`long long fract __satfractsidq` (*int* a)	[Runtime Function]
`short accum __satfractsiha` (*int* a)	[Runtime Function]
`accum __satfractsisa` (*int* a)	[Runtime Function]
`long accum __satfractsida` (*int* a)	[Runtime Function]
`long long accum __satfractsita` (*int* a)	[Runtime Function]
`unsigned short fract __satfractsiuqq` (*int* a)	[Runtime Function]

`unsigned fract __satfractsiuhq (`*int* `a)`	[Runtime Function]
`unsigned long fract __satfractsiusq (`*int* `a)`	[Runtime Function]
`unsigned long long fract __satfractsiudq (`*int* `a)`	[Runtime Function]
`unsigned short accum __satfractsiuha (`*int* `a)`	[Runtime Function]
`unsigned accum __satfractsiusa (`*int* `a)`	[Runtime Function]
`unsigned long accum __satfractsiuda (`*int* `a)`	[Runtime Function]
`unsigned long long accum __satfractsiuta (`*int* `a)`	[Runtime Function]
`short fract __satfractdiqq (`*long* `a)`	[Runtime Function]
`fract __satfractdihq (`*long* `a)`	[Runtime Function]
`long fract __satfractdisq (`*long* `a)`	[Runtime Function]
`long long fract __satfractdidq (`*long* `a)`	[Runtime Function]
`short accum __satfractdiha (`*long* `a)`	[Runtime Function]
`accum __satfractdisa (`*long* `a)`	[Runtime Function]
`long accum __satfractdida (`*long* `a)`	[Runtime Function]
`long long accum __satfractdita (`*long* `a)`	[Runtime Function]
`unsigned short fract __satfractdiuqq (`*long* `a)`	[Runtime Function]
`unsigned fract __satfractdiuhq (`*long* `a)`	[Runtime Function]
`unsigned long fract __satfractdiusq (`*long* `a)`	[Runtime Function]
`unsigned long long fract __satfractdiudq (`*long* `a)`	[Runtime Function]
`unsigned short accum __satfractdiuha (`*long* `a)`	[Runtime Function]
`unsigned accum __satfractdiusa (`*long* `a)`	[Runtime Function]
`unsigned long accum __satfractdiuda (`*long* `a)`	[Runtime Function]
`unsigned long long accum __satfractdiuta (`*long* `a)`	[Runtime Function]
`short fract __satfracttiqq (`*long long* `a)`	[Runtime Function]
`fract __satfracttihq (`*long long* `a)`	[Runtime Function]
`long fract __satfracttisq (`*long long* `a)`	[Runtime Function]
`long long fract __satfracttidq (`*long long* `a)`	[Runtime Function]
`short accum __satfracttiha (`*long long* `a)`	[Runtime Function]
`accum __satfracttisa (`*long long* `a)`	[Runtime Function]
`long accum __satfracttida (`*long long* `a)`	[Runtime Function]
`long long accum __satfracttita (`*long long* `a)`	[Runtime Function]
`unsigned short fract __satfracttiuqq (`*long long* `a)`	[Runtime Function]
`unsigned fract __satfracttiuhq (`*long long* `a)`	[Runtime Function]
`unsigned long fract __satfracttiusq (`*long long* `a)`	[Runtime Function]
`unsigned long long fract __satfracttiudq (`*long long* `a)`	[Runtime Function]
`unsigned short accum __satfracttiuha (`*long long* `a)`	[Runtime Function]
`unsigned accum __satfracttiusa (`*long long* `a)`	[Runtime Function]
`unsigned long accum __satfracttiuda (`*long long* `a)`	[Runtime Function]
`unsigned long long accum __satfracttiuta (`*long long* `a)`	[Runtime Function]
`short fract __satfractsfqq (`*float* `a)`	[Runtime Function]
`fract __satfractsfhq (`*float* `a)`	[Runtime Function]
`long fract __satfractsfsq (`*float* `a)`	[Runtime Function]
`long long fract __satfractsfdq (`*float* `a)`	[Runtime Function]
`short accum __satfractsfha (`*float* `a)`	[Runtime Function]
`accum __satfractsfsa (`*float* `a)`	[Runtime Function]
`long accum __satfractsfda (`*float* `a)`	[Runtime Function]
`long long accum __satfractsfta (`*float* `a)`	[Runtime Function]

`unsigned short fract __satfractsfuqq (`*float* a`)`	[Runtime Function]
`unsigned fract __satfractsfuhq (`*float* a`)`	[Runtime Function]
`unsigned long fract __satfractsfusq (`*float* a`)`	[Runtime Function]
`unsigned long long fract __satfractsfudq (`*float* a`)`	[Runtime Function]
`unsigned short accum __satfractsfuha (`*float* a`)`	[Runtime Function]
`unsigned accum __satfractsfusa (`*float* a`)`	[Runtime Function]
`unsigned long accum __satfractsfuda (`*float* a`)`	[Runtime Function]
`unsigned long long accum __satfractsfuta (`*float* a`)`	[Runtime Function]
`short fract __satfractdfqq (`*double* a`)`	[Runtime Function]
`fract __satfractdfhq (`*double* a`)`	[Runtime Function]
`long fract __satfractdfsq (`*double* a`)`	[Runtime Function]
`long long fract __satfractdfdq (`*double* a`)`	[Runtime Function]
`short accum __satfractdfha (`*double* a`)`	[Runtime Function]
`accum __satfractdfsa (`*double* a`)`	[Runtime Function]
`long accum __satfractdfda (`*double* a`)`	[Runtime Function]
`long long accum __satfractdfta (`*double* a`)`	[Runtime Function]
`unsigned short fract __satfractdfuqq (`*double* a`)`	[Runtime Function]
`unsigned fract __satfractdfuhq (`*double* a`)`	[Runtime Function]
`unsigned long fract __satfractdfusq (`*double* a`)`	[Runtime Function]
`unsigned long long fract __satfractdfudq (`*double* a`)`	[Runtime Function]
`unsigned short accum __satfractdfuha (`*double* a`)`	[Runtime Function]
`unsigned accum __satfractdfusa (`*double* a`)`	[Runtime Function]
`unsigned long accum __satfractdfuda (`*double* a`)`	[Runtime Function]
`unsigned long long accum __satfractdfuta (`*double* a`)`	[Runtime Function]

The functions convert from fractional and signed non-fractionals to fractionals, with saturation.

`unsigned char __fractunsqqqi (`*short fract* a`)`	[Runtime Function]
`unsigned short __fractunsqqhi (`*short fract* a`)`	[Runtime Function]
`unsigned int __fractunsqqsi (`*short fract* a`)`	[Runtime Function]
`unsigned long __fractunsqqdi (`*short fract* a`)`	[Runtime Function]
`unsigned long long __fractunsqqti (`*short fract* a`)`	[Runtime Function]
`unsigned char __fractunshqqi (`*fract* a`)`	[Runtime Function]
`unsigned short __fractunshqhi (`*fract* a`)`	[Runtime Function]
`unsigned int __fractunshqsi (`*fract* a`)`	[Runtime Function]
`unsigned long __fractunshqdi (`*fract* a`)`	[Runtime Function]
`unsigned long long __fractunshqti (`*fract* a`)`	[Runtime Function]
`unsigned char __fractunssqqi (`*long fract* a`)`	[Runtime Function]
`unsigned short __fractunssqhi (`*long fract* a`)`	[Runtime Function]
`unsigned int __fractunssqsi (`*long fract* a`)`	[Runtime Function]
`unsigned long __fractunssqdi (`*long fract* a`)`	[Runtime Function]
`unsigned long long __fractunssqti (`*long fract* a`)`	[Runtime Function]
`unsigned char __fractunsdqqi (`*long long fract* a`)`	[Runtime Function]
`unsigned short __fractunsdqhi (`*long long fract* a`)`	[Runtime Function]
`unsigned int __fractunsdqsi (`*long long fract* a`)`	[Runtime Function]
`unsigned long __fractunsdqdi (`*long long fract* a`)`	[Runtime Function]
`unsigned long long __fractunsdqti (`*long long fract* a`)`	[Runtime Function]

unsigned char __fractunshaqi (*short accum* a) [Runtime Function]
unsigned short __fractunshahi (*short accum* a) [Runtime Function]
unsigned int __fractunshasi (*short accum* a) [Runtime Function]
unsigned long __fractunshadi (*short accum* a) [Runtime Function]
unsigned long long __fractunshati (*short accum* a) [Runtime Function]
unsigned char __fractunssaqi (*accum* a) [Runtime Function]
unsigned short __fractunssahi (*accum* a) [Runtime Function]
unsigned int __fractunssasi (*accum* a) [Runtime Function]
unsigned long __fractunssadi (*accum* a) [Runtime Function]
unsigned long long __fractunssati (*accum* a) [Runtime Function]
unsigned char __fractunsdaqi (*long accum* a) [Runtime Function]
unsigned short __fractunsdahi (*long accum* a) [Runtime Function]
unsigned int __fractunsdasi (*long accum* a) [Runtime Function]
unsigned long __fractunsdadi (*long accum* a) [Runtime Function]
unsigned long long __fractunsdati (*long accum* a) [Runtime Function]
unsigned char __fractunstaqi (*long long accum* a) [Runtime Function]
unsigned short __fractunstahi (*long long accum* a) [Runtime Function]
unsigned int __fractunstasi (*long long accum* a) [Runtime Function]
unsigned long __fractunstadi (*long long accum* a) [Runtime Function]
unsigned long long __fractunstati (*long long accum* a) [Runtime Function]
unsigned char __fractunsuqqi (*unsigned short fract* a) [Runtime Function]
unsigned short __fractunsuqhi (*unsigned short fract* a) [Runtime Function]
unsigned int __fractunsuqsi (*unsigned short fract* a) [Runtime Function]
unsigned long __fractunsuqdi (*unsigned short fract* a) [Runtime Function]
unsigned long long __fractunsuqti (*unsigned short fract* a) [Runtime Function]
unsigned char __fractunsuhqi (*unsigned fract* a) [Runtime Function]
unsigned short __fractunsuhhi (*unsigned fract* a) [Runtime Function]
unsigned int __fractunsuhsi (*unsigned fract* a) [Runtime Function]
unsigned long __fractunsuhdi (*unsigned fract* a) [Runtime Function]
unsigned long long __fractunsuhti (*unsigned fract* a) [Runtime Function]
unsigned char __fractunsusqi (*unsigned long fract* a) [Runtime Function]
unsigned short __fractunsushi (*unsigned long fract* a) [Runtime Function]
unsigned int __fractunsussi (*unsigned long fract* a) [Runtime Function]
unsigned long __fractunsusdi (*unsigned long fract* a) [Runtime Function]
unsigned long long __fractunsusti (*unsigned long fract* a) [Runtime Function]
unsigned char __fractunsudqi (*unsigned long long fract* a) [Runtime Function]
unsigned short __fractunsudhi (*unsigned long long fract* a) [Runtime Function]
unsigned int __fractunsudsi (*unsigned long long fract* a) [Runtime Function]
unsigned long __fractunsuddi (*unsigned long long fract* a) [Runtime Function]
unsigned long long __fractunsudti (*unsigned long long fract* a) [Runtime Function]
unsigned char __fractunsuhaqi (*unsigned short accum* a) [Runtime Function]
unsigned short __fractunsuhahi (*unsigned short accum* a) [Runtime Function]
unsigned int __fractunsuhasi (*unsigned short accum* a) [Runtime Function]

unsigned long __fractunsuhadi (*unsigned short accum* a) [Runtime Function]
unsigned long long __fractunsuhati (*unsigned short accum* a) [Runtime Function]
unsigned char __fractunsusaqi (*unsigned accum* a) [Runtime Function]
unsigned short __fractunsusahi (*unsigned accum* a) [Runtime Function]
unsigned int __fractunsusasi (*unsigned accum* a) [Runtime Function]
unsigned long __fractunsusadi (*unsigned accum* a) [Runtime Function]
unsigned long long __fractunsusati (*unsigned accum* a) [Runtime Function]
unsigned char __fractunsudaqi (*unsigned long accum* a) [Runtime Function]
unsigned short __fractunsudahi (*unsigned long accum* a) [Runtime Function]
unsigned int __fractunsudasi (*unsigned long accum* a) [Runtime Function]
unsigned long __fractunsudadi (*unsigned long accum* a) [Runtime Function]
unsigned long long __fractunsudati (*unsigned long accum* a) [Runtime Function]
unsigned char __fractunsutaqi (*unsigned long long accum* a) [Runtime Function]
unsigned short __fractunsutahi (*unsigned long long accum* a) [Runtime Function]
unsigned int __fractunsutasi (*unsigned long long accum* a) [Runtime Function]
unsigned long __fractunsutadi (*unsigned long long accum* a) [Runtime Function]
unsigned long long __fractunsutati (*unsigned long long accum* a) [Runtime Function]
short fract __fractunsqiqq (*unsigned char* a) [Runtime Function]
fract __fractunsqihq (*unsigned char* a) [Runtime Function]
long fract __fractunsqisq (*unsigned char* a) [Runtime Function]
long long fract __fractunsqidq (*unsigned char* a) [Runtime Function]
short accum __fractunsqiha (*unsigned char* a) [Runtime Function]
accum __fractunsqisa (*unsigned char* a) [Runtime Function]
long accum __fractunsqida (*unsigned char* a) [Runtime Function]
long long accum __fractunsqita (*unsigned char* a) [Runtime Function]
unsigned short fract __fractunsqiuqq (*unsigned char* a) [Runtime Function]
unsigned fract __fractunsqiuhq (*unsigned char* a) [Runtime Function]
unsigned long fract __fractunsqiusq (*unsigned char* a) [Runtime Function]
unsigned long long fract __fractunsqiudq (*unsigned char* a) [Runtime Function]
unsigned short accum __fractunsqiuha (*unsigned char* a) [Runtime Function]
unsigned accum __fractunsqiusa (*unsigned char* a) [Runtime Function]
unsigned long accum __fractunsqiuda (*unsigned char* a) [Runtime Function]
unsigned long long accum __fractunsqiuta (*unsigned char* a) [Runtime Function]
short fract __fractunshiqq (*unsigned short* a) [Runtime Function]
fract __fractunshihq (*unsigned short* a) [Runtime Function]
long fract __fractunshisq (*unsigned short* a) [Runtime Function]
long long fract __fractunshidq (*unsigned short* a) [Runtime Function]
short accum __fractunshiha (*unsigned short* a) [Runtime Function]
accum __fractunshisa (*unsigned short* a) [Runtime Function]

`long accum __fractunshida (`*unsigned short* `a)`	[Runtime Function]
`long long accum __fractunshita (`*unsigned short* `a)`	[Runtime Function]
`unsigned short fract __fractunshiuqq (`*unsigned short* `a)`	[Runtime Function]
`unsigned fract __fractunshiuhq (`*unsigned short* `a)`	[Runtime Function]
`unsigned long fract __fractunshiusq (`*unsigned short* `a)`	[Runtime Function]
`unsigned long long fract __fractunshiudq (`*unsigned short* `a)`	[Runtime Function]
`unsigned short accum __fractunshiuha (`*unsigned short* `a)`	[Runtime Function]
`unsigned accum __fractunshiusa (`*unsigned short* `a)`	[Runtime Function]
`unsigned long accum __fractunshiuda (`*unsigned short* `a)`	[Runtime Function]
`unsigned long long accum __fractunshiuta (`*unsigned short* `a)`	[Runtime Function]
`short fract __fractunssiqq (`*unsigned int* `a)`	[Runtime Function]
`fract __fractunssihq (`*unsigned int* `a)`	[Runtime Function]
`long fract __fractunssisq (`*unsigned int* `a)`	[Runtime Function]
`long long fract __fractunssidq (`*unsigned int* `a)`	[Runtime Function]
`short accum __fractunssiha (`*unsigned int* `a)`	[Runtime Function]
`accum __fractunssisa (`*unsigned int* `a)`	[Runtime Function]
`long accum __fractunssida (`*unsigned int* `a)`	[Runtime Function]
`long long accum __fractunssita (`*unsigned int* `a)`	[Runtime Function]
`unsigned short fract __fractunssiuqq (`*unsigned int* `a)`	[Runtime Function]
`unsigned fract __fractunssiuhq (`*unsigned int* `a)`	[Runtime Function]
`unsigned long fract __fractunssiusq (`*unsigned int* `a)`	[Runtime Function]
`unsigned long long fract __fractunssiudq (`*unsigned int* `a)`	[Runtime Function]
`unsigned short accum __fractunssiuha (`*unsigned int* `a)`	[Runtime Function]
`unsigned accum __fractunssiusa (`*unsigned int* `a)`	[Runtime Function]
`unsigned long accum __fractunssiuda (`*unsigned int* `a)`	[Runtime Function]
`unsigned long long accum __fractunssiuta (`*unsigned int* `a)`	[Runtime Function]
`short fract __fractunsdiqq (`*unsigned long* `a)`	[Runtime Function]
`fract __fractunsdihq (`*unsigned long* `a)`	[Runtime Function]
`long fract __fractunsdisq (`*unsigned long* `a)`	[Runtime Function]
`long long fract __fractunsdidq (`*unsigned long* `a)`	[Runtime Function]
`short accum __fractunsdiha (`*unsigned long* `a)`	[Runtime Function]
`accum __fractunsdisa (`*unsigned long* `a)`	[Runtime Function]
`long accum __fractunsdida (`*unsigned long* `a)`	[Runtime Function]
`long long accum __fractunsdita (`*unsigned long* `a)`	[Runtime Function]
`unsigned short fract __fractunsdiuqq (`*unsigned long* `a)`	[Runtime Function]
`unsigned fract __fractunsdiuhq (`*unsigned long* `a)`	[Runtime Function]
`unsigned long fract __fractunsdiusq (`*unsigned long* `a)`	[Runtime Function]
`unsigned long long fract __fractunsdiudq (`*unsigned long* `a)`	[Runtime Function]
`unsigned short accum __fractunsdiuha (`*unsigned long* `a)`	[Runtime Function]
`unsigned accum __fractunsdiusa (`*unsigned long* `a)`	[Runtime Function]
`unsigned long accum __fractunsdiuda (`*unsigned long* `a)`	[Runtime Function]

unsigned long long accum __fractunsdiuta (*unsigned long* a)   [Runtime Function]
short fract __fractunstiqq (*unsigned long long* a)   [Runtime Function]
fract __fractunstihq (*unsigned long long* a)   [Runtime Function]
long fract __fractunstisq (*unsigned long long* a)   [Runtime Function]
long long fract __fractunstidq (*unsigned long long* a)   [Runtime Function]
short accum __fractunstiha (*unsigned long long* a)   [Runtime Function]
accum __fractunstisa (*unsigned long long* a)   [Runtime Function]
long accum __fractunstida (*unsigned long long* a)   [Runtime Function]
long long accum __fractunstita (*unsigned long long* a)   [Runtime Function]
unsigned short fract __fractunstiuqq (*unsigned long long* a)   [Runtime Function]
unsigned fract __fractunstiuhq (*unsigned long long* a)   [Runtime Function]
unsigned long fract __fractunstiusq (*unsigned long long* a)   [Runtime Function]
unsigned long long fract __fractunstiudq (*unsigned long long* a)   [Runtime Function]
unsigned short accum __fractunstiuha (*unsigned long long* a)   [Runtime Function]
unsigned accum __fractunstiusa (*unsigned long long* a)   [Runtime Function]
unsigned long accum __fractunstiuda (*unsigned long long* a)   [Runtime Function]
unsigned long long accum __fractunstiuta (*unsigned long long* a)   [Runtime Function]

    These functions convert from fractionals to unsigned non-fractionals; and from unsigned non-fractionals to fractionals, without saturation.

short fract __satfractunsqiqq (*unsigned char* a)   [Runtime Function]
fract __satfractunsqihq (*unsigned char* a)   [Runtime Function]
long fract __satfractunsqisq (*unsigned char* a)   [Runtime Function]
long long fract __satfractunsqidq (*unsigned char* a)   [Runtime Function]
short accum __satfractunsqiha (*unsigned char* a)   [Runtime Function]
accum __satfractunsqisa (*unsigned char* a)   [Runtime Function]
long accum __satfractunsqida (*unsigned char* a)   [Runtime Function]
long long accum __satfractunsqita (*unsigned char* a)   [Runtime Function]
unsigned short fract __satfractunsqiuqq (*unsigned char* a)   [Runtime Function]
unsigned fract __satfractunsqiuhq (*unsigned char* a)   [Runtime Function]
unsigned long fract __satfractunsqiusq (*unsigned char* a)   [Runtime Function]
unsigned long long fract __satfractunsqiudq (*unsigned char* a)   [Runtime Function]
unsigned short accum __satfractunsqiuha (*unsigned char* a)   [Runtime Function]
unsigned accum __satfractunsqiusa (*unsigned char* a)   [Runtime Function]
unsigned long accum __satfractunsqiuda (*unsigned char* a)   [Runtime Function]

`unsigned long long accum __satfractunsqiuta` (*unsigned char* a)	[Runtime Function]
`short fract __satfractunshiqq` (*unsigned short* a)	[Runtime Function]
`fract __satfractunshihq` (*unsigned short* a)	[Runtime Function]
`long fract __satfractunshisq` (*unsigned short* a)	[Runtime Function]
`long long fract __satfractunshidq` (*unsigned short* a)	[Runtime Function]
`short accum __satfractunshiha` (*unsigned short* a)	[Runtime Function]
`accum __satfractunshisa` (*unsigned short* a)	[Runtime Function]
`long accum __satfractunshida` (*unsigned short* a)	[Runtime Function]
`long long accum __satfractunshita` (*unsigned short* a)	[Runtime Function]
`unsigned short fract __satfractunshiuqq` (*unsigned short* a)	[Runtime Function]
`unsigned fract __satfractunshiuhq` (*unsigned short* a)	[Runtime Function]
`unsigned long fract __satfractunshiusq` (*unsigned short* a)	[Runtime Function]
`unsigned long long fract __satfractunshiudq` (*unsigned short* a)	[Runtime Function]
`unsigned short accum __satfractunshiuha` (*unsigned short* a)	[Runtime Function]
`unsigned accum __satfractunshiusa` (*unsigned short* a)	[Runtime Function]
`unsigned long accum __satfractunshiuda` (*unsigned short* a)	[Runtime Function]
`unsigned long long accum __satfractunshiuta` (*unsigned short* a)	[Runtime Function]
`short fract __satfractunssiqq` (*unsigned int* a)	[Runtime Function]
`fract __satfractunssihq` (*unsigned int* a)	[Runtime Function]
`long fract __satfractunssisq` (*unsigned int* a)	[Runtime Function]
`long long fract __satfractunssidq` (*unsigned int* a)	[Runtime Function]
`short accum __satfractunssiha` (*unsigned int* a)	[Runtime Function]
`accum __satfractunssisa` (*unsigned int* a)	[Runtime Function]
`long accum __satfractunssida` (*unsigned int* a)	[Runtime Function]
`long long accum __satfractunssita` (*unsigned int* a)	[Runtime Function]
`unsigned short fract __satfractunssiuqq` (*unsigned int* a)	[Runtime Function]
`unsigned fract __satfractunssiuhq` (*unsigned int* a)	[Runtime Function]
`unsigned long fract __satfractunssiusq` (*unsigned int* a)	[Runtime Function]
`unsigned long long fract __satfractunssiudq` (*unsigned int* a)	[Runtime Function]
`unsigned short accum __satfractunssiuha` (*unsigned int* a)	[Runtime Function]
`unsigned accum __satfractunssiusa` (*unsigned int* a)	[Runtime Function]
`unsigned long accum __satfractunssiuda` (*unsigned int* a)	[Runtime Function]
`unsigned long long accum __satfractunssiuta` (*unsigned int* a)	[Runtime Function]
`short fract __satfractunsdiqq` (*unsigned long* a)	[Runtime Function]
`fract __satfractunsdihq` (*unsigned long* a)	[Runtime Function]
`long fract __satfractunsdisq` (*unsigned long* a)	[Runtime Function]

`long long fract __satfractunsdidq` (*unsigned long* a)	[Runtime Function]
`short accum __satfractunsdiha` (*unsigned long* a)	[Runtime Function]
`accum __satfractunsdisa` (*unsigned long* a)	[Runtime Function]
`long accum __satfractunsdida` (*unsigned long* a)	[Runtime Function]
`long long accum __satfractunsdita` (*unsigned long* a)	[Runtime Function]
`unsigned short fract __satfractunsdiuqq` (*unsigned long* a)	[Runtime Function]
`unsigned fract __satfractunsdiuhq` (*unsigned long* a)	[Runtime Function]
`unsigned long fract __satfractunsdiusq` (*unsigned long* a)	[Runtime Function]
`unsigned long long fract __satfractunsdiudq` (*unsigned long* a)	[Runtime Function]
`unsigned short accum __satfractunsdiuha` (*unsigned long* a)	[Runtime Function]
`unsigned accum __satfractunsdiusa` (*unsigned long* a)	[Runtime Function]
`unsigned long accum __satfractunsdiuda` (*unsigned long* a)	[Runtime Function]
`unsigned long long accum __satfractunsdiuta` (*unsigned long* a)	[Runtime Function]
`short fract __satfractunstiqq` (*unsigned long long* a)	[Runtime Function]
`fract __satfractunstihq` (*unsigned long long* a)	[Runtime Function]
`long fract __satfractunstisq` (*unsigned long long* a)	[Runtime Function]
`long long fract __satfractunstidq` (*unsigned long long* a)	[Runtime Function]
`short accum __satfractunstiha` (*unsigned long long* a)	[Runtime Function]
`accum __satfractunstisa` (*unsigned long long* a)	[Runtime Function]
`long accum __satfractunstida` (*unsigned long long* a)	[Runtime Function]
`long long accum __satfractunstita` (*unsigned long long* a)	[Runtime Function]
`unsigned short fract __satfractunstiuqq` (*unsigned long long* a)	[Runtime Function]
`unsigned fract __satfractunstiuhq` (*unsigned long long* a)	[Runtime Function]
`unsigned long fract __satfractunstiusq` (*unsigned long long* a)	[Runtime Function]
`unsigned long long fract __satfractunstiudq` (*unsigned long long* a)	[Runtime Function]
`unsigned short accum __satfractunstiuha` (*unsigned long long* a)	[Runtime Function]
`unsigned accum __satfractunstiusa` (*unsigned long long* a)	[Runtime Function]
`unsigned long accum __satfractunstiuda` (*unsigned long long* a)	[Runtime Function]
`unsigned long long accum __satfractunstiuta` (*unsigned long long* a)	[Runtime Function]

These functions convert from unsigned non-fractionals to fractionals, with saturation.

4.5 Language-independent routines for exception handling

document me!

`_Unwind_DeleteException`

Chapter 4: The GCC low-level runtime library   57

```
_Unwind_Find_FDE
_Unwind_ForcedUnwind
_Unwind_GetGR
_Unwind_GetIP
_Unwind_GetLanguageSpecificData
_Unwind_GetRegionStart
_Unwind_GetTextRelBase
_Unwind_GetDataRelBase
_Unwind_RaiseException
_Unwind_Resume
_Unwind_SetGR
_Unwind_SetIP
_Unwind_FindEnclosingFunction
_Unwind_SjLj_Register
_Unwind_SjLj_Unregister
_Unwind_SjLj_RaiseException
_Unwind_SjLj_ForcedUnwind
_Unwind_SjLj_Resume
__deregister_frame
__deregister_frame_info
__deregister_frame_info_bases
__register_frame
__register_frame_info
__register_frame_info_bases
__register_frame_info_table
__register_frame_info_table_bases
__register_frame_table
```

4.6 Miscellaneous runtime library routines

4.6.1 Cache control functions

void __clear_cache (char *beg, char *end)   [Runtime Function]
    This function clears the instruction cache between *beg* and *end*.

4.6.2 Split stack functions and variables

void * __splitstack_find (void *segment_arg, void *sp,   [Runtime Function]
    size_t len, void **next_segment, void **next_sp, void **initial_sp)
    When using '-fsplit-stack', this call may be used to iterate over the stack segments.
    It may be called like this:

```
void *next_segment = NULL;
void *next_sp = NULL;
void *initial_sp = NULL;
void *stack;
size_t stack_size;
while ((stack = __splitstack_find (next_segment, next_sp,
                                   &stack_size, &next_segment,
                                   &next_sp, &initial_sp))
       != NULL)
  {
    /* Stack segment starts at stack and is
       stack_size bytes long.  */
  }
```

There is no way to iterate over the stack segments of a different thread. However, what is permitted is for one thread to call this with the *segment_arg* and *sp* arguments NULL, to pass *next_segment*, *next_sp*, and *initial_sp* to a different thread, and then to suspend one way or another. A different thread may run the subsequent `__splitstack_find` iterations. Of course, this will only work if the first thread is suspended while the second thread is calling `__splitstack_find`. If not, the second thread could be looking at the stack while it is changing, and anything could happen.

`__morestack_segments` [Variable]
`__morestack_current_segment` [Variable]
`__morestack_initial_sp` [Variable]

Internal variables used by the '-fsplit-stack' implementation.

5 Language Front Ends in GCC

The interface to front ends for languages in GCC, and in particular the `tree` structure (see Chapter 11 [GENERIC], page 153), was initially designed for C, and many aspects of it are still somewhat biased towards C and C-like languages. It is, however, reasonably well suited to other procedural languages, and front ends for many such languages have been written for GCC.

Writing a compiler as a front end for GCC, rather than compiling directly to assembler or generating C code which is then compiled by GCC, has several advantages:

- GCC front ends benefit from the support for many different target machines already present in GCC.
- GCC front ends benefit from all the optimizations in GCC. Some of these, such as alias analysis, may work better when GCC is compiling directly from source code then when it is compiling from generated C code.
- Better debugging information is generated when compiling directly from source code than when going via intermediate generated C code.

Because of the advantages of writing a compiler as a GCC front end, GCC front ends have also been created for languages very different from those for which GCC was designed, such as the declarative logic/functional language Mercury. For these reasons, it may also be useful to implement compilers created for specialized purposes (for example, as part of a research project) as GCC front ends.

6 Source Tree Structure and Build System

This chapter describes the structure of the GCC source tree, and how GCC is built. The user documentation for building and installing GCC is in a separate manual (http://gcc.gnu.org/install/), with which it is presumed that you are familiar.

6.1 Configure Terms and History

The configure and build process has a long and colorful history, and can be confusing to anyone who doesn't know why things are the way they are. While there are other documents which describe the configuration process in detail, here are a few things that everyone working on GCC should know.

There are three system names that the build knows about: the machine you are building on (*build*), the machine that you are building for (*host*), and the machine that GCC will produce code for (*target*). When you configure GCC, you specify these with '--build=', '--host=', and '--target='.

Specifying the host without specifying the build should be avoided, as `configure` may (and once did) assume that the host you specify is also the build, which may not be true.

If build, host, and target are all the same, this is called a *native*. If build and host are the same but target is different, this is called a *cross*. If build, host, and target are all different this is called a *canadian* (for obscure reasons dealing with Canada's political party and the background of the person working on the build at that time). If host and target are the same, but build is different, you are using a cross-compiler to build a native for a different system. Some people call this a *host-x-host*, *crossed native*, or *cross-built native*. If build and target are the same, but host is different, you are using a cross compiler to build a cross compiler that produces code for the machine you're building on. This is rare, so there is no common way of describing it. There is a proposal to call this a *crossback*.

If build and host are the same, the GCC you are building will also be used to build the target libraries (like `libstdc++`). If build and host are different, you must have already built and installed a cross compiler that will be used to build the target libraries (if you configured with '--target=foo-bar', this compiler will be called `foo-bar-gcc`).

In the case of target libraries, the machine you're building for is the machine you specified with '--target'. So, build is the machine you're building on (no change there), host is the machine you're building for (the target libraries are built for the target, so host is the target you specified), and target doesn't apply (because you're not building a compiler, you're building libraries). The configure/make process will adjust these variables as needed. It also sets $with_cross_host to the original '--host' value in case you need it.

The `libiberty` support library is built up to three times: once for the host, once for the target (even if they are the same), and once for the build if build and host are different. This allows it to be used by all programs which are generated in the course of the build process.

6.2 Top Level Source Directory

The top level source directory in a GCC distribution contains several files and directories that are shared with other software distributions such as that of GNU Binutils. It also contains several subdirectories that contain parts of GCC and its runtime libraries:

'boehm-gc'
: The Boehm conservative garbage collector, optionally used as part of the ObjC runtime library when configured with '--enable-objc-gc'.

'config'
: Autoconf macros and Makefile fragments used throughout the tree.

'contrib'
: Contributed scripts that may be found useful in conjunction with GCC. One of these, 'contrib/texi2pod.pl', is used to generate man pages from Texinfo manuals as part of the GCC build process.

'fixincludes'
: The support for fixing system headers to work with GCC. See 'fixincludes/README' for more information. The headers fixed by this mechanism are installed in 'libsubdir/include-fixed'. Along with those headers, 'README-fixinc' is also installed, as 'libsubdir/include-fixed/README'.

'gcc'
: The main sources of GCC itself (except for runtime libraries), including optimizers, support for different target architectures, language front ends, and testsuites. See Section 6.3 [The 'gcc' Subdirectory], page 63, for details.

'gnattools'
: Support tools for GNAT.

'include'
: Headers for the libiberty library.

'intl'
: GNU libintl, from GNU gettext, for systems which do not include it in libc.

'libada'
: The Ada runtime library.

'libatomic'
: The runtime support library for atomic operations (e.g. for __sync and __atomic).

'libcpp'
: The C preprocessor library.

'libdecnumber'
: The Decimal Float support library.

'libffi'
: The libffi library, used as part of the Go runtime library.

'libgcc'
: The GCC runtime library.

'libgfortran'
: The Fortran runtime library.

'libgo'
: The Go runtime library. The bulk of this library is mirrored from the master Go repository.

'libgomp'
: The GNU Offloading and Multi Processing Runtime Library.

'libiberty'
: The libiberty library, used for portability and for some generally useful data structures and algorithms. See Section "Introduction" in GNU libiberty, for more information about this library.

'libitm'
: The runtime support library for transactional memory.

'libobjc'   The Objective-C and Objective-C++ runtime library.

'libquadmath'
            The runtime support library for quad-precision math operations.

'libssp'   The Stack protector runtime library.

'libstdc++-v3'
            The C++ runtime library.

'lto-plugin'
            Plugin used by the linker if link-time optimizations are enabled.

'maintainer-scripts'
            Scripts used by the gccadmin account on gcc.gnu.org.

'zlib'   The zlib compression library, used for compressing and uncompressing GCC's intermediate language in LTO object files.

The build system in the top level directory, including how recursion into subdirectories works and how building runtime libraries for multilibs is handled, is documented in a separate manual, included with GNU Binutils. See Section "GNU configure and build system" in The GNU configure and build system, for details.

6.3 The 'gcc' Subdirectory

The 'gcc' directory contains many files that are part of the C sources of GCC, other files used as part of the configuration and build process, and subdirectories including documentation and a testsuite. The files that are sources of GCC are documented in a separate chapter. See Chapter 9 [Passes and Files of the Compiler], page 123.

6.3.1 Subdirectories of 'gcc'

The 'gcc' directory contains the following subdirectories:

'language' Subdirectories for various languages. Directories containing a file 'config-lang.in' are language subdirectories. The contents of the subdirectories 'c' (for C), 'cp' (for C++), 'objc' (for Objective-C), 'objcp' (for Objective-C++), and 'lto' (for LTO) are documented in this manual (see Chapter 9 [Passes and Files of the Compiler], page 123); those for other languages are not. See Section 6.3.8 [Anatomy of a Language Front End], page 71, for details of the files in these directories.

'common'   Source files shared between the compiler drivers (such as gcc) and the compilers proper (such as 'cc1'). If an architecture defines target hooks shared between those places, it also has a subdirectory in 'common/config'. See Section 18.1 [Target Structure], page 461.

'config'   Configuration files for supported architectures and operating systems. See Section 6.3.9 [Anatomy of a Target Back End], page 75, for details of the files in this directory.

'doc'   Texinfo documentation for GCC, together with automatically generated man pages and support for converting the installation manual to HTML. See Section 6.3.7 [Documentation], page 69.

'ginclude'   System headers installed by GCC, mainly those required by the C standard of freestanding implementations. See Section 6.3.6 [Headers Installed by GCC], page 68, for details of when these and other headers are installed.

'po'   Message catalogs with translations of messages produced by GCC into various languages, 'language.po'. This directory also contains 'gcc.pot', the template for these message catalogues, 'exgettext', a wrapper around gettext to extract the messages from the GCC sources and create 'gcc.pot', which is run by 'make gcc.pot', and 'EXCLUDES', a list of files from which messages should not be extracted.

'testsuite' The GCC testsuites (except for those for runtime libraries). See Chapter 7 [Testsuites], page 79.

6.3.2 Configuration in the 'gcc' Directory

The 'gcc' directory is configured with an Autoconf-generated script 'configure'. The 'configure' script is generated from 'configure.ac' and 'aclocal.m4'. From the files 'configure.ac' and 'acconfig.h', Autoheader generates the file 'config.in'. The file 'cstamp-h.in' is used as a timestamp.

6.3.2.1 Scripts Used by 'configure'

'configure' uses some other scripts to help in its work:

- The standard GNU 'config.sub' and 'config.guess' files, kept in the top level directory, are used.
- The file 'config.gcc' is used to handle configuration specific to the particular target machine. The file 'config.build' is used to handle configuration specific to the particular build machine. The file 'config.host' is used to handle configuration specific to the particular host machine. (In general, these should only be used for features that cannot reasonably be tested in Autoconf feature tests.) See Section 6.3.2.2 [The 'config.build'; 'config.host'; and 'config.gcc' Files], page 64, for details of the contents of these files.
- Each language subdirectory has a file 'language/config-lang.in' that is used for front-end-specific configuration. See Section 6.3.8.2 [The Front End 'config-lang.in' File], page 73, for details of this file.
- A helper script 'configure.frag' is used as part of creating the output of 'configure'.

6.3.2.2 The 'config.build'; 'config.host'; and 'config.gcc' Files

The 'config.build' file contains specific rules for particular systems which GCC is built on. This should be used as rarely as possible, as the behavior of the build system can always be detected by autoconf.

The 'config.host' file contains specific rules for particular systems which GCC will run on. This is rarely needed.

Chapter 6: Source Tree Structure and Build System   65

The 'config.gcc' file contains specific rules for particular systems which GCC will generate code for. This is usually needed.

Each file has a list of the shell variables it sets, with descriptions, at the top of the file.

FIXME: document the contents of these files, and what variables should be set to control build, host and target configuration.

6.3.2.3 Files Created by `configure`

Here we spell out what files will be set up by 'configure' in the 'gcc' directory. Some other files are created as temporary files in the configuration process, and are not used in the subsequent build; these are not documented.

- 'Makefile' is constructed from 'Makefile.in', together with the host and target fragments (see Chapter 20 [Makefile Fragments], page 647) 't-*target*' and 'x-*host*' from 'config', if any, and language Makefile fragments '*language*/Make-lang.in'.

- 'auto-host.h' contains information about the host machine determined by 'configure'. If the host machine is different from the build machine, then 'auto-build.h' is also created, containing such information about the build machine.

- 'config.status' is a script that may be run to recreate the current configuration.

- 'configargs.h' is a header containing details of the arguments passed to 'configure' to configure GCC, and of the thread model used.

- 'cstamp-h' is used as a timestamp.

- If a language 'config-lang.in' file (see Section 6.3.8.2 [The Front End 'config-lang.in' File], page 73) sets outputs, then the files listed in outputs there are also generated.

The following configuration headers are created from the Makefile, using 'mkconfig.sh', rather than directly by 'configure'. 'config.h', 'bconfig.h' and 'tconfig.h' all contain the 'xm-*machine*.h' header, if any, appropriate to the host, build and target machines respectively, the configuration headers for the target, and some definitions; for the host and build machines, these include the autoconfigured headers generated by 'configure'. The other configuration headers are determined by 'config.gcc'. They also contain the typedefs for rtx, rtvec and tree.

- 'config.h', for use in programs that run on the host machine.

- 'bconfig.h', for use in programs that run on the build machine.

- 'tconfig.h', for use in programs and libraries for the target machine.

- 'tm_p.h', which includes the header '*machine*-protos.h' that contains prototypes for functions in the target '*machine*.c' file. The header '*machine*-protos.h' can include prototypes of functions that use rtl and tree data structures inside appropriate #ifdef RTX_CODE and #ifdef TREE_CODE conditional code segments. The '*machine*-protos.h' is included after the 'rtl.h' and/or 'tree.h' would have been included. The 'tm_p.h' also includes the header 'tm-preds.h' which is generated by 'genpreds' program during the build to define the declarations and inline functions for the predicate functions.

6.3.3 Build System in the 'gcc' Directory

FIXME: describe the build system, including what is built in what stages. Also list the various source files that are used in the build process but aren't source files of GCC itself and so aren't documented below (see Chapter 9 [Passes], page 123).

6.3.4 Makefile Targets

These targets are available from the 'gcc' directory:

all
: This is the default target. Depending on what your build/host/target configuration is, it coordinates all the things that need to be built.

doc
: Produce info-formatted documentation and man pages. Essentially it calls 'make man' and 'make info'.

dvi
: Produce DVI-formatted documentation.

pdf
: Produce PDF-formatted documentation.

html
: Produce HTML-formatted documentation.

man
: Generate man pages.

info
: Generate info-formatted pages.

mostlyclean
: Delete the files made while building the compiler.

clean
: That, and all the other files built by 'make all'.

distclean
: That, and all the files created by configure.

maintainer-clean
: Distclean plus any file that can be generated from other files. Note that additional tools may be required beyond what is normally needed to build GCC.

srcextra
: Generates files in the source directory that are not version-controlled but should go into a release tarball.

srcinfo
srcman
: Copies the info-formatted and manpage documentation into the source directory usually for the purpose of generating a release tarball.

install
: Installs GCC.

uninstall
: Deletes installed files, though this is not supported.

check
: Run the testsuite. This creates a 'testsuite' subdirectory that has various '.sum' and '.log' files containing the results of the testing. You can run subsets with, for example, 'make check-gcc'. You can specify specific tests by setting RUNTESTFLAGS to be the name of the '.exp' file, optionally followed by (for some tests) an equals and a file wildcard, like:

    ```
    make check-gcc RUNTESTFLAGS="execute.exp=19980413-*"
    ```

    Note that running the testsuite may require additional tools be installed, such as Tcl or DejaGnu.

Chapter 6: Source Tree Structure and Build System

The toplevel tree from which you start GCC compilation is not the GCC directory, but rather a complex Makefile that coordinates the various steps of the build, including bootstrapping the compiler and using the new compiler to build target libraries.

When GCC is configured for a native configuration, the default action for `make` is to do a full three-stage bootstrap. This means that GCC is built three times—once with the native compiler, once with the native-built compiler it just built, and once with the compiler it built the second time. In theory, the last two should produce the same results, which 'make compare' can check. Each stage is configured separately and compiled into a separate directory, to minimize problems due to ABI incompatibilities between the native compiler and GCC.

If you do a change, rebuilding will also start from the first stage and "bubble" up the change through the three stages. Each stage is taken from its build directory (if it had been built previously), rebuilt, and copied to its subdirectory. This will allow you to, for example, continue a bootstrap after fixing a bug which causes the stage2 build to crash. It does not provide as good coverage of the compiler as bootstrapping from scratch, but it ensures that the new code is syntactically correct (e.g., that you did not use GCC extensions by mistake), and avoids spurious bootstrap comparison failures[1].

Other targets available from the top level include:

`bootstrap-lean`
> Like `bootstrap`, except that the various stages are removed once they're no longer needed. This saves disk space.

`bootstrap2`
`bootstrap2-lean`
> Performs only the first two stages of bootstrap. Unlike a three-stage bootstrap, this does not perform a comparison to test that the compiler is running properly. Note that the disk space required by a "lean" bootstrap is approximately independent of the number of stages.

`stageN-bubble` (*N* = 1...4, `profile`, `feedback`)
> Rebuild all the stages up to *N*, with the appropriate flags, "bubbling" the changes as described above.

`all-stageN` (*N* = 1...4, `profile`, `feedback`)
> Assuming that stage *N* has already been built, rebuild it with the appropriate flags. This is rarely needed.

`cleanstrap`
> Remove everything ('make clean') and rebuilds ('make bootstrap').

`compare`
> Compares the results of stages 2 and 3. This ensures that the compiler is running properly, since it should produce the same object files regardless of how it itself was compiled.

`profiledbootstrap`
> Builds a compiler with profiling feedback information. In this case, the second and third stages are named 'profile' and 'feedback', respectively. For more information, see the installation instructions.

---

[1] Except if the compiler was buggy and miscompiled some of the files that were not modified. In this case, it's best to use `make restrap`.

restrap   Restart a bootstrap, so that everything that was not built with the system compiler is rebuilt.

stage*N*-start (*N* = 1...4, profile, feedback)
For each package that is bootstrapped, rename directories so that, for example, 'gcc' points to the stage*N* GCC, compiled with the stage*N-1* GCC[2].

You will invoke this target if you need to test or debug the stage*N* GCC. If you only need to execute GCC (but you need not run 'make' either to rebuild it or to run test suites), you should be able to work directly in the 'stage*N*-gcc' directory. This makes it easier to debug multiple stages in parallel.

stage   For each package that is bootstrapped, relocate its build directory to indicate its stage. For example, if the 'gcc' directory points to the stage2 GCC, after invoking this target it will be renamed to 'stage2-gcc'.

If you wish to use non-default GCC flags when compiling the stage2 and stage3 compilers, set BOOT_CFLAGS on the command line when doing 'make'.

Usually, the first stage only builds the languages that the compiler is written in: typically, C and maybe Ada. If you are debugging a miscompilation of a different stage2 front-end (for example, of the Fortran front-end), you may want to have front-ends for other languages in the first stage as well. To do so, set STAGE1_LANGUAGES on the command line when doing 'make'.

For example, in the aforementioned scenario of debugging a Fortran front-end miscompilation caused by the stage1 compiler, you may need a command like

    make stage2-bubble STAGE1_LANGUAGES=c,fortran

Alternatively, you can use per-language targets to build and test languages that are not enabled by default in stage1. For example, make f951 will build a Fortran compiler even in the stage1 build directory.

6.3.5 Library Source Files and Headers under the 'gcc' Directory

FIXME: list here, with explanation, all the C source files and headers under the 'gcc' directory that aren't built into the GCC executable but rather are part of runtime libraries and object files, such as 'crtstuff.c' and 'unwind-dw2.c'. See Section 6.3.6 [Headers Installed by GCC], page 68, for more information about the 'ginclude' directory.

6.3.6 Headers Installed by GCC

In general, GCC expects the system C library to provide most of the headers to be used with it. However, GCC will fix those headers if necessary to make them work with GCC, and will install some headers required of freestanding implementations. These headers are installed in '*libsubdir*/include'. Headers for non-C runtime libraries are also installed by GCC; these are not documented here. (FIXME: document them somewhere.)

Several of the headers GCC installs are in the 'ginclude' directory. These headers, 'iso646.h', 'stdarg.h', 'stdbool.h', and 'stddef.h', are installed in '*libsubdir*/include', unless the target Makefile fragment (see Section 20.1 [Target Fragment], page 647) overrides this by setting USER_H.

---

[2] Customarily, the system compiler is also termed the 'stage0' GCC.

In addition to these headers and those generated by fixing system headers to work with GCC, some other headers may also be installed in 'libsubdir/include'. 'config.gcc' may set `extra_headers`; this specifies additional headers under 'config' to be installed on some systems.

GCC installs its own version of `<float.h>`, from 'ginclude/float.h'. This is done to cope with command-line options that change the representation of floating point numbers.

GCC also installs its own version of `<limits.h>`; this is generated from 'glimits.h', together with 'limitx.h' and 'limity.h' if the system also has its own version of `<limits.h>`. (GCC provides its own header because it is required of ISO C freestanding implementations, but needs to include the system header from its own header as well because other standards such as POSIX specify additional values to be defined in `<limits.h>`.) The system's `<limits.h>` header is used via 'libsubdir/include/syslimits.h', which is copied from 'gsyslimits.h' if it does not need fixing to work with GCC; if it needs fixing, 'syslimits.h' is the fixed copy.

GCC can also install `<tgmath.h>`. It will do this when 'config.gcc' sets `use_gcc_tgmath` to yes.

6.3.7 Building Documentation

The main GCC documentation is in the form of manuals in Texinfo format. These are installed in Info format; DVI versions may be generated by 'make dvi', PDF versions by 'make pdf', and HTML versions by 'make html'. In addition, some man pages are generated from the Texinfo manuals, there are some other text files with miscellaneous documentation, and runtime libraries have their own documentation outside the 'gcc' directory. FIXME: document the documentation for runtime libraries somewhere.

6.3.7.1 Texinfo Manuals

The manuals for GCC as a whole, and the C and C++ front ends, are in files 'doc/*.texi'. Other front ends have their own manuals in files 'language/*.texi'. Common files 'doc/include/*.texi' are provided which may be included in multiple manuals; the following files are in 'doc/include':

'fdl.texi'
    The GNU Free Documentation License.

'funding.texi'
    The section "Funding Free Software".

'gcc-common.texi'
    Common definitions for manuals.

'gpl_v3.texi'
    The GNU General Public License.

'texinfo.tex'
    A copy of 'texinfo.tex' known to work with the GCC manuals.

DVI-formatted manuals are generated by 'make dvi', which uses `texi2dvi` (via the Makefile macro `$(TEXI2DVI)`). PDF-formatted manuals are generated by 'make pdf', which uses `texi2pdf` (via the Makefile macro `$(TEXI2PDF)`). HTML formatted manuals are generated by '`make html`'. Info manuals are generated by '`make info`' (which is run as part of a bootstrap); this generates the manuals in the source directory, using `makeinfo` via the Makefile macro `$(MAKEINFO)`, and they are included in release distributions.

Manuals are also provided on the GCC web site, in both HTML and PostScript forms. This is done via the script '`maintainer-scripts/update_web_docs_svn`'. Each manual to be provided online must be listed in the definition of `MANUALS` in that file; a file '`name.texi`' must only appear once in the source tree, and the output manual must have the same name as the source file. (However, other Texinfo files, included in manuals but not themselves the root files of manuals, may have names that appear more than once in the source tree.) The manual file '`name.texi`' should only include other files in its own directory or in '`doc/include`'. HTML manuals will be generated by '`makeinfo --html`', PostScript manuals by `texi2dvi` and `dvips`, and PDF manuals by `texi2pdf`. All Texinfo files that are parts of manuals must be version-controlled, even if they are generated files, for the generation of online manuals to work.

The installation manual, '`doc/install.texi`', is also provided on the GCC web site. The HTML version is generated by the script '`doc/install.texi2html`'.

6.3.7.2 Man Page Generation

Because of user demand, in addition to full Texinfo manuals, man pages are provided which contain extracts from those manuals. These man pages are generated from the Texinfo manuals using '`contrib/texi2pod.pl`' and `pod2man`. (The man page for g++, '`cp/g++.1`', just contains a '`.so`' reference to '`gcc.1`', but all the other man pages are generated from Texinfo manuals.)

Because many systems may not have the necessary tools installed to generate the man pages, they are only generated if the '`configure`' script detects that recent enough tools are installed, and the Makefiles allow generating man pages to fail without aborting the build. Man pages are also included in release distributions. They are generated in the source directory.

Magic comments in Texinfo files starting '`@c man`' control what parts of a Texinfo file go into a man page. Only a subset of Texinfo is supported by '`texi2pod.pl`', and it may be necessary to add support for more Texinfo features to this script when generating new man pages. To improve the man page output, some special Texinfo macros are provided in '`doc/include/gcc-common.texi`' which '`texi2pod.pl`' understands:

`@gcctabopt`
: Use in the form '`@table @gcctabopt`' for tables of options, where for printed output the effect of '`@code`' is better than that of '`@option`' but for man page output a different effect is wanted.

`@gccoptlist`
: Use for summary lists of options in manuals.

`@gol`
: Use at the end of each line inside '`@gccoptlist`'. This is necessary to avoid problems with differences in how the '`@gccoptlist`' macro is handled by different Texinfo formatters.

FIXME: describe the '`texi2pod.pl`' input language and magic comments in more detail.

6.3.7.3 Miscellaneous Documentation

In addition to the formal documentation that is installed by GCC, there are several other text files in the 'gcc' subdirectory with miscellaneous documentation:

'ABOUT-GCC-NLS'
: Notes on GCC's Native Language Support. FIXME: this should be part of this manual rather than a separate file.

'ABOUT-NLS'
: Notes on the Free Translation Project.

'COPYING'
'COPYING3'
: The GNU General Public License, Versions 2 and 3.

'COPYING.LIB'
'COPYING3.LIB'
: The GNU Lesser General Public License, Versions 2.1 and 3.

'*ChangeLog*'
'*/ChangeLog*'
: Change log files for various parts of GCC.

'LANGUAGES'
: Details of a few changes to the GCC front-end interface. FIXME: the information in this file should be part of general documentation of the front-end interface in this manual.

'ONEWS'
: Information about new features in old versions of GCC. (For recent versions, the information is on the GCC web site.)

'README.Portability'
: Information about portability issues when writing code in GCC. FIXME: why isn't this part of this manual or of the GCC Coding Conventions?

FIXME: document such files in subdirectories, at least 'config', 'c', 'cp', 'objc', 'testsuite'.

6.3.8 Anatomy of a Language Front End

A front end for a language in GCC has the following parts:

- A directory '*language*' under 'gcc' containing source files for that front end. See Section 6.3.8.1 [The Front End '*language*' Directory], page 72, for details.
- A mention of the language in the list of supported languages in 'gcc/doc/install.texi'.
- A mention of the name under which the language's runtime library is recognized by '--enable-shared=*package*' in the documentation of that option in 'gcc/doc/install.texi'.
- A mention of any special prerequisites for building the front end in the documentation of prerequisites in 'gcc/doc/install.texi'.
- Details of contributors to that front end in 'gcc/doc/contrib.texi'. If the details are in that front end's own manual then there should be a link to that manual's list in 'contrib.texi'.

- Information about support for that language in 'gcc/doc/frontends.texi'.
- Information about standards for that language, and the front end's support for them, in 'gcc/doc/standards.texi'. This may be a link to such information in the front end's own manual.
- Details of source file suffixes for that language and '-x lang' options supported, in 'gcc/doc/invoke.texi'.
- Entries in default_compilers in 'gcc.c' for source file suffixes for that language.
- Preferably testsuites, which may be under 'gcc/testsuite' or runtime library directories. FIXME: document somewhere how to write testsuite harnesses.
- Probably a runtime library for the language, outside the 'gcc' directory. FIXME: document this further.
- Details of the directories of any runtime libraries in 'gcc/doc/sourcebuild.texi'.
- Check targets in 'Makefile.def' for the top-level 'Makefile' to check just the compiler or the compiler and runtime library for the language.

If the front end is added to the official GCC source repository, the following are also necessary:

- At least one Bugzilla component for bugs in that front end and runtime libraries. This category needs to be added to the Bugzilla database.
- Normally, one or more maintainers of that front end listed in 'MAINTAINERS'.
- Mentions on the GCC web site in 'index.html' and 'frontends.html', with any relevant links on 'readings.html'. (Front ends that are not an official part of GCC may also be listed on 'frontends.html', with relevant links.)
- A news item on 'index.html', and possibly an announcement on the gcc-announce@gcc.gnu.org mailing list.
- The front end's manuals should be mentioned in 'maintainer-scripts/update_web_docs_svn' (see Section 6.3.7.1 [Texinfo Manuals], page 69) and the online manuals should be linked to from 'onlinedocs/index.html'.
- Any old releases or CVS repositories of the front end, before its inclusion in GCC, should be made available on the GCC FTP site ftp://gcc.gnu.org/pub/gcc/old-releases/.
- The release and snapshot script 'maintainer-scripts/gcc_release' should be updated to generate appropriate tarballs for this front end.
- If this front end includes its own version files that include the current date, 'maintainer-scripts/update_version' should be updated accordingly.

6.3.8.1 The Front End 'language' Directory

A front end 'language' directory contains the source files of that front end (but not of any runtime libraries, which should be outside the 'gcc' directory). This includes documentation, and possibly some subsidiary programs built alongside the front end. Certain files are special and other parts of the compiler depend on their names:

'config-lang.in'
: This file is required in all language subdirectories. See Section 6.3.8.2 [The Front End 'config-lang.in' File], page 73, for details of its contents

'Make-lang.in'
: This file is required in all language subdirectories. See Section 6.3.8.3 [The Front End 'Make-lang.in' File], page 74, for details of its contents.

'lang.opt'
: This file registers the set of switches that the front end accepts on the command line, and their '--help' text. See Chapter 8 [Options], page 115.

'lang-specs.h'
: This file provides entries for default_compilers in 'gcc.c' which override the default of giving an error that a compiler for that language is not installed.

'language-tree.def'
: This file, which need not exist, defines any language-specific tree codes.

6.3.8.2 The Front End 'config-lang.in' File

Each language subdirectory contains a 'config-lang.in' file. This file is a shell script that may define some variables describing the language:

language
: This definition must be present, and gives the name of the language for some purposes such as arguments to '--enable-languages'.

lang_requires
: If defined, this variable lists (space-separated) language front ends other than C that this front end requires to be enabled (with the names given being their language settings). For example, the Obj-C++ front end depends on the C++ and ObjC front ends, so sets 'lang_requires="objc c++"'.

subdir_requires
: If defined, this variable lists (space-separated) front end directories other than C that this front end requires to be present. For example, the Objective-C++ front end uses source files from the C++ and Objective-C front ends, so sets 'subdir_requires="cp objc"'.

target_libs
: If defined, this variable lists (space-separated) targets in the top level 'Makefile' to build the runtime libraries for this language, such as target-libobjc.

lang_dirs
: If defined, this variable lists (space-separated) top level directories (parallel to 'gcc'), apart from the runtime libraries, that should not be configured if this front end is not built.

build_by_default
: If defined to 'no', this language front end is not built unless enabled in a '--enable-languages' argument. Otherwise, front ends are built by default, subject to any special logic in 'configure.ac' (as is present to disable the Ada front end if the Ada compiler is not already installed).

boot_language
: If defined to 'yes', this front end is built in stage1 of the bootstrap. This is only relevant to front ends written in their own languages.

compilers
: If defined, a space-separated list of compiler executables that will be run by the driver. The names here will each end with '\$(exeext)'.

outputs
: If defined, a space-separated list of files that should be generated by 'configure' substituting values in them. This mechanism can be used to create a file 'language/Makefile' from 'language/Makefile.in', but this is deprecated, building everything from the single 'gcc/Makefile' is preferred.

gtfiles
: If defined, a space-separated list of files that should be scanned by 'gengtype.c' to generate the garbage collection tables and routines for this language. This excludes the files that are common to all front ends. See Chapter 23 [Type Information], page 655.

6.3.8.3 The Front End 'Make-lang.in' File

Each language subdirectory contains a 'Make-lang.in' file. It contains targets *lang.hook* (where *lang* is the setting of language in 'config-lang.in') for the following values of *hook*, and any other Makefile rules required to build those targets (which may if necessary use other Makefiles specified in outputs in 'config-lang.in', although this is deprecated). It also adds any testsuite targets that can use the standard rule in 'gcc/Makefile.in' to the variable lang_checks.

all.cross
start.encap
rest.encap
: FIXME: exactly what goes in each of these targets?

tags
: Build an etags 'TAGS' file in the language subdirectory in the source tree.

info
: Build info documentation for the front end, in the build directory. This target is only called by 'make bootstrap' if a suitable version of makeinfo is available, so does not need to check for this, and should fail if an error occurs.

dvi
: Build DVI documentation for the front end, in the build directory. This should be done using $(TEXI2DVI), with appropriate '-I' arguments pointing to directories of included files.

pdf
: Build PDF documentation for the front end, in the build directory. This should be done using $(TEXI2PDF), with appropriate '-I' arguments pointing to directories of included files.

html
: Build HTML documentation for the front end, in the build directory.

man
: Build generated man pages for the front end from Texinfo manuals (see Section 6.3.7.2 [Man Page Generation], page 70), in the build directory. This target is only called if the necessary tools are available, but should ignore errors so as not to stop the build if errors occur; man pages are optional and the tools involved may be installed in a broken way.

install-common
: Install everything that is part of the front end, apart from the compiler executables listed in compilers in 'config-lang.in'.

`install-info`
: Install info documentation for the front end, if it is present in the source directory. This target should have dependencies on info files that should be installed.

`install-man`
: Install man pages for the front end. This target should ignore errors.

`install-plugin`
: Install headers needed for plugins.

`srcextra` Copies its dependencies into the source directory. This generally should be used for generated files such as Bison output files which are not version-controlled, but should be included in any release tarballs. This target will be executed during a bootstrap if '`--enable-generated-files-in-srcdir`' was specified as a '`configure`' option.

`srcinfo`
`srcman` Copies its dependencies into the source directory. These targets will be executed during a bootstrap if '`--enable-generated-files-in-srcdir`' was specified as a '`configure`' option.

`uninstall`
: Uninstall files installed by installing the compiler. This is currently documented not to be supported, so the hook need not do anything.

`mostlyclean`
`clean`
`distclean`
`maintainer-clean`
: The language parts of the standard GNU '`*clean`' targets. See Section "Standard Targets for Users" in *GNU Coding Standards*, for details of the standard targets. For GCC, `maintainer-clean` should delete all generated files in the source directory that are not version-controlled, but should not delete anything that is.

'Make-lang.in' must also define a variable `lang_OBJS` to a list of host object files that are used by that language.

6.3.9 Anatomy of a Target Back End

A back end for a target architecture in GCC has the following parts:

- A directory '*machine*' under '`gcc/config`', containing a machine description '*machine*.md' file (see Chapter 17 [Machine Descriptions], page 327), header files '*machine*.h' and '*machine*-protos.h' and a source file '*machine*.c' (see Chapter 18 [Target Description Macros and Functions], page 461), possibly a target Makefile fragment '`t-`*machine*' (see Section 20.1 [The Target Makefile Fragment], page 647), and maybe some other files. The names of these files may be changed from the defaults given by explicit specifications in '`config.gcc`'.

- If necessary, a file '*machine*-modes.def' in the '*machine*' directory, containing additional machine modes to represent condition codes. See Section 18.15 [Condition Code], page 552, for further details.

- An optional '`machine.opt`' file in the '`machine`' directory, containing a list of target-specific options. You can also add other option files using the `extra_options` variable in '`config.gcc`'. See Chapter 8 [Options], page 115.
- Entries in '`config.gcc`' (see Section 6.3.2.2 [The '`config.gcc`' File], page 64) for the systems with this target architecture.
- Documentation in '`gcc/doc/invoke.texi`' for any command-line options supported by this target (see Section 18.3 [Run-time Target Specification], page 468). This means both entries in the summary table of options and details of the individual options.
- Documentation in '`gcc/doc/extend.texi`' for any target-specific attributes supported (see Section 18.24 [Defining target-specific uses of `__attribute__`], page 613), including where the same attribute is already supported on some targets, which are enumerated in the manual.
- Documentation in '`gcc/doc/extend.texi`' for any target-specific pragmas supported.
- Documentation in '`gcc/doc/extend.texi`' of any target-specific built-in functions supported.
- Documentation in '`gcc/doc/extend.texi`' of any target-specific format checking styles supported.
- Documentation in '`gcc/doc/md.texi`' of any target-specific constraint letters (see Section 17.8.5 [Constraints for Particular Machines], page 347).
- A note in '`gcc/doc/contrib.texi`' under the person or people who contributed the target support.
- Entries in '`gcc/doc/install.texi`' for all target triplets supported with this target architecture, giving details of any special notes about installation for this target, or saying that there are no special notes if there are none.
- Possibly other support outside the '`gcc`' directory for runtime libraries. FIXME: reference docs for this. The `libstdc++` porting manual needs to be installed as info for this to work, or to be a chapter of this manual.

GCC uses the macro `IN_TARGET_CODE` to distinguish between machine-specific '`.c`' and '`.cc`' files and machine-independent '`.c`' and '`.cc`' files. Machine-specific files should use the directive:

```
#define IN_TARGET_CODE 1
```

before including `config.h`.

If the back end is added to the official GCC source repository, the following are also necessary:

- An entry for the target architecture in '`readings.html`' on the GCC web site, with any relevant links.
- Details of the properties of the back end and target architecture in '`backends.html`' on the GCC web site.
- A news item about the contribution of support for that target architecture, in '`index.html`' on the GCC web site.
- Normally, one or more maintainers of that target listed in '`MAINTAINERS`'. Some existing architectures may be unmaintained, but it would be unusual to add support for a target that does not have a maintainer when support is added.

- Target triplets covering all 'config.gcc' stanzas for the target, in the list in 'contrib/config-list.mk'.

7 Testsuites

GCC contains several testsuites to help maintain compiler quality. Most of the runtime libraries and language front ends in GCC have testsuites. Currently only the C language testsuites are documented here; FIXME: document the others.

7.1 Idioms Used in Testsuite Code

In general, C testcases have a trailing '-*n*.c', starting with '-1.c', in case other testcases with similar names are added later. If the test is a test of some well-defined feature, it should have a name referring to that feature such as '*feature*-1.c'. If it does not test a well-defined feature but just happens to exercise a bug somewhere in the compiler, and a bug report has been filed for this bug in the GCC bug database, 'pr*bug-number*-1.c' is the appropriate form of name. Otherwise (for miscellaneous bugs not filed in the GCC bug database), and previously more generally, test cases are named after the date on which they were added. This allows people to tell at a glance whether a test failure is because of a recently found bug that has not yet been fixed, or whether it may be a regression, but does not give any other information about the bug or where discussion of it may be found. Some other language testsuites follow similar conventions.

In the 'gcc.dg' testsuite, it is often necessary to test that an error is indeed a hard error and not just a warning—for example, where it is a constraint violation in the C standard, which must become an error with '-pedantic-errors'. The following idiom, where the first line shown is line *line* of the file and the line that generates the error, is used for this:

```
/* { dg-bogus "warning" "warning in place of error" } */
/* { dg-error "regexp" "message" { target *-*-* } line } */
```

It may be necessary to check that an expression is an integer constant expression and has a certain value. To check that *E* has value *V*, an idiom similar to the following is used:

```
char x[((E) == (V) ? 1 : -1)];
```

In 'gcc.dg' tests, __typeof__ is sometimes used to make assertions about the types of expressions. See, for example, 'gcc.dg/c99-condexpr-1.c'. The more subtle uses depend on the exact rules for the types of conditional expressions in the C standard; see, for example, 'gcc.dg/c99-intconst-1.c'.

It is useful to be able to test that optimizations are being made properly. This cannot be done in all cases, but it can be done where the optimization will lead to code being optimized away (for example, where flow analysis or alias analysis should show that certain code cannot be called) or to functions not being called because they have been expanded as built-in functions. Such tests go in 'gcc.c-torture/execute'. Where code should be optimized away, a call to a nonexistent function such as link_failure () may be inserted; a definition

```
#ifndef __OPTIMIZE__
void
link_failure (void)
{
  abort ();
}
#endif
```

will also be needed so that linking still succeeds when the test is run without optimization.
When all calls to a built-in function should have been optimized and no calls to the non-built-in version of the function should remain, that function may be defined as `static` to call `abort ()` (although redeclaring a function as static may not work on all targets).

All testcases must be portable. Target-specific testcases must have appropriate code to avoid causing failures on unsupported systems; unfortunately, the mechanisms for this differ by directory.

FIXME: discuss non-C testsuites here.

7.2 Directives used within DejaGnu tests

7.2.1 Syntax and Descriptions of test directives

Test directives appear within comments in a test source file and begin with `dg-`. Some of these are defined within DejaGnu and others are local to the GCC testsuite.

The order in which test directives appear in a test can be important: directives local to GCC sometimes override information used by the DejaGnu directives, which know nothing about the GCC directives, so the DejaGnu directives must precede GCC directives.

Several test directives include selectors (see Section 7.2.2 [Selectors], page 84) which are usually preceded by the keyword `target` or `xfail`.

7.2.1.1 Specify how to build the test

`{ dg-do do-what-keyword [{ target/xfail selector }] }`

> *do-what-keyword* specifies how the test is compiled and whether it is executed. It is one of:
>
> **preprocess**
> > Compile with '-E' to run only the preprocessor.
>
> **compile** Compile with '-S' to produce an assembly code file.
>
> **assemble** Compile with '-c' to produce a relocatable object file.
>
> **link** Compile, assemble, and link to produce an executable file.
>
> **run** Produce and run an executable file, which is expected to return an exit code of 0.
>
> The default is `compile`. That can be overridden for a set of tests by redefining `dg-do-what-default` within the `.exp` file for those tests.
>
> If the directive includes the optional '{ target *selector* }' then the test is skipped unless the target system matches the *selector*.
>
> If *do-what-keyword* is `run` and the directive includes the optional '{ xfail *selector* }' and the selector is met then the test is expected to fail. The `xfail` clause is ignored for other values of *do-what-keyword*; those tests can use directive `dg-xfail-if`.

7.2.1.2 Specify additional compiler options

`{ dg-options` *options* `[{ target` *selector* `}] }`
: This DejaGnu directive provides a list of compiler options, to be used if the target system matches *selector*, that replace the default options used for this set of tests.

`{ dg-add-options` *feature* `... }`
: Add any compiler options that are needed to access certain features. This directive does nothing on targets that enable the features by default, or that don't provide them at all. It must come after all `dg-options` directives. For supported values of *feature* see Section 7.2.4 [Add Options], page 100.

`{ dg-additional-options` *options* `[{ target` *selector* `}] }`
: This directive provides a list of compiler options, to be used if the target system matches *selector*, that are added to the default options used for this set of tests.

7.2.1.3 Modify the test timeout value

The normal timeout limit, in seconds, is found by searching the following in order:

- the value defined by an earlier `dg-timeout` directive in the test
- variable *tool_timeout* defined by the set of tests
- *gcc,timeout* set in the target board
- 300

`{ dg-timeout` *n* `[{target` *selector* `}] }`
: Set the time limit for the compilation and for the execution of the test to the specified number of seconds.

`{ dg-timeout-factor` *x* `[{ target` *selector* `}] }`
: Multiply the normal time limit for compilation and execution of the test by the specified floating-point factor.

7.2.1.4 Skip a test for some targets

`{ dg-skip-if` *comment* `{` *selector* `}` `[{` *include-opts* `}` `[{` *exclude-opts* `}]] }`
: Arguments *include-opts* and *exclude-opts* are lists in which each element is a string of zero or more GCC options. Skip the test if all of the following conditions are met:

  - the test system is included in *selector*
  - for at least one of the option strings in *include-opts*, every option from that string is in the set of options with which the test would be compiled; use '"*"' for an *include-opts* list that matches any options; that is the default if *include-opts* is not specified
  - for each of the option strings in *exclude-opts*, at least one option from that string is not in the set of options with which the test would be compiled; use '""' for an empty *exclude-opts* list; that is the default if *exclude-opts* is not specified

For example, to skip a test if option `-Os` is present:

```
            /* { dg-skip-if "" { *-*-* } { "-Os" } { "" } } */
```
To skip a test if both options -O2 and -g are present:
```
            /* { dg-skip-if "" { *-*-* } { "-O2 -g" } { "" } } */
```
To skip a test if either -O2 or -O3 is present:
```
            /* { dg-skip-if "" { *-*-* } { "-O2" "-O3" } { "" } } */
```
To skip a test unless option -Os is present:
```
            /* { dg-skip-if "" { *-*-* } { "*" } { "-Os" } } */
```
To skip a test if either -O2 or -O3 is used with -g but not if -fpic is also present:
```
            /* { dg-skip-if "" { *-*-* } { "-O2 -g" "-O3 -g" } { "-fpic" } } */
```

{ dg-require-effective-target *keyword* [{ *selector* }] }
: Skip the test if the test target, including current multilib flags, is not covered by the effective-target keyword. If the directive includes the optional '{ *selector* }' then the effective-target test is only performed if the target system matches the *selector*. This directive must appear after any dg-do directive in the test and before any dg-additional-sources directive. See Section 7.2.3 [Effective-Target Keywords], page 84.

{ dg-require-*support* args }
: Skip the test if the target does not provide the required support. These directives must appear after any dg-do directive in the test and before any dg-additional-sources directive. They require at least one argument, which can be an empty string if the specific procedure does not examine the argument. See Section 7.2.5 [Require Support], page 102, for a complete list of these directives.

7.2.1.5 Expect a test to fail for some targets

{ dg-xfail-if *comment* { *selector* } [{ *include-opts* } [{ *exclude-opts* }]] }
: Expect the test to fail if the conditions (which are the same as for dg-skip-if) are met. This does not affect the execute step.

{ dg-xfail-run-if *comment* { *selector* } [{ *include-opts* } [{ *exclude-opts* }]] }
: Expect the execute step of a test to fail if the conditions (which are the same as for dg-skip-if) are met.

7.2.1.6 Expect the test executable to fail

{ dg-shouldfail *comment* [{ *selector* } [{ *include-opts* } [{ *exclude-opts* }]]] }
: Expect the test executable to return a nonzero exit status if the conditions (which are the same as for dg-skip-if) are met.

7.2.1.7 Verify compiler messages

{ dg-error *regexp* [*comment* [{ target/xfail *selector* } [*line*]]] }
: This DejaGnu directive appears on a source line that is expected to get an error message, or else specifies the source line associated with the message. If there is no message for that line or if the text of that message is not matched by *regexp* then the check fails and *comment* is included in the FAIL message. The check does not look for the string 'error' unless it is part of *regexp*.

`{ dg-warning regexp [comment [{ target/xfail selector } [line] ]] }`
> This DejaGnu directive appears on a source line that is expected to get a warning message, or else specifies the source line associated with the message. If there is no message for that line or if the text of that message is not matched by *regexp* then the check fails and *comment* is included in the `FAIL` message. The check does not look for the string 'warning' unless it is part of *regexp*.

`{ dg-message regexp [comment [{ target/xfail selector } [line] ]] }`
> The line is expected to get a message other than an error or warning. If there is no message for that line or if the text of that message is not matched by *regexp* then the check fails and *comment* is included in the `FAIL` message.

`{ dg-bogus regexp [comment [{ target/xfail selector } [line] ]] }`
> This DejaGnu directive appears on a source line that should not get a message matching *regexp*, or else specifies the source line associated with the bogus message. It is usually used with 'xfail' to indicate that the message is a known problem for a particular set of targets.

`{ dg-line linenumvar }`
> This DejaGnu directive sets the variable *linenumvar* to the line number of the source line. The variable *linenumvar* can then be used in subsequent `dg-error`, `dg-warning`, `dg-message` and `dg-bogus` directives. For example:
>
> ```
> int a;   /* { dg-line first_def_a } */
> float a; /* { dg-error "conflicting types of" } */
> /* { dg-message "previous declaration of" "" { target *-*-* } first_def_a } */
> ```

`{ dg-excess-errors comment [{ target/xfail selector }] }`
> This DejaGnu directive indicates that the test is expected to fail due to compiler messages that are not handled by 'dg-error', 'dg-warning' or 'dg-bogus'. For this directive 'xfail' has the same effect as 'target'.

`{ dg-prune-output regexp }`
> Prune messages matching *regexp* from the test output.

7.2.1.8 Verify output of the test executable

`{ dg-output regexp [{ target/xfail selector }] }`
> This DejaGnu directive compares *regexp* to the combined output that the test executable writes to 'stdout' and 'stderr'.

7.2.1.9 Specify additional files for a test

`{ dg-additional-files "filelist" }`
> Specify additional files, other than source files, that must be copied to the system where the compiler runs.

`{ dg-additional-sources "filelist" }`
> Specify additional source files to appear in the compile line following the main test file.

7.2.1.10 Add checks at the end of a test

`{ dg-final { `*`local-directive`*` } }`

> This DejaGnu directive is placed within a comment anywhere in the source file and is processed after the test has been compiled and run. Multiple 'dg-final' commands are processed in the order in which they appear in the source file. See Section 7.2.6 [Final Actions], page 103, for a list of directives that can be used within dg-final.

7.2.2 Selecting targets to which a test applies

Several test directives include *selector*s to limit the targets for which a test is run or to declare that a test is expected to fail on particular targets.

A selector is:

- one or more target triplets, possibly including wildcard characters; use '*-*-*' to match any target
- a single effective-target keyword (see Section 7.2.3 [Effective-Target Keywords], page 84)
- a logical expression

Depending on the context, the selector specifies whether a test is skipped and reported as unsupported or is expected to fail. A context that allows either 'target' or 'xfail' also allows '{ target *selector1* xfail *selector2* }' to skip the test for targets that don't match *selector1* and the test to fail for targets that match *selector2*.

A selector expression appears within curly braces and uses a single logical operator: one of '!', '&&', or '||'. An operand is another selector expression, an effective-target keyword, a single target triplet, or a list of target triplets within quotes or curly braces. For example:

```
{ target { ! "hppa*-*-* ia64*-*-*" } }
{ target { powerpc*-*-* && lp64 } }
{ xfail { lp64 || vect_no_align } }
```

7.2.3 Keywords describing target attributes

Effective-target keywords identify sets of targets that support particular functionality. They are used to limit tests to be run only for particular targets, or to specify that particular sets of targets are expected to fail some tests.

Effective-target keywords are defined in 'lib/target-supports.exp' in the GCC testsuite, with the exception of those that are documented as being local to a particular test directory.

The 'effective target' takes into account all of the compiler options with which the test will be compiled, including the multilib options. By convention, keywords ending in _nocache can also include options specified for the particular test in an earlier dg-options or dg-add-options directive.

7.2.3.1 Data type sizes

ilp32   Target has 32-bit `int`, `long`, and pointers.

lp64   Target has 32-bit `int`, 64-bit `long` and pointers.

llp64
: Target has 32-bit `int` and `long`, 64-bit `long long` and pointers.

double64
: Target has 64-bit `double`.

double64plus
: Target has `double` that is 64 bits or longer.

longdouble128
: Target has 128-bit `long double`.

int32plus
: Target has `int` that is at 32 bits or longer.

int16
: Target has `int` that is 16 bits or shorter.

long_neq_int
: Target has `int` and `long` with different sizes.

large_double
: Target supports `double` that is longer than `float`.

large_long_double
: Target supports `long double` that is longer than `double`.

ptr32plus
: Target has pointers that are 32 bits or longer.

size32plus
: Target supports array and structure sizes that are 32 bits or longer.

4byte_wchar_t
: Target has `wchar_t` that is at least 4 bytes.

floatn
: Target has the `_Floatn` type.

floatnx
: Target has the `_Floatnx` type.

floatn_runtime
: Target has the `_Floatn` type, including runtime support for any options added with `dg-add-options`.

floatnx_runtime
: Target has the `_Floatnx` type, including runtime support for any options added with `dg-add-options`.

floatn_nx_runtime
: Target has runtime support for any options added with `dg-add-options` for any `_Floatn` or `_Floatnx` type.

7.2.3.2 Fortran-specific attributes

fortran_integer_16
: Target supports Fortran `integer` that is 16 bytes or longer.

fortran_real_10
: Target supports Fortran `real` that is 10 bytes or longer.

`fortran_real_16`
> Target supports Fortran `real` that is 16 bytes or longer.

`fortran_large_int`
> Target supports Fortran `integer` kinds larger than `integer(8)`.

`fortran_large_real`
> Target supports Fortran `real` kinds larger than `real(8)`.

7.2.3.3 Vector-specific attributes

`vect_align_stack_vars`
> The target's ABI allows stack variables to be aligned to the preferred vector alignment.

`vect_condition`
> Target supports vector conditional operations.

`vect_cond_mixed`
> Target supports vector conditional operations where comparison operands have different type from the value operands.

`vect_double`
> Target supports hardware vectors of `double`.

`vect_element_align_preferred`
> The target's preferred vector alignment is the same as the element alignment.

`vect_float`
> Target supports hardware vectors of `float` when '-funsafe-math-optimizations' is in effect.

`vect_float_strict`
> Target supports hardware vectors of `float` when '-funsafe-math-optimizations' is not in effect. This implies `vect_float`.

`vect_int` Target supports hardware vectors of `int`.

`vect_long`
> Target supports hardware vectors of `long`.

`vect_long_long`
> Target supports hardware vectors of `long long`.

`vect_fully_masked`
> Target supports fully-masked (also known as fully-predicated) loops, so that vector loops can handle partial as well as full vectors.

`vect_masked_store`
> Target supports vector masked stores.

`vect_scatter_store`
> Target supports vector scatter stores.

`vect_aligned_arrays`
> Target aligns arrays to vector alignment boundary.

`vect_hw_misalign`
: Target supports a vector misalign access.

`vect_no_align`
: Target does not support a vector alignment mechanism.

`vect_peeling_profitable`
: Target might require to peel loops for alignment purposes.

`vect_no_int_min_max`
: Target does not support a vector min and max instruction on `int`.

`vect_no_int_add`
: Target does not support a vector add instruction on `int`.

`vect_no_bitwise`
: Target does not support vector bitwise instructions.

`vect_char_mult`
: Target supports `vector char` multiplication.

`vect_short_mult`
: Target supports `vector short` multiplication.

`vect_int_mult`
: Target supports `vector int` multiplication.

`vect_long_mult`
: Target supports 64 bit `vector long` multiplication.

`vect_extract_even_odd`
: Target supports vector even/odd element extraction.

`vect_extract_even_odd_wide`
: Target supports vector even/odd element extraction of vectors with elements `SImode` or larger.

`vect_interleave`
: Target supports vector interleaving.

`vect_strided`
: Target supports vector interleaving and extract even/odd.

`vect_strided_wide`
: Target supports vector interleaving and extract even/odd for wide element types.

`vect_perm`
: Target supports vector permutation.

`vect_perm_byte`
: Target supports permutation of vectors with 8-bit elements.

`vect_perm_short`
: Target supports permutation of vectors with 16-bit elements.

`vect_perm3_byte`
: Target supports permutation of vectors with 8-bit elements, and for the default vector length it is possible to permute:

    { a0, a1, a2, b0, b1, b2, ... }

  to:

    { a0, a0, a0, b0, b0, b0, ... }
    { a1, a1, a1, b1, b1, b1, ... }
    { a2, a2, a2, b2, b2, b2, ... }

  using only two-vector permutes, regardless of how long the sequence is.

`vect_perm3_int`
: Like `vect_perm3_byte`, but for 32-bit elements.

`vect_perm3_short`
: Like `vect_perm3_byte`, but for 16-bit elements.

`vect_shift`
: Target supports a hardware vector shift operation.

`vect_unaligned_possible`
: Target prefers vectors to have an alignment greater than element alignment, but also allows unaligned vector accesses in some circumstances.

`vect_variable_length`
: Target has variable-length vectors.

`vect_widen_sum_hi_to_si`
: Target supports a vector widening summation of `short` operands into `int` results, or can promote (unpack) from `short` to `int`.

`vect_widen_sum_qi_to_hi`
: Target supports a vector widening summation of `char` operands into `short` results, or can promote (unpack) from `char` to `short`.

`vect_widen_sum_qi_to_si`
: Target supports a vector widening summation of `char` operands into `int` results.

`vect_widen_mult_qi_to_hi`
: Target supports a vector widening multiplication of `char` operands into `short` results, or can promote (unpack) from `char` to `short` and perform non-widening multiplication of `short`.

`vect_widen_mult_hi_to_si`
: Target supports a vector widening multiplication of `short` operands into `int` results, or can promote (unpack) from `short` to `int` and perform non-widening multiplication of `int`.

`vect_widen_mult_si_to_di_pattern`
: Target supports a vector widening multiplication of `int` operands into `long` results.

`vect_sdot_qi`
: Target supports a vector dot-product of `signed char`.

`vect_udot_qi`
: Target supports a vector dot-product of `unsigned char`.

`vect_sdot_hi`
: Target supports a vector dot-product of `signed short`.

`vect_udot_hi`
: Target supports a vector dot-product of `unsigned short`.

`vect_pack_trunc`
: Target supports a vector demotion (packing) of `short` to `char` and from `int` to `short` using modulo arithmetic.

`vect_unpack`
: Target supports a vector promotion (unpacking) of `char` to `short` and from `char` to `int`.

`vect_intfloat_cvt`
: Target supports conversion from `signed int` to `float`.

`vect_uintfloat_cvt`
: Target supports conversion from `unsigned int` to `float`.

`vect_floatint_cvt`
: Target supports conversion from `float` to `signed int`.

`vect_floatuint_cvt`
: Target supports conversion from `float` to `unsigned int`.

`vect_intdouble_cvt`
: Target supports conversion from `signed int` to `double`.

`vect_doubleint_cvt`
: Target supports conversion from `double` to `signed int`.

`vect_max_reduc`
: Target supports max reduction for vectors.

`vect_sizes_16B_8B`
: Target supports 16- and 8-bytes vectors.

`vect_sizes_32B_16B`
: Target supports 32- and 16-bytes vectors.

`vect_logical_reduc`
: Target supports AND, IOR and XOR reduction on vectors.

`vect_fold_extract_last`
: Target supports the `fold_extract_last` optab.

7.2.3.4 Thread Local Storage attributes

`tls`
: Target supports thread-local storage.

`tls_native`
: Target supports native (rather than emulated) thread-local storage.

`tls_runtime`
: Test system supports executing TLS executables.

7.2.3.5 Decimal floating point attributes

dfp
: Targets supports compiling decimal floating point extension to C.

dfp_nocache
: Including the options used to compile this particular test, the target supports compiling decimal floating point extension to C.

dfprt
: Test system can execute decimal floating point tests.

dfprt_nocache
: Including the options used to compile this particular test, the test system can execute decimal floating point tests.

hard_dfp
: Target generates decimal floating point instructions with current options.

7.2.3.6 ARM-specific attributes

arm32
: ARM target generates 32-bit code.

arm_eabi
: ARM target adheres to the ABI for the ARM Architecture.

arm_fp_ok
: ARM target defines __ARM_FP using -mfloat-abi=softfp or equivalent options. Some multilibs may be incompatible with these options.

arm_hf_eabi
: ARM target adheres to the VFP and Advanced SIMD Register Arguments variant of the ABI for the ARM Architecture (as selected with -mfloat-abi=hard).

arm_softfloat
: ARM target uses the soft-float ABI with no floating-point instructions used whatsoever (as selected with -mfloat-abi=soft).

arm_hard_vfp_ok
: ARM target supports -mfpu=vfp -mfloat-abi=hard. Some multilibs may be incompatible with these options.

arm_iwmmxt_ok
: ARM target supports -mcpu=iwmmxt. Some multilibs may be incompatible with this option.

arm_neon
: ARM target supports generating NEON instructions.

arm_tune_string_ops_prefer_neon
: Test CPU tune supports inlining string operations with NEON instructions.

arm_neon_hw
: Test system supports executing NEON instructions.

arm_neonv2_hw
: Test system supports executing NEON v2 instructions.

arm_neon_ok
: ARM Target supports -mfpu=neon -mfloat-abi=softfp or compatible options. Some multilibs may be incompatible with these options.

`arm_neon_ok_no_float_abi`
: ARM Target supports NEON with -mfpu=neon, but without any -mfloat-abi= option. Some multilibs may be incompatible with this option.

`arm_neonv2_ok`
: ARM Target supports -mfpu=neon-vfpv4 -mfloat-abi=softfp or compatible options. Some multilibs may be incompatible with these options.

`arm_fp16_ok`
: Target supports options to generate VFP half-precision floating-point instructions. Some multilibs may be incompatible with these options. This test is valid for ARM only.

`arm_fp16_hw`
: Target supports executing VFP half-precision floating-point instructions. This test is valid for ARM only.

`arm_neon_fp16_ok`
: ARM Target supports -mfpu=neon-fp16 -mfloat-abi=softfp or compatible options, including -mfp16-format=ieee if necessary to obtain the __fp16 type. Some multilibs may be incompatible with these options.

`arm_neon_fp16_hw`
: Test system supports executing Neon half-precision float instructions. (Implies previous.)

`arm_fp16_alternative_ok`
: ARM target supports the ARM FP16 alternative format. Some multilibs may be incompatible with the options needed.

`arm_fp16_none_ok`
: ARM target supports specifying none as the ARM FP16 format.

`arm_thumb1_ok`
: ARM target generates Thumb-1 code for -mthumb.

`arm_thumb2_ok`
: ARM target generates Thumb-2 code for -mthumb.

`arm_vfp_ok`
: ARM target supports -mfpu=vfp -mfloat-abi=softfp. Some multilibs may be incompatible with these options.

`arm_vfp3_ok`
: ARM target supports -mfpu=vfp3 -mfloat-abi=softfp. Some multilibs may be incompatible with these options.

`arm_v8_vfp_ok`
: ARM target supports -mfpu=fp-armv8 -mfloat-abi=softfp. Some multilibs may be incompatible with these options.

`arm_v8_neon_ok`
: ARM target supports -mfpu=neon-fp-armv8 -mfloat-abi=softfp. Some multilibs may be incompatible with these options.

`arm_v8_1a_neon_ok`
> ARM target supports options to generate ARMv8.1-A Adv.SIMD instructions. Some multilibs may be incompatible with these options.

`arm_v8_1a_neon_hw`
> ARM target supports executing ARMv8.1-A Adv.SIMD instructions. Some multilibs may be incompatible with the options needed. Implies arm_v8_1a_neon_ok.

`arm_acq_rel`
> ARM target supports acquire-release instructions.

`arm_v8_2a_fp16_scalar_ok`
> ARM target supports options to generate instructions for ARMv8.2-A and scalar instructions from the FP16 extension. Some multilibs may be incompatible with these options.

`arm_v8_2a_fp16_scalar_hw`
> ARM target supports executing instructions for ARMv8.2-A and scalar instructions from the FP16 extension. Some multilibs may be incompatible with these options. Implies arm_v8_2a_fp16_neon_ok.

`arm_v8_2a_fp16_neon_ok`
> ARM target supports options to generate instructions from ARMv8.2-A with the FP16 extension. Some multilibs may be incompatible with these options. Implies arm_v8_2a_fp16_scalar_ok.

`arm_v8_2a_fp16_neon_hw`
> ARM target supports executing instructions from ARMv8.2-A with the FP16 extension. Some multilibs may be incompatible with these options. Implies arm_v8_2a_fp16_neon_ok and arm_v8_2a_fp16_scalar_hw.

`arm_v8_2a_dotprod_neon_ok`
> ARM target supports options to generate instructions from ARMv8.2-A with the Dot Product extension. Some multilibs may be incompatible with these options.

`arm_v8_2a_dotprod_neon_hw`
> ARM target supports executing instructions from ARMv8.2-A with the Dot Product extension. Some multilibs may be incompatible with these options. Implies arm_v8_2a_dotprod_neon_ok.

`arm_fp16fml_neon_ok`
> ARM target supports extensions to generate the `VFMAL` and `VFMLS` half-precision floating-point instructions available from ARMv8.2-A and onwards. Some multilibs may be incompatible with these options.

`arm_prefer_ldrd_strd`
> ARM target prefers `LDRD` and `STRD` instructions over `LDM` and `STM` instructions.

`arm_thumb1_movt_ok`
> ARM target generates Thumb-1 code for `-mthumb` with `MOVW` and `MOVT` instructions available.

`arm_thumb1_cbz_ok`
: ARM target generates Thumb-1 code for -mthumb with CBZ and CBNZ instructions available.

`arm_divmod_simode`
: ARM target for which divmod transform is disabled, if it supports hardware div instruction.

`arm_cmse_ok`
: ARM target supports ARMv8-M Security Extensions, enabled by the -mcmse option.

`arm_coproc1_ok`
: ARM target supports the following coprocessor instructions: CDP, LDC, STC, MCR and MRC.

`arm_coproc2_ok`
: ARM target supports all the coprocessor instructions also listed as supported in [arm_coproc1_ok], page 93 in addition to the following: CDP2, LDC2, LDC21, STC2, STC21, MCR2 and MRC2.

`arm_coproc3_ok`
: ARM target supports all the coprocessor instructions also listed as supported in [arm_coproc2_ok], page 93 in addition the following: MCRR and MRRC.

`arm_coproc4_ok`
: ARM target supports all the coprocessor instructions also listed as supported in [arm_coproc3_ok], page 93 in addition the following: MCRR2 and MRRC2.

7.2.3.7 AArch64-specific attributes

`aarch64_asm_<ext>_ok`
: AArch64 assembler supports the architecture extension ext via the .arch_extension pseudo-op.

`aarch64_tiny`
: AArch64 target which generates instruction sequences for tiny memory model.

`aarch64_small`
: AArch64 target which generates instruction sequences for small memory model.

`aarch64_large`
: AArch64 target which generates instruction sequences for large memory model.

`aarch64_little_endian`
: AArch64 target which generates instruction sequences for little endian.

`aarch64_big_endian`
: AArch64 target which generates instruction sequences for big endian.

`aarch64_small_fpic`
: Binutils installed on test system supports relocation types required by -fpic for AArch64 small memory model.

7.2.3.8 MIPS-specific attributes

`mips64`   MIPS target supports 64-bit instructions.

`nomips16` MIPS target does not produce MIPS16 code.

`mips16_attribute`
: MIPS target can generate MIPS16 code.

`mips_loongson`
: MIPS target is a Loongson-2E or -2F target using an ABI that supports the Loongson vector modes.

`mips_msa` MIPS target supports -mmsa, MIPS SIMD Architecture (MSA).

`mips_newabi_large_long_double`
: MIPS target supports `long double` larger than `double` when using the new ABI.

`mpaired_single`
: MIPS target supports -mpaired-single.

7.2.3.9 PowerPC-specific attributes

`dfp_hw`   PowerPC target supports executing hardware DFP instructions.

`p8vector_hw`
: PowerPC target supports executing VSX instructions (ISA 2.07).

`powerpc64`
: Test system supports executing 64-bit instructions.

`powerpc_altivec`
: PowerPC target supports AltiVec.

`powerpc_altivec_ok`
: PowerPC target supports -maltivec.

`powerpc_eabi_ok`
: PowerPC target supports -meabi.

`powerpc_elfv2`
: PowerPC target supports -mabi=elfv2.

`powerpc_fprs`
: PowerPC target supports floating-point registers.

`powerpc_hard_double`
: PowerPC target supports hardware double-precision floating-point.

`powerpc_htm_ok`
: PowerPC target supports -mhtm

`powerpc_p8vector_ok`
: PowerPC target supports -mpower8-vector

`powerpc_popcntb_ok`
: PowerPC target supports the `popcntb` instruction, indicating that this target supports -mcpu=power5.

Chapter 7: Testsuites 95

`powerpc_ppu_ok`
: PowerPC target supports `-mcpu=cell`.

`powerpc_spe`
: PowerPC target supports PowerPC SPE.

`powerpc_spe_nocache`
: Including the options used to compile this particular test, the PowerPC target supports PowerPC SPE.

`powerpc_spu`
: PowerPC target supports PowerPC SPU.

`powerpc_vsx_ok`
: PowerPC target supports `-mvsx`.

`powerpc_405_nocache`
: Including the options used to compile this particular test, the PowerPC target supports PowerPC 405.

`ppc_recip_hw`
: PowerPC target supports executing reciprocal estimate instructions.

`spu_auto_overlay`
: SPU target has toolchain that supports automatic overlay generation.

`vmx_hw`
: PowerPC target supports executing AltiVec instructions.

`vsx_hw`
: PowerPC target supports executing VSX instructions (ISA 2.06).

7.2.3.10 Other hardware attributes

`autoincdec`
: Target supports autoincrement/decrement addressing.

`avx`
: Target supports compiling `avx` instructions.

`avx_runtime`
: Target supports the execution of `avx` instructions.

`avx2`
: Target supports compiling `avx2` instructions.

`avx2_runtime`
: Target supports the execution of `avx2` instructions.

`avx512f`
: Target supports compiling `avx512f` instructions.

`avx512f_runtime`
: Target supports the execution of `avx512f` instructions.

`cell_hw`
: Test system can execute AltiVec and Cell PPU instructions.

`coldfire_fpu`
: Target uses a ColdFire FPU.

`divmod`
: Target supporting hardware divmod insn or divmod libcall.

`divmod_simode`
: Target supporting hardware divmod insn or divmod libcall for SImode.

`hard_float`
: Target supports FPU instructions.

`non_strict_align`
: Target does not require strict alignment.

`pie_copyreloc`
: The x86-64 target linker supports PIE with copy reloc.

`rdrand`
: Target supports x86 `rdrand` instruction.

`sqrt_insn`
: Target has a square root instruction that the compiler can generate.

`sse`
: Target supports compiling `sse` instructions.

`sse_runtime`
: Target supports the execution of `sse` instructions.

`sse2`
: Target supports compiling `sse2` instructions.

`sse2_runtime`
: Target supports the execution of `sse2` instructions.

`sync_char_short`
: Target supports atomic operations on `char` and `short`.

`sync_int_long`
: Target supports atomic operations on `int` and `long`.

`ultrasparc_hw`
: Test environment appears to run executables on a simulator that accepts only `EM_SPARC` executables and chokes on `EM_SPARC32PLUS` or `EM_SPARCV9` executables.

`vect_cmdline_needed`
: Target requires a command line argument to enable a SIMD instruction set.

`xorsign`
: Target supports the xorsign optab expansion.

7.2.3.11 Environment attributes

`c`
: The language for the compiler under test is C.

`c++`
: The language for the compiler under test is C++.

`c99_runtime`
: Target provides a full C99 runtime.

`correct_iso_cpp_string_wchar_protos`
: Target `string.h` and `wchar.h` headers provide C++ required overloads for `strchr` etc. functions.

`dummy_wcsftime`
: Target uses a dummy `wcsftime` function that always returns zero.

`fd_truncate`
: Target can truncate a file from a file descriptor, as used by 'libgfortran/io/unix.c:fd_truncate'; i.e. `ftruncate` or `chsize`.

`freestanding`
: Target is 'freestanding' as defined in section 4 of the C99 standard. Effectively, it is a target which supports no extra headers or libraries other than what is considered essential.

`gettimeofday`
: Target supports `gettimeofday`.

`init_priority`
: Target supports constructors with initialization priority arguments.

`inttypes_types`
: Target has the basic signed and unsigned types in `inttypes.h`. This is for tests that GCC's notions of these types agree with those in the header, as some systems have only `inttypes.h`.

`lax_strtofp`
: Target might have errors of a few ULP in string to floating-point conversion functions and overflow is not always detected correctly by those functions.

`mempcpy` Target provides `mempcpy` function.

`mmap` Target supports `mmap`.

`newlib` Target supports Newlib.

`pow10` Target provides `pow10` function.

`pthread` Target can compile using `pthread.h` with no errors or warnings.

`pthread_h`
: Target has `pthread.h`.

`run_expensive_tests`
: Expensive testcases (usually those that consume excessive amounts of CPU time) should be run on this target. This can be enabled by setting the `GCC_TEST_RUN_EXPENSIVE` environment variable to a non-empty string.

`simulator`
: Test system runs executables on a simulator (i.e. slowly) rather than hardware (i.e. fast).

`signal` Target has `signal.h`.

`stabs` Target supports the stabs debugging format.

`stdint_types`
: Target has the basic signed and unsigned C types in `stdint.h`. This will be obsolete when GCC ensures a working `stdint.h` for all targets.

`stpcpy` Target provides `stpcpy` function.

`trampolines`
: Target supports trampolines.

`uclibc` Target supports uClibc.

`unwrapped`
: Target does not use a status wrapper.

`vxworks_kernel`
: Target is a VxWorks kernel.

`vxworks_rtp`
: Target is a VxWorks RTP.

`wchar`   Target supports wide characters.

7.2.3.12 Other attributes

`automatic_stack_alignment`
: Target supports automatic stack alignment.

`branch_cost`
: Target supports '`-branch-cost=N`'.

`cxa_atexit`
: Target uses `__cxa_atexit`.

`default_packed`
: Target has packed layout of structure members by default.

`fgraphite`
: Target supports Graphite optimizations.

`fixed_point`
: Target supports fixed-point extension to C.

`fopenacc`   Target supports OpenACC via '`-fopenacc`'.

`fopenmp`   Target supports OpenMP via '`-fopenmp`'.

`fpic`   Target supports '`-fpic`' and '`-fPIC`'.

`freorder`   Target supports '`-freorder-blocks-and-partition`'.

`fstack_protector`
: Target supports '`-fstack-protector`'.

`gas`   Target uses GNU as.

`gc_sections`
: Target supports '`--gc-sections`'.

`gld`   Target uses GNU ld.

`keeps_null_pointer_checks`
: Target keeps null pointer checks, either due to the use of '`-fno-delete-null-pointer-checks`' or hardwired into the target.

`lto`   Compiler has been configured to support link-time optimization (LTO).

`naked_functions`
: Target supports the `naked` function attribute.

`named_sections`
: Target supports named sections.

`natural_alignment_32`
: Target uses natural alignment (aligned to type size) for types of 32 bits or less.

`target_natural_alignment_64`
: Target uses natural alignment (aligned to type size) for types of 64 bits or less.

`nonpic`   Target does not generate PIC by default.

`pie_enabled`
: Target generates PIE by default.

`pcc_bitfield_type_matters`
: Target defines `PCC_BITFIELD_TYPE_MATTERS`.

`pe_aligned_commons`
: Target supports '`-mpe-aligned-commons`'.

`pie`   Target supports '`-pie`', '`-fpie`' and '`-fPIE`'.

`rdynamic`   Target supports '`-rdynamic`'.

`section_anchors`
: Target supports section anchors.

`short_enums`
: Target defaults to short enums.

`stack_size`
: Target has limited stack size. The stack size limit can be obtained using the `STACK_SIZE` macro defined by [dg-add-options feature `stack_size`], page 102.

`static`   Target supports '`-static`'.

`static_libgfortran`
: Target supports statically linking '`libgfortran`'.

`string_merging`
: Target supports merging string constants at link time.

`ucn`   Target supports compiling and assembling UCN.

`ucn_nocache`
: Including the options used to compile this particular test, the target supports compiling and assembling UCN.

`unaligned_stack`
: Target does not guarantee that its `STACK_BOUNDARY` is greater than or equal to the required vector alignment.

`vector_alignment_reachable`
: Vector alignment is reachable for types of 32 bits or less.

`vector_alignment_reachable_for_64bit`
: Vector alignment is reachable for types of 64 bits or less.

`wchar_t_char16_t_compatible`
: Target supports `wchar_t` that is compatible with `char16_t`.

`wchar_t_char32_t_compatible`
: Target supports `wchar_t` that is compatible with `char32_t`.

`comdat_group`
: Target uses comdat groups.

`weak_undefined`
: Target supports weak undefined symbols.

`word_mode_no_slow_unalign`
: Target does not have slow unaligned access when doing word size accesses.

7.2.3.13 Local to tests in `gcc.target/i386`

`3dnow`   Target supports compiling `3dnow` instructions.

`aes`   Target supports compiling `aes` instructions.

`fma4`   Target supports compiling `fma4` instructions.

`ms_hook_prologue`
: Target supports attribute `ms_hook_prologue`.

`pclmul`   Target supports compiling `pclmul` instructions.

`sse3`   Target supports compiling `sse3` instructions.

`sse4`   Target supports compiling `sse4` instructions.

`sse4a`   Target supports compiling `sse4a` instructions.

`ssse3`   Target supports compiling `ssse3` instructions.

`vaes`   Target supports compiling `vaes` instructions.

`vpclmul` Target supports compiling `vpclmul` instructions.

`xop`   Target supports compiling `xop` instructions.

7.2.3.14 Local to tests in `gcc.target/spu/ea`

`ealib`   Target `__ea` library functions are available.

7.2.3.15 Local to tests in `gcc.test-framework`

`no`   Always returns 0.

`yes`   Always returns 1.

7.2.4 Features for `dg-add-options`

The supported values of *feature* for directive `dg-add-options` are:

`arm_fp`   `__ARM_FP` definition. Only ARM targets support this feature, and only then in certain modes; see the [arm_fp_ok effective target keyword], page 90.

`arm_neon`   NEON support. Only ARM targets support this feature, and only then in certain modes; see the [arm_neon_ok effective target keyword], page 90.

`arm_fp16`   VFP half-precision floating point support. This does not select the FP16 format; for that, use [arm_fp16_ieee], page 101 or [arm_fp16_alternative], page 101 instead. This feature is only supported by ARM targets and then only in certain modes; see the [arm_fp16_ok effective target keyword], page 91.

`arm_fp16_ieee`
     ARM IEEE 754-2008 format VFP half-precision floating point support. This feature is only supported by ARM targets and then only in certain modes; see the [arm_fp16_ok effective target keyword], page 91.

`arm_fp16_alternative`
     ARM Alternative format VFP half-precision floating point support. This feature is only supported by ARM targets and then only in certain modes; see the [arm_fp16_ok effective target keyword], page 91.

`arm_neon_fp16`
     NEON and half-precision floating point support. Only ARM targets support this feature, and only then in certain modes; see the [arm_neon_fp16_ok effective target keyword], page 91.

`arm_vfp3`   arm vfp3 floating point support; see the [arm_vfp3_ok effective target keyword], page 91.

`arm_v8_1a_neon`
     Add options for ARMv8.1-A with Adv.SIMD support, if this is supported by the target; see the [arm_v8_1a_neon_ok], page 92 effective target keyword.

`arm_v8_2a_fp16_scalar`
     Add options for ARMv8.2-A with scalar FP16 support, if this is supported by the target; see the [arm_v8_2a_fp16_scalar_ok], page 92 effective target keyword.

`arm_v8_2a_fp16_neon`
     Add options for ARMv8.2-A with Adv.SIMD FP16 support, if this is supported by the target; see the [arm_v8_2a_fp16_neon_ok], page 92 effective target keyword.

`arm_v8_2a_dotprod_neon`
     Add options for ARMv8.2-A with Adv.SIMD Dot Product support, if this is supported by the target; see the [arm_v8_2a_dotprod_neon_ok], page 92 effective target keyword.

`arm_fp16fml_neon`
     Add options to enable generation of the `VFMAL` and `VFMSL` instructions, if this is supported by the target; see the [arm_fp16fml_neon_ok], page 92 effective target keyword.

`bind_pic_locally`
     Add the target-specific flags needed to enable functions to bind locally when using pic/PIC passes in the testsuite.

`c99_runtime`
: Add the target-specific flags needed to access the C99 runtime.

`float`*n*
: Add the target-specific flags needed to use the _Float*n* type.

`float`*n*`x`
: Add the target-specific flags needed to use the _Float*n*x type.

`ieee`
: Add the target-specific flags needed to enable full IEEE compliance mode.

`mips16_attribute`
: `mips16` function attributes. Only MIPS targets support this feature, and only then in certain modes.

`stack_size`
: Add the flags needed to define macro STACK_SIZE and set it to the stack size limit associated with the [`stack_size` effective target], page 99.

`tls`
: Add the target-specific flags needed to use thread-local storage.

7.2.5 Variants of `dg-require-support`

A few of the `dg-require` directives take arguments.

`dg-require-iconv` *codeset*
: Skip the test if the target does not support iconv. *codeset* is the codeset to convert to.

`dg-require-profiling` *profopt*
: Skip the test if the target does not support profiling with option *profopt*.

`dg-require-stack-check` *check*
: Skip the test if the target does not support the -fstack-check option. If *check* is "", support for -fstack-check is checked, for -fstack-check=("*check*") otherwise.

`dg-require-stack-size` *size*
: Skip the test if the target does not support a stack size of *size*.

`dg-require-visibility` *vis*
: Skip the test if the target does not support the `visibility` attribute. If *vis* is "", support for `visibility("hidden")` is checked, for `visibility("vis")` otherwise.

The original `dg-require` directives were defined before there was support for effective-target keywords. The directives that do not take arguments could be replaced with effective-target keywords.

`dg-require-alias ""`
: Skip the test if the target does not support the 'alias' attribute.

`dg-require-ascii-locale ""`
: Skip the test if the host does not support an ASCII locale.

`dg-require-compat-dfp ""`
: Skip this test unless both compilers in a 'compat' testsuite support decimal floating point.

`dg-require-cxa-atexit ""`
> Skip the test if the target does not support `__cxa_atexit`. This is equivalent to `dg-require-effective-target cxa_atexit`.

`dg-require-dll ""`
> Skip the test if the target does not support DLL attributes.

`dg-require-fork ""`
> Skip the test if the target does not support `fork`.

`dg-require-gc-sections ""`
> Skip the test if the target's linker does not support the `--gc-sections` flags. This is equivalent to `dg-require-effective-target gc-sections`.

`dg-require-host-local ""`
> Skip the test if the host is remote, rather than the same as the build system. Some tests are incompatible with DejaGnu's handling of remote hosts, which involves copying the source file to the host and compiling it with a relative path and `"-o a.out"`.

`dg-require-mkfifo ""`
> Skip the test if the target does not support `mkfifo`.

`dg-require-named-sections ""`
> Skip the test is the target does not support named sections. This is equivalent to `dg-require-effective-target named_sections`.

`dg-require-weak ""`
> Skip the test if the target does not support weak symbols.

`dg-require-weak-override ""`
> Skip the test if the target does not support overriding weak symbols.

7.2.6 Commands for use in `dg-final`

The GCC testsuite defines the following directives to be used within `dg-final`.

7.2.6.1 Scan a particular file

`scan-file filename regexp [{ target/xfail selector }]`
> Passes if *regexp* matches text in *filename*.

`scan-file-not filename regexp [{ target/xfail selector }]`
> Passes if *regexp* does not match text in *filename*.

`scan-module module regexp [{ target/xfail selector }]`
> Passes if *regexp* matches in Fortran module *module*.

7.2.6.2 Scan the assembly output

`scan-assembler regex [{ target/xfail selector }]`
> Passes if *regex* matches text in the test's assembler output.

`scan-assembler-not regex [{ target/xfail selector }]`
> Passes if *regex* does not match text in the test's assembler output.

`scan-assembler-times` *regex num* `[{ target/xfail` *selector* `}]`
> Passes if *regex* is matched exactly *num* times in the test's assembler output.

`scan-assembler-dem` *regex* `[{ target/xfail` *selector* `}]`
> Passes if *regex* matches text in the test's demangled assembler output.

`scan-assembler-dem-not` *regex* `[{ target/xfail` *selector* `}]`
> Passes if *regex* does not match text in the test's demangled assembler output.

`scan-hidden` *symbol* `[{ target/xfail` *selector* `}]`
> Passes if *symbol* is defined as a hidden symbol in the test's assembly output.

`scan-not-hidden` *symbol* `[{ target/xfail` *selector* `}]`
> Passes if *symbol* is not defined as a hidden symbol in the test's assembly output.

7.2.6.3 Scan optimization dump files

These commands are available for *kind* of `tree`, `rtl`, and `ipa`.

`scan-`*kind*`-dump` *regex suffix* `[{ target/xfail` *selector* `}]`
> Passes if *regex* matches text in the dump file with suffix *suffix*.

`scan-`*kind*`-dump-not` *regex suffix* `[{ target/xfail` *selector* `}]`
> Passes if *regex* does not match text in the dump file with suffix *suffix*.

`scan-`*kind*`-dump-times` *regex num suffix* `[{ target/xfail` *selector* `}]`
> Passes if *regex* is found exactly *num* times in the dump file with suffix *suffix*.

`scan-`*kind*`-dump-dem` *regex suffix* `[{ target/xfail` *selector* `}]`
> Passes if *regex* matches demangled text in the dump file with suffix *suffix*.

`scan-`*kind*`-dump-dem-not` *regex suffix* `[{ target/xfail` *selector* `}]`
> Passes if *regex* does not match demangled text in the dump file with suffix *suffix*.

7.2.6.4 Verify that an output files exists or not

`output-exists` `[{ target/xfail` *selector* `}]`
> Passes if compiler output file exists.

`output-exists-not` `[{ target/xfail` *selector* `}]`
> Passes if compiler output file does not exist.

7.2.6.5 Check for LTO tests

`scan-symbol` *regexp* `[{ target/xfail` *selector* `}]`
> Passes if the pattern is present in the final executable.

7.2.6.6 Checks for gcov tests

`run-gcov` *sourcefile*
> Check line counts in `gcov` tests.

`run-gcov` `[branches] [calls] {` *opts sourcefile* `}`
> Check branch and/or call counts, in addition to line counts, in `gcov` tests.

Chapter 7: Testsuites   105

7.2.6.7 Clean up generated test files

Usually the test-framework removes files that were generated during testing. If a testcase, for example, uses any dumping mechanism to inspect a passes dump file, the testsuite recognized the dump option passed to the tool and schedules a final cleanup to remove these files.

There are, however, following additional cleanup directives that can be used to annotate a testcase "manually".

`cleanup-coverage-files`
> Removes coverage data files generated for this test.

`cleanup-modules "list-of-extra-modules"`
> Removes Fortran module files generated for this test, excluding the module names listed in keep-modules. Cleaning up module files is usually done automatically by the testsuite by looking at the source files and removing the modules after the test has been executed.
>
> ```
> module MoD1
> end module MoD1
> module Mod2
> end module Mod2
> module moD3
> end module moD3
> module mod4
> end module mod4
> ! { dg-final { cleanup-modules "mod1 mod2" } } ! redundant
> ! { dg-final { keep-modules "mod3 mod4" } }
> ```

`keep-modules "list-of-modules-not-to-delete"`
> Whitespace separated list of module names that should not be deleted by cleanup-modules. If the list of modules is empty, all modules defined in this file are kept.
>
> ```
> module maybe_unneeded
> end module maybe_unneeded
> module keep1
> end module keep1
> module keep2
> end module keep2
> ! { dg-final { keep-modules "keep1 keep2" } } ! just keep these two
> ! { dg-final { keep-modules "" } } ! keep all
> ```

`dg-keep-saved-temps "list of suffixes-not-to-delete"`
> Whitespace separated list of suffixes that should not be deleted automatically in a testcase that uses '-save-temps'.
>
> ```
> // { dg-options "-save-temps -fpch-preprocess -I." }
> int main() { return 0; }
> // { dg-keep-saved-temps ".s" } ! just keep assembler file
> // { dg-keep-saved-temps ".s" ".i" } ! ... and .i
> // { dg-keep-saved-temps ".ii" ".o" } ! or just .ii and .o
> ```

`cleanup-profile-file`
> Removes profiling files generated for this test.

`cleanup-repo-files`
> Removes files generated for this test for '-frepo'.

7.3 Ada Language Testsuites

The Ada testsuite includes executable tests from the ACATS testsuite, publicly available at http://www.ada-auth.org/acats.html.

These tests are integrated in the GCC testsuite in the 'ada/acats' directory, and enabled automatically when running make check, assuming the Ada language has been enabled when configuring GCC.

You can also run the Ada testsuite independently, using make check-ada, or run a subset of the tests by specifying which chapter to run, e.g.:

```
$ make check-ada CHAPTERS="c3 c9"
```

The tests are organized by directory, each directory corresponding to a chapter of the Ada Reference Manual. So for example, 'c9' corresponds to chapter 9, which deals with tasking features of the language.

The tests are run using two sh scripts: 'run_acats' and 'run_all.sh'. To run the tests using a simulator or a cross target, see the small customization section at the top of 'run_all.sh'.

These tests are run using the build tree: they can be run without doing a make install.

7.4 C Language Testsuites

GCC contains the following C language testsuites, in the 'gcc/testsuite' directory:

'gcc.dg'
: This contains tests of particular features of the C compiler, using the more modern 'dg' harness. Correctness tests for various compiler features should go here if possible.

  Magic comments determine whether the file is preprocessed, compiled, linked or run. In these tests, error and warning message texts are compared against expected texts or regular expressions given in comments. These tests are run with the options '-ansi -pedantic' unless other options are given in the test. Except as noted below they are not run with multiple optimization options.

'gcc.dg/compat'
: This subdirectory contains tests for binary compatibility using 'lib/compat.exp', which in turn uses the language-independent support (see Section 7.8 [Support for testing binary compatibility], page 110).

'gcc.dg/cpp'
: This subdirectory contains tests of the preprocessor.

'gcc.dg/debug'
: This subdirectory contains tests for debug formats. Tests in this subdirectory are run for each debug format that the compiler supports.

'gcc.dg/format'
: This subdirectory contains tests of the '-Wformat' format checking. Tests in this directory are run with and without '-DWIDE'.

'gcc.dg/noncompile'
: This subdirectory contains tests of code that should not compile and does not need any special compilation options. They are run with multiple optimization options, since sometimes invalid code crashes the compiler with optimization.

'gcc.dg/special'
: FIXME: describe this.

'gcc.c-torture'
: This contains particular code fragments which have historically broken easily. These tests are run with multiple optimization options, so tests for features which only break at some optimization levels belong here. This also contains tests to check that certain optimizations occur. It might be worthwhile to separate the correctness tests cleanly from the code quality tests, but it hasn't been done yet.

'gcc.c-torture/compat'
: FIXME: describe this.

  This directory should probably not be used for new tests.

'gcc.c-torture/compile'
: This testsuite contains test cases that should compile, but do not need to link or run. These test cases are compiled with several different combinations of optimization options. All warnings are disabled for these test cases, so this directory is not suitable if you wish to test for the presence or absence of compiler warnings. While special options can be set, and tests disabled on specific platforms, by the use of '.x' files, mostly these test cases should not contain platform dependencies. FIXME: discuss how defines such as STACK_SIZE are used.

'gcc.c-torture/execute'
: This testsuite contains test cases that should compile, link and run; otherwise the same comments as for 'gcc.c-torture/compile' apply.

'gcc.c-torture/execute/ieee'
: This contains tests which are specific to IEEE floating point.

'gcc.c-torture/unsorted'
: FIXME: describe this.

  This directory should probably not be used for new tests.

'gcc.misc-tests'
: This directory contains C tests that require special handling. Some of these tests have individual expect files, and others share special-purpose expect files:

  'bprob*.c'
  : Test '-fbranch-probabilities' using 'gcc.misc-tests/bprob.exp', which in turn uses the generic, language-independent framework (see Section 7.7 [Support for testing profile-directed optimizations], page 109).

  'gcov*.c'
  : Test gcov output using 'gcov.exp', which in turn uses the language-independent support (see Section 7.6 [Support for testing gcov], page 108).

  'i386-pf-*.c'
  : Test i386-specific support for data prefetch using 'i386-prefetch.exp'.

`gcc.test-framework`

'dg-*.c' Test the testsuite itself using 'gcc.test-framework/test-framework.exp'.

FIXME: merge in 'testsuite/README.gcc' and discuss the format of test cases and magic comments more.

7.5 Support for testing link-time optimizations

Tests for link-time optimizations usually require multiple source files that are compiled separately, perhaps with different sets of options. There are several special-purpose test directives used for these tests.

{ dg-lto-do *do-what-keyword* }

do-what-keyword specifies how the test is compiled and whether it is executed. It is one of:

assemble   Compile with '-c' to produce a relocatable object file.

link   Compile, assemble, and link to produce an executable file.

run   Produce and run an executable file, which is expected to return an exit code of 0.

The default is assemble. That can be overridden for a set of tests by redefining dg-do-what-default within the .exp file for those tests.

Unlike dg-do, dg-lto-do does not support an optional 'target' or 'xfail' list. Use dg-skip-if, dg-xfail-if, or dg-xfail-run-if.

{ dg-lto-options { { *options* } [{ *options* }] } [{ target *selector* }]}

This directive provides a list of one or more sets of compiler options to override *LTO_OPTIONS*. Each test will be compiled and run with each of these sets of options.

{ dg-extra-ld-options *options* [{ target *selector* }]}

This directive adds *options* to the linker options used.

{ dg-suppress-ld-options *options* [{ target *selector* }]}

This directive removes *options* from the set of linker options used.

7.6 Support for testing `gcov`

Language-independent support for testing `gcov`, and for checking that branch profiling produces expected values, is provided by the expect file 'lib/gcov.exp'. `gcov` tests also rely on procedures in 'lib/gcc-dg.exp' to compile and run the test program. A typical `gcov` test contains the following DejaGnu commands within comments:

```
{ dg-options "-fprofile-arcs -ftest-coverage" }
{ dg-do run { target native } }
{ dg-final { run-gcov sourcefile } }
```

Checks of `gcov` output can include line counts, branch percentages, and call return percentages. All of these checks are requested via commands that appear in comments in the test's source file. Commands to check line counts are processed by default. Commands to check branch percentages and call return percentages are processed if the run-gcov command has arguments branches or calls, respectively. For example, the following specifies checking both, as well as passing '-b' to `gcov`:

```
{ dg-final { run-gcov branches calls { -b sourcefile } } }
```

A line count command appears within a comment on the source line that is expected to get the specified count and has the form count(*cnt*). A test should only check line counts for lines that will get the same count for any architecture.

Commands to check branch percentages (branch) and call return percentages (returns) are very similar to each other. A beginning command appears on or before the first of a range of lines that will report the percentage, and the ending command follows that range of lines. The beginning command can include a list of percentages, all of which are expected to be found within the range. A range is terminated by the next command of the same kind. A command branch(end) or returns(end) marks the end of a range without starting a new one. For example:

```
if (i > 10 && j > i && j < 20)    /* branch(27 50 75) */
                                  /* branch(end) */
  foo (i, j);
```

For a call return percentage, the value specified is the percentage of calls reported to return. For a branch percentage, the value is either the expected percentage or 100 minus that value, since the direction of a branch can differ depending on the target or the optimization level.

Not all branches and calls need to be checked. A test should not check for branches that might be optimized away or replaced with predicated instructions. Don't check for calls inserted by the compiler or ones that might be inlined or optimized away.

A single test can check for combinations of line counts, branch percentages, and call return percentages. The command to check a line count must appear on the line that will report that count, but commands to check branch percentages and call return percentages can bracket the lines that report them.

7.7 Support for testing profile-directed optimizations

The file 'profopt.exp' provides language-independent support for checking correct execution of a test built with profile-directed optimization. This testing requires that a test program be built and executed twice. The first time it is compiled to generate profile data, and the second time it is compiled to use the data that was generated during the first execution. The second execution is to verify that the test produces the expected results.

To check that the optimization actually generated better code, a test can be built and run a third time with normal optimizations to verify that the performance is better with the profile-directed optimizations. 'profopt.exp' has the beginnings of this kind of support.

'profopt.exp' provides generic support for profile-directed optimizations. Each set of tests that uses it provides information about a specific optimization:

tool tool being tested, e.g., gcc

profile_option
    options used to generate profile data

feedback_option
    options used to optimize using that profile data

prof_ext suffix of profile data files

PROFOPT_OPTIONS
: list of options with which to run each test, similar to the lists for torture tests

`{ dg-final-generate { local-directive } }`
: This directive is similar to dg-final, but the *local-directive* is run after the generation of profile data.

`{ dg-final-use { local-directive } }`
: The *local-directive* is run after the profile data have been used.

7.8 Support for testing binary compatibility

The file 'compat.exp' provides language-independent support for binary compatibility testing. It supports testing interoperability of two compilers that follow the same ABI, or of multiple sets of compiler options that should not affect binary compatibility. It is intended to be used for testsuites that complement ABI testsuites.

A test supported by this framework has three parts, each in a separate source file: a main program and two pieces that interact with each other to split up the functionality being tested.

'`testname_main.suffix`'
: Contains the main program, which calls a function in file '`testname_x.suffix`'.

'`testname_x.suffix`'
: Contains at least one call to a function in '`testname_y.suffix`'.

'`testname_y.suffix`'
: Shares data with, or gets arguments from, '`testname_x.suffix`'.

Within each test, the main program and one functional piece are compiled by the GCC under test. The other piece can be compiled by an alternate compiler. If no alternate compiler is specified, then all three source files are all compiled by the GCC under test. You can specify pairs of sets of compiler options. The first element of such a pair specifies options used with the GCC under test, and the second element of the pair specifies options used with the alternate compiler. Each test is compiled with each pair of options.

'compat.exp' defines default pairs of compiler options. These can be overridden by defining the environment variable COMPAT_OPTIONS as:

    COMPAT_OPTIONS="[list [list {tst1} {alt1}]
        ...[list {tstn} {altn}]]"

where *tsti* and *alti* are lists of options, with *tsti* used by the compiler under test and *alti* used by the alternate compiler. For example, with [list [list {-g -O0} {-O3}] [list {-fpic} {-fPIC -O2}]], the test is first built with '-g -O0' by the compiler under test and with '-O3' by the alternate compiler. The test is built a second time using '-fpic' by the compiler under test and '-fPIC -O2' by the alternate compiler.

An alternate compiler is specified by defining an environment variable to be the full pathname of an installed compiler; for C define ALT_CC_UNDER_TEST, and for C++ define ALT_CXX_UNDER_TEST. These will be written to the 'site.exp' file used by DejaGnu. The default is to build each test with the compiler under test using the first of each pair of compiler options from COMPAT_OPTIONS. When ALT_CC_UNDER_TEST or ALT_CXX_UNDER_TEST is same, each test is built using the compiler under test but with combinations of the options from COMPAT_OPTIONS.

Chapter 7: Testsuites 111

To run only the C++ compatibility suite using the compiler under test and another version of GCC using specific compiler options, do the following from '*objdir/gcc*':

```
rm site.exp
make -k \
  ALT_CXX_UNDER_TEST=${alt_prefix}/bin/g++ \
  COMPAT_OPTIONS="lists as shown above" \
  check-c++ \
  RUNTESTFLAGS="compat.exp"
```

A test that fails when the source files are compiled with different compilers, but passes when the files are compiled with the same compiler, demonstrates incompatibility of the generated code or runtime support. A test that fails for the alternate compiler but passes for the compiler under test probably tests for a bug that was fixed in the compiler under test but is present in the alternate compiler.

The binary compatibility tests support a small number of test framework commands that appear within comments in a test file.

dg-require-*
: These commands can be used in '*testname_main.suffix*' to skip the test if specific support is not available on the target.

dg-options
: The specified options are used for compiling this particular source file, appended to the options from COMPAT_OPTIONS. When this command appears in '*testname_main.suffix*' the options are also used to link the test program.

dg-xfail-if
: This command can be used in a secondary source file to specify that compilation is expected to fail for particular options on particular targets.

7.9 Support for torture testing using multiple options

Throughout the compiler testsuite there are several directories whose tests are run multiple times, each with a different set of options. These are known as torture tests. '`lib/torture-options.exp`' defines procedures to set up these lists:

torture-init
: Initialize use of torture lists.

set-torture-options
: Set lists of torture options to use for tests with and without loops. Optionally combine a set of torture options with a set of other options, as is done with Objective-C runtime options.

torture-finish
: Finalize use of torture lists.

The '`.exp`' file for a set of tests that use torture options must include calls to these three procedures if:

- It calls `gcc-dg-runtest` and overrides *DG_TORTURE_OPTIONS*.
- It calls *${tool}*-`torture` or *${tool}*-`torture-execute`, where *tool* is `c`, `fortran`, or `objc`.

- It calls `dg-pch`.

It is not necessary for a '.exp' file that calls `gcc-dg-runtest` to call the torture procedures if the tests should use the list in *DG_TORTURE_OPTIONS* defined in 'gcc-dg.exp'.

Most uses of torture options can override the default lists by defining *TORTURE_OPTIONS* or add to the default list by defining *ADDITIONAL_TORTURE_OPTIONS*. Define these in a '.dejagnurc' file or add them to the 'site.exp' file; for example

```
set ADDITIONAL_TORTURE_OPTIONS  [list \
  { -O2 -ftree-loop-linear } \
  { -O2 -fpeel-loops } ]
```

7.10 Support for testing GIMPLE passes

As of gcc 7, C functions can be tagged with `__GIMPLE` to indicate that the function body will be GIMPLE, rather than C. The compiler requires the option '-fgimple' to enable this functionality. For example:

```
/* { dg-do compile } */
/* { dg-options "-O -fgimple" } */

void __GIMPLE (startwith ("dse2")) foo ()
{
  int a;

bb_2:
  if (a > 4)
    goto bb_3;
  else
    goto bb_4;

bb_3:
  a_2 = 10;
  goto bb_5;

bb_4:
  a_3 = 20;

bb_5:
  a_1 = __PHI (bb_3: a_2, bb_4: a_3);
  a_4 = a_1 + 4;

  return;
}
```

The `startwith` argument indicates at which pass to begin.

Use the dump modifier -gimple (e.g. '-fdump-tree-all-gimple') to make tree dumps more closely follow the format accepted by the GIMPLE parser.

Example DejaGnu tests of GIMPLE can be seen in the source tree at 'gcc/testsuite/gcc.dg/gimplefe-*.c'.

The `__GIMPLE` parser is integrated with the C tokenizer and preprocessor, so it should be possible to use macros to build out test coverage.

7.11 Support for testing RTL passes

As of gcc 7, C functions can be tagged with `__RTL` to indicate that the function body will be RTL, rather than C. For example:

```
double __RTL (startwith ("ira")) test (struct foo *f, const struct bar *b)
{
  (function "test"
     [...snip; various directives go in here...]
  ) ;; function "test"
}
```

The `startwith` argument indicates at which pass to begin.

The parser expects the RTL body to be in the format emitted by this dumping function:

```
DEBUG_FUNCTION void
print_rtx_function (FILE *outfile, function *fn, bool compact);
```

when "compact" is true. So you can capture RTL in the correct format from the debugger using:

```
(gdb) print_rtx_function (stderr, cfun, true);
```

and copy and paste the output into the body of the C function.

Example DejaGnu tests of RTL can be seen in the source tree under 'gcc/testsuite/gcc.dg/rtl'.

The `__RTL` parser is not integrated with the C tokenizer or preprocessor, and works simply by reading the relevant lines within the braces. In particular, the RTL body must be on separate lines from the enclosing braces, and the preprocessor is not usable within it.

8 Option specification files

Most GCC command-line options are described by special option definition files, the names of which conventionally end in .opt. This chapter describes the format of these files.

8.1 Option file format

Option files are a simple list of records in which each field occupies its own line and in which the records themselves are separated by blank lines. Comments may appear on their own line anywhere within the file and are preceded by semicolons. Whitespace is allowed before the semicolon.

The files can contain the following types of record:

- A language definition record. These records have two fields: the string 'Language' and the name of the language. Once a language has been declared in this way, it can be used as an option property. See Section 8.2 [Option properties], page 117.

- A target specific save record to save additional information. These records have two fields: the string 'TargetSave', and a declaration type to go in the cl_target_option structure.

- A variable record to define a variable used to store option information. These records have two fields: the string 'Variable', and a declaration of the type and name of the variable, optionally with an initializer (but without any trailing ';'). These records may be used for variables used for many options where declaring the initializer in a single option definition record, or duplicating it in many records, would be inappropriate, or for variables set in option handlers rather than referenced by Var properties.

- A variable record to define a variable used to store option information. These records have two fields: the string 'TargetVariable', and a declaration of the type and name of the variable, optionally with an initializer (but without any trailing ';'). 'TargetVariable' is a combination of 'Variable' and 'TargetSave' records in that the variable is defined in the gcc_options structure, but these variables are also stored in the cl_target_option structure. The variables are saved in the target save code and restored in the target restore code.

- A variable record to record any additional files that the 'options.h' file should include. This is useful to provide enumeration or structure definitions needed for target variables. These records have two fields: the string 'HeaderInclude' and the name of the include file.

- A variable record to record any additional files that the 'options.c' or 'options-save.c' file should include. This is useful to provide inline functions needed for target variables and/or #ifdef sequences to properly set up the initialization. These records have two fields: the string 'SourceInclude' and the name of the include file.

- An enumeration record to define a set of strings that may be used as arguments to an option or options. These records have three fields: the string 'Enum', a space-separated list of properties and help text used to describe the set of strings in '--help' output. Properties use the same format as option properties; the following are valid:

Name(*name*)
: This property is required; *name* must be a name (suitable for use in C identifiers) used to identify the set of strings in `Enum` option properties.

Type(*type*)
: This property is required; *type* is the C type for variables set by options using this enumeration together with `Var`.

UnknownError(*message*)
: The message *message* will be used as an error message if the argument is invalid; for enumerations without `UnknownError`, a generic error message is used. *message* should contain a single '%qs' format, which will be used to format the invalid argument.

- An enumeration value record to define one of the strings in a set given in an 'Enum' record. These records have two fields: the string 'EnumValue' and a space-separated list of properties. Properties use the same format as option properties; the following are valid:

Enum(*name*)
: This property is required; *name* says which 'Enum' record this 'EnumValue' record corresponds to.

String(*string*)
: This property is required; *string* is the string option argument being described by this record.

Value(*value*)
: This property is required; it says what value (representable as `int`) should be used for the given string.

Canonical
: This property is optional. If present, it says the present string is the canonical one among all those with the given value. Other strings yielding that value will be mapped to this one so specs do not need to handle them.

DriverOnly
: This property is optional. If present, the present string will only be accepted by the driver. This is used for cases such as '-march=native' that are processed by the driver so that 'gcc -v' shows how the options chosen depended on the system on which the compiler was run.

- An option definition record. These records have the following fields:
  1. the name of the option, with the leading "-" removed
  2. a space-separated list of option properties (see Section 8.2 [Option properties], page 117)
  3. the help text to use for '--help' (omitted if the second field contains the `Undocumented` property).

By default, all options beginning with "f", "W" or "m" are implicitly assumed to take a "no-" form. This form should not be listed separately. If an option beginning with one of these letters does not have a "no-" form, you can use the `RejectNegative` property to reject it.

Chapter 8: Option specification files 117

The help text is automatically line-wrapped before being displayed. Normally the name of the option is printed on the left-hand side of the output and the help text is printed on the right. However, if the help text contains a tab character, the text to the left of the tab is used instead of the option's name and the text to the right of the tab forms the help text. This allows you to elaborate on what type of argument the option takes.

- A target mask record. These records have one field of the form 'Mask(*x*)'. The options-processing script will automatically allocate a bit in `target_flags` (see Section 18.3 [Run-time Target], page 468) for each mask name *x* and set the macro MASK_*x* to the appropriate bitmask. It will also declare a TARGET_*x* macro that has the value 1 when bit MASK_*x* is set and 0 otherwise.

  They are primarily intended to declare target masks that are not associated with user options, either because these masks represent internal switches or because the options are not available on all configurations and yet the masks always need to be defined.

8.2 Option properties

The second field of an option record can specify any of the following properties. When an option takes an argument, it is enclosed in parentheses following the option property name. The parser that handles option files is quite simplistic, and will be tricked by any nested parentheses within the argument text itself; in this case, the entire option argument can be wrapped in curly braces within the parentheses to demarcate it, e.g.:

    Condition({defined (USE_CYGWIN_LIBSTDCXX_WRAPPERS)})

Common
: The option is available for all languages and targets.

Target
: The option is available for all languages but is target-specific.

Driver
: The option is handled by the compiler driver using code not shared with the compilers proper ('cc1' etc.).

language
: The option is available when compiling for the given language.

  It is possible to specify several different languages for the same option. Each *language* must have been declared by an earlier Language record. See Section 8.1 [Option file format], page 115.

RejectDriver
: The option is only handled by the compilers proper ('cc1' etc.) and should not be accepted by the driver.

RejectNegative
: The option does not have a "no-" form. All options beginning with "f", "W" or "m" are assumed to have a "no-" form unless this property is used.

Negative(*othername*)
: The option will turn off another option *othername*, which is the option name with the leading "-" removed. This chain action will propagate through the Negative property of the option to be turned off.

  As a consequence, if you have a group of mutually-exclusive options, their Negative properties should form a circular chain. For example, if options '-a', '-b' and '-c' are mutually exclusive, their respective Negative properties should be 'Negative(b)', 'Negative(c)' and 'Negative(a)'.

`Joined`
`Separate`   The option takes a mandatory argument. `Joined` indicates that the option and argument can be included in the same `argv` entry (as with `-mflush-func=`*name*, for example). `Separate` indicates that the option and argument can be separate `argv` entries (as with `-o`). An option is allowed to have both of these properties.

`JoinedOrMissing`
   The option takes an optional argument. If the argument is given, it will be part of the same `argv` entry as the option itself.

   This property cannot be used alongside `Joined` or `Separate`.

`MissingArgError(`*message*`)`
   For an option marked `Joined` or `Separate`, the message *message* will be used as an error message if the mandatory argument is missing; for options without `MissingArgError`, a generic error message is used. *message* should contain a single '%qs' format, which will be used to format the name of the option passed.

`Args(`*n*`)`   For an option marked `Separate`, indicate that it takes *n* arguments. The default is 1.

`UInteger`   The option's argument is a non-negative integer. The option parser will check and convert the argument before passing it to the relevant option handler. `UInteger` should also be used on options like `-falign-loops` where both `-falign-loops` and `-falign-loops=`*n* are supported to make sure the saved options are given a full integer.

`ToLower`   The option's argument should be converted to lowercase as part of putting it in canonical form, and before comparing with the strings indicated by any `Enum` property.

`NoDriverArg`
   For an option marked `Separate`, the option only takes an argument in the compiler proper, not in the driver. This is for compatibility with existing options that are used both directly and via '`-Wp,`'; new options should not have this property.

`Var(`*var*`)`   The state of this option should be stored in variable *var* (actually a macro for `global_options.x_`*var*). The way that the state is stored depends on the type of option:

   - If the option uses the `Mask` or `InverseMask` properties, *var* is the integer variable that contains the mask.

   - If the option is a normal on/off switch, *var* is an integer variable that is nonzero when the option is enabled. The options parser will set the variable to 1 when the positive form of the option is used and 0 when the "no-" form is used.

   - If the option takes an argument and has the `UInteger` property, *var* is an integer variable that stores the value of the argument.

   - If the option takes an argument and has the `Enum` property, *var* is a variable (type given in the `Type` property of the '`Enum`' record whose `Name` property

Chapter 8: Option specification files 119

> has the same argument as the `Enum` property of this option) that stores the
> value of the argument.

- If the option has the `Defer` property, *var* is a pointer to a
  `VEC(cl_deferred_option,heap)` that stores the option for later
  processing. (*var* is declared with type `void *` and needs to be cast to
  `VEC(cl_deferred_option,heap)` before use.)

- Otherwise, if the option takes an argument, *var* is a pointer to the argument
  string. The pointer will be null if the argument is optional and wasn't given.

The option-processing script will usually zero-initialize *var*. You can modify
this behavior using `Init`.

`Var(`*var*`,` *set*`)`
> The option controls an integer variable *var* and is active when *var* equals *set*.
> The option parser will set *var* to *set* when the positive form of the option is
> used and `!`*set* when the "no-" form is used.
>
> *var* is declared in the same way as for the single-argument form described above.

`Init(`*value*`)`
> The variable specified by the `Var` property should be statically initialized to
> *value*. If more than one option using the same variable specifies `Init`, all must
> specify the same initializer.

`Mask(`*name*`)`
> The option is associated with a bit in the `target_flags` variable (see
> Section 18.3 [Run-time Target], page 468) and is active when that bit is set.
> You may also specify `Var` to select a variable other than `target_flags`.
>
> The options-processing script will automatically allocate a unique bit for the
> option. If the option is attached to 'target_flags', the script will set the
> macro `MASK_`*name* to the appropriate bitmask. It will also declare a `TARGET_`
> *name* macro that has the value 1 when the option is active and 0 otherwise. If
> you use `Var` to attach the option to a different variable, the bitmask macro with
> be called `OPTION_MASK_`*name*.

`InverseMask(`*othername*`)`
`InverseMask(`*othername*`,` *thisname*`)`
> The option is the inverse of another option that has the `Mask(`*othername*`)` property. If *thisname* is given, the options-processing script will declare a `TARGET_`
> *thisname* macro that is 1 when the option is active and 0 otherwise.

`Enum(`*name*`)`
> The option's argument is a string from the set of strings associated with the
> corresponding 'Enum' record. The string is checked and converted to the integer
> specified in the corresponding 'EnumValue' record before being passed to option
> handlers.

`Defer`
> The option should be stored in a vector, specified with `Var`, for later processing.

`Alias(`*opt*`)`
`Alias(`*opt*`, `*arg*`)`
`Alias(`*opt*`, `*posarg*`, `*negarg*`)`

> The option is an alias for '-*opt*' (or the negative form of that option, depending on `NegativeAlias`). In the first form, any argument passed to the alias is considered to be passed to '-*opt*', and '-*opt*' is considered to be negated if the alias is used in negated form. In the second form, the alias may not be negated or have an argument, and *posarg* is considered to be passed as an argument to '-*opt*'. In the third form, the alias may not have an argument, if the alias is used in the positive form then *posarg* is considered to be passed to '-*opt*', and if the alias is used in the negative form then *negarg* is considered to be passed to '-*opt*'.
>
> Aliases should not specify `Var` or `Mask` or `UInteger`. Aliases should normally specify the same languages as the target of the alias; the flags on the target will be used to determine any diagnostic for use of an option for the wrong language, while those on the alias will be used to identify what command-line text is the option and what text is any argument to that option.
>
> When an `Alias` definition is used for an option, driver specs do not need to handle it and no 'OPT_' enumeration value is defined for it; only the canonical form of the option will be seen in those places.

`NegativeAlias`
> For an option marked with `Alias(`*opt*`)`, the option is considered to be an alias for the positive form of '-*opt*' if negated and for the negative form of '-*opt*' if not negated. `NegativeAlias` may not be used with the forms of `Alias` taking more than one argument.

`Ignore`
> This option is ignored apart from printing any warning specified using `Warn`. The option will not be seen by specs and no 'OPT_' enumeration value is defined for it.

`SeparateAlias`
> For an option marked with `Joined`, `Separate` and `Alias`, the option only acts as an alias when passed a separate argument; with a joined argument it acts as a normal option, with an 'OPT_' enumeration value. This is for compatibility with the Java '-d' option and should not be used for new options.

`Warn(`*message*`)`
> If this option is used, output the warning *message*. *message* is a format string, either taking a single operand with a '%qs' format which is the option name, or not taking any operands, which is passed to the 'warning' function. If an alias is marked `Warn`, the target of the alias must not also be marked `Warn`.

`Report`
> The state of the option should be printed by '-fverbose-asm'.

`Warning`
> This is a warning option and should be shown as such in '--help' output. This flag does not currently affect anything other than '--help'.

Optimization
: This is an optimization option. It should be shown as such in '`--help`' output, and any associated variable named using `Var` should be saved and restored when the optimization level is changed with `optimize` attributes.

PerFunction
: This is an option that can be overridden on a per-function basis. `Optimization` implies `PerFunction`, but options that do not affect executable code generation may use this flag instead, so that the option is not taken into account in ways that might affect executable code generation.

Undocumented
: The option is deliberately missing documentation and should not be included in the '`--help`' output.

Condition(*cond*)
: The option should only be accepted if preprocessor condition *cond* is true. Note that any C declarations associated with the option will be present even if *cond* is false; *cond* simply controls whether the option is accepted and whether it is printed in the '`--help`' output.

Save
: Build the `cl_target_option` structure to hold a copy of the option, add the functions `cl_target_option_save` and `cl_target_option_restore` to save and restore the options.

SetByCombined
: The option may also be set by a combined option such as '`-ffast-math`'. This causes the `gcc_options` struct to have a field `frontend_set_name`, where *name* is the name of the field holding the value of this option (without the leading `x_`). This gives the front end a way to indicate that the value has been set explicitly and should not be changed by the combined option. For example, some front ends use this to prevent '`-ffast-math`' and '`-fno-fast-math`' from changing the value of '`-fmath-errno`' for languages that do not use `errno`.

EnabledBy(*opt*)
EnabledBy(*opt* || *opt2*)
EnabledBy(*opt* && *opt2*)
: If not explicitly set, the option is set to the value of '*-opt*'; multiple options can be given, separated by ||. The third form using && specifies that the option is only set if both *opt* and *opt2* are set. The options *opt* and *opt2* must have the `Common` property; otherwise, use `LangEnabledBy`.

LangEnabledBy(*language*, *opt*)
LangEnabledBy(*language*, *opt*, *posarg*, *negarg*)
: When compiling for the given language, the option is set to the value of '*-opt*', if not explicitly set. *opt* can be also a list of || separated options. In the second form, if *opt* is used in the positive form then *posarg* is considered to be passed to the option, and if *opt* is used in the negative form then *negarg* is considered to be passed to the option. It is possible to specify several different languages. Each *language* must have been declared by an earlier `Language` record. See Section 8.1 [Option file format], page 115.

NoDWARFRecord
: The option is omitted from the producer string written by '-grecord-gcc-switches'.

PchIgnore
: Even if this is a target option, this option will not be recorded / compared to determine if a precompiled header file matches.

CPP(*var*)
: The state of this option should be kept in sync with the preprocessor option *var*. If this property is set, then properties Var and Init must be set as well.

CppReason(*CPP_W_Enum*)
: This warning option corresponds to cpplib.h warning reason code *CPP_W_Enum*. This should only be used for warning options of the C-family front-ends.

9 Passes and Files of the Compiler

This chapter is dedicated to giving an overview of the optimization and code generation passes of the compiler. In the process, it describes some of the language front end interface, though this description is no where near complete.

9.1 Parsing pass

The language front end is invoked only once, via `lang_hooks.parse_file`, to parse the entire input. The language front end may use any intermediate language representation deemed appropriate. The C front end uses GENERIC trees (see Chapter 11 [GENERIC], page 153), plus a double handful of language specific tree codes defined in 'c-common.def'. The Fortran front end uses a completely different private representation.

At some point the front end must translate the representation used in the front end to a representation understood by the language-independent portions of the compiler. Current practice takes one of two forms. The C front end manually invokes the gimplifier (see Chapter 12 [GIMPLE], page 199) on each function, and uses the gimplifier callbacks to convert the language-specific tree nodes directly to GIMPLE before passing the function off to be compiled. The Fortran front end converts from a private representation to GENERIC, which is later lowered to GIMPLE when the function is compiled. Which route to choose probably depends on how well GENERIC (plus extensions) can be made to match up with the source language and necessary parsing data structures.

BUG: Gimplification must occur before nested function lowering, and nested function lowering must be done by the front end before passing the data off to cgraph.

TODO: Cgraph should control nested function lowering. It would only be invoked when it is certain that the outer-most function is used.

TODO: Cgraph needs a gimplify_function callback. It should be invoked when (1) it is certain that the function is used, (2) warning flags specified by the user require some amount of compilation in order to honor, (3) the language indicates that semantic analysis is not complete until gimplification occurs. Hum... this sounds overly complicated. Perhaps we should just have the front end gimplify always; in most cases it's only one function call.

The front end needs to pass all function definitions and top level declarations off to the middle-end so that they can be compiled and emitted to the object file. For a simple procedural language, it is usually most convenient to do this as each top level declaration or definition is seen. There is also a distinction to be made between generating functional code and generating complete debug information. The only thing that is absolutely required for functional code is that function and data *definitions* be passed to the middle-end. For complete debug information, function, data and type declarations should all be passed as well.

In any case, the front end needs each complete top-level function or data declaration, and each data definition should be passed to `rest_of_decl_compilation`. Each complete type definition should be passed to `rest_of_type_compilation`. Each function definition should be passed to `cgraph_finalize_function`.

TODO: I know rest_of_compilation currently has all sorts of RTL generation semantics. I plan to move all code generation bits (both Tree and RTL) to compile_function. Should we hide cgraph from the front ends and move back to rest_of_compilation as the official interface? Possibly we should rename all three interfaces such that the names match in some meaningful way and that is more descriptive than "rest_of".

The middle-end will, at its option, emit the function and data definitions immediately or queue them for later processing.

9.2 Gimplification pass

Gimplification is a whimsical term for the process of converting the intermediate representation of a function into the GIMPLE language (see Chapter 12 [GIMPLE], page 199). The term stuck, and so words like "gimplification", "gimplify", "gimplifier" and the like are sprinkled throughout this section of code.

While a front end may certainly choose to generate GIMPLE directly if it chooses, this can be a moderately complex process unless the intermediate language used by the front end is already fairly simple. Usually it is easier to generate GENERIC trees plus extensions and let the language-independent gimplifier do most of the work.

The main entry point to this pass is `gimplify_function_tree` located in 'gimplify.c'. From here we process the entire function gimplifying each statement in turn. The main workhorse for this pass is `gimplify_expr`. Approximately everything passes through here at least once, and it is from here that we invoke the `lang_hooks.gimplify_expr` callback.

The callback should examine the expression in question and return `GS_UNHANDLED` if the expression is not a language specific construct that requires attention. Otherwise it should alter the expression in some way to such that forward progress is made toward producing valid GIMPLE. If the callback is certain that the transformation is complete and the expression is valid GIMPLE, it should return `GS_ALL_DONE`. Otherwise it should return `GS_OK`, which will cause the expression to be processed again. If the callback encounters an error during the transformation (because the front end is relying on the gimplification process to finish semantic checks), it should return `GS_ERROR`.

9.3 Pass manager

The pass manager is located in 'passes.c', 'tree-optimize.c' and 'tree-pass.h'. It processes passes as described in 'passes.def'. Its job is to run all of the individual passes in the correct order, and take care of standard bookkeeping that applies to every pass.

The theory of operation is that each pass defines a structure that represents everything we need to know about that pass—when it should be run, how it should be run, what intermediate language form or on-the-side data structures it needs. We register the pass to be run in some particular order, and the pass manager arranges for everything to happen in the correct order.

The actuality doesn't completely live up to the theory at present. Command-line switches and `timevar_id_t` enumerations must still be defined elsewhere. The pass manager validates constraints but does not attempt to (re-)generate data structures or lower intermediate language form based on the requirements of the next pass. Nevertheless, what is present is useful, and a far sight better than nothing at all.

Each pass should have a unique name. Each pass may have its own dump file (for GCC debugging purposes). Passes with a name starting with a star do not dump anything. Sometimes passes are supposed to share a dump file / option name. To still give these unique names, you can use a prefix that is delimited by a space from the part that is used for the dump file / option name. E.g. When the pass name is "ud dce", the name used for dump file/options is "dce".

TODO: describe the global variables set up by the pass manager, and a brief description of how a new pass should use it. I need to look at what info RTL passes use first...

9.4 Tree SSA passes

The following briefly describes the Tree optimization passes that are run after gimplification and what source files they are located in.

- Remove useless statements

  This pass is an extremely simple sweep across the gimple code in which we identify obviously dead code and remove it. Here we do things like simplify `if` statements with constant conditions, remove exception handling constructs surrounding code that obviously cannot throw, remove lexical bindings that contain no variables, and other assorted simplistic cleanups. The idea is to get rid of the obvious stuff quickly rather than wait until later when it's more work to get rid of it. This pass is located in 'tree-cfg.c' and described by **pass_remove_useless_stmts**.

- OpenMP lowering

  If OpenMP generation ('-fopenmp') is enabled, this pass lowers OpenMP constructs into GIMPLE.

  Lowering of OpenMP constructs involves creating replacement expressions for local variables that have been mapped using data sharing clauses, exposing the control flow of most synchronization directives and adding region markers to facilitate the creation of the control flow graph. The pass is located in 'omp-low.c' and is described by **pass_lower_omp**.

- OpenMP expansion

  If OpenMP generation ('-fopenmp') is enabled, this pass expands parallel regions into their own functions to be invoked by the thread library. The pass is located in 'omp-low.c' and is described by **pass_expand_omp**.

- Lower control flow

  This pass flattens `if` statements (COND_EXPR) and moves lexical bindings (BIND_EXPR) out of line. After this pass, all `if` statements will have exactly two `goto` statements in its **then** and **else** arms. Lexical binding information for each statement will be found in TREE_BLOCK rather than being inferred from its position under a BIND_EXPR. This pass is found in 'gimple-low.c' and is described by **pass_lower_cf**.

- Lower exception handling control flow

  This pass decomposes high-level exception handling constructs (TRY_FINALLY_EXPR and TRY_CATCH_EXPR) into a form that explicitly represents the control flow involved. After this pass, **lookup_stmt_eh_region** will return a non-negative number for any statement that may have EH control flow semantics; examine **tree_can_throw_internal** or **tree_can_throw_external** for exact semantics. Exact control flow may be extracted from **foreach_reachable_handler**. The EH region nesting tree is defined in 'except.h' and built in 'except.c'. The lowering pass itself is in 'tree-eh.c' and is described by **pass_lower_eh**.

- Build the control flow graph

  This pass decomposes a function into basic blocks and creates all of the edges that connect them. It is located in 'tree-cfg.c' and is described by `pass_build_cfg`.

- Find all referenced variables

  This pass walks the entire function and collects an array of all variables referenced in the function, `referenced_vars`. The index at which a variable is found in the array is used as a UID for the variable within this function. This data is needed by the SSA rewriting routines. The pass is located in 'tree-dfa.c' and is described by `pass_referenced_vars`.

- Enter static single assignment form

  This pass rewrites the function such that it is in SSA form. After this pass, all `is_gimple_reg` variables will be referenced by `SSA_NAME`, and all occurrences of other variables will be annotated with `VDEFS` and `VUSES`; PHI nodes will have been inserted as necessary for each basic block. This pass is located in 'tree-ssa.c' and is described by `pass_build_ssa`.

- Warn for uninitialized variables

  This pass scans the function for uses of `SSA_NAME`s that are fed by default definition. For non-parameter variables, such uses are uninitialized. The pass is run twice, before and after optimization (if turned on). In the first pass we only warn for uses that are positively uninitialized; in the second pass we warn for uses that are possibly uninitialized. The pass is located in 'tree-ssa.c' and is defined by `pass_early_warn_uninitialized` and `pass_late_warn_uninitialized`.

- Dead code elimination

  This pass scans the function for statements without side effects whose result is unused. It does not do memory life analysis, so any value that is stored in memory is considered used. The pass is run multiple times throughout the optimization process. It is located in 'tree-ssa-dce.c' and is described by `pass_dce`.

- Dominator optimizations

  This pass performs trivial dominator-based copy and constant propagation, expression simplification, and jump threading. It is run multiple times throughout the optimization process. It is located in 'tree-ssa-dom.c' and is described by `pass_dominator`.

- Forward propagation of single-use variables

  This pass attempts to remove redundant computation by substituting variables that are used once into the expression that uses them and seeing if the result can be simplified. It is located in 'tree-ssa-forwprop.c' and is described by `pass_forwprop`.

- Copy Renaming

  This pass attempts to change the name of compiler temporaries involved in copy operations such that SSA->normal can coalesce the copy away. When compiler temporaries are copies of user variables, it also renames the compiler temporary to the user variable resulting in better use of user symbols. It is located in 'tree-ssa-copyrename.c' and is described by `pass_copyrename`.

- PHI node optimizations

  This pass recognizes forms of PHI inputs that can be represented as conditional expressions and rewrites them into straight line code. It is located in 'tree-ssa-phiopt.c' and is described by **pass_phiopt**.

- May-alias optimization

  This pass performs a flow sensitive SSA-based points-to analysis. The resulting may-alias, must-alias, and escape analysis information is used to promote variables from in-memory addressable objects to non-aliased variables that can be renamed into SSA form. We also update the **VDEF/VUSE** memory tags for non-renameable aggregates so that we get fewer false kills. The pass is located in 'tree-ssa-alias.c' and is described by **pass_may_alias**.

  Interprocedural points-to information is located in 'tree-ssa-structalias.c' and described by **pass_ipa_pta**.

- Profiling

  This pass instruments the function in order to collect runtime block and value profiling data. Such data may be fed back into the compiler on a subsequent run so as to allow optimization based on expected execution frequencies. The pass is located in 'tree-profile.c' and is described by **pass_ipa_tree_profile**.

- Static profile estimation

  This pass implements series of heuristics to guess propababilities of branches. The resulting predictions are turned into edge profile by propagating branches across the control flow graphs. The pass is located in 'tree-profile.c' and is described by **pass_profile**.

- Lower complex arithmetic

  This pass rewrites complex arithmetic operations into their component scalar arithmetic operations. The pass is located in 'tree-complex.c' and is described by **pass_lower_complex**.

- Scalar replacement of aggregates

  This pass rewrites suitable non-aliased local aggregate variables into a set of scalar variables. The resulting scalar variables are rewritten into SSA form, which allows subsequent optimization passes to do a significantly better job with them. The pass is located in 'tree-sra.c' and is described by **pass_sra**.

- Dead store elimination

  This pass eliminates stores to memory that are subsequently overwritten by another store, without any intervening loads. The pass is located in 'tree-ssa-dse.c' and is described by **pass_dse**.

- Tail recursion elimination

  This pass transforms tail recursion into a loop. It is located in 'tree-tailcall.c' and is described by **pass_tail_recursion**.

- Forward store motion

  This pass sinks stores and assignments down the flowgraph closer to their use point. The pass is located in 'tree-ssa-sink.c' and is described by **pass_sink_code**.

- Partial redundancy elimination

    This pass eliminates partially redundant computations, as well as performing load motion. The pass is located in 'tree-ssa-pre.c' and is described by `pass_pre`.

    Just before partial redundancy elimination, if '-funsafe-math-optimizations' is on, GCC tries to convert divisions to multiplications by the reciprocal. The pass is located in 'tree-ssa-math-opts.c' and is described by `pass_cse_reciprocal`.

- Full redundancy elimination

    This is a simpler form of PRE that only eliminates redundancies that occur on all paths. It is located in 'tree-ssa-pre.c' and described by `pass_fre`.

- Loop optimization

    The main driver of the pass is placed in 'tree-ssa-loop.c' and described by `pass_loop`.

    The optimizations performed by this pass are:

    Loop invariant motion. This pass moves only invariants that would be hard to handle on RTL level (function calls, operations that expand to nontrivial sequences of insns). With '-funswitch-loops' it also moves operands of conditions that are invariant out of the loop, so that we can use just trivial invariantness analysis in loop unswitching. The pass also includes store motion. The pass is implemented in 'tree-ssa-loop-im.c'.

    Canonical induction variable creation. This pass creates a simple counter for number of iterations of the loop and replaces the exit condition of the loop using it, in case when a complicated analysis is necessary to determine the number of iterations. Later optimizations then may determine the number easily. The pass is implemented in 'tree-ssa-loop-ivcanon.c'.

    Induction variable optimizations. This pass performs standard induction variable optimizations, including strength reduction, induction variable merging and induction variable elimination. The pass is implemented in 'tree-ssa-loop-ivopts.c'.

    Loop unswitching. This pass moves the conditional jumps that are invariant out of the loops. To achieve this, a duplicate of the loop is created for each possible outcome of conditional jump(s). The pass is implemented in 'tree-ssa-loop-unswitch.c'.

    Loop splitting. If a loop contains a conditional statement that is always true for one part of the iteration space and false for the other this pass splits the loop into two, one dealing with one side the other only with the other, thereby removing one inner-loop conditional. The pass is implemented in 'tree-ssa-loop-split.c'.

    The optimizations also use various utility functions contained in 'tree-ssa-loop-manip.c', 'cfgloop.c', 'cfgloopanal.c' and 'cfgloopmanip.c'.

    Vectorization. This pass transforms loops to operate on vector types instead of scalar types. Data parallelism across loop iterations is exploited to group data elements from consecutive iterations into a vector and operate on them in parallel. Depending on available target support the loop is conceptually unrolled by a factor VF (vectorization factor), which is the number of elements operated upon in parallel in each iteration, and the VF copies of each scalar operation are fused to form a vector operation. Additional loop transformations such as peeling and versioning may take place to align the number of iterations, and to align the memory accesses in the loop. The pass is implemented in 'tree-vectorizer.c' (the main driver), 'tree-vect-loop.c' and 'tree-vect-loop-manip.c' (loop specific parts and general loop utilities), 'tree-vect-slp' (loop-aware SLP functionality), 'tree-vect-stmts.c' and 'tree-vect-data-refs.c'. Analysis of data references is in 'tree-data-ref.c'.

SLP Vectorization. This pass performs vectorization of straight-line code. The pass is implemented in 'tree-vectorizer.c' (the main driver), 'tree-vect-slp.c', 'tree-vect-stmts.c' and 'tree-vect-data-refs.c'.

Autoparallelization. This pass splits the loop iteration space to run into several threads. The pass is implemented in 'tree-parloops.c'.

Graphite is a loop transformation framework based on the polyhedral model. Graphite stands for Gimple Represented as Polyhedra. The internals of this infrastructure are documented in http://gcc.gnu.org/wiki/Graphite. The passes working on this representation are implemented in the various 'graphite-*' files.

- Tree level if-conversion for vectorizer

  This pass applies if-conversion to simple loops to help vectorizer. We identify if convertible loops, if-convert statements and merge basic blocks in one big block. The idea is to present loop in such form so that vectorizer can have one to one mapping between statements and available vector operations. This pass is located in 'tree-if-conv.c' and is described by **pass_if_conversion**.

- Conditional constant propagation

  This pass relaxes a lattice of values in order to identify those that must be constant even in the presence of conditional branches. The pass is located in 'tree-ssa-ccp.c' and is described by **pass_ccp**.

  A related pass that works on memory loads and stores, and not just register values, is located in 'tree-ssa-ccp.c' and described by **pass_store_ccp**.

- Conditional copy propagation

  This is similar to constant propagation but the lattice of values is the "copy-of" relation. It eliminates redundant copies from the code. The pass is located in 'tree-ssa-copy.c' and described by **pass_copy_prop**.

  A related pass that works on memory copies, and not just register copies, is located in 'tree-ssa-copy.c' and described by **pass_store_copy_prop**.

- Value range propagation

  This transformation is similar to constant propagation but instead of propagating single constant values, it propagates known value ranges. The implementation is based on Patterson's range propagation algorithm (Accurate Static Branch Prediction by Value Range Propagation, J. R. C. Patterson, PLDI '95). In contrast to Patterson's algorithm, this implementation does not propagate branch probabilities nor it uses more than a single range per SSA name. This means that the current implementation cannot be used for branch prediction (though adapting it would not be difficult). The pass is located in 'tree-vrp.c' and is described by **pass_vrp**.

- Folding built-in functions

  This pass simplifies built-in functions, as applicable, with constant arguments or with inferable string lengths. It is located in 'tree-ssa-ccp.c' and is described by **pass_fold_builtins**.

- Split critical edges

  This pass identifies critical edges and inserts empty basic blocks such that the edge is no longer critical. The pass is located in 'tree-cfg.c' and is described by `pass_split_crit_edges`.

- Control dependence dead code elimination

  This pass is a stronger form of dead code elimination that can eliminate unnecessary control flow statements. It is located in 'tree-ssa-dce.c' and is described by `pass_cd_dce`.

- Tail call elimination

  This pass identifies function calls that may be rewritten into jumps. No code transformation is actually applied here, but the data and control flow problem is solved. The code transformation requires target support, and so is delayed until RTL. In the meantime `CALL_EXPR_TAILCALL` is set indicating the possibility. The pass is located in 'tree-tailcall.c' and is described by `pass_tail_calls`. The RTL transformation is handled by `fixup_tail_calls` in 'calls.c'.

- Warn for function return without value

  For non-void functions, this pass locates return statements that do not specify a value and issues a warning. Such a statement may have been injected by falling off the end of the function. This pass is run last so that we have as much time as possible to prove that the statement is not reachable. It is located in 'tree-cfg.c' and is described by `pass_warn_function_return`.

- Leave static single assignment form

  This pass rewrites the function such that it is in normal form. At the same time, we eliminate as many single-use temporaries as possible, so the intermediate language is no longer GIMPLE, but GENERIC. The pass is located in 'tree-outof-ssa.c' and is described by `pass_del_ssa`.

- Merge PHI nodes that feed into one another

  This is part of the CFG cleanup passes. It attempts to join PHI nodes from a forwarder CFG block into another block with PHI nodes. The pass is located in 'tree-cfgcleanup.c' and is described by `pass_merge_phi`.

- Return value optimization

  If a function always returns the same local variable, and that local variable is an aggregate type, then the variable is replaced with the return value for the function (i.e., the function's DECL_RESULT). This is equivalent to the C++ named return value optimization applied to GIMPLE. The pass is located in 'tree-nrv.c' and is described by `pass_nrv`.

- Return slot optimization

  If a function returns a memory object and is called as `var = foo()`, this pass tries to change the call so that the address of `var` is sent to the caller to avoid an extra memory copy. This pass is located in tree-nrv.c and is described by `pass_return_slot`.

- Optimize calls to `__builtin_object_size`

  This is a propagation pass similar to CCP that tries to remove calls to `__builtin_object_size` when the size of the object can be computed at compile-time. This pass is located in 'tree-object-size.c' and is described by `pass_object_sizes`.

Chapter 9: Passes and Files of the Compiler   131

- Loop invariant motion

  This pass removes expensive loop-invariant computations out of loops. The pass is located in 'tree-ssa-loop.c' and described by **pass_lim**.

- Loop nest optimizations

  This is a family of loop transformations that works on loop nests. It includes loop interchange, scaling, skewing and reversal and they are all geared to the optimization of data locality in array traversals and the removal of dependencies that hamper optimizations such as loop parallelization and vectorization. The pass is located in 'tree-loop-linear.c' and described by **pass_linear_transform**.

- Removal of empty loops

  This pass removes loops with no code in them. The pass is located in 'tree-ssa-loop-ivcanon.c' and described by **pass_empty_loop**.

- Unrolling of small loops

  This pass completely unrolls loops with few iterations. The pass is located in 'tree-ssa-loop-ivcanon.c' and described by **pass_complete_unroll**.

- Predictive commoning

  This pass makes the code reuse the computations from the previous iterations of the loops, especially loads and stores to memory. It does so by storing the values of these computations to a bank of temporary variables that are rotated at the end of loop. To avoid the need for this rotation, the loop is then unrolled and the copies of the loop body are rewritten to use the appropriate version of the temporary variable. This pass is located in 'tree-predcom.c' and described by **pass_predcom**.

- Array prefetching

  This pass issues prefetch instructions for array references inside loops. The pass is located in 'tree-ssa-loop-prefetch.c' and described by **pass_loop_prefetch**.

- Reassociation

  This pass rewrites arithmetic expressions to enable optimizations that operate on them, like redundancy elimination and vectorization. The pass is located in 'tree-ssa-reassoc.c' and described by **pass_reassoc**.

- Optimization of **stdarg** functions

  This pass tries to avoid the saving of register arguments into the stack on entry to **stdarg** functions. If the function doesn't use any **va_start** macros, no registers need to be saved. If **va_start** macros are used, the **va_list** variables don't escape the function, it is only necessary to save registers that will be used in **va_arg** macros. For instance, if **va_arg** is only used with integral types in the function, floating point registers don't need to be saved. This pass is located in **tree-stdarg.c** and described by **pass_stdarg**.

9.5 RTL passes

The following briefly describes the RTL generation and optimization passes that are run after the Tree optimization passes.

- RTL generation

  The source files for RTL generation include 'stmt.c', 'calls.c', 'expr.c', 'explow.c', 'expmed.c', 'function.c', 'optabs.c' and 'emit-rtl.c'. Also, the file 'insn-emit.c', generated from the machine description by the program `genemit`, is used in this pass. The header file 'expr.h' is used for communication within this pass.

The header files 'insn-flags.h' and 'insn-codes.h', generated from the machine description by the programs `genflags` and `gencodes`, tell this pass which standard names are available for use and which patterns correspond to them.

- Generation of exception landing pads

    This pass generates the glue that handles communication between the exception handling library routines and the exception handlers within the function. Entry points in the function that are invoked by the exception handling library are called *landing pads*. The code for this pass is located in 'except.c'.

- Control flow graph cleanup

    This pass removes unreachable code, simplifies jumps to next, jumps to jump, jumps across jumps, etc. The pass is run multiple times. For historical reasons, it is occasionally referred to as the "jump optimization pass". The bulk of the code for this pass is in 'cfgcleanup.c', and there are support routines in 'cfgrtl.c' and 'jump.c'.

- Forward propagation of single-def values

    This pass attempts to remove redundant computation by substituting variables that come from a single definition, and seeing if the result can be simplified. It performs copy propagation and addressing mode selection. The pass is run twice, with values being propagated into loops only on the second run. The code is located in 'fwprop.c'.

- Common subexpression elimination

    This pass removes redundant computation within basic blocks, and optimizes addressing modes based on cost. The pass is run twice. The code for this pass is located in 'cse.c'.

- Global common subexpression elimination

    This pass performs two different types of GCSE depending on whether you are optimizing for size or not (LCM based GCSE tends to increase code size for a gain in speed, while Morel-Renvoise based GCSE does not). When optimizing for size, GCSE is done using Morel-Renvoise Partial Redundancy Elimination, with the exception that it does not try to move invariants out of loops—that is left to the loop optimization pass. If MR PRE GCSE is done, code hoisting (aka unification) is also done, as well as load motion. If you are optimizing for speed, LCM (lazy code motion) based GCSE is done. LCM is based on the work of Knoop, Ruthing, and Steffen. LCM based GCSE also does loop invariant code motion. We also perform load and store motion when optimizing for speed. Regardless of which type of GCSE is used, the GCSE pass also performs global constant and copy propagation. The source file for this pass is 'gcse.c', and the LCM routines are in 'lcm.c'.

- Loop optimization

    This pass performs several loop related optimizations. The source files 'cfgloopanal.c' and 'cfgloopmanip.c' contain generic loop analysis and manipulation code. Initialization and finalization of loop structures is handled by 'loop-init.c'. A loop invariant motion pass is implemented in 'loop-invariant.c'. Basic block level optimizations—unrolling, and peeling loops— are implemented in 'loop-unroll.c'. Replacing of the exit condition of loops by special machine-dependent instructions is handled by 'loop-doloop.c'.

- Jump bypassing

  This pass is an aggressive form of GCSE that transforms the control flow graph of a function by propagating constants into conditional branch instructions. The source file for this pass is 'gcse.c'.

- If conversion

  This pass attempts to replace conditional branches and surrounding assignments with arithmetic, boolean value producing comparison instructions, and conditional move instructions. In the very last invocation after reload/LRA, it will generate predicated instructions when supported by the target. The code is located in 'ifcvt.c'.

- Web construction

  This pass splits independent uses of each pseudo-register. This can improve effect of the other transformation, such as CSE or register allocation. The code for this pass is located in 'web.c'.

- Instruction combination

  This pass attempts to combine groups of two or three instructions that are related by data flow into single instructions. It combines the RTL expressions for the instructions by substitution, simplifies the result using algebra, and then attempts to match the result against the machine description. The code is located in 'combine.c'.

- Mode switching optimization

  This pass looks for instructions that require the processor to be in a specific "mode" and minimizes the number of mode changes required to satisfy all users. What these modes are, and what they apply to are completely target-specific. The code for this pass is located in 'mode-switching.c'.

- Modulo scheduling

  This pass looks at innermost loops and reorders their instructions by overlapping different iterations. Modulo scheduling is performed immediately before instruction scheduling. The code for this pass is located in 'modulo-sched.c'.

- Instruction scheduling

  This pass looks for instructions whose output will not be available by the time that it is used in subsequent instructions. Memory loads and floating point instructions often have this behavior on RISC machines. It re-orders instructions within a basic block to try to separate the definition and use of items that otherwise would cause pipeline stalls. This pass is performed twice, before and after register allocation. The code for this pass is located in 'haifa-sched.c', 'sched-deps.c', 'sched-ebb.c', 'sched-rgn.c' and 'sched-vis.c'.

- Register allocation

  These passes make sure that all occurrences of pseudo registers are eliminated, either by allocating them to a hard register, replacing them by an equivalent expression (e.g. a constant) or by placing them on the stack. This is done in several subpasses:

  - The integrated register allocator (IRA). It is called integrated because coalescing, register live range splitting, and hard register preferencing are done on-the-fly during coloring. It also has better integration with the reload/LRA pass. Pseudo-registers spilled by the allocator or the reload/LRA have still a chance to get hard-registers if the reload/LRA evicts some pseudo-registers from hard-registers. The allocator helps to choose better pseudos for spilling based on their live ranges and to coalesce stack slots allocated for the spilled pseudo-registers. IRA is a regional register allocator which is transformed into Chaitin-Briggs allocator if there is one region. By default, IRA chooses regions using register pressure but the user can force it to use one region or regions corresponding to all loops.

Source files of the allocator are 'ira.c', 'ira-build.c', 'ira-costs.c', 'ira-conflicts.c', 'ira-color.c', 'ira-emit.c', 'ira-lives', plus header files 'ira.h' and 'ira-int.h' used for the communication between the allocator and the rest of the compiler and between the IRA files.

- Reloading. This pass renumbers pseudo registers with the hardware registers numbers they were allocated. Pseudo registers that did not get hard registers are replaced with stack slots. Then it finds instructions that are invalid because a value has failed to end up in a register, or has ended up in a register of the wrong kind. It fixes up these instructions by reloading the problematical values temporarily into registers. Additional instructions are generated to do the copying.

  The reload pass also optionally eliminates the frame pointer and inserts instructions to save and restore call-clobbered registers around calls.

  Source files are 'reload.c' and 'reload1.c', plus the header 'reload.h' used for communication between them.

- This pass is a modern replacement of the reload pass. Source files are 'lra.c', 'lra-assign.c', 'lra-coalesce.c', 'lra-constraints.c', 'lra-eliminations.c', 'lra-lives.c', 'lra-remat.c', 'lra-spills.c', the header 'lra-int.h' used for communication between them, and the header 'lra.h' used for communication between LRA and the rest of compiler.

  Unlike the reload pass, intermediate LRA decisions are reflected in RTL as much as possible. This reduces the number of target-dependent macros and hooks, leaving instruction constraints as the primary source of control.

  LRA is run on targets for which TARGET_LRA_P returns true.

- Basic block reordering

  This pass implements profile guided code positioning. If profile information is not available, various types of static analysis are performed to make the predictions normally coming from the profile feedback (IE execution frequency, branch probability, etc). It is implemented in the file 'bb-reorder.c', and the various prediction routines are in 'predict.c'.

- Variable tracking

  This pass computes where the variables are stored at each position in code and generates notes describing the variable locations to RTL code. The location lists are then generated according to these notes to debug information if the debugging information format supports location lists. The code is located in 'var-tracking.c'.

- Delayed branch scheduling

  This optional pass attempts to find instructions that can go into the delay slots of other instructions, usually jumps and calls. The code for this pass is located in 'reorg.c'.

Chapter 9: Passes and Files of the Compiler   135

- Branch shortening

  On many RISC machines, branch instructions have a limited range. Thus, longer sequences of instructions must be used for long branches. In this pass, the compiler figures out what how far each instruction will be from each other instruction, and therefore whether the usual instructions, or the longer sequences, must be used for each branch. The code for this pass is located in 'final.c'.

- Register-to-stack conversion

  Conversion from usage of some hard registers to usage of a register stack may be done at this point. Currently, this is supported only for the floating-point registers of the Intel 80387 coprocessor. The code for this pass is located in 'reg-stack.c'.

- Final

  This pass outputs the assembler code for the function. The source files are 'final.c' plus 'insn-output.c'; the latter is generated automatically from the machine description by the tool 'genoutput'. The header file 'conditions.h' is used for communication between these files.

- Debugging information output

  This is run after final because it must output the stack slot offsets for pseudo registers that did not get hard registers. Source files are 'dbxout.c' for DBX symbol table format, 'dwarfout.c' for DWARF symbol table format, files 'dwarf2out.c' and 'dwarf2asm.c' for DWARF2 symbol table format, and 'vmsdbgout.c' for VMS debug symbol table format.

9.6 Optimization info

This section is describes dump infrastructure which is common to both pass dumps as well as optimization dumps. The goal for this infrastructure is to provide both gcc developers and users detailed information about various compiler transformations and optimizations.

9.6.1 Dump setup

A dump_manager class is defined in 'dumpfile.h'. Various passes register dumping pass-specific information via dump_register in 'passes.c'. During the registration, an optimization pass can select its optimization group (see Section 9.6.2 [Optimization groups], page 135). After that optimization information corresponding to the entire group (presumably from multiple passes) can be output via command-line switches. Note that if a pass does not fit into any of the pre-defined groups, it can select OPTGROUP_NONE.

Note that in general, a pass need not know its dump output file name, whether certain flags are enabled, etc. However, for legacy reasons, passes could also call dump_begin which returns a stream in case the particular pass has optimization dumps enabled. A pass could call dump_end when the dump has ended. These methods should go away once all the passes are converted to use the new dump infrastructure.

The recommended way to setup the dump output is via dump_start and dump_end.

9.6.2 Optimization groups

The optimization passes are grouped into several categories. Currently defined categories in 'dumpfile.h' are

OPTGROUP_IPA
: IPA optimization passes. Enabled by '-ipa'

OPTGROUP_LOOP
: Loop optimization passes. Enabled by '-loop'.

OPTGROUP_INLINE
: Inlining passes. Enabled by '-inline'.

OPTGROUP_OMP
: OMP (Offloading and Multi Processing) passes. Enabled by '-omp'.

OPTGROUP_VEC
: Vectorization passes. Enabled by '-vec'.

OPTGROUP_OTHER
: All other optimization passes which do not fall into one of the above.

OPTGROUP_ALL
: All optimization passes. Enabled by '-optall'.

By using groups a user could selectively enable optimization information only for a group of passes. By default, the optimization information for all the passes is dumped.

9.6.3 Dump files and streams

There are two separate output streams available for outputting optimization information from passes. Note that both these streams accept **stderr** and **stdout** as valid streams and thus it is possible to dump output to standard output or error. This is specially handy for outputting all available information in a single file by redirecting **stderr**.

pstream
: This stream is for pass-specific dump output. For example, '-fdump-tree-vect=foo.v' dumps tree vectorization pass output into the given file name 'foo.v'. If the file name is not provided, the default file name is based on the source file and pass number. Note that one could also use special file names **stdout** and **stderr** for dumping to standard output and standard error respectively.

alt_stream
: This steam is used for printing optimization specific output in response to the '-fopt-info'. Again a file name can be given. If the file name is not given, it defaults to **stderr**.

9.6.4 Dump output verbosity

The dump verbosity has the following options

'optimized'
: Print information when an optimization is successfully applied. It is up to a pass to decide which information is relevant. For example, the vectorizer passes print the source location of loops which got successfully vectorized.

'missed'
: Print information about missed optimizations. Individual passes control which information to include in the output. For example,

```
gcc -O2 -ftree-vectorize -fopt-info-vec-missed
```
will print information about missed optimization opportunities from vectorization passes on stderr.

'`note`' Print verbose information about optimizations, such as certain transformations, more detailed messages about decisions etc.

'`all`' Print detailed optimization information. This includes *optimized*, *missed*, and *note*.

9.6.5 Dump types

`dump_printf`
: This is a generic method for doing formatted output. It takes an additional argument `dump_kind` which signifies the type of dump. This method outputs information only when the dumps are enabled for this particular `dump_kind`. Note that the caller doesn't need to know if the particular dump is enabled or not, or even the file name. The caller only needs to decide which dump output information is relevant, and under what conditions. This determines the associated flags.

  Consider the following example from '`loop-unroll.c`' where an informative message about a loop (along with its location) is printed when any of the following flags is enabled

  - optimization messages
  - RTL dumps
  - detailed dumps

  ```
  int report_flags = MSG_OPTIMIZED_LOCATIONS | TDF_RTL | TDF_DETAILS;
  dump_printf_loc (report_flags, locus,
                   "loop turned into non-loop; it never loops.\n");
  ```

`dump_basic_block`
: Output basic block.

`dump_generic_expr`
: Output generic expression.

`dump_gimple_stmt`
: Output gimple statement.

  Note that the above methods also have variants prefixed with `_loc`, such as `dump_printf_loc`, which are similar except they also output the source location information.

9.6.6 Dump examples

```
gcc -O3 -fopt-info-missed=missed.all
```
outputs missed optimization report from all the passes into '`missed.all`'.

As another example,
```
gcc -O3 -fopt-info-inline-optimized-missed=inline.txt
```
will output information about missed optimizations as well as optimized locations from all the inlining passes into '`inline.txt`'.

If the *filename* is provided, then the dumps from all the applicable optimizations are concatenated into the '`filename`'. Otherwise the dump is output onto 'stderr'. If *options* is omitted, it defaults to '`optimized-optall`', which means dump all information about successful optimizations from all the passes. In the following example, the optimization information is output on to 'stderr'.

```
gcc -O3 -fopt-info
```

Note that '`-fopt-info-vec-missed`' behaves the same as '`-fopt-info-missed-vec`'. The order of the optimization group names and message types listed after '`-fopt-info`' does not matter.

As another example, consider

```
gcc -fopt-info-vec-missed=vec.miss -fopt-info-loop-optimized=loop.opt
```

Here the two output file names '`vec.miss`' and '`loop.opt`' are in conflict since only one output file is allowed. In this case, only the first option takes effect and the subsequent options are ignored. Thus only the '`vec.miss`' is produced which containts dumps from the vectorizer about missed opportunities.

10 Sizes and offsets as runtime invariants

GCC allows the size of a hardware register to be a runtime invariant rather than a compile-time constant. This in turn means that various sizes and offsets must also be runtime invariants rather than compile-time constants, such as:

- the size of a general `machine_mode` (see Section 14.6 [Machine Modes], page 261);
- the size of a spill slot;
- the offset of something within a stack frame;
- the number of elements in a vector;
- the size and offset of a `mem` rtx (see Section 14.8 [Regs and Memory], page 272); and
- the byte offset in a `subreg` rtx (see Section 14.8 [Regs and Memory], page 272).

The motivating example is the Arm SVE ISA, whose vector registers can be any multiple of 128 bits between 128 and 2048 inclusive. The compiler normally produces code that works for all SVE register sizes, with the actual size only being known at runtime.

GCC's main representation of such runtime invariants is the `poly_int` class. This chapter describes what `poly_int` does, lists the available operations, and gives some general usage guidelines.

10.1 Overview of `poly_int`

We define indeterminates x_1, ..., x_n whose values are only known at runtime and use polynomials of the form:

    c0 + c1 * x1 + ... + cn * xn

to represent a size or offset whose value might depend on some of these indeterminates. The coefficients c_0, ..., c_n are always known at compile time, with the c_0 term being the "constant" part that does not depend on any runtime value.

GCC uses the `poly_int` class to represent these coefficients. The class has two template parameters: the first specifies the number of coefficients ($n + 1$) and the second specifies the type of the coefficients. For example, '`poly_int<2, unsigned short>`' represents a polynomial with two coefficients (and thus one indeterminate), with each coefficient having type `unsigned short`. When n is 0, the class degenerates to a single compile-time constant c_0.

The number of coefficients needed for compilation is a fixed property of each target and is specified by the configuration macro `NUM_POLY_INT_COEFFS`. The default value is 1, since most targets do not have such runtime invariants. Targets that need a different value should #define the macro in their '`cpu-modes.def`' file. See Section 6.3.9 [Back End], page 75.

`poly_int` makes the simplifying requirement that each indeterminate must be a nonnegative integer. An indeterminate value of 0 should usually represent the minimum possible runtime value, with c_0 specifying the value in that case.

For example, when targetting the Arm SVE ISA, the single indeterminate represents the number of 128-bit blocks in a vector *beyond the minimum length of 128 bits*. Thus the number of 64-bit doublewords in a vector is $2 + 2 * x_1$. If an aggregate has a single SVE vector and 16 additional bytes, its total size is $32 + 16 * x_1$ bytes.

The header file '`poly-int-types.h`' provides typedefs for the most common forms of `poly_int`, all having `NUM_POLY_INT_COEFFS` coefficients:

`poly_uint16`
: a 'poly_int' with `unsigned short` coefficients.

`poly_int64`
: a 'poly_int' with `HOST_WIDE_INT` coefficients.

`poly_uint64`
: a 'poly_int' with `unsigned HOST_WIDE_INT` coefficients.

`poly_offset_int`
: a 'poly_int' with `offset_int` coefficients.

`poly_wide_int`
: a 'poly_int' with `wide_int` coefficients.

`poly_widest_int`
: a 'poly_int' with `widest_int` coefficients.

Since the main purpose of `poly_int` is to represent sizes and offsets, the last two typedefs are only rarely used.

10.2 Consequences of using `poly_int`

The two main consequences of using polynomial sizes and offsets are that:

- there is no total ordering between the values at compile time, and
- some operations might yield results that cannot be expressed as a `poly_int`.

For example, if x is a runtime invariant, we cannot tell at compile time whether:

```
3 + 4x <= 1 + 5x
```

since the condition is false when $x <= 1$ and true when $x >= 2$.

Similarly, `poly_int` cannot represent the result of:

```
(3 + 4x) * (1 + 5x)
```

since it cannot (and in practice does not need to) store powers greater than one. It also cannot represent the result of:

```
(3 + 4x) / (1 + 5x)
```

The following sections describe how we deal with these restrictions.

As described earlier, a `poly_int<1, T>` has no indeterminates and so degenerates to a compile-time constant of type T. It would be possible in that case to do all normal arithmetic on the T, and to compare the T using the normal C++ operators. We deliberately prevent target-independent code from doing this, since the compiler needs to support other `poly_int<n, T>` as well, regardless of the current target's `NUM_POLY_INT_COEFFS`.

However, it would be very artificial to force target-specific code to follow these restrictions if the target has no runtime indeterminates. There is therefore an implicit conversion from `poly_int<1, T>` to T when compiling target-specific translation units.

10.3 Comparisons involving `poly_int`

In general we need to compare sizes and offsets in two situations: those in which the values need to be ordered, and those in which the values can be unordered. More loosely, the distinction is often between values that have a definite link (usually because they refer to the same underlying register or memory location) and values that have no definite link. An example of the former is the relationship between the inner and outer sizes of a subreg, where we must know at compile time whether the subreg is paradoxical, partial, or complete. An example of the latter is alias analysis: we might want to check whether two arbitrary memory references overlap.

Referring back to the examples in the previous section, it makes sense to ask whether a memory reference of size '3 + 4x' overlaps one of size '1 + 5x', but it does not make sense to have a subreg in which the outer mode has '3 + 4x' bytes and the inner mode has '1 + 5x' bytes (or vice versa). Such subregs are always invalid and should trigger an internal compiler error if formed.

The underlying operators are the same in both cases, but the distinction affects how they are used.

10.3.1 Comparison functions for `poly_int`

`poly_int` provides the following routines for checking whether a particular condition "may be" (might be) true:

```
maybe_lt  maybe_le  maybe_eq  maybe_ge  maybe_gt
                    maybe_ne
```

The functions have their natural meaning:

'`maybe_lt(a, b)`'
>   Return true if a might be less than b.

'`maybe_le(a, b)`'
>   Return true if a might be less than or equal to b.

'`maybe_eq(a, b)`'
>   Return true if a might be equal to b.

'`maybe_ne(a, b)`'
>   Return true if a might not be equal to b.

'`maybe_ge(a, b)`'
>   Return true if a might be greater than or equal to b.

'`maybe_gt(a, b)`'
>   Return true if a might be greater than b.

For readability, `poly_int` also provides "known" inverses of these functions:

```
known_lt (a, b) == !maybe_ge (a, b)
known_le (a, b) == !maybe_gt (a, b)
known_eq (a, b) == !maybe_ne (a, b)
known_ge (a, b) == !maybe_lt (a, b)
known_gt (a, b) == !maybe_le (a, b)
known_ne (a, b) == !maybe_eq (a, b)
```

10.3.2 Properties of the `poly_int` comparisons

All "maybe" relations except `maybe_ne` are transitive, so for example:

```
maybe_lt (a, b) && maybe_lt (b, c) implies maybe_lt (a, c)
```

for all *a*, *b* and *c*. `maybe_lt`, `maybe_gt` and `maybe_ne` are irreflexive, so for example:

```
!maybe_lt (a, a)
```

is true for all *a*. `maybe_le`, `maybe_eq` and `maybe_ge` are reflexive, so for example:

```
maybe_le (a, a)
```

is true for all *a*. `maybe_eq` and `maybe_ne` are symmetric, so:

```
maybe_eq (a, b) == maybe_eq (b, a)
maybe_ne (a, b) == maybe_ne (b, a)
```

for all *a* and *b*. In addition:

```
maybe_le (a, b) == maybe_lt (a, b) || maybe_eq (a, b)
maybe_ge (a, b) == maybe_gt (a, b) || maybe_eq (a, b)
maybe_lt (a, b) == maybe_gt (b, a)
maybe_le (a, b) == maybe_ge (b, a)
```

However:

```
maybe_le (a, b) && maybe_le (b, a) does not imply !maybe_ne (a, b) [== known_eq (a, b)]
maybe_ge (a, b) && maybe_ge (b, a) does not imply !maybe_ne (a, b) [== known_eq (a, b)]
```

One example is again '$a == 3 + 4x$' and '$b == 1 + 5x$', where 'maybe_le (a, b)', 'maybe_ge (a, b)' and 'maybe_ne (a, b)' all hold. `maybe_le` and `maybe_ge` are therefore not antisymmetric and do not form a partial order.

From the above, it follows that:

- All "known" relations except `known_ne` are transitive.
- `known_lt`, `known_ne` and `known_gt` are irreflexive.
- `known_le`, `known_eq` and `known_ge` are reflexive.

Also:

```
known_lt (a, b) == known_gt (b, a)
known_le (a, b) == known_ge (b, a)
known_lt (a, b) implies !known_lt (b, a)   [asymmetry]
known_gt (a, b) implies !known_gt (b, a)
known_le (a, b) && known_le (b, a) == known_eq (a, b) [== !maybe_ne (a, b)]
known_ge (a, b) && known_ge (b, a) == known_eq (a, b) [== !maybe_ne (a, b)]
```

`known_le` and `known_ge` are therefore antisymmetric and are partial orders. However:

```
known_le (a, b) does not imply known_lt (a, b) || known_eq (a, b)
known_ge (a, b) does not imply known_gt (a, b) || known_eq (a, b)
```

For example, '`known_le (4, 4 + 4x)`' holds because the runtime indeterminate x is a nonnegative integer, but neither `known_lt (4, 4 + 4x)` nor `known_eq (4, 4 + 4x)` hold.

10.3.3 Comparing potentially-unordered `poly_ints`

In cases where there is no definite link between two `poly_ints`, we can usually make a conservatively-correct assumption. For example, the conservative assumption for alias analysis is that two references *might* alias.

One way of checking whether [*begin1*, *end1*) might overlap [*begin2*, *end2*) using the `poly_int` comparisons is:

```
maybe_gt (end1, begin2) && maybe_gt (end2, begin1)
```
and another (equivalent) way is:
```
!(known_le (end1, begin2) || known_le (end2, begin1))
```
However, in this particular example, it is better to use the range helper functions instead. See Section 10.3.6 [Range checks on `poly_int`s], page 144.

10.3.4 Comparing ordered `poly_int`s

In cases where there is a definite link between two `poly_int`s, such as the outer and inner sizes of subregs, we usually require the sizes to be ordered by the `known_le` partial order. `poly_int` provides the following utility functions for ordered values:

`ordered_p (a, b)`
: Return true if *a* and *b* are ordered by the `known_le` partial order.

`ordered_min (a, b)`
: Assert that *a* and *b* are ordered by `known_le` and return the minimum of the two. When using this function, please add a comment explaining why the values are known to be ordered.

`ordered_max (a, b)`
: Assert that *a* and *b* are ordered by `known_le` and return the maximum of the two. When using this function, please add a comment explaining why the values are known to be ordered.

For example, if a subreg has an outer mode of size *outer* and an inner mode of size *inner*:
- the subreg is complete if known_eq (*inner*, *outer*)
- otherwise, the subreg is paradoxical if known_le (*inner*, *outer*)
- otherwise, the subreg is partial if known_le (*outer*, *inner*)
- otherwise, the subreg is ill-formed

Thus the subreg is only valid if `ordered_p (outer, inner)` is true. If this condition is already known to be true then:
- the subreg is complete if known_eq (*inner*, *outer*)
- the subreg is paradoxical if maybe_lt (*inner*, *outer*)
- the subreg is partial if maybe_lt (*outer*, *inner*)

with the three conditions being mutually exclusive.

Code that checks whether a subreg is valid would therefore generally check whether `ordered_p` holds (in addition to whatever other checks are required for subreg validity). Code that is dealing with existing subregs can assert that `ordered_p` holds and use either of the classifications above.

10.3.5 Checking for a `poly_int` marker value

It is sometimes useful to have a special "marker value" that is not meant to be taken literally. For example, some code uses a size of -1 to represent an unknown size, rather than having to carry around a separate boolean to say whether the size is known.

The best way of checking whether something is a marker value is `known_eq`. Conversely the best way of checking whether something is *not* a marker value is `maybe_ne`.

Thus in the size example just mentioned, 'known_eq (size, -1)' would check for an unknown size and 'maybe_ne (size, -1)' would check for a known size.

10.3.6 Range checks on `poly_ints`

As well as the core comparisons (see Section 10.3.1 [Comparison functions for `poly_int`], page 141), `poly_int` provides utilities for various kinds of range check. In each case the range is represented by a start position and a size rather than a start position and an end position; this is because the former is used much more often than the latter in GCC. Also, the sizes can be -1 (or all ones for unsigned sizes) to indicate a range with a known start position but an unknown size. All other sizes must be nonnegative. A range of size 0 does not contain anything or overlap anything.

'known_size_p (*size*)'
: Return true if *size* represents a known range size, false if it is -1 or all ones (for signed and unsigned types respectively).

'ranges_maybe_overlap_p (*pos1*, *size1*, *pos2*, *size2*)'
: Return true if the range described by *pos1* and *size1* *might* overlap the range described by *pos2* and *size2* (in other words, return true if we cannot prove that the ranges are disjoint).

'ranges_known_overlap_p (*pos1*, *size1*, *pos2*, *size2*)'
: Return true if the range described by *pos1* and *size1* is known to overlap the range described by *pos2* and *size2*.

'known_subrange_p (*pos1*, *size1*, *pos2*, *size2*)'
: Return true if the range described by *pos1* and *size1* is known to be contained in the range described by *pos2* and *size2*.

'maybe_in_range_p (*value*, *pos*, *size*)'
: Return true if *value* *might* be in the range described by *pos* and *size* (in other words, return true if we cannot prove that *value* is outside that range).

'known_in_range_p (*value*, *pos*, *size*)'
: Return true if *value* is known to be in the range described by *pos* and *size*.

'endpoint_representable_p (*pos*, *size*)'
: Return true if the range described by *pos* and *size* is open-ended or if the endpoint (*pos* + *size*) is representable in the same type as *pos* and *size*. The function returns false if adding *size* to *pos* makes conceptual sense but could overflow.

There is also a `poly_int` version of the `IN_RANGE_P` macro:

'coeffs_in_range_p (*x*, *lower*, *upper*)'
: Return true if every coefficient of *x* is in the inclusive range [*lower*, *upper*]. This function can be useful when testing whether an operation would cause the values of coefficients to overflow.

  Note that the function does not indicate whether *x* itself is in the given range. *x* can be either a constant or a `poly_int`.

Chapter 10: Sizes and offsets as runtime invariants 145

10.3.7 Sorting `poly_ints`

`poly_int` provides the following routine for sorting:

'`compare_sizes_for_sort (a, b)`'
>Compare a and b in reverse lexicographical order (that is, compare the highest-indexed coefficients first). This can be useful when sorting data structures, since it has the effect of separating constant and non-constant values. If all values are nonnegative, the constant values come first.
>
>Note that the values do not necessarily end up in numerical order. For example, '`1 + 1x`' would come after '`100`' in the sort order, but may well be less than '`100`' at run time.

10.4 Arithmetic on `poly_ints`

Addition, subtraction, negation and bit inversion all work normally for `poly_int`s. Multiplication by a constant multiplier and left shifting by a constant shift amount also work normally. General multiplication of two `poly_int`s is not supported and is not useful in practice.

Other operations are only conditionally supported: the operation might succeed or might fail, depending on the inputs.

This section describes both types of operation.

10.4.1 Using `poly_int` with C++ arithmetic operators

The following C++ expressions are supported, where p1 and p2 are `poly_int`s and where c1 and c2 are scalars:

```
-p1
~p1

p1 + p2
p1 + c2
c1 + p2

p1 - p2
p1 - c2
c1 - p2

c1 * p2
p1 * c2

p1 << c2

p1 += p2
p1 += c2

p1 -= p2
p1 -= c2

p1 *= c2
p1 <<= c2
```

These arithmetic operations handle integer ranks in a similar way to C++. The main difference is that every coefficient narrower than `HOST_WIDE_INT` promotes to `HOST_WIDE_INT`, whereas in C++ everything narrower than `int` promotes to `int`. For example:

```
poly_uint16      + int          -> poly_int64
unsigned int     + poly_uint16  -> poly_int64
poly_int64       + int          -> poly_int64
poly_int32       + poly_uint64  -> poly_uint64
uint64           + poly_int64   -> poly_uint64
poly_offset_int  + int32        -> poly_offset_int
offset_int       + poly_uint16  -> poly_offset_int
```

In the first two examples, both coefficients are narrower than HOST_WIDE_INT, so the result has coefficients of type HOST_WIDE_INT. In the other examples, the coefficient with the highest rank "wins".

If one of the operands is wide_int or poly_wide_int, the rules are the same as for wide_int arithmetic.

10.4.2 wi arithmetic on poly_ints

As well as the C++ operators, poly_int supports the following wi routines:

```
wi::neg (p1, &overflow)

wi::add (p1, p2)
wi::add (p1, c2)
wi::add (c1, p1)
wi::add (p1, p2, sign, &overflow)

wi::sub (p1, p2)
wi::sub (p1, c2)
wi::sub (c1, p1)
wi::sub (p1, p2, sign, &overflow)

wi::mul (p1, c2)
wi::mul (c1, p1)
wi::mul (p1, c2, sign, &overflow)

wi::lshift (p1, c2)
```

These routines just check whether overflow occurs on any individual coefficient; it is not possible to know at compile time whether the final runtime value would overflow.

10.4.3 Division of poly_ints

Division of poly_ints is possible for certain inputs. The functions for division return true if the operation is possible and in most cases return the results by pointer. The routines are:

'multiple_p (a, b)'
'multiple_p (a, b, &quotient)'
>   Return true if a is an exact multiple of b, storing the result in *quotient* if so. There are overloads for various combinations of polynomial and constant a, b and *quotient*.

'constant_multiple_p (a, b)'
'constant_multiple_p (a, b, &quotient)'
>   Like multiple_p, but also test whether the multiple is a compile-time constant.

'can_div_trunc_p (a, b, &quotient)'
'can_div_trunc_p (a, b, &quotient, &remainder)'
> Return true if we can calculate 'trunc (a / b)' at compile time, storing the result in *quotient* and *remainder* if so.

'can_div_away_from_zero_p (a, b, &quotient)'
> Return true if we can calculate 'a / b' at compile time, rounding away from zero. Store the result in *quotient* if so.
>
> Note that this is true if and only if `can_div_trunc_p` is true. The only difference is in the rounding of the result.

There is also an asserting form of division:

'exact_div (a, b)'
> Assert that *a* is a multiple of *b* and return 'a / b'. The result is a `poly_int` if *a* is a `poly_int`.

10.4.4 Other `poly_int` arithmetic

There are tentative routines for other operations besides division:

'can_ior_p (a, b, &result)'
> Return true if we can calculate 'a | b' at compile time, storing the result in *result* if so.

Also, ANDs with a value '(1 << y) - 1' or its inverse can be treated as alignment operations. See Section 10.5 [Alignment of poly_ints], page 147.

In addition, the following miscellaneous routines are available:

'coeff_gcd (a)'
> Return the greatest common divisor of all nonzero coefficients in *a*, or zero if *a* is known to be zero.

'common_multiple (a, b)'
> Return a value that is a multiple of both *a* and *b*, where one value is a `poly_int` and the other is a scalar. The result will be the least common multiple for some indeterminate values but not necessarily for all.

'force_common_multiple (a, b)'
> Return a value that is a multiple of both `poly_int` *a* and `poly_int` *b*, asserting that such a value exists. The result will be the least common multiple for some indeterminate values but not necessarily for all.
>
> When using this routine, please add a comment explaining why the assertion is known to hold.

Please add any other operations that you find to be useful.

10.5 Alignment of `poly_ints`

`poly_int` provides various routines for aligning values and for querying misalignments. In each case the alignment must be a power of 2.

`can_align_p (value, align)`
: Return true if we can align *value* up or down to the nearest multiple of *align* at compile time. The answer is the same for both directions.

`can_align_down (value, align, &aligned)`
: Return true if `can_align_p`; if so, set *aligned* to the greatest aligned value that is less than or equal to *value*.

`can_align_up (value, align, &aligned)`
: Return true if `can_align_p`; if so, set *aligned* to the lowest aligned value that is greater than or equal to *value*.

`known_equal_after_align_down (a, b, align)`
: Return true if we can align *a* and *b* down to the nearest *align* boundary at compile time and if the two results are equal.

`known_equal_after_align_up (a, b, align)`
: Return true if we can align *a* and *b* up to the nearest *align* boundary at compile time and if the two results are equal.

`aligned_lower_bound (value, align)`
: Return a result that is no greater than *value* and that is aligned to *align*. The result will the closest aligned value for some indeterminate values but not necessarily for all.

    For example, suppose we are allocating an object of *size* bytes in a downward-growing stack whose current limit is given by *limit*. If the object requires *align* bytes of alignment, the new stack limit is given by:

    ```
    aligned_lower_bound (limit - size, align)
    ```

`aligned_upper_bound (value, align)`
: Likewise return a result that is no less than *value* and that is aligned to *align*. This is the routine that would be used for upward-growing stacks in the scenario just described.

`known_misalignment (value, align, &misalign)`
: Return true if we can calculate the misalignment of *value* with respect to *align* at compile time, storing the result in *misalign* if so.

`known_alignment (value)`
: Return the minimum alignment that *value* is known to have (in other words, the largest alignment that can be guaranteed whatever the values of the indeterminates turn out to be). Return 0 if *value* is known to be 0.

`force_align_down (value, align)`
: Assert that *value* can be aligned down to *align* at compile time and return the result. When using this routine, please add a comment explaining why the assertion is known to hold.

`force_align_up (value, align)`
: Likewise, but aligning up.

`force_align_down_and_div (value, align)`
: Divide the result of `force_align_down` by *align*. Again, please add a comment explaining why the assertion in `force_align_down` is known to hold.

'`force_align_up_and_div (value, align)`'
: Likewise for `force_align_up`.

'`force_get_misalignment (value, align)`'
: Assert that we can calculate the misalignment of *value* with respect to *align* at compile time and return the misalignment. When using this function, please add a comment explaining why the assertion is known to hold.

10.6 Computing bounds on `poly_ints`

`poly_int` also provides routines for calculating lower and upper bounds:

'`constant_lower_bound (a)`'
: Assert that *a* is nonnegative and return the smallest value it can have.

'`lower_bound (a, b)`'
: Return a value that is always less than or equal to both *a* and *b*. It will be the greatest such value for some indeterminate values but necessarily for all.

'`upper_bound (a, b)`'
: Return a value that is always greater than or equal to both *a* and *b*. It will be the least such value for some indeterminate values but necessarily for all.

10.7 Converting `poly_ints`

A `poly_int<n, T>` can be constructed from up to n individual T coefficients, with the remaining coefficients being implicitly zero. In particular, this means that every `poly_int<n, T>` can be constructed from a single scalar T, or something compatible with T.

Also, a `poly_int<n, T>` can be constructed from a `poly_int<n, U>` if T can be constructed from U.

The following functions provide other forms of conversion, or test whether such a conversion would succeed.

'`value.is_constant ()`'
: Return true if `poly_int` *value* is a compile-time constant.

'`value.is_constant (&c1)`'
: Return true if `poly_int` *value* is a compile-time constant, storing it in *c1* if so. *c1* must be able to hold all constant values of *value* without loss of precision.

'`value.to_constant ()`'
: Assert that *value* is a compile-time constant and return its value. When using this function, please add a comment explaining why the condition is known to hold (for example, because an earlier phase of analysis rejected non-constants).

'`value.to_shwi (&p2)`'
: Return true if '`poly_int<N, T>`' *value* can be represented without loss of precision as a '`poly_int<N, HOST_WIDE_INT>`', storing it in that form in *p2* if so.

'`value.to_uhwi (&p2)`'
: Return true if '`poly_int<N, T>`' *value* can be represented without loss of precision as a '`poly_int<N, unsigned HOST_WIDE_INT>`', storing it in that form in *p2* if so.

`value.force_shwi ()`
: Forcibly convert each coefficient of `poly_int<N, T>` value to HOST_WIDE_INT, truncating any that are out of range. Return the result as a `poly_int<N, HOST_WIDE_INT>`.

`value.force_uhwi ()`
: Forcibly convert each coefficient of `poly_int<N, T>` value to unsigned HOST_WIDE_INT, truncating any that are out of range. Return the result as a `poly_int<N, unsigned HOST_WIDE_INT>`.

`wi::shwi (value, precision)`
: Return a poly_int with the same value as value, but with the coefficients converted from HOST_WIDE_INT to wide_int. precision specifies the precision of the wide_int cofficients; if this is wider than a HOST_WIDE_INT, the coefficients of value will be sign-extended to fit.

`wi::uhwi (value, precision)`
: Like wi::shwi, except that value has coefficients of type unsigned HOST_WIDE_INT. If precision is wider than a HOST_WIDE_INT, the coefficients of value will be zero-extended to fit.

`wi::sext (value, precision)`
: Return a poly_int of the same type as value, sign-extending every coefficient from the low precision bits. This in effect applies wi::sext to each coefficient individually.

`wi::zext (value, precision)`
: Like wi::sext, but for zero extension.

`poly_wide_int::from (value, precision, sign)`
: Convert value to a poly_wide_int in which each coefficient has precision bits. Extend the coefficients according to sign if the coefficients have fewer bits.

`poly_offset_int::from (value, sign)`
: Convert value to a poly_offset_int, extending its coefficients according to sign if they have fewer bits than offset_int.

`poly_widest_int::from (value, sign)`
: Convert value to a poly_widest_int, extending its coefficients according to sign if they have fewer bits than widest_int.

10.8 Miscellaneous poly_int routines

`print_dec (value, file, sign)`
`print_dec (value, file)`
: Print value to file as a decimal value, interpreting the coefficients according to sign. The final argument is optional if value has an inherent sign; for example, poly_int64 values print as signed by default and poly_uint64 values print as unsigned by default.

  This is a simply a poly_int version of a wide-int routine.

10.9 Guidelines for using `poly_int`

One of the main design goals of `poly_int` was to make it easy to write target-independent code that handles variable-sized registers even when the current target has fixed-sized registers. There are two aspects to this:

- The set of `poly_int` operations should be complete enough that the question in most cases becomes "Can we do this operation on these particular `poly_int` values? If not, bail out" rather than "Are these `poly_int` values constant? If so, do the operation, otherwise bail out".

- If target-independent code compiles and runs correctly on a target with one value of `NUM_POLY_INT_COEFFS`, and if the code does not use asserting functions like `to_constant`, it is reasonable to assume that the code also works on targets with other values of `NUM_POLY_INT_COEFFS`. There is no need to check this during everyday development.

So the general principle is: if target-independent code is dealing with a `poly_int` value, it is better to operate on it as a `poly_int` if at all possible, choosing conservatively-correct behavior if a particular operation fails. For example, the following code handles an index `pos` into a sequence of vectors that each have `nunits` elements:

```
/* Calculate which vector contains the result, and which lane of
   that vector we need.  */
if (!can_div_trunc_p (pos, nunits, &vec_entry, &vec_index))
  {
    if (dump_enabled_p ())
      dump_printf_loc (MSG_MISSED_OPTIMIZATION, vect_location,
                       "Cannot determine which vector holds the"
                       " final result.\n");
    return false;
  }
```

However, there are some contexts in which operating on a `poly_int` is not possible or does not make sense. One example is when handling static initializers, since no current target supports the concept of a variable-length static initializer. In these situations, a reasonable fallback is:

```
if (poly_value.is_constant (&const_value))
  {
    ...
    /* Operate on const_value.  */
    ...
  }
else
  {
    ...
    /* Conservatively correct fallback.  */
    ...
  }
```

`poly_int` also provides some asserting functions like `to_constant`. Please only use these functions if there is a good theoretical reason to believe that the assertion cannot fire. For example, if some work is divided into an analysis phase and an implementation phase, the analysis phase might reject inputs that are not `is_constant`, in which case the implementation phase can reasonably use `to_constant` on the remaining inputs. The assertions should not be used to discover whether a condition ever occurs "in the field"; in other words, they should not be used to restrict code to constants at first, with the intention of only implementing a `poly_int` version if a user hits the assertion.

If a particular asserting function like `to_constant` is needed more than once for the same reason, it is probably worth adding a helper function or macro for that situation, so that the justification only needs to be given once. For example:

```
/* Return the size of an element in a vector of size SIZE, given that
   the vector has NELTS elements.  The return value is in the same units
   as SIZE (either bits or bytes).

   to_constant () is safe in this situation because vector elements are
   always constant-sized scalars.  */
#define vector_element_size(SIZE, NELTS) \
  (exact_div (SIZE, NELTS).to_constant ())
```

Target-specific code in 'config/*cpu*' only needs to handle non-constant `poly_int`s if `NUM_POLY_INT_COEFFS` is greater than one. For other targets, `poly_int` degenerates to a compile-time constant and is often interchangable with a normal scalar integer. There are two main exceptions:

- Sometimes an explicit cast to an integer type might be needed, such as to resolve ambiguities in a ?: expression, or when passing values through ... to things like print functions.

- Target macros are included in target-independent code and so do not have access to the implicit conversion to a scalar integer. If this becomes a problem for a particular target macro, the possible solutions, in order of preference, are:
  - Convert the target macro to a target hook (for all targets).
  - Put the target's implementation of the target macro in its '*cpu*.c' file and call it from the target macro in the '*cpu*.h' file.
  - Add `to_constant ()` calls where necessary. The previous option is preferable because it will help with any future conversion of the macro to a hook.

11 GENERIC

The purpose of GENERIC is simply to provide a language-independent way of representing an entire function in trees. To this end, it was necessary to add a few new tree codes to the back end, but almost everything was already there. If you can express it with the codes in `gcc/tree.def`, it's GENERIC.

Early on, there was a great deal of debate about how to think about statements in a tree IL. In GENERIC, a statement is defined as any expression whose value, if any, is ignored. A statement will always have `TREE_SIDE_EFFECTS` set (or it will be discarded), but a non-statement expression may also have side effects. A `CALL_EXPR`, for instance.

It would be possible for some local optimizations to work on the GENERIC form of a function; indeed, the adapted tree inliner works fine on GENERIC, but the current compiler performs inlining after lowering to GIMPLE (a restricted form described in the next section). Indeed, currently the frontends perform this lowering before handing off to `tree_rest_of_compilation`, but this seems inelegant.

11.1 Deficiencies

There are many places in which this document is incomplet and incorrekt. It is, as of yet, only *preliminary* documentation.

11.2 Overview

The central data structure used by the internal representation is the **tree**. These nodes, while all of the C type **tree**, are of many varieties. A **tree** is a pointer type, but the object to which it points may be of a variety of types. From this point forward, we will refer to trees in ordinary type, rather than in **this font**, except when talking about the actual C type **tree**.

You can tell what kind of node a particular tree is by using the `TREE_CODE` macro. Many, many macros take trees as input and return trees as output. However, most macros require a certain kind of tree node as input. In other words, there is a type-system for trees, but it is not reflected in the C type-system.

For safety, it is useful to configure GCC with '`--enable-checking`'. Although this results in a significant performance penalty (since all tree types are checked at run-time), and is therefore inappropriate in a release version, it is extremely helpful during the development process.

Many macros behave as predicates. Many, although not all, of these predicates end in '`_P`'. Do not rely on the result type of these macros being of any particular type. You may, however, rely on the fact that the type can be compared to 0, so that statements like

```
if (TEST_P (t) && !TEST_P (y))
  x = 1;
```

and

```
int i = (TEST_P (t) != 0);
```

are legal. Macros that return `int` values now may be changed to return **tree** values, or other pointers in the future. Even those that continue to return `int` may return multiple nonzero codes where previously they returned only zero and one. Therefore, you should not write code like

```
if (TEST_P (t) == 1)
```
as this code is not guaranteed to work correctly in the future.

You should not take the address of values returned by the macros or functions described here. In particular, no guarantee is given that the values are lvalues.

In general, the names of macros are all in uppercase, while the names of functions are entirely in lowercase. There are rare exceptions to this rule. You should assume that any macro or function whose name is made up entirely of uppercase letters may evaluate its arguments more than once. You may assume that a macro or function whose name is made up entirely of lowercase letters will evaluate its arguments only once.

The `error_mark_node` is a special tree. Its tree code is ERROR_MARK, but since there is only ever one node with that code, the usual practice is to compare the tree against `error_mark_node`. (This test is just a test for pointer equality.) If an error has occurred during front-end processing the flag `errorcount` will be set. If the front end has encountered code it cannot handle, it will issue a message to the user and set `sorrycount`. When these flags are set, any macro or function which normally returns a tree of a particular kind may instead return the `error_mark_node`. Thus, if you intend to do any processing of erroneous code, you must be prepared to deal with the `error_mark_node`.

Occasionally, a particular tree slot (like an operand to an expression, or a particular field in a declaration) will be referred to as "reserved for the back end". These slots are used to store RTL when the tree is converted to RTL for use by the GCC back end. However, if that process is not taking place (e.g., if the front end is being hooked up to an intelligent editor), then those slots may be used by the back end presently in use.

If you encounter situations that do not match this documentation, such as tree nodes of types not mentioned here, or macros documented to return entities of a particular kind that instead return entities of some different kind, you have found a bug, either in the front end or in the documentation. Please report these bugs as you would any other bug.

11.2.1 Trees

All GENERIC trees have two fields in common. First, TREE_CHAIN is a pointer that can be used as a singly-linked list to other trees. The other is TREE_TYPE. Many trees store the type of an expression or declaration in this field.

These are some other functions for handling trees:

tree_size
: Return the number of bytes a tree takes.

build0
build1
build2
build3
build4
build5
build6
: These functions build a tree and supply values to put in each parameter. The basic signature is 'code, type, [operands]'. code is the TREE_CODE, and type is a tree representing the TREE_TYPE. These are followed by the operands, each of which is also a tree.

11.2.2 Identifiers

An `IDENTIFIER_NODE` represents a slightly more general concept than the standard C or C++ concept of identifier. In particular, an `IDENTIFIER_NODE` may contain a '$', or other extraordinary characters.

There are never two distinct `IDENTIFIER_NODE`s representing the same identifier. Therefore, you may use pointer equality to compare `IDENTIFIER_NODE`s, rather than using a routine like `strcmp`. Use `get_identifier` to obtain the unique `IDENTIFIER_NODE` for a supplied string.

You can use the following macros to access identifiers:

`IDENTIFIER_POINTER`
> The string represented by the identifier, represented as a `char*`. This string is always `NUL`-terminated, and contains no embedded `NUL` characters.

`IDENTIFIER_LENGTH`
> The length of the string returned by `IDENTIFIER_POINTER`, not including the trailing `NUL`. This value of `IDENTIFIER_LENGTH (x)` is always the same as `strlen (IDENTIFIER_POINTER (x))`.

`IDENTIFIER_OPNAME_P`
> This predicate holds if the identifier represents the name of an overloaded operator. In this case, you should not depend on the contents of either the `IDENTIFIER_POINTER` or the `IDENTIFIER_LENGTH`.

`IDENTIFIER_TYPENAME_P`
> This predicate holds if the identifier represents the name of a user-defined conversion operator. In this case, the `TREE_TYPE` of the `IDENTIFIER_NODE` holds the type to which the conversion operator converts.

11.2.3 Containers

Two common container data structures can be represented directly with tree nodes. A `TREE_LIST` is a singly linked list containing two trees per node. These are the `TREE_PURPOSE` and `TREE_VALUE` of each node. (Often, the `TREE_PURPOSE` contains some kind of tag, or additional information, while the `TREE_VALUE` contains the majority of the payload. In other cases, the `TREE_PURPOSE` is simply `NULL_TREE`, while in still others both the `TREE_PURPOSE` and `TREE_VALUE` are of equal stature.) Given one `TREE_LIST` node, the next node is found by following the `TREE_CHAIN`. If the `TREE_CHAIN` is `NULL_TREE`, then you have reached the end of the list.

A `TREE_VEC` is a simple vector. The `TREE_VEC_LENGTH` is an integer (not a tree) giving the number of nodes in the vector. The nodes themselves are accessed using the `TREE_VEC_ELT` macro, which takes two arguments. The first is the `TREE_VEC` in question; the second is an integer indicating which element in the vector is desired. The elements are indexed from zero.

11.3 Types

All types have corresponding tree nodes. However, you should not assume that there is exactly one tree node corresponding to each type. There are often multiple nodes corresponding to the same type.

For the most part, different kinds of types have different tree codes. (For example, pointer types use a `POINTER_TYPE` code while arrays use an `ARRAY_TYPE` code.) However, pointers to member functions use the `RECORD_TYPE` code. Therefore, when writing a `switch` statement that depends on the code associated with a particular type, you should take care to handle pointers to member functions under the `RECORD_TYPE` case label.

The following functions and macros deal with cv-qualification of types:

`TYPE_MAIN_VARIANT`
> This macro returns the unqualified version of a type. It may be applied to an unqualified type, but it is not always the identity function in that case.

A few other macros and functions are usable with all types:

`TYPE_SIZE`
> The number of bits required to represent the type, represented as an `INTEGER_CST`. For an incomplete type, `TYPE_SIZE` will be `NULL_TREE`.

`TYPE_ALIGN`
> The alignment of the type, in bits, represented as an `int`.

`TYPE_NAME`
> This macro returns a declaration (in the form of a `TYPE_DECL`) for the type. (Note this macro does *not* return an `IDENTIFIER_NODE`, as you might expect, given its name!) You can look at the `DECL_NAME` of the `TYPE_DECL` to obtain the actual name of the type. The `TYPE_NAME` will be `NULL_TREE` for a type that is not a built-in type, the result of a typedef, or a named class type.

`TYPE_CANONICAL`
> This macro returns the "canonical" type for the given type node. Canonical types are used to improve performance in the C++ and Objective-C++ front ends by allowing efficient comparison between two type nodes in `same_type_p`: if the `TYPE_CANONICAL` values of the types are equal, the types are equivalent; otherwise, the types are not equivalent. The notion of equivalence for canonical types is the same as the notion of type equivalence in the language itself. For instance,
>
> When `TYPE_CANONICAL` is `NULL_TREE`, there is no canonical type for the given type node. In this case, comparison between this type and any other type requires the compiler to perform a deep, "structural" comparison to see if the two type nodes have the same form and properties.
>
> The canonical type for a node is always the most fundamental type in the equivalence class of types. For instance, `int` is its own canonical type. A typedef `I` of `int` will have `int` as its canonical type. Similarly, `I*` and a typedef `IP` (defined to `I*`) will has `int*` as their canonical type. When building a new type node, be sure to set `TYPE_CANONICAL` to the appropriate canonical type. If the new type is a compound type (built from other types), and any of those other types require structural equality, use `SET_TYPE_STRUCTURAL_EQUALITY` to ensure that the new type also requires structural equality. Finally, if for some reason you cannot guarantee that `TYPE_CANONICAL` will point to the canonical type, use `SET_TYPE_STRUCTURAL_EQUALITY` to make sure that the new type–and any type constructed based on it–requires structural equality. If you suspect

Chapter 11: GENERIC

that the canonical type system is miscomparing types, pass --param verify-canonical-types=1 to the compiler or configure with --enable-checking to force the compiler to verify its canonical-type comparisons against the structural comparisons; the compiler will then print any warnings if the canonical types miscompare.

TYPE_STRUCTURAL_EQUALITY_P
: This predicate holds when the node requires structural equality checks, e.g., when TYPE_CANONICAL is NULL_TREE.

SET_TYPE_STRUCTURAL_EQUALITY
: This macro states that the type node it is given requires structural equality checks, e.g., it sets TYPE_CANONICAL to NULL_TREE.

same_type_p
: This predicate takes two types as input, and holds if they are the same type. For example, if one type is a typedef for the other, or both are typedefs for the same type. This predicate also holds if the two trees given as input are simply copies of one another; i.e., there is no difference between them at the source level, but, for whatever reason, a duplicate has been made in the representation. You should never use == (pointer equality) to compare types; always use same_type_p instead.

Detailed below are the various kinds of types, and the macros that can be used to access them. Although other kinds of types are used elsewhere in G++, the types described here are the only ones that you will encounter while examining the intermediate representation.

VOID_TYPE
: Used to represent the void type.

INTEGER_TYPE
: Used to represent the various integral types, including char, short, int, long, and long long. This code is not used for enumeration types, nor for the bool type. The TYPE_PRECISION is the number of bits used in the representation, represented as an unsigned int. (Note that in the general case this is not the same value as TYPE_SIZE; suppose that there were a 24-bit integer type, but that alignment requirements for the ABI required 32-bit alignment. Then, TYPE_SIZE would be an INTEGER_CST for 32, while TYPE_PRECISION would be 24.) The integer type is unsigned if TYPE_UNSIGNED holds; otherwise, it is signed.

    The TYPE_MIN_VALUE is an INTEGER_CST for the smallest integer that may be represented by this type. Similarly, the TYPE_MAX_VALUE is an INTEGER_CST for the largest integer that may be represented by this type.

REAL_TYPE
: Used to represent the float, double, and long double types. The number of bits in the floating-point representation is given by TYPE_PRECISION, as in the INTEGER_TYPE case.

FIXED_POINT_TYPE
: Used to represent the short _Fract, _Fract, long _Fract, long long _Fract, short _Accum, _Accum, long _Accum, and long long _Accum types. The num-

ber of bits in the fixed-point representation is given by `TYPE_PRECISION`, as in the `INTEGER_TYPE` case. There may be padding bits, fractional bits and integral bits. The number of fractional bits is given by `TYPE_FBIT`, and the number of integral bits is given by `TYPE_IBIT`. The fixed-point type is unsigned if `TYPE_UNSIGNED` holds; otherwise, it is signed. The fixed-point type is saturating if `TYPE_SATURATING` holds; otherwise, it is not saturating.

`COMPLEX_TYPE`

Used to represent GCC built-in `__complex__` data types. The `TREE_TYPE` is the type of the real and imaginary parts.

`ENUMERAL_TYPE`

Used to represent an enumeration type. The `TYPE_PRECISION` gives (as an `int`), the number of bits used to represent the type. If there are no negative enumeration constants, `TYPE_UNSIGNED` will hold. The minimum and maximum enumeration constants may be obtained with `TYPE_MIN_VALUE` and `TYPE_MAX_VALUE`, respectively; each of these macros returns an `INTEGER_CST`.

The actual enumeration constants themselves may be obtained by looking at the `TYPE_VALUES`. This macro will return a `TREE_LIST`, containing the constants. The `TREE_PURPOSE` of each node will be an `IDENTIFIER_NODE` giving the name of the constant; the `TREE_VALUE` will be an `INTEGER_CST` giving the value assigned to that constant. These constants will appear in the order in which they were declared. The `TREE_TYPE` of each of these constants will be the type of enumeration type itself.

`BOOLEAN_TYPE`

Used to represent the `bool` type.

`POINTER_TYPE`

Used to represent pointer types, and pointer to data member types. The `TREE_TYPE` gives the type to which this type points.

`REFERENCE_TYPE`

Used to represent reference types. The `TREE_TYPE` gives the type to which this type refers.

`FUNCTION_TYPE`

Used to represent the type of non-member functions and of static member functions. The `TREE_TYPE` gives the return type of the function. The `TYPE_ARG_TYPES` are a `TREE_LIST` of the argument types. The `TREE_VALUE` of each node in this list is the type of the corresponding argument; the `TREE_PURPOSE` is an expression for the default argument value, if any. If the last node in the list is `void_list_node` (a `TREE_LIST` node whose `TREE_VALUE` is the `void_type_node`), then functions of this type do not take variable arguments. Otherwise, they do take a variable number of arguments.

Note that in C (but not in C++) a function declared like `void f()` is an unprototyped function taking a variable number of arguments; the `TYPE_ARG_TYPES` of such a function will be `NULL`.

METHOD_TYPE

> Used to represent the type of a non-static member function. Like a FUNCTION_TYPE, the return type is given by the TREE_TYPE. The type of *this, i.e., the class of which functions of this type are a member, is given by the TYPE_METHOD_BASETYPE. The TYPE_ARG_TYPES is the parameter list, as for a FUNCTION_TYPE, and includes the this argument.

ARRAY_TYPE

> Used to represent array types. The TREE_TYPE gives the type of the elements in the array. If the array-bound is present in the type, the TYPE_DOMAIN is an INTEGER_TYPE whose TYPE_MIN_VALUE and TYPE_MAX_VALUE will be the lower and upper bounds of the array, respectively. The TYPE_MIN_VALUE will always be an INTEGER_CST for zero, while the TYPE_MAX_VALUE will be one less than the number of elements in the array, i.e., the highest value which may be used to index an element in the array.

RECORD_TYPE

> Used to represent struct and class types, as well as pointers to member functions and similar constructs in other languages. TYPE_FIELDS contains the items contained in this type, each of which can be a FIELD_DECL, VAR_DECL, CONST_DECL, or TYPE_DECL. You may not make any assumptions about the ordering of the fields in the type or whether one or more of them overlap.

UNION_TYPE

> Used to represent union types. Similar to RECORD_TYPE except that all FIELD_DECL nodes in TYPE_FIELD start at bit position zero.

QUAL_UNION_TYPE

> Used to represent part of a variant record in Ada. Similar to UNION_TYPE except that each FIELD_DECL has a DECL_QUALIFIER field, which contains a boolean expression that indicates whether the field is present in the object. The type will only have one field, so each field's DECL_QUALIFIER is only evaluated if none of the expressions in the previous fields in TYPE_FIELDS are nonzero. Normally these expressions will reference a field in the outer object using a PLACEHOLDER_EXPR.

LANG_TYPE

> This node is used to represent a language-specific type. The front end must handle it.

OFFSET_TYPE

> This node is used to represent a pointer-to-data member. For a data member X::m the TYPE_OFFSET_BASETYPE is X and the TREE_TYPE is the type of m.

There are variables whose values represent some of the basic types. These include:

void_type_node
> A node for void.

integer_type_node
> A node for int.

`unsigned_type_node`.
: A node for `unsigned int`.

`char_type_node`.
: A node for `char`.

It may sometimes be useful to compare one of these variables with a type in hand, using `same_type_p`.

11.4 Declarations

This section covers the various kinds of declarations that appear in the internal representation, except for declarations of functions (represented by `FUNCTION_DECL` nodes), which are described in Section 11.8 [Functions], page 184.

11.4.1 Working with declarations

Some macros can be used with any kind of declaration. These include:

`DECL_NAME`
: This macro returns an `IDENTIFIER_NODE` giving the name of the entity.

`TREE_TYPE`
: This macro returns the type of the entity declared.

`EXPR_FILENAME`
: This macro returns the name of the file in which the entity was declared, as a `char*`. For an entity declared implicitly by the compiler (like `__builtin_memcpy`), this will be the string `"<internal>"`.

`EXPR_LINENO`
: This macro returns the line number at which the entity was declared, as an `int`.

`DECL_ARTIFICIAL`
: This predicate holds if the declaration was implicitly generated by the compiler. For example, this predicate will hold of an implicitly declared member function, or of the `TYPE_DECL` implicitly generated for a class type. Recall that in C++ code like:

    ```
    struct S {};
    ```

    is roughly equivalent to C code like:

    ```
    struct S {};
    typedef struct S S;
    ```

    The implicitly generated `typedef` declaration is represented by a `TYPE_DECL` for which `DECL_ARTIFICIAL` holds.

The various kinds of declarations include:

`LABEL_DECL`
: These nodes are used to represent labels in function bodies. For more information, see Section 11.8 [Functions], page 184. These nodes only appear in block scopes.

CONST_DECL

> These nodes are used to represent enumeration constants. The value of the constant is given by `DECL_INITIAL` which will be an `INTEGER_CST` with the same type as the `TREE_TYPE` of the `CONST_DECL`, i.e., an `ENUMERAL_TYPE`.

RESULT_DECL

> These nodes represent the value returned by a function. When a value is assigned to a `RESULT_DECL`, that indicates that the value should be returned, via bitwise copy, by the function. You can use `DECL_SIZE` and `DECL_ALIGN` on a `RESULT_DECL`, just as with a `VAR_DECL`.

TYPE_DECL

> These nodes represent `typedef` declarations. The `TREE_TYPE` is the type declared to have the name given by `DECL_NAME`. In some cases, there is no associated name.

VAR_DECL These nodes represent variables with namespace or block scope, as well as static data members. The `DECL_SIZE` and `DECL_ALIGN` are analogous to `TYPE_SIZE` and `TYPE_ALIGN`. For a declaration, you should always use the `DECL_SIZE` and `DECL_ALIGN` rather than the `TYPE_SIZE` and `TYPE_ALIGN` given by the `TREE_TYPE`, since special attributes may have been applied to the variable to give it a particular size and alignment. You may use the predicates `DECL_THIS_STATIC` or `DECL_THIS_EXTERN` to test whether the storage class specifiers `static` or `extern` were used to declare a variable.

> If this variable is initialized (but does not require a constructor), the `DECL_INITIAL` will be an expression for the initializer. The initializer should be evaluated, and a bitwise copy into the variable performed. If the `DECL_INITIAL` is the `error_mark_node`, there is an initializer, but it is given by an explicit statement later in the code; no bitwise copy is required.

> GCC provides an extension that allows either automatic variables, or global variables, to be placed in particular registers. This extension is being used for a particular `VAR_DECL` if `DECL_REGISTER` holds for the `VAR_DECL`, and if `DECL_ASSEMBLER_NAME` is not equal to `DECL_NAME`. In that case, `DECL_ASSEMBLER_NAME` is the name of the register into which the variable will be placed.

PARM_DECL

> Used to represent a parameter to a function. Treat these nodes similarly to `VAR_DECL` nodes. These nodes only appear in the `DECL_ARGUMENTS` for a `FUNCTION_DECL`.

> The `DECL_ARG_TYPE` for a `PARM_DECL` is the type that will actually be used when a value is passed to this function. It may be a wider type than the `TREE_TYPE` of the parameter; for example, the ordinary type might be `short` while the `DECL_ARG_TYPE` is `int`.

DEBUG_EXPR_DECL

> Used to represent an anonymous debug-information temporary created to hold an expression as it is optimized away, so that its value can be referenced in debug bind statements.

FIELD_DECL
: These nodes represent non-static data members. The `DECL_SIZE` and `DECL_ALIGN` behave as for `VAR_DECL` nodes. The position of the field within the parent record is specified by a combination of three attributes. `DECL_FIELD_OFFSET` is the position, counting in bytes, of the `DECL_OFFSET_ALIGN`-bit sized word containing the bit of the field closest to the beginning of the structure. `DECL_FIELD_BIT_OFFSET` is the bit offset of the first bit of the field within this word; this may be nonzero even for fields that are not bit-fields, since `DECL_OFFSET_ALIGN` may be greater than the natural alignment of the field's type.

    If `DECL_C_BIT_FIELD` holds, this field is a bit-field. In a bit-field, `DECL_BIT_FIELD_TYPE` also contains the type that was originally specified for it, while `DECL_TYPE` may be a modified type with lesser precision, according to the size of the bit field.

NAMESPACE_DECL
: Namespaces provide a name hierarchy for other declarations. They appear in the `DECL_CONTEXT` of other _DECL nodes.

11.4.2 Internal structure

DECL nodes are represented internally as a hierarchy of structures.

11.4.2.1 Current structure hierarchy

struct tree_decl_minimal
: This is the minimal structure to inherit from in order for common DECL macros to work. The fields it contains are a unique ID, source location, context, and name.

struct tree_decl_common
: This structure inherits from struct tree_decl_minimal. It contains fields that most DECL nodes need, such as a field to store alignment, machine mode, size, and attributes.

struct tree_field_decl
: This structure inherits from struct tree_decl_common. It is used to represent FIELD_DECL.

struct tree_label_decl
: This structure inherits from struct tree_decl_common. It is used to represent LABEL_DECL.

struct tree_translation_unit_decl
: This structure inherits from struct tree_decl_common. It is used to represent TRANSLATION_UNIT_DECL.

struct tree_decl_with_rtl
: This structure inherits from struct tree_decl_common. It contains a field to store the low-level RTL associated with a DECL node.

struct tree_result_decl
: This structure inherits from struct tree_decl_with_rtl. It is used to represent RESULT_DECL.

`struct tree_const_decl`
> This structure inherits from `struct tree_decl_with_rtl`. It is used to represent CONST_DECL.

`struct tree_parm_decl`
> This structure inherits from `struct tree_decl_with_rtl`. It is used to represent PARM_DECL.

`struct tree_decl_with_vis`
> This structure inherits from `struct tree_decl_with_rtl`. It contains fields necessary to store visibility information, as well as a section name and assembler name.

`struct tree_var_decl`
> This structure inherits from `struct tree_decl_with_vis`. It is used to represent VAR_DECL.

`struct tree_function_decl`
> This structure inherits from `struct tree_decl_with_vis`. It is used to represent FUNCTION_DECL.

11.4.2.2 Adding new DECL node types

Adding a new DECL tree consists of the following steps

Add a new tree code for the DECL node
> For language specific DECL nodes, there is a '.def' file in each frontend directory where the tree code should be added. For DECL nodes that are part of the middle-end, the code should be added to 'tree.def'.

Create a new structure type for the DECL node
> These structures should inherit from one of the existing structures in the language hierarchy by using that structure as the first member.
>
> ```
> struct tree_foo_decl
> {
>    struct tree_decl_with_vis common;
> }
> ```
>
> Would create a structure name tree_foo_decl that inherits from `struct tree_decl_with_vis`.
>
> For language specific DECL nodes, this new structure type should go in the appropriate '.h' file. For DECL nodes that are part of the middle-end, the structure type should go in 'tree.h'.

Add a member to the tree structure enumerator for the node
> For garbage collection and dynamic checking purposes, each DECL node structure type is required to have a unique enumerator value specified with it. For language specific DECL nodes, this new enumerator value should go in the appropriate '.def' file. For DECL nodes that are part of the middle-end, the enumerator values are specified in 'treestruct.def'.

Update `union tree_node`
: In order to make your new structure type usable, it must be added to `union tree_node`. For language specific DECL nodes, a new entry should be added to the appropriate '.h' file of the form

    ```
    struct tree_foo_decl GTY ((tag ("TS_VAR_DECL"))) foo_decl;
    ```

    For DECL nodes that are part of the middle-end, the additional member goes directly into `union tree_node` in 'tree.h'.

Update dynamic checking info
: In order to be able to check whether accessing a named portion of `union tree_node` is legal, and whether a certain DECL node contains one of the enumerated DECL node structures in the hierarchy, a simple lookup table is used. This lookup table needs to be kept up to date with the tree structure hierarchy, or else checking and containment macros will fail inappropriately.

    For language specific DECL nodes, their is an `init_ts` function in an appropriate '.c' file, which initializes the lookup table. Code setting up the table for new DECL nodes should be added there. For each DECL tree code and enumerator value representing a member of the inheritance hierarchy, the table should contain 1 if that tree code inherits (directly or indirectly) from that member. Thus, a FOO_DECL node derived from `struct decl_with_rtl`, and enumerator value TS_FOO_DECL, would be set up as follows

    ```
    tree_contains_struct[FOO_DECL][TS_FOO_DECL] = 1;
    tree_contains_struct[FOO_DECL][TS_DECL_WRTL] = 1;
    tree_contains_struct[FOO_DECL][TS_DECL_COMMON] = 1;
    tree_contains_struct[FOO_DECL][TS_DECL_MINIMAL] = 1;
    ```

    For DECL nodes that are part of the middle-end, the setup code goes into 'tree.c'.

Add macros to access any new fields and flags
: Each added field or flag should have a macro that is used to access it, that performs appropriate checking to ensure only the right type of DECL nodes access the field.

    These macros generally take the following form

    ```
    #define FOO_DECL_FIELDNAME(NODE) FOO_DECL_CHECK(NODE)->foo_decl.fieldname
    ```

    However, if the structure is simply a base class for further structures, something like the following should be used

    ```
    #define BASE_STRUCT_CHECK(T) CONTAINS_STRUCT_CHECK(T, TS_BASE_STRUCT)
    #define BASE_STRUCT_FIELDNAME(NODE) \
       (BASE_STRUCT_CHECK(NODE)->base_struct.fieldname
    ```

    Reading them from the generated 'all-tree.def' file (which in turn includes all the 'tree.def' files), 'gencheck.c' is used during GCC's build to generate the *_CHECK macros for all tree codes.

11.5 Attributes in trees

Attributes, as specified using the `__attribute__` keyword, are represented internally as a TREE_LIST. The TREE_PURPOSE is the name of the attribute, as an IDENTIFIER_NODE. The TREE_VALUE is a TREE_LIST of the arguments of the attribute, if any, or NULL_TREE if there are no arguments; the arguments are stored as the `TREE_VALUE` of successive entries in the list, and may be identifiers or expressions. The `TREE_CHAIN` of the attribute is the next attribute in a list of attributes applying to the same declaration or type, or `NULL_TREE` if there are no further attributes in the list.

Attributes may be attached to declarations and to types; these attributes may be accessed with the following macros. All attributes are stored in this way, and many also cause other changes to the declaration or type or to other internal compiler data structures.

tree `DECL_ATTRIBUTES` (*tree* `decl`)   [Tree Macro]
: This macro returns the attributes on the declaration *decl*.

tree `TYPE_ATTRIBUTES` (*tree* `type`)   [Tree Macro]
: This macro returns the attributes on the type *type*.

11.6 Expressions

The internal representation for expressions is for the most part quite straightforward. However, there are a few facts that one must bear in mind. In particular, the expression "tree" is actually a directed acyclic graph. (For example there may be many references to the integer constant zero throughout the source program; many of these will be represented by the same expression node.) You should not rely on certain kinds of node being shared, nor should you rely on certain kinds of nodes being unshared.

The following macros can be used with all expression nodes:

`TREE_TYPE`
: Returns the type of the expression. This value may not be precisely the same type that would be given the expression in the original program.

In what follows, some nodes that one might expect to always have type `bool` are documented to have either integral or boolean type. At some point in the future, the C front end may also make use of this same intermediate representation, and at this point these nodes will certainly have integral type. The previous sentence is not meant to imply that the C++ front end does not or will not give these nodes integral type.

Below, we list the various kinds of expression nodes. Except where noted otherwise, the operands to an expression are accessed using the `TREE_OPERAND` macro. For example, to access the first operand to a binary plus expression `expr`, use:

```
TREE_OPERAND (expr, 0)
```

As this example indicates, the operands are zero-indexed.

11.6.1 Constant expressions

The table below begins with constants, moves on to unary expressions, then proceeds to binary expressions, and concludes with various other kinds of expressions:

`INTEGER_CST`
: These nodes represent integer constants. Note that the type of these constants is obtained with `TREE_TYPE`; they are not always of type `int`. In particular, `char` constants are represented with `INTEGER_CST` nodes. The value of the integer constant `e` is represented in an array of HOST_WIDE_INT. There are enough

elements in the array to represent the value without taking extra elements for redundant 0s or -1. The number of elements used to represent e is available via `TREE_INT_CST_NUNITS`. Element i can be extracted by using `TREE_INT_CST_ELT (e, i)`. `TREE_INT_CST_LOW` is a shorthand for `TREE_INT_CST_ELT (e, 0)`.

The functions `tree_fits_shwi_p` and `tree_fits_uhwi_p` can be used to tell if the value is small enough to fit in a signed HOST_WIDE_INT or an unsigned HOST_WIDE_INT respectively. The value can then be extracted using `tree_to_shwi` and `tree_to_uhwi`.

`REAL_CST`

FIXME: Talk about how to obtain representations of this constant, do comparisons, and so forth.

`FIXED_CST`

These nodes represent fixed-point constants. The type of these constants is obtained with `TREE_TYPE`. `TREE_FIXED_CST_PTR` points to a `struct fixed_value`; `TREE_FIXED_CST` returns the structure itself. `struct fixed_value` contains `data` with the size of two `HOST_BITS_PER_WIDE_INT` and `mode` as the associated fixed-point machine mode for `data`.

`COMPLEX_CST`

These nodes are used to represent complex number constants, that is a `__complex__` whose parts are constant nodes. The `TREE_REALPART` and `TREE_IMAGPART` return the real and the imaginary parts respectively.

`VECTOR_CST`

These nodes are used to represent vector constants. Each vector constant v is treated as a specific instance of an arbitrary-length sequence that itself contains 'VECTOR_CST_NPATTERNS (v)' interleaved patterns. Each pattern has the form:

    { base0, base1, base1 + step, base1 + step * 2, ... }

The first three elements in each pattern are enough to determine the values of the other elements. However, if all *step*s are zero, only the first two elements are needed. If in addition each *base1* is equal to the corresponding *base0*, only the first element in each pattern is needed. The number of encoded elements per pattern is given by 'VECTOR_CST_NELTS_PER_PATTERN (v)'.

For example, the constant:

    { 0, 1, 2, 6, 3, 8, 4, 10, 5, 12, 6, 14, 7, 16, 8, 18 }

is interpreted as an interleaving of the sequences:

    { 0, 2, 3, 4, 5, 6, 7, 8 }
    { 1, 6, 8, 10, 12, 14, 16, 18 }

where the sequences are represented by the following patterns:

    base0 == 0, base1 == 2, step == 1
    base0 == 1, base1 == 6, step == 2

In this case:

    VECTOR_CST_NPATTERNS (v) == 2
    VECTOR_CST_NELTS_PER_PATTERN (v) == 3

The vector is therefore encoded using the first 6 elements ('{ 0, 1, 2, 6, 3, 8 }'), with the remaining 10 elements being implicit extensions of them.

Chapter 11: GENERIC 167

Sometimes this scheme can create two possible encodings of the same vector. For example { 0, 1 } could be seen as two patterns with one element each or one pattern with two elements (*base0* and *base1*). The canonical encoding is always the one with the fewest patterns or (if both encodings have the same number of petterns) the one with the fewest encoded elements.

'vector_cst_encoding_nelts (*v*)' gives the total number of encoded elements in *v*, which is 6 in the example above. VECTOR_CST_ENCODED_ELTS (*v*) gives a pointer to the elements encoded in *v* and VECTOR_CST_ENCODED_ELT (*v*, *i*) accesses the value of encoded element *i*.

'VECTOR_CST_DUPLICATE_P (*v*)' is true if *v* simply contains repeated instances of 'VECTOR_CST_NPATTERNS (*v*)' values. This is a shorthand for testing 'VECTOR_CST_NELTS_PER_PATTERN (*v*) == 1'.

'VECTOR_CST_STEPPED_P (*v*)' is true if at least one pattern in *v* has a nonzero step. This is a shorthand for testing 'VECTOR_CST_NELTS_PER_PATTERN (*v*) == 3'.

The utility function vector_cst_elt gives the value of an arbitrary index as a tree. vector_cst_int_elt gives the same value as a wide_int.

STRING_CST

These nodes represent string-constants. The TREE_STRING_LENGTH returns the length of the string, as an int. The TREE_STRING_POINTER is a char* containing the string itself. The string may not be NUL-terminated, and it may contain embedded NUL characters. Therefore, the TREE_STRING_LENGTH includes the trailing NUL if it is present.

For wide string constants, the TREE_STRING_LENGTH is the number of bytes in the string, and the TREE_STRING_POINTER points to an array of the bytes of the string, as represented on the target system (that is, as integers in the target endianness). Wide and non-wide string constants are distinguished only by the TREE_TYPE of the STRING_CST.

FIXME: The formats of string constants are not well-defined when the target system bytes are not the same width as host system bytes.

POLY_INT_CST

These nodes represent invariants that depend on some target-specific runtime parameters. They consist of NUM_POLY_INT_COEFFS coefficients, with the first coefficient being the constant term and the others being multipliers that are applied to the runtime parameters.

POLY_INT_CST_ELT (*x*, *i*) references coefficient number *i* of POLY_INT_CST node *x*. Each coefficient is an INTEGER_CST.

11.6.2 References to storage

ARRAY_REF

These nodes represent array accesses. The first operand is the array; the second is the index. To calculate the address of the memory accessed, you must scale the index by the size of the type of the array elements. The type of these expressions must be the type of a component of the array. The third and fourth operands are used after gimplification to represent the lower bound and component size but should not be used directly; call `array_ref_low_bound` and `array_ref_element_size` instead.

ARRAY_RANGE_REF

These nodes represent access to a range (or "slice") of an array. The operands are the same as that for `ARRAY_REF` and have the same meanings. The type of these expressions must be an array whose component type is the same as that of the first operand. The range of that array type determines the amount of data these expressions access.

TARGET_MEM_REF

These nodes represent memory accesses whose address directly map to an addressing mode of the target architecture. The first argument is `TMR_SYMBOL` and must be a `VAR_DECL` of an object with a fixed address. The second argument is `TMR_BASE` and the third one is `TMR_INDEX`. The fourth argument is `TMR_STEP` and must be an `INTEGER_CST`. The fifth argument is `TMR_OFFSET` and must be an `INTEGER_CST`. Any of the arguments may be NULL if the appropriate component does not appear in the address. Address of the `TARGET_MEM_REF` is determined in the following way.

```
&TMR_SYMBOL + TMR_BASE + TMR_INDEX * TMR_STEP + TMR_OFFSET
```

The sixth argument is the reference to the original memory access, which is preserved for the purposes of the RTL alias analysis. The seventh argument is a tag representing the results of tree level alias analysis.

ADDR_EXPR

These nodes are used to represent the address of an object. (These expressions will always have pointer or reference type.) The operand may be another expression, or it may be a declaration.

As an extension, GCC allows users to take the address of a label. In this case, the operand of the `ADDR_EXPR` will be a `LABEL_DECL`. The type of such an expression is `void*`.

If the object addressed is not an lvalue, a temporary is created, and the address of the temporary is used.

INDIRECT_REF

These nodes are used to represent the object pointed to by a pointer. The operand is the pointer being dereferenced; it will always have pointer or reference type.

MEM_REF

These nodes are used to represent the object pointed to by a pointer offset by a constant. The first operand is the pointer being dereferenced; it will always have pointer or reference type. The second operand is a pointer constant. Its type is specifying the type to be used for type-based alias analysis.

COMPONENT_REF

These nodes represent non-static data member accesses. The first operand is the object (rather than a pointer to it); the second operand is the `FIELD_DECL` for the data member. The third operand represents the byte offset of the field, but should not be used directly; call `component_ref_field_offset` instead.

Chapter 11: GENERIC

11.6.3 Unary and Binary Expressions

NEGATE_EXPR

These nodes represent unary negation of the single operand, for both integer and floating-point types. The type of negation can be determined by looking at the type of the expression.

The behavior of this operation on signed arithmetic overflow is controlled by the `flag_wrapv` and `flag_trapv` variables.

ABS_EXPR   These nodes represent the absolute value of the single operand, for both integer and floating-point types. This is typically used to implement the `abs`, `labs` and `llabs` builtins for integer types, and the `fabs`, `fabsf` and `fabsl` builtins for floating point types. The type of abs operation can be determined by looking at the type of the expression.

This node is not used for complex types. To represent the modulus or complex abs of a complex value, use the `BUILT_IN_CABS`, `BUILT_IN_CABSF` or `BUILT_IN_CABSL` builtins, as used to implement the C99 `cabs`, `cabsf` and `cabsl` built-in functions.

BIT_NOT_EXPR

These nodes represent bitwise complement, and will always have integral type. The only operand is the value to be complemented.

TRUTH_NOT_EXPR

These nodes represent logical negation, and will always have integral (or boolean) type. The operand is the value being negated. The type of the operand and that of the result are always of `BOOLEAN_TYPE` or `INTEGER_TYPE`.

PREDECREMENT_EXPR
PREINCREMENT_EXPR
POSTDECREMENT_EXPR
POSTINCREMENT_EXPR

These nodes represent increment and decrement expressions. The value of the single operand is computed, and the operand incremented or decremented. In the case of `PREDECREMENT_EXPR` and `PREINCREMENT_EXPR`, the value of the expression is the value resulting after the increment or decrement; in the case of `POSTDECREMENT_EXPR` and `POSTINCREMENT_EXPR` is the value before the increment or decrement occurs. The type of the operand, like that of the result, will be either integral, boolean, or floating-point.

FIX_TRUNC_EXPR

These nodes represent conversion of a floating-point value to an integer. The single operand will have a floating-point type, while the complete expression will have an integral (or boolean) type. The operand is rounded towards zero.

FLOAT_EXPR

These nodes represent conversion of an integral (or boolean) value to a floating-point value. The single operand will have integral type, while the complete expression will have a floating-point type.

FIXME: How is the operand supposed to be rounded? Is this dependent on '-mieee'?

`COMPLEX_EXPR`
: These nodes are used to represent complex numbers constructed from two expressions of the same (integer or real) type. The first operand is the real part and the second operand is the imaginary part.

`CONJ_EXPR`
: These nodes represent the conjugate of their operand.

`REALPART_EXPR`
`IMAGPART_EXPR`
: These nodes represent respectively the real and the imaginary parts of complex numbers (their sole argument).

`NON_LVALUE_EXPR`
: These nodes indicate that their one and only operand is not an lvalue. A back end can treat these identically to the single operand.

`NOP_EXPR`
: These nodes are used to represent conversions that do not require any code-generation. For example, conversion of a `char*` to an `int*` does not require any code be generated; such a conversion is represented by a `NOP_EXPR`. The single operand is the expression to be converted. The conversion from a pointer to a reference is also represented with a `NOP_EXPR`.

`CONVERT_EXPR`
: These nodes are similar to `NOP_EXPR`s, but are used in those situations where code may need to be generated. For example, if an `int*` is converted to an `int` code may need to be generated on some platforms. These nodes are never used for C++-specific conversions, like conversions between pointers to different classes in an inheritance hierarchy. Any adjustments that need to be made in such cases are always indicated explicitly. Similarly, a user-defined conversion is never represented by a `CONVERT_EXPR`; instead, the function calls are made explicit.

`FIXED_CONVERT_EXPR`
: These nodes are used to represent conversions that involve fixed-point values. For example, from a fixed-point value to another fixed-point value, from an integer to a fixed-point value, from a fixed-point value to an integer, from a floating-point value to a fixed-point value, or from a fixed-point value to a floating-point value.

`LSHIFT_EXPR`
`RSHIFT_EXPR`
: These nodes represent left and right shifts, respectively. The first operand is the value to shift; it will always be of integral type. The second operand is an expression for the number of bits by which to shift. Right shift should be treated as arithmetic, i.e., the high-order bits should be zero-filled when the expression has unsigned type and filled with the sign bit when the expression has signed type. Note that the result is undefined if the second operand is larger than or equal to the first operand's type size. Unlike most nodes, these can have a vector as first operand and a scalar as second operand.

BIT_IOR_EXPR
BIT_XOR_EXPR
BIT_AND_EXPR

> These nodes represent bitwise inclusive or, bitwise exclusive or, and bitwise and, respectively. Both operands will always have integral type.

TRUTH_ANDIF_EXPR
TRUTH_ORIF_EXPR

> These nodes represent logical "and" and logical "or", respectively. These operators are not strict; i.e., the second operand is evaluated only if the value of the expression is not determined by evaluation of the first operand. The type of the operands and that of the result are always of BOOLEAN_TYPE or INTEGER_TYPE.

TRUTH_AND_EXPR
TRUTH_OR_EXPR
TRUTH_XOR_EXPR

> These nodes represent logical and, logical or, and logical exclusive or. They are strict; both arguments are always evaluated. There are no corresponding operators in C or C++, but the front end will sometimes generate these expressions anyhow, if it can tell that strictness does not matter. The type of the operands and that of the result are always of BOOLEAN_TYPE or INTEGER_TYPE.

POINTER_PLUS_EXPR

> This node represents pointer arithmetic. The first operand is always a pointer/reference type. The second operand is always an unsigned integer type compatible with sizetype. This and POINTER_DIFF_EXPR are the only binary arithmetic operators that can operate on pointer types.

POINTER_DIFF_EXPR

> This node represents pointer subtraction. The two operands always have pointer/reference type. It returns a signed integer of the same precision as the pointers. The behavior is undefined if the difference of the two pointers, seen as infinite precision non-negative integers, does not fit in the result type. The result does not depend on the pointer type, it is not divided by the size of the pointed-to type.

PLUS_EXPR
MINUS_EXPR
MULT_EXPR

> These nodes represent various binary arithmetic operations. Respectively, these operations are addition, subtraction (of the second operand from the first) and multiplication. Their operands may have either integral or floating type, but there will never be case in which one operand is of floating type and the other is of integral type.
>
> The behavior of these operations on signed arithmetic overflow is controlled by the `flag_wrapv` and `flag_trapv` variables.

MULT_HIGHPART_EXPR

> This node represents the "high-part" of a widening multiplication. For an integral type with b bits of precision, the result is the most significant b bits of the full $2b$ product.

`RDIV_EXPR`
: This node represents a floating point division operation.

`TRUNC_DIV_EXPR`
`FLOOR_DIV_EXPR`
`CEIL_DIV_EXPR`
`ROUND_DIV_EXPR`
: These nodes represent integer division operations that return an integer result. `TRUNC_DIV_EXPR` rounds towards zero, `FLOOR_DIV_EXPR` rounds towards negative infinity, `CEIL_DIV_EXPR` rounds towards positive infinity and `ROUND_DIV_EXPR` rounds to the closest integer. Integer division in C and C++ is truncating, i.e. `TRUNC_DIV_EXPR`.

   The behavior of these operations on signed arithmetic overflow, when dividing the minimum signed integer by minus one, is controlled by the `flag_wrapv` and `flag_trapv` variables.

`TRUNC_MOD_EXPR`
`FLOOR_MOD_EXPR`
`CEIL_MOD_EXPR`
`ROUND_MOD_EXPR`
: These nodes represent the integer remainder or modulus operation. The integer modulus of two operands a and b is defined as a - (a/b)*b where the division calculated using the corresponding division operator. Hence for `TRUNC_MOD_EXPR` this definition assumes division using truncation towards zero, i.e. `TRUNC_DIV_EXPR`. Integer remainder in C and C++ uses truncating division, i.e. `TRUNC_MOD_EXPR`.

`EXACT_DIV_EXPR`
: The `EXACT_DIV_EXPR` code is used to represent integer divisions where the numerator is known to be an exact multiple of the denominator. This allows the backend to choose between the faster of `TRUNC_DIV_EXPR`, `CEIL_DIV_EXPR` and `FLOOR_DIV_EXPR` for the current target.

`LT_EXPR`
`LE_EXPR`
`GT_EXPR`
`GE_EXPR`
`EQ_EXPR`
`NE_EXPR`
: These nodes represent the less than, less than or equal to, greater than, greater than or equal to, equal, and not equal comparison operators. The first and second operands will either be both of integral type, both of floating type or both of vector type. The result type of these expressions will always be of integral, boolean or signed integral vector type. These operations return the result type's zero value for false, the result type's one value for true, and a vector whose elements are zero (false) or minus one (true) for vectors.

   For floating point comparisons, if we honor IEEE NaNs and either operand is NaN, then `NE_EXPR` always returns true and the remaining operators always return false. On some targets, comparisons against an IEEE NaN, other than equality and inequality, may generate a floating point exception.

Chapter 11: GENERIC   173

ORDERED_EXPR
UNORDERED_EXPR

These nodes represent non-trapping ordered and unordered comparison operators. These operations take two floating point operands and determine whether they are ordered or unordered relative to each other. If either operand is an IEEE NaN, their comparison is defined to be unordered, otherwise the comparison is defined to be ordered. The result type of these expressions will always be of integral or boolean type. These operations return the result type's zero value for false, and the result type's one value for true.

UNLT_EXPR
UNLE_EXPR
UNGT_EXPR
UNGE_EXPR
UNEQ_EXPR
LTGT_EXPR

These nodes represent the unordered comparison operators. These operations take two floating point operands and determine whether the operands are unordered or are less than, less than or equal to, greater than, greater than or equal to, or equal respectively. For example, UNLT_EXPR returns true if either operand is an IEEE NaN or the first operand is less than the second. With the possible exception of LTGT_EXPR, all of these operations are guaranteed not to generate a floating point exception. The result type of these expressions will always be of integral or boolean type. These operations return the result type's zero value for false, and the result type's one value for true.

MODIFY_EXPR

These nodes represent assignment. The left-hand side is the first operand; the right-hand side is the second operand. The left-hand side will be a VAR_DECL, INDIRECT_REF, COMPONENT_REF, or other lvalue.

These nodes are used to represent not only assignment with '=' but also compound assignments (like '+='), by reduction to '=' assignment. In other words, the representation for 'i += 3' looks just like that for 'i = i + 3'.

INIT_EXPR

These nodes are just like MODIFY_EXPR, but are used only when a variable is initialized, rather than assigned to subsequently. This means that we can assume that the target of the initialization is not used in computing its own value; any reference to the lhs in computing the rhs is undefined.

COMPOUND_EXPR

These nodes represent comma-expressions. The first operand is an expression whose value is computed and thrown away prior to the evaluation of the second operand. The value of the entire expression is the value of the second operand.

COND_EXPR

These nodes represent ?: expressions. The first operand is of boolean or integral type. If it evaluates to a nonzero value, the second operand should be evaluated, and returned as the value of the expression. Otherwise, the third operand is evaluated, and returned as the value of the expression.

The second operand must have the same type as the entire expression, unless it unconditionally throws an exception or calls a noreturn function, in which case it should have void type. The same constraints apply to the third operand. This allows array bounds checks to be represented conveniently as (i >= 0 && i < 10) ? i : abort().

As a GNU extension, the C language front-ends allow the second operand of the ?: operator may be omitted in the source. For example, x ? : 3 is equivalent to x ? x : 3, assuming that x is an expression without side-effects. In the tree representation, however, the second operand is always present, possibly protected by SAVE_EXPR if the first argument does cause side-effects.

CALL_EXPR

These nodes are used to represent calls to functions, including non-static member functions. CALL_EXPRs are implemented as expression nodes with a variable number of operands. Rather than using TREE_OPERAND to extract them, it is preferable to use the specialized accessor macros and functions that operate specifically on CALL_EXPR nodes.

CALL_EXPR_FN returns a pointer to the function to call; it is always an expression whose type is a POINTER_TYPE.

The number of arguments to the call is returned by call_expr_nargs, while the arguments themselves can be accessed with the CALL_EXPR_ARG macro. The arguments are zero-indexed and numbered left-to-right. You can iterate over the arguments using FOR_EACH_CALL_EXPR_ARG, as in:

```
tree call, arg;
call_expr_arg_iterator iter;
FOR_EACH_CALL_EXPR_ARG (arg, iter, call)
  /* arg is bound to successive arguments of call. */
  ...;
```

For non-static member functions, there will be an operand corresponding to the this pointer. There will always be expressions corresponding to all of the arguments, even if the function is declared with default arguments and some arguments are not explicitly provided at the call sites.

CALL_EXPRs also have a CALL_EXPR_STATIC_CHAIN operand that is used to implement nested functions. This operand is otherwise null.

CLEANUP_POINT_EXPR

These nodes represent full-expressions. The single operand is an expression to evaluate. Any destructor calls engendered by the creation of temporaries during the evaluation of that expression should be performed immediately after the expression is evaluated.

CONSTRUCTOR

These nodes represent the brace-enclosed initializers for a structure or an array. They contain a sequence of component values made out of a vector of constructor_elt, which is a (INDEX, VALUE) pair.

If the TREE_TYPE of the CONSTRUCTOR is a RECORD_TYPE, UNION_TYPE or QUAL_UNION_TYPE then the INDEX of each node in the sequence will be a FIELD_DECL and the VALUE will be the expression used to initialize that field.

If the TREE_TYPE of the CONSTRUCTOR is an ARRAY_TYPE, then the INDEX of each node in the sequence will be an INTEGER_CST or a RANGE_EXPR of two INTEGER_CSTs. A single INTEGER_CST indicates which element of the array is being assigned to. A RANGE_EXPR indicates an inclusive range of elements to initialize. In both cases the VALUE is the corresponding initializer. It is re-evaluated for each element of a RANGE_EXPR. If the INDEX is NULL_TREE, then the initializer is for the next available array element.

In the front end, you should not depend on the fields appearing in any particular order. However, in the middle end, fields must appear in declaration order. You should not assume that all fields will be represented. Unrepresented fields will be cleared (zeroed), unless the CONSTRUCTOR_NO_CLEARING flag is set, in which case their value becomes undefined.

COMPOUND_LITERAL_EXPR

These nodes represent ISO C99 compound literals. The COMPOUND_LITERAL_EXPR_DECL_EXPR is a DECL_EXPR containing an anonymous VAR_DECL for the unnamed object represented by the compound literal; the DECL_INITIAL of that VAR_DECL is a CONSTRUCTOR representing the brace-enclosed list of initializers in the compound literal. That anonymous VAR_DECL can also be accessed directly by the COMPOUND_LITERAL_EXPR_DECL macro.

SAVE_EXPR

A SAVE_EXPR represents an expression (possibly involving side-effects) that is used more than once. The side-effects should occur only the first time the expression is evaluated. Subsequent uses should just reuse the computed value. The first operand to the SAVE_EXPR is the expression to evaluate. The side-effects should be executed where the SAVE_EXPR is first encountered in a depth-first preorder traversal of the expression tree.

TARGET_EXPR

A TARGET_EXPR represents a temporary object. The first operand is a VAR_DECL for the temporary variable. The second operand is the initializer for the temporary. The initializer is evaluated and, if non-void, copied (bitwise) into the temporary. If the initializer is void, that means that it will perform the initialization itself.

Often, a TARGET_EXPR occurs on the right-hand side of an assignment, or as the second operand to a comma-expression which is itself the right-hand side of an assignment, etc. In this case, we say that the TARGET_EXPR is "normal"; otherwise, we say it is "orphaned". For a normal TARGET_EXPR the temporary variable should be treated as an alias for the left-hand side of the assignment, rather than as a new temporary variable.

The third operand to the TARGET_EXPR, if present, is a cleanup-expression (i.e., destructor call) for the temporary. If this expression is orphaned, then this expression must be executed when the statement containing this expression is complete. These cleanups must always be executed in the order opposite to that in which they were encountered. Note that if a temporary is created on one branch of a conditional operator (i.e., in the second or third operand to a COND_EXPR), the cleanup must be run only if that branch is actually executed.

VA_ARG_EXPR

> This node is used to implement support for the C/C++ variable argument-list mechanism. It represents expressions like va_arg (ap, type). Its TREE_TYPE yields the tree representation for type and its sole argument yields the representation for ap.

ANNOTATE_EXPR

> This node is used to attach markers to an expression. The first operand is the annotated expression, the second is an INTEGER_CST with a value from enum annot_expr_kind, the third is an INTEGER_CST.

11.6.4 Vectors

VEC_DUPLICATE_EXPR

> This node has a single operand and represents a vector in which every element is equal to that operand.

VEC_SERIES_EXPR

> This node represents a vector formed from a scalar base and step, given as the first and second operands respectively. Element *i* of the result is equal to 'base + i*step'.
>
> This node is restricted to integral types, in order to avoid specifying the rounding behavior for floating-point types.

VEC_LSHIFT_EXPR
VEC_RSHIFT_EXPR

> These nodes represent whole vector left and right shifts, respectively. The first operand is the vector to shift; it will always be of vector type. The second operand is an expression for the number of bits by which to shift. Note that the result is undefined if the second operand is larger than or equal to the first operand's type size.

VEC_WIDEN_MULT_HI_EXPR
VEC_WIDEN_MULT_LO_EXPR

> These nodes represent widening vector multiplication of the high and low parts of the two input vectors, respectively. Their operands are vectors that contain the same number of elements (N) of the same integral type. The result is a vector that contains half as many elements, of an integral type whose size is twice as wide. In the case of VEC_WIDEN_MULT_HI_EXPR the high N/2 elements of the two vector are multiplied to produce the vector of N/2 products. In the case of VEC_WIDEN_MULT_LO_EXPR the low N/2 elements of the two vector are multiplied to produce the vector of N/2 products.

VEC_UNPACK_HI_EXPR
VEC_UNPACK_LO_EXPR

> These nodes represent unpacking of the high and low parts of the input vector, respectively. The single operand is a vector that contains N elements of the same integral or floating point type. The result is a vector that contains half as many elements, of an integral or floating point type whose size is twice as wide. In the case of VEC_UNPACK_HI_EXPR the high N/2 elements of the vector

are extracted and widened (promoted). In the case of `VEC_UNPACK_LO_EXPR` the low N/2 elements of the vector are extracted and widened (promoted).

`VEC_UNPACK_FLOAT_HI_EXPR`
`VEC_UNPACK_FLOAT_LO_EXPR`

These nodes represent unpacking of the high and low parts of the input vector, where the values are converted from fixed point to floating point. The single operand is a vector that contains N elements of the same integral type. The result is a vector that contains half as many elements of a floating point type whose size is twice as wide. In the case of `VEC_UNPACK_HI_EXPR` the high N/2 elements of the vector are extracted, converted and widened. In the case of `VEC_UNPACK_LO_EXPR` the low N/2 elements of the vector are extracted, converted and widened.

`VEC_PACK_TRUNC_EXPR`

This node represents packing of truncated elements of the two input vectors into the output vector. Input operands are vectors that contain the same number of elements of the same integral or floating point type. The result is a vector that contains twice as many elements of an integral or floating point type whose size is half as wide. The elements of the two vectors are demoted and merged (concatenated) to form the output vector.

`VEC_PACK_SAT_EXPR`

This node represents packing of elements of the two input vectors into the output vector using saturation. Input operands are vectors that contain the same number of elements of the same integral type. The result is a vector that contains twice as many elements of an integral type whose size is half as wide. The elements of the two vectors are demoted and merged (concatenated) to form the output vector.

`VEC_PACK_FIX_TRUNC_EXPR`

This node represents packing of elements of the two input vectors into the output vector, where the values are converted from floating point to fixed point. Input operands are vectors that contain the same number of elements of a floating point type. The result is a vector that contains twice as many elements of an integral type whose size is half as wide. The elements of the two vectors are merged (concatenated) to form the output vector.

`VEC_COND_EXPR`

These nodes represent ?: expressions. The three operands must be vectors of the same size and number of elements. The second and third operands must have the same type as the entire expression. The first operand is of signed integral vector type. If an element of the first operand evaluates to a zero value, the corresponding element of the result is taken from the third operand. If it evaluates to a minus one value, it is taken from the second operand. It should never evaluate to any other value currently, but optimizations should not rely on that property. In contrast with a `COND_EXPR`, all operands are always evaluated.

`SAD_EXPR` This node represents the Sum of Absolute Differences operation. The three operands must be vectors of integral types. The first and second operand must have the same type. The size of the vector element of the third operand must be at lease twice of the size of the vector element of the first and second one. The SAD is calculated between the first and second operands, added to the third operand, and returned.

11.7 Statements

Most statements in GIMPLE are assignment statements, represented by `GIMPLE_ASSIGN`. No other C expressions can appear at statement level; a reference to a volatile object is converted into a `GIMPLE_ASSIGN`.

There are also several varieties of complex statements.

11.7.1 Basic Statements

ASM_EXPR

> Used to represent an inline assembly statement. For an inline assembly statement like:
>
> ```
> asm ("mov x, y");
> ```
>
> The `ASM_STRING` macro will return a `STRING_CST` node for `"mov x, y"`. If the original statement made use of the extended-assembly syntax, then `ASM_OUTPUTS`, `ASM_INPUTS`, and `ASM_CLOBBERS` will be the outputs, inputs, and clobbers for the statement, represented as `STRING_CST` nodes. The extended-assembly syntax looks like:
>
> ```
> asm ("fsinx %1,%0" : "=f" (result) : "f" (angle));
> ```
>
> The first string is the `ASM_STRING`, containing the instruction template. The next two strings are the output and inputs, respectively; this statement has no clobbers. As this example indicates, "plain" assembly statements are merely a special case of extended assembly statements; they have no cv-qualifiers, outputs, inputs, or clobbers. All of the strings will be `NUL`-terminated, and will contain no embedded `NUL`-characters.
>
> If the assembly statement is declared `volatile`, or if the statement was not an extended assembly statement, and is therefore implicitly volatile, then the predicate `ASM_VOLATILE_P` will hold of the `ASM_EXPR`.

DECL_EXPR

> Used to represent a local declaration. The `DECL_EXPR_DECL` macro can be used to obtain the entity declared. This declaration may be a `LABEL_DECL`, indicating that the label declared is a local label. (As an extension, GCC allows the declaration of labels with scope.) In C, this declaration may be a `FUNCTION_DECL`, indicating the use of the GCC nested function extension. For more information, see Section 11.8 [Functions], page 184.

LABEL_EXPR

> Used to represent a label. The `LABEL_DECL` declared by this statement can be obtained with the `LABEL_EXPR_LABEL` macro. The `IDENTIFIER_NODE` giving the name of the label can be obtained from the `LABEL_DECL` with `DECL_NAME`.

GOTO_EXPR

> Used to represent a `goto` statement. The GOTO_DESTINATION will usually be a LABEL_DECL. However, if the "computed goto" extension has been used, the GOTO_DESTINATION will be an arbitrary expression indicating the destination. This expression will always have pointer type.

RETURN_EXPR

> Used to represent a `return` statement. Operand 0 represents the value to return. It should either be the RESULT_DECL for the containing function, or a MODIFY_EXPR or INIT_EXPR setting the function's RESULT_DECL. It will be NULL_TREE if the statement was just
>
> > `return;`

LOOP_EXPR

> These nodes represent "infinite" loops. The LOOP_EXPR_BODY represents the body of the loop. It should be executed forever, unless an EXIT_EXPR is encountered.

EXIT_EXPR

> These nodes represent conditional exits from the nearest enclosing LOOP_EXPR. The single operand is the condition; if it is nonzero, then the loop should be exited. An EXIT_EXPR will only appear within a LOOP_EXPR.

SWITCH_STMT

> Used to represent a `switch` statement. The SWITCH_STMT_COND is the expression on which the switch is occurring. See the documentation for an IF_STMT for more information on the representation used for the condition. The SWITCH_STMT_BODY is the body of the switch statement. The SWITCH_STMT_TYPE is the original type of switch expression as given in the source, before any compiler conversions.

CASE_LABEL_EXPR

> Use to represent a `case` label, range of `case` labels, or a `default` label. If CASE_LOW is NULL_TREE, then this is a `default` label. Otherwise, if CASE_HIGH is NULL_TREE, then this is an ordinary `case` label. In this case, CASE_LOW is an expression giving the value of the label. Both CASE_LOW and CASE_HIGH are INTEGER_CST nodes. These values will have the same type as the condition expression in the switch statement.
>
> Otherwise, if both CASE_LOW and CASE_HIGH are defined, the statement is a range of case labels. Such statements originate with the extension that allows users to write things of the form:
>
> > `case 2 ... 5:`
>
> The first value will be CASE_LOW, while the second will be CASE_HIGH.

DEBUG_BEGIN_STMT

> Marks the beginning of a source statement, for purposes of debug information generation.

11.7.2 Blocks

Block scopes and the variables they declare in GENERIC are expressed using the BIND_EXPR code, which in previous versions of GCC was primarily used for the C statement-expression extension.

Variables in a block are collected into BIND_EXPR_VARS in declaration order through their TREE_CHAIN field. Any runtime initialization is moved out of DECL_INITIAL and into a statement in the controlled block. When gimplifying from C or C++, this initialization replaces the DECL_STMT. These variables will never require cleanups. The scope of these variables is just the body

Variable-length arrays (VLAs) complicate this process, as their size often refers to variables initialized earlier in the block and their initialization involves an explicit stack allocation. To handle this, we add an indirection and replace them with a pointer to stack space allocated by means of alloca. In most cases, we also arrange for this space to be reclaimed when the enclosing BIND_EXPR is exited, the exception to this being when there is an explicit call to alloca in the source code, in which case the stack is left depressed on exit of the BIND_EXPR.

A C++ program will usually contain more BIND_EXPRs than there are syntactic blocks in the source code, since several C++ constructs have implicit scopes associated with them. On the other hand, although the C++ front end uses pseudo-scopes to handle cleanups for objects with destructors, these don't translate into the GIMPLE form; multiple declarations at the same level use the same BIND_EXPR.

11.7.3 Statement Sequences

Multiple statements at the same nesting level are collected into a STATEMENT_LIST. Statement lists are modified and traversed using the interface in 'tree-iterator.h'.

11.7.4 Empty Statements

Whenever possible, statements with no effect are discarded. But if they are nested within another construct which cannot be discarded for some reason, they are instead replaced with an empty statement, generated by build_empty_stmt. Initially, all empty statements were shared, after the pattern of the Java front end, but this caused a lot of trouble in practice.

An empty statement is represented as (void)0.

11.7.5 Jumps

Other jumps are expressed by either GOTO_EXPR or RETURN_EXPR.

The operand of a GOTO_EXPR must be either a label or a variable containing the address to jump to.

The operand of a RETURN_EXPR is either NULL_TREE, RESULT_DECL, or a MODIFY_EXPR which sets the return value. It would be nice to move the MODIFY_EXPR into a separate statement, but the special return semantics in expand_return make that difficult. It may still happen in the future, perhaps by moving most of that logic into expand_assignment.

11.7.6 Cleanups

Destructors for local C++ objects and similar dynamic cleanups are represented in GIMPLE by a `TRY_FINALLY_EXPR`. `TRY_FINALLY_EXPR` has two operands, both of which are a sequence of statements to execute. The first sequence is executed. When it completes the second sequence is executed.

The first sequence may complete in the following ways:

1. Execute the last statement in the sequence and fall off the end.
2. Execute a goto statement (`GOTO_EXPR`) to an ordinary label outside the sequence.
3. Execute a return statement (`RETURN_EXPR`).
4. Throw an exception. This is currently not explicitly represented in GIMPLE.

The second sequence is not executed if the first sequence completes by calling `setjmp` or `exit` or any other function that does not return. The second sequence is also not executed if the first sequence completes via a non-local goto or a computed goto (in general the compiler does not know whether such a goto statement exits the first sequence or not, so we assume that it doesn't).

After the second sequence is executed, if it completes normally by falling off the end, execution continues wherever the first sequence would have continued, by falling off the end, or doing a goto, etc.

`TRY_FINALLY_EXPR` complicates the flow graph, since the cleanup needs to appear on every edge out of the controlled block; this reduces the freedom to move code across these edges. Therefore, the EH lowering pass which runs before most of the optimization passes eliminates these expressions by explicitly adding the cleanup to each edge. Rethrowing the exception is represented using `RESX_EXPR`.

11.7.7 OpenMP

All the statements starting with `OMP_` represent directives and clauses used by the OpenMP API http://www.openmp.org/.

`OMP_PARALLEL`

> Represents `#pragma omp parallel [clause1 ... clauseN]`. It has four operands:
>
> Operand `OMP_PARALLEL_BODY` is valid while in GENERIC and High GIMPLE forms. It contains the body of code to be executed by all the threads. During GIMPLE lowering, this operand becomes NULL and the body is emitted linearly after `OMP_PARALLEL`.
>
> Operand `OMP_PARALLEL_CLAUSES` is the list of clauses associated with the directive.
>
> Operand `OMP_PARALLEL_FN` is created by `pass_lower_omp`, it contains the `FUNCTION_DECL` for the function that will contain the body of the parallel region.
>
> Operand `OMP_PARALLEL_DATA_ARG` is also created by `pass_lower_omp`. If there are shared variables to be communicated to the children threads, this operand will contain the `VAR_DECL` that contains all the shared values and variables.

OMP_FOR

Represents #pragma omp for [clause1 ... clauseN]. It has six operands:

Operand OMP_FOR_BODY contains the loop body.

Operand OMP_FOR_CLAUSES is the list of clauses associated with the directive.

Operand OMP_FOR_INIT is the loop initialization code of the form VAR = N1.

Operand OMP_FOR_COND is the loop conditional expression of the form VAR {<,>,<=,>=} N2.

Operand OMP_FOR_INCR is the loop index increment of the form VAR {+=,-=} INCR.

Operand OMP_FOR_PRE_BODY contains side-effect code from operands OMP_FOR_INIT, OMP_FOR_COND and OMP_FOR_INC. These side-effects are part of the OMP_FOR block but must be evaluated before the start of loop body.

The loop index variable VAR must be a signed integer variable, which is implicitly private to each thread. Bounds N1 and N2 and the increment expression INCR are required to be loop invariant integer expressions that are evaluated without any synchronization. The evaluation order, frequency of evaluation and side-effects are unspecified by the standard.

OMP_SECTIONS

Represents #pragma omp sections [clause1 ... clauseN].

Operand OMP_SECTIONS_BODY contains the sections body, which in turn contains a set of OMP_SECTION nodes for each of the concurrent sections delimited by #pragma omp section.

Operand OMP_SECTIONS_CLAUSES is the list of clauses associated with the directive.

OMP_SECTION

Section delimiter for OMP_SECTIONS.

OMP_SINGLE

Represents #pragma omp single.

Operand OMP_SINGLE_BODY contains the body of code to be executed by a single thread.

Operand OMP_SINGLE_CLAUSES is the list of clauses associated with the directive.

OMP_MASTER

Represents #pragma omp master.

Operand OMP_MASTER_BODY contains the body of code to be executed by the master thread.

OMP_ORDERED

Represents #pragma omp ordered.

Operand OMP_ORDERED_BODY contains the body of code to be executed in the sequential order dictated by the loop index variable.

OMP_CRITICAL

Represents #pragma omp critical [name].

Chapter 11: GENERIC   183

> Operand `OMP_CRITICAL_BODY` is the critical section.
>
> Operand `OMP_CRITICAL_NAME` is an optional identifier to label the critical section.

`OMP_RETURN`
> This does not represent any OpenMP directive, it is an artificial marker to indicate the end of the body of an OpenMP. It is used by the flow graph (`tree-cfg.c`) and OpenMP region building code (`omp-low.c`).

`OMP_CONTINUE`
> Similarly, this instruction does not represent an OpenMP directive, it is used by `OMP_FOR` (and similar codes) as well as `OMP_SECTIONS` to mark the place where the code needs to loop to the next iteration, or the next section, respectively.
>
> In some cases, `OMP_CONTINUE` is placed right before `OMP_RETURN`. But if there are cleanups that need to occur right after the looping body, it will be emitted between `OMP_CONTINUE` and `OMP_RETURN`.

`OMP_ATOMIC`
> Represents `#pragma omp atomic`.
>
> Operand 0 is the address at which the atomic operation is to be performed.
>
> Operand 1 is the expression to evaluate. The gimplifier tries three alternative code generation strategies. Whenever possible, an atomic update built-in is used. If that fails, a compare-and-swap loop is attempted. If that also fails, a regular critical section around the expression is used.

`OMP_CLAUSE`
> Represents clauses associated with one of the `OMP_` directives. Clauses are represented by separate subcodes defined in 'tree.h'. Clauses codes can be one of: `OMP_CLAUSE_PRIVATE`, `OMP_CLAUSE_SHARED`, `OMP_CLAUSE_FIRSTPRIVATE`, `OMP_CLAUSE_LASTPRIVATE`, `OMP_CLAUSE_COPYIN`, `OMP_CLAUSE_COPYPRIVATE`, `OMP_CLAUSE_IF`, `OMP_CLAUSE_NUM_THREADS`, `OMP_CLAUSE_SCHEDULE`, `OMP_CLAUSE_NOWAIT`, `OMP_CLAUSE_ORDERED`, `OMP_CLAUSE_DEFAULT`, `OMP_CLAUSE_REDUCTION`, `OMP_CLAUSE_COLLAPSE`, `OMP_CLAUSE_UNTIED`, `OMP_CLAUSE_FINAL`, and `OMP_CLAUSE_MERGEABLE`. Each code represents the corresponding OpenMP clause.
>
> Clauses associated with the same directive are chained together via `OMP_CLAUSE_CHAIN`. Those clauses that accept a list of variables are restricted to exactly one, accessed with `OMP_CLAUSE_VAR`. Therefore, multiple variables under the same clause C need to be represented as multiple C clauses chained together. This facilitates adding new clauses during compilation.

11.7.8 OpenACC

All the statements starting with `OACC_` represent directives and clauses used by the OpenACC API https://www.openacc.org.

`OACC_CACHE`
> Represents `#pragma acc cache (var ...)`.

`OACC_DATA`
> Represents `#pragma acc data [clause1 ... clauseN]`.

`OACC_DECLARE`
: Represents `#pragma acc declare [clause1 ... clauseN]`.

`OACC_ENTER_DATA`
: Represents `#pragma acc enter data [clause1 ... clauseN]`.

`OACC_EXIT_DATA`
: Represents `#pragma acc exit data [clause1 ... clauseN]`.

`OACC_HOST_DATA`
: Represents `#pragma acc host_data [clause1 ... clauseN]`.

`OACC_KERNELS`
: Represents `#pragma acc kernels [clause1 ... clauseN]`.

`OACC_LOOP`
: Represents `#pragma acc loop [clause1 ... clauseN]`.

  See the description of the `OMP_FOR` code.

`OACC_PARALLEL`
: Represents `#pragma acc parallel [clause1 ... clauseN]`.

`OACC_UPDATE`
: Represents `#pragma acc update [clause1 ... clauseN]`.

11.8 Functions

A function is represented by a `FUNCTION_DECL` node. It stores the basic pieces of the function such as body, parameters, and return type as well as information on the surrounding context, visibility, and linkage.

11.8.1 Function Basics

A function has four core parts: the name, the parameters, the result, and the body. The following macros and functions access these parts of a `FUNCTION_DECL` as well as other basic features:

`DECL_NAME`
: This macro returns the unqualified name of the function, as an `IDENTIFIER_NODE`. For an instantiation of a function template, the `DECL_NAME` is the unqualified name of the template, not something like `f<int>`. The value of `DECL_NAME` is undefined when used on a constructor, destructor, overloaded operator, or type-conversion operator, or any function that is implicitly generated by the compiler. See below for macros that can be used to distinguish these cases.

`DECL_ASSEMBLER_NAME`
: This macro returns the mangled name of the function, also an `IDENTIFIER_NODE`. This name does not contain leading underscores on systems that prefix all identifiers with underscores. The mangled name is computed in the same way on all platforms; if special processing is required to deal with the object file format used on a particular platform, it is the responsibility of the back end to perform those modifications. (Of course, the back end should not modify `DECL_ASSEMBLER_NAME` itself.)

Using `DECL_ASSEMBLER_NAME` will cause additional memory to be allocated (for the mangled name of the entity) so it should be used only when emitting assembly code. It should not be used within the optimizers to determine whether or not two declarations are the same, even though some of the existing optimizers do use it in that way. These uses will be removed over time.

`DECL_ARGUMENTS`
> This macro returns the `PARM_DECL` for the first argument to the function. Subsequent `PARM_DECL` nodes can be obtained by following the `TREE_CHAIN` links.

`DECL_RESULT`
> This macro returns the `RESULT_DECL` for the function.

`DECL_SAVED_TREE`
> This macro returns the complete body of the function.

`TREE_TYPE`
> This macro returns the `FUNCTION_TYPE` or `METHOD_TYPE` for the function.

`DECL_INITIAL`
> A function that has a definition in the current translation unit will have a non-`NULL` `DECL_INITIAL`. However, back ends should not make use of the particular value given by `DECL_INITIAL`.
>
> It should contain a tree of `BLOCK` nodes that mirrors the scopes that variables are bound in the function. Each block contains a list of decls declared in a basic block, a pointer to a chain of blocks at the next lower scope level, then a pointer to the next block at the same level and a backpointer to the parent `BLOCK` or `FUNCTION_DECL`. So given a function as follows:
>
> ```
> void foo()
> {
>   int a;
>   {
>     int b;
>   }
>   int c;
> }
> ```
>
> you would get the following:
>
> ```
> tree foo = FUNCTION_DECL;
> tree decl_a = VAR_DECL;
> tree decl_b = VAR_DECL;
> tree decl_c = VAR_DECL;
> tree block_a = BLOCK;
> tree block_b = BLOCK;
> tree block_c = BLOCK;
> BLOCK_VARS(block_a) = decl_a;
> BLOCK_SUBBLOCKS(block_a) = block_b;
> BLOCK_CHAIN(block_a) = block_c;
> BLOCK_SUPERCONTEXT(block_a) = foo;
> BLOCK_VARS(block_b) = decl_b;
> BLOCK_SUPERCONTEXT(block_b) = block_a;
> BLOCK_VARS(block_c) = decl_c;
> BLOCK_SUPERCONTEXT(block_c) = foo;
> DECL_INITIAL(foo) = block_a;
> ```

11.8.2 Function Properties

To determine the scope of a function, you can use the `DECL_CONTEXT` macro. This macro will return the class (either a `RECORD_TYPE` or a `UNION_TYPE`) or namespace (a `NAMESPACE_DECL`) of which the function is a member. For a virtual function, this macro returns the class in which the function was actually defined, not the base class in which the virtual declaration occurred.

In C, the `DECL_CONTEXT` for a function maybe another function. This representation indicates that the GNU nested function extension is in use. For details on the semantics of nested functions, see the GCC Manual. The nested function can refer to local variables in its containing function. Such references are not explicitly marked in the tree structure; back ends must look at the `DECL_CONTEXT` for the referenced `VAR_DECL`. If the `DECL_CONTEXT` for the referenced `VAR_DECL` is not the same as the function currently being processed, and neither `DECL_EXTERNAL` nor `TREE_STATIC` hold, then the reference is to a local variable in a containing function, and the back end must take appropriate action.

`DECL_EXTERNAL`
: This predicate holds if the function is undefined.

`TREE_PUBLIC`
: This predicate holds if the function has external linkage.

`TREE_STATIC`
: This predicate holds if the function has been defined.

`TREE_THIS_VOLATILE`
: This predicate holds if the function does not return normally.

`TREE_READONLY`
: This predicate holds if the function can only read its arguments.

`DECL_PURE_P`
: This predicate holds if the function can only read its arguments, but may also read global memory.

`DECL_VIRTUAL_P`
: This predicate holds if the function is virtual.

`DECL_ARTIFICIAL`
: This macro holds if the function was implicitly generated by the compiler, rather than explicitly declared. In addition to implicitly generated class member functions, this macro holds for the special functions created to implement static initialization and destruction, to compute run-time type information, and so forth.

`DECL_FUNCTION_SPECIFIC_TARGET`
: This macro returns a tree node that holds the target options that are to be used to compile this particular function or `NULL_TREE` if the function is to be compiled with the target options specified on the command line.

`DECL_FUNCTION_SPECIFIC_OPTIMIZATION`
: This macro returns a tree node that holds the optimization options that are to be used to compile this particular function or `NULL_TREE` if the function is to be compiled with the optimization options specified on the command line.

11.9 Language-dependent trees

Front ends may wish to keep some state associated with various GENERIC trees while parsing. To support this, trees provide a set of flags that may be used by the front end. They are accessed using `TREE_LANG_FLAG_n` where 'n' is currently 0 through 6.

If necessary, a front end can use some language-dependent tree codes in its GENERIC representation, so long as it provides a hook for converting them to GIMPLE and doesn't expect them to work with any (hypothetical) optimizers that run before the conversion to GIMPLE. The intermediate representation used while parsing C and C++ looks very little like GENERIC, but the C and C++ gimplifier hooks are perfectly happy to take it as input and spit out GIMPLE.

11.10 C and C++ Trees

This section documents the internal representation used by GCC to represent C and C++ source programs. When presented with a C or C++ source program, GCC parses the program, performs semantic analysis (including the generation of error messages), and then produces the internal representation described here. This representation contains a complete representation for the entire translation unit provided as input to the front end. This representation is then typically processed by a code-generator in order to produce machine code, but could also be used in the creation of source browsers, intelligent editors, automatic documentation generators, interpreters, and any other programs needing the ability to process C or C++ code.

This section explains the internal representation. In particular, it documents the internal representation for C and C++ source constructs, and the macros, functions, and variables that can be used to access these constructs. The C++ representation is largely a superset of the representation used in the C front end. There is only one construct used in C that does not appear in the C++ front end and that is the GNU "nested function" extension. Many of the macros documented here do not apply in C because the corresponding language constructs do not appear in C.

The C and C++ front ends generate a mix of GENERIC trees and ones specific to C and C++. These language-specific trees are higher-level constructs than the ones in GENERIC to make the parser's job easier. This section describes those trees that aren't part of GENERIC as well as aspects of GENERIC trees that are treated in a language-specific manner.

If you are developing a "back end", be it is a code-generator or some other tool, that uses this representation, you may occasionally find that you need to ask questions not easily answered by the functions and macros available here. If that situation occurs, it is quite likely that GCC already supports the functionality you desire, but that the interface is simply not documented here. In that case, you should ask the GCC maintainers (via mail to gcc@gcc.gnu.org) about documenting the functionality you require. Similarly, if you find yourself writing functions that do not deal directly with your back end, but instead might be useful to other people using the GCC front end, you should submit your patches for inclusion in GCC.

11.10.1 Types for C++

In C++, an array type is not qualified; rather the type of the array elements is qualified. This situation is reflected in the intermediate representation. The macros described here will always examine the qualification of the underlying element type when applied to an array type. (If the element type is itself an array, then the recursion continues until a non-array type is found, and the qualification of this type is examined.) So, for example, `CP_TYPE_CONST_P` will hold of the type `const int ()[7]`, denoting an array of seven `int`s.

The following functions and macros deal with cv-qualification of types:

`cp_type_quals`
: This function returns the set of type qualifiers applied to this type. This value is `TYPE_UNQUALIFIED` if no qualifiers have been applied. The `TYPE_QUAL_CONST` bit is set if the type is `const`-qualified. The `TYPE_QUAL_VOLATILE` bit is set if the type is `volatile`-qualified. The `TYPE_QUAL_RESTRICT` bit is set if the type is `restrict`-qualified.

`CP_TYPE_CONST_P`
: This macro holds if the type is `const`-qualified.

`CP_TYPE_VOLATILE_P`
: This macro holds if the type is `volatile`-qualified.

`CP_TYPE_RESTRICT_P`
: This macro holds if the type is `restrict`-qualified.

`CP_TYPE_CONST_NON_VOLATILE_P`
: This predicate holds for a type that is `const`-qualified, but *not* `volatile`-qualified; other cv-qualifiers are ignored as well: only the `const`-ness is tested.

A few other macros and functions are usable with all types:

`TYPE_SIZE`
: The number of bits required to represent the type, represented as an `INTEGER_CST`. For an incomplete type, `TYPE_SIZE` will be `NULL_TREE`.

`TYPE_ALIGN`
: The alignment of the type, in bits, represented as an `int`.

`TYPE_NAME`
: This macro returns a declaration (in the form of a `TYPE_DECL`) for the type. (Note this macro does *not* return an `IDENTIFIER_NODE`, as you might expect, given its name!) You can look at the `DECL_NAME` of the `TYPE_DECL` to obtain the actual name of the type. The `TYPE_NAME` will be `NULL_TREE` for a type that is not a built-in type, the result of a typedef, or a named class type.

`CP_INTEGRAL_TYPE`
: This predicate holds if the type is an integral type. Notice that in C++, enumerations are *not* integral types.

`ARITHMETIC_TYPE_P`
: This predicate holds if the type is an integral type (in the C++ sense) or a floating point type.

`CLASS_TYPE_P`
: This predicate holds for a class-type.

`TYPE_BUILT_IN`
: This predicate holds for a built-in type.

Chapter 11: GENERIC

`TYPE_PTRDATAMEM_P`
: This predicate holds if the type is a pointer to data member.

`TYPE_PTR_P`
: This predicate holds if the type is a pointer type, and the pointee is not a data member.

`TYPE_PTRFN_P`
: This predicate holds for a pointer to function type.

`TYPE_PTROB_P`
: This predicate holds for a pointer to object type. Note however that it does not hold for the generic pointer to object type `void *`. You may use `TYPE_PTROBV_P` to test for a pointer to object type as well as `void *`.

The table below describes types specific to C and C++ as well as language-dependent info about GENERIC types.

`POINTER_TYPE`
: Used to represent pointer types, and pointer to data member types. If `TREE_TYPE` is a pointer to data member type, then `TYPE_PTRDATAMEM_P` will hold. For a pointer to data member type of the form 'T X::*', `TYPE_PTRMEM_CLASS_TYPE` will be the type X, while `TYPE_PTRMEM_POINTED_TO_TYPE` will be the type T.

`RECORD_TYPE`
: Used to represent `struct` and `class` types in C and C++. If `TYPE_PTRMEMFUNC_P` holds, then this type is a pointer-to-member type. In that case, the `TYPE_PTRMEMFUNC_FN_TYPE` is a `POINTER_TYPE` pointing to a `METHOD_TYPE`. The `METHOD_TYPE` is the type of a function pointed to by the pointer-to-member function. If `TYPE_PTRMEMFUNC_P` does not hold, this type is a class type. For more information, see Section 11.10.3 [Classes], page 191.

`UNKNOWN_TYPE`
: This node is used to represent a type the knowledge of which is insufficient for a sound processing.

`TYPENAME_TYPE`
: Used to represent a construct of the form `typename T::A`. The `TYPE_CONTEXT` is T; the `TYPE_NAME` is an `IDENTIFIER_NODE` for A. If the type is specified via a template-id, then `TYPENAME_TYPE_FULLNAME` yields a `TEMPLATE_ID_EXPR`. The `TREE_TYPE` is non-NULL if the node is implicitly generated in support for the implicit typename extension; in which case the `TREE_TYPE` is a type node for the base-class.

`TYPEOF_TYPE`
: Used to represent the `__typeof__` extension. The `TYPE_FIELDS` is the expression the type of which is being represented.

11.10.2 Namespaces

The root of the entire intermediate representation is the variable `global_namespace`. This is the namespace specified with `::` in C++ source code. All other namespaces, types, variables, functions, and so forth can be found starting with this namespace.

However, except for the fact that it is distinguished as the root of the representation, the global namespace is no different from any other namespace. Thus, in what follows, we describe namespaces generally, rather than the global namespace in particular.

A namespace is represented by a `NAMESPACE_DECL` node.

The following macros and functions can be used on a `NAMESPACE_DECL`:

DECL_NAME

> This macro is used to obtain the `IDENTIFIER_NODE` corresponding to the unqualified name of the name of the namespace (see Section 11.2.2 [Identifiers], page 155). The name of the global namespace is '::', even though in C++ the global namespace is unnamed. However, you should use comparison with `global_namespace`, rather than `DECL_NAME` to determine whether or not a namespace is the global one. An unnamed namespace will have a `DECL_NAME` equal to `anonymous_namespace_name`. Within a single translation unit, all unnamed namespaces will have the same name.

DECL_CONTEXT

> This macro returns the enclosing namespace. The `DECL_CONTEXT` for the `global_namespace` is `NULL_TREE`.

DECL_NAMESPACE_ALIAS

> If this declaration is for a namespace alias, then `DECL_NAMESPACE_ALIAS` is the namespace for which this one is an alias.
>
> Do not attempt to use `cp_namespace_decls` for a namespace which is an alias. Instead, follow `DECL_NAMESPACE_ALIAS` links until you reach an ordinary, non-alias, namespace, and call `cp_namespace_decls` there.

DECL_NAMESPACE_STD_P

> This predicate holds if the namespace is the special `::std` namespace.

cp_namespace_decls

> This function will return the declarations contained in the namespace, including types, overloaded functions, other namespaces, and so forth. If there are no declarations, this function will return `NULL_TREE`. The declarations are connected through their `TREE_CHAIN` fields.
>
> Although most entries on this list will be declarations, `TREE_LIST` nodes may also appear. In this case, the `TREE_VALUE` will be an `OVERLOAD`. The value of the `TREE_PURPOSE` is unspecified; back ends should ignore this value. As with the other kinds of declarations returned by `cp_namespace_decls`, the `TREE_CHAIN` will point to the next declaration in this list.
>
> For more information on the kinds of declarations that can occur on this list, See Section 11.4 [Declarations], page 160. Some declarations will not appear on this list. In particular, no `FIELD_DECL`, `LABEL_DECL`, or `PARM_DECL` nodes will appear here.
>
> This function cannot be used with namespaces that have `DECL_NAMESPACE_ALIAS` set.

11.10.3 Classes

Besides namespaces, the other high-level scoping construct in C++ is the class. (Throughout this manual the term *class* is used to mean the types referred to in the ANSI/ISO C++ Standard as classes; these include types defined with the `class`, `struct`, and `union` keywords.)

A class type is represented by either a `RECORD_TYPE` or a `UNION_TYPE`. A class declared with the `union` tag is represented by a `UNION_TYPE`, while classes declared with either the `struct` or the `class` tag are represented by `RECORD_TYPE`s. You can use the `CLASSTYPE_DECLARED_CLASS` macro to discern whether or not a particular type is a `class` as opposed to a `struct`. This macro will be true only for classes declared with the `class` tag.

Almost all members are available on the `TYPE_FIELDS` list. Given one member, the next can be found by following the `TREE_CHAIN`. You should not depend in any way on the order in which fields appear on this list. All nodes on this list will be 'DECL' nodes. A `FIELD_DECL` is used to represent a non-static data member, a `VAR_DECL` is used to represent a static data member, and a `TYPE_DECL` is used to represent a type. Note that the `CONST_DECL` for an enumeration constant will appear on this list, if the enumeration type was declared in the class. (Of course, the `TYPE_DECL` for the enumeration type will appear here as well.) There are no entries for base classes on this list. In particular, there is no `FIELD_DECL` for the "base-class portion" of an object. If a function member is overloaded, each of the overloaded functions appears; no `OVERLOAD` nodes appear on the `TYPE_FIELDS` list. Implicitly declared functions (including default constructors, copy constructors, assignment operators, and destructors) will appear on this list as well.

The `TYPE_VFIELD` is a compiler-generated field used to point to virtual function tables. It may or may not appear on the `TYPE_FIELDS` list. However, back ends should handle the `TYPE_VFIELD` just like all the entries on the `TYPE_FIELDS` list.

Every class has an associated *binfo*, which can be obtained with `TYPE_BINFO`. Binfos are used to represent base-classes. The binfo given by `TYPE_BINFO` is the degenerate case, whereby every class is considered to be its own base-class. The base binfos for a particular binfo are held in a vector, whose length is obtained with `BINFO_N_BASE_BINFOS`. The base binfos themselves are obtained with `BINFO_BASE_BINFO` and `BINFO_BASE_ITERATE`. To add a new binfo, use `BINFO_BASE_APPEND`. The vector of base binfos can be obtained with `BINFO_BASE_BINFOS`, but normally you do not need to use that. The class type associated with a binfo is given by `BINFO_TYPE`. It is not always the case that `BINFO_TYPE (TYPE_BINFO (x))`, because of typedefs and qualified types. Neither is it the case that `TYPE_BINFO (BINFO_TYPE (y))` is the same binfo as y. The reason is that if y is a binfo representing a base-class B of a derived class D, then `BINFO_TYPE (y)` will be B, and `TYPE_BINFO (BINFO_TYPE (y))` will be B as its own base-class, rather than as a base-class of D.

The access to a base type can be found with `BINFO_BASE_ACCESS`. This will produce `access_public_node`, `access_private_node` or `access_protected_node`. If bases are always public, `BINFO_BASE_ACCESSES` may be NULL.

`BINFO_VIRTUAL_P` is used to specify whether the binfo is inherited virtually or not. The other flags, `BINFO_FLAG_0` to `BINFO_FLAG_6`, can be used for language specific use.

The following macros can be used on a tree node representing a class-type.

LOCAL_CLASS_P
: This predicate holds if the class is local class *i.e.* declared inside a function body.

TYPE_POLYMORPHIC_P
: This predicate holds if the class has at least one virtual function (declared or inherited).

TYPE_HAS_DEFAULT_CONSTRUCTOR
: This predicate holds whenever its argument represents a class-type with default constructor.

CLASSTYPE_HAS_MUTABLE
TYPE_HAS_MUTABLE_P
: These predicates hold for a class-type having a mutable data member.

CLASSTYPE_NON_POD_P
: This predicate holds only for class-types that are not PODs.

TYPE_HAS_NEW_OPERATOR
: This predicate holds for a class-type that defines `operator new`.

TYPE_HAS_ARRAY_NEW_OPERATOR
: This predicate holds for a class-type for which `operator new[]` is defined.

TYPE_OVERLOADS_CALL_EXPR
: This predicate holds for class-type for which the function call `operator()` is overloaded.

TYPE_OVERLOADS_ARRAY_REF
: This predicate holds for a class-type that overloads `operator[]`

TYPE_OVERLOADS_ARROW
: This predicate holds for a class-type for which `operator->` is overloaded.

11.10.4 Functions for C++

A function is represented by a `FUNCTION_DECL` node. A set of overloaded functions is sometimes represented by an `OVERLOAD` node.

An `OVERLOAD` node is not a declaration, so none of the 'DECL_' macros should be used on an `OVERLOAD`. An `OVERLOAD` node is similar to a `TREE_LIST`. Use `OVL_CURRENT` to get the function associated with an `OVERLOAD` node; use `OVL_NEXT` to get the next `OVERLOAD` node in the list of overloaded functions. The macros `OVL_CURRENT` and `OVL_NEXT` are actually polymorphic; you can use them to work with `FUNCTION_DECL` nodes as well as with overloads. In the case of a `FUNCTION_DECL`, `OVL_CURRENT` will always return the function itself, and `OVL_NEXT` will always be `NULL_TREE`.

To determine the scope of a function, you can use the `DECL_CONTEXT` macro. This macro will return the class (either a `RECORD_TYPE` or a `UNION_TYPE`) or namespace (a `NAMESPACE_DECL`) of which the function is a member. For a virtual function, this macro returns the class in which the function was actually defined, not the base class in which the virtual declaration occurred.

If a friend function is defined in a class scope, the `DECL_FRIEND_CONTEXT` macro can be used to determine the class in which it was defined. For example, in

Chapter 11: GENERIC   193

```
class C { friend void f() {} };
```

the `DECL_CONTEXT` for `f` will be the `global_namespace`, but the `DECL_FRIEND_CONTEXT` will be the `RECORD_TYPE` for C.

The following macros and functions can be used on a `FUNCTION_DECL`:

`DECL_MAIN_P`
> This predicate holds for a function that is the program entry point ::code.

`DECL_LOCAL_FUNCTION_P`
> This predicate holds if the function was declared at block scope, even though it has a global scope.

`DECL_ANTICIPATED`
> This predicate holds if the function is a built-in function but its prototype is not yet explicitly declared.

`DECL_EXTERN_C_FUNCTION_P`
> This predicate holds if the function is declared as an 'extern "C"' function.

`DECL_LINKONCE_P`
> This macro holds if multiple copies of this function may be emitted in various translation units. It is the responsibility of the linker to merge the various copies. Template instantiations are the most common example of functions for which `DECL_LINKONCE_P` holds; G++ instantiates needed templates in all translation units which require them, and then relies on the linker to remove duplicate instantiations.
>
> FIXME: This macro is not yet implemented.

`DECL_FUNCTION_MEMBER_P`
> This macro holds if the function is a member of a class, rather than a member of a namespace.

`DECL_STATIC_FUNCTION_P`
> This predicate holds if the function a static member function.

`DECL_NONSTATIC_MEMBER_FUNCTION_P`
> This macro holds for a non-static member function.

`DECL_CONST_MEMFUNC_P`
> This predicate holds for a `const`-member function.

`DECL_VOLATILE_MEMFUNC_P`
> This predicate holds for a `volatile`-member function.

`DECL_CONSTRUCTOR_P`
> This macro holds if the function is a constructor.

`DECL_NONCONVERTING_P`
> This predicate holds if the constructor is a non-converting constructor.

`DECL_COMPLETE_CONSTRUCTOR_P`
> This predicate holds for a function which is a constructor for an object of a complete type.

DECL_BASE_CONSTRUCTOR_P
: This predicate holds for a function which is a constructor for a base class sub-object.

DECL_COPY_CONSTRUCTOR_P
: This predicate holds for a function which is a copy-constructor.

DECL_DESTRUCTOR_P
: This macro holds if the function is a destructor.

DECL_COMPLETE_DESTRUCTOR_P
: This predicate holds if the function is the destructor for an object a complete type.

DECL_OVERLOADED_OPERATOR_P
: This macro holds if the function is an overloaded operator.

DECL_CONV_FN_P
: This macro holds if the function is a type-conversion operator.

DECL_GLOBAL_CTOR_P
: This predicate holds if the function is a file-scope initialization function.

DECL_GLOBAL_DTOR_P
: This predicate holds if the function is a file-scope finalization function.

DECL_THUNK_P
: This predicate holds if the function is a thunk.

  These functions represent stub code that adjusts the `this` pointer and then jumps to another function. When the jumped-to function returns, control is transferred directly to the caller, without returning to the thunk. The first parameter to the thunk is always the `this` pointer; the thunk should add THUNK_DELTA to this value. (The THUNK_DELTA is an `int`, not an INTEGER_CST.)

  Then, if THUNK_VCALL_OFFSET (an INTEGER_CST) is nonzero the adjusted `this` pointer must be adjusted again. The complete calculation is given by the following pseudo-code:

  ```
  this += THUNK_DELTA
  if (THUNK_VCALL_OFFSET)
    this += (*((ptrdiff_t **) this))[THUNK_VCALL_OFFSET]
  ```

  Finally, the thunk should jump to the location given by DECL_INITIAL; this will always be an expression for the address of a function.

DECL_NON_THUNK_FUNCTION_P
: This predicate holds if the function is *not* a thunk function.

GLOBAL_INIT_PRIORITY
: If either DECL_GLOBAL_CTOR_P or DECL_GLOBAL_DTOR_P holds, then this gives the initialization priority for the function. The linker will arrange that all functions for which DECL_GLOBAL_CTOR_P holds are run in increasing order of priority before `main` is called. When the program exits, all functions for which DECL_GLOBAL_DTOR_P holds are run in the reverse order.

TYPE_RAISES_EXCEPTIONS
: This macro returns the list of exceptions that a (member-)function can raise. The returned list, if non NULL, is comprised of nodes whose TREE_VALUE represents a type.

TYPE_NOTHROW_P
: This predicate holds when the exception-specification of its arguments is of the form '()'.

DECL_ARRAY_DELETE_OPERATOR_P
: This predicate holds if the function an overloaded operator delete[].

11.10.5 Statements for C++

A function that has a definition in the current translation unit will have a non-NULL DECL_INITIAL. However, back ends should not make use of the particular value given by DECL_INITIAL.

The DECL_SAVED_TREE macro will give the complete body of the function.

11.10.5.1 Statements

There are tree nodes corresponding to all of the source-level statement constructs, used within the C and C++ frontends. These are enumerated here, together with a list of the various macros that can be used to obtain information about them. There are a few macros that can be used with all statements:

STMT_IS_FULL_EXPR_P
: In C++, statements normally constitute "full expressions"; temporaries created during a statement are destroyed when the statement is complete. However, G++ sometimes represents expressions by statements; these statements will not have STMT_IS_FULL_EXPR_P set. Temporaries created during such statements should be destroyed when the innermost enclosing statement with STMT_IS_FULL_EXPR_P set is exited.

Here is the list of the various statement nodes, and the macros used to access them. This documentation describes the use of these nodes in non-template functions (including instantiations of template functions). In template functions, the same nodes are used, but sometimes in slightly different ways.

Many of the statements have substatements. For example, a while loop will have a body, which is itself a statement. If the substatement is NULL_TREE, it is considered equivalent to a statement consisting of a single ;, i.e., an expression statement in which the expression has been omitted. A substatement may in fact be a list of statements, connected via their TREE_CHAINs. So, you should always process the statement tree by looping over substatements, like this:

```
void process_stmt (stmt)
     tree stmt;
{
  while (stmt)
    {
      switch (TREE_CODE (stmt))
        {
        case IF_STMT:
```

```
              process_stmt (THEN_CLAUSE (stmt));
              /* More processing here.  */
              break;

            ...
          }

          stmt = TREE_CHAIN (stmt);
        }
    }
```

In other words, while the `then` clause of an `if` statement in C++ can be only one statement (although that one statement may be a compound statement), the intermediate representation will sometimes use several statements chained together.

BREAK_STMT

>   Used to represent a `break` statement. There are no additional fields.

CLEANUP_STMT

>   Used to represent an action that should take place upon exit from the enclosing scope. Typically, these actions are calls to destructors for local objects, but back ends cannot rely on this fact. If these nodes are in fact representing such destructors, CLEANUP_DECL will be the VAR_DECL destroyed. Otherwise, CLEANUP_DECL will be NULL_TREE. In any case, the CLEANUP_EXPR is the expression to execute. The cleanups executed on exit from a scope should be run in the reverse order of the order in which the associated CLEANUP_STMTs were encountered.

CONTINUE_STMT

>   Used to represent a `continue` statement. There are no additional fields.

CTOR_STMT

>   Used to mark the beginning (if CTOR_BEGIN_P holds) or end (if CTOR_END_P holds of the main body of a constructor. See also SUBOBJECT for more information on how to use these nodes.

DO_STMT

>   Used to represent a `do` loop. The body of the loop is given by DO_BODY while the termination condition for the loop is given by DO_COND. The condition for a `do`-statement is always an expression.

EMPTY_CLASS_EXPR

>   Used to represent a temporary object of a class with no data whose address is never taken. (All such objects are interchangeable.) The TREE_TYPE represents the type of the object.

EXPR_STMT

>   Used to represent an expression statement. Use EXPR_STMT_EXPR to obtain the expression.

FOR_STMT

>   Used to represent a `for` statement. The FOR_INIT_STMT is the initialization statement for the loop. The FOR_COND is the termination condition. The FOR_EXPR is the expression executed right before the FOR_COND on each loop iteration;

often, this expression increments a counter. The body of the loop is given by FOR_BODY. Note that FOR_INIT_STMT and FOR_BODY return statements, while FOR_COND and FOR_EXPR return expressions.

HANDLER

Used to represent a C++ `catch` block. The HANDLER_TYPE is the type of exception that will be caught by this handler; it is equal (by pointer equality) to NULL if this handler is for all types. HANDLER_PARMS is the DECL_STMT for the catch parameter, and HANDLER_BODY is the code for the block itself.

IF_STMT

Used to represent an `if` statement. The IF_COND is the expression.

If the condition is a TREE_LIST, then the TREE_PURPOSE is a statement (usually a DECL_STMT). Each time the condition is evaluated, the statement should be executed. Then, the TREE_VALUE should be used as the conditional expression itself. This representation is used to handle C++ code like this:

C++ distinguishes between this and COND_EXPR for handling templates.

```
if (int i = 7) ...
```

where there is a new local variable (or variables) declared within the condition.

The THEN_CLAUSE represents the statement given by the `then` condition, while the ELSE_CLAUSE represents the statement given by the `else` condition.

SUBOBJECT

In a constructor, these nodes are used to mark the point at which a subobject of `this` is fully constructed. If, after this point, an exception is thrown before a CTOR_STMT with CTOR_END_P set is encountered, the SUBOBJECT_CLEANUP must be executed. The cleanups must be executed in the reverse order in which they appear.

SWITCH_STMT

Used to represent a `switch` statement. The SWITCH_STMT_COND is the expression on which the switch is occurring. See the documentation for an IF_STMT for more information on the representation used for the condition. The SWITCH_STMT_BODY is the body of the switch statement. The SWITCH_STMT_TYPE is the original type of switch expression as given in the source, before any compiler conversions.

TRY_BLOCK

Used to represent a `try` block. The body of the try block is given by TRY_STMTS. Each of the catch blocks is a HANDLER node. The first handler is given by TRY_HANDLERS. Subsequent handlers are obtained by following the TREE_CHAIN link from one handler to the next. The body of the handler is given by HANDLER_BODY.

If CLEANUP_P holds of the TRY_BLOCK, then the TRY_HANDLERS will not be a HANDLER node. Instead, it will be an expression that should be executed if an exception is thrown in the try block. It must rethrow the exception after executing that code. And, if an exception is thrown while the expression is executing, `terminate` must be called.

USING_STMT
> Used to represent a `using` directive. The namespace is given by `USING_STMT_NAMESPACE`, which will be a NAMESPACE_DECL. This node is needed inside template functions, to implement using directives during instantiation.

WHILE_STMT
> Used to represent a `while` loop. The `WHILE_COND` is the termination condition for the loop. See the documentation for an `IF_STMT` for more information on the representation used for the condition.
>
> The `WHILE_BODY` is the body of the loop.

11.10.6 C++ Expressions

This section describes expressions specific to the C and C++ front ends.

TYPEID_EXPR
> Used to represent a `typeid` expression.

NEW_EXPR
VEC_NEW_EXPR
> Used to represent a call to `new` and `new[]` respectively.

DELETE_EXPR
VEC_DELETE_EXPR
> Used to represent a call to `delete` and `delete[]` respectively.

MEMBER_REF
> Represents a reference to a member of a class.

THROW_EXPR
> Represents an instance of `throw` in the program. Operand 0, which is the expression to throw, may be `NULL_TREE`.

AGGR_INIT_EXPR
> An `AGGR_INIT_EXPR` represents the initialization as the return value of a function call, or as the result of a constructor. An `AGGR_INIT_EXPR` will only appear as a full-expression, or as the second operand of a `TARGET_EXPR`. `AGGR_INIT_EXPR`s have a representation similar to that of `CALL_EXPR`s. You can use the `AGGR_INIT_EXPR_FN` and `AGGR_INIT_EXPR_ARG` macros to access the function to call and the arguments to pass.
>
> If `AGGR_INIT_VIA_CTOR_P` holds of the `AGGR_INIT_EXPR`, then the initialization is via a constructor call. The address of the `AGGR_INIT_EXPR_SLOT` operand, which is always a `VAR_DECL`, is taken, and this value replaces the first argument in the argument list.
>
> In either case, the expression is void.

11.11 Java Trees

12 GIMPLE

GIMPLE is a three-address representation derived from GENERIC by breaking down GENERIC expressions into tuples of no more than 3 operands (with some exceptions like function calls). GIMPLE was heavily influenced by the SIMPLE IL used by the McCAT compiler project at McGill University, though we have made some different choices. For one thing, SIMPLE doesn't support `goto`.

Temporaries are introduced to hold intermediate values needed to compute complex expressions. Additionally, all the control structures used in GENERIC are lowered into conditional jumps, lexical scopes are removed and exception regions are converted into an on the side exception region tree.

The compiler pass which converts GENERIC into GIMPLE is referred to as the 'gimplifier'. The gimplifier works recursively, generating GIMPLE tuples out of the original GENERIC expressions.

One of the early implementation strategies used for the GIMPLE representation was to use the same internal data structures used by front ends to represent parse trees. This simplified implementation because we could leverage existing functionality and interfaces. However, GIMPLE is a much more restrictive representation than abstract syntax trees (AST), therefore it does not require the full structural complexity provided by the main tree data structure.

The GENERIC representation of a function is stored in the `DECL_SAVED_TREE` field of the associated `FUNCTION_DECL` tree node. It is converted to GIMPLE by a call to `gimplify_function_tree`.

If a front end wants to include language-specific tree codes in the tree representation which it provides to the back end, it must provide a definition of `LANG_HOOKS_GIMPLIFY_EXPR` which knows how to convert the front end trees to GIMPLE. Usually such a hook will involve much of the same code for expanding front end trees to RTL. This function can return fully lowered GIMPLE, or it can return GENERIC trees and let the main gimplifier lower them the rest of the way; this is often simpler. GIMPLE that is not fully lowered is known as "High GIMPLE" and consists of the IL before the pass `pass_lower_cf`. High GIMPLE contains some container statements like lexical scopes (represented by `GIMPLE_BIND`) and nested expressions (e.g., `GIMPLE_TRY`), while "Low GIMPLE" exposes all of the implicit jumps for control and exception expressions directly in the IL and EH region trees.

The C and C++ front ends currently convert directly from front end trees to GIMPLE, and hand that off to the back end rather than first converting to GENERIC. Their gimplifier hooks know about all the _STMT nodes and how to convert them to GENERIC forms. There was some work done on a genericization pass which would run first, but the existence of `STMT_EXPR` meant that in order to convert all of the C statements into GENERIC equivalents would involve walking the entire tree anyway, so it was simpler to lower all the way. This might change in the future if someone writes an optimization pass which would work better with higher-level trees, but currently the optimizers all expect GIMPLE.

You can request to dump a C-like representation of the GIMPLE form with the flag '-fdump-tree-gimple'.

12.1 Tuple representation

GIMPLE instructions are tuples of variable size divided in two groups: a header describing the instruction and its locations, and a variable length body with all the operands. Tuples are organized into a hierarchy with 3 main classes of tuples.

12.1.1 `gimple` (gsbase)

This is the root of the hierarchy, it holds basic information needed by most GIMPLE statements. There are some fields that may not be relevant to every GIMPLE statement, but those were moved into the base structure to take advantage of holes left by other fields (thus making the structure more compact). The structure takes 4 words (32 bytes) on 64 bit hosts:

Field	Size (bits)
code	8
subcode	16
no_warning	1
visited	1
nontemporal_move	1
plf	2
modified	1
has_volatile_ops	1
references_memory_p	1
uid	32
location	32
num_ops	32
bb	64
block	63
Total size	32 bytes

- **code** Main identifier for a GIMPLE instruction.

- **subcode** Used to distinguish different variants of the same basic instruction or provide flags applicable to a given code. The subcode flags field has different uses depending on the code of the instruction, but mostly it distinguishes instructions of the same family. The most prominent use of this field is in assignments, where subcode indicates the operation done on the RHS of the assignment. For example, a = b + c is encoded as GIMPLE_ASSIGN <PLUS_EXPR, a, b, c>.

- **no_warning** Bitflag to indicate whether a warning has already been issued on this statement.

- **visited** General purpose "visited" marker. Set and cleared by each pass when needed.

- **nontemporal_move** Bitflag used in assignments that represent non-temporal moves. Although this bitflag is only used in assignments, it was moved into the base to take advantage of the bit holes left by the previous fields.

- **plf** Pass Local Flags. This 2-bit mask can be used as general purpose markers by any pass. Passes are responsible for clearing and setting these two flags accordingly.

- **modified** Bitflag to indicate whether the statement has been modified. Used mainly by the operand scanner to determine when to re-scan a statement for operands.

- `has_volatile_ops` Bitflag to indicate whether this statement contains operands that have been marked volatile.
- `references_memory_p` Bitflag to indicate whether this statement contains memory references (i.e., its operands are either global variables, or pointer dereferences or anything that must reside in memory).
- `uid` This is an unsigned integer used by passes that want to assign IDs to every statement. These IDs must be assigned and used by each pass.
- `location` This is a `location_t` identifier to specify source code location for this statement. It is inherited from the front end.
- `num_ops` Number of operands that this statement has. This specifies the size of the operand vector embedded in the tuple. Only used in some tuples, but it is declared in the base tuple to take advantage of the 32-bit hole left by the previous fields.
- `bb` Basic block holding the instruction.
- `block` Lexical block holding this statement. Also used for debug information generation.

12.1.2 gimple_statement_with_ops

This tuple is actually split in two: `gimple_statement_with_ops_base` and `gimple_statement_with_ops`. This is needed to accommodate the way the operand vector is allocated. The operand vector is defined to be an array of 1 element. So, to allocate a dynamic number of operands, the memory allocator (`gimple_alloc`) simply allocates enough memory to hold the structure itself plus N - 1 operands which run "off the end" of the structure. For example, to allocate space for a tuple with 3 operands, `gimple_alloc` reserves `sizeof (struct gimple_statement_with_ops) + 2 * sizeof (tree)` bytes.

On the other hand, several fields in this tuple need to be shared with the `gimple_statement_with_memory_ops` tuple. So, these common fields are placed in `gimple_statement_with_ops_base` which is then inherited from the other two tuples.

gsbase	256
def_ops	64
use_ops	64
op	num_ops * 64
Total size	48 + 8 * num_ops bytes

- `gsbase` Inherited from `struct gimple`.
- `def_ops` Array of pointers into the operand array indicating all the slots that contain a variable written-to by the statement. This array is also used for immediate use chaining. Note that it would be possible to not rely on this array, but the changes required to implement this are pretty invasive.
- `use_ops` Similar to `def_ops` but for variables read by the statement.
- `op` Array of trees with `num_ops` slots.

12.1.3 gimple_statement_with_memory_ops

This tuple is essentially identical to `gimple_statement_with_ops`, except that it contains 4 additional fields to hold vectors related memory stores and loads. Similar to the previous case, the structure is split in two to accommodate for the operand vector (`gimple_statement_with_memory_ops_base` and `gimple_statement_with_memory_ops`).

Field	Size (bits)
gsbase	256
def_ops	64
use_ops	64
vdef_ops	64
vuse_ops	64
stores	64
loads	64
op	num_ops * 64
Total size	80 + 8 * num_ops bytes

- `vdef_ops` Similar to `def_ops` but for VDEF operators. There is one entry per memory symbol written by this statement. This is used to maintain the memory SSA use-def and def-def chains.

- `vuse_ops` Similar to `use_ops` but for VUSE operators. There is one entry per memory symbol loaded by this statement. This is used to maintain the memory SSA use-def chains.

- `stores` Bitset with all the UIDs for the symbols written-to by the statement. This is different than `vdef_ops` in that all the affected symbols are mentioned in this set. If memory partitioning is enabled, the `vdef_ops` vector will refer to memory partitions. Furthermore, no SSA information is stored in this set.

- `loads` Similar to `stores`, but for memory loads. (Note that there is some amount of redundancy here, it should be possible to reduce memory utilization further by removing these sets).

All the other tuples are defined in terms of these three basic ones. Each tuple will add some fields.

12.2 Class hierarchy of GIMPLE statements

The following diagram shows the C++ inheritance hierarchy of statement kinds, along with their relationships to `GSS_` values (layouts) and `GIMPLE_` values (codes):

```
gimple
  |    layout: GSS_BASE
  |    used for 4 codes: GIMPLE_ERROR_MARK
  |                      GIMPLE_NOP
  |                      GIMPLE_OMP_SECTIONS_SWITCH
  |                      GIMPLE_PREDICT
  |
  + gimple_statement_with_ops_base
  |  |    (no GSS layout)
  |  |
  |  + gimple_statement_with_ops
  |  |  |    layout: GSS_WITH_OPS
  |  |  |
  |  |  + gcond
  |  |  |    code: GIMPLE_COND
  |  |  |
  |  |  + gdebug
```

```
|   |   |   |     code: GIMPLE_DEBUG
|   |   |   |
|   |   | + ggoto
|   |   | |   code: GIMPLE_GOTO
|   |   | |
|   |   | + glabel
|   |   | |   code: GIMPLE_LABEL
|   |   | |
|   |   | + gswitch
|   |   |     code: GIMPLE_SWITCH
|   |   |
|   | + gimple_statement_with_memory_ops_base
|   |   |     layout: GSS_WITH_MEM_OPS_BASE
|   |   |
|   |   + gimple_statement_with_memory_ops
|   |   |   |  layout: GSS_WITH_MEM_OPS
|   |   |   |
|   |   |   + gassign
|   |   |   |   code GIMPLE_ASSIGN
|   |   |   |
|   |   |   + greturn
|   |   |       code GIMPLE_RETURN
|   |   |
|   |   + gcall
|   |   |     layout: GSS_CALL, code: GIMPLE_CALL
|   |   |
|   |   + gasm
|   |   |     layout: GSS_ASM, code: GIMPLE_ASM
|   |   |
|   |   + gtransaction
|   |         layout: GSS_TRANSACTION, code: GIMPLE_TRANSACTION
|
+ gimple_statement_omp
|   |     layout: GSS_OMP.  Used for code GIMPLE_OMP_SECTION
|   |
|   + gomp_critical
|   |     layout: GSS_OMP_CRITICAL, code: GIMPLE_OMP_CRITICAL
|   |
|   + gomp_for
|   |     layout: GSS_OMP_FOR, code: GIMPLE_OMP_FOR
|   |
|   + gomp_parallel_layout
|   |   |  layout: GSS_OMP_PARALLEL_LAYOUT
|   |   |
|   |   + gimple_statement_omp_taskreg
|   |   |   |
|   |   |   + gomp_parallel
|   |   |   |     code: GIMPLE_OMP_PARALLEL
|   |   |   |
|   |   |   + gomp_task
|   |   |         code: GIMPLE_OMP_TASK
|   |   |
|   |   + gimple_statement_omp_target
|   |         code: GIMPLE_OMP_TARGET
|   |
|   + gomp_sections
|   |     layout: GSS_OMP_SECTIONS, code: GIMPLE_OMP_SECTIONS
|   |
```

```
   |    + gimple_statement_omp_single_layout
   |    |       layout: GSS_OMP_SINGLE_LAYOUT
   |    |
   |      + gomp_single
   |      |      code: GIMPLE_OMP_SINGLE
   |      |
   |      + gomp_teams
   |             code: GIMPLE_OMP_TEAMS
   |
 + gbind
 |        layout: GSS_BIND, code: GIMPLE_BIND
 |
 + gcatch
 |        layout: GSS_CATCH, code: GIMPLE_CATCH
 |
 + geh_filter
 |        layout: GSS_EH_FILTER, code: GIMPLE_EH_FILTER
 |
 + geh_else
 |        layout: GSS_EH_ELSE, code: GIMPLE_EH_ELSE
 |
 + geh_mnt
 |        layout: GSS_EH_MNT, code: GIMPLE_EH_MUST_NOT_THROW
 |
 + gphi
 |        layout: GSS_PHI, code: GIMPLE_PHI
 |
 + gimple_statement_eh_ctrl
 |    |    layout: GSS_EH_CTRL
 |    |
 |    + gresx
 |    |      code: GIMPLE_RESX
 |    |
 |    + geh_dispatch
 |           code: GIMPLE_EH_DISPATCH
 |
 + gtry
 |        layout: GSS_TRY, code: GIMPLE_TRY
 |
 + gimple_statement_wce
 |        layout: GSS_WCE, code: GIMPLE_WITH_CLEANUP_EXPR
 |
 + gomp_continue
 |        layout: GSS_OMP_CONTINUE, code: GIMPLE_OMP_CONTINUE
 |
 + gomp_atomic_load
 |        layout: GSS_OMP_ATOMIC_LOAD, code: GIMPLE_OMP_ATOMIC_LOAD
 |
 + gimple_statement_omp_atomic_store_layout
      |    layout: GSS_OMP_ATOMIC_STORE_LAYOUT,
      |    code: GIMPLE_OMP_ATOMIC_STORE
      |
      + gomp_atomic_store
      |       code: GIMPLE_OMP_ATOMIC_STORE
      |
      + gomp_return
              code: GIMPLE_OMP_RETURN
```

12.3 GIMPLE instruction set

The following table briefly describes the GIMPLE instruction set.

Instruction	High GIMPLE	Low GIMPLE
GIMPLE_ASM	x	x
GIMPLE_ASSIGN	x	x
GIMPLE_BIND	x	
GIMPLE_CALL	x	x
GIMPLE_CATCH	x	
GIMPLE_COND	x	x
GIMPLE_DEBUG	x	x
GIMPLE_EH_FILTER	x	
GIMPLE_GOTO	x	x
GIMPLE_LABEL	x	x
GIMPLE_NOP	x	x
GIMPLE_OMP_ATOMIC_LOAD	x	x
GIMPLE_OMP_ATOMIC_STORE	x	x
GIMPLE_OMP_CONTINUE	x	x
GIMPLE_OMP_CRITICAL	x	x
GIMPLE_OMP_FOR	x	x
GIMPLE_OMP_MASTER	x	x
GIMPLE_OMP_ORDERED	x	x
GIMPLE_OMP_PARALLEL	x	x
GIMPLE_OMP_RETURN	x	x
GIMPLE_OMP_SECTION	x	x
GIMPLE_OMP_SECTIONS	x	x
GIMPLE_OMP_SECTIONS_SWITCH	x	x
GIMPLE_OMP_SINGLE	x	x
GIMPLE_PHI		x
GIMPLE_RESX		x
GIMPLE_RETURN	x	x
GIMPLE_SWITCH	x	x
GIMPLE_TRY	x	

12.4 Exception Handling

Other exception handling constructs are represented using `GIMPLE_TRY_CATCH`. `GIMPLE_TRY_CATCH` has two operands. The first operand is a sequence of statements to execute. If executing these statements does not throw an exception, then the second operand is ignored. Otherwise, if an exception is thrown, then the second operand of the `GIMPLE_TRY_CATCH` is checked. The second operand may have the following forms:

1. A sequence of statements to execute. When an exception occurs, these statements are executed, and then the exception is rethrown.
2. A sequence of `GIMPLE_CATCH` statements. Each `GIMPLE_CATCH` has a list of applicable exception types and handler code. If the thrown exception matches one of the caught types, the associated handler code is executed. If the handler code falls off the bottom, execution continues after the original `GIMPLE_TRY_CATCH`.

3. A `GIMPLE_EH_FILTER` statement. This has a list of permitted exception types, and code to handle a match failure. If the thrown exception does not match one of the allowed types, the associated match failure code is executed. If the thrown exception does match, it continues unwinding the stack looking for the next handler.

Currently throwing an exception is not directly represented in GIMPLE, since it is implemented by calling a function. At some point in the future we will want to add some way to express that the call will throw an exception of a known type.

Just before running the optimizers, the compiler lowers the high-level EH constructs above into a set of 'goto's, magic labels, and EH regions. Continuing to unwind at the end of a cleanup is represented with a `GIMPLE_RESX`.

12.5 Temporaries

When gimplification encounters a subexpression that is too complex, it creates a new temporary variable to hold the value of the subexpression, and adds a new statement to initialize it before the current statement. These special temporaries are known as 'expression temporaries', and are allocated using `get_formal_tmp_var`. The compiler tries to always evaluate identical expressions into the same temporary, to simplify elimination of redundant calculations.

We can only use expression temporaries when we know that it will not be reevaluated before its value is used, and that it will not be otherwise modified[1]. Other temporaries can be allocated using `get_initialized_tmp_var` or `create_tmp_var`.

Currently, an expression like `a = b + 5` is not reduced any further. We tried converting it to something like

```
T1 = b + 5;
a = T1;
```

but this bloated the representation for minimal benefit. However, a variable which must live in memory cannot appear in an expression; its value is explicitly loaded into a temporary first. Similarly, storing the value of an expression to a memory variable goes through a temporary.

12.6 Operands

In general, expressions in GIMPLE consist of an operation and the appropriate number of simple operands; these operands must either be a GIMPLE rvalue (`is_gimple_val`), i.e. a constant or a register variable. More complex operands are factored out into temporaries, so that

```
a = b + c + d
```

becomes

```
T1 = b + c;
a = T1 + d;
```

The same rule holds for arguments to a `GIMPLE_CALL`.

The target of an assignment is usually a variable, but can also be a `MEM_REF` or a compound lvalue as described below.

---

[1] These restrictions are derived from those in Morgan 4.8.

12.6.1 Compound Expressions

The left-hand side of a C comma expression is simply moved into a separate statement.

12.6.2 Compound Lvalues

Currently compound lvalues involving array and structure field references are not broken down; an expression like `a.b[2] = 42` is not reduced any further (though complex array subscripts are). This restriction is a workaround for limitations in later optimizers; if we were to convert this to

```
T1 = &a.b;
T1[2] = 42;
```

alias analysis would not remember that the reference to `T1[2]` came by way of `a.b`, so it would think that the assignment could alias another member of `a`; this broke `struct-alias-1.c`. Future optimizer improvements may make this limitation unnecessary.

12.6.3 Conditional Expressions

A C ?: expression is converted into an `if` statement with each branch assigning to the same temporary. So,

```
a = b ? c : d;
```

becomes

```
if (b == 1)
  T1 = c;
else
  T1 = d;
a = T1;
```

The GIMPLE level if-conversion pass re-introduces ?: expression, if appropriate. It is used to vectorize loops with conditions using vector conditional operations.

Note that in GIMPLE, `if` statements are represented using `GIMPLE_COND`, as described below.

12.6.4 Logical Operators

Except when they appear in the condition operand of a `GIMPLE_COND`, logical 'and' and 'or' operators are simplified as follows: `a = b && c` becomes

```
T1 = (bool)b;
if (T1 == true)
  T1 = (bool)c;
a = T1;
```

Note that `T1` in this example cannot be an expression temporary, because it has two different assignments.

12.6.5 Manipulating operands

All gimple operands are of type `tree`. But only certain types of trees are allowed to be used as operand tuples. Basic validation is controlled by the function `get_gimple_rhs_class`, which given a tree code, returns an `enum` with the following values of type `enum gimple_rhs_class`

- `GIMPLE_INVALID_RHS` The tree cannot be used as a GIMPLE operand.
- `GIMPLE_TERNARY_RHS` The tree is a valid GIMPLE ternary operation.

- `GIMPLE_BINARY_RHS` The tree is a valid GIMPLE binary operation.
- `GIMPLE_UNARY_RHS` The tree is a valid GIMPLE unary operation.
- `GIMPLE_SINGLE_RHS` The tree is a single object, that cannot be split into simpler operands (for instance, `SSA_NAME`, `VAR_DECL`, `COMPONENT_REF`, etc).

  This operand class also acts as an escape hatch for tree nodes that may be flattened out into the operand vector, but would need more than two slots on the RHS. For instance, a `COND_EXPR` expression of the form (a op b) ? x : y could be flattened out on the operand vector using 4 slots, but it would also require additional processing to distinguish c = a op b from c = a op b ? x : y. Something similar occurs with `ASSERT_EXPR`. In time, these special case tree expressions should be flattened into the operand vector.

For tree nodes in the categories `GIMPLE_TERNARY_RHS`, `GIMPLE_BINARY_RHS` and `GIMPLE_UNARY_RHS`, they cannot be stored inside tuples directly. They first need to be flattened and separated into individual components. For instance, given the GENERIC expression

    a = b + c

its tree representation is:

    MODIFY_EXPR <VAR_DECL <a>, PLUS_EXPR <VAR_DECL <b>, VAR_DECL <c>>>

In this case, the GIMPLE form for this statement is logically identical to its GENERIC form but in GIMPLE, the `PLUS_EXPR` on the RHS of the assignment is not represented as a tree, instead the two operands are taken out of the `PLUS_EXPR` sub-tree and flattened into the GIMPLE tuple as follows:

    GIMPLE_ASSIGN <PLUS_EXPR, VAR_DECL <a>, VAR_DECL <b>, VAR_DECL <c>>

12.6.6 Operand vector allocation

The operand vector is stored at the bottom of the three tuple structures that accept operands. This means, that depending on the code of a given statement, its operand vector will be at different offsets from the base of the structure. To access tuple operands use the following accessors

unsigned gimple_num_ops (*gimple g*)   [GIMPLE function]
    Returns the number of operands in statement G.

tree gimple_op (*gimple g, unsigned i*)   [GIMPLE function]
    Returns operand I from statement G.

tree * gimple_ops (*gimple g*)   [GIMPLE function]
    Returns a pointer into the operand vector for statement G. This is computed using an internal table called `gimple_ops_offset_[]`. This table is indexed by the gimple code of G.

    When the compiler is built, this table is filled-in using the sizes of the structures used by each statement code defined in gimple.def. Since the operand vector is at the bottom of the structure, for a gimple code C the offset is computed as sizeof (struct-of C) - sizeof (tree).

    This mechanism adds one memory indirection to every access when using `gimple_op()`, if this becomes a bottleneck, a pass can choose to memoize the result from `gimple_ops()` and use that to access the operands.

12.6.7 Operand validation

When adding a new operand to a gimple statement, the operand will be validated according to what each tuple accepts in its operand vector. These predicates are called by the `gimple_name_set_...()`. Each tuple will use one of the following predicates (Note, this list is not exhaustive):

bool **is_gimple_val** (*tree t*) [GIMPLE function]
: Returns true if t is a "GIMPLE value", which are all the non-addressable stack variables (variables for which `is_gimple_reg` returns true) and constants (expressions for which `is_gimple_min_invariant` returns true).

bool **is_gimple_addressable** (*tree t*) [GIMPLE function]
: Returns true if t is a symbol or memory reference whose address can be taken.

bool **is_gimple_asm_val** (*tree t*) [GIMPLE function]
: Similar to `is_gimple_val` but it also accepts hard registers.

bool **is_gimple_call_addr** (*tree t*) [GIMPLE function]
: Return true if t is a valid expression to use as the function called by a `GIMPLE_CALL`.

bool **is_gimple_mem_ref_addr** (*tree t*) [GIMPLE function]
: Return true if t is a valid expression to use as first operand of a `MEM_REF` expression.

bool **is_gimple_constant** (*tree t*) [GIMPLE function]
: Return true if t is a valid gimple constant.

bool **is_gimple_min_invariant** (*tree t*) [GIMPLE function]
: Return true if t is a valid minimal invariant. This is different from constants, in that the specific value of t may not be known at compile time, but it is known that it doesn't change (e.g., the address of a function local variable).

bool **is_gimple_ip_invariant** (*tree t*) [GIMPLE function]
: Return true if t is an interprocedural invariant. This means that t is a valid invariant in all functions (e.g. it can be an address of a global variable but not of a local one).

bool **is_gimple_ip_invariant_address** (*tree t*) [GIMPLE function]
: Return true if t is an `ADDR_EXPR` that does not change once the program is running (and which is valid in all functions).

12.6.8 Statement validation

bool **is_gimple_assign** (*gimple g*) [GIMPLE function]
: Return true if the code of g is `GIMPLE_ASSIGN`.

bool **is_gimple_call** (*gimple g*) [GIMPLE function]
: Return true if the code of g is `GIMPLE_CALL`.

bool **is_gimple_debug** (*gimple g*) [GIMPLE function]
: Return true if the code of g is `GIMPLE_DEBUG`.

bool **gimple_assign_cast_p** (*const_gimple g*) [GIMPLE function]
: Return true if g is a `GIMPLE_ASSIGN` that performs a type cast operation.

bool gimple_debug_bind_p (*gimple g*) [GIMPLE function]
: Return true if g is a `GIMPLE_DEBUG` that binds the value of an expression to a variable.

bool is_gimple_omp (*gimple g*) [GIMPLE function]
: Return true if g is any of the OpenMP codes.

gimple_debug_begin_stmt_p (*gimple g*) [GIMPLE function]
: Return true if g is a `GIMPLE_DEBUG` that marks the beginning of a source statement.

gimple_debug_inline_entry_p (*gimple g*) [GIMPLE function]
: Return true if g is a `GIMPLE_DEBUG` that marks the entry point of an inlined function.

gimple_debug_nonbind_marker_p (*gimple g*) [GIMPLE function]
: Return true if g is a `GIMPLE_DEBUG` that marks a program location, without any variable binding.

12.7 Manipulating GIMPLE statements

This section documents all the functions available to handle each of the GIMPLE instructions.

12.7.1 Common accessors

The following are common accessors for gimple statements.

enum gimple_code gimple_code (*gimple g*) [GIMPLE function]
: Return the code for statement G.

basic_block gimple_bb (*gimple g*) [GIMPLE function]
: Return the basic block to which statement G belongs to.

tree gimple_block (*gimple g*) [GIMPLE function]
: Return the lexical scope block holding statement G.

tree gimple_expr_type (*gimple stmt*) [GIMPLE function]
: Return the type of the main expression computed by STMT. Return `void_type_node` if STMT computes nothing. This will only return something meaningful for `GIMPLE_ASSIGN`, `GIMPLE_COND` and `GIMPLE_CALL`. For all other tuple codes, it will return `void_type_node`.

enum tree_code gimple_expr_code (*gimple stmt*) [GIMPLE function]
: Return the tree code for the expression computed by STMT. This is only meaningful for `GIMPLE_CALL`, `GIMPLE_ASSIGN` and `GIMPLE_COND`. If STMT is `GIMPLE_CALL`, it will return `CALL_EXPR`. For `GIMPLE_COND`, it returns the code of the comparison predicate. For `GIMPLE_ASSIGN` it returns the code of the operation performed by the RHS of the assignment.

void gimple_set_block (*gimple g, tree block*) [GIMPLE function]
: Set the lexical scope block of G to BLOCK.

location_t gimple_locus (*gimple g*) [GIMPLE function]
: Return locus information for statement G.

Chapter 12: GIMPLE 211

void gimple_set_locus (*gimple g, location_t locus*) [GIMPLE function]
Set locus information for statement G.

bool gimple_locus_empty_p (*gimple g*) [GIMPLE function]
Return true if G does not have locus information.

bool gimple_no_warning_p (*gimple stmt*) [GIMPLE function]
Return true if no warnings should be emitted for statement STMT.

void gimple_set_visited (*gimple stmt, bool visited_p*) [GIMPLE function]
Set the visited status on statement STMT to VISITED_P.

bool gimple_visited_p (*gimple stmt*) [GIMPLE function]
Return the visited status on statement STMT.

void gimple_set_plf (*gimple stmt, enum plf_mask plf, bool val_p*) [GIMPLE function]
Set pass local flag PLF on statement STMT to VAL_P.

unsigned int gimple_plf (*gimple stmt, enum plf_mask plf*) [GIMPLE function]
Return the value of pass local flag PLF on statement STMT.

bool gimple_has_ops (*gimple g*) [GIMPLE function]
Return true if statement G has register or memory operands.

bool gimple_has_mem_ops (*gimple g*) [GIMPLE function]
Return true if statement G has memory operands.

unsigned gimple_num_ops (*gimple g*) [GIMPLE function]
Return the number of operands for statement G.

tree * gimple_ops (*gimple g*) [GIMPLE function]
Return the array of operands for statement G.

tree gimple_op (*gimple g, unsigned i*) [GIMPLE function]
Return operand I for statement G.

tree * gimple_op_ptr (*gimple g, unsigned i*) [GIMPLE function]
Return a pointer to operand I for statement G.

void gimple_set_op (*gimple g, unsigned i, tree op*) [GIMPLE function]
Set operand I of statement G to OP.

bitmap gimple_addresses_taken (*gimple stmt*) [GIMPLE function]
Return the set of symbols that have had their address taken by STMT.

struct def_optype_d * gimple_def_ops (*gimple g*) [GIMPLE function]
Return the set of DEF operands for statement G.

void gimple_set_def_ops (*gimple g, struct def_optype_d *def*) [GIMPLE function]
Set DEF to be the set of DEF operands for statement G.

`struct use_optype_d * gimple_use_ops` (*gimple g*) [GIMPLE function]
: Return the set of USE operands for statement G.

`void gimple_set_use_ops` (*gimple g, struct use_optype_d *use*) [GIMPLE function]
: Set USE to be the set of USE operands for statement G.

`struct voptype_d * gimple_vuse_ops` (*gimple g*) [GIMPLE function]
: Return the set of VUSE operands for statement G.

`void gimple_set_vuse_ops` (*gimple g, struct voptype_d *ops*) [GIMPLE function]
: Set OPS to be the set of VUSE operands for statement G.

`struct voptype_d * gimple_vdef_ops` (*gimple g*) [GIMPLE function]
: Return the set of VDEF operands for statement G.

`void gimple_set_vdef_ops` (*gimple g, struct voptype_d *ops*) [GIMPLE function]
: Set OPS to be the set of VDEF operands for statement G.

`bitmap gimple_loaded_syms` (*gimple g*) [GIMPLE function]
: Return the set of symbols loaded by statement G. Each element of the set is the DECL_UID of the corresponding symbol.

`bitmap gimple_stored_syms` (*gimple g*) [GIMPLE function]
: Return the set of symbols stored by statement G. Each element of the set is the DECL_UID of the corresponding symbol.

`bool gimple_modified_p` (*gimple g*) [GIMPLE function]
: Return true if statement G has operands and the modified field has been set.

`bool gimple_has_volatile_ops` (*gimple stmt*) [GIMPLE function]
: Return true if statement STMT contains volatile operands.

`void gimple_set_has_volatile_ops` (*gimple stmt, bool volatilep*) [GIMPLE function]
: Return true if statement STMT contains volatile operands.

`void update_stmt` (*gimple s*) [GIMPLE function]
: Mark statement S as modified, and update it.

`void update_stmt_if_modified` (*gimple s*) [GIMPLE function]
: Update statement S if it has been marked modified.

`gimple gimple_copy` (*gimple stmt*) [GIMPLE function]
: Return a deep copy of statement STMT.

12.8 Tuple specific accessors

12.8.1 `GIMPLE_ASM`

`gasm *gimple_build_asm_vec` (*const char *string, vec<tree,*   [GIMPLE function]
    *va_gc> *inputs, vec<tree, va_gc> *outputs, vec<tree, va_gc> *clobbers,*
    *vec<tree, va_gc> *labels*)
    Build a `GIMPLE_ASM` statement. This statement is used for building in-line assembly constructs. `STRING` is the assembly code. `INPUTS`, `OUTPUTS`, `CLOBBERS` and `LABELS` are the inputs, outputs, clobbered registers and labels.

`unsigned gimple_asm_ninputs` (*const gasm *g*)   [GIMPLE function]
    Return the number of input operands for `GIMPLE_ASM` G.

`unsigned gimple_asm_noutputs` (*const gasm *g*)   [GIMPLE function]
    Return the number of output operands for `GIMPLE_ASM` G.

`unsigned gimple_asm_nclobbers` (*const gasm *g*)   [GIMPLE function]
    Return the number of clobber operands for `GIMPLE_ASM` G.

`tree gimple_asm_input_op` (*const gasm *g, unsigned index*)   [GIMPLE function]
    Return input operand `INDEX` of `GIMPLE_ASM` G.

`void gimple_asm_set_input_op` (*gasm *g, unsigned index,*   [GIMPLE function]
    tree in_op)
    Set `IN_OP` to be input operand `INDEX` in `GIMPLE_ASM` G.

`tree gimple_asm_output_op` (*const gasm *g, unsigned index*)   [GIMPLE function]
    Return output operand `INDEX` of `GIMPLE_ASM` G.

`void gimple_asm_set_output_op` (*gasm *g, unsigned index,*   [GIMPLE function]
    tree out_op)
    Set `OUT_OP` to be output operand `INDEX` in `GIMPLE_ASM` G.

`tree gimple_asm_clobber_op` (*const gasm *g, unsigned index*)   [GIMPLE function]
    Return clobber operand `INDEX` of `GIMPLE_ASM` G.

`void gimple_asm_set_clobber_op` (*gasm *g, unsigned index,*   [GIMPLE function]
    tree clobber_op)
    Set `CLOBBER_OP` to be clobber operand `INDEX` in `GIMPLE_ASM` G.

`const char * gimple_asm_string` (*const gasm *g*)   [GIMPLE function]
    Return the string representing the assembly instruction in `GIMPLE_ASM` G.

`bool gimple_asm_volatile_p` (*const gasm *g*)   [GIMPLE function]
    Return true if `G` is an asm statement marked volatile.

`void gimple_asm_set_volatile` (*gasm *g, bool volatile_p*)   [GIMPLE function]
    Mark asm statement `G` as volatile or non-volatile based on `VOLATILE_P`.

12.8.2 GIMPLE_ASSIGN

`gassign *gimple_build_assign` (*tree lhs, tree rhs*) [GIMPLE function]
Build a `GIMPLE_ASSIGN` statement. The left-hand side is an lvalue passed in lhs. The right-hand side can be either a unary or binary tree expression. The expression tree rhs will be flattened and its operands assigned to the corresponding operand slots in the new statement. This function is useful when you already have a tree expression that you want to convert into a tuple. However, try to avoid building expression trees for the sole purpose of calling this function. If you already have the operands in separate trees, it is better to use `gimple_build_assign` with `enum tree_code` argument and separate arguments for each operand.

`gassign *gimple_build_assign` (*tree lhs, enum tree_code subcode, tree op1, tree op2, tree op3*) [GIMPLE function]
This function is similar to two operand `gimple_build_assign`, but is used to build a `GIMPLE_ASSIGN` statement when the operands of the right-hand side of the assignment are already split into different operands.

The left-hand side is an lvalue passed in lhs. Subcode is the `tree_code` for the right-hand side of the assignment. Op1, op2 and op3 are the operands.

`gassign *gimple_build_assign` (*tree lhs, enum tree_code subcode, tree op1, tree op2*) [GIMPLE function]
Like the above 5 operand `gimple_build_assign`, but with the last argument NULL - this overload should not be used for `GIMPLE_TERNARY_RHS` assignments.

`gassign *gimple_build_assign` (*tree lhs, enum tree_code subcode, tree op1*) [GIMPLE function]
Like the above 4 operand `gimple_build_assign`, but with the last argument NULL - this overload should be used only for `GIMPLE_UNARY_RHS` and `GIMPLE_SINGLE_RHS` assignments.

`gimple gimplify_assign` (*tree dst, tree src, gimple_seq *seq_p*) [GIMPLE function]
Build a new `GIMPLE_ASSIGN` tuple and append it to the end of *SEQ_P.

DST/SRC are the destination and source respectively. You can pass ungimplified trees in DST or SRC, in which case they will be converted to a gimple operand if necessary.

This function returns the newly created `GIMPLE_ASSIGN` tuple.

`enum tree_code gimple_assign_rhs_code` (*gimple g*) [GIMPLE function]
Return the code of the expression computed on the RHS of assignment statement G.

`enum gimple_rhs_class gimple_assign_rhs_class` (*gimple g*) [GIMPLE function]
Return the gimple rhs class of the code for the expression computed on the rhs of assignment statement G. This will never return `GIMPLE_INVALID_RHS`.

`tree gimple_assign_lhs` (*gimple g*) [GIMPLE function]
Return the LHS of assignment statement G.

`tree * gimple_assign_lhs_ptr (gimple g)` [GIMPLE function]
: Return a pointer to the LHS of assignment statement G.

`tree gimple_assign_rhs1 (gimple g)` [GIMPLE function]
: Return the first operand on the RHS of assignment statement G.

`tree * gimple_assign_rhs1_ptr (gimple g)` [GIMPLE function]
: Return the address of the first operand on the RHS of assignment statement G.

`tree gimple_assign_rhs2 (gimple g)` [GIMPLE function]
: Return the second operand on the RHS of assignment statement G.

`tree * gimple_assign_rhs2_ptr (gimple g)` [GIMPLE function]
: Return the address of the second operand on the RHS of assignment statement G.

`tree gimple_assign_rhs3 (gimple g)` [GIMPLE function]
: Return the third operand on the RHS of assignment statement G.

`tree * gimple_assign_rhs3_ptr (gimple g)` [GIMPLE function]
: Return the address of the third operand on the RHS of assignment statement G.

`void gimple_assign_set_lhs (gimple g, tree lhs)` [GIMPLE function]
: Set LHS to be the LHS operand of assignment statement G.

`void gimple_assign_set_rhs1 (gimple g, tree rhs)` [GIMPLE function]
: Set RHS to be the first operand on the RHS of assignment statement G.

`void gimple_assign_set_rhs2 (gimple g, tree rhs)` [GIMPLE function]
: Set RHS to be the second operand on the RHS of assignment statement G.

`void gimple_assign_set_rhs3 (gimple g, tree rhs)` [GIMPLE function]
: Set RHS to be the third operand on the RHS of assignment statement G.

`bool gimple_assign_cast_p (const_gimple s)` [GIMPLE function]
: Return true if S is a type-cast assignment.

12.8.3 GIMPLE_BIND

`gbind *gimple_build_bind (tree vars, gimple_seq body)` [GIMPLE function]
: Build a GIMPLE_BIND statement with a list of variables in VARS and a body of statements in sequence BODY.

`tree gimple_bind_vars (const gbind *g)` [GIMPLE function]
: Return the variables declared in the GIMPLE_BIND statement G.

`void gimple_bind_set_vars (gbind *g, tree vars)` [GIMPLE function]
: Set VARS to be the set of variables declared in the GIMPLE_BIND statement G.

`void gimple_bind_append_vars (gbind *g, tree vars)` [GIMPLE function]
: Append VARS to the set of variables declared in the GIMPLE_BIND statement G.

`gimple_seq gimple_bind_body (gbind *g)` [GIMPLE function]
: Return the GIMPLE sequence contained in the GIMPLE_BIND statement G.

void gimple_bind_set_body (*gbind *g, gimple_seq seq*) [GIMPLE function]
: Set SEQ to be sequence contained in the GIMPLE_BIND statement G.

void gimple_bind_add_stmt (*gbind *gs, gimple stmt*) [GIMPLE function]
: Append a statement to the end of a GIMPLE_BIND's body.

void gimple_bind_add_seq (*gbind *gs, gimple_seq seq*) [GIMPLE function]
: Append a sequence of statements to the end of a GIMPLE_BIND's body.

tree gimple_bind_block (*const gbind *g*) [GIMPLE function]
: Return the TREE_BLOCK node associated with GIMPLE_BIND statement G. This is analogous to the BIND_EXPR_BLOCK field in trees.

void gimple_bind_set_block (*gbind *g, tree block*) [GIMPLE function]
: Set BLOCK to be the TREE_BLOCK node associated with GIMPLE_BIND statement G.

12.8.4 GIMPLE_CALL

gcall *gimple_build_call (*tree fn, unsigned nargs, ...*) [GIMPLE function]
: Build a GIMPLE_CALL statement to function FN. The argument FN must be either a FUNCTION_DECL or a gimple call address as determined by is_gimple_call_addr. NARGS are the number of arguments. The rest of the arguments follow the argument NARGS, and must be trees that are valid as rvalues in gimple (i.e., each operand is validated with is_gimple_operand).

gcall *gimple_build_call_from_tree (*tree call_expr, tree fnptrtype*) [GIMPLE function]
: Build a GIMPLE_CALL from a CALL_EXPR node. The arguments and the function are taken from the expression directly. The type of the GIMPLE_CALL is set from the second parameter passed by a caller. This routine assumes that call_expr is already in GIMPLE form. That is, its operands are GIMPLE values and the function call needs no further simplification. All the call flags in call_expr are copied over to the new GIMPLE_CALL.

gcall *gimple_build_call_vec (*tree fn, vec<tree> args*) [GIMPLE function]
: Identical to gimple_build_call but the arguments are stored in a vec<tree>.

tree gimple_call_lhs (*gimple g*) [GIMPLE function]
: Return the LHS of call statement G.

tree * gimple_call_lhs_ptr (*gimple g*) [GIMPLE function]
: Return a pointer to the LHS of call statement G.

void gimple_call_set_lhs (*gimple g, tree lhs*) [GIMPLE function]
: Set LHS to be the LHS operand of call statement G.

tree gimple_call_fn (*gimple g*) [GIMPLE function]
: Return the tree node representing the function called by call statement G.

void gimple_call_set_fn (*gcall *g, tree fn*) [GIMPLE function]
: Set FN to be the function called by call statement G. This has to be a gimple value specifying the address of the called function.

Chapter 12: GIMPLE   217

tree gimple_call_fndecl (*gimple g*)   [GIMPLE function]
    If a given GIMPLE_CALL's callee is a FUNCTION_DECL, return it. Otherwise return NULL.
    This function is analogous to get_callee_fndecl in GENERIC.

tree gimple_call_set_fndecl (*gimple g, tree fndecl*)   [GIMPLE function]
    Set the called function to FNDECL.

tree gimple_call_return_type (*const gcall *g*)   [GIMPLE function]
    Return the type returned by call statement G.

tree gimple_call_chain (*gimple g*)   [GIMPLE function]
    Return the static chain for call statement G.

void gimple_call_set_chain (*gcall *g, tree chain*)   [GIMPLE function]
    Set CHAIN to be the static chain for call statement G.

unsigned gimple_call_num_args (*gimple g*)   [GIMPLE function]
    Return the number of arguments used by call statement G.

tree gimple_call_arg (*gimple g, unsigned index*)   [GIMPLE function]
    Return the argument at position INDEX for call statement G. The first argument is 0.

tree * gimple_call_arg_ptr (*gimple g, unsigned index*)   [GIMPLE function]
    Return a pointer to the argument at position INDEX for call statement G.

void gimple_call_set_arg (*gimple g, unsigned index, tree*   [GIMPLE function]
    arg)
    Set ARG to be the argument at position INDEX for call statement G.

void gimple_call_set_tail (*gcall *s*)   [GIMPLE function]
    Mark call statement S as being a tail call (i.e., a call just before the exit of a function).
    These calls are candidate for tail call optimization.

bool gimple_call_tail_p (*gcall *s*)   [GIMPLE function]
    Return true if GIMPLE_CALL S is marked as a tail call.

bool gimple_call_noreturn_p (*gimple s*)   [GIMPLE function]
    Return true if S is a noreturn call.

gimple gimple_call_copy_skip_args (*gcall *stmt, bitmap*   [GIMPLE function]
    args_to_skip)
    Build a GIMPLE_CALL identical to STMT but skipping the arguments in the positions
    marked by the set ARGS_TO_SKIP.

12.8.5 GIMPLE_CATCH

gcatch *gimple_build_catch (*tree types, gimple_seq handler*)   [GIMPLE function]
    Build a GIMPLE_CATCH statement. TYPES are the tree types this catch handles.
    HANDLER is a sequence of statements with the code for the handler.

tree gimple_catch_types (*const gcatch *g*)   [GIMPLE function]
    Return the types handled by GIMPLE_CATCH statement G.

`tree * gimple_catch_types_ptr` (*gcatch *g*) [GIMPLE function]
: Return a pointer to the types handled by GIMPLE_CATCH statement G.

`gimple_seq gimple_catch_handler` (*gcatch *g*) [GIMPLE function]
: Return the GIMPLE sequence representing the body of the handler of GIMPLE_CATCH statement G.

`void gimple_catch_set_types` (*gcatch *g, tree t*) [GIMPLE function]
: Set T to be the set of types handled by GIMPLE_CATCH G.

`void gimple_catch_set_handler` (*gcatch *g, gimple_seq handler*) [GIMPLE function]
: Set HANDLER to be the body of GIMPLE_CATCH G.

12.8.6 GIMPLE_COND

`gcond *gimple_build_cond` (*enum tree_code pred_code, tree lhs, tree rhs, tree t_label, tree f_label*) [GIMPLE function]
: Build a GIMPLE_COND statement. A GIMPLE_COND statement compares LHS and RHS and if the condition in PRED_CODE is true, jump to the label in t_label, otherwise jump to the label in f_label. PRED_CODE are relational operator tree codes like EQ_EXPR, LT_EXPR, LE_EXPR, NE_EXPR, etc.

`gcond *gimple_build_cond_from_tree` (*tree cond, tree t_label, tree f_label*) [GIMPLE function]
: Build a GIMPLE_COND statement from the conditional expression tree COND. T_LABEL and F_LABEL are as in `gimple_build_cond`.

`enum tree_code gimple_cond_code` (*gimple g*) [GIMPLE function]
: Return the code of the predicate computed by conditional statement G.

`void gimple_cond_set_code` (*gcond *g, enum tree_code code*) [GIMPLE function]
: Set CODE to be the predicate code for the conditional statement G.

`tree gimple_cond_lhs` (*gimple g*) [GIMPLE function]
: Return the LHS of the predicate computed by conditional statement G.

`void gimple_cond_set_lhs` (*gcond *g, tree lhs*) [GIMPLE function]
: Set LHS to be the LHS operand of the predicate computed by conditional statement G.

`tree gimple_cond_rhs` (*gimple g*) [GIMPLE function]
: Return the RHS operand of the predicate computed by conditional G.

`void gimple_cond_set_rhs` (*gcond *g, tree rhs*) [GIMPLE function]
: Set RHS to be the RHS operand of the predicate computed by conditional statement G.

`tree gimple_cond_true_label` (*const gcond *g*) [GIMPLE function]
: Return the label used by conditional statement G when its predicate evaluates to true.

`void gimple_cond_set_true_label` (*gcond *g, tree label*) [GIMPLE function]
: Set LABEL to be the label used by conditional statement G when its predicate evaluates to true.

Chapter 12: GIMPLE   219

void gimple_cond_set_false_label (*gcond *g, tree label*) [GIMPLE function]
:   Set LABEL to be the label used by conditional statement G when its predicate evaluates to false.

tree gimple_cond_false_label (*const gcond *g*) [GIMPLE function]
:   Return the label used by conditional statement G when its predicate evaluates to false.

void gimple_cond_make_false (*gcond *g*) [GIMPLE function]
:   Set the conditional COND_STMT to be of the form 'if (1 == 0)'.

void gimple_cond_make_true (*gcond *g*) [GIMPLE function]
:   Set the conditional COND_STMT to be of the form 'if (1 == 1)'.

12.8.7 GIMPLE_DEBUG

gdebug *gimple_build_debug_bind (*tree var, tree value, gimple stmt*) [GIMPLE function]
:   Build a GIMPLE_DEBUG statement with GIMPLE_DEBUG_BIND subcode. The effect of this statement is to tell debug information generation machinery that the value of user variable var is given by value at that point, and to remain with that value until var runs out of scope, a dynamically-subsequent debug bind statement overrides the binding, or conflicting values reach a control flow merge point. Even if components of the value expression change afterwards, the variable is supposed to retain the same value, though not necessarily the same location.

    It is expected that var be most often a tree for automatic user variables (VAR_DECL or PARM_DECL) that satisfy the requirements for gimple registers, but it may also be a tree for a scalarized component of a user variable (ARRAY_REF, COMPONENT_REF), or a debug temporary (DEBUG_EXPR_DECL).

    As for value, it can be an arbitrary tree expression, but it is recommended that it be in a suitable form for a gimple assignment RHS. It is not expected that user variables that could appear as var ever appear in value, because in the latter we'd have their SSA_NAMEs instead, but even if they were not in SSA form, user variables appearing in value are to be regarded as part of the executable code space, whereas those in var are to be regarded as part of the source code space. There is no way to refer to the value bound to a user variable within a value expression.

    If value is GIMPLE_DEBUG_BIND_NOVALUE, debug information generation machinery is informed that the variable var is unbound, i.e., that its value is indeterminate, which sometimes means it is really unavailable, and other times that the compiler could not keep track of it.

    Block and location information for the newly-created stmt are taken from stmt, if given.

tree gimple_debug_bind_get_var (*gimple stmt*) [GIMPLE function]
:   Return the user variable var that is bound at stmt.

tree gimple_debug_bind_get_value (*gimple stmt*) [GIMPLE function]
:   Return the value expression that is bound to a user variable at stmt.

tree * gimple_debug_bind_get_value_ptr (*gimple stmt*)   [GIMPLE function]
: Return a pointer to the value expression that is bound to a user variable at `stmt`.

void gimple_debug_bind_set_var (*gimple stmt, tree var*)   [GIMPLE function]
: Modify the user variable bound at `stmt` to *var*.

void gimple_debug_bind_set_value (*gimple stmt, tree var*)   [GIMPLE function]
: Modify the value bound to the user variable bound at `stmt` to *value*.

void gimple_debug_bind_reset_value (*gimple stmt*)   [GIMPLE function]
: Modify the value bound to the user variable bound at `stmt` so that the variable becomes unbound.

bool gimple_debug_bind_has_value_p (*gimple stmt*)   [GIMPLE function]
: Return `TRUE` if `stmt` binds a user variable to a value, and `FALSE` if it unbinds the variable.

gimple gimple_build_debug_begin_stmt (*tree block, location_t location*)   [GIMPLE function]
: Build a `GIMPLE_DEBUG` statement with `GIMPLE_DEBUG_BEGIN_STMT` subcode. The effect of this statement is to tell debug information generation machinery that the user statement at the given `location` and `block` starts at the point at which the statement is inserted. The intent is that side effects (e.g. variable bindings) of all prior user statements are observable, and that none of the side effects of subsequent user statements are.

gimple gimple_build_debug_inline_entry (*tree block, location_t location*)   [GIMPLE function]
: Build a `GIMPLE_DEBUG` statement with `GIMPLE_DEBUG_INLINE_ENTRY` subcode. The effect of this statement is to tell debug information generation machinery that a function call at `location` underwent inline substitution, that `block` is the enclosing lexical block created for the substitution, and that at the point of the program in which the stmt is inserted, all parameters for the inlined function are bound to the respective arguments, and none of the side effects of its stmts are observable.

12.8.8 GIMPLE_EH_FILTER

geh_filter *gimple_build_eh_filter (*tree types, gimple_seq failure*)   [GIMPLE function]
: Build a `GIMPLE_EH_FILTER` statement. `TYPES` are the filter's types. `FAILURE` is a sequence with the filter's failure action.

tree gimple_eh_filter_types (*gimple g*)   [GIMPLE function]
: Return the types handled by `GIMPLE_EH_FILTER` statement G.

tree * gimple_eh_filter_types_ptr (*gimple g*)   [GIMPLE function]
: Return a pointer to the types handled by `GIMPLE_EH_FILTER` statement G.

gimple_seq gimple_eh_filter_failure (*gimple g*)   [GIMPLE function]
: Return the sequence of statement to execute when `GIMPLE_EH_FILTER` statement fails.

Chapter 12: GIMPLE

void gimple_eh_filter_set_types (*geh_filter *g, tree types*) [GIMPLE function]
: Set TYPES to be the set of types handled by GIMPLE_EH_FILTER G.

void gimple_eh_filter_set_failure (*geh_filter *g,* [GIMPLE function]
   gimple_seq failure)
: Set FAILURE to be the sequence of statements to execute on failure for GIMPLE_EH_FILTER G.

tree gimple_eh_must_not_throw_fndecl (*geh_mnt* [GIMPLE function]
   *eh_mnt_stmt)
: Get the function decl to be called by the MUST_NOT_THROW region.

void gimple_eh_must_not_throw_set_fndecl (*geh_mnt* [GIMPLE function]
   *eh_mnt_stmt, tree decl)
: Set the function decl to be called by GS to DECL.

12.8.9 GIMPLE_LABEL

glabel *gimple_build_label (*tree label*) [GIMPLE function]
: Build a GIMPLE_LABEL statement with corresponding to the tree label, LABEL.

tree gimple_label_label (*const glabel *g*) [GIMPLE function]
: Return the LABEL_DECL node used by GIMPLE_LABEL statement G.

void gimple_label_set_label (*glabel *g, tree label*) [GIMPLE function]
: Set LABEL to be the LABEL_DECL node used by GIMPLE_LABEL statement G.

12.8.10 GIMPLE_GOTO

ggoto *gimple_build_goto (*tree dest*) [GIMPLE function]
: Build a GIMPLE_GOTO statement to label DEST.

tree gimple_goto_dest (*gimple g*) [GIMPLE function]
: Return the destination of the unconditional jump G.

void gimple_goto_set_dest (*ggoto *g, tree dest*) [GIMPLE function]
: Set DEST to be the destination of the unconditional jump G.

12.8.11 GIMPLE_NOP

gimple gimple_build_nop (*void*) [GIMPLE function]
: Build a GIMPLE_NOP statement.

bool gimple_nop_p (*gimple g*) [GIMPLE function]
: Returns TRUE if statement G is a GIMPLE_NOP.

12.8.12 GIMPLE_OMP_ATOMIC_LOAD

gomp_atomic_load *gimple_build_omp_atomic_load (*tree* [GIMPLE function]
   lhs, tree rhs)
: Build a GIMPLE_OMP_ATOMIC_LOAD statement. LHS is the left-hand side of the assignment. RHS is the right-hand side of the assignment.

void gimple_omp_atomic_load_set_lhs (*gomp_atomic_load*   [GIMPLE function]
    *g, tree lhs)
    Set the LHS of an atomic load.

tree gimple_omp_atomic_load_lhs (*const*   [GIMPLE function]
    *gomp_atomic_load *g*)
    Get the LHS of an atomic load.

void gimple_omp_atomic_load_set_rhs (*gomp_atomic_load*   [GIMPLE function]
    *g, tree rhs)
    Set the RHS of an atomic set.

tree gimple_omp_atomic_load_rhs (*const*   [GIMPLE function]
    *gomp_atomic_load *g*)
    Get the RHS of an atomic set.

12.8.13 GIMPLE_OMP_ATOMIC_STORE

gomp_atomic_store *gimple_build_omp_atomic_store ([GIMPLE function]
    tree val)
    Build a GIMPLE_OMP_ATOMIC_STORE statement. VAL is the value to be stored.

void gimple_omp_atomic_store_set_val ([GIMPLE function]
    *gomp_atomic_store *g, tree val*)
    Set the value being stored in an atomic store.

tree gimple_omp_atomic_store_val (*const*   [GIMPLE function]
    *gomp_atomic_store *g*)
    Return the value being stored in an atomic store.

12.8.14 GIMPLE_OMP_CONTINUE

gomp_continue *gimple_build_omp_continue (*tree*   [GIMPLE function]
    control_def, tree control_use)
    Build a GIMPLE_OMP_CONTINUE statement. CONTROL_DEF is the definition of the control variable. CONTROL_USE is the use of the control variable.

tree gimple_omp_continue_control_def (*const*   [GIMPLE function]
    *gomp_continue *s*)
    Return the definition of the control variable on a GIMPLE_OMP_CONTINUE in S.

tree gimple_omp_continue_control_def_ptr ([GIMPLE function]
    *gomp_continue *s*)
    Same as above, but return the pointer.

tree gimple_omp_continue_set_control_def ([GIMPLE function]
    *gomp_continue *s*)
    Set the control variable definition for a GIMPLE_OMP_CONTINUE statement in S.

tree gimple_omp_continue_control_use (*const*   [GIMPLE function]
    *gomp_continue *s*)
    Return the use of the control variable on a GIMPLE_OMP_CONTINUE in S.

Chapter 12: GIMPLE   223

> `tree gimple_omp_continue_control_use_ptr (`   [GIMPLE function]
>   *gomp_continue *s*)
>   Same as above, but return the pointer.

> `tree gimple_omp_continue_set_control_use (`   [GIMPLE function]
>   *gomp_continue *s*)
>   Set the control variable use for a `GIMPLE_OMP_CONTINUE` statement in `S`.

12.8.15 GIMPLE_OMP_CRITICAL

> `gomp_critical *gimple_build_omp_critical (` *gimple_seq*   [GIMPLE function]
>   *body, tree name*)
>   Build a `GIMPLE_OMP_CRITICAL` statement. `BODY` is the sequence of statements for which only one thread can execute. `NAME` is an optional identifier for this critical block.

> `tree gimple_omp_critical_name (` *const gomp_critical *g*)   [GIMPLE function]
>   Return the name associated with `OMP_CRITICAL` statement `G`.

> `tree * gimple_omp_critical_name_ptr (` *gomp_critical *g*)   [GIMPLE function]
>   Return a pointer to the name associated with `OMP` critical statement `G`.

> `void gimple_omp_critical_set_name (` *gomp_critical *g,*   [GIMPLE function]
>   *tree name*)
>   Set `NAME` to be the name associated with `OMP` critical statement `G`.

12.8.16 GIMPLE_OMP_FOR

> `gomp_for *gimple_build_omp_for (`*gimple_seq body, tree*   [GIMPLE function]
>   *clauses, tree index, tree initial, tree final, tree incr, gimple_seq pre_body, enum tree_code omp_for_cond*)
>   Build a `GIMPLE_OMP_FOR` statement. `BODY` is sequence of statements inside the for loop. `CLAUSES`, are any of the loop construct's clauses. `PRE_BODY` is the sequence of statements that are loop invariant. `INDEX` is the index variable. `INITIAL` is the initial value of `INDEX`. `FINAL` is final value of `INDEX`. `OMP_FOR_COND` is the predicate used to compare `INDEX` and `FINAL`. `INCR` is the increment expression.

> `tree gimple_omp_for_clauses (`*gimple g*)   [GIMPLE function]
>   Return the clauses associated with `OMP_FOR G`.

> `tree * gimple_omp_for_clauses_ptr (`*gimple g*)   [GIMPLE function]
>   Return a pointer to the `OMP_FOR G`.

> `void gimple_omp_for_set_clauses (`*gimple g, tree clauses*)   [GIMPLE function]
>   Set `CLAUSES` to be the list of clauses associated with `OMP_FOR G`.

> `tree gimple_omp_for_index (`*gimple g*)   [GIMPLE function]
>   Return the index variable for `OMP_FOR G`.

> `tree * gimple_omp_for_index_ptr (`*gimple g*)   [GIMPLE function]
>   Return a pointer to the index variable for `OMP_FOR G`.

`void gimple_omp_for_set_index` (*gimple g, tree index*)   [GIMPLE function]
> Set `INDEX` to be the index variable for `OMP_FOR` G.

`tree gimple_omp_for_initial` (*gimple g*)   [GIMPLE function]
> Return the initial value for `OMP_FOR` G.

`tree * gimple_omp_for_initial_ptr` (*gimple g*)   [GIMPLE function]
> Return a pointer to the initial value for `OMP_FOR` G.

`void gimple_omp_for_set_initial` (*gimple g, tree initial*)   [GIMPLE function]
> Set `INITIAL` to be the initial value for `OMP_FOR` G.

`tree gimple_omp_for_final` (*gimple g*)   [GIMPLE function]
> Return the final value for `OMP_FOR` G.

`tree * gimple_omp_for_final_ptr` (*gimple g*)   [GIMPLE function]
> turn a pointer to the final value for `OMP_FOR` G.

`void gimple_omp_for_set_final` (*gimple g, tree final*)   [GIMPLE function]
> Set `FINAL` to be the final value for `OMP_FOR` G.

`tree gimple_omp_for_incr` (*gimple g*)   [GIMPLE function]
> Return the increment value for `OMP_FOR` G.

`tree * gimple_omp_for_incr_ptr` (*gimple g*)   [GIMPLE function]
> Return a pointer to the increment value for `OMP_FOR` G.

`void gimple_omp_for_set_incr` (*gimple g, tree incr*)   [GIMPLE function]
> Set `INCR` to be the increment value for `OMP_FOR` G.

`gimple_seq gimple_omp_for_pre_body` (*gimple g*)   [GIMPLE function]
> Return the sequence of statements to execute before the `OMP_FOR` statement G starts.

`void gimple_omp_for_set_pre_body` (*gimple g, gimple_seq pre_body*)   [GIMPLE function]
> Set `PRE_BODY` to be the sequence of statements to execute before the `OMP_FOR` statement G starts.

`void gimple_omp_for_set_cond` (*gimple g, enum tree_code cond*)   [GIMPLE function]
> Set `COND` to be the condition code for `OMP_FOR` G.

`enum tree_code gimple_omp_for_cond` (*gimple g*)   [GIMPLE function]
> Return the condition code associated with `OMP_FOR` G.

12.8.17 GIMPLE_OMP_MASTER

`gimple gimple_build_omp_master` (*gimple_seq body*)   [GIMPLE function]
> Build a `GIMPLE_OMP_MASTER` statement. BODY is the sequence of statements to be executed by just the master.

12.8.18 GIMPLE_OMP_ORDERED

gimple gimple_build_omp_ordered (*gimple_seq body*) [GIMPLE function]
    Build a GIMPLE_OMP_ORDERED statement.

BODY is the sequence of statements inside a loop that will executed in sequence.

12.8.19 GIMPLE_OMP_PARALLEL

gomp_parallel *gimple_build_omp_parallel (*gimple_seq* [GIMPLE function]
    body, tree clauses, tree child_fn, tree data_arg)
    Build a GIMPLE_OMP_PARALLEL statement.

BODY is sequence of statements which are executed in parallel. CLAUSES, are the OMP parallel construct's clauses. CHILD_FN is the function created for the parallel threads to execute. DATA_ARG are the shared data argument(s).

bool gimple_omp_parallel_combined_p (*gimple g*) [GIMPLE function]
    Return true if OMP parallel statement G has the GF_OMP_PARALLEL_COMBINED flag set.

void gimple_omp_parallel_set_combined_p (*gimple g*) [GIMPLE function]
    Set the GF_OMP_PARALLEL_COMBINED field in OMP parallel statement G.

gimple_seq gimple_omp_body (*gimple g*) [GIMPLE function]
    Return the body for the OMP statement G.

void gimple_omp_set_body (*gimple g, gimple_seq body*) [GIMPLE function]
    Set BODY to be the body for the OMP statement G.

tree gimple_omp_parallel_clauses (*gimple g*) [GIMPLE function]
    Return the clauses associated with OMP_PARALLEL G.

tree * gimple_omp_parallel_clauses_ptr (*gomp_parallel* [GIMPLE function]
    **g*)
    Return a pointer to the clauses associated with OMP_PARALLEL G.

void gimple_omp_parallel_set_clauses (*gomp_parallel* [GIMPLE function]
    **g, tree clauses*)
    Set CLAUSES to be the list of clauses associated with OMP_PARALLEL G.

tree gimple_omp_parallel_child_fn (*const gomp_parallel* [GIMPLE function]
    **g*)
    Return the child function used to hold the body of OMP_PARALLEL G.

tree * gimple_omp_parallel_child_fn_ptr ([GIMPLE function]
    *gomp_parallel *g*)
    Return a pointer to the child function used to hold the body of OMP_PARALLEL G.

void gimple_omp_parallel_set_child_fn (*gomp_parallel* [GIMPLE function]
    **g, tree child_fn*)
    Set CHILD_FN to be the child function for OMP_PARALLEL G.

`tree gimple_omp_parallel_data_arg (` *const gomp_parallel*   [GIMPLE function]
    *g)
    Return the artificial argument used to send variables and values from the parent to the children threads in OMP_PARALLEL G.

`tree * gimple_omp_parallel_data_arg_ptr (`   [GIMPLE function]
    gomp_parallel *g)
    Return a pointer to the data argument for OMP_PARALLEL G.

`void gimple_omp_parallel_set_data_arg (` *gomp_parallel*   [GIMPLE function]
    *g, tree data_arg)
    Set DATA_ARG to be the data argument for OMP_PARALLEL G.

12.8.20 GIMPLE_OMP_RETURN

`gimple gimple_build_omp_return` (*bool wait_p*)   [GIMPLE function]
    Build a GIMPLE_OMP_RETURN statement. WAIT_P is true if this is a non-waiting return.

`void gimple_omp_return_set_nowait` (*gimple s*)   [GIMPLE function]
    Set the nowait flag on GIMPLE_OMP_RETURN statement S.

`bool gimple_omp_return_nowait_p` (*gimple g*)   [GIMPLE function]
    Return true if OMP return statement G has the GF_OMP_RETURN_NOWAIT flag set.

12.8.21 GIMPLE_OMP_SECTION

`gimple gimple_build_omp_section` (*gimple_seq body*)   [GIMPLE function]
    Build a GIMPLE_OMP_SECTION statement for a sections statement.

    BODY is the sequence of statements in the section.

`bool gimple_omp_section_last_p` (*gimple g*)   [GIMPLE function]
    Return true if OMP section statement G has the GF_OMP_SECTION_LAST flag set.

`void gimple_omp_section_set_last` (*gimple g*)   [GIMPLE function]
    Set the GF_OMP_SECTION_LAST flag on G.

12.8.22 GIMPLE_OMP_SECTIONS

`gomp_sections *gimple_build_omp_sections (` *gimple_seq*   [GIMPLE function]
    body, tree clauses)
    Build a GIMPLE_OMP_SECTIONS statement. BODY is a sequence of section statements. CLAUSES are any of the OMP sections construct's clauses: private, firstprivate, lastprivate, reduction, and nowait.

`gimple gimple_build_omp_sections_switch` (*void*)   [GIMPLE function]
    Build a GIMPLE_OMP_SECTIONS_SWITCH statement.

`tree gimple_omp_sections_control` (*gimple g*)   [GIMPLE function]
    Return the control variable associated with the GIMPLE_OMP_SECTIONS in G.

tree * gimple_omp_sections_control_ptr (*gimple g*)   [GIMPLE function]
: Return a pointer to the clauses associated with the `GIMPLE_OMP_SECTIONS` in G.

void gimple_omp_sections_set_control (*gimple g, tree control*)   [GIMPLE function]
: Set `CONTROL` to be the set of clauses associated with the `GIMPLE_OMP_SECTIONS` in G.

tree gimple_omp_sections_clauses (*gimple g*)   [GIMPLE function]
: Return the clauses associated with `OMP_SECTIONS` G.

tree * gimple_omp_sections_clauses_ptr (*gimple g*)   [GIMPLE function]
: Return a pointer to the clauses associated with `OMP_SECTIONS` G.

void gimple_omp_sections_set_clauses (*gimple g, tree clauses*)   [GIMPLE function]
: Set `CLAUSES` to be the set of clauses associated with `OMP_SECTIONS` G.

12.8.23 GIMPLE_OMP_SINGLE

gomp_single *gimple_build_omp_single (*gimple_seq body, tree clauses*)   [GIMPLE function]
: Build a `GIMPLE_OMP_SINGLE` statement. BODY is the sequence of statements that will be executed once. CLAUSES are any of the OMP single construct's clauses: private, firstprivate, copyprivate, nowait.

tree gimple_omp_single_clauses (*gimple g*)   [GIMPLE function]
: Return the clauses associated with `OMP_SINGLE` G.

tree * gimple_omp_single_clauses_ptr (*gimple g*)   [GIMPLE function]
: Return a pointer to the clauses associated with `OMP_SINGLE` G.

void gimple_omp_single_set_clauses (*gomp_single *g, tree clauses*)   [GIMPLE function]
: Set `CLAUSES` to be the clauses associated with `OMP_SINGLE` G.

12.8.24 GIMPLE_PHI

unsigned gimple_phi_capacity (*gimple g*)   [GIMPLE function]
: Return the maximum number of arguments supported by `GIMPLE_PHI` G.

unsigned gimple_phi_num_args (*gimple g*)   [GIMPLE function]
: Return the number of arguments in `GIMPLE_PHI` G. This must always be exactly the number of incoming edges for the basic block holding G.

tree gimple_phi_result (*gimple g*)   [GIMPLE function]
: Return the SSA name created by `GIMPLE_PHI` G.

tree * gimple_phi_result_ptr (*gimple g*)   [GIMPLE function]
: Return a pointer to the SSA name created by `GIMPLE_PHI` G.

void gimple_phi_set_result (*gphi *g, tree result*)   [GIMPLE function]
: Set `RESULT` to be the SSA name created by `GIMPLE_PHI` G.

`struct phi_arg_d * gimple_phi_arg` (*gimple g, index*)   [GIMPLE function]
: Return the PHI argument corresponding to incoming edge INDEX for GIMPLE_PHI G.

`void gimple_phi_set_arg` (*gphi *g, index, struct phi_arg_d * phiarg*)   [GIMPLE function]
: Set PHIARG to be the argument corresponding to incoming edge INDEX for GIMPLE_PHI G.

12.8.25 GIMPLE_RESX

`gresx *gimple_build_resx` (*int region*)   [GIMPLE function]
: Build a GIMPLE_RESX statement which is a statement. This statement is a placeholder for _Unwind_Resume before we know if a function call or a branch is needed. REGION is the exception region from which control is flowing.

`int gimple_resx_region` (*const gresx *g*)   [GIMPLE function]
: Return the region number for GIMPLE_RESX G.

`void gimple_resx_set_region` (*gresx *g, int region*)   [GIMPLE function]
: Set REGION to be the region number for GIMPLE_RESX G.

12.8.26 GIMPLE_RETURN

`greturn *gimple_build_return` (*tree retval*)   [GIMPLE function]
: Build a GIMPLE_RETURN statement whose return value is retval.

`tree gimple_return_retval` (*const greturn *g*)   [GIMPLE function]
: Return the return value for GIMPLE_RETURN G.

`void gimple_return_set_retval` (*greturn *g, tree retval*)   [GIMPLE function]
: Set RETVAL to be the return value for GIMPLE_RETURN G.

12.8.27 GIMPLE_SWITCH

`gswitch *gimple_build_switch` (*tree index, tree default_label, vec<tree> *args*)   [GIMPLE function]
: Build a GIMPLE_SWITCH statement. INDEX is the index variable to switch on, and DEFAULT_LABEL represents the default label. ARGS is a vector of CASE_LABEL_EXPR trees that contain the non-default case labels. Each label is a tree of code CASE_LABEL_EXPR.

`unsigned gimple_switch_num_labels` (*const gswitch *g*)   [GIMPLE function]
: Return the number of labels associated with the switch statement G.

`void gimple_switch_set_num_labels` (*gswitch *g, unsigned nlabels*)   [GIMPLE function]
: Set NLABELS to be the number of labels for the switch statement G.

`tree gimple_switch_index` (*const gswitch *g*)   [GIMPLE function]
: Return the index variable used by the switch statement G.

Chapter 12: GIMPLE

void gimple_switch_set_index (*gswitch *g, tree index*) [GIMPLE function]
: Set INDEX to be the index variable for switch statement G.

tree gimple_switch_label (*const gswitch *g, unsigned index*) [GIMPLE function]
: Return the label numbered INDEX. The default label is 0, followed by any labels in a switch statement.

void gimple_switch_set_label (*gswitch *g, unsigned index, tree label*) [GIMPLE function]
: Set the label number INDEX to LABEL. 0 is always the default label.

tree gimple_switch_default_label (*const gswitch *g*) [GIMPLE function]
: Return the default label for a switch statement.

void gimple_switch_set_default_label (*gswitch *g, tree label*) [GIMPLE function]
: Set the default label for a switch statement.

12.8.28 GIMPLE_TRY

gtry *gimple_build_try (*gimple_seq eval, gimple_seq cleanup, unsigned int kind*) [GIMPLE function]
: Build a GIMPLE_TRY statement. EVAL is a sequence with the expression to evaluate. CLEANUP is a sequence of statements to run at clean-up time. KIND is the enumeration value GIMPLE_TRY_CATCH if this statement denotes a try/catch construct or GIMPLE_TRY_FINALLY if this statement denotes a try/finally construct.

enum gimple_try_flags gimple_try_kind (*gimple g*) [GIMPLE function]
: Return the kind of try block represented by GIMPLE_TRY G. This is either GIMPLE_TRY_CATCH or GIMPLE_TRY_FINALLY.

bool gimple_try_catch_is_cleanup (*gimple g*) [GIMPLE function]
: Return the GIMPLE_TRY_CATCH_IS_CLEANUP flag.

gimple_seq gimple_try_eval (*gimple g*) [GIMPLE function]
: Return the sequence of statements used as the body for GIMPLE_TRY G.

gimple_seq gimple_try_cleanup (*gimple g*) [GIMPLE function]
: Return the sequence of statements used as the cleanup body for GIMPLE_TRY G.

void gimple_try_set_catch_is_cleanup (*gimple g, bool catch_is_cleanup*) [GIMPLE function]
: Set the GIMPLE_TRY_CATCH_IS_CLEANUP flag.

void gimple_try_set_eval (*gtry *g, gimple_seq eval*) [GIMPLE function]
: Set EVAL to be the sequence of statements to use as the body for GIMPLE_TRY G.

void gimple_try_set_cleanup (*gtry *g, gimple_seq cleanup*) [GIMPLE function]
: Set CLEANUP to be the sequence of statements to use as the cleanup body for GIMPLE_TRY G.

12.8.29 `GIMPLE_WITH_CLEANUP_EXPR`

`gimple gimple_build_wce` (*gimple_seq cleanup*) [GIMPLE function]
    Build a `GIMPLE_WITH_CLEANUP_EXPR` statement. `CLEANUP` is the clean-up expression.

`gimple_seq gimple_wce_cleanup` (*gimple g*) [GIMPLE function]
    Return the cleanup sequence for cleanup statement `G`.

`void gimple_wce_set_cleanup` (*gimple g, gimple_seq cleanup*) [GIMPLE function]
    Set `CLEANUP` to be the cleanup sequence for `G`.

`bool gimple_wce_cleanup_eh_only` (*gimple g*) [GIMPLE function]
    Return the `CLEANUP_EH_ONLY` flag for a `WCE` tuple.

`void gimple_wce_set_cleanup_eh_only` (*gimple g, bool eh_only_p*) [GIMPLE function]
    Set the `CLEANUP_EH_ONLY` flag for a `WCE` tuple.

12.9 GIMPLE sequences

GIMPLE sequences are the tuple equivalent of `STATEMENT_LIST`'s used in `GENERIC`. They are used to chain statements together, and when used in conjunction with sequence iterators, provide a framework for iterating through statements.

GIMPLE sequences are of type struct `gimple_sequence`, but are more commonly passed by reference to functions dealing with sequences. The type for a sequence pointer is `gimple_seq` which is the same as struct `gimple_sequence *`. When declaring a local sequence, you can define a local variable of type struct `gimple_sequence`. When declaring a sequence allocated on the garbage collected heap, use the function `gimple_seq_alloc` documented below.

There are convenience functions for iterating through sequences in the section entitled Sequence Iterators.

Below is a list of functions to manipulate and query sequences.

`void gimple_seq_add_stmt` (*gimple_seq *seq, gimple g*) [GIMPLE function]
    Link a gimple statement to the end of the sequence *`SEQ` if `G` is not `NULL`. If *`SEQ` is `NULL`, allocate a sequence before linking.

`void gimple_seq_add_seq` (*gimple_seq *dest, gimple_seq src*) [GIMPLE function]
    Append sequence `SRC` to the end of sequence *`DEST` if `SRC` is not `NULL`. If *`DEST` is `NULL`, allocate a new sequence before appending.

`gimple_seq gimple_seq_deep_copy` (*gimple_seq src*) [GIMPLE function]
    Perform a deep copy of sequence `SRC` and return the result.

`gimple_seq gimple_seq_reverse` (*gimple_seq seq*) [GIMPLE function]
    Reverse the order of the statements in the sequence `SEQ`. Return `SEQ`.

`gimple gimple_seq_first` (*gimple_seq s*) [GIMPLE function]
    Return the first statement in sequence `S`.

Chapter 12: GIMPLE 231

`gimple gimple_seq_last` (*gimple_seq s*) [GIMPLE function]
    Return the last statement in sequence `S`.

`void gimple_seq_set_last` (*gimple_seq s, gimple last*) [GIMPLE function]
    Set the last statement in sequence `S` to the statement in `LAST`.

`void gimple_seq_set_first` (*gimple_seq s, gimple first*) [GIMPLE function]
    Set the first statement in sequence `S` to the statement in `FIRST`.

`void gimple_seq_init` (*gimple_seq s*) [GIMPLE function]
    Initialize sequence `S` to an empty sequence.

`gimple_seq gimple_seq_alloc` (*void*) [GIMPLE function]
    Allocate a new sequence in the garbage collected store and return it.

`void gimple_seq_copy` (*gimple_seq dest, gimple_seq src*) [GIMPLE function]
    Copy the sequence `SRC` into the sequence `DEST`.

`bool gimple_seq_empty_p` (*gimple_seq s*) [GIMPLE function]
    Return true if the sequence `S` is empty.

`gimple_seq bb_seq` (*basic_block bb*) [GIMPLE function]
    Returns the sequence of statements in `BB`.

`void set_bb_seq` (*basic_block bb, gimple_seq seq*) [GIMPLE function]
    Sets the sequence of statements in `BB` to `SEQ`.

`bool gimple_seq_singleton_p` (*gimple_seq seq*) [GIMPLE function]
    Determine whether `SEQ` contains exactly one statement.

12.10 Sequence iterators

Sequence iterators are convenience constructs for iterating through statements in a sequence. Given a sequence `SEQ`, here is a typical use of gimple sequence iterators:

```
gimple_stmt_iterator gsi;

for (gsi = gsi_start (seq); !gsi_end_p (gsi); gsi_next (&gsi))
  {
    gimple g = gsi_stmt (gsi);
    /* Do something with gimple statement G.  */
  }
```

Backward iterations are possible:

```
for (gsi = gsi_last (seq); !gsi_end_p (gsi); gsi_prev (&gsi))
```

Forward and backward iterations on basic blocks are possible with `gsi_start_bb` and `gsi_last_bb`.

In the documentation below we sometimes refer to enum `gsi_iterator_update`. The valid options for this enumeration are:

- `GSI_NEW_STMT` Only valid when a single statement is added. Move the iterator to it.
- `GSI_SAME_STMT` Leave the iterator at the same statement.
- `GSI_CONTINUE_LINKING` Move iterator to whatever position is suitable for linking other statements in the same direction.

Below is a list of the functions used to manipulate and use statement iterators.

`gimple_stmt_iterator gsi_start` (*gimple_seq seq*) [GIMPLE function]
: Return a new iterator pointing to the sequence SEQ's first statement. If SEQ is empty, the iterator's basic block is NULL. Use `gsi_start_bb` instead when the iterator needs to always have the correct basic block set.

`gimple_stmt_iterator gsi_start_bb` (*basic_block bb*) [GIMPLE function]
: Return a new iterator pointing to the first statement in basic block BB.

`gimple_stmt_iterator gsi_last` (*gimple_seq seq*) [GIMPLE function]
: Return a new iterator initially pointing to the last statement of sequence SEQ. If SEQ is empty, the iterator's basic block is NULL. Use `gsi_last_bb` instead when the iterator needs to always have the correct basic block set.

`gimple_stmt_iterator gsi_last_bb` (*basic_block bb*) [GIMPLE function]
: Return a new iterator pointing to the last statement in basic block BB.

`bool gsi_end_p` (*gimple_stmt_iterator i*) [GIMPLE function]
: Return TRUE if at the end of I.

`bool gsi_one_before_end_p` (*gimple_stmt_iterator i*) [GIMPLE function]
: Return TRUE if we're one statement before the end of I.

`void gsi_next` (*gimple_stmt_iterator *i*) [GIMPLE function]
: Advance the iterator to the next gimple statement.

`void gsi_prev` (*gimple_stmt_iterator *i*) [GIMPLE function]
: Advance the iterator to the previous gimple statement.

`gimple gsi_stmt` (*gimple_stmt_iterator i*) [GIMPLE function]
: Return the current stmt.

`gimple_stmt_iterator gsi_after_labels` (*basic_block bb*) [GIMPLE function]
: Return a block statement iterator that points to the first non-label statement in block BB.

`gimple * gsi_stmt_ptr` (*gimple_stmt_iterator *i*) [GIMPLE function]
: Return a pointer to the current stmt.

`basic_block gsi_bb` (*gimple_stmt_iterator i*) [GIMPLE function]
: Return the basic block associated with this iterator.

`gimple_seq gsi_seq` (*gimple_stmt_iterator i*) [GIMPLE function]
: Return the sequence associated with this iterator.

`void gsi_remove` (*gimple_stmt_iterator *i, bool remove_eh_info*) [GIMPLE function]
: Remove the current stmt from the sequence. The iterator is updated to point to the next statement. When REMOVE_EH_INFO is true we remove the statement pointed to by iterator I from the EH tables. Otherwise we do not modify the EH tables. Generally, REMOVE_EH_INFO should be true when the statement is going to be removed from the IL and not reinserted elsewhere.

Chapter 12: GIMPLE

void gsi_link_seq_before (*gimple_stmt_iterator *i,* [GIMPLE function]
    gimple_seq seq, enum gsi_iterator_update mode)
> Links the sequence of statements SEQ before the statement pointed by iterator I. MODE indicates what to do with the iterator after insertion (see enum `gsi_iterator_update` above).

void gsi_link_before (*gimple_stmt_iterator *i, gimple g,* [GIMPLE function]
    enum gsi_iterator_update mode)
> Links statement G before the statement pointed-to by iterator I. Updates iterator I according to MODE.

void gsi_link_seq_after (*gimple_stmt_iterator *i,* [GIMPLE function]
    gimple_seq seq, enum gsi_iterator_update mode)
> Links sequence SEQ after the statement pointed-to by iterator I. MODE is as in `gsi_insert_after`.

void gsi_link_after (*gimple_stmt_iterator *i, gimple g, enum* [GIMPLE function]
    gsi_iterator_update mode)
> Links statement G after the statement pointed-to by iterator I. MODE is as in `gsi_insert_after`.

gimple_seq gsi_split_seq_after (*gimple_stmt_iterator i*) [GIMPLE function]
> Move all statements in the sequence after I to a new sequence. Return this new sequence.

gimple_seq gsi_split_seq_before (*gimple_stmt_iterator *i*) [GIMPLE function]
> Move all statements in the sequence before I to a new sequence. Return this new sequence.

void gsi_replace (*gimple_stmt_iterator *i, gimple stmt, bool* [GIMPLE function]
    update_eh_info)
> Replace the statement pointed-to by I to STMT. If UPDATE_EH_INFO is true, the exception handling information of the original statement is moved to the new statement.

void gsi_insert_before (*gimple_stmt_iterator *i, gimple* [GIMPLE function]
    stmt, enum gsi_iterator_update mode)
> Insert statement STMT before the statement pointed-to by iterator I, update STMT's basic block and scan it for new operands. MODE specifies how to update iterator I after insertion (see enum `gsi_iterator_update`).

void gsi_insert_seq_before (*gimple_stmt_iterator *i,* [GIMPLE function]
    gimple_seq seq, enum gsi_iterator_update mode)
> Like `gsi_insert_before`, but for all the statements in SEQ.

void gsi_insert_after (*gimple_stmt_iterator *i, gimple stmt,* [GIMPLE function]
    enum gsi_iterator_update mode)
> Insert statement STMT after the statement pointed-to by iterator I, update STMT's basic block and scan it for new operands. MODE specifies how to update iterator I after insertion (see enum `gsi_iterator_update`).

void gsi_insert_seq_after (*gimple_stmt_iterator *i,*   [GIMPLE function]
        gimple_seq seq, enum gsi_iterator_update mode)
    Like `gsi_insert_after`, but for all the statements in SEQ.

gimple_stmt_iterator gsi_for_stmt (*gimple stmt*)   [GIMPLE function]
    Finds iterator for STMT.

void gsi_move_after (*gimple_stmt_iterator *from,*   [GIMPLE function]
        *gimple_stmt_iterator *to*)
    Move the statement at FROM so it comes right after the statement at TO.

void gsi_move_before (*gimple_stmt_iterator *from,*   [GIMPLE function]
        *gimple_stmt_iterator *to*)
    Move the statement at FROM so it comes right before the statement at TO.

void gsi_move_to_bb_end (*gimple_stmt_iterator *from,*   [GIMPLE function]
        basic_block bb)
    Move the statement at FROM to the end of basic block BB.

void gsi_insert_on_edge (*edge e, gimple stmt*)   [GIMPLE function]
    Add STMT to the pending list of edge E. No actual insertion is made until a call to `gsi_commit_edge_inserts`() is made.

void gsi_insert_seq_on_edge (*edge e, gimple_seq seq*)   [GIMPLE function]
    Add the sequence of statements in SEQ to the pending list of edge E. No actual insertion is made until a call to `gsi_commit_edge_inserts`() is made.

basic_block gsi_insert_on_edge_immediate (*edge e,*   [GIMPLE function]
        gimple stmt)
    Similar to `gsi_insert_on_edge`+`gsi_commit_edge_inserts`. If a new block has to be created, it is returned.

void gsi_commit_one_edge_insert (*edge e, basic_block*   [GIMPLE function]
        **new_bb*)
    Commit insertions pending at edge E. If a new block is created, set NEW_BB to this block, otherwise set it to NULL.

void gsi_commit_edge_inserts (*void*)   [GIMPLE function]
    This routine will commit all pending edge insertions, creating any new basic blocks which are necessary.

12.11 Adding a new GIMPLE statement code

The first step in adding a new GIMPLE statement code, is modifying the file `gimple.def`, which contains all the GIMPLE codes. Then you must add a corresponding gimple subclass located in `gimple.h`. This in turn, will require you to add a corresponding GTY tag in `gsstruct.def`, and code to handle this tag in `gss_for_code` which is located in `gimple.c`.

In order for the garbage collector to know the size of the structure you created in `gimple.h`, you need to add a case to handle your new GIMPLE statement in `gimple_size` which is located in `gimple.c`.

You will probably want to create a function to build the new gimple statement in `gimple.c`. The function should be called `gimple_build_new-tuple-name`, and should return the new tuple as a pointer to the appropriate gimple subclass.

If your new statement requires accessors for any members or operands it may have, put simple inline accessors in `gimple.h` and any non-trivial accessors in `gimple.c` with a corresponding prototype in `gimple.h`.

You should add the new statement subclass to the class hierarchy diagram in `gimple.texi`.

12.12 Statement and operand traversals

There are two functions available for walking statements and sequences: `walk_gimple_stmt` and `walk_gimple_seq`, accordingly, and a third function for walking the operands in a statement: `walk_gimple_op`.

tree walk_gimple_stmt (*gimple_stmt_iterator *gsi,*   [GIMPLE function]
    walk_stmt_fn callback_stmt, walk_tree_fn callback_op, struct walk_stmt_info *wi)

This function is used to walk the current statement in `GSI`, optionally using traversal state stored in `WI`. If `WI` is `NULL`, no state is kept during the traversal.

The callback `CALLBACK_STMT` is called. If `CALLBACK_STMT` returns true, it means that the callback function has handled all the operands of the statement and it is not necessary to walk its operands.

If `CALLBACK_STMT` is `NULL` or it returns false, `CALLBACK_OP` is called on each operand of the statement via `walk_gimple_op`. If `walk_gimple_op` returns non-`NULL` for any operand, the remaining operands are not scanned.

The return value is that returned by the last call to `walk_gimple_op`, or `NULL_TREE` if no `CALLBACK_OP` is specified.

tree walk_gimple_op (*gimple stmt, walk_tree_fn callback_op,*   [GIMPLE function]
    struct walk_stmt_info *wi)

Use this function to walk the operands of statement `STMT`. Every operand is walked via `walk_tree` with optional state information in `WI`.

`CALLBACK_OP` is called on each operand of `STMT` via `walk_tree`. Additional parameters to `walk_tree` must be stored in `WI`. For each operand `OP`, `walk_tree` is called as:

    `walk_tree (&OP, CALLBACK_OP, WI, PSET)`

If `CALLBACK_OP` returns non-`NULL` for an operand, the remaining operands are not scanned. The return value is that returned by the last call to `walk_tree`, or `NULL_TREE` if no `CALLBACK_OP` is specified.

tree walk_gimple_seq (*gimple_seq seq, walk_stmt_fn*   [GIMPLE function]
    callback_stmt, walk_tree_fn callback_op, struct walk_stmt_info *wi)

This function walks all the statements in the sequence `SEQ` calling `walk_gimple_stmt` on each one. `WI` is as in `walk_gimple_stmt`. If `walk_gimple_stmt` returns non-`NULL`, the walk is stopped and the value returned. Otherwise, all the statements are walked and `NULL_TREE` returned.

13 Analysis and Optimization of GIMPLE tuples

GCC uses three main intermediate languages to represent the program during compilation: GENERIC, GIMPLE and RTL. GENERIC is a language-independent representation generated by each front end. It is used to serve as an interface between the parser and optimizer. GENERIC is a common representation that is able to represent programs written in all the languages supported by GCC.

GIMPLE and RTL are used to optimize the program. GIMPLE is used for target and language independent optimizations (e.g., inlining, constant propagation, tail call elimination, redundancy elimination, etc). Much like GENERIC, GIMPLE is a language independent, tree based representation. However, it differs from GENERIC in that the GIMPLE grammar is more restrictive: expressions contain no more than 3 operands (except function calls), it has no control flow structures and expressions with side-effects are only allowed on the right hand side of assignments. See the chapter describing GENERIC and GIMPLE for more details.

This chapter describes the data structures and functions used in the GIMPLE optimizers (also known as "tree optimizers" or "middle end"). In particular, it focuses on all the macros, data structures, functions and programming constructs needed to implement optimization passes for GIMPLE.

13.1 Annotations

The optimizers need to associate attributes with variables during the optimization process. For instance, we need to know whether a variable has aliases. All these attributes are stored in data structures called annotations which are then linked to the field `ann` in `struct tree_common`.

13.2 SSA Operands

Almost every GIMPLE statement will contain a reference to a variable or memory location. Since statements come in different shapes and sizes, their operands are going to be located at various spots inside the statement's tree. To facilitate access to the statement's operands, they are organized into lists associated inside each statement's annotation. Each element in an operand list is a pointer to a `VAR_DECL`, `PARM_DECL` or `SSA_NAME` tree node. This provides a very convenient way of examining and replacing operands.

Data flow analysis and optimization is done on all tree nodes representing variables. Any node for which `SSA_VAR_P` returns nonzero is considered when scanning statement operands. However, not all `SSA_VAR_P` variables are processed in the same way. For the purposes of optimization, we need to distinguish between references to local scalar variables and references to globals, statics, structures, arrays, aliased variables, etc. The reason is simple, the compiler can gather complete data flow information for a local scalar. On the other hand, a global variable may be modified by a function call, it may not be possible to keep track of all the elements of an array or the fields of a structure, etc.

The operand scanner gathers two kinds of operands: *real* and *virtual*. An operand for which `is_gimple_reg` returns true is considered real, otherwise it is a virtual operand. We also distinguish between uses and definitions. An operand is used if its value is loaded by the statement (e.g., the operand at the RHS of an assignment). If the statement assigns a new value to the operand, the operand is considered a definition (e.g., the operand at the LHS of an assignment).

Virtual and real operands also have very different data flow properties. Real operands are unambiguous references to the full object that they represent. For instance, given

```
{
  int a, b;
  a = b
}
```

Since a and b are non-aliased locals, the statement a = b will have one real definition and one real use because variable a is completely modified with the contents of variable b. Real definition are also known as *killing definitions*. Similarly, the use of b reads all its bits.

In contrast, virtual operands are used with variables that can have a partial or ambiguous reference. This includes structures, arrays, globals, and aliased variables. In these cases, we have two types of definitions. For globals, structures, and arrays, we can determine from a statement whether a variable of these types has a killing definition. If the variable does, then the statement is marked as having a *must definition* of that variable. However, if a statement is only defining a part of the variable (i.e. a field in a structure), or if we know that a statement might define the variable but we cannot say for sure, then we mark that statement as having a *may definition*. For instance, given

```
{
  int a, b, *p;

  if (...)
    p = &a;
  else
    p = &b;
  *p = 5;
  return *p;
}
```

The assignment *p = 5 may be a definition of a or b. If we cannot determine statically where p is pointing to at the time of the store operation, we create virtual definitions to mark that statement as a potential definition site for a and b. Memory loads are similarly marked with virtual use operands. Virtual operands are shown in tree dumps right before the statement that contains them. To request a tree dump with virtual operands, use the '-vops' option to '-fdump-tree':

```
{
  int a, b, *p;

  if (...)
    p = &a;
  else
    p = &b;
  # a = VDEF <a>
  # b = VDEF <b>
  *p = 5;

  # VUSE <a>
  # VUSE <b>
  return *p;
}
```

Notice that VDEF operands have two copies of the referenced variable. This indicates that this is not a killing definition of that variable. In this case we refer to it as a *may definition* or *aliased store*. The presence of the second copy of the variable in the VDEF operand will become important when the function is converted into SSA form. This will be used to link all the non-killing definitions to prevent optimizations from making incorrect assumptions about them.

Operands are updated as soon as the statement is finished via a call to `update_stmt`. If statement elements are changed via SET_USE or SET_DEF, then no further action is required (i.e., those macros take care of updating the statement). If changes are made by manipulating the statement's tree directly, then a call must be made to `update_stmt` when complete. Calling one of the `bsi_insert` routines or `bsi_replace` performs an implicit call to `update_stmt`.

13.2.1 Operand Iterators And Access Routines

Operands are collected by 'tree-ssa-operands.c'. They are stored inside each statement's annotation and can be accessed through either the operand iterators or an access routine.

The following access routines are available for examining operands:

1. SINGLE_SSA_{USE,DEF,TREE}_OPERAND: These accessors will return NULL unless there is exactly one operand matching the specified flags. If there is exactly one operand, the operand is returned as either a tree, def_operand_p, or use_operand_p.
   ```
   tree t = SINGLE_SSA_TREE_OPERAND (stmt, flags);
   use_operand_p u = SINGLE_SSA_USE_OPERAND (stmt, SSA_ALL_VIRTUAL_USES);
   def_operand_p d = SINGLE_SSA_DEF_OPERAND (stmt, SSA_OP_ALL_DEFS);
   ```

2. ZERO_SSA_OPERANDS: This macro returns true if there are no operands matching the specified flags.
   ```
   if (ZERO_SSA_OPERANDS (stmt, SSA_OP_ALL_VIRTUALS))
     return;
   ```

3. NUM_SSA_OPERANDS: This macro Returns the number of operands matching 'flags'. This actually executes a loop to perform the count, so only use this if it is really needed.
   ```
   int count = NUM_SSA_OPERANDS (stmt, flags)
   ```

If you wish to iterate over some or all operands, use the FOR_EACH_SSA_{USE,DEF,TREE}_OPERAND iterator. For example, to print all the operands for a statement:
```
void
print_ops (tree stmt)
{
  ssa_op_iter;
  tree var;

  FOR_EACH_SSA_TREE_OPERAND (var, stmt, iter, SSA_OP_ALL_OPERANDS)
    print_generic_expr (stderr, var, TDF_SLIM);
}
```

How to choose the appropriate iterator:

1. Determine whether you are need to see the operand pointers, or just the trees, and choose the appropriate macro:

Need	Macro:
use_operand_p	FOR_EACH_SSA_USE_OPERAND

```
        def_operand_p    FOR_EACH_SSA_DEF_OPERAND
        tree             FOR_EACH_SSA_TREE_OPERAND
```

2. You need to declare a variable of the type you are interested in, and an ssa_op_iter structure which serves as the loop controlling variable.

3. Determine which operands you wish to use, and specify the flags of those you are interested in. They are documented in 'tree-ssa-operands.h':

```
#define SSA_OP_USE          0x01   /* Real USE operands. */
#define SSA_OP_DEF          0x02   /* Real DEF operands. */
#define SSA_OP_VUSE         0x04   /* VUSE operands. */
#define SSA_OP_VDEF         0x08   /* VDEF operands. */

/* These are commonly grouped operand flags.  */
#define SSA_OP_VIRTUAL_USES (SSA_OP_VUSE)
#define SSA_OP_VIRTUAL_DEFS (SSA_OP_VDEF)
#define SSA_OP_ALL_VIRTUALS    (SSA_OP_VIRTUAL_USES | SSA_OP_VIRTUAL_DEFS)
#define SSA_OP_ALL_USES (SSA_OP_VIRTUAL_USES | SSA_OP_USE)
#define SSA_OP_ALL_DEFS (SSA_OP_VIRTUAL_DEFS | SSA_OP_DEF)
#define SSA_OP_ALL_OPERANDS (SSA_OP_ALL_USES | SSA_OP_ALL_DEFS)
```

So if you want to look at the use pointers for all the USE and VUSE operands, you would do something like:

```
use_operand_p use_p;
ssa_op_iter iter;

FOR_EACH_SSA_USE_OPERAND (use_p, stmt, iter, (SSA_OP_USE | SSA_OP_VUSE))
  {
    process_use_ptr (use_p);
  }
```

The TREE macro is basically the same as the USE and DEF macros, only with the use or def dereferenced via USE_FROM_PTR (use_p) and DEF_FROM_PTR (def_p). Since we aren't using operand pointers, use and defs flags can be mixed.

```
tree var;
ssa_op_iter iter;

FOR_EACH_SSA_TREE_OPERAND (var, stmt, iter, SSA_OP_VUSE)
  {
    print_generic_expr (stderr, var, TDF_SLIM);
  }
```

VDEFs are broken into two flags, one for the DEF portion (SSA_OP_VDEF) and one for the USE portion (SSA_OP_VUSE).

There are many examples in the code, in addition to the documentation in 'tree-ssa-operands.h' and 'ssa-iterators.h'.

There are also a couple of variants on the stmt iterators regarding PHI nodes.

FOR_EACH_PHI_ARG Works exactly like FOR_EACH_SSA_USE_OPERAND, except it works over PHI arguments instead of statement operands.

```
/* Look at every virtual PHI use.  */
FOR_EACH_PHI_ARG (use_p, phi_stmt, iter, SSA_OP_VIRTUAL_USES)
{
  my_code;
}

/* Look at every real PHI use.  */
```

Chapter 13: Analysis and Optimization of GIMPLE tuples

```
    FOR_EACH_PHI_ARG (use_p, phi_stmt, iter, SSA_OP_USES)
      my_code;

    /* Look at every PHI use.  */
    FOR_EACH_PHI_ARG (use_p, phi_stmt, iter, SSA_OP_ALL_USES)
      my_code;
```

FOR_EACH_PHI_OR_STMT_{USE,DEF} works exactly like FOR_EACH_SSA_{USE,DEF}_OPERAND, except it will function on either a statement or a PHI node. These should be used when it is appropriate but they are not quite as efficient as the individual FOR_EACH_PHI and FOR_EACH_SSA routines.

```
    FOR_EACH_PHI_OR_STMT_USE (use_operand_p, stmt, iter, flags)
      {
         my_code;
      }

    FOR_EACH_PHI_OR_STMT_DEF (def_operand_p, phi, iter, flags)
      {
         my_code;
      }
```

13.2.2 Immediate Uses

Immediate use information is now always available. Using the immediate use iterators, you may examine every use of any SSA_NAME. For instance, to change each use of ssa_var to ssa_var2 and call fold_stmt on each stmt after that is done:

```
    use_operand_p imm_use_p;
    imm_use_iterator iterator;
    tree ssa_var, stmt;


    FOR_EACH_IMM_USE_STMT (stmt, iterator, ssa_var)
      {
        FOR_EACH_IMM_USE_ON_STMT (imm_use_p, iterator)
          SET_USE (imm_use_p, ssa_var_2);
        fold_stmt (stmt);
      }
```

There are 2 iterators which can be used. FOR_EACH_IMM_USE_FAST is used when the immediate uses are not changed, i.e., you are looking at the uses, but not setting them.

If they do get changed, then care must be taken that things are not changed under the iterators, so use the FOR_EACH_IMM_USE_STMT and FOR_EACH_IMM_USE_ON_STMT iterators. They attempt to preserve the sanity of the use list by moving all the uses for a statement into a controlled position, and then iterating over those uses. Then the optimization can manipulate the stmt when all the uses have been processed. This is a little slower than the FAST version since it adds a placeholder element and must sort through the list a bit for each statement. This placeholder element must be also be removed if the loop is terminated early. The macro BREAK_FROM_IMM_USE_SAFE is provided to do this :

```
    FOR_EACH_IMM_USE_STMT (stmt, iterator, ssa_var)
      {
        if (stmt == last_stmt)
          BREAK_FROM_SAFE_IMM_USE (iter);

        FOR_EACH_IMM_USE_ON_STMT (imm_use_p, iterator)
          SET_USE (imm_use_p, ssa_var_2);
```

```
        fold_stmt (stmt);
    }
```

There are checks in `verify_ssa` which verify that the immediate use list is up to date, as well as checking that an optimization didn't break from the loop without using this macro. It is safe to simply 'break'; from a `FOR_EACH_IMM_USE_FAST` traverse.

Some useful functions and macros:

1. `has_zero_uses (ssa_var)` : Returns true if there are no uses of `ssa_var`.
2. `has_single_use (ssa_var)` : Returns true if there is only a single use of `ssa_var`.
3. `single_imm_use (ssa_var, use_operand_p *ptr, tree *stmt)` : Returns true if there is only a single use of `ssa_var`, and also returns the use pointer and statement it occurs in, in the second and third parameters.
4. `num_imm_uses (ssa_var)` : Returns the number of immediate uses of `ssa_var`. It is better not to use this if possible since it simply utilizes a loop to count the uses.
5. `PHI_ARG_INDEX_FROM_USE (use_p)` : Given a use within a PHI node, return the index number for the use. An assert is triggered if the use isn't located in a PHI node.
6. `USE_STMT (use_p)` : Return the statement a use occurs in.

Note that uses are not put into an immediate use list until their statement is actually inserted into the instruction stream via a `bsi_*` routine.

It is also still possible to utilize lazy updating of statements, but this should be used only when absolutely required. Both alias analysis and the dominator optimizations currently do this.

When lazy updating is being used, the immediate use information is out of date and cannot be used reliably. Lazy updating is achieved by simply marking statements modified via calls to `gimple_set_modified` instead of `update_stmt`. When lazy updating is no longer required, all the modified statements must have `update_stmt` called in order to bring them up to date. This must be done before the optimization is finished, or `verify_ssa` will trigger an abort.

This is done with a simple loop over the instruction stream:

```
block_stmt_iterator bsi;
basic_block bb;
FOR_EACH_BB (bb)
  {
    for (bsi = bsi_start (bb); !bsi_end_p (bsi); bsi_next (&bsi))
      update_stmt_if_modified (bsi_stmt (bsi));
  }
```

13.3 Static Single Assignment

Most of the tree optimizers rely on the data flow information provided by the Static Single Assignment (SSA) form. We implement the SSA form as described in *R. Cytron, J. Ferrante, B. Rosen, M. Wegman, and K. Zadeck. Efficiently Computing Static Single Assignment Form and the Control Dependence Graph. ACM Transactions on Programming Languages and Systems, 13(4):451-490, October 1991.*

The SSA form is based on the premise that program variables are assigned in exactly one location in the program. Multiple assignments to the same variable create new versions of that variable. Naturally, actual programs are seldom in SSA form initially because variables tend to be assigned multiple times. The compiler modifies the program representation so that every time a variable is assigned in the code, a new version of the variable is created. Different versions of the same variable are distinguished by subscripting the variable name with its version number. Variables used in the right-hand side of expressions are renamed so that their version number matches that of the most recent assignment.

We represent variable versions using `SSA_NAME` nodes. The renaming process in 'tree-ssa.c' wraps every real and virtual operand with an `SSA_NAME` node which contains the version number and the statement that created the `SSA_NAME`. Only definitions and virtual definitions may create new `SSA_NAME` nodes.

Sometimes, flow of control makes it impossible to determine the most recent version of a variable. In these cases, the compiler inserts an artificial definition for that variable called *PHI function* or *PHI node*. This new definition merges all the incoming versions of the variable to create a new name for it. For instance,

```
if (...)
   a_1 = 5;
else if (...)
   a_2 = 2;
else
   a_3 = 13;

# a_4 = PHI <a_1, a_2, a_3>
return a_4;
```

Since it is not possible to determine which of the three branches will be taken at runtime, we don't know which of `a_1`, `a_2` or `a_3` to use at the return statement. So, the SSA renamer creates a new version `a_4` which is assigned the result of "merging" `a_1`, `a_2` and `a_3`. Hence, PHI nodes mean "one of these operands. I don't know which".

The following functions can be used to examine PHI nodes

`gimple_phi_result (phi)` [Function]
   Returns the `SSA_NAME` created by PHI node *phi* (i.e., *phi*'s LHS).

`gimple_phi_num_args (phi)` [Function]
   Returns the number of arguments in *phi*. This number is exactly the number of incoming edges to the basic block holding *phi*.

`gimple_phi_arg (phi, i)` [Function]
   Returns *i*th argument of *phi*.

`gimple_phi_arg_edge (phi, i)` [Function]
   Returns the incoming edge for the *i*th argument of *phi*.

`gimple_phi_arg_def (phi, i)` [Function]
   Returns the `SSA_NAME` for the *i*th argument of *phi*.

13.3.1 Preserving the SSA form

Some optimization passes make changes to the function that invalidate the SSA property. This can happen when a pass has added new symbols or changed the program so that variables that were previously aliased aren't anymore. Whenever something like this happens, the affected symbols must be renamed into SSA form again. Transformations that emit new code or replicate existing statements will also need to update the SSA form.

Since GCC implements two different SSA forms for register and virtual variables, keeping the SSA form up to date depends on whether you are updating register or virtual names. In both cases, the general idea behind incremental SSA updates is similar: when new SSA names are created, they typically are meant to replace other existing names in the program.

For instance, given the following code:

```
1   L0:
2   x_1 = PHI (0, x_5)
3   if (x_1 < 10)
4     if (x_1 > 7)
5       y_2 = 0
6     else
7       y_3 = x_1 + x_7
8     endif
9     x_5 = x_1 + 1
10    goto L0;
11  endif
```

Suppose that we insert new names x_10 and x_11 (lines 4 and 8).

```
1   L0:
2   x_1 = PHI (0, x_5)
3   if (x_1 < 10)
4     x_10 = ...
5     if (x_1 > 7)
6       y_2 = 0
7     else
8       x_11 = ...
9       y_3 = x_1 + x_7
10    endif
11    x_5 = x_1 + 1
12    goto L0;
13  endif
```

We want to replace all the uses of x_1 with the new definitions of x_10 and x_11. Note that the only uses that should be replaced are those at lines 5, 9 and 11. Also, the use of x_7 at line 9 should *not* be replaced (this is why we cannot just mark symbol x for renaming).

Additionally, we may need to insert a PHI node at line 11 because that is a merge point for x_10 and x_11. So the use of x_1 at line 11 will be replaced with the new PHI node. The insertion of PHI nodes is optional. They are not strictly necessary to preserve the SSA form, and depending on what the caller inserted, they may not even be useful for the optimizers.

Updating the SSA form is a two step process. First, the pass has to identify which names need to be updated and/or which symbols need to be renamed into SSA form for the first time. When new names are introduced to replace existing names in the program, the mapping between the old and the new names are registered by calling `register_new_name_mapping` (note that if your pass creates new code by duplicating basic blocks, the call to `tree_duplicate_bb` will set up the necessary mappings automatically).

After the replacement mappings have been registered and new symbols marked for renaming, a call to `update_ssa` makes the registered changes. This can be done with an explicit call or by creating TODO flags in the `tree_opt_pass` structure for your pass. There are several TODO flags that control the behavior of `update_ssa`:

- `TODO_update_ssa`. Update the SSA form inserting PHI nodes for newly exposed symbols and virtual names marked for updating. When updating real names, only insert PHI nodes for a real name O_j in blocks reached by all the new and old definitions for O_j. If the iterated dominance frontier for O_j is not pruned, we may end up inserting PHI nodes in blocks that have one or more edges with no incoming definition for O_j. This would lead to uninitialized warnings for O_j's symbol.

- `TODO_update_ssa_no_phi`. Update the SSA form without inserting any new PHI nodes at all. This is used by passes that have either inserted all the PHI nodes themselves or passes that need only to patch use-def and def-def chains for virtuals (e.g., DCE).

- `TODO_update_ssa_full_phi`. Insert PHI nodes everywhere they are needed. No pruning of the IDF is done. This is used by passes that need the PHI nodes for O_j even if it means that some arguments will come from the default definition of O_j's symbol (e.g., `pass_linear_transform`).

  WARNING: If you need to use this flag, chances are that your pass may be doing something wrong. Inserting PHI nodes for an old name where not all edges carry a new replacement may lead to silent codegen errors or spurious uninitialized warnings.

- `TODO_update_ssa_only_virtuals`. Passes that update the SSA form on their own may want to delegate the updating of virtual names to the generic updater. Since FUD chains are easier to maintain, this simplifies the work they need to do. NOTE: If this flag is used, any OLD->NEW mappings for real names are explicitly destroyed and only the symbols marked for renaming are processed.

13.3.2 Examining `SSA_NAME` nodes

The following macros can be used to examine `SSA_NAME` nodes

SSA_NAME_DEF_STMT (*var*) [Macro]

Returns the statement *s* that creates the `SSA_NAME` *var*. If *s* is an empty statement (i.e., `IS_EMPTY_STMT (s)` returns `true`), it means that the first reference to this variable is a USE or a VUSE.

SSA_NAME_VERSION (*var*) [Macro]

Returns the version number of the `SSA_NAME` object *var*.

13.3.3 Walking the dominator tree

void walk_dominator_tree (*walk_data*, *bb*) [Tree SSA function]

This function walks the dominator tree for the current CFG calling a set of callback functions defined in *struct dom_walk_data* in 'domwalk.h'. The call back functions you need to define give you hooks to execute custom code at various points during traversal:

1. Once to initialize any local data needed while processing *bb* and its children. This local data is pushed into an internal stack which is automatically pushed and popped as the walker traverses the dominator tree.

2. Once before traversing all the statements in the *bb*.

3. Once for every statement inside *bb*.

4. Once after traversing all the statements and before recursing into *bb*'s dominator children.

5. It then recurses into all the dominator children of *bb*.
6. After recursing into all the dominator children of *bb* it can, optionally, traverse every statement in *bb* again (i.e., repeating steps 2 and 3).
7. Once after walking the statements in *bb* and *bb*'s dominator children. At this stage, the block local data stack is popped.

13.4 Alias analysis

Alias analysis in GIMPLE SSA form consists of two pieces. First the virtual SSA web ties conflicting memory accesses and provides a SSA use-def chain and SSA immediate-use chains for walking possibly dependent memory accesses. Second an alias-oracle can be queried to disambiguate explicit and implicit memory references.

1. Memory SSA form.

   All statements that may use memory have exactly one accompanied use of a virtual SSA name that represents the state of memory at the given point in the IL.

   All statements that may define memory have exactly one accompanied definition of a virtual SSA name using the previous state of memory and defining the new state of memory after the given point in the IL.

   ```
   int i;
   int foo (void)
   {
     # .MEM_3 = VDEF <.MEM_2(D)>
     i = 1;
     # VUSE <.MEM_3>
     return i;
   }
   ```

   The virtual SSA names in this case are .MEM_2(D) and .MEM_3. The store to the global variable i defines .MEM_3 invalidating .MEM_2(D). The load from i uses that new state .MEM_3.

   The virtual SSA web serves as constraints to SSA optimizers preventing illegitimate code-motion and optimization. It also provides a way to walk related memory statements.

2. Points-to and escape analysis.

   Points-to analysis builds a set of constraints from the GIMPLE SSA IL representing all pointer operations and facts we do or do not know about pointers. Solving this set of constraints yields a conservatively correct solution for each pointer variable in the program (though we are only interested in SSA name pointers) as to what it may possibly point to.

   This points-to solution for a given SSA name pointer is stored in the `pt_solution` sub-structure of the `SSA_NAME_PTR_INFO` record. The following accessor functions are available:

   - `pt_solution_includes`
   - `pt_solutions_intersect`

   Points-to analysis also computes the solution for two special set of pointers, `ESCAPED` and `CALLUSED`. Those represent all memory that has escaped the scope of analysis or that is used by pure or nested const calls.

3. Type-based alias analysis

   Type-based alias analysis is frontend dependent though generic support is provided by the middle-end in `alias.c`. TBAA code is used by both tree optimizers and RTL optimizers.

   Every language that wishes to perform language-specific alias analysis should define a function that computes, given a `tree` node, an alias set for the node. Nodes in different alias sets are not allowed to alias. For an example, see the C front-end function `c_get_alias_set`.

4. Tree alias-oracle

   The tree alias-oracle provides means to disambiguate two memory references and memory references against statements. The following queries are available:

   - `refs_may_alias_p`
   - `ref_maybe_used_by_stmt_p`
   - `stmt_may_clobber_ref_p`

   In addition to those two kind of statement walkers are available walking statements related to a reference ref. `walk_non_aliased_vuses` walks over dominating memory defining statements and calls back if the statement does not clobber ref providing the non-aliased VUSE. The walk stops at the first clobbering statement or if asked to. `walk_aliased_vdefs` walks over dominating memory defining statements and calls back on each statement clobbering ref providing its aliasing VDEF. The walk stops if asked to.

13.5 Memory model

The memory model used by the middle-end models that of the C/C++ languages. The middle-end has the notion of an effective type of a memory region which is used for type-based alias analysis.

The following is a refinement of ISO C99 6.5/6, clarifying the block copy case to follow common sense and extending the concept of a dynamic effective type to objects with a declared type as required for C++.

```
The effective type of an object for an access to its stored value is
the declared type of the object or the effective type determined by
a previous store to it.  If a value is stored into an object through
an lvalue having a type that is not a character type, then the
type of the lvalue becomes the effective type of the object for that
access and for subsequent accesses that do not modify the stored value.
If a value is copied into an object using memcpy or memmove,
or is copied as an array of character type, then the effective type
of the modified object for that access and for subsequent accesses that
do not modify the value is undetermined.  For all other accesses to an
object, the effective type of the object is simply the type of the
lvalue used for the access.
```

14 RTL Representation

The last part of the compiler work is done on a low-level intermediate representation called Register Transfer Language. In this language, the instructions to be output are described, pretty much one by one, in an algebraic form that describes what the instruction does.

RTL is inspired by Lisp lists. It has both an internal form, made up of structures that point at other structures, and a textual form that is used in the machine description and in printed debugging dumps. The textual form uses nested parentheses to indicate the pointers in the internal form.

14.1 RTL Object Types

RTL uses five kinds of objects: expressions, integers, wide integers, strings and vectors. Expressions are the most important ones. An RTL expression ("RTX", for short) is a C structure, but it is usually referred to with a pointer; a type that is given the typedef name `rtx`.

An integer is simply an `int`; their written form uses decimal digits. A wide integer is an integral object whose type is `HOST_WIDE_INT`; their written form uses decimal digits.

A string is a sequence of characters. In core it is represented as a `char *` in usual C fashion, and it is written in C syntax as well. However, strings in RTL may never be null. If you write an empty string in a machine description, it is represented in core as a null pointer rather than as a pointer to a null character. In certain contexts, these null pointers instead of strings are valid. Within RTL code, strings are most commonly found inside `symbol_ref` expressions, but they appear in other contexts in the RTL expressions that make up machine descriptions.

In a machine description, strings are normally written with double quotes, as you would in C. However, strings in machine descriptions may extend over many lines, which is invalid C, and adjacent string constants are not concatenated as they are in C. Any string constant may be surrounded with a single set of parentheses. Sometimes this makes the machine description easier to read.

There is also a special syntax for strings, which can be useful when C code is embedded in a machine description. Wherever a string can appear, it is also valid to write a C-style brace block. The entire brace block, including the outermost pair of braces, is considered to be the string constant. Double quote characters inside the braces are not special. Therefore, if you write string constants in the C code, you need not escape each quote character with a backslash.

A vector contains an arbitrary number of pointers to expressions. The number of elements in the vector is explicitly present in the vector. The written form of a vector consists of square brackets ('[...]') surrounding the elements, in sequence and with whitespace separating them. Vectors of length zero are not created; null pointers are used instead.

Expressions are classified by *expression codes* (also called RTX codes). The expression code is a name defined in 'rtl.def', which is also (in uppercase) a C enumeration constant. The possible expression codes and their meanings are machine-independent. The code of an RTX can be extracted with the macro `GET_CODE (x)` and altered with `PUT_CODE (x, newcode)`.

The expression code determines how many operands the expression contains, and what kinds of objects they are. In RTL, unlike Lisp, you cannot tell by looking at an operand what kind of object it is. Instead, you must know from its context—from the expression code of the containing expression. For example, in an expression of code `subreg`, the first operand is to be regarded as an expression and the second operand as a polynomial integer. In an expression of code `plus`, there are two operands, both of which are to be regarded as expressions. In a `symbol_ref` expression, there is one operand, which is to be regarded as a string.

Expressions are written as parentheses containing the name of the expression type, its flags and machine mode if any, and then the operands of the expression (separated by spaces).

Expression code names in the 'md' file are written in lowercase, but when they appear in C code they are written in uppercase. In this manual, they are shown as follows: `const_int`.

In a few contexts a null pointer is valid where an expression is normally wanted. The written form of this is (nil).

14.2 RTL Classes and Formats

The various expression codes are divided into several *classes*, which are represented by single characters. You can determine the class of an RTX code with the macro `GET_RTX_CLASS (code)`. Currently, 'rtl.def' defines these classes:

RTX_OBJ   An RTX code that represents an actual object, such as a register (REG) or a memory location (MEM, SYMBOL_REF). LO_SUM) is also included; instead, SUBREG and STRICT_LOW_PART are not in this class, but in class x.

RTX_CONST_OBJ
    An RTX code that represents a constant object. HIGH is also included in this class.

RTX_COMPARE
    An RTX code for a non-symmetric comparison, such as GEU or LT.

RTX_COMM_COMPARE
    An RTX code for a symmetric (commutative) comparison, such as EQ or ORDERED.

RTX_UNARY
    An RTX code for a unary arithmetic operation, such as NEG, NOT, or ABS. This category also includes value extension (sign or zero) and conversions between integer and floating point.

RTX_COMM_ARITH
    An RTX code for a commutative binary operation, such as PLUS or AND. NE and EQ are comparisons, so they have class <.

RTX_BIN_ARITH
    An RTX code for a non-commutative binary operation, such as MINUS, DIV, or ASHIFTRT.

Chapter 14: RTL Representation

`RTX_BITFIELD_OPS`
: An RTX code for a bit-field operation. Currently only `ZERO_EXTRACT` and `SIGN_EXTRACT`. These have three inputs and are lvalues (so they can be used for insertion as well). See Section 14.11 [Bit-Fields], page 284.

`RTX_TERNARY`
: An RTX code for other three input operations. Currently only `IF_THEN_ELSE`, `VEC_MERGE`, `SIGN_EXTRACT`, `ZERO_EXTRACT`, and `FMA`.

`RTX_INSN`
: An RTX code for an entire instruction: `INSN`, `JUMP_INSN`, and `CALL_INSN`. See Section 14.19 [Insns], page 294.

`RTX_MATCH`
: An RTX code for something that matches in insns, such as `MATCH_DUP`. These only occur in machine descriptions.

`RTX_AUTOINC`
: An RTX code for an auto-increment addressing mode, such as `POST_INC`. 'XEXP (x, 0)' gives the auto-modified register.

`RTX_EXTRA`
: All other RTX codes. This category includes the remaining codes used only in machine descriptions (`DEFINE_*`, etc.). It also includes all the codes describing side effects (`SET`, `USE`, `CLOBBER`, etc.) and the non-insns that may appear on an insn chain, such as `NOTE`, `BARRIER`, and `CODE_LABEL`. `SUBREG` is also part of this class.

For each expression code, 'rtl.def' specifies the number of contained objects and their kinds using a sequence of characters called the *format* of the expression code. For example, the format of `subreg` is 'ep'.

These are the most commonly used format characters:

e
: An expression (actually a pointer to an expression).

i
: An integer.

w
: A wide integer.

s
: A string.

E
: A vector of expressions.

A few other format characters are used occasionally:

u
: 'u' is equivalent to 'e' except that it is printed differently in debugging dumps. It is used for pointers to insns.

n
: 'n' is equivalent to 'i' except that it is printed differently in debugging dumps. It is used for the line number or code number of a `note` insn.

S
: 'S' indicates a string which is optional. In the RTL objects in core, 'S' is equivalent to 's', but when the object is read, from an 'md' file, the string value of this operand may be omitted. An omitted string is taken to be the null string.

V   'V' indicates a vector which is optional. In the RTL objects in core, 'V' is equivalent to 'E', but when the object is read from an 'md' file, the vector value of this operand may be omitted. An omitted vector is effectively the same as a vector of no elements.

B   'B' indicates a pointer to basic block structure.

p   A polynomial integer. At present this is used only for SUBREG_BYTE.

0   '0' means a slot whose contents do not fit any normal category. '0' slots are not printed at all in dumps, and are often used in special ways by small parts of the compiler.

There are macros to get the number of operands and the format of an expression code:

GET_RTX_LENGTH (*code*)
: Number of operands of an RTX of code *code*.

GET_RTX_FORMAT (*code*)
: The format of an RTX of code *code*, as a C string.

Some classes of RTX codes always have the same format. For example, it is safe to assume that all comparison operations have format ee.

1   All codes of this class have format e.

<
c
2   All codes of these classes have format ee.

b
3   All codes of these classes have format eee.

i   All codes of this class have formats that begin with iuueiee. See Section 14.19 [Insns], page 294. Note that not all RTL objects linked onto an insn chain are of class i.

o
m
x   You can make no assumptions about the format of these codes.

14.3 Access to Operands

Operands of expressions are accessed using the macros XEXP, XINT, XWINT and XSTR. Each of these macros takes two arguments: an expression-pointer (RTX) and an operand number (counting from zero). Thus,

    XEXP (x, 2)

accesses operand 2 of expression x, as an expression.

    XINT (x, 2)

accesses the same operand as an integer. XSTR, used in the same fashion, would access it as a string.

Any operand can be accessed as an integer, as an expression or as a string. You must choose the correct method of access for the kind of value actually stored in the operand.

You would do this based on the expression code of the containing expression. That is also how you would know how many operands there are.

For example, if x is an `int_list` expression, you know that it has two operands which can be correctly accessed as XINT (x, 0) and XEXP (x, 1). Incorrect accesses like XEXP (x, 0) and XINT (x, 1) would compile, but would trigger an internal compiler error when rtl checking is enabled. Nothing stops you from writing XEXP (x, 28) either, but this will access memory past the end of the expression with unpredictable results.

Access to operands which are vectors is more complicated. You can use the macro XVEC to get the vector-pointer itself, or the macros XVECEXP and XVECLEN to access the elements and length of a vector.

XVEC (*exp*, *idx*)
: Access the vector-pointer which is operand number *idx* in *exp*.

XVECLEN (*exp*, *idx*)
: Access the length (number of elements) in the vector which is in operand number *idx* in *exp*. This value is an `int`.

XVECEXP (*exp*, *idx*, *eltnum*)
: Access element number *eltnum* in the vector which is in operand number *idx* in *exp*. This value is an RTX.

    It is up to you to make sure that *eltnum* is not negative and is less than XVECLEN (*exp*, *idx*).

All the macros defined in this section expand into lvalues and therefore can be used to assign the operands, lengths and vector elements as well as to access them.

14.4 Access to Special Operands

Some RTL nodes have special annotations associated with them.

MEM

> MEM_ALIAS_SET (x)
> : If 0, x is not in any alias set, and may alias anything. Otherwise, x can only alias MEMs in a conflicting alias set. This value is set in a language-dependent manner in the front-end, and should not be altered in the back-end. In some front-ends, these numbers may correspond in some way to types, or other language-level entities, but they need not, and the back-end makes no such assumptions. These set numbers are tested with `alias_sets_conflict_p`.
>
> MEM_EXPR (x)
> : If this register is known to hold the value of some user-level declaration, this is that tree node. It may also be a COMPONENT_REF, in which case this is some field reference, and TREE_OPERAND (x, 0) contains the declaration, or another COMPONENT_REF, or null if there is no compile-time object associated with the reference.
>
> MEM_OFFSET_KNOWN_P (x)
> : True if the offset of the memory reference from MEM_EXPR is known. 'MEM_OFFSET (x)' provides the offset if so.

MEM_OFFSET (*x*)
: The offset from the start of MEM_EXPR. The value is only valid if 'MEM_OFFSET_KNOWN_P (*x*)' is true.

MEM_SIZE_KNOWN_P (*x*)
: True if the size of the memory reference is known. 'MEM_SIZE (*x*)' provides its size if so.

MEM_SIZE (*x*)
: The size in bytes of the memory reference. This is mostly relevant for BLKmode references as otherwise the size is implied by the mode. The value is only valid if 'MEM_SIZE_KNOWN_P (*x*)' is true.

MEM_ALIGN (*x*)
: The known alignment in bits of the memory reference.

MEM_ADDR_SPACE (*x*)
: The address space of the memory reference. This will commonly be zero for the generic address space.

REG

ORIGINAL_REGNO (*x*)
: This field holds the number the register "originally" had; for a pseudo register turned into a hard reg this will hold the old pseudo register number.

REG_EXPR (*x*)
: If this register is known to hold the value of some user-level declaration, this is that tree node.

REG_OFFSET (*x*)
: If this register is known to hold the value of some user-level declaration, this is the offset into that logical storage.

SYMBOL_REF

SYMBOL_REF_DECL (*x*)
: If the symbol_ref *x* was created for a VAR_DECL or a FUNCTION_DECL, that tree is recorded here. If this value is null, then *x* was created by back end code generation routines, and there is no associated front end symbol table entry.

    SYMBOL_REF_DECL may also point to a tree of class 'c', that is, some sort of constant. In this case, the symbol_ref is an entry in the per-file constant pool; again, there is no associated front end symbol table entry.

SYMBOL_REF_CONSTANT (*x*)
: If 'CONSTANT_POOL_ADDRESS_P (*x*)' is true, this is the constant pool entry for *x*. It is null otherwise.

SYMBOL_REF_DATA (*x*)
: A field of opaque type used to store SYMBOL_REF_DECL or SYMBOL_REF_CONSTANT.

SYMBOL_REF_FLAGS (x)
: In a `symbol_ref`, this is used to communicate various predicates about the symbol. Some of these are common enough to be computed by common code, some are specific to the target. The common bits are:

SYMBOL_FLAG_FUNCTION
: Set if the symbol refers to a function.

SYMBOL_FLAG_LOCAL
: Set if the symbol is local to this "module". See `TARGET_BINDS_LOCAL_P`.

SYMBOL_FLAG_EXTERNAL
: Set if this symbol is not defined in this translation unit. Note that this is not the inverse of `SYMBOL_FLAG_LOCAL`.

SYMBOL_FLAG_SMALL
: Set if the symbol is located in the small data section. See `TARGET_IN_SMALL_DATA_P`.

SYMBOL_REF_TLS_MODEL (x)
: This is a multi-bit field accessor that returns the `tls_model` to be used for a thread-local storage symbol. It returns zero for non-thread-local symbols.

SYMBOL_FLAG_HAS_BLOCK_INFO
: Set if the symbol has `SYMBOL_REF_BLOCK` and `SYMBOL_REF_BLOCK_OFFSET` fields.

SYMBOL_FLAG_ANCHOR
: Set if the symbol is used as a section anchor. "Section anchors" are symbols that have a known position within an `object_block` and that can be used to access nearby members of that block. They are used to implement '-fsection-anchors'.

    If this flag is set, then `SYMBOL_FLAG_HAS_BLOCK_INFO` will be too.

Bits beginning with `SYMBOL_FLAG_MACH_DEP` are available for the target's use.

SYMBOL_REF_BLOCK (x)
: If 'SYMBOL_REF_HAS_BLOCK_INFO_P (x)', this is the 'object_block' structure to which the symbol belongs, or `NULL` if it has not been assigned a block.

SYMBOL_REF_BLOCK_OFFSET (x)
: If 'SYMBOL_REF_HAS_BLOCK_INFO_P (x)', this is the offset of x from the first object in 'SYMBOL_REF_BLOCK (x)'. The value is negative if x has not yet been assigned to a block, or it has not been given an offset within that block.

14.5 Flags in an RTL Expression

RTL expressions contain several flags (one-bit bit-fields) that are used in certain types of expression. Most often they are accessed with the following macros, which expand into lvalues.

CROSSING_JUMP_P (*x*)
: Nonzero in a `jump_insn` if it crosses between hot and cold sections, which could potentially be very far apart in the executable. The presence of this flag indicates to other optimizations that this branching instruction should not be "collapsed" into a simpler branching construct. It is used when the optimization to partition basic blocks into hot and cold sections is turned on.

CONSTANT_POOL_ADDRESS_P (*x*)
: Nonzero in a `symbol_ref` if it refers to part of the current function's constant pool. For most targets these addresses are in a `.rodata` section entirely separate from the function, but for some targets the addresses are close to the beginning of the function. In either case GCC assumes these addresses can be addressed directly, perhaps with the help of base registers. Stored in the `unchanging` field and printed as '/u'.

INSN_ANNULLED_BRANCH_P (*x*)
: In a `jump_insn`, `call_insn`, or `insn` indicates that the branch is an annulling one. See the discussion under `sequence` below. Stored in the `unchanging` field and printed as '/u'.

INSN_DELETED_P (*x*)
: In an `insn`, `call_insn`, `jump_insn`, `code_label`, `jump_table_data`, `barrier`, or `note`, nonzero if the insn has been deleted. Stored in the `volatil` field and printed as '/v'.

INSN_FROM_TARGET_P (*x*)
: In an `insn` or `jump_insn` or `call_insn` in a delay slot of a branch, indicates that the insn is from the target of the branch. If the branch insn has INSN_ANNULLED_BRANCH_P set, this insn will only be executed if the branch is taken. For annulled branches with INSN_FROM_TARGET_P clear, the insn will be executed only if the branch is not taken. When INSN_ANNULLED_BRANCH_P is not set, this insn will always be executed. Stored in the `in_struct` field and printed as '/s'.

LABEL_PRESERVE_P (*x*)
: In a `code_label` or `note`, indicates that the label is referenced by code or data not visible to the RTL of a given function. Labels referenced by a non-local goto will have this bit set. Stored in the `in_struct` field and printed as '/s'.

LABEL_REF_NONLOCAL_P (*x*)
: In `label_ref` and `reg_label` expressions, nonzero if this is a reference to a non-local label. Stored in the `volatil` field and printed as '/v'.

MEM_KEEP_ALIAS_SET_P (*x*)
: In `mem` expressions, 1 if we should keep the alias set for this mem unchanged when we access a component. Set to 1, for example, when we are already in a non-addressable component of an aggregate. Stored in the `jump` field and printed as '/j'.

MEM_VOLATILE_P (*x*)

In `mem`, `asm_operands`, and `asm_input` expressions, nonzero for volatile memory references. Stored in the `volatil` field and printed as '/v'.

MEM_NOTRAP_P (*x*)

In `mem`, nonzero for memory references that will not trap. Stored in the `call` field and printed as '/c'.

MEM_POINTER (*x*)

Nonzero in a `mem` if the memory reference holds a pointer. Stored in the `frame_related` field and printed as '/f'.

MEM_READONLY_P (*x*)

Nonzero in a `mem`, if the memory is statically allocated and read-only.

Read-only in this context means never modified during the lifetime of the program, not necessarily in ROM or in write-disabled pages. A common example of the later is a shared library's global offset table. This table is initialized by the runtime loader, so the memory is technically writable, but after control is transferred from the runtime loader to the application, this memory will never be subsequently modified.

Stored in the `unchanging` field and printed as '/u'.

PREFETCH_SCHEDULE_BARRIER_P (*x*)

In a `prefetch`, indicates that the prefetch is a scheduling barrier. No other INSNs will be moved over it. Stored in the `volatil` field and printed as '/v'.

REG_FUNCTION_VALUE_P (*x*)

Nonzero in a `reg` if it is the place in which this function's value is going to be returned. (This happens only in a hard register.) Stored in the `return_val` field and printed as '/i'.

REG_POINTER (*x*)

Nonzero in a `reg` if the register holds a pointer. Stored in the `frame_related` field and printed as '/f'.

REG_USERVAR_P (*x*)

In a `reg`, nonzero if it corresponds to a variable present in the user's source code. Zero for temporaries generated internally by the compiler. Stored in the `volatil` field and printed as '/v'.

The same hard register may be used also for collecting the values of functions called by this one, but REG_FUNCTION_VALUE_P is zero in this kind of use.

RTL_CONST_CALL_P (*x*)

In a `call_insn` indicates that the insn represents a call to a const function. Stored in the `unchanging` field and printed as '/u'.

RTL_PURE_CALL_P (*x*)

In a `call_insn` indicates that the insn represents a call to a pure function. Stored in the `return_val` field and printed as '/i'.

RTL_CONST_OR_PURE_CALL_P (*x*)

In a `call_insn`, true if RTL_CONST_CALL_P or RTL_PURE_CALL_P is true.

RTL_LOOPING_CONST_OR_PURE_CALL_P (x)
: In a `call_insn` indicates that the insn represents a possibly infinite looping call to a const or pure function. Stored in the `call` field and printed as '/c'. Only true if one of RTL_CONST_CALL_P or RTL_PURE_CALL_P is true.

RTX_FRAME_RELATED_P (x)
: Nonzero in an `insn`, `call_insn`, `jump_insn`, `barrier`, or `set` which is part of a function prologue and sets the stack pointer, sets the frame pointer, or saves a register. This flag should also be set on an instruction that sets up a temporary register to use in place of the frame pointer. Stored in the `frame_related` field and printed as '/f'.

    In particular, on RISC targets where there are limits on the sizes of immediate constants, it is sometimes impossible to reach the register save area directly from the stack pointer. In that case, a temporary register is used that is near enough to the register save area, and the Canonical Frame Address, i.e., DWARF2's logical frame pointer, register must (temporarily) be changed to be this temporary register. So, the instruction that sets this temporary register must be marked as RTX_FRAME_RELATED_P.

    If the marked instruction is overly complex (defined in terms of what `dwarf2out_frame_debug_expr` can handle), you will also have to create a REG_FRAME_RELATED_EXPR note and attach it to the instruction. This note should contain a simple expression of the computation performed by this instruction, i.e., one that `dwarf2out_frame_debug_expr` can handle.

    This flag is required for exception handling support on targets with RTL prologues.

SCHED_GROUP_P (x)
: During instruction scheduling, in an `insn`, `call_insn`, `jump_insn` or `jump_table_data`, indicates that the previous insn must be scheduled together with this insn. This is used to ensure that certain groups of instructions will not be split up by the instruction scheduling pass, for example, `use` insns before a `call_insn` may not be separated from the `call_insn`. Stored in the `in_struct` field and printed as '/s'.

SET_IS_RETURN_P (x)
: For a `set`, nonzero if it is for a return. Stored in the `jump` field and printed as '/j'.

SIBLING_CALL_P (x)
: For a `call_insn`, nonzero if the insn is a sibling call. Stored in the `jump` field and printed as '/j'.

STRING_POOL_ADDRESS_P (x)
: For a `symbol_ref` expression, nonzero if it addresses this function's string constant pool. Stored in the `frame_related` field and printed as '/f'.

SUBREG_PROMOTED_UNSIGNED_P (x)
: Returns a value greater then zero for a `subreg` that has SUBREG_PROMOTED_VAR_P nonzero if the object being referenced is kept zero-extended, zero if it is kept sign-extended, and less then zero if it is extended some other way via

the `ptr_extend` instruction. Stored in the `unchanging` field and `volatil` field, printed as '/u' and '/v'. This macro may only be used to get the value it may not be used to change the value. Use `SUBREG_PROMOTED_UNSIGNED_SET` to change the value.

SUBREG_PROMOTED_UNSIGNED_SET (x)

Set the `unchanging` and `volatil` fields in a `subreg` to reflect zero, sign, or other extension. If `volatil` is zero, then `unchanging` as nonzero means zero extension and as zero means sign extension. If `volatil` is nonzero then some other type of extension was done via the `ptr_extend` instruction.

SUBREG_PROMOTED_VAR_P (x)

Nonzero in a `subreg` if it was made when accessing an object that was promoted to a wider mode in accord with the `PROMOTED_MODE` machine description macro (see Section 18.5 [Storage Layout], page 472). In this case, the mode of the `subreg` is the declared mode of the object and the mode of `SUBREG_REG` is the mode of the register that holds the object. Promoted variables are always either sign- or zero-extended to the wider mode on every assignment. Stored in the `in_struct` field and printed as '/s'.

SYMBOL_REF_USED (x)

In a `symbol_ref`, indicates that x has been used. This is normally only used to ensure that x is only declared external once. Stored in the `used` field.

SYMBOL_REF_WEAK (x)

In a `symbol_ref`, indicates that x has been declared weak. Stored in the `return_val` field and printed as '/i'.

SYMBOL_REF_FLAG (x)

In a `symbol_ref`, this is used as a flag for machine-specific purposes. Stored in the `volatil` field and printed as '/v'.

Most uses of `SYMBOL_REF_FLAG` are historic and may be subsumed by `SYMBOL_REF_FLAGS`. Certainly use of `SYMBOL_REF_FLAGS` is mandatory if the target requires more than one bit of storage.

These are the fields to which the above macros refer:

call   In a `mem`, 1 means that the memory reference will not trap.

In a `call`, 1 means that this pure or const call may possibly infinite loop.

In an RTL dump, this flag is represented as '/c'.

frame_related

In an `insn` or `set` expression, 1 means that it is part of a function prologue and sets the stack pointer, sets the frame pointer, saves a register, or sets up a temporary register to use in place of the frame pointer.

In `reg` expressions, 1 means that the register holds a pointer.

In `mem` expressions, 1 means that the memory reference holds a pointer.

In `symbol_ref` expressions, 1 means that the reference addresses this function's string constant pool.

In an RTL dump, this flag is represented as '/f'.

`in_struct`
> In `reg` expressions, it is 1 if the register has its entire life contained within the test expression of some loop.
>
> In `subreg` expressions, 1 means that the `subreg` is accessing an object that has had its mode promoted from a wider mode.
>
> In `label_ref` expressions, 1 means that the referenced label is outside the innermost loop containing the insn in which the `label_ref` was found.
>
> In `code_label` expressions, it is 1 if the label may never be deleted. This is used for labels which are the target of non-local gotos. Such a label that would have been deleted is replaced with a `note` of type `NOTE_INSN_DELETED_LABEL`.
>
> In an `insn` during dead-code elimination, 1 means that the insn is dead code.
>
> In an `insn` or `jump_insn` during reorg for an insn in the delay slot of a branch, 1 means that this insn is from the target of the branch.
>
> In an `insn` during instruction scheduling, 1 means that this insn must be scheduled as part of a group together with the previous insn.
>
> In an RTL dump, this flag is represented as '/s'.

`return_val`
> In `reg` expressions, 1 means the register contains the value to be returned by the current function. On machines that pass parameters in registers, the same register number may be used for parameters as well, but this flag is not set on such uses.
>
> In `symbol_ref` expressions, 1 means the referenced symbol is weak.
>
> In `call` expressions, 1 means the call is pure.
>
> In an RTL dump, this flag is represented as '/i'.

`jump`
> In a `mem` expression, 1 means we should keep the alias set for this mem unchanged when we access a component.
>
> In a `set`, 1 means it is for a return.
>
> In a `call_insn`, 1 means it is a sibling call.
>
> In a `jump_insn`, 1 means it is a crossing jump.
>
> In an RTL dump, this flag is represented as '/j'.

`unchanging`
> In `reg` and `mem` expressions, 1 means that the value of the expression never changes.
>
> In `subreg` expressions, it is 1 if the `subreg` references an unsigned object whose mode has been promoted to a wider mode.
>
> In an `insn` or `jump_insn` in the delay slot of a branch instruction, 1 means an annulling branch should be used.
>
> In a `symbol_ref` expression, 1 means that this symbol addresses something in the per-function constant pool.
>
> In a `call_insn` 1 means that this instruction is a call to a const function.
>
> In an RTL dump, this flag is represented as '/u'.

Chapter 14: RTL Representation   261

used   This flag is used directly (without an access macro) at the end of RTL generation
                for a function, to count the number of times an expression appears in insns.
                Expressions that appear more than once are copied, according to the rules for
                shared structure (see Section 14.21 [Sharing], page 304).

                For a reg, it is used directly (without an access macro) by the leaf register
                renumbering code to ensure that each register is only renumbered once.

                In a symbol_ref, it indicates that an external declaration for the symbol has
                already been written.

volatil   In a mem, asm_operands, or asm_input expression, it is 1 if the memory refer-
                ence is volatile. Volatile memory references may not be deleted, reordered or
                combined.

                In a symbol_ref expression, it is used for machine-specific purposes.

                In a reg expression, it is 1 if the value is a user-level variable. 0 indicates an
                internal compiler temporary.

                In an insn, 1 means the insn has been deleted.

                In label_ref and reg_label expressions, 1 means a reference to a non-local
                label.

                In prefetch expressions, 1 means that the containing insn is a scheduling bar-
                rier.

                In an RTL dump, this flag is represented as '/v'.

14.6 Machine Modes

A machine mode describes a size of data object and the representation used for it. In the
C code, machine modes are represented by an enumeration type, machine_mode, defined
in 'machmode.def'. Each RTL expression has room for a machine mode and so do certain
kinds of tree expressions (declarations and types, to be precise).

In debugging dumps and machine descriptions, the machine mode of an RTL expression
is written after the expression code with a colon to separate them. The letters 'mode' which
appear at the end of each machine mode name are omitted. For example, (reg:SI 38) is
a reg expression with machine mode SImode. If the mode is VOIDmode, it is not written at
all.

Here is a table of machine modes. The term "byte" below refers to an object of BITS_
PER_UNIT bits (see Section 18.5 [Storage Layout], page 472).

BImode   "Bit" mode represents a single bit, for predicate registers.

QImode   "Quarter-Integer" mode represents a single byte treated as an integer.

HImode   "Half-Integer" mode represents a two-byte integer.

PSImode   "Partial Single Integer" mode represents an integer which occupies four bytes
                but which doesn't really use all four. On some machines, this is the right mode
                to use for pointers.

SImode   "Single Integer" mode represents a four-byte integer.

`PDImode` "Partial Double Integer" mode represents an integer which occupies eight bytes but which doesn't really use all eight. On some machines, this is the right mode to use for certain pointers.

`DImode` "Double Integer" mode represents an eight-byte integer.

`TImode` "Tetra Integer" (?) mode represents a sixteen-byte integer.

`OImode` "Octa Integer" (?) mode represents a thirty-two-byte integer.

`XImode` "Hexadeca Integer" (?) mode represents a sixty-four-byte integer.

`QFmode` "Quarter-Floating" mode represents a quarter-precision (single byte) floating point number.

`HFmode` "Half-Floating" mode represents a half-precision (two byte) floating point number.

`TQFmode` "Three-Quarter-Floating" (?) mode represents a three-quarter-precision (three byte) floating point number.

`SFmode` "Single Floating" mode represents a four byte floating point number. In the common case, of a processor with IEEE arithmetic and 8-bit bytes, this is a single-precision IEEE floating point number; it can also be used for double-precision (on processors with 16-bit bytes) and single-precision VAX and IBM types.

`DFmode` "Double Floating" mode represents an eight byte floating point number. In the common case, of a processor with IEEE arithmetic and 8-bit bytes, this is a double-precision IEEE floating point number.

`XFmode` "Extended Floating" mode represents an IEEE extended floating point number. This mode only has 80 meaningful bits (ten bytes). Some processors require such numbers to be padded to twelve bytes, others to sixteen; this mode is used for either.

`SDmode` "Single Decimal Floating" mode represents a four byte decimal floating point number (as distinct from conventional binary floating point).

`DDmode` "Double Decimal Floating" mode represents an eight byte decimal floating point number.

`TDmode` "Tetra Decimal Floating" mode represents a sixteen byte decimal floating point number all 128 of whose bits are meaningful.

`TFmode` "Tetra Floating" mode represents a sixteen byte floating point number all 128 of whose bits are meaningful. One common use is the IEEE quad-precision format.

`QQmode` "Quarter-Fractional" mode represents a single byte treated as a signed fractional number. The default format is "s.7".

`HQmode` "Half-Fractional" mode represents a two-byte signed fractional number. The default format is "s.15".

`SQmode` "Single Fractional" mode represents a four-byte signed fractional number. The default format is "s.31".

`DQmode`   "Double Fractional" mode represents an eight-byte signed fractional number. The default format is "s.63".

`TQmode`   "Tetra Fractional" mode represents a sixteen-byte signed fractional number. The default format is "s.127".

`UQQmode` "Unsigned Quarter-Fractional" mode represents a single byte treated as an unsigned fractional number. The default format is ".8".

`UHQmode` "Unsigned Half-Fractional" mode represents a two-byte unsigned fractional number. The default format is ".16".

`USQmode` "Unsigned Single Fractional" mode represents a four-byte unsigned fractional number. The default format is ".32".

`UDQmode` "Unsigned Double Fractional" mode represents an eight-byte unsigned fractional number. The default format is ".64".

`UTQmode` "Unsigned Tetra Fractional" mode represents a sixteen-byte unsigned fractional number. The default format is ".128".

`HAmode`   "Half-Accumulator" mode represents a two-byte signed accumulator. The default format is "s8.7".

`SAmode`   "Single Accumulator" mode represents a four-byte signed accumulator. The default format is "s16.15".

`DAmode`   "Double Accumulator" mode represents an eight-byte signed accumulator. The default format is "s32.31".

`TAmode`   "Tetra Accumulator" mode represents a sixteen-byte signed accumulator. The default format is "s64.63".

`UHAmode` "Unsigned Half-Accumulator" mode represents a two-byte unsigned accumulator. The default format is "8.8".

`USAmode` "Unsigned Single Accumulator" mode represents a four-byte unsigned accumulator. The default format is "16.16".

`UDAmode` "Unsigned Double Accumulator" mode represents an eight-byte unsigned accumulator. The default format is "32.32".

`UTAmode` "Unsigned Tetra Accumulator" mode represents a sixteen-byte unsigned accumulator. The default format is "64.64".

`CCmode`   "Condition Code" mode represents the value of a condition code, which is a machine-specific set of bits used to represent the result of a comparison operation. Other machine-specific modes may also be used for the condition code. These modes are not used on machines that use `cc0` (see Section 18.15 [Condition Code], page 552).

`BLKmode` "Block" mode represents values that are aggregates to which none of the other modes apply. In RTL, only memory references can have this mode, and only if they appear in string-move or vector instructions. On machines which have no such instructions, `BLKmode` will not appear in RTL.

`VOIDmode` Void mode means the absence of a mode or an unspecified mode. For example, RTL expressions of code `const_int` have mode `VOIDmode` because they can be taken to have whatever mode the context requires. In debugging dumps of RTL, `VOIDmode` is expressed by the absence of any mode.

`QCmode, HCmode, SCmode, DCmode, XCmode, TCmode`
: These modes stand for a complex number represented as a pair of floating point values. The floating point values are in `QFmode`, `HFmode`, `SFmode`, `DFmode`, `XFmode`, and `TFmode`, respectively.

`CQImode, CHImode, CSImode, CDImode, CTImode, COImode, CPSImode`
: These modes stand for a complex number represented as a pair of integer values. The integer values are in `QImode`, `HImode`, `SImode`, `DImode`, `TImode`, `OImode`, and `PSImode`, respectively.

`BND32mode BND64mode`
: These modes stand for bounds for pointer of 32 and 64 bit size respectively. Mode size is double pointer mode size.

The machine description defines `Pmode` as a C macro which expands into the machine mode used for addresses. Normally this is the mode whose size is `BITS_PER_WORD`, `SImode` on 32-bit machines.

The only modes which a machine description *must* support are `QImode`, and the modes corresponding to `BITS_PER_WORD`, `FLOAT_TYPE_SIZE` and `DOUBLE_TYPE_SIZE`. The compiler will attempt to use `DImode` for 8-byte structures and unions, but this can be prevented by overriding the definition of `MAX_FIXED_MODE_SIZE`. Alternatively, you can have the compiler use `TImode` for 16-byte structures and unions. Likewise, you can arrange for the C type `short int` to avoid using `HImode`.

Very few explicit references to machine modes remain in the compiler and these few references will soon be removed. Instead, the machine modes are divided into mode classes. These are represented by the enumeration type `enum mode_class` defined in 'machmode.h'. The possible mode classes are:

`MODE_INT` Integer modes. By default these are `BImode`, `QImode`, `HImode`, `SImode`, `DImode`, `TImode`, and `OImode`.

`MODE_PARTIAL_INT`
: The "partial integer" modes, `PQImode`, `PHImode`, `PSImode` and `PDImode`.

`MODE_FLOAT`
: Floating point modes. By default these are `QFmode`, `HFmode`, `TQFmode`, `SFmode`, `DFmode`, `XFmode` and `TFmode`.

`MODE_DECIMAL_FLOAT`
: Decimal floating point modes. By default these are `SDmode`, `DDmode` and `TDmode`.

`MODE_FRACT`
: Signed fractional modes. By default these are `QQmode`, `HQmode`, `SQmode`, `DQmode` and `TQmode`.

`MODE_UFRACT`
: Unsigned fractional modes. By default these are `UQQmode`, `UHQmode`, `USQmode`, `UDQmode` and `UTQmode`.

MODE_ACCUM
: Signed accumulator modes. By default these are HAmode, SAmode, DAmode and TAmode.

MODE_UACCUM
: Unsigned accumulator modes. By default these are UHAmode, USAmode, UDAmode and UTAmode.

MODE_COMPLEX_INT
: Complex integer modes. (These are not currently implemented).

MODE_COMPLEX_FLOAT
: Complex floating point modes. By default these are QCmode, HCmode, SCmode, DCmode, XCmode, and TCmode.

MODE_FUNCTION
: Algol or Pascal function variables including a static chain. (These are not currently implemented).

MODE_CC
: Modes representing condition code values. These are CCmode plus any CC_MODE modes listed in the '*machine-modes.def*'. See Section 17.12 [Jump Patterns], page 419, also see Section 18.15 [Condition Code], page 552.

MODE_POINTER_BOUNDS
: Pointer bounds modes. Used to represent values of pointer bounds type. Operations in these modes may be executed as NOPs depending on hardware features and environment setup.

MODE_RANDOM
: This is a catchall mode class for modes which don't fit into the above classes. Currently VOIDmode and BLKmode are in MODE_RANDOM.

machmode.h also defines various wrapper classes that combine a `machine_mode` with a static assertion that a particular condition holds. The classes are:

scalar_int_mode
: A mode that has class MODE_INT or MODE_PARTIAL_INT.

scalar_float_mode
: A mode that has class MODE_FLOAT or MODE_DECIMAL_FLOAT.

scalar_mode
: A mode that holds a single numerical value. In practice this means that the mode is a `scalar_int_mode`, is a `scalar_float_mode`, or has class MODE_FRACT, MODE_UFRACT, MODE_ACCUM, MODE_UACCUM or MODE_POINTER_BOUNDS.

complex_mode
: A mode that has class MODE_COMPLEX_INT or MODE_COMPLEX_FLOAT.

fixed_size_mode
: A mode whose size is known at compile time.

Named modes use the most constrained of the available wrapper classes, if one exists, otherwise they use `machine_mode`. For example, QImode is a `scalar_int_mode`, SFmode is a `scalar_float_mode` and BLKmode is a plain `machine_mode`. It is possible to refer to any mode as a raw `machine_mode` by adding the `E_` prefix, where E stands for "enumeration". For example, the raw `machine_mode` names of the modes just mentioned are `E_QImode`, `E_SFmode` and `E_BLKmode` respectively.

The wrapper classes implicitly convert to `machine_mode` and to any wrapper class that represents a more general condition; for example `scalar_int_mode` and `scalar_float_mode` both convert to `scalar_mode` and all three convert to `fixed_size_mode`. The classes act like `machine_mode`s that accept only certain named modes.

'machmode.h' also defines a template class `opt_mode<T>` that holds a T or nothing, where T can be either `machine_mode` or one of the wrapper classes above. The main operations on an `opt_mode<T>` x are as follows:

'x.exists ()'
: Return true if x holds a mode rather than nothing.

'x.exists (&y)'
: Return true if x holds a mode rather than nothing, storing the mode in y if so. y must be assignment-compatible with T.

'x.require ()'
: Assert that x holds a mode rather than nothing and return that mode.

'x = y'
: Set x to y, where y is a T or implicitly converts to a T.

The default constructor sets an `opt_mode<T>` to nothing. There is also a constructor that takes an initial value of type T.

It is possible to use the 'is-a.h' accessors on a `machine_mode` or machine mode wrapper x:

'is_a <T> (x)'
: Return true if x meets the conditions for wrapper class T.

'is_a <T> (x, &y)'
: Return true if x meets the conditions for wrapper class T, storing it in y if so. y must be assignment-compatible with T.

'as_a <T> (x)'
: Assert that x meets the conditions for wrapper class T and return it as a T.

'dyn_cast <T> (x)'
: Return an `opt_mode<T>` that holds x if x meets the conditions for wrapper class T and that holds nothing otherwise.

The purpose of these wrapper classes is to give stronger static type checking. For example, if a function takes a `scalar_int_mode`, a caller that has a general `machine_mode` must either check or assert that the code is indeed a scalar integer first, using one of the functions above.

The wrapper classes are normal C++ classes, with user-defined constructors. Sometimes it is useful to have a POD version of the same type, particularly if the type appears in a union. The template class `pod_mode<T>` provides a POD version of wrapper class T. It is assignment-compatible with T and implicitly converts to both `machine_mode` and T.

Here are some C macros that relate to machine modes:

Chapter 14: RTL Representation   267

GET_MODE (x)
: Returns the machine mode of the RTX x.

PUT_MODE (x, newmode)
: Alters the machine mode of the RTX x to be newmode.

NUM_MACHINE_MODES
: Stands for the number of machine modes available on the target machine. This is one greater than the largest numeric value of any machine mode.

GET_MODE_NAME (m)
: Returns the name of mode m as a string.

GET_MODE_CLASS (m)
: Returns the mode class of mode m.

GET_MODE_WIDER_MODE (m)
: Returns the next wider natural mode. For example, the expression GET_MODE_WIDER_MODE (QImode) returns HImode.

GET_MODE_SIZE (m)
: Returns the size in bytes of a datum of mode m.

GET_MODE_BITSIZE (m)
: Returns the size in bits of a datum of mode m.

GET_MODE_IBIT (m)
: Returns the number of integral bits of a datum of fixed-point mode m.

GET_MODE_FBIT (m)
: Returns the number of fractional bits of a datum of fixed-point mode m.

GET_MODE_MASK (m)
: Returns a bitmask containing 1 for all bits in a word that fit within mode m. This macro can only be used for modes whose bitsize is less than or equal to HOST_BITS_PER_INT.

GET_MODE_ALIGNMENT (m)
: Return the required alignment, in bits, for an object of mode m.

GET_MODE_UNIT_SIZE (m)
: Returns the size in bytes of the subunits of a datum of mode m. This is the same as GET_MODE_SIZE except in the case of complex modes. For them, the unit size is the size of the real or imaginary part.

GET_MODE_NUNITS (m)
: Returns the number of units contained in a mode, i.e., GET_MODE_SIZE divided by GET_MODE_UNIT_SIZE.

GET_CLASS_NARROWEST_MODE (c)
: Returns the narrowest mode in mode class c.

The following 3 variables are defined on every target. They can be used to allocate buffers that are guaranteed to be large enough to hold any value that can be represented on the target. The first two can be overridden by defining them in the target's mode.def file, however, the value must be a constant that can determined very early in the compilation process. The third symbol cannot be overridden.

`BITS_PER_UNIT`
> The number of bits in an addressable storage unit (byte). If you do not define this, the default is 8.

`MAX_BITSIZE_MODE_ANY_INT`
> The maximum bitsize of any mode that is used in integer math. This should be overridden by the target if it uses large integers as containers for larger vectors but otherwise never uses the contents to compute integer values.

`MAX_BITSIZE_MODE_ANY_MODE`
> The bitsize of the largest mode on the target. The default value is the largest mode size given in the mode definition file, which is always correct for targets whose modes have a fixed size. Targets that might increase the size of a mode beyond this default should define `MAX_BITSIZE_MODE_ANY_MODE` to the actual upper limit in 'machine-modes.def'.

The global variables `byte_mode` and `word_mode` contain modes whose classes are `MODE_INT` and whose bitsizes are either `BITS_PER_UNIT` or `BITS_PER_WORD`, respectively. On 32-bit machines, these are `QImode` and `SImode`, respectively.

14.7 Constant Expression Types

The simplest RTL expressions are those that represent constant values.

`(const_int i)`
> This type of expression represents the integer value *i*. *i* is customarily accessed with the macro `INTVAL` as in `INTVAL (exp)`, which is equivalent to `XWINT (exp, 0)`.
>
> Constants generated for modes with fewer bits than in `HOST_WIDE_INT` must be sign extended to full width (e.g., with `gen_int_mode`). For constants for modes with more bits than in `HOST_WIDE_INT` the implied high order bits of that constant are copies of the top bit. Note however that values are neither inherently signed nor inherently unsigned; where necessary, signedness is determined by the rtl operation instead.
>
> There is only one expression object for the integer value zero; it is the value of the variable `const0_rtx`. Likewise, the only expression for integer value one is found in `const1_rtx`, the only expression for integer value two is found in `const2_rtx`, and the only expression for integer value negative one is found in `constm1_rtx`. Any attempt to create an expression of code `const_int` and value zero, one, two or negative one will return `const0_rtx`, `const1_rtx`, `const2_rtx` or `constm1_rtx` as appropriate.
>
> Similarly, there is only one object for the integer whose value is `STORE_FLAG_VALUE`. It is found in `const_true_rtx`. If `STORE_FLAG_VALUE` is one, `const_true_rtx` and `const1_rtx` will point to the same object. If `STORE_FLAG_VALUE` is −1, `const_true_rtx` and `constm1_rtx` will point to the same object.

(const_double:*m i0 i1 ...*)
: This represents either a floating-point constant of mode *m* or (on older ports that do not define TARGET_SUPPORTS_WIDE_INT) an integer constant too large to fit into HOST_BITS_PER_WIDE_INT bits but small enough to fit within twice that number of bits. In the latter case, *m* will be VOIDmode. For integral values constants for modes with more bits than twice the number in HOST_WIDE_INT the implied high order bits of that constant are copies of the top bit of CONST_DOUBLE_HIGH. Note however that integral values are neither inherently signed nor inherently unsigned; where necessary, signedness is determined by the rtl operation instead.

    On more modern ports, CONST_DOUBLE only represents floating point values. New ports define TARGET_SUPPORTS_WIDE_INT to make this designation.

    If *m* is VOIDmode, the bits of the value are stored in *i0* and *i1*. *i0* is customarily accessed with the macro CONST_DOUBLE_LOW and *i1* with CONST_DOUBLE_HIGH.

    If the constant is floating point (regardless of its precision), then the number of integers used to store the value depends on the size of REAL_VALUE_TYPE (see Section 18.22 [Floating Point], page 611). The integers represent a floating point number, but not precisely in the target machine's or host machine's floating point format. To convert them to the precise bit pattern used by the target machine, use the macro REAL_VALUE_TO_TARGET_DOUBLE and friends (see Section 18.20.2 [Data Output], page 579).

(const_wide_int:*m nunits elt0 ...*)
: This contains an array of HOST_WIDE_INTs that is large enough to hold any constant that can be represented on the target. This form of rtl is only used on targets that define TARGET_SUPPORTS_WIDE_INT to be nonzero and then CONST_DOUBLEs are only used to hold floating-point values. If the target leaves TARGET_SUPPORTS_WIDE_INT defined as 0, CONST_WIDE_INTs are not used and CONST_DOUBLEs are as they were before.

    The values are stored in a compressed format. The higher-order 0s or -1s are not represented if they are just the logical sign extension of the number that is represented.

CONST_WIDE_INT_VEC (*code*)
: Returns the entire array of HOST_WIDE_INTs that are used to store the value. This macro should be rarely used.

CONST_WIDE_INT_NUNITS (*code*)
: The number of HOST_WIDE_INTs used to represent the number. Note that this generally is smaller than the number of HOST_WIDE_INTs implied by the mode size.

CONST_WIDE_INT_NUNITS (*code,i*)
: Returns the *i*th element of the array. Element 0 is contains the low order bits of the constant.

(const_fixed:*m ...*)
: Represents a fixed-point constant of mode *m*. The operand is a data structure of type struct fixed_value and is accessed with the macro CONST_FIXED_

VALUE. The high part of data is accessed with `CONST_FIXED_VALUE_HIGH`; the low part is accessed with `CONST_FIXED_VALUE_LOW`.

`(const_poly_int:m [c0 c1 ...])`

Represents a `poly_int`-style polynomial integer with coefficients $c0, c1, \ldots$. The coefficients are `wide_int`-based integers rather than rtxes. `CONST_POLY_INT_COEFFS` gives the values of individual coefficients (which is mostly only useful in low-level routines) and `const_poly_int_value` gives the full `poly_int` value.

`(const_vector:m [x0 x1 ...])`

Represents a vector constant. The values in square brackets are elements of the vector, which are always `const_int`, `const_wide_int`, `const_double` or `const_fixed` expressions.

Each vector constant v is treated as a specific instance of an arbitrary-length sequence that itself contains 'CONST_VECTOR_NPATTERNS (v)' interleaved patterns. Each pattern has the form:

```
{ base0, base1, base1 + step, base1 + step * 2, ... }
```

The first three elements in each pattern are enough to determine the values of the other elements. However, if all *steps* are zero, only the first two elements are needed. If in addition each *base1* is equal to the corresponding *base0*, only the first element in each pattern is needed. The number of determining elements per pattern is given by 'CONST_VECTOR_NELTS_PER_PATTERN (v)'.

For example, the constant:

```
{ 0, 1, 2, 6, 3, 8, 4, 10, 5, 12, 6, 14, 7, 16, 8, 18 }
```

is interpreted as an interleaving of the sequences:

```
{ 0, 2, 3, 4, 5, 6, 7, 8 }
{ 1, 6, 8, 10, 12, 14, 16, 18 }
```

where the sequences are represented by the following patterns:

```
base0 == 0, base1 == 2, step == 1
base0 == 1, base1 == 6, step == 2
```

In this case:

```
CONST_VECTOR_NPATTERNS (v) == 2
CONST_VECTOR_NELTS_PER_PATTERN (v) == 3
```

Thus the first 6 elements ('{ 0, 1, 2, 6, 3, 8 }') are enough to determine the whole sequence; we refer to them as the "encoded" elements. They are the only elements present in the square brackets for variable-length `const_vectors` (i.e. for `const_vectors` whose mode m has a variable number of elements). However, as a convenience to code that needs to handle both `const_vectors` and `parallels`, all elements are present in the square brackets for fixed-length `const_vectors`; the encoding scheme simply reduces the amount of work involved in processing constants that follow a regular pattern.

Sometimes this scheme can create two possible encodings of the same vector. For example { 0, 1 } could be seen as two patterns with one element each or one pattern with two elements (*base0* and *base1*). The canonical encoding is always the one with the fewest patterns or (if both encodings have the same number of petterns) the one with the fewest encoded elements.

Chapter 14: RTL Representation 271

'const_vector_encoding_nelts (v)' gives the total number of encoded elements in v, which is 6 in the example above. CONST_VECTOR_ENCODED_ELT (v, i) accesses the value of encoded element i.

'CONST_VECTOR_DUPLICATE_P (v)' is true if v simply contains repeated instances of 'CONST_VECTOR_NPATTERNS (v)' values. This is a shorthand for testing 'CONST_VECTOR_NELTS_PER_PATTERN (v) == 1'.

'CONST_VECTOR_STEPPED_P (v)' is true if at least one pattern in v has a nonzero step. This is a shorthand for testing 'CONST_VECTOR_NELTS_PER_PATTERN (v) == 3'.

CONST_VECTOR_NUNITS (v) gives the total number of elements in v; it is a shorthand for getting the number of units in 'GET_MODE (v)'.

The utility function const_vector_elt gives the value of an arbitrary element as an rtx. const_vector_int_elt gives the same value as a wide_int.

(const_string str)

Represents a constant string with value str. Currently this is used only for insn attributes (see Section 17.19 [Insn Attributes], page 434) since constant strings in C are placed in memory.

(symbol_ref:mode symbol)

Represents the value of an assembler label for data. symbol is a string that describes the name of the assembler label. If it starts with a '*', the label is the rest of symbol not including the '*'. Otherwise, the label is symbol, usually prefixed with '_'.

The symbol_ref contains a mode, which is usually Pmode. Usually that is the only mode for which a symbol is directly valid.

(label_ref:mode label)

Represents the value of an assembler label for code. It contains one operand, an expression, which must be a code_label or a note of type NOTE_INSN_DELETED_LABEL that appears in the instruction sequence to identify the place where the label should go.

The reason for using a distinct expression type for code label references is so that jump optimization can distinguish them.

The label_ref contains a mode, which is usually Pmode. Usually that is the only mode for which a label is directly valid.

(const:m exp)

Represents a constant that is the result of an assembly-time arithmetic computation. The operand, exp, contains only const_int, symbol_ref, label_ref or unspec expressions, combined with plus and minus. Any such unspecs are target-specific and typically represent some form of relocation operator. m should be a valid address mode.

(high:m exp)

Represents the high-order bits of exp, usually a symbol_ref. The number of bits is machine-dependent and is normally the number of bits specified in an instruction that initializes the high order bits of a register. It is used with `lo_sum` to represent the typical two-instruction sequence used in RISC machines to reference a global memory location.

m should be `Pmode`.

The macro `CONST0_RTX (mode)` refers to an expression with value 0 in mode *mode*. If mode *mode* is of mode class `MODE_INT`, it returns `const0_rtx`. If mode *mode* is of mode class `MODE_FLOAT`, it returns a `CONST_DOUBLE` expression in mode *mode*. Otherwise, it returns a `CONST_VECTOR` expression in mode *mode*. Similarly, the macro `CONST1_RTX (mode)` refers to an expression with value 1 in mode *mode* and similarly for `CONST2_RTX`. The `CONST1_RTX` and `CONST2_RTX` macros are undefined for vector modes.

14.8 Registers and Memory

Here are the RTL expression types for describing access to machine registers and to main memory.

(`reg:m n`) For small values of the integer *n* (those that are less than `FIRST_PSEUDO_REGISTER`), this stands for a reference to machine register number *n*: a *hard register*. For larger values of *n*, it stands for a temporary value or *pseudo register*. The compiler's strategy is to generate code assuming an unlimited number of such pseudo registers, and later convert them into hard registers or into memory references.

m is the machine mode of the reference. It is necessary because machines can generally refer to each register in more than one mode. For example, a register may contain a full word but there may be instructions to refer to it as a half word or as a single byte, as well as instructions to refer to it as a floating point number of various precisions.

Even for a register that the machine can access in only one mode, the mode must always be specified.

The symbol `FIRST_PSEUDO_REGISTER` is defined by the machine description, since the number of hard registers on the machine is an invariant characteristic of the machine. Note, however, that not all of the machine registers must be general registers. All the machine registers that can be used for storage of data are given hard register numbers, even those that can be used only in certain instructions or can hold only certain types of data.

A hard register may be accessed in various modes throughout one function, but each pseudo register is given a natural mode and is accessed only in that mode. When it is necessary to describe an access to a pseudo register using a nonnatural mode, a `subreg` expression is used.

A `reg` expression with a machine mode that specifies more than one word of data may actually stand for several consecutive registers. If in addition the register number specifies a hardware register, then it actually represents several consecutive hardware registers starting with the specified one.

Each pseudo register number used in a function's RTL code is represented by a unique `reg` expression.

Chapter 14: RTL Representation

Some pseudo register numbers, those within the range of FIRST_VIRTUAL_REGISTER to LAST_VIRTUAL_REGISTER only appear during the RTL generation phase and are eliminated before the optimization phases. These represent locations in the stack frame that cannot be determined until RTL generation for the function has been completed. The following virtual register numbers are defined:

VIRTUAL_INCOMING_ARGS_REGNUM

> This points to the first word of the incoming arguments passed on the stack. Normally these arguments are placed there by the caller, but the callee may have pushed some arguments that were previously passed in registers.
>
> When RTL generation is complete, this virtual register is replaced by the sum of the register given by ARG_POINTER_REGNUM and the value of FIRST_PARM_OFFSET.

VIRTUAL_STACK_VARS_REGNUM

> If FRAME_GROWS_DOWNWARD is defined to a nonzero value, this points to immediately above the first variable on the stack. Otherwise, it points to the first variable on the stack.
>
> VIRTUAL_STACK_VARS_REGNUM is replaced with the sum of the register given by FRAME_POINTER_REGNUM and the value TARGET_STARTING_FRAME_OFFSET.

VIRTUAL_STACK_DYNAMIC_REGNUM

> This points to the location of dynamically allocated memory on the stack immediately after the stack pointer has been adjusted by the amount of memory desired.
>
> This virtual register is replaced by the sum of the register given by STACK_POINTER_REGNUM and the value STACK_DYNAMIC_OFFSET.

VIRTUAL_OUTGOING_ARGS_REGNUM

> This points to the location in the stack at which outgoing arguments should be written when the stack is pre-pushed (arguments pushed using push insns should always use STACK_POINTER_REGNUM).
>
> This virtual register is replaced by the sum of the register given by STACK_POINTER_REGNUM and the value STACK_POINTER_OFFSET.

(subreg:*m1 reg:m2 bytenum*)

> subreg expressions are used to refer to a register in a machine mode other than its natural one, or to refer to one register of a multi-part reg that actually refers to several registers.
>
> Each pseudo register has a natural mode. If it is necessary to operate on it in a different mode, the register must be enclosed in a subreg.
>
> There are currently three supported types for the first operand of a subreg:
>
> - pseudo registers This is the most common case. Most subregs have pseudo regs as their first operand.

- mem subregs of mem were common in earlier versions of GCC and are still supported. During the reload pass these are replaced by plain mems. On machines that do not do instruction scheduling, use of subregs of mem are still used, but this is no longer recommended. Such subregs are considered to be `register_operands` rather than `memory_operands` before and during reload. Because of this, the scheduling passes cannot properly schedule instructions with subregs of mem, so for machines that do scheduling, subregs of mem should never be used. To support this, the combine and recog passes have explicit code to inhibit the creation of subregs of mem when `INSN_SCHEDULING` is defined.

  The use of subregs of mem after the reload pass is an area that is not well understood and should be avoided. There is still some code in the compiler to support this, but this code has possibly rotted. This use of subregs is discouraged and will most likely not be supported in the future.

- hard registers It is seldom necessary to wrap hard registers in subregs; such registers would normally reduce to a single reg rtx. This use of subregs is discouraged and may not be supported in the future.

subregs of subregs are not supported. Using `simplify_gen_subreg` is the recommended way to avoid this problem.

subregs come in two distinct flavors, each having its own usage and rules:

Paradoxical subregs

> When $m1$ is strictly wider than $m2$, the subreg expression is called *paradoxical*. The canonical test for this class of subreg is:
>
> `paradoxical_subreg_p (m1, m2)`
>
> Paradoxical subregs can be used as both lvalues and rvalues. When used as an lvalue, the low-order bits of the source value are stored in *reg* and the high-order bits are discarded. When used as an rvalue, the low-order bits of the subreg are taken from *reg* while the high-order bits may or may not be defined.
>
> The high-order bits of rvalues are defined in the following circumstances:
>
> - subregs of mem When $m2$ is smaller than a word, the macro `LOAD_EXTEND_OP`, can control how the high-order bits are defined.
> - subreg of regs The upper bits are defined when `SUBREG_PROMOTED_VAR_P` is true. `SUBREG_PROMOTED_UNSIGNED_P` describes what the upper bits hold. Such subregs usually represent local variables, register variables and parameter pseudo variables that have been promoted to a wider mode.
>
> *bytenum* is always zero for a paradoxical subreg, even on big-endian targets.
>
> For example, the paradoxical subreg:
>
> `(set (subreg:SI (reg:HI x) 0) y)`

stores the lower 2 bytes of *y* in *x* and discards the upper 2 bytes. A subsequent:

    `(set z (subreg:SI (reg:HI x) 0))`

would set the lower two bytes of *z* to *y* and set the upper two bytes to an unknown value assuming `SUBREG_PROMOTED_VAR_P` is false.

Normal subregs

When *m1* is at least as narrow as *m2* the `subreg` expression is called *normal*.

Normal `subreg`s restrict consideration to certain bits of *reg*. For this purpose, *reg* is divided into individually-addressable blocks in which each block has:

    `REGMODE_NATURAL_SIZE (m2)`

bytes. Usually the value is `UNITS_PER_WORD`; that is, most targets usually treat each word of a register as being independently addressable.

There are two types of normal `subreg`. If *m1* is known to be no bigger than a block, the `subreg` refers to the least-significant part (or *lowpart*) of one block of *reg*. If *m1* is known to be larger than a block, the `subreg` refers to two or more complete blocks.

When used as an lvalue, `subreg` is a block-based accessor. Storing to a `subreg` modifies all the blocks of *reg* that overlap the `subreg`, but it leaves the other blocks of *reg* alone.

When storing to a normal `subreg` that is smaller than a block, the other bits of the referenced block are usually left in an undefined state. This laxity makes it easier to generate efficient code for such instructions. To represent an instruction that preserves all the bits outside of those in the `subreg`, use `strict_low_part` or `zero_extract` around the `subreg`.

bytenum must identify the offset of the first byte of the `subreg` from the start of *reg*, assuming that *reg* is laid out in memory order. The memory order of bytes is defined by two target macros, `WORDS_BIG_ENDIAN` and `BYTES_BIG_ENDIAN`:

- `WORDS_BIG_ENDIAN`, if set to 1, says that byte number zero is part of the most significant word; otherwise, it is part of the least significant word.

- `BYTES_BIG_ENDIAN`, if set to 1, says that byte number zero is the most significant byte within a word; otherwise, it is the least significant byte within a word.

On a few targets, `FLOAT_WORDS_BIG_ENDIAN` disagrees with `WORDS_BIG_ENDIAN`. However, most parts of the compiler treat floating point values as if they had the same endianness as integer values. This works because they handle them solely as a collection of integer values, with no particular numerical value. Only real.c and the runtime libraries care about `FLOAT_WORDS_BIG_ENDIAN`.

Thus,

    `(subreg:HI (reg:SI x) 2)`

on a `BYTES_BIG_ENDIAN`, 'UNITS_PER_WORD == 4' target is the same as

    `(subreg:HI (reg:SI x) 0)`

on a little-endian, 'UNITS_PER_WORD == 4' target. Both **subregs** access the lower two bytes of register *x*.

Note that the byte offset is a polynomial integer; it may not be a compile-time constant on targets with variable-sized modes. However, the restrictions above mean that there are only a certain set of acceptable offsets for a given combination of *m1* and *m2*. The compiler can always tell which blocks a valid subreg occupies, and whether the subreg is a lowpart of a block.

A `MODE_PARTIAL_INT` mode behaves as if it were as wide as the corresponding `MODE_INT` mode, except that it has an unknown number of undefined bits. For example:

    `(subreg:PSI (reg:SI 0) 0)`

accesses the whole of '`(reg:SI 0)`', but the exact relationship between the PSImode value and the SImode value is not defined. If we assume 'REGMODE_NATURAL_SIZE (DImode) <= 4', then the following two **subregs**:

    `(subreg:PSI (reg:DI 0) 0)`
    `(subreg:PSI (reg:DI 0) 4)`

represent independent 4-byte accesses to the two halves of '`(reg:DI 0)`'. Both **subregs** have an unknown number of undefined bits.

If 'REGMODE_NATURAL_SIZE (PSImode) <= 2' then these two **subregs**:

    `(subreg:HI (reg:PSI 0) 0)`
    `(subreg:HI (reg:PSI 0) 2)`

represent independent 2-byte accesses that together span the whole of '`(reg:PSI 0)`'. Storing to the first **subreg** does not affect the value of the second, and vice versa. '`(reg:PSI 0)`' has an unknown number of undefined bits, so the assignment:

    `(set (subreg:HI (reg:PSI 0) 0) (reg:HI 4))`

does not guarantee that '`(subreg:HI (reg:PSI 0) 0)`' has the value '`(reg:HI 4)`'.

The rules above apply to both pseudo *regs* and hard *regs*. If the semantics are not correct for particular combinations of *m1*, *m2* and hard *reg*, the target-specific code must ensure that those combinations are never used. For example:

    `TARGET_CAN_CHANGE_MODE_CLASS (m2, m1, class)`

must be false for every class *class* that includes *reg*.

GCC must be able to determine at compile time whether a subreg is paradoxical, whether it occupies a whole number of blocks, or whether it is a lowpart of a block. This means that certain combinations of variable-sized mode are not permitted. For example, if *m2* holds *n* SI values, where *n* is greater than zero, it is not possible to form a DI subreg of it; such a **subreg** would be paradoxical when *n* is 1 but not when *n* is greater than 1.

The first operand of a `subreg` expression is customarily accessed with the `SUBREG_REG` macro and the second operand is customarily accessed with the `SUBREG_BYTE` macro.

It has been several years since a platform in which `BYTES_BIG_ENDIAN` not equal to `WORDS_BIG_ENDIAN` has been tested. Anyone wishing to support such a platform in the future may be confronted with code rot.

(scratch:*m*)
: This represents a scratch register that will be required for the execution of a single instruction and not used subsequently. It is converted into a `reg` by either the local register allocator or the reload pass.

  `scratch` is usually present inside a `clobber` operation (see Section 14.15 [Side Effects], page 287).

(cc0)
: This refers to the machine's condition code register. It has no operands and may not have a machine mode. There are two ways to use it:

  - To stand for a complete set of condition code flags. This is best on most machines, where each comparison sets the entire series of flags.

    With this technique, (cc0) may be validly used in only two contexts: as the destination of an assignment (in test and compare instructions) and in comparison operators comparing against zero (`const_int` with value zero; that is to say, const0_rtx).

  - To stand for a single flag that is the result of a single condition. This is useful on machines that have only a single flag bit, and in which comparison instructions must specify the condition to test.

    With this technique, (cc0) may be validly used in only two contexts: as the destination of an assignment (in test and compare instructions) where the source is a comparison operator, and as the first operand of `if_then_else` (in a conditional branch).

  There is only one expression object of code cc0; it is the value of the variable cc0_rtx. Any attempt to create an expression of code cc0 will return cc0_rtx.

  Instructions can set the condition code implicitly. On many machines, nearly all instructions set the condition code based on the value that they compute or store. It is not necessary to record these actions explicitly in the RTL because the machine description includes a prescription for recognizing the instructions that do so (by means of the macro `NOTICE_UPDATE_CC`). See Section 18.15 [Condition Code], page 552. Only instructions whose sole purpose is to set the condition code, and instructions that use the condition code, need mention (cc0).

  On some machines, the condition code register is given a register number and a `reg` is used instead of (cc0). This is usually the preferable approach if only a small subset of instructions modify the condition code. Other machines store condition codes in general registers; in such cases a pseudo register should be used.

  Some machines, such as the SPARC and RS/6000, have two sets of arithmetic instructions, one that sets and one that does not set the condition code. This is best handled by normally generating the instruction that does not set the condition code, and making a pattern that both performs the arithmetic and sets the condition code register (which would not be (cc0) in this case). For examples, search for 'addcc' and 'andcc' in 'sparc.md'.

(pc) This represents the machine's program counter. It has no operands and may not have a machine mode. (pc) may be validly used only in certain specific contexts in jump instructions.

There is only one expression object of code pc; it is the value of the variable pc_rtx. Any attempt to create an expression of code pc will return pc_rtx.

All instructions that do not jump alter the program counter implicitly by incrementing it, but there is no need to mention this in the RTL.

(mem:m addr alias)
This RTX represents a reference to main memory at an address represented by the expression addr. m specifies how large a unit of memory is accessed. alias specifies an alias set for the reference. In general two items are in different alias sets if they cannot reference the same memory address.

The construct (mem:BLK (scratch)) is considered to alias all other memories. Thus it may be used as a memory barrier in epilogue stack deallocation patterns.

(concatm rtx rtx)
This RTX represents the concatenation of two other RTXs. This is used for complex values. It should only appear in the RTL attached to declarations and during RTL generation. It should not appear in the ordinary insn chain.

(concatnm [rtx ...])
This RTX represents the concatenation of all the rtx to make a single value. Like concat, this should only appear in declarations, and not in the insn chain.

14.9 RTL Expressions for Arithmetic

Unless otherwise specified, all the operands of arithmetic expressions must be valid for mode m. An operand is valid for mode m if it has mode m, or if it is a const_int or const_double and m is a mode of class MODE_INT.

For commutative binary operations, constants should be placed in the second operand.

(plus:m x y)
(ss_plus:m x y)
(us_plus:m x y)

These three expressions all represent the sum of the values represented by x and y carried out in machine mode m. They differ in their behavior on overflow of integer modes. plus wraps round modulo the width of m; ss_plus saturates at the maximum signed value representable in m; us_plus saturates at the maximum unsigned value.

(lo_sum:m x y)
This expression represents the sum of x and the low-order bits of y. It is used with high (see Section 14.7 [Constants], page 268) to represent the typical

Chapter 14: RTL Representation

two-instruction sequence used in RISC machines to reference a global memory location.

The number of low order bits is machine-dependent but is normally the number of bits in a `Pmode` item minus the number of bits set by `high`.

m should be `Pmode`.

(minus:*m x y*)
(ss_minus:*m x y*)
(us_minus:*m x y*)

These three expressions represent the result of subtracting *y* from *x*, carried out in mode *M*. Behavior on overflow is the same as for the three variants of `plus` (see above).

(compare:*m x y*)

Represents the result of subtracting *y* from *x* for purposes of comparison. The result is computed without overflow, as if with infinite precision.

Of course, machines cannot really subtract with infinite precision. However, they can pretend to do so when only the sign of the result will be used, which is the case when the result is stored in the condition code. And that is the *only* way this kind of expression may validly be used: as a value to be stored in the condition codes, either (cc0) or a register. See Section 14.10 [Comparisons], page 282.

The mode *m* is not related to the modes of *x* and *y*, but instead is the mode of the condition code value. If (cc0) is used, it is `VOIDmode`. Otherwise it is some mode in class `MODE_CC`, often `CCmode`. See Section 18.15 [Condition Code], page 552. If *m* is `VOIDmode` or `CCmode`, the operation returns sufficient information (in an unspecified format) so that any comparison operator can be applied to the result of the `COMPARE` operation. For other modes in class `MODE_CC`, the operation only returns a subset of this information.

Normally, *x* and *y* must have the same mode. Otherwise, `compare` is valid only if the mode of *x* is in class `MODE_INT` and *y* is a `const_int` or `const_double` with mode `VOIDmode`. The mode of *x* determines what mode the comparison is to be done in; thus it must not be `VOIDmode`.

If one of the operands is a constant, it should be placed in the second operand and the comparison code adjusted as appropriate.

A `compare` specifying two `VOIDmode` constants is not valid since there is no way to know in what mode the comparison is to be performed; the comparison must either be folded during the compilation or the first operand must be loaded into a register while its mode is still known.

(neg:*m x*)
(ss_neg:*m x*)
(us_neg:*m x*)

These two expressions represent the negation (subtraction from zero) of the value represented by *x*, carried out in mode *m*. They differ in the behavior on overflow of integer modes. In the case of `neg`, the negation of the operand may be a number not representable in mode *m*, in which case it is truncated to *m*. `ss_neg` and `us_neg` ensure that an out-of-bounds result saturates to the maximum or minimum signed or unsigned value.

(`mult:`*m x y*)
(`ss_mult:`*m x y*)
(`us_mult:`*m x y*)

> Represents the signed product of the values represented by *x* and *y* carried out in machine mode *m*. `ss_mult` and `us_mult` ensure that an out-of-bounds result saturates to the maximum or minimum signed or unsigned value.
>
> Some machines support a multiplication that generates a product wider than the operands. Write the pattern for this as
>
> > (`mult:`*m* (`sign_extend:`*m x*) (`sign_extend:`*m y*))
>
> where *m* is wider than the modes of *x* and *y*, which need not be the same.
>
> For unsigned widening multiplication, use the same idiom, but with `zero_extend` instead of `sign_extend`.

(`fma:`*m x y z*)

> Represents the `fma`, `fmaf`, and `fmal` builtin functions, which compute '*x* * *y* + *z*' without doing an intermediate rounding step.

(`div:`*m x y*)
(`ss_div:`*m x y*)

> Represents the quotient in signed division of *x* by *y*, carried out in machine mode *m*. If *m* is a floating point mode, it represents the exact quotient; otherwise, the integerized quotient. `ss_div` ensures that an out-of-bounds result saturates to the maximum or minimum signed value.
>
> Some machines have division instructions in which the operands and quotient widths are not all the same; you should represent such instructions using `truncate` and `sign_extend` as in,
>
> > (`truncate:`*m1* (`div:`*m2 x* (`sign_extend:`*m2 y*)))

(`udiv:`*m x y*)
(`us_div:`*m x y*)

> Like `div` but represents unsigned division. `us_div` ensures that an out-of-bounds result saturates to the maximum or minimum unsigned value.

(`mod:`*m x y*)
(`umod:`*m x y*)

> Like `div` and `udiv` but represent the remainder instead of the quotient.

(`smin:`*m x y*)
(`smax:`*m x y*)

> Represents the smaller (for `smin`) or larger (for `smax`) of *x* and *y*, interpreted as signed values in mode *m*. When used with floating point, if both operands are zeros, or if either operand is NaN, then it is unspecified which of the two operands is returned as the result.

(`umin:`*m x y*)
(`umax:`*m x y*)

> Like `smin` and `smax`, but the values are interpreted as unsigned integers.

(not:*m x*) Represents the bitwise complement of the value represented by *x*, carried out in mode *m*, which must be a fixed-point machine mode.

(and:*m x y*)
:   Represents the bitwise logical-and of the values represented by *x* and *y*, carried out in machine mode *m*, which must be a fixed-point machine mode.

(ior:*m x y*)
:   Represents the bitwise inclusive-or of the values represented by *x* and *y*, carried out in machine mode *m*, which must be a fixed-point mode.

(xor:*m x y*)
:   Represents the bitwise exclusive-or of the values represented by *x* and *y*, carried out in machine mode *m*, which must be a fixed-point mode.

(ashift:*m x c*)
(ss_ashift:*m x c*)
(us_ashift:*m x c*)
:   These three expressions represent the result of arithmetically shifting *x* left by *c* places. They differ in their behavior on overflow of integer modes. An **ashift** operation is a plain shift with no special behavior in case of a change in the sign bit; **ss_ashift** and **us_ashift** saturates to the minimum or maximum representable value if any of the bits shifted out differs from the final sign bit.

    x have mode *m*, a fixed-point machine mode. *c* be a fixed-point mode or be a constant with mode **VOIDmode**; which mode is determined by the mode called for in the machine description entry for the left-shift instruction. For example, on the VAX, the mode of *c* is **QImode** regardless of *m*.

(lshiftrt:*m x c*)
(ashiftrt:*m x c*)
:   Like **ashift** but for right shift. Unlike the case for left shift, these two operations are distinct.

(rotate:*m x c*)
(rotatert:*m x c*)
:   Similar but represent left and right rotate. If *c* is a constant, use **rotate**.

(abs:*m x*)

(ss_abs:*m x*)
:   Represents the absolute value of *x*, computed in mode *m*. **ss_abs** ensures that an out-of-bounds result saturates to the maximum signed value.

(sqrt:*m x*)
:   Represents the square root of *x*, computed in mode *m*. Most often *m* will be a floating point mode.

(ffs:*m x*) Represents one plus the index of the least significant 1-bit in *x*, represented as an integer of mode *m*. (The value is zero if *x* is zero.) The mode of *x* must be *m* or **VOIDmode**.

(clrsb:*m x*)
:   Represents the number of redundant leading sign bits in *x*, represented as an integer of mode *m*, starting at the most significant bit position. This is one less

than the number of leading sign bits (either 0 or 1), with no special cases. The mode of x must be m or VOIDmode.

(clz:m x) Represents the number of leading 0-bits in x, represented as an integer of mode m, starting at the most significant bit position. If x is zero, the value is determined by CLZ_DEFINED_VALUE_AT_ZERO (see Section 18.30 [Misc], page 621). Note that this is one of the few expressions that is not invariant under widening. The mode of x must be m or VOIDmode.

(ctz:m x) Represents the number of trailing 0-bits in x, represented as an integer of mode m, starting at the least significant bit position. If x is zero, the value is determined by CTZ_DEFINED_VALUE_AT_ZERO (see Section 18.30 [Misc], page 621). Except for this case, ctz(x) is equivalent to ffs(x) - 1. The mode of x must be m or VOIDmode.

(popcount:m x)
　　Represents the number of 1-bits in x, represented as an integer of mode m. The mode of x must be m or VOIDmode.

(parity:m x)
　　Represents the number of 1-bits modulo 2 in x, represented as an integer of mode m. The mode of x must be m or VOIDmode.

(bswap:m x)
　　Represents the value x with the order of bytes reversed, carried out in mode m, which must be a fixed-point machine mode. The mode of x must be m or VOIDmode.

14.10 Comparison Operations

Comparison operators test a relation on two operands and are considered to represent a machine-dependent nonzero value described by, but not necessarily equal to, STORE_FLAG_VALUE (see Section 18.30 [Misc], page 621) if the relation holds, or zero if it does not, for comparison operators whose results have a 'MODE_INT' mode, FLOAT_STORE_FLAG_VALUE (see Section 18.30 [Misc], page 621) if the relation holds, or zero if it does not, for comparison operators that return floating-point values, and a vector of either VECTOR_STORE_FLAG_VALUE (see Section 18.30 [Misc], page 621) if the relation holds, or of zeros if it does not, for comparison operators that return vector results. The mode of the comparison operation is independent of the mode of the data being compared. If the comparison operation is being tested (e.g., the first operand of an if_then_else), the mode must be VOIDmode.

There are two ways that comparison operations may be used. The comparison operators may be used to compare the condition codes (cc0) against zero, as in (eq (cc0) (const_int 0)). Such a construct actually refers to the result of the preceding instruction in which the condition codes were set. The instruction setting the condition code must be adjacent to the instruction using the condition code; only note insns may separate them.

Alternatively, a comparison operation may directly compare two data objects. The mode of the comparison is determined by the operands; they must both be valid for a common machine mode. A comparison with both operands constant would be invalid as the machine mode could not be deduced from it, but such a comparison should never exist in RTL due to constant folding.

In the example above, if (cc0) were last set to (compare x y), the comparison operation is identical to (eq x y). Usually only one style of comparisons is supported on a particular machine, but the combine pass will try to merge the operations to produce the eq shown in case it exists in the context of the particular insn involved.

Inequality comparisons come in two flavors, signed and unsigned. Thus, there are distinct expression codes gt and gtu for signed and unsigned greater-than. These can produce different results for the same pair of integer values: for example, 1 is signed greater-than −1 but not unsigned greater-than, because −1 when regarded as unsigned is actually 0xffffffff which is greater than 1.

The signed comparisons are also used for floating point values. Floating point comparisons are distinguished by the machine modes of the operands.

(eq:*m x y*)
: STORE_FLAG_VALUE if the values represented by *x* and *y* are equal, otherwise 0.

(ne:*m x y*)
: STORE_FLAG_VALUE if the values represented by *x* and *y* are not equal, otherwise 0.

(gt:*m x y*)
: STORE_FLAG_VALUE if the *x* is greater than *y*. If they are fixed-point, the comparison is done in a signed sense.

(gtu:*m x y*)
: Like gt but does unsigned comparison, on fixed-point numbers only.

(lt:*m x y*)
(ltu:*m x y*)
: Like gt and gtu but test for "less than".

(ge:*m x y*)
(geu:*m x y*)
: Like gt and gtu but test for "greater than or equal".

(le:*m x y*)
(leu:*m x y*)
: Like gt and gtu but test for "less than or equal".

(if_then_else *cond then else*)
: This is not a comparison operation but is listed here because it is always used in conjunction with a comparison operation. To be precise, *cond* is a comparison expression. This expression represents a choice, according to *cond*, between the value represented by *then* and the one represented by *else*.

  On most machines, if_then_else expressions are valid only to express conditional jumps.

(cond [*test1 value1 test2 value2* ...] *default*)
: Similar to if_then_else, but more general. Each of *test1*, *test2*, ... is performed in turn. The result of this expression is the *value* corresponding to the first nonzero test, or *default* if none of the tests are nonzero expressions.

  This is currently not valid for instruction patterns and is supported only for insn attributes. See Section 17.19 [Insn Attributes], page 434.

14.11 Bit-Fields

Special expression codes exist to represent bit-field instructions.

(sign_extract:*m loc size pos*)
> This represents a reference to a sign-extended bit-field contained or starting in *loc* (a memory or register reference). The bit-field is *size* bits wide and starts at bit *pos*. The compilation option `BITS_BIG_ENDIAN` says which end of the memory unit *pos* counts from.
>
> If *loc* is in memory, its mode must be a single-byte integer mode. If *loc* is in a register, the mode to use is specified by the operand of the `insv` or `extv` pattern (see Section 17.9 [Standard Names], page 382) and is usually a full-word integer mode, which is the default if none is specified.
>
> The mode of *pos* is machine-specific and is also specified in the `insv` or `extv` pattern.
>
> The mode *m* is the same as the mode that would be used for *loc* if it were a register.
>
> A `sign_extract` can not appear as an lvalue, or part thereof, in RTL.

(zero_extract:*m loc size pos*)
> Like `sign_extract` but refers to an unsigned or zero-extended bit-field. The same sequence of bits are extracted, but they are filled to an entire word with zeros instead of by sign-extension.
>
> Unlike `sign_extract`, this type of expressions can be lvalues in RTL; they may appear on the left side of an assignment, indicating insertion of a value into the specified bit-field.

14.12 Vector Operations

All normal RTL expressions can be used with vector modes; they are interpreted as operating on each part of the vector independently. Additionally, there are a few new expressions to describe specific vector operations.

(vec_merge:*m vec1 vec2 items*)
> This describes a merge operation between two vectors. The result is a vector of mode *m*; its elements are selected from either *vec1* or *vec2*. Which elements are selected is described by *items*, which is a bit mask represented by a `const_int`; a zero bit indicates the corresponding element in the result vector is taken from *vec2* while a set bit indicates it is taken from *vec1*.

(vec_select:*m vec1 selection*)
> This describes an operation that selects parts of a vector. *vec1* is the source vector, and *selection* is a `parallel` that contains a `const_int` for each of the subparts of the result vector, giving the number of the source subpart that should be stored into it. The result mode *m* is either the submode for a single element of *vec1* (if only one subpart is selected), or another vector mode with that element submode (if multiple subparts are selected).

Chapter 14: RTL Representation 285

(vec_concat:*m x1 x2*)
: Describes a vector concat operation. The result is a concatenation of the vectors or scalars *x1* and *x2*; its length is the sum of the lengths of the two inputs.

(vec_duplicate:*m x*)
: This operation converts a scalar into a vector or a small vector into a larger one by duplicating the input values. The output vector mode must have the same submodes as the input vector mode or the scalar modes, and the number of output parts must be an integer multiple of the number of input parts.

(vec_series:*m base step*)
: This operation creates a vector in which element *i* is equal to '*base* + *i**step'. *m* must be a vector integer mode.

14.13 Conversions

All conversions between machine modes must be represented by explicit conversion operations. For example, an expression which is the sum of a byte and a full word cannot be written as (plus:SI (reg:QI 34) (reg:SI 80)) because the plus operation requires two operands of the same machine mode. Therefore, the byte-sized operand is enclosed in a conversion operation, as in

  (plus:SI (sign_extend:SI (reg:QI 34)) (reg:SI 80))

The conversion operation is not a mere placeholder, because there may be more than one way of converting from a given starting mode to the desired final mode. The conversion operation code says how to do it.

For all conversion operations, *x* must not be VOIDmode because the mode in which to do the conversion would not be known. The conversion must either be done at compile-time or *x* must be placed into a register.

(sign_extend:*m x*)
: Represents the result of sign-extending the value *x* to machine mode *m*. *m* must be a fixed-point mode and *x* a fixed-point value of a mode narrower than *m*.

(zero_extend:*m x*)
: Represents the result of zero-extending the value *x* to machine mode *m*. *m* must be a fixed-point mode and *x* a fixed-point value of a mode narrower than *m*.

(float_extend:*m x*)
: Represents the result of extending the value *x* to machine mode *m*. *m* must be a floating point mode and *x* a floating point value of a mode narrower than *m*.

(truncate:*m x*)
: Represents the result of truncating the value *x* to machine mode *m*. *m* must be a fixed-point mode and *x* a fixed-point value of a mode wider than *m*.

(ss_truncate:*m x*)
: Represents the result of truncating the value *x* to machine mode *m*, using signed saturation in the case of overflow. Both *m* and the mode of *x* must be fixed-point modes.

(us_truncate:*m x*)

> Represents the result of truncating the value *x* to machine mode *m*, using unsigned saturation in the case of overflow. Both *m* and the mode of *x* must be fixed-point modes.

(float_truncate:*m x*)

> Represents the result of truncating the value *x* to machine mode *m*. *m* must be a floating point mode and *x* a floating point value of a mode wider than *m*.

(float:*m x*)

> Represents the result of converting fixed point value *x*, regarded as signed, to floating point mode *m*.

(unsigned_float:*m x*)

> Represents the result of converting fixed point value *x*, regarded as unsigned, to floating point mode *m*.

(fix:*m x*) When *m* is a floating-point mode, represents the result of converting floating point value *x* (valid for mode *m*) to an integer, still represented in floating point mode *m*, by rounding towards zero.

> When *m* is a fixed-point mode, represents the result of converting floating point value *x* to mode *m*, regarded as signed. How rounding is done is not specified, so this operation may be used validly in compiling C code only for integer-valued operands.

(unsigned_fix:*m x*)

> Represents the result of converting floating point value *x* to fixed point mode *m*, regarded as unsigned. How rounding is done is not specified.

(fract_convert:*m x*)

> Represents the result of converting fixed-point value *x* to fixed-point mode *m*, signed integer value *x* to fixed-point mode *m*, floating-point value *x* to fixed-point mode *m*, fixed-point value *x* to integer mode *m* regarded as signed, or fixed-point value *x* to floating-point mode *m*. When overflows or underflows happen, the results are undefined.

(sat_fract:*m x*)

> Represents the result of converting fixed-point value *x* to fixed-point mode *m*, signed integer value *x* to fixed-point mode *m*, or floating-point value *x* to fixed-point mode *m*. When overflows or underflows happen, the results are saturated to the maximum or the minimum.

(unsigned_fract_convert:*m x*)

> Represents the result of converting fixed-point value *x* to integer mode *m* regarded as unsigned, or unsigned integer value *x* to fixed-point mode *m*. When overflows or underflows happen, the results are undefined.

(unsigned_sat_fract:*m x*)

> Represents the result of converting unsigned integer value *x* to fixed-point mode *m*. When overflows or underflows happen, the results are saturated to the maximum or the minimum.

14.14 Declarations

Declaration expression codes do not represent arithmetic operations but rather state assertions about their operands.

(strict_low_part (subreg:m (reg:n r) 0))

> This expression code is used in only one context: as the destination operand of a set expression. In addition, the operand of this expression must be a non-paradoxical subreg expression.
>
> The presence of strict_low_part says that the part of the register which is meaningful in mode n, but is not part of mode m, is not to be altered. Normally, an assignment to such a subreg is allowed to have undefined effects on the rest of the register when m is smaller than 'REGMODE_NATURAL_SIZE (n)'.

14.15 Side Effect Expressions

The expression codes described so far represent values, not actions. But machine instructions never produce values; they are meaningful only for their side effects on the state of the machine. Special expression codes are used to represent side effects.

The body of an instruction is always one of these side effect codes; the codes described above, which represent values, appear only as the operands of these.

(set lval x)

> Represents the action of storing the value of x into the place represented by lval. lval must be an expression representing a place that can be stored in: reg (or subreg, strict_low_part or zero_extract), mem, pc, parallel, or cc0.
>
> If lval is a reg, subreg or mem, it has a machine mode; then x must be valid for that mode.
>
> If lval is a reg whose machine mode is less than the full width of the register, then it means that the part of the register specified by the machine mode is given the specified value and the rest of the register receives an undefined value. Likewise, if lval is a subreg whose machine mode is narrower than the mode of the register, the rest of the register can be changed in an undefined way.
>
> If lval is a strict_low_part of a subreg, then the part of the register specified by the machine mode of the subreg is given the value x and the rest of the register is not changed.
>
> If lval is a zero_extract, then the referenced part of the bit-field (a memory or register reference) specified by the zero_extract is given the value x and the rest of the bit-field is not changed. Note that sign_extract can not appear in lval.
>
> If lval is (cc0), it has no machine mode, and x may be either a compare expression or a value that may have any mode. The latter case represents a "test" instruction. The expression (set (cc0) (reg:m n)) is equivalent to (set (cc0) (compare (reg:m n) (const_int 0))). Use the former expression to save space during the compilation.
>
> If lval is a parallel, it is used to represent the case of a function returning a structure in multiple registers. Each element of the parallel is an expr_list

whose first operand is a `reg` and whose second operand is a `const_int` representing the offset (in bytes) into the structure at which the data in that register corresponds. The first element may be null to indicate that the structure is also passed partly in memory.

If *lval* is `(pc)`, we have a jump instruction, and the possibilities for *x* are very limited. It may be a `label_ref` expression (unconditional jump). It may be an `if_then_else` (conditional jump), in which case either the second or the third operand must be `(pc)` (for the case which does not jump) and the other of the two must be a `label_ref` (for the case which does jump). *x* may also be a `mem` or `(plus:SI (pc) y)`, where *y* may be a `reg` or a `mem`; these unusual patterns are used to represent jumps through branch tables.

If *lval* is neither `(cc0)` nor `(pc)`, the mode of *lval* must not be `VOIDmode` and the mode of *x* must be valid for the mode of *lval*.

lval is customarily accessed with the `SET_DEST` macro and *x* with the `SET_SRC` macro.

`(return)` As the sole expression in a pattern, represents a return from the current function, on machines where this can be done with one instruction, such as VAXen. On machines where a multi-instruction "epilogue" must be executed in order to return from the function, returning is done by jumping to a label which precedes the epilogue, and the `return` expression code is never used.

Inside an `if_then_else` expression, represents the value to be placed in `pc` to return to the caller.

Note that an insn pattern of `(return)` is logically equivalent to `(set (pc) (return))`, but the latter form is never used.

`(simple_return)`
Like `(return)`, but truly represents only a function return, while `(return)` may represent an insn that also performs other functions of the function epilogue. Like `(return)`, this may also occur in conditional jumps.

`(call function nargs)`
Represents a function call. *function* is a `mem` expression whose address is the address of the function to be called. *nargs* is an expression which can be used for two purposes: on some machines it represents the number of bytes of stack argument; on others, it represents the number of argument registers.

Each machine has a standard machine mode which *function* must have. The machine description defines macro `FUNCTION_MODE` to expand into the requisite mode name. The purpose of this mode is to specify what kind of addressing is allowed, on machines where the allowed kinds of addressing depend on the machine mode being addressed.

`(clobber x)`
Represents the storing or possible storing of an unpredictable, undescribed value into *x*, which must be a `reg`, `scratch`, `parallel` or `mem` expression.

One place this is used is in string instructions that store standard values into particular hard registers. It may not be worth the trouble to describe the values that are stored, but it is essential to inform the compiler that the registers will be altered, lest it attempt to keep data in them across the string instruction.

If x is (mem:BLK (const_int 0)) or (mem:BLK (scratch)), it means that all memory locations must be presumed clobbered. If x is a parallel, it has the same meaning as a parallel in a set expression.

Note that the machine description classifies certain hard registers as "call-clobbered". All function call instructions are assumed by default to clobber these registers, so there is no need to use clobber expressions to indicate this fact. Also, each function call is assumed to have the potential to alter any memory location, unless the function is declared const.

If the last group of expressions in a parallel are each a clobber expression whose arguments are reg or match_scratch (see Section 17.4 [RTL Template], page 329) expressions, the combiner phase can add the appropriate clobber expressions to an insn it has constructed when doing so will cause a pattern to be matched.

This feature can be used, for example, on a machine that whose multiply and add instructions don't use an MQ register but which has an add-accumulate instruction that does clobber the MQ register. Similarly, a combined instruction might require a temporary register while the constituent instructions might not.

When a clobber expression for a register appears inside a parallel with other side effects, the register allocator guarantees that the register is unoccupied both before and after that insn if it is a hard register clobber. For pseudo-register clobber, the register allocator and the reload pass do not assign the same hard register to the clobber and the input operands if there is an insn alternative containing the '&' constraint (see Section 17.8.4 [Modifiers], page 346) for the clobber and the hard register is in register classes of the clobber in the alternative. You can clobber either a specific hard register, a pseudo register, or a scratch expression; in the latter two cases, GCC will allocate a hard register that is available there for use as a temporary.

For instructions that require a temporary register, you should use scratch instead of a pseudo-register because this will allow the combiner phase to add the clobber when required. You do this by coding (clobber (match_scratch ...)). If you do clobber a pseudo register, use one which appears nowhere else—generate a new one each time. Otherwise, you may confuse CSE.

There is one other known use for clobbering a pseudo register in a parallel: when one of the input operands of the insn is also clobbered by the insn. In this case, using the same pseudo register in the clobber and elsewhere in the insn produces the expected results.

(use x) Represents the use of the value of x. It indicates that the value in x at this point in the program is needed, even though it may not be apparent why this is so. Therefore, the compiler will not attempt to delete previous instructions whose only effect is to store a value in x. x must be a reg expression.

In some situations, it may be tempting to add a use of a register in a parallel to describe a situation where the value of a special register will modify the behavior of the instruction. A hypothetical example might be a pattern for an

addition that can either wrap around or use saturating addition depending on
the value of a special control register:

```
(parallel [(set (reg:SI 2) (unspec:SI [(reg:SI 3)
                                       (reg:SI 4)] 0))
           (use (reg:SI 1))])
```

This will not work, several of the optimizers only look at expressions locally; it
is very likely that if you have multiple insns with identical inputs to the unspec,
they will be optimized away even if register 1 changes in between.

This means that use can *only* be used to describe that the register is live. You
should think twice before adding use statements, more often you will want to
use unspec instead. The use RTX is most commonly useful to describe that
a fixed register is implicitly used in an insn. It is also safe to use in patterns
where the compiler knows for other reasons that the result of the whole pattern
is variable, such as 'movmem*m*' or 'call' patterns.

During the reload phase, an insn that has a use as pattern can carry a reg_equal
note. These use insns will be deleted before the reload phase exits.

During the delayed branch scheduling phase, x may be an insn. This indicates
that x previously was located at this place in the code and its data dependencies
need to be taken into account. These use insns will be deleted before the delayed
branch scheduling phase exits.

(parallel [*x0 x1* ...])

Represents several side effects performed in parallel. The square brackets stand
for a vector; the operand of parallel is a vector of expressions. *x0*, *x1* and so
on are individual side effect expressions—expressions of code set, call, return,
simple_return, clobber or use.

"In parallel" means that first all the values used in the individual side-effects are
computed, and second all the actual side-effects are performed. For example,

```
(parallel [(set (reg:SI 1) (mem:SI (reg:SI 1)))
           (set (mem:SI (reg:SI 1)) (reg:SI 1))])
```

says unambiguously that the values of hard register 1 and the memory location
addressed by it are interchanged. In both places where (reg:SI 1) appears as
a memory address it refers to the value in register 1 *before* the execution of the
insn.

It follows that it is *incorrect* to use parallel and expect the result of one set
to be available for the next one. For example, people sometimes attempt to
represent a jump-if-zero instruction this way:

```
(parallel [(set (cc0) (reg:SI 34))
           (set (pc) (if_then_else
                        (eq (cc0) (const_int 0))
                        (label_ref ...)
                        (pc)))])
```

But this is incorrect, because it says that the jump condition depends on the
condition code value *before* this instruction, not on the new value that is set by
this instruction.

Peephole optimization, which takes place together with final assembly code
output, can produce insns whose patterns consist of a parallel whose elements

Chapter 14: RTL Representation 291

are the operands needed to output the resulting assembler code—often `reg`, `mem` or constant expressions. This would not be well-formed RTL at any other stage in compilation, but it is OK then because no further optimization remains to be done. However, the definition of the macro `NOTICE_UPDATE_CC`, if any, must deal with such insns if you define any peephole optimizations.

`(cond_exec [cond expr])`

Represents a conditionally executed expression. The *expr* is executed only if the *cond* is nonzero. The *cond* expression must not have side-effects, but the *expr* may very well have side-effects.

`(sequence [insns ...])`

Represents a sequence of insns. If a `sequence` appears in the chain of insns, then each of the *insns* that appears in the sequence must be suitable for appearing in the chain of insns, i.e. must satisfy the `INSN_P` predicate.

After delay-slot scheduling is completed, an insn and all the insns that reside in its delay slots are grouped together into a `sequence`. The insn requiring the delay slot is the first insn in the vector; subsequent insns are to be placed in the delay slot.

`INSN_ANNULLED_BRANCH_P` is set on an insn in a delay slot to indicate that a branch insn should be used that will conditionally annul the effect of the insns in the delay slots. In such a case, `INSN_FROM_TARGET_P` indicates that the insn is from the target of the branch and should be executed only if the branch is taken; otherwise the insn should be executed only if the branch is not taken. See Section 17.19.8 [Delay Slots], page 443.

Some back ends also use `sequence` objects for purposes other than delay-slot groups. This is not supported in the common parts of the compiler, which treat such sequences as delay-slot groups.

DWARF2 Call Frame Address (CFA) adjustments are sometimes also expressed using `sequence` objects as the value of a `RTX_FRAME_RELATED_P` note. This only happens if the CFA adjustments cannot be easily derived from the pattern of the instruction to which the note is attached. In such cases, the value of the note is used instead of best-guesing the semantics of the instruction. The back end can attach notes containing a `sequence` of `set` patterns that express the effect of the parent instruction.

These expression codes appear in place of a side effect, as the body of an insn, though strictly speaking they do not always describe side effects as such:

`(asm_input s)`

Represents literal assembler code as described by the string *s*.

`(unspec [operands ...] index)`
`(unspec_volatile [operands ...] index)`

Represents a machine-specific operation on *operands*. *index* selects between multiple machine-specific operations. `unspec_volatile` is used for volatile operations and operations that may trap; `unspec` is used for other operations.

These codes may appear inside a `pattern` of an insn, inside a `parallel`, or inside an expression.

(addr_vec:m [lr0 lr1 ...])
: Represents a table of jump addresses. The vector elements lr0, etc., are `label_ref` expressions. The mode m specifies how much space is given to each address; normally m would be Pmode.

(addr_diff_vec:m base [lr0 lr1 ...] min max flags)
: Represents a table of jump addresses expressed as offsets from base. The vector elements lr0, etc., are `label_ref` expressions and so is base. The mode m specifies how much space is given to each address-difference. min and max are set up by branch shortening and hold a label with a minimum and a maximum address, respectively. flags indicates the relative position of base, min and max to the containing insn and of min and max to base. See rtl.def for details.

(prefetch:m addr rw locality)
: Represents prefetch of memory at address addr. Operand rw is 1 if the prefetch is for data to be written, 0 otherwise; targets that do not support write prefetches should treat this as a normal prefetch. Operand locality specifies the amount of temporal locality; 0 if there is none or 1, 2, or 3 for increasing levels of temporal locality; targets that do not support locality hints should ignore this.

  This insn is used to minimize cache-miss latency by moving data into a cache before it is accessed. It should use only non-faulting data prefetch instructions.

14.16 Embedded Side-Effects on Addresses

Six special side-effect expression codes appear as memory addresses.

(pre_dec:m x)
: Represents the side effect of decrementing x by a standard amount and represents also the value that x has after being decremented. x must be a `reg` or `mem`, but most machines allow only a `reg`. m must be the machine mode for pointers on the machine in use. The amount x is decremented by is the length in bytes of the machine mode of the containing memory reference of which this expression serves as the address. Here is an example of its use:

    (mem:DF (pre_dec:SI (reg:SI 39)))

  This says to decrement pseudo register 39 by the length of a DFmode value and use the result to address a DFmode value.

(pre_inc:m x)
: Similar, but specifies incrementing x instead of decrementing it.

(post_dec:m x)
: Represents the same side effect as `pre_dec` but a different value. The value represented here is the value x has *before* being decremented.

(post_inc:m x)
: Similar, but specifies incrementing x instead of decrementing it.

(post_modify:m x y)
: Represents the side effect of setting x to y and represents x before x is modified. x must be a `reg` or `mem`, but most machines allow only a `reg`. m must be the machine mode for pointers on the machine in use.

The expression *y* must be one of three forms: (plus:*m x z*), (minus:*m x z*), or (plus:*m x i*), where *z* is an index register and *i* is a constant.

Here is an example of its use:

```
(mem:SF (post_modify:SI (reg:SI 42) (plus (reg:SI 42)
                                          (reg:SI 48))))
```

This says to modify pseudo register 42 by adding the contents of pseudo register 48 to it, after the use of what ever 42 points to.

(pre_modify:*m x expr*)

    Similar except side effects happen before the use.

These embedded side effect expressions must be used with care. Instruction patterns may not use them. Until the 'flow' pass of the compiler, they may occur only to represent pushes onto the stack. The 'flow' pass finds cases where registers are incremented or decremented in one instruction and used as an address shortly before or after; these cases are then transformed to use pre- or post-increment or -decrement.

If a register used as the operand of these expressions is used in another address in an insn, the original value of the register is used. Uses of the register outside of an address are not permitted within the same insn as a use in an embedded side effect expression because such insns behave differently on different machines and hence must be treated as ambiguous and disallowed.

An instruction that can be represented with an embedded side effect could also be represented using parallel containing an additional set to describe how the address register is altered. This is not done because machines that allow these operations at all typically allow them wherever a memory address is called for. Describing them as additional parallel stores would require doubling the number of entries in the machine description.

14.17 Assembler Instructions as Expressions

The RTX code asm_operands represents a value produced by a user-specified assembler instruction. It is used to represent an asm statement with arguments. An asm statement with a single output operand, like this:

```
asm ("foo %1,%2,%0" : "=a" (outputvar) : "g" (x + y), "di" (*z));
```

is represented using a single asm_operands RTX which represents the value that is stored in outputvar:

```
(set rtx-for-outputvar
     (asm_operands "foo %1,%2,%0" "a" 0
                   [rtx-for-addition-result rtx-for-*z]
                   [(asm_input:m1 "g")
                    (asm_input:m2 "di")]))
```

Here the operands of the asm_operands RTX are the assembler template string, the output-operand's constraint, the index-number of the output operand among the output operands specified, a vector of input operand RTX's, and a vector of input-operand modes and constraints. The mode *m1* is the mode of the sum x+y; *m2* is that of *z.

When an asm statement has multiple output values, its insn has several such set RTX's inside of a parallel. Each set contains an asm_operands; all of these share the same assembler template and vectors, but each contains the constraint for the respective output operand. They are also distinguished by the output-operand index number, which is 0, 1, ... for successive output operands.

14.18 Variable Location Debug Information in RTL

Variable tracking relies on `MEM_EXPR` and `REG_EXPR` annotations to determine what user variables memory and register references refer to.

Variable tracking at assignments uses these notes only when they refer to variables that live at fixed locations (e.g., addressable variables, global non-automatic variables). For variables whose location may vary, it relies on the following types of notes.

(var_location:*mode var exp stat*)
: Binds variable *var*, a tree, to value *exp*, an RTL expression. It appears only in `NOTE_INSN_VAR_LOCATION` and `DEBUG_INSNs`, with slightly different meanings. *mode*, if present, represents the mode of *exp*, which is useful if it is a modeless expression. *stat* is only meaningful in notes, indicating whether the variable is known to be initialized or uninitialized.

(debug_expr:*mode decl*)
: Stands for the value bound to the `DEBUG_EXPR_DECL` *decl*, that points back to it, within value expressions in `VAR_LOCATION` nodes.

(debug_implicit_ptr:*mode decl*)
: Stands for the location of a *decl* that is no longer addressable.

(entry_value:*mode decl*)
: Stands for the value a *decl* had at the entry point of the containing function.

(debug_parameter_ref:*mode decl*)
: Refers to a parameter that was completely optimized out.

(debug_marker:*mode*)
: Marks a program location. With `VOIDmode`, it stands for the beginning of a statement, a recommended inspection point logically after all prior side effects, and before any subsequent side effects. With `BLKmode`, it indicates an inline entry point: the lexical block encoded in the `INSN_LOCATION` is the enclosing block that encloses the inlined function.

14.19 Insns

The RTL representation of the code for a function is a doubly-linked chain of objects called *insns*. Insns are expressions with special codes that are used for no other purpose. Some insns are actual instructions; others represent dispatch tables for `switch` statements; others represent labels to jump to or various sorts of declarative information.

In addition to its own specific data, each insn must have a unique id-number that distinguishes it from all other insns in the current function (after delayed branch scheduling, copies of an insn with the same id-number may be present in multiple places in a function, but these copies will always be identical and will only appear inside a `sequence`), and chain pointers to the preceding and following insns. These three fields occupy the same position in every insn, independent of the expression code of the insn. They could be accessed with `XEXP` and `XINT`, but instead three special macros are always used:

`INSN_UID (i)`
: Accesses the unique id of insn *i*.

PREV_INSN (*i*)
: Accesses the chain pointer to the insn preceding *i*. If *i* is the first insn, this is a null pointer.

NEXT_INSN (*i*)
: Accesses the chain pointer to the insn following *i*. If *i* is the last insn, this is a null pointer.

The first insn in the chain is obtained by calling `get_insns`; the last insn is the result of calling `get_last_insn`. Within the chain delimited by these insns, the NEXT_INSN and PREV_INSN pointers must always correspond: if *insn* is not the first insn,

        NEXT_INSN (PREV_INSN (*insn*)) == *insn*

is always true and if *insn* is not the last insn,

        PREV_INSN (NEXT_INSN (*insn*)) == *insn*

is always true.

After delay slot scheduling, some of the insns in the chain might be **sequence** expressions, which contain a vector of insns. The value of NEXT_INSN in all but the last of these insns is the next insn in the vector; the value of NEXT_INSN of the last insn in the vector is the same as the value of NEXT_INSN for the **sequence** in which it is contained. Similar rules apply for PREV_INSN.

This means that the above invariants are not necessarily true for insns inside **sequence** expressions. Specifically, if *insn* is the first insn in a **sequence**, NEXT_INSN (PREV_INSN (*insn*)) is the insn containing the **sequence** expression, as is the value of PREV_INSN (NEXT_INSN (*insn*)) if *insn* is the last insn in the **sequence** expression. You can use these expressions to find the containing **sequence** expression.

Every insn has one of the following expression codes:

insn
: The expression code **insn** is used for instructions that do not jump and do not do function calls. **sequence** expressions are always contained in insns with code **insn** even if one of those insns should jump or do function calls.

    Insns with code **insn** have four additional fields beyond the three mandatory ones listed above. These four are described in a table below.

jump_insn
: The expression code **jump_insn** is used for instructions that may jump (or, more generally, may contain **label_ref** expressions to which **pc** can be set in that instruction). If there is an instruction to return from the current function, it is recorded as a **jump_insn**.

    jump_insn insns have the same extra fields as **insn** insns, accessed in the same way and in addition contain a field JUMP_LABEL which is defined once jump optimization has completed.

    For simple conditional and unconditional jumps, this field contains the **code_label** to which this insn will (possibly conditionally) branch. In a more complex jump, JUMP_LABEL records one of the labels that the insn refers to; other jump target labels are recorded as REG_LABEL_TARGET notes. The exception is **addr_vec** and **addr_diff_vec**, where JUMP_LABEL is NULL_RTX and the only way to find the labels is to scan the entire body of the insn.

Return insns count as jumps, but their JUMP_LABEL is RETURN or SIMPLE_RETURN.

`call_insn`

The expression code `call_insn` is used for instructions that may do function calls. It is important to distinguish these instructions because they imply that certain registers and memory locations may be altered unpredictably.

`call_insn` insns have the same extra fields as `insn` insns, accessed in the same way and in addition contain a field `CALL_INSN_FUNCTION_USAGE`, which contains a list (chain of `expr_list` expressions) containing `use`, `clobber` and sometimes `set` expressions that denote hard registers and `mems` used or clobbered by the called function.

A `mem` generally points to a stack slot in which arguments passed to the libcall by reference (see Section 18.9.7 [Register Arguments], page 518) are stored. If the argument is caller-copied (see Section 18.9.7 [Register Arguments], page 518), the stack slot will be mentioned in `clobber` and `use` entries; if it's callee-copied, only a `use` will appear, and the `mem` may point to addresses that are not stack slots.

Registers occurring inside a `clobber` in this list augment registers specified in `CALL_USED_REGISTERS` (see Section 18.7.1 [Register Basics], page 487).

If the list contains a `set` involving two registers, it indicates that the function returns one of its arguments. Such a `set` may look like a no-op if the same register holds the argument and the return value.

`code_label`

A `code_label` insn represents a label that a jump insn can jump to. It contains two special fields of data in addition to the three standard ones. `CODE_LABEL_NUMBER` is used to hold the *label number*, a number that identifies this label uniquely among all the labels in the compilation (not just in the current function). Ultimately, the label is represented in the assembler output as an assembler label, usually of the form 'L*n*' where *n* is the label number.

When a `code_label` appears in an RTL expression, it normally appears within a `label_ref` which represents the address of the label, as a number.

Besides as a `code_label`, a label can also be represented as a `note` of type `NOTE_INSN_DELETED_LABEL`.

The field `LABEL_NUSES` is only defined once the jump optimization phase is completed. It contains the number of times this label is referenced in the current function.

The field `LABEL_KIND` differentiates four different types of labels: `LABEL_NORMAL`, `LABEL_STATIC_ENTRY`, `LABEL_GLOBAL_ENTRY`, and `LABEL_WEAK_ENTRY`. The only labels that do not have type `LABEL_NORMAL` are *alternate entry points* to the current function. These may be static (visible only in the containing translation unit), global (exposed to all translation units), or weak (global, but can be overridden by another symbol with the same name).

Much of the compiler treats all four kinds of label identically. Some of it needs to know whether or not a label is an alternate entry point; for this purpose, the macro LABEL_ALT_ENTRY_P is provided. It is equivalent to testing whether 'LABEL_KIND (label) == LABEL_NORMAL'. The only place that cares about the distinction between static, global, and weak alternate entry points, besides the front-end code that creates them, is the function output_alternate_entry_point, in 'final.c'.

To set the kind of a label, use the SET_LABEL_KIND macro.

jump_table_data
: A jump_table_data insn is a placeholder for the jump-table data of a casesi or tablejump insn. They are placed after a tablejump_p insn. A jump_table_data insn is not part o a basic blockm but it is associated with the basic block that ends with the tablejump_p insn. The PATTERN of a jump_table_data is always either an addr_vec or an addr_diff_vec, and a jump_table_data insn is always preceded by a code_label. The tablejump_p insn refers to that code_label via its JUMP_LABEL.

barrier
: Barriers are placed in the instruction stream when control cannot flow past them. They are placed after unconditional jump instructions to indicate that the jumps are unconditional and after calls to volatile functions, which do not return (e.g., exit). They contain no information beyond the three standard fields.

note
: note insns are used to represent additional debugging and declarative information. They contain two nonstandard fields, an integer which is accessed with the macro NOTE_LINE_NUMBER and a string accessed with NOTE_SOURCE_FILE.

    If NOTE_LINE_NUMBER is positive, the note represents the position of a source line and NOTE_SOURCE_FILE is the source file name that the line came from. These notes control generation of line number data in the assembler output.

    Otherwise, NOTE_LINE_NUMBER is not really a line number but a code with one of the following values (and NOTE_SOURCE_FILE must contain a null pointer):

    NOTE_INSN_DELETED
    : Such a note is completely ignorable. Some passes of the compiler delete insns by altering them into notes of this kind.

    NOTE_INSN_DELETED_LABEL
    : This marks what used to be a code_label, but was not used for other purposes than taking its address and was transformed to mark that no code jumps to it.

    NOTE_INSN_BLOCK_BEG
    NOTE_INSN_BLOCK_END
    : These types of notes indicate the position of the beginning and end of a level of scoping of variable names. They control the output of debugging information.

    NOTE_INSN_EH_REGION_BEG
    NOTE_INSN_EH_REGION_END
    : These types of notes indicate the position of the beginning and end of a level of scoping for exception handling. NOTE_EH_HANDLER identifies which region is associated with these notes.

NOTE_INSN_FUNCTION_BEG
: Appears at the start of the function body, after the function prologue.

NOTE_INSN_VAR_LOCATION
: This note is used to generate variable location debugging information. It indicates that the user variable in its `VAR_LOCATION` operand is at the location given in the RTL expression, or holds a value that can be computed by evaluating the RTL expression from that static point in the program up to the next such note for the same user variable.

NOTE_INSN_BEGIN_STMT
: This note is used to generate `is_stmt` markers in line number debuggign information. It indicates the beginning of a user statement.

NOTE_INSN_INLINE_ENTRY
: This note is used to generate `entry_pc` for inlined subroutines in debugging information. It indicates an inspection point at which all arguments for the inlined function have been bound, and before its first statement.

These codes are printed symbolically when they appear in debugging dumps.

`debug_insn`

The expression code `debug_insn` is used for pseudo-instructions that hold debugging information for variable tracking at assignments (see '-fvar-tracking-assignments' option). They are the RTL representation of GIMPLE_DEBUG statements (Section 12.8.7 [GIMPLE_DEBUG], page 219), with a `VAR_LOCATION` operand that binds a user variable tree to an RTL representation of the `value` in the corresponding statement. A DEBUG_EXPR in it stands for the value bound to the corresponding DEBUG_EXPR_DECL.

GIMPLE_DEBUG_BEGIN_STMT and GIMPLE_DEBUG_INLINE_ENTRY are expanded to RTL as a DEBUG_INSN with a DEBUG_MARKER PATTERN; the difference is the RTL mode: the former's DEBUG_MARKER is VOIDmode, whereas the latter is BLKmode; information about the inlined function can be taken from the lexical block encoded in the INSN_LOCATION. These DEBUG_INSNs, that do not carry VAR_LOCATION information, just DEBUG_MARKERs, can be detected by testing DEBUG_MARKER_INSN_P, whereas those that do can be recognized as DEBUG_BIND_INSN_P.

Throughout optimization passes, DEBUG_INSNs are not reordered with respect to each other, particularly during scheduling. Binding information is kept in pseudo-instruction form, so that, unlike notes, it gets the same treatment and adjustments that regular instructions would. It is the variable tracking pass that turns these pseudo-instructions into NOTE_INSN_VAR_LOCATION, NOTE_INSN_BEGIN_STMT and NOTE_INSN_INLINE_ENTRY notes, analyzing control flow, value equivalences and changes to registers and memory referenced in value expressions, propagating the values of debug temporaries and determining expressions that can be used to compute the value of each user variable at as many points (ranges, actually) in the program as possible.

Unlike `NOTE_INSN_VAR_LOCATION`, the value expression in an `INSN_VAR_LOCATION` denotes a value at that specific point in the program, rather than an expression that can be evaluated at any later point before an overriding `VAR_LOCATION` is encountered. E.g., if a user variable is bound to a `REG` and then a subsequent insn modifies the `REG`, the note location would keep mapping the user variable to the register across the insn, whereas the insn location would keep the variable bound to the value, so that the variable tracking pass would emit another location note for the variable at the point in which the register is modified.

The machine mode of an insn is normally `VOIDmode`, but some phases use the mode for various purposes.

The common subexpression elimination pass sets the mode of an insn to `QImode` when it is the first insn in a block that has already been processed.

The second Haifa scheduling pass, for targets that can multiple issue, sets the mode of an insn to `TImode` when it is believed that the instruction begins an issue group. That is, when the instruction cannot issue simultaneously with the previous. This may be relied on by later passes, in particular machine-dependent reorg.

Here is a table of the extra fields of `insn`, `jump_insn` and `call_insn` insns:

PATTERN (*i*)
> An expression for the side effect performed by this insn. This must be one of the following codes: `set`, `call`, `use`, `clobber`, `return`, `simple_return`, `asm_input`, `asm_output`, `addr_vec`, `addr_diff_vec`, `trap_if`, `unspec`, `unspec_volatile`, `parallel`, `cond_exec`, or `sequence`. If it is a `parallel`, each element of the `parallel` must be one these codes, except that `parallel` expressions cannot be nested and `addr_vec` and `addr_diff_vec` are not permitted inside a `parallel` expression.

INSN_CODE (*i*)
> An integer that says which pattern in the machine description matches this insn, or −1 if the matching has not yet been attempted.
>
> Such matching is never attempted and this field remains −1 on an insn whose pattern consists of a single `use`, `clobber`, `asm_input`, `addr_vec` or `addr_diff_vec` expression.
>
> Matching is also never attempted on insns that result from an `asm` statement. These contain at least one `asm_operands` expression. The function `asm_noperands` returns a non-negative value for such insns.
>
> In the debugging output, this field is printed as a number followed by a symbolic representation that locates the pattern in the 'md' file as some small positive or negative offset from a named pattern.

LOG_LINKS (*i*)
> A list (chain of `insn_list` expressions) giving information about dependencies between instructions within a basic block. Neither a jump nor a label may come between the related insns. These are only used by the schedulers and by combine. This is a deprecated data structure. Def-use and use-def chains are now preferred.

REG_NOTES (i)

> A list (chain of `expr_list`, `insn_list` and `int_list` expressions) giving miscellaneous information about the insn. It is often information pertaining to the registers used in this insn.

The `LOG_LINKS` field of an insn is a chain of `insn_list` expressions. Each of these has two operands: the first is an insn, and the second is another `insn_list` expression (the next one in the chain). The last `insn_list` in the chain has a null pointer as second operand. The significant thing about the chain is which insns appear in it (as first operands of `insn_list` expressions). Their order is not significant.

This list is originally set up by the flow analysis pass; it is a null pointer until then. Flow only adds links for those data dependencies which can be used for instruction combination. For each insn, the flow analysis pass adds a link to insns which store into registers values that are used for the first time in this insn.

The `REG_NOTES` field of an insn is a chain similar to the `LOG_LINKS` field but it includes `expr_list` and `int_list` expressions in addition to `insn_list` expressions. There are several kinds of register notes, which are distinguished by the machine mode, which in a register note is really understood as being an `enum reg_note`. The first operand *op* of the note is data whose meaning depends on the kind of note.

The macro `REG_NOTE_KIND (x)` returns the kind of register note. Its counterpart, the macro `PUT_REG_NOTE_KIND (x, newkind)` sets the register note type of *x* to be *newkind*.

Register notes are of three classes: They may say something about an input to an insn, they may say something about an output of an insn, or they may create a linkage between two insns. There are also a set of values that are only used in `LOG_LINKS`.

These register notes annotate inputs to an insn:

REG_DEAD
> The value in *op* dies in this insn; that is to say, altering the value immediately after this insn would not affect the future behavior of the program.
>
> It does not follow that the register *op* has no useful value after this insn since *op* is not necessarily modified by this insn. Rather, no subsequent instruction uses the contents of *op*.

REG_UNUSED
> The register *op* being set by this insn will not be used in a subsequent insn. This differs from a `REG_DEAD` note, which indicates that the value in an input will not be used subsequently. These two notes are independent; both may be present for the same register.

REG_INC
> The register *op* is incremented (or decremented; at this level there is no distinction) by an embedded side effect inside this insn. This means it appears in a `post_inc`, `pre_inc`, `post_dec` or `pre_dec` expression.

REG_NONNEG
> The register *op* is known to have a nonnegative value when this insn is reached. This is used so that decrement and branch until zero instructions, such as the m68k dbra, can be matched.
>
> The `REG_NONNEG` note is added to insns only if the machine description has a 'decrement_and_branch_until_zero' pattern.

REG_LABEL_OPERAND

> This insn uses *op*, a `code_label` or a `note` of type `NOTE_INSN_DELETED_LABEL`, but is not a `jump_insn`, or it is a `jump_insn` that refers to the operand as an ordinary operand. The label may still eventually be a jump target, but if so in an indirect jump in a subsequent insn. The presence of this note allows jump optimization to be aware that *op* is, in fact, being used, and flow optimization to build an accurate flow graph.

REG_LABEL_TARGET

> This insn is a `jump_insn` but not an `addr_vec` or `addr_diff_vec`. It uses *op*, a `code_label` as a direct or indirect jump target. Its purpose is similar to that of `REG_LABEL_OPERAND`. This note is only present if the insn has multiple targets; the last label in the insn (in the highest numbered insn-field) goes into the `JUMP_LABEL` field and does not have a `REG_LABEL_TARGET` note. See Section 14.19 [Insns], page 294.

REG_SETJMP

> Appears attached to each `CALL_INSN` to `setjmp` or a related function.

The following notes describe attributes of outputs of an insn:

REG_EQUIV
REG_EQUAL

> This note is only valid on an insn that sets only one register and indicates that that register will be equal to *op* at run time; the scope of this equivalence differs between the two types of notes. The value which the insn explicitly copies into the register may look different from *op*, but they will be equal at run time. If the output of the single `set` is a `strict_low_part` or `zero_extract` expression, the note refers to the register that is contained in its first operand.
>
> For `REG_EQUIV`, the register is equivalent to *op* throughout the entire function, and could validly be replaced in all its occurrences by *op*. ("Validly" here refers to the data flow of the program; simple replacement may make some insns invalid.) For example, when a constant is loaded into a register that is never assigned any other value, this kind of note is used.
>
> When a parameter is copied into a pseudo-register at entry to a function, a note of this kind records that the register is equivalent to the stack slot where the parameter was passed. Although in this case the register may be set by other insns, it is still valid to replace the register by the stack slot throughout the function.
>
> A `REG_EQUIV` note is also used on an instruction which copies a register parameter into a pseudo-register at entry to a function, if there is a stack slot where that parameter could be stored. Although other insns may set the pseudo-register, it is valid for the compiler to replace the pseudo-register by stack slot throughout the function, provided the compiler ensures that the stack slot is properly initialized by making the replacement in the initial copy instruction as well. This is used on machines for which the calling convention allocates stack space for register parameters. See `REG_PARM_STACK_SPACE` in Section 18.9.6 [Stack Arguments], page 516.

In the case of `REG_EQUAL`, the register that is set by this insn will be equal to *op* at run time at the end of this insn but not necessarily elsewhere in the function. In this case, *op* is typically an arithmetic expression. For example, when a sequence of insns such as a library call is used to perform an arithmetic operation, this kind of note is attached to the insn that produces or copies the final value.

These two notes are used in different ways by the compiler passes. `REG_EQUAL` is used by passes prior to register allocation (such as common subexpression elimination and loop optimization) to tell them how to think of that value. `REG_EQUIV` notes are used by register allocation to indicate that there is an available substitute expression (either a constant or a `mem` expression for the location of a parameter on the stack) that may be used in place of a register if insufficient registers are available.

Except for stack homes for parameters, which are indicated by a `REG_EQUIV` note and are not useful to the early optimization passes and pseudo registers that are equivalent to a memory location throughout their entire life, which is not detected until later in the compilation, all equivalences are initially indicated by an attached `REG_EQUAL` note. In the early stages of register allocation, a `REG_EQUAL` note is changed into a `REG_EQUIV` note if *op* is a constant and the insn represents the only set of its destination register.

Thus, compiler passes prior to register allocation need only check for `REG_EQUAL` notes and passes subsequent to register allocation need only check for `REG_EQUIV` notes.

These notes describe linkages between insns. They occur in pairs: one insn has one of a pair of notes that points to a second insn, which has the inverse note pointing back to the first insn.

`REG_CC_SETTER`
`REG_CC_USER`

> On machines that use cc0, the insns which set and use cc0 set and use cc0 are adjacent. However, when branch delay slot filling is done, this may no longer be true. In this case a `REG_CC_USER` note will be placed on the insn setting cc0 to point to the insn using cc0 and a `REG_CC_SETTER` note will be placed on the insn using cc0 to point to the insn setting cc0.

These values are only used in the `LOG_LINKS` field, and indicate the type of dependency that each link represents. Links which indicate a data dependence (a read after write dependence) do not use any code, they simply have mode `VOIDmode`, and are printed without any descriptive text.

`REG_DEP_TRUE`

> This indicates a true dependence (a read after write dependence).

`REG_DEP_OUTPUT`

> This indicates an output dependence (a write after write dependence).

`REG_DEP_ANTI`

> This indicates an anti dependence (a write after read dependence).

Chapter 14: RTL Representation 303

These notes describe information gathered from gcov profile data. They are stored in the `REG_NOTES` field of an insn.

REG_BR_PROB

This is used to specify the ratio of branches to non-branches of a branch insn according to the profile data. The note is represented as an `int_list` expression whose integer value is an encoding of `profile_probability` type. `profile_probability` provide member function `from_reg_br_prob_note` and `to_reg_br_prob_note` to extract and store the probability into the RTL encoding.

REG_BR_PRED

These notes are found in JUMP insns after delayed branch scheduling has taken place. They indicate both the direction and the likelihood of the JUMP. The format is a bitmask of ATTR_FLAG_* values.

REG_FRAME_RELATED_EXPR

This is used on an RTX_FRAME_RELATED_P insn wherein the attached expression is used in place of the actual insn pattern. This is done in cases where the pattern is either complex or misleading.

The note REG_CALL_NOCF_CHECK is used in conjunction with the '-fcf-protection=branch' option. The note is set if a `nocf_check` attribute is specified for a function type or a pointer to function type. The note is stored in the `REG_NOTES` field of an insn.

REG_CALL_NOCF_CHECK

Users have control through the `nocf_check` attribute to identify which calls to a function should be skipped from control-flow instrumentation when the option '-fcf-protection=branch' is specified. The compiler puts a REG_CALL_NOCF_CHECK note on each CALL_INSN instruction that has a function type marked with a `nocf_check` attribute.

For convenience, the machine mode in an `insn_list` or `expr_list` is printed using these symbolic codes in debugging dumps.

The only difference between the expression codes `insn_list` and `expr_list` is that the first operand of an `insn_list` is assumed to be an insn and is printed in debugging dumps as the insn's unique id; the first operand of an `expr_list` is printed in the ordinary way as an expression.

14.20 RTL Representation of Function-Call Insns

Insns that call subroutines have the RTL expression code `call_insn`. These insns must satisfy special rules, and their bodies must use a special RTL expression code, `call`.

A `call` expression has two operands, as follows:

    (call (mem:fm addr) nbytes)

Here *nbytes* is an operand that represents the number of bytes of argument data being passed to the subroutine, *fm* is a machine mode (which must equal as the definition of the `FUNCTION_MODE` macro in the machine description) and *addr* represents the address of the subroutine.

For a subroutine that returns no value, the `call` expression as shown above is the entire body of the insn, except that the insn might also contain `use` or `clobber` expressions.

For a subroutine that returns a value whose mode is not `BLKmode`, the value is returned in a hard register. If this register's number is *r*, then the body of the call insn looks like this:

```
(set (reg:m r)
     (call (mem:fm addr) nbytes))
```

This RTL expression makes it clear (to the optimizer passes) that the appropriate register receives a useful value in this insn.

When a subroutine returns a `BLKmode` value, it is handled by passing to the subroutine the address of a place to store the value. So the call insn itself does not "return" any value, and it has the same RTL form as a call that returns nothing.

On some machines, the call instruction itself clobbers some register, for example to contain the return address. `call_insn` insns on these machines should have a body which is a `parallel` that contains both the `call` expression and `clobber` expressions that indicate which registers are destroyed. Similarly, if the call instruction requires some register other than the stack pointer that is not explicitly mentioned in its RTL, a `use` subexpression should mention that register.

Functions that are called are assumed to modify all registers listed in the configuration macro `CALL_USED_REGISTERS` (see Section 18.7.1 [Register Basics], page 487) and, with the exception of `const` functions and library calls, to modify all of memory.

Insns containing just `use` expressions directly precede the `call_insn` insn to indicate which registers contain inputs to the function. Similarly, if registers other than those in `CALL_USED_REGISTERS` are clobbered by the called function, insns containing a single `clobber` follow immediately after the call to indicate which registers.

14.21 Structure Sharing Assumptions

The compiler assumes that certain kinds of RTL expressions are unique; there do not exist two distinct objects representing the same value. In other cases, it makes an opposite assumption: that no RTL expression object of a certain kind appears in more than one place in the containing structure.

These assumptions refer to a single function; except for the RTL objects that describe global variables and external functions, and a few standard objects such as small integer constants, no RTL objects are common to two functions.

- Each pseudo-register has only a single `reg` object to represent it, and therefore only a single machine mode.
- For any symbolic label, there is only one `symbol_ref` object referring to it.
- All `const_int` expressions with equal values are shared.
- All `const_poly_int` expressions with equal modes and values are shared.
- There is only one `pc` expression.
- There is only one `cc0` expression.
- There is only one `const_double` expression with value 0 for each floating point mode. Likewise for values 1 and 2.
- There is only one `const_vector` expression with value 0 for each vector mode, be it an integer or a double constant vector.

- No `label_ref` or `scratch` appears in more than one place in the RTL structure; in other words, it is safe to do a tree-walk of all the insns in the function and assume that each time a `label_ref` or `scratch` is seen it is distinct from all others that are seen.
- Only one `mem` object is normally created for each static variable or stack slot, so these objects are frequently shared in all the places they appear. However, separate but equal objects for these variables are occasionally made.
- When a single `asm` statement has multiple output operands, a distinct `asm_operands` expression is made for each output operand. However, these all share the vector which contains the sequence of input operands. This sharing is used later on to test whether two `asm_operands` expressions come from the same statement, so all optimizations must carefully preserve the sharing if they copy the vector at all.
- No RTL object appears in more than one place in the RTL structure except as described above. Many passes of the compiler rely on this by assuming that they can modify RTL objects in place without unwanted side-effects on other insns.
- During initial RTL generation, shared structure is freely introduced. After all the RTL for a function has been generated, all shared structure is copied by `unshare_all_rtl` in 'emit-rtl.c', after which the above rules are guaranteed to be followed.
- During the combiner pass, shared structure within an insn can exist temporarily. However, the shared structure is copied before the combiner is finished with the insn. This is done by calling `copy_rtx_if_shared`, which is a subroutine of `unshare_all_rtl`.

14.22 Reading RTL

To read an RTL object from a file, call `read_rtx`. It takes one argument, a stdio stream, and returns a single RTL object. This routine is defined in 'read-rtl.c'. It is not available in the compiler itself, only the various programs that generate the compiler back end from the machine description.

People frequently have the idea of using RTL stored as text in a file as an interface between a language front end and the bulk of GCC. This idea is not feasible.

GCC was designed to use RTL internally only. Correct RTL for a given program is very dependent on the particular target machine. And the RTL does not contain all the information about the program.

The proper way to interface GCC to a new language front end is with the "tree" data structure, described in the files 'tree.h' and 'tree.def'. The documentation for this structure (see Chapter 11 [GENERIC], page 153) is incomplete.

15 Control Flow Graph

A control flow graph (CFG) is a data structure built on top of the intermediate code representation (the RTL or GIMPLE instruction stream) abstracting the control flow behavior of a function that is being compiled. The CFG is a directed graph where the vertices represent basic blocks and edges represent possible transfer of control flow from one basic block to another. The data structures used to represent the control flow graph are defined in 'basic-block.h'.

In GCC, the representation of control flow is maintained throughout the compilation process, from constructing the CFG early in `pass_build_cfg` to `pass_free_cfg` (see 'passes.def'). The CFG takes various different modes and may undergo extensive manipulations, but the graph is always valid between its construction and its release. This way, transfer of information such as data flow, a measured profile, or the loop tree, can be propagated through the passes pipeline, and even from GIMPLE to RTL.

Often the CFG may be better viewed as integral part of instruction chain, than structure built on the top of it. Updating the compiler's intermediate representation for instructions can not be easily done without proper maintenance of the CFG simultaneously.

15.1 Basic Blocks

A basic block is a straight-line sequence of code with only one entry point and only one exit. In GCC, basic blocks are represented using the `basic_block` data type.

Special basic blocks represent possible entry and exit points of a function. These blocks are called `ENTRY_BLOCK_PTR` and `EXIT_BLOCK_PTR`. These blocks do not contain any code.

The `BASIC_BLOCK` array contains all basic blocks in an unspecified order. Each `basic_block` structure has a field that holds a unique integer identifier `index` that is the index of the block in the `BASIC_BLOCK` array. The total number of basic blocks in the function is `n_basic_blocks`. Both the basic block indices and the total number of basic blocks may vary during the compilation process, as passes reorder, create, duplicate, and destroy basic blocks. The index for any block should never be greater than `last_basic_block`. The indices 0 and 1 are special codes reserved for `ENTRY_BLOCK` and `EXIT_BLOCK`, the indices of `ENTRY_BLOCK_PTR` and `EXIT_BLOCK_PTR`.

Two pointer members of the `basic_block` structure are the pointers `next_bb` and `prev_bb`. These are used to keep doubly linked chain of basic blocks in the same order as the underlying instruction stream. The chain of basic blocks is updated transparently by the provided API for manipulating the CFG. The macro `FOR_EACH_BB` can be used to visit all the basic blocks in lexicographical order, except `ENTRY_BLOCK` and `EXIT_BLOCK`. The macro `FOR_ALL_BB` also visits all basic blocks in lexicographical order, including `ENTRY_BLOCK` and `EXIT_BLOCK`.

The functions `post_order_compute` and `inverted_post_order_compute` can be used to compute topological orders of the CFG. The orders are stored as vectors of basic block indices. The `BASIC_BLOCK` array can be used to iterate each basic block by index. Dominator traversals are also possible using `walk_dominator_tree`. Given two basic blocks A and B, block A dominates block B if A is *always* executed before B.

Each `basic_block` also contains pointers to the first instruction (the *head*) and the last instruction (the *tail*) or *end* of the instruction stream contained in a basic block. In fact, since the `basic_block` data type is used to represent blocks in both major intermediate representations of GCC (GIMPLE and RTL), there are pointers to the head and end of a basic block for both representations, stored in intermediate representation specific data in the il field of struct `basic_block_def`.

For RTL, these pointers are `BB_HEAD` and `BB_END`.

In the RTL representation of a function, the instruction stream contains not only the "real" instructions, but also *notes* or *insn notes* (to distinguish them from *reg notes*). Any function that moves or duplicates the basic blocks needs to take care of updating of these notes. Many of these notes expect that the instruction stream consists of linear regions, so updating can sometimes be tedious. All types of insn notes are defined in '`insn-notes.def`'.

In the RTL function representation, the instructions contained in a basic block always follow a `NOTE_INSN_BASIC_BLOCK`, but zero or more `CODE_LABEL` nodes can precede the block note. A basic block ends with a control flow instruction or with the last instruction before the next `CODE_LABEL` or `NOTE_INSN_BASIC_BLOCK`. By definition, a `CODE_LABEL` cannot appear in the middle of the instruction stream of a basic block.

In addition to notes, the jump table vectors are also represented as "pseudo-instructions" inside the insn stream. These vectors never appear in the basic block and should always be placed just after the table jump instructions referencing them. After removing the table-jump it is often difficult to eliminate the code computing the address and referencing the vector, so cleaning up these vectors is postponed until after liveness analysis. Thus the jump table vectors may appear in the insn stream unreferenced and without any purpose. Before any edge is made *fall-thru*, the existence of such construct in the way needs to be checked by calling `can_fallthru` function.

For the GIMPLE representation, the PHI nodes and statements contained in a basic block are in a `gimple_seq` pointed to by the basic block intermediate language specific pointers. Abstract containers and iterators are used to access the PHI nodes and statements in a basic blocks. These iterators are called *GIMPLE statement iterators* (GSIs). Grep for ^gsi in the various '`gimple-*`' and '`tree-*`' files. There is a `gimple_stmt_iterator` type for iterating over all kinds of statement, and a `gphi_iterator` subclass for iterating over PHI nodes. The following snippet will pretty-print all PHI nodes the statements of the current function in the GIMPLE representation.

```
basic_block bb;

FOR_EACH_BB (bb)
  {
    gphi_iterator pi;
    gimple_stmt_iterator si;

    for (pi = gsi_start_phis (bb); !gsi_end_p (pi); gsi_next (&pi))
      {
        gphi *phi = pi.phi ();
        print_gimple_stmt (dump_file, phi, 0, TDF_SLIM);
      }
    for (si = gsi_start_bb (bb); !gsi_end_p (si); gsi_next (&si))
      {
        gimple stmt = gsi_stmt (si);
        print_gimple_stmt (dump_file, stmt, 0, TDF_SLIM);
      }
  }
```

15.2 Edges

Edges represent possible control flow transfers from the end of some basic block A to the head of another basic block B. We say that A is a predecessor of B, and B is a successor of A. Edges are represented in GCC with the `edge` data type. Each `edge` acts as a link between two basic blocks: The `src` member of an edge points to the predecessor basic block of the `dest` basic block. The members `preds` and `succs` of the `basic_block` data type point to type-safe vectors of edges to the predecessors and successors of the block.

When walking the edges in an edge vector, *edge iterators* should be used. Edge iterators are constructed using the `edge_iterator` data structure and several methods are available to operate on them:

`ei_start` This function initializes an `edge_iterator` that points to the first edge in a vector of edges.

`ei_last` This function initializes an `edge_iterator` that points to the last edge in a vector of edges.

`ei_end_p` This predicate is `true` if an `edge_iterator` represents the last edge in an edge vector.

`ei_one_before_end_p`
    This predicate is `true` if an `edge_iterator` represents the second last edge in an edge vector.

`ei_next` This function takes a pointer to an `edge_iterator` and makes it point to the next edge in the sequence.

`ei_prev` This function takes a pointer to an `edge_iterator` and makes it point to the previous edge in the sequence.

`ei_edge` This function returns the `edge` currently pointed to by an `edge_iterator`.

`ei_safe_safe`
    This function returns the `edge` currently pointed to by an `edge_iterator`, but returns `NULL` if the iterator is pointing at the end of the sequence. This function has been provided for existing code makes the assumption that a `NULL` edge indicates the end of the sequence.

The convenience macro `FOR_EACH_EDGE` can be used to visit all of the edges in a sequence of predecessor or successor edges. It must not be used when an element might be removed during the traversal, otherwise elements will be missed. Here is an example of how to use the macro.

```
edge e;
edge_iterator ei;

FOR_EACH_EDGE (e, ei, bb->succs)
  {
    if (e->flags & EDGE_FALLTHRU)
      break;
  }
```

There are various reasons why control flow may transfer from one block to another. One possibility is that some instruction, for example a `CODE_LABEL`, in a linearized instruction stream just always starts a new basic block. In this case a *fall-thru* edge links the basic block to the first following basic block. But there are several other reasons why edges may be created. The `flags` field of the `edge` data type is used to store information about the type of edge we are dealing with. Each edge is of one of the following types:

jump No type flags are set for edges corresponding to jump instructions. These edges are used for unconditional or conditional jumps and in RTL also for table jumps. They are the easiest to manipulate as they may be freely redirected when the flow graph is not in SSA form.

fall-thru Fall-thru edges are present in case where the basic block may continue execution to the following one without branching. These edges have the `EDGE_FALLTHRU` flag set. Unlike other types of edges, these edges must come into the basic block immediately following in the instruction stream. The function `force_nonfallthru` is available to insert an unconditional jump in the case that redirection is needed. Note that this may require creation of a new basic block.

exception handling

Exception handling edges represent possible control transfers from a trapping instruction to an exception handler. The definition of "trapping" varies. In C++, only function calls can throw, but for Ada exceptions like division by zero or segmentation fault are defined and thus each instruction possibly throwing this kind of exception needs to be handled as control flow instruction. Exception edges have the `EDGE_ABNORMAL` and `EDGE_EH` flags set.

When updating the instruction stream it is easy to change possibly trapping instruction to non-trapping, by simply removing the exception edge. The opposite conversion is difficult, but should not happen anyway. The edges can be eliminated via `purge_dead_edges` call.

In the RTL representation, the destination of an exception edge is specified by `REG_EH_REGION` note attached to the insn. In case of a trapping call the `EDGE_ABNORMAL_CALL` flag is set too. In the GIMPLE representation, this extra flag is not set.

In the RTL representation, the predicate `may_trap_p` may be used to check whether instruction still may trap or not. For the tree representation, the `tree_could_trap_p` predicate is available, but this predicate only checks for possible memory traps, as in dereferencing an invalid pointer location.

sibling calls

Sibling calls or tail calls terminate the function in a non-standard way and thus an edge to the exit must be present. `EDGE_SIBCALL` and `EDGE_ABNORMAL` are set in such case. These edges only exist in the RTL representation.

computed jumps

Computed jumps contain edges to all labels in the function referenced from the code. All those edges have `EDGE_ABNORMAL` flag set. The edges used to represent computed jumps often cause compile time performance problems, since functions consisting of many taken labels and many computed jumps may have *very* dense flow graphs, so these edges need to be handled with special

Chapter 15: Control Flow Graph   311

care. During the earlier stages of the compilation process, GCC tries to avoid
such dense flow graphs by factoring computed jumps. For example, given the
following series of jumps,
```
goto *x;
[ ... ]

goto *x;
[ ... ]

goto *x;
[ ... ]
```
factoring the computed jumps results in the following code sequence which has
a much simpler flow graph:
```
goto y;
[ ... ]

goto y;
[ ... ]

goto y;
[ ... ]

y:
   goto *x;
```
However, the classic problem with this transformation is that it has a runtime
cost in there resulting code: An extra jump. Therefore, the computed jumps
are un-factored in the later passes of the compiler (in the pass called `pass_duplicate_computed_gotos`). Be aware of that when you work on passes in
that area. There have been numerous examples already where the compile time
for code with unfactored computed jumps caused some serious headaches.

nonlocal goto handlers

GCC allows nested functions to return into caller using a `goto` to a label passed
to as an argument to the callee. The labels passed to nested functions contain
special code to cleanup after function call. Such sections of code are referred to
as "nonlocal goto receivers". If a function contains such nonlocal goto receivers,
an edge from the call to the label is created with the `EDGE_ABNORMAL` and `EDGE_ABNORMAL_CALL` flags set.

function entry points

By definition, execution of function starts at basic block 0, so there is always
an edge from the `ENTRY_BLOCK_PTR` to basic block 0. There is no GIMPLE
representation for alternate entry points at this moment. In RTL, alternate
entry points are specified by `CODE_LABEL` with `LABEL_ALTERNATE_NAME` defined.
This feature is currently used for multiple entry point prologues and is limited
to post-reload passes only. This can be used by back-ends to emit alternate
prologues for functions called from different contexts. In future full support for
multiple entry functions defined by Fortran 90 needs to be implemented.

function exits

In the pre-reload representation a function terminates after the last instruction
in the insn chain and no explicit return instructions are used. This corresponds

to the fall-thru edge into exit block. After reload, optimal RTL epilogues are used that use explicit (conditional) return instructions that are represented by edges with no flags set.

15.3 Profile information

In many cases a compiler must make a choice whether to trade speed in one part of code for speed in another, or to trade code size for code speed. In such cases it is useful to know information about how often some given block will be executed. That is the purpose for maintaining profile within the flow graph. GCC can handle profile information obtained through *profile feedback*, but it can also estimate branch probabilities based on statics and heuristics.

The feedback based profile is produced by compiling the program with instrumentation, executing it on a train run and reading the numbers of executions of basic blocks and edges back to the compiler while re-compiling the program to produce the final executable. This method provides very accurate information about where a program spends most of its time on the train run. Whether it matches the average run of course depends on the choice of train data set, but several studies have shown that the behavior of a program usually changes just marginally over different data sets.

When profile feedback is not available, the compiler may be asked to attempt to predict the behavior of each branch in the program using a set of heuristics (see 'predict.def' for details) and compute estimated frequencies of each basic block by propagating the probabilities over the graph.

Each `basic_block` contains two integer fields to represent profile information: `frequency` and `count`. The `frequency` is an estimation how often is basic block executed within a function. It is represented as an integer scaled in the range from 0 to `BB_FREQ_BASE`. The most frequently executed basic block in function is initially set to `BB_FREQ_BASE` and the rest of frequencies are scaled accordingly. During optimization, the frequency of the most frequent basic block can both decrease (for instance by loop unrolling) or grow (for instance by cross-jumping optimization), so scaling sometimes has to be performed multiple times.

The `count` contains hard-counted numbers of execution measured during training runs and is nonzero only when profile feedback is available. This value is represented as the host's widest integer (typically a 64 bit integer) of the special type `gcov_type`.

Most optimization passes can use only the frequency information of a basic block, but a few passes may want to know hard execution counts. The frequencies should always match the counts after scaling, however during updating of the profile information numerical error may accumulate into quite large errors.

Each edge also contains a branch probability field: an integer in the range from 0 to `REG_BR_PROB_BASE`. It represents probability of passing control from the end of the `src` basic block to the `dest` basic block, i.e. the probability that control will flow along this edge. The `EDGE_FREQUENCY` macro is available to compute how frequently a given edge is taken. There is a `count` field for each edge as well, representing same information as for a basic block.

The basic block frequencies are not represented in the instruction stream, but in the RTL representation the edge frequencies are represented for conditional jumps (via the `REG_BR_`

PROB macro) since they are used when instructions are output to the assembly file and the flow graph is no longer maintained.

The probability that control flow arrives via a given edge to its destination basic block is called *reverse probability* and is not directly represented, but it may be easily computed from frequencies of basic blocks.

Updating profile information is a delicate task that can unfortunately not be easily integrated with the CFG manipulation API. Many of the functions and hooks to modify the CFG, such as `redirect_edge_and_branch`, do not have enough information to easily update the profile, so updating it is in the majority of cases left up to the caller. It is difficult to uncover bugs in the profile updating code, because they manifest themselves only by producing worse code, and checking profile consistency is not possible because of numeric error accumulation. Hence special attention needs to be given to this issue in each pass that modifies the CFG.

It is important to point out that `REG_BR_PROB_BASE` and `BB_FREQ_BASE` are both set low enough to be possible to compute second power of any frequency or probability in the flow graph, it is not possible to even square the `count` field, as modern CPUs are fast enough to execute 2^{32} operations quickly.

15.4 Maintaining the CFG

An important task of each compiler pass is to keep both the control flow graph and all profile information up-to-date. Reconstruction of the control flow graph after each pass is not an option, since it may be very expensive and lost profile information cannot be reconstructed at all.

GCC has two major intermediate representations, and both use the `basic_block` and `edge` data types to represent control flow. Both representations share as much of the CFG maintenance code as possible. For each representation, a set of *hooks* is defined so that each representation can provide its own implementation of CFG manipulation routines when necessary. These hooks are defined in 'cfghooks.h'. There are hooks for almost all common CFG manipulations, including block splitting and merging, edge redirection and creating and deleting basic blocks. These hooks should provide everything you need to maintain and manipulate the CFG in both the RTL and `GIMPLE` representation.

At the moment, the basic block boundaries are maintained transparently when modifying instructions, so there rarely is a need to move them manually (such as in case someone wants to output instruction outside basic block explicitly).

In the RTL representation, each instruction has a `BLOCK_FOR_INSN` value that represents pointer to the basic block that contains the instruction. In the `GIMPLE` representation, the function `gimple_bb` returns a pointer to the basic block containing the queried statement.

When changes need to be applied to a function in its `GIMPLE` representation, *GIMPLE statement iterators* should be used. These iterators provide an integrated abstraction of the flow graph and the instruction stream. Block statement iterators are constructed using the `gimple_stmt_iterator` data structure and several modifiers are available, including the following:

`gsi_start`

> This function initializes a `gimple_stmt_iterator` that points to the first non-empty statement in a basic block.

`gsi_last`   This function initializes a `gimple_stmt_iterator` that points to the last statement in a basic block.

`gsi_end_p`
               This predicate is `true` if a `gimple_stmt_iterator` represents the end of a basic block.

`gsi_next`   This function takes a `gimple_stmt_iterator` and makes it point to its successor.

`gsi_prev`   This function takes a `gimple_stmt_iterator` and makes it point to its predecessor.

`gsi_insert_after`
               This function inserts a statement after the `gimple_stmt_iterator` passed in. The final parameter determines whether the statement iterator is updated to point to the newly inserted statement, or left pointing to the original statement.

`gsi_insert_before`
               This function inserts a statement before the `gimple_stmt_iterator` passed in. The final parameter determines whether the statement iterator is updated to point to the newly inserted statement, or left pointing to the original statement.

`gsi_remove`
               This function removes the `gimple_stmt_iterator` passed in and rechains the remaining statements in a basic block, if any.

In the RTL representation, the macros `BB_HEAD` and `BB_END` may be used to get the head and end `rtx` of a basic block. No abstract iterators are defined for traversing the insn chain, but you can just use `NEXT_INSN` and `PREV_INSN` instead. See Section 14.19 [Insns], page 294.

Usually a code manipulating pass simplifies the instruction stream and the flow of control, possibly eliminating some edges. This may for example happen when a conditional jump is replaced with an unconditional jump. Updating of edges is not transparent and each optimization pass is required to do so manually. However only few cases occur in practice. The pass may call `purge_dead_edges` on a given basic block to remove superfluous edges, if any.

Another common scenario is redirection of branch instructions, but this is best modeled as redirection of edges in the control flow graph and thus use of `redirect_edge_and_branch` is preferred over more low level functions, such as `redirect_jump` that operate on RTL chain only. The CFG hooks defined in 'cfghooks.h' should provide the complete API required for manipulating and maintaining the CFG.

It is also possible that a pass has to insert control flow instruction into the middle of a basic block, thus creating an entry point in the middle of the basic block, which is impossible by definition: The block must be split to make sure it only has one entry point, i.e. the head of the basic block. The CFG hook `split_block` may be used when an instruction in the middle of a basic block has to become the target of a jump or branch instruction.

For a global optimizer, a common operation is to split edges in the flow graph and insert instructions on them. In the RTL representation, this can be easily done using the `insert_insn_on_edge` function that emits an instruction "on the edge", caching it for a later `commit_edge_insertions` call that will take care of moving the inserted instructions off the edge into the instruction stream contained in a basic block. This includes the creation of new basic blocks where needed. In the GIMPLE representation, the equivalent functions are `gsi_insert_on_edge` which inserts a block statement iterator on an edge, and `gsi_commit_edge_inserts` which flushes the instruction to actual instruction stream.

While debugging the optimization pass, the `verify_flow_info` function may be useful to find bugs in the control flow graph updating code.

15.5 Liveness information

Liveness information is useful to determine whether some register is "live" at given point of program, i.e. that it contains a value that may be used at a later point in the program. This information is used, for instance, during register allocation, as the pseudo registers only need to be assigned to a unique hard register or to a stack slot if they are live. The hard registers and stack slots may be freely reused for other values when a register is dead.

Liveness information is available in the back end starting with `pass_df_initialize` and ending with `pass_df_finish`. Three flavors of live analysis are available: With LR, it is possible to determine at any point P in the function if the register may be used on some path from P to the end of the function. With UR, it is possible to determine if there is a path from the beginning of the function to P that defines the variable. LIVE is the intersection of the LR and UR and a variable is live at P if there is both an assignment that reaches it from the beginning of the function and a use that can be reached on some path from P to the end of the function.

In general LIVE is the most useful of the three. The macros DF_[LR,UR,LIVE]_[IN,OUT] can be used to access this information. The macros take a basic block number and return a bitmap that is indexed by the register number. This information is only guaranteed to be up to date after calls are made to `df_analyze`. See the file `df-core.c` for details on using the dataflow.

The liveness information is stored partly in the RTL instruction stream and partly in the flow graph. Local information is stored in the instruction stream: Each instruction may contain REG_DEAD notes representing that the value of a given register is no longer needed, or REG_UNUSED notes representing that the value computed by the instruction is never used. The second is useful for instructions computing multiple values at once.

16 Analysis and Representation of Loops

GCC provides extensive infrastructure for work with natural loops, i.e., strongly connected components of CFG with only one entry block. This chapter describes representation of loops in GCC, both on GIMPLE and in RTL, as well as the interfaces to loop-related analyses (induction variable analysis and number of iterations analysis).

16.1 Loop representation

This chapter describes the representation of loops in GCC, and functions that can be used to build, modify and analyze this representation. Most of the interfaces and data structures are declared in 'cfgloop.h'. Loop structures are analyzed and this information disposed or updated at the discretion of individual passes. Still most of the generic CFG manipulation routines are aware of loop structures and try to keep them up-to-date. By this means an increasing part of the compilation pipeline is setup to maintain loop structure across passes to allow attaching meta information to individual loops for consumption by later passes.

In general, a natural loop has one entry block (header) and possibly several back edges (latches) leading to the header from the inside of the loop. Loops with several latches may appear if several loops share a single header, or if there is a branching in the middle of the loop. The representation of loops in GCC however allows only loops with a single latch. During loop analysis, headers of such loops are split and forwarder blocks are created in order to disambiguate their structures. Heuristic based on profile information and structure of the induction variables in the loops is used to determine whether the latches correspond to sub-loops or to control flow in a single loop. This means that the analysis sometimes changes the CFG, and if you run it in the middle of an optimization pass, you must be able to deal with the new blocks. You may avoid CFG changes by passing LOOPS_MAY_HAVE_MULTIPLE_LATCHES flag to the loop discovery, note however that most other loop manipulation functions will not work correctly for loops with multiple latch edges (the functions that only query membership of blocks to loops and subloop relationships, or enumerate and test loop exits, can be expected to work).

Body of the loop is the set of blocks that are dominated by its header, and reachable from its latch against the direction of edges in CFG. The loops are organized in a containment hierarchy (tree) such that all the loops immediately contained inside loop L are the children of L in the tree. This tree is represented by the struct loops structure. The root of this tree is a fake loop that contains all blocks in the function. Each of the loops is represented in a struct loop structure. Each loop is assigned an index (num field of the struct loop structure), and the pointer to the loop is stored in the corresponding field of the larray vector in the loops structure. The indices do not have to be continuous, there may be empty (NULL) entries in the larray created by deleting loops. Also, there is no guarantee on the relative order of a loop and its subloops in the numbering. The index of a loop never changes.

The entries of the larray field should not be accessed directly. The function get_loop returns the loop description for a loop with the given index. number_of_loops function returns number of loops in the function. To traverse all loops, use FOR_EACH_LOOP macro. The flags argument of the macro is used to determine the direction of traversal and the set of loops visited. Each loop is guaranteed to be visited exactly once, regardless of the changes to the loop tree, and the loops may be removed during the traversal. The newly created loops are never traversed, if they need to be visited, this must be done separately after their creation. The `FOR_EACH_LOOP` macro allocates temporary variables. If the `FOR_EACH_LOOP` loop were ended using break or goto, they would not be released; `FOR_EACH_LOOP_BREAK` macro must be used instead.

Each basic block contains the reference to the innermost loop it belongs to (`loop_father`). For this reason, it is only possible to have one `struct loops` structure initialized at the same time for each CFG. The global variable `current_loops` contains the `struct loops` structure. Many of the loop manipulation functions assume that dominance information is up-to-date.

The loops are analyzed through `loop_optimizer_init` function. The argument of this function is a set of flags represented in an integer bitmask. These flags specify what other properties of the loop structures should be calculated/enforced and preserved later:

- `LOOPS_MAY_HAVE_MULTIPLE_LATCHES`: If this flag is set, no changes to CFG will be performed in the loop analysis, in particular, loops with multiple latch edges will not be disambiguated. If a loop has multiple latches, its latch block is set to NULL. Most of the loop manipulation functions will not work for loops in this shape. No other flags that require CFG changes can be passed to loop_optimizer_init.

- `LOOPS_HAVE_PREHEADERS`: Forwarder blocks are created in such a way that each loop has only one entry edge, and additionally, the source block of this entry edge has only one successor. This creates a natural place where the code can be moved out of the loop, and ensures that the entry edge of the loop leads from its immediate super-loop.

- `LOOPS_HAVE_SIMPLE_LATCHES`: Forwarder blocks are created to force the latch block of each loop to have only one successor. This ensures that the latch of the loop does not belong to any of its sub-loops, and makes manipulation with the loops significantly easier. Most of the loop manipulation functions assume that the loops are in this shape. Note that with this flag, the "normal" loop without any control flow inside and with one exit consists of two basic blocks.

- `LOOPS_HAVE_MARKED_IRREDUCIBLE_REGIONS`: Basic blocks and edges in the strongly connected components that are not natural loops (have more than one entry block) are marked with `BB_IRREDUCIBLE_LOOP` and `EDGE_IRREDUCIBLE_LOOP` flags. The flag is not set for blocks and edges that belong to natural loops that are in such an irreducible region (but it is set for the entry and exit edges of such a loop, if they lead to/from this region).

- `LOOPS_HAVE_RECORDED_EXITS`: The lists of exits are recorded and updated for each loop. This makes some functions (e.g., `get_loop_exit_edges`) more efficient. Some functions (e.g., `single_exit`) can be used only if the lists of exits are recorded.

These properties may also be computed/enforced later, using functions `create_preheaders`, `force_single_succ_latches`, `mark_irreducible_loops` and `record_loop_exits`. The properties can be queried using `loops_state_satisfies_p`.

The memory occupied by the loops structures should be freed with `loop_optimizer_finalize` function. When loop structures are setup to be preserved across passes this function reduces the information to be kept up-to-date to a minimum (only `LOOPS_MAY_HAVE_MULTIPLE_LATCHES` set).

The CFG manipulation functions in general do not update loop structures. Specialized versions that additionally do so are provided for the most common tasks. On GIMPLE,

Chapter 16: Analysis and Representation of Loops

`cleanup_tree_cfg_loop` function can be used to cleanup CFG while updating the loops structures if `current_loops` is set.

At the moment loop structure is preserved from the start of GIMPLE loop optimizations until the end of RTL loop optimizations. During this time a loop can be tracked by its `struct loop` and number.

16.2 Loop querying

The functions to query the information about loops are declared in 'cfgloop.h'. Some of the information can be taken directly from the structures. `loop_father` field of each basic block contains the innermost loop to that the block belongs. The most useful fields of loop structure (that are kept up-to-date at all times) are:

- `header`, `latch`: Header and latch basic blocks of the loop.
- `num_nodes`: Number of basic blocks in the loop (including the basic blocks of the sub-loops).
- `outer`, `inner`, `next`: The super-loop, the first sub-loop, and the sibling of the loop in the loops tree.

There are other fields in the loop structures, many of them used only by some of the passes, or not updated during CFG changes; in general, they should not be accessed directly.

The most important functions to query loop structures are:

- `loop_depth`: The depth of the loop in the loops tree, i.e., the number of super-loops of the loop.
- `flow_loops_dump`: Dumps the information about loops to a file.
- `verify_loop_structure`: Checks consistency of the loop structures.
- `loop_latch_edge`: Returns the latch edge of a loop.
- `loop_preheader_edge`: If loops have preheaders, returns the preheader edge of a loop.
- `flow_loop_nested_p`: Tests whether loop is a sub-loop of another loop.
- `flow_bb_inside_loop_p`: Tests whether a basic block belongs to a loop (including its sub-loops).
- `find_common_loop`: Finds the common super-loop of two loops.
- `superloop_at_depth`: Returns the super-loop of a loop with the given depth.
- `tree_num_loop_insns`, `num_loop_insns`: Estimates the number of insns in the loop, on GIMPLE and on RTL.
- `loop_exit_edge_p`: Tests whether edge is an exit from a loop.
- `mark_loop_exit_edges`: Marks all exit edges of all loops with `EDGE_LOOP_EXIT` flag.
- `get_loop_body`, `get_loop_body_in_dom_order`, `get_loop_body_in_bfs_order`: Enumerates the basic blocks in the loop in depth-first search order in reversed CFG, ordered by dominance relation, and breath-first search order, respectively.
- `single_exit`: Returns the single exit edge of the loop, or `NULL` if the loop has more than one exit. You can only use this function if LOOPS_HAVE_MARKED_SINGLE_EXITS property is used.
- `get_loop_exit_edges`: Enumerates the exit edges of a loop.

- `just_once_each_iteration_p`: Returns true if the basic block is executed exactly once during each iteration of a loop (that is, it does not belong to a sub-loop, and it dominates the latch of the loop).

16.3 Loop manipulation

The loops tree can be manipulated using the following functions:

- `flow_loop_tree_node_add`: Adds a node to the tree.
- `flow_loop_tree_node_remove`: Removes a node from the tree.
- `add_bb_to_loop`: Adds a basic block to a loop.
- `remove_bb_from_loops`: Removes a basic block from loops.

Most low-level CFG functions update loops automatically. The following functions handle some more complicated cases of CFG manipulations:

- `remove_path`: Removes an edge and all blocks it dominates.
- `split_loop_exit_edge`: Splits exit edge of the loop, ensuring that PHI node arguments remain in the loop (this ensures that loop-closed SSA form is preserved). Only useful on GIMPLE.

Finally, there are some higher-level loop transformations implemented. While some of them are written so that they should work on non-innermost loops, they are mostly untested in that case, and at the moment, they are only reliable for the innermost loops:

- `create_iv`: Creates a new induction variable. Only works on GIMPLE. `standard_iv_increment_position` can be used to find a suitable place for the iv increment.
- `duplicate_loop_to_header_edge`, `tree_duplicate_loop_to_header_edge`: These functions (on RTL and on GIMPLE) duplicate the body of the loop prescribed number of times on one of the edges entering loop header, thus performing either loop unrolling or loop peeling. `can_duplicate_loop_p` (`can_unroll_loop_p` on GIMPLE) must be true for the duplicated loop.
- `loop_version`: This function creates a copy of a loop, and a branch before them that selects one of them depending on the prescribed condition. This is useful for optimizations that need to verify some assumptions in runtime (one of the copies of the loop is usually left unchanged, while the other one is transformed in some way).
- `tree_unroll_loop`: Unrolls the loop, including peeling the extra iterations to make the number of iterations divisible by unroll factor, updating the exit condition, and removing the exits that now cannot be taken. Works only on GIMPLE.

16.4 Loop-closed SSA form

Throughout the loop optimizations on tree level, one extra condition is enforced on the SSA form: No SSA name is used outside of the loop in that it is defined. The SSA form satisfying this condition is called "loop-closed SSA form" – LCSSA. To enforce LCSSA, PHI nodes must be created at the exits of the loops for the SSA names that are used outside of them. Only the real operands (not virtual SSA names) are held in LCSSA, in order to save memory.

There are various benefits of LCSSA:

Chapter 16: Analysis and Representation of Loops   321

- Many optimizations (value range analysis, final value replacement) are interested in the values that are defined in the loop and used outside of it, i.e., exactly those for that we create new PHI nodes.

- In induction variable analysis, it is not necessary to specify the loop in that the analysis should be performed – the scalar evolution analysis always returns the results with respect to the loop in that the SSA name is defined.

- It makes updating of SSA form during loop transformations simpler. Without LCSSA, operations like loop unrolling may force creation of PHI nodes arbitrarily far from the loop, while in LCSSA, the SSA form can be updated locally. However, since we only keep real operands in LCSSA, we cannot use this advantage (we could have local updating of real operands, but it is not much more efficient than to use generic SSA form updating for it as well; the amount of changes to SSA is the same).

However, it also means LCSSA must be updated. This is usually straightforward, unless you create a new value in loop and use it outside, or unless you manipulate loop exit edges (functions are provided to make these manipulations simple). `rewrite_into_loop_closed_ssa` is used to rewrite SSA form to LCSSA, and `verify_loop_closed_ssa` to check that the invariant of LCSSA is preserved.

16.5 Scalar evolutions

Scalar evolutions (SCEV) are used to represent results of induction variable analysis on GIMPLE. They enable us to represent variables with complicated behavior in a simple and consistent way (we only use it to express values of polynomial induction variables, but it is possible to extend it). The interfaces to SCEV analysis are declared in 'tree-scalar-evolution.h'. To use scalar evolutions analysis, `scev_initialize` must be used. To stop using SCEV, `scev_finalize` should be used. SCEV analysis caches results in order to save time and memory. This cache however is made invalid by most of the loop transformations, including removal of code. If such a transformation is performed, `scev_reset` must be called to clean the caches.

Given an SSA name, its behavior in loops can be analyzed using the `analyze_scalar_evolution` function. The returned SCEV however does not have to be fully analyzed and it may contain references to other SSA names defined in the loop. To resolve these (potentially recursive) references, `instantiate_parameters` or `resolve_mixers` functions must be used. `instantiate_parameters` is useful when you use the results of SCEV only for some analysis, and when you work with whole nest of loops at once. It will try replacing all SSA names by their SCEV in all loops, including the super-loops of the current loop, thus providing a complete information about the behavior of the variable in the loop nest. `resolve_mixers` is useful if you work with only one loop at a time, and if you possibly need to create code based on the value of the induction variable. It will only resolve the SSA names defined in the current loop, leaving the SSA names defined outside unchanged, even if their evolution in the outer loops is known.

The SCEV is a normal tree expression, except for the fact that it may contain several special tree nodes. One of them is `SCEV_NOT_KNOWN`, used for SSA names whose value cannot be expressed. The other one is `POLYNOMIAL_CHREC`. Polynomial chrec has three arguments – base, step and loop (both base and step may contain further polynomial chrecs). Type of the expression and of base and step must be the same. A variable has evolution `POLYNOMIAL_`

CHREC(base, step, loop) if it is (in the specified loop) equivalent to x_1 in the following example

```
while (...)
  {
    x_1 = phi (base, x_2);
    x_2 = x_1 + step;
  }
```

Note that this includes the language restrictions on the operations. For example, if we compile C code and x has signed type, then the overflow in addition would cause undefined behavior, and we may assume that this does not happen. Hence, the value with this SCEV cannot overflow (which restricts the number of iterations of such a loop).

In many cases, one wants to restrict the attention just to affine induction variables. In this case, the extra expressive power of SCEV is not useful, and may complicate the optimizations. In this case, `simple_iv` function may be used to analyze a value – the result is a loop-invariant base and step.

16.6 IV analysis on RTL

The induction variable on RTL is simple and only allows analysis of affine induction variables, and only in one loop at once. The interface is declared in 'cfgloop.h'. Before analyzing induction variables in a loop L, `iv_analysis_loop_init` function must be called on L. After the analysis (possibly calling `iv_analysis_loop_init` for several loops) is finished, `iv_analysis_done` should be called. The following functions can be used to access the results of the analysis:

- `iv_analyze`: Analyzes a single register used in the given insn. If no use of the register in this insn is found, the following insns are scanned, so that this function can be called on the insn returned by get_condition.
- `iv_analyze_result`: Analyzes result of the assignment in the given insn.
- `iv_analyze_expr`: Analyzes a more complicated expression. All its operands are analyzed by `iv_analyze`, and hence they must be used in the specified insn or one of the following insns.

The description of the induction variable is provided in `struct rtx_iv`. In order to handle subregs, the representation is a bit complicated; if the value of the `extend` field is not UNKNOWN, the value of the induction variable in the i-th iteration is

```
delta + mult * extend_{extend_mode} (subreg_{mode} (base + i * step)),
```

with the following exception: if `first_special` is true, then the value in the first iteration (when i is zero) is `delta + mult * base`. However, if `extend` is equal to UNKNOWN, then `first_special` must be false, `delta` 0, `mult` 1 and the value in the i-th iteration is

```
subreg_{mode} (base + i * step)
```

The function `get_iv_value` can be used to perform these calculations.

16.7 Number of iterations analysis

Both on GIMPLE and on RTL, there are functions available to determine the number of iterations of a loop, with a similar interface. The number of iterations of a loop in GCC is defined as the number of executions of the loop latch. In many cases, it is not possible to determine the number of iterations unconditionally – the determined number is correct only if some assumptions are satisfied. The analysis tries to verify these conditions using the information contained in the program; if it fails, the conditions are returned together with the result. The following information and conditions are provided by the analysis:

- `assumptions`: If this condition is false, the rest of the information is invalid.
- `noloop_assumptions` on RTL, `may_be_zero` on GIMPLE: If this condition is true, the loop exits in the first iteration.
- `infinite`: If this condition is true, the loop is infinite. This condition is only available on RTL. On GIMPLE, conditions for finiteness of the loop are included in `assumptions`.
- `niter_expr` on RTL, `niter` on GIMPLE: The expression that gives number of iterations. The number of iterations is defined as the number of executions of the loop latch.

Both on GIMPLE and on RTL, it necessary for the induction variable analysis framework to be initialized (SCEV on GIMPLE, loop-iv on RTL). On GIMPLE, the results are stored to `struct tree_niter_desc` structure. Number of iterations before the loop is exited through a given exit can be determined using `number_of_iterations_exit` function. On RTL, the results are returned in `struct niter_desc` structure. The corresponding function is named `check_simple_exit`. There are also functions that pass through all the exits of a loop and try to find one with easy to determine number of iterations – `find_loop_niter` on GIMPLE and `find_simple_exit` on RTL. Finally, there are functions that provide the same information, but additionally cache it, so that repeated calls to number of iterations are not so costly – `number_of_latch_executions` on GIMPLE and `get_simple_loop_desc` on RTL.

Note that some of these functions may behave slightly differently than others – some of them return only the expression for the number of iterations, and fail if there are some assumptions. The function `number_of_latch_executions` works only for single-exit loops. The function `number_of_cond_exit_executions` can be used to determine number of executions of the exit condition of a single-exit loop (i.e., the `number_of_latch_executions` increased by one).

On GIMPLE, below constraint flags affect semantics of some APIs of number of iterations analyzer:

- `LOOP_C_INFINITE`: If this constraint flag is set, the loop is known to be infinite. APIs like `number_of_iterations_exit` can return false directly without doing any analysis.
- `LOOP_C_FINITE`: If this constraint flag is set, the loop is known to be finite, in other words, loop's number of iterations can be computed with `assumptions` be true.

Generally, the constraint flags are set/cleared by consumers which are loop optimizers. It's also the consumers' responsibility to set/clear constraints correctly. Failing to do that might result in hard to track down bugs in scev/niter consumers. One typical use case is vectorizer: it drives number of iterations analyzer by setting `LOOP_C_FINITE` and vectorizes possibly infinite loop by versioning loop with analysis result. In return, constraints set by consumers can also help number of iterations analyzer in following optimizers. For example, `niter` of a loop versioned under `assumptions` is valid unconditionally.

Other constraints may be added in the future, for example, a constraint indicating that loops' latch must roll thus `may_be_zero` would be false unconditionally.

16.8 Data Dependency Analysis

The code for the data dependence analysis can be found in 'tree-data-ref.c' and its interface and data structures are described in 'tree-data-ref.h'. The function that computes the data dependences for all the array and pointer references for a given loop is compute_data_dependences_for_loop. This function is currently used by the linear loop transform and the vectorization passes. Before calling this function, one has to allocate two vectors: a first vector will contain the set of data references that are contained in the analyzed loop body, and the second vector will contain the dependence relations between the data references. Thus if the vector of data references is of size n, the vector containing the dependence relations will contain n*n elements. However if the analyzed loop contains side effects, such as calls that potentially can interfere with the data references in the current analyzed loop, the analysis stops while scanning the loop body for data references, and inserts a single chrec_dont_know in the dependence relation array.

The data references are discovered in a particular order during the scanning of the loop body: the loop body is analyzed in execution order, and the data references of each statement are pushed at the end of the data reference array. Two data references syntactically occur in the program in the same order as in the array of data references. This syntactic order is important in some classical data dependence tests, and mapping this order to the elements of this array avoids costly queries to the loop body representation.

Three types of data references are currently handled: ARRAY_REF, INDIRECT_REF and COMPONENT_REF. The data structure for the data reference is data_reference, where data_reference_p is a name of a pointer to the data reference structure. The structure contains the following elements:

- base_object_info: Provides information about the base object of the data reference and its access functions. These access functions represent the evolution of the data reference in the loop relative to its base, in keeping with the classical meaning of the data reference access function for the support of arrays. For example, for a reference a.b[i][j], the base object is a.b and the access functions, one for each array subscript, are: {i_init, + i_step}_1, {j_init, +, j_step}_2.

- first_location_in_loop: Provides information about the first location accessed by the data reference in the loop and about the access function used to represent evolution relative to this location. This data is used to support pointers, and is not used for arrays (for which we have base objects). Pointer accesses are represented as a one-dimensional access that starts from the first location accessed in the loop. For example:

        for1 i
          for2 j
            *((int *)p + i + j) = a[i][j];

The access function of the pointer access is {0, + 4B}_for2 relative to p + i. The access functions of the array are {i_init, + i_step}_for1 and {j_init, +, j_step}_for2 relative to a.

Usually, the object the pointer refers to is either unknown, or we cannot prove that the access is confined to the boundaries of a certain object.

Two data references can be compared only if at least one of these two representations has all its fields filled for both data references.

The current strategy for data dependence tests is as follows: If both a and b are represented as arrays, compare a.base_object and b.base_object; if they are equal, apply dependence tests (use access functions based on base_objects). Else if both a and b are represented as pointers, compare a.first_location and b.first_location; if they are equal, apply dependence tests (use access functions based on first location). However, if a and b are represented differently, only try to prove that the bases are definitely different.

- Aliasing information.
- Alignment information.

The structure describing the relation between two data references is data_dependence_relation and the shorter name for a pointer to such a structure is ddr_p. This structure contains:

- a pointer to each data reference,
- a tree node are_dependent that is set to chrec_known if the analysis has proved that there is no dependence between these two data references, chrec_dont_know if the analysis was not able to determine any useful result and potentially there could exist a dependence between these data references, and are_dependent is set to NULL_TREE if there exist a dependence relation between the data references, and the description of this dependence relation is given in the subscripts, dir_vects, and dist_vects arrays,
- a boolean that determines whether the dependence relation can be represented by a classical distance vector,
- an array subscripts that contains a description of each subscript of the data references. Given two array accesses a subscript is the tuple composed of the access functions for a given dimension. For example, given A[f1][f2][f3] and B[g1][g2][g3], there are three subscripts: (f1, g1), (f2, g2), (f3, g3).
- two arrays dir_vects and dist_vects that contain classical representations of the data dependences under the form of direction and distance dependence vectors,
- an array of loops loop_nest that contains the loops to which the distance and direction vectors refer to.

Several functions for pretty printing the information extracted by the data dependence analysis are available: dump_ddrs prints with a maximum verbosity the details of a data dependence relations array, dump_dist_dir_vectors prints only the classical distance and direction vectors for a data dependence relations array, and dump_data_references prints the details of the data references contained in a data reference array.

17 Machine Descriptions

A machine description has two parts: a file of instruction patterns ('.md' file) and a C header file of macro definitions.

The '.md' file for a target machine contains a pattern for each instruction that the target machine supports (or at least each instruction that is worth telling the compiler about). It may also contain comments. A semicolon causes the rest of the line to be a comment, unless the semicolon is inside a quoted string.

See the next chapter for information on the C header file.

17.1 Overview of How the Machine Description is Used

There are three main conversions that happen in the compiler:

1. The front end reads the source code and builds a parse tree.
2. The parse tree is used to generate an RTL insn list based on named instruction patterns.
3. The insn list is matched against the RTL templates to produce assembler code.

For the generate pass, only the names of the insns matter, from either a named define_insn or a define_expand. The compiler will choose the pattern with the right name and apply the operands according to the documentation later in this chapter, without regard for the RTL template or operand constraints. Note that the names the compiler looks for are hard-coded in the compiler—it will ignore unnamed patterns and patterns with names it doesn't know about, but if you don't provide a named pattern it needs, it will abort.

If a define_insn is used, the template given is inserted into the insn list. If a define_expand is used, one of three things happens, based on the condition logic. The condition logic may manually create new insns for the insn list, say via emit_insn(), and invoke DONE. For certain named patterns, it may invoke FAIL to tell the compiler to use an alternate way of performing that task. If it invokes neither DONE nor FAIL, the template given in the pattern is inserted, as if the define_expand were a define_insn.

Once the insn list is generated, various optimization passes convert, replace, and rearrange the insns in the insn list. This is where the define_split and define_peephole patterns get used, for example.

Finally, the insn list's RTL is matched up with the RTL templates in the define_insn patterns, and those patterns are used to emit the final assembly code. For this purpose, each named define_insn acts like it's unnamed, since the names are ignored.

17.2 Everything about Instruction Patterns

A define_insn expression is used to define instruction patterns to which insns may be matched. A define_insn expression contains an incomplete RTL expression, with pieces to be filled in later, operand constraints that restrict how the pieces can be filled in, and an output template or C code to generate the assembler output.

A define_insn is an RTL expression containing four or five operands:

1. An optional name. The presence of a name indicates that this instruction pattern can perform a certain standard job for the RTL-generation pass of the compiler. This pass

knows certain names and will use the instruction patterns with those names, if the names are defined in the machine description.

The absence of a name is indicated by writing an empty string where the name should go. Nameless instruction patterns are never used for generating RTL code, but they may permit several simpler insns to be combined later on.

Names that are not thus known and used in RTL-generation have no effect; they are equivalent to no name at all.

For the purpose of debugging the compiler, you may also specify a name beginning with the '*' character. Such a name is used only for identifying the instruction in RTL dumps; it is equivalent to having a nameless pattern for all other purposes. Names beginning with the '*' character are not required to be unique.

2. The *RTL template*: This is a vector of incomplete RTL expressions which describe the semantics of the instruction (see Section 17.4 [RTL Template], page 329). It is incomplete because it may contain `match_operand`, `match_operator`, and `match_dup` expressions that stand for operands of the instruction.

   If the vector has multiple elements, the RTL template is treated as a `parallel` expression.

3. The condition: This is a string which contains a C expression. When the compiler attempts to match RTL against a pattern, the condition is evaluated. If the condition evaluates to `true`, the match is permitted. The condition may be an empty string, which is treated as always `true`.

   For a named pattern, the condition may not depend on the data in the insn being matched, but only the target-machine-type flags. The compiler needs to test these conditions during initialization in order to learn exactly which named instructions are available in a particular run.

   For nameless patterns, the condition is applied only when matching an individual insn, and only after the insn has matched the pattern's recognition template. The insn's operands may be found in the vector `operands`.

   An instruction condition cannot become more restrictive as compilation progresses. If the condition accepts a particular RTL instruction at one stage of compilation, it must continue to accept that instruction until the final pass. For example, '!reload_completed' and 'can_create_pseudo_p ()' are both invalid instruction conditions, because they are true during the earlier RTL passes and false during the later ones. For the same reason, if a condition accepts an instruction before register allocation, it cannot later try to control register allocation by excluding certain register or value combinations.

   Although a condition cannot become more restrictive as compilation progresses, the condition for a nameless pattern *can* become more permissive. For example, a nameless instruction can require 'reload_completed' to be true, in which case it only matches after register allocation.

4. The *output template* or *output statement*: This is either a string, or a fragment of C code which returns a string.

   When simple substitution isn't general enough, you can specify a piece of C code to compute the output. See Section 17.6 [Output Statement], page 334.

5. The *insn attributes*: This is an optional vector containing the values of attributes for insns matching this pattern (see Section 17.19 [Insn Attributes], page 434).

17.3 Example of `define_insn`

Here is an example of an instruction pattern, taken from the machine description for the 68000/68020.

```
(define_insn "tstsi"
  [(set (cc0)
        (match_operand:SI 0 "general_operand" "rm"))]
  ""
  "*
{
  if (TARGET_68020 || ! ADDRESS_REG_P (operands[0]))
    return \"tstl %0\";
  return \"cmpl #0,%0\";
}")
```

This can also be written using braced strings:

```
(define_insn "tstsi"
  [(set (cc0)
        (match_operand:SI 0 "general_operand" "rm"))]
  ""
  {
    if (TARGET_68020 || ! ADDRESS_REG_P (operands[0]))
      return "tstl %0";
    return "cmpl #0,%0";
  })
```

This describes an instruction which sets the condition codes based on the value of a general operand. It has no condition, so any insn with an RTL description of the form shown may be matched to this pattern. The name 'tstsi' means "test a SImode value" and tells the RTL generation pass that, when it is necessary to test such a value, an insn to do so can be constructed using this pattern.

The output control string is a piece of C code which chooses which output template to return based on the kind of operand and the specific type of CPU for which code is being generated.

'"rm"' is an operand constraint. Its meaning is explained below.

17.4 RTL Template

The RTL template is used to define which insns match the particular pattern and how to find their operands. For named patterns, the RTL template also says how to construct an insn from specified operands.

Construction involves substituting specified operands into a copy of the template. Matching involves determining the values that serve as the operands in the insn being matched. Both of these activities are controlled by special expression types that direct matching and substitution of the operands.

`(match_operand:`*m n predicate constraint*`)`
> This expression is a placeholder for operand number *n* of the insn. When constructing an insn, operand number *n* will be substituted at this point. When matching an insn, whatever appears at this position in the insn will be taken

as operand number *n*; but it must satisfy *predicate* or this instruction pattern will not match at all.

Operand numbers must be chosen consecutively counting from zero in each instruction pattern. There may be only one `match_operand` expression in the pattern for each operand number. Usually operands are numbered in the order of appearance in `match_operand` expressions. In the case of a `define_expand`, any operand numbers used only in `match_dup` expressions have higher values than all other operand numbers.

predicate is a string that is the name of a function that accepts two arguments, an expression and a machine mode. See Section 17.7 [Predicates], page 336. During matching, the function will be called with the putative operand as the expression and *m* as the mode argument (if *m* is not specified, `VOIDmode` will be used, which normally causes *predicate* to accept any mode). If it returns zero, this instruction pattern fails to match. *predicate* may be an empty string; then it means no test is to be done on the operand, so anything which occurs in this position is valid.

Most of the time, *predicate* will reject modes other than *m*—but not always. For example, the predicate `address_operand` uses *m* as the mode of memory ref that the address should be valid for. Many predicates accept `const_int` nodes even though their mode is `VOIDmode`.

constraint controls reloading and the choice of the best register class to use for a value, as explained later (see Section 17.8 [Constraints], page 340). If the constraint would be an empty string, it can be omitted.

People are often unclear on the difference between the constraint and the predicate. The predicate helps decide whether a given insn matches the pattern. The constraint plays no role in this decision; instead, it controls various decisions in the case of an insn which does match.

`(match_scratch:`*m n constraint*`)`
> This expression is also a placeholder for operand number *n* and indicates that operand must be a `scratch` or `reg` expression.
>
> When matching patterns, this is equivalent to
>
> > `(match_operand:`*m n* `"scratch_operand"` *constraint*`)`
>
> but, when generating RTL, it produces a (`scratch:`*m*) expression.
>
> If the last few expressions in a `parallel` are `clobber` expressions whose operands are either a hard register or `match_scratch`, the combiner can add or delete them when necessary. See Section 14.15 [Side Effects], page 287.

`(match_dup` *n*`)`
> This expression is also a placeholder for operand number *n*. It is used when the operand needs to appear more than once in the insn.
>
> In construction, `match_dup` acts just like `match_operand`: the operand is substituted into the insn being constructed. But in matching, `match_dup` behaves differently. It assumes that operand number *n* has already been determined by a `match_operand` appearing earlier in the recognition template, and it matches only an identical-looking expression.

Note that `match_dup` should not be used to tell the compiler that a particular register is being used for two operands (example: `add` that adds one register to another; the second register is both an input operand and the output operand). Use a matching constraint (see Section 17.8.1 [Simple Constraints], page 340) for those. `match_dup` is for the cases where one operand is used in two places in the template, such as an instruction that computes both a quotient and a remainder, where the opcode takes two input operands but the RTL template has to refer to each of those twice; once for the quotient pattern and once for the remainder pattern.

(`match_operator`:*m n predicate* [*operands*...])

This pattern is a kind of placeholder for a variable RTL expression code.

When constructing an insn, it stands for an RTL expression whose expression code is taken from that of operand *n*, and whose operands are constructed from the patterns *operands*.

When matching an expression, it matches an expression if the function *predicate* returns nonzero on that expression *and* the patterns *operands* match the operands of the expression.

Suppose that the function `commutative_operator` is defined as follows, to match any expression whose operator is one of the commutative arithmetic operators of RTL and whose mode is *mode*:

```
int
commutative_integer_operator (x, mode)
    rtx x;
    machine_mode mode;
{
  enum rtx_code code = GET_CODE (x);
  if (GET_MODE (x) != mode)
    return 0;
  return (GET_RTX_CLASS (code) == RTX_COMM_ARITH
          || code == EQ || code == NE);
}
```

Then the following pattern will match any RTL expression consisting of a commutative operator applied to two general operands:

```
(match_operator:SI 3 "commutative_operator"
  [(match_operand:SI 1 "general_operand" "g")
   (match_operand:SI 2 "general_operand" "g")])
```

Here the vector [*operands*...] contains two patterns because the expressions to be matched all contain two operands.

When this pattern does match, the two operands of the commutative operator are recorded as operands 1 and 2 of the insn. (This is done by the two instances of `match_operand`.) Operand 3 of the insn will be the entire commutative expression: use `GET_CODE (operands[3])` to see which commutative operator was used.

The machine mode *m* of `match_operator` works like that of `match_operand`: it is passed as the second argument to the predicate function, and that function is solely responsible for deciding whether the expression to be matched "has" that mode.

When constructing an insn, argument 3 of the gen-function will specify the operation (i.e. the expression code) for the expression to be made. It should be an RTL expression, whose expression code is copied into a new expression whose operands are arguments 1 and 2 of the gen-function. The subexpressions of argument 3 are not used; only its expression code matters.

When `match_operator` is used in a pattern for matching an insn, it usually best if the operand number of the `match_operator` is higher than that of the actual operands of the insn. This improves register allocation because the register allocator often looks at operands 1 and 2 of insns to see if it can do register tying.

There is no way to specify constraints in `match_operator`. The operand of the insn which corresponds to the `match_operator` never has any constraints because it is never reloaded as a whole. However, if parts of its *operands* are matched by `match_operand` patterns, those parts may have constraints of their own.

`(match_op_dup:m n[operands...])`

Like `match_dup`, except that it applies to operators instead of operands. When constructing an insn, operand number *n* will be substituted at this point. But in matching, `match_op_dup` behaves differently. It assumes that operand number *n* has already been determined by a `match_operator` appearing earlier in the recognition template, and it matches only an identical-looking expression.

`(match_parallel n predicate [subpat...])`

This pattern is a placeholder for an insn that consists of a `parallel` expression with a variable number of elements. This expression should only appear at the top level of an insn pattern.

When constructing an insn, operand number *n* will be substituted at this point. When matching an insn, it matches if the body of the insn is a `parallel` expression with at least as many elements as the vector of *subpat* expressions in the `match_parallel`, if each *subpat* matches the corresponding element of the `parallel`, *and* the function *predicate* returns nonzero on the `parallel` that is the body of the insn. It is the responsibility of the predicate to validate elements of the `parallel` beyond those listed in the `match_parallel`.

A typical use of `match_parallel` is to match load and store multiple expressions, which can contain a variable number of elements in a `parallel`. For example,

```
(define_insn ""
  [(match_parallel 0 "load_multiple_operation"
     [(set (match_operand:SI 1 "gpc_reg_operand" "=r")
           (match_operand:SI 2 "memory_operand" "m"))
      (use (reg:SI 179))
      (clobber (reg:SI 179))])]
  ""
  "loadm 0,0,%1,%2")
```

This example comes from 'a29k.md'. The function `load_multiple_operation` is defined in 'a29k.c' and checks that subsequent elements in the `parallel` are the same as the `set` in the pattern, except that they are referencing subsequent registers and memory locations.

An insn that matches this pattern might look like:

```
(parallel
 [(set (reg:SI 20) (mem:SI (reg:SI 100)))
  (use (reg:SI 179))
  (clobber (reg:SI 179))
  (set (reg:SI 21)
       (mem:SI (plus:SI (reg:SI 100)
                        (const_int 4))))
  (set (reg:SI 22)
       (mem:SI (plus:SI (reg:SI 100)
                        (const_int 8))))])
```

(match_par_dup n [subpat...])
: Like match_op_dup, but for match_parallel instead of match_operator.

17.5 Output Templates and Operand Substitution

The *output template* is a string which specifies how to output the assembler code for an instruction pattern. Most of the template is a fixed string which is output literally. The character '%' is used to specify where to substitute an operand; it can also be used to identify places where different variants of the assembler require different syntax.

In the simplest case, a '%' followed by a digit *n* says to output operand *n* at that point in the string.

'%' followed by a letter and a digit says to output an operand in an alternate fashion. Four letters have standard, built-in meanings described below. The machine description macro PRINT_OPERAND can define additional letters with nonstandard meanings.

'%c*digit*' can be used to substitute an operand that is a constant value without the syntax that normally indicates an immediate operand.

'%n*digit*' is like '%c*digit*' except that the value of the constant is negated before printing.

'%a*digit*' can be used to substitute an operand as if it were a memory reference, with the actual operand treated as the address. This may be useful when outputting a "load address" instruction, because often the assembler syntax for such an instruction requires you to write the operand as if it were a memory reference.

'%l*digit*' is used to substitute a label_ref into a jump instruction.

'%=' outputs a number which is unique to each instruction in the entire compilation. This is useful for making local labels to be referred to more than once in a single template that generates multiple assembler instructions.

'%' followed by a punctuation character specifies a substitution that does not use an operand. Only one case is standard: '%%' outputs a '%' into the assembler code. Other nonstandard cases can be defined in the PRINT_OPERAND macro. You must also define which punctuation characters are valid with the PRINT_OPERAND_PUNCT_VALID_P macro.

The template may generate multiple assembler instructions. Write the text for the instructions, with '\;' between them.

When the RTL contains two operands which are required by constraint to match each other, the output template must refer only to the lower-numbered operand. Matching operands are not always identical, and the rest of the compiler arranges to put the proper RTL expression for printing into the lower-numbered operand.

One use of nonstandard letters or punctuation following '%' is to distinguish between different assembler languages for the same machine; for example, Motorola syntax versus MIT syntax for the 68000. Motorola syntax requires periods in most opcode names, while MIT syntax does not. For example, the opcode 'movel' in MIT syntax is 'move.l' in Motorola syntax. The same file of patterns is used for both kinds of output syntax, but the character sequence '%.' is used in each place where Motorola syntax wants a period. The PRINT_OPERAND macro for Motorola syntax defines the sequence to output a period; the macro for MIT syntax defines it to do nothing.

As a special case, a template consisting of the single character # instructs the compiler to first split the insn, and then output the resulting instructions separately. This helps eliminate redundancy in the output templates. If you have a define_insn that needs to emit multiple assembler instructions, and there is a matching define_split already defined, then you can simply use # as the output template instead of writing an output template that emits the multiple assembler instructions.

Note that # only has an effect while generating assembly code; it does not affect whether a split occurs earlier. An associated define_split must exist and it must be suitable for use after register allocation.

If the macro ASSEMBLER_DIALECT is defined, you can use construct of the form '{option0|option1|option2}' in the templates. These describe multiple variants of assembler language syntax. See Section 18.20.7 [Instruction Output], page 595.

17.6 C Statements for Assembler Output

Often a single fixed template string cannot produce correct and efficient assembler code for all the cases that are recognized by a single instruction pattern. For example, the opcodes may depend on the kinds of operands; or some unfortunate combinations of operands may require extra machine instructions.

If the output control string starts with a '@', then it is actually a series of templates, each on a separate line. (Blank lines and leading spaces and tabs are ignored.) The templates correspond to the pattern's constraint alternatives (see Section 17.8.2 [Multi-Alternative], page 345). For example, if a target machine has a two-address add instruction 'addr' to add into a register and another 'addm' to add a register to memory, you might write this pattern:

```
(define_insn "addsi3"
  [(set (match_operand:SI 0 "general_operand" "=r,m")
        (plus:SI (match_operand:SI 1 "general_operand" "0,0")
                 (match_operand:SI 2 "general_operand" "g,r")))]
  ""
  "@
   addr %2,%0
   addm %2,%0")
```

If the output control string starts with a '*', then it is not an output template but rather a piece of C program that should compute a template. It should execute a return statement to return the template-string you want. Most such templates use C string literals, which require doublequote characters to delimit them. To include these doublequote characters in the string, prefix each one with '\'.

If the output control string is written as a brace block instead of a double-quoted string, it is automatically assumed to be C code. In that case, it is not necessary to put in a leading asterisk, or to escape the doublequotes surrounding C string literals.

The operands may be found in the array `operands`, whose C data type is `rtx []`.

It is very common to select different ways of generating assembler code based on whether an immediate operand is within a certain range. Be careful when doing this, because the result of `INTVAL` is an integer on the host machine. If the host machine has more bits in an `int` than the target machine has in the mode in which the constant will be used, then some of the bits you get from `INTVAL` will be superfluous. For proper results, you must carefully disregard the values of those bits.

It is possible to output an assembler instruction and then go on to output or compute more of them, using the subroutine `output_asm_insn`. This receives two arguments: a template-string and a vector of operands. The vector may be `operands`, or it may be another array of `rtx` that you declare locally and initialize yourself.

When an insn pattern has multiple alternatives in its constraints, often the appearance of the assembler code is determined mostly by which alternative was matched. When this is so, the C code can test the variable `which_alternative`, which is the ordinal number of the alternative that was actually satisfied (0 for the first, 1 for the second alternative, etc.).

For example, suppose there are two opcodes for storing zero, 'clrreg' for registers and 'clrmem' for memory locations. Here is how a pattern could use `which_alternative` to choose between them:

```
(define_insn ""
  [(set (match_operand:SI 0 "general_operand" "=r,m")
        (const_int 0))]
  ""
  {
  return (which_alternative == 0
          ? "clrreg %0" : "clrmem %0");
  })
```

The example above, where the assembler code to generate was *solely* determined by the alternative, could also have been specified as follows, having the output control string start with a '@':

```
(define_insn ""
  [(set (match_operand:SI 0 "general_operand" "=r,m")
        (const_int 0))]
  ""
  "@
   clrreg %0
   clrmem %0")
```

If you just need a little bit of C code in one (or a few) alternatives, you can use '*' inside of a '@' multi-alternative template:

```
(define_insn ""
  [(set (match_operand:SI 0 "general_operand" "=r,<,m")
        (const_int 0))]
  ""
  "@
   clrreg %0
   * return stack_mem_p (operands[0]) ? \"push 0\" : \"clrmem %0\";
   clrmem %0")
```

17.7 Predicates

A predicate determines whether a `match_operand` or `match_operator` expression matches, and therefore whether the surrounding instruction pattern will be used for that combination of operands. GCC has a number of machine-independent predicates, and you can define machine-specific predicates as needed. By convention, predicates used with `match_operand` have names that end in '`_operand`', and those used with `match_operator` have names that end in '`_operator`'.

All predicates are boolean functions (in the mathematical sense) of two arguments: the RTL expression that is being considered at that position in the instruction pattern, and the machine mode that the `match_operand` or `match_operator` specifies. In this section, the first argument is called *op* and the second argument *mode*. Predicates can be called from C as ordinary two-argument functions; this can be useful in output templates or other machine-specific code.

Operand predicates can allow operands that are not actually acceptable to the hardware, as long as the constraints give reload the ability to fix them up (see Section 17.8 [Constraints], page 340). However, GCC will usually generate better code if the predicates specify the requirements of the machine instructions as closely as possible. Reload cannot fix up operands that must be constants ("immediate operands"); you must use a predicate that allows only constants, or else enforce the requirement in the extra condition.

Most predicates handle their *mode* argument in a uniform manner. If *mode* is `VOIDmode` (unspecified), then *op* can have any mode. If *mode* is anything else, then *op* must have the same mode, unless *op* is a `CONST_INT` or integer `CONST_DOUBLE`. These RTL expressions always have `VOIDmode`, so it would be counterproductive to check that their mode matches. Instead, predicates that accept `CONST_INT` and/or integer `CONST_DOUBLE` check that the value stored in the constant will fit in the requested mode.

Predicates with this behavior are called *normal*. `genrecog` can optimize the instruction recognizer based on knowledge of how normal predicates treat modes. It can also diagnose certain kinds of common errors in the use of normal predicates; for instance, it is almost always an error to use a normal predicate without specifying a mode.

Predicates that do something different with their *mode* argument are called *special*. The generic predicates `address_operand` and `pmode_register_operand` are special predicates. `genrecog` does not do any optimizations or diagnosis when special predicates are used.

17.7.1 Machine-Independent Predicates

These are the generic predicates available to all back ends. They are defined in '`recog.c`'. The first category of predicates allow only constant, or *immediate*, operands.

`immediate_operand` [Function]
> This predicate allows any sort of constant that fits in *mode*. It is an appropriate choice for instructions that take operands that must be constant.

`const_int_operand` [Function]
> This predicate allows any `CONST_INT` expression that fits in *mode*. It is an appropriate choice for an immediate operand that does not allow a symbol or label.

`const_double_operand`   [Function]
>   This predicate accepts any `CONST_DOUBLE` expression that has exactly *mode*. If *mode* is `VOIDmode`, it will also accept `CONST_INT`. It is intended for immediate floating point constants.

The second category of predicates allow only some kind of machine register.

`register_operand`   [Function]
>   This predicate allows any `REG` or `SUBREG` expression that is valid for *mode*. It is often suitable for arithmetic instruction operands on a RISC machine.

`pmode_register_operand`   [Function]
>   This is a slight variant on `register_operand` which works around a limitation in the machine-description reader.
>
>   > (match_operand *n* "pmode_register_operand" *constraint*)
>
>   means exactly what
>
>   > (match_operand:P *n* "register_operand" *constraint*)
>
>   would mean, if the machine-description reader accepted ':P' mode suffixes. Unfortunately, it cannot, because `Pmode` is an alias for some other mode, and might vary with machine-specific options. See Section 18.30 [Misc], page 621.

`scratch_operand`   [Function]
>   This predicate allows hard registers and `SCRATCH` expressions, but not pseudo-registers. It is used internally by `match_scratch`; it should not be used directly.

The third category of predicates allow only some kind of memory reference.

`memory_operand`   [Function]
>   This predicate allows any valid reference to a quantity of mode *mode* in memory, as determined by the weak form of `GO_IF_LEGITIMATE_ADDRESS` (see Section 18.13 [Addressing Modes], page 542).

`address_operand`   [Function]
>   This predicate is a little unusual; it allows any operand that is a valid expression for the *address* of a quantity of mode *mode*, again determined by the weak form of `GO_IF_LEGITIMATE_ADDRESS`. To first order, if '(mem:*mode* (*exp*))' is acceptable to `memory_operand`, then *exp* is acceptable to `address_operand`. Note that *exp* does not necessarily have the mode *mode*.

`indirect_operand`   [Function]
>   This is a stricter form of `memory_operand` which allows only memory references with a `general_operand` as the address expression. New uses of this predicate are discouraged, because `general_operand` is very permissive, so it's hard to tell what an `indirect_operand` does or does not allow. If a target has different requirements for memory operands for different instructions, it is better to define target-specific predicates which enforce the hardware's requirements explicitly.

push_operand   [Function]
:   This predicate allows a memory reference suitable for pushing a value onto the stack. This will be a MEM which refers to stack_pointer_rtx, with a side-effect in its address expression (see Section 14.16 [Incdec], page 292); which one is determined by the STACK_PUSH_CODE macro (see Section 18.9.1 [Frame Layout], page 504).

pop_operand   [Function]
:   This predicate allows a memory reference suitable for popping a value off the stack. Again, this will be a MEM referring to stack_pointer_rtx, with a side-effect in its address expression. However, this time STACK_POP_CODE is expected.

The fourth category of predicates allow some combination of the above operands.

nonmemory_operand   [Function]
:   This predicate allows any immediate or register operand valid for *mode*.

nonimmediate_operand   [Function]
:   This predicate allows any register or memory operand valid for *mode*.

general_operand   [Function]
:   This predicate allows any immediate, register, or memory operand valid for *mode*.

Finally, there are two generic operator predicates.

comparison_operator   [Function]
:   This predicate matches any expression which performs an arithmetic comparison in *mode*; that is, COMPARISON_P is true for the expression code.

ordered_comparison_operator   [Function]
:   This predicate matches any expression which performs an arithmetic comparison in *mode* and whose expression code is valid for integer modes; that is, the expression code will be one of eq, ne, lt, ltu, le, leu, gt, gtu, ge, geu.

17.7.2 Defining Machine-Specific Predicates

Many machines have requirements for their operands that cannot be expressed precisely using the generic predicates. You can define additional predicates using define_predicate and define_special_predicate expressions. These expressions have three operands:

- The name of the predicate, as it will be referred to in match_operand or match_operator expressions.
- An RTL expression which evaluates to true if the predicate allows the operand *op*, false if it does not. This expression can only use the following RTL codes:

    MATCH_OPERAND
    :   When written inside a predicate expression, a MATCH_OPERAND expression evaluates to true if the predicate it names would allow *op*. The operand number and constraint are ignored. Due to limitations in genrecog, you can only refer to generic predicates and predicates that have already been defined.

MATCH_CODE

> This expression evaluates to true if *op* or a specified subexpression of *op* has one of a given list of RTX codes.
>
> The first operand of this expression is a string constant containing a comma-separated list of RTX code names (in lower case). These are the codes for which the `MATCH_CODE` will be true.
>
> The second operand is a string constant which indicates what subexpression of *op* to examine. If it is absent or the empty string, *op* itself is examined. Otherwise, the string constant must be a sequence of digits and/or lowercase letters. Each character indicates a subexpression to extract from the current expression; for the first character this is *op*, for the second and subsequent characters it is the result of the previous character. A digit *n* extracts 'XEXP (*e, n*)'; a letter *l* extracts 'XVECEXP (*e*, 0, *n*)' where *n* is the alphabetic ordinal of *l* (0 for 'a', 1 for 'b', and so on). The `MATCH_CODE` then examines the RTX code of the subexpression extracted by the complete string. It is not possible to extract components of an `rtvec` that is not at position 0 within its RTX object.

MATCH_TEST

> This expression has one operand, a string constant containing a C expression. The predicate's arguments, *op* and *mode*, are available with those names in the C expression. The `MATCH_TEST` evaluates to true if the C expression evaluates to a nonzero value. `MATCH_TEST` expressions must not have side effects.

AND
IOR
NOT
IF_THEN_ELSE

> The basic 'MATCH_' expressions can be combined using these logical operators, which have the semantics of the C operators '&&', '||', '!', and '? :' respectively. As in Common Lisp, you may give an `AND` or `IOR` expression an arbitrary number of arguments; this has exactly the same effect as writing a chain of two-argument `AND` or `IOR` expressions.

- An optional block of C code, which should execute 'return true' if the predicate is found to match and 'return false' if it does not. It must not have any side effects. The predicate arguments, *op* and *mode*, are available with those names.

If a code block is present in a predicate definition, then the RTL expression must evaluate to true *and* the code block must execute 'return true' for the predicate to allow the operand. The RTL expression is evaluated first; do not re-check anything in the code block that was checked in the RTL expression.

The program `genrecog` scans `define_predicate` and `define_special_predicate` expressions to determine which RTX codes are possibly allowed. You should always make this explicit in the RTL predicate expression, using `MATCH_OPERAND` and `MATCH_CODE`.

Here is an example of a simple predicate definition, from the IA64 machine description:

```
;; True if op is a SYMBOL_REF which refers to the sdata section.
(define_predicate "small_addr_symbolic_operand"
  (and (match_code "symbol_ref")
       (match_test "SYMBOL_REF_SMALL_ADDR_P (op)")))
```

And here is another, showing the use of the C block.

```
;; True if op is a register operand that is (or could be) a GR reg.
(define_predicate "gr_register_operand"
  (match_operand 0 "register_operand")
{
  unsigned int regno;
  if (GET_CODE (op) == SUBREG)
    op = SUBREG_REG (op);

  regno = REGNO (op);
  return (regno >= FIRST_PSEUDO_REGISTER || GENERAL_REGNO_P (regno));
})
```

Predicates written with define_predicate automatically include a test that *mode* is VOIDmode, or *op* has the same mode as *mode*, or *op* is a CONST_INT or CONST_DOUBLE. They do *not* check specifically for integer CONST_DOUBLE, nor do they test that the value of either kind of constant fits in the requested mode. This is because target-specific predicates that take constants usually have to do more stringent value checks anyway. If you need the exact same treatment of CONST_INT or CONST_DOUBLE that the generic predicates provide, use a MATCH_OPERAND subexpression to call const_int_operand, const_double_operand, or immediate_operand.

Predicates written with define_special_predicate do not get any automatic mode checks, and are treated as having special mode handling by genrecog.

The program genpreds is responsible for generating code to test predicates. It also writes a header file containing function declarations for all machine-specific predicates. It is not necessary to declare these predicates in 'cpu-protos.h'.

17.8 Operand Constraints

Each match_operand in an instruction pattern can specify constraints for the operands allowed. The constraints allow you to fine-tune matching within the set of operands allowed by the predicate.

Constraints can say whether an operand may be in a register, and which kinds of register; whether the operand can be a memory reference, and which kinds of address; whether the operand may be an immediate constant, and which possible values it may have. Constraints can also require two operands to match. Side-effects aren't allowed in operands of inline asm, unless '<' or '>' constraints are used, because there is no guarantee that the side-effects will happen exactly once in an instruction that can update the addressing register.

17.8.1 Simple Constraints

The simplest kind of constraint is a string full of letters, each of which describes one kind of operand that is permitted. Here are the letters that are allowed:

whitespace
> Whitespace characters are ignored and can be inserted at any position except the first. This enables each alternative for different operands to be visually

aligned in the machine description even if they have different number of constraints and modifiers.

'm' A memory operand is allowed, with any kind of address that the machine supports in general. Note that the letter used for the general memory constraint can be re-defined by a back end using the TARGET_MEM_CONSTRAINT macro.

'o' A memory operand is allowed, but only if the address is *offsettable*. This means that adding a small integer (actually, the width in bytes of the operand, as determined by its machine mode) may be added to the address and the result is also a valid memory address.

For example, an address which is constant is offsettable; so is an address that is the sum of a register and a constant (as long as a slightly larger constant is also within the range of address-offsets supported by the machine); but an autoincrement or autodecrement address is not offsettable. More complicated indirect/indexed addresses may or may not be offsettable depending on the other addressing modes that the machine supports.

Note that in an output operand which can be matched by another operand, the constraint letter 'o' is valid only when accompanied by both '<' (if the target machine has predecrement addressing) and '>' (if the target machine has preincrement addressing).

'V' A memory operand that is not offsettable. In other words, anything that would fit the 'm' constraint but not the 'o' constraint.

'<' A memory operand with autodecrement addressing (either predecrement or postdecrement) is allowed. In inline asm this constraint is only allowed if the operand is used exactly once in an instruction that can handle the side-effects. Not using an operand with '<' in constraint string in the inline asm pattern at all or using it in multiple instructions isn't valid, because the side-effects wouldn't be performed or would be performed more than once. Furthermore, on some targets the operand with '<' in constraint string must be accompanied by special instruction suffixes like %U0 instruction suffix on PowerPC or %P0 on IA-64.

'>' A memory operand with autoincrement addressing (either preincrement or postincrement) is allowed. In inline asm the same restrictions as for '<' apply.

'r' A register operand is allowed provided that it is in a general register.

'i' An immediate integer operand (one with constant value) is allowed. This includes symbolic constants whose values will be known only at assembly time or later.

'n' An immediate integer operand with a known numeric value is allowed. Many systems cannot support assembly-time constants for operands less than a word wide. Constraints for these operands should use 'n' rather than 'i'.

'I', 'J', 'K', ... 'P'
Other letters in the range 'I' through 'P' may be defined in a machine-dependent fashion to permit immediate integer operands with explicit integer values in

specified ranges. For example, on the 68000, 'I' is defined to stand for the range of values 1 to 8. This is the range permitted as a shift count in the shift instructions.

'E'
An immediate floating operand (expression code `const_double`) is allowed, but only if the target floating point format is the same as that of the host machine (on which the compiler is running).

'F'
An immediate floating operand (expression code `const_double` or `const_vector`) is allowed.

'G', 'H'
'G' and 'H' may be defined in a machine-dependent fashion to permit immediate floating operands in particular ranges of values.

's'
An immediate integer operand whose value is not an explicit integer is allowed.

This might appear strange; if an insn allows a constant operand with a value not known at compile time, it certainly must allow any known value. So why use 's' instead of 'i'? Sometimes it allows better code to be generated.

For example, on the 68000 in a fullword instruction it is possible to use an immediate operand; but if the immediate value is between −128 and 127, better code results from loading the value into a register and using the register. This is because the load into the register can be done with a 'moveq' instruction. We arrange for this to happen by defining the letter 'K' to mean "any integer outside the range −128 to 127", and then specifying 'Ks' in the operand constraints.

'g'
Any register, memory or immediate integer operand is allowed, except for registers that are not general registers.

'X'
Any operand whatsoever is allowed, even if it does not satisfy `general_operand`. This is normally used in the constraint of a `match_scratch` when certain alternatives will not actually require a scratch register.

'0', '1', '2', ... '9'
An operand that matches the specified operand number is allowed. If a digit is used together with letters within the same alternative, the digit should come last.

This number is allowed to be more than a single digit. If multiple digits are encountered consecutively, they are interpreted as a single decimal integer. There is scant chance for ambiguity, since to-date it has never been desirable that '10' be interpreted as matching either operand 1 *or* operand 0. Should this be desired, one can use multiple alternatives instead.

This is called a *matching constraint* and what it really means is that the assembler has only a single operand that fills two roles considered separate in the RTL insn. For example, an add insn has two input operands and one output operand in the RTL, but on most CISC machines an add instruction really has only two operands, one of them an input-output operand:

```
addl #35,r12
```

Matching constraints are used in these circumstances. More precisely, the two operands that match must include one input-only operand and one output-only operand. Moreover, the digit must be a smaller number than the number of the operand that uses it in the constraint.

For operands to match in a particular case usually means that they are identical-looking RTL expressions. But in a few special cases specific kinds of dissimilarity are allowed. For example, *x as an input operand will match *x++ as an output operand. For proper results in such cases, the output template should always use the output-operand's number when printing the operand.

'p' An operand that is a valid memory address is allowed. This is for "load address" and "push address" instructions.

'p' in the constraint must be accompanied by `address_operand` as the predicate in the `match_operand`. This predicate interprets the mode specified in the `match_operand` as the mode of the memory reference for which the address would be valid.

other-letters

Other letters can be defined in machine-dependent fashion to stand for particular classes of registers or other arbitrary operand types. 'd', 'a' and 'f' are defined on the 68000/68020 to stand for data, address and floating point registers.

In order to have valid assembler code, each operand must satisfy its constraint. But a failure to do so does not prevent the pattern from applying to an insn. Instead, it directs the compiler to modify the code so that the constraint will be satisfied. Usually this is done by copying an operand into a register.

Contrast, therefore, the two instruction patterns that follow:

```
(define_insn ""
  [(set (match_operand:SI 0 "general_operand" "=r")
        (plus:SI (match_dup 0)
                 (match_operand:SI 1 "general_operand" "r")))]
  ""
  "...")
```

which has two operands, one of which must appear in two places, and

```
(define_insn ""
  [(set (match_operand:SI 0 "general_operand" "=r")
        (plus:SI (match_operand:SI 1 "general_operand" "0")
                 (match_operand:SI 2 "general_operand" "r")))]
  ""
  "...")
```

which has three operands, two of which are required by a constraint to be identical. If we are considering an insn of the form

```
(insn n prev next
   (set (reg:SI 3)
        (plus:SI (reg:SI 6) (reg:SI 109)))
   ...)
```

the first pattern would not apply at all, because this insn does not contain two identical subexpressions in the right place. The pattern would say, "That does not look like an add instruction; try other patterns". The second pattern would say, "Yes, that's an add instruction, but there is something wrong with it". It would direct the reload pass of the compiler to generate additional insns to make the constraint true. The results might look like this:

```
(insn n2 prev n
  (set (reg:SI 3) (reg:SI 6))
  ...)

(insn n n2 next
  (set (reg:SI 3)
       (plus:SI (reg:SI 3) (reg:SI 109)))
  ...)
```

It is up to you to make sure that each operand, in each pattern, has constraints that can handle any RTL expression that could be present for that operand. (When multiple alternatives are in use, each pattern must, for each possible combination of operand expressions, have at least one alternative which can handle that combination of operands.) The constraints don't need to *allow* any possible operand—when this is the case, they do not constrain—but they must at least point the way to reloading any possible operand so that it will fit.

- If the constraint accepts whatever operands the predicate permits, there is no problem: reloading is never necessary for this operand.

  For example, an operand whose constraints permit everything except registers is safe provided its predicate rejects registers.

  An operand whose predicate accepts only constant values is safe provided its constraints include the letter 'i'. If any possible constant value is accepted, then nothing less than 'i' will do; if the predicate is more selective, then the constraints may also be more selective.

- Any operand expression can be reloaded by copying it into a register. So if an operand's constraints allow some kind of register, it is certain to be safe. It need not permit all classes of registers; the compiler knows how to copy a register into another register of the proper class in order to make an instruction valid.

- A nonoffsettable memory reference can be reloaded by copying the address into a register. So if the constraint uses the letter 'o', all memory references are taken care of.

- A constant operand can be reloaded by allocating space in memory to hold it as preinitialized data. Then the memory reference can be used in place of the constant. So if the constraint uses the letters 'o' or 'm', constant operands are not a problem.

- If the constraint permits a constant and a pseudo register used in an insn was not allocated to a hard register and is equivalent to a constant, the register will be replaced with the constant. If the predicate does not permit a constant and the insn is re-recognized for some reason, the compiler will crash. Thus the predicate must always recognize any objects allowed by the constraint.

If the operand's predicate can recognize registers, but the constraint does not permit them, it can make the compiler crash. When this operand happens to be a register, the reload pass will be stymied, because it does not know how to copy a register temporarily into memory.

If the predicate accepts a unary operator, the constraint applies to the operand. For example, the MIPS processor at ISA level 3 supports an instruction which adds two registers in `SImode` to produce a `DImode` result, but only if the registers are correctly sign extended. This predicate for the input operands accepts a `sign_extend` of an `SImode` register. Write the constraint to indicate the type of register that is required for the operand of the `sign_extend`.

17.8.2 Multiple Alternative Constraints

Sometimes a single instruction has multiple alternative sets of possible operands. For example, on the 68000, a logical-or instruction can combine register or an immediate value into memory, or it can combine any kind of operand into a register; but it cannot combine one memory location into another.

These constraints are represented as multiple alternatives. An alternative can be described by a series of letters for each operand. The overall constraint for an operand is made from the letters for this operand from the first alternative, a comma, the letters for this operand from the second alternative, a comma, and so on until the last alternative. All operands for a single instruction must have the same number of alternatives. Here is how it is done for fullword logical-or on the 68000:

```
(define_insn "iorsi3"
  [(set (match_operand:SI 0 "general_operand" "=m,d")
        (ior:SI (match_operand:SI 1 "general_operand" "%0,0")
                (match_operand:SI 2 "general_operand" "dKs,dmKs")))]
  ...)
```

The first alternative has 'm' (memory) for operand 0, '0' for operand 1 (meaning it must match operand 0), and 'dKs' for operand 2. The second alternative has 'd' (data register) for operand 0, '0' for operand 1, and 'dmKs' for operand 2. The '=' and '%' in the constraints apply to all the alternatives; their meaning is explained in the next section (see Section 17.8.3 [Class Preferences], page 346).

If all the operands fit any one alternative, the instruction is valid. Otherwise, for each alternative, the compiler counts how many instructions must be added to copy the operands so that that alternative applies. The alternative requiring the least copying is chosen. If two alternatives need the same amount of copying, the one that comes first is chosen. These choices can be altered with the '?' and '!' characters:

?   Disparage slightly the alternative that the '?' appears in, as a choice when no alternative applies exactly. The compiler regards this alternative as one unit more costly for each '?' that appears in it.

!   Disparage severely the alternative that the '!' appears in. This alternative can still be used if it fits without reloading, but if reloading is needed, some other alternative will be used.

^   This constraint is analogous to '?' but it disparages slightly the alternative only if the operand with the '^' needs a reload.

$ This constraint is analogous to '!' but it disparages severely the alternative only if the operand with the '$' needs a reload.

When an insn pattern has multiple alternatives in its constraints, often the appearance of the assembler code is determined mostly by which alternative was matched. When this is so, the C code for writing the assembler code can use the variable `which_alternative`, which is the ordinal number of the alternative that was actually satisfied (0 for the first, 1 for the second alternative, etc.). See Section 17.6 [Output Statement], page 334.

17.8.3 Register Class Preferences

The operand constraints have another function: they enable the compiler to decide which kind of hardware register a pseudo register is best allocated to. The compiler examines the constraints that apply to the insns that use the pseudo register, looking for the machine-dependent letters such as 'd' and 'a' that specify classes of registers. The pseudo register is put in whichever class gets the most "votes". The constraint letters 'g' and 'r' also vote: they vote in favor of a general register. The machine description says which registers are considered general.

Of course, on some machines all registers are equivalent, and no register classes are defined. Then none of this complexity is relevant.

17.8.4 Constraint Modifier Characters

Here are constraint modifier characters.

'=' Means that this operand is written to by this instruction: the previous value is discarded and replaced by new data.

'+' Means that this operand is both read and written by the instruction.

When the compiler fixes up the operands to satisfy the constraints, it needs to know which operands are read by the instruction and which are written by it. '=' identifies an operand which is only written; '+' identifies an operand that is both read and written; all other operands are assumed to only be read.

If you specify '=' or '+' in a constraint, you put it in the first character of the constraint string.

'&' Means (in a particular alternative) that this operand is an *earlyclobber* operand, which is written before the instruction is finished using the input operands. Therefore, this operand may not lie in a register that is read by the instruction or as part of any memory address.

'&' applies only to the alternative in which it is written. In constraints with multiple alternatives, sometimes one alternative requires '&' while others do not. See, for example, the '`movdf`' insn of the 68000.

A operand which is read by the instruction can be tied to an earlyclobber operand if its only use as an input occurs before the early result is written. Adding alternatives of this form often allows GCC to produce better code when only some of the read operands can be affected by the earlyclobber. See, for example, the '`mulsi3`' insn of the ARM.

Furthermore, if the *earlyclobber* operand is also a read/write operand, then that operand is written only after it's used.

'&' does not obviate the need to write '=' or '+'. As *earlyclobber* operands are always written, a read-only *earlyclobber* operand is ill-formed and will be rejected by the compiler.

'%' Declares the instruction to be commutative for this operand and the following operand. This means that the compiler may interchange the two operands if that is the cheapest way to make all operands fit the constraints. '%' applies to all alternatives and must appear as the first character in the constraint. Only read-only operands can use '%'.

This is often used in patterns for addition instructions that really have only two operands: the result must go in one of the arguments. Here for example, is how the 68000 halfword-add instruction is defined:

```
(define_insn "addhi3"
  [(set (match_operand:HI 0 "general_operand" "=m,r")
        (plus:HI (match_operand:HI 1 "general_operand" "%0,0")
                 (match_operand:HI 2 "general_operand" "di,g")))]
  ...)
```

GCC can only handle one commutative pair in an asm; if you use more, the compiler may fail. Note that you need not use the modifier if the two alternatives are strictly identical; this would only waste time in the reload pass. The modifier is not operational after register allocation, so the result of define_peephole2 and define_splits performed after reload cannot rely on '%' to make the intended insn match.

'#' Says that all following characters, up to the next comma, are to be ignored as a constraint. They are significant only for choosing register preferences.

'*' Says that the following character should be ignored when choosing register preferences. '*' has no effect on the meaning of the constraint as a constraint, and no effect on reloading. For LRA '*' additionally disparages slightly the alternative if the following character matches the operand.

Here is an example: the 68000 has an instruction to sign-extend a halfword in a data register, and can also sign-extend a value by copying it into an address register. While either kind of register is acceptable, the constraints on an address-register destination are less strict, so it is best if register allocation makes an address register its goal. Therefore, '*' is used so that the 'd' constraint letter (for data register) is ignored when computing register preferences.

```
(define_insn "extendhisi2"
  [(set (match_operand:SI 0 "general_operand" "=*d,a")
        (sign_extend:SI
         (match_operand:HI 1 "general_operand" "0,g")))]
  ...)
```

17.8.5 Constraints for Particular Machines

Whenever possible, you should use the general-purpose constraint letters in asm arguments, since they will convey meaning more readily to people reading your code. Failing that, use the constraint letters that usually have very similar meanings across architectures. The most commonly used constraints are 'm' and 'r' (for memory and general-purpose registers respectively; see Section 17.8.1 [Simple Constraints], page 340), and 'I', usually the letter indicating the most common immediate-constant format.

Each architecture defines additional constraints. These constraints are used by the compiler itself for instruction generation, as well as for asm statements; therefore, some of the constraints are not particularly useful for asm. Here is a summary of some of the machine-dependent constraints available on some particular machines; it includes both constraints that are useful for asm and constraints that aren't. The compiler source file mentioned in the table heading for each architecture is the definitive reference for the meanings of that architecture's constraints.

AArch64 family—'config/aarch64/constraints.md'

	k	The stack pointer register (SP)
	w	Floating point register, Advanced SIMD vector register or SVE vector register
	Upl	One of the low eight SVE predicate registers (P0 to P7)
	Upa	Any of the SVE predicate registers (P0 to P15)
	I	Integer constant that is valid as an immediate operand in an ADD instruction
	J	Integer constant that is valid as an immediate operand in a SUB instruction (once negated)
	K	Integer constant that can be used with a 32-bit logical instruction
	L	Integer constant that can be used with a 64-bit logical instruction
	M	Integer constant that is valid as an immediate operand in a 32-bit MOV pseudo instruction. The MOV may be assembled to one of several different machine instructions depending on the value
	N	Integer constant that is valid as an immediate operand in a 64-bit MOV pseudo instruction
	S	An absolute symbolic address or a label reference
	Y	Floating point constant zero
	Z	Integer constant zero
	Ush	The high part (bits 12 and upwards) of the pc-relative address of a symbol within 4GB of the instruction
	Q	A memory address which uses a single base register with no offset
	Ump	A memory address suitable for a load/store pair instruction in SI, DI, SF and DF modes

ARC —'config/arc/constraints.md'

	q	Registers usable in ARCompact 16-bit instructions: r0-r3, r12-r15. This constraint can only match when the '-mq' option is in effect.
	e	Registers usable as base-regs of memory addresses in ARCompact 16-bit memory instructions: r0-r3, r12-r15, sp. This constraint can only match when the '-mq' option is in effect.
	D	ARC FPX (dpfp) 64-bit registers. D0, D1.
	I	A signed 12-bit integer constant.

Cal		constant for arithmetic/logical operations. This might be any constant that can be put into a long immediate by the assmbler or linker without involving a PIC relocation.
K		A 3-bit unsigned integer constant.
L		A 6-bit unsigned integer constant.
CnL		One's complement of a 6-bit unsigned integer constant.
CmL		Two's complement of a 6-bit unsigned integer constant.
M		A 5-bit unsigned integer constant.
O		A 7-bit unsigned integer constant.
P		A 8-bit unsigned integer constant.
H		Any const_double value.

ARM family—'config/arm/constraints.md'

h	In Thumb state, the core registers r8-r15.
k	The stack pointer register.
l	In Thumb State the core registers r0-r7. In ARM state this is an alias for the r constraint.
t	VFP floating-point registers s0-s31. Used for 32 bit values.
w	VFP floating-point registers d0-d31 and the appropriate subset d0-d15 based on command line options. Used for 64 bit values only. Not valid for Thumb1.
y	The iWMMX co-processor registers.
z	The iWMMX GR registers.
G	The floating-point constant 0.0
I	Integer that is valid as an immediate operand in a data processing instruction. That is, an integer in the range 0 to 255 rotated by a multiple of 2
J	Integer in the range −4095 to 4095
K	Integer that satisfies constraint 'I' when inverted (ones complement)
L	Integer that satisfies constraint 'I' when negated (twos complement)
M	Integer in the range 0 to 32
Q	A memory reference where the exact address is in a single register ("m" is preferable for **asm** statements)
R	An item in the constant pool
S	A symbol in the text segment of the current file

Uv		A memory reference suitable for VFP load/store insns (reg+constant offset)
Uy		A memory reference suitable for iWMMXt load/store instructions.
Uq		A memory reference suitable for the ARMv4 ldrsb instruction.

AVR family—'config/avr/constraints.md'

l	Registers from r0 to r15
a	Registers from r16 to r23
d	Registers from r16 to r31
w	Registers from r24 to r31. These registers can be used in 'adiw' command
e	Pointer register (r26–r31)
b	Base pointer register (r28–r31)
q	Stack pointer register (SPH:SPL)
t	Temporary register r0
x	Register pair X (r27:r26)
y	Register pair Y (r29:r28)
z	Register pair Z (r31:r30)
I	Constant greater than −1, less than 64
J	Constant greater than −64, less than 1
K	Constant integer 2
L	Constant integer 0
M	Constant that fits in 8 bits
N	Constant integer −1
O	Constant integer 8, 16, or 24
P	Constant integer 1
G	A floating point constant 0.0
Q	A memory address based on Y or Z pointer with displacement.

Blackfin family—'config/bfin/constraints.md'

a	P register
d	D register
z	A call clobbered P register.
q*n*	A single register. If *n* is in the range 0 to 7, the corresponding D register. If it is A, then the register P0.
D	Even-numbered D register

W	Odd-numbered D register
e	Accumulator register.
A	Even-numbered accumulator register.
B	Odd-numbered accumulator register.
b	I register
v	B register
f	M register
c	Registers used for circular buffering, i.e. I, B, or L registers.
C	The CC register.
t	LT0 or LT1.
k	LC0 or LC1.
u	LB0 or LB1.
x	Any D, P, B, M, I or L register.
y	Additional registers typically used only in prologues and epilogues: RETS, RETN, RETI, RETX, RETE, ASTAT, SEQSTAT and USP.
w	Any register except accumulators or CC.
Ksh	Signed 16 bit integer (in the range −32768 to 32767)
Kuh	Unsigned 16 bit integer (in the range 0 to 65535)
Ks7	Signed 7 bit integer (in the range −64 to 63)
Ku7	Unsigned 7 bit integer (in the range 0 to 127)
Ku5	Unsigned 5 bit integer (in the range 0 to 31)
Ks4	Signed 4 bit integer (in the range −8 to 7)
Ks3	Signed 3 bit integer (in the range −3 to 4)
Ku3	Unsigned 3 bit integer (in the range 0 to 7)
P*n*	Constant *n*, where *n* is a single-digit constant in the range 0 to 4.
PA	An integer equal to one of the MACFLAG_XXX constants that is suitable for use with either accumulator.
PB	An integer equal to one of the MACFLAG_XXX constants that is suitable for use only with accumulator A1.
M1	Constant 255.
M2	Constant 65535.
J	An integer constant with exactly a single bit set.
L	An integer constant with all bits set except exactly one.
H	

	Q	Any SYMBOL_REF.

CR16 Architecture—'config/cr16/cr16.h'

	b	Registers from r0 to r14 (registers without stack pointer)
	t	Register from r0 to r11 (all 16-bit registers)
	p	Register from r12 to r15 (all 32-bit registers)
	I	Signed constant that fits in 4 bits
	J	Signed constant that fits in 5 bits
	K	Signed constant that fits in 6 bits
	L	Unsigned constant that fits in 4 bits
	M	Signed constant that fits in 32 bits
	N	Check for 64 bits wide constants for add/sub instructions
	G	Floating point constant that is legal for store immediate

Epiphany—'config/epiphany/constraints.md'

	U16	An unsigned 16-bit constant.
	K	An unsigned 5-bit constant.
	L	A signed 11-bit constant.
	Cm1	A signed 11-bit constant added to −1. Can only match when the '-m1reg-*reg*' option is active.
	Cl1	Left-shift of −1, i.e., a bit mask with a block of leading ones, the rest being a block of trailing zeroes. Can only match when the '-m1reg-*reg*' option is active.
	Cr1	Right-shift of −1, i.e., a bit mask with a trailing block of ones, the rest being zeroes. Or to put it another way, one less than a power of two. Can only match when the '-m1reg-*reg*' option is active.
	Cal	Constant for arithmetic/logical operations. This is like i, except that for position independent code, no symbols / expressions needing relocations are allowed.
	Csy	Symbolic constant for call/jump instruction.
	Rcs	The register class usable in short insns. This is a register class constraint, and can thus drive register allocation. This constraint won't match unless '-mprefer-short-insn-regs' is in effect.
	Rsc	The the register class of registers that can be used to hold a sibcall call address. I.e., a caller-saved register.
	Rct	Core control register class.
	Rgs	The register group usable in short insns. This constraint does not use a register class, so that it only passively matches suitable registers, and doesn't drive register allocation.

Car		Constant suitable for the addsi3_r pattern. This is a valid offset For byte, halfword, or word addressing.
Rra		Matches the return address if it can be replaced with the link register.
Rcc		Matches the integer condition code register.
Sra		Matches the return address if it is in a stack slot.
Cfm		Matches control register values to switch fp mode, which are encapsulated in UNSPEC_FP_MODE.

FRV—'config/frv/frv.h'

a	Register in the class ACC_REGS (acc0 to acc7).
b	Register in the class EVEN_ACC_REGS (acc0 to acc7).
c	Register in the class CC_REGS (fcc0 to fcc3 and icc0 to icc3).
d	Register in the class GPR_REGS (gr0 to gr63).
e	Register in the class EVEN_REGS (gr0 to gr63). Odd registers are excluded not in the class but through the use of a machine mode larger than 4 bytes.
f	Register in the class FPR_REGS (fr0 to fr63).
h	Register in the class FEVEN_REGS (fr0 to fr63). Odd registers are excluded not in the class but through the use of a machine mode larger than 4 bytes.
l	Register in the class LR_REG (the lr register).
q	Register in the class QUAD_REGS (gr2 to gr63). Register numbers not divisible by 4 are excluded not in the class but through the use of a machine mode larger than 8 bytes.
t	Register in the class ICC_REGS (icc0 to icc3).
u	Register in the class FCC_REGS (fcc0 to fcc3).
v	Register in the class ICR_REGS (cc4 to cc7).
w	Register in the class FCR_REGS (cc0 to cc3).
x	Register in the class QUAD_FPR_REGS (fr0 to fr63). Register numbers not divisible by 4 are excluded not in the class but through the use of a machine mode larger than 8 bytes.
z	Register in the class SPR_REGS (lcr and lr).
A	Register in the class QUAD_ACC_REGS (acc0 to acc7).
B	Register in the class ACCG_REGS (accg0 to accg7).
C	Register in the class CR_REGS (cc0 to cc7).
G	Floating point constant zero

I	6-bit signed integer constant	
J	10-bit signed integer constant	
L	16-bit signed integer constant	
M	16-bit unsigned integer constant	
N	12-bit signed integer constant that is negative—i.e. in the range of -2048 to -1	
O	Constant zero	
P	12-bit signed integer constant that is greater than zero—i.e. in the range of 1 to 2047.	

FT32—'config/ft32/constraints.md'

A	An absolute address
B	An offset address
W	A register indirect memory operand
e	An offset address.
f	An offset address.
O	The constant zero or one
I	A 16-bit signed constant ($-32768 \ldots 32767$)
w	A bitfield mask suitable for bext or bins
x	An inverted bitfield mask suitable for bext or bins
L	A 16-bit unsigned constant, multiple of 4 ($0 \ldots 65532$)
S	A 20-bit signed constant ($-524288 \ldots 524287$)
b	A constant for a bitfield width ($1 \ldots 16$)
KA	A 10-bit signed constant ($-512 \ldots 511$)

Hewlett-Packard PA-RISC—'config/pa/pa.h'

a	General register 1
f	Floating point register
q	Shift amount register
x	Floating point register (deprecated)
y	Upper floating point register (32-bit), floating point register (64-bit)
Z	Any register
I	Signed 11-bit integer constant
J	Signed 14-bit integer constant
K	Integer constant that can be deposited with a `zdepi` instruction

L		Signed 5-bit integer constant
M		Integer constant 0
N		Integer constant that can be loaded with a `ldil` instruction
O		Integer constant whose value plus one is a power of 2
P		Integer constant that can be used for `and` operations in `depi` and `extru` instructions
S		Integer constant 31
U		Integer constant 63
G		Floating-point constant 0.0
A		A `lo_sum` data-linkage-table memory operand
Q		A memory operand that can be used as the destination operand of an integer store instruction
R		A scaled or unscaled indexed memory operand
T		A memory operand for floating-point loads and stores
W		A register indirect memory operand

Intel IA-64—'config/ia64/ia64.h'

a	General register `r0` to `r3` for `addl` instruction
b	Branch register
c	Predicate register ('c' as in "conditional")
d	Application register residing in M-unit
e	Application register residing in I-unit
f	Floating-point register
m	Memory operand. If used together with '<' or '>', the operand can have postincrement and postdecrement which require printing with '%Pn' on IA-64.
G	Floating-point constant 0.0 or 1.0
I	14-bit signed integer constant
J	22-bit signed integer constant
K	8-bit signed integer constant for logical instructions
L	8-bit adjusted signed integer constant for compare pseudo-ops
M	6-bit unsigned integer constant for shift counts
N	9-bit signed integer constant for load and store postincrements
O	The constant zero
P	0 or -1 for `dep` instruction

Q	Non-volatile memory for floating-point loads and stores
R	Integer constant in the range 1 to 4 for `shladd` instruction
S	Memory operand except postincrement and postdecrement. This is now roughly the same as 'm' when not used together with '<' or '>'.

M32C—'config/m32c/m32c.c'

Rsp	
Rfb	
Rsb	'$sp', '$fb', '$sb'.
Rcr	Any control register, when they're 16 bits wide (nothing if control registers are 24 bits wide)
Rcl	Any control register, when they're 24 bits wide.
R0w	
R1w	
R2w	
R3w	$r0, $r1, $r2, $r3.
R02	$r0 or $r2, or $r2r0 for 32 bit values.
R13	$r1 or $r3, or $r3r1 for 32 bit values.
Rdi	A register that can hold a 64 bit value.
Rhl	$r0 or $r1 (registers with addressable high/low bytes)
R23	$r2 or $r3
Raa	Address registers
Raw	Address registers when they're 16 bits wide.
Ral	Address registers when they're 24 bits wide.
Rqi	Registers that can hold QI values.
Rad	Registers that can be used with displacements ($a0, $a1, $sb).
Rsi	Registers that can hold 32 bit values.
Rhi	Registers that can hold 16 bit values.
Rhc	Registers chat can hold 16 bit values, including all control registers.
Rra	$r0 through R1, plus $a0 and $a1.
Rfl	The flags register.
Rmm	The memory-based pseudo-registers $mem0 through $mem15.
Rpi	Registers that can hold pointers (16 bit registers for r8c, m16c; 24 bit registers for m32cm, m32c).
Rpa	Matches multiple registers in a PARALLEL to form a larger register. Used to match function return values.

Chapter 17: Machine Descriptions

Is3	−8 ... 7
IS1	−128 ... 127
IS2	−32768 ... 32767
IU2	0 ... 65535
In4	−8 ... −1 or 1 ... 8
In5	−16 ... −1 or 1 ... 16
In6	−32 ... −1 or 1 ... 32
IM2	−65536 ... −1
Ilb	An 8 bit value with exactly one bit set.
Ilw	A 16 bit value with exactly one bit set.
Sd	The common src/dest memory addressing modes.
Sa	Memory addressed using $a0 or $a1.
Si	Memory addressed with immediate addresses.
Ss	Memory addressed using the stack pointer ($sp).
Sf	Memory addressed using the frame base register ($fb).
Ss	Memory addressed using the small base register ($sb).
S1	$r1h

MicroBlaze—'config/microblaze/constraints.md'

d	A general register (r0 to r31).
z	A status register (rmsr, $fcc1 to $fcc7).

MIPS—'config/mips/constraints.md'

d	A general-purpose register. This is equivalent to r unless generating MIPS16 code, in which case the MIPS16 register set is used.
f	A floating-point register (if available).
h	Formerly the hi register. This constraint is no longer supported.
l	The lo register. Use this register to store values that are no bigger than a word.
x	The concatenated hi and lo registers. Use this register to store doubleword values.
c	A register suitable for use in an indirect jump. This will always be $25 for '-mabicalls'.
v	Register $3. Do not use this constraint in new code; it is retained only for compatibility with glibc.
y	Equivalent to r; retained for backwards compatibility.
z	A floating-point condition code register.

I		A signed 16-bit constant (for arithmetic instructions).
J		Integer zero.
K		An unsigned 16-bit constant (for logic instructions).
L		A signed 32-bit constant in which the lower 16 bits are zero. Such constants can be loaded using `lui`.
M		A constant that cannot be loaded using `lui`, `addiu` or `ori`.
N		A constant in the range -65535 to -1 (inclusive).
O		A signed 15-bit constant.
P		A constant in the range 1 to 65535 (inclusive).
G		Floating-point zero.
R		An address that can be used in a non-macro load or store.
ZC		A memory operand whose address is formed by a base register and offset that is suitable for use in instructions with the same addressing mode as `ll` and `sc`.
ZD		An address suitable for a `prefetch` instruction, or for any other instruction with the same addressing mode as `prefetch`.

Motorola 680x0—'config/m68k/constraints.md'

a	Address register
d	Data register
f	68881 floating-point register, if available
I	Integer in the range 1 to 8
J	16-bit signed number
K	Signed number whose magnitude is greater than 0x80
L	Integer in the range -8 to -1
M	Signed number whose magnitude is greater than 0x100
N	Range 24 to 31, rotatert:SI 8 to 1 expressed as rotate
O	16 (for rotate using swap)
P	Range 8 to 15, rotatert:HI 8 to 1 expressed as rotate
R	Numbers that mov3q can handle
G	Floating point constant that is not a 68881 constant
S	Operands that satisfy 'm' when -mpcrel is in effect
T	Operands that satisfy 's' when -mpcrel is not in effect
Q	Address register indirect addressing mode
U	Register offset addressing

Chapter 17: Machine Descriptions 359

W	const_call_operand	
Cs	symbol_ref or const	
Ci	const_int	
C0	const_int 0	
Cj	Range of signed numbers that don't fit in 16 bits	
Cmvq	Integers valid for mvq	
Capsw	Integers valid for a moveq followed by a swap	
Cmvz	Integers valid for mvz	
Cmvs	Integers valid for mvs	
Ap	push_operand	
Ac	Non-register operands allowed in clr	

Moxie—'config/moxie/constraints.md'

A	An absolute address
B	An offset address
W	A register indirect memory operand
I	A constant in the range of 0 to 255.
N	A constant in the range of 0 to −255.

MSP430–'config/msp430/constraints.md'

R12	Register R12.
R13	Register R13.
K	Integer constant 1.
L	Integer constant -1^20..1^19.
M	Integer constant 1-4.
Ya	Memory references which do not require an extended MOVX instruction.
Yl	Memory reference, labels only.
Ys	Memory reference, stack only.

NDS32—'config/nds32/constraints.md'

w	LOW register class $r0 to $r7 constraint for V3/V3M ISA.
l	LOW register class $r0 to $r7.
d	MIDDLE register class $r0 to $r11, $r16 to $r19.
h	HIGH register class $r12 to $r14, $r20 to $r31.
t	Temporary assist register $ta (i.e. $r15).

k	Stack register $sp.
Iu03	Unsigned immediate 3-bit value.
In03	Negative immediate 3-bit value in the range of -7–0.
Iu04	Unsigned immediate 4-bit value.
Is05	Signed immediate 5-bit value.
Iu05	Unsigned immediate 5-bit value.
In05	Negative immediate 5-bit value in the range of -31–0.
Ip05	Unsigned immediate 5-bit value for movpi45 instruction with range 16–47.
Iu06	Unsigned immediate 6-bit value constraint for addri36.sp instruction.
Iu08	Unsigned immediate 8-bit value.
Iu09	Unsigned immediate 9-bit value.
Is10	Signed immediate 10-bit value.
Is11	Signed immediate 11-bit value.
Is15	Signed immediate 15-bit value.
Iu15	Unsigned immediate 15-bit value.
Ic15	A constant which is not in the range of imm15u but ok for bclr instruction.
Ie15	A constant which is not in the range of imm15u but ok for bset instruction.
It15	A constant which is not in the range of imm15u but ok for btgl instruction.
Ii15	A constant whose compliment value is in the range of imm15u and ok for bitci instruction.
Is16	Signed immediate 16-bit value.
Is17	Signed immediate 17-bit value.
Is19	Signed immediate 19-bit value.
Is20	Signed immediate 20-bit value.
Ihig	The immediate value that can be simply set high 20-bit.
Izeb	The immediate value 0xff.
Izeh	The immediate value 0xffff.
Ixls	The immediate value 0x01.
Ix11	The immediate value 0x7ff.
Ibms	The immediate value with power of 2.

Chapter 17: Machine Descriptions 361

        `Ifex`   The immediate value with power of 2 minus 1.

        `U33`   Memory constraint for 333 format.

        `U45`   Memory constraint for 45 format.

        `U37`   Memory constraint for 37 format.

Nios II family—'`config/nios2/constraints.md`'

    `I`   Integer that is valid as an immediate operand in an instruction taking a signed 16-bit number. Range −32768 to 32767.

    `J`   Integer that is valid as an immediate operand in an instruction taking an unsigned 16-bit number. Range 0 to 65535.

    `K`   Integer that is valid as an immediate operand in an instruction taking only the upper 16-bits of a 32-bit number. Range 32-bit numbers with the lower 16-bits being 0.

    `L`   Integer that is valid as an immediate operand for a shift instruction. Range 0 to 31.

    `M`   Integer that is valid as an immediate operand for only the value 0. Can be used in conjunction with the format modifier `z` to use `r0` instead of `0` in the assembly output.

    `N`   Integer that is valid as an immediate operand for a custom instruction opcode. Range 0 to 255.

    `P`   An immediate operand for R2 andchi/andci instructions.

    `S`   Matches immediates which are addresses in the small data section and therefore can be added to `gp` as a 16-bit immediate to re-create their 32-bit value.

    `U`   Matches constants suitable as an operand for the rdprs and cache instructions.

    `v`   A memory operand suitable for Nios II R2 load/store exclusive instructions.

    `w`   A memory operand suitable for load/store IO and cache instructions.

    `T`   A `const` wrapped `UNSPEC` expression, representing a supported PIC or TLS relocation.

PDP-11—'`config/pdp11/constraints.md`'

    `a`   Floating point registers AC0 through AC3. These can be loaded from/to memory with a single instruction.

    `d`   Odd numbered general registers (R1, R3, R5). These are used for 16-bit multiply operations.

    `f`   Any of the floating point registers (AC0 through AC5).

    `G`   Floating point constant 0.

I	An integer constant that fits in 16 bits.
J	An integer constant whose low order 16 bits are zero.
K	An integer constant that does not meet the constraints for codes 'I' or 'J'.
L	The integer constant 1.
M	The integer constant −1.
N	The integer constant 0.
O	Integer constants −4 through −1 and 1 through 4; shifts by these amounts are handled as multiple single-bit shifts rather than a single variable-length shift.
Q	A memory reference which requires an additional word (address or offset) after the opcode.
R	A memory reference that is encoded within the opcode.

PowerPC and IBM RS6000—'config/rs6000/constraints.md'

b	Address base register
d	Floating point register (containing 64-bit value)
f	Floating point register (containing 32-bit value)
v	Altivec vector register

wa	Any VSX register if the '-mvsx' option was used or NO_REGS.
	
	When using any of the register constraints (wa, wd, wf, wg, wh, wi, wj, wk, wl, wm, wo, wp, wq, ws, wt, wu, wv, ww, or wy) that take VSX registers, you must use %x<n> in the template so that the correct register is used. Otherwise the register number output in the assembly file will be incorrect if an Altivec register is an operand of a VSX instruction that expects VSX register numbering.
	
	```\nasm ("xvadddp %x0,%x1,%x2"\n : "=wa" (v1)\n : "wa" (v2), "wa" (v3));\n```
	is correct, but:
	```\nasm ("xvadddp %0,%1,%2"\n : "=wa" (v1)\n : "wa" (v2), "wa" (v3));\n```
	is not correct.
	
	If an instruction only takes Altivec registers, you do not want to use %x<n>.
	
	```\nasm ("xsaddqp %0,%1,%2"\n : "=v" (v1)\n : "v" (v2), "v" (v3));\n```
	is correct because the **xsaddqp** instruction only takes Altivec registers, while:

Chapter 17: Machine Descriptions

```
asm ("xsaddqp %x0,%x1,%x2"
     : "=v" (v1)
     : "v" (v2), "v" (v3));
```

is incorrect.

wb	Altivec register if '-mcpu=power9' is used or NO_REGS.
wd	VSX vector register to hold vector double data or NO_REGS.
we	VSX register if the '-mcpu=power9' and '-m64' options were used or NO_REGS.
wf	VSX vector register to hold vector float data or NO_REGS.
wg	If '-mmfpgpr' was used, a floating point register or NO_REGS.
wh	Floating point register if direct moves are available, or NO_REGS.
wi	FP or VSX register to hold 64-bit integers for VSX insns or NO_REGS.
wj	FP or VSX register to hold 64-bit integers for direct moves or NO_REGS.
wk	FP or VSX register to hold 64-bit doubles for direct moves or NO_REGS.
wl	Floating point register if the LFIWAX instruction is enabled or NO_REGS.
wm	VSX register if direct move instructions are enabled, or NO_REGS.
wn	No register (NO_REGS).
wo	VSX register to use for ISA 3.0 vector instructions, or NO_REGS.
wp	VSX register to use for IEEE 128-bit floating point TFmode, or NO_REGS.
wq	VSX register to use for IEEE 128-bit floating point, or NO_REGS.
wr	General purpose register if 64-bit instructions are enabled or NO_REGS.
ws	VSX vector register to hold scalar double values or NO_REGS.
wt	VSX vector register to hold 128 bit integer or NO_REGS.
wu	Altivec register to use for float/32-bit int loads/stores or NO_REGS.
wv	Altivec register to use for double loads/stores or NO_REGS.
ww	FP or VSX register to perform float operations under '-mvsx' or NO_REGS.
wx	Floating point register if the STFIWX instruction is enabled or NO_REGS.
wy	FP or VSX register to perform ISA 2.07 float ops or NO_REGS.

wz	Floating point register if the LFIWZX instruction is enabled or NO_REGS.
wA	Address base register if 64-bit instructions are enabled or NO_REGS.
wB	Signed 5-bit constant integer that can be loaded into an altivec register.
wD	Int constant that is the element number of the 64-bit scalar in a vector.
wE	Vector constant that can be loaded with the XXSPLTIB instruction.
wF	Memory operand suitable for power9 fusion load/stores.
wG	Memory operand suitable for TOC fusion memory references.
wH	Altivec register if '-mvsx-small-integer'.
wI	Floating point register if '-mvsx-small-integer'.
wJ	FP register if '-mvsx-small-integer' and '-mpower9-vector'.
wK	Altivec register if '-mvsx-small-integer' and '-mpower9-vector'.
wL	Int constant that is the element number that the MFVSRLD instruction. targets.
wM	Match vector constant with all 1's if the XXLORC instruction is available.
wO	A memory operand suitable for the ISA 3.0 vector d-form instructions.
wQ	A memory address that will work with the lq and stq instructions.
wS	Vector constant that can be loaded with XXSPLTIB & sign extension.
h	'MQ', 'CTR', or 'LINK' register
c	'CTR' register
l	'LINK' register
x	'CR' register (condition register) number 0
y	'CR' register (condition register)
z	'XER[CA]' carry bit (part of the XER register)
I	Signed 16-bit constant
J	Unsigned 16-bit constant shifted left 16 bits (use 'L' instead for SImode constants)
K	Unsigned 16-bit constant
L	Signed 16-bit constant shifted left 16 bits

Chapter 17: Machine Descriptions   365

M	Constant larger than 31
N	Exact power of 2
O	Zero
P	Constant whose negation is a signed 16-bit constant
G	Floating point constant that can be loaded into a register with one instruction per word
H	Integer/Floating point constant that can be loaded into a register using three instructions

m	Memory operand. Normally, m does not allow addresses that update the base register. If '<' or '>' constraint is also used, they are allowed and therefore on PowerPC targets in that case it is only safe to use 'm<>' in an asm statement if that asm statement accesses the operand exactly once. The asm statement must also use '%U<*opno*>' as a placeholder for the "update" flag in the corresponding load or store instruction. For example:
	`asm ("st%U0 %1,%0" : "=m<>" (mem) : "r" (val));`
	is correct but:
	`asm ("st %1,%0" : "=m<>" (mem) : "r" (val));`
	is not.

es	A "stable" memory operand; that is, one which does not include any automodification of the base register. This used to be useful when 'm' allowed automodification of the base register, but as those are now only allowed when '<' or '>' is used, 'es' is basically the same as 'm' without '<' and '>'.
Q	Memory operand that is an offset from a register (it is usually better to use 'm' or 'es' in asm statements)
Z	Memory operand that is an indexed or indirect from a register (it is usually better to use 'm' or 'es' in asm statements)
R	AIX TOC entry
a	Address operand that is an indexed or indirect from a register ('p' is preferable for asm statements)
U	System V Release 4 small data area reference
W	Vector constant that does not require memory
j	Vector constant that is all zeros.

RL78—'config/rl78/constraints.md'

Int3	An integer constant in the range 1 ... 7.
Int8	An integer constant in the range 0 ... 255.
J	An integer constant in the range −255 ... 0

K	The integer constant 1.
L	The integer constant -1.
M	The integer constant 0.
N	The integer constant 2.
O	The integer constant -2.
P	An integer constant in the range 1 ... 15.
Qbi	The built-in compare types–eq, ne, gtu, ltu, geu, and leu.
Qsc	The synthetic compare types–gt, lt, ge, and le.
Wab	A memory reference with an absolute address.
Wbc	A memory reference using BC as a base register, with an optional offset.
Wca	A memory reference using AX, BC, DE, or HL for the address, for calls.
Wcv	A memory reference using any 16-bit register pair for the address, for calls.
Wd2	A memory reference using DE as a base register, with an optional offset.
Wde	A memory reference using DE as a base register, without any offset.
Wfr	Any memory reference to an address in the far address space.
Wh1	A memory reference using HL as a base register, with an optional one-byte offset.
Whb	A memory reference using HL as a base register, with B or C as the index register.
Whl	A memory reference using HL as a base register, without any offset.
Ws1	A memory reference using SP as a base register, with an optional one-byte offset.
Y	Any memory reference to an address in the near address space.
A	The AX register.
B	The BC register.
D	The DE register.
R	A through L registers.
S	The SP register.
T	The HL register.
Z08W	The 16-bit R8 register.
Z10W	The 16-bit R10 register.

Zint	The registers reserved for interrupts (R24 to R31).	
a	The A register.	
b	The B register.	
c	The C register.	
d	The D register.	
e	The E register.	
h	The H register.	
l	The L register.	
v	The virtual registers.	
w	The PSW register.	
x	The X register.	

RISC-V—'config/riscv/constraints.md'

f	A floating-point register (if availiable).
I	An I-type 12-bit signed immediate.
J	Integer zero.
K	A 5-bit unsigned immediate for CSR access instructions.
A	An address that is held in a general-purpose register.

RX—'config/rx/constraints.md'

Q	An address which does not involve register indirect addressing or pre/post increment/decrement addressing.
Symbol	A symbol reference.
Int08	A constant in the range −256 to 255, inclusive.
Sint08	A constant in the range −128 to 127, inclusive.
Sint16	A constant in the range −32768 to 32767, inclusive.
Sint24	A constant in the range −8388608 to 8388607, inclusive.
Uint04	A constant in the range 0 to 15, inclusive.

S/390 and zSeries—'config/s390/s390.h'

a	Address register (general purpose register except r0)
c	Condition code register
d	Data register (arbitrary general purpose register)
f	Floating-point register
I	Unsigned 8-bit constant (0–255)
J	Unsigned 12-bit constant (0–4095)

K	Signed 16-bit constant (−32768–32767)
L	Value appropriate as displacement.
	(0..4095)
	for short displacement
	(−524288..524287)
	for long displacement
M	Constant integer with a value of 0x7fffffff.
N	Multiple letter constraint followed by 4 parameter letters.
	0..9: number of the part counting from most to least significant
	H,Q: mode of the part
	D,S,H: mode of the containing operand
	0,F: value of the other parts (F—all bits set)
	The constraint matches if the specified part of a constant has a value different from its other parts.
Q	Memory reference without index register and with short displacement.
R	Memory reference with index register and short displacement.
S	Memory reference without index register but with long displacement.
T	Memory reference with index register and long displacement.
U	Pointer with short displacement.
W	Pointer with long displacement.
Y	Shift count operand.

SPARC—'config/sparc/sparc.h'

f	Floating-point register on the SPARC-V8 architecture and lower floating-point register on the SPARC-V9 architecture.
e	Floating-point register. It is equivalent to 'f' on the SPARC-V8 architecture and contains both lower and upper floating-point registers on the SPARC-V9 architecture.
c	Floating-point condition code register.
d	Lower floating-point register. It is only valid on the SPARC-V9 architecture when the Visual Instruction Set is available.
b	Floating-point register. It is only valid on the SPARC-V9 architecture when the Visual Instruction Set is available.
h	64-bit global or out register for the SPARC-V8+ architecture.

C		The constant all-ones, for floating-point.
A		Signed 5-bit constant
D		A vector constant
I		Signed 13-bit constant
J		Zero
K		32-bit constant with the low 12 bits clear (a constant that can be loaded with the `sethi` instruction)
L		A constant in the range supported by `movcc` instructions (11-bit signed immediate)
M		A constant in the range supported by `movrcc` instructions (10-bit signed immediate)
N		Same as 'K', except that it verifies that bits that are not in the lower 32-bit range are all zero. Must be used instead of 'K' for modes wider than `SImode`
O		The constant 4096
G		Floating-point zero
H		Signed 13-bit constant, sign-extended to 32 or 64 bits
P		The constant -1
Q		Floating-point constant whose integral representation can be moved into an integer register using a single sethi instruction
R		Floating-point constant whose integral representation can be moved into an integer register using a single mov instruction
S		Floating-point constant whose integral representation can be moved into an integer register using a high/lo_sum instruction sequence
T		Memory address aligned to an 8-byte boundary
U		Even register
W		Memory address for 'e' constraint registers
w		Memory address with only a base register
Y		Vector zero

SPU—'config/spu/spu.h'

a		An immediate which can be loaded with the il/ila/ilh/ilhu instructions. const_int is treated as a 64 bit value.
c		An immediate for and/xor/or instructions. const_int is treated as a 64 bit value.
d		An immediate for the `iohl` instruction. const_int is treated as a 64 bit value.

f	An immediate which can be loaded with `fsmbi`.
A	An immediate which can be loaded with the il/ila/ilh/ilhu instructions. const_int is treated as a 32 bit value.
B	An immediate for most arithmetic instructions. const_int is treated as a 32 bit value.
C	An immediate for and/xor/or instructions. const_int is treated as a 32 bit value.
D	An immediate for the `iohl` instruction. const_int is treated as a 32 bit value.
I	A constant in the range [−64, 63] for shift/rotate instructions.
J	An unsigned 7-bit constant for conversion/nop/channel instructions.
K	A signed 10-bit constant for most arithmetic instructions.
M	A signed 16 bit immediate for `stop`.
N	An unsigned 16-bit constant for `iohl` and `fsmbi`.
O	An unsigned 7-bit constant whose 3 least significant bits are 0.
P	An unsigned 3-bit constant for 16-byte rotates and shifts
R	Call operand, reg, for indirect calls
S	Call operand, symbol, for relative calls.
T	Call operand, const_int, for absolute calls.
U	An immediate which can be loaded with the il/ila/ilh/ilhu instructions. const_int is sign extended to 128 bit.
W	An immediate for shift and rotate instructions. const_int is treated as a 32 bit value.
Y	An immediate for and/xor/or instructions. const_int is sign extended as a 128 bit.
Z	An immediate for the `iohl` instruction. const_int is sign extended to 128 bit.

TI C6X family—'`config/c6x/constraints.md`'

a	Register file A (A0–A31).
b	Register file B (B0–B31).
A	Predicate registers in register file A (A0–A2 on C64X and higher, A1 and A2 otherwise).
B	Predicate registers in register file B (B0–B2).
C	A call-used register in register file B (B0–B9, B16–B31).
Da	Register file A, excluding predicate registers (A3–A31, plus A0 if not C64X or higher).

Db	Register file B, excluding predicate registers (B3–B31).
Iu4	Integer constant in the range 0 ... 15.
Iu5	Integer constant in the range 0 ... 31.
In5	Integer constant in the range −31 ... 0.
Is5	Integer constant in the range −16 ... 15.
I5x	Integer constant that can be the operand of an ADDA or a SUBA insn.
IuB	Integer constant in the range 0 ... 65535.
IsB	Integer constant in the range −32768 ... 32767.
IsC	Integer constant in the range -2^{20} ... $2^{20} - 1$.
Jc	Integer constant that is a valid mask for the clr instruction.
Js	Integer constant that is a valid mask for the set instruction.
Q	Memory location with A base register.
R	Memory location with B base register.
S0	On C64x+ targets, a GP-relative small data reference.
S1	Any kind of `SYMBOL_REF`, for use in a call address.
Si	Any kind of immediate operand, unless it matches the S0 constraint.
T	Memory location with B base register, but not using a long offset.
W	A memory operand with an address that cannot be used in an unaligned access.
Z	Register B14 (aka DP).

TILE-Gx—'`config/tilegx/constraints.md`'

R00	
R01	
R02	
R03	
R04	
R05	
R06	
R07	
R08	
R09	
R10	Each of these represents a register constraint for an individual register, from r0 to r10.
I	Signed 8-bit integer constant.
J	Signed 16-bit integer constant.

K	Unsigned 16-bit integer constant.
L	Integer constant that fits in one signed byte when incremented by one (−129 ... 126).
m	Memory operand. If used together with '<' or '>', the operand can have postincrement which requires printing with '%In' and '%in' on TILE-Gx. For example: `asm ("st_add %I0,%1,%i0" : "=m<>" (*mem) : "r" (val));`
M	A bit mask suitable for the BFINS instruction.
N	Integer constant that is a byte tiled out eight times.
O	The integer zero constant.
P	Integer constant that is a sign-extended byte tiled out as four shorts.
Q	Integer constant that fits in one signed byte when incremented (−129 ... 126), but excluding -1.
S	Integer constant that has all 1 bits consecutive and starting at bit 0.
T	A 16-bit fragment of a got, tls, or pc-relative reference.
U	Memory operand except postincrement. This is roughly the same as 'm' when not used together with '<' or '>'.
W	An 8-element vector constant with identical elements.
Y	A 4-element vector constant with identical elements.
Z0	The integer constant 0xffffffff.
Z1	The integer constant 0xffffffff00000000.

TILEPro—'config/tilepro/constraints.md'

R00	
R01	
R02	
R03	
R04	
R05	
R06	
R07	
R08	
R09	
R10	Each of these represents a register constraint for an individual register, from r0 to r10.
I	Signed 8-bit integer constant.
J	Signed 16-bit integer constant.
K	Nonzero integer constant with low 16 bits zero.

L	Integer constant that fits in one signed byte when incremented by one (−129 ... 126).
m	Memory operand. If used together with '<' or '>', the operand can have postincrement which requires printing with '%In' and '%in' on TILEPro. For example: `asm ("swadd %I0,%1,%i0" : "=m<>" (mem) : "r" (val));`
M	A bit mask suitable for the MM instruction.
N	Integer constant that is a byte tiled out four times.
O	The integer zero constant.
P	Integer constant that is a sign-extended byte tiled out as two shorts.
Q	Integer constant that fits in one signed byte when incremented (−129 ... 126), but excluding -1.
T	A symbolic operand, or a 16-bit fragment of a got, tls, or pc-relative reference.
U	Memory operand except postincrement. This is roughly the same as 'm' when not used together with '<' or '>'.
W	A 4-element vector constant with identical elements.
Y	A 2-element vector constant with identical elements.

Visium—'config/visium/constraints.md'

b	EAM register `mdb`
c	EAM register `mdc`
f	Floating point register
k	Register for sibcall optimization
l	General register, but not `r29`, `r30` and `r31`
t	Register `r1`
u	Register `r2`
v	Register `r3`
G	Floating-point constant 0.0
J	Integer constant in the range 0 .. 65535 (16-bit immediate)
K	Integer constant in the range 1 .. 31 (5-bit immediate)
L	Integer constant in the range −65535 .. −1 (16-bit negative immediate)
M	Integer constant −1
O	Integer constant 0
P	Integer constant 32

x86 family—'config/i386/constraints.md'

R	Legacy register—the eight integer registers available on all i386 processors (a, b, c, d, si, di, bp, sp).
q	Any register accessible as rl. In 32-bit mode, a, b, c, and d; in 64-bit mode, any integer register.
Q	Any register accessible as rh: a, b, c, and d.
l	Any register that can be used as the index in a base+index memory access: that is, any general register except the stack pointer.
a	The a register.
b	The b register.
c	The c register.
d	The d register.
S	The si register.
D	The di register.
A	The a and d registers. This class is used for instructions that return double word results in the ax:dx register pair. Single word values will be allocated either in ax or dx. For example on i386 the following implements rdtsc:

```
unsigned long long rdtsc (void)
{
  unsigned long long tick;
  __asm__ __volatile__("rdtsc":"=A"(tick));
  return tick;
}
```

This is not correct on x86-64 as it would allocate tick in either ax or dx. You have to use the following variant instead:

```
unsigned long long rdtsc (void)
{
  unsigned int tickl, tickh;
  __asm__ __volatile__("rdtsc":"=a"(tickl),"=d"(tickh));
  return ((unsigned long long)tickh << 32)|tickl;
}
```

U	The call-clobbered integer registers.
f	Any 80387 floating-point (stack) register.
t	Top of 80387 floating-point stack (%st(0)).
u	Second from top of 80387 floating-point stack (%st(1)).
Yk	Any mask register that can be used as a predicate, i.e. k1-k7.
k	Any mask register.
y	Any MMX register.
x	Any SSE register.

v	Any EVEX encodable SSE register (%xmm0-%xmm31).
w	Any bound register.
Yz	First SSE register (%xmm0).
Yi	Any SSE register, when SSE2 and inter-unit moves are enabled.
Yj	Any SSE register, when SSE2 and inter-unit moves from vector registers are enabled.
Ym	Any MMX register, when inter-unit moves are enabled.
Yn	Any MMX register, when inter-unit moves from vector registers are enabled.
Yp	Any integer register when `TARGET_PARTIAL_REG_STALL` is disabled.
Ya	Any integer register when zero extensions with `AND` are disabled.
Yb	Any register that can be used as the GOT base when calling `___tls_get_addr`: that is, any general register except `a` and `sp` registers, for '-fno-plt' if linker supports it. Otherwise, `b` register.
Yf	Any x87 register when 80387 floating-point arithmetic is enabled.
Yr	Lower SSE register when avoiding REX prefix and all SSE registers otherwise.
Yv	For AVX512VL, any EVEX-encodable SSE register (%xmm0-%xmm31), otherwise any SSE register.
Yh	Any EVEX-encodable SSE register, that has number factor of four.
Bf	Flags register operand.
Bg	GOT memory operand.
Bm	Vector memory operand.
Bc	Constant memory operand.
Bn	Memory operand without REX prefix.
Bs	Sibcall memory operand.
Bw	Call memory operand.
Bz	Constant call address operand.
BC	SSE constant -1 operand.
I	Integer constant in the range 0 ... 31, for 32-bit shifts.
J	Integer constant in the range 0 ... 63, for 64-bit shifts.
K	Signed 8-bit integer constant.
L	0xFF or 0xFFFF, for andsi as a zero-extending move.
M	0, 1, 2, or 3 (shifts for the `lea` instruction).
N	Unsigned 8-bit integer constant (for `in` and `out` instructions).

O	Integer constant in the range 0 ... 127, for 128-bit shifts.
G	Standard 80387 floating point constant.
C	SSE constant zero operand.
e	32-bit signed integer constant, or a symbolic reference known to fit that range (for immediate operands in sign-extending x86-64 instructions).
We	32-bit signed integer constant, or a symbolic reference known to fit that range (for sign-extending conversion operations that require non-VOIDmode immediate operands).
Wz	32-bit unsigned integer constant, or a symbolic reference known to fit that range (for zero-extending conversion operations that require non-VOIDmode immediate operands).
Wd	128-bit integer constant where both the high and low 64-bit word satisfy the e constraint.
Z	32-bit unsigned integer constant, or a symbolic reference known to fit that range (for immediate operands in zero-extending x86-64 instructions).
Tv	VSIB address operand.
Ts	Address operand without segment register.
Ti	MPX address operand without index.
Tb	MPX address operand without base.

Xstormy16—'config/stormy16/stormy16.h'

a	Register r0.
b	Register r1.
c	Register r2.
d	Register r8.
e	Registers r0 through r7.
t	Registers r0 and r1.
y	The carry register.
z	Registers r8 and r9.
I	A constant between 0 and 3 inclusive.
J	A constant that has exactly one bit set.
K	A constant that has exactly one bit clear.
L	A constant between 0 and 255 inclusive.
M	A constant between −255 and 0 inclusive.
N	A constant between −3 and 0 inclusive.

O	A constant between 1 and 4 inclusive.
P	A constant between −4 and −1 inclusive.
Q	A memory reference that is a stack push.
R	A memory reference that is a stack pop.
S	A memory reference that refers to a constant address of known value.
T	The register indicated by Rx (not implemented yet).
U	A constant that is not between 2 and 15 inclusive.
Z	The constant 0.

Xtensa—'config/xtensa/constraints.md'

a	General-purpose 32-bit register
b	One-bit boolean register
A	MAC16 40-bit accumulator register
I	Signed 12-bit integer constant, for use in MOVI instructions
J	Signed 8-bit integer constant, for use in ADDI instructions
K	Integer constant valid for BccI instructions
L	Unsigned constant valid for BccUI instructions

17.8.6 Disable insn alternatives using the `enabled` attribute

There are three insn attributes that may be used to selectively disable instruction alternatives:

`enabled` Says whether an alternative is available on the current subtarget.

`preferred_for_size`
    Says whether an enabled alternative should be used in code that is optimized for size.

`preferred_for_speed`
    Says whether an enabled alternative should be used in code that is optimized for speed.

All these attributes should use (const_int 1) to allow an alternative or (const_int 0) to disallow it. The attributes must be a static property of the subtarget; they cannot for example depend on the current operands, on the current optimization level, on the location of the insn within the body of a loop, on whether register allocation has finished, or on the current compiler pass.

The `enabled` attribute is a correctness property. It tells GCC to act as though the disabled alternatives were never defined in the first place. This is useful when adding new instructions to an existing pattern in cases where the new instructions are only available for certain cpu architecture levels (typically mapped to the `-march=` command-line option).

In contrast, the `preferred_for_size` and `preferred_for_speed` attributes are strong optimization hints rather than correctness properties. `preferred_for_size` tells GCC which alternatives to consider when adding or modifying an instruction that GCC wants to optimize for size. `preferred_for_speed` does the same thing for speed. Note that things like code motion can lead to cases where code optimized for size uses alternatives that are not preferred for size, and similarly for speed.

Although `define_insn`s can in principle specify the `enabled` attribute directly, it is often clearer to have subsidiary attributes for each architectural feature of interest. The `define_insn`s can then use these subsidiary attributes to say which alternatives require which features. The example below does this for `cpu_facility`.

E.g. the following two patterns could easily be merged using the `enabled` attribute:

```
(define_insn "*movdi_old"
  [(set (match_operand:DI 0 "register_operand" "=d")
        (match_operand:DI 1 "register_operand" " d"))]
  "!TARGET_NEW"
  "lgr %0,%1")

(define_insn "*movdi_new"
  [(set (match_operand:DI 0 "register_operand" "=d,f,d")
        (match_operand:DI 1 "register_operand" " d,d,f"))]
  "TARGET_NEW"
  "@
   lgr  %0,%1
   ldgr %0,%1
   lgdr %0,%1")
```

to:

```
(define_insn "*movdi_combined"
  [(set (match_operand:DI 0 "register_operand" "=d,f,d")
        (match_operand:DI 1 "register_operand" " d,d,f"))]
  ""
  "@
   lgr  %0,%1
   ldgr %0,%1
   lgdr %0,%1"
   [(set_attr "cpu_facility" "*,new,new")])
```

with the `enabled` attribute defined like this:

```
(define_attr "cpu_facility" "standard,new" (const_string "standard"))

(define_attr "enabled" ""
  (cond [(eq_attr "cpu_facility" "standard") (const_int 1)
         (and (eq_attr "cpu_facility" "new")
              (ne (symbol_ref "TARGET_NEW") (const_int 0)))
         (const_int 1)]
        (const_int 0)))
```

17.8.7 Defining Machine-Specific Constraints

Machine-specific constraints fall into two categories: register and non-register constraints. Within the latter category, constraints which allow subsets of all possible memory or address operands should be specially marked, to give `reload` more information.

Machine-specific constraints can be given names of arbitrary length, but they must be entirely composed of letters, digits, underscores ('_'), and angle brackets ('< >'). Like C identifiers, they must begin with a letter or underscore.

In order to avoid ambiguity in operand constraint strings, no constraint can have a name that begins with any other constraint's name. For example, if x is defined as a constraint name, xy may not be, and vice versa. As a consequence of this rule, no constraint may begin with one of the generic constraint letters: 'E F V X g i m n o p r s'.

Register constraints correspond directly to register classes. See Section 18.8 [Register Classes], page 493. There is thus not much flexibility in their definitions.

define_register_constraint *name regclass docstring* [MD Expression]
: All three arguments are string constants. *name* is the name of the constraint, as it will appear in `match_operand` expressions. If *name* is a multi-letter constraint its length shall be the same for all constraints starting with the same letter. *regclass* can be either the name of the corresponding register class (see Section 18.8 [Register Classes], page 493), or a C expression which evaluates to the appropriate register class. If it is an expression, it must have no side effects, and it cannot look at the operand. The usual use of expressions is to map some register constraints to `NO_REGS` when the register class is not available on a given subarchitecture.

    docstring is a sentence documenting the meaning of the constraint. Docstrings are explained further below.

Non-register constraints are more like predicates: the constraint definition gives a boolean expression which indicates whether the constraint matches.

define_constraint *name docstring exp* [MD Expression]
: The *name* and *docstring* arguments are the same as for `define_register_constraint`, but note that the docstring comes immediately after the name for these expressions. *exp* is an RTL expression, obeying the same rules as the RTL expressions in predicate definitions. See Section 17.7.2 [Defining Predicates], page 338, for details. If it evaluates true, the constraint matches; if it evaluates false, it doesn't. Constraint expressions should indicate which RTL codes they might match, just like predicate expressions.

    `match_test` C expressions have access to the following variables:

op	The RTL object defining the operand.
mode	The machine mode of *op*.
ival	'INTVAL (*op*)', if *op* is a `const_int`.
hval	'CONST_DOUBLE_HIGH (*op*)', if *op* is an integer `const_double`.
lval	'CONST_DOUBLE_LOW (*op*)', if *op* is an integer `const_double`.
rval	'CONST_DOUBLE_REAL_VALUE (*op*)', if *op* is a floating-point `const_double`.

    The *val* variables should only be used once another piece of the expression has verified that *op* is the appropriate kind of RTL object.

Most non-register constraints should be defined with `define_constraint`. The remaining two definition expressions are only appropriate for constraints that should be handled specially by `reload` if they fail to match.

`define_memory_constraint` *name docstring exp*   [MD Expression]

    Use this expression for constraints that match a subset of all memory operands: that is, `reload` can make them match by converting the operand to the form '(mem (reg X))', where X is a base register (from the register class specified by `BASE_REG_CLASS`, see Section 18.8 [Register Classes], page 493).

    For example, on the S/390, some instructions do not accept arbitrary memory references, but only those that do not make use of an index register. The constraint letter 'Q' is defined to represent a memory address of this type. If 'Q' is defined with `define_memory_constraint`, a 'Q' constraint can handle any memory operand, because `reload` knows it can simply copy the memory address into a base register if required. This is analogous to the way an 'o' constraint can handle any memory operand.

    The syntax and semantics are otherwise identical to `define_constraint`.

`define_special_memory_constraint` *name docstring exp*   [MD Expression]

    Use this expression for constraints that match a subset of all memory operands: that is, `reload` can not make them match by reloading the address as it is described for `define_memory_constraint` or such address reload is undesirable with the performance point of view.

    For example, `define_special_memory_constraint` can be useful if specifically aligned memory is necessary or desirable for some insn operand.

    The syntax and semantics are otherwise identical to `define_constraint`.

`define_address_constraint` *name docstring exp*   [MD Expression]

    Use this expression for constraints that match a subset of all address operands: that is, `reload` can make the constraint match by converting the operand to the form '(reg X)', again with X a base register.

    Constraints defined with `define_address_constraint` can only be used with the `address_operand` predicate, or machine-specific predicates that work the same way. They are treated analogously to the generic 'p' constraint.

    The syntax and semantics are otherwise identical to `define_constraint`.

For historical reasons, names beginning with the letters 'G H' are reserved for constraints that match only `const_doubles`, and names beginning with the letters 'I J K L M N O P' are reserved for constraints that match only `const_ints`. This may change in the future. For the time being, constraints with these names must be written in a stylized form, so that `genpreds` can tell you did it correctly:

```
(define_constraint "[GHIJKLMNOP]..."
  "doc..."
  (and (match_code "const_int")   ; const_double for G/H
       condition...))              ; usually a match_test
```

It is fine to use names beginning with other letters for constraints that match `const_doubles` or `const_ints`.

Each docstring in a constraint definition should be one or more complete sentences, marked up in Texinfo format. *They are currently unused.* In the future they will be copied into the GCC manual, in Section 17.8.5 [Machine Constraints], page 347, replacing the hand-maintained tables currently found in that section. Also, in the future the compiler may use this to give more helpful diagnostics when poor choice of `asm` constraints causes a reload failure.

If you put the pseudo-Texinfo directive '`@internal`' at the beginning of a docstring, then (in the future) it will appear only in the internals manual's version of the machine-specific constraint tables. Use this for constraints that should not appear in `asm` statements.

17.8.8 Testing constraints from C

It is occasionally useful to test a constraint from C code rather than implicitly via the constraint string in a `match_operand`. The generated file '`tm_p.h`' declares a few interfaces for working with constraints. At present these are defined for all constraints except g (which is equivalent to `general_operand`).

Some valid constraint names are not valid C identifiers, so there is a mangling scheme for referring to them from C. Constraint names that do not contain angle brackets or underscores are left unchanged. Underscores are doubled, each '`<`' is replaced with '`_l`', and each '`>`' with '`_g`'. Here are some examples:

Original	Mangled
x	x
P42x	P42x
P4_x	P4__x
P4>x	P4_gx
P4>>	P4_g_g
P4_g>	P4__g_g

Throughout this section, the variable *c* is either a constraint in the abstract sense, or a constant from `enum constraint_num`; the variable *m* is a mangled constraint name (usually as part of a larger identifier).

`constraint_num` [Enum]
> For each constraint except g, there is a corresponding enumeration constant: '`CONSTRAINT_`' plus the mangled name of the constraint. Functions that take an `enum constraint_num` as an argument expect one of these constants.

`inline bool satisfies_constraint_m` (*rtx exp*) [Function]
> For each non-register constraint *m* except g, there is one of these functions; it returns `true` if *exp* satisfies the constraint. These functions are only visible if '`rtl.h`' was included before '`tm_p.h`'.

`bool constraint_satisfied_p` (*rtx exp*, *enum constraint_num c*) [Function]
> Like the `satisfies_constraint_m` functions, but the constraint to test is given as an argument, *c*. If *c* specifies a register constraint, this function will always return `false`.

enum reg_class reg_class_for_constraint (*enum constraint_num*   [Function]
    c)

    Returns the register class associated with *c*. If *c* is not a register constraint, or those registers are not available for the currently selected subtarget, returns NO_REGS.

Here is an example use of satisfies_constraint_*m*. In peephole optimizations (see Section 17.18 [Peephole Definitions], page 430), operand constraint strings are ignored, so if there are relevant constraints, they must be tested in the C condition. In the example, the optimization is applied if operand 2 does *not* satisfy the 'K' constraint. (This is a simplified version of a peephole definition from the i386 machine description.)

```
(define_peephole2
  [(match_scratch:SI 3 "r")
   (set (match_operand:SI 0 "register_operand" "")
        (mult:SI (match_operand:SI 1 "memory_operand" "")
                 (match_operand:SI 2 "immediate_operand" "")))]

  "!satisfies_constraint_K (operands[2])"

  [(set (match_dup 3) (match_dup 1))
   (set (match_dup 0) (mult:SI (match_dup 3) (match_dup 2)))]

  "")
```

17.9 Standard Pattern Names For Generation

Here is a table of the instruction names that are meaningful in the RTL generation pass of the compiler. Giving one of these names to an instruction pattern tells the RTL generation pass that it can use the pattern to accomplish a certain task.

'mov*m*'   Here *m* stands for a two-letter machine mode name, in lowercase. This instruction pattern moves data with that machine mode from operand 1 to operand 0. For example, 'movsi' moves full-word data.

    If operand 0 is a subreg with mode *m* of a register whose own mode is wider than *m*, the effect of this instruction is to store the specified value in the part of the register that corresponds to mode *m*. Bits outside of *m*, but which are within the same target word as the subreg are undefined. Bits which are outside the target word are left unchanged.

    This class of patterns is special in several ways. First of all, each of these names up to and including full word size *must* be defined, because there is no other way to copy a datum from one place to another. If there are patterns accepting operands in larger modes, 'mov*m*' must be defined for integer modes of those sizes.

    Second, these patterns are not used solely in the RTL generation pass. Even the reload pass can generate move insns to copy values from stack slots into temporary registers. When it does so, one of the operands is a hard register and the other is an operand that can need to be reloaded into a register.

    Therefore, when given such a pair of operands, the pattern must generate RTL which needs no reloading and needs no temporary registers—no registers other than the operands. For example, if you support the pattern with a define_ expand, then in such a case the `define_expand` mustn't call `force_reg` or any other such function which might generate new pseudo registers.

This requirement exists even for subword modes on a RISC machine where fetching those modes from memory normally requires several insns and some temporary registers.

During reload a memory reference with an invalid address may be passed as an operand. Such an address will be replaced with a valid address later in the reload pass. In this case, nothing may be done with the address except to use it as it stands. If it is copied, it will not be replaced with a valid address. No attempt should be made to make such an address into a valid address and no routine (such as `change_address`) that will do so may be called. Note that `general_operand` will fail when applied to such an address.

The global variable `reload_in_progress` (which must be explicitly declared if required) can be used to determine whether such special handling is required.

The variety of operands that have reloads depends on the rest of the machine description, but typically on a RISC machine these can only be pseudo registers that did not get hard registers, while on other machines explicit memory references will get optional reloads.

If a scratch register is required to move an object to or from memory, it can be allocated using `gen_reg_rtx` prior to life analysis.

If there are cases which need scratch registers during or after reload, you must provide an appropriate secondary_reload target hook.

The macro `can_create_pseudo_p` can be used to determine if it is unsafe to create new pseudo registers. If this variable is nonzero, then it is unsafe to call `gen_reg_rtx` to allocate a new pseudo.

The constraints on a 'mov$m$' must permit moving any hard register to any other hard register provided that `TARGET_HARD_REGNO_MODE_OK` permits mode m in both registers and `TARGET_REGISTER_MOVE_COST` applied to their classes returns a value of 2.

It is obligatory to support floating point 'mov$m$' instructions into and out of any registers that can hold fixed point values, because unions and structures (which have modes SImode or DImode) can be in those registers and they may have floating point members.

There may also be a need to support fixed point 'mov$m$' instructions in and out of floating point registers. Unfortunately, I have forgotten why this was so, and I don't know whether it is still true. If `TARGET_HARD_REGNO_MODE_OK` rejects fixed point values in floating point registers, then the constraints of the fixed point 'mov$m$' instructions must be designed to avoid ever trying to reload into a floating point register.

'reload_in$m$'
'reload_out$m$'

These named patterns have been obsoleted by the target hook `secondary_reload`.

Like 'mov$m$', but used when a scratch register is required to move between operand 0 and operand 1. Operand 2 describes the scratch register. See the discussion of the SECONDARY_RELOAD_CLASS macro in see Section 18.8 [Register Classes], page 493.

There are special restrictions on the form of the match_operands used in these patterns. First, only the predicate for the reload operand is examined, i.e., reload_in examines operand 1, but not the predicates for operand 0 or 2. Second, there may be only one alternative in the constraints. Third, only a single register class letter may be used for the constraint; subsequent constraint letters are ignored. As a special exception, an empty constraint string matches the ALL_REGS register class. This may relieve ports of the burden of defining an ALL_REGS constraint letter just for these patterns.

'movstrict*m*'
: Like 'mov*m*' except that if operand 0 is a subreg with mode *m* of a register whose natural mode is wider, the 'movstrict*m*' instruction is guaranteed not to alter any of the register except the part which belongs to mode *m*.

'movmisalign*m*'
: This variant of a move pattern is designed to load or store a value from a memory address that is not naturally aligned for its mode. For a store, the memory will be in operand 0; for a load, the memory will be in operand 1. The other operand is guaranteed not to be a memory, so that it's easy to tell whether this is a load or store.

  This pattern is used by the autovectorizer, and when expanding a MISALIGNED_INDIRECT_REF expression.

'load_multiple'
: Load several consecutive memory locations into consecutive registers. Operand 0 is the first of the consecutive registers, operand 1 is the first memory location, and operand 2 is a constant: the number of consecutive registers.

  Define this only if the target machine really has such an instruction; do not define this if the most efficient way of loading consecutive registers from memory is to do them one at a time.

  On some machines, there are restrictions as to which consecutive registers can be stored into memory, such as particular starting or ending register numbers or only a range of valid counts. For those machines, use a define_expand (see Section 17.15 [Expander Definitions], page 423) and make the pattern fail if the restrictions are not met.

  Write the generated insn as a parallel with elements being a set of one register from the appropriate memory location (you may also need use or clobber elements). Use a match_parallel (see Section 17.4 [RTL Template], page 329) to recognize the insn. See 'rs6000.md' for examples of the use of this insn pattern.

'store_multiple'
: Similar to 'load_multiple', but store several consecutive registers into consecutive memory locations. Operand 0 is the first of the consecutive memory locations, operand 1 is the first register, and operand 2 is a constant: the number of consecutive registers.

'vec_load_lanes*mn*'
: Perform an interleaved load of several vectors from memory operand 1 into register operand 0. Both operands have mode *m*. The register operand is viewed as holding consecutive vectors of mode *n*, while the memory operand is a flat array that contains the same number of elements. The operation is equivalent to:

```
int c = GET_MODE_SIZE (m) / GET_MODE_SIZE (n);
for (j = 0; j < GET_MODE_NUNITS (n); j++)
  for (i = 0; i < c; i++)
    operand0[i][j] = operand1[j * c + i];
```

For example, 'vec_load_lanestiv4hi' loads 8 16-bit values from memory into a register of mode 'TI'. The register contains two consecutive vectors of mode 'V4HI'.

This pattern can only be used if:

TARGET_ARRAY_MODE_SUPPORTED_P (*n*, *c*)

is true. GCC assumes that, if a target supports this kind of instruction for some mode *n*, it also supports unaligned loads for vectors of mode *n*.

This pattern is not allowed to FAIL.

'vec_mask_load_lanes*mn*'
: Like 'vec_load_lanes*mn*', but takes an additional mask operand (operand 2) that specifies which elements of the destination vectors should be loaded. Other elements of the destination vectors are set to zero. The operation is equivalent to:

```
int c = GET_MODE_SIZE (m) / GET_MODE_SIZE (n);
for (j = 0; j < GET_MODE_NUNITS (n); j++)
  if (operand2[j])
    for (i = 0; i < c; i++)
      operand0[i][j] = operand1[j * c + i];
  else
    for (i = 0; i < c; i++)
      operand0[i][j] = 0;
```

This pattern is not allowed to FAIL.

'vec_store_lanes*mn*'
: Equivalent to 'vec_load_lanes*mn*', with the memory and register operands reversed. That is, the instruction is equivalent to:

```
int c = GET_MODE_SIZE (m) / GET_MODE_SIZE (n);
for (j = 0; j < GET_MODE_NUNITS (n); j++)
  for (i = 0; i < c; i++)
    operand0[j * c + i] = operand1[i][j];
```

for a memory operand 0 and register operand 1.

This pattern is not allowed to FAIL.

'vec_mask_store_lanes*mn*'
: Like 'vec_store_lanes*mn*', but takes an additional mask operand (operand 2) that specifies which elements of the source vectors should be stored. The operation is equivalent to:

```
int c = GET_MODE_SIZE (m) / GET_MODE_SIZE (n);
for (j = 0; j < GET_MODE_NUNITS (n); j++)
```

```
            if (operand2[j])
              for (i = 0; i < c; i++)
                operand0[j * c + i] = operand1[i][j];
```
This pattern is not allowed to FAIL.

'gather_load*m*'

Load several separate memory locations into a vector of mode *m*. Operand 1 is a scalar base address and operand 2 is a vector of offsets from that base. Operand 0 is a destination vector with the same number of elements as the offset. For each element index *i*:

- extend the offset element *i* to address width, using zero extension if operand 3 is 1 and sign extension if operand 3 is zero;
- multiply the extended offset by operand 4;
- add the result to the base; and
- load the value at that address into element *i* of operand 0.

The value of operand 3 does not matter if the offsets are already address width.

'mask_gather_load*m*'

Like 'gather_load*m*', but takes an extra mask operand as operand 5. Bit *i* of the mask is set if element *i* of the result should be loaded from memory and clear if element *i* of the result should be set to zero.

'scatter_store*m*'

Store a vector of mode *m* into several distinct memory locations. Operand 0 is a scalar base address and operand 1 is a vector of offsets from that base. Operand 4 is the vector of values that should be stored, which has the same number of elements as the offset. For each element index *i*:

- extend the offset element *i* to address width, using zero extension if operand 2 is 1 and sign extension if operand 2 is zero;
- multiply the extended offset by operand 3;
- add the result to the base; and
- store element *i* of operand 4 to that address.

The value of operand 2 does not matter if the offsets are already address width.

'mask_scatter_store*m*'

Like 'scatter_store*m*', but takes an extra mask operand as operand 5. Bit *i* of the mask is set if element *i* of the result should be stored to memory.

'vec_set*m*'

Set given field in the vector value. Operand 0 is the vector to modify, operand 1 is new value of field and operand 2 specify the field index.

'vec_extract*mn*'

Extract given field from the vector value. Operand 1 is the vector, operand 2 specify field index and operand 0 place to store value into. The *n* mode is the mode of the field or vector of fields that should be extracted, should be either element mode of the vector mode *m*, or a vector mode with the same element mode and smaller number of elements. If *n* is a vector mode, the index is counted in units of that mode.

'vec_init*mn*'
: Initialize the vector to given values. Operand 0 is the vector to initialize and operand 1 is parallel containing values for individual fields. The *n* mode is the mode of the elements, should be either element mode of the vector mode *m*, or a vector mode with the same element mode and smaller number of elements.

'vec_duplicate*m*'
: Initialize vector output operand 0 so that each element has the value given by scalar input operand 1. The vector has mode *m* and the scalar has the mode appropriate for one element of *m*.

    This pattern only handles duplicates of non-constant inputs. Constant vectors go through the mov*m* pattern instead.

    This pattern is not allowed to FAIL.

'vec_series*m*'
: Initialize vector output operand 0 so that element *i* is equal to operand 1 plus *i* times operand 2. In other words, create a linear series whose base value is operand 1 and whose step is operand 2.

    The vector output has mode *m* and the scalar inputs have the mode appropriate for one element of *m*. This pattern is not used for floating-point vectors, in order to avoid having to specify the rounding behavior for $i > 1$.

    This pattern is not allowed to FAIL.

while_ult*mn*
: Set operand 0 to a mask that is true while incrementing operand 1 gives a value that is less than operand 2. Operand 0 has mode *n* and operands 1 and 2 are scalar integers of mode *m*. The operation is equivalent to:

    ```
    operand0[0] = operand1 < operand2;
    for (i = 1; i < GET_MODE_NUNITS (n); i++)
      operand0[i] = operand0[i - 1] && (operand1 + i < operand2);
    ```

'vec_cmp*mn*'
: Output a vector comparison. Operand 0 of mode *n* is the destination for predicate in operand 1 which is a signed vector comparison with operands of mode *m* in operands 2 and 3. Predicate is computed by element-wise evaluation of the vector comparison with a truth value of all-ones and a false value of all-zeros.

'vec_cmpu*mn*'
: Similar to vec_cmp*mn* but perform unsigned vector comparison.

'vec_cmpeq*mn*'
: Similar to vec_cmp*mn* but perform equality or non-equality vector comparison only. If vec_cmp*mn* or vec_cmpu*mn* instruction pattern is supported, it will be preferred over vec_cmpeq*mn*, so there is no need to define this instruction pattern if the others are supported.

'vcond*mn*'
: Output a conditional vector move. Operand 0 is the destination to receive a combination of operand 1 and operand 2, which are of mode *m*, dependent on the outcome of the predicate in operand 3 which is a signed vector comparison with operands of mode *n* in operands 4 and 5. The modes *m* and *n* should have

the same size. Operand 0 will be set to the value *op1 & msk | op2 & ~msk* where *msk* is computed by element-wise evaluation of the vector comparison with a truth value of all-ones and a false value of all-zeros.

'vcondu*mn*'

Similar to vcond*mn* but performs unsigned vector comparison.

'vcondeq*mn*'

Similar to vcond*mn* but performs equality or non-equality vector comparison only. If vcond*mn* or vcondu*mn* instruction pattern is supported, it will be preferred over vcondeq*mn*, so there is no need to define this instruction pattern if the others are supported.

'vcond_mask_*mn*'

Similar to vcond*mn* but operand 3 holds a pre-computed result of vector comparison.

'maskload*mn*'

Perform a masked load of vector from memory operand 1 of mode *m* into register operand 0. Mask is provided in register operand 2 of mode *n*.

This pattern is not allowed to FAIL.

'maskstore*mn*'

Perform a masked store of vector from register operand 1 of mode *m* into memory operand 0. Mask is provided in register operand 2 of mode *n*.

This pattern is not allowed to FAIL.

'vec_perm*m*'

Output a (variable) vector permutation. Operand 0 is the destination to receive elements from operand 1 and operand 2, which are of mode *m*. Operand 3 is the *selector*. It is an integral mode vector of the same width and number of elements as mode *m*.

The input elements are numbered from 0 in operand 1 through $2*N-1$ in operand 2. The elements of the selector must be computed modulo $2*N$. Note that if rtx_equal_p(operand1, operand2), this can be implemented with just operand 1 and selector elements modulo N.

In order to make things easy for a number of targets, if there is no 'vec_perm' pattern for mode *m*, but there is for mode *q* where *q* is a vector of QImode of the same width as *m*, the middle-end will lower the mode *m* VEC_PERM_EXPR to mode *q*.

See also TARGET_VECTORIZER_VEC_PERM_CONST, which performs the analogous operation for constant selectors.

'push*m*1'

Output a push instruction. Operand 0 is value to push. Used only when PUSH_ROUNDING is defined. For historical reason, this pattern may be missing and in such case an mov expander is used instead, with a MEM expression forming the push operation. The mov expander method is deprecated.

'add*m*3'

Add operand 2 and operand 1, storing the result in operand 0. All operands must have mode *m*. This can be used even on two-address machines, by means of constraints requiring operands 1 and 0 to be the same location.

'ssadd*m*3', 'usadd*m*3'
'sub*m*3', 'sssub*m*3', 'ussub*m*3'
'mul*m*3', 'ssmul*m*3', 'usmul*m*3'
'div*m*3', 'ssdiv*m*3'
'udiv*m*3', 'usdiv*m*3'
'mod*m*3', 'umod*m*3'
'umin*m*3', 'umax*m*3'
'and*m*3', 'ior*m*3', 'xor*m*3'

    Similar, for other arithmetic operations.

'addv*m*4'
    Like add*m*3 but takes a `code_label` as operand 3 and emits code to jump to it if signed overflow occurs during the addition. This pattern is used to implement the built-in functions performing signed integer addition with overflow checking.

'subv*m*4', 'mulv*m*4'
    Similar, for other signed arithmetic operations.

'uaddv*m*4'
    Like addv*m*4 but for unsigned addition. That is to say, the operation is the same as signed addition but the jump is taken only on unsigned overflow.

'usubv*m*4', 'umulv*m*4'
    Similar, for other unsigned arithmetic operations.

'addptr*m*3'
    Like add*m*3 but is guaranteed to only be used for address calculations. The expanded code is not allowed to clobber the condition code. It only needs to be defined if add*m*3 sets the condition code. If adds used for address calculations and normal adds are not compatible it is required to expand a distinct pattern (e.g. using an unspec). The pattern is used by LRA to emit address calculations. add*m*3 is used if addptr*m*3 is not defined.

'fma*m*4'
    Multiply operand 2 and operand 1, then add operand 3, storing the result in operand 0 without doing an intermediate rounding step. All operands must have mode *m*. This pattern is used to implement the `fma`, `fmaf`, and `fmal` builtin functions from the ISO C99 standard.

'fms*m*4'
    Like fma*m*4, except operand 3 subtracted from the product instead of added to the product. This is represented in the rtl as
        (fma:*m* *op1* *op2* (neg:*m* *op3*))

'fnma*m*4'
    Like fma*m*4 except that the intermediate product is negated before being added to operand 3. This is represented in the rtl as
        (fma:*m* (neg:*m* *op1*) *op2* *op3*)

'fnms*m*4'
    Like fms*m*4 except that the intermediate product is negated before subtracting operand 3. This is represented in the rtl as
        (fma:*m* (neg:*m* *op1*) *op2* (neg:*m* *op3*))

'smin*m*3', 'smax*m*3'
    Signed minimum and maximum operations. When used with floating point, if both operands are zeros, or if either operand is `NaN`, then it is unspecified which of the two operands is returned as the result.

'fmin*m*3', 'fmax*m*3'
: IEEE-conformant minimum and maximum operations. If one operand is a quiet NaN, then the other operand is returned. If both operands are quiet NaN, then a quiet NaN is returned. In the case when gcc supports signaling NaN (-fsignaling-nans) an invalid floating point exception is raised and a quiet NaN is returned.

    All operands have mode *m*, which is a scalar or vector floating-point mode. These patterns are not allowed to FAIL.

'reduc_smin_scal_*m*', 'reduc_smax_scal_*m*'
: Find the signed minimum/maximum of the elements of a vector. The vector is operand 1, and operand 0 is the scalar result, with mode equal to the mode of the elements of the input vector.

'reduc_umin_scal_*m*', 'reduc_umax_scal_*m*'
: Find the unsigned minimum/maximum of the elements of a vector. The vector is operand 1, and operand 0 is the scalar result, with mode equal to the mode of the elements of the input vector.

'reduc_plus_scal_*m*'
: Compute the sum of the elements of a vector. The vector is operand 1, and operand 0 is the scalar result, with mode equal to the mode of the elements of the input vector.

'reduc_and_scal_*m*'
'reduc_ior_scal_*m*'
'reduc_xor_scal_*m*'
: Compute the bitwise AND/IOR/XOR reduction of the elements of a vector of mode *m*. Operand 1 is the vector input and operand 0 is the scalar result. The mode of the scalar result is the same as one element of *m*.

extract_last_*m*
: Find the last set bit in mask operand 1 and extract the associated element of vector operand 2. Store the result in scalar operand 0. Operand 2 has vector mode *m* while operand 0 has the mode appropriate for one element of *m*. Operand 1 has the usual mask mode for vectors of mode *m*; see TARGET_VECTORIZE_GET_MASK_MODE.

fold_extract_last_*m*
: If any bits of mask operand 2 are set, find the last set bit, extract the associated element from vector operand 3, and store the result in operand 0. Store operand 1 in operand 0 otherwise. Operand 3 has mode *m* and operands 0 and 1 have the mode appropriate for one element of *m*. Operand 2 has the usual mask mode for vectors of mode *m*; see TARGET_VECTORIZE_GET_MASK_MODE.

fold_left_plus_*m*
: Take scalar operand 1 and successively add each element from vector operand 2. Store the result in scalar operand 0. The vector has mode *m* and the scalars have the mode appropriate for one element of *m*. The operation is strictly in-order: there is no reassociation.

'sdot_prod*m*'

'udot_prod*m*'

> Compute the sum of the products of two signed/unsigned elements. Operand 1 and operand 2 are of the same mode. Their product, which is of a wider mode, is computed and added to operand 3. Operand 3 is of a mode equal or wider than the mode of the product. The result is placed in operand 0, which is of the same mode as operand 3.

'ssad*m*'

'usad*m*'

> Compute the sum of absolute differences of two signed/unsigned elements. Operand 1 and operand 2 are of the same mode. Their absolute difference, which is of a wider mode, is computed and added to operand 3. Operand 3 is of a mode equal or wider than the mode of the absolute difference. The result is placed in operand 0, which is of the same mode as operand 3.

'widen_ssum*m*3'

'widen_usum*m*3'

> Operands 0 and 2 are of the same mode, which is wider than the mode of operand 1. Add operand 1 to operand 2 and place the widened result in operand 0. (This is used express accumulation of elements into an accumulator of a wider mode.)

'vec_shl_insert_*m*'

> Shift the elements in vector input operand 1 left one element (i.e. away from element 0) and fill the vacated element 0 with the scalar in operand 2. Store the result in vector output operand 0. Operands 0 and 1 have mode *m* and operand 2 has the mode appropriate for one element of *m*.

'vec_shr_*m*'

> Whole vector right shift in bits, i.e. towards element 0. Operand 1 is a vector to be shifted. Operand 2 is an integer shift amount in bits. Operand 0 is where the resulting shifted vector is stored. The output and input vectors should have the same modes.

'vec_pack_trunc_*m*'

> Narrow (demote) and merge the elements of two vectors. Operands 1 and 2 are vectors of the same mode having N integral or floating point elements of size S. Operand 0 is the resulting vector in which 2*N elements of size N/2 are concatenated after narrowing them down using truncation.

'vec_pack_ssat_*m*', 'vec_pack_usat_*m*'

> Narrow (demote) and merge the elements of two vectors. Operands 1 and 2 are vectors of the same mode having N integral elements of size S. Operand 0 is the resulting vector in which the elements of the two input vectors are concatenated after narrowing them down using signed/unsigned saturating arithmetic.

'vec_pack_sfix_trunc_*m*', 'vec_pack_ufix_trunc_*m*'

> Narrow, convert to signed/unsigned integral type and merge the elements of two vectors. Operands 1 and 2 are vectors of the same mode having N floating point elements of size S. Operand 0 is the resulting vector in which 2*N elements of size N/2 are concatenated.

'vec_unpacks_hi_m', 'vec_unpacks_lo_m'
: Extract and widen (promote) the high/low part of a vector of signed integral or floating point elements. The input vector (operand 1) has N elements of size S. Widen (promote) the high/low elements of the vector using signed or floating point extension and place the resulting N/2 values of size 2*S in the output vector (operand 0).

'vec_unpacku_hi_m', 'vec_unpacku_lo_m'
: Extract and widen (promote) the high/low part of a vector of unsigned integral elements. The input vector (operand 1) has N elements of size S. Widen (promote) the high/low elements of the vector using zero extension and place the resulting N/2 values of size 2*S in the output vector (operand 0).

'vec_unpacks_float_hi_m', 'vec_unpacks_float_lo_m'
'vec_unpacku_float_hi_m', 'vec_unpacku_float_lo_m'
: Extract, convert to floating point type and widen the high/low part of a vector of signed/unsigned integral elements. The input vector (operand 1) has N elements of size S. Convert the high/low elements of the vector using floating point conversion and place the resulting N/2 values of size 2*S in the output vector (operand 0).

'vec_widen_umult_hi_m', 'vec_widen_umult_lo_m'
'vec_widen_smult_hi_m', 'vec_widen_smult_lo_m'
'vec_widen_umult_even_m', 'vec_widen_umult_odd_m'
'vec_widen_smult_even_m', 'vec_widen_smult_odd_m'
: Signed/Unsigned widening multiplication. The two inputs (operands 1 and 2) are vectors with N signed/unsigned elements of size S. Multiply the high/low or even/odd elements of the two vectors, and put the N/2 products of size 2*S in the output vector (operand 0). A target shouldn't implement even/odd pattern pair if it is less efficient than lo/hi one.

'vec_widen_ushiftl_hi_m', 'vec_widen_ushiftl_lo_m'
'vec_widen_sshiftl_hi_m', 'vec_widen_sshiftl_lo_m'
: Signed/Unsigned widening shift left. The first input (operand 1) is a vector with N signed/unsigned elements of size S. Operand 2 is a constant. Shift the high/low elements of operand 1, and put the N/2 results of size 2*S in the output vector (operand 0).

'mulhisi3'
: Multiply operands 1 and 2, which have mode HImode, and store a SImode product in operand 0.

'mulqihi3', 'mulsidi3'
: Similar widening-multiplication instructions of other widths.

'umulqihi3', 'umulhisi3', 'umulsidi3'
: Similar widening-multiplication instructions that do unsigned multiplication.

'usmulqihi3', 'usmulhisi3', 'usmulsidi3'
: Similar widening-multiplication instructions that interpret the first operand as unsigned and the second operand as signed, then do a signed multiplication.

'smul*m*3_highpart'
: Perform a signed multiplication of operands 1 and 2, which have mode *m*, and store the most significant half of the product in operand 0. The least significant half of the product is discarded.

'umul*m*3_highpart'
: Similar, but the multiplication is unsigned.

'madd*mn*4'
: Multiply operands 1 and 2, sign-extend them to mode *n*, add operand 3, and store the result in operand 0. Operands 1 and 2 have mode *m* and operands 0 and 3 have mode *n*. Both modes must be integer or fixed-point modes and *n* must be twice the size of *m*.

    In other words, madd*mn*4 is like mul*mn*3 except that it also adds operand 3.

    These instructions are not allowed to FAIL.

'umadd*mn*4'
: Like madd*mn*4, but zero-extend the multiplication operands instead of sign-extending them.

'ssmadd*mn*4'
: Like madd*mn*4, but all involved operations must be signed-saturating.

'usmadd*mn*4'
: Like umadd*mn*4, but all involved operations must be unsigned-saturating.

'msub*mn*4'
: Multiply operands 1 and 2, sign-extend them to mode *n*, subtract the result from operand 3, and store the result in operand 0. Operands 1 and 2 have mode *m* and operands 0 and 3 have mode *n*. Both modes must be integer or fixed-point modes and *n* must be twice the size of *m*.

    In other words, msub*mn*4 is like mul*mn*3 except that it also subtracts the result from operand 3.

    These instructions are not allowed to FAIL.

'umsub*mn*4'
: Like msub*mn*4, but zero-extend the multiplication operands instead of sign-extending them.

'ssmsub*mn*4'
: Like msub*mn*4, but all involved operations must be signed-saturating.

'usmsub*mn*4'
: Like umsub*mn*4, but all involved operations must be unsigned-saturating.

'divmod*m*4'
: Signed division that produces both a quotient and a remainder. Operand 1 is divided by operand 2 to produce a quotient stored in operand 0 and a remainder stored in operand 3.

    For machines with an instruction that produces both a quotient and a remainder, provide a pattern for 'divmod*m*4' but do not provide patterns for 'div*m*3' and 'mod*m*3'. This allows optimization in the relatively common case when both the quotient and remainder are computed.

If an instruction that just produces a quotient or just a remainder exists and is more efficient than the instruction that produces both, write the output routine of 'divmod*m*4' to call `find_reg_note` and look for a `REG_UNUSED` note on the quotient or remainder and generate the appropriate instruction.

'udivmod*m*4'
: Similar, but does unsigned division.

'ashl*m*3', 'ssashl*m*3', 'usashl*m*3'
: Arithmetic-shift operand 1 left by a number of bits specified by operand 2, and store the result in operand 0. Here *m* is the mode of operand 0 and operand 1; operand 2's mode is specified by the instruction pattern, and the compiler will convert the operand to that mode before generating the instruction. The shift or rotate expander or instruction pattern should explicitly specify the mode of the operand 2, it should never be `VOIDmode`. The meaning of out-of-range shift counts can optionally be specified by `TARGET_SHIFT_TRUNCATION_MASK`. See [TARGET_SHIFT_TRUNCATION_MASK], page 624. Operand 2 is always a scalar type.

'ashr*m*3', 'lshr*m*3', 'rotl*m*3', 'rotr*m*3'
: Other shift and rotate instructions, analogous to the ashl*m*3 instructions. Operand 2 is always a scalar type.

'vashl*m*3', 'vashr*m*3', 'vlshr*m*3', 'vrotl*m*3', 'vrotr*m*3'
: Vector shift and rotate instructions that take vectors as operand 2 instead of a scalar type.

'bswap*m*2'
: Reverse the order of bytes of operand 1 and store the result in operand 0.

'neg*m*2', 'ssneg*m*2', 'usneg*m*2'
: Negate operand 1 and store the result in operand 0.

'negv*m*3'
: Like neg*m*2 but takes a `code_label` as operand 2 and emits code to jump to it if signed overflow occurs during the negation.

'abs*m*2'
: Store the absolute value of operand 1 into operand 0.

'sqrt*m*2'
: Store the square root of operand 1 into operand 0. Both operands have mode *m*, which is a scalar or vector floating-point mode.

  This pattern is not allowed to `FAIL`.

'rsqrt*m*2'
: Store the reciprocal of the square root of operand 1 into operand 0. Both operands have mode *m*, which is a scalar or vector floating-point mode.

  On most architectures this pattern is only approximate, so either its C condition or the `TARGET_OPTAB_SUPPORTED_P` hook should check for the appropriate math flags. (Using the C condition is more direct, but using `TARGET_OPTAB_SUPPORTED_P` can be useful if a target-specific built-in also uses the 'rsqrt*m*2' pattern.)

  This pattern is not allowed to `FAIL`.

'fmod*m*3'
: Store the remainder of dividing operand 1 by operand 2 into operand 0, rounded towards zero to an integer. All operands have mode *m*, which is a scalar or vector floating-point mode.

This pattern is not allowed to FAIL.

'remainder*m*3'
: Store the remainder of dividing operand 1 by operand 2 into operand 0, rounded to the nearest integer. All operands have mode *m*, which is a scalar or vector floating-point mode.

    This pattern is not allowed to FAIL.

'scalb*m*3'
: Raise FLT_RADIX to the power of operand 2, multiply it by operand 1, and store the result in operand 0. All operands have mode *m*, which is a scalar or vector floating-point mode.

    This pattern is not allowed to FAIL.

'ldexp*m*3'
: Raise 2 to the power of operand 2, multiply it by operand 1, and store the result in operand 0. Operands 0 and 1 have mode *m*, which is a scalar or vector floating-point mode. Operand 2's mode has the same number of elements as *m* and each element is wide enough to store an int. The integers are signed.

    This pattern is not allowed to FAIL.

'cos*m*2'
: Store the cosine of operand 1 into operand 0. Both operands have mode *m*, which is a scalar or vector floating-point mode.

    This pattern is not allowed to FAIL.

'sin*m*2'
: Store the sine of operand 1 into operand 0. Both operands have mode *m*, which is a scalar or vector floating-point mode.

    This pattern is not allowed to FAIL.

'sincos*m*3'
: Store the cosine of operand 2 into operand 0 and the sine of operand 2 into operand 1. All operands have mode *m*, which is a scalar or vector floating-point mode.

    Targets that can calculate the sine and cosine simultaneously can implement this pattern as opposed to implementing individual **sin*m*2** and **cos*m*2** patterns. The **sin** and **cos** built-in functions will then be expanded to the **sincos*m*3** pattern, with one of the output values left unused.

'tan*m*2'
: Store the tangent of operand 1 into operand 0. Both operands have mode *m*, which is a scalar or vector floating-point mode.

    This pattern is not allowed to FAIL.

'asin*m*2'
: Store the arc sine of operand 1 into operand 0. Both operands have mode *m*, which is a scalar or vector floating-point mode.

    This pattern is not allowed to FAIL.

'acos*m*2'
: Store the arc cosine of operand 1 into operand 0. Both operands have mode *m*, which is a scalar or vector floating-point mode.

    This pattern is not allowed to FAIL.

'atan*m*2'
: Store the arc tangent of operand 1 into operand 0. Both operands have mode *m*, which is a scalar or vector floating-point mode.

    This pattern is not allowed to FAIL.

'exp$m$2'   Raise e (the base of natural logarithms) to the power of operand 1 and store the result in operand 0. Both operands have mode m, which is a scalar or vector floating-point mode.

This pattern is not allowed to FAIL.

'expm1m2'   Raise e (the base of natural logarithms) to the power of operand 1, subtract 1, and store the result in operand 0. Both operands have mode m, which is a scalar or vector floating-point mode.

For inputs close to zero, the pattern is expected to be more accurate than a separate exp$m$2 and sub$m$3 would be.

This pattern is not allowed to FAIL.

'exp10m2'   Raise 10 to the power of operand 1 and store the result in operand 0. Both operands have mode m, which is a scalar or vector floating-point mode.

This pattern is not allowed to FAIL.

'exp2m2'   Raise 2 to the power of operand 1 and store the result in operand 0. Both operands have mode m, which is a scalar or vector floating-point mode.

This pattern is not allowed to FAIL.

'log$m$2'   Store the natural logarithm of operand 1 into operand 0. Both operands have mode m, which is a scalar or vector floating-point mode.

This pattern is not allowed to FAIL.

'log1pm2'   Add 1 to operand 1, compute the natural logarithm, and store the result in operand 0. Both operands have mode m, which is a scalar or vector floating-point mode.

For inputs close to zero, the pattern is expected to be more accurate than a separate add$m$3 and log$m$2 would be.

This pattern is not allowed to FAIL.

'log10m2'   Store the base-10 logarithm of operand 1 into operand 0. Both operands have mode m, which is a scalar or vector floating-point mode.

This pattern is not allowed to FAIL.

'log2m2'   Store the base-2 logarithm of operand 1 into operand 0. Both operands have mode m, which is a scalar or vector floating-point mode.

This pattern is not allowed to FAIL.

'logb$m$2'   Store the base-FLT_RADIX logarithm of operand 1 into operand 0. Both operands have mode m, which is a scalar or vector floating-point mode.

This pattern is not allowed to FAIL.

'significand$m$2'

Store the significand of floating-point operand 1 in operand 0. Both operands have mode m, which is a scalar or vector floating-point mode.

This pattern is not allowed to FAIL.

'pow$m$3'   Store the value of operand 1 raised to the exponent operand 2 into operand 0. All operands have mode m, which is a scalar or vector floating-point mode.

This pattern is not allowed to FAIL.

'atan2*m*3'   Store the arc tangent (inverse tangent) of operand 1 divided by operand 2 into operand 0, using the signs of both arguments to determine the quadrant of the result. All operands have mode *m*, which is a scalar or vector floating-point mode.

This pattern is not allowed to FAIL.

'floor*m*2'   Store the largest integral value not greater than operand 1 in operand 0. Both operands have mode *m*, which is a scalar or vector floating-point mode. If '-ffp-int-builtin-inexact' is in effect, the "inexact" exception may be raised for noninteger operands; otherwise, it may not.

This pattern is not allowed to FAIL.

'btrunc*m*2'

Round operand 1 to an integer, towards zero, and store the result in operand 0. Both operands have mode *m*, which is a scalar or vector floating-point mode. If '-ffp-int-builtin-inexact' is in effect, the "inexact" exception may be raised for noninteger operands; otherwise, it may not.

This pattern is not allowed to FAIL.

'round*m*2'   Round operand 1 to the nearest integer, rounding away from zero in the event of a tie, and store the result in operand 0. Both operands have mode *m*, which is a scalar or vector floating-point mode. If '-ffp-int-builtin-inexact' is in effect, the "inexact" exception may be raised for noninteger operands; otherwise, it may not.

This pattern is not allowed to FAIL.

'ceil*m*2'   Store the smallest integral value not less than operand 1 in operand 0. Both operands have mode *m*, which is a scalar or vector floating-point mode. If '-ffp-int-builtin-inexact' is in effect, the "inexact" exception may be raised for noninteger operands; otherwise, it may not.

This pattern is not allowed to FAIL.

'nearbyint*m*2'

Round operand 1 to an integer, using the current rounding mode, and store the result in operand 0. Do not raise an inexact condition when the result is different from the argument. Both operands have mode *m*, which is a scalar or vector floating-point mode.

This pattern is not allowed to FAIL.

'rint*m*2'   Round operand 1 to an integer, using the current rounding mode, and store the result in operand 0. Raise an inexact condition when the result is different from the argument. Both operands have mode *m*, which is a scalar or vector floating-point mode.

This pattern is not allowed to FAIL.

'lrint*mn*2'

Convert operand 1 (valid for floating point mode *m*) to fixed point mode *n* as a signed number according to the current rounding mode and store in operand 0 (which has mode *n*).

'lround*mn*2'
: Convert operand 1 (valid for floating point mode *m*) to fixed point mode *n* as a signed number rounding to nearest and away from zero and store in operand 0 (which has mode *n*).

'lfloor*mn*2'
: Convert operand 1 (valid for floating point mode *m*) to fixed point mode *n* as a signed number rounding down and store in operand 0 (which has mode *n*).

'lceil*mn*2'
: Convert operand 1 (valid for floating point mode *m*) to fixed point mode *n* as a signed number rounding up and store in operand 0 (which has mode *n*).

'copysign*m*3'
: Store a value with the magnitude of operand 1 and the sign of operand 2 into operand 0. All operands have mode *m*, which is a scalar or vector floating-point mode.

  This pattern is not allowed to **FAIL**.

'ffs*m*2'
: Store into operand 0 one plus the index of the least significant 1-bit of operand 1. If operand 1 is zero, store zero.

  m is either a scalar or vector integer mode. When it is a scalar, operand 1 has mode *m* but operand 0 can have whatever scalar integer mode is suitable for the target. The compiler will insert conversion instructions as necessary (typically to convert the result to the same width as `int`). When *m* is a vector, both operands must have mode *m*.

  This pattern is not allowed to **FAIL**.

'clrsb*m*2'
: Count leading redundant sign bits. Store into operand 0 the number of redundant sign bits in operand 1, starting at the most significant bit position. A redundant sign bit is defined as any sign bit after the first. As such, this count will be one less than the count of leading sign bits.

  m is either a scalar or vector integer mode. When it is a scalar, operand 1 has mode *m* but operand 0 can have whatever scalar integer mode is suitable for the target. The compiler will insert conversion instructions as necessary (typically to convert the result to the same width as `int`). When *m* is a vector, both operands must have mode *m*.

  This pattern is not allowed to **FAIL**.

'clz*m*2'
: Store into operand 0 the number of leading 0-bits in operand 1, starting at the most significant bit position. If operand 1 is 0, the `CLZ_DEFINED_VALUE_AT_ZERO` (see Section 18.30 [Misc], page 621) macro defines if the result is undefined or has a useful value.

  m is either a scalar or vector integer mode. When it is a scalar, operand 1 has mode *m* but operand 0 can have whatever scalar integer mode is suitable for the target. The compiler will insert conversion instructions as necessary (typically to convert the result to the same width as `int`). When *m* is a vector, both operands must have mode *m*.

  This pattern is not allowed to **FAIL**.

'ctz*m*2'   Store into operand 0 the number of trailing 0-bits in operand 1, starting at the least significant bit position. If operand 1 is 0, the CTZ_DEFINED_VALUE_AT_ZERO (see Section 18.30 [Misc], page 621) macro defines if the result is undefined or has a useful value.

m is either a scalar or vector integer mode. When it is a scalar, operand 1 has mode *m* but operand 0 can have whatever scalar integer mode is suitable for the target. The compiler will insert conversion instructions as necessary (typically to convert the result to the same width as int). When *m* is a vector, both operands must have mode *m*.

This pattern is not allowed to FAIL.

'popcount*m*2'   Store into operand 0 the number of 1-bits in operand 1.

m is either a scalar or vector integer mode. When it is a scalar, operand 1 has mode *m* but operand 0 can have whatever scalar integer mode is suitable for the target. The compiler will insert conversion instructions as necessary (typically to convert the result to the same width as int). When *m* is a vector, both operands must have mode *m*.

This pattern is not allowed to FAIL.

'parity*m*2'   Store into operand 0 the parity of operand 1, i.e. the number of 1-bits in operand 1 modulo 2.

m is either a scalar or vector integer mode. When it is a scalar, operand 1 has mode *m* but operand 0 can have whatever scalar integer mode is suitable for the target. The compiler will insert conversion instructions as necessary (typically to convert the result to the same width as int). When *m* is a vector, both operands must have mode *m*.

This pattern is not allowed to FAIL.

'one_cpl*m*2'   Store the bitwise-complement of operand 1 into operand 0.

'movmem*m*'   Block move instruction. The destination and source blocks of memory are the first two operands, and both are mem:BLKs with an address in mode Pmode.

The number of bytes to move is the third operand, in mode *m*. Usually, you specify Pmode for *m*. However, if you can generate better code knowing the range of valid lengths is smaller than those representable in a full Pmode pointer, you should provide a pattern with a mode corresponding to the range of values you can handle efficiently (e.g., QImode for values in the range 0–127; note we avoid numbers that appear negative) and also a pattern with Pmode.

The fourth operand is the known shared alignment of the source and destination, in the form of a const_int rtx. Thus, if the compiler knows that both source and destination are word-aligned, it may provide the value 4 for this operand.

Optional operands 5 and 6 specify expected alignment and size of block respectively. The expected alignment differs from alignment in operand 4 in a way that the blocks are not required to be aligned according to it in all cases. This expected alignment is also in bytes, just like operand 4. Expected size, when unknown, is set to (`const_int -1`).

Descriptions of multiple movmem*m* patterns can only be beneficial if the patterns for smaller modes have fewer restrictions on their first, second and fourth operands. Note that the mode *m* in movmem*m* does not impose any restriction on the mode of individually moved data units in the block.

These patterns need not give special consideration to the possibility that the source and destination strings might overlap.

'movstr'   String copy instruction, with `stpcpy` semantics. Operand 0 is an output operand in mode `Pmode`. The addresses of the destination and source strings are operands 1 and 2, and both are `mem:BLK`s with addresses in mode `Pmode`. The execution of the expansion of this pattern should store in operand 0 the address in which the `NUL` terminator was stored in the destination string.

This patern has also several optional operands that are same as in `setmem`.

'setmem*m*'   Block set instruction. The destination string is the first operand, given as a `mem:BLK` whose address is in mode `Pmode`. The number of bytes to set is the second operand, in mode *m*. The value to initialize the memory with is the third operand. Targets that only support the clearing of memory should reject any value that is not the constant 0. See 'movmem*m*' for a discussion of the choice of mode.

The fourth operand is the known alignment of the destination, in the form of a `const_int` rtx. Thus, if the compiler knows that the destination is word-aligned, it may provide the value 4 for this operand.

Optional operands 5 and 6 specify expected alignment and size of block respectively. The expected alignment differs from alignment in operand 4 in a way that the blocks are not required to be aligned according to it in all cases. This expected alignment is also in bytes, just like operand 4. Expected size, when unknown, is set to (`const_int -1`). Operand 7 is the minimal size of the block and operand 8 is the maximal size of the block (NULL if it can not be represented as CONST_INT). Operand 9 is the probable maximal size (i.e. we can not rely on it for correctness, but it can be used for choosing proper code sequence for a given size).

The use for multiple setmem*m* is as for movmem*m*.

'cmpstrn*m*'

String compare instruction, with five operands. Operand 0 is the output; it has mode *m*. The remaining four operands are like the operands of 'movmem*m*'. The two memory blocks specified are compared byte by byte in lexicographic order starting at the beginning of each string. The instruction is not allowed to prefetch more than one byte at a time since either string may end in the first byte and reading past that may access an invalid page or segment and cause a fault. The comparison terminates early if the fetched bytes are different or if they are equal to zero. The effect of the instruction is to store a value in operand 0 whose sign indicates the result of the comparison.

'cmpstr*m*' String compare instruction, without known maximum length. Operand 0 is the output; it has mode *m*. The second and third operand are the blocks of memory to be compared; both are `mem:BLK` with an address in mode `Pmode`.

The fourth operand is the known shared alignment of the source and destination, in the form of a `const_int` rtx. Thus, if the compiler knows that both source and destination are word-aligned, it may provide the value 4 for this operand.

The two memory blocks specified are compared byte by byte in lexicographic order starting at the beginning of each string. The instruction is not allowed to prefetch more than one byte at a time since either string may end in the first byte and reading past that may access an invalid page or segment and cause a fault. The comparison will terminate when the fetched bytes are different or if they are equal to zero. The effect of the instruction is to store a value in operand 0 whose sign indicates the result of the comparison.

'cmpmem*m*' Block compare instruction, with five operands like the operands of 'cmpstr*m*'. The two memory blocks specified are compared byte by byte in lexicographic order starting at the beginning of each block. Unlike 'cmpstr*m*' the instruction can prefetch any bytes in the two memory blocks. Also unlike 'cmpstr*m*' the comparison will not stop if both bytes are zero. The effect of the instruction is to store a value in operand 0 whose sign indicates the result of the comparison.

'strlen*m*' Compute the length of a string, with three operands. Operand 0 is the result (of mode *m*), operand 1 is a `mem` referring to the first character of the string, operand 2 is the character to search for (normally zero), and operand 3 is a constant describing the known alignment of the beginning of the string.

'float*mn*2'
Convert signed integer operand 1 (valid for fixed point mode *m*) to floating point mode *n* and store in operand 0 (which has mode *n*).

'floatuns*mn*2'
Convert unsigned integer operand 1 (valid for fixed point mode *m*) to floating point mode *n* and store in operand 0 (which has mode *n*).

'fix*mn*2' Convert operand 1 (valid for floating point mode *m*) to fixed point mode *n* as a signed number and store in operand 0 (which has mode *n*). This instruction's result is defined only when the value of operand 1 is an integer.

If the machine description defines this pattern, it also needs to define the `ftrunc` pattern.

'fixuns*mn*2'
Convert operand 1 (valid for floating point mode *m*) to fixed point mode *n* as an unsigned number and store in operand 0 (which has mode *n*). This instruction's result is defined only when the value of operand 1 is an integer.

'ftrunc*m*2'
Convert operand 1 (valid for floating point mode *m*) to an integer value, still represented in floating point mode *m*, and store it in operand 0 (valid for floating point mode *m*).

'fix_truncmn2'
: Like 'fixmn2' but works for any floating point value of mode *m* by converting the value to an integer.

'fixuns_truncmn2'
: Like 'fixunsmn2' but works for any floating point value of mode *m* by converting the value to an integer.

'truncmn2'
: Truncate operand 1 (valid for mode *m*) to mode *n* and store in operand 0 (which has mode *n*). Both modes must be fixed point or both floating point.

'extendmn2'
: Sign-extend operand 1 (valid for mode *m*) to mode *n* and store in operand 0 (which has mode *n*). Both modes must be fixed point or both floating point.

'zero_extendmn2'
: Zero-extend operand 1 (valid for mode *m*) to mode *n* and store in operand 0 (which has mode *n*). Both modes must be fixed point.

'fractmn2'
: Convert operand 1 of mode *m* to mode *n* and store in operand 0 (which has mode *n*). Mode *m* and mode *n* could be fixed-point to fixed-point, signed integer to fixed-point, fixed-point to signed integer, floating-point to fixed-point, or fixed-point to floating-point. When overflows or underflows happen, the results are undefined.

'satfractmn2'
: Convert operand 1 of mode *m* to mode *n* and store in operand 0 (which has mode *n*). Mode *m* and mode *n* could be fixed-point to fixed-point, signed integer to fixed-point, or floating-point to fixed-point. When overflows or underflows happen, the instruction saturates the results to the maximum or the minimum.

'fractunsmn2'
: Convert operand 1 of mode *m* to mode *n* and store in operand 0 (which has mode *n*). Mode *m* and mode *n* could be unsigned integer to fixed-point, or fixed-point to unsigned integer. When overflows or underflows happen, the results are undefined.

'satfractunsmn2'
: Convert unsigned integer operand 1 of mode *m* to fixed-point mode *n* and store in operand 0 (which has mode *n*). When overflows or underflows happen, the instruction saturates the results to the maximum or the minimum.

'extvm'
: Extract a bit-field from register operand 1, sign-extend it, and store it in operand 0. Operand 2 specifies the width of the field in bits and operand 3 the starting bit, which counts from the most significant bit if 'BITS_BIG_ENDIAN' is true and from the least significant bit otherwise.

    Operands 0 and 1 both have mode *m*. Operands 2 and 3 have a target-specific mode.

'extv*m*misalign*m*'

Extract a bit-field from memory operand 1, sign extend it, and store it in operand 0. Operand 2 specifies the width in bits and operand 3 the starting bit. The starting bit is always somewhere in the first byte of operand 1; it counts from the most significant bit if 'BITS_BIG_ENDIAN' is true and from the least significant bit otherwise.

Operand 0 has mode *m* while operand 1 has BLK mode. Operands 2 and 3 have a target-specific mode.

The instruction must not read beyond the last byte of the bit-field.

'extzv*m*' Like 'extv*m*' except that the bit-field value is zero-extended.

'extzv*m*misalign*m*'

Like 'extv*m*misalign*m*' except that the bit-field value is zero-extended.

'insv*m*' Insert operand 3 into a bit-field of register operand 0. Operand 1 specifies the width of the field in bits and operand 2 the starting bit, which counts from the most significant bit if 'BITS_BIG_ENDIAN' is true and from the least significant bit otherwise.

Operands 0 and 3 both have mode *m*. Operands 1 and 2 have a target-specific mode.

'insv*m*misalign*m*'

Insert operand 3 into a bit-field of memory operand 0. Operand 1 specifies the width of the field in bits and operand 2 the starting bit. The starting bit is always somewhere in the first byte of operand 0; it counts from the most significant bit if 'BITS_BIG_ENDIAN' is true and from the least significant bit otherwise.

Operand 3 has mode *m* while operand 0 has BLK mode. Operands 1 and 2 have a target-specific mode.

The instruction must not read or write beyond the last byte of the bit-field.

'extv' Extract a bit-field from operand 1 (a register or memory operand), where operand 2 specifies the width in bits and operand 3 the starting bit, and store it in operand 0. Operand 0 must have mode word_mode. Operand 1 may have mode byte_mode or word_mode; often word_mode is allowed only for registers. Operands 2 and 3 must be valid for word_mode.

The RTL generation pass generates this instruction only with constants for operands 2 and 3 and the constant is never zero for operand 2.

The bit-field value is sign-extended to a full word integer before it is stored in operand 0.

This pattern is deprecated; please use 'extv*m*' and extv*m*misalign*m* instead.

'extzv' Like 'extv' except that the bit-field value is zero-extended.

This pattern is deprecated; please use 'extzv*m*' and extzv*m*misalign*m* instead.

'insv' Store operand 3 (which must be valid for word_mode) into a bit-field in operand 0, where operand 1 specifies the width in bits and operand 2 the starting bit.

Operand 0 may have mode `byte_mode` or `word_mode`; often `word_mode` is allowed only for registers. Operands 1 and 2 must be valid for `word_mode`.

The RTL generation pass generates this instruction only with constants for operands 1 and 2 and the constant is never zero for operand 1.

This pattern is deprecated; please use 'insv*m*' and `insvmisalign`*m* instead.

'mov*mode*cc'

Conditionally move operand 2 or operand 3 into operand 0 according to the comparison in operand 1. If the comparison is true, operand 2 is moved into operand 0, otherwise operand 3 is moved.

The mode of the operands being compared need not be the same as the operands being moved. Some machines, sparc64 for example, have instructions that conditionally move an integer value based on the floating point condition codes and vice versa.

If the machine does not have conditional move instructions, do not define these patterns.

'add*mode*cc'

Similar to 'mov*mode*cc' but for conditional addition. Conditionally move operand 2 or (operands 2 + operand 3) into operand 0 according to the comparison in operand 1. If the comparison is false, operand 2 is moved into operand 0, otherwise (operand 2 + operand 3) is moved.

'cond_add*mode*'
'cond_sub*mode*'
'cond_and*mode*'
'cond_ior*mode*'
'cond_xor*mode*'
'cond_smin*mode*'
'cond_smax*mode*'
'cond_umin*mode*'
'cond_umax*mode*'

Perform an elementwise operation on vector operands 2 and 3, under the control of the vector mask in operand 1, and store the result in operand 0. This is equivalent to:

```
for (i = 0; i < GET_MODE_NUNITS (n); i++)
  op0[i] = op1[i] ? op2[i] op op3[i] : op2[i];
```

where, for example, *op* is + for 'cond_add*mode*'.

When defined for floating-point modes, the contents of 'op3[i]' are not interpreted if *op1[i]* is false, just like they would not be in a normal C '?:' condition.

Operands 0, 2 and 3 all have mode *m*, while operand 1 has the mode returned by `TARGET_VECTORIZE_GET_MASK_MODE`.

'neg*mode*cc'

Similar to 'mov*mode*cc' but for conditional negation. Conditionally move the negation of operand 2 or the unchanged operand 3 into operand 0 according to the comparison in operand 1. If the comparison is true, the negation of operand 2 is moved into operand 0, otherwise operand 3 is moved.

'notmodecc'
: Similar to 'negmodecc' but for conditional complement. Conditionally move the bitwise complement of operand 2 or the unchanged operand 3 into operand 0 according to the comparison in operand 1. If the comparison is true, the complement of operand 2 is moved into operand 0, otherwise operand 3 is moved.

'cstoremode4'
: Store zero or nonzero in operand 0 according to whether a comparison is true. Operand 1 is a comparison operator. Operand 2 and operand 3 are the first and second operand of the comparison, respectively. You specify the mode that operand 0 must have when you write the match_operand expression. The compiler automatically sees which mode you have used and supplies an operand of that mode.

  The value stored for a true condition must have 1 as its low bit, or else must be negative. Otherwise the instruction is not suitable and you should omit it from the machine description. You describe to the compiler exactly which value is stored by defining the macro STORE_FLAG_VALUE (see Section 18.30 [Misc], page 621). If a description cannot be found that can be used for all the possible comparison operators, you should pick one and use a define_expand to map all results onto the one you chose.

  These operations may FAIL, but should do so only in relatively uncommon cases; if they would FAIL for common cases involving integer comparisons, it is best to restrict the predicates to not allow these operands. Likewise if a given comparison operator will always fail, independent of the operands (for floating-point modes, the ordered_comparison_operator predicate is often useful in this case).

  If this pattern is omitted, the compiler will generate a conditional branch—for example, it may copy a constant one to the target and branching around an assignment of zero to the target—or a libcall. If the predicate for operand 1 only rejects some operators, it will also try reordering the operands and/or inverting the result value (e.g. by an exclusive OR). These possibilities could be cheaper or equivalent to the instructions used for the 'cstoremode4' pattern followed by those required to convert a positive result from STORE_FLAG_VALUE to 1; in this case, you can and should make operand 1's predicate reject some operators in the 'cstoremode4' pattern, or remove the pattern altogether from the machine description.

'cbranchmode4'
: Conditional branch instruction combined with a compare instruction. Operand 0 is a comparison operator. Operand 1 and operand 2 are the first and second operands of the comparison, respectively. Operand 3 is the code_label to jump to.

'jump'
: A jump inside a function; an unconditional branch. Operand 0 is the code_label to jump to. This pattern name is mandatory on all machines.

'call'   Subroutine call instruction returning no value. Operand 0 is the function to call; operand 1 is the number of bytes of arguments pushed as a `const_int`; operand 2 is the number of registers used as operands.

On most machines, operand 2 is not actually stored into the RTL pattern. It is supplied for the sake of some RISC machines which need to put this information into the assembler code; they can put it in the RTL instead of operand 1.

Operand 0 should be a `mem` RTX whose address is the address of the function. Note, however, that this address can be a `symbol_ref` expression even if it would not be a legitimate memory address on the target machine. If it is also not a valid argument for a call instruction, the pattern for this operation should be a `define_expand` (see Section 17.15 [Expander Definitions], page 423) that places the address into a register and uses that register in the call instruction.

'call_value'
Subroutine call instruction returning a value. Operand 0 is the hard register in which the value is returned. There are three more operands, the same as the three operands of the 'call' instruction (but with numbers increased by one).

Subroutines that return `BLKmode` objects use the 'call' insn.

'call_pop', 'call_value_pop'
Similar to 'call' and 'call_value', except used if defined and if `RETURN_POPS_ARGS` is nonzero. They should emit a `parallel` that contains both the function call and a `set` to indicate the adjustment made to the frame pointer.

For machines where `RETURN_POPS_ARGS` can be nonzero, the use of these patterns increases the number of functions for which the frame pointer can be eliminated, if desired.

'untyped_call'
Subroutine call instruction returning a value of any type. Operand 0 is the function to call; operand 1 is a memory location where the result of calling the function is to be stored; operand 2 is a `parallel` expression where each element is a `set` expression that indicates the saving of a function return value into the result block.

This instruction pattern should be defined to support `__builtin_apply` on machines where special instructions are needed to call a subroutine with arbitrary arguments or to save the value returned. This instruction pattern is required on machines that have multiple registers that can hold a return value (i.e. `FUNCTION_VALUE_REGNO_P` is true for more than one register).

'return'   Subroutine return instruction. This instruction pattern name should be defined only if a single instruction can do all the work of returning from a function.

Like the '`movm`' patterns, this pattern is also used after the RTL generation phase. In this case it is to support machines where multiple instructions are usually needed to return from a function, but some class of functions only requires one instruction to implement a return. Normally, the applicable functions are those which do not need to save any registers or allocate stack space.

It is valid for this pattern to expand to an instruction using `simple_return` if no epilogue is required.

'simple_return'
: Subroutine return instruction. This instruction pattern name should be defined only if a single instruction can do all the work of returning from a function on a path where no epilogue is required. This pattern is very similar to the `return` instruction pattern, but it is emitted only by the shrink-wrapping optimization on paths where the function prologue has not been executed, and a function return should occur without any of the effects of the epilogue. Additional uses may be introduced on paths where both the prologue and the epilogue have executed.

For such machines, the condition specified in this pattern should only be true when `reload_completed` is nonzero and the function's epilogue would only be a single instruction. For machines with register windows, the routine `leaf_function_p` may be used to determine if a register window push is required.

Machines that have conditional return instructions should define patterns such as

```
(define_insn ""
  [(set (pc)
        (if_then_else (match_operator
                          0 "comparison_operator"
                          [(cc0) (const_int 0)])
                      (return)
                      (pc)))]
  "condition"
  "...")
```

where *condition* would normally be the same condition specified on the named 'return' pattern.

'untyped_return'
: Untyped subroutine return instruction. This instruction pattern should be defined to support `__builtin_return` on machines where special instructions are needed to return a value of any type.

Operand 0 is a memory location where the result of calling a function with `__builtin_apply` is stored; operand 1 is a `parallel` expression where each element is a `set` expression that indicates the restoring of a function return value from the result block.

'nop'
: No-op instruction. This instruction pattern name should always be defined to output a no-op in assembler code. (`const_int 0`) will do as an RTL pattern.

'indirect_jump'
: An instruction to jump to an address which is operand zero. This pattern name is mandatory on all machines.

'casesi'
: Instruction to jump through a dispatch table, including bounds checking. This instruction takes five operands:

  1. The index to dispatch on, which has mode `SImode`.
  2. The lower bound for indices in the table, an integer constant.
  3. The total range of indices in the table—the largest index minus the smallest one (both inclusive).

    4. A label that precedes the table itself.
    5. A label to jump to if the index has a value outside the bounds.

    The table is an `addr_vec` or `addr_diff_vec` inside of a `jump_table_data`. The number of elements in the table is one plus the difference between the upper bound and the lower bound.

'tablejump'
    Instruction to jump to a variable address. This is a low-level capability which can be used to implement a dispatch table when there is no 'casesi' pattern.

    This pattern requires two operands: the address or offset, and a label which should immediately precede the jump table. If the macro CASE_VECTOR_PC_RELATIVE evaluates to a nonzero value then the first operand is an offset which counts from the address of the table; otherwise, it is an absolute address to jump to. In either case, the first operand has mode Pmode.

    The 'tablejump' insn is always the last insn before the jump table it uses. Its assembler code normally has no need to use the second operand, but you should incorporate it in the RTL pattern so that the jump optimizer will not delete the table as unreachable code.

'decrement_and_branch_until_zero'
    Conditional branch instruction that decrements a register and jumps if the register is nonzero. Operand 0 is the register to decrement and test; operand 1 is the label to jump to if the register is nonzero. See Section 17.13 [Looping Patterns], page 420.

    This optional instruction pattern is only used by the combiner, typically for loops reversed by the loop optimizer when strength reduction is enabled.

'doloop_end'
    Conditional branch instruction that decrements a register and jumps if the register is nonzero. Operand 0 is the register to decrement and test; operand 1 is the label to jump to if the register is nonzero. See Section 17.13 [Looping Patterns], page 420.

    This optional instruction pattern should be defined for machines with low-overhead looping instructions as the loop optimizer will try to modify suitable loops to utilize it. The target hook TARGET_CAN_USE_DOLOOP_P controls the conditions under which low-overhead loops can be used.

'doloop_begin'
    Companion instruction to `doloop_end` required for machines that need to perform some initialization, such as loading a special counter register. Operand 1 is the associated `doloop_end` pattern and operand 0 is the register that it decrements.

    If initialization insns do not always need to be emitted, use a `define_expand` (see Section 17.15 [Expander Definitions], page 423) and make it fail.

'canonicalize_funcptr_for_compare'
    Canonicalize the function pointer in operand 1 and store the result into operand 0.

Chapter 17: Machine Descriptions

Operand 0 is always a `reg` and has mode `Pmode`; operand 1 may be a `reg`, `mem`, `symbol_ref`, `const_int`, etc and also has mode `Pmode`.

Canonicalization of a function pointer usually involves computing the address of the function which would be called if the function pointer were used in an indirect call.

Only define this pattern if function pointers on the target machine can have different values but still call the same function when used in an indirect call.

'`save_stack_block`'
'`save_stack_function`'
'`save_stack_nonlocal`'
'`restore_stack_block`'
'`restore_stack_function`'
'`restore_stack_nonlocal`'

Most machines save and restore the stack pointer by copying it to or from an object of mode `Pmode`. Do not define these patterns on such machines.

Some machines require special handling for stack pointer saves and restores. On those machines, define the patterns corresponding to the non-standard cases by using a `define_expand` (see Section 17.15 [Expander Definitions], page 423) that produces the required insns. The three types of saves and restores are:

1. '`save_stack_block`' saves the stack pointer at the start of a block that allocates a variable-sized object, and '`restore_stack_block`' restores the stack pointer when the block is exited.

2. '`save_stack_function`' and '`restore_stack_function`' do a similar job for the outermost block of a function and are used when the function allocates variable-sized objects or calls `alloca`. Only the epilogue uses the restored stack pointer, allowing a simpler save or restore sequence on some machines.

3. '`save_stack_nonlocal`' is used in functions that contain labels branched to by nested functions. It saves the stack pointer in such a way that the inner function can use '`restore_stack_nonlocal`' to restore the stack pointer. The compiler generates code to restore the frame and argument pointer registers, but some machines require saving and restoring additional data such as register window information or stack backchains. Place insns in these patterns to save and restore any such required data.

When saving the stack pointer, operand 0 is the save area and operand 1 is the stack pointer. The mode used to allocate the save area defaults to `Pmode` but you can override that choice by defining the `STACK_SAVEAREA_MODE` macro (see Section 18.5 [Storage Layout], page 472). You must specify an integral mode, or `VOIDmode` if no save area is needed for a particular type of save (either because no save is needed or because a machine-specific save area can be used). Operand 0 is the stack pointer and operand 1 is the save area for restore operations. If '`save_stack_block`' is defined, operand 0 must not be `VOIDmode` since these saves can be arbitrarily nested.

A save area is a `mem` that is at a constant offset from `virtual_stack_vars_rtx` when the stack pointer is saved for use by nonlocal gotos and a `reg` in the other two cases.

'`allocate_stack`'

Subtract (or add if `STACK_GROWS_DOWNWARD` is undefined) operand 1 from the stack pointer to create space for dynamically allocated data.

Store the resultant pointer to this space into operand 0. If you are allocating space from the main stack, do this by emitting a move insn to copy `virtual_stack_dynamic_rtx` to operand 0. If you are allocating the space elsewhere, generate code to copy the location of the space to operand 0. In the latter case, you must ensure this space gets freed when the corresponding space on the main stack is free.

Do not define this pattern if all that must be done is the subtraction. Some machines require other operations such as stack probes or maintaining the back chain. Define this pattern to emit those operations in addition to updating the stack pointer.

'`check_stack`'

If stack checking (see Section 18.9.3 [Stack Checking], page 510) cannot be done on your system by probing the stack, define this pattern to perform the needed check and signal an error if the stack has overflowed. The single operand is the address in the stack farthest from the current stack pointer that you need to validate. Normally, on platforms where this pattern is needed, you would obtain the stack limit from a global or thread-specific variable or register.

'`probe_stack_address`'

If stack checking (see Section 18.9.3 [Stack Checking], page 510) can be done on your system by probing the stack but without the need to actually access it, define this pattern and signal an error if the stack has overflowed. The single operand is the memory address in the stack that needs to be probed.

'`probe_stack`'

If stack checking (see Section 18.9.3 [Stack Checking], page 510) can be done on your system by probing the stack but doing it with a "store zero" instruction is not valid or optimal, define this pattern to do the probing differently and signal an error if the stack has overflowed. The single operand is the memory reference in the stack that needs to be probed.

'`nonlocal_goto`'

Emit code to generate a non-local goto, e.g., a jump from one function to a label in an outer function. This pattern has four arguments, each representing a value to be used in the jump. The first argument is to be loaded into the frame pointer, the second is the address to branch to (code to dispatch to the actual label), the third is the address of a location where the stack is saved, and the last is the address of the label, to be placed in the location for the incoming static chain.

On most machines you need not define this pattern, since GCC will already generate the correct code, which is to load the frame pointer and static chain,

Chapter 17: Machine Descriptions   411

'nonlocal_goto_receiver'
: restore the stack (using the 'restore_stack_nonlocal' pattern, if defined), and jump indirectly to the dispatcher. You need only define this pattern if this code will not work on your machine.

'nonlocal_goto_receiver'
: This pattern, if defined, contains code needed at the target of a nonlocal goto after the code already generated by GCC. You will not normally need to define this pattern. A typical reason why you might need this pattern is if some value, such as a pointer to a global table, must be restored when the frame pointer is restored. Note that a nonlocal goto only occurs within a unit-of-translation, so a global table pointer that is shared by all functions of a given module need not be restored. There are no arguments.

'exception_receiver'
: This pattern, if defined, contains code needed at the site of an exception handler that isn't needed at the site of a nonlocal goto. You will not normally need to define this pattern. A typical reason why you might need this pattern is if some value, such as a pointer to a global table, must be restored after control flow is branched to the handler of an exception. There are no arguments.

'builtin_setjmp_setup'
: This pattern, if defined, contains additional code needed to initialize the `jmp_buf`. You will not normally need to define this pattern. A typical reason why you might need this pattern is if some value, such as a pointer to a global table, must be restored. Though it is preferred that the pointer value be recalculated if possible (given the address of a label for instance). The single argument is a pointer to the `jmp_buf`. Note that the buffer is five words long and that the first three are normally used by the generic mechanism.

'builtin_setjmp_receiver'
: This pattern, if defined, contains code needed at the site of a built-in setjmp that isn't needed at the site of a nonlocal goto. You will not normally need to define this pattern. A typical reason why you might need this pattern is if some value, such as a pointer to a global table, must be restored. It takes one argument, which is the label to which builtin_longjmp transferred control; this pattern may be emitted at a small offset from that label.

'builtin_longjmp'
: This pattern, if defined, performs the entire action of the longjmp. You will not normally need to define this pattern unless you also define `builtin_setjmp_setup`. The single argument is a pointer to the `jmp_buf`.

'eh_return'
: This pattern, if defined, affects the way `__builtin_eh_return`, and thence the call frame exception handling library routines, are built. It is intended to handle non-trivial actions needed along the abnormal return path.

  The address of the exception handler to which the function should return is passed as operand to this pattern. It will normally need to copied by the pattern to some special register or memory location. If the pattern needs to determine the location of the target call frame in order to do so, it may use `EH_RETURN_STACKADJ_RTX`, if defined; it will have already been assigned.

If this pattern is not defined, the default action will be to simply copy the return address to `EH_RETURN_HANDLER_RTX`. Either that macro or this pattern needs to be defined if call frame exception handling is to be used.

'`prologue`'
: This pattern, if defined, emits RTL for entry to a function. The function entry is responsible for setting up the stack frame, initializing the frame pointer register, saving callee saved registers, etc.

  Using a prologue pattern is generally preferred over defining `TARGET_ASM_FUNCTION_PROLOGUE` to emit assembly code for the prologue.

  The `prologue` pattern is particularly useful for targets which perform instruction scheduling.

'`window_save`'
: This pattern, if defined, emits RTL for a register window save. It should be defined if the target machine has register windows but the window events are decoupled from calls to subroutines. The canonical example is the SPARC architecture.

'`epilogue`'
: This pattern emits RTL for exit from a function. The function exit is responsible for deallocating the stack frame, restoring callee saved registers and emitting the return instruction.

  Using an epilogue pattern is generally preferred over defining `TARGET_ASM_FUNCTION_EPILOGUE` to emit assembly code for the epilogue.

  The `epilogue` pattern is particularly useful for targets which perform instruction scheduling or which have delay slots for their return instruction.

'`sibcall_epilogue`'
: This pattern, if defined, emits RTL for exit from a function without the final branch back to the calling function. This pattern will be emitted before any sibling call (aka tail call) sites.

  The `sibcall_epilogue` pattern must not clobber any arguments used for parameter passing or any stack slots for arguments passed to the current function.

'`trap`'
: This pattern, if defined, signals an error, typically by causing some kind of signal to be raised.

'`ctrapMM4`'
: Conditional trap instruction. Operand 0 is a piece of RTL which performs a comparison, and operands 1 and 2 are the arms of the comparison. Operand 3 is the trap code, an integer.

  A typical `ctrap` pattern looks like

  ```
  (define_insn "ctrapsi4"
    [(trap_if (match_operator 0 "trap_operator"
               [(match_operand 1 "register_operand")
                (match_operand 2 "immediate_operand")])
              (match_operand 3 "const_int_operand" "i"))]
    ""
    "...")
  ```

'prefetch'
: This pattern, if defined, emits code for a non-faulting data prefetch instruction. Operand 0 is the address of the memory to prefetch. Operand 1 is a constant 1 if the prefetch is preparing for a write to the memory address, or a constant 0 otherwise. Operand 2 is the expected degree of temporal locality of the data and is a value between 0 and 3, inclusive; 0 means that the data has no temporal locality, so it need not be left in the cache after the access; 3 means that the data has a high degree of temporal locality and should be left in all levels of cache possible; 1 and 2 mean, respectively, a low or moderate degree of temporal locality.

    Targets that do not support write prefetches or locality hints can ignore the values of operands 1 and 2.

'blockage'
: This pattern defines a pseudo insn that prevents the instruction scheduler and other passes from moving instructions and using register equivalences across the boundary defined by the blockage insn. This needs to be an UNSPEC_VOLATILE pattern or a volatile ASM.

'memory_blockage'
: This pattern, if defined, represents a compiler memory barrier, and will be placed at points across which RTL passes may not propagate memory accesses. This instruction needs to read and write volatile BLKmode memory. It does not need to generate any machine instruction. If this pattern is not defined, the compiler falls back to emitting an instruction corresponding to `asm volatile ("" ::: "memory")`.

'memory_barrier'
: If the target memory model is not fully synchronous, then this pattern should be defined to an instruction that orders both loads and stores before the instruction with respect to loads and stores after the instruction. This pattern has no operands.

'sync_compare_and_swap*mode*'
: This pattern, if defined, emits code for an atomic compare-and-swap operation. Operand 1 is the memory on which the atomic operation is performed. Operand 2 is the "old" value to be compared against the current contents of the memory location. Operand 3 is the "new" value to store in the memory if the compare succeeds. Operand 0 is the result of the operation; it should contain the contents of the memory before the operation. If the compare succeeds, this should obviously be a copy of operand 2.

    This pattern must show that both operand 0 and operand 1 are modified.

    This pattern must issue any memory barrier instructions such that all memory operations before the atomic operation occur before the atomic operation and all memory operations after the atomic operation occur after the atomic operation.

    For targets where the success or failure of the compare-and-swap operation is available via the status flags, it is possible to avoid a separate compare operation and issue the subsequent branch or store-flag operation immediately after the compare-and-swap. To this end, GCC will look for a MODE_CC set in the output of sync_compare_and_swap*mode*; if the machine description includes such a set, the target should also define special cbranchcc4 and/or cstorecc4 instructions. GCC will then be able to take the destination of the MODE_CC set and pass it to the cbranchcc4 or cstorecc4 pattern as the first operand of the comparison (the second will be (const_int 0)).

For targets where the operating system may provide support for this operation via library calls, the sync_compare_and_swap_optab may be initialized to a function with the same interface as the __sync_val_compare_and_swap_*n* built-in. If the entire set of *__sync* builtins are supported via library calls, the target can initialize all of the optabs at once with init_sync_libfuncs. For the purposes of C++11 std::atomic::is_lock_free, it is assumed that these library calls do *not* use any kind of interruptable locking.

'sync_add*mode*', 'sync_sub*mode*'
'sync_ior*mode*', 'sync_and*mode*'
'sync_xor*mode*', 'sync_nand*mode*'

> These patterns emit code for an atomic operation on memory. Operand 0 is the memory on which the atomic operation is performed. Operand 1 is the second operand to the binary operator.
>
> This pattern must issue any memory barrier instructions such that all memory operations before the atomic operation occur before the atomic operation and all memory operations after the atomic operation occur after the atomic operation.
>
> If these patterns are not defined, the operation will be constructed from a compare-and-swap operation, if defined.

'sync_old_add*mode*', 'sync_old_sub*mode*'
'sync_old_ior*mode*', 'sync_old_and*mode*'
'sync_old_xor*mode*', 'sync_old_nand*mode*'

> These patterns emit code for an atomic operation on memory, and return the value that the memory contained before the operation. Operand 0 is the result value, operand 1 is the memory on which the atomic operation is performed, and operand 2 is the second operand to the binary operator.
>
> This pattern must issue any memory barrier instructions such that all memory operations before the atomic operation occur before the atomic operation and all memory operations after the atomic operation occur after the atomic operation.
>
> If these patterns are not defined, the operation will be constructed from a compare-and-swap operation, if defined.

'sync_new_add*mode*', 'sync_new_sub*mode*'
'sync_new_ior*mode*', 'sync_new_and*mode*'
'sync_new_xor*mode*', 'sync_new_nand*mode*'

> These patterns are like their sync_old_*op* counterparts, except that they return the value that exists in the memory location after the operation, rather than before the operation.

'sync_lock_test_and_set*mode*'

This pattern takes two forms, based on the capabilities of the target. In either case, operand 0 is the result of the operand, operand 1 is the memory on which the atomic operation is performed, and operand 2 is the value to set in the lock.

In the ideal case, this operation is an atomic exchange operation, in which the previous value in memory operand is copied into the result operand, and the value operand is stored in the memory operand.

For less capable targets, any value operand that is not the constant 1 should be rejected with `FAIL`. In this case the target may use an atomic test-and-set bit operation. The result operand should contain 1 if the bit was previously set and 0 if the bit was previously clear. The true contents of the memory operand are implementation defined.

This pattern must issue any memory barrier instructions such that the pattern as a whole acts as an acquire barrier, that is all memory operations after the pattern do not occur until the lock is acquired.

If this pattern is not defined, the operation will be constructed from a compare-and-swap operation, if defined.

'sync_lock_release*mode*'

This pattern, if defined, releases a lock set by `sync_lock_test_and_set`*mode*. Operand 0 is the memory that contains the lock; operand 1 is the value to store in the lock.

If the target doesn't implement full semantics for `sync_lock_test_and_set`*mode*, any value operand which is not the constant 0 should be rejected with `FAIL`, and the true contents of the memory operand are implementation defined.

This pattern must issue any memory barrier instructions such that the pattern as a whole acts as a release barrier, that is the lock is released only after all previous memory operations have completed.

If this pattern is not defined, then a `memory_barrier` pattern will be emitted, followed by a store of the value to the memory operand.

'atomic_compare_and_swap*mode*'

This pattern, if defined, emits code for an atomic compare-and-swap operation with memory model semantics. Operand 2 is the memory on which the atomic operation is performed. Operand 0 is an output operand which is set to true or false based on whether the operation succeeded. Operand 1 is an output operand which is set to the contents of the memory before the operation was attempted. Operand 3 is the value that is expected to be in memory. Operand 4 is the value to put in memory if the expected value is found there. Operand 5 is set to 1 if this compare and swap is to be treated as a weak operation. Operand 6 is the memory model to be used if the operation is a success. Operand 7 is the memory model to be used if the operation fails.

If memory referred to in operand 2 contains the value in operand 3, then operand 4 is stored in memory pointed to by operand 2 and fencing based on the memory model in operand 6 is issued.

If memory referred to in operand 2 does not contain the value in operand 3, then fencing based on the memory model in operand 7 is issued.

If a target does not support weak compare-and-swap operations, or the port elects not to implement weak operations, the argument in operand 5 can be ignored. Note a strong implementation must be provided.

If this pattern is not provided, the `__atomic_compare_exchange` built-in functions will utilize the legacy `sync_compare_and_swap` pattern with an `__ATOMIC_SEQ_CST` memory model.

'atomic_load*mode*'

> This pattern implements an atomic load operation with memory model semantics. Operand 1 is the memory address being loaded from. Operand 0 is the result of the load. Operand 2 is the memory model to be used for the load operation.
>
> If not present, the `__atomic_load` built-in function will either resort to a normal load with memory barriers, or a compare-and-swap operation if a normal load would not be atomic.

'atomic_store*mode*'

> This pattern implements an atomic store operation with memory model semantics. Operand 0 is the memory address being stored to. Operand 1 is the value to be written. Operand 2 is the memory model to be used for the operation.
>
> If not present, the `__atomic_store` built-in function will attempt to perform a normal store and surround it with any required memory fences. If the store would not be atomic, then an `__atomic_exchange` is attempted with the result being ignored.

'atomic_exchange*mode*'

> This pattern implements an atomic exchange operation with memory model semantics. Operand 1 is the memory location the operation is performed on. Operand 0 is an output operand which is set to the original value contained in the memory pointed to by operand 1. Operand 2 is the value to be stored. Operand 3 is the memory model to be used.
>
> If this pattern is not present, the built-in function `__atomic_exchange` will attempt to preform the operation with a compare and swap loop.

'atomic_add*mode*', 'atomic_sub*mode*'
'atomic_or*mode*', 'atomic_and*mode*'
'atomic_xor*mode*', 'atomic_nand*mode*'

> These patterns emit code for an atomic operation on memory with memory model semantics. Operand 0 is the memory on which the atomic operation is performed. Operand 1 is the second operand to the binary operator. Operand 2 is the memory model to be used by the operation.
>
> If these patterns are not defined, attempts will be made to use legacy `sync` patterns, or equivalent patterns which return a result. If none of these are available a compare-and-swap loop will be used.

Chapter 17: Machine Descriptions   417

'atomic_fetch_add*mode*', 'atomic_fetch_sub*mode*'
'atomic_fetch_or*mode*', 'atomic_fetch_and*mode*'
'atomic_fetch_xor*mode*', 'atomic_fetch_nand*mode*'

>   These patterns emit code for an atomic operation on memory with memory model semantics, and return the original value. Operand 0 is an output operand which contains the value of the memory location before the operation was performed. Operand 1 is the memory on which the atomic operation is performed. Operand 2 is the second operand to the binary operator. Operand 3 is the memory model to be used by the operation.
>
>   If these patterns are not defined, attempts will be made to use legacy `sync` patterns. If none of these are available a compare-and-swap loop will be used.

'atomic_add_fetch*mode*', 'atomic_sub_fetch*mode*'
'atomic_or_fetch*mode*', 'atomic_and_fetch*mode*'
'atomic_xor_fetch*mode*', 'atomic_nand_fetch*mode*'

>   These patterns emit code for an atomic operation on memory with memory model semantics and return the result after the operation is performed. Operand 0 is an output operand which contains the value after the operation. Operand 1 is the memory on which the atomic operation is performed. Operand 2 is the second operand to the binary operator. Operand 3 is the memory model to be used by the operation.
>
>   If these patterns are not defined, attempts will be made to use legacy `sync` patterns, or equivalent patterns which return the result before the operation followed by the arithmetic operation required to produce the result. If none of these are available a compare-and-swap loop will be used.

'atomic_test_and_set'

>   This pattern emits code for `__builtin_atomic_test_and_set`. Operand 0 is an output operand which is set to true if the previous previous contents of the byte was "set", and false otherwise. Operand 1 is the `QImode` memory to be modified. Operand 2 is the memory model to be used.
>
>   The specific value that defines "set" is implementation defined, and is normally based on what is performed by the native atomic test and set instruction.

'atomic_bit_test_and_set*mode*'
'atomic_bit_test_and_complement*mode*'
'atomic_bit_test_and_reset*mode*'

>   These patterns emit code for an atomic bitwise operation on memory with memory model semantics, and return the original value of the specified bit. Operand 0 is an output operand which contains the value of the specified bit from the memory location before the operation was performed. Operand 1 is the memory on which the atomic operation is performed. Operand 2 is the bit within the operand, starting with least significant bit. Operand 3 is the memory model to be used by the operation. Operand 4 is a flag - it is `const1_rtx` if operand 0 should contain the original value of the specified bit in the least significant bit of the operand, and `const0_rtx` if the bit should be in its original position in the operand. `atomic_bit_test_and_set`*mode* atomically sets the specified bit after remembering its original value, `atomic_bit_test_and_complement`*mode*

inverts the specified bit and `atomic_bit_test_and_reset`*mode* clears the specified bit.

If these patterns are not defined, attempts will be made to use `atomic_fetch_or`*mode*, `atomic_fetch_xor`*mode* or `atomic_fetch_and`*mode* instruction patterns, or their `sync` counterparts. If none of these are available a compare-and-swap loop will be used.

'`mem_thread_fence`'
: This pattern emits code required to implement a thread fence with memory model semantics. Operand 0 is the memory model to be used.

    For the `__ATOMIC_RELAXED` model no instructions need to be issued and this expansion is not invoked.

    The compiler always emits a compiler memory barrier regardless of what expanding this pattern produced.

    If this pattern is not defined, the compiler falls back to expanding the `memory_barrier` pattern, then to emitting `__sync_synchronize` library call, and finally to just placing a compiler memory barrier.

'`get_thread_pointer`*mode*'
'`set_thread_pointer`*mode*'
: These patterns emit code that reads/sets the TLS thread pointer. Currently, these are only needed if the target needs to support the `__builtin_thread_pointer` and `__builtin_set_thread_pointer` builtins.

    The get/set patterns have a single output/input operand respectively, with *mode* intended to be `Pmode`.

'`stack_protect_set`'
: This pattern, if defined, moves a `ptr_mode` value from the memory in operand 1 to the memory in operand 0 without leaving the value in a register afterward. This is to avoid leaking the value some place that an attacker might use to rewrite the stack guard slot after having clobbered it.

    If this pattern is not defined, then a plain move pattern is generated.

'`stack_protect_test`'
: This pattern, if defined, compares a `ptr_mode` value from the memory in operand 1 with the memory in operand 0 without leaving the value in a register afterward and branches to operand 2 if the values were equal.

    If this pattern is not defined, then a plain compare pattern and conditional branch pattern is used.

'`clear_cache`'
: This pattern, if defined, flushes the instruction cache for a region of memory. The region is bounded to by the Pmode pointers in operand 0 inclusive and operand 1 exclusive.

    If this pattern is not defined, a call to the library function `__clear_cache` is used.

17.10 When the Order of Patterns Matters

Sometimes an insn can match more than one instruction pattern. Then the pattern that appears first in the machine description is the one used. Therefore, more specific patterns (patterns that will match fewer things) and faster instructions (those that will produce better code when they do match) should usually go first in the description.

In some cases the effect of ordering the patterns can be used to hide a pattern when it is not valid. For example, the 68000 has an instruction for converting a fullword to floating point and another for converting a byte to floating point. An instruction converting an integer to floating point could match either one. We put the pattern to convert the fullword first to make sure that one will be used rather than the other. (Otherwise a large integer might be generated as a single-byte immediate quantity, which would not work.) Instead of using this pattern ordering it would be possible to make the pattern for convert-a-byte smart enough to deal properly with any constant value.

17.11 Interdependence of Patterns

In some cases machines support instructions identical except for the machine mode of one or more operands. For example, there may be "sign-extend halfword" and "sign-extend byte" instructions whose patterns are

```
(set (match_operand:SI 0 ...)
     (extend:SI (match_operand:HI 1 ...)))

(set (match_operand:SI 0 ...)
     (extend:SI (match_operand:QI 1 ...)))
```

Constant integers do not specify a machine mode, so an instruction to extend a constant value could match either pattern. The pattern it actually will match is the one that appears first in the file. For correct results, this must be the one for the widest possible mode (HImode, here). If the pattern matches the QImode instruction, the results will be incorrect if the constant value does not actually fit that mode.

Such instructions to extend constants are rarely generated because they are optimized away, but they do occasionally happen in nonoptimized compilations.

If a constraint in a pattern allows a constant, the reload pass may replace a register with a constant permitted by the constraint in some cases. Similarly for memory references. Because of this substitution, you should not provide separate patterns for increment and decrement instructions. Instead, they should be generated from the same pattern that supports register-register add insns by examining the operands and generating the appropriate machine instruction.

17.12 Defining Jump Instruction Patterns

GCC does not assume anything about how the machine realizes jumps. The machine description should define a single pattern, usually a `define_expand`, which expands to all the required insns.

Usually, this would be a comparison insn to set the condition code and a separate branch insn testing the condition code and branching or not according to its value. For many machines, however, separating compares and branches is limiting, which is why the more flexible approach with one `define_expand` is used in GCC. The machine description becomes clearer for architectures that have compare-and-branch instructions but no condition code. It also works better when different sets of comparison operators are supported by different kinds of conditional branches (e.g. integer vs. floating-point), or by conditional branches with respect to conditional stores.

Two separate insns are always used if the machine description represents a condition code register using the legacy RTL expression (cc0), and on most machines that use a separate condition code register (see Section 18.15 [Condition Code], page 552). For machines that use (cc0), in fact, the set and use of the condition code must be separate and adjacent[1], thus allowing flags in `cc_status` to be used (see Section 18.15 [Condition Code], page 552) and so that the comparison and branch insns could be located from each other by using the functions `prev_cc0_setter` and `next_cc0_user`.

Even in this case having a single entry point for conditional branches is advantageous, because it handles equally well the case where a single comparison instruction records the results of both signed and unsigned comparison of the given operands (with the branch insns coming in distinct signed and unsigned flavors) as in the x86 or SPARC, and the case where there are distinct signed and unsigned compare instructions and only one set of conditional branch instructions as in the PowerPC.

17.13 Defining Looping Instruction Patterns

Some machines have special jump instructions that can be utilized to make loops more efficient. A common example is the 68000 'dbra' instruction which performs a decrement of a register and a branch if the result was greater than zero. Other machines, in particular digital signal processors (DSPs), have special block repeat instructions to provide low-overhead loop support. For example, the TI TMS320C3x/C4x DSPs have a block repeat instruction that loads special registers to mark the top and end of a loop and to count the number of loop iterations. This avoids the need for fetching and executing a 'dbra'-like instruction and avoids pipeline stalls associated with the jump.

GCC has three special named patterns to support low overhead looping. They are 'decrement_and_branch_until_zero', 'doloop_begin', and 'doloop_end'. The first pattern, 'decrement_and_branch_until_zero', is not emitted during RTL generation but may be emitted during the instruction combination phase. This requires the assistance of the loop optimizer, using information collected during strength reduction, to reverse a loop to count down to zero. Some targets also require the loop optimizer to add a REG_NONNEG note to indicate that the iteration count is always positive. This is needed if the target performs a signed loop termination test. For example, the 68000 uses a pattern similar to the following for its `dbra` instruction:

---

[1] `note` insns can separate them, though.

```
(define_insn "decrement_and_branch_until_zero"
  [(set (pc)
        (if_then_else
          (ge (plus:SI (match_operand:SI 0 "general_operand" "+d*am")
                       (const_int -1))
              (const_int 0))
          (label_ref (match_operand 1 "" ""))
          (pc)))
   (set (match_dup 0)
        (plus:SI (match_dup 0)
                 (const_int -1)))]
  "find_reg_note (insn, REG_NONNEG, 0)"
  "...")
```

Note that since the insn is both a jump insn and has an output, it must deal with its own reloads, hence the 'm' constraints. Also note that since this insn is generated by the instruction combination phase combining two sequential insns together into an implicit parallel insn, the iteration counter needs to be biased by the same amount as the decrement operation, in this case -1. Note that the following similar pattern will not be matched by the combiner.

```
(define_insn "decrement_and_branch_until_zero"
  [(set (pc)
        (if_then_else
          (ge (match_operand:SI 0 "general_operand" "+d*am")
              (const_int 1))
          (label_ref (match_operand 1 "" ""))
          (pc)))
   (set (match_dup 0)
        (plus:SI (match_dup 0)
                 (const_int -1)))]
  "find_reg_note (insn, REG_NONNEG, 0)"
  "...")
```

The other two special looping patterns, 'doloop_begin' and 'doloop_end', are emitted by the loop optimizer for certain well-behaved loops with a finite number of loop iterations using information collected during strength reduction.

The 'doloop_end' pattern describes the actual looping instruction (or the implicit looping operation) and the 'doloop_begin' pattern is an optional companion pattern that can be used for initialization needed for some low-overhead looping instructions.

Note that some machines require the actual looping instruction to be emitted at the top of the loop (e.g., the TMS320C3x/C4x DSPs). Emitting the true RTL for a looping instruction at the top of the loop can cause problems with flow analysis. So instead, a dummy doloop insn is emitted at the end of the loop. The machine dependent reorg pass checks for the presence of this doloop insn and then searches back to the top of the loop, where it inserts the true looping insn (provided there are no instructions in the loop which would cause problems). Any additional labels can be emitted at this point. In addition, if the desired special iteration counter register was not allocated, this machine dependent reorg pass could emit a traditional compare and jump instruction pair.

The essential difference between the 'decrement_and_branch_until_zero' and the 'doloop_end' patterns is that the loop optimizer allocates an additional pseudo register for the latter as an iteration counter. This pseudo register cannot be used within the loop (i.e., general induction variables cannot be derived from it), however, in many cases the loop induction variable may become redundant and removed by the flow pass.

17.14 Canonicalization of Instructions

There are often cases where multiple RTL expressions could represent an operation performed by a single machine instruction. This situation is most commonly encountered with logical, branch, and multiply-accumulate instructions. In such cases, the compiler attempts to convert these multiple RTL expressions into a single canonical form to reduce the number of insn patterns required.

In addition to algebraic simplifications, following canonicalizations are performed:

- For commutative and comparison operators, a constant is always made the second operand. If a machine only supports a constant as the second operand, only patterns that match a constant in the second operand need be supplied.

- For associative operators, a sequence of operators will always chain to the left; for instance, only the left operand of an integer plus can itself be a plus. and, ior, xor, plus, mult, smin, smax, umin, and umax are associative when applied to integers, and sometimes to floating-point.

- For these operators, if only one operand is a neg, not, mult, plus, or minus expression, it will be the first operand.

- In combinations of neg, mult, plus, and minus, the neg operations (if any) will be moved inside the operations as far as possible. For instance, (neg (mult A B)) is canonicalized as (mult (neg A) B), but (plus (mult (neg B) C) A) is canonicalized as (minus A (mult B C)).

- For the compare operator, a constant is always the second operand if the first argument is a condition code register or (cc0).

- For instructions that inherently set a condition code register, the compare operator is always written as the first RTL expression of the parallel instruction pattern. For example,

```
(define_insn ""
  [(set (reg:CCZ FLAGS_REG)
(compare:CCZ
  (plus:SI
    (match_operand:SI 1 "register_operand" "%r")
    (match_operand:SI 2 "register_operand" "r"))
  (const_int 0)))
   (set (match_operand:SI 0 "register_operand" "=r")
(plus:SI (match_dup 1) (match_dup 2)))]
  ""
  "addl %0, %1, %2")
```

- An operand of neg, not, mult, plus, or minus is made the first operand under the same conditions as above.

- (ltu (plus a b) b) is converted to (ltu (plus a b) a). Likewise with geu instead of ltu.

- (minus x (const_int n)) is converted to (plus x (const_int -n)).

- Within address computations (i.e., inside mem), a left shift is converted into the appropriate multiplication by a power of two.

- De Morgan's Law is used to move bitwise negation inside a bitwise logical-and or logical-or operation. If this results in only one operand being a not expression, it will be the first one.

A machine that has an instruction that performs a bitwise logical-and of one operand with the bitwise negation of the other should specify the pattern for that instruction as

```
(define_insn ""
  [(set (match_operand:m 0 ...)
        (and:m (not:m (match_operand:m 1 ...))
               (match_operand:m 2 ...)))]
  "..."
  "...")
```

Similarly, a pattern for a "NAND" instruction should be written

```
(define_insn ""
  [(set (match_operand:m 0 ...)
        (ior:m (not:m (match_operand:m 1 ...))
               (not:m (match_operand:m 2 ...))))]
  "..."
  "...")
```

In both cases, it is not necessary to include patterns for the many logically equivalent RTL expressions.

- The only possible RTL expressions involving both bitwise exclusive-or and bitwise negation are (xor:m x y) and (not:m (xor:m x y)).
- The sum of three items, one of which is a constant, will only appear in the form
    (plus:m (plus:m x y) constant)
- Equality comparisons of a group of bits (usually a single bit) with zero will be written using zero_extract rather than the equivalent and or sign_extract operations.
- (sign_extend:m1 (mult:m2 (sign_extend:m2 x) (sign_extend:m2 y))) is converted to (mult:m1 (sign_extend:m1 x) (sign_extend:m1 y)), and likewise for zero_extend.
- (sign_extend:m1 (mult:m2 (ashiftrt:m2 x s) (sign_extend:m2 y))) is converted to (mult:m1 (sign_extend:m1 (ashiftrt:m2 x s)) (sign_extend:m1 y)), and likewise for patterns using zero_extend and lshiftrt. If the second operand of mult is also a shift, then that is extended also. This transformation is only applied when it can be proven that the original operation had sufficient precision to prevent overflow.

Further canonicalization rules are defined in the function commutative_operand_precedence in 'gcc/rtlanal.c'.

17.15 Defining RTL Sequences for Code Generation

On some target machines, some standard pattern names for RTL generation cannot be handled with single insn, but a sequence of RTL insns can represent them. For these target machines, you can write a define_expand to specify how to generate the sequence of RTL.

A define_expand is an RTL expression that looks almost like a define_insn; but, unlike the latter, a define_expand is used only for RTL generation and it can produce more than one RTL insn.

A define_expand RTX has four operands:

- The name. Each define_expand must have a name, since the only use for it is to refer to it by name.

- The RTL template. This is a vector of RTL expressions representing a sequence of separate instructions. Unlike `define_insn`, there is no implicit surrounding PARALLEL.

- The condition, a string containing a C expression. This expression is used to express how the availability of this pattern depends on subclasses of target machine, selected by command-line options when GCC is run. This is just like the condition of a `define_insn` that has a standard name. Therefore, the condition (if present) may not depend on the data in the insn being matched, but only the target-machine-type flags. The compiler needs to test these conditions during initialization in order to learn exactly which named instructions are available in a particular run.

- The preparation statements, a string containing zero or more C statements which are to be executed before RTL code is generated from the RTL template.

  Usually these statements prepare temporary registers for use as internal operands in the RTL template, but they can also generate RTL insns directly by calling routines such as `emit_insn`, etc. Any such insns precede the ones that come from the RTL template.

- Optionally, a vector containing the values of attributes. See Section 17.19 [Insn Attributes], page 434.

Every RTL insn emitted by a `define_expand` must match some `define_insn` in the machine description. Otherwise, the compiler will crash when trying to generate code for the insn or trying to optimize it.

The RTL template, in addition to controlling generation of RTL insns, also describes the operands that need to be specified when this pattern is used. In particular, it gives a predicate for each operand.

A true operand, which needs to be specified in order to generate RTL from the pattern, should be described with a `match_operand` in its first occurrence in the RTL template. This enters information on the operand's predicate into the tables that record such things. GCC uses the information to preload the operand into a register if that is required for valid RTL code. If the operand is referred to more than once, subsequent references should use `match_dup`.

The RTL template may also refer to internal "operands" which are temporary registers or labels used only within the sequence made by the `define_expand`. Internal operands are substituted into the RTL template with `match_dup`, never with `match_operand`. The values of the internal operands are not passed in as arguments by the compiler when it requests use of this pattern. Instead, they are computed within the pattern, in the preparation statements. These statements compute the values and store them into the appropriate elements of `operands` so that `match_dup` can find them.

There are two special macros defined for use in the preparation statements: DONE and FAIL. Use them with a following semicolon, as a statement.

DONE   Use the DONE macro to end RTL generation for the pattern. The only RTL insns resulting from the pattern on this occasion will be those already emitted by explicit calls to `emit_insn` within the preparation statements; the RTL template will not be generated.

Chapter 17: Machine Descriptions   425

FAIL   Make the pattern fail on this occasion. When a pattern fails, it means that the
            pattern was not truly available. The calling routines in the compiler will try
            other strategies for code generation using other patterns.

            Failure is currently supported only for binary (addition, multiplication, shifting,
            etc.) and bit-field (`extv`, `extzv`, and `insv`) operations.

If the preparation falls through (invokes neither DONE nor FAIL), then the `define_expand`
acts like a `define_insn` in that the RTL template is used to generate the insn.

The RTL template is not used for matching, only for generating the initial insn list. If
the preparation statement always invokes DONE or FAIL, the RTL template may be reduced
to a simple list of operands, such as this example:

```
(define_expand "addsi3"
  [(match_operand:SI 0 "register_operand" "")
   (match_operand:SI 1 "register_operand" "")
   (match_operand:SI 2 "register_operand" "")]
  ""
  "
{
  handle_add (operands[0], operands[1], operands[2]);
  DONE;
}")
```

Here is an example, the definition of left-shift for the SPUR chip:

```
(define_expand "ashlsi3"
  [(set (match_operand:SI 0 "register_operand" "")
        (ashift:SI
          (match_operand:SI 1 "register_operand" "")
          (match_operand:SI 2 "nonmemory_operand" "")))]
  ""
  "
{
  if (GET_CODE (operands[2]) != CONST_INT
      || (unsigned) INTVAL (operands[2]) > 3)
    FAIL;
}")
```

This example uses `define_expand` so that it can generate an RTL insn for shifting when the
shift-count is in the supported range of 0 to 3 but fail in other cases where machine insns
aren't available. When it fails, the compiler tries another strategy using different patterns
(such as a library call).

If the compiler were able to handle nontrivial condition strings in patterns with names,
then it would be possible to use a `define_insn` in that case. Here is another case (zero-
extension on the 68000) which makes more use of the power of `define_expand`:

```
(define_expand "zero_extendhisi2"
  [(set (match_operand:SI 0 "general_operand" "")
        (const_int 0))
   (set (strict_low_part
          (subreg:HI
            (match_dup 0)
            0))
        (match_operand:HI 1 "general_operand" ""))]
  ""
  "operands[1] = make_safe_from (operands[1], operands[0]);")
```

Here two RTL insns are generated, one to clear the entire output operand and the other to copy the input operand into its low half. This sequence is incorrect if the input operand refers to [the old value of] the output operand, so the preparation statement makes sure this isn't so. The function `make_safe_from` copies the `operands[1]` into a temporary register if it refers to `operands[0]`. It does this by emitting another RTL insn.

Finally, a third example shows the use of an internal operand. Zero-extension on the SPUR chip is done by `and`-ing the result against a halfword mask. But this mask cannot be represented by a `const_int` because the constant value is too large to be legitimate on this machine. So it must be copied into a register with `force_reg` and then the register used in the `and`.

```
(define_expand "zero_extendhisi2"
  [(set (match_operand:SI 0 "register_operand" "")
        (and:SI (subreg:SI
                  (match_operand:HI 1 "register_operand" "")
                  0)
                (match_dup 2)))]
  ""
  "operands[2]
     = force_reg (SImode, GEN_INT (65535)); ")
```

Note: If the `define_expand` is used to serve a standard binary or unary arithmetic operation or a bit-field operation, then the last insn it generates must not be a `code_label`, `barrier` or `note`. It must be an `insn`, `jump_insn` or `call_insn`. If you don't need a real insn at the end, emit an insn to copy the result of the operation into itself. Such an insn will generate no code, but it can avoid problems in the compiler.

17.16 Defining How to Split Instructions

There are two cases where you should specify how to split a pattern into multiple insns. On machines that have instructions requiring delay slots (see Section 17.19.8 [Delay Slots], page 443) or that have instructions whose output is not available for multiple cycles (see Section 17.19.9 [Processor pipeline description], page 444), the compiler phases that optimize these cases need to be able to move insns into one-instruction delay slots. However, some insns may generate more than one machine instruction. These insns cannot be placed into a delay slot.

Often you can rewrite the single insn as a list of individual insns, each corresponding to one machine instruction. The disadvantage of doing so is that it will cause the compilation to be slower and require more space. If the resulting insns are too complex, it may also suppress some optimizations. The compiler splits the insn if there is a reason to believe that it might improve instruction or delay slot scheduling.

The insn combiner phase also splits putative insns. If three insns are merged into one insn with a complex expression that cannot be matched by some `define_insn` pattern, the combiner phase attempts to split the complex pattern into two insns that are recognized. Usually it can break the complex pattern into two patterns by splitting out some subexpression. However, in some other cases, such as performing an addition of a large constant in two insns on a RISC machine, the way to split the addition into two insns is machine-dependent.

The `define_split` definition tells the compiler how to split a complex insn into several simpler insns. It looks like this:

Chapter 17: Machine Descriptions

```
(define_split
  [insn-pattern]
  "condition"
  [new-insn-pattern-1
   new-insn-pattern-2
   ...]
  "preparation-statements")
```

insn-pattern is a pattern that needs to be split and *condition* is the final condition to be tested, as in a `define_insn`. When an insn matching *insn-pattern* and satisfying *condition* is found, it is replaced in the insn list with the insns given by *new-insn-pattern-1*, *new-insn-pattern-2*, etc.

The *preparation-statements* are similar to those statements that are specified for `define_expand` (see Section 17.15 [Expander Definitions], page 423) and are executed before the new RTL is generated to prepare for the generated code or emit some insns whose pattern is not fixed. Unlike those in `define_expand`, however, these statements must not generate any new pseudo-registers. Once reload has completed, they also must not allocate any space in the stack frame.

Patterns are matched against *insn-pattern* in two different circumstances. If an insn needs to be split for delay slot scheduling or insn scheduling, the insn is already known to be valid, which means that it must have been matched by some `define_insn` and, if `reload_completed` is nonzero, is known to satisfy the constraints of that `define_insn`. In that case, the new insn patterns must also be insns that are matched by some `define_insn` and, if `reload_completed` is nonzero, must also satisfy the constraints of those definitions.

As an example of this usage of `define_split`, consider the following example from 'a29k.md', which splits a `sign_extend` from HImode to SImode into a pair of shift insns:

```
(define_split
  [(set (match_operand:SI 0 "gen_reg_operand" "")
        (sign_extend:SI (match_operand:HI 1 "gen_reg_operand" "")))]
  ""
  [(set (match_dup 0)
        (ashift:SI (match_dup 1)
                   (const_int 16)))
   (set (match_dup 0)
        (ashiftrt:SI (match_dup 0)
                     (const_int 16)))]
  "
{ operands[1] = gen_lowpart (SImode, operands[1]); }")
```

When the combiner phase tries to split an insn pattern, it is always the case that the pattern is *not* matched by any `define_insn`. The combiner pass first tries to split a single `set` expression and then the same `set` expression inside a `parallel`, but followed by a `clobber` of a pseudo-reg to use as a scratch register. In these cases, the combiner expects exactly two new insn patterns to be generated. It will verify that these patterns match some `define_insn` definitions, so you need not do this test in the `define_split` (of course, there is no point in writing a `define_split` that will never produce insns that match).

Here is an example of this use of `define_split`, taken from 'rs6000.md':

```
(define_split
  [(set (match_operand:SI 0 "gen_reg_operand" "")
        (plus:SI (match_operand:SI 1 "gen_reg_operand" "")
                 (match_operand:SI 2 "non_add_cint_operand" "")))]
  ""
```

```
      [(set (match_dup 0) (plus:SI (match_dup 1) (match_dup 3)))
       (set (match_dup 0) (plus:SI (match_dup 0) (match_dup 4)))]
  "
  {
    int low = INTVAL (operands[2]) & 0xffff;
    int high = (unsigned) INTVAL (operands[2]) >> 16;

    if (low & 0x8000)
      high++, low |= 0xffff0000;

    operands[3] = GEN_INT (high << 16);
    operands[4] = GEN_INT (low);
  }")
```

Here the predicate `non_add_cint_operand` matches any `const_int` that is *not* a valid operand of a single add insn. The add with the smaller displacement is written so that it can be substituted into the address of a subsequent operation.

An example that uses a scratch register, from the same file, generates an equality comparison of a register and a large constant:

```
(define_split
  [(set (match_operand:CC 0 "cc_reg_operand" "")
        (compare:CC (match_operand:SI 1 "gen_reg_operand" "")
                    (match_operand:SI 2 "non_short_cint_operand" "")))
   (clobber (match_operand:SI 3 "gen_reg_operand" ""))]
  "find_single_use (operands[0], insn, 0)
   && (GET_CODE (*find_single_use (operands[0], insn, 0)) == EQ
       || GET_CODE (*find_single_use (operands[0], insn, 0)) == NE)"
  [(set (match_dup 3) (xor:SI (match_dup 1) (match_dup 4)))
   (set (match_dup 0) (compare:CC (match_dup 3) (match_dup 5)))]
  "
  {
    /* Get the constant we are comparing against, C, and see what it
       looks like sign-extended to 16 bits.  Then see what constant
       could be XOR'ed with C to get the sign-extended value.  */

    int c = INTVAL (operands[2]);
    int sextc = (c << 16) >> 16;
    int xorv = c ^ sextc;

    operands[4] = GEN_INT (xorv);
    operands[5] = GEN_INT (sextc);
  }")
```

To avoid confusion, don't write a single `define_split` that accepts some insns that match some `define_insn` as well as some insns that don't. Instead, write two separate `define_split` definitions, one for the insns that are valid and one for the insns that are not valid.

The splitter is allowed to split jump instructions into sequence of jumps or create new jumps in while splitting non-jump instructions. As the control flow graph and branch prediction information needs to be updated, several restriction apply.

Splitting of jump instruction into sequence that over by another jump instruction is always valid, as compiler expect identical behavior of new jump. When new sequence contains multiple jump instructions or new labels, more assistance is needed. Splitter is required to create only unconditional jumps, or simple conditional jump instructions. Additionally it must attach a `REG_BR_PROB` note to each conditional jump. A global variable `split_branch_probability` holds the probability of the original branch in case it was a simple conditional jump, −1 otherwise. To simplify recomputing of edge frequencies, the new sequence is required to have only forward jumps to the newly created labels.

For the common case where the pattern of a define_split exactly matches the pattern of a define_insn, use `define_insn_and_split`. It looks like this:

```
(define_insn_and_split
  [insn-pattern]
  "condition"
  "output-template"
  "split-condition"
  [new-insn-pattern-1
   new-insn-pattern-2
   ...]
  "preparation-statements"
  [insn-attributes])
```

insn-pattern, *condition*, *output-template*, and *insn-attributes* are used as in `define_insn`. The *new-insn-pattern* vector and the *preparation-statements* are used as in a `define_split`. The *split-condition* is also used as in `define_split`, with the additional behavior that if the condition starts with '&&', the condition used for the split will be the constructed as a logical "and" of the split condition with the insn condition. For example, from i386.md:

```
(define_insn_and_split "zero_extendhisi2_and"
  [(set (match_operand:SI 0 "register_operand" "=r")
     (zero_extend:SI (match_operand:HI 1 "register_operand" "0")))
   (clobber (reg:CC 17))]
  "TARGET_ZERO_EXTEND_WITH_AND && !optimize_size"
  "#"
  "&& reload_completed"
  [(parallel [(set (match_dup 0)
                   (and:SI (match_dup 0) (const_int 65535)))
              (clobber (reg:CC 17))])]
  ""
  [(set_attr "type" "alu1")])
```

In this case, the actual split condition will be 'TARGET_ZERO_EXTEND_WITH_AND && !optimize_size && reload_completed'.

The `define_insn_and_split` construction provides exactly the same functionality as two separate `define_insn` and `define_split` patterns. It exists for compactness, and as a maintenance tool to prevent having to ensure the two patterns' templates match.

17.17 Including Patterns in Machine Descriptions.

The `include` pattern tells the compiler tools where to look for patterns that are in files other than in the file '.md'. This is used only at build time and there is no preprocessing allowed.

It looks like:

```
(include
  pathname)
```

For example:

```
(include "filestuff")
```

Where *pathname* is a string that specifies the location of the file, specifies the include file to be in 'gcc/config/target/filestuff'. The directory 'gcc/config/target' is regarded as the default directory.

Machine descriptions may be split up into smaller more manageable subsections and placed into subdirectories.

By specifying:

```
(include "BOGUS/filestuff")
```

the include file is specified to be in 'gcc/config/target/BOGUS/filestuff'.

Specifying an absolute path for the include file such as;

```
(include "/u2/BOGUS/filestuff")
```

is permitted but is not encouraged.

17.17.1 RTL Generation Tool Options for Directory Search

The '-I*dir*' option specifies directories to search for machine descriptions. For example:

```
genrecog -I/p1/abc/proc1 -I/p2/abcd/pro2 target.md
```

Add the directory *dir* to the head of the list of directories to be searched for header files. This can be used to override a system machine definition file, substituting your own version, since these directories are searched before the default machine description file directories. If you use more than one '-I' option, the directories are scanned in left-to-right order; the standard default directory come after.

17.18 Machine-Specific Peephole Optimizers

In addition to instruction patterns the 'md' file may contain definitions of machine-specific peephole optimizations.

The combiner does not notice certain peephole optimizations when the data flow in the program does not suggest that it should try them. For example, sometimes two consecutive insns related in purpose can be combined even though the second one does not appear to use a register computed in the first one. A machine-specific peephole optimizer can detect such opportunities.

There are two forms of peephole definitions that may be used. The original `define_peephole` is run at assembly output time to match insns and substitute assembly text. Use of `define_peephole` is deprecated.

A newer `define_peephole2` matches insns and substitutes new insns. The `peephole2` pass is run after register allocation but before scheduling, which may result in much better code for targets that do scheduling.

17.18.1 RTL to Text Peephole Optimizers

A definition looks like this:

```
(define_peephole
  [insn-pattern-1
   insn-pattern-2
   ...]
  "condition"
  "template"
  "optional-insn-attributes")
```

The last string operand may be omitted if you are not using any machine-specific information in this machine description. If present, it must obey the same rules as in a `define_insn`.

In this skeleton, *insn-pattern-1* and so on are patterns to match consecutive insns. The optimization applies to a sequence of insns when *insn-pattern-1* matches the first one, *insn-pattern-2* matches the next, and so on.

Each of the insns matched by a peephole must also match a `define_insn`. Peepholes are checked only at the last stage just before code generation, and only optionally. Therefore, any insn which would match a peephole but no `define_insn` will cause a crash in code generation in an unoptimized compilation, or at various optimization stages.

The operands of the insns are matched with `match_operands`, `match_operator`, and `match_dup`, as usual. What is not usual is that the operand numbers apply to all the insn patterns in the definition. So, you can check for identical operands in two insns by using `match_operand` in one insn and `match_dup` in the other.

The operand constraints used in `match_operand` patterns do not have any direct effect on the applicability of the peephole, but they will be validated afterward, so make sure your constraints are general enough to apply whenever the peephole matches. If the peephole matches but the constraints are not satisfied, the compiler will crash.

It is safe to omit constraints in all the operands of the peephole; or you can write constraints which serve as a double-check on the criteria previously tested.

Once a sequence of insns matches the patterns, the *condition* is checked. This is a C expression which makes the final decision whether to perform the optimization (we do so if the expression is nonzero). If *condition* is omitted (in other words, the string is empty) then the optimization is applied to every sequence of insns that matches the patterns.

The defined peephole optimizations are applied after register allocation is complete. Therefore, the peephole definition can check which operands have ended up in which kinds of registers, just by looking at the operands.

The way to refer to the operands in *condition* is to write `operands[i]` for operand number *i* (as matched by `(match_operand i ...)`). Use the variable `insn` to refer to the last of the insns being matched; use `prev_active_insn` to find the preceding insns.

When optimizing computations with intermediate results, you can use *condition* to match only when the intermediate results are not used elsewhere. Use the C expression `dead_or_set_p (insn, op)`, where *insn* is the insn in which you expect the value to be used for the last time (from the value of `insn`, together with use of `prev_nonnote_insn`), and *op* is the intermediate value (from `operands[i]`).

Applying the optimization means replacing the sequence of insns with one new insn. The *template* controls ultimate output of assembler code for this combined insn. It works exactly like the template of a `define_insn`. Operand numbers in this template are the same ones used in matching the original sequence of insns.

The result of a defined peephole optimizer does not need to match any of the insn patterns in the machine description; it does not even have an opportunity to match them. The peephole optimizer definition itself serves as the insn pattern to control how the insn is output.

Defined peephole optimizers are run as assembler code is being output, so the insns they produce are never combined or rearranged in any way.

Here is an example, taken from the 68000 machine description:

```
(define_peephole
  [(set (reg:SI 15) (plus:SI (reg:SI 15) (const_int 4)))
   (set (match_operand:DF 0 "register_operand" "=f")
        (match_operand:DF 1 "register_operand" "ad"))]
  "FP_REG_P (operands[0]) && ! FP_REG_P (operands[1])"
{
  rtx xoperands[2];
  xoperands[1] = gen_rtx_REG (SImode, REGNO (operands[1]) + 1);
#ifdef MOTOROLA
  output_asm_insn ("move.l %1,(sp)", xoperands);
  output_asm_insn ("move.l %1,-(sp)", operands);
  return "fmove.d (sp)+,%0";
#else
  output_asm_insn ("movel %1,sp@", xoperands);
  output_asm_insn ("movel %1,sp@-", operands);
  return "fmoved sp@+,%0";
#endif
})
```

The effect of this optimization is to change

```
jbsr _foobar
addql #4,sp
movel d1,sp@-
movel d0,sp@-
fmoved sp@+,fp0
```

into

```
jbsr _foobar
movel d1,sp@
movel d0,sp@-
fmoved sp@+,fp0
```

insn-pattern-1 and so on look *almost* like the second operand of `define_insn`. There is one important difference: the second operand of `define_insn` consists of one or more RTX's enclosed in square brackets. Usually, there is only one: then the same action can be written as an element of a `define_peephole`. But when there are multiple actions in a `define_insn`, they are implicitly enclosed in a `parallel`. Then you must explicitly write the `parallel`, and the square brackets within it, in the `define_peephole`. Thus, if an insn pattern looks like this,

```
(define_insn "divmodsi4"
  [(set (match_operand:SI 0 "general_operand" "=d")
        (div:SI (match_operand:SI 1 "general_operand" "0")
                (match_operand:SI 2 "general_operand" "dmsK")))
   (set (match_operand:SI 3 "general_operand" "=d")
        (mod:SI (match_dup 1) (match_dup 2)))]
  "TARGET_68020"
```

Chapter 17: Machine Descriptions

```
    "divsl%.1 %2,%3:%0")
```

then the way to mention this insn in a peephole is as follows:

```
(define_peephole
  [...
   (parallel
     [(set (match_operand:SI 0 "general_operand" "=d")
           (div:SI (match_operand:SI 1 "general_operand" "0")
                   (match_operand:SI 2 "general_operand" "dmsK")))
      (set (match_operand:SI 3 "general_operand" "=d")
           (mod:SI (match_dup 1) (match_dup 2)))])
   ...]
  ...)
```

17.18.2 RTL to RTL Peephole Optimizers

The `define_peephole2` definition tells the compiler how to substitute one sequence of instructions for another sequence, what additional scratch registers may be needed and what their lifetimes must be.

```
(define_peephole2
  [insn-pattern-1
   insn-pattern-2
   ...]
  "condition"
  [new-insn-pattern-1
   new-insn-pattern-2
   ...]
  "preparation-statements")
```

The definition is almost identical to `define_split` (see Section 17.16 [Insn Splitting], page 426) except that the pattern to match is not a single instruction, but a sequence of instructions.

It is possible to request additional scratch registers for use in the output template. If appropriate registers are not free, the pattern will simply not match.

Scratch registers are requested with a `match_scratch` pattern at the top level of the input pattern. The allocated register (initially) will be dead at the point requested within the original sequence. If the scratch is used at more than a single point, a `match_dup` pattern at the top level of the input pattern marks the last position in the input sequence at which the register must be available.

Here is an example from the IA-32 machine description:

```
(define_peephole2
  [(match_scratch:SI 2 "r")
   (parallel [(set (match_operand:SI 0 "register_operand" "")
                   (match_operator:SI 3 "arith_or_logical_operator"
                     [(match_dup 0)
                      (match_operand:SI 1 "memory_operand" "")]))
              (clobber (reg:CC 17))])]
  "! optimize_size && ! TARGET_READ_MODIFY"
  [(set (match_dup 2) (match_dup 1))
   (parallel [(set (match_dup 0)
                   (match_op_dup 3 [(match_dup 0) (match_dup 2)]))
              (clobber (reg:CC 17))])]
  "")
```

This pattern tries to split a load from its use in the hopes that we'll be able to schedule around the memory load latency. It allocates a single `SImode` register of class `GENERAL_REGS` (`"r"`) that needs to be live only at the point just before the arithmetic.

A real example requiring extended scratch lifetimes is harder to come by, so here's a silly made-up example:

```
(define_peephole2
  [(match_scratch:SI 4 "r")
   (set (match_operand:SI 0 "" "") (match_operand:SI 1 "" ""))
   (set (match_operand:SI 2 "" "") (match_dup 1))
   (match_dup 4)
   (set (match_operand:SI 3 "" "") (match_dup 1))]
  "/* determine 1 does not overlap 0 and 2 */"
  [(set (match_dup 4) (match_dup 1))
   (set (match_dup 0) (match_dup 4))
   (set (match_dup 2) (match_dup 4))
   (set (match_dup 3) (match_dup 4))]
  "")
```

If we had not added the (`match_dup 4`) in the middle of the input sequence, it might have been the case that the register we chose at the beginning of the sequence is killed by the first or second `set`.

17.19 Instruction Attributes

In addition to describing the instruction supported by the target machine, the 'md' file also defines a group of *attributes* and a set of values for each. Every generated insn is assigned a value for each attribute. One possible attribute would be the effect that the insn has on the machine's condition code. This attribute can then be used by `NOTICE_UPDATE_CC` to track the condition codes.

17.19.1 Defining Attributes and their Values

The `define_attr` expression is used to define each attribute required by the target machine. It looks like:

    (define_attr name list-of-values default)

name is a string specifying the name of the attribute being defined. Some attributes are used in a special way by the rest of the compiler. The `enabled` attribute can be used to conditionally enable or disable insn alternatives (see Section 17.8.6 [Disable Insn Alternatives], page 377). The `predicable` attribute, together with a suitable `define_cond_exec` (see Section 17.20 [Conditional Execution], page 450), can be used to automatically generate conditional variants of instruction patterns. The `mnemonic` attribute can be used to check for the instruction mnemonic (see Section 17.19.7 [Mnemonic Attribute], page 442). The compiler internally uses the names `ce_enabled` and `nonce_enabled`, so they should not be used elsewhere as alternative names.

list-of-values is either a string that specifies a comma-separated list of values that can be assigned to the attribute, or a null string to indicate that the attribute takes numeric values.

default is an attribute expression that gives the value of this attribute for insns that match patterns whose definition does not include an explicit value for this attribute. See Section 17.19.4 [Attr Example], page 440, for more information on the handling of defaults.

See Section 17.19.6 [Constant Attributes], page 442, for information on attributes that do not depend on any particular insn.

For each defined attribute, a number of definitions are written to the 'insn-attr.h' file. For cases where an explicit set of values is specified for an attribute, the following are defined:

- A '#define' is written for the symbol 'HAVE_ATTR_*name*'.
- An enumerated class is defined for '*attr_name*' with elements of the form '*upper-name*_*upper-value*' where the attribute name and value are first converted to uppercase.
- A function 'get_attr_*name*' is defined that is passed an insn and returns the attribute value for that insn.

For example, if the following is present in the 'md' file:

```
(define_attr "type" "branch,fp,load,store,arith" ...)
```

the following lines will be written to the file 'insn-attr.h'.

```
#define HAVE_ATTR_type 1
enum attr_type {TYPE_BRANCH, TYPE_FP, TYPE_LOAD,
                TYPE_STORE, TYPE_ARITH};
extern enum attr_type get_attr_type ();
```

If the attribute takes numeric values, no **enum** type will be defined and the function to obtain the attribute's value will return **int**.

There are attributes which are tied to a specific meaning. These attributes are not free to use for other purposes:

length   The `length` attribute is used to calculate the length of emitted code chunks. This is especially important when verifying branch distances. See Section 17.19.5 [Insn Lengths], page 441.

enabled The `enabled` attribute can be defined to prevent certain alternatives of an insn definition from being used during code generation. See Section 17.8.6 [Disable Insn Alternatives], page 377.

mnemonic The `mnemonic` attribute can be defined to implement instruction specific checks in e.g. the pipeline description. See Section 17.19.7 [Mnemonic Attribute], page 442.

For each of these special attributes, the corresponding 'HAVE_ATTR_*name*' '#define' is also written when the attribute is not defined; in that case, it is defined as '0'.

Another way of defining an attribute is to use:

```
(define_enum_attr "attr" "enum" default)
```

This works in just the same way as **define_attr**, except that the list of values is taken from a separate enumeration called *enum* (see [define_enum], page 455). This form allows you to use the same list of values for several attributes without having to repeat the list each time. For example:

```
(define_enum "processor" [
  model_a
  model_b
  ...
])
```

```
(define_enum_attr "arch" "processor"
  (const (symbol_ref "target_arch")))
(define_enum_attr "tune" "processor"
  (const (symbol_ref "target_tune")))
```

defines the same attributes as:

```
(define_attr "arch" "model_a,model_b,..."
  (const (symbol_ref "target_arch")))
(define_attr "tune" "model_a,model_b,..."
  (const (symbol_ref "target_tune")))
```

but without duplicating the processor list. The second example defines two separate C enums (`attr_arch` and `attr_tune`) whereas the first defines a single C enum (`processor`).

17.19.2 Attribute Expressions

RTL expressions used to define attributes use the codes described above plus a few specific to attribute definitions, to be discussed below. Attribute value expressions must have one of the following forms:

`(const_int i)`
> The integer *i* specifies the value of a numeric attribute. *i* must be non-negative.
>
> The value of a numeric attribute can be specified either with a `const_int`, or as an integer represented as a string in `const_string`, `eq_attr` (see below), `attr`, `symbol_ref`, simple arithmetic expressions, and `set_attr` overrides on specific instructions (see Section 17.19.3 [Tagging Insns], page 438).

`(const_string value)`
> The string *value* specifies a constant attribute value. If *value* is specified as '"*"', it means that the default value of the attribute is to be used for the insn containing this expression. '"*"' obviously cannot be used in the *default* expression of a `define_attr`.
>
> If the attribute whose value is being specified is numeric, *value* must be a string containing a non-negative integer (normally `const_int` would be used in this case). Otherwise, it must contain one of the valid values for the attribute.

`(if_then_else test true-value false-value)`
> *test* specifies an attribute test, whose format is defined below. The value of this expression is *true-value* if *test* is true, otherwise it is *false-value*.

`(cond [test1 value1 ...] default)`
> The first operand of this expression is a vector containing an even number of expressions and consisting of pairs of *test* and *value* expressions. The value of the `cond` expression is that of the *value* corresponding to the first true *test* expression. If none of the *test* expressions are true, the value of the `cond` expression is that of the *default* expression.

test expressions can have one of the following forms:

`(const_int i)`
> This test is true if *i* is nonzero and false otherwise.

`(not `*`test`*`)`

`(ior `*`test1 test2`*`)`

`(and `*`test1 test2`*`)`

> These tests are true if the indicated logical function is true.

`(match_operand:`*`m n pred constraints`*`)`

> This test is true if operand *n* of the insn whose attribute value is being determined has mode *m* (this part of the test is ignored if *m* is `VOIDmode`) and the function specified by the string *pred* returns a nonzero value when passed operand *n* and mode *m* (this part of the test is ignored if *pred* is the null string).
>
> The *constraints* operand is ignored and should be the null string.

`(match_test `*`c-expr`*`)`

> The test is true if C expression *c-expr* is true. In non-constant attributes, *c-expr* has access to the following variables:
>
> *insn*   The rtl instruction under test.
>
> *which_alternative*
> > The `define_insn` alternative that *insn* matches. See Section 17.6 [Output Statement], page 334.
>
> *operands*   An array of *insn*'s rtl operands.
>
> *c-expr* behaves like the condition in a C `if` statement, so there is no need to explicitly convert the expression into a boolean 0 or 1 value. For example, the following two tests are equivalent:
> ```
> (match_test "x & 2")
> (match_test "(x & 2) != 0")
> ```

`(le `*`arith1 arith2`*`)`

`(leu `*`arith1 arith2`*`)`

`(lt `*`arith1 arith2`*`)`

`(ltu `*`arith1 arith2`*`)`

`(gt `*`arith1 arith2`*`)`

`(gtu `*`arith1 arith2`*`)`

`(ge `*`arith1 arith2`*`)`

`(geu `*`arith1 arith2`*`)`

`(ne `*`arith1 arith2`*`)`

`(eq `*`arith1 arith2`*`)`

> These tests are true if the indicated comparison of the two arithmetic expressions is true. Arithmetic expressions are formed with `plus`, `minus`, `mult`, `div`, `mod`, `abs`, `neg`, `and`, `ior`, `xor`, `not`, `ashift`, `lshiftrt`, and `ashiftrt` expressions.
>
> `const_int` and `symbol_ref` are always valid terms (see Section 17.19.5 [Insn Lengths], page 441, for additional forms). `symbol_ref` is a string denoting a C expression that yields an `int` when evaluated by the 'get_attr_...' routine. It should normally be a global variable.

`(eq_attr `*`name value`*`)`

> *name* is a string specifying the name of an attribute.

value is a string that is either a valid value for attribute *name*, a comma-separated list of values, or '!' followed by a value or list. If *value* does not begin with a '!', this test is true if the value of the *name* attribute of the current insn is in the list specified by *value*. If *value* begins with a '!', this test is true if the attribute's value is *not* in the specified list.

For example,

```
(eq_attr "type" "load,store")
```

is equivalent to

```
(ior (eq_attr "type" "load") (eq_attr "type" "store"))
```

If *name* specifies an attribute of 'alternative', it refers to the value of the compiler variable which_alternative (see Section 17.6 [Output Statement], page 334) and the values must be small integers. For example,

```
(eq_attr "alternative" "2,3")
```

is equivalent to

```
(ior (eq (symbol_ref "which_alternative") (const_int 2))
     (eq (symbol_ref "which_alternative") (const_int 3)))
```

Note that, for most attributes, an `eq_attr` test is simplified in cases where the value of the attribute being tested is known for all insns matching a particular pattern. This is by far the most common case.

(attr_flag *name*)

The value of an `attr_flag` expression is true if the flag specified by *name* is true for the `insn` currently being scheduled.

name is a string specifying one of a fixed set of flags to test. Test the flags **forward** and **backward** to determine the direction of a conditional branch.

This example describes a conditional branch delay slot which can be nullified for forward branches that are taken (annul-true) or for backward branches which are not taken (annul-false).

```
(define_delay (eq_attr "type" "cbranch")
  [(eq_attr "in_branch_delay" "true")
   (and (eq_attr "in_branch_delay" "true")
        (attr_flag "forward"))
   (and (eq_attr "in_branch_delay" "true")
        (attr_flag "backward"))])
```

The `forward` and `backward` flags are false if the current `insn` being scheduled is not a conditional branch.

`attr_flag` is only used during delay slot scheduling and has no meaning to other passes of the compiler.

(attr *name*)

The value of another attribute is returned. This is most useful for numeric attributes, as `eq_attr` and `attr_flag` produce more efficient code for non-numeric attributes.

17.19.3 Assigning Attribute Values to Insns

The value assigned to an attribute of an insn is primarily determined by which pattern is matched by that insn (or which `define_peephole` generated it). Every `define_insn` and

Chapter 17: Machine Descriptions   439

`define_peephole` can have an optional last argument to specify the values of attributes for
matching insns. The value of any attribute not specified in a particular insn is set to the
default value for that attribute, as specified in its `define_attr`. Extensive use of default
values for attributes permits the specification of the values for only one or two attributes
in the definition of most insn patterns, as seen in the example in the next section.

The optional last argument of `define_insn` and `define_peephole` is a vector of expressions, each of which defines the value for a single attribute. The most general way of
assigning an attribute's value is to use a `set` expression whose first operand is an `attr`
expression giving the name of the attribute being set. The second operand of the `set` is
an attribute expression (see Section 17.19.2 [Expressions], page 436) giving the value of the
attribute.

When the attribute value depends on the 'alternative' attribute (i.e., which is the
applicable alternative in the constraint of the insn), the `set_attr_alternative` expression
can be used. It allows the specification of a vector of attribute expressions, one for each
alternative.

When the generality of arbitrary attribute expressions is not required, the simpler `set_attr` expression can be used, which allows specifying a string giving either a single attribute
value or a list of attribute values, one for each alternative.

The form of each of the above specifications is shown below. In each case, *name* is a
string specifying the attribute to be set.

(set_attr *name value-string*)

> *value-string* is either a string giving the desired attribute value, or a string
> containing a comma-separated list giving the values for succeeding alternatives.
> The number of elements must match the number of alternatives in the constraint
> of the insn pattern.
>
> Note that it may be useful to specify '*' for some alternative, in which case the
> attribute will assume its default value for insns matching that alternative.

(set_attr_alternative *name* [*value1 value2* ...])

> Depending on the alternative of the insn, the value will be one of the specified
> values. This is a shorthand for using a `cond` with tests on the 'alternative'
> attribute.

(set (attr *name*) *value*)

> The first operand of this `set` must be the special RTL expression `attr`, whose
> sole operand is a string giving the name of the attribute being set. *value* is the
> value of the attribute.

The following shows three different ways of representing the same attribute value specification:

```
(set_attr "type" "load,store,arith")

(set_attr_alternative "type"
                     [(const_string "load") (const_string "store")
                      (const_string "arith")])

(set (attr "type")
     (cond [(eq_attr "alternative" "1") (const_string "load")
```

```
            (eq_attr "alternative" "2") (const_string "store")]
         (const_string "arith")))
```

The `define_asm_attributes` expression provides a mechanism to specify the attributes assigned to insns produced from an `asm` statement. It has the form:

```
(define_asm_attributes [attr-sets])
```

where *attr-sets* is specified the same as for both the `define_insn` and the `define_peephole` expressions.

These values will typically be the "worst case" attribute values. For example, they might indicate that the condition code will be clobbered.

A specification for a `length` attribute is handled specially. The way to compute the length of an `asm` insn is to multiply the length specified in the expression `define_asm_attributes` by the number of machine instructions specified in the `asm` statement, determined by counting the number of semicolons and newlines in the string. Therefore, the value of the `length` attribute specified in a `define_asm_attributes` should be the maximum possible length of a single machine instruction.

17.19.4 Example of Attribute Specifications

The judicious use of defaulting is important in the efficient use of insn attributes. Typically, insns are divided into *types* and an attribute, customarily called `type`, is used to represent this value. This attribute is normally used only to define the default value for other attributes. An example will clarify this usage.

Assume we have a RISC machine with a condition code and in which only full-word operations are performed in registers. Let us assume that we can divide all insns into loads, stores, (integer) arithmetic operations, floating point operations, and branches.

Here we will concern ourselves with determining the effect of an insn on the condition code and will limit ourselves to the following possible effects: The condition code can be set unpredictably (clobbered), not be changed, be set to agree with the results of the operation, or only changed if the item previously set into the condition code has been modified.

Here is part of a sample 'md' file for such a machine:

```
(define_attr "type" "load,store,arith,fp,branch" (const_string "arith"))

(define_attr "cc" "clobber,unchanged,set,change0"
             (cond [(eq_attr "type" "load")
                        (const_string "change0")
                    (eq_attr "type" "store,branch")
                        (const_string "unchanged")
                    (eq_attr "type" "arith")
                        (if_then_else (match_operand:SI 0 "" "")
                                      (const_string "set")
                                      (const_string "clobber"))]
                   (const_string "clobber")))

(define_insn ""
  [(set (match_operand:SI 0 "general_operand" "=r,r,m")
        (match_operand:SI 1 "general_operand" "r,m,r"))]
  ""
  "@
   move %0,%1
   load %0,%1
```

```
        store %0,%1"
  [(set_attr "type" "arith,load,store")])
```

Note that we assume in the above example that arithmetic operations performed on quantities smaller than a machine word clobber the condition code since they will set the condition code to a value corresponding to the full-word result.

17.19.5 Computing the Length of an Insn

For many machines, multiple types of branch instructions are provided, each for different length branch displacements. In most cases, the assembler will choose the correct instruction to use. However, when the assembler cannot do so, GCC can when a special attribute, the `length` attribute, is defined. This attribute must be defined to have numeric values by specifying a null string in its `define_attr`.

In the case of the `length` attribute, two additional forms of arithmetic terms are allowed in test expressions:

`(match_dup n)`
: This refers to the address of operand n of the current insn, which must be a `label_ref`.

`(pc)`
: For non-branch instructions and backward branch instructions, this refers to the address of the current insn. But for forward branch instructions, this refers to the address of the next insn, because the length of the current insn is to be computed.

For normal insns, the length will be determined by value of the `length` attribute. In the case of `addr_vec` and `addr_diff_vec` insn patterns, the length is computed as the number of vectors multiplied by the size of each vector.

Lengths are measured in addressable storage units (bytes).

Note that it is possible to call functions via the `symbol_ref` mechanism to compute the length of an insn. However, if you use this mechanism you must provide dummy clauses to express the maximum length without using the function call. You can an example of this in the `pa` machine description for the `call_symref` pattern.

The following macros can be used to refine the length computation:

`ADJUST_INSN_LENGTH (insn, length)`
: If defined, modifies the length assigned to instruction *insn* as a function of the context in which it is used. *length* is an lvalue that contains the initially computed length of the insn and should be updated with the correct length of the insn.

  This macro will normally not be required. A case in which it is required is the ROMP. On this machine, the size of an `addr_vec` insn must be increased by two to compensate for the fact that alignment may be required.

The routine that returns `get_attr_length` (the value of the `length` attribute) can be used by the output routine to determine the form of the branch instruction to be written, as the example below illustrates.

As an example of the specification of variable-length branches, consider the IBM 360. If we adopt the convention that a register will be set to the starting address of a function, we can jump to labels within 4k of the start using a four-byte instruction. Otherwise, we need a six-byte sequence to load the address from memory and then branch to it.

On such a machine, a pattern for a branch instruction might be specified as follows:
```
(define_insn "jump"
  [(set (pc)
        (label_ref (match_operand 0 "" "")))]
  ""
{
   return (get_attr_length (insn) == 4
           ? "b %l0" : "l r15,=a(%l0); br r15");
}
  [(set (attr "length")
        (if_then_else (lt (match_dup 0) (const_int 4096))
                      (const_int 4)
                      (const_int 6)))])
```

17.19.6 Constant Attributes

A special form of `define_attr`, where the expression for the default value is a `const` expression, indicates an attribute that is constant for a given run of the compiler. Constant attributes may be used to specify which variety of processor is used. For example,
```
(define_attr "cpu" "m88100,m88110,m88000"
 (const
  (cond [(symbol_ref "TARGET_88100") (const_string "m88100")
         (symbol_ref "TARGET_88110") (const_string "m88110")]
        (const_string "m88000"))))

(define_attr "memory" "fast,slow"
 (const
  (if_then_else (symbol_ref "TARGET_FAST_MEM")
                (const_string "fast")
                (const_string "slow"))))
```

The routine generated for constant attributes has no parameters as it does not depend on any particular insn. RTL expressions used to define the value of a constant attribute may use the `symbol_ref` form, but may not use either the `match_operand` form or `eq_attr` forms involving insn attributes.

17.19.7 Mnemonic Attribute

The `mnemonic` attribute is a string type attribute holding the instruction mnemonic for an insn alternative. The attribute values will automatically be generated by the machine description parser if there is an attribute definition in the md file:
```
(define_attr "mnemonic" "unknown" (const_string "unknown"))
```
The default value can be freely chosen as long as it does not collide with any of the instruction mnemonics. This value will be used whenever the machine description parser is not able to determine the mnemonic string. This might be the case for output templates containing more than a single instruction as in `"mvcle\t%0,%1,0\;jo\t.-4"`.

The `mnemonic` attribute set is not generated automatically if the instruction string is generated via C code.

An existing `mnemonic` attribute set in an insn definition will not be overriden by the md file parser. That way it is possible to manually set the instruction mnemonics for the cases where the md file parser fails to determine it automatically.

The `mnemonic` attribute is useful for dealing with instruction specific properties in the pipeline description without defining additional insn attributes.

```
(define_attr "ooo_expanded" ""
  (cond [(eq_attr "mnemonic" "dlr,dsgr,d,dsgf,stam,dsgfr,dlgr")
         (const_int 1)]
        (const_int 0)))
```

17.19.8 Delay Slot Scheduling

The insn attribute mechanism can be used to specify the requirements for delay slots, if any, on a target machine. An instruction is said to require a *delay slot* if some instructions that are physically after the instruction are executed as if they were located before it. Classic examples are branch and call instructions, which often execute the following instruction before the branch or call is performed.

On some machines, conditional branch instructions can optionally *annul* instructions in the delay slot. This means that the instruction will not be executed for certain branch outcomes. Both instructions that annul if the branch is true and instructions that annul if the branch is false are supported.

Delay slot scheduling differs from instruction scheduling in that determining whether an instruction needs a delay slot is dependent only on the type of instruction being generated, not on data flow between the instructions. See the next section for a discussion of data-dependent instruction scheduling.

The requirement of an insn needing one or more delay slots is indicated via the `define_delay` expression. It has the following form:

```
(define_delay test
              [delay-1 annul-true-1 annul-false-1
               delay-2 annul-true-2 annul-false-2
               ...])
```

test is an attribute test that indicates whether this `define_delay` applies to a particular insn. If so, the number of required delay slots is determined by the length of the vector specified as the second argument. An insn placed in delay slot *n* must satisfy attribute test *delay-n*. *annul-true-n* is an attribute test that specifies which insns may be annulled if the branch is true. Similarly, *annul-false-n* specifies which insns in the delay slot may be annulled if the branch is false. If annulling is not supported for that delay slot, `(nil)` should be coded.

For example, in the common case where branch and call insns require a single delay slot, which may contain any insn other than a branch or call, the following would be placed in the 'md' file:

```
(define_delay (eq_attr "type" "branch,call")
              [(eq_attr "type" "!branch,call") (nil) (nil)])
```

Multiple `define_delay` expressions may be specified. In this case, each such expression specifies different delay slot requirements and there must be no insn for which tests in two `define_delay` expressions are both true.

For example, if we have a machine that requires one delay slot for branches but two for calls, no delay slot can contain a branch or call insn, and any valid insn in the delay slot for the branch can be annulled if the branch is true, we might represent this as follows:

```
(define_delay (eq_attr "type" "branch")
   [(eq_attr "type" "!branch,call")
```

```
            (eq_attr "type" "!branch,call")
            (nil)])

    (define_delay (eq_attr "type" "call")
                  [(eq_attr "type" "!branch,call") (nil) (nil)
                   (eq_attr "type" "!branch,call") (nil) (nil)])
```

17.19.9 Specifying processor pipeline description

To achieve better performance, most modern processors (super-pipelined, superscalar RISC, and VLIW processors) have many *functional units* on which several instructions can be executed simultaneously. An instruction starts execution if its issue conditions are satisfied. If not, the instruction is stalled until its conditions are satisfied. Such *interlock (pipeline) delay* causes interruption of the fetching of successor instructions (or demands nop instructions, e.g. for some MIPS processors).

There are two major kinds of interlock delays in modern processors. The first one is a data dependence delay determining *instruction latency time*. The instruction execution is not started until all source data have been evaluated by prior instructions (there are more complex cases when the instruction execution starts even when the data are not available but will be ready in given time after the instruction execution start). Taking the data dependence delays into account is simple. The data dependence (true, output, and anti-dependence) delay between two instructions is given by a constant. In most cases this approach is adequate. The second kind of interlock delays is a reservation delay. The reservation delay means that two instructions under execution will be in need of shared processors resources, i.e. buses, internal registers, and/or functional units, which are reserved for some time. Taking this kind of delay into account is complex especially for modern RISC processors.

The task of exploiting more processor parallelism is solved by an instruction scheduler. For a better solution to this problem, the instruction scheduler has to have an adequate description of the processor parallelism (or *pipeline description*). GCC machine descriptions describe processor parallelism and functional unit reservations for groups of instructions with the aid of *regular expressions*.

The GCC instruction scheduler uses a *pipeline hazard recognizer* to figure out the possibility of the instruction issue by the processor on a given simulated processor cycle. The pipeline hazard recognizer is automatically generated from the processor pipeline description. The pipeline hazard recognizer generated from the machine description is based on a deterministic finite state automaton (DFA): the instruction issue is possible if there is a transition from one automaton state to another one. This algorithm is very fast, and furthermore, its speed is not dependent on processor complexity[2].

The rest of this section describes the directives that constitute an automaton-based processor pipeline description. The order of these constructions within the machine description file is not important.

The following optional construction describes names of automata generated and used for the pipeline hazards recognition. Sometimes the generated finite state automaton used

---

[2] However, the size of the automaton depends on processor complexity. To limit this effect, machine descriptions can split orthogonal parts of the machine description among several automata: but then, since each of these must be stepped independently, this does cause a small decrease in the algorithm's performance.

Chapter 17: Machine Descriptions   445

by the pipeline hazard recognizer is large. If we use more than one automaton and bind
functional units to the automata, the total size of the automata is usually less than the
size of the single automaton. If there is no one such construction, only one finite state
automaton is generated.

    `(define_automaton automata-names)`

automata-names is a string giving names of the automata. The names are separated by
commas. All the automata should have unique names. The automaton name is used in the
constructions `define_cpu_unit` and `define_query_cpu_unit`.

Each processor functional unit used in the description of instruction reservations should
be described by the following construction.

    `(define_cpu_unit unit-names [automaton-name])`

unit-names is a string giving the names of the functional units separated by commas.
Don't use name '`nothing`', it is reserved for other goals.

automaton-name is a string giving the name of the automaton with which the unit is
bound. The automaton should be described in construction `define_automaton`. You should
give *automaton-name*, if there is a defined automaton.

The assignment of units to automata are constrained by the uses of the units in insn
reservations. The most important constraint is: if a unit reservation is present on a particular cycle of an alternative for an insn reservation, then some unit from the same automaton
must be present on the same cycle for the other alternatives of the insn reservation. The
rest of the constraints are mentioned in the description of the subsequent constructions.

The following construction describes CPU functional units analogously to `define_cpu_unit`. The reservation of such units can be queried for an automaton state. The instruction
scheduler never queries reservation of functional units for given automaton state. So as
a rule, you don't need this construction. This construction could be used for future code
generation goals (e.g. to generate VLIW insn templates).

    `(define_query_cpu_unit unit-names [automaton-name])`

unit-names is a string giving names of the functional units separated by commas.

automaton-name is a string giving the name of the automaton with which the unit is
bound.

The following construction is the major one to describe pipeline characteristics of an
instruction.

    `(define_insn_reservation insn-name default_latency`
                             `condition regexp)`

default_latency is a number giving latency time of the instruction. There is an important
difference between the old description and the automaton based pipeline description. The
latency time is used for all dependencies when we use the old description. In the automaton based pipeline description, the given latency time is only used for true dependencies.
The cost of anti-dependencies is always zero and the cost of output dependencies is the
difference between latency times of the producing and consuming insns (if the difference is
negative, the cost is considered to be zero). You can always change the default costs for
any description by using the target hook `TARGET_SCHED_ADJUST_COST` (see Section 18.17
[Scheduling], page 562).

insn-name is a string giving the internal name of the insn. The internal names are
used in constructions `define_bypass` and in the automaton description file generated for

debugging. The internal name has nothing in common with the names in `define_insn`. It is a good practice to use insn classes described in the processor manual.

condition defines what RTL insns are described by this construction. You should remember that you will be in trouble if *condition* for two or more different `define_insn_reservation` constructions is TRUE for an insn. In this case what reservation will be used for the insn is not defined. Such cases are not checked during generation of the pipeline hazards recognizer because in general recognizing that two conditions may have the same value is quite difficult (especially if the conditions contain `symbol_ref`). It is also not checked during the pipeline hazard recognizer work because it would slow down the recognizer considerably.

regexp is a string describing the reservation of the cpu's functional units by the instruction. The reservations are described by a regular expression according to the following syntax:

```
regexp = regexp "," oneof
       | oneof

oneof = oneof "|" allof
      | allof

allof = allof "+" repeat
      | repeat

repeat = element "*" number
       | element

element = cpu_function_unit_name
        | reservation_name
        | result_name
        | "nothing"
        | "(" regexp ")"
```

- ',' is used for describing the start of the next cycle in the reservation.
- '|' is used for describing a reservation described by the first regular expression **or** a reservation described by the second regular expression **or** etc.
- '+' is used for describing a reservation described by the first regular expression **and** a reservation described by the second regular expression **and** etc.
- '*' is used for convenience and simply means a sequence in which the regular expression are repeated *number* times with cycle advancing (see ',').
- '`cpu_function_unit_name`' denotes reservation of the named functional unit.
- '`reservation_name`' — see description of construction '`define_reservation`'.
- '`nothing`' denotes no unit reservations.

Sometimes unit reservations for different insns contain common parts. In such case, you can simplify the pipeline description by describing the common part by the following construction

```
(define_reservation reservation-name regexp)
```

reservation-name is a string giving name of *regexp*. Functional unit names and reservation names are in the same name space. So the reservation names should be different from the functional unit names and can not be the reserved name '`nothing`'.

The following construction is used to describe exceptions in the latency time for given instruction pair. This is so called bypasses.

```
(define_bypass number out_insn_names in_insn_names
               [guard])
```

number defines when the result generated by the instructions given in string *out_insn_names* will be ready for the instructions given in string *in_insn_names*. Each of these strings is a comma-separated list of filename-style globs and they refer to the names of `define_insn_reservations`. For example:

```
(define_bypass 1 "cpu1_load_*, cpu1_store_*" "cpu1_load_*")
```

defines a bypass between instructions that start with 'cpu1_load_' or 'cpu1_store_' and those that start with 'cpu1_load_'.

guard is an optional string giving the name of a C function which defines an additional guard for the bypass. The function will get the two insns as parameters. If the function returns zero the bypass will be ignored for this case. The additional guard is necessary to recognize complicated bypasses, e.g. when the consumer is only an address of insn 'store' (not a stored value).

If there are more one bypass with the same output and input insns, the chosen bypass is the first bypass with a guard in description whose guard function returns nonzero. If there is no such bypass, then bypass without the guard function is chosen.

The following five constructions are usually used to describe VLIW processors, or more precisely, to describe a placement of small instructions into VLIW instruction slots. They can be used for RISC processors, too.

```
(exclusion_set unit-names unit-names)
(presence_set unit-names patterns)
(final_presence_set unit-names patterns)
(absence_set unit-names patterns)
(final_absence_set unit-names patterns)
```

unit-names is a string giving names of functional units separated by commas.

patterns is a string giving patterns of functional units separated by comma. Currently pattern is one unit or units separated by white-spaces.

The first construction ('`exclusion_set`') means that each functional unit in the first string can not be reserved simultaneously with a unit whose name is in the second string and vice versa. For example, the construction is useful for describing processors (e.g. some SPARC processors) with a fully pipelined floating point functional unit which can execute simultaneously only single floating point insns or only double floating point insns.

The second construction ('`presence_set`') means that each functional unit in the first string can not be reserved unless at least one of pattern of units whose names are in the second string is reserved. This is an asymmetric relation. For example, it is useful for description that VLIW 'slot1' is reserved after 'slot0' reservation. We could describe it by the following construction

```
(presence_set "slot1" "slot0")
```

Or 'slot1' is reserved only after 'slot0' and unit 'b0' reservation. In this case we could write

```
(presence_set "slot1" "slot0 b0")
```

The third construction ('`final_presence_set`') is analogous to '`presence_set`'. The difference between them is when checking is done. When an instruction is issued in given automaton state reflecting all current and planned unit reservations, the automaton state is changed. The first state is a source state, the second one is a result state. Checking for 'presence_set' is done on the source state reservation, checking for 'final_presence_set' is done on the result reservation. This construction is useful to describe a reservation which is actually two subsequent reservations. For example, if we use

> (presence_set "slot1" "slot0")

the following insn will be never issued (because 'slot1' requires 'slot0' which is absent in the source state).

> (define_reservation "insn_and_nop" "slot0 + slot1")

but it can be issued if we use analogous 'final_presence_set'.

The forth construction ('absence_set') means that each functional unit in the first string can be reserved only if each pattern of units whose names are in the second string is not reserved. This is an asymmetric relation (actually 'exclusion_set' is analogous to this one but it is symmetric). For example it might be useful in a VLIW description to say that 'slot0' cannot be reserved after either 'slot1' or 'slot2' have been reserved. This can be described as:

> (absence_set "slot0" "slot1, slot2")

Or 'slot2' can not be reserved if 'slot0' and unit 'b0' are reserved or 'slot1' and unit 'b1' are reserved. In this case we could write

> (absence_set "slot2" "slot0 b0, slot1 b1")

All functional units mentioned in a set should belong to the same automaton.

The last construction ('final_absence_set') is analogous to 'absence_set' but checking is done on the result (state) reservation. See comments for 'final_presence_set'.

You can control the generator of the pipeline hazard recognizer with the following construction.

> (automata_option *options*)

options is a string giving options which affect the generated code. Currently there are the following options:

- *no-minimization* makes no minimization of the automaton. This is only worth to do when we are debugging the description and need to look more accurately at reservations of states.
- *time* means printing time statistics about the generation of automata.
- *stats* means printing statistics about the generated automata such as the number of DFA states, NDFA states and arcs.
- *v* means a generation of the file describing the result automata. The file has suffix '.dfa' and can be used for the description verification and debugging.
- *w* means a generation of warning instead of error for non-critical errors.
- *no-comb-vect* prevents the automaton generator from generating two data structures and comparing them for space efficiency. Using a comb vector to represent transitions may be better, but it can be very expensive to construct. This option is useful if the build process spends an unacceptably long time in genautomata.
- *ndfa* makes nondeterministic finite state automata. This affects the treatment of operator '|' in the regular expressions. The usual treatment of the operator is to try the

first alternative and, if the reservation is not possible, the second alternative. The nondeterministic treatment means trying all alternatives, some of them may be rejected by reservations in the subsequent insns.

- *collapse-ndfa* modifies the behavior of the generator when producing an automaton. An additional state transition to collapse a nondeterministic NDFA state to a deterministic DFA state is generated. It can be triggered by passing `const0_rtx` to state_transition. In such an automaton, cycle advance transitions are available only for these collapsed states. This option is useful for ports that want to use the `ndfa` option, but also want to use `define_query_cpu_unit` to assign units to insns issued in a cycle.

- *progress* means output of a progress bar showing how many states were generated so far for automaton being processed. This is useful during debugging a DFA description. If you see too many generated states, you could interrupt the generator of the pipeline hazard recognizer and try to figure out a reason for generation of the huge automaton.

As an example, consider a superscalar RISC machine which can issue three insns (two integer insns and one floating point insn) on the cycle but can finish only two insns. To describe this, we define the following functional units.

```
(define_cpu_unit "i0_pipeline, i1_pipeline, f_pipeline")
(define_cpu_unit "port0, port1")
```

All simple integer insns can be executed in any integer pipeline and their result is ready in two cycles. The simple integer insns are issued into the first pipeline unless it is reserved, otherwise they are issued into the second pipeline. Integer division and multiplication insns can be executed only in the second integer pipeline and their results are ready correspondingly in 9 and 4 cycles. The integer division is not pipelined, i.e. the subsequent integer division insn can not be issued until the current division insn finished. Floating point insns are fully pipelined and their results are ready in 3 cycles. Where the result of a floating point insn is used by an integer insn, an additional delay of one cycle is incurred. To describe all of this we could specify

```
(define_cpu_unit "div")

(define_insn_reservation "simple" 2 (eq_attr "type" "int")
                         "(i0_pipeline | i1_pipeline), (port0 | port1)")

(define_insn_reservation "mult" 4 (eq_attr "type" "mult")
                         "i1_pipeline, nothing*2, (port0 | port1)")

(define_insn_reservation "div" 9 (eq_attr "type" "div")
                         "i1_pipeline, div*7, div + (port0 | port1)")

(define_insn_reservation "float" 3 (eq_attr "type" "float")
                         "f_pipeline, nothing, (port0 | port1))

(define_bypass 4 "float" "simple,mult,div")
```

To simplify the description we could describe the following reservation

```
(define_reservation "finish" "port0|port1")
```

and use it in all `define_insn_reservation` as in the following construction

```
(define_insn_reservation "simple" 2 (eq_attr "type" "int")
                         "(i0_pipeline | i1_pipeline), finish")
```

17.20 Conditional Execution

A number of architectures provide for some form of conditional execution, or predication. The hallmark of this feature is the ability to nullify most of the instructions in the instruction set. When the instruction set is large and not entirely symmetric, it can be quite tedious to describe these forms directly in the '.md' file. An alternative is the `define_cond_exec` template.

```
(define_cond_exec
  [predicate-pattern]
  "condition"
  "output-template"
  "optional-insn-attribues")
```

predicate-pattern is the condition that must be true for the insn to be executed at runtime and should match a relational operator. One can use `match_operator` to match several relational operators at once. Any `match_operand` operands must have no more than one alternative.

condition is a C expression that must be true for the generated pattern to match.

output-template is a string similar to the `define_insn` output template (see Section 17.5 [Output Template], page 333), except that the '*' and '@' special cases do not apply. This is only useful if the assembly text for the predicate is a simple prefix to the main insn. In order to handle the general case, there is a global variable `current_insn_predicate` that will contain the entire predicate if the current insn is predicated, and will otherwise be NULL.

optional-insn-attributes is an optional vector of attributes that gets appended to the insn attributes of the produced cond_exec rtx. It can be used to add some distinguishing attribute to cond_exec rtxs produced that way. An example usage would be to use this attribute in conjunction with attributes on the main pattern to disable particular alternatives under certain conditions.

When `define_cond_exec` is used, an implicit reference to the `predicable` instruction attribute is made. See Section 17.19 [Insn Attributes], page 434. This attribute must be a boolean (i.e. have exactly two elements in its *list-of-values*), with the possible values being **no** and **yes**. The default and all uses in the insns must be a simple constant, not a complex expressions. It may, however, depend on the alternative, by using a comma-separated list of values. If that is the case, the port should also define an `enabled` attribute (see Section 17.8.6 [Disable Insn Alternatives], page 377), which should also allow only **no** and **yes** as its values.

For each `define_insn` for which the `predicable` attribute is true, a new `define_insn` pattern will be generated that matches a predicated version of the instruction. For example,

```
(define_insn "addsi"
  [(set (match_operand:SI 0 "register_operand" "r")
        (plus:SI (match_operand:SI 1 "register_operand" "r")
                 (match_operand:SI 2 "register_operand" "r")))]
  "test1"
  "add %2,%1,%0")

(define_cond_exec
  [(ne (match_operand:CC 0 "register_operand" "c")
       (const_int 0))]
  "test2"
  "(%0)")
```

generates a new pattern
```
(define_insn ""
  [(cond_exec
     (ne (match_operand:CC 3 "register_operand" "c") (const_int 0))
     (set (match_operand:SI 0 "register_operand" "r")
          (plus:SI (match_operand:SI 1 "register_operand" "r")
                   (match_operand:SI 2 "register_operand" "r"))))]
  "(test2) && (test1)"
  "(%3) add %2,%1,%0")
```

17.21 RTL Templates Transformations

For some hardware architectures there are common cases when the RTL templates for the instructions can be derived from the other RTL templates using simple transformations. E.g., 'i386.md' contains an RTL template for the ordinary sub instruction— *subsi_1, and for the sub instruction with subsequent zero-extension—*subsi_1_zext. Such cases can be easily implemented by a single meta-template capable of generating a modified case based on the initial one:

```
(define_subst "name"
  [input-template]
  "condition"
  [output-template])
```

input-template is a pattern describing the source RTL template, which will be transformed.

condition is a C expression that is conjunct with the condition from the input-template to generate a condition to be used in the output-template.

output-template is a pattern that will be used in the resulting template.

define_subst mechanism is tightly coupled with the notion of the subst attribute (see Section 17.23.4 [Subst Iterators], page 460). The use of define_subst is triggered by a reference to a subst attribute in the transforming RTL template. This reference initiates duplication of the source RTL template and substitution of the attributes with their values. The source RTL template is left unchanged, while the copy is transformed by define_subst. This transformation can fail in the case when the source RTL template is not matched against the input-template of the define_subst. In such case the copy is deleted.

define_subst can be used only in define_insn and define_expand, it cannot be used in other expressions (e.g. in define_insn_and_split).

17.21.1 define_subst Example

To illustrate how define_subst works, let us examine a simple template transformation.

Suppose there are two kinds of instructions: one that touches flags and the other that does not. The instructions of the second type could be generated with the following define_subst:

```
(define_subst "add_clobber_subst"
  [(set (match_operand:SI 0 "" "")
        (match_operand:SI 1 "" ""))]
  ""
  [(set (match_dup 0)
        (match_dup 1))
   (clobber (reg:CC FLAGS_REG))]
```

This `define_subst` can be applied to any RTL pattern containing `set` of mode SI and generates a copy with clobber when it is applied.

Assume there is an RTL template for a `max` instruction to be used in `define_subst` mentioned above:

```
(define_insn "maxsi"
  [(set (match_operand:SI 0 "register_operand" "=r")
        (max:SI
          (match_operand:SI 1 "register_operand" "r")
          (match_operand:SI 2 "register_operand" "r")))]
  ""
  "max\t{%2, %1, %0|%0, %1, %2}"
  [...])
```

To mark the RTL template for `define_subst` application, subst-attributes are used. They should be declared in advance:

```
(define_subst_attr "add_clobber_name" "add_clobber_subst" "_noclobber" "_clobber")
```

Here 'add_clobber_name' is the attribute name, 'add_clobber_subst' is the name of the corresponding `define_subst`, the third argument ('_noclobber') is the attribute value that would be substituted into the unchanged version of the source RTL template, and the last argument ('_clobber') is the value that would be substituted into the second, transformed, version of the RTL template.

Once the subst-attribute has been defined, it should be used in RTL templates which need to be processed by the `define_subst`. So, the original RTL template should be changed:

```
(define_insn "maxsi<add_clobber_name>"
  [(set (match_operand:SI 0 "register_operand" "=r")
        (max:SI
          (match_operand:SI 1 "register_operand" "r")
          (match_operand:SI 2 "register_operand" "r")))]
  ""
  "max\t{%2, %1, %0|%0, %1, %2}"
  [...])
```

The result of the `define_subst` usage would look like the following:

```
(define_insn "maxsi_noclobber"
  [(set (match_operand:SI 0 "register_operand" "=r")
        (max:SI
          (match_operand:SI 1 "register_operand" "r")
          (match_operand:SI 2 "register_operand" "r")))]
  ""
  "max\t{%2, %1, %0|%0, %1, %2}"
  [...])
(define_insn "maxsi_clobber"
  [(set (match_operand:SI 0 "register_operand" "=r")
        (max:SI
          (match_operand:SI 1 "register_operand" "r")
          (match_operand:SI 2 "register_operand" "r")))
   (clobber (reg:CC FLAGS_REG))]
  ""
  "max\t{%2, %1, %0|%0, %1, %2}"
  [...])
```

17.21.2 Pattern Matching in `define_subst`

All expressions, allowed in `define_insn` or `define_expand`, are allowed in the input-template of `define_subst`, except `match_par_dup`, `match_scratch`, `match_parallel`. The meanings of expressions in the input-template were changed:

`match_operand` matches any expression (possibly, a subtree in RTL-template), if modes of the `match_operand` and this expression are the same, or mode of the `match_operand` is VOIDmode, or this expression is `match_dup`, `match_op_dup`. If the expression is `match_operand` too, and predicate of `match_operand` from the input pattern is not empty, then the predicates are compared. That can be used for more accurate filtering of accepted RTL-templates.

`match_operator` matches common operators (like `plus`, `minus`), `unspec`, `unspec_volatile` operators and `match_operator`s from the original pattern if the modes match and `match_operator` from the input pattern has the same number of operands as the operator from the original pattern.

17.21.3 Generation of output template in `define_subst`

If all necessary checks for `define_subst` application pass, a new RTL-pattern, based on the output-template, is created to replace the old template. Like in input-patterns, meanings of some RTL expressions are changed when they are used in output-patterns of a `define_subst`. Thus, `match_dup` is used for copying the whole expression from the original pattern, which matched corresponding `match_operand` from the input pattern.

`match_dup N` is used in the output template to be replaced with the expression from the original pattern, which matched `match_operand N` from the input pattern. As a consequence, `match_dup` cannot be used to point to `match_operand`s from the output pattern, it should always refer to a `match_operand` from the input pattern.

In the output template one can refer to the expressions from the original pattern and create new ones. For instance, some operands could be added by means of standard `match_operand`.

After replacing `match_dup` with some RTL-subtree from the original pattern, it could happen that several `match_operand`s in the output pattern have the same indexes. It is unknown, how many and what indexes would be used in the expression which would replace `match_dup`, so such conflicts in indexes are inevitable. To overcome this issue, `match_operand`s and `match_operator`s, which were introduced into the output pattern, are renumerated when all `match_dup`s are replaced.

Number of alternatives in `match_operand`s introduced into the output template M could differ from the number of alternatives in the original pattern N, so in the resultant pattern there would be N*M alternatives. Thus, constraints from the original pattern would be duplicated N times, constraints from the output pattern would be duplicated M times, producing all possible combinations.

17.22 Constant Definitions

Using literal constants inside instruction patterns reduces legibility and can be a maintenance problem.

To overcome this problem, you may use the `define_constants` expression. It contains a vector of name-value pairs. From that point on, wherever any of the names appears in

the MD file, it is as if the corresponding value had been written instead. You may use
`define_constants` multiple times; each appearance adds more constants to the table. It
is an error to redefine a constant with a different value.

To come back to the a29k load multiple example, instead of

```
(define_insn ""
  [(match_parallel 0 "load_multiple_operation"
     [(set (match_operand:SI 1 "gpc_reg_operand" "=r")
           (match_operand:SI 2 "memory_operand" "m"))
      (use (reg:SI 179))
      (clobber (reg:SI 179))])]
  ""
  "loadm 0,0,%1,%2")
```

You could write:

```
(define_constants [
    (R_BP 177)
    (R_FC 178)
    (R_CR 179)
    (R_Q  180)
])

(define_insn ""
  [(match_parallel 0 "load_multiple_operation"
     [(set (match_operand:SI 1 "gpc_reg_operand" "=r")
           (match_operand:SI 2 "memory_operand" "m"))
      (use (reg:SI R_CR))
      (clobber (reg:SI R_CR))])]
  ""
  "loadm 0,0,%1,%2")
```

The constants that are defined with a define_constant are also output in the insn-codes.h
header file as #defines.

You can also use the machine description file to define enumerations. Like the constants
defined by `define_constant`, these enumerations are visible to both the machine description
file and the main C code.

The syntax is as follows:

```
(define_c_enum "name" [
  value0
  value1
  ...
  valuen
])
```

This definition causes the equivalent of the following C code to appear in
'insn-constants.h':

```
enum name {
  value0 = 0,
  value1 = 1,
  ...
  valuen = n
};
#define NUM_cname_VALUES (n + 1)
```

where *cname* is the capitalized form of *name*. It also makes each *valuei* available in the
machine description file, just as if it had been declared with:

Chapter 17: Machine Descriptions 455

```
(define_constants [(valuei i)])
```

Each *valuei* is usually an upper-case identifier and usually begins with *cname*.

You can split the enumeration definition into as many statements as you like. The above example is directly equivalent to:

```
(define_c_enum "name" [value0])
(define_c_enum "name" [value1])
...
(define_c_enum "name" [valuen])
```

Splitting the enumeration helps to improve the modularity of each individual .md file. For example, if a port defines its synchronization instructions in a separate 'sync.md' file, it is convenient to define all synchronization-specific enumeration values in 'sync.md' rather than in the main '.md' file.

Some enumeration names have special significance to GCC:

unspecv   If an enumeration called **unspecv** is defined, GCC will use it when printing out **unspec_volatile** expressions. For example:

```
(define_c_enum "unspecv" [
  UNSPECV_BLOCKAGE
])
```

causes GCC to print '(unspec_volatile ... 0)' as:

```
(unspec_volatile ... UNSPECV_BLOCKAGE)
```

unspec   If an enumeration called **unspec** is defined, GCC will use it when printing out **unspec** expressions. GCC will also use it when printing out **unspec_volatile** expressions unless an **unspecv** enumeration is also defined. You can therefore decide whether to keep separate enumerations for volatile and non-volatile expressions or whether to use the same enumeration for both.

Another way of defining an enumeration is to use **define_enum**:

```
(define_enum "name" [
  value0
  value1
  ...
  valuen
])
```

This directive implies:

```
(define_c_enum "name" [
  cname_cvalue0
  cname_cvalue1
  ...
  cname_cvaluen
])
```

where *cvaluei* is the capitalized form of *valuei*. However, unlike **define_c_enum**, the enumerations defined by **define_enum** can be used in attribute specifications (see [define_enum_attr], page 435).

17.23 Iterators

Ports often need to define similar patterns for more than one machine mode or for more than one rtx code. GCC provides some simple iterator facilities to make this process easier.

17.23.1 Mode Iterators

Ports often need to define similar patterns for two or more different modes. For example:

- If a processor has hardware support for both single and double floating-point arithmetic, the SFmode patterns tend to be very similar to the DFmode ones.
- If a port uses SImode pointers in one configuration and DImode pointers in another, it will usually have very similar SImode and DImode patterns for manipulating pointers.

Mode iterators allow several patterns to be instantiated from one '.md' file template. They can be used with any type of rtx-based construct, such as a define_insn, define_split, or define_peephole2.

17.23.1.1 Defining Mode Iterators

The syntax for defining a mode iterator is:

```
(define_mode_iterator name [(mode1 "cond1") ... (moden "condn")])
```

This allows subsequent '.md' file constructs to use the mode suffix :*name*. Every construct that does so will be expanded *n* times, once with every use of :*name* replaced by :*mode1*, once with every use replaced by :*mode2*, and so on. In the expansion for a particular *modei*, every C condition will also require that *condi* be true.

For example:

```
(define_mode_iterator P [(SI "Pmode == SImode") (DI "Pmode == DImode")])
```

defines a new mode suffix :P. Every construct that uses :P will be expanded twice, once with every :P replaced by :SI and once with every :P replaced by :DI. The :SI version will only apply if Pmode == SImode and the :DI version will only apply if Pmode == DImode.

As with other '.md' conditions, an empty string is treated as "always true". (*mode* "") can also be abbreviated to *mode*. For example:

```
(define_mode_iterator GPR [SI (DI "TARGET_64BIT")])
```

means that the :DI expansion only applies if TARGET_64BIT but that the :SI expansion has no such constraint.

Iterators are applied in the order they are defined. This can be significant if two iterators are used in a construct that requires substitutions. See Section 17.23.1.2 [Substitutions], page 456.

17.23.1.2 Substitution in Mode Iterators

If an '.md' file construct uses mode iterators, each version of the construct will often need slightly different strings or modes. For example:

- When a define_expand defines several addm3 patterns (see Section 17.9 [Standard Names], page 382), each expander will need to use the appropriate mode name for *m*.
- When a define_insn defines several instruction patterns, each instruction will often use a different assembler mnemonic.
- When a define_insn requires operands with different modes, using an iterator for one of the operand modes usually requires a specific mode for the other operand(s).

GCC supports such variations through a system of "mode attributes". There are two standard attributes: mode, which is the name of the mode in lower case, and MODE, which is the same thing in upper case. You can define other attributes using:

```
(define_mode_attr name [(mode1 "value1") ... (moden "valuen")])
```
where *name* is the name of the attribute and *valuei* is the value associated with *modei*.

When GCC replaces some *:iterator* with *:mode*, it will scan each string and mode in the pattern for sequences of the form `<iterator:attr>`, where *attr* is the name of a mode attribute. If the attribute is defined for *mode*, the whole `<...>` sequence will be replaced by the appropriate attribute value.

For example, suppose an '.md' file has:
```
(define_mode_iterator P [(SI "Pmode == SImode") (DI "Pmode == DImode")])
(define_mode_attr load [(SI "lw") (DI "ld")])
```

If one of the patterns that uses :P contains the string `"<P:load>\t%0,%1"`, the SI version of that pattern will use `"lw\t%0,%1"` and the DI version will use `"ld\t%0,%1"`.

Here is an example of using an attribute for a mode:
```
(define_mode_iterator LONG [SI DI])
(define_mode_attr SHORT [(SI "HI") (DI "SI")])
(define_insn ...
   (sign_extend:LONG (match_operand:<LONG:SHORT> ...)) ...)
```

The `iterator:` prefix may be omitted, in which case the substitution will be attempted for every iterator expansion.

17.23.1.3 Mode Iterator Examples

Here is an example from the MIPS port. It defines the following modes and attributes (among others):
```
(define_mode_iterator GPR [SI (DI "TARGET_64BIT")])
(define_mode_attr d [(SI "") (DI "d")])
```

and uses the following template to define both subsi3 and subdi3:
```
(define_insn "sub<mode>3"
  [(set (match_operand:GPR 0 "register_operand" "=d")
        (minus:GPR (match_operand:GPR 1 "register_operand" "d")
                   (match_operand:GPR 2 "register_operand" "d")))]
  ""
  "<d>subu\t%0,%1,%2"
  [(set_attr "type" "arith")
   (set_attr "mode" "<MODE>")])
```

This is exactly equivalent to:
```
(define_insn "subsi3"
  [(set (match_operand:SI 0 "register_operand" "=d")
        (minus:SI (match_operand:SI 1 "register_operand" "d")
                  (match_operand:SI 2 "register_operand" "d")))]
  ""
  "subu\t%0,%1,%2"
  [(set_attr "type" "arith")
   (set_attr "mode" "SI")])

(define_insn "subdi3"
  [(set (match_operand:DI 0 "register_operand" "=d")
        (minus:DI (match_operand:DI 1 "register_operand" "d")
                  (match_operand:DI 2 "register_operand" "d")))]
  ""
  "dsubu\t%0,%1,%2"
  [(set_attr "type" "arith")
   (set_attr "mode" "DI")])
```

17.23.2 Code Iterators

Code iterators operate in a similar way to mode iterators. See Section 17.23.1 [Mode Iterators], page 456.

The construct:

```
(define_code_iterator name [(code1 "cond1") ... (coden "condn")])
```

defines a pseudo rtx code *name* that can be instantiated as *codei* if condition *condi* is true. Each *codei* must have the same rtx format. See Section 14.2 [RTL Classes], page 250.

As with mode iterators, each pattern that uses *name* will be expanded *n* times, once with all uses of *name* replaced by *code1*, once with all uses replaced by *code2*, and so on. See Section 17.23.1.1 [Defining Mode Iterators], page 456.

It is possible to define attributes for codes as well as for modes. There are two standard code attributes: `code`, the name of the code in lower case, and `CODE`, the name of the code in upper case. Other attributes are defined using:

```
(define_code_attr name [(code1 "value1") ... (coden "valuen")])
```

Here's an example of code iterators in action, taken from the MIPS port:

```
(define_code_iterator any_cond [unordered ordered unlt unge uneq ltgt unle ungt
                                eq ne gt ge lt le gtu geu ltu leu])

(define_expand "b<code>"
  [(set (pc)
        (if_then_else (any_cond:CC (cc0)
                                   (const_int 0))
                      (label_ref (match_operand 0 ""))
                      (pc)))]
  ""
{
  gen_conditional_branch (operands, <CODE>);
  DONE;
})
```

This is equivalent to:

```
(define_expand "bunordered"
  [(set (pc)
        (if_then_else (unordered:CC (cc0)
                                    (const_int 0))
                      (label_ref (match_operand 0 ""))
                      (pc)))]
  ""
{
  gen_conditional_branch (operands, UNORDERED);
  DONE;
})

(define_expand "bordered"
  [(set (pc)
        (if_then_else (ordered:CC (cc0)
                                  (const_int 0))
                      (label_ref (match_operand 0 ""))
                      (pc)))]
  ""
{
  gen_conditional_branch (operands, ORDERED);
  DONE;
```

```
      })

    ...
```

17.23.3 Int Iterators

Int iterators operate in a similar way to code iterators. See Section 17.23.2 [Code Iterators], page 458.

The construct:

```
    (define_int_iterator name [(int1 "cond1") ... (intn "condn")])
```

defines a pseudo integer constant *name* that can be instantiated as *inti* if condition *condi* is true. Each *int* must have the same rtx format. See Section 14.2 [RTL Classes], page 250. Int iterators can appear in only those rtx fields that have 'i' as the specifier. This means that each *int* has to be a constant defined using define_constant or define_c_enum.

As with mode and code iterators, each pattern that uses *name* will be expanded *n* times, once with all uses of *name* replaced by *int1*, once with all uses replaced by *int2*, and so on. See Section 17.23.1.1 [Defining Mode Iterators], page 456.

It is possible to define attributes for ints as well as for codes and modes. Attributes are defined using:

```
    (define_int_attr name [(int1 "value1") ... (intn "valuen")])
```

Here's an example of int iterators in action, taken from the ARM port:

```
    (define_int_iterator QABSNEG [UNSPEC_VQABS UNSPEC_VQNEG])

    (define_int_attr absneg [(UNSPEC_VQABS "abs") (UNSPEC_VQNEG "neg")])

    (define_insn "neon_vq<absneg><mode>"
      [(set (match_operand:VDQIW 0 "s_register_operand" "=w")
    (unspec:VDQIW [(match_operand:VDQIW 1 "s_register_operand" "w")
            (match_operand:SI 2 "immediate_operand" "i")]
           QABSNEG))]
      "TARGET_NEON"
      "vq<absneg>.<V_s_elem>\t%<V_reg>0, %<V_reg>1"
      [(set_attr "type" "neon_vqneg_vqabs")]
    )
```

This is equivalent to:

```
    (define_insn "neon_vqabs<mode>"
      [(set (match_operand:VDQIW 0 "s_register_operand" "=w")
    (unspec:VDQIW [(match_operand:VDQIW 1 "s_register_operand" "w")
            (match_operand:SI 2 "immediate_operand" "i")]
           UNSPEC_VQABS))]
      "TARGET_NEON"
      "vqabs.<V_s_elem>\t%<V_reg>0, %<V_reg>1"
      [(set_attr "type" "neon_vqneg_vqabs")]
    )

    (define_insn "neon_vqneg<mode>"
      [(set (match_operand:VDQIW 0 "s_register_operand" "=w")
    (unspec:VDQIW [(match_operand:VDQIW 1 "s_register_operand" "w")
            (match_operand:SI 2 "immediate_operand" "i")]
           UNSPEC_VQNEG))]
      "TARGET_NEON"
      "vqneg.<V_s_elem>\t%<V_reg>0, %<V_reg>1"
```

```
      [(set_attr "type" "neon_vqneg_vqabs")]
)
```

17.23.4 Subst Iterators

Subst iterators are special type of iterators with the following restrictions: they could not be declared explicitly, they always have only two values, and they do not have explicit dedicated name. Subst-iterators are triggered only when corresponding subst-attribute is used in RTL-pattern.

Subst iterators transform templates in the following way: the templates are duplicated, the subst-attributes in these templates are replaced with the corresponding values, and a new attribute is implicitly added to the given `define_insn`/`define_expand`. The name of the added attribute matches the name of `define_subst`. Such attributes are declared implicitly, and it is not allowed to have a `define_attr` named as a `define_subst`.

Each subst iterator is linked to a `define_subst`. It is declared implicitly by the first appearance of the corresponding `define_subst_attr`, and it is not allowed to define it explicitly.

Declarations of subst-attributes have the following syntax:

```
(define_subst_attr "name"
  "subst-name"
  "no-subst-value"
  "subst-applied-value")
```

name is a string with which the given subst-attribute could be referred to.

subst-name shows which `define_subst` should be applied to an RTL-template if the given subst-attribute is present in the RTL-template.

no-subst-value is a value with which subst-attribute would be replaced in the first copy of the original RTL-template.

subst-applied-value is a value with which subst-attribute would be replaced in the second copy of the original RTL-template.

18 Target Description Macros and Functions

In addition to the file '`machine.md`', a machine description includes a C header file conventionally given the name '`machine.h`' and a C source file named '`machine.c`'. The header file defines numerous macros that convey the information about the target machine that does not fit into the scheme of the '.md' file. The file '`tm.h`' should be a link to '`machine.h`'. The header file '`config.h`' includes '`tm.h`' and most compiler source files include '`config.h`'. The source file defines a variable `targetm`, which is a structure containing pointers to functions and data relating to the target machine. '`machine.c`' should also contain their definitions, if they are not defined elsewhere in GCC, and other functions called through the macros defined in the '.h' file.

18.1 The Global `targetm` Variable

struct gcc_target targetm   [Variable]

The target '.c' file must define the global `targetm` variable which contains pointers to functions and data relating to the target machine. The variable is declared in '`target.h`'; '`target-def.h`' defines the macro `TARGET_INITIALIZER` which is used to initialize the variable, and macros for the default initializers for elements of the structure. The '.c' file should override those macros for which the default definition is inappropriate. For example:

```
#include "target.h"
#include "target-def.h"

/* Initialize the GCC target structure.  */

#undef TARGET_COMP_TYPE_ATTRIBUTES
#define TARGET_COMP_TYPE_ATTRIBUTES machine_comp_type_attributes

struct gcc_target targetm = TARGET_INITIALIZER;
```

Where a macro should be defined in the '.c' file in this manner to form part of the `targetm` structure, it is documented below as a "Target Hook" with a prototype. Many macros will change in future from being defined in the '.h' file to being part of the `targetm` structure.

Similarly, there is a `targetcm` variable for hooks that are specific to front ends for C-family languages, documented as "C Target Hook". This is declared in '`c-family/c-target.h`', the initializer `TARGETCM_INITIALIZER` in '`c-family/c-target-def.h`'. If targets initialize `targetcm` themselves, they should set `target_has_targetcm=yes` in '`config.gcc`'; otherwise a default definition is used.

Similarly, there is a `targetm_common` variable for hooks that are shared between the compiler driver and the compilers proper, documented as "Common Target Hook". This is declared in '`common/common-target.h`', the initializer `TARGETM_COMMON_INITIALIZER` in '`common/common-target-def.h`'. If targets initialize `targetm_common` themselves, they should set `target_has_targetm_common=yes` in '`config.gcc`'; otherwise a default definition is used.

18.2 Controlling the Compilation Driver, 'gcc'

You can control the compilation driver.

DRIVER_SELF_SPECS [Macro]

A list of specs for the driver itself. It should be a suitable initializer for an array of strings, with no surrounding braces.

The driver applies these specs to its own command line between loading default 'specs' files (but not command-line specified ones) and choosing the multilib directory or running any subcommands. It applies them in the order given, so each spec can depend on the options added by earlier ones. It is also possible to remove options using '%<*option*'* in the usual way.

This macro can be useful when a port has several interdependent target options. It provides a way of standardizing the command line so that the other specs are easier to write.

Do not define this macro if it does not need to do anything.

OPTION_DEFAULT_SPECS [Macro]

A list of specs used to support configure-time default options (i.e. '--with' options) in the driver. It should be a suitable initializer for an array of structures, each containing two strings, without the outermost pair of surrounding braces.

The first item in the pair is the name of the default. This must match the code in 'config.gcc' for the target. The second item is a spec to apply if a default with this name was specified. The string '%(VALUE)' in the spec will be replaced by the value of the default everywhere it occurs.

The driver will apply these specs to its own command line between loading default 'specs' files and processing DRIVER_SELF_SPECS, using the same mechanism as DRIVER_SELF_SPECS.

Do not define this macro if it does not need to do anything.

CPP_SPEC [Macro]

A C string constant that tells the GCC driver program options to pass to CPP. It can also specify how to translate options you give to GCC into options for GCC to pass to the CPP.

Do not define this macro if it does not need to do anything.

CPLUSPLUS_CPP_SPEC [Macro]

This macro is just like CPP_SPEC, but is used for C++, rather than C. If you do not define this macro, then the value of CPP_SPEC (if any) will be used instead.

CC1_SPEC [Macro]

A C string constant that tells the GCC driver program options to pass to cc1, cc1plus, f771, and the other language front ends. It can also specify how to translate options you give to GCC into options for GCC to pass to front ends.

Do not define this macro if it does not need to do anything.

Chapter 18: Target Description Macros and Functions 463

CC1PLUS_SPEC [Macro]

> A C string constant that tells the GCC driver program options to pass to `cc1plus`. It can also specify how to translate options you give to GCC into options for GCC to pass to the `cc1plus`.
>
> Do not define this macro if it does not need to do anything. Note that everything defined in CC1_SPEC is already passed to `cc1plus` so there is no need to duplicate the contents of CC1_SPEC in CC1PLUS_SPEC.

ASM_SPEC [Macro]

> A C string constant that tells the GCC driver program options to pass to the assembler. It can also specify how to translate options you give to GCC into options for GCC to pass to the assembler. See the file 'sun3.h' for an example of this.
>
> Do not define this macro if it does not need to do anything.

ASM_FINAL_SPEC [Macro]

> A C string constant that tells the GCC driver program how to run any programs which cleanup after the normal assembler. Normally, this is not needed. See the file 'mips.h' for an example of this.
>
> Do not define this macro if it does not need to do anything.

AS_NEEDS_DASH_FOR_PIPED_INPUT [Macro]

> Define this macro, with no value, if the driver should give the assembler an argument consisting of a single dash, '-', to instruct it to read from its standard input (which will be a pipe connected to the output of the compiler proper). This argument is given after any '-o' option specifying the name of the output file.
>
> If you do not define this macro, the assembler is assumed to read its standard input if given no non-option arguments. If your assembler cannot read standard input at all, use a '%{pipe:%e}' construct; see 'mips.h' for instance.

LINK_SPEC [Macro]

> A C string constant that tells the GCC driver program options to pass to the linker. It can also specify how to translate options you give to GCC into options for GCC to pass to the linker.
>
> Do not define this macro if it does not need to do anything.

LIB_SPEC [Macro]

> Another C string constant used much like `LINK_SPEC`. The difference between the two is that `LIB_SPEC` is used at the end of the command given to the linker.
>
> If this macro is not defined, a default is provided that loads the standard C library from the usual place. See 'gcc.c'.

LIBGCC_SPEC [Macro]

> Another C string constant that tells the GCC driver program how and when to place a reference to 'libgcc.a' into the linker command line. This constant is placed both before and after the value of `LIB_SPEC`.
>
> If this macro is not defined, the GCC driver provides a default that passes the string '-lgcc' to the linker.

REAL_LIBGCC_SPEC   [Macro]
    By default, if ENABLE_SHARED_LIBGCC is defined, the LIBGCC_SPEC is not directly
    used by the driver program but is instead modified to refer to different versions of
    'libgcc.a' depending on the values of the command line flags '-static', '-shared',
    '-static-libgcc', and '-shared-libgcc'. On targets where these modifications are
    inappropriate, define REAL_LIBGCC_SPEC instead. REAL_LIBGCC_SPEC tells the driver
    how to place a reference to 'libgcc' on the link command line, but, unlike LIBGCC_
    SPEC, it is used unmodified.

USE_LD_AS_NEEDED   [Macro]
    A macro that controls the modifications to LIBGCC_SPEC mentioned in REAL_LIBGCC_
    SPEC. If nonzero, a spec will be generated that uses '--as-needed' or equivalent
    options and the shared 'libgcc' in place of the static exception handler library, when
    linking without any of -static, -static-libgcc, or -shared-libgcc.

LINK_EH_SPEC   [Macro]
    If defined, this C string constant is added to LINK_SPEC. When USE_LD_AS_NEEDED
    is zero or undefined, it also affects the modifications to LIBGCC_SPEC mentioned in
    REAL_LIBGCC_SPEC.

STARTFILE_SPEC   [Macro]
    Another C string constant used much like LINK_SPEC. The difference between the
    two is that STARTFILE_SPEC is used at the very beginning of the command given to
    the linker.

    If this macro is not defined, a default is provided that loads the standard C startup
    file from the usual place. See 'gcc.c'.

ENDFILE_SPEC   [Macro]
    Another C string constant used much like LINK_SPEC. The difference between the
    two is that ENDFILE_SPEC is used at the very end of the command given to the linker.

    Do not define this macro if it does not need to do anything.

THREAD_MODEL_SPEC   [Macro]
    GCC -v will print the thread model GCC was configured to use. However, this doesn't
    work on platforms that are multilibbed on thread models, such as AIX 4.3. On such
    platforms, define THREAD_MODEL_SPEC such that it evaluates to a string without blanks
    that names one of the recognized thread models. %*, the default value of this macro,
    will expand to the value of thread_file set in 'config.gcc'.

SYSROOT_SUFFIX_SPEC   [Macro]
    Define this macro to add a suffix to the target sysroot when GCC is configured with
    a sysroot. This will cause GCC to search for usr/lib, et al, within sysroot+suffix.

SYSROOT_HEADERS_SUFFIX_SPEC   [Macro]
    Define this macro to add a headers_suffix to the target sysroot when GCC is configured
    with a sysroot. This will cause GCC to pass the updated sysroot+headers_suffix to
    CPP, causing it to search for usr/include, et al, within sysroot+headers_suffix.

Chapter 18: Target Description Macros and Functions 465

EXTRA_SPECS [Macro]

Define this macro to provide additional specifications to put in the 'specs' file that can be used in various specifications like CC1_SPEC.

The definition should be an initializer for an array of structures, containing a string constant, that defines the specification name, and a string constant that provides the specification.

Do not define this macro if it does not need to do anything.

EXTRA_SPECS is useful when an architecture contains several related targets, which have various ..._SPECS which are similar to each other, and the maintainer would like one central place to keep these definitions.

For example, the PowerPC System V.4 targets use EXTRA_SPECS to define either _CALL_SYSV when the System V calling sequence is used or _CALL_AIX when the older AIX-based calling sequence is used.

The 'config/rs6000/rs6000.h' target file defines:

```
#define EXTRA_SPECS \
  { "cpp_sysv_default", CPP_SYSV_DEFAULT },

#define CPP_SYS_DEFAULT ""
```

The 'config/rs6000/sysv.h' target file defines:

```
#undef CPP_SPEC
#define CPP_SPEC \
"%{posix: -D_POSIX_SOURCE } \
%{mcall-sysv: -D_CALL_SYSV } \
%{!mcall-sysv: %(cpp_sysv_default) } \
%{msoft-float: -D_SOFT_FLOAT} %{mcpu=403: -D_SOFT_FLOAT}"

#undef CPP_SYSV_DEFAULT
#define CPP_SYSV_DEFAULT "-D_CALL_SYSV"
```

while the 'config/rs6000/eabiaix.h' target file defines CPP_SYSV_DEFAULT as:

```
#undef CPP_SYSV_DEFAULT
#define CPP_SYSV_DEFAULT "-D_CALL_AIX"
```

LINK_LIBGCC_SPECIAL_1 [Macro]

Define this macro if the driver program should find the library 'libgcc.a'. If you do not define this macro, the driver program will pass the argument '-lgcc' to tell the linker to do the search.

LINK_GCC_C_SEQUENCE_SPEC [Macro]

The sequence in which libgcc and libc are specified to the linker. By default this is %G %L %G.

POST_LINK_SPEC [Macro]

Define this macro to add additional steps to be executed after linker. The default value of this macro is empty string.

LINK_COMMAND_SPEC [Macro]

A C string constant giving the complete command line need to execute the linker. When you do this, you will need to update your port each time a change is made to the link command line within 'gcc.c'. Therefore, define this macro only if you need to completely redefine the command line for invoking the linker and there is no other way to accomplish the effect you need. Overriding this macro may be avoidable by overriding LINK_GCC_C_SEQUENCE_SPEC instead.

bool TARGET_ALWAYS_STRIP_DOTDOT [Common Target Hook]
True if '..' components should always be removed from directory names computed relative to GCC's internal directories, false (default) if such components should be preserved and directory names containing them passed to other tools such as the linker.

MULTILIB_DEFAULTS [Macro]
Define this macro as a C expression for the initializer of an array of string to tell the driver program which options are defaults for this target and thus do not need to be handled specially when using MULTILIB_OPTIONS.

Do not define this macro if MULTILIB_OPTIONS is not defined in the target makefile fragment or if none of the options listed in MULTILIB_OPTIONS are set by default. See Section 20.1 [Target Fragment], page 647.

RELATIVE_PREFIX_NOT_LINKDIR [Macro]
Define this macro to tell gcc that it should only translate a '-B' prefix into a '-L' linker option if the prefix indicates an absolute file name.

MD_EXEC_PREFIX [Macro]
If defined, this macro is an additional prefix to try after STANDARD_EXEC_PREFIX. MD_EXEC_PREFIX is not searched when the compiler is built as a cross compiler. If you define MD_EXEC_PREFIX, then be sure to add it to the list of directories used to find the assembler in 'configure.ac'.

STANDARD_STARTFILE_PREFIX [Macro]
Define this macro as a C string constant if you wish to override the standard choice of libdir as the default prefix to try when searching for startup files such as 'crt0.o'. STANDARD_STARTFILE_PREFIX is not searched when the compiler is built as a cross compiler.

STANDARD_STARTFILE_PREFIX_1 [Macro]
Define this macro as a C string constant if you wish to override the standard choice of /lib as a prefix to try after the default prefix when searching for startup files such as 'crt0.o'. STANDARD_STARTFILE_PREFIX_1 is not searched when the compiler is built as a cross compiler.

STANDARD_STARTFILE_PREFIX_2 [Macro]
Define this macro as a C string constant if you wish to override the standard choice of /lib as yet another prefix to try after the default prefix when searching for startup files such as 'crt0.o'. STANDARD_STARTFILE_PREFIX_2 is not searched when the compiler is built as a cross compiler.

MD_STARTFILE_PREFIX [Macro]
If defined, this macro supplies an additional prefix to try after the standard prefixes. MD_EXEC_PREFIX is not searched when the compiler is built as a cross compiler.

Chapter 18: Target Description Macros and Functions 467

MD_STARTFILE_PREFIX_1 [Macro]
: If defined, this macro supplies yet another prefix to try after the standard prefixes. It is not searched when the compiler is built as a cross compiler.

INIT_ENVIRONMENT [Macro]
: Define this macro as a C string constant if you wish to set environment variables for programs called by the driver, such as the assembler and loader. The driver passes the value of this macro to `putenv` to initialize the necessary environment variables.

LOCAL_INCLUDE_DIR [Macro]
: Define this macro as a C string constant if you wish to override the standard choice of '/usr/local/include' as the default prefix to try when searching for local header files. LOCAL_INCLUDE_DIR comes before NATIVE_SYSTEM_HEADER_DIR (set in 'config.gcc', normally '/usr/include') in the search order.

  Cross compilers do not search either '/usr/local/include' or its replacement.

NATIVE_SYSTEM_HEADER_COMPONENT [Macro]
: The "component" corresponding to NATIVE_SYSTEM_HEADER_DIR. See INCLUDE_DEFAULTS, below, for the description of components. If you do not define this macro, no component is used.

INCLUDE_DEFAULTS [Macro]
: Define this macro if you wish to override the entire default search path for include files. For a native compiler, the default search path usually consists of GCC_INCLUDE_DIR, LOCAL_INCLUDE_DIR, GPLUSPLUS_INCLUDE_DIR, and NATIVE_SYSTEM_HEADER_DIR. In addition, GPLUSPLUS_INCLUDE_DIR and GCC_INCLUDE_DIR are defined automatically by 'Makefile', and specify private search areas for GCC. The directory GPLUSPLUS_INCLUDE_DIR is used only for C++ programs.

  The definition should be an initializer for an array of structures. Each array element should have four elements: the directory name (a string constant), the component name (also a string constant), a flag for C++-only directories, and a flag showing that the includes in the directory don't need to be wrapped in extern 'C' when compiling C++. Mark the end of the array with a null element.

  The component name denotes what GNU package the include file is part of, if any, in all uppercase letters. For example, it might be 'GCC' or 'BINUTILS'. If the package is part of a vendor-supplied operating system, code the component name as '0'.

  For example, here is the definition used for VAX/VMS:

  ```
  #define INCLUDE_DEFAULTS \
  {                                         \
    { "GNU_GXX_INCLUDE:", "G++", 1, 1},     \
    { "GNU_CC_INCLUDE:", "GCC", 0, 0},      \
    { "SYS$SYSROOT:[SYSLIB.]", 0, 0, 0},    \
    { ".", 0, 0, 0},                        \
    { 0, 0, 0, 0}                           \
  }
  ```

Here is the order of prefixes tried for exec files:

1. Any prefixes specified by the user with '-B'.

2. The environment variable `GCC_EXEC_PREFIX` or, if `GCC_EXEC_PREFIX` is not set and the compiler has not been installed in the configure-time *prefix*, the location in which the compiler has actually been installed.
3. The directories specified by the environment variable `COMPILER_PATH`.
4. The macro `STANDARD_EXEC_PREFIX`, if the compiler has been installed in the configured-time *prefix*.
5. The location '/usr/libexec/gcc/', but only if this is a native compiler.
6. The location '/usr/lib/gcc/', but only if this is a native compiler.
7. The macro `MD_EXEC_PREFIX`, if defined, but only if this is a native compiler.

Here is the order of prefixes tried for startfiles:

1. Any prefixes specified by the user with '-B'.
2. The environment variable `GCC_EXEC_PREFIX` or its automatically determined value based on the installed toolchain location.
3. The directories specified by the environment variable `LIBRARY_PATH` (or port-specific name; native only, cross compilers do not use this).
4. The macro `STANDARD_EXEC_PREFIX`, but only if the toolchain is installed in the configured *prefix* or this is a native compiler.
5. The location '/usr/lib/gcc/', but only if this is a native compiler.
6. The macro `MD_EXEC_PREFIX`, if defined, but only if this is a native compiler.
7. The macro `MD_STARTFILE_PREFIX`, if defined, but only if this is a native compiler, or we have a target system root.
8. The macro `MD_STARTFILE_PREFIX_1`, if defined, but only if this is a native compiler, or we have a target system root.
9. The macro `STANDARD_STARTFILE_PREFIX`, with any sysroot modifications. If this path is relative it will be prefixed by `GCC_EXEC_PREFIX` and the machine suffix or `STANDARD_EXEC_PREFIX` and the machine suffix.
10. The macro `STANDARD_STARTFILE_PREFIX_1`, but only if this is a native compiler, or we have a target system root. The default for this macro is '/lib/'.
11. The macro `STANDARD_STARTFILE_PREFIX_2`, but only if this is a native compiler, or we have a target system root. The default for this macro is '/usr/lib/'.

18.3 Run-time Target Specification

Here are run-time target specifications.

`TARGET_CPU_CPP_BUILTINS ()` [Macro]

This function-like macro expands to a block of code that defines built-in preprocessor macros and assertions for the target CPU, using the functions `builtin_define`, `builtin_define_std` and `builtin_assert`. When the front end calls this macro it provides a trailing semicolon, and since it has finished command line option processing your code can use those results freely.

`builtin_assert` takes a string in the form you pass to the command-line option '-A', such as `cpu=mips`, and creates the assertion. `builtin_define` takes a string in the form accepted by option '-D' and unconditionally defines the macro.

builtin_define_std takes a string representing the name of an object-like macro. If it doesn't lie in the user's namespace, builtin_define_std defines it unconditionally. Otherwise, it defines a version with two leading underscores, and another version with two leading and trailing underscores, and defines the original only if an ISO standard was not requested on the command line. For example, passing unix defines __unix, __unix__ and possibly unix; passing _mips defines __mips, __mips__ and possibly _mips, and passing _ABI64 defines only _ABI64.

You can also test for the C dialect being compiled. The variable c_language is set to one of clk_c, clk_cplusplus or clk_objective_c. Note that if we are preprocessing assembler, this variable will be clk_c but the function-like macro preprocessing_asm_p() will return true, so you might want to check for that first. If you need to check for strict ANSI, the variable flag_iso can be used. The function-like macro preprocessing_trad_p() can be used to check for traditional preprocessing.

TARGET_OS_CPP_BUILTINS () [Macro]

Similarly to TARGET_CPU_CPP_BUILTINS but this macro is optional and is used for the target operating system instead.

TARGET_OBJFMT_CPP_BUILTINS () [Macro]

Similarly to TARGET_CPU_CPP_BUILTINS but this macro is optional and is used for the target object format. 'elfos.h' uses this macro to define __ELF__, so you probably do not need to define it yourself.

extern int target_flags [Variable]

This variable is declared in 'options.h', which is included before any target-specific headers.

int TARGET_DEFAULT_TARGET_FLAGS [Common Target Hook]

This variable specifies the initial value of target_flags. Its default setting is 0.

bool TARGET_HANDLE_OPTION (*struct gcc_options *opts,*** [Common Target Hook]
*struct gcc_options *opts_set, const struct cl_decoded_option *decoded, location_t loc***)**

This hook is called whenever the user specifies one of the target-specific options described by the '.opt' definition files (see Chapter 8 [Options], page 115). It has the opportunity to do some option-specific processing and should return true if the option is valid. The default definition does nothing but return true.

decoded specifies the option and its arguments. *opts* and *opts_set* are the gcc_options structures to be used for storing option state, and *loc* is the location at which the option was passed (UNKNOWN_LOCATION except for options passed via attributes).

bool TARGET_HANDLE_C_OPTION (*size_t code, const char *arg, int*** [C Target Hook]
*value***)**

This target hook is called whenever the user specifies one of the target-specific C language family options described by the '.opt' definition files(see Chapter 8 [Options], page 115). It has the opportunity to do some option-specific processing and should return true if the option is valid. The arguments are like for TARGET_HANDLE_OPTION. The default definition does nothing but return false.

In general, you should use `TARGET_HANDLE_OPTION` to handle options. However, if processing an option requires routines that are only available in the C (and related language) front ends, then you should use `TARGET_HANDLE_C_OPTION` instead.

tree TARGET_OBJC_CONSTRUCT_STRING_OBJECT (*tree string*)   [C Target Hook]
Targets may provide a string object type that can be used within and between C, C++ and their respective Objective-C dialects. A string object might, for example, embed encoding and length information. These objects are considered opaque to the compiler and handled as references. An ideal implementation makes the composition of the string object match that of the Objective-C `NSString` (`NXString` for GNUStep), allowing efficient interworking between C-only and Objective-C code. If a target implements string objects then this hook should return a reference to such an object constructed from the normal 'C' string representation provided in *string*. At present, the hook is used by Objective-C only, to obtain a common-format string object when the target provides one.

void TARGET_OBJC_DECLARE_UNRESOLVED_CLASS_REFERENCE   [C Target Hook]
    (*const char *classname*)
Declare that Objective C class *classname* is referenced by the current TU.

void TARGET_OBJC_DECLARE_CLASS_DEFINITION (*const char*   [C Target Hook]
    *classname)
Declare that Objective C class *classname* is defined by the current TU.

bool TARGET_STRING_OBJECT_REF_TYPE_P (*const_tree*   [C Target Hook]
    stringref)
If a target implements string objects then this hook should return **true** if *stringref* is a valid reference to such an object.

void TARGET_CHECK_STRING_OBJECT_FORMAT_ARG (*tree*   [C Target Hook]
    format_arg, *tree args_list*)
If a target implements string objects then this hook should should provide a facility to check the function arguments in *args_list* against the format specifiers in *format_arg* where the type of *format_arg* is one recognized as a valid string reference type.

void TARGET_OVERRIDE_OPTIONS_AFTER_CHANGE (*void*)   [Target Hook]
This target function is similar to the hook `TARGET_OPTION_OVERRIDE` but is called when the optimize level is changed via an attribute or pragma or when it is reset at the end of the code affected by the attribute or pragma. It is not called at the beginning of compilation when `TARGET_OPTION_OVERRIDE` is called so if you want to perform these actions then, you should have `TARGET_OPTION_OVERRIDE` call `TARGET_OVERRIDE_OPTIONS_AFTER_CHANGE`.

C_COMMON_OVERRIDE_OPTIONS   [Macro]
This is similar to the `TARGET_OPTION_OVERRIDE` hook but is only used in the C language frontends (C, Objective-C, C++, Objective-C++) and so can be used to alter option flag variables which only exist in those frontends.

const struct default_options *   [Common Target Hook]
  TARGET_OPTION_OPTIMIZATION_TABLE

  Some machines may desire to change what optimizations are performed for various optimization levels. This variable, if defined, describes options to enable at particular sets of optimization levels. These options are processed once just after the optimization level is determined and before the remainder of the command options have been parsed, so may be overridden by other options passed explicitly.

  This processing is run once at program startup and when the optimization options are changed via `#pragma GCC optimize` or by using the `optimize` attribute.

void TARGET_OPTION_INIT_STRUCT (*struct gcc_options*   [Common Target Hook]
  opts)

  Set target-dependent initial values of fields in *opts*.

void TARGET_OPTION_DEFAULT_PARAMS (*void*)   [Common Target Hook]

  Set target-dependent default values for '--param' settings, using calls to `set_default_param_value`.

SWITCHABLE_TARGET   [Macro]

  Some targets need to switch between substantially different subtargets during compilation. For example, the MIPS target has one subtarget for the traditional MIPS architecture and another for MIPS16. Source code can switch between these two subarchitectures using the `mips16` and `nomips16` attributes.

  Such subtargets can differ in things like the set of available registers, the set of available instructions, the costs of various operations, and so on. GCC caches a lot of this type of information in global variables, and recomputing them for each subtarget takes a significant amount of time. The compiler therefore provides a facility for maintaining several versions of the global variables and quickly switching between them; see 'target-globals.h' for details.

  Define this macro to 1 if your target needs this facility. The default is 0.

bool TARGET_FLOAT_EXCEPTIONS_ROUNDING_SUPPORTED_P (*void*)   [Target Hook]

  Returns true if the target supports IEEE 754 floating-point exceptions and rounding modes, false otherwise. This is intended to relate to the `float` and `double` types, but not necessarily `long double`. By default, returns true if the `adddf3` instruction pattern is available and false otherwise, on the assumption that hardware floating point supports exceptions and rounding modes but software floating point does not.

18.4 Defining data structures for per-function information.

If the target needs to store information on a per-function basis, GCC provides a macro and a couple of variables to allow this. Note, just using statics to store the information is a bad idea, since GCC supports nested functions, so you can be halfway through encoding one function when another one comes along.

  GCC defines a data structure called `struct function` which contains all of the data specific to an individual function. This structure contains a field called `machine` whose type is `struct machine_function *`, which can be used by targets to point to their own specific data.

If a target needs per-function specific data it should define the type `struct machine_function` and also the macro `INIT_EXPANDERS`. This macro should be used to initialize the function pointer `init_machine_status`. This pointer is explained below.

One typical use of per-function, target specific data is to create an RTX to hold the register containing the function's return address. This RTX can then be used to implement the `__builtin_return_address` function, for level 0.

Note—earlier implementations of GCC used a single data area to hold all of the per-function information. Thus when processing of a nested function began the old per-function data had to be pushed onto a stack, and when the processing was finished, it had to be popped off the stack. GCC used to provide function pointers called `save_machine_status` and `restore_machine_status` to handle the saving and restoring of the target specific information. Since the single data area approach is no longer used, these pointers are no longer supported.

INIT_EXPANDERS [Macro]

> Macro called to initialize any target specific information. This macro is called once per function, before generation of any RTL has begun. The intention of this macro is to allow the initialization of the function pointer `init_machine_status`.

void (*)(struct function *) init_machine_status [Variable]

> If this function pointer is non-NULL it will be called once per function, before function compilation starts, in order to allow the target to perform any target specific initialization of the `struct function` structure. It is intended that this would be used to initialize the `machine` of that structure.
>
> `struct machine_function` structures are expected to be freed by GC. Generally, any memory that they reference must be allocated by using GC allocation, including the structure itself.

18.5 Storage Layout

Note that the definitions of the macros in this table which are sizes or alignments measured in bits do not need to be constant. They can be C expressions that refer to static variables, such as the `target_flags`. See Section 18.3 [Run-time Target], page 468.

BITS_BIG_ENDIAN [Macro]

> Define this macro to have the value 1 if the most significant bit in a byte has the lowest number; otherwise define it to have the value zero. This means that bit-field instructions count from the most significant bit. If the machine has no bit-field instructions, then this must still be defined, but it doesn't matter which value it is defined to. This macro need not be a constant.
>
> This macro does not affect the way structure fields are packed into bytes or words; that is controlled by `BYTES_BIG_ENDIAN`.

BYTES_BIG_ENDIAN [Macro]

> Define this macro to have the value 1 if the most significant byte in a word has the lowest number. This macro need not be a constant.

Chapter 18: Target Description Macros and Functions 473

WORDS_BIG_ENDIAN [Macro]

Define this macro to have the value 1 if, in a multiword object, the most significant word has the lowest number. This applies to both memory locations and registers; see REG_WORDS_BIG_ENDIAN if the order of words in memory is not the same as the order in registers. This macro need not be a constant.

REG_WORDS_BIG_ENDIAN [Macro]

On some machines, the order of words in a multiword object differs between registers in memory. In such a situation, define this macro to describe the order of words in a register. The macro WORDS_BIG_ENDIAN controls the order of words in memory.

FLOAT_WORDS_BIG_ENDIAN [Macro]

Define this macro to have the value 1 if DFmode, XFmode or TFmode floating point numbers are stored in memory with the word containing the sign bit at the lowest address; otherwise define it to have the value 0. This macro need not be a constant.

You need not define this macro if the ordering is the same as for multi-word integers.

BITS_PER_WORD [Macro]

Number of bits in a word. If you do not define this macro, the default is BITS_PER_UNIT * UNITS_PER_WORD.

MAX_BITS_PER_WORD [Macro]

Maximum number of bits in a word. If this is undefined, the default is BITS_PER_WORD. Otherwise, it is the constant value that is the largest value that BITS_PER_WORD can have at run-time.

UNITS_PER_WORD [Macro]

Number of storage units in a word; normally the size of a general-purpose register, a power of two from 1 or 8.

MIN_UNITS_PER_WORD [Macro]

Minimum number of units in a word. If this is undefined, the default is UNITS_PER_WORD. Otherwise, it is the constant value that is the smallest value that UNITS_PER_WORD can have at run-time.

POINTER_SIZE [Macro]

Width of a pointer, in bits. You must specify a value no wider than the width of Pmode. If it is not equal to the width of Pmode, you must define POINTERS_EXTEND_UNSIGNED. If you do not specify a value the default is BITS_PER_WORD.

POINTERS_EXTEND_UNSIGNED [Macro]

A C expression that determines how pointers should be extended from ptr_mode to either Pmode or word_mode. It is greater than zero if pointers should be zero-extended, zero if they should be sign-extended, and negative if some other sort of conversion is needed. In the last case, the extension is done by the target's ptr_extend instruction.

You need not define this macro if the ptr_mode, Pmode and word_mode are all the same width.

PROMOTE_MODE (*m*, *unsignedp*, *type*) [Macro]

A macro to update *m* and *unsignedp* when an object whose type is *type* and which has the specified mode and signedness is to be stored in a register. This macro is only called when *type* is a scalar type.

On most RISC machines, which only have operations that operate on a full register, define this macro to set *m* to `word_mode` if *m* is an integer mode narrower than `BITS_PER_WORD`. In most cases, only integer modes should be widened because wider-precision floating-point operations are usually more expensive than their narrower counterparts.

For most machines, the macro definition does not change *unsignedp*. However, some machines, have instructions that preferentially handle either signed or unsigned quantities of certain modes. For example, on the DEC Alpha, 32-bit loads from memory and 32-bit add instructions sign-extend the result to 64 bits. On such machines, set *unsignedp* according to which kind of extension is more efficient.

Do not define this macro if it would never modify *m*.

enum flt_eval_method TARGET_C_EXCESS_PRECISION (*enum excess_precision_type* type) [Target Hook]

Return a value, with the same meaning as the C99 macro `FLT_EVAL_METHOD` that describes which excess precision should be applied. *type* is either `EXCESS_PRECISION_TYPE_IMPLICIT`, `EXCESS_PRECISION_TYPE_FAST`, or `EXCESS_PRECISION_TYPE_STANDARD`. For `EXCESS_PRECISION_TYPE_IMPLICIT`, the target should return which precision and range operations will be implictly evaluated in regardless of the excess precision explicitly added. For `EXCESS_PRECISION_TYPE_STANDARD` and `EXCESS_PRECISION_TYPE_FAST`, the target should return the explicit excess precision that should be added depending on the value set for '-fexcess-precision=[standard|fast]'. Note that unpredictable explicit excess precision does not make sense, so a target should never return `FLT_EVAL_METHOD_UNPREDICTABLE` when *type* is `EXCESS_PRECISION_TYPE_STANDARD` or `EXCESS_PRECISION_TYPE_FAST`.

machine_mode TARGET_PROMOTE_FUNCTION_MODE (*const_tree* type, *machine_mode* mode, *int* *punsignedp, *const_tree* funtype, *int* for_return) [Target Hook]

Like `PROMOTE_MODE`, but it is applied to outgoing function arguments or function return values. The target hook should return the new mode and possibly change *punsignedp* if the promotion should change signedness. This function is called only for scalar *or pointer* types.

for_return allows to distinguish the promotion of arguments and return values. If it is 1, a return value is being promoted and `TARGET_FUNCTION_VALUE` must perform the same promotions done here. If it is 2, the returned mode should be that of the register in which an incoming parameter is copied, or the outgoing result is computed; then the hook should return the same mode as `promote_mode`, though the signedness may be different.

type can be NULL when promoting function arguments of libcalls.

The default is to not promote arguments and return values. You can also define the hook to `default_promote_function_mode_always_promote` if you would like to apply the same rules given by `PROMOTE_MODE`.

Chapter 18: Target Description Macros and Functions 475

PARM_BOUNDARY [Macro]

Normal alignment required for function parameters on the stack, in bits. All stack parameters receive at least this much alignment regardless of data type. On most machines, this is the same as the size of an integer.

STACK_BOUNDARY [Macro]

Define this macro to the minimum alignment enforced by hardware for the stack pointer on this machine. The definition is a C expression for the desired alignment (measured in bits). This value is used as a default if PREFERRED_STACK_BOUNDARY is not defined. On most machines, this should be the same as PARM_BOUNDARY.

PREFERRED_STACK_BOUNDARY [Macro]

Define this macro if you wish to preserve a certain alignment for the stack pointer, greater than what the hardware enforces. The definition is a C expression for the desired alignment (measured in bits). This macro must evaluate to a value equal to or larger than STACK_BOUNDARY.

INCOMING_STACK_BOUNDARY [Macro]

Define this macro if the incoming stack boundary may be different from PREFERRED_STACK_BOUNDARY. This macro must evaluate to a value equal to or larger than STACK_BOUNDARY.

FUNCTION_BOUNDARY [Macro]

Alignment required for a function entry point, in bits.

BIGGEST_ALIGNMENT [Macro]

Biggest alignment that any data type can require on this machine, in bits. Note that this is not the biggest alignment that is supported, just the biggest alignment that, when violated, may cause a fault.

HOST_WIDE_INT TARGET_ABSOLUTE_BIGGEST_ALIGNMENT [Target Hook]

If defined, this target hook specifies the absolute biggest alignment that a type or variable can have on this machine, otherwise, BIGGEST_ALIGNMENT is used.

MALLOC_ABI_ALIGNMENT [Macro]

Alignment, in bits, a C conformant malloc implementation has to provide. If not defined, the default value is BITS_PER_WORD.

ATTRIBUTE_ALIGNED_VALUE [Macro]

Alignment used by the __attribute__ ((aligned)) construct. If not defined, the default value is BIGGEST_ALIGNMENT.

MINIMUM_ATOMIC_ALIGNMENT [Macro]

If defined, the smallest alignment, in bits, that can be given to an object that can be referenced in one operation, without disturbing any nearby object. Normally, this is BITS_PER_UNIT, but may be larger on machines that don't have byte or half-word store operations.

BIGGEST_FIELD_ALIGNMENT [Macro]

Biggest alignment that any structure or union field can require on this machine, in bits. If defined, this overrides BIGGEST_ALIGNMENT for structure and union fields only, unless the field alignment has been set by the `__attribute__ ((aligned (n)))` construct.

ADJUST_FIELD_ALIGN (*field*, *type*, *computed*) [Macro]
    An expression for the alignment of a structure field *field* of type *type* if the alignment computed in the usual way (including applying of `BIGGEST_ALIGNMENT` and `BIGGEST_FIELD_ALIGNMENT` to the alignment) is *computed*. It overrides alignment only if the field alignment has not been set by the `__attribute__ ((aligned (n)))` construct. Note that *field* may be `NULL_TREE` in case we just query for the minimum alignment of a field of type *type* in structure context.

MAX_STACK_ALIGNMENT [Macro]
    Biggest stack alignment guaranteed by the backend. Use this macro to specify the maximum alignment of a variable on stack.

    If not defined, the default value is `STACK_BOUNDARY`.

MAX_OFILE_ALIGNMENT [Macro]
    Biggest alignment supported by the object file format of this machine. Use this macro to limit the alignment which can be specified using the `__attribute__ ((aligned (n)))` construct. If not defined, the default value is `BIGGEST_ALIGNMENT`.

    On systems that use ELF, the default (in 'config/elfos.h') is the largest supported 32-bit ELF section alignment representable on a 32-bit host e.g. '(((uint64_t) 1 << 28) * 8)'. On 32-bit ELF the largest supported section alignment in bits is '(0x80000000 * 8)', but this is not representable on 32-bit hosts.

HOST_WIDE_INT TARGET_STATIC_RTX_ALIGNMENT (*machine_mode mode*) [Target Hook]
    This hook returns the preferred alignment in bits for a statically-allocated rtx, such as a constant pool entry. *mode* is the mode of the rtx. The default implementation returns 'GET_MODE_ALIGNMENT (*mode*)'.

DATA_ALIGNMENT (*type*, *basic-align*) [Macro]
    If defined, a C expression to compute the alignment for a variable in the static store. *type* is the data type, and *basic-align* is the alignment that the object would ordinarily have. The value of this macro is used instead of that alignment to align the object.

    If this macro is not defined, then *basic-align* is used.

    One use of this macro is to increase alignment of medium-size data to make it all fit in fewer cache lines. Another is to cause character arrays to be word-aligned so that `strcpy` calls that copy constants to character arrays can be done inline.

DATA_ABI_ALIGNMENT (*type*, *basic-align*) [Macro]
    Similar to `DATA_ALIGNMENT`, but for the cases where the ABI mandates some alignment increase, instead of optimization only purposes. E.g. AMD x86-64 psABI says that variables with array type larger than 15 bytes must be aligned to 16 byte boundaries.

    If this macro is not defined, then *basic-align* is used.

HOST_WIDE_INT TARGET_CONSTANT_ALIGNMENT (*const_tree*   [Target Hook]
     constant, *HOST_WIDE_INT* `basic_align`)

    This hook returns the alignment in bits of a constant that is being placed in memory. *constant* is the constant and *basic_align* is the alignment that the object would ordinarily have.

    The default definition just returns *basic_align*.

    The typical use of this hook is to increase alignment for string constants to be word aligned so that `strcpy` calls that copy constants can be done inline. The function `constant_alignment_word_strings` provides such a definition.

LOCAL_ALIGNMENT (*type*, *basic-align*)   [Macro]

    If defined, a C expression to compute the alignment for a variable in the local store. *type* is the data type, and *basic-align* is the alignment that the object would ordinarily have. The value of this macro is used instead of that alignment to align the object.

    If this macro is not defined, then *basic-align* is used.

    One use of this macro is to increase alignment of medium-size data to make it all fit in fewer cache lines.

    If the value of this macro has a type, it should be an unsigned type.

HOST_WIDE_INT TARGET_VECTOR_ALIGNMENT (*const_tree* *type*)   [Target Hook]

    This hook can be used to define the alignment for a vector of type *type*, in order to comply with a platform ABI. The default is to require natural alignment for vector types. The alignment returned by this hook must be a power-of-two multiple of the default alignment of the vector element type.

STACK_SLOT_ALIGNMENT (*type*, *mode*, *basic-align*)   [Macro]

    If defined, a C expression to compute the alignment for stack slot. *type* is the data type, *mode* is the widest mode available, and *basic-align* is the alignment that the slot would ordinarily have. The value of this macro is used instead of that alignment to align the slot.

    If this macro is not defined, then *basic-align* is used when *type* is NULL. Otherwise, LOCAL_ALIGNMENT will be used.

    This macro is to set alignment of stack slot to the maximum alignment of all possible modes which the slot may have.

    If the value of this macro has a type, it should be an unsigned type.

LOCAL_DECL_ALIGNMENT (*decl*)   [Macro]

    If defined, a C expression to compute the alignment for a local variable *decl*.

    If this macro is not defined, then LOCAL_ALIGNMENT (TREE_TYPE (*decl*), DECL_ALIGN (*decl*)) is used.

    One use of this macro is to increase alignment of medium-size data to make it all fit in fewer cache lines.

    If the value of this macro has a type, it should be an unsigned type.

MINIMUM_ALIGNMENT (*exp*, *mode*, *align*) [Macro]

If defined, a C expression to compute the minimum required alignment for dynamic stack realignment purposes for *exp* (a type or decl), *mode*, assuming normal alignment *align*.

If this macro is not defined, then *align* will be used.

EMPTY_FIELD_BOUNDARY [Macro]

Alignment in bits to be given to a structure bit-field that follows an empty field such as `int : 0;`.

If `PCC_BITFIELD_TYPE_MATTERS` is true, it overrides this macro.

STRUCTURE_SIZE_BOUNDARY [Macro]

Number of bits which any structure or union's size must be a multiple of. Each structure or union's size is rounded up to a multiple of this.

If you do not define this macro, the default is the same as `BITS_PER_UNIT`.

STRICT_ALIGNMENT [Macro]

Define this macro to be the value 1 if instructions will fail to work if given data not on the nominal alignment. If instructions will merely go slower in that case, define this macro as 0.

PCC_BITFIELD_TYPE_MATTERS [Macro]

Define this if you wish to imitate the way many other C compilers handle alignment of bit-fields and the structures that contain them.

The behavior is that the type written for a named bit-field (`int`, `short`, or other integer type) imposes an alignment for the entire structure, as if the structure really did contain an ordinary field of that type. In addition, the bit-field is placed within the structure so that it would fit within such a field, not crossing a boundary for it.

Thus, on most machines, a named bit-field whose type is written as `int` would not cross a four-byte boundary, and would force four-byte alignment for the whole structure. (The alignment used may not be four bytes; it is controlled by the other alignment parameters.)

An unnamed bit-field will not affect the alignment of the containing structure.

If the macro is defined, its definition should be a C expression; a nonzero value for the expression enables this behavior.

Note that if this macro is not defined, or its value is zero, some bit-fields may cross more than one alignment boundary. The compiler can support such references if there are 'insv', 'extv', and 'extzv' insns that can directly reference memory.

The other known way of making bit-fields work is to define `STRUCTURE_SIZE_BOUNDARY` as large as `BIGGEST_ALIGNMENT`. Then every structure can be accessed with fullwords.

Unless the machine has bit-field instructions or you define `STRUCTURE_SIZE_BOUNDARY` that way, you must define `PCC_BITFIELD_TYPE_MATTERS` to have a nonzero value.

If your aim is to make GCC use the same conventions for laying out bit-fields as are used by another compiler, here is how to investigate what the other compiler does. Compile and run this program:

```
            struct foo1
            {
              char x;
              char :0;
              char y;
            };

            struct foo2
            {
              char x;
              int :0;
              char y;
            };

            main ()
            {
              printf ("Size of foo1 is %d\n",
                      sizeof (struct foo1));
              printf ("Size of foo2 is %d\n",
                      sizeof (struct foo2));
              exit (0);
            }
```

If this prints 2 and 5, then the compiler's behavior is what you would get from `PCC_BITFIELD_TYPE_MATTERS`.

BITFIELD_NBYTES_LIMITED [Macro]

Like `PCC_BITFIELD_TYPE_MATTERS` except that its effect is limited to aligning a bitfield within the structure.

bool TARGET_ALIGN_ANON_BITFIELD (*void*) [Target Hook]

When `PCC_BITFIELD_TYPE_MATTERS` is true this hook will determine whether unnamed bitfields affect the alignment of the containing structure. The hook should return true if the structure should inherit the alignment requirements of an unnamed bitfield's type.

bool TARGET_NARROW_VOLATILE_BITFIELD (*void*) [Target Hook]

This target hook should return `true` if accesses to volatile bitfields should use the narrowest mode possible. It should return `false` if these accesses should use the bitfield container type.

The default is `false`.

bool TARGET_MEMBER_TYPE_FORCES_BLK (*const_tree* `field`, [Target Hook]
    machine_mode `mode`)

Return true if a structure, union or array containing *field* should be accessed using BLKMODE.

If *field* is the only field in the structure, *mode* is its mode, otherwise *mode* is VOIDmode. *mode* is provided in the case where structures of one field would require the structure's mode to retain the field's mode.

Normally, this is not needed.

`ROUND_TYPE_ALIGN (type, computed, specified)` [Macro]
: Define this macro as an expression for the alignment of a type (given by *type* as a tree node) if the alignment computed in the usual way is *computed* and the alignment explicitly specified was *specified*.

    The default is to use *specified* if it is larger; otherwise, use the smaller of *computed* and `BIGGEST_ALIGNMENT`

`MAX_FIXED_MODE_SIZE` [Macro]
: An integer expression for the size in bits of the largest integer machine mode that should actually be used. All integer machine modes of this size or smaller can be used for structures and unions with the appropriate sizes. If this macro is undefined, `GET_MODE_BITSIZE (DImode)` is assumed.

`STACK_SAVEAREA_MODE (save_level)` [Macro]
: If defined, an expression of type `machine_mode` that specifies the mode of the save area operand of a `save_stack_level` named pattern (see Section 17.9 [Standard Names], page 382). *save_level* is one of `SAVE_BLOCK`, `SAVE_FUNCTION`, or `SAVE_NONLOCAL` and selects which of the three named patterns is having its mode specified.

    You need not define this macro if it always returns `Pmode`. You would most commonly define this macro if the `save_stack_level` patterns need to support both a 32- and a 64-bit mode.

`STACK_SIZE_MODE` [Macro]
: If defined, an expression of type `machine_mode` that specifies the mode of the size increment operand of an `allocate_stack` named pattern (see Section 17.9 [Standard Names], page 382).

    You need not define this macro if it always returns `word_mode`. You would most commonly define this macro if the `allocate_stack` pattern needs to support both a 32- and a 64-bit mode.

`scalar_int_mode TARGET_LIBGCC_CMP_RETURN_MODE (void)` [Target Hook]
: This target hook should return the mode to be used for the return value of compare instructions expanded to libgcc calls. If not defined `word_mode` is returned which is the right choice for a majority of targets.

`scalar_int_mode TARGET_LIBGCC_SHIFT_COUNT_MODE (void)` [Target Hook]
: This target hook should return the mode to be used for the shift count operand of shift instructions expanded to libgcc calls. If not defined `word_mode` is returned which is the right choice for a majority of targets.

`scalar_int_mode TARGET_UNWIND_WORD_MODE (void)` [Target Hook]
: Return machine mode to be used for `_Unwind_Word` type. The default is to use `word_mode`.

`bool TARGET_MS_BITFIELD_LAYOUT_P (const_tree record_type)` [Target Hook]
: This target hook returns `true` if bit-fields in the given *record_type* are to be laid out following the rules of Microsoft Visual C/C++, namely: (i) a bit-field won't share the same storage unit with the previous bit-field if their underlying types have different

sizes, and the bit-field will be aligned to the highest alignment of the underlying types of itself and of the previous bit-field; (ii) a zero-sized bit-field will affect the alignment of the whole enclosing structure, even if it is unnamed; except that (iii) a zero-sized bit-field will be disregarded unless it follows another bit-field of nonzero size. If this hook returns `true`, other macros that control bit-field layout are ignored.

When a bit-field is inserted into a packed record, the whole size of the underlying type is used by one or more same-size adjacent bit-fields (that is, if its long:3, 32 bits is used in the record, and any additional adjacent long bit-fields are packed into the same chunk of 32 bits. However, if the size changes, a new field of that size is allocated). In an unpacked record, this is the same as using alignment, but not equivalent when packing.

If both MS bit-fields and '`__attribute__((packed))`' are used, the latter will take precedence. If '`__attribute__((packed))`' is used on a single field when MS bit-fields are in use, it will take precedence for that field, but the alignment of the rest of the structure may affect its placement.

bool TARGET_DECIMAL_FLOAT_SUPPORTED_P (*void*) [Target Hook]
Returns true if the target supports decimal floating point.

bool TARGET_FIXED_POINT_SUPPORTED_P (*void*) [Target Hook]
Returns true if the target supports fixed-point arithmetic.

void TARGET_EXPAND_TO_RTL_HOOK (*void*) [Target Hook]
This hook is called just before expansion into rtl, allowing the target to perform additional initializations or analysis before the expansion. For example, the rs6000 port uses it to allocate a scratch stack slot for use in copying SDmode values between memory and floating point registers whenever the function being expanded has any SDmode usage.

void TARGET_INSTANTIATE_DECLS (*void*) [Target Hook]
This hook allows the backend to perform additional instantiations on rtl that are not actually in any insns yet, but will be later.

const char * TARGET_MANGLE_TYPE (*const_tree* **type**) [Target Hook]
If your target defines any fundamental types, or any types your target uses should be mangled differently from the default, define this hook to return the appropriate encoding for these types as part of a C++ mangled name. The *type* argument is the tree structure representing the type to be mangled. The hook may be applied to trees which are not target-specific fundamental types; it should return NULL for all such types, as well as arguments it does not recognize. If the return value is not NULL, it must point to a statically-allocated string constant.

Target-specific fundamental types might be new fundamental types or qualified versions of ordinary fundamental types. Encode new fundamental types as '**u** *n* **name**', where *name* is the name used for the type in source code, and *n* is the length of *name* in decimal. Encode qualified versions of ordinary types as '**U** *n* **name** *code*', where *name* is the name used for the type qualifier in source code, *n* is the length of *name* as above, and *code* is the code used to represent the unqualified version of this type.

(See `write_builtin_type` in 'cp/mangle.c' for the list of codes.) In both cases the spaces are for clarity; do not include any spaces in your string.

This hook is applied to types prior to typedef resolution. If the mangled name for a particular type depends only on that type's main variant, you can perform typedef resolution yourself using `TYPE_MAIN_VARIANT` before mangling.

The default version of this hook always returns `NULL`, which is appropriate for a target that does not define any new fundamental types.

18.6 Layout of Source Language Data Types

These macros define the sizes and other characteristics of the standard basic data types used in programs being compiled. Unlike the macros in the previous section, these apply to specific features of C and related languages, rather than to fundamental aspects of storage layout.

`INT_TYPE_SIZE` [Macro]

    A C expression for the size in bits of the type `int` on the target machine. If you don't define this, the default is one word.

`SHORT_TYPE_SIZE` [Macro]

    A C expression for the size in bits of the type `short` on the target machine. If you don't define this, the default is half a word. (If this would be less than one storage unit, it is rounded up to one unit.)

`LONG_TYPE_SIZE` [Macro]

    A C expression for the size in bits of the type `long` on the target machine. If you don't define this, the default is one word.

`ADA_LONG_TYPE_SIZE` [Macro]

    On some machines, the size used for the Ada equivalent of the type `long` by a native Ada compiler differs from that used by C. In that situation, define this macro to be a C expression to be used for the size of that type. If you don't define this, the default is the value of `LONG_TYPE_SIZE`.

`LONG_LONG_TYPE_SIZE` [Macro]

    A C expression for the size in bits of the type `long long` on the target machine. If you don't define this, the default is two words. If you want to support GNU Ada on your machine, the value of this macro must be at least 64.

`CHAR_TYPE_SIZE` [Macro]

    A C expression for the size in bits of the type `char` on the target machine. If you don't define this, the default is `BITS_PER_UNIT`.

`BOOL_TYPE_SIZE` [Macro]

    A C expression for the size in bits of the C++ type `bool` and C99 type `_Bool` on the target machine. If you don't define this, and you probably shouldn't, the default is `CHAR_TYPE_SIZE`.

`FLOAT_TYPE_SIZE` [Macro]

    A C expression for the size in bits of the type `float` on the target machine. If you don't define this, the default is one word.

`DOUBLE_TYPE_SIZE` [Macro]
: A C expression for the size in bits of the type `double` on the target machine. If you don't define this, the default is two words.

`LONG_DOUBLE_TYPE_SIZE` [Macro]
: A C expression for the size in bits of the type `long double` on the target machine. If you don't define this, the default is two words.

`SHORT_FRACT_TYPE_SIZE` [Macro]
: A C expression for the size in bits of the type `short _Fract` on the target machine. If you don't define this, the default is `BITS_PER_UNIT`.

`FRACT_TYPE_SIZE` [Macro]
: A C expression for the size in bits of the type `_Fract` on the target machine. If you don't define this, the default is `BITS_PER_UNIT * 2`.

`LONG_FRACT_TYPE_SIZE` [Macro]
: A C expression for the size in bits of the type `long _Fract` on the target machine. If you don't define this, the default is `BITS_PER_UNIT * 4`.

`LONG_LONG_FRACT_TYPE_SIZE` [Macro]
: A C expression for the size in bits of the type `long long _Fract` on the target machine. If you don't define this, the default is `BITS_PER_UNIT * 8`.

`SHORT_ACCUM_TYPE_SIZE` [Macro]
: A C expression for the size in bits of the type `short _Accum` on the target machine. If you don't define this, the default is `BITS_PER_UNIT * 2`.

`ACCUM_TYPE_SIZE` [Macro]
: A C expression for the size in bits of the type `_Accum` on the target machine. If you don't define this, the default is `BITS_PER_UNIT * 4`.

`LONG_ACCUM_TYPE_SIZE` [Macro]
: A C expression for the size in bits of the type `long _Accum` on the target machine. If you don't define this, the default is `BITS_PER_UNIT * 8`.

`LONG_LONG_ACCUM_TYPE_SIZE` [Macro]
: A C expression for the size in bits of the type `long long _Accum` on the target machine. If you don't define this, the default is `BITS_PER_UNIT * 16`.

`LIBGCC2_GNU_PREFIX` [Macro]
: This macro corresponds to the `TARGET_LIBFUNC_GNU_PREFIX` target hook and should be defined if that hook is overriden to be true. It causes function names in libgcc to be changed to use a `__gnu_` prefix for their name rather than the default `__`. A port which uses this macro should also arrange to use 't-gnu-prefix' in the libgcc 'config.host'.

`WIDEST_HARDWARE_FP_SIZE` [Macro]
: A C expression for the size in bits of the widest floating-point format supported by the hardware. If you define this macro, you must specify a value less than or equal to the value of `LONG_DOUBLE_TYPE_SIZE`. If you do not define this macro, the value of `LONG_DOUBLE_TYPE_SIZE` is the default.

DEFAULT_SIGNED_CHAR [Macro]

An expression whose value is 1 or 0, according to whether the type `char` should be signed or unsigned by default. The user can always override this default with the options '`-fsigned-char`' and '`-funsigned-char`'.

bool TARGET_DEFAULT_SHORT_ENUMS (*void*) [Target Hook]

This target hook should return true if the compiler should give an `enum` type only as many bytes as it takes to represent the range of possible values of that type. It should return false if all `enum` types should be allocated like `int`.

The default is to return false.

SIZE_TYPE [Macro]

A C expression for a string describing the name of the data type to use for size values. The typedef name `size_t` is defined using the contents of the string.

The string can contain more than one keyword. If so, separate them with spaces, and write first any length keyword, then `unsigned` if appropriate, and finally `int`. The string must exactly match one of the data type names defined in the function `c_common_nodes_and_builtins` in the file '`c-family/c-common.c`'. You may not omit `int` or change the order—that would cause the compiler to crash on startup.

If you don't define this macro, the default is `"long unsigned int"`.

SIZETYPE [Macro]

GCC defines internal types (`sizetype`, `ssizetype`, `bitsizetype` and `sbitsizetype`) for expressions dealing with size. This macro is a C expression for a string describing the name of the data type from which the precision of `sizetype` is extracted.

The string has the same restrictions as `SIZE_TYPE` string.

If you don't define this macro, the default is `SIZE_TYPE`.

PTRDIFF_TYPE [Macro]

A C expression for a string describing the name of the data type to use for the result of subtracting two pointers. The typedef name `ptrdiff_t` is defined using the contents of the string. See `SIZE_TYPE` above for more information.

If you don't define this macro, the default is `"long int"`.

WCHAR_TYPE [Macro]

A C expression for a string describing the name of the data type to use for wide characters. The typedef name `wchar_t` is defined using the contents of the string. See `SIZE_TYPE` above for more information.

If you don't define this macro, the default is `"int"`.

WCHAR_TYPE_SIZE [Macro]

A C expression for the size in bits of the data type for wide characters. This is used in `cpp`, which cannot make use of `WCHAR_TYPE`.

WINT_TYPE [Macro]

A C expression for a string describing the name of the data type to use for wide characters passed to `printf` and returned from `getwc`. The typedef name `wint_t` is defined using the contents of the string. See `SIZE_TYPE` above for more information.

If you don't define this macro, the default is `"unsigned int"`.

Chapter 18: Target Description Macros and Functions   485

INTMAX_TYPE   [Macro]

    A C expression for a string describing the name of the data type that can represent any value of any standard or extended signed integer type. The typedef name `intmax_t` is defined using the contents of the string. See `SIZE_TYPE` above for more information.

    If you don't define this macro, the default is the first of "int", "long int", or "long long int" that has as much precision as `long long int`.

UINTMAX_TYPE   [Macro]

    A C expression for a string describing the name of the data type that can represent any value of any standard or extended unsigned integer type. The typedef name `uintmax_t` is defined using the contents of the string. See `SIZE_TYPE` above for more information.

    If you don't define this macro, the default is the first of "unsigned int", "long unsigned int", or "long long unsigned int" that has as much precision as `long long unsigned int`.

SIG_ATOMIC_TYPE   [Macro]
INT8_TYPE   [Macro]
INT16_TYPE   [Macro]
INT32_TYPE   [Macro]
INT64_TYPE   [Macro]
UINT8_TYPE   [Macro]
UINT16_TYPE   [Macro]
UINT32_TYPE   [Macro]
UINT64_TYPE   [Macro]
INT_LEAST8_TYPE   [Macro]
INT_LEAST16_TYPE   [Macro]
INT_LEAST32_TYPE   [Macro]
INT_LEAST64_TYPE   [Macro]
UINT_LEAST8_TYPE   [Macro]
UINT_LEAST16_TYPE   [Macro]
UINT_LEAST32_TYPE   [Macro]
UINT_LEAST64_TYPE   [Macro]
INT_FAST8_TYPE   [Macro]
INT_FAST16_TYPE   [Macro]
INT_FAST32_TYPE   [Macro]
INT_FAST64_TYPE   [Macro]
UINT_FAST8_TYPE   [Macro]
UINT_FAST16_TYPE   [Macro]
UINT_FAST32_TYPE   [Macro]
UINT_FAST64_TYPE   [Macro]
INTPTR_TYPE   [Macro]
UINTPTR_TYPE   [Macro]

    C expressions for the standard types `sig_atomic_t`, `int8_t`, `int16_t`, `int32_t`, `int64_t`, `uint8_t`, `uint16_t`, `uint32_t`, `uint64_t`, `int_least8_t`, `int_least16_t`, `int_least32_t`, `int_least64_t`, `uint_least8_t`, `uint_least16_t`, `uint_least32_t`, `uint_least64_t`, `int_fast8_t`, `int_fast16_t`, `int_fast32_t`, `int_fast64_t`, uint_fast8_t, uint_fast16_t, uint_fast32_t, uint_fast64_t, intptr_t, and uintptr_t. See SIZE_TYPE above for more information.

If any of these macros evaluates to a null pointer, the corresponding type is not supported; if GCC is configured to provide <stdint.h> in such a case, the header provided may not conform to C99, depending on the type in question. The defaults for all of these macros are null pointers.

TARGET_PTRMEMFUNC_VBIT_LOCATION [Macro]

The C++ compiler represents a pointer-to-member-function with a struct that looks like:

```
struct {
  union {
    void (*fn)();
    ptrdiff_t vtable_index;
  };
  ptrdiff_t delta;
};
```

The C++ compiler must use one bit to indicate whether the function that will be called through a pointer-to-member-function is virtual. Normally, we assume that the low-order bit of a function pointer must always be zero. Then, by ensuring that the vtable_index is odd, we can distinguish which variant of the union is in use. But, on some platforms function pointers can be odd, and so this doesn't work. In that case, we use the low-order bit of the `delta` field, and shift the remainder of the `delta` field to the left.

GCC will automatically make the right selection about where to store this bit using the `FUNCTION_BOUNDARY` setting for your platform. However, some platforms such as ARM/Thumb have `FUNCTION_BOUNDARY` set such that functions always start at even addresses, but the lowest bit of pointers to functions indicate whether the function at that address is in ARM or Thumb mode. If this is the case of your architecture, you should define this macro to `ptrmemfunc_vbit_in_delta`.

In general, you should not have to define this macro. On architectures in which function addresses are always even, according to `FUNCTION_BOUNDARY`, GCC will automatically define this macro to `ptrmemfunc_vbit_in_pfn`.

TARGET_VTABLE_USES_DESCRIPTORS [Macro]

Normally, the C++ compiler uses function pointers in vtables. This macro allows the target to change to use "function descriptors" instead. Function descriptors are found on targets for whom a function pointer is actually a small data structure. Normally the data structure consists of the actual code address plus a data pointer to which the function's data is relative.

If vtables are used, the value of this macro should be the number of words that the function descriptor occupies.

TARGET_VTABLE_ENTRY_ALIGN [Macro]

By default, the vtable entries are void pointers, the so the alignment is the same as pointer alignment. The value of this macro specifies the alignment of the vtable entry in bits. It should be defined only when special alignment is necessary. */

`TARGET_VTABLE_DATA_ENTRY_DISTANCE` [Macro]

There are a few non-descriptor entries in the vtable at offsets below zero. If these entries must be padded (say, to preserve the alignment specified by `TARGET_VTABLE_ENTRY_ALIGN`), set this to the number of words in each data entry.

18.7 Register Usage

This section explains how to describe what registers the target machine has, and how (in general) they can be used.

The description of which registers a specific instruction can use is done with register classes; see Section 18.8 [Register Classes], page 493. For information on using registers to access a stack frame, see Section 18.9.4 [Frame Registers], page 512. For passing values in registers, see Section 18.9.7 [Register Arguments], page 518. For returning values in registers, see Section 18.9.8 [Scalar Return], page 525.

18.7.1 Basic Characteristics of Registers

Registers have various characteristics.

`FIRST_PSEUDO_REGISTER` [Macro]

Number of hardware registers known to the compiler. They receive numbers 0 through `FIRST_PSEUDO_REGISTER-1`; thus, the first pseudo register's number really is assigned the number `FIRST_PSEUDO_REGISTER`.

`FIXED_REGISTERS` [Macro]

An initializer that says which registers are used for fixed purposes all throughout the compiled code and are therefore not available for general allocation. These would include the stack pointer, the frame pointer (except on machines where that can be used as a general register when no frame pointer is needed), the program counter on machines where that is considered one of the addressable registers, and any other numbered register with a standard use.

This information is expressed as a sequence of numbers, separated by commas and surrounded by braces. The nth number is 1 if register n is fixed, 0 otherwise.

The table initialized from this macro, and the table initialized by the following one, may be overridden at run time either automatically, by the actions of the macro `CONDITIONAL_REGISTER_USAGE`, or by the user with the command options '-ffixed-*reg*', '-fcall-used-*reg*' and '-fcall-saved-*reg*'.

`CALL_USED_REGISTERS` [Macro]

Like `FIXED_REGISTERS` but has 1 for each register that is clobbered (in general) by function calls as well as for fixed registers. This macro therefore identifies the registers that are not available for general allocation of values that must live across function calls.

If a register has 0 in `CALL_USED_REGISTERS`, the compiler automatically saves it on function entry and restores it on function exit, if the register is used within the function.

CALL_REALLY_USED_REGISTERS [Macro]
    Like CALL_USED_REGISTERS except this macro doesn't require that the entire set of FIXED_REGISTERS be included. (CALL_USED_REGISTERS must be a superset of FIXED_REGISTERS). This macro is optional. If not specified, it defaults to the value of CALL_USED_REGISTERS.

bool TARGET_HARD_REGNO_CALL_PART_CLOBBERED (*unsigned int regno*, *machine_mode* mode) [Target Hook]
    This hook should return true if *regno* is partly call-saved and partly call-clobbered, and if a value of mode *mode* would be partly clobbered by a call. For example, if the low 32 bits of *regno* are preserved across a call but higher bits are clobbered, this hook should return true for a 64-bit mode but false for a 32-bit mode.

    The default implementation returns false, which is correct for targets that don't have partly call-clobbered registers.

void TARGET_CONDITIONAL_REGISTER_USAGE (*void*) [Target Hook]
    This hook may conditionally modify five variables fixed_regs, call_used_regs, global_regs, reg_names, and reg_class_contents, to take into account any dependence of these register sets on target flags. The first three of these are of type char [] (interpreted as boolean vectors). global_regs is a const char *[], and reg_class_contents is a HARD_REG_SET. Before the macro is called, fixed_regs, call_used_regs, reg_class_contents, and reg_names have been initialized from FIXED_REGISTERS, CALL_USED_REGISTERS, REG_CLASS_CONTENTS, and REGISTER_NAMES, respectively. global_regs has been cleared, and any '-ffixed-*reg*', '-fcall-used-*reg*' and '-fcall-saved-*reg*' command options have been applied.

    If the usage of an entire class of registers depends on the target flags, you may indicate this to GCC by using this macro to modify fixed_regs and call_used_regs to 1 for each of the registers in the classes which should not be used by GCC. Also make define_register_constraints return NO_REGS for constraints that shouldn't be used.

    (However, if this class is not included in GENERAL_REGS and all of the insn patterns whose constraints permit this class are controlled by target switches, then GCC will automatically avoid using these registers when the target switches are opposed to them.)

INCOMING_REGNO (*out*) [Macro]
    Define this macro if the target machine has register windows. This C expression returns the register number as seen by the called function corresponding to the register number *out* as seen by the calling function. Return *out* if register number *out* is not an outbound register.

OUTGOING_REGNO (*in*) [Macro]
    Define this macro if the target machine has register windows. This C expression returns the register number as seen by the calling function corresponding to the register number *in* as seen by the called function. Return *in* if register number *in* is not an inbound register.

LOCAL_REGNO (*regno*)   [Macro]

> Define this macro if the target machine has register windows. This C expression returns true if the register is call-saved but is in the register window. Unlike most call-saved registers, such registers need not be explicitly restored on function exit or during non-local gotos.

PC_REGNUM   [Macro]

> If the program counter has a register number, define this as that register number. Otherwise, do not define it.

18.7.2 Order of Allocation of Registers

Registers are allocated in order.

REG_ALLOC_ORDER   [Macro]

> If defined, an initializer for a vector of integers, containing the numbers of hard registers in the order in which GCC should prefer to use them (from most preferred to least).
>
> If this macro is not defined, registers are used lowest numbered first (all else being equal).
>
> One use of this macro is on machines where the highest numbered registers must always be saved and the save-multiple-registers instruction supports only sequences of consecutive registers. On such machines, define REG_ALLOC_ORDER to be an initializer that lists the highest numbered allocable register first.

ADJUST_REG_ALLOC_ORDER   [Macro]

> A C statement (sans semicolon) to choose the order in which to allocate hard registers for pseudo-registers local to a basic block.
>
> Store the desired register order in the array `reg_alloc_order`. Element 0 should be the register to allocate first; element 1, the next register; and so on.
>
> The macro body should not assume anything about the contents of `reg_alloc_order` before execution of the macro.
>
> On most machines, it is not necessary to define this macro.

HONOR_REG_ALLOC_ORDER   [Macro]

> Normally, IRA tries to estimate the costs for saving a register in the prologue and restoring it in the epilogue. This discourages it from using call-saved registers. If a machine wants to ensure that IRA allocates registers in the order given by REG_ALLOC_ORDER even if some call-saved registers appear earlier than call-used ones, then define this macro as a C expression to nonzero. Default is 0.

IRA_HARD_REGNO_ADD_COST_MULTIPLIER (*regno*)   [Macro]

> In some case register allocation order is not enough for the Integrated Register Allocator (IRA) to generate a good code. If this macro is defined, it should return a floating point value based on *regno*. The cost of using *regno* for a pseudo will be increased by approximately the pseudo's usage frequency times the value returned by this macro. Not defining this macro is equivalent to having it always return 0.0.
>
> On most machines, it is not necessary to define this macro.

18.7.3 How Values Fit in Registers

This section discusses the macros that describe which kinds of values (specifically, which machine modes) each register can hold, and how many consecutive registers are needed for a given mode.

unsigned int TARGET_HARD_REGNO_NREGS (*unsigned int* **regno**, *machine_mode* **mode**) [Target Hook]

    This hook returns the number of consecutive hard registers, starting at register number *regno*, required to hold a value of mode *mode*. This hook must never return zero, even if a register cannot hold the requested mode - indicate that with TARGET_HARD_REGNO_MODE_OK and/or TARGET_CAN_CHANGE_MODE_CLASS instead.

    The default definition returns the number of words in *mode*.

HARD_REGNO_NREGS_HAS_PADDING (*regno*, *mode*) [Macro]

    A C expression that is nonzero if a value of mode *mode*, stored in memory, ends with padding that causes it to take up more space than in registers starting at register number *regno* (as determined by multiplying GCC's notion of the size of the register when containing this mode by the number of registers returned by TARGET_HARD_REGNO_NREGS). By default this is zero.

    For example, if a floating-point value is stored in three 32-bit registers but takes up 128 bits in memory, then this would be nonzero.

    This macros only needs to be defined if there are cases where subreg_get_info would otherwise wrongly determine that a subreg can be represented by an offset to the register number, when in fact such a subreg would contain some of the padding not stored in registers and so not be representable.

HARD_REGNO_NREGS_WITH_PADDING (*regno*, *mode*) [Macro]

    For values of *regno* and *mode* for which HARD_REGNO_NREGS_HAS_PADDING returns nonzero, a C expression returning the greater number of registers required to hold the value including any padding. In the example above, the value would be four.

REGMODE_NATURAL_SIZE (*mode*) [Macro]

    Define this macro if the natural size of registers that hold values of mode *mode* is not the word size. It is a C expression that should give the natural size in bytes for the specified mode. It is used by the register allocator to try to optimize its results. This happens for example on SPARC 64-bit where the natural size of floating-point registers is still 32-bit.

bool TARGET_HARD_REGNO_MODE_OK (*unsigned int* **regno**, *machine_mode* **mode**) [Target Hook]

    This hook returns true if it is permissible to store a value of mode *mode* in hard register number *regno* (or in several registers starting with that one). The default definition returns true unconditionally.

    You need not include code to check for the numbers of fixed registers, because the allocation mechanism considers them to be always occupied.

    On some machines, double-precision values must be kept in even/odd register pairs. You can implement that by defining this hook to reject odd register numbers for such modes.

The minimum requirement for a mode to be OK in a register is that the 'mov*mode*' instruction pattern support moves between the register and other hard register in the same class and that moving a value into the register and back out not alter it.

Since the same instruction used to move word_mode will work for all narrower integer modes, it is not necessary on any machine for this hook to distinguish between these modes, provided you define patterns 'movhi', etc., to take advantage of this. This is useful because of the interaction between TARGET_HARD_REGNO_MODE_OK and TARGET_MODES_TIEABLE_P; it is very desirable for all integer modes to be tieable.

Many machines have special registers for floating point arithmetic. Often people assume that floating point machine modes are allowed only in floating point registers. This is not true. Any registers that can hold integers can safely *hold* a floating point machine mode, whether or not floating arithmetic can be done on it in those registers. Integer move instructions can be used to move the values.

On some machines, though, the converse is true: fixed-point machine modes may not go in floating registers. This is true if the floating registers normalize any value stored in them, because storing a non-floating value there would garble it. In this case, TARGET_HARD_REGNO_MODE_OK should reject fixed-point machine modes in floating registers. But if the floating registers do not automatically normalize, if you can store any bit pattern in one and retrieve it unchanged without a trap, then any machine mode may go in a floating register, so you can define this hook to say so.

The primary significance of special floating registers is rather that they are the registers acceptable in floating point arithmetic instructions. However, this is of no concern to TARGET_HARD_REGNO_MODE_OK. You handle it by writing the proper constraints for those instructions.

On some machines, the floating registers are especially slow to access, so that it is better to store a value in a stack frame than in such a register if floating point arithmetic is not being done. As long as the floating registers are not in class GENERAL_REGS, they will not be used unless some pattern's constraint asks for one.

HARD_REGNO_RENAME_OK (*from, to*) [Macro]

A C expression that is nonzero if it is OK to rename a hard register *from* to another hard register *to*.

One common use of this macro is to prevent renaming of a register to another register that is not saved by a prologue in an interrupt handler.

The default is always nonzero.

bool TARGET_MODES_TIEABLE_P (*machine_mode mode1,* [Target Hook]
     machine_mode mode2)

This hook returns true if a value of mode *mode1* is accessible in mode *mode2* without copying.

If TARGET_HARD_REGNO_MODE_OK (*r, mode1*) and TARGET_HARD_REGNO_MODE_OK (*r, mode2*) are always the same for any *r*, then TARGET_MODES_TIEABLE_P (*mode1, mode2*) should be true. If they differ for any *r*, you should define this hook to return false unless some other mechanism ensures the accessibility of the value in a narrower mode.

You should define this hook to return true in as many cases as possible since doing so will allow GCC to perform better register allocation. The default definition returns true unconditionally.

bool TARGET_HARD_REGNO_SCRATCH_OK (*unsigned int regno*)   [Target Hook]

This target hook should return `true` if it is OK to use a hard register *regno* as scratch reg in peephole2.

One common use of this macro is to prevent using of a register that is not saved by a prologue in an interrupt handler.

The default version of this hook always returns `true`.

AVOID_CCMODE_COPIES   [Macro]

Define this macro if the compiler should avoid copies to/from `CCmode` registers. You should only define this macro if support for copying to/from `CCmode` is incomplete.

18.7.4 Handling Leaf Functions

On some machines, a leaf function (i.e., one which makes no calls) can run more efficiently if it does not make its own register window. Often this means it is required to receive its arguments in the registers where they are passed by the caller, instead of the registers where they would normally arrive.

The special treatment for leaf functions generally applies only when other conditions are met; for example, often they may use only those registers for its own variables and temporaries. We use the term "leaf function" to mean a function that is suitable for this special handling, so that functions with no calls are not necessarily "leaf functions".

GCC assigns register numbers before it knows whether the function is suitable for leaf function treatment. So it needs to renumber the registers in order to output a leaf function. The following macros accomplish this.

LEAF_REGISTERS   [Macro]

Name of a char vector, indexed by hard register number, which contains 1 for a register that is allowable in a candidate for leaf function treatment.

If leaf function treatment involves renumbering the registers, then the registers marked here should be the ones before renumbering—those that GCC would ordinarily allocate. The registers which will actually be used in the assembler code, after renumbering, should not be marked with 1 in this vector.

Define this macro only if the target machine offers a way to optimize the treatment of leaf functions.

LEAF_REG_REMAP (*regno*)   [Macro]

A C expression whose value is the register number to which *regno* should be renumbered, when a function is treated as a leaf function.

If *regno* is a register number which should not appear in a leaf function before renumbering, then the expression should yield -1, which will cause the compiler to abort.

Define this macro only if the target machine offers a way to optimize the treatment of leaf functions, and registers need to be renumbered to do this.

Chapter 18: Target Description Macros and Functions 493

`TARGET_ASM_FUNCTION_PROLOGUE` and `TARGET_ASM_FUNCTION_EPILOGUE` must usually treat leaf functions specially. They can test the C variable `current_function_is_leaf` which is nonzero for leaf functions. `current_function_is_leaf` is set prior to local register allocation and is valid for the remaining compiler passes. They can also test the C variable `current_function_uses_only_leaf_regs` which is nonzero for leaf functions which only use leaf registers. `current_function_uses_only_leaf_regs` is valid after all passes that modify the instructions have been run and is only useful if `LEAF_REGISTERS` is defined.

18.7.5 Registers That Form a Stack

There are special features to handle computers where some of the "registers" form a stack. Stack registers are normally written by pushing onto the stack, and are numbered relative to the top of the stack.

Currently, GCC can only handle one group of stack-like registers, and they must be consecutively numbered. Furthermore, the existing support for stack-like registers is specific to the 80387 floating point coprocessor. If you have a new architecture that uses stack-like registers, you will need to do substantial work on 'reg-stack.c' and write your machine description to cooperate with it, as well as defining these macros.

`STACK_REGS` [Macro]
    Define this if the machine has any stack-like registers.

`STACK_REG_COVER_CLASS` [Macro]
    This is a cover class containing the stack registers. Define this if the machine has any stack-like registers.

`FIRST_STACK_REG` [Macro]
    The number of the first stack-like register. This one is the top of the stack.

`LAST_STACK_REG` [Macro]
    The number of the last stack-like register. This one is the bottom of the stack.

18.8 Register Classes

On many machines, the numbered registers are not all equivalent. For example, certain registers may not be allowed for indexed addressing; certain registers may not be allowed in some instructions. These machine restrictions are described to the compiler using *register classes*.

You define a number of register classes, giving each one a name and saying which of the registers belong to it. Then you can specify register classes that are allowed as operands to particular instruction patterns.

In general, each register will belong to several classes. In fact, one class must be named `ALL_REGS` and contain all the registers. Another class must be named `NO_REGS` and contain no registers. Often the union of two classes will be another class; however, this is not required.

One of the classes must be named `GENERAL_REGS`. There is nothing terribly special about the name, but the operand constraint letters 'r' and 'g' specify this class. If `GENERAL_REGS` is the same as `ALL_REGS`, just define it as a macro which expands to `ALL_REGS`.

Order the classes so that if class *x* is contained in class *y* then *x* has a lower class number than *y*.

The way classes other than `GENERAL_REGS` are specified in operand constraints is through machine-dependent operand constraint letters. You can define such letters to correspond to various classes, then use them in operand constraints.

You must define the narrowest register classes for allocatable registers, so that each class either has no subclasses, or that for some mode, the move cost between registers within the class is cheaper than moving a register in the class to or from memory (see Section 18.16 [Costs], page 556).

You should define a class for the union of two classes whenever some instruction allows both classes. For example, if an instruction allows either a floating point (coprocessor) register or a general register for a certain operand, you should define a class `FLOAT_OR_GENERAL_REGS` which includes both of them. Otherwise you will get suboptimal code, or even internal compiler errors when reload cannot find a register in the class computed via `reg_class_subunion`.

You must also specify certain redundant information about the register classes: for each class, which classes contain it and which ones are contained in it; for each pair of classes, the largest class contained in their union.

When a value occupying several consecutive registers is expected in a certain class, all the registers used must belong to that class. Therefore, register classes cannot be used to enforce a requirement for a register pair to start with an even-numbered register. The way to specify this requirement is with `TARGET_HARD_REGNO_MODE_OK`.

Register classes used for input-operands of bitwise-and or shift instructions have a special requirement: each such class must have, for each fixed-point machine mode, a subclass whose registers can transfer that mode to or from memory. For example, on some machines, the operations for single-byte values (`QImode`) are limited to certain registers. When this is so, each register class that is used in a bitwise-and or shift instruction must have a subclass consisting of registers from which single-byte values can be loaded or stored. This is so that `PREFERRED_RELOAD_CLASS` can always have a possible value to return.

`enum reg_class` [Data type]
> An enumerated type that must be defined with all the register class names as enumerated values. `NO_REGS` must be first. `ALL_REGS` must be the last register class, followed by one more enumerated value, `LIM_REG_CLASSES`, which is not a register class but rather tells how many classes there are.
>
> Each register class has a number, which is the value of casting the class name to type `int`. The number serves as an index in many of the tables described below.

`N_REG_CLASSES` [Macro]
> The number of distinct register classes, defined as follows:
> ```
> #define N_REG_CLASSES (int) LIM_REG_CLASSES
> ```

`REG_CLASS_NAMES` [Macro]
> An initializer containing the names of the register classes as C string constants. These names are used in writing some of the debugging dumps.

Chapter 18: Target Description Macros and Functions   495

`REG_CLASS_CONTENTS`   [Macro]

　　An initializer containing the contents of the register classes, as integers which are bit masks. The nth integer specifies the contents of class n. The way the integer *mask* is interpreted is that register r is in the class if `mask & (1 << r)` is 1.

　　When the machine has more than 32 registers, an integer does not suffice. Then the integers are replaced by sub-initializers, braced groupings containing several integers. Each sub-initializer must be suitable as an initializer for the type `HARD_REG_SET` which is defined in 'hard-reg-set.h'. In this situation, the first integer in each sub-initializer corresponds to registers 0 through 31, the second integer to registers 32 through 63, and so on.

`REGNO_REG_CLASS (regno)`   [Macro]

　　A C expression whose value is a register class containing hard register *regno*. In general there is more than one such class; choose a class which is *minimal*, meaning that no smaller class also contains the register.

`BASE_REG_CLASS`   [Macro]

　　A macro whose definition is the name of the class to which a valid base register must belong. A base register is one used in an address which is the register value plus a displacement.

`MODE_BASE_REG_CLASS (mode)`   [Macro]

　　This is a variation of the `BASE_REG_CLASS` macro which allows the selection of a base register in a mode dependent manner. If *mode* is VOIDmode then it should return the same value as `BASE_REG_CLASS`.

`MODE_BASE_REG_REG_CLASS (mode)`   [Macro]

　　A C expression whose value is the register class to which a valid base register must belong in order to be used in a base plus index register address. You should define this macro if base plus index addresses have different requirements than other base register uses.

`MODE_CODE_BASE_REG_CLASS (mode, address_space, outer_code,`   [Macro]
　　　　`index_code)`

　　A C expression whose value is the register class to which a valid base register for a memory reference in mode *mode* to address space *address_space* must belong. *outer_code* and *index_code* define the context in which the base register occurs. *outer_code* is the code of the immediately enclosing expression (MEM for the top level of an address, ADDRESS for something that occurs in an address_operand). *index_code* is the code of the corresponding index expression if *outer_code* is PLUS; SCRATCH otherwise.

`INDEX_REG_CLASS`   [Macro]

　　A macro whose definition is the name of the class to which a valid index register must belong. An index register is one used in an address where its value is either multiplied by a scale factor or added to another register (as well as added to a displacement).

`REGNO_OK_FOR_BASE_P (num)`   [Macro]

　　A C expression which is nonzero if register number *num* is suitable for use as a base register in operand addresses.

REGNO_MODE_OK_FOR_BASE_P (*num*, *mode*) [Macro]

A C expression that is just like REGNO_OK_FOR_BASE_P, except that that expression may examine the mode of the memory reference in *mode*. You should define this macro if the mode of the memory reference affects whether a register may be used as a base register. If you define this macro, the compiler will use it instead of REGNO_OK_FOR_BASE_P. The mode may be VOIDmode for addresses that appear outside a MEM, i.e., as an address_operand.

REGNO_MODE_OK_FOR_REG_BASE_P (*num*, *mode*) [Macro]

A C expression which is nonzero if register number *num* is suitable for use as a base register in base plus index operand addresses, accessing memory in mode *mode*. It may be either a suitable hard register or a pseudo register that has been allocated such a hard register. You should define this macro if base plus index addresses have different requirements than other base register uses.

Use of this macro is deprecated; please use the more general REGNO_MODE_CODE_OK_FOR_BASE_P.

REGNO_MODE_CODE_OK_FOR_BASE_P (*num*, *mode*, *address_space*, [Macro]
    outer_code, *index_code*)

A C expression which is nonzero if register number *num* is suitable for use as a base register in operand addresses, accessing memory in mode *mode* in address space *address_space*. This is similar to REGNO_MODE_OK_FOR_BASE_P, except that that expression may examine the context in which the register appears in the memory reference. *outer_code* is the code of the immediately enclosing expression (MEM if at the top level of the address, ADDRESS for something that occurs in an address_operand). *index_code* is the code of the corresponding index expression if *outer_code* is PLUS; SCRATCH otherwise. The mode may be VOIDmode for addresses that appear outside a MEM, i.e., as an address_operand.

REGNO_OK_FOR_INDEX_P (*num*) [Macro]

A C expression which is nonzero if register number *num* is suitable for use as an index register in operand addresses. It may be either a suitable hard register or a pseudo register that has been allocated such a hard register.

The difference between an index register and a base register is that the index register may be scaled. If an address involves the sum of two registers, neither one of them scaled, then either one may be labeled the "base" and the other the "index"; but whichever labeling is used must fit the machine's constraints of which registers may serve in each capacity. The compiler will try both labelings, looking for one that is valid, and will reload one or both registers only if neither labeling works.

reg_class_t TARGET_PREFERRED_RENAME_CLASS (*reg_class_t* [Target Hook]
    rclass)

A target hook that places additional preference on the register class to use when it is necessary to rename a register in class *rclass* to another class, or perhaps *NO_REGS*, if no preferred register class is found or hook preferred_rename_class is not implemented. Sometimes returning a more restrictive class makes better code. For example, on ARM, thumb-2 instructions using LO_REGS may be smaller than instruc-

Chapter 18: Target Description Macros and Functions 497

tions using `GENERIC_REGS`. By returning `LO_REGS` from `preferred_rename_class`, code size can be reduced.

`reg_class_t` **TARGET_PREFERRED_RELOAD_CLASS** (*rtx x*, *reg_class_t* [Target Hook]
    rclass)

> A target hook that places additional restrictions on the register class to use when it is necessary to copy value *x* into a register in class *rclass*. The value is a register class; perhaps *rclass*, or perhaps another, smaller class.
>
> The default version of this hook always returns value of `rclass` argument.
>
> Sometimes returning a more restrictive class makes better code. For example, on the 68000, when *x* is an integer constant that is in range for a 'moveq' instruction, the value of this macro is always `DATA_REGS` as long as *rclass* includes the data registers. Requiring a data register guarantees that a 'moveq' will be used.
>
> One case where `TARGET_PREFERRED_RELOAD_CLASS` must not return *rclass* is if *x* is a legitimate constant which cannot be loaded into some register class. By returning `NO_REGS` you can force *x* into a memory location. For example, rs6000 can load immediate values into general-purpose registers, but does not have an instruction for loading an immediate value into a floating-point register, so `TARGET_PREFERRED_RELOAD_CLASS` returns `NO_REGS` when *x* is a floating-point constant. If the constant can't be loaded into any kind of register, code generation will be better if `TARGET_LEGITIMATE_CONSTANT_P` makes the constant illegitimate instead of using `TARGET_PREFERRED_RELOAD_CLASS`.
>
> If an insn has pseudos in it after register allocation, reload will go through the alternatives and call repeatedly `TARGET_PREFERRED_RELOAD_CLASS` to find the best one. Returning `NO_REGS`, in this case, makes reload add a ! in front of the constraint: the x86 back-end uses this feature to discourage usage of 387 registers when math is done in the SSE registers (and vice versa).

PREFERRED_RELOAD_CLASS (*x*, *class*) [Macro]

> A C expression that places additional restrictions on the register class to use when it is necessary to copy value *x* into a register in class *class*. The value is a register class; perhaps *class*, or perhaps another, smaller class. On many machines, the following definition is safe:
>
>   #define PREFERRED_RELOAD_CLASS(X,CLASS) CLASS
>
> Sometimes returning a more restrictive class makes better code. For example, on the 68000, when *x* is an integer constant that is in range for a 'moveq' instruction, the value of this macro is always `DATA_REGS` as long as *class* includes the data registers. Requiring a data register guarantees that a 'moveq' will be used.
>
> One case where `PREFERRED_RELOAD_CLASS` must not return *class* is if *x* is a legitimate constant which cannot be loaded into some register class. By returning `NO_REGS` you can force *x* into a memory location. For example, rs6000 can load immediate values into general-purpose registers, but does not have an instruction for loading an immediate value into a floating-point register, so `PREFERRED_RELOAD_CLASS` returns `NO_REGS` when *x* is a floating-point constant. If the constant cannot be loaded into any kind of register, code generation will be better if `TARGET_LEGITIMATE_CONSTANT_P` makes the constant illegitimate instead of using `TARGET_PREFERRED_RELOAD_CLASS`.

If an insn has pseudos in it after register allocation, reload will go through the alternatives and call repeatedly `PREFERRED_RELOAD_CLASS` to find the best one. Returning `NO_REGS`, in this case, makes reload add a ! in front of the constraint: the x86 backend uses this feature to discourage usage of 387 registers when math is done in the SSE registers (and vice versa).

`reg_class_t` TARGET_PREFERRED_OUTPUT_RELOAD_CLASS (*rtx x,*   [Target Hook]
    reg_class_t `rclass`)

Like `TARGET_PREFERRED_RELOAD_CLASS`, but for output reloads instead of input reloads.

The default version of this hook always returns value of `rclass` argument.

You can also use `TARGET_PREFERRED_OUTPUT_RELOAD_CLASS` to discourage reload from using some alternatives, like `TARGET_PREFERRED_RELOAD_CLASS`.

LIMIT_RELOAD_CLASS (*mode, class*)   [Macro]

A C expression that places additional restrictions on the register class to use when it is necessary to be able to hold a value of mode *mode* in a reload register for which class *class* would ordinarily be used.

Unlike `PREFERRED_RELOAD_CLASS`, this macro should be used when there are certain modes that simply cannot go in certain reload classes.

The value is a register class; perhaps *class*, or perhaps another, smaller class.

Don't define this macro unless the target machine has limitations which require the macro to do something nontrivial.

`reg_class_t` TARGET_SECONDARY_RELOAD (*bool* `in_p`, *rtx x,*   [Target Hook]
    reg_class_t `reload_class`, *machine_mode* `reload_mode`,
    secondary_reload_info *`sri`)

Many machines have some registers that cannot be copied directly to or from memory or even from other types of registers. An example is the 'MQ' register, which on most machines, can only be copied to or from general registers, but not memory. Below, we shall be using the term 'intermediate register' when a move operation cannot be performed directly, but has to be done by copying the source into the intermediate register first, and then copying the intermediate register to the destination. An intermediate register always has the same mode as source and destination. Since it holds the actual value being copied, reload might apply optimizations to re-use an intermediate register and eliding the copy from the source when it can determine that the intermediate register still holds the required value.

Another kind of secondary reload is required on some machines which allow copying all registers to and from memory, but require a scratch register for stores to some memory locations (e.g., those with symbolic address on the RT, and those with certain symbolic address on the SPARC when compiling PIC). Scratch registers need not have the same mode as the value being copied, and usually hold a different value than that being copied. Special patterns in the md file are needed to describe how the copy is performed with the help of the scratch register; these patterns also describe the number, register class(es) and mode(s) of the scratch register(s).

In some cases, both an intermediate and a scratch register are required.

For input reloads, this target hook is called with nonzero *in_p*, and *x* is an rtx that needs to be copied to a register of class *reload_class* in *reload_mode*. For output reloads, this target hook is called with zero *in_p*, and a register of class *reload_class* needs to be copied to rtx *x* in *reload_mode*.

If copying a register of *reload_class* from/to *x* requires an intermediate register, the hook `secondary_reload` should return the register class required for this intermediate register. If no intermediate register is required, it should return NO_REGS. If more than one intermediate register is required, describe the one that is closest in the copy chain to the reload register.

If scratch registers are needed, you also have to describe how to perform the copy from/to the reload register to/from this closest intermediate register. Or if no intermediate register is required, but still a scratch register is needed, describe the copy from/to the reload register to/from the reload operand *x*.

You do this by setting `sri->icode` to the instruction code of a pattern in the md file which performs the move. Operands 0 and 1 are the output and input of this copy, respectively. Operands from operand 2 onward are for scratch operands. These scratch operands must have a mode, and a single-register-class output constraint.

When an intermediate register is used, the `secondary_reload` hook will be called again to determine how to copy the intermediate register to/from the reload operand *x*, so your hook must also have code to handle the register class of the intermediate operand.

x might be a pseudo-register or a `subreg` of a pseudo-register, which could either be in a hard register or in memory. Use `true_regnum` to find out; it will return −1 if the pseudo is in memory and the hard register number if it is in a register.

Scratch operands in memory (constraint "=m" / "=&m") are currently not supported. For the time being, you will have to continue to use `TARGET_SECONDARY_MEMORY_NEEDED` for that purpose.

`copy_cost` also uses this target hook to find out how values are copied. If you want it to include some extra cost for the need to allocate (a) scratch register(s), set `sri->extra_cost` to the additional cost. Or if two dependent moves are supposed to have a lower cost than the sum of the individual moves due to expected fortuitous scheduling and/or special forwarding logic, you can set `sri->extra_cost` to a negative amount.

SECONDARY_RELOAD_CLASS (*class*, *mode*, *x*) [Macro]
SECONDARY_INPUT_RELOAD_CLASS (*class*, *mode*, *x*) [Macro]
SECONDARY_OUTPUT_RELOAD_CLASS (*class*, *mode*, *x*) [Macro]

These macros are obsolete, new ports should use the target hook `TARGET_SECONDARY_RELOAD` instead.

These are obsolete macros, replaced by the `TARGET_SECONDARY_RELOAD` target hook. Older ports still define these macros to indicate to the reload phase that it may need to allocate at least one register for a reload in addition to the register to contain the data. Specifically, if copying *x* to a register *class* in *mode* requires an intermediate register, you were supposed to define `SECONDARY_INPUT_RELOAD_CLASS` to return the largest register class all of whose registers can be used as intermediate registers or scratch registers.

If copying a register *class* in *mode* to *x* requires an intermediate or scratch register, `SECONDARY_OUTPUT_RELOAD_CLASS` was supposed to be defined be defined to return the largest register class required. If the requirements for input and output reloads were the same, the macro `SECONDARY_RELOAD_CLASS` should have been used instead of defining both macros identically.

The values returned by these macros are often `GENERAL_REGS`. Return `NO_REGS` if no spare register is needed; i.e., if *x* can be directly copied to or from a register of *class* in *mode* without requiring a scratch register. Do not define this macro if it would always return `NO_REGS`.

If a scratch register is required (either with or without an intermediate register), you were supposed to define patterns for 'reload_in*m*' or 'reload_out*m*', as required (see Section 17.9 [Standard Names], page 382. These patterns, which were normally implemented with a `define_expand`, should be similar to the 'mov*m*' patterns, except that operand 2 is the scratch register.

These patterns need constraints for the reload register and scratch register that contain a single register class. If the original reload register (whose class is *class*) can meet the constraint given in the pattern, the value returned by these macros is used for the class of the scratch register. Otherwise, two additional reload registers are required. Their classes are obtained from the constraints in the insn pattern.

x might be a pseudo-register or a `subreg` of a pseudo-register, which could either be in a hard register or in memory. Use `true_regnum` to find out; it will return −1 if the pseudo is in memory and the hard register number if it is in a register.

These macros should not be used in the case where a particular class of registers can only be copied to memory and not to another class of registers. In that case, secondary reload registers are not needed and would not be helpful. Instead, a stack location must be used to perform the copy and the mov*m* pattern should use memory as an intermediate storage. This case often occurs between floating-point and general registers.

`bool` **TARGET_SECONDARY_MEMORY_NEEDED** (*machine_mode* `mode`, [Target Hook]
     reg_class_t `class1`, *reg_class_t* `class2`)

Certain machines have the property that some registers cannot be copied to some other registers without using memory. Define this hook on those machines to return true if objects of mode *m* in registers of *class1* can only be copied to registers of class *class2* by storing a register of *class1* into memory and loading that memory location into a register of *class2*. The default definition returns false for all inputs.

SECONDARY_MEMORY_NEEDED_RTX (*mode*) [Macro]

Normally when `TARGET_SECONDARY_MEMORY_NEEDED` is defined, the compiler allocates a stack slot for a memory location needed for register copies. If this macro is defined, the compiler instead uses the memory location defined by this macro.

Do not define this macro if you do not define `TARGET_SECONDARY_MEMORY_NEEDED`.

machine_mode TARGET_SECONDARY_MEMORY_NEEDED_MODE [Target Hook]
(*machine_mode mode*)

If `TARGET_SECONDARY_MEMORY_NEEDED` tells the compiler to use memory when moving between two particular registers of mode *mode*, this hook specifies the mode that the memory should have.

The default depends on `TARGET_LRA_P`. Without LRA, the default is to use a word-sized mode for integral modes that are smaller than a a word. This is right thing to do on most machines because it ensures that all bits of the register are copied and prevents accesses to the registers in a narrower mode, which some machines prohibit for floating-point registers.

However, this default behavior is not correct on some machines, such as the DEC Alpha, that store short integers in floating-point registers differently than in integer registers. On those machines, the default widening will not work correctly and you must define this hook to suppress that widening in some cases. See the file 'alpha.c' for details.

With LRA, the default is to use *mode* unmodified.

void TARGET_SELECT_EARLY_REMAT_MODES (*sbitmap modes*) [Target Hook]

On some targets, certain modes cannot be held in registers around a standard ABI call and are relatively expensive to spill to the stack. The early rematerialization pass can help in such cases by aggressively recomputing values after calls, so that they don't need to be spilled.

This hook returns the set of such modes by setting the associated bits in *modes*. The default implementation selects no modes, which has the effect of disabling the early rematerialization pass.

bool TARGET_CLASS_LIKELY_SPILLED_P (*reg_class_t rclass*) [Target Hook]

A target hook which returns `true` if pseudos that have been assigned to registers of class *rclass* would likely be spilled because registers of *rclass* are needed for spill registers.

The default version of this target hook returns `true` if *rclass* has exactly one register and `false` otherwise. On most machines, this default should be used. For generally register-starved machines, such as i386, or machines with right register constraints, such as SH, this hook can be used to avoid excessive spilling.

This hook is also used by some of the global intra-procedural code transformations to throttle code motion, to avoid increasing register pressure.

unsigned char TARGET_CLASS_MAX_NREGS (*reg_class_t rclass,* [Target Hook]
machine_mode mode)

A target hook returns the maximum number of consecutive registers of class *rclass* needed to hold a value of mode *mode*.

This is closely related to the macro `TARGET_HARD_REGNO_NREGS`. In fact, the value returned by `TARGET_CLASS_MAX_NREGS (rclass, mode)` target hook should be the maximum value of `TARGET_HARD_REGNO_NREGS (regno, mode)` for all *regno* values in the class *rclass*.

This target hook helps control the handling of multiple-word values in the reload pass. The default version of this target hook returns the size of *mode* in words.

CLASS_MAX_NREGS (*class*, *mode*) [Macro]

    A C expression for the maximum number of consecutive registers of class *class* needed to hold a value of mode *mode*.

    This is closely related to the macro `TARGET_HARD_REGNO_NREGS`. In fact, the value of the macro `CLASS_MAX_NREGS (class, mode)` should be the maximum value of `TARGET_HARD_REGNO_NREGS (regno, mode)` for all *regno* values in the class *class*.

    This macro helps control the handling of multiple-word values in the reload pass.

bool TARGET_CAN_CHANGE_MODE_CLASS (*machine_mode* `from`, [Target Hook]
    machine_mode `to`, *reg_class_t* `rclass`)

    This hook returns true if it is possible to bitcast values held in registers of class *rclass* from mode *from* to mode *to* and if doing so preserves the low-order bits that are common to both modes. The result is only meaningful if *rclass* has registers that can hold both `from` and `to`. The default implementation returns true.

    As an example of when such bitcasting is invalid, loading 32-bit integer or floating-point objects into floating-point registers on Alpha extends them to 64 bits. Therefore loading a 64-bit object and then storing it as a 32-bit object does not store the low-order 32 bits, as would be the case for a normal register. Therefore, 'alpha.h' defines `TARGET_CAN_CHANGE_MODE_CLASS` to return:

        `(GET_MODE_SIZE (from) == GET_MODE_SIZE (to)`
        `|| !reg_classes_intersect_p (FLOAT_REGS, rclass))`

    Even if storing from a register in mode *to* would be valid, if both *from* and `raw_reg_mode` for *rclass* are wider than `word_mode`, then we must prevent *to* narrowing the mode. This happens when the middle-end assumes that it can load or store pieces of an *N*-word pseudo, and that the pseudo will eventually be allocated to *N* `word_mode` hard registers. Failure to prevent this kind of mode change will result in the entire `raw_reg_mode` being modified instead of the partial value that the middle-end intended.

reg_class_t TARGET_IRA_CHANGE_PSEUDO_ALLOCNO_CLASS (*int*, [Target Hook]
    reg_class_t, *reg_class_t*)

    A target hook which can change allocno class for given pseudo from allocno and best class calculated by IRA.

    The default version of this target hook always returns given class.

bool TARGET_LRA_P (*void*) [Target Hook]

    A target hook which returns true if we use LRA instead of reload pass. The default version of this target hook returns true. New ports should use LRA, and existing ports are encouraged to convert.

int TARGET_REGISTER_PRIORITY (*int*) [Target Hook]

    A target hook which returns the register priority number to which the register *hard_regno* belongs to. The bigger the number, the more preferable the hard register usage (when all other conditions are the same). This hook can be used to prefer some hard register over others in LRA. For example, some x86-64 register usage needs additional prefix which makes instructions longer. The hook can return lower priority number for such registers make them less favorable and as result making the generated code smaller. The default version of this target hook returns always zero.

bool TARGET_REGISTER_USAGE_LEVELING_P (*void*) [Target Hook]
: A target hook which returns true if we need register usage leveling. That means if a few hard registers are equally good for the assignment, we choose the least used hard register. The register usage leveling may be profitable for some targets. Don't use the usage leveling for targets with conditional execution or targets with big register files as it hurts if-conversion and cross-jumping optimizations. The default version of this target hook returns always false.

bool TARGET_DIFFERENT_ADDR_DISPLACEMENT_P (*void*) [Target Hook]
: A target hook which returns true if an address with the same structure can have different maximal legitimate displacement. For example, the displacement can depend on memory mode or on operand combinations in the insn. The default version of this target hook returns always false.

bool TARGET_CANNOT_SUBSTITUTE_MEM_EQUIV_P (*rtx* `subst`) [Target Hook]
: A target hook which returns `true` if *subst* can't substitute safely pseudos with equivalent memory values during register allocation. The default version of this target hook returns `false`. On most machines, this default should be used. For generally machines with non orthogonal register usage for addressing, such as SH, this hook can be used to avoid excessive spilling.

bool TARGET_LEGITIMIZE_ADDRESS_DISPLACEMENT (*rtx* [Target Hook]
          *offset1, *rtx* *offset2, *poly_int64* `orig_offset`, *machine_mode* `mode`)
: This hook tries to split address offset *orig_offset* into two parts: one that should be added to the base address to create a local anchor point, and an additional offset that can be applied to the anchor to address a value of mode *mode*. The idea is that the local anchor could be shared by other accesses to nearby locations.

    The hook returns true if it succeeds, storing the offset of the anchor from the base in *offset1* and the offset of the final address from the anchor in *offset2*. The default implementation returns false.

reg_class_t TARGET_SPILL_CLASS (*reg_class_t*, `machine_mode`) [Target Hook]
: This hook defines a class of registers which could be used for spilling pseudos of the given mode and class, or `NO_REGS` if only memory should be used. Not defining this hook is equivalent to returning `NO_REGS` for all inputs.

bool TARGET_ADDITIONAL_ALLOCNO_CLASS_P (*reg_class_t*) [Target Hook]
: This hook should return `true` if given class of registers should be an allocno class in any way. Usually RA uses only one register class from all classes containing the same register set. In some complicated cases, you need to have two or more such classes as allocno ones for RA correct work. Not defining this hook is equivalent to returning `false` for all inputs.

scalar_int_mode TARGET_CSTORE_MODE (*enum insn_code* `icode`) [Target Hook]
: This hook defines the machine mode to use for the boolean result of conditional store patterns. The ICODE argument is the instruction code for the cstore being performed. Not definiting this hook is the same as accepting the mode encoded into operand 0 of the cstore expander patterns.

int TARGET_COMPUTE_PRESSURE_CLASSES (*enum reg_class*   [Target Hook]
    pressure_classes)

    A target hook which lets a backend compute the set of pressure classes to be used by those optimization passes which take register pressure into account, as opposed to letting IRA compute them. It returns the number of register classes stored in the array *pressure_classes*.

18.9 Stack Layout and Calling Conventions

This describes the stack layout and calling conventions.

18.9.1 Basic Stack Layout

Here is the basic stack layout.

STACK_GROWS_DOWNWARD   [Macro]

    Define this macro to be true if pushing a word onto the stack moves the stack pointer to a smaller address, and false otherwise.

STACK_PUSH_CODE   [Macro]

    This macro defines the operation used when something is pushed on the stack. In RTL, a push operation will be (set (mem (STACK_PUSH_CODE (reg sp))) ...)

    The choices are PRE_DEC, POST_DEC, PRE_INC, and POST_INC. Which of these is correct depends on the stack direction and on whether the stack pointer points to the last item on the stack or whether it points to the space for the next item on the stack.

    The default is PRE_DEC when STACK_GROWS_DOWNWARD is true, which is almost always right, and PRE_INC otherwise, which is often wrong.

FRAME_GROWS_DOWNWARD   [Macro]

    Define this macro to nonzero value if the addresses of local variable slots are at negative offsets from the frame pointer.

ARGS_GROW_DOWNWARD   [Macro]

    Define this macro if successive arguments to a function occupy decreasing addresses on the stack.

HOST_WIDE_INT TARGET_STARTING_FRAME_OFFSET (*void*)   [Target Hook]

    This hook returns the offset from the frame pointer to the first local variable slot to be allocated. If FRAME_GROWS_DOWNWARD, it is the offset to *end* of the first slot allocated, otherwise it is the offset to *beginning* of the first slot allocated. The default implementation returns 0.

STACK_ALIGNMENT_NEEDED   [Macro]

    Define to zero to disable final alignment of the stack during reload. The nonzero default for this macro is suitable for most ports.

    On ports where TARGET_STARTING_FRAME_OFFSET is nonzero or where there is a register save block following the local block that doesn't require alignment to STACK_BOUNDARY, it may be beneficial to disable stack alignment and do it in the backend.

Chapter 18: Target Description Macros and Functions 505

STACK_POINTER_OFFSET [Macro]

    Offset from the stack pointer register to the first location at which outgoing arguments are placed. If not specified, the default value of zero is used. This is the proper value for most machines.

    If `ARGS_GROW_DOWNWARD`, this is the offset to the location above the first location at which outgoing arguments are placed.

FIRST_PARM_OFFSET (*fundecl*) [Macro]

    Offset from the argument pointer register to the first argument's address. On some machines it may depend on the data type of the function.

    If `ARGS_GROW_DOWNWARD`, this is the offset to the location above the first argument's address.

STACK_DYNAMIC_OFFSET (*fundecl*) [Macro]

    Offset from the stack pointer register to an item dynamically allocated on the stack, e.g., by `alloca`.

    The default value for this macro is `STACK_POINTER_OFFSET` plus the length of the outgoing arguments. The default is correct for most machines. See 'function.c' for details.

INITIAL_FRAME_ADDRESS_RTX [Macro]

    A C expression whose value is RTL representing the address of the initial stack frame. This address is passed to `RETURN_ADDR_RTX` and `DYNAMIC_CHAIN_ADDRESS`. If you don't define this macro, a reasonable default value will be used. Define this macro in order to make frame pointer elimination work in the presence of `__builtin_frame_address (count)` and `__builtin_return_address (count)` for `count` not equal to zero.

DYNAMIC_CHAIN_ADDRESS (*frameaddr*) [Macro]

    A C expression whose value is RTL representing the address in a stack frame where the pointer to the caller's frame is stored. Assume that *frameaddr* is an RTL expression for the address of the stack frame itself.

    If you don't define this macro, the default is to return the value of *frameaddr*—that is, the stack frame address is also the address of the stack word that points to the previous frame.

SETUP_FRAME_ADDRESSES [Macro]

    A C expression that produces the machine-specific code to setup the stack so that arbitrary frames can be accessed. For example, on the SPARC, we must flush all of the register windows to the stack before we can access arbitrary stack frames. You will seldom need to define this macro. The default is to do nothing.

rtx TARGET_BUILTIN_SETJMP_FRAME_VALUE (*void*) [Target Hook]

    This target hook should return an rtx that is used to store the address of the current frame into the built in `setjmp` buffer. The default value, `virtual_stack_vars_rtx`, is correct for most machines. One reason you may need to define this target hook is if `hard_frame_pointer_rtx` is the appropriate value on your machine.

FRAME_ADDR_RTX (*frameaddr*) [Macro]

    A C expression whose value is RTL representing the value of the frame address for the current frame. *frameaddr* is the frame pointer of the current frame. This is used for __builtin_frame_address. You need only define this macro if the frame address is not the same as the frame pointer. Most machines do not need to define it.

RETURN_ADDR_RTX (*count*, *frameaddr*) [Macro]

    A C expression whose value is RTL representing the value of the return address for the frame *count* steps up from the current frame, after the prologue. *frameaddr* is the frame pointer of the *count* frame, or the frame pointer of the *count* − 1 frame if RETURN_ADDR_IN_PREVIOUS_FRAME is nonzero.

    The value of the expression must always be the correct address when *count* is zero, but may be NULL_RTX if there is no way to determine the return address of other frames.

RETURN_ADDR_IN_PREVIOUS_FRAME [Macro]

    Define this macro to nonzero value if the return address of a particular stack frame is accessed from the frame pointer of the previous stack frame. The zero default for this macro is suitable for most ports.

INCOMING_RETURN_ADDR_RTX [Macro]

    A C expression whose value is RTL representing the location of the incoming return address at the beginning of any function, before the prologue. This RTL is either a REG, indicating that the return value is saved in 'REG', or a MEM representing a location in the stack.

    You only need to define this macro if you want to support call frame debugging information like that provided by DWARF 2.

    If this RTL is a REG, you should also define DWARF_FRAME_RETURN_COLUMN to DWARF_FRAME_REGNUM (REGNO).

DWARF_ALT_FRAME_RETURN_COLUMN [Macro]

    A C expression whose value is an integer giving a DWARF 2 column number that may be used as an alternative return column. The column must not correspond to any gcc hard register (that is, it must not be in the range of DWARF_FRAME_REGNUM).

    This macro can be useful if DWARF_FRAME_RETURN_COLUMN is set to a general register, but an alternative column needs to be used for signal frames. Some targets have also used different frame return columns over time.

DWARF_ZERO_REG [Macro]

    A C expression whose value is an integer giving a DWARF 2 register number that is considered to always have the value zero. This should only be defined if the target has an architected zero register, and someone decided it was a good idea to use that register number to terminate the stack backtrace. New ports should avoid this.

void TARGET_DWARF_HANDLE_FRAME_UNSPEC (*const char *label*, [Target Hook]
    rtx pattern, *int index*)

    This target hook allows the backend to emit frame-related insns that contain UNSPECs or UNSPEC_VOLATILEs. The DWARF 2 call frame debugging info engine will invoke it on insns of the form

Chapter 18: Target Description Macros and Functions 507

```
          (set (reg) (unspec [...] UNSPEC_INDEX))
```
and
```
          (set (reg) (unspec_volatile [...] UNSPECV_INDEX)).
```
to let the backend emit the call frame instructions. *label* is the CFI label attached to the insn, *pattern* is the pattern of the insn and *index* is UNSPEC_INDEX or UNSPECV_INDEX.

unsigned int TARGET_DWARF_POLY_INDETERMINATE_VALUE   [Target Hook]
(*unsigned int i, unsigned int *factor, int *offset*)

Express the value of poly_int indeterminate *i* as a DWARF expression, with *i* counting from 1. Return the number of a DWARF register *R* and set '*factor*' and '*offset*' such that the value of the indeterminate is:

    value_of(R) / factor - offset

A target only needs to define this hook if it sets 'NUM_POLY_INT_COEFFS' to a value greater than 1.

INCOMING_FRAME_SP_OFFSET   [Macro]

A C expression whose value is an integer giving the offset, in bytes, from the value of the stack pointer register to the top of the stack frame at the beginning of any function, before the prologue. The top of the frame is defined to be the value of the stack pointer in the previous frame, just before the call instruction.

You only need to define this macro if you want to support call frame debugging information like that provided by DWARF 2.

DEFAULT_INCOMING_FRAME_SP_OFFSET   [Macro]

Like INCOMING_FRAME_SP_OFFSET, but must be the same for all functions of the same ABI, and when using GAS .cfi_* directives must also agree with the default CFI GAS emits. Define this macro only if INCOMING_FRAME_SP_OFFSET can have different values between different functions of the same ABI or when INCOMING_FRAME_SP_OFFSET does not agree with GAS default CFI.

ARG_POINTER_CFA_OFFSET (*fundecl*)   [Macro]

A C expression whose value is an integer giving the offset, in bytes, from the argument pointer to the canonical frame address (cfa). The final value should coincide with that calculated by INCOMING_FRAME_SP_OFFSET. Which is unfortunately not usable during virtual register instantiation.

The default value for this macro is FIRST_PARM_OFFSET (fundecl) + crtl->args.pretend_args_size, which is correct for most machines; in general, the arguments are found immediately before the stack frame. Note that this is not the case on some targets that save registers into the caller's frame, such as SPARC and rs6000, and so such targets need to define this macro.

You only need to define this macro if the default is incorrect, and you want to support call frame debugging information like that provided by DWARF 2.

FRAME_POINTER_CFA_OFFSET (*fundecl*)   [Macro]

If defined, a C expression whose value is an integer giving the offset in bytes from the frame pointer to the canonical frame address (cfa). The final value should coincide with that calculated by INCOMING_FRAME_SP_OFFSET.

Normally the CFA is calculated as an offset from the argument pointer, via `ARG_POINTER_CFA_OFFSET`, but if the argument pointer is variable due to the ABI, this may not be possible. If this macro is defined, it implies that the virtual register instantiation should be based on the frame pointer instead of the argument pointer. Only one of `FRAME_POINTER_CFA_OFFSET` and `ARG_POINTER_CFA_OFFSET` should be defined.

CFA_FRAME_BASE_OFFSET (*fundecl*) [Macro]

If defined, a C expression whose value is an integer giving the offset in bytes from the canonical frame address (cfa) to the frame base used in DWARF 2 debug information. The default is zero. A different value may reduce the size of debug information on some ports.

18.9.2 Exception Handling Support

EH_RETURN_DATA_REGNO (*N*) [Macro]

A C expression whose value is the *N*th register number used for data by exception handlers, or `INVALID_REGNUM` if fewer than *N* registers are usable.

The exception handling library routines communicate with the exception handlers via a set of agreed upon registers. Ideally these registers should be call-clobbered; it is possible to use call-saved registers, but may negatively impact code size. The target must support at least 2 data registers, but should define 4 if there are enough free registers.

You must define this macro if you want to support call frame exception handling like that provided by DWARF 2.

EH_RETURN_STACKADJ_RTX [Macro]

A C expression whose value is RTL representing a location in which to store a stack adjustment to be applied before function return. This is used to unwind the stack to an exception handler's call frame. It will be assigned zero on code paths that return normally.

Typically this is a call-clobbered hard register that is otherwise untouched by the epilogue, but could also be a stack slot.

Do not define this macro if the stack pointer is saved and restored by the regular prolog and epilog code in the call frame itself; in this case, the exception handling library routines will update the stack location to be restored in place. Otherwise, you must define this macro if you want to support call frame exception handling like that provided by DWARF 2.

EH_RETURN_HANDLER_RTX [Macro]

A C expression whose value is RTL representing a location in which to store the address of an exception handler to which we should return. It will not be assigned on code paths that return normally.

Typically this is the location in the call frame at which the normal return address is stored. For targets that return by popping an address off the stack, this might be a memory address just below the *target* call frame rather than inside the current call frame. If defined, `EH_RETURN_STACKADJ_RTX` will have already been assigned, so it may be used to calculate the location of the target call frame.

Some targets have more complex requirements than storing to an address calculable during initial code generation. In that case the `eh_return` instruction pattern should be used instead.

If you want to support call frame exception handling, you must define either this macro or the `eh_return` instruction pattern.

RETURN_ADDR_OFFSET [Macro]

If defined, an integer-valued C expression for which rtl will be generated to add it to the exception handler address before it is searched in the exception handling tables, and to subtract it again from the address before using it to return to the exception handler.

ASM_PREFERRED_EH_DATA_FORMAT (*code, global*) [Macro]

This macro chooses the encoding of pointers embedded in the exception handling sections. If at all possible, this should be defined such that the exception handling section will not require dynamic relocations, and so may be read-only.

code is 0 for data, 1 for code labels, 2 for function pointers. *global* is true if the symbol may be affected by dynamic relocations. The macro should return a combination of the `DW_EH_PE_*` defines as found in 'dwarf2.h'.

If this macro is not defined, pointers will not be encoded but represented directly.

ASM_MAYBE_OUTPUT_ENCODED_ADDR_RTX (*file, encoding, size, addr, done*) [Macro]

This macro allows the target to emit whatever special magic is required to represent the encoding chosen by `ASM_PREFERRED_EH_DATA_FORMAT`. Generic code takes care of pc-relative and indirect encodings; this must be defined if the target uses text-relative or data-relative encodings.

This is a C statement that branches to *done* if the format was handled. *encoding* is the format chosen, *size* is the number of bytes that the format occupies, *addr* is the `SYMBOL_REF` to be emitted.

MD_FALLBACK_FRAME_STATE_FOR (*context, fs*) [Macro]

This macro allows the target to add CPU and operating system specific code to the call frame unwinder for use when there is no unwind data available. The most common reason to implement this macro is to unwind through signal frames.

This macro is called from `uw_frame_state_for` in 'unwind-dw2.c', 'unwind-dw2-xtensa.c' and 'unwind-ia64.c'. *context* is an `_Unwind_Context`; *fs* is an `_Unwind_FrameState`. Examine `context->ra` for the address of the code being executed and `context->cfa` for the stack pointer value. If the frame can be decoded, the register save addresses should be updated in *fs* and the macro should evaluate to `_URC_NO_REASON`. If the frame cannot be decoded, the macro should evaluate to `_URC_END_OF_STACK`.

For proper signal handling in Java this macro is accompanied by `MAKE_THROW_FRAME`, defined in 'libjava/include/*-signal.h' headers.

MD_HANDLE_UNWABI (*context, fs*) [Macro]
: This macro allows the target to add operating system specific code to the call-frame unwinder to handle the IA-64 .unwabi unwinding directive, usually used for signal or interrupt frames.

    This macro is called from uw_update_context in libgcc's 'unwind-ia64.c'. *context* is an _Unwind_Context; *fs* is an _Unwind_FrameState. Examine fs->unwabi for the abi and context in the .unwabi directive. If the .unwabi directive can be handled, the register save addresses should be updated in *fs*.

TARGET_USES_WEAK_UNWIND_INFO [Macro]
: A C expression that evaluates to true if the target requires unwind info to be given comdat linkage. Define it to be 1 if comdat linkage is necessary. The default is 0.

18.9.3 Specifying How Stack Checking is Done

GCC will check that stack references are within the boundaries of the stack, if the option '-fstack-check' is specified, in one of three ways:

1. If the value of the STACK_CHECK_BUILTIN macro is nonzero, GCC will assume that you have arranged for full stack checking to be done at appropriate places in the configuration files. GCC will not do other special processing.

2. If STACK_CHECK_BUILTIN is zero and the value of the STACK_CHECK_STATIC_BUILTIN macro is nonzero, GCC will assume that you have arranged for static stack checking (checking of the static stack frame of functions) to be done at appropriate places in the configuration files. GCC will only emit code to do dynamic stack checking (checking on dynamic stack allocations) using the third approach below.

3. If neither of the above are true, GCC will generate code to periodically "probe" the stack pointer using the values of the macros defined below.

If neither STACK_CHECK_BUILTIN nor STACK_CHECK_STATIC_BUILTIN is defined, GCC will change its allocation strategy for large objects if the option '-fstack-check' is specified: they will always be allocated dynamically if their size exceeds STACK_CHECK_MAX_VAR_SIZE bytes.

STACK_CHECK_BUILTIN [Macro]
: A nonzero value if stack checking is done by the configuration files in a machine-dependent manner. You should define this macro if stack checking is required by the ABI of your machine or if you would like to do stack checking in some more efficient way than the generic approach. The default value of this macro is zero.

STACK_CHECK_STATIC_BUILTIN [Macro]
: A nonzero value if static stack checking is done by the configuration files in a machine-dependent manner. You should define this macro if you would like to do static stack checking in some more efficient way than the generic approach. The default value of this macro is zero.

STACK_CHECK_PROBE_INTERVAL_EXP [Macro]
: An integer specifying the interval at which GCC must generate stack probe instructions, defined as 2 raised to this integer. You will normally define this macro so that the interval be no larger than the size of the "guard pages" at the end of a stack area. The default value of 12 (4096-byte interval) is suitable for most systems.

STACK_CHECK_MOVING_SP [Macro]

An integer which is nonzero if GCC should move the stack pointer page by page when doing probes. This can be necessary on systems where the stack pointer contains the bottom address of the memory area accessible to the executing thread at any point in time. In this situation an alternate signal stack is required in order to be able to recover from a stack overflow. The default value of this macro is zero.

STACK_CHECK_PROTECT [Macro]

The number of bytes of stack needed to recover from a stack overflow, for languages where such a recovery is supported. The default value of 4KB/8KB with the `setjmp/longjmp`-based exception handling mechanism and 8KB/12KB with other exception handling mechanisms should be adequate for most architectures and operating systems.

The following macros are relevant only if neither STACK_CHECK_BUILTIN nor STACK_CHECK_STATIC_BUILTIN is defined; you can omit them altogether in the opposite case.

STACK_CHECK_MAX_FRAME_SIZE [Macro]

The maximum size of a stack frame, in bytes. GCC will generate probe instructions in non-leaf functions to ensure at least this many bytes of stack are available. If a stack frame is larger than this size, stack checking will not be reliable and GCC will issue a warning. The default is chosen so that GCC only generates one instruction on most systems. You should normally not change the default value of this macro.

STACK_CHECK_FIXED_FRAME_SIZE [Macro]

GCC uses this value to generate the above warning message. It represents the amount of fixed frame used by a function, not including space for any callee-saved registers, temporaries and user variables. You need only specify an upper bound for this amount and will normally use the default of four words.

STACK_CHECK_MAX_VAR_SIZE [Macro]

The maximum size, in bytes, of an object that GCC will place in the fixed area of the stack frame when the user specifies '`-fstack-check`'. GCC computed the default from the values of the above macros and you will normally not need to override that default.

bool TARGET_STACK_CLASH_PROTECTION_FINAL_DYNAMIC_PROBE [Target Hook]
(*rtx* `residual`)

Some targets make optimistic assumptions about the state of stack probing when they emit their prologues. On such targets a probe into the end of any dynamically allocated space is likely required for safety against stack clash style attacks. Define this variable to return nonzero if such a probe is required or zero otherwise. You need not define this macro if it would always have the value zero.

18.9.4 Registers That Address the Stack Frame

This discusses registers that address the stack frame.

STACK_POINTER_REGNUM [Macro]

    The register number of the stack pointer register, which must also be a fixed register according to FIXED_REGISTERS. On most machines, the hardware determines which register this is.

FRAME_POINTER_REGNUM [Macro]

    The register number of the frame pointer register, which is used to access automatic variables in the stack frame. On some machines, the hardware determines which register this is. On other machines, you can choose any register you wish for this purpose.

HARD_FRAME_POINTER_REGNUM [Macro]

    On some machines the offset between the frame pointer and starting offset of the automatic variables is not known until after register allocation has been done (for example, because the saved registers are between these two locations). On those machines, define FRAME_POINTER_REGNUM the number of a special, fixed register to be used internally until the offset is known, and define HARD_FRAME_POINTER_REGNUM to be the actual hard register number used for the frame pointer.

    You should define this macro only in the very rare circumstances when it is not possible to calculate the offset between the frame pointer and the automatic variables until after register allocation has been completed. When this macro is defined, you must also indicate in your definition of ELIMINABLE_REGS how to eliminate FRAME_POINTER_REGNUM into either HARD_FRAME_POINTER_REGNUM or STACK_POINTER_REGNUM.

    Do not define this macro if it would be the same as FRAME_POINTER_REGNUM.

ARG_POINTER_REGNUM [Macro]

    The register number of the arg pointer register, which is used to access the function's argument list. On some machines, this is the same as the frame pointer register. On some machines, the hardware determines which register this is. On other machines, you can choose any register you wish for this purpose. If this is not the same register as the frame pointer register, then you must mark it as a fixed register according to FIXED_REGISTERS, or arrange to be able to eliminate it (see Section 18.9.5 [Elimination], page 514).

HARD_FRAME_POINTER_IS_FRAME_POINTER [Macro]

    Define this to a preprocessor constant that is nonzero if hard_frame_pointer_rtx and frame_pointer_rtx should be the same. The default definition is '(HARD_FRAME_POINTER_REGNUM == FRAME_POINTER_REGNUM)'; you only need to define this macro if that definition is not suitable for use in preprocessor conditionals.

HARD_FRAME_POINTER_IS_ARG_POINTER [Macro]

    Define this to a preprocessor constant that is nonzero if hard_frame_pointer_rtx and arg_pointer_rtx should be the same. The default definition is '(HARD_FRAME_POINTER_REGNUM == ARG_POINTER_REGNUM)'; you only need to define this macro if that definition is not suitable for use in preprocessor conditionals.

Chapter 18: Target Description Macros and Functions 513

RETURN_ADDRESS_POINTER_REGNUM [Macro]

> The register number of the return address pointer register, which is used to access the current function's return address from the stack. On some machines, the return address is not at a fixed offset from the frame pointer or stack pointer or argument pointer. This register can be defined to point to the return address on the stack, and then be converted by `ELIMINABLE_REGS` into either the frame pointer or stack pointer.
>
> Do not define this macro unless there is no other way to get the return address from the stack.

STATIC_CHAIN_REGNUM [Macro]
STATIC_CHAIN_INCOMING_REGNUM [Macro]

> Register numbers used for passing a function's static chain pointer. If register windows are used, the register number as seen by the called function is `STATIC_CHAIN_INCOMING_REGNUM`, while the register number as seen by the calling function is `STATIC_CHAIN_REGNUM`. If these registers are the same, `STATIC_CHAIN_INCOMING_REGNUM` need not be defined.
>
> The static chain register need not be a fixed register.
>
> If the static chain is passed in memory, these macros should not be defined; instead, the `TARGET_STATIC_CHAIN` hook should be used.

rtx TARGET_STATIC_CHAIN (*const_tree* `fndecl_or_type`, *bool* [Target Hook]
    `incoming_p`)

> This hook replaces the use of `STATIC_CHAIN_REGNUM` et al for targets that may use different static chain locations for different nested functions. This may be required if the target has function attributes that affect the calling conventions of the function and those calling conventions use different static chain locations.
>
> The default version of this hook uses `STATIC_CHAIN_REGNUM` et al.
>
> If the static chain is passed in memory, this hook should be used to provide rtx giving `mem` expressions that denote where they are stored. Often the `mem` expression as seen by the caller will be at an offset from the stack pointer and the `mem` expression as seen by the callee will be at an offset from the frame pointer. The variables `stack_pointer_rtx`, `frame_pointer_rtx`, and `arg_pointer_rtx` will have been initialized and should be used to refer to those items.

DWARF_FRAME_REGISTERS [Macro]

> This macro specifies the maximum number of hard registers that can be saved in a call frame. This is used to size data structures used in DWARF2 exception handling.
>
> Prior to GCC 3.0, this macro was needed in order to establish a stable exception handling ABI in the face of adding new hard registers for ISA extensions. In GCC 3.0 and later, the EH ABI is insulated from changes in the number of hard registers. Nevertheless, this macro can still be used to reduce the runtime memory requirements of the exception handling routines, which can be substantial if the ISA contains a lot of registers that are not call-saved.
>
> If this macro is not defined, it defaults to `FIRST_PSEUDO_REGISTER`.

PRE_GCC3_DWARF_FRAME_REGISTERS [Macro]

This macro is similar to `DWARF_FRAME_REGISTERS`, but is provided for backward compatibility in pre GCC 3.0 compiled code.

If this macro is not defined, it defaults to `DWARF_FRAME_REGISTERS`.

DWARF_REG_TO_UNWIND_COLUMN (*regno*) [Macro]

Define this macro if the target's representation for dwarf registers is different than the internal representation for unwind column. Given a dwarf register, this macro should return the internal unwind column number to use instead.

DWARF_FRAME_REGNUM (*regno*) [Macro]

Define this macro if the target's representation for dwarf registers used in .eh_frame or .debug_frame is different from that used in other debug info sections. Given a GCC hard register number, this macro should return the .eh_frame register number. The default is `DBX_REGISTER_NUMBER (regno)`.

DWARF2_FRAME_REG_OUT (*regno*, *for_eh*) [Macro]

Define this macro to map register numbers held in the call frame info that GCC has collected using `DWARF_FRAME_REGNUM` to those that should be output in .debug_frame (*for_eh* is zero) and .eh_frame (*for_eh* is nonzero). The default is to return *regno*.

REG_VALUE_IN_UNWIND_CONTEXT [Macro]

Define this macro if the target stores register values as `_Unwind_Word` type in unwind context. It should be defined if target register size is larger than the size of `void *`. The default is to store register values as `void *` type.

ASSUME_EXTENDED_UNWIND_CONTEXT [Macro]

Define this macro to be 1 if the target always uses extended unwind context with version, args_size and by_value fields. If it is undefined, it will be defined to 1 when `REG_VALUE_IN_UNWIND_CONTEXT` is defined and 0 otherwise.

DWARF_LAZY_REGISTER_VALUE (*regno*, *value*) [Macro]

Define this macro if the target has pseudo DWARF registers whose values need to be computed lazily on demand by the unwinder (such as when referenced in a CFA expression). The macro returns true if *regno* is such a register and stores its value in '*value*' if so.

18.9.5 Eliminating Frame Pointer and Arg Pointer

This is about eliminating the frame pointer and arg pointer.

bool TARGET_FRAME_POINTER_REQUIRED (*void*) [Target Hook]

This target hook should return **true** if a function must have and use a frame pointer. This target hook is called in the reload pass. If its return value is **true** the function will have a frame pointer.

This target hook can in principle examine the current function and decide according to the facts, but on most machines the constant **false** or the constant **true** suffices. Use **false** when the machine allows code to be generated with no frame pointer, and doing so saves some time or space. Use **true** when there is no possible advantage to avoiding a frame pointer.

In certain cases, the compiler does not know how to produce valid code without a frame pointer. The compiler recognizes those cases and automatically gives the function a frame pointer regardless of what `targetm.frame_pointer_required` returns. You don't need to worry about them.

In a function that does not require a frame pointer, the frame pointer register can be allocated for ordinary usage, unless you mark it as a fixed register. See `FIXED_REGISTERS` for more information.

Default return value is `false`.

ELIMINABLE_REGS [Macro]

This macro specifies a table of register pairs used to eliminate unneeded registers that point into the stack frame.

The definition of this macro is a list of structure initializations, each of which specifies an original and replacement register.

On some machines, the position of the argument pointer is not known until the compilation is completed. In such a case, a separate hard register must be used for the argument pointer. This register can be eliminated by replacing it with either the frame pointer or the argument pointer, depending on whether or not the frame pointer has been eliminated.

In this case, you might specify:

```
#define ELIMINABLE_REGS  \
{{ARG_POINTER_REGNUM, STACK_POINTER_REGNUM}, \
 {ARG_POINTER_REGNUM, FRAME_POINTER_REGNUM}, \
 {FRAME_POINTER_REGNUM, STACK_POINTER_REGNUM}}
```

Note that the elimination of the argument pointer with the stack pointer is specified first since that is the preferred elimination.

bool TARGET_CAN_ELIMINATE (*const int* `from_reg`, *const int* `to_reg`) [Target Hook]

This target hook should return `true` if the compiler is allowed to try to replace register number *from_reg* with register number *to_reg*. This target hook will usually be `true`, since most of the cases preventing register elimination are things that the compiler already knows about.

Default return value is `true`.

INITIAL_ELIMINATION_OFFSET (*from-reg*, *to-reg*, *offset-var*) [Macro]

This macro returns the initial difference between the specified pair of registers. The value would be computed from information such as the result of `get_frame_size ()` and the tables of registers `df_regs_ever_live_p` and `call_used_regs`.

void TARGET_COMPUTE_FRAME_LAYOUT (*void*) [Target Hook]

This target hook is called once each time the frame layout needs to be recalculated. The calculations can be cached by the target and can then be used by `INITIAL_ELIMINATION_OFFSET` instead of re-computing the layout on every invocation of that hook. This is particularly useful for targets that have an expensive frame layout function. Implementing this callback is optional.

18.9.6 Passing Function Arguments on the Stack

The macros in this section control how arguments are passed on the stack. See the following section for other macros that control passing certain arguments in registers.

bool TARGET_PROMOTE_PROTOTYPES (*const_tree fntype*) [Target Hook]
> This target hook returns **true** if an argument declared in a prototype as an integral type smaller than **int** should actually be passed as an **int**. In addition to avoiding errors in certain cases of mismatch, it also makes for better code on certain machines. The default is to not promote prototypes.

PUSH_ARGS [Macro]
> A C expression. If nonzero, push insns will be used to pass outgoing arguments. If the target machine does not have a push instruction, set it to zero. That directs GCC to use an alternate strategy: to allocate the entire argument block and then store the arguments into it. When PUSH_ARGS is nonzero, PUSH_ROUNDING must be defined too.

PUSH_ARGS_REVERSED [Macro]
> A C expression. If nonzero, function arguments will be evaluated from last to first, rather than from first to last. If this macro is not defined, it defaults to PUSH_ARGS on targets where the stack and args grow in opposite directions, and 0 otherwise.

PUSH_ROUNDING (*npushed*) [Macro]
> A C expression that is the number of bytes actually pushed onto the stack when an instruction attempts to push *npushed* bytes.
>
> On some machines, the definition
>
> ```
> #define PUSH_ROUNDING(BYTES) (BYTES)
> ```
>
> will suffice. But on other machines, instructions that appear to push one byte actually push two bytes in an attempt to maintain alignment. Then the definition should be
>
> ```
> #define PUSH_ROUNDING(BYTES) (((BYTES) + 1) & ~1)
> ```
>
> If the value of this macro has a type, it should be an unsigned type.

ACCUMULATE_OUTGOING_ARGS [Macro]
> A C expression. If nonzero, the maximum amount of space required for outgoing arguments will be computed and placed into crtl->outgoing_args_size. No space will be pushed onto the stack for each call; instead, the function prologue should increase the stack frame size by this amount.
>
> Setting both PUSH_ARGS and ACCUMULATE_OUTGOING_ARGS is not proper.

REG_PARM_STACK_SPACE (*fndecl*) [Macro]
> Define this macro if functions should assume that stack space has been allocated for arguments even when their values are passed in registers.
>
> The value of this macro is the size, in bytes, of the area reserved for arguments passed in registers for the function represented by *fndecl*, which can be zero if GCC is calling a library function. The argument *fndecl* can be the FUNCTION_DECL, or the type itself of the function.
>
> This space can be allocated by the caller, or be a part of the machine-dependent stack frame: OUTGOING_REG_PARM_STACK_SPACE says which.

`INCOMING_REG_PARM_STACK_SPACE (fndecl)` [Macro]

    Like `REG_PARM_STACK_SPACE`, but for incoming register arguments. Define this macro if space guaranteed when compiling a function body is different to space required when making a call, a situation that can arise with K&R style function definitions.

`OUTGOING_REG_PARM_STACK_SPACE (fntype)` [Macro]

    Define this to a nonzero value if it is the responsibility of the caller to allocate the area reserved for arguments passed in registers when calling a function of *fntype*. *fntype* may be NULL if the function called is a library function.

    If `ACCUMULATE_OUTGOING_ARGS` is defined, this macro controls whether the space for these arguments counts in the value of `crtl->outgoing_args_size`.

`STACK_PARMS_IN_REG_PARM_AREA` [Macro]

    Define this macro if `REG_PARM_STACK_SPACE` is defined, but the stack parameters don't skip the area specified by it.

    Normally, when a parameter is not passed in registers, it is placed on the stack beyond the `REG_PARM_STACK_SPACE` area. Defining this macro suppresses this behavior and causes the parameter to be passed on the stack in its natural location.

`poly_int64 TARGET_RETURN_POPS_ARGS (tree fundecl, tree funtype, poly_int64 size)` [Target Hook]

    This target hook returns the number of bytes of its own arguments that a function pops on returning, or 0 if the function pops no arguments and the caller must therefore pop them all after the function returns.

    fundecl is a C variable whose value is a tree node that describes the function in question. Normally it is a node of type `FUNCTION_DECL` that describes the declaration of the function. From this you can obtain the `DECL_ATTRIBUTES` of the function.

    funtype is a C variable whose value is a tree node that describes the function in question. Normally it is a node of type `FUNCTION_TYPE` that describes the data type of the function. From this it is possible to obtain the data types of the value and arguments (if known).

    When a call to a library function is being considered, *fundecl* will contain an identifier node for the library function. Thus, if you need to distinguish among various library functions, you can do so by their names. Note that "library function" in this context means a function used to perform arithmetic, whose name is known specially in the compiler and was not mentioned in the C code being compiled.

    size is the number of bytes of arguments passed on the stack. If a variable number of bytes is passed, it is zero, and argument popping will always be the responsibility of the calling function.

    On the VAX, all functions always pop their arguments, so the definition of this macro is *size*. On the 68000, using the standard calling convention, no functions pop their arguments, so the value of the macro is always 0 in this case. But an alternative calling convention is available in which functions that take a fixed number of arguments pop them but other functions (such as `printf`) pop nothing (the caller pops all). When this convention is in use, *funtype* is examined to determine whether a function takes a fixed number of arguments.

CALL_POPS_ARGS (*cum*)   [Macro]

A C expression that should indicate the number of bytes a call sequence pops off the stack. It is added to the value of RETURN_POPS_ARGS when compiling a function call.

cum is the variable in which all arguments to the called function have been accumulated.

On certain architectures, such as the SH5, a call trampoline is used that pops certain registers off the stack, depending on the arguments that have been passed to the function. Since this is a property of the call site, not of the called function, RETURN_POPS_ARGS is not appropriate.

18.9.7 Passing Arguments in Registers

This section describes the macros which let you control how various types of arguments are passed in registers or how they are arranged in the stack.

rtx TARGET_FUNCTION_ARG (*cumulative_args_t* ca, *machine_mode*   [Target Hook]
     mode, *const_tree* type, *bool* named)

Return an RTX indicating whether a function argument is passed in a register and if so, which register.

The arguments are *ca*, which summarizes all the previous arguments; *mode*, the machine mode of the argument; *type*, the data type of the argument as a tree node or 0 if that is not known (which happens for C support library functions); and *named*, which is true for an ordinary argument and false for nameless arguments that correspond to '...' in the called function's prototype. *type* can be an incomplete type if a syntax error has previously occurred.

The return value is usually either a reg RTX for the hard register in which to pass the argument, or zero to pass the argument on the stack.

The return value can be a const_int which means argument is passed in a target specific slot with specified number. Target hooks should be used to store or load argument in such case. See TARGET_STORE_BOUNDS_FOR_ARG and TARGET_LOAD_BOUNDS_FOR_ARG for more information.

The value of the expression can also be a parallel RTX. This is used when an argument is passed in multiple locations. The mode of the parallel should be the mode of the entire argument. The parallel holds any number of expr_list pairs; each one describes where part of the argument is passed. In each expr_list the first operand must be a reg RTX for the hard register in which to pass this part of the argument, and the mode of the register RTX indicates how large this part of the argument is. The second operand of the expr_list is a const_int which gives the offset in bytes into the entire argument of where this part starts. As a special exception the first expr_list in the parallel RTX may have a first operand of zero. This indicates that the entire argument is also stored on the stack.

The last time this hook is called, it is called with MODE == VOIDmode, and its result is passed to the call or call_value pattern as operands 2 and 3 respectively.

The usual way to make the ISO library 'stdarg.h' work on a machine where some arguments are usually passed in registers, is to cause nameless arguments to be passed on the stack instead. This is done by making TARGET_FUNCTION_ARG return 0 whenever *named* is false.

Chapter 18: Target Description Macros and Functions 519

You may use the hook `targetm.calls.must_pass_in_stack` in the definition of this macro to determine if this argument is of a type that must be passed in the stack. If `REG_PARM_STACK_SPACE` is not defined and `TARGET_FUNCTION_ARG` returns nonzero for such an argument, the compiler will abort. If `REG_PARM_STACK_SPACE` is defined, the argument will be computed in the stack and then loaded into a register.

bool TARGET_MUST_PASS_IN_STACK (*machine_mode* `mode`, [Target Hook]
    const_tree `type`)

This target hook should return `true` if we should not pass *type* solely in registers. The file 'expr.h' defines a definition that is usually appropriate, refer to 'expr.h' for additional documentation.

rtx TARGET_FUNCTION_INCOMING_ARG (*cumulative_args_t* `ca`, [Target Hook]
    machine_mode `mode`, *const_tree* `type`, *bool* `named`)

Define this hook if the caller and callee on the target have different views of where arguments are passed. Also define this hook if there are functions that are never directly called, but are invoked by the hardware and which have nonstandard calling conventions.

In this case `TARGET_FUNCTION_ARG` computes the register in which the caller passes the value, and `TARGET_FUNCTION_INCOMING_ARG` should be defined in a similar fashion to tell the function being called where the arguments will arrive.

`TARGET_FUNCTION_INCOMING_ARG` can also return arbitrary address computation using hard register, which can be forced into a register, so that it can be used to pass special arguments.

If `TARGET_FUNCTION_INCOMING_ARG` is not defined, `TARGET_FUNCTION_ARG` serves both purposes.

bool TARGET_USE_PSEUDO_PIC_REG (*void*) [Target Hook]

This hook should return 1 in case pseudo register should be created for pic_offset_table_rtx during function expand.

void TARGET_INIT_PIC_REG (*void*) [Target Hook]

Perform a target dependent initialization of pic_offset_table_rtx. This hook is called at the start of register allocation.

int TARGET_ARG_PARTIAL_BYTES (*cumulative_args_t* `cum`, [Target Hook]
    machine_mode `mode`, *tree* `type`, *bool* `named`)

This target hook returns the number of bytes at the beginning of an argument that must be put in registers. The value must be zero for arguments that are passed entirely in registers or that are entirely pushed on the stack.

On some machines, certain arguments must be passed partially in registers and partially in memory. On these machines, typically the first few words of arguments are passed in registers, and the rest on the stack. If a multi-word argument (a **double** or a structure) crosses that boundary, its first few words must be passed in registers and the rest must be pushed. This macro tells the compiler when this occurs, and how many bytes should go in registers.

TARGET_FUNCTION_ARG for these arguments should return the first register to be used by the caller for this argument; likewise TARGET_FUNCTION_INCOMING_ARG, for the called function.

bool TARGET_PASS_BY_REFERENCE (*cumulative_args_t* cum,   [Target Hook]
    machine_mode mode, *const_tree* type, *bool* named)

This target hook should return **true** if an argument at the position indicated by *cum* should be passed by reference. This predicate is queried after target independent reasons for being passed by reference, such as TREE_ADDRESSABLE (type).

If the hook returns true, a copy of that argument is made in memory and a pointer to the argument is passed instead of the argument itself. The pointer is passed in whatever way is appropriate for passing a pointer to that type.

bool TARGET_CALLEE_COPIES (*cumulative_args_t* cum,   [Target Hook]
    machine_mode mode, *const_tree* type, *bool* named)

The function argument described by the parameters to this hook is known to be passed by reference. The hook should return true if the function argument should be copied by the callee instead of copied by the caller.

For any argument for which the hook returns true, if it can be determined that the argument is not modified, then a copy need not be generated.

The default version of this hook always returns false.

CUMULATIVE_ARGS   [Macro]

A C type for declaring a variable that is used as the first argument of TARGET_FUNCTION_ARG and other related values. For some target machines, the type **int** suffices and can hold the number of bytes of argument so far.

There is no need to record in CUMULATIVE_ARGS anything about the arguments that have been passed on the stack. The compiler has other variables to keep track of that. For target machines on which all arguments are passed on the stack, there is no need to store anything in CUMULATIVE_ARGS; however, the data structure must exist and should not be empty, so use **int**.

OVERRIDE_ABI_FORMAT (*fndecl*)   [Macro]

If defined, this macro is called before generating any code for a function, but after the *cfun* descriptor for the function has been created. The back end may use this macro to update *cfun* to reflect an ABI other than that which would normally be used by default. If the compiler is generating code for a compiler-generated function, *fndecl* may be **NULL**.

INIT_CUMULATIVE_ARGS (*cum*, *fntype*, *libname*, *fndecl*,   [Macro]
    n_named_args)

A C statement (sans semicolon) for initializing the variable *cum* for the state at the beginning of the argument list. The variable has type CUMULATIVE_ARGS. The value of *fntype* is the tree node for the data type of the function which will receive the args, or 0 if the args are to a compiler support library function. For direct calls that are not libcalls, *fndecl* contain the declaration node of the function. *fndecl* is also set when INIT_CUMULATIVE_ARGS is used to find arguments for the function being compiled. *n_named_args* is set to the number of named arguments, including a structure return address if it is passed as a parameter, when making a call. When processing incoming arguments, *n_named_args* is set to −1.

When processing a call to a compiler support library function, *libname* identifies which one. It is a `symbol_ref` rtx which contains the name of the function, as a string. *libname* is 0 when an ordinary C function call is being processed. Thus, each time this macro is called, either *libname* or *fntype* is nonzero, but never both of them at once.

INIT_CUMULATIVE_LIBCALL_ARGS (*cum*, *mode*, *libname*) [Macro]
Like `INIT_CUMULATIVE_ARGS` but only used for outgoing libcalls, it gets a `MODE` argument instead of *fntype*, that would be `NULL`. *indirect* would always be zero, too. If this macro is not defined, `INIT_CUMULATIVE_ARGS (cum, NULL_RTX, libname, 0)` is used instead.

INIT_CUMULATIVE_INCOMING_ARGS (*cum*, *fntype*, *libname*) [Macro]
Like `INIT_CUMULATIVE_ARGS` but overrides it for the purposes of finding the arguments for the function being compiled. If this macro is undefined, `INIT_CUMULATIVE_ARGS` is used instead.

The value passed for *libname* is always 0, since library routines with special calling conventions are never compiled with GCC. The argument *libname* exists for symmetry with `INIT_CUMULATIVE_ARGS`.

void TARGET_FUNCTION_ARG_ADVANCE (*cumulative_args_t* **ca**, [Target Hook]
        machine_mode **mode**, *const_tree* **type**, *bool* **named**)
This hook updates the summarizer variable pointed to by *ca* to advance past an argument in the argument list. The values *mode*, *type* and *named* describe that argument. Once this is done, the variable *cum* is suitable for analyzing the *following* argument with `TARGET_FUNCTION_ARG`, etc.

This hook need not do anything if the argument in question was passed on the stack. The compiler knows how to track the amount of stack space used for arguments without any special help.

HOST_WIDE_INT TARGET_FUNCTION_ARG_OFFSET (*machine_mode* [Target Hook]
        mode, *const_tree* **type**)
This hook returns the number of bytes to add to the offset of an argument of type *type* and mode *mode* when passed in memory. This is needed for the SPU, which passes `char` and `short` arguments in the preferred slot that is in the middle of the quad word instead of starting at the top. The default implementation returns 0.

pad_direction TARGET_FUNCTION_ARG_PADDING (*machine_mode* [Target Hook]
        mode, *const_tree* **type**)
This hook determines whether, and in which direction, to pad out an argument of mode *mode* and type *type*. It returns `PAD_UPWARD` to insert padding above the argument, `PAD_DOWNWARD` to insert padding below the argument, or `PAD_NONE` to inhibit padding.

The *amount* of padding is not controlled by this hook, but by `TARGET_FUNCTION_ARG_ROUND_BOUNDARY`. It is always just enough to reach the next multiple of that boundary.

This hook has a default definition that is right for most systems. For little-endian machines, the default is to pad upward. For big-endian machines, the default is to pad downward for an argument of constant size shorter than an `int`, and upward otherwise.

PAD_VARARGS_DOWN [Macro]

If defined, a C expression which determines whether the default implementation of va_arg will attempt to pad down before reading the next argument, if that argument is smaller than its aligned space as controlled by `PARM_BOUNDARY`. If this macro is not defined, all such arguments are padded down if `BYTES_BIG_ENDIAN` is true.

BLOCK_REG_PADDING (mode, type, first) [Macro]

Specify padding for the last element of a block move between registers and memory. *first* is nonzero if this is the only element. Defining this macro allows better control of register function parameters on big-endian machines, without using `PARALLEL` rtl. In particular, `MUST_PASS_IN_STACK` need not test padding and mode of types in registers, as there is no longer a "wrong" part of a register; For example, a three byte aggregate may be passed in the high part of a register if so required.

unsigned int TARGET_FUNCTION_ARG_BOUNDARY (*machine_mode mode*, *const_tree type*) [Target Hook]

This hook returns the alignment boundary, in bits, of an argument with the specified mode and type. The default hook returns `PARM_BOUNDARY` for all arguments.

unsigned int TARGET_FUNCTION_ARG_ROUND_BOUNDARY (*machine_mode mode*, *const_tree type*) [Target Hook]

Normally, the size of an argument is rounded up to `PARM_BOUNDARY`, which is the default value for this hook. You can define this hook to return a different value if an argument size must be rounded to a larger value.

FUNCTION_ARG_REGNO_P (regno) [Macro]

A C expression that is nonzero if *regno* is the number of a hard register in which function arguments are sometimes passed. This does *not* include implicit arguments such as the static chain and the structure-value address. On many machines, no registers can be used for this purpose since all function arguments are pushed on the stack.

bool TARGET_SPLIT_COMPLEX_ARG (*const_tree type*) [Target Hook]

This hook should return true if parameter of type *type* are passed as two scalar parameters. By default, GCC will attempt to pack complex arguments into the target's word size. Some ABIs require complex arguments to be split and treated as their individual components. For example, on AIX64, complex floats should be passed in a pair of floating point registers, even though a complex float would fit in one 64-bit floating point register.

The default value of this hook is `NULL`, which is treated as always false.

tree TARGET_BUILD_BUILTIN_VA_LIST (*void*) [Target Hook]

This hook returns a type node for `va_list` for the target. The default version of the hook returns `void*`.

int TARGET_ENUM_VA_LIST_P (*int* `idx`, *const char* `**pname`, *tree* [Target Hook]
 `*ptree`)

> This target hook is used in function `c_common_nodes_and_builtins` to iterate through the target specific builtin types for va_list. The variable *idx* is used as iterator. *pname* has to be a pointer to a `const char *` and *ptree* a pointer to a `tree` typed variable. The arguments *pname* and *ptree* are used to store the result of this macro and are set to the name of the va_list builtin type and its internal type. If the return value of this macro is zero, then there is no more element. Otherwise the *IDX* should be increased for the next call of this macro to iterate through all types.

tree TARGET_FN_ABI_VA_LIST (*tree* `fndecl`) [Target Hook]

> This hook returns the va_list type of the calling convention specified by *fndecl*. The default version of this hook returns `va_list_type_node`.

tree TARGET_CANONICAL_VA_LIST_TYPE (*tree* `type`) [Target Hook]

> This hook returns the va_list type of the calling convention specified by the type of *type*. If *type* is not a valid va_list type, it returns `NULL_TREE`.

tree TARGET_GIMPLIFY_VA_ARG_EXPR (*tree* `valist`, *tree* `type`, [Target Hook]
 gimple_seq `*pre_p`, *gimple_seq* `*post_p`)

> This hook performs target-specific gimplification of `VA_ARG_EXPR`. The first two parameters correspond to the arguments to `va_arg`; the latter two are as in `gimplify.c:gimplify_expr`.

bool TARGET_VALID_POINTER_MODE (*scalar_int_mode* `mode`) [Target Hook]

> Define this to return nonzero if the port can handle pointers with machine mode *mode*. The default version of this hook returns true for both `ptr_mode` and `Pmode`.

bool TARGET_REF_MAY_ALIAS_ERRNO (*struct ao_ref* `*ref`) [Target Hook]

> Define this to return nonzero if the memory reference *ref* may alias with the system C library errno location. The default version of this hook assumes the system C library errno location is either a declaration of type int or accessed by dereferencing a pointer to int.

bool TARGET_SCALAR_MODE_SUPPORTED_P (*scalar_mode* `mode`) [Target Hook]

> Define this to return nonzero if the port is prepared to handle insns involving scalar mode *mode*. For a scalar mode to be considered supported, all the basic arithmetic and comparisons must work.
>
> The default version of this hook returns true for any mode required to handle the basic C types (as defined by the port). Included here are the double-word arithmetic supported by the code in 'optabs.c'.

bool TARGET_VECTOR_MODE_SUPPORTED_P (*machine_mode* `mode`) [Target Hook]

> Define this to return nonzero if the port is prepared to handle insns involving vector mode *mode*. At the very least, it must have move patterns for this mode.

opt_machine_mode TARGET_ARRAY_MODE (*machine_mode* `mode`, [Target Hook]
 unsigned HOST_WIDE_INT `nelems`)

> Return the mode that GCC should use for an array that has *nelems* elements, with each element having mode *mode*. Return no mode if the target has no special requirements. In the latter case, GCC looks for an integer mode of the appropriate size

if available and uses BLKmode otherwise. Usually the search for the integer mode is limited to `MAX_FIXED_MODE_SIZE`, but the `TARGET_ARRAY_MODE_SUPPORTED_P` hook allows a larger mode to be used in specific cases.

The main use of this hook is to specify that an array of vectors should also have a vector mode. The default implementation returns no mode.

bool TARGET_ARRAY_MODE_SUPPORTED_P (*machine_mode* `mode`, [Target Hook] *unsigned HOST_WIDE_INT* `nelems`)

Return true if GCC should try to use a scalar mode to store an array of *nelems* elements, given that each element has mode *mode*. Returning true here overrides the usual `MAX_FIXED_MODE` limit and allows GCC to use any defined integer mode.

One use of this hook is to support vector load and store operations that operate on several homogeneous vectors. For example, ARM NEON has operations like:

```
int8x8x3_t vld3_s8 (const int8_t *)
```

where the return type is defined as:

```
typedef struct int8x8x3_t
{
  int8x8_t val[3];
} int8x8x3_t;
```

If this hook allows `val` to have a scalar mode, then `int8x8x3_t` can have the same mode. GCC can then store `int8x8x3_t`s in registers rather than forcing them onto the stack.

bool TARGET_LIBGCC_FLOATING_MODE_SUPPORTED_P [Target Hook] (*scalar_float_mode* `mode`)

Define this to return nonzero if libgcc provides support for the floating-point mode *mode*, which is known to pass `TARGET_SCALAR_MODE_SUPPORTED_P`. The default version of this hook returns true for all of `SFmode`, `DFmode`, `XFmode` and `TFmode`, if such modes exist.

opt_scalar_float_mode TARGET_FLOATN_MODE (*int* `n`, *bool* [Target Hook] `extended`)

Define this to return the machine mode to use for the type `_Floatn`, if *extended* is false, or the type `_Floatnx`, if *extended* is true. If such a type is not supported, return `opt_scalar_float_mode ()`. The default version of this hook returns `SFmode` for `_Float32`, `DFmode` for `_Float64` and `_Float32x` and `TFmode` for `_Float128`, if those modes exist and satisfy the requirements for those types and pass `TARGET_SCALAR_MODE_SUPPORTED_P` and `TARGET_LIBGCC_FLOATING_MODE_SUPPORTED_P`; for `_Float64x`, it returns the first of `XFmode` and `TFmode` that exists and satisfies the same requirements; for other types, it returns `opt_scalar_float_mode ()`. The hook is only called for values of *n* and *extended* that are valid according to ISO/IEC TS 18661-3:2015; that is, *n* is one of 32, 64, 128, or, if *extended* is false, 16 or greater than 128 and a multiple of 32.

bool TARGET_FLOATN_BUILTIN_P (*int* `func`) [Target Hook]

Define this to return true if the `_Floatn` and `_Floatnx` built-in functions should implicitly enable the built-in function without the `__builtin_` prefix in addition to the normal built-in function with the `__builtin_` prefix. The default is to only enable

Chapter 18: Target Description Macros and Functions   525

built-in functions without the `__builtin_` prefix for the GNU C langauge. In strict ANSI/ISO mode, the built-in function without the `__builtin_` prefix is not enabled. The argument `FUNC` is the `enum built_in_function` id of the function to be enabled.

bool TARGET_SMALL_REGISTER_CLASSES_FOR_MODE_P   [Target Hook]
   (*machine_mode* `mode`)

Define this to return nonzero for machine modes for which the port has small register classes. If this target hook returns nonzero for a given *mode*, the compiler will try to minimize the lifetime of registers in *mode*. The hook may be called with `VOIDmode` as argument. In this case, the hook is expected to return nonzero if it returns nonzero for any mode.

On some machines, it is risky to let hard registers live across arbitrary insns. Typically, these machines have instructions that require values to be in specific registers (like an accumulator), and reload will fail if the required hard register is used for another purpose across such an insn.

Passes before reload do not know which hard registers will be used in an instruction, but the machine modes of the registers set or used in the instruction are already known. And for some machines, register classes are small for, say, integer registers but not for floating point registers. For example, the AMD x86-64 architecture requires specific registers for the legacy x86 integer instructions, but there are many SSE registers for floating point operations. On such targets, a good strategy may be to return nonzero from this hook for `INTEGRAL_MODE_P` machine modes but zero for the SSE register classes.

The default version of this hook returns false for any mode. It is always safe to redefine this hook to return with a nonzero value. But if you unnecessarily define it, you will reduce the amount of optimizations that can be performed in some cases. If you do not define this hook to return a nonzero value when it is required, the compiler will run out of spill registers and print a fatal error message.

18.9.8 How Scalar Function Values Are Returned

This section discusses the macros that control returning scalars as values—values that can fit in registers.

rtx TARGET_FUNCTION_VALUE (*const_tree* `ret_type`, *const_tree*   [Target Hook]
   `fn_decl_or_type`, *bool* `outgoing`)

Define this to return an RTX representing the place where a function returns or receives a value of data type *ret_type*, a tree node representing a data type. *fn_decl_or_type* is a tree node representing `FUNCTION_DECL` or `FUNCTION_TYPE` of a function being called. If *outgoing* is false, the hook should compute the register in which the caller will see the return value. Otherwise, the hook should return an RTX representing the place where a function returns a value.

On many machines, only `TYPE_MODE (ret_type)` is relevant. (Actually, on most machines, scalar values are returned in the same place regardless of mode.) The value of the expression is usually a `reg` RTX for the hard register where the return value is stored. The value can also be a `parallel` RTX, if the return value is in multiple places. See `TARGET_FUNCTION_ARG` for an explanation of the `parallel` form.

Note that the callee will populate every location specified in the `parallel`, but if the first element of the `parallel` contains the whole return value, callers will use that element as the canonical location and ignore the others. The m68k port uses this type of `parallel` to return pointers in both '%a0' (the canonical location) and '%d0'.

If `TARGET_PROMOTE_FUNCTION_RETURN` returns true, you must apply the same promotion rules specified in `PROMOTE_MODE` if valtype is a scalar type.

If the precise function being called is known, func is a tree node (`FUNCTION_DECL`) for it; otherwise, func is a null pointer. This makes it possible to use a different value-returning convention for specific functions when all their calls are known.

Some target machines have "register windows" so that the register in which a function returns its value is not the same as the one in which the caller sees the value. For such machines, you should return different RTX depending on outgoing.

`TARGET_FUNCTION_VALUE` is not used for return values with aggregate data types, because these are returned in another way. See `TARGET_STRUCT_VALUE_RTX` and related macros, below.

FUNCTION_VALUE (*valtype*, *func*) [Macro]

> This macro has been deprecated. Use `TARGET_FUNCTION_VALUE` for a new target instead.

LIBCALL_VALUE (*mode*) [Macro]

> A C expression to create an RTX representing the place where a library function returns a value of mode mode.
>
> Note that "library function" in this context means a compiler support routine, used to perform arithmetic, whose name is known specially by the compiler and was not mentioned in the C code being compiled.

rtx TARGET_LIBCALL_VALUE (*machine_mode mode*, *const_rtx fun*) [Target Hook]

> Define this hook if the back-end needs to know the name of the libcall function in order to determine where the result should be returned.
>
> The mode of the result is given by mode and the name of the called library function is given by fun. The hook should return an RTX representing the place where the library function result will be returned.
>
> If this hook is not defined, then LIBCALL_VALUE will be used.

FUNCTION_VALUE_REGNO_P (*regno*) [Macro]

> A C expression that is nonzero if regno is the number of a hard register in which the values of called function may come back.
>
> A register whose use for returning values is limited to serving as the second of a pair (for a value of type `double`, say) need not be recognized by this macro. So for most machines, this definition suffices:
>
>   #define FUNCTION_VALUE_REGNO_P(N) ((N) == 0)
>
> If the machine has register windows, so that the caller and the called function use different registers for the return value, this macro should recognize only the caller's register numbers.
>
> This macro has been deprecated. Use `TARGET_FUNCTION_VALUE_REGNO_P` for a new target instead.

bool TARGET_FUNCTION_VALUE_REGNO_P (*const unsigned int* [Target Hook]
    regno)

> A target hook that return **true** if *regno* is the number of a hard register in which the values of called function may come back.
>
> A register whose use for returning values is limited to serving as the second of a pair (for a value of type **double**, say) need not be recognized by this target hook.
>
> If the machine has register windows, so that the caller and the called function use different registers for the return value, this target hook should recognize only the caller's register numbers.
>
> If this hook is not defined, then FUNCTION_VALUE_REGNO_P will be used.

APPLY_RESULT_SIZE [Macro]

> Define this macro if 'untyped_call' and 'untyped_return' need more space than is implied by FUNCTION_VALUE_REGNO_P for saving and restoring an arbitrary return value.

bool TARGET_OMIT_STRUCT_RETURN_REG [Target Hook]

> Normally, when a function returns a structure by memory, the address is passed as an invisible pointer argument, but the compiler also arranges to return the address from the function like it would a normal pointer return value. Define this to true if that behavior is undesirable on your target.

bool TARGET_RETURN_IN_MSB (*const_tree* **type**) [Target Hook]

> This hook should return true if values of type *type* are returned at the most significant end of a register (in other words, if they are padded at the least significant end). You can assume that *type* is returned in a register; the caller is required to check this.
>
> Note that the register provided by TARGET_FUNCTION_VALUE must be able to hold the complete return value. For example, if a 1-, 2- or 3-byte structure is returned at the most significant end of a 4-byte register, TARGET_FUNCTION_VALUE should provide an SImode rtx.

18.9.9 How Large Values Are Returned

When a function value's mode is BLKmode (and in some other cases), the value is not returned according to TARGET_FUNCTION_VALUE (see Section 18.9.8 [Scalar Return], page 525). Instead, the caller passes the address of a block of memory in which the value should be stored. This address is called the *structure value address*.

This section describes how to control returning structure values in memory.

bool TARGET_RETURN_IN_MEMORY (*const_tree* **type**, *const_tree* [Target Hook]
    fntype)

> This target hook should return a nonzero value to say to return the function value in memory, just as large structures are always returned. Here *type* will be the data type of the value, and *fntype* will be the type of the function doing the returning, or NULL for libcalls.
>
> Note that values of mode BLKmode must be explicitly handled by this function. Also, the option '-fpcc-struct-return' takes effect regardless of this macro. On most

systems, it is possible to leave the hook undefined; this causes a default definition to be used, whose value is the constant 1 for BLKmode values, and 0 otherwise.

Do not use this hook to indicate that structures and unions should always be returned in memory. You should instead use DEFAULT_PCC_STRUCT_RETURN to indicate this.

DEFAULT_PCC_STRUCT_RETURN [Macro]

Define this macro to be 1 if all structure and union return values must be in memory. Since this results in slower code, this should be defined only if needed for compatibility with other compilers or with an ABI. If you define this macro to be 0, then the conventions used for structure and union return values are decided by the TARGET_RETURN_IN_MEMORY target hook.

If not defined, this defaults to the value 1.

rtx TARGET_STRUCT_VALUE_RTX (*tree* **fndecl**, *int* **incoming**) [Target Hook]

This target hook should return the location of the structure value address (normally a mem or reg), or 0 if the address is passed as an "invisible" first argument. Note that *fndecl* may be NULL, for libcalls. You do not need to define this target hook if the address is always passed as an "invisible" first argument.

On some architectures the place where the structure value address is found by the called function is not the same place that the caller put it. This can be due to register windows, or it could be because the function prologue moves it to a different place. *incoming* is 1 or 2 when the location is needed in the context of the called function, and 0 in the context of the caller.

If *incoming* is nonzero and the address is to be found on the stack, return a mem which refers to the frame pointer. If *incoming* is 2, the result is being used to fetch the structure value address at the beginning of a function. If you need to emit adjusting code, you should do it at this point.

PCC_STATIC_STRUCT_RETURN [Macro]

Define this macro if the usual system convention on the target machine for returning structures and unions is for the called function to return the address of a static variable containing the value.

Do not define this if the usual system convention is for the caller to pass an address to the subroutine.

This macro has effect in '-fpcc-struct-return' mode, but it does nothing when you use '-freg-struct-return' mode.

fixed_size_mode TARGET_GET_RAW_RESULT_MODE (*int* **regno**) [Target Hook]

This target hook returns the mode to be used when accessing raw return registers in __builtin_return. Define this macro if the value in *reg_raw_mode* is not correct.

fixed_size_mode TARGET_GET_RAW_ARG_MODE (*int* **regno**) [Target Hook]

This target hook returns the mode to be used when accessing raw argument registers in __builtin_apply_args. Define this macro if the value in *reg_raw_mode* is not correct.

bool TARGET_EMPTY_RECORD_P (*const_tree* **type**) [Target Hook]

This target hook returns true if the type is an empty record. The default is to return false.

void TARGET_WARN_PARAMETER_PASSING_ABI (*cumulative_args_t*   [Target Hook]
    ca, *tree type*)

This target hook warns about the change in empty class parameter passing ABI.

18.9.10 Caller-Saves Register Allocation

If you enable it, GCC can save registers around function calls. This makes it possible to use call-clobbered registers to hold variables that must live across calls.

HARD_REGNO_CALLER_SAVE_MODE (*regno*, *nregs*)   [Macro]

A C expression specifying which mode is required for saving *nregs* of a pseudo-register in call-clobbered hard register *regno*. If *regno* is unsuitable for caller save, VOIDmode should be returned. For most machines this macro need not be defined since GCC will select the smallest suitable mode.

18.9.11 Function Entry and Exit

This section describes the macros that output function entry (*prologue*) and exit (*epilogue*) code.

void TARGET_ASM_PRINT_PATCHABLE_FUNCTION_ENTRY (*FILE*   [Target Hook]
    *file, *unsigned HOST_WIDE_INT patch_area_size*, *bool record_p*)

Generate a patchable area at the function start, consisting of *patch_area_size* NOP instructions. If the target supports named sections and if *record_p* is true, insert a pointer to the current location in the table of patchable functions. The default implementation of the hook places the table of pointers in the special section named __patchable_function_entries.

void TARGET_ASM_FUNCTION_PROLOGUE (*FILE* *file)   [Target Hook]

If defined, a function that outputs the assembler code for entry to a function. The prologue is responsible for setting up the stack frame, initializing the frame pointer register, saving registers that must be saved, and allocating *size* additional bytes of storage for the local variables. *file* is a stdio stream to which the assembler code should be output.

The label for the beginning of the function need not be output by this macro. That has already been done when the macro is run.

To determine which registers to save, the macro can refer to the array regs_ever_live: element r is nonzero if hard register r is used anywhere within the function. This implies the function prologue should save register r, provided it is not one of the call-used registers. (TARGET_ASM_FUNCTION_EPILOGUE must likewise use regs_ever_live.)

On machines that have "register windows", the function entry code does not save on the stack the registers that are in the windows, even if they are supposed to be preserved by function calls; instead it takes appropriate steps to "push" the register stack, if any non-call-used registers are used in the function.

On machines where functions may or may not have frame-pointers, the function entry code must vary accordingly; it must set up the frame pointer if one is wanted, and not otherwise. To determine whether a frame pointer is in wanted, the macro can refer to the variable `frame_pointer_needed`. The variable's value will be 1 at run time in a function that needs a frame pointer. See Section 18.9.5 [Elimination], page 514.

The function entry code is responsible for allocating any stack space required for the function. This stack space consists of the regions listed below. In most cases, these regions are allocated in the order listed, with the last listed region closest to the top of the stack (the lowest address if `STACK_GROWS_DOWNWARD` is defined, and the highest address if it is not defined). You can use a different order for a machine if doing so is more convenient or required for compatibility reasons. Except in cases where required by standard or by a debugger, there is no reason why the stack layout used by GCC need agree with that used by other compilers for a machine.

void TARGET_ASM_FUNCTION_END_PROLOGUE (*FILE *file*)   [Target Hook]
> If defined, a function that outputs assembler code at the end of a prologue. This should be used when the function prologue is being emitted as RTL, and you have some extra assembler that needs to be emitted. See [prologue instruction pattern], page 412.

void TARGET_ASM_FUNCTION_BEGIN_EPILOGUE (*FILE *file*)   [Target Hook]
> If defined, a function that outputs assembler code at the start of an epilogue. This should be used when the function epilogue is being emitted as RTL, and you have some extra assembler that needs to be emitted. See [epilogue instruction pattern], page 412.

void TARGET_ASM_FUNCTION_EPILOGUE (*FILE *file*)   [Target Hook]
> If defined, a function that outputs the assembler code for exit from a function. The epilogue is responsible for restoring the saved registers and stack pointer to their values when the function was called, and returning control to the caller. This macro takes the same argument as the macro `TARGET_ASM_FUNCTION_PROLOGUE`, and the registers to restore are determined from `regs_ever_live` and `CALL_USED_REGISTERS` in the same way.
>
> On some machines, there is a single instruction that does all the work of returning from the function. On these machines, give that instruction the name 'return' and do not define the macro `TARGET_ASM_FUNCTION_EPILOGUE` at all.
>
> Do not define a pattern named 'return' if you want the `TARGET_ASM_FUNCTION_EPILOGUE` to be used. If you want the target switches to control whether return instructions or epilogues are used, define a 'return' pattern with a validity condition that tests the target switches appropriately. If the 'return' pattern's validity condition is false, epilogues will be used.
>
> On machines where functions may or may not have frame-pointers, the function exit code must vary accordingly. Sometimes the code for these two cases is completely different. To determine whether a frame pointer is wanted, the macro can refer to the variable `frame_pointer_needed`. The variable's value will be 1 when compiling a function that needs a frame pointer.
>
> Normally, `TARGET_ASM_FUNCTION_PROLOGUE` and `TARGET_ASM_FUNCTION_EPILOGUE` must treat leaf functions specially. The C variable `current_function_is_leaf` is nonzero for such a function. See Section 18.7.4 [Leaf Functions], page 492.

Chapter 18: Target Description Macros and Functions 531

On some machines, some functions pop their arguments on exit while others leave that for the caller to do. For example, the 68020 when given '-mrtd' pops arguments in functions that take a fixed number of arguments.

Your definition of the macro RETURN_POPS_ARGS decides which functions pop their own arguments. TARGET_ASM_FUNCTION_EPILOGUE needs to know what was decided. The number of bytes of the current function's arguments that this function should pop is available in crtl->args.pops_args. See Section 18.9.8 [Scalar Return], page 525.

- A region of crtl->args.pretend_args_size bytes of uninitialized space just underneath the first argument arriving on the stack. (This may not be at the very start of the allocated stack region if the calling sequence has pushed anything else since pushing the stack arguments. But usually, on such machines, nothing else has been pushed yet, because the function prologue itself does all the pushing.) This region is used on machines where an argument may be passed partly in registers and partly in memory, and, in some cases to support the features in <stdarg.h>.

- An area of memory used to save certain registers used by the function. The size of this area, which may also include space for such things as the return address and pointers to previous stack frames, is machine-specific and usually depends on which registers have been used in the function. Machines with register windows often do not require a save area.

- A region of at least *size* bytes, possibly rounded up to an allocation boundary, to contain the local variables of the function. On some machines, this region and the save area may occur in the opposite order, with the save area closer to the top of the stack.

- Optionally, when ACCUMULATE_OUTGOING_ARGS is defined, a region of crtl->outgoing_args_size bytes to be used for outgoing argument lists of the function. See Section 18.9.6 [Stack Arguments], page 516.

EXIT_IGNORE_STACK [Macro]

Define this macro as a C expression that is nonzero if the return instruction or the function epilogue ignores the value of the stack pointer; in other words, if it is safe to delete an instruction to adjust the stack pointer before a return from the function. The default is 0.

Note that this macro's value is relevant only for functions for which frame pointers are maintained. It is never safe to delete a final stack adjustment in a function that has no frame pointer, and the compiler knows this regardless of EXIT_IGNORE_STACK.

EPILOGUE_USES (*regno*) [Macro]

Define this macro as a C expression that is nonzero for registers that are used by the epilogue or the 'return' pattern. The stack and frame pointer registers are already assumed to be used as needed.

EH_USES (*regno*) [Macro]

Define this macro as a C expression that is nonzero for registers that are used by the exception handling mechanism, and so should be considered live on entry to an exception edge.

`void` **TARGET_ASM_OUTPUT_MI_THUNK** (*FILE* `*file`, *tree*   [Target Hook]
    `thunk_fndecl`, *HOST_WIDE_INT* `delta`, *HOST_WIDE_INT*
    `vcall_offset`, *tree* `function`)

  A function that outputs the assembler code for a thunk function, used to implement C++ virtual function calls with multiple inheritance. The thunk acts as a wrapper around a virtual function, adjusting the implicit object parameter before handing control off to the real function.

  First, emit code to add the integer *delta* to the location that contains the incoming first argument. Assume that this argument contains a pointer, and is the one used to pass the `this` pointer in C++. This is the incoming argument *before* the function prologue, e.g. '%o0' on a sparc. The addition must preserve the values of all other incoming arguments.

  Then, if *vcall_offset* is nonzero, an additional adjustment should be made after adding `delta`. In particular, if *p* is the adjusted pointer, the following adjustment should be made:

    `p += (*((ptrdiff_t **)p))[vcall_offset/sizeof(ptrdiff_t)]`

  After the additions, emit code to jump to *function*, which is a `FUNCTION_DECL`. This is a direct pure jump, not a call, and does not touch the return address. Hence returning from *FUNCTION* will return to whoever called the current 'thunk'.

  The effect must be as if *function* had been called directly with the adjusted first argument. This macro is responsible for emitting all of the code for a thunk function; `TARGET_ASM_FUNCTION_PROLOGUE` and `TARGET_ASM_FUNCTION_EPILOGUE` are not invoked.

  The *thunk_fndecl* is redundant. (*delta* and *function* have already been extracted from it.) It might possibly be useful on some targets, but probably not.

  If you do not define this macro, the target-independent code in the C++ front end will generate a less efficient heavyweight thunk that calls *function* instead of jumping to it. The generic approach does not support varargs.

`bool` **TARGET_ASM_CAN_OUTPUT_MI_THUNK** (*const_tree*   [Target Hook]
    `thunk_fndecl`, *HOST_WIDE_INT* `delta`, *HOST_WIDE_INT*
    `vcall_offset`, *const_tree* `function`)

  A function that returns true if TARGET_ASM_OUTPUT_MI_THUNK would be able to output the assembler code for the thunk function specified by the arguments it is passed, and false otherwise. In the latter case, the generic approach will be used by the C++ front end, with the limitations previously exposed.

18.9.12 Generating Code for Profiling

These macros will help you generate code for profiling.

FUNCTION_PROFILER (`file`, `labelno`)   [Macro]

  A C statement or compound statement to output to *file* some assembler code to call the profiling subroutine `mcount`.

  The details of how `mcount` expects to be called are determined by your operating system environment, not by GCC. To figure them out, compile a small program for profiling using the system's installed C compiler and look at the assembler code that results.

Older implementations of `mcount` expect the address of a counter variable to be loaded into some register. The name of this variable is 'LP' followed by the number *labelno*, so you would generate the name using 'LP%d' in a `fprintf`.

PROFILE_HOOK [Macro]

A C statement or compound statement to output to *file* some assembly code to call the profiling subroutine `mcount` even the target does not support profiling.

NO_PROFILE_COUNTERS [Macro]

Define this macro to be an expression with a nonzero value if the `mcount` subroutine on your system does not need a counter variable allocated for each function. This is true for almost all modern implementations. If you define this macro, you must not use the *labelno* argument to `FUNCTION_PROFILER`.

PROFILE_BEFORE_PROLOGUE [Macro]

Define this macro if the code for function profiling should come before the function prologue. Normally, the profiling code comes after.

bool **TARGET_KEEP_LEAF_WHEN_PROFILED** (*void*) [Target Hook]

This target hook returns true if the target wants the leaf flag for the current function to stay true even if it calls mcount. This might make sense for targets using the leaf flag only to determine whether a stack frame needs to be generated or not and for which the call to mcount is generated before the function prologue.

18.9.13 Permitting tail calls

bool **TARGET_FUNCTION_OK_FOR_SIBCALL** (*tree decl*, *tree exp*) [Target Hook]

True if it is OK to do sibling call optimization for the specified call expression *exp*. *decl* will be the called function, or `NULL` if this is an indirect call.

It is not uncommon for limitations of calling conventions to prevent tail calls to functions outside the current unit of translation, or during PIC compilation. The hook is used to enforce these restrictions, as the `sibcall` md pattern can not fail, or fall over to a "normal" call. The criteria for successful sibling call optimization may vary greatly between different architectures.

void **TARGET_EXTRA_LIVE_ON_ENTRY** (*bitmap regs*) [Target Hook]

Add any hard registers to *regs* that are live on entry to the function. This hook only needs to be defined to provide registers that cannot be found by examination of FUNCTION_ARG_REGNO_P, the callee saved registers, STATIC_CHAIN_INCOMING_REGNUM, STATIC_CHAIN_REGNUM, TARGET_STRUCT_VALUE_RTX, FRAME_POINTER_REGNUM, EH_USES, FRAME_POINTER_REGNUM, ARG_POINTER_REGNUM, and the PIC_OFFSET_TABLE_REGNUM.

void **TARGET_SET_UP_BY_PROLOGUE** (*struct hard_reg_set_container* [Target Hook] ***)

This hook should add additional registers that are computed by the prologue to the hard regset for shrink-wrapping optimization purposes.

bool TARGET_WARN_FUNC_RETURN (*tree*) [Target Hook]
: True if a function's return statements should be checked for matching the function's return type. This includes checking for falling off the end of a non-void function. Return false if no such check should be made.

18.9.14 Shrink-wrapping separate components

The prologue may perform a variety of target dependent tasks such as saving callee-saved registers, saving the return address, aligning the stack, creating a stack frame, initializing the PIC register, setting up the static chain, etc.

On some targets some of these tasks may be independent of others and thus may be shrink-wrapped separately. These independent tasks are referred to as components and are handled generically by the target independent parts of GCC.

Using the following hooks those prologue or epilogue components can be shrink-wrapped separately, so that the initialization (and possibly teardown) those components do is not done as frequently on execution paths where this would unnecessary.

What exactly those components are is up to the target code; the generic code treats them abstractly, as a bit in an `sbitmap`. These `sbitmap`s are allocated by the `shrink_wrap.get_separate_components` and `shrink_wrap.components_for_bb` hooks, and deallocated by the generic code.

sbitmap TARGET_SHRINK_WRAP_GET_SEPARATE_COMPONENTS (*void*) [Target Hook]
: This hook should return an `sbitmap` with the bits set for those components that can be separately shrink-wrapped in the current function. Return NULL if the current function should not get any separate shrink-wrapping. Don't define this hook if it would always return NULL. If it is defined, the other hooks in this group have to be defined as well.

sbitmap TARGET_SHRINK_WRAP_COMPONENTS_FOR_BB (*basic_block*) [Target Hook]
: This hook should return an `sbitmap` with the bits set for those components where either the prologue component has to be executed before the `basic_block`, or the epilogue component after it, or both.

void TARGET_SHRINK_WRAP_DISQUALIFY_COMPONENTS (*sbitmap components*, *edge e*, *sbitmap edge_components*, *bool is_prologue*) [Target Hook]
: This hook should clear the bits in the *components* bitmap for those components in *edge_components* that the target cannot handle on edge *e*, where *is_prologue* says if this is for a prologue or an epilogue instead.

void TARGET_SHRINK_WRAP_EMIT_PROLOGUE_COMPONENTS (*sbitmap*) [Target Hook]
: Emit prologue insns for the components indicated by the parameter.

void TARGET_SHRINK_WRAP_EMIT_EPILOGUE_COMPONENTS (*sbitmap*) [Target Hook]
: Emit epilogue insns for the components indicated by the parameter.

void **TARGET_SHRINK_WRAP_SET_HANDLED_COMPONENTS** (*sbitmap*) [Target Hook]
    Mark the components in the parameter as handled, so that the `prologue` and `epilogue` named patterns know to ignore those components. The target code should not hang on to the `sbitmap`, it will be deleted after this call.

18.9.15 Stack smashing protection

tree **TARGET_STACK_PROTECT_GUARD** (*void*) [Target Hook]
    This hook returns a `DECL` node for the external variable to use for the stack protection guard. This variable is initialized by the runtime to some random value and is used to initialize the guard value that is placed at the top of the local stack frame. The type of this variable must be `ptr_type_node`.

    The default version of this hook creates a variable called '`__stack_chk_guard`', which is normally defined in '`libgcc2.c`'.

tree **TARGET_STACK_PROTECT_FAIL** (*void*) [Target Hook]
    This hook returns a `CALL_EXPR` that alerts the runtime that the stack protect guard variable has been modified. This expression should involve a call to a `noreturn` function.

    The default version of this hook invokes a function called '`__stack_chk_fail`', taking no arguments. This function is normally defined in '`libgcc2.c`'.

bool **TARGET_STACK_PROTECT_RUNTIME_ENABLED_P** (*void*) [Target Hook]
    Returns true if the target wants GCC's default stack protect runtime support, otherwise return false. The default implementation always returns true.

bool **TARGET_SUPPORTS_SPLIT_STACK** (*bool* `report`, struct *gcc_options* `*opts`) [Common Target Hook]
    Whether this target supports splitting the stack when the options described in *opts* have been passed. This is called after options have been parsed, so the target may reject splitting the stack in some configurations. The default version of this hook returns false. If *report* is true, this function may issue a warning or error; if *report* is false, it must simply return a value

18.9.16 Miscellaneous register hooks

bool **TARGET_CALL_FUSAGE_CONTAINS_NON_CALLEE_CLOBBERS** [Target Hook]
    Set to true if each call that binds to a local definition explicitly clobbers or sets all non-fixed registers modified by performing the call. That is, by the call pattern itself, or by code that might be inserted by the linker (e.g. stubs, veneers, branch islands), but not including those modifiable by the callee. The affected registers may be mentioned explicitly in the call pattern, or included as clobbers in CALL_INSN_FUNCTION_USAGE. The default version of this hook is set to false. The purpose of this hook is to enable the fipa-ra optimization.

18.10 Implementing the Varargs Macros

GCC comes with an implementation of `<varargs.h>` and `<stdarg.h>` that work without change on machines that pass arguments on the stack. Other machines require their own implementations of varargs, and the two machine independent header files must have conditionals to include it.

ISO `<stdarg.h>` differs from traditional `<varargs.h>` mainly in the calling convention for `va_start`. The traditional implementation takes just one argument, which is the variable in which to store the argument pointer. The ISO implementation of `va_start` takes an additional second argument. The user is supposed to write the last named argument of the function here.

However, `va_start` should not use this argument. The way to find the end of the named arguments is with the built-in functions described below.

`__builtin_saveregs ()` [Macro]

    Use this built-in function to save the argument registers in memory so that the varargs mechanism can access them. Both ISO and traditional versions of `va_start` must use `__builtin_saveregs`, unless you use `TARGET_SETUP_INCOMING_VARARGS` (see below) instead.

    On some machines, `__builtin_saveregs` is open-coded under the control of the target hook `TARGET_EXPAND_BUILTIN_SAVEREGS`. On other machines, it calls a routine written in assembler language, found in 'libgcc2.c'.

    Code generated for the call to `__builtin_saveregs` appears at the beginning of the function, as opposed to where the call to `__builtin_saveregs` is written, regardless of what the code is. This is because the registers must be saved before the function starts to use them for its own purposes.

`__builtin_next_arg (lastarg)` [Macro]

    This builtin returns the address of the first anonymous stack argument, as type `void *`. If `ARGS_GROW_DOWNWARD`, it returns the address of the location above the first anonymous stack argument. Use it in `va_start` to initialize the pointer for fetching arguments from the stack. Also use it in `va_start` to verify that the second parameter *lastarg* is the last named argument of the current function.

`__builtin_classify_type (object)` [Macro]

    Since each machine has its own conventions for which data types are passed in which kind of register, your implementation of `va_arg` has to embody these conventions. The easiest way to categorize the specified data type is to use `__builtin_classify_type` together with `sizeof` and `__alignof__`.

    `__builtin_classify_type` ignores the value of *object*, considering only its data type. It returns an integer describing what kind of type that is—integer, floating, pointer, structure, and so on.

    The file 'typeclass.h' defines an enumeration that you can use to interpret the values of `__builtin_classify_type`.

These machine description macros help implement varargs:

`rtx TARGET_EXPAND_BUILTIN_SAVEREGS (void)` [Target Hook]

    If defined, this hook produces the machine-specific code for a call to `__builtin_saveregs`. This code will be moved to the very beginning of the function, before any parameter access are made. The return value of this function should be an RTX that contains the value to use as the return of `__builtin_saveregs`.

void TARGET_SETUP_INCOMING_VARARGS (*cumulative_args_t* [Target Hook]
    args_so_far, *machine_mode* mode, *tree* type, *int* *pretend_args_size*, *int* second_time)

    This target hook offers an alternative to using __builtin_saveregs and defining the hook TARGET_EXPAND_BUILTIN_SAVEREGS. Use it to store the anonymous register arguments into the stack so that all the arguments appear to have been passed consecutively on the stack. Once this is done, you can use the standard implementation of varargs that works for machines that pass all their arguments on the stack.

    The argument *args_so_far* points to the CUMULATIVE_ARGS data structure, containing the values that are obtained after processing the named arguments. The arguments *mode* and *type* describe the last named argument—its machine mode and its data type as a tree node.

    The target hook should do two things: first, push onto the stack all the argument registers *not* used for the named arguments, and second, store the size of the data thus pushed into the int-valued variable pointed to by *pretend_args_size*. The value that you store here will serve as additional offset for setting up the stack frame.

    Because you must generate code to push the anonymous arguments at compile time without knowing their data types, TARGET_SETUP_INCOMING_VARARGS is only useful on machines that have just a single category of argument register and use it uniformly for all data types.

    If the argument *second_time* is nonzero, it means that the arguments of the function are being analyzed for the second time. This happens for an inline function, which is not actually compiled until the end of the source file. The hook TARGET_SETUP_INCOMING_VARARGS should not generate any instructions in this case.

bool TARGET_STRICT_ARGUMENT_NAMING (*cumulative_args_t* ca) [Target Hook]
    Define this hook to return true if the location where a function argument is passed depends on whether or not it is a named argument.

    This hook controls how the *named* argument to TARGET_FUNCTION_ARG is set for varargs and stdarg functions. If this hook returns true, the *named* argument is always true for named arguments, and false for unnamed arguments. If it returns false, but TARGET_PRETEND_OUTGOING_VARARGS_NAMED returns true, then all arguments are treated as named. Otherwise, all named arguments except the last are treated as named.

    You need not define this hook if it always returns false.

void TARGET_CALL_ARGS (*rtx*, *tree*) [Target Hook]
    While generating RTL for a function call, this target hook is invoked once for each argument passed to the function, either a register returned by TARGET_FUNCTION_ARG or a memory location. It is called just before the point where argument registers are stored. The type of the function to be called is also passed as the second argument; it is NULL_TREE for libcalls. The TARGET_END_CALL_ARGS hook is invoked just after the code to copy the return reg has been emitted. This functionality can be used to perform special setup of call argument registers if a target needs it. For functions without arguments, the hook is called once with pc_rtx passed instead of an argument register. Most ports do not need to implement anything for this hook.

void **TARGET_END_CALL_ARGS** (*void*)   [Target Hook]

    This target hook is invoked while generating RTL for a function call, just after the point where the return reg is copied into a pseudo. It signals that all the call argument and return registers for the just emitted call are now no longer in use. Most ports do not need to implement anything for this hook.

bool **TARGET_PRETEND_OUTGOING_VARARGS_NAMED**   [Target Hook]

    (*cumulative_args_t* `ca`)

    If you need to conditionally change ABIs so that one works with `TARGET_SETUP_INCOMING_VARARGS`, but the other works like neither `TARGET_SETUP_INCOMING_VARARGS` nor `TARGET_STRICT_ARGUMENT_NAMING` was defined, then define this hook to return `true` if `TARGET_SETUP_INCOMING_VARARGS` is used, `false` otherwise. Otherwise, you should not define this hook.

rtx **TARGET_LOAD_BOUNDS_FOR_ARG** (*rtx* `slot`, *rtx* `arg`, *rtx*   [Target Hook]

    `slot_no`)

    This hook is used by expand pass to emit insn to load bounds of *arg* passed in *slot*. Expand pass uses this hook in case bounds of *arg* are not passed in register. If *slot* is a memory, then bounds are loaded as for regular pointer loaded from memory. If *slot* is not a memory then *slot_no* is an integer constant holding number of the target dependent special slot which should be used to obtain bounds. Hook returns RTX holding loaded bounds.

void **TARGET_STORE_BOUNDS_FOR_ARG** (*rtx* `arg`, *rtx* `slot`, *rtx*   [Target Hook]

    `bounds`, *rtx* `slot_no`)

    This hook is used by expand pass to emit insns to store *bounds* of *arg* passed in *slot*. Expand pass uses this hook in case *bounds* of *arg* are not passed in register. If *slot* is a memory, then *bounds* are stored as for regular pointer stored in memory. If *slot* is not a memory then *slot_no* is an integer constant holding number of the target dependent special slot which should be used to store *bounds*.

rtx **TARGET_LOAD_RETURNED_BOUNDS** (*rtx* `slot`)   [Target Hook]

    This hook is used by expand pass to emit insn to load bounds returned by function call in *slot*. Hook returns RTX holding loaded bounds.

void **TARGET_STORE_RETURNED_BOUNDS** (*rtx* `slot`, *rtx* `bounds`)   [Target Hook]

    This hook is used by expand pass to emit insn to store *bounds* returned by function call into *slot*.

rtx **TARGET_CHKP_FUNCTION_VALUE_BOUNDS** (*const_tree* `ret_type`,   [Target Hook]

    const_tree `fn_decl_or_type`, *bool* `outgoing`)

    Define this to return an RTX representing the place where a function returns bounds for returned pointers. Arguments meaning is similar to `TARGET_FUNCTION_VALUE`.

void **TARGET_SETUP_INCOMING_VARARG_BOUNDS** (*cumulative_args_t*   [Target Hook]

    `args_so_far`, *machine_mode* `mode`, *tree* `type`, *int* `*pretend_args_size`, *int* `second_time`)

    Use it to store bounds for anonymous register arguments stored into the stack. Arguments meaning is similar to `TARGET_SETUP_INCOMING_VARARGS`.

18.11 Trampolines for Nested Functions

A *trampoline* is a small piece of code that is created at run time when the address of a nested function is taken. It normally resides on the stack, in the stack frame of the containing function. These macros tell GCC how to generate code to allocate and initialize a trampoline.

The instructions in the trampoline must do two things: load a constant address into the static chain register, and jump to the real address of the nested function. On CISC machines such as the m68k, this requires two instructions, a move immediate and a jump. Then the two addresses exist in the trampoline as word-long immediate operands. On RISC machines, it is often necessary to load each address into a register in two parts. Then pieces of each address form separate immediate operands.

The code generated to initialize the trampoline must store the variable parts—the static chain value and the function address—into the immediate operands of the instructions. On a CISC machine, this is simply a matter of copying each address to a memory reference at the proper offset from the start of the trampoline. On a RISC machine, it may be necessary to take out pieces of the address and store them separately.

void **TARGET_ASM_TRAMPOLINE_TEMPLATE** (*FILE *f*) [Target Hook]

> This hook is called by `assemble_trampoline_template` to output, on the stream *f*, assembler code for a block of data that contains the constant parts of a trampoline. This code should not include a label—the label is taken care of automatically.
>
> If you do not define this hook, it means no template is needed for the target. Do not define this hook on systems where the block move code to copy the trampoline into place would be larger than the code to generate it on the spot.

TRAMPOLINE_SECTION [Macro]

> Return the section into which the trampoline template is to be placed (see Section 18.18 [Sections], page 570). The default value is `readonly_data_section`.

TRAMPOLINE_SIZE [Macro]

> A C expression for the size in bytes of the trampoline, as an integer.

TRAMPOLINE_ALIGNMENT [Macro]

> Alignment required for trampolines, in bits.
>
> If you don't define this macro, the value of `FUNCTION_ALIGNMENT` is used for aligning trampolines.

void **TARGET_TRAMPOLINE_INIT** (*rtx m_tramp*, *tree fndecl*, *rtx static_chain*) [Target Hook]

> This hook is called to initialize a trampoline. *m_tramp* is an RTX for the memory block for the trampoline; *fndecl* is the `FUNCTION_DECL` for the nested function; *static_chain* is an RTX for the static chain value that should be passed to the function when it is called.
>
> If the target defines `TARGET_ASM_TRAMPOLINE_TEMPLATE`, then the first thing this hook should do is emit a block move into *m_tramp* from the memory block returned by `assemble_trampoline_template`. Note that the block move need only cover the

constant parts of the trampoline. If the target isolates the variable parts of the trampoline to the end, not all `TRAMPOLINE_SIZE` bytes need be copied.

If the target requires any other actions, such as flushing caches or enabling stack execution, these actions should be performed after initializing the trampoline proper.

`rtx` **TARGET_TRAMPOLINE_ADJUST_ADDRESS** (*rtx addr*) [Target Hook]
This hook should perform any machine-specific adjustment in the address of the trampoline. Its argument contains the address of the memory block that was passed to `TARGET_TRAMPOLINE_INIT`. In case the address to be used for a function call should be different from the address at which the template was stored, the different address should be returned; otherwise *addr* should be returned unchanged. If this hook is not defined, *addr* will be used for function calls.

`int` **TARGET_CUSTOM_FUNCTION_DESCRIPTORS** [Target Hook]
This hook should be defined to a power of 2 if the target will benefit from the use of custom descriptors for nested functions instead of the standard trampolines. Such descriptors are created at run time on the stack and made up of data only, but they are non-standard so the generated code must be prepared to deal with them. This hook should be defined to 0 if the target uses function descriptors for its standard calling sequence, like for example HP-PA or IA-64. Using descriptors for nested functions eliminates the need for trampolines that reside on the stack and require it to be made executable.

The value of the macro is used to parameterize the run-time identification scheme implemented to distinguish descriptors from function addresses: it gives the number of bytes by which their address is misaligned compared with function addresses. The value of 1 will generally work, unless it is already reserved by the target for another purpose, like for example on ARM.

Implementing trampolines is difficult on many machines because they have separate instruction and data caches. Writing into a stack location fails to clear the memory in the instruction cache, so when the program jumps to that location, it executes the old contents.

Here are two possible solutions. One is to clear the relevant parts of the instruction cache whenever a trampoline is set up. The other is to make all trampolines identical, by having them jump to a standard subroutine. The former technique makes trampoline execution faster; the latter makes initialization faster.

To clear the instruction cache when a trampoline is initialized, define the following macro.

CLEAR_INSN_CACHE (*beg*, *end*) [Macro]
If defined, expands to a C expression clearing the *instruction cache* in the specified interval. The definition of this macro would typically be a series of `asm` statements. Both *beg* and *end* are both pointer expressions.

To use a standard subroutine, define the following macro. In addition, you must make sure that the instructions in a trampoline fill an entire cache line with identical instructions, or else ensure that the beginning of the trampoline code is always aligned at the same point in its cache line. Look in 'm68k.h' as a guide.

Chapter 18: Target Description Macros and Functions

TRANSFER_FROM_TRAMPOLINE [Macro]

Define this macro if trampolines need a special subroutine to do their work. The macro should expand to a series of `asm` statements which will be compiled with GCC. They go in a library function named `__transfer_from_trampoline`.

If you need to avoid executing the ordinary prologue code of a compiled C function when you jump to the subroutine, you can do so by placing a special label of your own in the assembler code. Use one `asm` statement to generate an assembler label, and another to make the label global. Then trampolines can use that label to jump directly to your special assembler code.

18.12 Implicit Calls to Library Routines

Here is an explanation of implicit calls to library routines.

DECLARE_LIBRARY_RENAMES [Macro]

This macro, if defined, should expand to a piece of C code that will get expanded when compiling functions for libgcc.a. It can be used to provide alternate names for GCC's internal library functions if there are ABI-mandated names that the compiler should provide.

void TARGET_INIT_LIBFUNCS (*void*) [Target Hook]

This hook should declare additional library routines or rename existing ones, using the functions `set_optab_libfunc` and `init_one_libfunc` defined in 'optabs.c'. `init_optabs` calls this macro after initializing all the normal library routines.

The default is to do nothing. Most ports don't need to define this hook.

bool TARGET_LIBFUNC_GNU_PREFIX [Target Hook]

If false (the default), internal library routines start with two underscores. If set to true, these routines start with `__gnu_` instead. E.g., `__muldi3` changes to `__gnu_muldi3`. This currently only affects functions defined in 'libgcc2.c'. If this is set to true, the 'tm.h' file must also `#define LIBGCC2_GNU_PREFIX`.

FLOAT_LIB_COMPARE_RETURNS_BOOL (*mode, comparison*) [Macro]

This macro should return `true` if the library routine that implements the floating point comparison operator *comparison* in mode *mode* will return a boolean, and *false* if it will return a tristate.

GCC's own floating point libraries return tristates from the comparison operators, so the default returns false always. Most ports don't need to define this macro.

TARGET_LIB_INT_CMP_BIASED [Macro]

This macro should evaluate to `true` if the integer comparison functions (like `__cmpdi2`) return 0 to indicate that the first operand is smaller than the second, 1 to indicate that they are equal, and 2 to indicate that the first operand is greater than the second. If this macro evaluates to `false` the comparison functions return −1, 0, and 1 instead of 0, 1, and 2. If the target uses the routines in 'libgcc.a', you do not need to define this macro.

`TARGET_HAS_NO_HW_DIVIDE` [Macro]
> This macro should be defined if the target has no hardware divide instructions. If this macro is defined, GCC will use an algorithm which make use of simple logical and arithmetic operations for 64-bit division. If the macro is not defined, GCC will use an algorithm which make use of a 64-bit by 32-bit divide primitive.

`TARGET_EDOM` [Macro]
> The value of `EDOM` on the target machine, as a C integer constant expression. If you don't define this macro, GCC does not attempt to deposit the value of `EDOM` into `errno` directly. Look in '/usr/include/errno.h' to find the value of `EDOM` on your system.
>
> If you do not define `TARGET_EDOM`, then compiled code reports domain errors by calling the library function and letting it report the error. If mathematical functions on your system use `matherr` when there is an error, then you should leave `TARGET_EDOM` undefined so that `matherr` is used normally.

`GEN_ERRNO_RTX` [Macro]
> Define this macro as a C expression to create an rtl expression that refers to the global "variable" `errno`. (On certain systems, `errno` may not actually be a variable.) If you don't define this macro, a reasonable default is used.

`bool TARGET_LIBC_HAS_FUNCTION (enum function_class fn_class)` [Target Hook]
> This hook determines whether a function from a class of functions *fn_class* is present at the runtime.

`NEXT_OBJC_RUNTIME` [Macro]
> Set this macro to 1 to use the "NeXT" Objective-C message sending conventions by default. This calling convention involves passing the object, the selector and the method arguments all at once to the method-lookup library function. This is the usual setting when targeting Darwin/Mac OS X systems, which have the NeXT runtime installed.
>
> If the macro is set to 0, the "GNU" Objective-C message sending convention will be used by default. This convention passes just the object and the selector to the method-lookup function, which returns a pointer to the method.
>
> In either case, it remains possible to select code-generation for the alternate scheme, by means of compiler command line switches.

18.13 Addressing Modes

This is about addressing modes.

`HAVE_PRE_INCREMENT` [Macro]
`HAVE_PRE_DECREMENT` [Macro]
`HAVE_POST_INCREMENT` [Macro]
`HAVE_POST_DECREMENT` [Macro]
> A C expression that is nonzero if the machine supports pre-increment, pre-decrement, post-increment, or post-decrement addressing respectively.

Chapter 18: Target Description Macros and Functions 543

HAVE_PRE_MODIFY_DISP [Macro]
HAVE_POST_MODIFY_DISP [Macro]
: A C expression that is nonzero if the machine supports pre- or post-address side-effect generation involving constants other than the size of the memory operand.

HAVE_PRE_MODIFY_REG [Macro]
HAVE_POST_MODIFY_REG [Macro]
: A C expression that is nonzero if the machine supports pre- or post-address side-effect generation involving a register displacement.

CONSTANT_ADDRESS_P (x) [Macro]
: A C expression that is 1 if the RTX x is a constant which is a valid address. On most machines the default definition of (CONSTANT_P (x) && GET_CODE (x) != CONST_DOUBLE) is acceptable, but a few machines are more restrictive as to which constant addresses are supported.

CONSTANT_P (x) [Macro]
: CONSTANT_P, which is defined by target-independent code, accepts integer-values expressions whose values are not explicitly known, such as symbol_ref, label_ref, and high expressions and const arithmetic expressions, in addition to const_int and const_double expressions.

MAX_REGS_PER_ADDRESS [Macro]
: A number, the maximum number of registers that can appear in a valid memory address. Note that it is up to you to specify a value equal to the maximum number that TARGET_LEGITIMATE_ADDRESS_P would ever accept.

bool TARGET_LEGITIMATE_ADDRESS_P (*machine_mode* mode, *rtx* x, [Target Hook]
       bool strict)
: A function that returns whether x (an RTX) is a legitimate memory address on the target machine for a memory operand of mode *mode*.

  Legitimate addresses are defined in two variants: a strict variant and a non-strict one. The *strict* parameter chooses which variant is desired by the caller.

  The strict variant is used in the reload pass. It must be defined so that any pseudo-register that has not been allocated a hard register is considered a memory reference. This is because in contexts where some kind of register is required, a pseudo-register with no hard register must be rejected. For non hard registers, the strict variant should look up the reg_renumber array; it should then proceed using the hard register number in the array, or treat the pseudo as a memory reference if the array holds -1.

  The non-strict variant is used in other passes. It must be defined to accept all pseudo-registers in every context where some kind of register is required.

  Normally, constant addresses which are the sum of a symbol_ref and an integer are stored inside a const RTX to mark them as constant. Therefore, there is no need to recognize such sums specifically as legitimate addresses. Normally you would simply recognize any const as legitimate.

  Usually PRINT_OPERAND_ADDRESS is not prepared to handle constant sums that are not marked with const. It assumes that a naked plus indicates indexing. If so, then you *must* reject such naked constant sums as illegitimate addresses, so that none of them will be given to PRINT_OPERAND_ADDRESS.

On some machines, whether a symbolic address is legitimate depends on the section that the address refers to. On these machines, define the target hook TARGET_ENCODE_SECTION_INFO to store the information into the symbol_ref, and then check for it here. When you see a const, you will have to look inside it to find the symbol_ref in order to determine the section. See Section 18.20 [Assembler Format], page 576.

Some ports are still using a deprecated legacy substitute for this hook, the GO_IF_LEGITIMATE_ADDRESS macro. This macro has this syntax:

```
#define GO_IF_LEGITIMATE_ADDRESS (mode, x, label)
```

and should goto label if the address x is a valid address on the target machine for a memory operand of mode mode.

Compiler source files that want to use the strict variant of this macro define the macro REG_OK_STRICT. You should use an #ifdef REG_OK_STRICT conditional to define the strict variant in that case and the non-strict variant otherwise.

Using the hook is usually simpler because it limits the number of files that are recompiled when changes are made.

TARGET_MEM_CONSTRAINT [Macro]

A single character to be used instead of the default 'm' character for general memory addresses. This defines the constraint letter which matches the memory addresses accepted by TARGET_LEGITIMATE_ADDRESS_P. Define this macro if you want to support new address formats in your back end without changing the semantics of the 'm' constraint. This is necessary in order to preserve functionality of inline assembly constructs using the 'm' constraint.

FIND_BASE_TERM (x) [Macro]

A C expression to determine the base term of address x, or to provide a simplified version of x from which 'alias.c' can easily find the base term. This macro is used in only two places: find_base_value and find_base_term in 'alias.c'.

It is always safe for this macro to not be defined. It exists so that alias analysis can understand machine-dependent addresses.

The typical use of this macro is to handle addresses containing a label_ref or symbol_ref within an UNSPEC.

rtx TARGET_LEGITIMIZE_ADDRESS (*rtx x, rtx oldx, machine_mode mode*) [Target Hook]

This hook is given an invalid memory address x for an operand of mode mode and should try to return a valid memory address.

x will always be the result of a call to break_out_memory_refs, and oldx will be the operand that was given to that function to produce x.

The code of the hook should not alter the substructure of x. If it transforms x into a more legitimate form, it should return the new x.

It is not necessary for this hook to come up with a legitimate address, with the exception of native TLS addresses (see Section 18.25 [Emulated TLS], page 616). The

Chapter 18: Target Description Macros and Functions 545

compiler has standard ways of doing so in all cases. In fact, if the target supports only emulated TLS, it is safe to omit this hook or make it return *x* if it cannot find a valid way to legitimize the address. But often a machine-dependent strategy can generate better code.

LEGITIMIZE_RELOAD_ADDRESS (*x*, *mode*, *opnum*, *type*, *ind_levels*, *win*) [Macro]
A C compound statement that attempts to replace *x*, which is an address that needs reloading, with a valid memory address for an operand of mode *mode*. *win* will be a C statement label elsewhere in the code. It is not necessary to define this macro, but it might be useful for performance reasons.

For example, on the i386, it is sometimes possible to use a single reload register instead of two by reloading a sum of two pseudo registers into a register. On the other hand, for number of RISC processors offsets are limited so that often an intermediate address needs to be generated in order to address a stack slot. By defining **LEGITIMIZE_RELOAD_ADDRESS** appropriately, the intermediate addresses generated for adjacent some stack slots can be made identical, and thus be shared.

Note: This macro should be used with caution. It is necessary to know something of how reload works in order to effectively use this, and it is quite easy to produce macros that build in too much knowledge of reload internals.

Note: This macro must be able to reload an address created by a previous invocation of this macro. If it fails to handle such addresses then the compiler may generate incorrect code or abort.

The macro definition should use `push_reload` to indicate parts that need reloading; *opnum*, *type* and *ind_levels* are usually suitable to be passed unaltered to `push_reload`.

The code generated by this macro must not alter the substructure of *x*. If it transforms *x* into a more legitimate form, it should assign *x* (which will always be a C variable) a new value. This also applies to parts that you change indirectly by calling `push_reload`.

The macro definition may use `strict_memory_address_p` to test if the address has become legitimate.

If you want to change only a part of *x*, one standard way of doing this is to use `copy_rtx`. Note, however, that it unshares only a single level of rtl. Thus, if the part to be changed is not at the top level, you'll need to replace first the top level. It is not necessary for this macro to come up with a legitimate address; but often a machine-dependent strategy can generate better code.

bool TARGET_MODE_DEPENDENT_ADDRESS_P (*const_rtx* **addr**, [Target Hook]
 addr_space_t **addrspace**)
This hook returns **true** if memory address *addr* in address space *addrspace* can have different meanings depending on the machine mode of the memory reference it is used for or if the address is valid for some modes but not others.

Autoincrement and autodecrement addresses typically have mode-dependent effects because the amount of the increment or decrement is the size of the operand being addressed. Some machines have other mode-dependent addresses. Many RISC machines have no mode-dependent addresses.

You may assume that *addr* is a valid address for the machine.

The default version of this hook returns `false`.

bool **TARGET_LEGITIMATE_CONSTANT_P** (*machine_mode* `mode`, *rtx* `x`)   [Target Hook]

This hook returns true if *x* is a legitimate constant for a *mode*-mode immediate operand on the target machine. You can assume that *x* satisfies `CONSTANT_P`, so you need not check this.

The default definition returns true.

rtx **TARGET_DELEGITIMIZE_ADDRESS** (*rtx* `x`)   [Target Hook]

This hook is used to undo the possibly obfuscating effects of the `LEGITIMIZE_ADDRESS` and `LEGITIMIZE_RELOAD_ADDRESS` target macros. Some backend implementations of these macros wrap symbol references inside an `UNSPEC` rtx to represent PIC or similar addressing modes. This target hook allows GCC's optimizers to understand the semantics of these opaque `UNSPEC`s by converting them back into their original form.

bool **TARGET_CONST_NOT_OK_FOR_DEBUG_P** (*rtx* `x`)   [Target Hook]

This hook should return true if *x* should not be emitted into debug sections.

bool **TARGET_CANNOT_FORCE_CONST_MEM** (*machine_mode* `mode`, *rtx* `x`)   [Target Hook]

This hook should return true if *x* is of a form that cannot (or should not) be spilled to the constant pool. *mode* is the mode of *x*.

The default version of this hook returns false.

The primary reason to define this hook is to prevent reload from deciding that a non-legitimate constant would be better reloaded from the constant pool instead of spilling and reloading a register holding the constant. This restriction is often true of addresses of TLS symbols for various targets.

bool **TARGET_USE_BLOCKS_FOR_CONSTANT_P** (*machine_mode* `mode`, *const_rtx* `x`)   [Target Hook]

This hook should return true if pool entries for constant *x* can be placed in an `object_block` structure. *mode* is the mode of *x*.

The default version returns false for all constants.

bool **TARGET_USE_BLOCKS_FOR_DECL_P** (*const_tree* `decl`)   [Target Hook]

This hook should return true if pool entries for *decl* should be placed in an `object_block` structure.

The default version returns true for all decls.

tree **TARGET_BUILTIN_RECIPROCAL** (*tree* `fndecl`)   [Target Hook]

This hook should return the DECL of a function that implements the reciprocal of the machine-specific builtin function *fndecl*, or `NULL_TREE` if such a function is not available.

Chapter 18: Target Description Macros and Functions 547

tree TARGET_VECTORIZE_BUILTIN_MASK_FOR_LOAD (*void*)   [Target Hook]

This hook should return the DECL of a function *f* that given an address *addr* as an argument returns a mask *m* that can be used to extract from two vectors the relevant data that resides in *addr* in case *addr* is not properly aligned.

The autovectorizer, when vectorizing a load operation from an address *addr* that may be unaligned, will generate two vector loads from the two aligned addresses around *addr*. It then generates a `REALIGN_LOAD` operation to extract the relevant data from the two loaded vectors. The first two arguments to `REALIGN_LOAD`, *v1* and *v2*, are the two vectors, each of size *VS*, and the third argument, *OFF*, defines how the data will be extracted from these two vectors: if *OFF* is 0, then the returned vector is *v2*; otherwise, the returned vector is composed from the last *VS-OFF* elements of *v1* concatenated to the first *OFF* elements of *v2*.

If this hook is defined, the autovectorizer will generate a call to *f* (using the DECL tree that this hook returns) and will use the return value of *f* as the argument *OFF* to `REALIGN_LOAD`. Therefore, the mask *m* returned by *f* should comply with the semantics expected by `REALIGN_LOAD` described above. If this hook is not defined, then *addr* will be used as the argument *OFF* to `REALIGN_LOAD`, in which case the low $\log 2(VS) - 1$ bits of *addr* will be considered.

int TARGET_VECTORIZE_BUILTIN_VECTORIZATION_COST (*enum*   [Target Hook]
    vect_cost_for_stmt `type_of_cost`, *tree* `vectype`, *int* `misalign`)

Returns cost of different scalar or vector statements for vectorization cost model. For vector memory operations the cost may depend on type (*vectype*) and misalignment value (*misalign*).

HOST_WIDE_INT   [Target Hook]
    TARGET_VECTORIZE_PREFERRED_VECTOR_ALIGNMENT (*const_tree* `type`)

This hook returns the preferred alignment in bits for accesses to vectors of type *type* in vectorized code. This might be less than or greater than the ABI-defined value returned by `TARGET_VECTOR_ALIGNMENT`. It can be equal to the alignment of a single element, in which case the vectorizer will not try to optimize for alignment.

The default hook returns `TYPE_ALIGN (type)`, which is correct for most targets.

bool TARGET_VECTORIZE_VECTOR_ALIGNMENT_REACHABLE   [Target Hook]
    (*const_tree* `type`, *bool* `is_packed`)

Return true if vector alignment is reachable (by peeling N iterations) for the given scalar type *type*. *is_packed* is false if the scalar access using *type* is known to be naturally aligned.

bool TARGET_VECTORIZE_VEC_PERM_CONST (*machine_mode* `mode`,   [Target Hook]
    rtx `output`, *rtx* `in0`, *rtx* `in1`, *const vec_perm_indices* `&sel`)

This hook is used to test whether the target can permute up to two vectors of mode *mode* using the permutation vector `sel`, and also to emit such a permutation. In the former case *in0*, *in1* and *out* are all null. In the latter case *in0* and *in1* are the source vectors and *out* is the destination vector; all three are registers of mode *mode*. *in1* is the same as *in0* if *sel* describes a permutation on one vector instead of two.

Return true if the operation is possible, emitting instructions for it if rtxes are provided.

If the hook returns false for a mode with multibyte elements, GCC will try the equivalent byte operation. If that also fails, it will try forcing the selector into a register and using the *vec_permmode* instruction pattern. There is no need for the hook to handle these two implementation approaches itself.

`tree` **TARGET_VECTORIZE_BUILTIN_CONVERSION** (*unsigned* `code`, [Target Hook]
     tree `dest_type`, *tree* `src_type`)

This hook should return the DECL of a function that implements conversion of the input vector of type *src_type* to type *dest_type*. The value of *code* is one of the enumerators in `enum tree_code` and specifies how the conversion is to be applied (truncation, rounding, etc.).

If this hook is defined, the autovectorizer will use the `TARGET_VECTORIZE_BUILTIN_CONVERSION` target hook when vectorizing conversion. Otherwise, it will return `NULL_TREE`.

`tree` **TARGET_VECTORIZE_BUILTIN_VECTORIZED_FUNCTION** [Target Hook]
     (*unsigned* `code`, *tree* `vec_type_out`, *tree* `vec_type_in`)

This hook should return the decl of a function that implements the vectorized variant of the function with the `combined_fn` code *code* or `NULL_TREE` if such a function is not available. The return type of the vectorized function shall be of vector type *vec_type_out* and the argument types should be *vec_type_in*.

`tree` **TARGET_VECTORIZE_BUILTIN_MD_VECTORIZED_FUNCTION** [Target Hook]
     (*tree* `fndecl`, *tree* `vec_type_out`, *tree* `vec_type_in`)

This hook should return the decl of a function that implements the vectorized variant of target built-in function `fndecl`. The return type of the vectorized function shall be of vector type *vec_type_out* and the argument types should be *vec_type_in*.

`bool` **TARGET_VECTORIZE_SUPPORT_VECTOR_MISALIGNMENT** [Target Hook]
     (*machine_mode* `mode`, *const_tree* `type`, *int* `misalignment`, *bool* `is_packed`)

This hook should return true if the target supports misaligned vector store/load of a specific factor denoted in the *misalignment* parameter. The vector store/load should be of machine mode *mode* and the elements in the vectors should be of type *type*. *is_packed* parameter is true if the memory access is defined in a packed struct.

`machine_mode` **TARGET_VECTORIZE_PREFERRED_SIMD_MODE** [Target Hook]
     (*scalar_mode* `mode`)

This hook should return the preferred mode for vectorizing scalar mode *mode*. The default is equal to `word_mode`, because the vectorizer can do some transformations even in absence of specialized SIMD hardware.

`machine_mode` **TARGET_VECTORIZE_SPLIT_REDUCTION** [Target Hook]
     (*machine_mode*)

This hook should return the preferred mode to split the final reduction step on *mode* to. The reduction is then carried out reducing upper against lower halves of vectors recursively until the specified mode is reached. The default is *mode* which means no splitting.

Chapter 18: Target Description Macros and Functions 549

void TARGET_VECTORIZE_AUTOVECTORIZE_VECTOR_SIZES [Target Hook]
(*vector_sizes* *`sizes`*)

If the mode returned by `TARGET_VECTORIZE_PREFERRED_SIMD_MODE` is not the only one that is worth considering, this hook should add all suitable vector sizes to *sizes*, in order of decreasing preference. The first one should be the size of `TARGET_VECTORIZE_PREFERRED_SIMD_MODE`.

The hook does not need to do anything if the vector returned by `TARGET_VECTORIZE_PREFERRED_SIMD_MODE` is the only one relevant for autovectorization. The default implementation does nothing.

opt_machine_mode TARGET_VECTORIZE_GET_MASK_MODE [Target Hook]
(*poly_uint64* `nunits`, *poly_uint64* `length`)

A vector mask is a value that holds one boolean result for every element in a vector. This hook returns the machine mode that should be used to represent such a mask when the vector in question is *length* bytes long and contains *nunits* elements. The hook returns an empty `opt_machine_mode` if no such mode exists.

The default implementation returns the mode of an integer vector that is *length* bytes long and that contains *nunits* elements, if such a mode exists.

bool TARGET_VECTORIZE_EMPTY_MASK_IS_EXPENSIVE (*unsigned* [Target Hook]
`ifn`)

This hook returns true if masked internal function *ifn* (really of type `internal_fn`) should be considered expensive when the mask is all zeros. GCC can then try to branch around the instruction instead.

void * TARGET_VECTORIZE_INIT_COST (*struct loop* *`loop_info`*) [Target Hook]

This hook should initialize target-specific data structures in preparation for modeling the costs of vectorizing a loop or basic block. The default allocates three unsigned integers for accumulating costs for the prologue, body, and epilogue of the loop or basic block. If *loop_info* is non-NULL, it identifies the loop being vectorized; otherwise a single block is being vectorized.

unsigned TARGET_VECTORIZE_ADD_STMT_COST (*void* *`data`*, *int* [Target Hook]
`count`, *enum vect_cost_for_stmt* `kind`, *struct _stmt_vec_info* *`stmt_info`*, *int*
`misalign`, *enum vect_cost_model_location* `where`)

This hook should update the target specific *data* in response to adding *count* copies of the given *kind* of statement to a loop or basic block. The default adds the builtin vectorizer cost for the copies of the statement to the accumulator specified by *where*, (the prologue, body, or epilogue) and returns the amount added. The return value should be viewed as a tentative cost that may later be revised.

void TARGET_VECTORIZE_FINISH_COST (*void* *`data`*, *unsigned* [Target Hook]
`prologue_cost`, *unsigned* *`body_cost`*, *unsigned* *`epilogue_cost`*)

This hook should complete calculations of the cost of vectorizing a loop or basic block based on *data*, and return the prologue, body, and epilogue costs as unsigned integers. The default returns the value of the three accumulators.

void TARGET_VECTORIZE_DESTROY_COST_DATA (*void* `*data`) [Target Hook]
   This hook should release *data* and any related data structures allocated by TARGET_VECTORIZE_INIT_COST. The default releases the accumulator.

tree TARGET_VECTORIZE_BUILTIN_GATHER (*const_tree* [Target Hook]
      `mem_vectype`, *const_tree* `index_type`, *int* `scale`)
   Target builtin that implements vector gather operation. *mem_vectype* is the vector type of the load and *index_type* is scalar type of the index, scaled by *scale*. The default is `NULL_TREE` which means to not vectorize gather loads.

tree TARGET_VECTORIZE_BUILTIN_SCATTER (*const_tree* `vectype`, [Target Hook]
      const_tree `index_type`, *int* `scale`)
   Target builtin that implements vector scatter operation. *vectype* is the vector type of the store and *index_type* is scalar type of the index, scaled by *scale*. The default is `NULL_TREE` which means to not vectorize scatter stores.

int TARGET_SIMD_CLONE_COMPUTE_VECSIZE_AND_SIMDLEN (*struct* [Target Hook]
      cgraph_node *, *struct cgraph_simd_clone* *, **tree**, **int**)
   This hook should set *vecsize_mangle*, *vecsize_int*, *vecsize_float* fields in *simd_clone* structure pointed by *clone_info* argument and also *simdlen* field if it was previously 0. The hook should return 0 if SIMD clones shouldn't be emitted, or number of *vecsize_mangle* variants that should be emitted.

void TARGET_SIMD_CLONE_ADJUST (*struct cgraph_node* *) [Target Hook]
   This hook should add implicit `attribute(target("..."))` attribute to SIMD clone *node* if needed.

int TARGET_SIMD_CLONE_USABLE (*struct cgraph_node* *) [Target Hook]
   This hook should return -1 if SIMD clone *node* shouldn't be used in vectorized loops in current function, or non-negative number if it is usable. In that case, the smaller the number is, the more desirable it is to use it.

int TARGET_SIMT_VF (*void*) [Target Hook]
   Return number of threads in SIMT thread group on the target.

bool TARGET_GOACC_VALIDATE_DIMS (*tree* `decl`, *int* `*dims`, *int* [Target Hook]
      `fn_level`)
   This hook should check the launch dimensions provided for an OpenACC compute region, or routine. Defaulted values are represented as -1 and non-constant values as 0. The *fn_level* is negative for the function corresponding to the compute region. For a routine is is the outermost level at which partitioned execution may be spawned. The hook should verify non-default values. If DECL is NULL, global defaults are being validated and unspecified defaults should be filled in. Diagnostics should be issued as appropriate. Return true, if changes have been made. You must override this hook to provide dimensions larger than 1.

int TARGET_GOACC_DIM_LIMIT (*int* `axis`) [Target Hook]
   This hook should return the maximum size of a particular dimension, or zero if unbounded.

bool TARGET_GOACC_FORK_JOIN (*gcall *call, const int *dims, bool*   [Target Hook]
    is_fork)
    This hook can be used to convert IFN_GOACC_FORK and IFN_GOACC_JOIN function calls to target-specific gimple, or indicate whether they should be retained. It is executed during the oacc_device_lower pass. It should return true, if the call should be retained. It should return false, if it is to be deleted (either because target-specific gimple has been inserted before it, or there is no need for it). The default hook returns false, if there are no RTL expanders for them.

void TARGET_GOACC_REDUCTION (*gcall *call*)   [Target Hook]
    This hook is used by the oacc_transform pass to expand calls to the GOACC_REDUCTION internal function, into a sequence of gimple instructions. *call* is gimple statement containing the call to the function. This hook removes statement *call* after the expanded sequence has been inserted. This hook is also responsible for allocating any storage for reductions when necessary.

18.14 Anchored Addresses

GCC usually addresses every static object as a separate entity. For example, if we have:

```
static int a, b, c;
int foo (void) { return a + b + c; }
```

the code for `foo` will usually calculate three separate symbolic addresses: those of `a`, `b` and `c`. On some targets, it would be better to calculate just one symbolic address and access the three variables relative to it. The equivalent pseudocode would be something like:

```
int foo (void)
{
  register int *xr = &x;
  return xr[&a - &x] + xr[&b - &x] + xr[&c - &x];
}
```

(which isn't valid C). We refer to shared addresses like `x` as "section anchors". Their use is controlled by '-fsection-anchors'.

The hooks below describe the target properties that GCC needs to know in order to make effective use of section anchors. It won't use section anchors at all unless either `TARGET_MIN_ANCHOR_OFFSET` or `TARGET_MAX_ANCHOR_OFFSET` is set to a nonzero value.

HOST_WIDE_INT TARGET_MIN_ANCHOR_OFFSET   [Target Hook]
    The minimum offset that should be applied to a section anchor. On most targets, it should be the smallest offset that can be applied to a base register while still giving a legitimate address for every mode. The default value is 0.

HOST_WIDE_INT TARGET_MAX_ANCHOR_OFFSET   [Target Hook]
    Like `TARGET_MIN_ANCHOR_OFFSET`, but the maximum (inclusive) offset that should be applied to section anchors. The default value is 0.

void TARGET_ASM_OUTPUT_ANCHOR (*rtx x*)   [Target Hook]
    Write the assembly code to define section anchor *x*, which is a `SYMBOL_REF` for which 'SYMBOL_REF_ANCHOR_P (*x*)' is true. The hook is called with the assembly output position set to the beginning of `SYMBOL_REF_BLOCK` (*x*).

If `ASM_OUTPUT_DEF` is available, the hook's default definition uses it to define the symbol as '. + SYMBOL_REF_BLOCK_OFFSET (x)'. If `ASM_OUTPUT_DEF` is not available, the hook's default definition is `NULL`, which disables the use of section anchors altogether.

bool **TARGET_USE_ANCHORS_FOR_SYMBOL_P** (*const_rtx x*)　　　　　　　　[Target Hook]
Return true if GCC should attempt to use anchors to access `SYMBOL_REF` x. You can assume 'SYMBOL_REF_HAS_BLOCK_INFO_P (x)' and '!SYMBOL_REF_ANCHOR_P (x)'.

The default version is correct for most targets, but you might need to intercept this hook to handle things like target-specific attributes or target-specific sections.

18.15 Condition Code Status

The macros in this section can be split in two families, according to the two ways of representing condition codes in GCC.

The first representation is the so called (cc0) representation (see Section 17.12 [Jump Patterns], page 419), where all instructions can have an implicit clobber of the condition codes. The second is the condition code register representation, which provides better schedulability for architectures that do have a condition code register, but on which most instructions do not affect it. The latter category includes most RISC machines.

The implicit clobbering poses a strong restriction on the placement of the definition and use of the condition code. In the past the definition and use were always adjacent. However, recent changes to support trapping arithmetic may result in the definition and user being in different blocks. Thus, there may be a `NOTE_INSN_BASIC_BLOCK` between them. Additionally, the definition may be the source of exception handling edges.

These restrictions can prevent important optimizations on some machines. For example, on the IBM RS/6000, there is a delay for taken branches unless the condition code register is set three instructions earlier than the conditional branch. The instruction scheduler cannot perform this optimization if it is not permitted to separate the definition and use of the condition code register.

For this reason, it is possible and suggested to use a register to represent the condition code for new ports. If there is a specific condition code register in the machine, use a hard register. If the condition code or comparison result can be placed in any general register, or if there are multiple condition registers, use a pseudo register. Registers used to store the condition code value will usually have a mode that is in class `MODE_CC`.

Alternatively, you can use `BImode` if the comparison operator is specified already in the compare instruction. In this case, you are not interested in most macros in this section.

18.15.1 Representation of condition codes using (cc0)

The file 'conditions.h' defines a variable `cc_status` to describe how the condition code was computed (in case the interpretation of the condition code depends on the instruction that it was set by). This variable contains the RTL expressions on which the condition code is currently based, and several standard flags.

Sometimes additional machine-specific flags must be defined in the machine description header file. It can also add additional machine-specific information by defining `CC_STATUS_MDEP`.

Chapter 18: Target Description Macros and Functions

CC_STATUS_MDEP [Macro]

C code for a data type which is used for declaring the `mdep` component of `cc_status`. It defaults to `int`.

This macro is not used on machines that do not use `cc0`.

CC_STATUS_MDEP_INIT [Macro]

A C expression to initialize the `mdep` field to "empty". The default definition does nothing, since most machines don't use the field anyway. If you want to use the field, you should probably define this macro to initialize it.

This macro is not used on machines that do not use `cc0`.

NOTICE_UPDATE_CC (*exp*, *insn*) [Macro]

A C compound statement to set the components of `cc_status` appropriately for an insn *insn* whose body is *exp*. It is this macro's responsibility to recognize insns that set the condition code as a byproduct of other activity as well as those that explicitly set (cc0).

This macro is not used on machines that do not use `cc0`.

If there are insns that do not set the condition code but do alter other machine registers, this macro must check to see whether they invalidate the expressions that the condition code is recorded as reflecting. For example, on the 68000, insns that store in address registers do not set the condition code, which means that usually `NOTICE_UPDATE_CC` can leave `cc_status` unaltered for such insns. But suppose that the previous insn set the condition code based on location 'a4@(102)' and the current insn stores a new value in 'a4'. Although the condition code is not changed by this, it will no longer be true that it reflects the contents of 'a4@(102)'. Therefore, `NOTICE_UPDATE_CC` must alter `cc_status` in this case to say that nothing is known about the condition code value.

The definition of `NOTICE_UPDATE_CC` must be prepared to deal with the results of peephole optimization: insns whose patterns are `parallel` RTXs containing various `reg`, `mem` or constants which are just the operands. The RTL structure of these insns is not sufficient to indicate what the insns actually do. What `NOTICE_UPDATE_CC` should do when it sees one is just to run `CC_STATUS_INIT`.

A possible definition of `NOTICE_UPDATE_CC` is to call a function that looks at an attribute (see Section 17.19 [Insn Attributes], page 434) named, for example, 'cc'. This avoids having detailed information about patterns in two places, the 'md' file and in `NOTICE_UPDATE_CC`.

18.15.2 Representation of condition codes using registers

SELECT_CC_MODE (*op*, *x*, *y*) [Macro]

On many machines, the condition code may be produced by other instructions than compares, for example the branch can use directly the condition code set by a subtract instruction. However, on some machines when the condition code is set this way some bits (such as the overflow bit) are not set in the same way as a test instruction, so that a different branch instruction must be used for some conditional branches. When this happens, use the machine mode of the condition code register to record different formats of the condition code register. Modes can also be used to record which compare instruction (e.g. a signed or an unsigned comparison) produced the condition codes.

If other modes than CCmode are required, add them to 'machine-modes.def' and define SELECT_CC_MODE to choose a mode given an operand of a compare. This is needed because the modes have to be chosen not only during RTL generation but also, for example, by instruction combination. The result of SELECT_CC_MODE should be consistent with the mode used in the patterns; for example to support the case of the add on the SPARC discussed above, we have the pattern

```
(define_insn ""
  [(set (reg:CCNZ 0)
        (compare:CCNZ
          (plus:SI (match_operand:SI 0 "register_operand" "%r")
                   (match_operand:SI 1 "arith_operand" "rI"))
          (const_int 0)))]
  ""
  "...")
```

together with a SELECT_CC_MODE that returns CCNZmode for comparisons whose argument is a plus:

```
#define SELECT_CC_MODE(OP,X,Y) \
  (GET_MODE_CLASS (GET_MODE (X)) == MODE_FLOAT            \
   ? ((OP == LT || OP == LE || OP == GT || OP == GE)      \
      ? CCFPEmode : CCFPmode)                             \
   : ((GET_CODE (X) == PLUS || GET_CODE (X) == MINUS      \
       || GET_CODE (X) == NEG || GET_CODE (x) == ASHIFT)  \
      ? CCNZmode : CCmode))
```

Another reason to use modes is to retain information on which operands were used by the comparison; see REVERSIBLE_CC_MODE later in this section.

You should define this macro if and only if you define extra CC modes in 'machine-modes.def'.

void **TARGET_CANONICALIZE_COMPARISON** (*int *code, rtx *op0, rtx *op1, bool op0_preserve_value*)   [Target Hook]

On some machines not all possible comparisons are defined, but you can convert an invalid comparison into a valid one. For example, the Alpha does not have a GT comparison, but you can use an LT comparison instead and swap the order of the operands.

On such machines, implement this hook to do any required conversions. *code* is the initial comparison code and *op0* and *op1* are the left and right operands of the comparison, respectively. If *op0_preserve_value* is true the implementation is not allowed to change the value of *op0* since the value might be used in RTXs which aren't comparisons. E.g. the implementation is not allowed to swap operands in that case.

GCC will not assume that the comparison resulting from this macro is valid but will see if the resulting insn matches a pattern in the 'md' file.

You need not to implement this hook if it would never change the comparison code or operands.

REVERSIBLE_CC_MODE (*mode*) [Macro]

A C expression whose value is one if it is always safe to reverse a comparison whose mode is *mode*. If SELECT_CC_MODE can ever return *mode* for a floating-point inequality comparison, then REVERSIBLE_CC_MODE (*mode*) must be zero.

You need not define this macro if it would always returns zero or if the floating-point format is anything other than IEEE_FLOAT_FORMAT. For example, here is the definition used on the SPARC, where floating-point inequality comparisons are given either CCFPEmode or CCFPmode:

```
#define REVERSIBLE_CC_MODE(MODE) \
  ((MODE) != CCFPEmode && (MODE) != CCFPmode)
```

REVERSE_CONDITION (*code*, *mode*) [Macro]

A C expression whose value is reversed condition code of the *code* for comparison done in CC_MODE *mode*. The macro is used only in case REVERSIBLE_CC_MODE (*mode*) is nonzero. Define this macro in case machine has some non-standard way how to reverse certain conditionals. For instance in case all floating point conditions are non-trapping, compiler may freely convert unordered compares to ordered ones. Then definition may look like:

```
#define REVERSE_CONDITION(CODE, MODE) \
  ((MODE) != CCFPmode ? reverse_condition (CODE) \
   : reverse_condition_maybe_unordered (CODE))
```

bool TARGET_FIXED_CONDITION_CODE_REGS (*unsigned int *p1*, [Target Hook]
    *unsigned int *p2*)

On targets which do not use (cc0), and which use a hard register rather than a pseudo-register to hold condition codes, the regular CSE passes are often not able to identify cases in which the hard register is set to a common value. Use this hook to enable a small pass which optimizes such cases. This hook should return true to enable this pass, and it should set the integers to which its arguments point to the hard register numbers used for condition codes. When there is only one such register, as is true on most systems, the integer pointed to by *p2* should be set to INVALID_REGNUM.

The default version of this hook returns false.

machine_mode TARGET_CC_MODES_COMPATIBLE (*machine_mode m1*, [Target Hook]
    machine_mode m2)

On targets which use multiple condition code modes in class MODE_CC, it is sometimes the case that a comparison can be validly done in more than one mode. On such a system, define this target hook to take two mode arguments and to return a mode in which both comparisons may be validly done. If there is no such mode, return VOIDmode.

The default version of this hook checks whether the modes are the same. If they are, it returns that mode. If they are different, it returns VOIDmode.

unsigned int TARGET_FLAGS_REGNUM [Target Hook]

If the target has a dedicated flags register, and it needs to use the post-reload comparison elimination pass, then this value should be set appropriately.

18.16 Describing Relative Costs of Operations

These macros let you describe the relative speed of various operations on the target machine.

REGISTER_MOVE_COST (*mode*, *from*, *to*) [Macro]

    A C expression for the cost of moving data of mode *mode* from a register in class *from* to one in class *to*. The classes are expressed using the enumeration values such as GENERAL_REGS. A value of 2 is the default; other values are interpreted relative to that.

    It is not required that the cost always equal 2 when *from* is the same as *to*; on some machines it is expensive to move between registers if they are not general registers.

    If reload sees an insn consisting of a single `set` between two hard registers, and if REGISTER_MOVE_COST applied to their classes returns a value of 2, reload does not check to ensure that the constraints of the insn are met. Setting a cost of other than 2 will allow reload to verify that the constraints are met. You should do this if the 'mov*m*' pattern's constraints do not allow such copying.

    These macros are obsolete, new ports should use the target hook TARGET_REGISTER_MOVE_COST instead.

int TARGET_REGISTER_MOVE_COST (*machine_mode* *mode*, *reg_class_t* *from*, *reg_class_t* *to*) [Target Hook]

    This target hook should return the cost of moving data of mode *mode* from a register in class *from* to one in class *to*. The classes are expressed using the enumeration values such as GENERAL_REGS. A value of 2 is the default; other values are interpreted relative to that.

    It is not required that the cost always equal 2 when *from* is the same as *to*; on some machines it is expensive to move between registers if they are not general registers.

    If reload sees an insn consisting of a single `set` between two hard registers, and if TARGET_REGISTER_MOVE_COST applied to their classes returns a value of 2, reload does not check to ensure that the constraints of the insn are met. Setting a cost of other than 2 will allow reload to verify that the constraints are met. You should do this if the 'mov*m*' pattern's constraints do not allow such copying.

    The default version of this function returns 2.

MEMORY_MOVE_COST (*mode*, *class*, *in*) [Macro]

    A C expression for the cost of moving data of mode *mode* between a register of class *class* and memory; *in* is zero if the value is to be written to memory, nonzero if it is to be read in. This cost is relative to those in REGISTER_MOVE_COST. If moving between registers and memory is more expensive than between two registers, you should define this macro to express the relative cost.

    If you do not define this macro, GCC uses a default cost of 4 plus the cost of copying via a secondary reload register, if one is needed. If your machine requires a secondary reload register to copy between memory and a register of *class* but the reload mechanism is more complex than copying via an intermediate, define this macro to reflect the actual cost of the move.

    GCC defines the function `memory_move_secondary_cost` if secondary reloads are needed. It computes the costs due to copying via a secondary register. If your

Chapter 18: Target Description Macros and Functions   557

machine copies from memory using a secondary register in the conventional way but the default base value of 4 is not correct for your machine, define this macro to add some other value to the result of that function. The arguments to that function are the same as to this macro.

These macros are obsolete, new ports should use the target hook `TARGET_MEMORY_MOVE_COST` instead.

int `TARGET_MEMORY_MOVE_COST` (*machine_mode* `mode`, *reg_class_t*   [Target Hook]
    `rclass`, *bool* `in`)

This target hook should return the cost of moving data of mode *mode* between a register of class *rclass* and memory; *in* is `false` if the value is to be written to memory, `true` if it is to be read in. This cost is relative to those in `TARGET_REGISTER_MOVE_COST`. If moving between registers and memory is more expensive than between two registers, you should add this target hook to express the relative cost.

If you do not add this target hook, GCC uses a default cost of 4 plus the cost of copying via a secondary reload register, if one is needed. If your machine requires a secondary reload register to copy between memory and a register of *rclass* but the reload mechanism is more complex than copying via an intermediate, use this target hook to reflect the actual cost of the move.

GCC defines the function `memory_move_secondary_cost` if secondary reloads are needed. It computes the costs due to copying via a secondary register. If your machine copies from memory using a secondary register in the conventional way but the default base value of 4 is not correct for your machine, use this target hook to add some other value to the result of that function. The arguments to that function are the same as to this target hook.

`BRANCH_COST` (`speed_p`, `predictable_p`)   [Macro]

A C expression for the cost of a branch instruction. A value of 1 is the default; other values are interpreted relative to that. Parameter *speed_p* is true when the branch in question should be optimized for speed. When it is false, `BRANCH_COST` should return a value optimal for code size rather than performance. *predictable_p* is true for well-predicted branches. On many architectures the `BRANCH_COST` can be reduced then.

Here are additional macros which do not specify precise relative costs, but only that certain actions are more expensive than GCC would ordinarily expect.

`SLOW_BYTE_ACCESS`   [Macro]

Define this macro as a C expression which is nonzero if accessing less than a word of memory (i.e. a `char` or a `short`) is no faster than accessing a word of memory, i.e., if such access require more than one instruction or if there is no difference in cost between byte and (aligned) word loads.

When this macro is not defined, the compiler will access a field by finding the smallest containing object; when it is defined, a fullword load will be used if alignment permits. Unless bytes accesses are faster than word accesses, using word accesses is preferable since it may eliminate subsequent memory access if subsequent accesses occur to other fields in the same word of the structure, but to different bytes.

bool TARGET_SLOW_UNALIGNED_ACCESS (*machine_mode* `mode`, ⁣ ⁣ ⁣ ⁣ ⁣ ⁣ ⁣ ⁣ ⁣ ⁣ [Target Hook]
 unsigned int `align`)

    This hook returns true if memory accesses described by the *mode* and *alignment* parameters have a cost many times greater than aligned accesses, for example if they are emulated in a trap handler. This hook is invoked only for unaligned accesses, i.e. when `alignment < GET_MODE_ALIGNMENT (mode)`.

    When this hook returns true, the compiler will act as if `STRICT_ALIGNMENT` were true when generating code for block moves. This can cause significantly more instructions to be produced. Therefore, do not make this hook return true if unaligned accesses only add a cycle or two to the time for a memory access.

    The hook must return true whenever `STRICT_ALIGNMENT` is true. The default implementation returns `STRICT_ALIGNMENT`.

MOVE_RATIO (*speed*) ⁣ [Macro]

    The threshold of number of scalar memory-to-memory move insns, *below* which a sequence of insns should be generated instead of a string move insn or a library call. Increasing the value will always make code faster, but eventually incurs high cost in increased code size.

    Note that on machines where the corresponding move insn is a `define_expand` that emits a sequence of insns, this macro counts the number of such sequences.

    The parameter *speed* is true if the code is currently being optimized for speed rather than size.

    If you don't define this, a reasonable default is used.

bool TARGET_USE_BY_PIECES_INFRASTRUCTURE_P (*unsigned* ⁣ ⁣ ⁣ ⁣ ⁣ ⁣ [Target Hook]
 HOST_WIDE_INT `size`, *unsigned int* `alignment`, *enum by_pieces_operation* `op`, *bool* `speed_p`)

    GCC will attempt several strategies when asked to copy between two areas of memory, or to set, clear or store to memory, for example when copying a `struct`. The `by_pieces` infrastructure implements such memory operations as a sequence of load, store or move insns. Alternate strategies are to expand the `movmem` or `setmem` optabs, to emit a library call, or to emit unit-by-unit, loop-based operations.

    This target hook should return true if, for a memory operation with a given *size* and *alignment*, using the `by_pieces` infrastructure is expected to result in better code generation. Both *size* and *alignment* are measured in terms of storage units.

    The parameter *op* is one of: `CLEAR_BY_PIECES`, `MOVE_BY_PIECES`, `SET_BY_PIECES`, `STORE_BY_PIECES` or `COMPARE_BY_PIECES`. These describe the type of memory operation under consideration.

    The parameter *speed_p* is true if the code is currently being optimized for speed rather than size.

    Returning true for higher values of *size* can improve code generation for speed if the target does not provide an implementation of the `movmem` or `setmem` standard names, if the `movmem` or `setmem` implementation would be more expensive than a sequence of insns, or if the overhead of a library call would dominate that of the body of the memory operation.

Chapter 18: Target Description Macros and Functions 559

Returning true for higher values of `size` may also cause an increase in code size, for example where the number of insns emitted to perform a move would be greater than that of a library call.

`int TARGET_COMPARE_BY_PIECES_BRANCH_RATIO (`machine_mode [Target Hook]
      `mode`**`)`**
When expanding a block comparison in MODE, gcc can try to reduce the number of branches at the expense of more memory operations. This hook allows the target to override the default choice. It should return the factor by which branches should be reduced over the plain expansion with one comparison per *mode*-sized piece. A port can also prevent a particular mode from being used for block comparisons by returning a negative number from this hook.

`MOVE_MAX_PIECES` [Macro]
A C expression used by `move_by_pieces` to determine the largest unit a load or store used to copy memory is. Defaults to `MOVE_MAX`.

`STORE_MAX_PIECES` [Macro]
A C expression used by `store_by_pieces` to determine the largest unit a store used to memory is. Defaults to `MOVE_MAX_PIECES`, or two times the size of `HOST_WIDE_INT`, whichever is smaller.

`COMPARE_MAX_PIECES` [Macro]
A C expression used by `compare_by_pieces` to determine the largest unit a load or store used to compare memory is. Defaults to `MOVE_MAX_PIECES`.

`CLEAR_RATIO (`speed**`)`** [Macro]
The threshold of number of scalar move insns, *below* which a sequence of insns should be generated to clear memory instead of a string clear insn or a library call. Increasing the value will always make code faster, but eventually incurs high cost in increased code size.

The parameter *speed* is true if the code is currently being optimized for speed rather than size.

If you don't define this, a reasonable default is used.

`SET_RATIO (`speed**`)`** [Macro]
The threshold of number of scalar move insns, *below* which a sequence of insns should be generated to set memory to a constant value, instead of a block set insn or a library call. Increasing the value will always make code faster, but eventually incurs high cost in increased code size.

The parameter *speed* is true if the code is currently being optimized for speed rather than size.

If you don't define this, it defaults to the value of `MOVE_RATIO`.

`USE_LOAD_POST_INCREMENT (`mode**`)`** [Macro]
A C expression used to determine whether a load postincrement is a good thing to use for a given mode. Defaults to the value of `HAVE_POST_INCREMENT`.

`USE_LOAD_POST_DECREMENT (mode)` [Macro]
: A C expression used to determine whether a load postdecrement is a good thing to use for a given mode. Defaults to the value of `HAVE_POST_DECREMENT`.

`USE_LOAD_PRE_INCREMENT (mode)` [Macro]
: A C expression used to determine whether a load preincrement is a good thing to use for a given mode. Defaults to the value of `HAVE_PRE_INCREMENT`.

`USE_LOAD_PRE_DECREMENT (mode)` [Macro]
: A C expression used to determine whether a load predecrement is a good thing to use for a given mode. Defaults to the value of `HAVE_PRE_DECREMENT`.

`USE_STORE_POST_INCREMENT (mode)` [Macro]
: A C expression used to determine whether a store postincrement is a good thing to use for a given mode. Defaults to the value of `HAVE_POST_INCREMENT`.

`USE_STORE_POST_DECREMENT (mode)` [Macro]
: A C expression used to determine whether a store postdecrement is a good thing to use for a given mode. Defaults to the value of `HAVE_POST_DECREMENT`.

`USE_STORE_PRE_INCREMENT (mode)` [Macro]
: This macro is used to determine whether a store preincrement is a good thing to use for a given mode. Defaults to the value of `HAVE_PRE_INCREMENT`.

`USE_STORE_PRE_DECREMENT (mode)` [Macro]
: This macro is used to determine whether a store predecrement is a good thing to use for a given mode. Defaults to the value of `HAVE_PRE_DECREMENT`.

`NO_FUNCTION_CSE` [Macro]
: Define this macro to be true if it is as good or better to call a constant function address than to call an address kept in a register.

`LOGICAL_OP_NON_SHORT_CIRCUIT` [Macro]
: Define this macro if a non-short-circuit operation produced by '`fold_range_test ()`' is optimal. This macro defaults to true if `BRANCH_COST` is greater than or equal to the value 2.

`bool TARGET_OPTAB_SUPPORTED_P (int op, machine_mode mode1, machine_mode mode2, optimization_type opt_type)` [Target Hook]
: Return true if the optimizers should use optab *op* with modes *mode1* and *mode2* for optimization type *opt_type*. The optab is known to have an associated '.md' instruction whose C condition is true. *mode2* is only meaningful for conversion optabs; for direct optabs it is a copy of *mode1*.

    For example, when called with *op* equal to `rint_optab` and *mode1* equal to `DFmode`, the hook should say whether the optimizers should use optab `rintdf2`.

    The default hook returns true for all inputs.

`bool TARGET_RTX_COSTS (rtx x, machine_mode mode, int outer_code, int opno, int *total, bool speed)` [Target Hook]
: This target hook describes the relative costs of RTL expressions.

The cost may depend on the precise form of the expression, which is available for examination in *x*, and the fact that *x* appears as operand *opno* of an expression with rtx code *outer_code*. That is, the hook can assume that there is some rtx *y* such that 'GET_CODE (*y*) == outer_code' and such that either (a) 'XEXP (*y, opno*) == *x*' or (b) 'XVEC (*y, opno*)' contains *x*.

mode is *x*'s machine mode, or for cases like `const_int` that do not have a mode, the mode in which *x* is used.

In implementing this hook, you can use the construct COSTS_N_INSNS (*n*) to specify a cost equal to *n* fast instructions.

On entry to the hook, *total* contains a default estimate for the cost of the expression. The hook should modify this value as necessary. Traditionally, the default costs are COSTS_N_INSNS (5) for multiplications, COSTS_N_INSNS (7) for division and modulus operations, and COSTS_N_INSNS (1) for all other operations.

When optimizing for code size, i.e. when **speed** is false, this target hook should be used to estimate the relative size cost of an expression, again relative to COSTS_N_INSNS.

The hook returns true when all subexpressions of *x* have been processed, and false when `rtx_cost` should recurse.

int TARGET_ADDRESS_COST (*rtx address, machine_mode mode,*   [Target Hook]
    addr_space_t **as**, *bool* **speed**)

This hook computes the cost of an addressing mode that contains *address*. If not defined, the cost is computed from the *address* expression and the TARGET_RTX_COST hook.

For most CISC machines, the default cost is a good approximation of the true cost of the addressing mode. However, on RISC machines, all instructions normally have the same length and execution time. Hence all addresses will have equal costs.

In cases where more than one form of an address is known, the form with the lowest cost will be used. If multiple forms have the same, lowest, cost, the one that is the most complex will be used.

For example, suppose an address that is equal to the sum of a register and a constant is used twice in the same basic block. When this macro is not defined, the address will be computed in a register and memory references will be indirect through that register. On machines where the cost of the addressing mode containing the sum is no higher than that of a simple indirect reference, this will produce an additional instruction and possibly require an additional register. Proper specification of this macro eliminates this overhead for such machines.

This hook is never called with an invalid address.

On machines where an address involving more than one register is as cheap as an address computation involving only one register, defining TARGET_ADDRESS_COST to reflect this can cause two registers to be live over a region of code where only one would have been if TARGET_ADDRESS_COST were not defined in that manner. This effect should be considered in the definition of this macro. Equivalent costs should probably only be given to addresses with different numbers of registers on machines with lots of registers.

int TARGET_INSN_COST (*rtx_insn* *insn, *bool* speed) [Target Hook]
    This target hook describes the relative costs of RTL instructions.

    In implementing this hook, you can use the construct COSTS_N_INSNS (*n*) to specify a cost equal to *n* fast instructions.

    When optimizing for code size, i.e. when speed is false, this target hook should be used to estimate the relative size cost of an expression, again relative to COSTS_N_INSNS.

unsigned int TARGET_MAX_NOCE_IFCVT_SEQ_COST (*edge* e) [Target Hook]
    This hook returns a value in the same units as TARGET_RTX_COSTS, giving the maximum acceptable cost for a sequence generated by the RTL if-conversion pass when conditional execution is not available. The RTL if-conversion pass attempts to convert conditional operations that would require a branch to a series of unconditional operations and *movmodecc* insns. This hook returns the maximum cost of the unconditional instructions and the *movmodecc* insns. RTL if-conversion is cancelled if the cost of the converted sequence is greater than the value returned by this hook.

    e is the edge between the basic block containing the conditional branch to the basic block which would be executed if the condition were true.

    The default implementation of this hook uses the max-rtl-if-conversion-[un]predictable parameters if they are set, and uses a multiple of BRANCH_COST otherwise.

bool TARGET_NOCE_CONVERSION_PROFITABLE_P (*rtx_insn* *seq, [Target Hook]
    struct noce_if_info *if_info)
    This hook returns true if the instruction sequence seq is a good candidate as a replacement for the if-convertible sequence described in if_info.

bool TARGET_NO_SPECULATION_IN_DELAY_SLOTS_P (*void*) [Target Hook]
    This predicate controls the use of the eager delay slot filler to disallow speculatively executed instructions being placed in delay slots. Targets such as certain MIPS architectures possess both branches with and without delay slots. As the eager delay slot filler can decrease performance, disabling it is beneficial when ordinary branches are available. Use of delay slot branches filled using the basic filler is often still desirable as the delay slot can hide a pipeline bubble.

HOST_WIDE_INT TARGET_ESTIMATED_POLY_VALUE (*poly_int64* val) [Target Hook]
    Return an estimate of the runtime value of *val*, for use in things like cost calculations or profiling frequencies. The default implementation returns the lowest possible value of *val*.

18.17 Adjusting the Instruction Scheduler

The instruction scheduler may need a fair amount of machine-specific adjustment in order to produce good code. GCC provides several target hooks for this purpose. It is usually enough to define just a few of them: try the first ones in this list first.

int TARGET_SCHED_ISSUE_RATE (*void*) [Target Hook]
    This hook returns the maximum number of instructions that can ever issue at the same time on the target machine. The default is one. Although the insn scheduler

Chapter 18: Target Description Macros and Functions 563

can define itself the possibility of issue an insn on the same cycle, the value can serve as an additional constraint to issue insns on the same simulated processor cycle (see hooks 'TARGET_SCHED_REORDER' and 'TARGET_SCHED_REORDER2'). This value must be constant over the entire compilation. If you need it to vary depending on what the instructions are, you must use 'TARGET_SCHED_VARIABLE_ISSUE'.

int TARGET_SCHED_VARIABLE_ISSUE (FILE *file, int verbose, [Target Hook]
    rtx_insn *insn, int more)
This hook is executed by the scheduler after it has scheduled an insn from the ready list. It should return the number of insns which can still be issued in the current cycle. The default is 'more - 1' for insns other than CLOBBER and USE, which normally are not counted against the issue rate. You should define this hook if some insns take more machine resources than others, so that fewer insns can follow them in the same cycle. file is either a null pointer, or a stdio stream to write any debug output to. verbose is the verbose level provided by '-fsched-verbose-n'. insn is the instruction that was scheduled.

int TARGET_SCHED_ADJUST_COST (rtx_insn *insn, int dep_type1, [Target Hook]
    rtx_insn *dep_insn, int cost, unsigned int dw)
This function corrects the value of cost based on the relationship between insn and dep_insn through a dependence of type dep_type, and strength dw. It should return the new value. The default is to make no adjustment to cost. This can be used for example to specify to the scheduler using the traditional pipeline description that an output- or anti-dependence does not incur the same cost as a data-dependence. If the scheduler using the automaton based pipeline description, the cost of anti-dependence is zero and the cost of output-dependence is maximum of one and the difference of latency times of the first and the second insns. If these values are not acceptable, you could use the hook to modify them too. See also see Section 17.19.9 [Processor pipeline description], page 444.

int TARGET_SCHED_ADJUST_PRIORITY (rtx_insn *insn, int [Target Hook]
    priority)
This hook adjusts the integer scheduling priority priority of insn. It should return the new priority. Increase the priority to execute insn earlier, reduce the priority to execute insn later. Do not define this hook if you do not need to adjust the scheduling priorities of insns.

int TARGET_SCHED_REORDER (FILE *file, int verbose, rtx_insn [Target Hook]
    **ready, int *n_readyp, int clock)
This hook is executed by the scheduler after it has scheduled the ready list, to allow the machine description to reorder it (for example to combine two small instructions together on 'VLIW' machines). file is either a null pointer, or a stdio stream to write any debug output to. verbose is the verbose level provided by '-fsched-verbose-n'. ready is a pointer to the ready list of instructions that are ready to be scheduled. n_readyp is a pointer to the number of elements in the ready list. The scheduler reads the ready list in reverse order, starting with ready[*n_readyp − 1] and going to ready[0]. clock is the timer tick of the scheduler. You may modify the ready list and the number of ready insns. The return value is the number of insns that can issue this cycle; normally this is just issue_rate. See also 'TARGET_SCHED_REORDER2'.

`int` **TARGET_SCHED_REORDER2** (*FILE* `*file`, *int* `verbose`, *rtx_insn* [Target Hook]
  `**ready`, *int* `*n_readyp`, *int* `clock`)

  Like 'TARGET_SCHED_REORDER', but called at a different time. That function is called whenever the scheduler starts a new cycle. This one is called once per iteration over a cycle, immediately after 'TARGET_SCHED_VARIABLE_ISSUE'; it can reorder the ready list and return the number of insns to be scheduled in the same cycle. Defining this hook can be useful if there are frequent situations where scheduling one insn causes other insns to become ready in the same cycle. These other insns can then be taken into account properly.

`bool` **TARGET_SCHED_MACRO_FUSION_P** (*void*) [Target Hook]

  This hook is used to check whether target platform supports macro fusion.

`bool` **TARGET_SCHED_MACRO_FUSION_PAIR_P** (*rtx_insn* `*prev`, [Target Hook]
  rtx_insn `*curr`)

  This hook is used to check whether two insns should be macro fused for a target microarchitecture. If this hook returns true for the given insn pair (*prev* and *curr*), the scheduler will put them into a sched group, and they will not be scheduled apart. The two insns will be either two SET insns or a compare and a conditional jump and this hook should validate any dependencies needed to fuse the two insns together.

`void` **TARGET_SCHED_DEPENDENCIES_EVALUATION_HOOK** (*rtx_insn* [Target Hook]
  `*head`, *rtx_insn* `*tail`)

  This hook is called after evaluation forward dependencies of insns in chain given by two parameter values (*head* and *tail* correspondingly) but before insns scheduling of the insn chain. For example, it can be used for better insn classification if it requires analysis of dependencies. This hook can use backward and forward dependencies of the insn scheduler because they are already calculated.

`void` **TARGET_SCHED_INIT** (*FILE* `*file`, *int* `verbose`, *int* [Target Hook]
  `max_ready`)

  This hook is executed by the scheduler at the beginning of each block of instructions that are to be scheduled. *file* is either a null pointer, or a stdio stream to write any debug output to. *verbose* is the verbose level provided by '-fsched-verbose-n'. *max_ready* is the maximum number of insns in the current scheduling region that can be live at the same time. This can be used to allocate scratch space if it is needed, e.g. by 'TARGET_SCHED_REORDER'.

`void` **TARGET_SCHED_FINISH** (*FILE* `*file`, *int* `verbose`) [Target Hook]

  This hook is executed by the scheduler at the end of each block of instructions that are to be scheduled. It can be used to perform cleanup of any actions done by the other scheduling hooks. *file* is either a null pointer, or a stdio stream to write any debug output to. *verbose* is the verbose level provided by '-fsched-verbose-n'.

`void` **TARGET_SCHED_INIT_GLOBAL** (*FILE* `*file`, *int* `verbose`, *int* [Target Hook]
  `old_max_uid`)

  This hook is executed by the scheduler after function level initializations. *file* is either a null pointer, or a stdio stream to write any debug output to. *verbose* is the verbose level provided by '-fsched-verbose-n'. *old_max_uid* is the maximum insn uid when scheduling begins.

void TARGET_SCHED_FINISH_GLOBAL (*FILE *file*, *int verbose*)   [Target Hook]
: This is the cleanup hook corresponding to TARGET_SCHED_INIT_GLOBAL. *file* is either a null pointer, or a stdio stream to write any debug output to. *verbose* is the verbose level provided by '-fsched-verbose-n'.

rtx TARGET_SCHED_DFA_PRE_CYCLE_INSN (*void*)   [Target Hook]
: The hook returns an RTL insn. The automaton state used in the pipeline hazard recognizer is changed as if the insn were scheduled when the new simulated processor cycle starts. Usage of the hook may simplify the automaton pipeline description for some VLIW processors. If the hook is defined, it is used only for the automaton based pipeline description. The default is not to change the state when the new simulated processor cycle starts.

void TARGET_SCHED_INIT_DFA_PRE_CYCLE_INSN (*void*)   [Target Hook]
: The hook can be used to initialize data used by the previous hook.

rtx_insn * TARGET_SCHED_DFA_POST_CYCLE_INSN (*void*)   [Target Hook]
: The hook is analogous to 'TARGET_SCHED_DFA_PRE_CYCLE_INSN' but used to changed the state as if the insn were scheduled when the new simulated processor cycle finishes.

void TARGET_SCHED_INIT_DFA_POST_CYCLE_INSN (*void*)   [Target Hook]
: The hook is analogous to 'TARGET_SCHED_INIT_DFA_PRE_CYCLE_INSN' but used to initialize data used by the previous hook.

void TARGET_SCHED_DFA_PRE_ADVANCE_CYCLE (*void*)   [Target Hook]
: The hook to notify target that the current simulated cycle is about to finish. The hook is analogous to 'TARGET_SCHED_DFA_PRE_CYCLE_INSN' but used to change the state in more complicated situations - e.g., when advancing state on a single insn is not enough.

void TARGET_SCHED_DFA_POST_ADVANCE_CYCLE (*void*)   [Target Hook]
: The hook to notify target that new simulated cycle has just started. The hook is analogous to 'TARGET_SCHED_DFA_POST_CYCLE_INSN' but used to change the state in more complicated situations - e.g., when advancing state on a single insn is not enough.

int TARGET_SCHED_FIRST_CYCLE_MULTIPASS_DFA_LOOKAHEAD   [Target Hook]
  (*void*)
: This hook controls better choosing an insn from the ready insn queue for the DFA-based insn scheduler. Usually the scheduler chooses the first insn from the queue. If the hook returns a positive value, an additional scheduler code tries all permutations of 'TARGET_SCHED_FIRST_CYCLE_MULTIPASS_DFA_LOOKAHEAD ()' subsequent ready insns to choose an insn whose issue will result in maximal number of issued insns on the same cycle. For the VLIW processor, the code could actually solve the problem of packing simple insns into the VLIW insn. Of course, if the rules of VLIW packing are described in the automaton.

  This code also could be used for superscalar RISC processors. Let us consider a superscalar RISC processor with 3 pipelines. Some insns can be executed in pipelines *A* or *B*, some insns can be executed only in pipelines *B* or *C*, and one insn can be executed in pipeline B. The processor may issue the 1st insn into A and the 2nd one into B. In this case, the 3rd insn will wait for freeing B until the next cycle. If the scheduler issues the 3rd insn the first, the processor could issue all 3 insns per cycle.

Actually this code demonstrates advantages of the automaton based pipeline hazard recognizer. We try quickly and easy many insn schedules to choose the best one.

The default is no multipass scheduling.

int   [Target Hook]
TARGET_SCHED_FIRST_CYCLE_MULTIPASS_DFA_LOOKAHEAD_GUARD
(*rtx_insn* `*insn`, *int* `ready_index`)

This hook controls what insns from the ready insn queue will be considered for the multipass insn scheduling. If the hook returns zero for *insn*, the insn will be considered in multipass scheduling. Positive return values will remove *insn* from consideration on the current round of multipass scheduling. Negative return values will remove *insn* from consideration for given number of cycles. Backends should be careful about returning non-zero for highest priority instruction at position 0 in the ready list. *ready_index* is passed to allow backends make correct judgements.

The default is that any ready insns can be chosen to be issued.

void TARGET_SCHED_FIRST_CYCLE_MULTIPASS_BEGIN (*void*   [Target Hook]
`*data`, *signed char* `*ready_try`, *int* `n_ready`, *bool* `first_cycle_insn_p`)

This hook prepares the target backend for a new round of multipass scheduling.

void TARGET_SCHED_FIRST_CYCLE_MULTIPASS_ISSUE (*void*   [Target Hook]
`*data`, *signed char* `*ready_try`, *int* `n_ready`, *rtx_insn* `*insn`, *const void* `*prev_data`)

This hook is called when multipass scheduling evaluates instruction INSN.

void TARGET_SCHED_FIRST_CYCLE_MULTIPASS_BACKTRACK (*const*   [Target Hook]
void `*data`, *signed char* `*ready_try`, *int* `n_ready`)

This is called when multipass scheduling backtracks from evaluation of an instruction.

void TARGET_SCHED_FIRST_CYCLE_MULTIPASS_END (*const void*   [Target Hook]
`*data`)

This hook notifies the target about the result of the concluded current round of multipass scheduling.

void TARGET_SCHED_FIRST_CYCLE_MULTIPASS_INIT (*void* `*data`)   [Target Hook]
This hook initializes target-specific data used in multipass scheduling.

void TARGET_SCHED_FIRST_CYCLE_MULTIPASS_FINI (*void* `*data`)   [Target Hook]
This hook finalizes target-specific data used in multipass scheduling.

int TARGET_SCHED_DFA_NEW_CYCLE (*FILE* `*dump`, *int* `verbose`,   [Target Hook]
rtx_insn `*insn`, *int* `last_clock`, *int* `clock`, *int* `*sort_p`)

This hook is called by the insn scheduler before issuing *insn* on cycle *clock*. If the hook returns nonzero, *insn* is not issued on this processor cycle. Instead, the processor cycle is advanced. If **sort_p* is zero, the insn ready queue is not sorted on the new cycle start as usually. *dump* and *verbose* specify the file and verbosity level to use for debugging output. *last_clock* and *clock* are, respectively, the processor cycle on which the previous insn has been issued, and the current processor cycle.

bool TARGET_SCHED_IS_COSTLY_DEPENDENCE (*struct _dep *_dep,*   [Target Hook]
    int `cost`, *int* `distance`)

This hook is used to define which dependences are considered costly by the target, so costly that it is not advisable to schedule the insns that are involved in the dependence too close to one another. The parameters to this hook are as follows: The first parameter *_dep* is the dependence being evaluated. The second parameter *cost* is the cost of the dependence as estimated by the scheduler, and the third parameter *distance* is the distance in cycles between the two insns. The hook returns `true` if considering the distance between the two insns the dependence between them is considered costly by the target, and `false` otherwise.

Defining this hook can be useful in multiple-issue out-of-order machines, where (a) it's practically hopeless to predict the actual data/resource delays, however: (b) there's a better chance to predict the actual grouping that will be formed, and (c) correctly emulating the grouping can be very important. In such targets one may want to allow issuing dependent insns closer to one another—i.e., closer than the dependence distance; however, not in cases of "costly dependences", which this hooks allows to define.

void TARGET_SCHED_H_I_D_EXTENDED (*void*)   [Target Hook]

This hook is called by the insn scheduler after emitting a new instruction to the instruction stream. The hook notifies a target backend to extend its per instruction data structures.

void * TARGET_SCHED_ALLOC_SCHED_CONTEXT (*void*)   [Target Hook]

Return a pointer to a store large enough to hold target scheduling context.

void TARGET_SCHED_INIT_SCHED_CONTEXT (*void *tc, bool*   [Target Hook]
    `clean_p`)

Initialize store pointed to by *tc* to hold target scheduling context. It *clean_p* is true then initialize *tc* as if scheduler is at the beginning of the block. Otherwise, copy the current context into *tc*.

void TARGET_SCHED_SET_SCHED_CONTEXT (*void *tc*)   [Target Hook]

Copy target scheduling context pointed to by *tc* to the current context.

void TARGET_SCHED_CLEAR_SCHED_CONTEXT (*void *tc*)   [Target Hook]

Deallocate internal data in target scheduling context pointed to by *tc*.

void TARGET_SCHED_FREE_SCHED_CONTEXT (*void *tc*)   [Target Hook]

Deallocate a store for target scheduling context pointed to by *tc*.

int TARGET_SCHED_SPECULATE_INSN (*rtx_insn *`insn`, unsigned int*   [Target Hook]
    `dep_status`, *rtx **`new_pat`)

This hook is called by the insn scheduler when *insn* has only speculative dependencies and therefore can be scheduled speculatively. The hook is used to check if the pattern of *insn* has a speculative version and, in case of successful check, to generate that speculative pattern. The hook should return 1, if the instruction has a speculative form, or −1, if it doesn't. *request* describes the type of requested speculation. If the return value equals 1 then *new_pat* is assigned the generated speculative pattern.

bool **TARGET_SCHED_NEEDS_BLOCK_P** (*unsigned int* `dep_status`) [Target Hook]
This hook is called by the insn scheduler during generation of recovery code for *insn*. It should return `true`, if the corresponding check instruction should branch to recovery code, or `false` otherwise.

rtx **TARGET_SCHED_GEN_SPEC_CHECK** (*rtx_insn* *insn, *rtx_insn* [Target Hook]
*`label`, *unsigned int* `ds`)
This hook is called by the insn scheduler to generate a pattern for recovery check instruction. If *mutate_p* is zero, then *insn* is a speculative instruction for which the check should be generated. *label* is either a label of a basic block, where recovery code should be emitted, or a null pointer, when requested check doesn't branch to recovery code (a simple check). If *mutate_p* is nonzero, then a pattern for a branchy check corresponding to a simple check denoted by *insn* should be generated. In this case *label* can't be null.

void **TARGET_SCHED_SET_SCHED_FLAGS** (*struct spec_info_def* [Target Hook]
*`spec_info`)
This hook is used by the insn scheduler to find out what features should be enabled/used. The structure *spec_info should be filled in by the target. The structure describes speculation types that can be used in the scheduler.

bool **TARGET_SCHED_CAN_SPECULATE_INSN** (*rtx_insn* *insn) [Target Hook]
Some instructions should never be speculated by the schedulers, usually because the instruction is too expensive to get this wrong. Often such instructions have long latency, and often they are not fully modeled in the pipeline descriptions. This hook should return `false` if *insn* should not be speculated.

int **TARGET_SCHED_SMS_RES_MII** (*struct ddg* *g) [Target Hook]
This hook is called by the swing modulo scheduler to calculate a resource-based lower bound which is based on the resources available in the machine and the resources required by each instruction. The target backend can use *g* to calculate such bound. A very simple lower bound will be used in case this hook is not implemented: the total number of instructions divided by the issue rate.

bool **TARGET_SCHED_DISPATCH** (*rtx_insn* *insn, *int* `x`) [Target Hook]
This hook is called by Haifa Scheduler. It returns true if dispatch scheduling is supported in hardware and the condition specified in the parameter is true.

void **TARGET_SCHED_DISPATCH_DO** (*rtx_insn* *insn, *int* `x`) [Target Hook]
This hook is called by Haifa Scheduler. It performs the operation specified in its second parameter.

bool **TARGET_SCHED_EXPOSED_PIPELINE** [Target Hook]
True if the processor has an exposed pipeline, which means that not just the order of instructions is important for correctness when scheduling, but also the latencies of operations.

int TARGET_SCHED_REASSOCIATION_WIDTH (*unsigned int* `opc`,   [Target Hook]
    machine_mode `mode`)

This hook is called by tree reassociator to determine a level of parallelism required in output calculations chain.

void TARGET_SCHED_FUSION_PRIORITY (*rtx_insn* *insn, *int*   [Target Hook]
    *max_pri, *int* *fusion_pri, *int* *pri)

This hook is called by scheduling fusion pass. It calculates fusion priorities for each instruction passed in by parameter. The priorities are returned via pointer parameters.

insn is the instruction whose priorities need to be calculated. *max_pri* is the maximum priority can be returned in any cases. *fusion_pri* is the pointer parameter through which *insn*'s fusion priority should be calculated and returned. *pri* is the pointer parameter through which *insn*'s priority should be calculated and returned.

Same *fusion_pri* should be returned for instructions which should be scheduled together. Different *pri* should be returned for instructions with same *fusion_pri*. *fusion_pri* is the major sort key, *pri* is the minor sort key. All instructions will be scheduled according to the two priorities. All priorities calculated should be between 0 (exclusive) and *max_pri* (inclusive). To avoid false dependencies, *fusion_pri* of instructions which need to be scheduled together should be smaller than *fusion_pri* of irrelevant instructions.

Given below example:
```
ldr r10, [r1, 4]
add r4, r4, r10
ldr r15, [r2, 8]
sub r5, r5, r15
ldr r11, [r1, 0]
add r4, r4, r11
ldr r16, [r2, 12]
sub r5, r5, r16
```

On targets like ARM/AArch64, the two pairs of consecutive loads should be merged. Since peephole2 pass can't help in this case unless consecutive loads are actually next to each other in instruction flow. That's where this scheduling fusion pass works. This hook calculates priority for each instruction based on its fustion type, like:
```
ldr r10, [r1, 4]   ; fusion_pri=99,  pri=96
add r4, r4, r10    ; fusion_pri=100, pri=100
ldr r15, [r2, 8]   ; fusion_pri=98,  pri=92
sub r5, r5, r15    ; fusion_pri=100, pri=100
ldr r11, [r1, 0]   ; fusion_pri=99,  pri=100
add r4, r4, r11    ; fusion pri=100, pri=100
ldr r16, [r2, 12]  ; fusion_pri=98,  pri=88
sub r5, r5, r16    ; fusion_pri=100, pri=100
```

Scheduling fusion pass then sorts all ready to issue instructions according to the priorities. As a result, instructions of same fusion type will be pushed together in instruction flow, like:
```
ldr r11, [r1, 0]
ldr r10, [r1, 4]
ldr r15, [r2, 8]
ldr r16, [r2, 12]
add r4, r4, r10
```

```
    sub r5, r5, r15
    add r4, r4, r11
    sub r5, r5, r16
```

Now peephole2 pass can simply merge the two pairs of loads.

Since scheduling fusion pass relies on peephole2 to do real fusion work, it is only enabled by default when peephole2 is in effect.

This is firstly introduced on ARM/AArch64 targets, please refer to the hook implementation for how different fusion types are supported.

void **TARGET_EXPAND_DIVMOD_LIBFUNC** (*rtx libfunc,* [Target Hook]
        machine_mode mode, rtx op0, rtx op1, rtx *quot, rtx *rem)

Define this hook for enabling divmod transform if the port does not have hardware divmod insn but defines target-specific divmod libfuncs.

18.18 Dividing the Output into Sections (Texts, Data, . . .)

An object file is divided into sections containing different types of data. In the most common case, there are three sections: the *text section*, which holds instructions and read-only data; the *data section*, which holds initialized writable data; and the *bss section*, which holds uninitialized data. Some systems have other kinds of sections.

'varasm.c' provides several well-known sections, such as text_section, data_section and bss_section. The normal way of controlling a foo_section variable is to define the associated FOO_SECTION_ASM_OP macro, as described below. The macros are only read once, when 'varasm.c' initializes itself, so their values must be run-time constants. They may however depend on command-line flags.

Note: Some run-time files, such 'crtstuff.c', also make use of the FOO_SECTION_ASM_OP macros, and expect them to be string literals.

Some assemblers require a different string to be written every time a section is selected. If your assembler falls into this category, you should define the TARGET_ASM_INIT_SECTIONS hook and use get_unnamed_section to set up the sections.

You must always create a text_section, either by defining TEXT_SECTION_ASM_OP or by initializing text_section in TARGET_ASM_INIT_SECTIONS. The same is true of data_section and DATA_SECTION_ASM_OP. If you do not create a distinct readonly_data_section, the default is to reuse text_section.

All the other 'varasm.c' sections are optional, and are null if the target does not provide them.

TEXT_SECTION_ASM_OP [Macro]

A C expression whose value is a string, including spacing, containing the assembler operation that should precede instructions and read-only data. Normally "\t.text" is right.

HOT_TEXT_SECTION_NAME [Macro]

If defined, a C string constant for the name of the section containing most frequently executed functions of the program. If not defined, GCC will provide a default definition if the target supports named sections.

Chapter 18: Target Description Macros and Functions   571

UNLIKELY_EXECUTED_TEXT_SECTION_NAME   [Macro]

> If defined, a C string constant for the name of the section containing unlikely executed functions in the program.

DATA_SECTION_ASM_OP   [Macro]

> A C expression whose value is a string, including spacing, containing the assembler operation to identify the following data as writable initialized data. Normally `"\t.data"` is right.

SDATA_SECTION_ASM_OP   [Macro]

> If defined, a C expression whose value is a string, including spacing, containing the assembler operation to identify the following data as initialized, writable small data.

READONLY_DATA_SECTION_ASM_OP   [Macro]

> A C expression whose value is a string, including spacing, containing the assembler operation to identify the following data as read-only initialized data.

BSS_SECTION_ASM_OP   [Macro]

> If defined, a C expression whose value is a string, including spacing, containing the assembler operation to identify the following data as uninitialized global data. If not defined, and `ASM_OUTPUT_ALIGNED_BSS` not defined, uninitialized global data will be output in the data section if '-fno-common' is passed, otherwise `ASM_OUTPUT_COMMON` will be used.

SBSS_SECTION_ASM_OP   [Macro]

> If defined, a C expression whose value is a string, including spacing, containing the assembler operation to identify the following data as uninitialized, writable small data.

TLS_COMMON_ASM_OP   [Macro]

> If defined, a C expression whose value is a string containing the assembler operation to identify the following data as thread-local common data. The default is `".tls_common"`.

TLS_SECTION_ASM_FLAG   [Macro]

> If defined, a C expression whose value is a character constant containing the flag used to mark a section as a TLS section. The default is 'T'.

INIT_SECTION_ASM_OP   [Macro]

> If defined, a C expression whose value is a string, including spacing, containing the assembler operation to identify the following data as initialization code. If not defined, GCC will assume such a section does not exist. This section has no corresponding `init_section` variable; it is used entirely in runtime code.

FINI_SECTION_ASM_OP   [Macro]

> If defined, a C expression whose value is a string, including spacing, containing the assembler operation to identify the following data as finalization code. If not defined, GCC will assume such a section does not exist. This section has no corresponding `fini_section` variable; it is used entirely in runtime code.

INIT_ARRAY_SECTION_ASM_OP   [Macro]
      If defined, a C expression whose value is a string, including spacing, containing the
      assembler operation to identify the following data as part of the `.init_array` (or
      equivalent) section. If not defined, GCC will assume such a section does not exist.
      Do not define both this macro and INIT_SECTION_ASM_OP.

FINI_ARRAY_SECTION_ASM_OP   [Macro]
      If defined, a C expression whose value is a string, including spacing, containing the
      assembler operation to identify the following data as part of the `.fini_array` (or
      equivalent) section. If not defined, GCC will assume such a section does not exist.
      Do not define both this macro and FINI_SECTION_ASM_OP.

MACH_DEP_SECTION_ASM_FLAG   [Macro]
      If defined, a C expression whose value is a character constant containing the flag used
      to mark a machine-dependent section. This corresponds to the SECTION_MACH_DEP
      section flag.

CRT_CALL_STATIC_FUNCTION (section_op, function)   [Macro]
      If defined, an ASM statement that switches to a different section via *section_op*, calls
      function, and switches back to the text section. This is used in 'crtstuff.c' if INIT_
      SECTION_ASM_OP or FINI_SECTION_ASM_OP to calls to initialization and finalization
      functions from the init and fini sections. By default, this macro uses a simple function
      call. Some ports need hand-crafted assembly code to avoid dependencies on registers
      initialized in the function prologue or to ensure that constant pools don't end up too
      far way in the text section.

TARGET_LIBGCC_SDATA_SECTION   [Macro]
      If defined, a string which names the section into which small variables defined in
      crtstuff and libgcc should go. This is useful when the target has options for optimizing
      access to small data, and you want the crtstuff and libgcc routines to be conservative
      in what they expect of your application yet liberal in what your application expects.
      For example, for targets with a `.sdata` section (like MIPS), you could compile crtstuff
      with -G 0 so that it doesn't require small data support from your application, but use
      this macro to put small data into `.sdata` so that your application can access these
      variables whether it uses small data or not.

FORCE_CODE_SECTION_ALIGN   [Macro]
      If defined, an ASM statement that aligns a code section to some arbitrary boundary.
      This is used to force all fragments of the `.init` and `.fini` sections to have to same
      alignment and thus prevent the linker from having to add any padding.

JUMP_TABLES_IN_TEXT_SECTION   [Macro]
      Define this macro to be an expression with a nonzero value if jump tables (for
      `tablejump` insns) should be output in the text section, along with the assembler
      instructions. Otherwise, the readonly data section is used.
      This macro is irrelevant if there is no separate readonly data section.

void TARGET_ASM_INIT_SECTIONS (*void*)   [Target Hook]
      Define this hook if you need to do something special to set up the 'varasm.c' sections,
      or if your target has some special sections of its own that you need to create.

GCC calls this hook after processing the command line, but before writing any assembly code, and before calling any of the section-returning hooks described below.

int TARGET_ASM_RELOC_RW_MASK (*void*) [Target Hook]

Return a mask describing how relocations should be treated when selecting sections. Bit 1 should be set if global relocations should be placed in a read-write section; bit 0 should be set if local relocations should be placed in a read-write section.

The default version of this function returns 3 when '-fpic' is in effect, and 0 otherwise. The hook is typically redefined when the target cannot support (some kinds of) dynamic relocations in read-only sections even in executables.

section * TARGET_ASM_SELECT_SECTION (*tree exp, int reloc,* [Target Hook]
unsigned HOST_WIDE_INT align)

Return the section into which *exp* should be placed. You can assume that *exp* is either a VAR_DECL node or a constant of some sort. *reloc* indicates whether the initial value of *exp* requires link-time relocations. Bit 0 is set when variable contains local relocations only, while bit 1 is set for global relocations. *align* is the constant alignment in bits.

The default version of this function takes care of putting read-only variables in readonly_data_section.

See also USE_SELECT_SECTION_FOR_FUNCTIONS.

USE_SELECT_SECTION_FOR_FUNCTIONS [Macro]

Define this macro if you wish TARGET_ASM_SELECT_SECTION to be called for FUNCTION_DECLs as well as for variables and constants.

In the case of a FUNCTION_DECL, *reloc* will be zero if the function has been determined to be likely to be called, and nonzero if it is unlikely to be called.

void TARGET_ASM_UNIQUE_SECTION (*tree decl, int reloc*) [Target Hook]

Build up a unique section name, expressed as a STRING_CST node, and assign it to 'DECL_SECTION_NAME (*decl*)'. As with TARGET_ASM_SELECT_SECTION, *reloc* indicates whether the initial value of *exp* requires link-time relocations.

The default version of this function appends the symbol name to the ELF section name that would normally be used for the symbol. For example, the function foo would be placed in .text.foo. Whatever the actual target object format, this is often good enough.

section * TARGET_ASM_FUNCTION_RODATA_SECTION (*tree decl*) [Target Hook]

Return the readonly data section associated with 'DECL_SECTION_NAME (*decl*)'. The default version of this function selects .gnu.linkonce.r.name if the function's section is .gnu.linkonce.t.name, .rodata.name if function is in .text.name, and the normal readonly-data section otherwise.

const char * TARGET_ASM_MERGEABLE_RODATA_PREFIX [Target Hook]

Usually, the compiler uses the prefix ".rodata" to construct section names for mergeable constant data. Define this macro to override the string if a different section name should be used.

section * **TARGET_ASM_TM_CLONE_TABLE_SECTION** (*void*) [Target Hook]
: Return the section that should be used for transactional memory clone tables.

section * **TARGET_ASM_SELECT_RTX_SECTION** (*machine_mode* [Target Hook]
mode, *rtx* x, *unsigned HOST_WIDE_INT* align)
: Return the section into which a constant x, of mode *mode*, should be placed. You can assume that x is some kind of constant in RTL. The argument *mode* is redundant except in the case of a `const_int` rtx. *align* is the constant alignment in bits.

  The default version of this function takes care of putting symbolic constants in `flag_pic` mode in `data_section` and everything else in `readonly_data_section`.

tree **TARGET_MANGLE_DECL_ASSEMBLER_NAME** (*tree* decl, *tree* id) [Target Hook]
: Define this hook if you need to postprocess the assembler name generated by target-independent code. The *id* provided to this hook will be the computed name (e.g., the macro `DECL_NAME` of the *decl* in C, or the mangled name of the *decl* in C++). The return value of the hook is an `IDENTIFIER_NODE` for the appropriate mangled name on your target system. The default implementation of this hook just returns the *id* provided.

void **TARGET_ENCODE_SECTION_INFO** (*tree* decl, *rtx* rtl, *int* [Target Hook]
new_decl_p)
: Define this hook if references to a symbol or a constant must be treated differently depending on something about the variable or function named by the symbol (such as what section it is in).

  The hook is executed immediately after rtl has been created for *decl*, which may be a variable or function declaration or an entry in the constant pool. In either case, *rtl* is the rtl in question. Do *not* use `DECL_RTL (decl)` in this hook; that field may not have been initialized yet.

  In the case of a constant, it is safe to assume that the rtl is a `mem` whose address is a `symbol_ref`. Most decls will also have this form, but that is not guaranteed. Global register variables, for instance, will have a `reg` for their rtl. (Normally the right thing to do with such unusual rtl is leave it alone.)

  The *new_decl_p* argument will be true if this is the first time that `TARGET_ENCODE_SECTION_INFO` has been invoked on this decl. It will be false for subsequent invocations, which will happen for duplicate declarations. Whether or not anything must be done for the duplicate declaration depends on whether the hook examines `DECL_ATTRIBUTES`. *new_decl_p* is always true when the hook is called for a constant.

  The usual thing for this hook to do is to record flags in the `symbol_ref`, using `SYMBOL_REF_FLAG` or `SYMBOL_REF_FLAGS`. Historically, the name string was modified if it was necessary to encode more than one bit of information, but this practice is now discouraged; use `SYMBOL_REF_FLAGS`.

  The default definition of this hook, `default_encode_section_info` in 'varasm.c', sets a number of commonly-useful bits in `SYMBOL_REF_FLAGS`. Check whether the default does what you need before overriding it.

const char * **TARGET_STRIP_NAME_ENCODING** (*const char* *name) [Target Hook]
: Decode *name* and return the real name part, sans the characters that `TARGET_ENCODE_SECTION_INFO` may have added.

bool TARGET_IN_SMALL_DATA_P (*const_tree exp*) [Target Hook]
: Returns true if *exp* should be placed into a "small data" section. The default version of this hook always returns false.

bool TARGET_HAVE_SRODATA_SECTION [Target Hook]
: Contains the value true if the target places read-only "small data" into a separate section. The default value is false.

bool TARGET_PROFILE_BEFORE_PROLOGUE (*void*) [Target Hook]
: It returns true if target wants profile code emitted before prologue.

    The default version of this hook use the target macro PROFILE_BEFORE_PROLOGUE.

bool TARGET_BINDS_LOCAL_P (*const_tree exp*) [Target Hook]
: Returns true if *exp* names an object for which name resolution rules must resolve to the current "module" (dynamic shared library or executable image).

    The default version of this hook implements the name resolution rules for ELF, which has a looser model of global name binding than other currently supported object file formats.

bool TARGET_HAVE_TLS [Target Hook]
: Contains the value true if the target supports thread-local storage. The default value is false.

18.19 Position Independent Code

This section describes macros that help implement generation of position independent code. Simply defining these macros is not enough to generate valid PIC; you must also add support to the hook TARGET_LEGITIMATE_ADDRESS_P and to the macro PRINT_OPERAND_ADDRESS, as well as LEGITIMIZE_ADDRESS. You must modify the definition of 'movsi' to do something appropriate when the source operand contains a symbolic address. You may also need to alter the handling of switch statements so that they use relative addresses.

PIC_OFFSET_TABLE_REGNUM [Macro]
: The register number of the register used to address a table of static data addresses in memory. In some cases this register is defined by a processor's "application binary interface" (ABI). When this macro is defined, RTL is generated for this register once, as with the stack pointer and frame pointer registers. If this macro is not defined, it is up to the machine-dependent files to allocate such a register (if necessary). Note that this register must be fixed when in use (e.g. when flag_pic is true).

PIC_OFFSET_TABLE_REG_CALL_CLOBBERED [Macro]
: A C expression that is nonzero if the register defined by PIC_OFFSET_TABLE_REGNUM is clobbered by calls. If not defined, the default is zero. Do not define this macro if PIC_OFFSET_TABLE_REGNUM is not defined.

LEGITIMATE_PIC_OPERAND_P (*x*) [Macro]
: A C expression that is nonzero if *x* is a legitimate immediate operand on the target machine when generating position independent code. You can assume that *x* satisfies CONSTANT_P, so you need not check this. You can also assume *flag_pic* is true, so you need not check it either. You need not define this macro if all constants (including SYMBOL_REF) can be immediate operands when generating position independent code.

18.20 Defining the Output Assembler Language

This section describes macros whose principal purpose is to describe how to write instructions in assembler language—rather than what the instructions do.

18.20.1 The Overall Framework of an Assembler File

This describes the overall framework of an assembly file.

void TARGET_ASM_FILE_START (*void*) [Target Hook]

Output to `asm_out_file` any text which the assembler expects to find at the beginning of a file. The default behavior is controlled by two flags, documented below. Unless your target's assembler is quite unusual, if you override the default, you should call `default_file_start` at some point in your target hook. This lets other target files rely on these variables.

bool TARGET_ASM_FILE_START_APP_OFF [Target Hook]

If this flag is true, the text of the macro `ASM_APP_OFF` will be printed as the very first line in the assembly file, unless '-fverbose-asm' is in effect. (If that macro has been defined to the empty string, this variable has no effect.) With the normal definition of `ASM_APP_OFF`, the effect is to notify the GNU assembler that it need not bother stripping comments or extra whitespace from its input. This allows it to work a bit faster.

The default is false. You should not set it to true unless you have verified that your port does not generate any extra whitespace or comments that will cause GAS to issue errors in NO_APP mode.

bool TARGET_ASM_FILE_START_FILE_DIRECTIVE [Target Hook]

If this flag is true, `output_file_directive` will be called for the primary source file, immediately after printing `ASM_APP_OFF` (if that is enabled). Most ELF assemblers expect this to be done. The default is false.

void TARGET_ASM_FILE_END (*void*) [Target Hook]

Output to `asm_out_file` any text which the assembler expects to find at the end of a file. The default is to output nothing.

void file_end_indicate_exec_stack () [Function]

Some systems use a common convention, the '.note.GNU-stack' special section, to indicate whether or not an object file relies on the stack being executable. If your system uses this convention, you should define `TARGET_ASM_FILE_END` to this function. If you need to do other things in that hook, have your hook function call this function.

void TARGET_ASM_LTO_START (*void*) [Target Hook]

Output to `asm_out_file` any text which the assembler expects to find at the start of an LTO section. The default is to output nothing.

void TARGET_ASM_LTO_END (*void*) [Target Hook]

Output to `asm_out_file` any text which the assembler expects to find at the end of an LTO section. The default is to output nothing.

void TARGET_ASM_CODE_END (*void*)   [Target Hook]

> Output to `asm_out_file` any text which is needed before emitting unwind info and debug info at the end of a file. Some targets emit here PIC setup thunks that cannot be emitted at the end of file, because they couldn't have unwind info then. The default is to output nothing.

ASM_COMMENT_START   [Macro]

> A C string constant describing how to begin a comment in the target assembler language. The compiler assumes that the comment will end at the end of the line.

ASM_APP_ON   [Macro]

> A C string constant for text to be output before each `asm` statement or group of consecutive ones. Normally this is `"#APP"`, which is a comment that has no effect on most assemblers but tells the GNU assembler that it must check the lines that follow for all valid assembler constructs.

ASM_APP_OFF   [Macro]

> A C string constant for text to be output after each `asm` statement or group of consecutive ones. Normally this is `"#NO_APP"`, which tells the GNU assembler to resume making the time-saving assumptions that are valid for ordinary compiler output.

ASM_OUTPUT_SOURCE_FILENAME (*stream*, *name*)   [Macro]

> A C statement to output COFF information or DWARF debugging information which indicates that filename *name* is the current source file to the stdio stream *stream*.
>
> This macro need not be defined if the standard form of output for the file format in use is appropriate.

void TARGET_ASM_OUTPUT_SOURCE_FILENAME (*FILE *file*, *const*   [Target Hook]
        char *name)

> Output DWARF debugging information which indicates that filename *name* is the current source file to the stdio stream *file*.
>
> This target hook need not be defined if the standard form of output for the file format in use is appropriate.

void TARGET_ASM_OUTPUT_IDENT (*const char *name*)   [Target Hook]

> Output a string based on *name*, suitable for the '#ident' directive, or the equivalent directive or pragma in non-C-family languages. If this hook is not defined, nothing is output for the '#ident' directive.

OUTPUT_QUOTED_STRING (*stream*, *string*)   [Macro]

> A C statement to output the string *string* to the stdio stream *stream*. If you do not call the function `output_quoted_string` in your config files, GCC will only call it to output filenames to the assembler source. So you can use it to canonicalize the format of the filename using this macro.

void TARGET_ASM_NAMED_SECTION (*const char *name*, *unsigned int*   [Target Hook]
        flags, *tree decl*)

> Output assembly directives to switch to section *name*. The section should have attributes as specified by *flags*, which is a bit mask of the `SECTION_*` flags defined in 'output.h'. If *decl* is non-NULL, it is the VAR_DECL or FUNCTION_DECL with which this section is associated.

bool TARGET_ASM_ELF_FLAGS_NUMERIC (*unsigned int* `flags`,   [Target Hook]
      unsigned int `*num`)
: This hook can be used to encode ELF section flags for which no letter code has been defined in the assembler. It is called by `default_asm_named_section` whenever the section flags need to be emitted in the assembler output. If the hook returns true, then the numerical value for ELF section flags should be calculated from *flags* and saved in **num*; the value is printed out instead of the normal sequence of letter codes. If the hook is not defined, or if it returns false, then *num* is ignored and the traditional letter sequence is emitted.

section * TARGET_ASM_FUNCTION_SECTION (*tree* `decl`, *enum*   [Target Hook]
      node_frequency `freq`, *bool* `startup`, *bool* `exit`)
: Return preferred text (sub)section for function *decl*. Main purpose of this function is to separate cold, normal and hot functions. *startup* is true when function is known to be used only at startup (from static constructors or it is `main()`). *exit* is true when function is known to be used only at exit (from static destructors). Return NULL if function should go to default text section.

void TARGET_ASM_FUNCTION_SWITCHED_TEXT_SECTIONS (*FILE*   [Target Hook]
      `*file`, *tree* `decl`, *bool* `new_is_cold`)
: Used by the target to emit any assembler directives or additional labels needed when a function is partitioned between different sections. Output should be written to *file*. The function decl is available as *decl* and the new section is 'cold' if *new_is_cold* is `true`.

bool TARGET_HAVE_NAMED_SECTIONS   [Common Target Hook]
: This flag is true if the target supports `TARGET_ASM_NAMED_SECTION`. It must not be modified by command-line option processing.

bool TARGET_HAVE_SWITCHABLE_BSS_SECTIONS   [Target Hook]
: This flag is true if we can create zeroed data by switching to a BSS section and then using `ASM_OUTPUT_SKIP` to allocate the space. This is true on most ELF targets.

unsigned int TARGET_SECTION_TYPE_FLAGS (*tree* `decl`, *const*   [Target Hook]
      char `*name`, *int* `reloc`)
: Choose a set of section attributes for use by `TARGET_ASM_NAMED_SECTION` based on a variable or function decl, a section name, and whether or not the declaration's initializer may contain runtime relocations. *decl* may be null, in which case read-write data should be assumed.

  The default version of this function handles choosing code vs data, read-only vs read-write data, and `flag_pic`. You should only need to override this if your target has special flags that might be set via `__attribute__`.

int TARGET_ASM_RECORD_GCC_SWITCHES (*print_switch_type* `type`,   [Target Hook]
      const char `*text`)
: Provides the target with the ability to record the gcc command line switches that have been passed to the compiler, and options that are enabled. The *type* argument specifies what is being recorded. It can take the following values:

Chapter 18: Target Description Macros and Functions 579

SWITCH_TYPE_PASSED
: *text* is a command line switch that has been set by the user.

SWITCH_TYPE_ENABLED
: *text* is an option which has been enabled. This might be as a direct result of a command line switch, or because it is enabled by default or because it has been enabled as a side effect of a different command line switch. For example, the '-O2' switch enables various different individual optimization passes.

SWITCH_TYPE_DESCRIPTIVE
: *text* is either NULL or some descriptive text which should be ignored. If *text* is NULL then it is being used to warn the target hook that either recording is starting or ending. The first time *type* is SWITCH_TYPE_DESCRIPTIVE and *text* is NULL, the warning is for start up and the second time the warning is for wind down. This feature is to allow the target hook to make any necessary preparations before it starts to record switches and to perform any necessary tidying up after it has finished recording switches.

SWITCH_TYPE_LINE_START
: This option can be ignored by this target hook.

SWITCH_TYPE_LINE_END
: This option can be ignored by this target hook.

The hook's return value must be zero. Other return values may be supported in the future.

By default this hook is set to NULL, but an example implementation is provided for ELF based targets. Called *elf_record_gcc_switches*, it records the switches as ASCII text inside a new, string mergeable section in the assembler output file. The name of the new section is provided by the `TARGET_ASM_RECORD_GCC_SWITCHES_SECTION` target hook.

const char * TARGET_ASM_RECORD_GCC_SWITCHES_SECTION [Target Hook]
: This is the name of the section that will be created by the example ELF implementation of the TARGET_ASM_RECORD_GCC_SWITCHES target hook.

18.20.2 Output of Data

const char * TARGET_ASM_BYTE_OP [Target Hook]
const char * TARGET_ASM_ALIGNED_HI_OP [Target Hook]
const char * TARGET_ASM_ALIGNED_SI_OP [Target Hook]
const char * TARGET_ASM_ALIGNED_DI_OP [Target Hook]
const char * TARGET_ASM_ALIGNED_TI_OP [Target Hook]
const char * TARGET_ASM_UNALIGNED_HI_OP [Target Hook]
const char * TARGET_ASM_UNALIGNED_SI_OP [Target Hook]
const char * TARGET_ASM_UNALIGNED_DI_OP [Target Hook]
const char * TARGET_ASM_UNALIGNED_TI_OP [Target Hook]

These hooks specify assembly directives for creating certain kinds of integer object. The `TARGET_ASM_BYTE_OP` directive creates a byte-sized object, the `TARGET_ASM_`

ALIGNED_HI_OP one creates an aligned two-byte object, and so on. Any of the hooks may be NULL, indicating that no suitable directive is available.

The compiler will print these strings at the start of a new line, followed immediately by the object's initial value. In most cases, the string should contain a tab, a pseudo-op, and then another tab.

bool **TARGET_ASM_INTEGER** (*rtx* x, *unsigned int* size, *int* aligned_p) [Target Hook]

The `assemble_integer` function uses this hook to output an integer object. x is the object's value, *size* is its size in bytes and *aligned_p* indicates whether it is aligned. The function should return `true` if it was able to output the object. If it returns false, `assemble_integer` will try to split the object into smaller parts.

The default implementation of this hook will use the `TARGET_ASM_BYTE_OP` family of strings, returning `false` when the relevant string is NULL.

void **TARGET_ASM_DECL_END** (*void*) [Target Hook]

Define this hook if the target assembler requires a special marker to terminate an initialized variable declaration.

bool **TARGET_ASM_OUTPUT_ADDR_CONST_EXTRA** (*FILE* *file, *rtx* x) [Target Hook]

A target hook to recognize *rtx* patterns that `output_addr_const` can't deal with, and output assembly code to *file* corresponding to the pattern x. This may be used to allow machine-dependent UNSPECs to appear within constants.

If target hook fails to recognize a pattern, it must return `false`, so that a standard error message is printed. If it prints an error message itself, by calling, for example, `output_operand_lossage`, it may just return `true`.

ASM_OUTPUT_ASCII (*stream*, *ptr*, *len*) [Macro]

A C statement to output to the stdio stream *stream* an assembler instruction to assemble a string constant containing the *len* bytes at *ptr*. *ptr* will be a C expression of type `char *` and *len* a C expression of type `int`.

If the assembler has a .ascii pseudo-op as found in the Berkeley Unix assembler, do not define the macro `ASM_OUTPUT_ASCII`.

ASM_OUTPUT_FDESC (*stream*, *decl*, *n*) [Macro]

A C statement to output word *n* of a function descriptor for *decl*. This must be defined if `TARGET_VTABLE_USES_DESCRIPTORS` is defined, and is otherwise unused.

CONSTANT_POOL_BEFORE_FUNCTION [Macro]

You may define this macro as a C expression. You should define the expression to have a nonzero value if GCC should output the constant pool for a function before the code for the function, or a zero value if GCC should output the constant pool after the function. If you do not define this macro, the usual case, GCC will output the constant pool before the function.

ASM_OUTPUT_POOL_PROLOGUE (*file*, *funname*, *fundecl*, *size*) [Macro]

A C statement to output assembler commands to define the start of the constant pool for a function. *funname* is a string giving the name of the function. Should the return

Chapter 18: Target Description Macros and Functions   581

type of the function be required, it can be obtained via *fundecl*. *size* is the size, in bytes, of the constant pool that will be written immediately after this call.

If no constant-pool prefix is required, the usual case, this macro need not be defined.

ASM_OUTPUT_SPECIAL_POOL_ENTRY (*file*, *x*, *mode*, *align*, *labelno*,   [Macro]
        jumpto)

A C statement (with or without semicolon) to output a constant in the constant pool, if it needs special treatment. (This macro need not do anything for RTL expressions that can be output normally.)

The argument *file* is the standard I/O stream to output the assembler code on. *x* is the RTL expression for the constant to output, and *mode* is the machine mode (in case *x* is a 'const_int'). *align* is the required alignment for the value *x*; you should output an assembler directive to force this much alignment.

The argument *labelno* is a number to use in an internal label for the address of this pool entry. The definition of this macro is responsible for outputting the label definition at the proper place. Here is how to do this:

    (*targetm.asm_out.internal_label) (file, "LC", labelno);

When you output a pool entry specially, you should end with a `goto` to the label *jumpto*. This will prevent the same pool entry from being output a second time in the usual manner.

You need not define this macro if it would do nothing.

ASM_OUTPUT_POOL_EPILOGUE (*file funname fundecl size*)   [Macro]

A C statement to output assembler commands to at the end of the constant pool for a function. *funname* is a string giving the name of the function. Should the return type of the function be required, you can obtain it via *fundecl*. *size* is the size, in bytes, of the constant pool that GCC wrote immediately before this call.

If no constant-pool epilogue is required, the usual case, you need not define this macro.

IS_ASM_LOGICAL_LINE_SEPARATOR (*C*, *STR*)   [Macro]

Define this macro as a C expression which is nonzero if *C* is used as a logical line separator by the assembler. *STR* points to the position in the string where *C* was found; this can be used if a line separator uses multiple characters.

If you do not define this macro, the default is that only the character ';' is treated as a logical line separator.

`const char *` **TARGET_ASM_OPEN_PAREN**   [Target Hook]
`const char *` **TARGET_ASM_CLOSE_PAREN**   [Target Hook]

These target hooks are C string constants, describing the syntax in the assembler for grouping arithmetic expressions. If not overridden, they default to normal parentheses, which is correct for most assemblers.

These macros are provided by 'real.h' for writing the definitions of ASM_OUTPUT_DOUBLE and the like:

REAL_VALUE_TO_TARGET_SINGLE (*x*, *l*)   [Macro]
REAL_VALUE_TO_TARGET_DOUBLE (*x*, *l*)   [Macro]

`REAL_VALUE_TO_TARGET_LONG_DOUBLE (x, l)` [Macro]
`REAL_VALUE_TO_TARGET_DECIMAL32 (x, l)` [Macro]
`REAL_VALUE_TO_TARGET_DECIMAL64 (x, l)` [Macro]
`REAL_VALUE_TO_TARGET_DECIMAL128 (x, l)` [Macro]

These translate *x*, of type `REAL_VALUE_TYPE`, to the target's floating point representation, and store its bit pattern in the variable *l*. For `REAL_VALUE_TO_TARGET_SINGLE` and `REAL_VALUE_TO_TARGET_DECIMAL32`, this variable should be a simple `long int`. For the others, it should be an array of `long int`. The number of elements in this array is determined by the size of the desired target floating point data type: 32 bits of it go in each `long int` array element. Each array element holds 32 bits of the result, even if `long int` is wider than 32 bits on the host machine.

The array element values are designed so that you can print them out using `fprintf` in the order they should appear in the target machine's memory.

18.20.3 Output of Uninitialized Variables

Each of the macros in this section is used to do the whole job of outputting a single uninitialized variable.

`ASM_OUTPUT_COMMON (stream, name, size, rounded)` [Macro]

A C statement (sans semicolon) to output to the stdio stream *stream* the assembler definition of a common-label named *name* whose size is *size* bytes. The variable *rounded* is the size rounded up to whatever alignment the caller wants. It is possible that *size* may be zero, for instance if a struct with no other member than a zero-length array is defined. In this case, the backend must output a symbol definition that allocates at least one byte, both so that the address of the resulting object does not compare equal to any other, and because some object formats cannot even express the concept of a zero-sized common symbol, as that is how they represent an ordinary undefined external.

Use the expression `assemble_name (stream, name)` to output the name itself; before and after that, output the additional assembler syntax for defining the name, and a newline.

This macro controls how the assembler definitions of uninitialized common global variables are output.

`ASM_OUTPUT_ALIGNED_COMMON (stream, name, size, alignment)` [Macro]

Like `ASM_OUTPUT_COMMON` except takes the required alignment as a separate, explicit argument. If you define this macro, it is used in place of `ASM_OUTPUT_COMMON`, and gives you more flexibility in handling the required alignment of the variable. The alignment is specified as the number of bits.

`ASM_OUTPUT_ALIGNED_DECL_COMMON (stream, decl, name, size, alignment)` [Macro]

Like `ASM_OUTPUT_ALIGNED_COMMON` except that *decl* of the variable to be output, if there is one, or `NULL_TREE` if there is no corresponding variable. If you define this macro, GCC will use it in place of both `ASM_OUTPUT_COMMON` and `ASM_OUTPUT_ALIGNED_COMMON`. Define this macro when you need to see the variable's decl in order to chose what to output.

ASM_OUTPUT_ALIGNED_BSS (*stream*, *decl*, *name*, *size*, *alignment*) [Macro]

A C statement (sans semicolon) to output to the stdio stream *stream* the assembler definition of uninitialized global *decl* named *name* whose size is *size* bytes. The variable *alignment* is the alignment specified as the number of bits.

Try to use function **asm_output_aligned_bss** defined in file 'varasm.c' when defining this macro. If unable, use the expression **assemble_name (*stream*, *name*)** to output the name itself; before and after that, output the additional assembler syntax for defining the name, and a newline.

There are two ways of handling global BSS. One is to define this macro. The other is to have **TARGET_ASM_SELECT_SECTION** return a switchable BSS section (see [TARGET_HAVE_SWITCHABLE_BSS_SECTIONS], page 578). You do not need to do both.

Some languages do not have **common** data, and require a non-common form of global BSS in order to handle uninitialized globals efficiently. C++ is one example of this. However, if the target does not support global BSS, the front end may choose to make globals common in order to save space in the object file.

ASM_OUTPUT_LOCAL (*stream*, *name*, *size*, *rounded*) [Macro]

A C statement (sans semicolon) to output to the stdio stream *stream* the assembler definition of a local-common-label named *name* whose size is *size* bytes. The variable *rounded* is the size rounded up to whatever alignment the caller wants.

Use the expression **assemble_name (*stream*, *name*)** to output the name itself; before and after that, output the additional assembler syntax for defining the name, and a newline.

This macro controls how the assembler definitions of uninitialized static variables are output.

ASM_OUTPUT_ALIGNED_LOCAL (*stream*, *name*, *size*, *alignment*) [Macro]

Like **ASM_OUTPUT_LOCAL** except takes the required alignment as a separate, explicit argument. If you define this macro, it is used in place of **ASM_OUTPUT_LOCAL**, and gives you more flexibility in handling the required alignment of the variable. The alignment is specified as the number of bits.

ASM_OUTPUT_ALIGNED_DECL_LOCAL (*stream*, *decl*, *name*, *size*, *alignment*) [Macro]

Like **ASM_OUTPUT_ALIGNED_DECL** except that *decl* of the variable to be output, if there is one, or **NULL_TREE** if there is no corresponding variable. If you define this macro, GCC will use it in place of both **ASM_OUTPUT_DECL** and **ASM_OUTPUT_ALIGNED_DECL**. Define this macro when you need to see the variable's decl in order to chose what to output.

18.20.4 Output and Generation of Labels

This is about outputting labels.

ASM_OUTPUT_LABEL (*stream*, *name*) [Macro]

A C statement (sans semicolon) to output to the stdio stream *stream* the assembler definition of a label named *name*. Use the expression **assemble_name (*stream*, *name*) to output the name itself; before and after that, output the additional assembler syntax for defining the name, and a newline. A default definition of this macro is provided which is correct for most systems.

ASM_OUTPUT_FUNCTION_LABEL (*stream*, *name*, *decl*) [Macro]

A C statement (sans semicolon) to output to the stdio stream *stream* the assembler definition of a label named *name* of a function. Use the expression `assemble_name (stream, name)` to output the name itself; before and after that, output the additional assembler syntax for defining the name, and a newline. A default definition of this macro is provided which is correct for most systems.

If this macro is not defined, then the function name is defined in the usual manner as a label (by means of `ASM_OUTPUT_LABEL`).

ASM_OUTPUT_INTERNAL_LABEL (*stream*, *name*) [Macro]

Identical to `ASM_OUTPUT_LABEL`, except that *name* is known to refer to a compiler-generated label. The default definition uses `assemble_name_raw`, which is like `assemble_name` except that it is more efficient.

SIZE_ASM_OP [Macro]

A C string containing the appropriate assembler directive to specify the size of a symbol, without any arguments. On systems that use ELF, the default (in 'config/elfos.h') is '"\t.size\t"'; on other systems, the default is not to define this macro.

Define this macro only if it is correct to use the default definitions of `ASM_OUTPUT_SIZE_DIRECTIVE` and `ASM_OUTPUT_MEASURED_SIZE` for your system. If you need your own custom definitions of those macros, or if you do not need explicit symbol sizes at all, do not define this macro.

ASM_OUTPUT_SIZE_DIRECTIVE (*stream*, *name*, *size*) [Macro]

A C statement (sans semicolon) to output to the stdio stream *stream* a directive telling the assembler that the size of the symbol *name* is *size*. *size* is a `HOST_WIDE_INT`. If you define `SIZE_ASM_OP`, a default definition of this macro is provided.

ASM_OUTPUT_MEASURED_SIZE (*stream*, *name*) [Macro]

A C statement (sans semicolon) to output to the stdio stream *stream* a directive telling the assembler to calculate the size of the symbol *name* by subtracting its address from the current address.

If you define `SIZE_ASM_OP`, a default definition of this macro is provided. The default assumes that the assembler recognizes a special '.' symbol as referring to the current address, and can calculate the difference between this and another symbol. If your assembler does not recognize '.' or cannot do calculations with it, you will need to redefine `ASM_OUTPUT_MEASURED_SIZE` to use some other technique.

NO_DOLLAR_IN_LABEL [Macro]

Define this macro if the assembler does not accept the character '$' in label names. By default constructors and destructors in G++ have '$' in the identifiers. If this macro is defined, '.' is used instead.

Chapter 18: Target Description Macros and Functions 585

NO_DOT_IN_LABEL [Macro]

Define this macro if the assembler does not accept the character '.' in label names. By default constructors and destructors in G++ have names that use '.'. If this macro is defined, these names are rewritten to avoid '.'.

TYPE_ASM_OP [Macro]

A C string containing the appropriate assembler directive to specify the type of a symbol, without any arguments. On systems that use ELF, the default (in 'config/elfos.h') is '"\t.type\t"'; on other systems, the default is not to define this macro.

Define this macro only if it is correct to use the default definition of ASM_OUTPUT_TYPE_DIRECTIVE for your system. If you need your own custom definition of this macro, or if you do not need explicit symbol types at all, do not define this macro.

TYPE_OPERAND_FMT [Macro]

A C string which specifies (using printf syntax) the format of the second operand to TYPE_ASM_OP. On systems that use ELF, the default (in 'config/elfos.h') is '"@%s"'; on other systems, the default is not to define this macro.

Define this macro only if it is correct to use the default definition of ASM_OUTPUT_TYPE_DIRECTIVE for your system. If you need your own custom definition of this macro, or if you do not need explicit symbol types at all, do not define this macro.

ASM_OUTPUT_TYPE_DIRECTIVE (stream, type) [Macro]

A C statement (sans semicolon) to output to the stdio stream stream a directive telling the assembler that the type of the symbol name is type. type is a C string; currently, that string is always either '"function"' or '"object"', but you should not count on this.

If you define TYPE_ASM_OP and TYPE_OPERAND_FMT, a default definition of this macro is provided.

ASM_DECLARE_FUNCTION_NAME (stream, name, decl) [Macro]

A C statement (sans semicolon) to output to the stdio stream stream any text necessary for declaring the name name of a function which is being defined. This macro is responsible for outputting the label definition (perhaps using ASM_OUTPUT_FUNCTION_LABEL). The argument decl is the FUNCTION_DECL tree node representing the function.

If this macro is not defined, then the function name is defined in the usual manner as a label (by means of ASM_OUTPUT_FUNCTION_LABEL).

You may wish to use ASM_OUTPUT_TYPE_DIRECTIVE in the definition of this macro.

ASM_DECLARE_FUNCTION_SIZE (stream, name, decl) [Macro]

A C statement (sans semicolon) to output to the stdio stream stream any text necessary for declaring the size of a function which is being defined. The argument name is the name of the function. The argument decl is the FUNCTION_DECL tree node representing the function.

If this macro is not defined, then the function size is not defined.

You may wish to use ASM_OUTPUT_MEASURED_SIZE in the definition of this macro.

ASM_DECLARE_COLD_FUNCTION_NAME (*stream*, *name*, *decl*) [Macro]

> A C statement (sans semicolon) to output to the stdio stream *stream* any text necessary for declaring the name *name* of a cold function partition which is being defined. This macro is responsible for outputting the label definition (perhaps using `ASM_OUTPUT_FUNCTION_LABEL`). The argument *decl* is the `FUNCTION_DECL` tree node representing the function.
>
> If this macro is not defined, then the cold partition name is defined in the usual manner as a label (by means of `ASM_OUTPUT_LABEL`).
>
> You may wish to use `ASM_OUTPUT_TYPE_DIRECTIVE` in the definition of this macro.

ASM_DECLARE_COLD_FUNCTION_SIZE (*stream*, *name*, *decl*) [Macro]

> A C statement (sans semicolon) to output to the stdio stream *stream* any text necessary for declaring the size of a cold function partition which is being defined. The argument *name* is the name of the cold partition of the function. The argument *decl* is the `FUNCTION_DECL` tree node representing the function.
>
> If this macro is not defined, then the partition size is not defined.
>
> You may wish to use `ASM_OUTPUT_MEASURED_SIZE` in the definition of this macro.

ASM_DECLARE_OBJECT_NAME (*stream*, *name*, *decl*) [Macro]

> A C statement (sans semicolon) to output to the stdio stream *stream* any text necessary for declaring the name *name* of an initialized variable which is being defined. This macro must output the label definition (perhaps using `ASM_OUTPUT_LABEL`). The argument *decl* is the `VAR_DECL` tree node representing the variable.
>
> If this macro is not defined, then the variable name is defined in the usual manner as a label (by means of `ASM_OUTPUT_LABEL`).
>
> You may wish to use `ASM_OUTPUT_TYPE_DIRECTIVE` and/or `ASM_OUTPUT_SIZE_DIRECTIVE` in the definition of this macro.

void TARGET_ASM_DECLARE_CONSTANT_NAME (*FILE *file*, const char **name*, *const_tree expr*, *HOST_WIDE_INT size*) [Target Hook]

> A target hook to output to the stdio stream *file* any text necessary for declaring the name *name* of a constant which is being defined. This target hook is responsible for outputting the label definition (perhaps using `assemble_label`). The argument *exp* is the value of the constant, and *size* is the size of the constant in bytes. The *name* will be an internal label.
>
> The default version of this target hook, define the *name* in the usual manner as a label (by means of `assemble_label`).
>
> You may wish to use `ASM_OUTPUT_TYPE_DIRECTIVE` in this target hook.

ASM_DECLARE_REGISTER_GLOBAL (*stream*, *decl*, *regno*, *name*) [Macro]

> A C statement (sans semicolon) to output to the stdio stream *stream* any text necessary for claiming a register *regno* for a global variable *decl* with name *name*.
>
> If you don't define this macro, that is equivalent to defining it to do nothing.

ASM_FINISH_DECLARE_OBJECT (*stream*, *decl*, *toplevel*, *atend*) [Macro]

> A C statement (sans semicolon) to finish up declaring a variable name once the compiler has processed its initializer fully and thus has had a chance to determine the

Chapter 18: Target Description Macros and Functions   587

size of an array when controlled by an initializer. This is used on systems where it's necessary to declare something about the size of the object.

If you don't define this macro, that is equivalent to defining it to do nothing.

You may wish to use `ASM_OUTPUT_SIZE_DIRECTIVE` and/or `ASM_OUTPUT_MEASURED_SIZE` in the definition of this macro.

void **TARGET_ASM_GLOBALIZE_LABEL** (*FILE *stream*, *const char* [Target Hook]
        *name)
: This target hook is a function to output to the stdio stream *stream* some commands that will make the label *name* global; that is, available for reference from other files.

    The default implementation relies on a proper definition of `GLOBAL_ASM_OP`.

void **TARGET_ASM_GLOBALIZE_DECL_NAME** (*FILE *stream*, *tree* [Target Hook]
        decl)
: This target hook is a function to output to the stdio stream *stream* some commands that will make the name associated with *decl* global; that is, available for reference from other files.

    The default implementation uses the TARGET_ASM_GLOBALIZE_LABEL target hook.

void **TARGET_ASM_ASSEMBLE_UNDEFINED_DECL** (*FILE *stream*, [Target Hook]
        const char *name, *const_tree decl*)
: This target hook is a function to output to the stdio stream *stream* some commands that will declare the name associated with *decl* which is not defined in the current translation unit. Most assemblers do not require anything to be output in this case.

ASM_WEAKEN_LABEL (*stream*, *name*) [Macro]
: A C statement (sans semicolon) to output to the stdio stream *stream* some commands that will make the label *name* weak; that is, available for reference from other files but only used if no other definition is available. Use the expression `assemble_name (stream, name)` to output the name itself; before and after that, output the additional assembler syntax for making that name weak, and a newline.

    If you don't define this macro or `ASM_WEAKEN_DECL`, GCC will not support weak symbols and you should not define the `SUPPORTS_WEAK` macro.

ASM_WEAKEN_DECL (*stream*, *decl*, *name*, *value*) [Macro]
: Combines (and replaces) the function of `ASM_WEAKEN_LABEL` and `ASM_OUTPUT_WEAK_ALIAS`, allowing access to the associated function or variable *decl*. If *value* is not NULL, this C statement should output to the stdio stream *stream* assembler code which defines (equates) the weak symbol *name* to have the value *value*. If *value* is NULL, it should output commands to make *name* weak.

ASM_OUTPUT_WEAKREF (*stream*, *decl*, *name*, *value*) [Macro]
: Outputs a directive that enables *name* to be used to refer to symbol *value* with weak-symbol semantics. *decl* is the declaration of *name*.

SUPPORTS_WEAK [Macro]
: A preprocessor constant expression which evaluates to true if the target supports weak symbols.

If you don't define this macro, 'defaults.h' provides a default definition. If either ASM_WEAKEN_LABEL or ASM_WEAKEN_DECL is defined, the default definition is '1'; otherwise, it is '0'.

TARGET_SUPPORTS_WEAK [Macro]

A C expression which evaluates to true if the target supports weak symbols.

If you don't define this macro, 'defaults.h' provides a default definition. The default definition is '(SUPPORTS_WEAK)'. Define this macro if you want to control weak symbol support with a compiler flag such as '-melf'.

MAKE_DECL_ONE_ONLY (decl) [Macro]

A C statement (sans semicolon) to mark decl to be emitted as a public symbol such that extra copies in multiple translation units will be discarded by the linker. Define this macro if your object file format provides support for this concept, such as the 'COMDAT' section flags in the Microsoft Windows PE/COFF format, and this support requires changes to decl, such as putting it in a separate section.

SUPPORTS_ONE_ONLY [Macro]

A C expression which evaluates to true if the target supports one-only semantics.

If you don't define this macro, 'varasm.c' provides a default definition. If MAKE_DECL_ONE_ONLY is defined, the default definition is '1'; otherwise, it is '0'. Define this macro if you want to control one-only symbol support with a compiler flag, or if setting the DECL_ONE_ONLY flag is enough to mark a declaration to be emitted as one-only.

void TARGET_ASM_ASSEMBLE_VISIBILITY (tree decl, int visibility) [Target Hook]

This target hook is a function to output to asm_out_file some commands that will make the symbol(s) associated with decl have hidden, protected or internal visibility as specified by visibility.

TARGET_WEAK_NOT_IN_ARCHIVE_TOC [Macro]

A C expression that evaluates to true if the target's linker expects that weak symbols do not appear in a static archive's table of contents. The default is 0.

Leaving weak symbols out of an archive's table of contents means that, if a symbol will only have a definition in one translation unit and will have undefined references from other translation units, that symbol should not be weak. Defining this macro to be nonzero will thus have the effect that certain symbols that would normally be weak (explicit template instantiations, and vtables for polymorphic classes with noninline key methods) will instead be nonweak.

The C++ ABI requires this macro to be zero. Define this macro for targets where full C++ ABI compliance is impossible and where linker restrictions require weak symbols to be left out of a static archive's table of contents.

ASM_OUTPUT_EXTERNAL (stream, decl, name) [Macro]

A C statement (sans semicolon) to output to the stdio stream stream any text necessary for declaring the name of an external symbol named name which is referenced in this compilation but not defined. The value of decl is the tree node for the declaration.

This macro need not be defined if it does not need to output anything. The GNU assembler and most Unix assemblers don't require anything.

void TARGET_ASM_EXTERNAL_LIBCALL (*rtx symref*) [Target Hook]
This target hook is a function to output to *asm_out_file* an assembler pseudo-op to declare a library function name external. The name of the library function is given by *symref*, which is a `symbol_ref`.

void TARGET_ASM_MARK_DECL_PRESERVED (*const char *symbol*) [Target Hook]
This target hook is a function to output to *asm_out_file* an assembler directive to annotate *symbol* as used. The Darwin target uses the .no_dead_code_strip directive.

ASM_OUTPUT_LABELREF (*stream, name*) [Macro]
A C statement (sans semicolon) to output to the stdio stream *stream* a reference in assembler syntax to a label named *name*. This should add '_' to the front of the name, if that is customary on your operating system, as it is in most Berkeley Unix systems. This macro is used in `assemble_name`.

tree TARGET_MANGLE_ASSEMBLER_NAME (*const char *name*) [Target Hook]
Given a symbol *name*, perform same mangling as `varasm.c`'s `assemble_name`, but in memory rather than to a file stream, returning result as an IDENTIFIER_NODE. Required for correct LTO symtabs. The default implementation calls the TARGET_STRIP_NAME_ENCODING hook and then prepends the USER_LABEL_PREFIX, if any.

ASM_OUTPUT_SYMBOL_REF (*stream, sym*) [Macro]
A C statement (sans semicolon) to output a reference to SYMBOL_REF *sym*. If not defined, `assemble_name` will be used to output the name of the symbol. This macro may be used to modify the way a symbol is referenced depending on information encoded by TARGET_ENCODE_SECTION_INFO.

ASM_OUTPUT_LABEL_REF (*stream, buf*) [Macro]
A C statement (sans semicolon) to output a reference to *buf*, the result of ASM_GENERATE_INTERNAL_LABEL. If not defined, `assemble_name` will be used to output the name of the symbol. This macro is not used by `output_asm_label`, or the %l specifier that calls it; the intention is that this macro should be set when it is necessary to output a label differently when its address is being taken.

void TARGET_ASM_INTERNAL_LABEL (*FILE *stream, const char *prefix, unsigned long labelno*) [Target Hook]
A function to output to the stdio stream *stream* a label whose name is made from the string *prefix* and the number *labelno*.

It is absolutely essential that these labels be distinct from the labels used for user-level functions and variables. Otherwise, certain programs will have name conflicts with internal labels.

It is desirable to exclude internal labels from the symbol table of the object file. Most assemblers have a naming convention for labels that should be excluded; on many systems, the letter 'L' at the beginning of a label has this effect. You should find out what convention your system uses, and follow it.

The default version of this function utilizes ASM_GENERATE_INTERNAL_LABEL.

ASM_OUTPUT_DEBUG_LABEL (*stream*, *prefix*, *num*) [Macro]

> A C statement to output to the stdio stream *stream* a debug info label whose name is made from the string *prefix* and the number *num*. This is useful for VLIW targets, where debug info labels may need to be treated differently than branch target labels. On some systems, branch target labels must be at the beginning of instruction bundles, but debug info labels can occur in the middle of instruction bundles.
>
> If this macro is not defined, then (*targetm.asm_out.internal_label) will be used.

ASM_GENERATE_INTERNAL_LABEL (*string*, *prefix*, *num*) [Macro]

> A C statement to store into the string *string* a label whose name is made from the string *prefix* and the number *num*.
>
> This string, when output subsequently by assemble_name, should produce the output that (*targetm.asm_out.internal_label) would produce with the same *prefix* and *num*.
>
> If the string begins with '*', then assemble_name will output the rest of the string unchanged. It is often convenient for ASM_GENERATE_INTERNAL_LABEL to use '*' in this way. If the string doesn't start with '*', then ASM_OUTPUT_LABELREF gets to output the string, and may change it. (Of course, ASM_OUTPUT_LABELREF is also part of your machine description, so you should know what it does on your machine.)

ASM_FORMAT_PRIVATE_NAME (*outvar*, *name*, *number*) [Macro]

> A C expression to assign to *outvar* (which is a variable of type char *) a newly allocated string made from the string *name* and the number *number*, with some suitable punctuation added. Use alloca to get space for the string.
>
> The string will be used as an argument to ASM_OUTPUT_LABELREF to produce an assembler label for an internal static variable whose name is *name*. Therefore, the string must be such as to result in valid assembler code. The argument *number* is different each time this macro is executed; it prevents conflicts between similarly-named internal static variables in different scopes.
>
> Ideally this string should not be a valid C identifier, to prevent any conflict with the user's own symbols. Most assemblers allow periods or percent signs in assembler symbols; putting at least one of these between the name and the number will suffice.
>
> If this macro is not defined, a default definition will be provided which is correct for most systems.

ASM_OUTPUT_DEF (*stream*, *name*, *value*) [Macro]

> A C statement to output to the stdio stream *stream* assembler code which defines (equates) the symbol *name* to have the value *value*.
>
> If SET_ASM_OP is defined, a default definition is provided which is correct for most systems.

ASM_OUTPUT_DEF_FROM_DECLS (*stream*, *decl_of_name*, *decl_of_value*) [Macro]

> A C statement to output to the stdio stream *stream* assembler code which defines (equates) the symbol whose tree node is *decl_of_name* to have the value of the tree node *decl_of_value*. This macro will be used in preference to 'ASM_OUTPUT_DEF' if it is defined and if the tree nodes are available.

Chapter 18: Target Description Macros and Functions   591

If `SET_ASM_OP` is defined, a default definition is provided which is correct for most systems.

`TARGET_DEFERRED_OUTPUT_DEFS (decl_of_name, decl_of_value)`   [Macro]
A C statement that evaluates to true if the assembler code which defines (equates) the symbol whose tree node is *decl_of_name* to have the value of the tree node *decl_of_value* should be emitted near the end of the current compilation unit. The default is to not defer output of defines. This macro affects defines output by 'ASM_OUTPUT_DEF' and 'ASM_OUTPUT_DEF_FROM_DECLS'.

`ASM_OUTPUT_WEAK_ALIAS (stream, name, value)`   [Macro]
A C statement to output to the stdio stream *stream* assembler code which defines (equates) the weak symbol *name* to have the value *value*. If *value* is NULL, it defines *name* as an undefined weak symbol.

Define this macro if the target only supports weak aliases; define `ASM_OUTPUT_DEF` instead if possible.

`OBJC_GEN_METHOD_LABEL (buf, is_inst, class_name, cat_name,`   [Macro]
    `sel_name)`
Define this macro to override the default assembler names used for Objective-C methods.

The default name is a unique method number followed by the name of the class (e.g. '_1_Foo'). For methods in categories, the name of the category is also included in the assembler name (e.g. '_1_Foo_Bar').

These names are safe on most systems, but make debugging difficult since the method's selector is not present in the name. Therefore, particular systems define other ways of computing names.

buf is an expression of type `char *` which gives you a buffer in which to store the name; its length is as long as *class_name*, *cat_name* and *sel_name* put together, plus 50 characters extra.

The argument *is_inst* specifies whether the method is an instance method or a class method; *class_name* is the name of the class; *cat_name* is the name of the category (or NULL if the method is not in a category); and *sel_name* is the name of the selector.

On systems where the assembler can handle quoted names, you can use this macro to provide more human-readable names.

18.20.5 How Initialization Functions Are Handled

The compiled code for certain languages includes *constructors* (also called *initialization routines*)—functions to initialize data in the program when the program is started. These functions need to be called before the program is "started"—that is to say, before `main` is called.

Compiling some languages generates *destructors* (also called *termination routines*) that should be called when the program terminates.

To make the initialization and termination functions work, the compiler must output something in the assembler code to cause those functions to be called at the appropriate time. When you port the compiler to a new system, you need to specify how to do this.

There are two major ways that GCC currently supports the execution of initialization and termination functions. Each way has two variants. Much of the structure is common to all four variations.

The linker must build two lists of these functions—a list of initialization functions, called __CTOR_LIST__, and a list of termination functions, called __DTOR_LIST__.

Each list always begins with an ignored function pointer (which may hold 0, −1, or a count of the function pointers after it, depending on the environment). This is followed by a series of zero or more function pointers to constructors (or destructors), followed by a function pointer containing zero.

Depending on the operating system and its executable file format, either 'crtstuff.c' or 'libgcc2.c' traverses these lists at startup time and exit time. Constructors are called in reverse order of the list; destructors in forward order.

The best way to handle static constructors works only for object file formats which provide arbitrarily-named sections. A section is set aside for a list of constructors, and another for a list of destructors. Traditionally these are called '.ctors' and '.dtors'. Each object file that defines an initialization function also puts a word in the constructor section to point to that function. The linker accumulates all these words into one contiguous '.ctors' section. Termination functions are handled similarly.

This method will be chosen as the default by 'target-def.h' if TARGET_ASM_NAMED_SECTION is defined. A target that does not support arbitrary sections, but does support special designated constructor and destructor sections may define CTORS_SECTION_ASM_OP and DTORS_SECTION_ASM_OP to achieve the same effect.

When arbitrary sections are available, there are two variants, depending upon how the code in 'crtstuff.c' is called. On systems that support a *.init* section which is executed at program startup, parts of 'crtstuff.c' are compiled into that section. The program is linked by the gcc driver like this:

```
ld -o output_file crti.o crtbegin.o ... -lgcc crtend.o crtn.o
```

The prologue of a function (__init) appears in the .init section of 'crti.o'; the epilogue appears in 'crtn.o'. Likewise for the function __fini in the *.fini* section. Normally these files are provided by the operating system or by the GNU C library, but are provided by GCC for a few targets.

The objects 'crtbegin.o' and 'crtend.o' are (for most targets) compiled from 'crtstuff.c'. They contain, among other things, code fragments within the .init and .fini sections that branch to routines in the .text section. The linker will pull all parts of a section together, which results in a complete __init function that invokes the routines we need at startup.

To use this variant, you must define the INIT_SECTION_ASM_OP macro properly.

If no init section is available, when GCC compiles any function called main (or more accurately, any function designated as a program entry point by the language front end calling expand_main_function), it inserts a procedure call to __main as the first executable code after the function prologue. The __main function is defined in 'libgcc2.c' and runs the global constructors.

In file formats that don't support arbitrary sections, there are again two variants. In the simplest variant, the GNU linker (GNU ld) and an 'a.out' format must be used. In this case, `TARGET_ASM_CONSTRUCTOR` is defined to produce a `.stabs` entry of type 'N_SETT', referencing the name `__CTOR_LIST__`, and with the address of the void function containing the initialization code as its value. The GNU linker recognizes this as a request to add the value to a *set*; the values are accumulated, and are eventually placed in the executable as a vector in the format described above, with a leading (ignored) count and a trailing zero element. `TARGET_ASM_DESTRUCTOR` is handled similarly. Since no init section is available, the absence of `INIT_SECTION_ASM_OP` causes the compilation of `main` to call `__main` as above, starting the initialization process.

The last variant uses neither arbitrary sections nor the GNU linker. This is preferable when you want to do dynamic linking and when using file formats which the GNU linker does not support, such as 'ECOFF'. In this case, `TARGET_HAVE_CTORS_DTORS` is false, initialization and termination functions are recognized simply by their names. This requires an extra program in the linkage step, called `collect2`. This program pretends to be the linker, for use with GCC; it does its job by running the ordinary linker, but also arranges to include the vectors of initialization and termination functions. These functions are called via `__main` as described above. In order to use this method, `use_collect2` must be defined in the target in 'config.gcc'.

18.20.6 Macros Controlling Initialization Routines

Here are the macros that control how the compiler handles initialization and termination functions:

INIT_SECTION_ASM_OP [Macro]

If defined, a C string constant, including spacing, for the assembler operation to identify the following data as initialization code. If not defined, GCC will assume such a section does not exist. When you are using special sections for initialization and termination functions, this macro also controls how 'crtstuff.c' and 'libgcc2.c' arrange to run the initialization functions.

HAS_INIT_SECTION [Macro]

If defined, `main` will not call `__main` as described above. This macro should be defined for systems that control start-up code on a symbol-by-symbol basis, such as OSF/1, and should not be defined explicitly for systems that support `INIT_SECTION_ASM_OP`.

LD_INIT_SWITCH [Macro]

If defined, a C string constant for a switch that tells the linker that the following symbol is an initialization routine.

LD_FINI_SWITCH [Macro]

If defined, a C string constant for a switch that tells the linker that the following symbol is a finalization routine.

COLLECT_SHARED_INIT_FUNC (*stream*, *func*) [Macro]

If defined, a C statement that will write a function that can be automatically called when a shared library is loaded. The function should call *func*, which takes no arguments. If not defined, and the object format requires an explicit initialization function, then a function called `_GLOBAL__DI` will be generated.

This function and the following one are used by collect2 when linking a shared library that needs constructors or destructors, or has DWARF2 exception tables embedded in the code.

COLLECT_SHARED_FINI_FUNC (*stream*, *func*) [Macro]
If defined, a C statement that will write a function that can be automatically called when a shared library is unloaded. The function should call *func*, which takes no arguments. If not defined, and the object format requires an explicit finalization function, then a function called `_GLOBAL__DD` will be generated.

INVOKE__main [Macro]
If defined, `main` will call `__main` despite the presence of `INIT_SECTION_ASM_OP`. This macro should be defined for systems where the init section is not actually run automatically, but is still useful for collecting the lists of constructors and destructors.

SUPPORTS_INIT_PRIORITY [Macro]
If nonzero, the C++ `init_priority` attribute is supported and the compiler should emit instructions to control the order of initialization of objects. If zero, the compiler will issue an error message upon encountering an `init_priority` attribute.

bool TARGET_HAVE_CTORS_DTORS [Target Hook]
This value is true if the target supports some "native" method of collecting constructors and destructors to be run at startup and exit. It is false if we must use `collect2`.

void TARGET_ASM_CONSTRUCTOR (*rtx symbol*, *int priority*) [Target Hook]
If defined, a function that outputs assembler code to arrange to call the function referenced by *symbol* at initialization time.

Assume that *symbol* is a `SYMBOL_REF` for a function taking no arguments and with no return value. If the target supports initialization priorities, *priority* is a value between 0 and `MAX_INIT_PRIORITY`; otherwise it must be `DEFAULT_INIT_PRIORITY`.

If this macro is not defined by the target, a suitable default will be chosen if (1) the target supports arbitrary section names, (2) the target defines `CTORS_SECTION_ASM_OP`, or (3) `USE_COLLECT2` is not defined.

void TARGET_ASM_DESTRUCTOR (*rtx symbol*, *int priority*) [Target Hook]
This is like `TARGET_ASM_CONSTRUCTOR` but used for termination functions rather than initialization functions.

If `TARGET_HAVE_CTORS_DTORS` is true, the initialization routine generated for the generated object file will have static linkage.

If your system uses `collect2` as the means of processing constructors, then that program normally uses `nm` to scan an object file for constructor functions to be called.

On certain kinds of systems, you can define this macro to make `collect2` work faster (and, in some cases, make it work at all):

OBJECT_FORMAT_COFF [Macro]
Define this macro if the system uses COFF (Common Object File Format) object files, so that `collect2` can assume this format and scan object files directly for dynamic constructor/destructor functions.

Chapter 18: Target Description Macros and Functions 595

This macro is effective only in a native compiler; `collect2` as part of a cross compiler always uses `nm` for the target machine.

REAL_NM_FILE_NAME [Macro]

Define this macro as a C string constant containing the file name to use to execute `nm`. The default is to search the path normally for `nm`.

NM_FLAGS [Macro]

`collect2` calls `nm` to scan object files for static constructors and destructors and LTO info. By default, '-n' is passed. Define `NM_FLAGS` to a C string constant if other options are needed to get the same output format as GNU `nm -n` produces.

If your system supports shared libraries and has a program to list the dynamic dependencies of a given library or executable, you can define these macros to enable support for running initialization and termination functions in shared libraries:

LDD_SUFFIX [Macro]

Define this macro to a C string constant containing the name of the program which lists dynamic dependencies, like `ldd` under SunOS 4.

PARSE_LDD_OUTPUT (*ptr*) [Macro]

Define this macro to be C code that extracts filenames from the output of the program denoted by `LDD_SUFFIX`. *ptr* is a variable of type `char *` that points to the beginning of a line of output from `LDD_SUFFIX`. If the line lists a dynamic dependency, the code must advance *ptr* to the beginning of the filename on that line. Otherwise, it must set *ptr* to `NULL`.

SHLIB_SUFFIX [Macro]

Define this macro to a C string constant containing the default shared library extension of the target (e.g., '".so"'). `collect2` strips version information after this suffix when generating global constructor and destructor names. This define is only needed on targets that use `collect2` to process constructors and destructors.

18.20.7 Output of Assembler Instructions

This describes assembler instruction output.

REGISTER_NAMES [Macro]

A C initializer containing the assembler's names for the machine registers, each one as a C string constant. This is what translates register numbers in the compiler into assembler language.

ADDITIONAL_REGISTER_NAMES [Macro]

If defined, a C initializer for an array of structures containing a name and a register number. This macro defines additional names for hard registers, thus allowing the `asm` option in declarations to refer to registers using alternate names.

OVERLAPPING_REGISTER_NAMES [Macro]

If defined, a C initializer for an array of structures containing a name, a register number and a count of the number of consecutive machine registers the name overlaps. This macro defines additional names for hard registers, thus allowing the `asm` option in declarations to refer to registers using alternate names. Unlike `ADDITIONAL_REGISTER_NAMES`, this macro should be used when the register name implies multiple underlying registers.

This macro should be used when it is important that a clobber in an `asm` statement clobbers all the underlying values implied by the register name. For example, on ARM, clobbering the double-precision VFP register "d0" implies clobbering both single-precision registers "s0" and "s1".

`ASM_OUTPUT_OPCODE (stream, ptr)` [Macro]

Define this macro if you are using an unusual assembler that requires different names for the machine instructions.

The definition is a C statement or statements which output an assembler instruction opcode to the stdio stream *stream*. The macro-operand *ptr* is a variable of type `char *` which points to the opcode name in its "internal" form—the form that is written in the machine description. The definition should output the opcode name to *stream*, performing any translation you desire, and increment the variable *ptr* to point at the end of the opcode so that it will not be output twice.

In fact, your macro definition may process less than the entire opcode name, or more than the opcode name; but if you want to process text that includes '%'-sequences to substitute operands, you must take care of the substitution yourself. Just be sure to increment *ptr* over whatever text should not be output normally.

If you need to look at the operand values, they can be found as the elements of `recog_data.operand`.

If the macro definition does nothing, the instruction is output in the usual way.

`FINAL_PRESCAN_INSN (insn, opvec, noperands)` [Macro]

If defined, a C statement to be executed just prior to the output of assembler code for *insn*, to modify the extracted operands so they will be output differently.

Here the argument *opvec* is the vector containing the operands extracted from *insn*, and *noperands* is the number of elements of the vector which contain meaningful data for this insn. The contents of this vector are what will be used to convert the insn template into assembler code, so you can change the assembler output by changing the contents of the vector.

This macro is useful when various assembler syntaxes share a single file of instruction patterns; by defining this macro differently, you can cause a large class of instructions to be output differently (such as with rearranged operands). Naturally, variations in assembler syntax affecting individual insn patterns ought to be handled by writing conditional output routines in those patterns.

If this macro is not defined, it is equivalent to a null statement.

`void TARGET_ASM_FINAL_POSTSCAN_INSN (FILE *file, rtx_insn *insn, rtx *opvec, int noperands)` [Target Hook]

If defined, this target hook is a function which is executed just after the output of assembler code for *insn*, to change the mode of the assembler if necessary.

Here the argument *opvec* is the vector containing the operands extracted from *insn*, and *noperands* is the number of elements of the vector which contain meaningful data for this insn. The contents of this vector are what was used to convert the insn template into assembler code, so you can change the assembler mode by checking the contents of the vector.

PRINT_OPERAND (*stream*, *x*, *code*) [Macro]

A C compound statement to output to stdio stream *stream* the assembler syntax for an instruction operand *x*. *x* is an RTL expression.

code is a value that can be used to specify one of several ways of printing the operand. It is used when identical operands must be printed differently depending on the context. *code* comes from the '%' specification that was used to request printing of the operand. If the specification was just '%*digit*' then *code* is 0; if the specification was '%*ltr digit*' then *code* is the ASCII code for *ltr*.

If *x* is a register, this macro should print the register's name. The names can be found in an array `reg_names` whose type is `char *[]`. `reg_names` is initialized from `REGISTER_NAMES`.

When the machine description has a specification '%*punct*' (a '%' followed by a punctuation character), this macro is called with a null pointer for *x* and the punctuation character for *code*.

PRINT_OPERAND_PUNCT_VALID_P (*code*) [Macro]

A C expression which evaluates to true if *code* is a valid punctuation character for use in the `PRINT_OPERAND` macro. If `PRINT_OPERAND_PUNCT_VALID_P` is not defined, it means that no punctuation characters (except for the standard one, '%') are used in this way.

PRINT_OPERAND_ADDRESS (*stream*, *x*) [Macro]

A C compound statement to output to stdio stream *stream* the assembler syntax for an instruction operand that is a memory reference whose address is *x*. *x* is an RTL expression.

On some machines, the syntax for a symbolic address depends on the section that the address refers to. On these machines, define the hook `TARGET_ENCODE_SECTION_INFO` to store the information into the `symbol_ref`, and then check for it here. See Section 18.20 [Assembler Format], page 576.

DBR_OUTPUT_SEQEND (*file*) [Macro]

A C statement, to be executed after all slot-filler instructions have been output. If necessary, call `dbr_sequence_length` to determine the number of slots filled in a sequence (zero if not currently outputting a sequence), to decide how many no-ops to output, or whatever.

Don't define this macro if it has nothing to do, but it is helpful in reading assembly output if the extent of the delay sequence is made explicit (e.g. with white space).

Note that output routines for instructions with delay slots must be prepared to deal with not being output as part of a sequence (i.e. when the scheduling pass is not run, or when no slot fillers could be found.) The variable `final_sequence` is null when not processing a sequence, otherwise it contains the `sequence` rtx being output.

REGISTER_PREFIX [Macro]
LOCAL_LABEL_PREFIX [Macro]
USER_LABEL_PREFIX [Macro]
IMMEDIATE_PREFIX [Macro]

If defined, C string expressions to be used for the '%R', '%L', '%U', and '%I' options of `asm_fprintf` (see 'final.c'). These are useful when a single 'md' file must support multiple assembler formats. In that case, the various 'tm.h' files can define these macros differently.

ASM_FPRINTF_EXTENSIONS (*file*, *argptr*, *format*) [Macro]

If defined this macro should expand to a series of `case` statements which will be parsed inside the `switch` statement of the `asm_fprintf` function. This allows targets to define extra printf formats which may useful when generating their assembler statements. Note that uppercase letters are reserved for future generic extensions to asm_fprintf, and so are not available to target specific code. The output file is given by the parameter *file*. The varargs input pointer is *argptr* and the rest of the format string, starting the character after the one that is being switched upon, is pointed to by *format*.

ASSEMBLER_DIALECT [Macro]

If your target supports multiple dialects of assembler language (such as different opcodes), define this macro as a C expression that gives the numeric index of the assembler language dialect to use, with zero as the first variant.

If this macro is defined, you may use constructs of the form

'{option0|option1|option2...}'

in the output templates of patterns (see Section 17.5 [Output Template], page 333) or in the first argument of `asm_fprintf`. This construct outputs 'option0', 'option1', 'option2', etc., if the value of ASSEMBLER_DIALECT is zero, one, two, etc. Any special characters within these strings retain their usual meaning. If there are fewer alternatives within the braces than the value of ASSEMBLER_DIALECT, the construct outputs nothing. If it's needed to print curly braces or '|' character in assembler output directly, '%{', '%}' and '%|' can be used.

If you do not define this macro, the characters '{', '|' and '}' do not have any special meaning when used in templates or operands to `asm_fprintf`.

Define the macros REGISTER_PREFIX, LOCAL_LABEL_PREFIX, USER_LABEL_PREFIX and IMMEDIATE_PREFIX if you can express the variations in assembler language syntax with that mechanism. Define ASSEMBLER_DIALECT and use the '{option0|option1}' syntax if the syntax variant are larger and involve such things as different opcodes or operand order.

ASM_OUTPUT_REG_PUSH (*stream*, *regno*) [Macro]

A C expression to output to *stream* some assembler code which will push hard register number *regno* onto the stack. The code need not be optimal, since this macro is used only when profiling.

Chapter 18: Target Description Macros and Functions 599

ASM_OUTPUT_REG_POP (*stream*, *regno*) [Macro]

> A C expression to output to *stream* some assembler code which will pop hard register number *regno* off of the stack. The code need not be optimal, since this macro is used only when profiling.

18.20.8 Output of Dispatch Tables

This concerns dispatch tables.

ASM_OUTPUT_ADDR_DIFF_ELT (*stream*, *body*, *value*, *rel*) [Macro]

> A C statement to output to the stdio stream *stream* an assembler pseudo-instruction to generate a difference between two labels. *value* and *rel* are the numbers of two internal labels. The definitions of these labels are output using (*targetm.asm_out.internal_label), and they must be printed in the same way here. For example,
>
> ```
> fprintf (stream, "\t.word L%d-L%d\n",
>          value, rel)
> ```
>
> You must provide this macro on machines where the addresses in a dispatch table are relative to the table's own address. If defined, GCC will also use this macro on all machines when producing PIC. *body* is the body of the ADDR_DIFF_VEC; it is provided so that the mode and flags can be read.

ASM_OUTPUT_ADDR_VEC_ELT (*stream*, *value*) [Macro]

> This macro should be provided on machines where the addresses in a dispatch table are absolute.
>
> The definition should be a C statement to output to the stdio stream *stream* an assembler pseudo-instruction to generate a reference to a label. *value* is the number of an internal label whose definition is output using (*targetm.asm_out.internal_label). For example,
>
> ```
> fprintf (stream, "\t.word L%d\n", value)
> ```

ASM_OUTPUT_CASE_LABEL (*stream*, *prefix*, *num*, *table*) [Macro]

> Define this if the label before a jump-table needs to be output specially. The first three arguments are the same as for (*targetm.asm_out.internal_label); the fourth argument is the jump-table which follows (a jump_table_data containing an addr_vec or addr_diff_vec).
>
> This feature is used on system V to output a swbeg statement for the table.
>
> If this macro is not defined, these labels are output with (*targetm.asm_out.internal_label).

ASM_OUTPUT_CASE_END (*stream*, *num*, *table*) [Macro]

> Define this if something special must be output at the end of a jump-table. The definition should be a C statement to be executed after the assembler code for the table is written. It should write the appropriate code to stdio stream *stream*. The argument *table* is the jump-table insn, and *num* is the label-number of the preceding label.
>
> If this macro is not defined, nothing special is output at the end of the jump-table.

void TARGET_ASM_EMIT_UNWIND_LABEL (*FILE* `*stream`, *tree* `decl`, [Target Hook]
    int `for_eh`, *int* `empty`)
    This target hook emits a label at the beginning of each FDE. It should be defined on targets where FDEs need special labels, and it should write the appropriate label, for the FDE associated with the function declaration *decl*, to the stdio stream *stream*. The third argument, *for_eh*, is a boolean: true if this is for an exception table. The fourth argument, *empty*, is a boolean: true if this is a placeholder label for an omitted FDE.

    The default is that FDEs are not given nonlocal labels.

void TARGET_ASM_EMIT_EXCEPT_TABLE_LABEL (*FILE* `*stream`)   [Target Hook]
    This target hook emits a label at the beginning of the exception table. It should be defined on targets where it is desirable for the table to be broken up according to function.

    The default is that no label is emitted.

void TARGET_ASM_EMIT_EXCEPT_PERSONALITY (*rtx* `personality`)   [Target Hook]
    If the target implements `TARGET_ASM_UNWIND_EMIT`, this hook may be used to emit a directive to install a personality hook into the unwind info. This hook should not be used if dwarf2 unwind info is used.

void TARGET_ASM_UNWIND_EMIT (*FILE* `*stream`, *rtx_insn* `*insn`)   [Target Hook]
    This target hook emits assembly directives required to unwind the given instruction. This is only used when `TARGET_EXCEPT_UNWIND_INFO` returns `UI_TARGET`.

bool TARGET_ASM_UNWIND_EMIT_BEFORE_INSN   [Target Hook]
    True if the `TARGET_ASM_UNWIND_EMIT` hook should be called before the assembly for *insn* has been emitted, false if the hook should be called afterward.

18.20.9 Assembler Commands for Exception Regions

This describes commands marking the start and the end of an exception region.

EH_FRAME_SECTION_NAME   [Macro]
    If defined, a C string constant for the name of the section containing exception handling frame unwind information. If not defined, GCC will provide a default definition if the target supports named sections. 'crtstuff.c' uses this macro to switch to the appropriate section.

    You should define this symbol if your target supports DWARF 2 frame unwind information and the default definition does not work.

EH_FRAME_THROUGH_COLLECT2   [Macro]
    If defined, DWARF 2 frame unwind information will identified by specially named labels. The collect2 process will locate these labels and generate code to register the frames.

    This might be necessary, for instance, if the system linker will not place the eh_frames in-between the sentinals from 'crtstuff.c', or if the system linker does garbage collection and sections cannot be marked as not to be collected.

Chapter 18: Target Description Macros and Functions   601

EH_TABLES_CAN_BE_READ_ONLY   [Macro]

> Define this macro to 1 if your target is such that no frame unwind information encoding used with non-PIC code will ever require a runtime relocation, but the linker may not support merging read-only and read-write sections into a single read-write section.

MASK_RETURN_ADDR   [Macro]

> An rtx used to mask the return address found via RETURN_ADDR_RTX, so that it does not contain any extraneous set bits in it.

DWARF2_UNWIND_INFO   [Macro]

> Define this macro to 0 if your target supports DWARF 2 frame unwind information, but it does not yet work with exception handling. Otherwise, if your target supports this information (if it defines INCOMING_RETURN_ADDR_RTX and OBJECT_FORMAT_ELF), GCC will provide a default definition of 1.

enum unwind_info_type TARGET_EXCEPT_UNWIND_INFO   [Common Target Hook]
    (*struct gcc_options *opts*)

> This hook defines the mechanism that will be used for exception handling by the target. If the target has ABI specified unwind tables, the hook should return UI_TARGET. If the target is to use the setjmp/longjmp-based exception handling scheme, the hook should return UI_SJLJ. If the target supports DWARF 2 frame unwind information, the hook should return UI_DWARF2.
>
> A target may, if exceptions are disabled, choose to return UI_NONE. This may end up simplifying other parts of target-specific code. The default implementation of this hook never returns UI_NONE.
>
> Note that the value returned by this hook should be constant. It should not depend on anything except the command-line switches described by *opts*. In particular, the setting UI_SJLJ must be fixed at compiler start-up as C pre-processor macros and builtin functions related to exception handling are set up depending on this setting.
>
> The default implementation of the hook first honors the '--enable-sjlj-exceptions' configure option, then DWARF2_UNWIND_INFO, and finally defaults to UI_SJLJ. If DWARF2_UNWIND_INFO depends on command-line options, the target must define this hook so that *opts* is used correctly.

bool TARGET_UNWIND_TABLES_DEFAULT   [Common Target Hook]

> This variable should be set to true if the target ABI requires unwinding tables even when exceptions are not used. It must not be modified by command-line option processing.

DONT_USE_BUILTIN_SETJMP   [Macro]

> Define this macro to 1 if the setjmp/longjmp-based scheme should use the setjmp/longjmp functions from the C library instead of the __builtin_setjmp/__builtin_longjmp machinery.

JMP_BUF_SIZE   [Macro]

> This macro has no effect unless DONT_USE_BUILTIN_SETJMP is also defined. Define this macro if the default size of jmp_buf buffer for the setjmp/longjmp-based exception

handling mechanism is not large enough, or if it is much too large. The default size is `FIRST_PSEUDO_REGISTER * sizeof(void *)`.

DWARF_CIE_DATA_ALIGNMENT [Macro]

This macro need only be defined if the target might save registers in the function prologue at an offset to the stack pointer that is not aligned to `UNITS_PER_WORD`. The definition should be the negative minimum alignment if `STACK_GROWS_DOWNWARD` is true, and the positive minimum alignment otherwise. See Section 18.21.5 [DWARF], page 608. Only applicable if the target supports DWARF 2 frame unwind information.

bool TARGET_TERMINATE_DW2_EH_FRAME_INFO [Target Hook]

Contains the value true if the target should add a zero word onto the end of a Dwarf-2 frame info section when used for exception handling. Default value is false if `EH_FRAME_SECTION_NAME` is defined, and true otherwise.

rtx TARGET_DWARF_REGISTER_SPAN (rtx reg) [Target Hook]

Given a register, this hook should return a parallel of registers to represent where to find the register pieces. Define this hook if the register and its mode are represented in Dwarf in non-contiguous locations, or if the register should be represented in more than one register in Dwarf. Otherwise, this hook should return `NULL_RTX`. If not defined, the default is to return `NULL_RTX`.

machine_mode TARGET_DWARF_FRAME_REG_MODE (int regno) [Target Hook]

Given a register, this hook should return the mode which the corresponding Dwarf frame register should have. This is normally used to return a smaller mode than the raw mode to prevent call clobbered parts of a register altering the frame register size

void TARGET_INIT_DWARF_REG_SIZES_EXTRA (tree address) [Target Hook]

If some registers are represented in Dwarf-2 unwind information in multiple pieces, define this hook to fill in information about the sizes of those pieces in the table used by the unwinder at runtime. It will be called by `expand_builtin_init_dwarf_reg_sizes` after filling in a single size corresponding to each hard register; *address* is the address of the table.

bool TARGET_ASM_TTYPE (rtx sym) [Target Hook]

This hook is used to output a reference from a frame unwinding table to the type_info object identified by *sym*. It should return `true` if the reference was output. Returning `false` will cause the reference to be output using the normal Dwarf2 routines.

bool TARGET_ARM_EABI_UNWINDER [Target Hook]

This flag should be set to `true` on targets that use an ARM EABI based unwinding library, and `false` on other targets. This effects the format of unwinding tables, and how the unwinder in entered after running a cleanup. The default is `false`.

18.20.10 Assembler Commands for Alignment

This describes commands for alignment.

JUMP_ALIGN (label) [Macro]

The alignment (log base 2) to put in front of *label*, which is a common destination of jumps and has no fallthru incoming edge.

Chapter 18: Target Description Macros and Functions 603

This macro need not be defined if you don't want any special alignment to be done at such a time. Most machine descriptions do not currently define the macro.

Unless it's necessary to inspect the *label* parameter, it is better to set the variable *align_jumps* in the target's `TARGET_OPTION_OVERRIDE`. Otherwise, you should try to honor the user's selection in *align_jumps* in a JUMP_ALIGN implementation.

int TARGET_ASM_JUMP_ALIGN_MAX_SKIP (*rtx_insn *label*) [Target Hook]

The maximum number of bytes to skip before *label* when applying `JUMP_ALIGN`. This works only if `ASM_OUTPUT_MAX_SKIP_ALIGN` is defined.

LABEL_ALIGN_AFTER_BARRIER (*label*) [Macro]

The alignment (log base 2) to put in front of *label*, which follows a `BARRIER`.

This macro need not be defined if you don't want any special alignment to be done at such a time. Most machine descriptions do not currently define the macro.

int TARGET_ASM_LABEL_ALIGN_AFTER_BARRIER_MAX_SKIP [Target Hook]
    (*rtx_insn *label*)

The maximum number of bytes to skip before *label* when applying `LABEL_ALIGN_AFTER_BARRIER`. This works only if `ASM_OUTPUT_MAX_SKIP_ALIGN` is defined.

LOOP_ALIGN (*label*) [Macro]

The alignment (log base 2) to put in front of *label* that heads a frequently executed basic block (usually the header of a loop).

This macro need not be defined if you don't want any special alignment to be done at such a time. Most machine descriptions do not currently define the macro.

Unless it's necessary to inspect the *label* parameter, it is better to set the variable `align_loops` in the target's `TARGET_OPTION_OVERRIDE`. Otherwise, you should try to honor the user's selection in `align_loops` in a LOOP_ALIGN implementation.

int TARGET_ASM_LOOP_ALIGN_MAX_SKIP (*rtx_insn *label*) [Target Hook]

The maximum number of bytes to skip when applying `LOOP_ALIGN` to *label*. This works only if `ASM_OUTPUT_MAX_SKIP_ALIGN` is defined.

LABEL_ALIGN (*label*) [Macro]

The alignment (log base 2) to put in front of *label*. If `LABEL_ALIGN_AFTER_BARRIER` / `LOOP_ALIGN` specify a different alignment, the maximum of the specified values is used.

Unless it's necessary to inspect the *label* parameter, it is better to set the variable `align_labels` in the target's `TARGET_OPTION_OVERRIDE`. Otherwise, you should try to honor the user's selection in `align_labels` in a LABEL_ALIGN implementation.

int TARGET_ASM_LABEL_ALIGN_MAX_SKIP (*rtx_insn *label*) [Target Hook]

The maximum number of bytes to skip when applying `LABEL_ALIGN` to *label*. This works only if `ASM_OUTPUT_MAX_SKIP_ALIGN` is defined.

ASM_OUTPUT_SKIP (*stream, nbytes*) [Macro]

A C statement to output to the stdio stream *stream* an assembler instruction to advance the location counter by *nbytes* bytes. Those bytes should be zero when loaded. *nbytes* will be a C expression of type `unsigned HOST_WIDE_INT`.

`ASM_NO_SKIP_IN_TEXT` [Macro]
: Define this macro if `ASM_OUTPUT_SKIP` should not be used in the text section because it fails to put zeros in the bytes that are skipped. This is true on many Unix systems, where the pseudo–op to skip bytes produces no-op instructions rather than zeros when used in the text section.

`ASM_OUTPUT_ALIGN (stream, power)` [Macro]
: A C statement to output to the stdio stream *stream* an assembler command to advance the location counter to a multiple of 2 to the *power* bytes. *power* will be a C expression of type `int`.

`ASM_OUTPUT_ALIGN_WITH_NOP (stream, power)` [Macro]
: Like `ASM_OUTPUT_ALIGN`, except that the "nop" instruction is used for padding, if necessary.

`ASM_OUTPUT_MAX_SKIP_ALIGN (stream, power, max_skip)` [Macro]
: A C statement to output to the stdio stream *stream* an assembler command to advance the location counter to a multiple of 2 to the *power* bytes, but only if *max_skip* or fewer bytes are needed to satisfy the alignment request. *power* and *max_skip* will be a C expression of type `int`.

18.21 Controlling Debugging Information Format

This describes how to specify debugging information.

18.21.1 Macros Affecting All Debugging Formats

These macros affect all debugging formats.

`DBX_REGISTER_NUMBER (regno)` [Macro]
: A C expression that returns the DBX register number for the compiler register number *regno*. In the default macro provided, the value of this expression will be *regno* itself. But sometimes there are some registers that the compiler knows about and DBX does not, or vice versa. In such cases, some register may need to have one number in the compiler and another for DBX.

    If two registers have consecutive numbers inside GCC, and they can be used as a pair to hold a multiword value, then they *must* have consecutive numbers after renumbering with `DBX_REGISTER_NUMBER`. Otherwise, debuggers will be unable to access such a pair, because they expect register pairs to be consecutive in their own numbering scheme.

    If you find yourself defining `DBX_REGISTER_NUMBER` in way that does not preserve register pairs, then what you must do instead is redefine the actual register numbering scheme.

`DEBUGGER_AUTO_OFFSET (x)` [Macro]
: A C expression that returns the integer offset value for an automatic variable having address *x* (an RTL expression). The default computation assumes that *x* is based on the frame-pointer and gives the offset from the frame-pointer. This is required for targets that produce debugging output for DBX and allow the frame-pointer to be eliminated when the '-g' option is used.

Chapter 18: Target Description Macros and Functions

DEBUGGER_ARG_OFFSET (*offset*, *x*) [Macro]

    A C expression that returns the integer offset value for an argument having address *x* (an RTL expression). The nominal offset is *offset*.

PREFERRED_DEBUGGING_TYPE [Macro]

    A C expression that returns the type of debugging output GCC should produce when the user specifies just '-g'. Define this if you have arranged for GCC to support more than one format of debugging output. Currently, the allowable values are DBX_DEBUG, DWARF2_DEBUG, XCOFF_DEBUG, VMS_DEBUG, and VMS_AND_DWARF2_DEBUG.

    When the user specifies '-ggdb', GCC normally also uses the value of this macro to select the debugging output format, but with two exceptions. If DWARF2_DEBUGGING_INFO is defined, GCC uses the value DWARF2_DEBUG. Otherwise, if DBX_DEBUGGING_INFO is defined, GCC uses DBX_DEBUG.

    The value of this macro only affects the default debugging output; the user can always get a specific type of output by using '-gstabs', '-gdwarf-2', '-gxcoff', or '-gvms'.

18.21.2 Specific Options for DBX Output

These are specific options for DBX output.

DBX_DEBUGGING_INFO [Macro]

    Define this macro if GCC should produce debugging output for DBX in response to the '-g' option.

XCOFF_DEBUGGING_INFO [Macro]

    Define this macro if GCC should produce XCOFF format debugging output in response to the '-g' option. This is a variant of DBX format.

DEFAULT_GDB_EXTENSIONS [Macro]

    Define this macro to control whether GCC should by default generate GDB's extended version of DBX debugging information (assuming DBX-format debugging information is enabled at all). If you don't define the macro, the default is 1: always generate the extended information if there is any occasion to.

DEBUG_SYMS_TEXT [Macro]

    Define this macro if all .stabs commands should be output while in the text section.

ASM_STABS_OP [Macro]

    A C string constant, including spacing, naming the assembler pseudo op to use instead of "\t.stabs\t" to define an ordinary debugging symbol. If you don't define this macro, "\t.stabs\t" is used. This macro applies only to DBX debugging information format.

ASM_STABD_OP [Macro]

    A C string constant, including spacing, naming the assembler pseudo op to use instead of "\t.stabd\t" to define a debugging symbol whose value is the current location. If you don't define this macro, "\t.stabd\t" is used. This macro applies only to DBX debugging information format.

ASM_STABN_OP [Macro]

A C string constant, including spacing, naming the assembler pseudo op to use instead of `"\t.stabn\t"` to define a debugging symbol with no name. If you don't define this macro, `"\t.stabn\t"` is used. This macro applies only to DBX debugging information format.

DBX_NO_XREFS [Macro]

Define this macro if DBX on your system does not support the construct 'xs*tagname*'. On some systems, this construct is used to describe a forward reference to a structure named *tagname*. On other systems, this construct is not supported at all.

DBX_CONTIN_LENGTH [Macro]

A symbol name in DBX-format debugging information is normally continued (split into two separate `.stabs` directives) when it exceeds a certain length (by default, 80 characters). On some operating systems, DBX requires this splitting; on others, splitting must not be done. You can inhibit splitting by defining this macro with the value zero. You can override the default splitting-length by defining this macro as an expression for the length you desire.

DBX_CONTIN_CHAR [Macro]

Normally continuation is indicated by adding a '\' character to the end of a `.stabs` string when a continuation follows. To use a different character instead, define this macro as a character constant for the character you want to use. Do not define this macro if backslash is correct for your system.

DBX_STATIC_STAB_DATA_SECTION [Macro]

Define this macro if it is necessary to go to the data section before outputting the '.stabs' pseudo-op for a non-global static variable.

DBX_TYPE_DECL_STABS_CODE [Macro]

The value to use in the "code" field of the `.stabs` directive for a typedef. The default is N_LSYM.

DBX_STATIC_CONST_VAR_CODE [Macro]

The value to use in the "code" field of the `.stabs` directive for a static variable located in the text section. DBX format does not provide any "right" way to do this. The default is N_FUN.

DBX_REGPARM_STABS_CODE [Macro]

The value to use in the "code" field of the `.stabs` directive for a parameter passed in registers. DBX format does not provide any "right" way to do this. The default is N_RSYM.

DBX_REGPARM_STABS_LETTER [Macro]

The letter to use in DBX symbol data to identify a symbol as a parameter passed in registers. DBX format does not customarily provide any way to do this. The default is 'P'.

DBX_FUNCTION_FIRST [Macro]
Define this macro if the DBX information for a function and its arguments should precede the assembler code for the function. Normally, in DBX format, the debugging information entirely follows the assembler code.

DBX_BLOCKS_FUNCTION_RELATIVE [Macro]
Define this macro, with value 1, if the value of a symbol describing the scope of a block (N_LBRAC or N_RBRAC) should be relative to the start of the enclosing function. Normally, GCC uses an absolute address.

DBX_LINES_FUNCTION_RELATIVE [Macro]
Define this macro, with value 1, if the value of a symbol indicating the current line number (N_SLINE) should be relative to the start of the enclosing function. Normally, GCC uses an absolute address.

DBX_USE_BINCL [Macro]
Define this macro if GCC should generate N_BINCL and N_EINCL stabs for included header files, as on Sun systems. This macro also directs GCC to output a type number as a pair of a file number and a type number within the file. Normally, GCC does not generate N_BINCL or N_EINCL stabs, and it outputs a single number for a type number.

18.21.3 Open-Ended Hooks for DBX Format

These are hooks for DBX format.

DBX_OUTPUT_SOURCE_LINE (*stream*, *line*, *counter*) [Macro]
A C statement to output DBX debugging information before code for line number *line* of the current source file to the stdio stream *stream*. *counter* is the number of time the macro was invoked, including the current invocation; it is intended to generate unique labels in the assembly output.

This macro should not be defined if the default output is correct, or if it can be made correct by defining DBX_LINES_FUNCTION_RELATIVE.

NO_DBX_FUNCTION_END [Macro]
Some stabs encapsulation formats (in particular ECOFF), cannot handle the .stabs "",N_FUN,,0,0,Lscope-function-1 gdb dbx extension construct. On those machines, define this macro to turn this feature off without disturbing the rest of the gdb extensions.

NO_DBX_BNSYM_ENSYM [Macro]
Some assemblers cannot handle the .stabd BNSYM/ENSYM,0,0 gdb dbx extension construct. On those machines, define this macro to turn this feature off without disturbing the rest of the gdb extensions.

18.21.4 File Names in DBX Format

This describes file names in DBX format.

DBX_OUTPUT_MAIN_SOURCE_FILENAME (stream*,* name**)** [Macro]

A C statement to output DBX debugging information to the stdio stream *stream*, which indicates that file *name* is the main source file—the file specified as the input file for compilation. This macro is called only once, at the beginning of compilation.

This macro need not be defined if the standard form of output for DBX debugging information is appropriate.

It may be necessary to refer to a label equal to the beginning of the text section. You can use 'assemble_name (stream, ltext_label_name)' to do so. If you do this, you must also set the variable *used_ltext_label_name* to true.

NO_DBX_MAIN_SOURCE_DIRECTORY [Macro]

Define this macro, with value 1, if GCC should not emit an indication of the current directory for compilation and current source language at the beginning of the file.

NO_DBX_GCC_MARKER [Macro]

Define this macro, with value 1, if GCC should not emit an indication that this object file was compiled by GCC. The default is to emit an N_OPT stab at the beginning of every source file, with 'gcc2_compiled.' for the string and value 0.

DBX_OUTPUT_MAIN_SOURCE_FILE_END (stream*,* name**)** [Macro]

A C statement to output DBX debugging information at the end of compilation of the main source file *name*. Output should be written to the stdio stream *stream*.

If you don't define this macro, nothing special is output at the end of compilation, which is correct for most machines.

DBX_OUTPUT_NULL_N_SO_AT_MAIN_SOURCE_FILE_END [Macro]

Define this macro *instead of* defining DBX_OUTPUT_MAIN_SOURCE_FILE_END, if what needs to be output at the end of compilation is an N_SO stab with an empty string, whose value is the highest absolute text address in the file.

18.21.5 Macros for DWARF Output

Here are macros for DWARF output.

DWARF2_DEBUGGING_INFO [Macro]

Define this macro if GCC should produce dwarf version 2 format debugging output in response to the '-g' option.

    int TARGET_DWARF_CALLING_CONVENTION (*const_tree* [Target Hook]
        *function***)**

Define this to enable the dwarf attribute DW_AT_calling_convention to be emitted for each function. Instead of an integer return the enum value for the DW_CC_ tag.

To support optional call frame debugging information, you must also define INCOMING_RETURN_ADDR_RTX and either set RTX_FRAME_RELATED_P on the prologue insns if you use RTL for the prologue, or call dwarf2out_def_cfa and dwarf2out_reg_save as appropriate from TARGET_ASM_FUNCTION_PROLOGUE if you don't.

Chapter 18: Target Description Macros and Functions 609

DWARF2_FRAME_INFO [Macro]

Define this macro to a nonzero value if GCC should always output Dwarf 2 frame information. If `TARGET_EXCEPT_UNWIND_INFO` (see Section 18.20.9 [Exception Region Output], page 600) returns `UI_DWARF2`, and exceptions are enabled, GCC will output this information not matter how you define `DWARF2_FRAME_INFO`.

enum unwind_info_type TARGET_DEBUG_UNWIND_INFO (*void*) [Target Hook]

This hook defines the mechanism that will be used for describing frame unwind information to the debugger. Normally the hook will return `UI_DWARF2` if DWARF 2 debug information is enabled, and return `UI_NONE` otherwise.

A target may return `UI_DWARF2` even when DWARF 2 debug information is disabled in order to always output DWARF 2 frame information.

A target may return `UI_TARGET` if it has ABI specified unwind tables. This will suppress generation of the normal debug frame unwind information.

DWARF2_ASM_LINE_DEBUG_INFO [Macro]

Define this macro to be a nonzero value if the assembler can generate Dwarf 2 line debug info sections. This will result in much more compact line number tables, and hence is desirable if it works.

DWARF2_ASM_VIEW_DEBUG_INFO [Macro]

Define this macro to be a nonzero value if the assembler supports view assignment and verification in `.loc`. If it does not, but the user enables location views, the compiler may have to fallback to internal line number tables.

int TARGET_RESET_LOCATION_VIEW (*rtx_insn **) [Target Hook]

This hook, if defined, enables -ginternal-reset-location-views, and uses its result to override cases in which the estimated min insn length might be nonzero even when a PC advance (i.e., a view reset) cannot be taken for granted.

If the hook is defined, it must return a positive value to indicate the insn definitely advances the PC, and so the view number can be safely assumed to be reset; a negative value to mean the insn definitely does not advance the PC, and os the view number must not be reset; or zero to decide based on the estimated insn length.

If insn length is to be regarded as reliable, set the hook to `hook_int_rtx_insn_0`.

bool TARGET_WANT_DEBUG_PUB_SECTIONS [Target Hook]

True if the `.debug_pubtypes` and `.debug_pubnames` sections should be emitted. These sections are not used on most platforms, and in particular GDB does not use them.

bool TARGET_DELAY_SCHED2 [Target Hook]

True if sched2 is not to be run at its normal place. This usually means it will be run as part of machine-specific reorg.

bool TARGET_DELAY_VARTRACK [Target Hook]

True if vartrack is not to be run at its normal place. This usually means it will be run as part of machine-specific reorg.

`bool` `TARGET_NO_REGISTER_ALLOCATION` [Target Hook]
: True if register allocation and the passes following it should not be run. Usually true only for virtual assembler targets.

`ASM_OUTPUT_DWARF_DELTA (stream, size, label1, label2)` [Macro]
: A C statement to issue assembly directives that create a difference *lab1* minus *lab2*, using an integer of the given *size*.

`ASM_OUTPUT_DWARF_VMS_DELTA (stream, size, label1, label2)` [Macro]
: A C statement to issue assembly directives that create a difference between the two given labels in system defined units, e.g. instruction slots on IA64 VMS, using an integer of the given size.

`ASM_OUTPUT_DWARF_OFFSET (stream, size, label, offset, section)` [Macro]
: A C statement to issue assembly directives that create a section-relative reference to the given *label* plus *offset*, using an integer of the given *size*. The label is known to be defined in the given *section*.

`ASM_OUTPUT_DWARF_PCREL (stream, size, label)` [Macro]
: A C statement to issue assembly directives that create a self-relative reference to the given *label*, using an integer of the given *size*.

`ASM_OUTPUT_DWARF_DATAREL (stream, size, label)` [Macro]
: A C statement to issue assembly directives that create a reference to the given *label* relative to the dbase, using an integer of the given *size*.

`ASM_OUTPUT_DWARF_TABLE_REF (label)` [Macro]
: A C statement to issue assembly directives that create a reference to the DWARF table identifier *label* from the current section. This is used on some systems to avoid garbage collecting a DWARF table which is referenced by a function.

`void` `TARGET_ASM_OUTPUT_DWARF_DTPREL` (*FILE *file*, *int size*, *rtx x*) [Target Hook]
: If defined, this target hook is a function which outputs a DTP-relative reference to the given TLS symbol of the specified size.

18.21.6 Macros for VMS Debug Format

Here are macros for VMS debug format.

`VMS_DEBUGGING_INFO` [Macro]
: Define this macro if GCC should produce debugging output for VMS in response to the '-g' option. The default behavior for VMS is to generate minimal debug info for a traceback in the absence of '-g' unless explicitly overridden with '-g0'. This behavior is controlled by `TARGET_OPTION_OPTIMIZATION` and `TARGET_OPTION_OVERRIDE`.

18.22 Cross Compilation and Floating Point

While all modern machines use twos-complement representation for integers, there are a variety of representations for floating point numbers. This means that in a cross-compiler the representation of floating point numbers in the compiled program may be different from that used in the machine doing the compilation.

Because different representation systems may offer different amounts of range and precision, all floating point constants must be represented in the target machine's format. Therefore, the cross compiler cannot safely use the host machine's floating point arithmetic; it must emulate the target's arithmetic. To ensure consistency, GCC always uses emulation to work with floating point values, even when the host and target floating point formats are identical.

The following macros are provided by 'real.h' for the compiler to use. All parts of the compiler which generate or optimize floating-point calculations must use these macros. They may evaluate their operands more than once, so operands must not have side effects.

REAL_VALUE_TYPE [Macro]
> The C data type to be used to hold a floating point value in the target machine's format. Typically this is a struct containing an array of HOST_WIDE_INT, but all code should treat it as an opaque quantity.

HOST_WIDE_INT REAL_VALUE_FIX (*REAL_VALUE_TYPE x*) [Macro]
> Truncates *x* to a signed integer, rounding toward zero.

unsigned HOST_WIDE_INT REAL_VALUE_UNSIGNED_FIX (*REAL_VALUE_TYPE x*) [Macro]
> Truncates *x* to an unsigned integer, rounding toward zero. If *x* is negative, returns zero.

REAL_VALUE_TYPE REAL_VALUE_ATOF (*const char *string, machine_mode mode*) [Macro]
> Converts *string* into a floating point number in the target machine's representation for mode *mode*. This routine can handle both decimal and hexadecimal floating point constants, using the syntax defined by the C language for both.

int REAL_VALUE_NEGATIVE (*REAL_VALUE_TYPE x*) [Macro]
> Returns 1 if *x* is negative (including negative zero), 0 otherwise.

int REAL_VALUE_ISINF (*REAL_VALUE_TYPE x*) [Macro]
> Determines whether *x* represents infinity (positive or negative).

int REAL_VALUE_ISNAN (*REAL_VALUE_TYPE x*) [Macro]
> Determines whether *x* represents a "NaN" (not-a-number).

REAL_VALUE_TYPE REAL_VALUE_NEGATE (*REAL_VALUE_TYPE x*) [Macro]
> Returns the negative of the floating point value *x*.

REAL_VALUE_TYPE REAL_VALUE_ABS (*REAL_VALUE_TYPE x*) [Macro]
> Returns the absolute value of *x*.

18.23 Mode Switching Instructions

The following macros control mode switching optimizations:

OPTIMIZE_MODE_SWITCHING (*entity*) [Macro]

> Define this macro if the port needs extra instructions inserted for mode switching in an optimizing compilation.
>
> For an example, the SH4 can perform both single and double precision floating point operations, but to perform a single precision operation, the FPSCR PR bit has to be cleared, while for a double precision operation, this bit has to be set. Changing the PR bit requires a general purpose register as a scratch register, hence these FPSCR sets have to be inserted before reload, i.e. you cannot put this into instruction emitting or TARGET_MACHINE_DEPENDENT_REORG.
>
> You can have multiple entities that are mode-switched, and select at run time which entities actually need it. OPTIMIZE_MODE_SWITCHING should return nonzero for any *entity* that needs mode-switching. If you define this macro, you also have to define NUM_MODES_FOR_MODE_SWITCHING, TARGET_MODE_NEEDED, TARGET_MODE_PRIORITY and TARGET_MODE_EMIT. TARGET_MODE_AFTER, TARGET_MODE_ENTRY, and TARGET_MODE_EXIT are optional.

NUM_MODES_FOR_MODE_SWITCHING [Macro]

> If you define OPTIMIZE_MODE_SWITCHING, you have to define this as initializer for an array of integers. Each initializer element N refers to an entity that needs mode switching, and specifies the number of different modes that might need to be set for this entity. The position of the initializer in the initializer—starting counting at zero—determines the integer that is used to refer to the mode-switched entity in question. In macros that take mode arguments / yield a mode result, modes are represented as numbers $0 \ldots N - 1$. N is used to specify that no mode switch is needed / supplied.

void TARGET_MODE_EMIT (*int entity*, *int mode*, *int prev_mode*, HARD_REG_SET *regs_live*) [Target Hook]

> Generate one or more insns to set *entity* to *mode*. *hard_reg_live* is the set of hard registers live at the point where the insn(s) are to be inserted. *prev_moxde* indicates the mode to switch from. Sets of a lower numbered entity will be emitted before sets of a higher numbered entity to a mode of the same or lower priority.

int TARGET_MODE_NEEDED (*int entity*, *rtx_insn *insn*) [Target Hook]

> *entity* is an integer specifying a mode-switched entity. If OPTIMIZE_MODE_SWITCHING is defined, you must define this macro to return an integer value not larger than the corresponding element in NUM_MODES_FOR_MODE_SWITCHING, to denote the mode that *entity* must be switched into prior to the execution of *insn*.

int TARGET_MODE_AFTER (*int entity*, *int mode*, *rtx_insn *insn*) [Target Hook]

> *entity* is an integer specifying a mode-switched entity. If this macro is defined, it is evaluated for every *insn* during mode switching. It determines the mode that an insn results in (if different from the incoming mode).

Chapter 18: Target Description Macros and Functions 613

int TARGET_MODE_ENTRY (*int* `entity`) [Target Hook]
: If this macro is defined, it is evaluated for every *entity* that needs mode switching. It should evaluate to an integer, which is a mode that *entity* is assumed to be switched to at function entry. If `TARGET_MODE_ENTRY` is defined then `TARGET_MODE_EXIT` must be defined.

int TARGET_MODE_EXIT (*int* `entity`) [Target Hook]
: If this macro is defined, it is evaluated for every *entity* that needs mode switching. It should evaluate to an integer, which is a mode that *entity* is assumed to be switched to at function exit. If `TARGET_MODE_EXIT` is defined then `TARGET_MODE_ENTRY` must be defined.

int TARGET_MODE_PRIORITY (*int* `entity`, *int* `n`) [Target Hook]
: This macro specifies the order in which modes for *entity* are processed. 0 is the highest priority, `NUM_MODES_FOR_MODE_SWITCHING[`*entity*`] - 1` the lowest. The value of the macro should be an integer designating a mode for *entity*. For any fixed *entity*, `mode_priority` (*entity*, n) shall be a bijection in 0 ... `num_modes_for_mode_switching[`*entity*`] - 1`.

18.24 Defining target-specific uses of __attribute__

Target-specific attributes may be defined for functions, data and types. These are described using the following target hooks; they also need to be documented in 'extend.texi'.

const struct attribute_spec * TARGET_ATTRIBUTE_TABLE [Target Hook]
: If defined, this target hook points to an array of 'struct attribute_spec' (defined in 'tree-core.h') specifying the machine specific attributes for this target and some of the restrictions on the entities to which these attributes are applied and the arguments they take.

bool TARGET_ATTRIBUTE_TAKES_IDENTIFIER_P (*const_tree* `name`) [Target Hook]
: If defined, this target hook is a function which returns true if the machine-specific attribute named *name* expects an identifier given as its first argument to be passed on as a plain identifier, not subjected to name lookup. If this is not defined, the default is false for all machine-specific attributes.

int TARGET_COMP_TYPE_ATTRIBUTES (*const_tree* `type1`, *const_tree* [Target Hook]
    `type2`)
: If defined, this target hook is a function which returns zero if the attributes on *type1* and *type2* are incompatible, one if they are compatible, and two if they are nearly compatible (which causes a warning to be generated). If this is not defined, machine-specific attributes are supposed always to be compatible.

void TARGET_SET_DEFAULT_TYPE_ATTRIBUTES (*tree* `type`) [Target Hook]
: If defined, this target hook is a function which assigns default attributes to the newly defined *type*.

tree TARGET_MERGE_TYPE_ATTRIBUTES (*tree* `type1`, *tree* `type2`) [Target Hook]
: Define this target hook if the merging of type attributes needs special handling. If defined, the result is a list of the combined `TYPE_ATTRIBUTES` of *type1* and *type2*. It

is assumed that `comptypes` has already been called and returned 1. This function may call `merge_attributes` to handle machine-independent merging.

tree TARGET_MERGE_DECL_ATTRIBUTES (*tree olddecl*, *tree newdecl*) [Target Hook]

Define this target hook if the merging of decl attributes needs special handling. If defined, the result is a list of the combined DECL_ATTRIBUTES of *olddecl* and *newdecl*. *newdecl* is a duplicate declaration of *olddecl*. Examples of when this is needed are when one attribute overrides another, or when an attribute is nullified by a subsequent definition. This function may call `merge_attributes` to handle machine-independent merging.

If the only target-specific handling you require is 'dllimport' for Microsoft Windows targets, you should define the macro TARGET_DLLIMPORT_DECL_ATTRIBUTES to 1. The compiler will then define a function called `merge_dllimport_decl_attributes` which can then be defined as the expansion of TARGET_MERGE_DECL_ATTRIBUTES. You can also add `handle_dll_attribute` in the attribute table for your port to perform initial processing of the 'dllimport' and 'dllexport' attributes. This is done in 'i386/cygwin.h' and 'i386/i386.c', for example.

bool TARGET_VALID_DLLIMPORT_ATTRIBUTE_P (*const_tree decl*) [Target Hook]

decl is a variable or function with `__attribute__((dllimport))` specified. Use this hook if the target needs to add extra validation checks to `handle_dll_attribute`.

TARGET_DECLSPEC [Macro]

Define this macro to a nonzero value if you want to treat `__declspec(X)` as equivalent to `__attribute((X))`. By default, this behavior is enabled only for targets that define TARGET_DLLIMPORT_DECL_ATTRIBUTES. The current implementation of `__declspec` is via a built-in macro, but you should not rely on this implementation detail.

void TARGET_INSERT_ATTRIBUTES (*tree node*, *tree *attr_ptr*) [Target Hook]

Define this target hook if you want to be able to add attributes to a decl when it is being created. This is normally useful for back ends which wish to implement a pragma by using the attributes which correspond to the pragma's effect. The *node* argument is the decl which is being created. The *attr_ptr* argument is a pointer to the attribute list for this decl. The list itself should not be modified, since it may be shared with other decls, but attributes may be chained on the head of the list and *attr_ptr* modified to point to the new attributes, or a copy of the list may be made if further changes are needed.

bool TARGET_FUNCTION_ATTRIBUTE_INLINABLE_P (*const_tree fndecl*) [Target Hook]

This target hook returns `true` if it is OK to inline *fndecl* into the current function, despite its having target-specific attributes, `false` otherwise. By default, if a function has a target specific attribute attached to it, it will not be inlined.

bool TARGET_OPTION_VALID_ATTRIBUTE_P (*tree fndecl*, *tree name*, *tree args*, *int flags*) [Target Hook]

This hook is called to parse `attribute(target("..."))`, which allows setting target-specific options on individual functions. These function-specific options may differ

Chapter 18: Target Description Macros and Functions 615

from the options specified on the command line. The hook should return `true` if the options are valid.

The hook should set the `DECL_FUNCTION_SPECIFIC_TARGET` field in the function declaration to hold a pointer to a target-specific `struct cl_target_option` structure.

void **TARGET_OPTION_SAVE** (*struct cl_target_option* `*ptr`, *struct gcc_options* `*opts`) [Target Hook]

This hook is called to save any additional target-specific information in the `struct cl_target_option` structure for function-specific options from the `struct gcc_options` structure. See Section 8.1 [Option file format], page 115.

void **TARGET_OPTION_RESTORE** (*struct gcc_options* `*opts`, *struct cl_target_option* `*ptr`) [Target Hook]

This hook is called to restore any additional target-specific information in the `struct cl_target_option` structure for function-specific options to the `struct gcc_options` structure.

void **TARGET_OPTION_POST_STREAM_IN** (*struct cl_target_option* `*ptr`) [Target Hook]

This hook is called to update target-specific information in the `struct cl_target_option` structure after it is streamed in from LTO bytecode.

void **TARGET_OPTION_PRINT** (*FILE* `*file`, *int* `indent`, *struct cl_target_option* `*ptr`) [Target Hook]

This hook is called to print any additional target-specific information in the `struct cl_target_option` structure for function-specific options.

bool **TARGET_OPTION_PRAGMA_PARSE** (*tree* `args`, *tree* `pop_target`) [Target Hook]

This target hook parses the options for `#pragma GCC target`, which sets the target-specific options for functions that occur later in the input stream. The options accepted should be the same as those handled by the `TARGET_OPTION_VALID_ATTRIBUTE_P` hook.

void **TARGET_OPTION_OVERRIDE** (*void*) [Target Hook]

Sometimes certain combinations of command options do not make sense on a particular target machine. You can override the hook `TARGET_OPTION_OVERRIDE` to take account of this. This hooks is called once just after all the command options have been parsed.

Don't use this hook to turn on various extra optimizations for '-O'. That is what `TARGET_OPTION_OPTIMIZATION` is for.

If you need to do something whenever the optimization level is changed via the optimize attribute or pragma, see `TARGET_OVERRIDE_OPTIONS_AFTER_CHANGE`

bool **TARGET_OPTION_FUNCTION_VERSIONS** (*tree* `decl1`, *tree* `decl2`) [Target Hook]

This target hook returns `true` if *DECL1* and *DECL2* are versions of the same function. *DECL1* and *DECL2* are function versions if and only if they have the same function signature and different target specific attributes, that is, they are compiled for different target machines.

bool TARGET_CAN_INLINE_P (*tree* `caller`, *tree* `callee`) [Target Hook]
: This target hook returns `false` if the *caller* function cannot inline *callee*, based on target specific information. By default, inlining is not allowed if the callee function has function specific target options and the caller does not use the same options.

void TARGET_RELAYOUT_FUNCTION (*tree* `fndecl`) [Target Hook]
: This target hook fixes function *fndecl* after attributes are processed. Default does nothing. On ARM, the default function's alignment is updated with the attribute target.

18.25 Emulating TLS

For targets whose psABI does not provide Thread Local Storage via specific relocations and instruction sequences, an emulation layer is used. A set of target hooks allows this emulation layer to be configured for the requirements of a particular target. For instance the psABI may in fact specify TLS support in terms of an emulation layer.

The emulation layer works by creating a control object for every TLS object. To access the TLS object, a lookup function is provided which, when given the address of the control object, will return the address of the current thread's instance of the TLS object.

const char * TARGET_EMUTLS_GET_ADDRESS [Target Hook]
: Contains the name of the helper function that uses a TLS control object to locate a TLS instance. The default causes libgcc's emulated TLS helper function to be used.

const char * TARGET_EMUTLS_REGISTER_COMMON [Target Hook]
: Contains the name of the helper function that should be used at program startup to register TLS objects that are implicitly initialized to zero. If this is `NULL`, all TLS objects will have explicit initializers. The default causes libgcc's emulated TLS registration function to be used.

const char * TARGET_EMUTLS_VAR_SECTION [Target Hook]
: Contains the name of the section in which TLS control variables should be placed. The default of `NULL` allows these to be placed in any section.

const char * TARGET_EMUTLS_TMPL_SECTION [Target Hook]
: Contains the name of the section in which TLS initializers should be placed. The default of `NULL` allows these to be placed in any section.

const char * TARGET_EMUTLS_VAR_PREFIX [Target Hook]
: Contains the prefix to be prepended to TLS control variable names. The default of `NULL` uses a target-specific prefix.

const char * TARGET_EMUTLS_TMPL_PREFIX [Target Hook]
: Contains the prefix to be prepended to TLS initializer objects. The default of `NULL` uses a target-specific prefix.

tree TARGET_EMUTLS_VAR_FIELDS (*tree* `type`, *tree* `*name`) [Target Hook]
: Specifies a function that generates the FIELD_DECLs for a TLS control object type. *type* is the RECORD_TYPE the fields are for and *name* should be filled with the structure tag, if the default of `__emutls_object` is unsuitable. The default creates a type suitable for libgcc's emulated TLS function.

tree TARGET_EMUTLS_VAR_INIT (tree *var*, tree *decl*, tree [Target Hook]
    tmpl_addr)

> Specifies a function that generates the CONSTRUCTOR to initialize a TLS control object. *var* is the TLS control object, *decl* is the TLS object and *tmpl_addr* is the address of the initializer. The default initializes libgcc's emulated TLS control object.

bool TARGET_EMUTLS_VAR_ALIGN_FIXED [Target Hook]

> Specifies whether the alignment of TLS control variable objects is fixed and should not be increased as some backends may do to optimize single objects. The default is false.

bool TARGET_EMUTLS_DEBUG_FORM_TLS_ADDRESS [Target Hook]

> Specifies whether a DWARF DW_OP_form_tls_address location descriptor may be used to describe emulated TLS control objects.

18.26 Defining coprocessor specifics for MIPS targets.

The MIPS specification allows MIPS implementations to have as many as 4 coprocessors, each with as many as 32 private registers. GCC supports accessing these registers and transferring values between the registers and memory using asm-ized variables. For example:

```
register unsigned int cp0count asm ("c0r1");
unsigned int d;

d = cp0count + 3;
```

("c0r1" is the default name of register 1 in coprocessor 0; alternate names may be added as described below, or the default names may be overridden entirely in SUBTARGET_CONDITIONAL_REGISTER_USAGE.)

Coprocessor registers are assumed to be epilogue-used; sets to them will be preserved even if it does not appear that the register is used again later in the function.

Another note: according to the MIPS spec, coprocessor 1 (if present) is the FPU. One accesses COP1 registers through standard mips floating-point support; they are not included in this mechanism.

18.27 Parameters for Precompiled Header Validity Checking

void * TARGET_GET_PCH_VALIDITY (*size_t *sz*) [Target Hook]

> This hook returns a pointer to the data needed by TARGET_PCH_VALID_P and sets '*sz*' to the size of the data in bytes.

const char * TARGET_PCH_VALID_P (*const void *data*, *size_t sz*) [Target Hook]

> This hook checks whether the options used to create a PCH file are compatible with the current settings. It returns NULL if so and a suitable error message if not. Error messages will be presented to the user and must be localized using '_(*msg*)'.
>
> *data* is the data that was returned by TARGET_GET_PCH_VALIDITY when the PCH file was created and *sz* is the size of that data in bytes. It's safe to assume that the data was created by the same version of the compiler, so no format checking is needed.
>
> The default definition of default_pch_valid_p should be suitable for most targets.

`const char * ` **`TARGET_CHECK_PCH_TARGET_FLAGS`** (*int* *pch_flags*) [Target Hook]

> If this hook is nonnull, the default implementation of `TARGET_PCH_VALID_P` will use it to check for compatible values of `target_flags`. *pch_flags* specifies the value that `target_flags` had when the PCH file was created. The return value is the same as for `TARGET_PCH_VALID_P`.

`void ` **`TARGET_PREPARE_PCH_SAVE`** (*void*) [Target Hook]

> Called before writing out a PCH file. If the target has some garbage-collected data that needs to be in a particular state on PCH loads, it can use this hook to enforce that state. Very few targets need to do anything here.

18.28 C++ ABI parameters

`tree ` **`TARGET_CXX_GUARD_TYPE`** (*void*) [Target Hook]

> Define this hook to override the integer type used for guard variables. These are used to implement one-time construction of static objects. The default is long_long_integer_type_node.

`bool ` **`TARGET_CXX_GUARD_MASK_BIT`** (*void*) [Target Hook]

> This hook determines how guard variables are used. It should return `false` (the default) if the first byte should be used. A return value of `true` indicates that only the least significant bit should be used.

`tree ` **`TARGET_CXX_GET_COOKIE_SIZE`** (*tree* *type*) [Target Hook]

> This hook returns the size of the cookie to use when allocating an array whose elements have the indicated *type*. Assumes that it is already known that a cookie is needed. The default is `max(sizeof (size_t), alignof(type))`, as defined in section 2.7 of the IA64/Generic C++ ABI.

`bool ` **`TARGET_CXX_COOKIE_HAS_SIZE`** (*void*) [Target Hook]

> This hook should return `true` if the element size should be stored in array cookies. The default is to return `false`.

`int ` **`TARGET_CXX_IMPORT_EXPORT_CLASS`** (*tree* *type*, *int* *import_export*) [Target Hook]

> If defined by a backend this hook allows the decision made to export class *type* to be overruled. Upon entry *import_export* will contain 1 if the class is going to be exported, −1 if it is going to be imported and 0 otherwise. This function should return the modified value and perform any other actions necessary to support the backend's targeted operating system.

`bool ` **`TARGET_CXX_CDTOR_RETURNS_THIS`** (*void*) [Target Hook]

> This hook should return `true` if constructors and destructors return the address of the object created/destroyed. The default is to return `false`.

`bool ` **`TARGET_CXX_KEY_METHOD_MAY_BE_INLINE`** (*void*) [Target Hook]

> This hook returns true if the key method for a class (i.e., the method which, if defined in the current translation unit, causes the virtual table to be emitted) may be an inline

Chapter 18: Target Description Macros and Functions 619

function. Under the standard Itanium C++ ABI the key method may be an inline function so long as the function is not declared inline in the class definition. Under some variants of the ABI, an inline function can never be the key method. The default is to return `true`.

void **TARGET_CXX_DETERMINE_CLASS_DATA_VISIBILITY** (*tree decl*) [Target Hook]

decl is a virtual table, virtual table table, typeinfo object, or other similar implicit class data object that will be emitted with external linkage in this translation unit. No ELF visibility has been explicitly specified. If the target needs to specify a visibility other than that of the containing class, use this hook to set `DECL_VISIBILITY` and `DECL_VISIBILITY_SPECIFIED`.

bool **TARGET_CXX_CLASS_DATA_ALWAYS_COMDAT** (*void*) [Target Hook]

This hook returns true (the default) if virtual tables and other similar implicit class data objects are always COMDAT if they have external linkage. If this hook returns false, then class data for classes whose virtual table will be emitted in only one translation unit will not be COMDAT.

bool **TARGET_CXX_LIBRARY_RTTI_COMDAT** (*void*) [Target Hook]

This hook returns true (the default) if the RTTI information for the basic types which is defined in the C++ runtime should always be COMDAT, false if it should not be COMDAT.

bool **TARGET_CXX_USE_AEABI_ATEXIT** (*void*) [Target Hook]

This hook returns true if `__aeabi_atexit` (as defined by the ARM EABI) should be used to register static destructors when '-fuse-cxa-atexit' is in effect. The default is to return false to use `__cxa_atexit`.

bool **TARGET_CXX_USE_ATEXIT_FOR_CXA_ATEXIT** (*void*) [Target Hook]

This hook returns true if the target `atexit` function can be used in the same manner as `__cxa_atexit` to register C++ static destructors. This requires that `atexit`-registered functions in shared libraries are run in the correct order when the libraries are unloaded. The default is to return false.

void **TARGET_CXX_ADJUST_CLASS_AT_DEFINITION** (*tree type*) [Target Hook]

type is a C++ class (i.e., RECORD_TYPE or UNION_TYPE) that has just been defined. Use this hook to make adjustments to the class (eg, tweak visibility or perform any other required target modifications).

tree **TARGET_CXX_DECL_MANGLING_CONTEXT** (*const_tree decl*) [Target Hook]

Return target-specific mangling context of *decl* or `NULL_TREE`.

18.29 Adding support for named address spaces

The draft technical report of the ISO/IEC JTC1 S22 WG14 N1275 standards committee, *Programming Languages - C - Extensions to support embedded processors*, specifies a syntax for embedded processors to specify alternate address spaces. You can configure a GCC port to support section 5.1 of the draft report to add support for address spaces other than the default address space. These address spaces are new keywords that are similar to the `volatile` and `const` type attributes.

Pointers to named address spaces can have a different size than pointers to the generic address space.

For example, the SPU port uses the `__ea` address space to refer to memory in the host processor, rather than memory local to the SPU processor. Access to memory in the `__ea` address space involves issuing DMA operations to move data between the host processor and the local processor memory address space. Pointers in the `__ea` address space are either 32 bits or 64 bits based on the '-mea32' or '-mea64' switches (native SPU pointers are always 32 bits).

Internally, address spaces are represented as a small integer in the range 0 to 15 with address space 0 being reserved for the generic address space.

To register a named address space qualifier keyword with the C front end, the target may call the `c_register_addr_space` routine. For example, the SPU port uses the following to declare `__ea` as the keyword for named address space #1:

```
#define ADDR_SPACE_EA 1
c_register_addr_space ("__ea", ADDR_SPACE_EA);
```

scalar_int_mode TARGET_ADDR_SPACE_POINTER_MODE [Target Hook]
(*addr_space_t* **address_space**)
Define this to return the machine mode to use for pointers to *address_space* if the target supports named address spaces. The default version of this hook returns `ptr_mode`.

scalar_int_mode TARGET_ADDR_SPACE_ADDRESS_MODE [Target Hook]
(*addr_space_t* **address_space**)
Define this to return the machine mode to use for addresses in *address_space* if the target supports named address spaces. The default version of this hook returns `Pmode`.

bool TARGET_ADDR_SPACE_VALID_POINTER_MODE (*scalar_int_mode* [Target Hook]
mode, *addr_space_t* **as**)
Define this to return nonzero if the port can handle pointers with machine mode *mode* to address space *as*. This target hook is the same as the `TARGET_VALID_POINTER_MODE` target hook, except that it includes explicit named address space support. The default version of this hook returns true for the modes returned by either the `TARGET_ADDR_SPACE_POINTER_MODE` or `TARGET_ADDR_SPACE_ADDRESS_MODE` target hooks for the given address space.

bool TARGET_ADDR_SPACE_LEGITIMATE_ADDRESS_P [Target Hook]
(*machine_mode* **mode**, *rtx* **exp**, *bool* **strict**, *addr_space_t* **as**)
Define this to return true if *exp* is a valid address for mode *mode* in the named address space *as*. The *strict* parameter says whether strict addressing is in effect after reload has finished. This target hook is the same as the `TARGET_LEGITIMATE_ADDRESS_P` target hook, except that it includes explicit named address space support.

rtx TARGET_ADDR_SPACE_LEGITIMIZE_ADDRESS (*rtx x*, *rtx oldx*,   [Target Hook]
        machine_mode mode, *addr_space_t as*)
: Define this to modify an invalid address *x* to be a valid address with mode *mode* in the named address space *as*. This target hook is the same as the `TARGET_LEGITIMIZE_ADDRESS` target hook, except that it includes explicit named address space support.

bool TARGET_ADDR_SPACE_SUBSET_P (*addr_space_t subset*,   [Target Hook]
        addr_space_t superset)
: Define this to return whether the *subset* named address space is contained within the *superset* named address space. Pointers to a named address space that is a subset of another named address space will be converted automatically without a cast if used together in arithmetic operations. Pointers to a superset address space can be converted to pointers to a subset address space via explicit casts.

bool TARGET_ADDR_SPACE_ZERO_ADDRESS_VALID (*addr_space_t*   [Target Hook]
        as)
: Define this to modify the default handling of address 0 for the address space. Return true if 0 should be considered a valid address.

rtx TARGET_ADDR_SPACE_CONVERT (*rtx op*, *tree from_type*, *tree*   [Target Hook]
        to_type)
: Define this to convert the pointer expression represented by the RTL *op* with type *from_type* that points to a named address space to a new pointer expression with type *to_type* that points to a different named address space. When this hook it called, it is guaranteed that one of the two address spaces is a subset of the other, as determined by the `TARGET_ADDR_SPACE_SUBSET_P` target hook.

int TARGET_ADDR_SPACE_DEBUG (*addr_space_t as*)   [Target Hook]
: Define this to define how the address space is encoded in dwarf. The result is the value to be used with `DW_AT_address_class`.

void TARGET_ADDR_SPACE_DIAGNOSE_USAGE (*addr_space_t as*,   [Target Hook]
        location_t loc)
: Define this hook if the availability of an address space depends on command line options and some diagnostics should be printed when the address space is used. This hook is called during parsing and allows to emit a better diagnostic compared to the case where the address space was not registered with `c_register_addr_space`. *as* is the address space as registered with `c_register_addr_space`. *loc* is the location of the address space qualifier token. The default implementation does nothing.

18.30 Miscellaneous Parameters

Here are several miscellaneous parameters.

HAS_LONG_COND_BRANCH   [Macro]
: Define this boolean macro to indicate whether or not your architecture has conditional branches that can span all of memory. It is used in conjunction with an optimization that partitions hot and cold basic blocks into separate sections of the executable. If this macro is set to false, gcc will convert any conditional branches that attempt to cross between sections into unconditional branches or indirect jumps.

HAS_LONG_UNCOND_BRANCH   [Macro]
    Define this boolean macro to indicate whether or not your architecture has uncon-
    ditional branches that can span all of memory. It is used in conjunction with an
    optimization that partitions hot and cold basic blocks into separate sections of the
    executable. If this macro is set to false, gcc will convert any unconditional branches
    that attempt to cross between sections into indirect jumps.

CASE_VECTOR_MODE   [Macro]
    An alias for a machine mode name. This is the machine mode that elements of a
    jump-table should have.

CASE_VECTOR_SHORTEN_MODE (*min_offset*, *max_offset*, *body*)   [Macro]
    Optional: return the preferred mode for an `addr_diff_vec` when the minimum and
    maximum offset are known. If you define this, it enables extra code in branch short-
    ening to deal with `addr_diff_vec`. To make this work, you also have to define INSN_
    ALIGN and make the alignment for `addr_diff_vec` explicit. The *body* argument is
    provided so that the offset-unsigned and scale flags can be updated.

CASE_VECTOR_PC_RELATIVE   [Macro]
    Define this macro to be a C expression to indicate when jump-tables should contain
    relative addresses. You need not define this macro if jump-tables never contain relative
    addresses, or jump-tables should contain relative addresses only when '-fPIC' or
    '-fPIC' is in effect.

unsigned int TARGET_CASE_VALUES_THRESHOLD (*void*)   [Target Hook]
    This function return the smallest number of different values for which it is best to use
    a jump-table instead of a tree of conditional branches. The default is four for machines
    with a `casesi` instruction and five otherwise. This is best for most machines.

WORD_REGISTER_OPERATIONS   [Macro]
    Define this macro to 1 if operations between registers with integral mode smaller
    than a word are always performed on the entire register. To be more explicit, if you
    start with a pair of `word_mode` registers with known values and you do a subword,
    for example QImode, addition on the low part of the registers, then the compiler may
    consider that the result has a known value in `word_mode` too if the macro is defined
    to 1. Most RISC machines have this property and most CISC machines do not.

unsigned int TARGET_MIN_ARITHMETIC_PRECISION (*void*)   [Target Hook]
    On some RISC architectures with 64-bit registers, the processor also maintains 32-
    bit condition codes that make it possible to do real 32-bit arithmetic, although the
    operations are performed on the full registers.

    On such architectures, defining this hook to 32 tells the compiler to try using 32-
    bit arithmetical operations setting the condition codes instead of doing full 64-bit
    arithmetic.

    More generally, define this hook on RISC architectures if you want the compiler to
    try using arithmetical operations setting the condition codes with a precision lower
    than the word precision.

    You need not define this hook if WORD_REGISTER_OPERATIONS is not defined to 1.

LOAD_EXTEND_OP (*mem_mode*) [Macro]

Define this macro to be a C expression indicating when insns that read memory in *mem_mode*, an integral mode narrower than a word, set the bits outside of *mem_mode* to be either the sign-extension or the zero-extension of the data read. Return SIGN_EXTEND for values of *mem_mode* for which the insn sign-extends, ZERO_EXTEND for which it zero-extends, and UNKNOWN for other modes.

This macro is not called with *mem_mode* non-integral or with a width greater than or equal to BITS_PER_WORD, so you may return any value in this case. Do not define this macro if it would always return UNKNOWN. On machines where this macro is defined, you will normally define it as the constant SIGN_EXTEND or ZERO_EXTEND.

You may return a non-UNKNOWN value even if for some hard registers the sign extension is not performed, if for the REGNO_REG_CLASS of these hard registers TARGET_CAN_CHANGE_MODE_CLASS returns false when the *from* mode is *mem_mode* and the *to* mode is any integral mode larger than this but not larger than word_mode.

You must return UNKNOWN if for some hard registers that allow this mode, TARGET_CAN_CHANGE_MODE_CLASS says that they cannot change to word_mode, but that they can change to another integral mode that is larger then *mem_mode* but still smaller than word_mode.

SHORT_IMMEDIATES_SIGN_EXTEND [Macro]

Define this macro to 1 if loading short immediate values into registers sign extends.

unsigned int TARGET_MIN_DIVISIONS_FOR_RECIP_MUL [Target Hook]
  (*machine_mode* mode)

When '-ffast-math' is in effect, GCC tries to optimize divisions by the same divisor, by turning them into multiplications by the reciprocal. This target hook specifies the minimum number of divisions that should be there for GCC to perform the optimization for a variable of mode *mode*. The default implementation returns 3 if the machine has an instruction for the division, and 2 if it does not.

MOVE_MAX [Macro]

The maximum number of bytes that a single instruction can move quickly between memory and registers or between two memory locations.

MAX_MOVE_MAX [Macro]

The maximum number of bytes that a single instruction can move quickly between memory and registers or between two memory locations. If this is undefined, the default is MOVE_MAX. Otherwise, it is the constant value that is the largest value that MOVE_MAX can have at run-time.

SHIFT_COUNT_TRUNCATED [Macro]

A C expression that is nonzero if on this machine the number of bits actually used for the count of a shift operation is equal to the number of bits needed to represent the size of the object being shifted. When this macro is nonzero, the compiler will assume that it is safe to omit a sign-extend, zero-extend, and certain bitwise 'and' instructions that truncates the count of a shift operation. On machines that have instructions that act on bit-fields at variable positions, which may include 'bit test' instructions, a nonzero `SHIFT_COUNT_TRUNCATED` also enables deletion of truncations of the values that serve as arguments to bit-field instructions.

If both types of instructions truncate the count (for shifts) and position (for bit-field operations), or if no variable-position bit-field instructions exist, you should define this macro.

However, on some machines, such as the 80386 and the 680x0, truncation only applies to shift operations and not the (real or pretended) bit-field operations. Define `SHIFT_COUNT_TRUNCATED` to be zero on such machines. Instead, add patterns to the 'md' file that include the implied truncation of the shift instructions.

You need not define this macro if it would always have the value of zero.

unsigned HOST_WIDE_INT TARGET_SHIFT_TRUNCATION_MASK [Target Hook]
(*machine_mode* `mode`)

This function describes how the standard shift patterns for *mode* deal with shifts by negative amounts or by more than the width of the mode. See [shift patterns], page 394.

On many machines, the shift patterns will apply a mask *m* to the shift count, meaning that a fixed-width shift of *x* by *y* is equivalent to an arbitrary-width shift of *x* by *y* & *m*. If this is true for mode *mode*, the function should return *m*, otherwise it should return 0. A return value of 0 indicates that no particular behavior is guaranteed.

Note that, unlike `SHIFT_COUNT_TRUNCATED`, this function does *not* apply to general shift rtxes; it applies only to instructions that are generated by the named shift patterns.

The default implementation of this function returns `GET_MODE_BITSIZE (mode) - 1` if `SHIFT_COUNT_TRUNCATED` and 0 otherwise. This definition is always safe, but if `SHIFT_COUNT_TRUNCATED` is false, and some shift patterns nevertheless truncate the shift count, you may get better code by overriding it.

bool TARGET_TRULY_NOOP_TRUNCATION (*poly_uint64* `outprec`, [Target Hook]
poly_uint64 `inprec`)

This hook returns true if it is safe to "convert" a value of *inprec* bits to one of *outprec* bits (where *outprec* is smaller than *inprec*) by merely operating on it as if it had only *outprec* bits. The default returns true unconditionally, which is correct for most machines.

If `TARGET_MODES_TIEABLE_P` returns false for a pair of modes, suboptimal code can result if this hook returns true for the corresponding mode sizes. Making this hook return false in such cases may improve things.

int TARGET_MODE_REP_EXTENDED (*scalar_int_mode* `mode`, [Target Hook]
scalar_int_mode `rep_mode`)

The representation of an integral mode can be such that the values are always extended to a wider integral mode. Return `SIGN_EXTEND` if values of *mode* are represented in sign-extended form to *rep_mode*. Return `UNKNOWN` otherwise. (Currently, none of the targets use zero-extended representation this way so unlike `LOAD_EXTEND_OP`, `TARGET_MODE_REP_EXTENDED` is expected to return either `SIGN_EXTEND` or `UNKNOWN`. Also no target extends *mode* to *rep_mode* so that *rep_mode* is not the next widest integral mode and currently we take advantage of this fact.)

Similarly to `LOAD_EXTEND_OP` you may return a non-UNKNOWN value even if the extension is not performed on certain hard registers as long as for the `REGNO_REG_CLASS` of these hard registers `TARGET_CAN_CHANGE_MODE_CLASS` returns false.

Note that `TARGET_MODE_REP_EXTENDED` and `LOAD_EXTEND_OP` describe two related properties. If you define `TARGET_MODE_REP_EXTENDED (mode, word_mode)` you probably also want to define `LOAD_EXTEND_OP (mode)` to return the same type of extension.

In order to enforce the representation of mode, `TARGET_TRULY_NOOP_TRUNCATION` should return false when truncating to mode.

STORE_FLAG_VALUE [Macro]

A C expression describing the value returned by a comparison operator with an integral mode and stored by a store-flag instruction ('cstore*mode*4') when the condition is true. This description must apply to *all* the 'cstore*mode*4' patterns and all the comparison operators whose results have a `MODE_INT` mode.

A value of 1 or −1 means that the instruction implementing the comparison operator returns exactly 1 or −1 when the comparison is true and 0 when the comparison is false. Otherwise, the value indicates which bits of the result are guaranteed to be 1 when the comparison is true. This value is interpreted in the mode of the comparison operation, which is given by the mode of the first operand in the 'cstore*mode*4' pattern. Either the low bit or the sign bit of `STORE_FLAG_VALUE` be on. Presently, only those bits are used by the compiler.

If `STORE_FLAG_VALUE` is neither 1 or −1, the compiler will generate code that depends only on the specified bits. It can also replace comparison operators with equivalent operations if they cause the required bits to be set, even if the remaining bits are undefined. For example, on a machine whose comparison operators return an SImode value and where `STORE_FLAG_VALUE` is defined as '0x80000000', saying that just the sign bit is relevant, the expression

    (ne:SI (and:SI x (const_int power-of-2)) (const_int 0))

can be converted to

    (ashift:SI x (const_int n))

where *n* is the appropriate shift count to move the bit being tested into the sign bit.

There is no way to describe a machine that always sets the low-order bit for a true value, but does not guarantee the value of any other bits, but we do not know of any machine that has such an instruction. If you are trying to port GCC to such a machine, include an instruction to perform a logical and of the result with 1 in the pattern for the comparison operators and let us know at gcc@gcc.gnu.org.

Often, a machine will have multiple instructions that obtain a value from a comparison (or the condition codes). Here are rules to guide the choice of value for `STORE_FLAG_VALUE`, and hence the instructions to be used:

- Use the shortest sequence that yields a valid definition for `STORE_FLAG_VALUE`. It is more efficient for the compiler to "normalize" the value (convert it to, e.g., 1 or 0) than for the comparison operators to do so because there may be opportunities to combine the normalization with other operations.

- For equal-length sequences, use a value of 1 or −1, with −1 being slightly preferred on machines with expensive jumps and 1 preferred on other machines.

- As a second choice, choose a value of '0x80000001' if instructions exist that set both the sign and low-order bits but do not define the others.
- Otherwise, use a value of '0x80000000'.

Many machines can produce both the value chosen for STORE_FLAG_VALUE and its negation in the same number of instructions. On those machines, you should also define a pattern for those cases, e.g., one matching

    (set A (neg:m (ne:m B C)))

Some machines can also perform and or plus operations on condition code values with less instructions than the corresponding 'cstoremode4' insn followed by and or plus. On those machines, define the appropriate patterns. Use the names incscc and decscc, respectively, for the patterns which perform plus or minus operations on condition code values. See 'rs6000.md' for some examples. The GNU Superoptimizer can be used to find such instruction sequences on other machines.

If this macro is not defined, the default value, 1, is used. You need not define STORE_FLAG_VALUE if the machine has no store-flag instructions, or if the value generated by these instructions is 1.

FLOAT_STORE_FLAG_VALUE (*mode*) [Macro]

A C expression that gives a nonzero REAL_VALUE_TYPE value that is returned when comparison operators with floating-point results are true. Define this macro on machines that have comparison operations that return floating-point values. If there are no such operations, do not define this macro.

VECTOR_STORE_FLAG_VALUE (*mode*) [Macro]

A C expression that gives a rtx representing the nonzero true element for vector comparisons. The returned rtx should be valid for the inner mode of *mode* which is guaranteed to be a vector mode. Define this macro on machines that have vector comparison operations that return a vector result. If there are no such operations, do not define this macro. Typically, this macro is defined as const1_rtx or constm1_rtx. This macro may return NULL_RTX to prevent the compiler optimizing such vector comparison operations for the given mode.

CLZ_DEFINED_VALUE_AT_ZERO (*mode*, *value*) [Macro]
CTZ_DEFINED_VALUE_AT_ZERO (*mode*, *value*) [Macro]

A C expression that indicates whether the architecture defines a value for clz or ctz with a zero operand. A result of 0 indicates the value is undefined. If the value is defined for only the RTL expression, the macro should evaluate to 1; if the value applies also to the corresponding optab entry (which is normally the case if it expands directly into the corresponding RTL), then the macro should evaluate to 2. In the cases where the value is defined, *value* should be set to this value.

If this macro is not defined, the value of clz or ctz at zero is assumed to be undefined.

This macro must be defined if the target's expansion for ffs relies on a particular value to get correct results. Otherwise it is not necessary, though it may be used to optimize some corner cases, and to provide a default expansion for the ffs optab.

Note that regardless of this macro the "definedness" of clz and ctz at zero do *not* extend to the builtin functions visible to the user. Thus one may be free to adjust

Chapter 18: Target Description Macros and Functions 627

Pmode [Macro]

An alias for the machine mode for pointers. On most machines, define this to be the integer mode corresponding to the width of a hardware pointer; SImode on 32-bit machine or DImode on 64-bit machines. On some machines you must define this to be one of the partial integer modes, such as PSImode.

The width of Pmode must be at least as large as the value of POINTER_SIZE. If it is not equal, you must define the macro POINTERS_EXTEND_UNSIGNED to specify how pointers are extended to Pmode.

FUNCTION_MODE [Macro]

An alias for the machine mode used for memory references to functions being called, in call RTL expressions. On most CISC machines, where an instruction can begin at any byte address, this should be QImode. On most RISC machines, where all instructions have fixed size and alignment, this should be a mode with the same size and alignment as the machine instruction words - typically SImode or HImode.

STDC_0_IN_SYSTEM_HEADERS [Macro]

In normal operation, the preprocessor expands __STDC__ to the constant 1, to signify that GCC conforms to ISO Standard C. On some hosts, like Solaris, the system compiler uses a different convention, where __STDC__ is normally 0, but is 1 if the user specifies strict conformance to the C Standard.

Defining STDC_0_IN_SYSTEM_HEADERS makes GNU CPP follows the host convention when processing system header files, but when processing user files __STDC__ will always expand to 1.

const char * TARGET_C_PREINCLUDE (*void*) [C Target Hook]

Define this hook to return the name of a header file to be included at the start of all compilations, as if it had been included with #include <*file*>. If this hook returns NULL, or is not defined, or the header is not found, or if the user specifies '-ffreestanding' or '-nostdinc', no header is included.

This hook can be used together with a header provided by the system C library to implement ISO C requirements for certain macros to be predefined that describe properties of the whole implementation rather than just the compiler.

bool TARGET_CXX_IMPLICIT_EXTERN_C (*const char**) [C Target Hook]

Define this hook to add target-specific C++ implicit extern C functions. If this function returns true for the name of a file-scope function, that function implicitly gets extern "C" linkage rather than whatever language linkage the declaration would normally have. An example of such function is WinMain on Win32 targets.

NO_IMPLICIT_EXTERN_C [Macro]

Define this macro if the system header files support C++ as well as C. This macro inhibits the usual method of using system header files in C++, which is to pretend that the file's contents are enclosed in 'extern "C" {...}'.

REGISTER_TARGET_PRAGMAS () [Macro]

Define this macro if you want to implement any target-specific pragmas. If defined, it is a C expression which makes a series of calls to `c_register_pragma` or `c_register_pragma_with_expansion` for each pragma. The macro may also do any setup required for the pragmas.

The primary reason to define this macro is to provide compatibility with other compilers for the same target. In general, we discourage definition of target-specific pragmas for GCC.

If the pragma can be implemented by attributes then you should consider defining the target hook 'TARGET_INSERT_ATTRIBUTES' as well.

Preprocessor macros that appear on pragma lines are not expanded. All '#pragma' directives that do not match any registered pragma are silently ignored, unless the user specifies '-Wunknown-pragmas'.

void c_register_pragma (*const char *space, const char *name, void (*callback) (struct cpp_reader *)*) [Function]

void c_register_pragma_with_expansion (*const char *space, const char *name, void (*callback) (struct cpp_reader *)*) [Function]

Each call to `c_register_pragma` or `c_register_pragma_with_expansion` establishes one pragma. The *callback* routine will be called when the preprocessor encounters a pragma of the form

```
#pragma [space] name ...
```

space is the case-sensitive namespace of the pragma, or NULL to put the pragma in the global namespace. The callback routine receives *pfile* as its first argument, which can be passed on to cpplib's functions if necessary. You can lex tokens after the *name* by calling `pragma_lex`. Tokens that are not read by the callback will be silently ignored. The end of the line is indicated by a token of type CPP_EOF. Macro expansion occurs on the arguments of pragmas registered with `c_register_pragma_with_expansion` but not on the arguments of pragmas registered with `c_register_pragma`.

Note that the use of `pragma_lex` is specific to the C and C++ compilers. It will not work in the Java or Fortran compilers, or any other language compilers for that matter. Thus if `pragma_lex` is going to be called from target-specific code, it must only be done so when building the C and C++ compilers. This can be done by defining the variables `c_target_objs` and `cxx_target_objs` in the target entry in the 'config.gcc' file. These variables should name the target-specific, language-specific object file which contains the code that uses `pragma_lex`. Note it will also be necessary to add a rule to the makefile fragment pointed to by `tmake_file` that shows how to build this object file.

HANDLE_PRAGMA_PACK_WITH_EXPANSION [Macro]

Define this macro if macros should be expanded in the arguments of '#pragma pack'.

TARGET_DEFAULT_PACK_STRUCT [Macro]

If your target requires a structure packing default other than 0 (meaning the machine default), define this macro to the necessary value (in bytes). This must be a value that would also be valid to use with '#pragma pack()' (that is, a small power of two).

Chapter 18: Target Description Macros and Functions 629

DOLLARS_IN_IDENTIFIERS [Macro]

> Define this macro to control use of the character '$' in identifier names for the C family of languages. 0 means '$' is not allowed by default; 1 means it is allowed. 1 is the default; there is no need to define this macro in that case.

INSN_SETS_ARE_DELAYED (*insn*) [Macro]

> Define this macro as a C expression that is nonzero if it is safe for the delay slot scheduler to place instructions in the delay slot of *insn*, even if they appear to use a resource set or clobbered in *insn*. *insn* is always a `jump_insn` or an `insn`; GCC knows that every `call_insn` has this behavior. On machines where some `insn` or `jump_insn` is really a function call and hence has this behavior, you should define this macro.

> You need not define this macro if it would always return zero.

INSN_REFERENCES_ARE_DELAYED (*insn*) [Macro]

> Define this macro as a C expression that is nonzero if it is safe for the delay slot scheduler to place instructions in the delay slot of *insn*, even if they appear to set or clobber a resource referenced in *insn*. *insn* is always a `jump_insn` or an `insn`. On machines where some `insn` or `jump_insn` is really a function call and its operands are registers whose use is actually in the subroutine it calls, you should define this macro. Doing so allows the delay slot scheduler to move instructions which copy arguments into the argument registers into the delay slot of *insn*.

> You need not define this macro if it would always return zero.

MULTIPLE_SYMBOL_SPACES [Macro]

> Define this macro as a C expression that is nonzero if, in some cases, global symbols from one translation unit may not be bound to undefined symbols in another translation unit without user intervention. For instance, under Microsoft Windows symbols must be explicitly imported from shared libraries (DLLs).

> You need not define this macro if it would always evaluate to zero.

rtx_insn * TARGET_MD_ASM_ADJUST (*vec<rtx>&* outputs, [Target Hook]
     vec<rtx>& inputs, *vec<const char *>&* constraints, *vec<rtx>&* clobbers,
     HARD_REG_SET& clobbered_regs)

> This target hook may add *clobbers* to *clobbers* and *clobbered_regs* for any hard regs the port wishes to automatically clobber for an asm. The *outputs* and *inputs* may be inspected to avoid clobbering a register that is already used by the asm.

> It may modify the *outputs*, *inputs*, and *constraints* as necessary for other pre-processing. In this case the return value is a sequence of insns to emit after the asm.

MATH_LIBRARY [Macro]

> Define this macro as a C string constant for the linker argument to link in the system math library, minus the initial '"-l"', or '""' if the target does not have a separate math library.

> You need only define this macro if the default of '"m"' is wrong.

LIBRARY_PATH_ENV [Macro]
: Define this macro as a C string constant for the environment variable that specifies where the linker should look for libraries.

You need only define this macro if the default of '"LIBRARY_PATH"' is wrong.

TARGET_POSIX_IO [Macro]
: Define this macro if the target supports the following POSIX file functions, access, mkdir and file locking with fcntl / F_SETLKW. Defining `TARGET_POSIX_IO` will enable the test coverage code to use file locking when exiting a program, which avoids race conditions if the program has forked. It will also create directories at run-time for cross-profiling.

MAX_CONDITIONAL_EXECUTE [Macro]
: A C expression for the maximum number of instructions to execute via conditional execution instructions instead of a branch. A value of `BRANCH_COST+1` is the default if the machine does not use cc0, and 1 if it does use cc0.

IFCVT_MODIFY_TESTS (*ce_info*, *true_expr*, *false_expr*) [Macro]
: Used if the target needs to perform machine-dependent modifications on the conditionals used for turning basic blocks into conditionally executed code. *ce_info* points to a data structure, `struct ce_if_block`, which contains information about the currently processed blocks. *true_expr* and *false_expr* are the tests that are used for converting the then-block and the else-block, respectively. Set either *true_expr* or *false_expr* to a null pointer if the tests cannot be converted.

IFCVT_MODIFY_MULTIPLE_TESTS (*ce_info*, *bb*, *true_expr*, *false_expr*) [Macro]
: Like `IFCVT_MODIFY_TESTS`, but used when converting more complicated if-statements into conditions combined by **and** and **or** operations. *bb* contains the basic block that contains the test that is currently being processed and about to be turned into a condition.

IFCVT_MODIFY_INSN (*ce_info*, *pattern*, *insn*) [Macro]
: A C expression to modify the *PATTERN* of an *INSN* that is to be converted to conditional execution format. *ce_info* points to a data structure, `struct ce_if_block`, which contains information about the currently processed blocks.

IFCVT_MODIFY_FINAL (*ce_info*) [Macro]
: A C expression to perform any final machine dependent modifications in converting code to conditional execution. The involved basic blocks can be found in the `struct ce_if_block` structure that is pointed to by *ce_info*.

IFCVT_MODIFY_CANCEL (*ce_info*) [Macro]
: A C expression to cancel any machine dependent modifications in converting code to conditional execution. The involved basic blocks can be found in the `struct ce_if_block` structure that is pointed to by *ce_info*.

IFCVT_MACHDEP_INIT (*ce_info*) [Macro]
: A C expression to initialize any machine specific data for if-conversion of the if-block in the `struct ce_if_block` structure that is pointed to by *ce_info*.

void TARGET_MACHINE_DEPENDENT_REORG (*void*) [Target Hook]

If non-null, this hook performs a target-specific pass over the instruction stream. The compiler will run it at all optimization levels, just before the point at which it normally does delayed-branch scheduling.

The exact purpose of the hook varies from target to target. Some use it to do transformations that are necessary for correctness, such as laying out in-function constant pools or avoiding hardware hazards. Others use it as an opportunity to do some machine-dependent optimizations.

You need not implement the hook if it has nothing to do. The default definition is null.

void TARGET_INIT_BUILTINS (*void*) [Target Hook]

Define this hook if you have any machine-specific built-in functions that need to be defined. It should be a function that performs the necessary setup.

Machine specific built-in functions can be useful to expand special machine instructions that would otherwise not normally be generated because they have no equivalent in the source language (for example, SIMD vector instructions or prefetch instructions).

To create a built-in function, call the function `lang_hooks.builtin_function` which is defined by the language front end. You can use any type nodes set up by `build_common_tree_nodes`; only language front ends that use those two functions will call 'TARGET_INIT_BUILTINS'.

tree TARGET_BUILTIN_DECL (*unsigned* `code`, *bool* `initialize_p`) [Target Hook]

Define this hook if you have any machine-specific built-in functions that need to be defined. It should be a function that returns the builtin function declaration for the builtin function code *code*. If there is no such builtin and it cannot be initialized at this time if *initialize_p* is true the function should return `NULL_TREE`. If *code* is out of range the function should return `error_mark_node`.

rtx TARGET_EXPAND_BUILTIN (*tree* `exp`, *rtx* `target`, *rtx* `subtarget`, *machine_mode* `mode`, *int* `ignore`) [Target Hook]

Expand a call to a machine specific built-in function that was set up by 'TARGET INIT BUILTINS'. *exp* is the expression for the function call; the result should go to *target* if that is convenient, and have mode *mode* if that is convenient. *subtarget* may be used as the target for computing one of *exp*'s operands. *ignore* is nonzero if the value is to be ignored. This function should return the result of the call to the built-in function.

tree TARGET_BUILTIN_CHKP_FUNCTION (*unsigned* `fcode`) [Target Hook]

This hook allows target to redefine built-in functions used by Pointer Bounds Checker for code instrumentation. Hook should return fndecl of function implementing generic builtin whose code is passed in *fcode*. Currently following built-in functions are obtained using this hook:

__bounds_type __chkp_bndmk (*const void *lb, size_t*   [Built-in Function]
    size)
: Function code - BUILT_IN_CHKP_BNDMK. This built-in function is used by Pointer Bounds Checker to create bound values. *lb* holds low bound of the resulting bounds. *size* holds size of created bounds.

void __chkp_bndstx (*const void *ptr, __bounds_type b,*   [Built-in Function]
    const void **loc)
: Function code - BUILT_IN_CHKP_BNDSTX. This built-in function is used by Pointer Bounds Checker to store bounds *b* for pointer *ptr* when *ptr* is stored by address *loc*.

__bounds_type __chkp_bndldx (*const void **loc, const*   [Built-in Function]
    void *ptr)
: Function code - BUILT_IN_CHKP_BNDLDX. This built-in function is used by Pointer Bounds Checker to get bounds of pointer *ptr* loaded by address *loc*.

void __chkp_bndcl (*const void *ptr, __bounds_type b*)   [Built-in Function]
: Function code - BUILT_IN_CHKP_BNDCL. This built-in function is used by Pointer Bounds Checker to perform check for pointer *ptr* against lower bound of bounds *b*.

void __chkp_bndcu (*const void *ptr, __bounds_type b*)   [Built-in Function]
: Function code - BUILT_IN_CHKP_BNDCU. This built-in function is used by Pointer Bounds Checker to perform check for pointer *ptr* against upper bound of bounds *b*.

__bounds_type __chkp_bndret (*void *ptr*)   [Built-in Function]
: Function code - BUILT_IN_CHKP_BNDRET. This built-in function is used by Pointer Bounds Checker to obtain bounds returned by a call statement. *ptr* passed to built-in is `SSA_NAME` returned by the call.

__bounds_type __chkp_intersect (*__bounds_type b1,*   [Built-in Function]
    __bounds_type b2)
: Function code - BUILT_IN_CHKP_INTERSECT. This built-in function returns intersection of bounds *b1* and *b2*.

__bounds_type __chkp_narrow (*const void *ptr,*   [Built-in Function]
    __bounds_type b, size_t s)
: Function code - BUILT_IN_CHKP_NARROW. This built-in function returns intersection of bounds *b* and [*ptr*, *ptr* + *s* - 1].

size_t __chkp_sizeof (*const void *ptr*)   [Built-in Function]
: Function code - BUILT_IN_CHKP_SIZEOF. This built-in function returns size of object referenced by *ptr*. *ptr* is always `ADDR_EXPR` of `VAR_DECL`. This built-in is used by Pointer Bounds Checker when bounds of object cannot be computed statically (e.g. object has incomplete type).

const void *__chkp_extract_lower (*__bounds_type b*)   [Built-in Function]
: Function code - BUILT_IN_CHKP_EXTRACT_LOWER. This built-in function returns lower bound of bounds *b*.

const void *__chkp_extract_upper (__bounds_type b) [Built-in Function]
: Function code - BUILT_IN_CHKP_EXTRACT_UPPER. This built-in function returns upper bound of bounds b.

tree TARGET_CHKP_BOUND_TYPE (void) [Target Hook]
: Return type to be used for bounds

machine_mode TARGET_CHKP_BOUND_MODE (void) [Target Hook]
: Return mode to be used for bounds.

tree TARGET_CHKP_MAKE_BOUNDS_CONSTANT (HOST_WIDE_INT lb, HOST_WIDE_INT ub) [Target Hook]
: Return constant used to statically initialize constant bounds with specified lower bound lb and upper bounds ub.

int TARGET_CHKP_INITIALIZE_BOUNDS (tree var, tree lb, tree ub, tree *stmts) [Target Hook]
: Generate a list of statements stmts to initialize pointer bounds variable var with bounds lb and ub. Return the number of generated statements.

tree TARGET_RESOLVE_OVERLOADED_BUILTIN (unsigned int loc, tree fndecl, void *arglist) [Target Hook]
: Select a replacement for a machine specific built-in function that was set up by 'TARGET_INIT_BUILTINS'. This is done *before* regular type checking, and so allows the target to implement a crude form of function overloading. fndecl is the declaration of the built-in function. arglist is the list of arguments passed to the built-in function. The result is a complete expression that implements the operation, usually another CALL_EXPR. arglist really has type 'VEC(tree,gc)*'

tree TARGET_FOLD_BUILTIN (tree fndecl, int n_args, tree *argp, bool ignore) [Target Hook]
: Fold a call to a machine specific built-in function that was set up by 'TARGET_INIT_BUILTINS'. fndecl is the declaration of the built-in function. n_args is the number of arguments passed to the function; the arguments themselves are pointed to by argp. The result is another tree, valid for both GIMPLE and GENERIC, containing a simplified expression for the call's result. If ignore is true the value will be ignored.

bool TARGET_GIMPLE_FOLD_BUILTIN (gimple_stmt_iterator *gsi) [Target Hook]
: Fold a call to a machine specific built-in function that was set up by 'TARGET_INIT_BUILTINS'. gsi points to the gimple statement holding the function call. Returns true if any change was made to the GIMPLE stream.

int TARGET_COMPARE_VERSION_PRIORITY (tree decl1, tree decl2) [Target Hook]
: This hook is used to compare the target attributes in two functions to determine which function's features get higher priority. This is used during function multi-versioning to figure out the order in which two versions must be dispatched. A function version with a higher priority is checked for dispatching earlier. decl1 and decl2 are the two function decls that will be compared.

tree TARGET_GET_FUNCTION_VERSIONS_DISPATCHER (*void *decl*) [Target Hook]
: This hook is used to get the dispatcher function for a set of function versions. The dispatcher function is called to invoke the right function version at run-time. *decl* is one version from a set of semantically identical versions.

tree TARGET_GENERATE_VERSION_DISPATCHER_BODY (*void *arg*) [Target Hook]
: This hook is used to generate the dispatcher logic to invoke the right function version at run-time for a given set of function versions. *arg* points to the callgraph node of the dispatcher function whose body must be generated.

bool TARGET_CAN_USE_DOLOOP_P (*const widest_int &iterations,* [Target Hook]
  const widest_int &iterations_max, unsigned int loop_depth, bool entered_at_top)
: Return true if it is possible to use low-overhead loops (`doloop_end` and `doloop_begin`) for a particular loop. *iterations* gives the exact number of iterations, or 0 if not known. *iterations_max* gives the maximum number of iterations, or 0 if not known. *loop_depth* is the nesting depth of the loop, with 1 for innermost loops, 2 for loops that contain innermost loops, and so on. *entered_at_top* is true if the loop is only entered from the top.

    This hook is only used if `doloop_end` is available. The default implementation returns true. You can use `can_use_doloop_if_innermost` if the loop must be the innermost, and if there are no other restrictions.

const char * TARGET_INVALID_WITHIN_DOLOOP (*const rtx_insn *insn*) [Target Hook]
: Take an instruction in *insn* and return NULL if it is valid within a low-overhead loop, otherwise return a string explaining why doloop could not be applied.

    Many targets use special registers for low-overhead looping. For any instruction that clobbers these this function should return a string indicating the reason why the doloop could not be applied. By default, the RTL loop optimizer does not use a present doloop pattern for loops containing function calls or branch on table instructions.

bool TARGET_LEGITIMATE_COMBINED_INSN (*rtx_insn *insn*) [Target Hook]
: Take an instruction in *insn* and return `false` if the instruction is not appropriate as a combination of two or more instructions. The default is to accept all instructions.

bool TARGET_CAN_FOLLOW_JUMP (*const rtx_insn *follower, const rtx_insn *followee*) [Target Hook]
: FOLLOWER and FOLLOWEE are JUMP_INSN instructions; return true if FOLLOWER may be modified to follow FOLLOWEE; false, if it can't. For example, on some targets, certain kinds of branches can't be made to follow through a hot/cold partitioning.

bool TARGET_COMMUTATIVE_P (*const_rtx x, int outer_code*) [Target Hook]
: This target hook returns `true` if *x* is considered to be commutative. Usually, this is just COMMUTATIVE_P (*x*), but the HP PA doesn't consider PLUS to be commutative inside a MEM. *outer_code* is the rtx code of the enclosing rtl, if known, otherwise it is UNKNOWN.

rtx **TARGET_ALLOCATE_INITIAL_VALUE** (*rtx hard_reg*) [Target Hook]
: When the initial value of a hard register has been copied in a pseudo register, it is often not necessary to actually allocate another register to this pseudo register, because the original hard register or a stack slot it has been saved into can be used. `TARGET_ALLOCATE_INITIAL_VALUE` is called at the start of register allocation once for each hard register that had its initial value copied by using `get_func_hard_reg_initial_val` or `get_hard_reg_initial_val`. Possible values are `NULL_RTX`, if you don't want to do any special allocation, a `REG` rtx—that would typically be the hard register itself, if it is known not to be clobbered—or a `MEM`. If you are returning a `MEM`, this is only a hint for the allocator; it might decide to use another register anyways. You may use `current_function_is_leaf` or `REG_N_SETS` in the hook to determine if the hard register in question will not be clobbered. The default value of this hook is `NULL`, which disables any special allocation.

int **TARGET_UNSPEC_MAY_TRAP_P** (*const_rtx x, unsigned flags*) [Target Hook]
: This target hook returns nonzero if *x*, an `unspec` or `unspec_volatile` operation, might cause a trap. Targets can use this hook to enhance precision of analysis for `unspec` and `unspec_volatile` operations. You may call `may_trap_p_1` to analyze inner elements of *x* in which case *flags* should be passed along.

void **TARGET_SET_CURRENT_FUNCTION** (*tree decl*) [Target Hook]
: The compiler invokes this hook whenever it changes its current function context (`cfun`). You can define this function if the back end needs to perform any initialization or reset actions on a per-function basis. For example, it may be used to implement function attributes that affect register usage or code generation patterns. The argument *decl* is the declaration for the new function context, and may be null to indicate that the compiler has left a function context and is returning to processing at the top level. The default hook function does nothing.

    GCC sets `cfun` to a dummy function context during initialization of some parts of the back end. The hook function is not invoked in this situation; you need not worry about the hook being invoked recursively, or when the back end is in a partially-initialized state. `cfun` might be `NULL` to indicate processing at top level, outside of any function scope.

TARGET_OBJECT_SUFFIX [Macro]
: Define this macro to be a C string representing the suffix for object files on your target machine. If you do not define this macro, GCC will use '.o' as the suffix for object files.

TARGET_EXECUTABLE_SUFFIX [Macro]
: Define this macro to be a C string representing the suffix to be automatically added to executable files on your target machine. If you do not define this macro, GCC will use the null string as the suffix for executable files.

COLLECT_EXPORT_LIST [Macro]
: If defined, `collect2` will scan the individual object files specified on its command line and create an export list for the linker. Define this macro for systems like AIX, where the linker discards object files that are not referenced from `main` and uses export lists.

MODIFY_JNI_METHOD_CALL (*mdecl*) [Macro]

Define this macro to a C expression representing a variant of the method call *mdecl*, if Java Native Interface (JNI) methods must be invoked differently from other methods on your target. For example, on 32-bit Microsoft Windows, JNI methods must be invoked using the `stdcall` calling convention and this macro is then defined as this expression:

```
build_type_attribute_variant (mdecl,
                              build_tree_list
                              (get_identifier ("stdcall"),
                              NULL))
```

bool TARGET_CANNOT_MODIFY_JUMPS_P (*void*) [Target Hook]

This target hook returns `true` past the point in which new jump instructions could be created. On machines that require a register for every jump such as the SHmedia ISA of SH5, this point would typically be reload, so this target hook should be defined to a function such as:

```
static bool
cannot_modify_jumps_past_reload_p ()
{
  return (reload_completed || reload_in_progress);
}
```

reg_class_t TARGET_BRANCH_TARGET_REGISTER_CLASS (*void*) [Target Hook]

This target hook returns a register class for which branch target register optimizations should be applied. All registers in this class should be usable interchangeably. After reload, registers in this class will be re-allocated and loads will be hoisted out of loops and be subjected to inter-block scheduling.

bool TARGET_BRANCH_TARGET_REGISTER_CALLEE_SAVED (*bool* [Target Hook]
 after_prologue_epilogue_gen)

Branch target register optimization will by default exclude callee-saved registers that are not already live during the current function; if this target hook returns true, they will be included. The target code must than make sure that all target registers in the class returned by 'TARGET_BRANCH_TARGET_REGISTER_CLASS' that might need saving are saved. *after_prologue_epilogue_gen* indicates if prologues and epilogues have already been generated. Note, even if you only return true when *after_prologue_epilogue_gen* is false, you still are likely to have to make special provisions in `INITIAL_ELIMINATION_OFFSET` to reserve space for caller-saved target registers.

bool TARGET_HAVE_CONDITIONAL_EXECUTION (*void*) [Target Hook]

This target hook returns true if the target supports conditional execution. This target hook is required only when the target has several different modes and they have different conditional execution capability, such as ARM.

rtx TARGET_GEN_CCMP_FIRST (*rtx_insn* **prep_seq, *rtx_insn* [Target Hook]
 **gen_seq, *int* *code*, *tree* *op0*, *tree* *op1*)

This function prepares to emit a comparison insn for the first compare in a sequence of conditional comparisions. It returns an appropriate comparison with `CC` for passing to `gen_ccmp_next` or `cbranch_optab`. The insns to prepare the compare are saved in

Chapter 18: Target Description Macros and Functions 637

prep_seq and the compare insns are saved in *gen_seq*. They will be emitted when all the compares in the the conditional comparision are generated without error. *code* is the `rtx_code` of the compare for *op0* and *op1*.

rtx **TARGET_GEN_CCMP_NEXT** (*rtx_insn* `**prep_seq`, *rtx_insn* [Target Hook]
    `**gen_seq`, *rtx* `prev`, *int* `cmp_code`, *tree* `op0`, *tree* `op1`, *int* `bit_code`)

This function prepares to emit a conditional comparison within a sequence of conditional comparisons. It returns an appropriate comparison with CC for passing to `gen_ccmp_next` or `cbranch_optab`. The insns to prepare the compare are saved in *prep_seq* and the compare insns are saved in *gen_seq*. They will be emitted when all the compares in the conditional comparision are generated without error. The *prev* expression is the result of a prior call to `gen_ccmp_first` or `gen_ccmp_next`. It may return NULL if the combination of *prev* and this comparison is not supported, otherwise the result must be appropriate for passing to `gen_ccmp_next` or `cbranch_optab`. *code* is the `rtx_code` of the compare for *op0* and *op1*. *bit_code* is AND or IOR, which is the op on the compares.

unsigned **TARGET_LOOP_UNROLL_ADJUST** (*unsigned* `nunroll`, *struct* [Target Hook]
    loop `*loop`)

This target hook returns a new value for the number of times *loop* should be unrolled. The parameter *nunroll* is the number of times the loop is to be unrolled. The parameter *loop* is a pointer to the loop, which is going to be checked for unrolling. This target hook is required only when the target has special constraints like maximum number of memory accesses.

POWI_MAX_MULTS [Macro]

If defined, this macro is interpreted as a signed integer C expression that specifies the maximum number of floating point multiplications that should be emitted when expanding exponentiation by an integer constant inline. When this value is defined, exponentiation requiring more than this number of multiplications is implemented by calling the system library's `pow`, `powf` or `powl` routines. The default value places no upper bound on the multiplication count.

void **TARGET_EXTRA_INCLUDES** (*const char* `*sysroot`, *const char* [Macro]
    `*iprefix`, *int* `stdinc`)

This target hook should register any extra include files for the target. The parameter *stdinc* indicates if normal include files are present. The parameter *sysroot* is the system root directory. The parameter *iprefix* is the prefix for the gcc directory.

void **TARGET_EXTRA_PRE_INCLUDES** (*const char* `*sysroot`, *const char* [Macro]
    `*iprefix`, *int* `stdinc`)

This target hook should register any extra include files for the target before any standard headers. The parameter *stdinc* indicates if normal include files are present. The parameter *sysroot* is the system root directory. The parameter *iprefix* is the prefix for the gcc directory.

void **TARGET_OPTF** (*char* `*path`) [Macro]

This target hook should register special include paths for the target. The parameter *path* is the include to register. On Darwin systems, this is used for Framework includes, which have semantics that are different from '-I'.

bool *TARGET_USE_LOCAL_THUNK_ALIAS_P* (*tree* `fndecl`)   [Macro]
: This target macro returns `true` if it is safe to use a local alias for a virtual function *fndecl* when constructing thunks, `false` otherwise. By default, the macro returns `true` for all functions, if a target supports aliases (i.e. defines `ASM_OUTPUT_DEF`), `false` otherwise,

`TARGET_FORMAT_TYPES`   [Macro]
: If defined, this macro is the name of a global variable containing target-specific format checking information for the '-Wformat' option. The default is to have no target-specific format checks.

`TARGET_N_FORMAT_TYPES`   [Macro]
: If defined, this macro is the number of entries in `TARGET_FORMAT_TYPES`.

`TARGET_OVERRIDES_FORMAT_ATTRIBUTES`   [Macro]
: If defined, this macro is the name of a global variable containing target-specific format overrides for the '-Wformat' option. The default is to have no target-specific format overrides. If defined, `TARGET_FORMAT_TYPES` must be defined, too.

`TARGET_OVERRIDES_FORMAT_ATTRIBUTES_COUNT`   [Macro]
: If defined, this macro specifies the number of entries in `TARGET_OVERRIDES_FORMAT_ATTRIBUTES`.

`TARGET_OVERRIDES_FORMAT_INIT`   [Macro]
: If defined, this macro specifies the optional initialization routine for target specific customizations of the system printf and scanf formatter settings.

`const char *` TARGET_INVALID_ARG_FOR_UNPROTOTYPED_FN   [Target Hook]
(*const_tree* `typelist`, *const_tree* `funcdecl`, *const_tree* `val`)
: If defined, this macro returns the diagnostic message when it is illegal to pass argument *val* to function *funcdecl* with prototype *typelist*.

`const char *` TARGET_INVALID_CONVERSION (*const_tree*   [Target Hook]
`fromtype`, *const_tree* `totype`)
: If defined, this macro returns the diagnostic message when it is invalid to convert from *fromtype* to *totype*, or `NULL` if validity should be determined by the front end.

`const char *` TARGET_INVALID_UNARY_OP (*int* `op`, *const_tree*   [Target Hook]
`type`)
: If defined, this macro returns the diagnostic message when it is invalid to apply operation *op* (where unary plus is denoted by `CONVERT_EXPR`) to an operand of type *type*, or `NULL` if validity should be determined by the front end.

`const char *` TARGET_INVALID_BINARY_OP (*int* `op`, *const_tree*   [Target Hook]
`type1`, *const_tree* `type2`)
: If defined, this macro returns the diagnostic message when it is invalid to apply operation *op* to operands of types *type1* and *type2*, or `NULL` if validity should be determined by the front end.

tree TARGET_PROMOTED_TYPE (*const_tree* `type`) [Target Hook]
> If defined, this target hook returns the type to which values of *type* should be promoted when they appear in expressions, analogous to the integer promotions, or `NULL_TREE` to use the front end's normal promotion rules. This hook is useful when there are target-specific types with special promotion rules. This is currently used only by the C and C++ front ends.

tree TARGET_CONVERT_TO_TYPE (*tree* `type`, *tree* `expr`) [Target Hook]
> If defined, this hook returns the result of converting *expr* to *type*. It should return the converted expression, or `NULL_TREE` to apply the front end's normal conversion rules. This hook is useful when there are target-specific types with special conversion rules. This is currently used only by the C and C++ front ends.

OBJC_JBLEN [Macro]
> This macro determines the size of the objective C jump buffer for the NeXT runtime. By default, OBJC_JBLEN is defined to an innocuous value.

LIBGCC2_UNWIND_ATTRIBUTE [Macro]
> Define this macro if any target-specific attributes need to be attached to the functions in 'libgcc' that provide low-level support for call stack unwinding. It is used in declarations in 'unwind-generic.h' and the associated definitions of those functions.

void TARGET_UPDATE_STACK_BOUNDARY (*void*) [Target Hook]
> Define this macro to update the current function stack boundary if necessary.

rtx TARGET_GET_DRAP_RTX (*void*) [Target Hook]
> This hook should return an rtx for Dynamic Realign Argument Pointer (DRAP) if a different argument pointer register is needed to access the function's argument list due to stack realignment. Return NULL if no DRAP is needed.

bool TARGET_ALLOCATE_STACK_SLOTS_FOR_ARGS (*void*) [Target Hook]
> When optimization is disabled, this hook indicates whether or not arguments should be allocated to stack slots. Normally, GCC allocates stacks slots for arguments when not optimizing in order to make debugging easier. However, when a function is declared with `__attribute__((naked))`, there is no stack frame, and the compiler cannot safely move arguments from the registers in which they are passed to the stack. Therefore, this hook should return true in general, but false for naked functions. The default implementation always returns true.

unsigned HOST WIDE INT TARGET CONST ANCHOR [Target Hook]
> On some architectures it can take multiple instructions to synthesize a constant. If there is another constant already in a register that is close enough in value then it is preferable that the new constant is computed from this register using immediate addition or subtraction. We accomplish this through CSE. Besides the value of the constant we also add a lower and an upper constant anchor to the available expressions. These are then queried when encountering new constants. The anchors are computed by rounding the constant up and down to a multiple of the value of TARGET_CONST_ANCHOR. TARGET_CONST_ANCHOR should be the maximum positive value accepted by immediate-add plus one. We currently assume that the value of

TARGET_CONST_ANCHOR is a power of 2. For example, on MIPS, where add-immediate takes a 16-bit signed value, TARGET_CONST_ANCHOR is set to '0x8000'. The default value is zero, which disables this optimization.

unsigned HOST_WIDE_INT TARGET_ASAN_SHADOW_OFFSET (*void*) [Target Hook]
Return the offset bitwise ored into shifted address to get corresponding Address Sanitizer shadow memory address. NULL if Address Sanitizer is not supported by the target.

unsigned HOST_WIDE_INT TARGET_MEMMODEL_CHECK (*unsigned HOST_WIDE_INT val*) [Target Hook]
Validate target specific memory model mask bits. When NULL no target specific memory model bits are allowed.

unsigned char TARGET_ATOMIC_TEST_AND_SET_TRUEVAL [Target Hook]
This value should be set if the result written by `atomic_test_and_set` is not exactly 1, i.e. the `bool` `true`.

bool TARGET_HAS_IFUNC_P (*void*) [Target Hook]
It returns true if the target supports GNU indirect functions. The support includes the assembler, linker and dynamic linker. The default value of this hook is based on target's libc.

unsigned int TARGET_ATOMIC_ALIGN_FOR_MODE (*machine_mode mode*) [Target Hook]
If defined, this function returns an appropriate alignment in bits for an atomic object of machine_mode *mode*. If 0 is returned then the default alignment for the specified mode is used.

void TARGET_ATOMIC_ASSIGN_EXPAND_FENV (*tree *hold, tree *clear, tree *update*) [Target Hook]
ISO C11 requires atomic compound assignments that may raise floating-point exceptions to raise exceptions corresponding to the arithmetic operation whose result was successfully stored in a compare-and-exchange sequence. This requires code equivalent to calls to `feholdexcept`, `feclearexcept` and `feupdateenv` to be generated at appropriate points in the compare-and-exchange sequence. This hook should set *hold* to an expression equivalent to the call to `feholdexcept`, *clear* to an expression equivalent to the call to `feclearexcept` and *update* to an expression equivalent to the call to `feupdateenv`. The three expressions are NULL_TREE on entry to the hook and may be left as NULL_TREE if no code is required in a particular place. The default implementation leaves all three expressions as NULL_TREE. The `__atomic_feraiseexcept` function from `libatomic` may be of use as part of the code generated in *update*.

void TARGET_RECORD_OFFLOAD_SYMBOL (*tree*) [Target Hook]
Used when offloaded functions are seen in the compilation unit and no named sections are available. It is called once for each symbol that must be recorded in the offload function and variable table.

`char * ` **`TARGET_OFFLOAD_OPTIONS`** (*void*) [Target Hook]

Used when writing out the list of options into an LTO file. It should translate any relevant target-specific options (such as the ABI in use) into one of the '`-foffload`' options that exist as a common interface to express such options. It should return a string containing these options, separated by spaces, which the caller will free.

`TARGET_SUPPORTS_WIDE_INT` [Macro]

On older ports, large integers are stored in `CONST_DOUBLE` rtl objects. Newer ports define `TARGET_SUPPORTS_WIDE_INT` to be nonzero to indicate that large integers are stored in `CONST_WIDE_INT` rtl objects. The `CONST_WIDE_INT` allows very large integer constants to be represented. `CONST_DOUBLE` is limited to twice the size of the host's `HOST_WIDE_INT` representation.

Converting a port mostly requires looking for the places where `CONST_DOUBLE`s are used with `VOIDmode` and replacing that code with code that accesses `CONST_WIDE_INT`s. '"`grep -i const_double`"' at the port level gets you to 95% of the changes that need to be made. There are a few places that require a deeper look.

- There is no equivalent to `hval` and `lval` for `CONST_WIDE_INT`s. This would be difficult to express in the md language since there are a variable number of elements.

  Most ports only check that `hval` is either 0 or -1 to see if the value is small. As mentioned above, this will no longer be necessary since small constants are always `CONST_INT`. Of course there are still a few exceptions, the alpha's constraint used by the zap instruction certainly requires careful examination by C code. However, all the current code does is pass the hval and lval to C code, so evolving the c code to look at the `CONST_WIDE_INT` is not really a large change.

- Because there is no standard template that ports use to materialize constants, there is likely to be some futzing that is unique to each port in this code.

- The rtx costs may have to be adjusted to properly account for larger constants that are represented as `CONST_WIDE_INT`.

All and all it does not take long to convert ports that the maintainer is familiar with.

`void ` **`TARGET_RUN_TARGET_SELFTESTS`** (*void*) [Target Hook]

If selftests are enabled, run any selftests for this target.

19 Host Configuration

Most details about the machine and system on which the compiler is actually running are detected by the `configure` script. Some things are impossible for `configure` to detect; these are described in two ways, either by macros defined in a file named 'xm-*machine*.h' or by hook functions in the file specified by the *out_host_hook_obj* variable in 'config.gcc'. (The intention is that very few hosts will need a header file but nearly every fully supported host will need to override some hooks.)

If you need to define only a few macros, and they have simple definitions, consider using the `xm_defines` variable in your 'config.gcc' entry instead of creating a host configuration header. See Section 6.3.2.2 [System Config], page 64.

19.1 Host Common

Some things are just not portable, even between similar operating systems, and are too difficult for autoconf to detect. They get implemented using hook functions in the file specified by the *host_hook_obj* variable in 'config.gcc'.

void HOST_HOOKS_EXTRA_SIGNALS (*void*) [Host Hook]
: This host hook is used to set up handling for extra signals. The most common thing to do in this hook is to detect stack overflow.

void * HOST_HOOKS_GT_PCH_GET_ADDRESS (*size_t size, int fd*) [Host Hook]
: This host hook returns the address of some space that is likely to be free in some subsequent invocation of the compiler. We intend to load the PCH data at this address such that the data need not be relocated. The area should be able to hold *size* bytes. If the host uses `mmap`, *fd* is an open file descriptor that can be used for probing.

int HOST_HOOKS_GT_PCH_USE_ADDRESS (*void * address, size_t size, int fd, size_t offset*) [Host Hook]
: This host hook is called when a PCH file is about to be loaded. We want to load *size* bytes from *fd* at *offset* into memory at *address*. The given address will be the result of a previous invocation of HOST_HOOKS_GT_PCH_GET_ADDRESS. Return −1 if we couldn't allocate *size* bytes at *address*. Return 0 if the memory is allocated but the data is not loaded. Return 1 if the hook has performed everything.

  If the implementation uses reserved address space, free any reserved space beyond *size*, regardless of the return value. If no PCH will be loaded, this hook may be called with *size* zero, in which case all reserved address space should be freed.

  Do not try to handle values of *address* that could not have been returned by this executable; just return −1. Such values usually indicate an out-of-date PCH file (built by some other GCC executable), and such a PCH file won't work.

size_t HOST_HOOKS_GT_PCH_ALLOC_GRANULARITY (*void*); [Host Hook]
: This host hook returns the alignment required for allocating virtual memory. Usually this is the same as getpagesize, but on some hosts the alignment for reserving memory differs from the pagesize for committing memory.

19.2 Host Filesystem

GCC needs to know a number of things about the semantics of the host machine's filesystem. Filesystems with Unix and MS-DOS semantics are automatically detected. For other systems, you can define the following macros in 'xm-*machine*.h'.

HAVE_DOS_BASED_FILE_SYSTEM

> This macro is automatically defined by 'system.h' if the host file system obeys the semantics defined by MS-DOS instead of Unix. DOS file systems are case insensitive, file specifications may begin with a drive letter, and both forward slash and backslash ('/' and '\') are directory separators.

DIR_SEPARATOR
DIR_SEPARATOR_2

> If defined, these macros expand to character constants specifying separators for directory names within a file specification. 'system.h' will automatically give them appropriate values on Unix and MS-DOS file systems. If your file system is neither of these, define one or both appropriately in 'xm-*machine*.h'.
>
> However, operating systems like VMS, where constructing a pathname is more complicated than just stringing together directory names separated by a special character, should not define either of these macros.

PATH_SEPARATOR

> If defined, this macro should expand to a character constant specifying the separator for elements of search paths. The default value is a colon (':'). DOS-based systems usually, but not always, use semicolon (';').

VMS   Define this macro if the host system is VMS.

HOST_OBJECT_SUFFIX

> Define this macro to be a C string representing the suffix for object files on your host machine. If you do not define this macro, GCC will use '.o' as the suffix for object files.

HOST_EXECUTABLE_SUFFIX

> Define this macro to be a C string representing the suffix for executable files on your host machine. If you do not define this macro, GCC will use the null string as the suffix for executable files.

HOST_BIT_BUCKET

> A pathname defined by the host operating system, which can be opened as a file and written to, but all the information written is discarded. This is commonly known as a *bit bucket* or *null device*. If you do not define this macro, GCC will use '/dev/null' as the bit bucket. If the host does not support a bit bucket, define this macro to an invalid filename.

UPDATE_PATH_HOST_CANONICALIZE (*path*)

> If defined, a C statement (sans semicolon) that performs host-dependent canonicalization when a path used in a compilation driver or preprocessor is canonicalized. *path* is a malloc-ed path to be canonicalized. If the C statement does canonicalize *path* into a different buffer, the old path should be freed and the new buffer should have been allocated with malloc.

`DUMPFILE_FORMAT`
> Define this macro to be a C string representing the format to use for constructing the index part of debugging dump file names. The resultant string must fit in fifteen bytes. The full filename will be the concatenation of: the prefix of the assembler file name, the string resulting from applying this format to an index number, and a string unique to each dump file kind, e.g. 'rtl'.
>
> If you do not define this macro, GCC will use '.%02d.'. You should define this macro if using the default will create an invalid file name.

`DELETE_IF_ORDINARY`
> Define this macro to be a C statement (sans semicolon) that performs host-dependent removal of ordinary temp files in the compilation driver.
>
> If you do not define this macro, GCC will use the default version. You should define this macro if the default version does not reliably remove the temp file as, for example, on VMS which allows multiple versions of a file.

`HOST_LACKS_INODE_NUMBERS`
> Define this macro if the host filesystem does not report meaningful inode numbers in struct stat.

19.3 Host Misc

`FATAL_EXIT_CODE`
> A C expression for the status code to be returned when the compiler exits after serious errors. The default is the system-provided macro 'EXIT_FAILURE', or '1' if the system doesn't define that macro. Define this macro only if these defaults are incorrect.

`SUCCESS_EXIT_CODE`
> A C expression for the status code to be returned when the compiler exits without serious errors. (Warnings are not serious errors.) The default is the system-provided macro 'EXIT_SUCCESS', or '0' if the system doesn't define that macro. Define this macro only if these defaults are incorrect.

`USE_C_ALLOCA`
> Define this macro if GCC should use the C implementation of alloca provided by 'libiberty.a'. This only affects how some parts of the compiler itself allocate memory. It does not change code generation.
>
> When GCC is built with a compiler other than itself, the C alloca is always used. This is because most other implementations have serious bugs. You should define this macro only on a system where no stack-based alloca can possibly work. For instance, if a system has a small limit on the size of the stack, GCC's builtin alloca will not work reliably.

`COLLECT2_HOST_INITIALIZATION`
> If defined, a C statement (sans semicolon) that performs host-dependent initialization when collect2 is being initialized.

`GCC_DRIVER_HOST_INITIALIZATION`
> If defined, a C statement (sans semicolon) that performs host-dependent initialization when a compilation driver is being initialized.

HOST_LONG_LONG_FORMAT
: If defined, the string used to indicate an argument of type `long long` to functions like `printf`. The default value is `"ll"`.

HOST_LONG_FORMAT
: If defined, the string used to indicate an argument of type `long` to functions like `printf`. The default value is `"l"`.

HOST_PTR_PRINTF
: If defined, the string used to indicate an argument of type `void *` to functions like `printf`. The default value is `"%p"`.

In addition, if `configure` generates an incorrect definition of any of the macros in 'auto-host.h', you can override that definition in a host configuration header. If you need to do this, first see if it is possible to fix `configure`.

20 Makefile Fragments

When you configure GCC using the 'configure' script, it will construct the file 'Makefile' from the template file 'Makefile.in'. When it does this, it can incorporate makefile fragments from the 'config' directory. These are used to set Makefile parameters that are not amenable to being calculated by autoconf. The list of fragments to incorporate is set by 'config.gcc' (and occasionally 'config.build' and 'config.host'); See Section 6.3.2.2 [System Config], page 64.

Fragments are named either 't-*target*' or 'x-*host*', depending on whether they are relevant to configuring GCC to produce code for a particular target, or to configuring GCC to run on a particular host. Here *target* and *host* are mnemonics which usually have some relationship to the canonical system name, but no formal connection.

If these files do not exist, it means nothing needs to be added for a given target or host. Most targets need a few 't-*target*' fragments, but needing 'x-*host*' fragments is rare.

20.1 Target Makefile Fragments

Target makefile fragments can set these Makefile variables.

`LIBGCC2_CFLAGS`
: Compiler flags to use when compiling 'libgcc2.c'.

`LIB2FUNCS_EXTRA`
: A list of source file names to be compiled or assembled and inserted into 'libgcc.a'.

`CRTSTUFF_T_CFLAGS`
: Special flags used when compiling 'crtstuff.c'. See Section 18.20.5 [Initialization], page 591.

`CRTSTUFF_T_CFLAGS_S`
: Special flags used when compiling 'crtstuff.c' for shared linking. Used if you use 'crtbeginS.o' and 'crtendS.o' in EXTRA-PARTS. See Section 18.20.5 [Initialization], page 591.

`MULTILIB_OPTIONS`
: For some targets, invoking GCC in different ways produces objects that can not be linked together. For example, for some targets GCC produces both big and little endian code. For these targets, you must arrange for multiple versions of 'libgcc.a' to be compiled, one for each set of incompatible options. When GCC invokes the linker, it arranges to link in the right version of 'libgcc.a', based on the command line options used.

  The MULTILIB_OPTIONS macro lists the set of options for which special versions of 'libgcc.a' must be built. Write options that are mutually incompatible side by side, separated by a slash. Write options that may be used together separated by a space. The build procedure will build all combinations of compatible options.

  For example, if you set MULTILIB_OPTIONS to 'm68000/m68020 msoft-float', 'Makefile' will build special versions of 'libgcc.a' using the following sets of options: '`-m68000`', '`-m68020`', '`-msoft-float`', '`-m68000 -msoft-float`', and '`-m68020 -msoft-float`'.

`MULTILIB_DIRNAMES`
> If `MULTILIB_OPTIONS` is used, this variable specifies the directory names that should be used to hold the various libraries. Write one element in `MULTILIB_DIRNAMES` for each element in `MULTILIB_OPTIONS`. If `MULTILIB_DIRNAMES` is not used, the default value will be `MULTILIB_OPTIONS`, with all slashes treated as spaces.
>
> `MULTILIB_DIRNAMES` describes the multilib directories using GCC conventions and is applied to directories that are part of the GCC installation. When multilib-enabled, the compiler will add a subdirectory of the form *prefix/multilib* before each directory in the search path for libraries and crt files.
>
> For example, if `MULTILIB_OPTIONS` is set to '`m68000/m68020 msoft-float`', then the default value of `MULTILIB_DIRNAMES` is '`m68000 m68020 msoft-float`'. You may specify a different value if you desire a different set of directory names.

`MULTILIB_MATCHES`
> Sometimes the same option may be written in two different ways. If an option is listed in `MULTILIB_OPTIONS`, GCC needs to know about any synonyms. In that case, set `MULTILIB_MATCHES` to a list of items of the form '`option=option`' to describe all relevant synonyms. For example, '`m68000=mc68000 m68020=mc68020`'.

`MULTILIB_EXCEPTIONS`
> Sometimes when there are multiple sets of `MULTILIB_OPTIONS` being specified, there are combinations that should not be built. In that case, set `MULTILIB_EXCEPTIONS` to be all of the switch exceptions in shell case syntax that should not be built.
>
> For example the ARM processor cannot execute both hardware floating point instructions and the reduced size THUMB instructions at the same time, so there is no need to build libraries with both of these options enabled. Therefore `MULTILIB_EXCEPTIONS` is set to:
>
> ```
> *mthumb/*mhard-float*
> ```

`MULTILIB_REQUIRED`
> Sometimes when there are only a few combinations are required, it would be a big effort to come up with a `MULTILIB_EXCEPTIONS` list to cover all undesired ones. In such a case, just listing all the required combinations in `MULTILIB_REQUIRED` would be more straightforward.
>
> The way to specify the entries in `MULTILIB_REQUIRED` is same with the way used for `MULTILIB_EXCEPTIONS`, only this time what are required will be specified. Suppose there are multiple sets of `MULTILIB_OPTIONS` and only two combinations are required, one for ARMv7-M and one for ARMv7-R with hard floating-point ABI and FPU, the `MULTILIB_REQUIRED` can be set to:
>
> ```
> MULTILIB_REQUIRED =  mthumb/march=armv7-m
> MULTILIB_REQUIRED += march=armv7-r/mfloat-abi=hard/mfpu=vfpv3-d16
> ```

The `MULTILIB_REQUIRED` can be used together with `MULTILIB_EXCEPTIONS`. The option combinations generated from `MULTILIB_OPTIONS` will be filtered by `MULTILIB_EXCEPTIONS` and then by `MULTILIB_REQUIRED`.

`MULTILIB_REUSE`

> Sometimes it is desirable to reuse one existing multilib for different sets of options. Such kind of reuse can minimize the number of multilib variants. And for some targets it is better to reuse an existing multilib than to fall back to default multilib when there is no corresponding multilib. This can be done by adding reuse rules to `MULTILIB_REUSE`.
>
> A reuse rule is comprised of two parts connected by equality sign. The left part is the option set used to build multilib and the right part is the option set that will reuse this multilib. Both parts should only use options specified in `MULTILIB_OPTIONS` and the equality signs found in options name should be replaced with periods. An explicit period in the rule can be escaped by preceding it with a backslash. The order of options in the left part matters and should be same with those specified in `MULTILIB_REQUIRED` or aligned with the order in `MULTILIB_OPTIONS`. There is no such limitation for options in the right part as we don't build multilib from them.
>
> `MULTILIB_REUSE` is different from `MULTILIB_MATCHES` in that it sets up relations between two option sets rather than two options. Here is an example to demo how we reuse libraries built in Thumb mode for applications built in ARM mode:
>
> ```
> MULTILIB_REUSE = mthumb/march.armv7-r=marm/march.armv7-r
> ```
>
> Before the advent of `MULTILIB_REUSE`, GCC select multilib by comparing command line options with options used to build multilib. The `MULTILIB_REUSE` is complementary to that way. Only when the original comparison matches nothing it will work to see if it is OK to reuse some existing multilib.

`MULTILIB_EXTRA_OPTS`

> Sometimes it is desirable that when building multiple versions of 'libgcc.a' certain options should always be passed on to the compiler. In that case, set `MULTILIB_EXTRA_OPTS` to be the list of options to be used for all builds. If you set this, you should probably set `CRTSTUFF_T_CFLAGS` to a dash followed by it.

`MULTILIB_OSDIRNAMES`

> If `MULTILIB_OPTIONS` is used, this variable specifies a list of subdirectory names, that are used to modify the search path depending on the chosen multilib. Unlike `MULTILIB_DIRNAMES`, `MULTILIB_OSDIRNAMES` describes the multilib directories using operating systems conventions, and is applied to the directories such as `lib` or those in the `LIBRARY_PATH` environment variable. The format is either the same as of `MULTILIB_DIRNAMES`, or a set of mappings. When it is the same as `MULTILIB_DIRNAMES`, it describes the multilib directories using operating system conventions, rather than GCC conventions. When it is a set of mappings of the form *gccdir=osdir*, the left side gives the GCC convention and the right gives the equivalent OS defined location. If the *osdir* part begins with a '!', GCC will not search in the non-multilib directory and use exclusively the multilib directory. Otherwise, the compiler will examine the search path for

libraries and crt files twice; the first time it will add *multilib* to each directory in the search path, the second it will not.

For configurations that support both multilib and multiarch, `MULTILIB_OSDIRNAMES` also encodes the multiarch name, thus subsuming `MULTIARCH_DIRNAME`. The multiarch name is appended to each directory name, separated by a colon (e.g. '`../lib32:i386-linux-gnu`').

Each multiarch subdirectory will be searched before the corresponding OS multilib directory, for example '`/lib/i386-linux-gnu`' before '`/lib/../lib32`'. The multiarch name will also be used to modify the system header search path, as explained for `MULTIARCH_DIRNAME`.

`MULTIARCH_DIRNAME`
: This variable specifies the multiarch name for configurations that are multiarch-enabled but not multilibbed configurations.

    The multiarch name is used to augment the search path for libraries, crt files and system header files with additional locations. The compiler will add a multiarch subdirectory of the form *prefix*/*multiarch* before each directory in the library and crt search path. It will also add two directories `LOCAL_INCLUDE_DIR`/*multiarch* and `NATIVE_SYSTEM_HEADER_DIR`/*multiarch*) to the system header search path, respectively before `LOCAL_INCLUDE_DIR` and `NATIVE_SYSTEM_HEADER_DIR`.

    `MULTIARCH_DIRNAME` is not used for configurations that support both multilib and multiarch. In that case, multiarch names are encoded in `MULTILIB_OSDIRNAMES` instead.

    More documentation about multiarch can be found at https://wiki.debian.org/Multiarch.

`SPECS`
: Unfortunately, setting `MULTILIB_EXTRA_OPTS` is not enough, since it does not affect the build of target libraries, at least not the build of the default multilib. One possible work-around is to use `DRIVER_SELF_SPECS` to bring options from the '`specs`' file as if they had been passed in the compiler driver command line. However, you don't want to be adding these options after the toolchain is installed, so you can instead tweak the '`specs`' file that will be used during the toolchain build, while you still install the original, built-in '`specs`'. The trick is to set `SPECS` to some other filename (say '`specs.install`'), that will then be created out of the built-in specs, and introduce a '`Makefile`' rule to generate the '`specs`' file that's going to be used at build time out of your '`specs.install`'.

`T_CFLAGS`
: These are extra flags to pass to the C compiler. They are used both when building GCC, and when compiling things with the just-built GCC. This variable is deprecated and should not be used.

20.2 Host Makefile Fragments

The use of '`x-host`' fragments is discouraged. You should only use it for makefile dependencies.

21 collect2

GCC uses a utility called `collect2` on nearly all systems to arrange to call various initialization functions at start time.

The program `collect2` works by linking the program once and looking through the linker output file for symbols with particular names indicating they are constructor functions. If it finds any, it creates a new temporary '.c' file containing a table of them, compiles it, and links the program a second time including that file.

The actual calls to the constructors are carried out by a subroutine called `__main`, which is called (automatically) at the beginning of the body of `main` (provided `main` was compiled with GNU CC). Calling `__main` is necessary, even when compiling C code, to allow linking C and C++ object code together. (If you use '-nostdlib', you get an unresolved reference to `__main`, since it's defined in the standard GCC library. Include '-lgcc' at the end of your compiler command line to resolve this reference.)

The program `collect2` is installed as `ld` in the directory where the passes of the compiler are installed. When `collect2` needs to find the *real* `ld`, it tries the following file names:

- a hard coded linker file name, if GCC was configured with the '--with-ld' option.
- 'real-ld' in the directories listed in the compiler's search directories.
- 'real-ld' in the directories listed in the environment variable `PATH`.
- The file specified in the `REAL_LD_FILE_NAME` configuration macro, if specified.
- 'ld' in the compiler's search directories, except that `collect2` will not execute itself recursively.
- 'ld' in `PATH`.

"The compiler's search directories" means all the directories where `gcc` searches for passes of the compiler. This includes directories that you specify with '-B'.

Cross-compilers search a little differently:

- 'real-ld' in the compiler's search directories.
- '*target*-real-ld' in `PATH`.
- The file specified in the `REAL_LD_FILE_NAME` configuration macro, if specified.
- 'ld' in the compiler's search directories.
- '*target*-ld' in `PATH`.

`collect2` explicitly avoids running `ld` using the file name under which `collect2` itself was invoked. In fact, it remembers up a list of such names—in case one copy of `collect2` finds another copy (or version) of `collect2` installed as `ld` in a second place in the search path.

`collect2` searches for the utilities `nm` and `strip` using the same algorithm as above for `ld`.

22 Standard Header File Directories

`GCC_INCLUDE_DIR` means the same thing for native and cross. It is where GCC stores its private include files, and also where GCC stores the fixed include files. A cross compiled GCC runs `fixincludes` on the header files in '`$(tooldir)/include`'. (If the cross compilation header files need to be fixed, they must be installed before GCC is built. If the cross compilation header files are already suitable for GCC, nothing special need be done).

`GPLUSPLUS_INCLUDE_DIR` means the same thing for native and cross. It is where `g++` looks first for header files. The C++ library installs only target independent header files in that directory.

`LOCAL_INCLUDE_DIR` is used only by native compilers. GCC doesn't install anything there. It is normally '`/usr/local/include`'. This is where local additions to a packaged system should place header files.

`CROSS_INCLUDE_DIR` is used only by cross compilers. GCC doesn't install anything there.

`TOOL_INCLUDE_DIR` is used for both native and cross compilers. It is the place for other packages to install header files that GCC will use. For a cross-compiler, this is the equivalent of '`/usr/include`'. When you build a cross-compiler, `fixincludes` processes any header files in this directory.

23 Memory Management and Type Information

GCC uses some fairly sophisticated memory management techniques, which involve determining information about GCC's data structures from GCC's source code and using this information to perform garbage collection and implement precompiled headers.

A full C++ parser would be too complicated for this task, so a limited subset of C++ is interpreted and special markers are used to determine what parts of the source to look at. All `struct`, `union` and `template` structure declarations that define data structures that are allocated under control of the garbage collector must be marked. All global variables that hold pointers to garbage-collected memory must also be marked. Finally, all global variables that need to be saved and restored by a precompiled header must be marked. (The precompiled header mechanism can only save static variables if they're scalar. Complex data structures must be allocated in garbage-collected memory to be saved in a precompiled header.)

The full format of a marker is

```
GTY (([option] [(param)], [option] [(param)] ...))
```

but in most cases no options are needed. The outer double parentheses are still necessary, though: `GTY(())`. Markers can appear:

- In a structure definition, before the open brace;
- In a global variable declaration, after the keyword `static` or `extern`; and
- In a structure field definition, before the name of the field.

Here are some examples of marking simple data structures and globals.

```
struct GTY(()) tag
{
  fields...
};

typedef struct GTY(()) tag
{
  fields...
} *typename;

static GTY(()) struct tag *list;   /* points to GC memory */
static GTY(()) int counter;        /* save counter in a PCH */
```

The parser understands simple typedefs such as `typedef struct tag *name;` and `typedef int name;`. These don't need to be marked.

Since gengtype's understanding of C++ is limited, there are several constructs and declarations that are not supported inside classes/structures marked for automatic GC code generation. The following C++ constructs produce a `gengtype` error on structures/classes marked for automatic GC code generation:

- Type definitions inside classes/structures are not supported.
- Enumerations inside classes/structures are not supported.

If you have a class or structure using any of the above constructs, you need to mark that class as `GTY ((user))` and provide your own marking routines (see section Section 23.3 [User GC], page 660 for details).

It is always valid to include function definitions inside classes. Those are always ignored by `gengtype`, as it only cares about data members.

23.1 The Inside of a `GTY(())`

Sometimes the C code is not enough to fully describe the type structure. Extra information can be provided with `GTY` options and additional markers. Some options take a parameter, which may be either a string or a type name, depending on the parameter. If an option takes no parameter, it is acceptable either to omit the parameter entirely, or to provide an empty string as a parameter. For example, `GTY ((skip))` and `GTY ((skip ("")))` are equivalent.

When the parameter is a string, often it is a fragment of C code. Four special escapes may be used in these strings, to refer to pieces of the data structure being marked:

%h   The current structure.

%1   The structure that immediately contains the current structure.

%0   The outermost structure that contains the current structure.

%a   A partial expression of the form `[i1][i2]...` that indexes the array item currently being marked.

For instance, suppose that you have a structure of the form
```
struct A {
  ...
};
struct B {
  struct A foo[12];
};
```
and b is a variable of type `struct B`. When marking 'b.foo[11]', %h would expand to 'b.foo[11]', %0 and %1 would both expand to 'b', and %a would expand to '[11]'.

As in ordinary C, adjacent strings will be concatenated; this is helpful when you have a complicated expression.
```
GTY ((chain_next ("TREE_CODE (&%h.generic) == INTEGER_TYPE"
                  " ? TYPE_NEXT_VARIANT (&%h.generic)"
                  " : TREE_CHAIN (&%h.generic)")))
```

The available options are:

length ("*expression*")

There are two places the type machinery will need to be explicitly told the length of an array of non-atomic objects. The first case is when a structure ends in a variable-length array, like this:
```
struct GTY(()) rtvec_def {
  int num_elem;         /* number of elements */
  rtx GTY ((length ("%h.num_elem"))) elem[1];
};
```
In this case, the `length` option is used to override the specified array length (which should usually be 1). The parameter of the option is a fragment of C code that calculates the length.

The second case is when a structure or a global variable contains a pointer to an array, like this:
```
struct gimple_omp_for_iter * GTY((length ("%h.collapse"))) iter;
```
In this case, `iter` has been allocated by writing something like

Chapter 23: Memory Management and Type Information   657

```
                       x->iter = ggc_alloc_cleared_vec_gimple_omp_for_iter (collapse);
```
and the `collapse` provides the length of the field.

This second use of `length` also works on global variables, like:

`static GTY((length("reg_known_value_size"))) rtx *reg_known_value;`

Note that the `length` option is only meant for use with arrays of non-atomic objects, that is, objects that contain pointers pointing to other GTY-managed objects. For other GC-allocated arrays and strings you should use `atomic`.

`skip`

> If `skip` is applied to a field, the type machinery will ignore it. This is somewhat dangerous; the only safe use is in a union when one field really isn't ever used.

`for_user`

> Use this to mark types that need to be marked by user gc routines, but are not refered to in a template argument. So if you have some user gc type T1 and a non user gc type T2 you can give T2 the for_user option so that the marking functions for T1 can call non mangled functions to mark T2.

`desc ("expression")`
`tag ("constant")`
`default`

> The type machinery needs to be told which field of a `union` is currently active. This is done by giving each field a constant `tag` value, and then specifying a discriminator using `desc`. The value of the expression given by `desc` is compared against each `tag` value, each of which should be different. If no `tag` is matched, the field marked with `default` is used if there is one, otherwise no field in the union will be marked.
>
> In the `desc` option, the "current structure" is the union that it discriminates. Use %1 to mean the structure containing it. There are no escapes available to the `tag` option, since it is a constant.
>
> For example,
> ```
>     struct GTY(()) tree_binding
>     {
>       struct tree_common common;
>       union tree_binding_u {
>         tree GTY ((tag ("0"))) scope;
>         struct cp_binding_level * GTY ((tag ("1"))) level;
>       } GTY ((desc ("BINDING_HAS_LEVEL_P ((tree)&%0)"))) xscope;
>       tree value;
>     };
> ```
> In this example, the value of BINDING_HAS_LEVEL_P when applied to a `struct tree_binding *` is presumed to be 0 or 1. If 1, the type mechanism will treat the field `level` as being present and if 0, will treat the field `scope` as being present.
>
> The `desc` and `tag` options can also be used for inheritance to denote which subclass an instance is. See Section 23.2 [Inheritance and GTY], page 660 for more information.

`cache`
: When the `cache` option is applied to a global variable gt_clear_cache is called on that variable between the mark and sweep phases of garbage collection. The gt_clear_cache function is free to mark blocks as used, or to clear pointers in the variable.

`deletable`
: `deletable`, when applied to a global variable, indicates that when garbage collection runs, there's no need to mark anything pointed to by this variable, it can just be set to NULL instead. This is used to keep a list of free structures around for re-use.

`maybe_undef`
: When applied to a field, `maybe_undef` indicates that it's OK if the structure that this fields points to is never defined, so long as this field is always NULL. This is used to avoid requiring backends to define certain optional structures. It doesn't work with language frontends.

`nested_ptr (type, "to expression", "from expression")`
: The type machinery expects all pointers to point to the start of an object. Sometimes for abstraction purposes it's convenient to have a pointer which points inside an object. So long as it's possible to convert the original object to and from the pointer, such pointers can still be used. *type* is the type of the original object, the *to expression* returns the pointer given the original object, and the *from expression* returns the original object given the pointer. The pointer will be available using the %h escape.

`chain_next ("expression")`
`chain_prev ("expression")`
`chain_circular ("expression")`
: It's helpful for the type machinery to know if objects are often chained together in long lists; this lets it generate code that uses less stack space by iterating along the list instead of recursing down it. `chain_next` is an expression for the next item in the list, `chain_prev` is an expression for the previous item. For singly linked lists, use only `chain_next`; for doubly linked lists, use both. The machinery requires that taking the next item of the previous item gives the original item. `chain_circular` is similar to `chain_next`, but can be used for circular single linked lists.

`reorder ("function name")`
: Some data structures depend on the relative ordering of pointers. If the precompiled header machinery needs to change that ordering, it will call the function referenced by the `reorder` option, before changing the pointers in the object that's pointed to by the field the option applies to. The function must take four arguments, with the signature 'void *, void *, gt_pointer_operator, void *'. The first parameter is a pointer to the structure that contains the object being updated, or the object itself if there is no containing structure. The second parameter is a cookie that should be ignored. The third parameter is a routine that, given a pointer, will

Chapter 23: Memory Management and Type Information   659

update it to its correct new value. The fourth parameter is a cookie that must be passed to the second parameter.

PCH cannot handle data structures that depend on the absolute values of pointers. `reorder` functions can be expensive. When possible, it is better to depend on properties of the data, like an ID number or the hash of a string instead.

`atomic`

The `atomic` option can only be used with pointers. It informs the GC machinery that the memory that the pointer points to does not contain any pointers, and hence it should be treated by the GC and PCH machinery as an "atomic" block of memory that does not need to be examined when scanning memory for pointers. In particular, the machinery will not scan that memory for pointers to mark them as reachable (when marking pointers for GC) or to relocate them (when writing a PCH file).

The `atomic` option differs from the `skip` option. `atomic` keeps the memory under Garbage Collection, but makes the GC ignore the contents of the memory. `skip` is more drastic in that it causes the pointer and the memory to be completely ignored by the Garbage Collector. So, memory marked as `atomic` is automatically freed when no longer reachable, while memory marked as `skip` is not.

The `atomic` option must be used with great care, because all sorts of problem can occur if used incorrectly, that is, if the memory the pointer points to does actually contain a pointer.

Here is an example of how to use it:

```
struct GTY(()) my_struct {
  int number_of_elements;
  unsigned int * GTY ((atomic)) elements;
};
```

In this case, `elements` is a pointer under GC, and the memory it points to needs to be allocated using the Garbage Collector, and will be freed automatically by the Garbage Collector when it is no longer referenced. But the memory that the pointer points to is an array of `unsigned int` elements, and the GC must not try to scan it to find pointers to mark or relocate, which is why it is marked with the `atomic` option.

Note that, currently, global variables can not be marked with `atomic`; only fields of a struct can. This is a known limitation. It would be useful to be able to mark global pointers with `atomic` to make the PCH machinery aware of them so that they are saved and restored correctly to PCH files.

`special ("name")`

The `special` option is used to mark types that have to be dealt with by special case machinery. The parameter is the name of the special case. See 'gengtype.c' for further details. Avoid adding new special cases unless there is no other alternative.

`user`

The `user` option indicates that the code to mark structure fields is completely handled by user-provided routines. See section Section 23.3 [User GC], page 660 for details on what functions need to be provided.

23.2 Support for inheritance

gengtype has some support for simple class hierarchies. You can use this to have gengtype autogenerate marking routines, provided:

- There must be a concrete base class, with a discriminator expression that can be used to identify which subclass an instance is.
- Only single inheritance is used.
- None of the classes within the hierarchy are templates.

If your class hierarchy does not fit in this pattern, you must use Section 23.3 [User GC], page 660 instead.

The base class and its discriminator must be identified using the "desc" option. Each concrete subclass must use the "tag" option to identify which value of the discriminator it corresponds to.

Every class in the hierarchy must have a `GTY(())` marker, as gengtype will only attempt to parse classes that have such a marker[1].

```
class GTY((desc("%h.kind"), tag("0"))) example_base
{
public:
    int kind;
    tree a;
};

class GTY((tag("1"))) some_subclass : public example_base
{
public:
    tree b;
};

class GTY((tag("2"))) some_other_subclass : public example_base
{
public:
    tree c;
};
```

The generated marking routines for the above will contain a "switch" on "kind", visiting all appropriate fields. For example, if kind is 2, it will cast to "some_other_subclass" and visit fields a, b, and c.

23.3 Support for user-provided GC marking routines

The garbage collector supports types for which no automatic marking code is generated. For these types, the user is required to provide three functions: one to act as a marker for

---

[1] Classes lacking such a marker will not be identified as being part of the hierarchy, and so the marking routines will not handle them, leading to a assertion failure within the marking routines due to an unknown tag value (assuming that assertions are enabled).

garbage collection, and two functions to act as marker and pointer walker for pre-compiled headers.

Given a structure `struct GTY((user)) my_struct`, the following functions should be defined to mark `my_struct`:

```
void gt_ggc_mx (my_struct *p)
{
  /* This marks field 'fld'. */
  gt_ggc_mx (p->fld);
}

void gt_pch_nx (my_struct *p)
{
  /* This marks field 'fld'. */
  gt_pch_nx (tp->fld);
}

void gt_pch_nx (my_struct *p, gt_pointer_operator op, void *cookie)
{
  /* For every field 'fld', call the given pointer operator. */
  op (&(tp->fld), cookie);
}
```

In general, each marker `M` should call `M` for every pointer field in the structure. Fields that are not allocated in GC or are not pointers must be ignored.

For embedded lists (e.g., structures with a `next` or `prev` pointer), the marker must follow the chain and mark every element in it.

Note that the rules for the pointer walker `gt_pch_nx (my_struct *, gt_pointer_operator, void *)` are slightly different. In this case, the operation `op` must be applied to the *address* of every pointer field.

23.3.1 User-provided marking routines for template types

When a template type `TP` is marked with `GTY`, all instances of that type are considered user-provided types. This means that the individual instances of `TP` do not need to be marked with `GTY`. The user needs to provide template functions to mark all the fields of the type.

The following code snippets represent all the functions that need to be provided. Note that type `TP` may reference to more than one type. In these snippets, there is only one type `T`, but there could be more.

```
template<typename T>
void gt_ggc_mx (TP<T> *tp)
{
  extern void gt_ggc_mx (T&);

  /* This marks field 'fld' of type 'T'. */
  gt_ggc_mx (tp->fld);
}

template<typename T>
void gt_pch_nx (TP<T> *tp)
{
  extern void gt_pch_nx (T&);

  /* This marks field 'fld' of type 'T'. */
  gt_pch_nx (tp->fld);
```

```
}

template<typename T>
void gt_pch_nx (TP<T *> *tp, gt_pointer_operator op, void *cookie)
{
  /* For every field 'fld' of 'tp' with type 'T *', call the given
     pointer operator.  */
  op (&(tp->fld), cookie);
}

template<typename T>
void gt_pch_nx (TP<T> *tp, gt_pointer_operator, void *cookie)
{
  extern void gt_pch_nx (T *, gt_pointer_operator, void *);

  /* For every field 'fld' of 'tp' with type 'T', call the pointer
     walker for all the fields of T.  */
  gt_pch_nx (&(tp->fld), op, cookie);
}
```

Support for user-defined types is currently limited. The following restrictions apply:

1. Type TP and all the argument types T must be marked with GTY.
2. Type TP can only have type names in its argument list.
3. The pointer walker functions are different for TP<T> and TP<T *>. In the case of TP<T>, references to T must be handled by calling gt_pch_nx (which will, in turn, walk all the pointers inside fields of T). In the case of TP<T *>, references to T * must be handled by calling the op function on the address of the pointer (see the code snippets above).

23.4 Marking Roots for the Garbage Collector

In addition to keeping track of types, the type machinery also locates the global variables (*roots*) that the garbage collector starts at. Roots must be declared using one of the following syntaxes:

- extern GTY(([options])) type name;
- static GTY(([options])) type name;

The syntax

- GTY(([options])) type name;

is *not* accepted. There should be an extern declaration of such a variable in a header somewhere—mark that, not the definition. Or, if the variable is only used in one file, make it static.

23.5 Source Files Containing Type Information

Whenever you add GTY markers to a source file that previously had none, or create a new source file containing GTY markers, there are three things you need to do:

1. You need to add the file to the list of source files the type machinery scans. There are four cases:
    a. For a back-end file, this is usually done automatically; if not, you should add it to target_gtfiles in the appropriate port's entries in 'config.gcc'.

Chapter 23: Memory Management and Type Information

b. For files shared by all front ends, add the filename to the `GTFILES` variable in 'Makefile.in'.

c. For files that are part of one front end, add the filename to the `gtfiles` variable defined in the appropriate 'config-lang.in'. Headers should appear before non-headers in this list.

d. For files that are part of some but not all front ends, add the filename to the `gtfiles` variable of *all* the front ends that use it.

2. If the file was a header file, you'll need to check that it's included in the right place to be visible to the generated files. For a back-end header file, this should be done automatically. For a front-end header file, it needs to be included by the same file that includes 'gtype-*lang*.h'. For other header files, it needs to be included in 'gtype-desc.c', which is a generated file, so add it to `ifiles` in `open_base_file` in 'gengtype.c'.

For source files that aren't header files, the machinery will generate a header file that should be included in the source file you just changed. The file will be called 'gt-*path*.h' where *path* is the pathname relative to the 'gcc' directory with slashes replaced by -, so for example the header file to be included in 'cp/parser.c' is called 'gt-cp-parser.c'. The generated header file should be included after everything else in the source file. Don't forget to mention this file as a dependency in the 'Makefile'!

For language frontends, there is another file that needs to be included somewhere. It will be called 'gtype-*lang*.h', where *lang* is the name of the subdirectory the language is contained in.

Plugins can add additional root tables. Run the `gengtype` utility in plugin mode as `gengtype -P pluginout.h source-dir file-list plugin*.c` with your plugin files *plugin*.c* using `GTY` to generate the *pluginout.h* file. The GCC build tree is needed to be present in that mode.

23.6 How to invoke the garbage collector

The GCC garbage collector GGC is only invoked explicitly. In contrast with many other garbage collectors, it is not implicitly invoked by allocation routines when a lot of memory has been consumed. So the only way to have GGC reclaim storage is to call the `ggc_collect` function explicitly. This call is an expensive operation, as it may have to scan the entire heap. Beware that local variables (on the GCC call stack) are not followed by such an invocation (as many other garbage collectors do): you should reference all your data from static or external `GTY`-ed variables, and it is advised to call `ggc_collect` with a shallow call stack. The GGC is an exact mark and sweep garbage collector (so it does not scan the call stack for pointers). In practice GCC passes don't often call `ggc_collect` themselves, because it is called by the pass manager between passes.

At the time of the `ggc_collect` call all pointers in the GC-marked structures must be valid or `NULL`. In practice this means that there should not be uninitialized pointer fields in the structures even if your code never reads or writes those fields at a particular instance. One way to ensure this is to use cleared versions of allocators unless all the fields are initialized manually immediately after allocation.

23.7 Troubleshooting the garbage collector

With the current garbage collector implementation, most issues should show up as GCC compilation errors. Some of the most commonly encountered issues are described below.

- Gengtype does not produce allocators for a `GTY`-marked type. Gengtype checks if there is at least one possible path from GC roots to at least one instance of each type before outputting allocators. If there is no such path, the `GTY` markers will be ignored and no allocators will be output. Solve this by making sure that there exists at least one such path. If creating it is unfeasible or raises a "code smell", consider if you really must use GC for allocating such type.

- Link-time errors about undefined `gt_ggc_r_foo_bar` and similarly-named symbols. Check if your 'foo_bar' source file has `#include "gt-foo_bar.h"` as its very last line.

24 Plugins

GCC plugins are loadable modules that provide extra features to the compiler. Like GCC itself they can be distributed in source and binary forms.

GCC plugins provide developers with a rich subset of the GCC API to allow them to extend GCC as they see fit. Whether it is writing an additional optimization pass, transforming code, or analyzing information, plugins can be quite useful.

24.1 Loading Plugins

Plugins are supported on platforms that support '-ldl -rdynamic' as well as Windows/MinGW. They are loaded by the compiler using `dlopen` or equivalent and invoked at pre-determined locations in the compilation process.

Plugins are loaded with

'-fplugin=/path/to/*name.ext*' '-fplugin-arg-*name*-*key1*[=*value1*]'

Where *name* is the plugin name and *ext* is the platform-specific dynamic library extension. It should be `dll` on Windows/MinGW, `dylib` on Darwin/Mac OS X, and `so` on all other platforms. The plugin arguments are parsed by GCC and passed to respective plugins as key-value pairs. Multiple plugins can be invoked by specifying multiple '-fplugin' arguments.

A plugin can be simply given by its short name (no dots or slashes). When simply passing '-fplugin=*name*', the plugin is loaded from the 'plugin' directory, so '-fplugin=*name*' is the same as '-fplugin=`gcc -print-file-name=plugin`/*name.ext*', using backquote shell syntax to query the 'plugin' directory.

24.2 Plugin API

Plugins are activated by the compiler at specific events as defined in 'gcc-plugin.h'. For each event of interest, the plugin should call `register_callback` specifying the name of the event and address of the callback function that will handle that event.

The header 'gcc-plugin.h' must be the first gcc header to be included.

24.2.1 Plugin license check

Every plugin should define the global symbol `plugin_is_GPL_compatible` to assert that it has been licensed under a GPL-compatible license. If this symbol does not exist, the compiler will emit a fatal error and exit with the error message:

```
fatal error: plugin name is not licensed under a GPL-compatible license
name: undefined symbol: plugin_is_GPL_compatible
compilation terminated
```

The declared type of the symbol should be int, to match a forward declaration in 'gcc-plugin.h' that suppresses C++ mangling. It does not need to be in any allocated section, though. The compiler merely asserts that the symbol exists in the global scope. Something like this is enough:

```
int plugin_is_GPL_compatible;
```

24.2.2 Plugin initialization

Every plugin should export a function called `plugin_init` that is called right after the plugin is loaded. This function is responsible for registering all the callbacks required by the plugin and do any other required initialization.

This function is called from `compile_file` right before invoking the parser. The arguments to `plugin_init` are:

- `plugin_info`: Plugin invocation information.
- `version`: GCC version.

The `plugin_info` struct is defined as follows:

```
struct plugin_name_args
{
  char *base_name;              /* Short name of the plugin
                                   (filename without .so suffix). */
  const char *full_name;        /* Path to the plugin as specified with
                                   -fplugin=. */
  int argc;                     /* Number of arguments specified with
                                   -fplugin-arg-.... */
  struct plugin_argument *argv; /* Array of ARGC key-value pairs. */
  const char *version;          /* Version string provided by plugin. */
  const char *help;             /* Help string provided by plugin. */
}
```

If initialization fails, `plugin_init` must return a non-zero value. Otherwise, it should return 0.

The version of the GCC compiler loading the plugin is described by the following structure:

```
struct plugin_gcc_version
{
  const char *basever;
  const char *datestamp;
  const char *devphase;
  const char *revision;
  const char *configuration_arguments;
};
```

The function `plugin_default_version_check` takes two pointers to such structure and compare them field by field. It can be used by the plugin's `plugin_init` function.

The version of GCC used to compile the plugin can be found in the symbol `gcc_version` defined in the header 'plugin-version.h'. The recommended version check to perform looks like

```
#include "plugin-version.h"
...

int
plugin_init (struct plugin_name_args *plugin_info,
             struct plugin_gcc_version *version)
{
  if (!plugin_default_version_check (version, &gcc_version))
    return 1;

}
```

but you can also check the individual fields if you want a less strict check.

24.2.3 Plugin callbacks

Callback functions have the following prototype:

```
/* The prototype for a plugin callback function.
     gcc_data  - event-specific data provided by GCC
     user_data - plugin-specific data provided by the plug-in. */
typedef void (*plugin_callback_func)(void *gcc_data, void *user_data);
```

Callbacks can be invoked at the following pre-determined events:

```
enum plugin_event
{
  PLUGIN_START_PARSE_FUNCTION,  /* Called before parsing the body of a function. */
  PLUGIN_FINISH_PARSE_FUNCTION, /* After finishing parsing a function. */
  PLUGIN_PASS_MANAGER_SETUP,    /* To hook into pass manager. */
  PLUGIN_FINISH_TYPE,           /* After finishing parsing a type. */
  PLUGIN_FINISH_DECL,           /* After finishing parsing a declaration. */
  PLUGIN_FINISH_UNIT,           /* Useful for summary processing. */
  PLUGIN_PRE_GENERICIZE,        /* Allows to see low level AST in C and C++ frontends. */
  PLUGIN_FINISH,                /* Called before GCC exits. */
  PLUGIN_INFO,                  /* Information about the plugin. */
  PLUGIN_GGC_START,             /* Called at start of GCC Garbage Collection. */
  PLUGIN_GGC_MARKING,           /* Extend the GGC marking. */
  PLUGIN_GGC_END,               /* Called at end of GGC. */
  PLUGIN_REGISTER_GGC_ROOTS,    /* Register an extra GGC root table. */
  PLUGIN_ATTRIBUTES,            /* Called during attribute registration */
  PLUGIN_START_UNIT,            /* Called before processing a translation unit. */
  PLUGIN_PRAGMAS,               /* Called during pragma registration. */
  /* Called before first pass from all_passes. */
  PLUGIN_ALL_PASSES_START,
  /* Called after last pass from all_passes. */
  PLUGIN_ALL_PASSES_END,
  /* Called before first ipa pass. */
  PLUGIN_ALL_IPA_PASSES_START,
  /* Called after last ipa pass. */
  PLUGIN_ALL_IPA_PASSES_END,
  /* Allows to override pass gate decision for current_pass. */
  PLUGIN_OVERRIDE_GATE,
  /* Called before executing a pass. */
  PLUGIN_PASS_EXECUTION,
  /* Called before executing subpasses of a GIMPLE_PASS in
     execute_ipa_pass_list. */
  PLUGIN_EARLY_GIMPLE_PASSES_START,
  /* Called after executing subpasses of a GIMPLE_PASS in
     execute_ipa_pass_list. */
  PLUGIN_EARLY_GIMPLE_PASSES_END,
  /* Called when a pass is first instantiated. */
  PLUGIN_NEW_PASS,
 /* Called when a file is #include-d or given via the #line directive.
    This could happen many times.  The event data is the included file path,
    as a const char* pointer. */
  PLUGIN_INCLUDE_FILE,

  PLUGIN_EVENT_FIRST_DYNAMIC    /* Dummy event used for indexing callback
                                   array. */
};
```

In addition, plugins can also look up the enumerator of a named event, and / or generate new events dynamically, by calling the function `get_named_event_id`.

To register a callback, the plugin calls `register_callback` with the arguments:

- `char *name`: Plugin name.
- `int event`: The event code.
- `plugin_callback_func callback`: The function that handles `event`.
- `void *user_data`: Pointer to plugin-specific data.

For the *PLUGIN_PASS_MANAGER_SETUP*, *PLUGIN_INFO*, and *PLUGIN_REGISTER_GGC_ROOTS* pseudo-events the `callback` should be null, and the `user_data` is specific.

When the *PLUGIN_PRAGMAS* event is triggered (with a null pointer as data from GCC), plugins may register their own pragmas. Notice that pragmas are not available from 'lto1', so plugins used with -flto option to GCC during link-time optimization cannot use pragmas and do not even see functions like `c_register_pragma` or `pragma_lex`.

The *PLUGIN_INCLUDE_FILE* event, with a `const char*` file path as GCC data, is triggered for processing of #include or #line directives.

The *PLUGIN_FINISH* event is the last time that plugins can call GCC functions, notably emit diagnostics with `warning`, `error` etc.

24.3 Interacting with the pass manager

There needs to be a way to add/reorder/remove passes dynamically. This is useful for both analysis plugins (plugging in after a certain pass such as CFG or an IPA pass) and optimization plugins.

Basic support for inserting new passes or replacing existing passes is provided. A plugin registers a new pass with GCC by calling `register_callback` with the PLUGIN_PASS_MANAGER_SETUP event and a pointer to a `struct register_pass_info` object defined as follows

```
enum pass_positioning_ops
{
  PASS_POS_INSERT_AFTER,   // Insert after the reference pass.
  PASS_POS_INSERT_BEFORE,  // Insert before the reference pass.
  PASS_POS_REPLACE         // Replace the reference pass.
};

struct register_pass_info
{
  struct opt_pass *pass;            /* New pass provided by the plugin. */
  const char *reference_pass_name;  /* Name of the reference pass for hooking
                                       up the new pass. */
  int ref_pass_instance_number;     /* Insert the pass at the specified
                                       instance number of the reference pass. */
                                    /* Do it for every instance if it is 0. */
  enum pass_positioning_ops pos_op; /* how to insert the new pass. */
};


/* Sample plugin code that registers a new pass. */
int
plugin_init (struct plugin_name_args *plugin_info,
             struct plugin_gcc_version *version)
{
  struct register_pass_info pass_info;
```

Chapter 24: Plugins   669

```
      ...
      /* Code to fill in the pass_info object with new pass information.  */
      ...
      /* Register the new pass.  */
      register_callback (plugin_info->base_name, PLUGIN_PASS_MANAGER_SETUP, NULL, &pass_info);
      ...
    }
```

24.4 Interacting with the GCC Garbage Collector

Some plugins may want to be informed when GGC (the GCC Garbage Collector) is running. They can register callbacks for the `PLUGIN_GGC_START` and `PLUGIN_GGC_END` events (for which the callback is called with a null `gcc_data`) to be notified of the start or end of the GCC garbage collection.

Some plugins may need to have GGC mark additional data. This can be done by registering a callback (called with a null `gcc_data`) for the `PLUGIN_GGC_MARKING` event. Such callbacks can call the `ggc_set_mark` routine, preferably through the `ggc_mark` macro (and conversely, these routines should usually not be used in plugins outside of the `PLUGIN_GGC_MARKING` event). Plugins that wish to hold weak references to gc data may also use this event to drop weak references when the object is about to be collected. The `ggc_marked_p` function can be used to tell if an object is marked, or is about to be collected. The `gt_clear_cache` overloads which some types define may also be of use in managing weak references.

Some plugins may need to add extra GGC root tables, e.g. to handle their own GTY-ed data. This can be done with the `PLUGIN_REGISTER_GGC_ROOTS` pseudo-event with a null callback and the extra root table (of type `struct ggc_root_tab*`) as `user_data`. Running the `gengtype -p` *source-dir file-list plugin*.c ... utility generates these extra root tables.

You should understand the details of memory management inside GCC before using `PLUGIN_GGC_MARKING` or `PLUGIN_REGISTER_GGC_ROOTS`.

24.5 Giving information about a plugin

A plugin should give some information to the user about itself. This uses the following structure:

```
    struct plugin_info
    {
      const char *version;
      const char *help;
    };
```

Such a structure is passed as the `user_data` by the plugin's init routine using `register_callback` with the `PLUGIN_INFO` pseudo-event and a null callback.

24.6 Registering custom attributes or pragmas

For analysis (or other) purposes it is useful to be able to add custom attributes or pragmas.

The `PLUGIN_ATTRIBUTES` callback is called during attribute registration. Use the `register_attribute` function to register custom attributes.

```
/* Attribute handler callback */
static tree
handle_user_attribute (tree *node, tree name, tree args,
                       int flags, bool *no_add_attrs)
{
  return NULL_TREE;
}

/* Attribute definition */
static struct attribute_spec user_attr =
  { "user", 1, 1, false,  false, false, false, handle_user_attribute, NULL };

/* Plugin callback called during attribute registration.
Registered with register_callback (plugin_name, PLUGIN_ATTRIBUTES, register_attributes, NULL)
*/
static void
register_attributes (void *event_data, void *data)
{
  warning (0, G_("Callback to register attributes"));
  register_attribute (&user_attr);
}
```

The *PLUGIN_PRAGMAS* callback is called once during pragmas registration. Use the `c_register_pragma`, `c_register_pragma_with_data`, `c_register_pragma_with_expansion`, `c_register_pragma_with_expansion_and_data` functions to register custom pragmas and their handlers (which often want to call `pragma_lex`) from 'c-family/c-pragma.h'.

```
/* Plugin callback called during pragmas registration. Registered with
      register_callback (plugin_name, PLUGIN_PRAGMAS,
                         register_my_pragma, NULL);
*/
static void
register_my_pragma (void *event_data, void *data)
{
  warning (0, G_("Callback to register pragmas"));
  c_register_pragma ("GCCPLUGIN", "sayhello", handle_pragma_sayhello);
}
```

It is suggested to pass `"GCCPLUGIN"` (or a short name identifying your plugin) as the "space" argument of your pragma.

Pragmas registered with `c_register_pragma_with_expansion` or `c_register_pragma_with_expansion_and_data` support preprocessor expansions. For example:

```
#define NUMBER 10
#pragma GCCPLUGIN foothreshold (NUMBER)
```

24.7 Recording information about pass execution

The event PLUGIN_PASS_EXECUTION passes the pointer to the executed pass (the same as current_pass) as `gcc_data` to the callback. You can also inspect cfun to find out about which function this pass is executed for. Note that this event will only be invoked if the gate check (if applicable, modified by PLUGIN_OVERRIDE_GATE) succeeds. You can use other hooks, like PLUGIN_ALL_PASSES_START, PLUGIN_ALL_PASSES_END,

PLUGIN_ALL_IPA_PASSES_START, PLUGIN_ALL_IPA_PASSES_END, PLUGIN_EARLY_GIMPLE_ PASSES_START, and/or PLUGIN_EARLY_GIMPLE_PASSES_END to manipulate global state in your plugin(s) in order to get context for the pass execution.

24.8 Controlling which passes are being run

After the original gate function for a pass is called, its result - the gate status - is stored as an integer. Then the event PLUGIN_OVERRIDE_GATE is invoked, with a pointer to the gate status in the `gcc_data` parameter to the callback function. A nonzero value of the gate status means that the pass is to be executed. You can both read and write the gate status via the passed pointer.

24.9 Keeping track of available passes

When your plugin is loaded, you can inspect the various pass lists to determine what passes are available. However, other plugins might add new passes. Also, future changes to GCC might cause generic passes to be added after plugin loading. When a pass is first added to one of the pass lists, the event PLUGIN_NEW_PASS is invoked, with the callback parameter `gcc_data` pointing to the new pass.

24.10 Building GCC plugins

If plugins are enabled, GCC installs the headers needed to build a plugin (somewhere in the installation tree, e.g. under '/usr/local'). In particular a 'plugin/include' directory is installed, containing all the header files needed to build plugins.

On most systems, you can query this `plugin` directory by invoking `gcc -print-file-name=plugin` (replace if needed `gcc` with the appropriate program path).

Inside plugins, this `plugin` directory name can be queried by calling `default_plugin_dir_name ()`.

Plugins may know, when they are compiled, the GCC version for which 'plugin-version.h' is provided. The constant macros GCCPLUGIN_VERSION_MAJOR, GCCPLUGIN_VERSION_MINOR, GCCPLUGIN_VERSION_PATCHLEVEL, GCCPLUGIN_VERSION are integer numbers, so a plugin could ensure it is built for GCC 4.7 with

```
#if GCCPLUGIN_VERSION != 4007
#error this GCC plugin is for GCC 4.7
#endif
```

The following GNU Makefile excerpt shows how to build a simple plugin:

```
HOST_GCC=g++
TARGET_GCC=gcc
PLUGIN_SOURCE_FILES= plugin1.c plugin2.cc
GCCPLUGINS_DIR:= $(shell $(TARGET_GCC) -print-file-name=plugin)
CXXFLAGS+= -I$(GCCPLUGINS_DIR)/include -fPIC -fno-rtti -O2

plugin.so: $(PLUGIN_SOURCE_FILES)
   $(HOST_GCC) -shared $(CXXFLAGS) $^ -o $@
```

A single source file plugin may be built with `g++ -I`gcc -print-file-name=plugin`/include -fPIC -shared -fno-rtti -O2 plugin.c -o plugin.so`, using backquote shell syntax to query the 'plugin' directory.

Plugin support on Windows/MinGW has a number of limitations and additional requirements. When building a plugin on Windows we have to link an import library for the corresponding backend executable, for example, 'cc1.exe', 'cc1plus.exe', etc., in order to gain access to the symbols provided by GCC. This means that on Windows a plugin is language-specific, for example, for C, C++, etc. If you wish to use your plugin with multiple languages, then you will need to build multiple plugin libraries and either instruct your users on how to load the correct version or provide a compiler wrapper that does this automatically.

Additionally, on Windows the plugin library has to export the plugin_is_GPL_compatible and plugin_init symbols. If you do not wish to modify the source code of your plugin, then you can use the '-Wl,--export-all-symbols' option or provide a suitable DEF file. Alternatively, you can export just these two symbols by decorating them with __declspec(dllexport), for example:

```
#ifdef _WIN32
__declspec(dllexport)
#endif
int plugin_is_GPL_compatible;

#ifdef _WIN32
__declspec(dllexport)
#endif
int plugin_init (plugin_name_args *, plugin_gcc_version *)
```

The import libraries are installed into the plugin directory and their names are derived by appending the .a extension to the backend executable names, for example, 'cc1.exe.a', 'cc1plus.exe.a', etc. The following command line shows how to build the single source file plugin on Windows to be used with the C++ compiler:

```
g++ -I`gcc -print-file-name=plugin`/include -shared -Wl,--export-all-symbols \
  -o plugin.dll plugin.c `gcc -print-file-name=plugin`/cc1plus.exe.a
```

When a plugin needs to use gengtype, be sure that both 'gengtype' and 'gtype.state' have the same version as the GCC for which the plugin is built.

25 Link Time Optimization

Link Time Optimization (LTO) gives GCC the capability of dumping its internal representation (GIMPLE) to disk, so that all the different compilation units that make up a single executable can be optimized as a single module. This expands the scope of inter-procedural optimizations to encompass the whole program (or, rather, everything that is visible at link time).

25.1 Design Overview

Link time optimization is implemented as a GCC front end for a bytecode representation of GIMPLE that is emitted in special sections of .o files. Currently, LTO support is enabled in most ELF-based systems, as well as darwin, cygwin and mingw systems.

Since GIMPLE bytecode is saved alongside final object code, object files generated with LTO support are larger than regular object files. This "fat" object format makes it easy to integrate LTO into existing build systems, as one can, for instance, produce archives of the files. Additionally, one might be able to ship one set of fat objects which could be used both for development and the production of optimized builds. A, perhaps surprising, side effect of this feature is that any mistake in the toolchain leads to LTO information not being used (e.g. an older `libtool` calling `ld` directly). This is both an advantage, as the system is more robust, and a disadvantage, as the user is not informed that the optimization has been disabled.

The current implementation only produces "fat" objects, effectively doubling compilation time and increasing file sizes up to 5x the original size. This hides the problem that some tools, such as `ar` and `nm`, need to understand symbol tables of LTO sections. These tools were extended to use the plugin infrastructure, and with these problems solved, GCC will also support "slim" objects consisting of the intermediate code alone.

At the highest level, LTO splits the compiler in two. The first half (the "writer") produces a streaming representation of all the internal data structures needed to optimize and generate code. This includes declarations, types, the callgraph and the GIMPLE representation of function bodies.

When '-flto' is given during compilation of a source file, the pass manager executes all the passes in `all_lto_gen_passes`. Currently, this phase is composed of two IPA passes:

- `pass_ipa_lto_gimple_out` This pass executes the function `lto_output` in 'lto-streamer-out.c', which traverses the call graph encoding every reachable declaration, type and function. This generates a memory representation of all the file sections described below.

- `pass_ipa_lto_finish_out` This pass executes the function `produce_asm_for_decls` in 'lto-streamer-out.c', which takes the memory image built in the previous pass and encodes it in the corresponding ELF file sections.

The second half of LTO support is the "reader". This is implemented as the GCC front end 'lto1' in 'lto/lto.c'. When 'collect2' detects a link set of .o/.a files with LTO information and the '-flto' is enabled, it invokes 'lto1' which reads the set of files and aggregates them into a single translation unit for optimization. The main entry point for the reader is 'lto/lto.c':lto_main.

25.1.1 LTO modes of operation

One of the main goals of the GCC link-time infrastructure was to allow effective compilation of large programs. For this reason GCC implements two link-time compilation modes.

1. *LTO mode*, in which the whole program is read into the compiler at link-time and optimized in a similar way as if it were a single source-level compilation unit.

2. *WHOPR or partitioned mode*, designed to utilize multiple CPUs and/or a distributed compilation environment to quickly link large applications. WHOPR stands for WHOle Program optimizeR (not to be confused with the semantics of '-fwhole-program'). It partitions the aggregated callgraph from many different .o files and distributes the compilation of the sub-graphs to different CPUs.

   Note that distributed compilation is not implemented yet, but since the parallelism is facilitated via generating a `Makefile`, it would be easy to implement.

WHOPR splits LTO into three main stages:

1. Local generation (LGEN) This stage executes in parallel. Every file in the program is compiled into the intermediate language and packaged together with the local callgraph and summary information. This stage is the same for both the LTO and WHOPR compilation mode.

2. Whole Program Analysis (WPA) WPA is performed sequentially. The global call-graph is generated, and a global analysis procedure makes transformation decisions. The global call-graph is partitioned to facilitate parallel optimization during phase 3. The results of the WPA stage are stored into new object files which contain the partitions of program expressed in the intermediate language and the optimization decisions.

3. Local transformations (LTRANS) This stage executes in parallel. All the decisions made during phase 2 are implemented locally in each partitioned object file, and the final object code is generated. Optimizations which cannot be decided efficiently during the phase 2 may be performed on the local call-graph partitions.

WHOPR can be seen as an extension of the usual LTO mode of compilation. In LTO, WPA and LTRANS are executed within a single execution of the compiler, after the whole program has been read into memory.

When compiling in WHOPR mode, the callgraph is partitioned during the WPA stage. The whole program is split into a given number of partitions of roughly the same size. The compiler tries to minimize the number of references which cross partition boundaries. The main advantage of WHOPR is to allow the parallel execution of LTRANS stages, which are the most time-consuming part of the compilation process. Additionally, it avoids the need to load the whole program into memory.

25.2 LTO file sections

LTO information is stored in several ELF sections inside object files. Data structures and enum codes for sections are defined in 'lto-streamer.h'.

These sections are emitted from 'lto-streamer-out.c' and mapped in all at once from 'lto/lto.c':lto_file_read. The individual functions dealing with the reading/writing of each section are described below.

Chapter 25: Link Time Optimization

- Command line options (.gnu.lto_.opts)

  This section contains the command line options used to generate the object files. This is used at link time to determine the optimization level and other settings when they are not explicitly specified at the linker command line.

  Currently, GCC does not support combining LTO object files compiled with different set of the command line options into a single binary. At link time, the options given on the command line and the options saved on all the files in a link-time set are applied globally. No attempt is made at validating the combination of flags (other than the usual validation done by option processing). This is implemented in 'lto/lto.c':lto_read_all_file_options.

- Symbol table (.gnu.lto_.symtab)

  This table replaces the ELF symbol table for functions and variables represented in the LTO IL. Symbols used and exported by the optimized assembly code of "fat" objects might not match the ones used and exported by the intermediate code. This table is necessary because the intermediate code is less optimized and thus requires a separate symbol table.

  Additionally, the binary code in the "fat" object will lack a call to a function, since the call was optimized out at compilation time after the intermediate language was streamed out. In some special cases, the same optimization may not happen during link-time optimization. This would lead to an undefined symbol if only one symbol table was used.

  The symbol table is emitted in 'lto-streamer-out.c':produce_symtab.

- Global declarations and types (.gnu.lto_.decls)

  This section contains an intermediate language dump of all declarations and types required to represent the callgraph, static variables and top-level debug info.

  The contents of this section are emitted in 'lto-streamer-out.c':produce_asm_for_decls. Types and symbols are emitted in a topological order that preserves the sharing of pointers when the file is read back in ('lto.c':read_cgraph_and_symbols).

- The callgraph (.gnu.lto_.cgraph)

  This section contains the basic data structure used by the GCC inter-procedural optimization infrastructure. This section stores an annotated multi-graph which represents the functions and call sites as well as the variables, aliases and top-level asm statements.

  This section is emitted in 'lto-streamer-out.c':output_cgraph and read in 'lto-cgraph.c':input_cgraph.

- IPA references (.gnu.lto_.refs)

  This section contains references between function and static variables. It is emitted by 'lto-cgraph.c':output_refs and read by 'lto-cgraph.c':input_refs.

- Function bodies (.gnu.lto_.function_body.<name>)

  This section contains function bodies in the intermediate language representation. Every function body is in a separate section to allow copying of the section independently to different object files or reading the function on demand.

  Functions are emitted in 'lto-streamer-out.c':output_function and read in 'lto-streamer-in.c':input_function.

- Static variable initializers (`.gnu.lto_.vars`)

  This section contains all the symbols in the global variable pool. It is emitted by '`lto-cgraph.c`':output_varpool and read in '`lto-cgraph.c`':input_cgraph.

- Summaries and optimization summaries used by IPA passes (`.gnu.lto_.<xxx>`, where `<xxx>` is one of `jmpfuncs`, `pureconst` or `reference`)

  These sections are used by IPA passes that need to emit summary information during LTO generation to be read and aggregated at link time. Each pass is responsible for implementing two pass manager hooks: one for writing the summary and another for reading it in. The format of these sections is entirely up to each individual pass. The only requirement is that the writer and reader hooks agree on the format.

25.3 Using summary information in IPA passes

Programs are represented internally as a *callgraph* (a multi-graph where nodes are functions and edges are call sites) and a *varpool* (a list of static and external variables in the program).

The inter-procedural optimization is organized as a sequence of individual passes, which operate on the callgraph and the varpool. To make the implementation of WHOPR possible, every inter-procedural optimization pass is split into several stages that are executed at different times during WHOPR compilation:

- LGEN time
  1. *Generate summary* (`generate_summary` in `struct ipa_opt_pass_d`). This stage analyzes every function body and variable initializer is examined and stores relevant information into a pass-specific data structure.
  2. *Write summary* (`write_summary` in `struct ipa_opt_pass_d`). This stage writes all the pass-specific information generated by `generate_summary`. Summaries go into their own `LTO_section_*` sections that have to be declared in '`lto-streamer.h`':enum lto_section_type. A new section is created by calling `create_output_block` and data can be written using the `lto_output_*` routines.

- WPA time
  1. *Read summary* (`read_summary` in `struct ipa_opt_pass_d`). This stage reads all the pass-specific information in exactly the same order that it was written by `write_summary`.
  2. *Execute* (`execute` in `struct opt_pass`). This performs inter-procedural propagation. This must be done without actual access to the individual function bodies or variable initializers. Typically, this results in a transitive closure operation over the summary information of all the nodes in the callgraph.
  3. *Write optimization summary* (`write_optimization_summary` in `struct ipa_opt_pass_d`). This writes the result of the inter-procedural propagation into the object file. This can use the same data structures and helper routines used in `write_summary`.

- LTRANS time
  1. *Read optimization summary* (`read_optimization_summary` in `struct ipa_opt_pass_d`). The counterpart to `write_optimization_summary`. This reads the interprocedural optimization decisions in exactly the same format emitted by `write_optimization_summary`.

2. *Transform* (`function_transform` and `variable_transform` in `struct ipa_opt_pass_d`). The actual function bodies and variable initializers are updated based on the information passed down from the *Execute* stage.

The implementation of the inter-procedural passes are shared between LTO, WHOPR and classic non-LTO compilation.

- During the traditional file-by-file mode every pass executes its own *Generate summary*, *Execute*, and *Transform* stages within the single execution context of the compiler.
- In LTO compilation mode, every pass uses *Generate summary* and *Write summary* stages at compilation time, while the *Read summary*, *Execute*, and *Transform* stages are executed at link time.
- In WHOPR mode all stages are used.

To simplify development, the GCC pass manager differentiates between normal inter-procedural passes and small inter-procedural passes. A *small inter-procedural pass* (`SIMPLE_IPA_PASS`) is a pass that does everything at once and thus it can not be executed during WPA in WHOPR mode. It defines only the *Execute* stage and during this stage it accesses and modifies the function bodies. Such passes are useful for optimization at LGEN or LTRANS time and are used, for example, to implement early optimization before writing object files. The simple inter-procedural passes can also be used for easier prototyping and development of a new inter-procedural pass.

25.3.1 Virtual clones

One of the main challenges of introducing the WHOPR compilation mode was addressing the interactions between optimization passes. In LTO compilation mode, the passes are executed in a sequence, each of which consists of analysis (or *Generate summary*), propagation (or *Execute*) and *Transform* stages. Once the work of one pass is finished, the next pass sees the updated program representation and can execute. This makes the individual passes dependent on each other.

In WHOPR mode all passes first execute their *Generate summary* stage. Then summary writing marks the end of the LGEN stage. At WPA time, the summaries are read back into memory and all passes run the *Execute* stage. Optimization summaries are streamed and sent to LTRANS, where all the passes execute the *Transform* stage.

Most optimization passes split naturally into analysis, propagation and transformation stages. But some do not. The main problem arises when one pass performs changes and the following pass gets confused by seeing different callgraphs between the *Transform* stage and the *Generate summary* or *Execute* stage. This means that the passes are required to communicate their decisions with each other.

To facilitate this communication, the GCC callgraph infrastructure implements *virtual clones*, a method of representing the changes performed by the optimization passes in the callgraph without needing to update function bodies.

A *virtual clone* in the callgraph is a function that has no associated body, just a description of how to create its body based on a different function (which itself may be a virtual clone).

The description of function modifications includes adjustments to the function's signature (which allows, for example, removing or adding function arguments), substitutions to perform on the function body, and, for inlined functions, a pointer to the function that it will be inlined into.

It is also possible to redirect any edge of the callgraph from a function to its virtual clone. This implies updating of the call site to adjust for the new function signature.

Most of the transformations performed by inter-procedural optimizations can be represented via virtual clones. For instance, a constant propagation pass can produce a virtual clone of the function which replaces one of its arguments by a constant. The inliner can represent its decisions by producing a clone of a function whose body will be later integrated into a given function.

Using *virtual clones*, the program can be easily updated during the *Execute* stage, solving most of pass interactions problems that would otherwise occur during *Transform*.

Virtual clones are later materialized in the LTRANS stage and turned into real functions. Passes executed after the virtual clone were introduced also perform their *Transform* stage on new functions, so for a pass there is no significant difference between operating on a real function or a virtual clone introduced before its *Execute* stage.

Optimization passes then work on virtual clones introduced before their *Execute* stage as if they were real functions. The only difference is that clones are not visible during the *Generate Summary* stage.

To keep function summaries updated, the callgraph interface allows an optimizer to register a callback that is called every time a new clone is introduced as well as when the actual function or variable is generated or when a function or variable is removed. These hooks are registered in the *Generate summary* stage and allow the pass to keep its information intact until the *Execute* stage. The same hooks can also be registered during the *Execute* stage to keep the optimization summaries updated for the *Transform* stage.

25.3.2 IPA references

GCC represents IPA references in the callgraph. For a function or variable A, the *IPA reference* is a list of all locations where the address of A is taken and, when A is a variable, a list of all direct stores and reads to/from A. References represent an oriented multi-graph on the union of nodes of the callgraph and the varpool. See 'ipa-reference.c':ipa_reference_write_optimization_summary and 'ipa-reference.c':ipa_reference_read_optimization_summary for details.

25.3.3 Jump functions

Suppose that an optimization pass sees a function A and it knows the values of (some of) its arguments. The *jump function* describes the value of a parameter of a given function call in function A based on this knowledge.

Jump functions are used by several optimizations, such as the inter-procedural constant propagation pass and the devirtualization pass. The inliner also uses jump functions to perform inlining of callbacks.

25.4 Whole program assumptions, linker plugin and symbol visibilities

Link-time optimization gives relatively minor benefits when used alone. The problem is that propagation of inter-procedural information does not work well across functions and variables that are called or referenced by other compilation units (such as from a dynamically linked library). We say that such functions and variables are *externally visible*.

To make the situation even more difficult, many applications organize themselves as a set of shared libraries, and the default ELF visibility rules allow one to overwrite any externally visible symbol with a different symbol at runtime. This basically disables any optimizations across such functions and variables, because the compiler cannot be sure that the function body it is seeing is the same function body that will be used at runtime. Any function or variable not declared `static` in the sources degrades the quality of inter-procedural optimization.

To avoid this problem the compiler must assume that it sees the whole program when doing link-time optimization. Strictly speaking, the whole program is rarely visible even at link-time. Standard system libraries are usually linked dynamically or not provided with the link-time information. In GCC, the whole program option ('`-fwhole-program`') asserts that every function and variable defined in the current compilation unit is static, except for function `main` (note: at link time, the current unit is the union of all objects compiled with LTO). Since some functions and variables need to be referenced externally, for example by another DSO or from an assembler file, GCC also provides the function and variable attribute `externally_visible` which can be used to disable the effect of '`-fwhole-program`' on a specific symbol.

The whole program mode assumptions are slightly more complex in C++, where inline functions in headers are put into *COMDAT* sections. COMDAT function and variables can be defined by multiple object files and their bodies are unified at link-time and dynamic link-time. COMDAT functions are changed to local only when their address is not taken and thus un-sharing them with a library is not harmful. COMDAT variables always remain externally visible, however for readonly variables it is assumed that their initializers cannot be overwritten by a different value.

GCC provides the function and variable attribute `visibility` that can be used to specify the visibility of externally visible symbols (or alternatively an '`-fdefault-visibility`' command line option). ELF defines the `default`, `protected`, `hidden` and `internal` visibilities.

The most commonly used is visibility is `hidden`. It specifies that the symbol cannot be referenced from outside of the current shared library. Unfortunately, this information cannot be used directly by the link-time optimization in the compiler since the whole shared library also might contain non-LTO objects and those are not visible to the compiler.

GCC solves this problem using linker plugins. A *linker plugin* is an interface to the linker that allows an external program to claim the ownership of a given object file. The linker then performs the linking procedure by querying the plugin about the symbol table of the claimed objects and once the linking decisions are complete, the plugin is allowed to provide the final object file before the actual linking is made. The linker plugin obtains the symbol resolution information which specifies which symbols provided by the claimed objects are bound from the rest of a binary being linked.

GCC is designed to be independent of the rest of the toolchain and aims to support linkers without plugin support. For this reason it does not use the linker plugin by default. Instead, the object files are examined by `collect2` before being passed to the linker and objects found to have LTO sections are passed to `lto1` first. This mode does not work for library archives.

The decision on what object files from the archive are needed depends on the actual linking and thus GCC would have to implement the linker itself. The resolution information is missing too and thus GCC needs to make an educated guess based on '-fwhole-program'. Without the linker plugin GCC also assumes that symbols are declared hidden and not referred by non-LTO code by default.

25.5 Internal flags controlling lto1

The following flags are passed into lto1 and are not meant to be used directly from the command line.

- -fwpa This option runs the serial part of the link-time optimizer performing the interprocedural propagation (WPA mode). The compiler reads in summary information from all inputs and performs an analysis based on summary information only. It generates object files for subsequent runs of the link-time optimizer where individual object files are optimized using both summary information from the WPA mode and the actual function bodies. It then drives the LTRANS phase.

- -fltrans This option runs the link-time optimizer in the local-transformation (LTRANS) mode, which reads in output from a previous run of the LTO in WPA mode. In the LTRANS mode, LTO optimizes an object and produces the final assembly.

- -fltrans-output-list=file This option specifies a file to which the names of LTRANS output files are written. This option is only meaningful in conjunction with '-fwpa'.

- -fresolution=file This option specifies the linker resolution file. This option is only meaningful in conjunction with '-fwpa' and as option to pass through to the LTO linker plugin.

26 Match and Simplify

The GIMPLE and GENERIC pattern matching project match-and-simplify tries to address several issues.

1. unify expression simplifications currently spread and duplicated over separate files like fold-const.c, gimple-fold.c and builtins.c
2. allow for a cheap way to implement building and simplifying non-trivial GIMPLE expressions, avoiding the need to go through building and simplifying GENERIC via fold_buildN and then gimplifying via force_gimple_operand

To address these the project introduces a simple domain specific language to write expression simplifications from which code targeting GIMPLE and GENERIC is auto-generated. The GENERIC variant follows the fold_buildN API while for the GIMPLE variant and to address 2) new APIs are introduced.

26.1 GIMPLE API

tree `gimple_simplify` (*enum tree_code, tree, tree, gimple_seq *, tree (*)(tree)*)   [GIMPLE function]

tree `gimple_simplify` (*enum tree_code, tree, tree, tree, gimple_seq *, tree (*)(tree)*)   [GIMPLE function]

tree `gimple_simplify` (*enum tree_code, tree, tree, tree, tree, gimple_seq *, tree (*)(tree)*)   [GIMPLE function]

tree `gimple_simplify` (*enum built_in_function, tree, tree, gimple_seq *, tree (*)(tree)*)   [GIMPLE function]

tree `gimple_simplify` (*enum built_in_function, tree, tree, tree, gimple_seq *, tree (*)(tree)*)   [GIMPLE function]

tree `gimple_simplify` (*enum built_in_function, tree, tree, tree, tree, gimple_seq *, tree (*)(tree)*)   [GIMPLE function]

    The main GIMPLE API entry to the expression simplifications mimicing that of the GENERIC fold_{unary,binary,ternary} functions.

thus providing n-ary overloads for operation or function. The additional arguments are a gimple_seq where built statements are inserted on (if NULL then simplifications requiring new statements are not performed) and a valueization hook that can be used to tie simplifications to a SSA lattice.

In addition to those APIs `fold_stmt` is overloaded with a valueization hook:

`fold_stmt` (*gimple_stmt_iterator *, tree (*)(tree)*);   [bool]

    Ontop of these a `fold_buildN`-like API for GIMPLE is introduced:

tree `gimple_build` (*gimple_seq *, location_t, enum tree_code, tree, tree, tree (*valueize) (tree) = NULL*);   [GIMPLE function]

tree `gimple_build` (*gimple_seq *, location_t, enum tree_code, tree, tree, tree, tree (*valueize) (tree) = NULL*);   [GIMPLE function]

tree `gimple_build` (*gimple_seq *, location_t, enum tree_code, tree, tree, tree, tree, tree (*valueize) (tree) = NULL*);   [GIMPLE function]

tree gimple_build (*gimple_seq* *, *location_t*, *enum*   [GIMPLE function]
        built_in_function, *tree*, *tree*, *tree* (*valueize) (*tree*) = *NULL*);
tree gimple_build (*gimple_seq* *, *location_t*, *enum*   [GIMPLE function]
        built_in_function, *tree*, *tree*, *tree*, *tree* (*valueize) (*tree*) = *NULL*);
tree gimple_build (*gimple_seq* *, *location_t*, *enum*   [GIMPLE function]
        built_in_function, *tree*, *tree*, *tree*, *tree*, *tree* (*valueize) (*tree*) = *NULL*);
tree gimple_convert (*gimple_seq* *, *location_t*, *tree*, *tree*);   [GIMPLE function]

which is supposed to replace `force_gimple_operand (fold_buildN (...), ...)` and calls to `fold_convert`. Overloads without the `location_t` argument exist. Built statements are inserted on the provided sequence and simplification is performed using the optional valueization hook.

26.2 The Language

The language to write expression simplifications in resembles other domain-specific languages GCC uses. Thus it is lispy. Lets start with an example from the match.pd file:

        (simplify
          (bit_and @0 integer_all_onesp)
          @0)

This example contains all required parts of an expression simplification. A simplification is wrapped inside a (`simplify` ...) expression. That contains at least two operands - an expression that is matched with the GIMPLE or GENERIC IL and a replacement expression that is returned if the match was successful.

Expressions have an operator ID, `bit_and` in this case. Expressions can be lower-case tree codes with `_expr` stripped off or builtin function code names in all-caps, like `BUILT_IN_SQRT`.

`@n` denotes a so-called capture. It captures the operand and lets you refer to it in other places of the match-and-simplify. In the above example it is refered to in the replacement expression. Captures are @ followed by a number or an identifier.

        (simplify
          (bit_xor @0 @0)
          { build_zero_cst (type); })

In this example @0 is mentioned twice which constrains the matched expression to have two equal operands. Usually matches are constraint to equal types. If operands may be constants and conversions are involved matching by value might be preferred in which case use @@0 to denote a by value match and the specific operand you want to refer to in the result part. This example also introduces operands written in C code. These can be used in the expression replacements and are supposed to evaluate to a tree node which has to be a valid GIMPLE operand (so you cannot generate expressions in C code).

        (simplify
          (trunc_mod integer_zerop@0 @1)
          (if (!integer_zerop (@1))
            @0))

Here @0 captures the first operand of the trunc_mod expression which is also predicated with `integer_zerop`. Expression operands may be either expressions, predicates or captures. Captures can be unconstrained or capture expresions or predicates.

This example introduces an optional operand of simplify, the if-expression. This condition is evaluated after the expression matched in the IL and is required to evaluate to true to

Chapter 26: Match and Simplify 683

enable the replacement expression in the second operand position. The expression operand of the `if` is a standard C expression which may contain references to captures. The `if` has an optional third operand which may contain the replacement expression that is enabled when the condition evaluates to false.

A `if` expression can be used to specify a common condition for multiple simplify patterns, avoiding the need to repeat that multiple times:

```
(if (!TYPE_SATURATING (type)
     && !FLOAT_TYPE_P (type) && !FIXED_POINT_TYPE_P (type))
 (simplify
  (minus (plus @0 @1) @0)
  @1)
 (simplify
  (minus (minus @0 @1) @0)
  (negate @1)))
```

Note that `if`s in outer position do not have the optional else clause but instead have multiple then clauses.

Ifs can be nested.

There exists a `switch` expression which can be used to chain conditions avoiding nesting `if`s too much:

```
(simplify
 (simple_comparison @0 REAL_CST@1)
 (switch
  /* a CMP (-0) -> a CMP 0 */
  (if (REAL_VALUE_MINUS_ZERO (TREE_REAL_CST (@1)))
   (cmp @0 { build_real (TREE_TYPE (@1), dconst0); }))
  /* x != NaN is always true, other ops are always false. */
  (if (REAL_VALUE_ISNAN (TREE_REAL_CST (@1))
       && ! HONOR_SNANS (@1))
   { constant_boolean_node (cmp == NE_EXPR, type); })))
```

Is equal to

```
(simplify
 (simple_comparison @0 REAL_CST@1)
 (switch
  /* a CMP (-0) -> a CMP 0 */
  (if (REAL_VALUE_MINUS_ZERO (TREE_REAL_CST (@1)))
   (cmp @0 { build_real (TREE_TYPE (@1), dconst0); })
   /* x != NaN is always true, other ops are always false. */
   (if (REAL_VALUE_ISNAN (TREE_REAL_CST (@1))
        && ! HONOR_SNANS (@1))
    { constant_boolean_node (cmp == NE_EXPR, type); }))))
```

which has the second `if` in the else operand of the first. The `switch` expression takes `if` expressions as operands (which may not have else clauses) and as a last operand a replacement expression which should be enabled by default if no other condition evaluated to true.

Captures can also be used for capturing results of sub-expressions.

```
#if GIMPLE
(simplify
  (pointer_plus (addr@2 @0) INTEGER_CST_P@1)
  (if (is_gimple_min_invariant (@2)))
  {
    poly_int64 off;
```

```
        tree base = get_addr_base_and_unit_offset (@0, &off);
        off += tree_to_uhwi (@1);
        /* Now with that we should be able to simply write
           (addr (mem_ref (addr @base) (plus @off @1))) */
        build1 (ADDR_EXPR, type,
                build2 (MEM_REF, TREE_TYPE (TREE_TYPE (@2)),
                        build_fold_addr_expr (base),
                        build_int_cst (ptr_type_node, off)));
    })
#endif
```

In the above example, @2 captures the result of the expression (addr @0). For outermost expression only its type can be captured, and the keyword type is reserved for this purpose. The above example also gives a way to conditionalize patterns to only apply to GIMPLE or GENERIC by means of using the pre-defined preprocessor macros GIMPLE and GENERIC and using preprocessor directives.

```
(simplify
  (bit_and:c integral_op_p@0 (bit_ior:c (bit_not @0) @1))
  (bit_and @1 @0))
```

Here we introduce flags on match expressions. The flag used above, c, denotes that the expression should be also matched commutated. Thus the above match expression is really the following four match expressions:

```
(bit_and integral_op_p@0 (bit_ior (bit_not @0) @1))
(bit_and (bit_ior (bit_not @0) @1) integral_op_p@0)
(bit_and integral_op_p@0 (bit_ior @1 (bit_not @0)))
(bit_and (bit_ior @1 (bit_not @0)) integral_op_p@0)
```

Usual canonicalizations you know from GENERIC expressions are applied before matching, so for example constant operands always come second in commutative expressions.

The second supported flag is s which tells the code generator to fail the pattern if the expression marked with s does have more than one use. For example in

```
(simplify
  (pointer_plus (pointer_plus:s @0 @1) @3)
  (pointer_plus @0 (plus @1 @3)))
```

this avoids the association if (pointer_plus @0 @1) is used outside of the matched expression and thus it would stay live and not trivially removed by dead code elimination.

More features exist to avoid too much repetition.

```
(for op (plus pointer_plus minus bit_ior bit_xor)
  (simplify
    (op @0 integer_zerop)
    @0))
```

A for expression can be used to repeat a pattern for each operator specified, substituting op. for can be nested and a for can have multiple operators to iterate.

```
(for opa (plus minus)
     opb (minus plus)
  (for opc (plus minus)
    (simplify...
```

In this example the pattern will be repeated four times with opa, opb, opc being plus, minus, plus, plus, minus, minus, minus, plus, plus, minus, plus, minus.

To avoid repeating operator lists in for you can name them via

Chapter 26: Match and Simplify

```
(define_operator_list pmm plus minus mult)
```

and use them in `for` operator lists where they get expanded.

```
(for opa (pmm trunc_div)
 (simplify...
```

So this example iterates over `plus`, `minus`, `mult` and `trunc_div`.

Using operator lists can also remove the need to explicitly write a `for`. All operator list uses that appear in a `simplify` or `match` pattern in operator positions will implicitly be added to a new `for`. For example

```
(define_operator_list SQRT BUILT_IN_SQRTF BUILT_IN_SQRT BUILT_IN_SQRTL)
(define_operator_list POW BUILT_IN_POWF BUILT_IN_POW BUILT_IN_POWL)
(simplify
 (SQRT (POW @0 @1))
 (POW (abs @0) (mult @1 { built_real (TREE_TYPE (@1), dconsthalf); })))
```

is the same as

```
(for SQRT (BUILT_IN_SQRTF BUILT_IN_SQRT BUILT_IN_SQRTL)
     POW (BUILT_IN_POWF BUILT_IN_POW BUILT_IN_POWL)
 (simplify
  (SQRT (POW @0 @1))
  (POW (abs @0) (mult @1 { built_real (TREE_TYPE (@1), dconsthalf); }))))
```

`for`s and operator lists can include the special identifier `null` that matches nothing and can never be generated. This can be used to pad an operator list so that it has a standard form, even if there isn't a suitable operator for every form.

Another building block are `with` expressions in the result expression which nest the generated code in a new C block followed by its argument:

```
(simplify
 (convert (mult @0 @1))
 (with { tree utype = unsigned_type_for (type); }
  (convert (mult (convert:utype @0) (convert:utype @1)))))
```

This allows code nested in the `with` to refer to the declared variables. In the above case we use the feature to specify the type of a generated expression with the `:type` syntax where `type` needs to be an identifier that refers to the desired type. Usually the types of the generated result expressions are determined from the context, but sometimes like in the above case it is required that you specify them explicitly.

As intermediate conversions are often optional there is a way to avoid the need to repeat patterns both with and without such conversions. Namely you can mark a conversion as being optional with a `?`:

```
(simplify
 (eq (convert@0 @1) (convert? @2))
 (eq @1 (convert @2)))
```

which will match both `(eq (convert @1) (convert @2))` and `(eq (convert @1) @2)`. The optional converts are supposed to be all either present or not, thus `(eq (convert? @1) (convert? @2))` will result in two patterns only. If you want to match all four combinations you have access to two additional conditional converts as in `(eq (convert1? @1) (convert2? @2))`.

Predicates available from the GCC middle-end need to be made available explicitly via `define_predicates`:

```
(define_predicates
  integer_onep integer_zerop integer_all_onesp)
```

You can also define predicates using the pattern matching language and the `match` form:

```
(match negate_expr_p
 INTEGER_CST
 (if (TYPE_OVERFLOW_WRAPS (type)
     || may_negate_without_overflow_p (t))))
(match negate_expr_p
 (negate @0))
```

This shows that for `match` expressions there is `t` available which captures the outermost expression (something not possible in the `simplify` context). As you can see `match` has an identifier as first operand which is how you refer to the predicate in patterns. Multiple `match` for the same identifier add additional cases where the predicate matches.

Predicates can also match an expression in which case you need to provide a template specifying the identifier and where to get its operands from:

```
(match (logical_inverted_value @0)
 (eq @0 integer_zerop))
(match (logical_inverted_value @0)
 (bit_not truth_valued_p@0))
```

You can use the above predicate like

```
(simplify
 (bit_and @0 (logical_inverted_value @0))
 { build_zero_cst (type); })
```

Which will match a bitwise and of an operand with its logical inverted value.

Funding Free Software

If you want to have more free software a few years from now, it makes sense for you to help encourage people to contribute funds for its development. The most effective approach known is to encourage commercial redistributors to donate.

Users of free software systems can boost the pace of development by encouraging for-a-fee distributors to donate part of their selling price to free software developers—the Free Software Foundation, and others.

The way to convince distributors to do this is to demand it and expect it from them. So when you compare distributors, judge them partly by how much they give to free software development. Show distributors they must compete to be the one who gives the most.

To make this approach work, you must insist on numbers that you can compare, such as, "We will donate ten dollars to the Frobnitz project for each disk sold." Don't be satisfied with a vague promise, such as "A portion of the profits are donated," since it doesn't give a basis for comparison.

Even a precise fraction "of the profits from this disk" is not very meaningful, since creative accounting and unrelated business decisions can greatly alter what fraction of the sales price counts as profit. If the price you pay is $50, ten percent of the profit is probably less than a dollar; it might be a few cents, or nothing at all.

Some redistributors do development work themselves. This is useful too; but to keep everyone honest, you need to inquire how much they do, and what kind. Some kinds of development make much more long-term difference than others. For example, maintaining a separate version of a program contributes very little; maintaining the standard version of a program for the whole community contributes much. Easy new ports contribute little, since someone else would surely do them; difficult ports such as adding a new CPU to the GNU Compiler Collection contribute more; major new features or packages contribute the most.

By establishing the idea that supporting further development is "the proper thing to do" when distributing free software for a fee, we can assure a steady flow of resources into making more free software.

 Copyright © 1994 Free Software Foundation, Inc.
 Verbatim copying and redistribution of this section is permitted
 without royalty; alteration is not permitted.

The GNU Project and GNU/Linux

The GNU Project was launched in 1984 to develop a complete Unix-like operating system which is free software: the GNU system. (GNU is a recursive acronym for "GNU's Not Unix"; it is pronounced "guh-NEW".) Variants of the GNU operating system, which use the kernel Linux, are now widely used; though these systems are often referred to as "Linux", they are more accurately called GNU/Linux systems.

For more information, see:
```
http://www.gnu.org/
http://www.gnu.org/gnu/linux-and-gnu.html
```

GNU General Public License

Version 3, 29 June 2007

Copyright © 2007 Free Software Foundation, Inc. `http://fsf.org/`

Everyone is permitted to copy and distribute verbatim copies of this license document, but changing it is not allowed.

Preamble

The GNU General Public License is a free, copyleft license for software and other kinds of works.

The licenses for most software and other practical works are designed to take away your freedom to share and change the works. By contrast, the GNU General Public License is intended to guarantee your freedom to share and change all versions of a program–to make sure it remains free software for all its users. We, the Free Software Foundation, use the GNU General Public License for most of our software; it applies also to any other work released this way by its authors. You can apply it to your programs, too.

When we speak of free software, we are referring to freedom, not price. Our General Public Licenses are designed to make sure that you have the freedom to distribute copies of free software (and charge for them if you wish), that you receive source code or can get it if you want it, that you can change the software or use pieces of it in new free programs, and that you know you can do these things.

To protect your rights, we need to prevent others from denying you these rights or asking you to surrender the rights. Therefore, you have certain responsibilities if you distribute copies of the software, or if you modify it: responsibilities to respect the freedom of others.

For example, if you distribute copies of such a program, whether gratis or for a fee, you must pass on to the recipients the same freedoms that you received. You must make sure that they, too, receive or can get the source code. And you must show them these terms so they know their rights.

Developers that use the GNU GPL protect your rights with two steps: (1) assert copyright on the software, and (2) offer you this License giving you legal permission to copy, distribute and/or modify it.

For the developers' and authors' protection, the GPL clearly explains that there is no warranty for this free software. For both users' and authors' sake, the GPL requires that modified versions be marked as changed, so that their problems will not be attributed erroneously to authors of previous versions.

Some devices are designed to deny users access to install or run modified versions of the software inside them, although the manufacturer can do so. This is fundamentally incompatible with the aim of protecting users' freedom to change the software. The systematic pattern of such abuse occurs in the area of products for individuals to use, which is precisely where it is most unacceptable. Therefore, we have designed this version of the GPL to prohibit the practice for those products. If such problems arise substantially in other domains, we stand ready to extend this provision to those domains in future versions of the GPL, as needed to protect the freedom of users.

Finally, every program is threatened constantly by software patents. States should not allow patents to restrict development and use of software on general-purpose computers, but in those that do, we wish to avoid the special danger that patents applied to a free program could make it effectively proprietary. To prevent this, the GPL assures that patents cannot be used to render the program non-free.

The precise terms and conditions for copying, distribution and modification follow.

TERMS AND CONDITIONS

0. Definitions.

    "This License" refers to version 3 of the GNU General Public License.

    "Copyright" also means copyright-like laws that apply to other kinds of works, such as semiconductor masks.

    "The Program" refers to any copyrightable work licensed under this License. Each licensee is addressed as "you". "Licensees" and "recipients" may be individuals or organizations.

    To "modify" a work means to copy from or adapt all or part of the work in a fashion requiring copyright permission, other than the making of an exact copy. The resulting work is called a "modified version" of the earlier work or a work "based on" the earlier work.

    A "covered work" means either the unmodified Program or a work based on the Program.

    To "propagate" a work means to do anything with it that, without permission, would make you directly or secondarily liable for infringement under applicable copyright law, except executing it on a computer or modifying a private copy. Propagation includes copying, distribution (with or without modification), making available to the public, and in some countries other activities as well.

    To "convey" a work means any kind of propagation that enables other parties to make or receive copies. Mere interaction with a user through a computer network, with no transfer of a copy, is not conveying.

    An interactive user interface displays "Appropriate Legal Notices" to the extent that it includes a convenient and prominently visible feature that (1) displays an appropriate copyright notice, and (2) tells the user that there is no warranty for the work (except to the extent that warranties are provided), that licensees may convey the work under this License, and how to view a copy of this License. If the interface presents a list of user commands or options, such as a menu, a prominent item in the list meets this criterion.

1. Source Code.

    The "source code" for a work means the preferred form of the work for making modifications to it. "Object code" means any non-source form of a work.

    A "Standard Interface" means an interface that either is an official standard defined by a recognized standards body, or, in the case of interfaces specified for a particular programming language, one that is widely used among developers working in that language.

The "System Libraries" of an executable work include anything, other than the work as a whole, that (a) is included in the normal form of packaging a Major Component, but which is not part of that Major Component, and (b) serves only to enable use of the work with that Major Component, or to implement a Standard Interface for which an implementation is available to the public in source code form. A "Major Component", in this context, means a major essential component (kernel, window system, and so on) of the specific operating system (if any) on which the executable work runs, or a compiler used to produce the work, or an object code interpreter used to run it.

The "Corresponding Source" for a work in object code form means all the source code needed to generate, install, and (for an executable work) run the object code and to modify the work, including scripts to control those activities. However, it does not include the work's System Libraries, or general-purpose tools or generally available free programs which are used unmodified in performing those activities but which are not part of the work. For example, Corresponding Source includes interface definition files associated with source files for the work, and the source code for shared libraries and dynamically linked subprograms that the work is specifically designed to require, such as by intimate data communication or control flow between those subprograms and other parts of the work.

The Corresponding Source need not include anything that users can regenerate automatically from other parts of the Corresponding Source.

The Corresponding Source for a work in source code form is that same work.

2. Basic Permissions.

   All rights granted under this License are granted for the term of copyright on the Program, and are irrevocable provided the stated conditions are met. This License explicitly affirms your unlimited permission to run the unmodified Program. The output from running a covered work is covered by this License only if the output, given its content, constitutes a covered work. This License acknowledges your rights of fair use or other equivalent, as provided by copyright law.

   You may make, run and propagate covered works that you do not convey, without conditions so long as your license otherwise remains in force. You may convey covered works to others for the sole purpose of having them make modifications exclusively for you, or provide you with facilities for running those works, provided that you comply with the terms of this License in conveying all material for which you do not control copyright. Those thus making or running the covered works for you must do so exclusively on your behalf, under your direction and control, on terms that prohibit them from making any copies of your copyrighted material outside their relationship with you.

   Conveying under any other circumstances is permitted solely under the conditions stated below. Sublicensing is not allowed; section 10 makes it unnecessary.

3. Protecting Users' Legal Rights From Anti-Circumvention Law.

   No covered work shall be deemed part of an effective technological measure under any applicable law fulfilling obligations under article 11 of the WIPO copyright treaty adopted on 20 December 1996, or similar laws prohibiting or restricting circumvention of such measures.

When you convey a covered work, you waive any legal power to forbid circumvention of technological measures to the extent such circumvention is effected by exercising rights under this License with respect to the covered work, and you disclaim any intention to limit operation or modification of the work as a means of enforcing, against the work's users, your or third parties' legal rights to forbid circumvention of technological measures.

4. Conveying Verbatim Copies.

    You may convey verbatim copies of the Program's source code as you receive it, in any medium, provided that you conspicuously and appropriately publish on each copy an appropriate copyright notice; keep intact all notices stating that this License and any non-permissive terms added in accord with section 7 apply to the code; keep intact all notices of the absence of any warranty; and give all recipients a copy of this License along with the Program.

    You may charge any price or no price for each copy that you convey, and you may offer support or warranty protection for a fee.

5. Conveying Modified Source Versions.

    You may convey a work based on the Program, or the modifications to produce it from the Program, in the form of source code under the terms of section 4, provided that you also meet all of these conditions:

    a. The work must carry prominent notices stating that you modified it, and giving a relevant date.

    b. The work must carry prominent notices stating that it is released under this License and any conditions added under section 7. This requirement modifies the requirement in section 4 to "keep intact all notices".

    c. You must license the entire work, as a whole, under this License to anyone who comes into possession of a copy. This License will therefore apply, along with any applicable section 7 additional terms, to the whole of the work, and all its parts, regardless of how they are packaged. This License gives no permission to license the work in any other way, but it does not invalidate such permission if you have separately received it.

    d. If the work has interactive user interfaces, each must display Appropriate Legal Notices; however, if the Program has interactive interfaces that do not display Appropriate Legal Notices, your work need not make them do so.

    A compilation of a covered work with other separate and independent works, which are not by their nature extensions of the covered work, and which are not combined with it such as to form a larger program, in or on a volume of a storage or distribution medium, is called an "aggregate" if the compilation and its resulting copyright are not used to limit the access or legal rights of the compilation's users beyond what the individual works permit. Inclusion of a covered work in an aggregate does not cause this License to apply to the other parts of the aggregate.

6. Conveying Non-Source Forms.

    You may convey a covered work in object code form under the terms of sections 4 and 5, provided that you also convey the machine-readable Corresponding Source under the terms of this License, in one of these ways:

a. Convey the object code in, or embodied in, a physical product (including a physical distribution medium), accompanied by the Corresponding Source fixed on a durable physical medium customarily used for software interchange.

b. Convey the object code in, or embodied in, a physical product (including a physical distribution medium), accompanied by a written offer, valid for at least three years and valid for as long as you offer spare parts or customer support for that product model, to give anyone who possesses the object code either (1) a copy of the Corresponding Source for all the software in the product that is covered by this License, on a durable physical medium customarily used for software interchange, for a price no more than your reasonable cost of physically performing this conveying of source, or (2) access to copy the Corresponding Source from a network server at no charge.

c. Convey individual copies of the object code with a copy of the written offer to provide the Corresponding Source. This alternative is allowed only occasionally and noncommercially, and only if you received the object code with such an offer, in accord with subsection 6b.

d. Convey the object code by offering access from a designated place (gratis or for a charge), and offer equivalent access to the Corresponding Source in the same way through the same place at no further charge. You need not require recipients to copy the Corresponding Source along with the object code. If the place to copy the object code is a network server, the Corresponding Source may be on a different server (operated by you or a third party) that supports equivalent copying facilities, provided you maintain clear directions next to the object code saying where to find the Corresponding Source. Regardless of what server hosts the Corresponding Source, you remain obligated to ensure that it is available for as long as needed to satisfy these requirements.

e. Convey the object code using peer-to-peer transmission, provided you inform other peers where the object code and Corresponding Source of the work are being offered to the general public at no charge under subsection 6d.

A separable portion of the object code, whose source code is excluded from the Corresponding Source as a System Library, need not be included in conveying the object code work.

A "User Product" is either (1) a "consumer product", which means any tangible personal property which is normally used for personal, family, or household purposes, or (2) anything designed or sold for incorporation into a dwelling. In determining whether a product is a consumer product, doubtful cases shall be resolved in favor of coverage. For a particular product received by a particular user, "normally used" refers to a typical or common use of that class of product, regardless of the status of the particular user or of the way in which the particular user actually uses, or expects or is expected to use, the product. A product is a consumer product regardless of whether the product has substantial commercial, industrial or non-consumer uses, unless such uses represent the only significant mode of use of the product.

"Installation Information" for a User Product means any methods, procedures, authorization keys, or other information required to install and execute modified versions of a covered work in that User Product from a modified version of its Corresponding Source.

The information must suffice to ensure that the continued functioning of the modified object code is in no case prevented or interfered with solely because modification has been made.

If you convey an object code work under this section in, or with, or specifically for use in, a User Product, and the conveying occurs as part of a transaction in which the right of possession and use of the User Product is transferred to the recipient in perpetuity or for a fixed term (regardless of how the transaction is characterized), the Corresponding Source conveyed under this section must be accompanied by the Installation Information. But this requirement does not apply if neither you nor any third party retains the ability to install modified object code on the User Product (for example, the work has been installed in ROM).

The requirement to provide Installation Information does not include a requirement to continue to provide support service, warranty, or updates for a work that has been modified or installed by the recipient, or for the User Product in which it has been modified or installed. Access to a network may be denied when the modification itself materially and adversely affects the operation of the network or violates the rules and protocols for communication across the network.

Corresponding Source conveyed, and Installation Information provided, in accord with this section must be in a format that is publicly documented (and with an implementation available to the public in source code form), and must require no special password or key for unpacking, reading or copying.

7. Additional Terms.

    "Additional permissions" are terms that supplement the terms of this License by making exceptions from one or more of its conditions. Additional permissions that are applicable to the entire Program shall be treated as though they were included in this License, to the extent that they are valid under applicable law. If additional permissions apply only to part of the Program, that part may be used separately under those permissions, but the entire Program remains governed by this License without regard to the additional permissions.

    When you convey a copy of a covered work, you may at your option remove any additional permissions from that copy, or from any part of it. (Additional permissions may be written to require their own removal in certain cases when you modify the work.) You may place additional permissions on material, added by you to a covered work, for which you have or can give appropriate copyright permission.

    Notwithstanding any other provision of this License, for material you add to a covered work, you may (if authorized by the copyright holders of that material) supplement the terms of this License with terms:

    a. Disclaiming warranty or limiting liability differently from the terms of sections 15 and 16 of this License; or

    b. Requiring preservation of specified reasonable legal notices or author attributions in that material or in the Appropriate Legal Notices displayed by works containing it; or

    c. Prohibiting misrepresentation of the origin of that material, or requiring that modified versions of such material be marked in reasonable ways as different from the original version; or

d. Limiting the use for publicity purposes of names of licensors or authors of the material; or

e. Declining to grant rights under trademark law for use of some trade names, trademarks, or service marks; or

f. Requiring indemnification of licensors and authors of that material by anyone who conveys the material (or modified versions of it) with contractual assumptions of liability to the recipient, for any liability that these contractual assumptions directly impose on those licensors and authors.

All other non-permissive additional terms are considered "further restrictions" within the meaning of section 10. If the Program as you received it, or any part of it, contains a notice stating that it is governed by this License along with a term that is a further restriction, you may remove that term. If a license document contains a further restriction but permits relicensing or conveying under this License, you may add to a covered work material governed by the terms of that license document, provided that the further restriction does not survive such relicensing or conveying.

If you add terms to a covered work in accord with this section, you must place, in the relevant source files, a statement of the additional terms that apply to those files, or a notice indicating where to find the applicable terms.

Additional terms, permissive or non-permissive, may be stated in the form of a separately written license, or stated as exceptions; the above requirements apply either way.

8. Termination.

You may not propagate or modify a covered work except as expressly provided under this License. Any attempt otherwise to propagate or modify it is void, and will automatically terminate your rights under this License (including any patent licenses granted under the third paragraph of section 11).

However, if you cease all violation of this License, then your license from a particular copyright holder is reinstated (a) provisionally, unless and until the copyright holder explicitly and finally terminates your license, and (b) permanently, if the copyright holder fails to notify you of the violation by some reasonable means prior to 60 days after the cessation.

Moreover, your license from a particular copyright holder is reinstated permanently if the copyright holder notifies you of the violation by some reasonable means, this is the first time you have received notice of violation of this License (for any work) from that copyright holder, and you cure the violation prior to 30 days after your receipt of the notice.

Termination of your rights under this section does not terminate the licenses of parties who have received copies or rights from you under this License. If your rights have been terminated and not permanently reinstated, you do not qualify to receive new licenses for the same material under section 10.

9. Acceptance Not Required for Having Copies.

You are not required to accept this License in order to receive or run a copy of the Program. Ancillary propagation of a covered work occurring solely as a consequence of using peer-to-peer transmission to receive a copy likewise does not require acceptance.

However, nothing other than this License grants you permission to propagate or modify any covered work. These actions infringe copyright if you do not accept this License. Therefore, by modifying or propagating a covered work, you indicate your acceptance of this License to do so.

10. Automatic Licensing of Downstream Recipients.

    Each time you convey a covered work, the recipient automatically receives a license from the original licensors, to run, modify and propagate that work, subject to this License. You are not responsible for enforcing compliance by third parties with this License.

    An "entity transaction" is a transaction transferring control of an organization, or substantially all assets of one, or subdividing an organization, or merging organizations. If propagation of a covered work results from an entity transaction, each party to that transaction who receives a copy of the work also receives whatever licenses to the work the party's predecessor in interest had or could give under the previous paragraph, plus a right to possession of the Corresponding Source of the work from the predecessor in interest, if the predecessor has it or can get it with reasonable efforts.

    You may not impose any further restrictions on the exercise of the rights granted or affirmed under this License. For example, you may not impose a license fee, royalty, or other charge for exercise of rights granted under this License, and you may not initiate litigation (including a cross-claim or counterclaim in a lawsuit) alleging that any patent claim is infringed by making, using, selling, offering for sale, or importing the Program or any portion of it.

11. Patents.

    A "contributor" is a copyright holder who authorizes use under this License of the Program or a work on which the Program is based. The work thus licensed is called the contributor's "contributor version".

    A contributor's "essential patent claims" are all patent claims owned or controlled by the contributor, whether already acquired or hereafter acquired, that would be infringed by some manner, permitted by this License, of making, using, or selling its contributor version, but do not include claims that would be infringed only as a consequence of further modification of the contributor version. For purposes of this definition, "control" includes the right to grant patent sublicenses in a manner consistent with the requirements of this License.

    Each contributor grants you a non-exclusive, worldwide, royalty-free patent license under the contributor's essential patent claims, to make, use, sell, offer for sale, import and otherwise run, modify and propagate the contents of its contributor version.

    In the following three paragraphs, a "patent license" is any express agreement or commitment, however denominated, not to enforce a patent (such as an express permission to practice a patent or covenant not to sue for patent infringement). To "grant" such a patent license to a party means to make such an agreement or commitment not to enforce a patent against the party.

    If you convey a covered work, knowingly relying on a patent license, and the Corresponding Source of the work is not available for anyone to copy, free of charge and under the terms of this License, through a publicly available network server or other readily accessible means, then you must either (1) cause the Corresponding Source to be so available, or (2) arrange to deprive yourself of the benefit of the patent license for this particular work, or (3) arrange, in a manner consistent with the requirements of this License, to extend the patent license to downstream recipients. "Knowingly relying" means you have actual knowledge that, but for the patent license, your conveying the covered work in a country, or your recipient's use of the covered work in a country, would infringe one or more identifiable patents in that country that you have reason to believe are valid.

If, pursuant to or in connection with a single transaction or arrangement, you convey, or propagate by procuring conveyance of, a covered work, and grant a patent license to some of the parties receiving the covered work authorizing them to use, propagate, modify or convey a specific copy of the covered work, then the patent license you grant is automatically extended to all recipients of the covered work and works based on it.

A patent license is "discriminatory" if it does not include within the scope of its coverage, prohibits the exercise of, or is conditioned on the non-exercise of one or more of the rights that are specifically granted under this License. You may not convey a covered work if you are a party to an arrangement with a third party that is in the business of distributing software, under which you make payment to the third party based on the extent of your activity of conveying the work, and under which the third party grants, to any of the parties who would receive the covered work from you, a discriminatory patent license (a) in connection with copies of the covered work conveyed by you (or copies made from those copies), or (b) primarily for and in connection with specific products or compilations that contain the covered work, unless you entered into that arrangement, or that patent license was granted, prior to 28 March 2007.

Nothing in this License shall be construed as excluding or limiting any implied license or other defenses to infringement that may otherwise be available to you under applicable patent law.

12. No Surrender of Others' Freedom.

    If conditions are imposed on you (whether by court order, agreement or otherwise) that contradict the conditions of this License, they do not excuse you from the conditions of this License. If you cannot convey a covered work so as to satisfy simultaneously your obligations under this License and any other pertinent obligations, then as a consequence you may not convey it at all. For example, if you agree to terms that obligate you to collect a royalty for further conveying from those to whom you convey the Program, the only way you could satisfy both those terms and this License would be to refrain entirely from conveying the Program.

13. Use with the GNU Affero General Public License.

    Notwithstanding any other provision of this License, you have permission to link or combine any covered work with a work licensed under version 3 of the GNU Affero General Public License into a single combined work, and to convey the resulting work. The terms of this License will continue to apply to the part which is the covered work, but the special requirements of the GNU Affero General Public License, section 13, concerning interaction through a network will apply to the combination as such.

14. Revised Versions of this License.

The Free Software Foundation may publish revised and/or new versions of the GNU General Public License from time to time. Such new versions will be similar in spirit to the present version, but may differ in detail to address new problems or concerns.

Each version is given a distinguishing version number. If the Program specifies that a certain numbered version of the GNU General Public License "or any later version" applies to it, you have the option of following the terms and conditions either of that numbered version or of any later version published by the Free Software Foundation. If the Program does not specify a version number of the GNU General Public License, you may choose any version ever published by the Free Software Foundation.

If the Program specifies that a proxy can decide which future versions of the GNU General Public License can be used, that proxy's public statement of acceptance of a version permanently authorizes you to choose that version for the Program.

Later license versions may give you additional or different permissions. However, no additional obligations are imposed on any author or copyright holder as a result of your choosing to follow a later version.

15. Disclaimer of Warranty.

    THERE IS NO WARRANTY FOR THE PROGRAM, TO THE EXTENT PERMITTED BY APPLICABLE LAW. EXCEPT WHEN OTHERWISE STATED IN WRITING THE COPYRIGHT HOLDERS AND/OR OTHER PARTIES PROVIDE THE PROGRAM "AS IS" WITHOUT WARRANTY OF ANY KIND, EITHER EXPRESSED OR IMPLIED, INCLUDING, BUT NOT LIMITED TO, THE IMPLIED WARRANTIES OF MERCHANTABILITY AND FITNESS FOR A PARTICULAR PURPOSE. THE ENTIRE RISK AS TO THE QUALITY AND PERFORMANCE OF THE PROGRAM IS WITH YOU. SHOULD THE PROGRAM PROVE DEFECTIVE, YOU ASSUME THE COST OF ALL NECESSARY SERVICING, REPAIR OR CORRECTION.

16. Limitation of Liability.

    IN NO EVENT UNLESS REQUIRED BY APPLICABLE LAW OR AGREED TO IN WRITING WILL ANY COPYRIGHT HOLDER, OR ANY OTHER PARTY WHO MODIFIES AND/OR CONVEYS THE PROGRAM AS PERMITTED ABOVE, BE LIABLE TO YOU FOR DAMAGES, INCLUDING ANY GENERAL, SPECIAL, INCIDENTAL OR CONSEQUENTIAL DAMAGES ARISING OUT OF THE USE OR INABILITY TO USE THE PROGRAM (INCLUDING BUT NOT LIMITED TO LOSS OF DATA OR DATA BEING RENDERED INACCURATE OR LOSSES SUSTAINED BY YOU OR THIRD PARTIES OR A FAILURE OF THE PROGRAM TO OPERATE WITH ANY OTHER PROGRAMS), EVEN IF SUCH HOLDER OR OTHER PARTY HAS BEEN ADVISED OF THE POSSIBILITY OF SUCH DAMAGES.

17. Interpretation of Sections 15 and 16.

    If the disclaimer of warranty and limitation of liability provided above cannot be given local legal effect according to their terms, reviewing courts shall apply local law that most closely approximates an absolute waiver of all civil liability in connection with the Program, unless a warranty or assumption of liability accompanies a copy of the Program in return for a fee.

END OF TERMS AND CONDITIONS

How to Apply These Terms to Your New Programs

If you develop a new program, and you want it to be of the greatest possible use to the public, the best way to achieve this is to make it free software which everyone can redistribute and change under these terms.

To do so, attach the following notices to the program. It is safest to attach them to the start of each source file to most effectively state the exclusion of warranty; and each file should have at least the "copyright" line and a pointer to where the full notice is found.

```
one line to give the program's name and a brief idea of what it does.
Copyright (C) year name of author

This program is free software: you can redistribute it and/or modify
it under the terms of the GNU General Public License as published by
the Free Software Foundation, either version 3 of the License, or (at
your option) any later version.

This program is distributed in the hope that it will be useful, but
WITHOUT ANY WARRANTY; without even the implied warranty of
MERCHANTABILITY or FITNESS FOR A PARTICULAR PURPOSE.  See the GNU
General Public License for more details.

You should have received a copy of the GNU General Public License
along with this program.  If not, see http://www.gnu.org/licenses/.
```

Also add information on how to contact you by electronic and paper mail.

If the program does terminal interaction, make it output a short notice like this when it starts in an interactive mode:

```
program Copyright (C) year name of author
This program comes with ABSOLUTELY NO WARRANTY; for details type 'show w'.
This is free software, and you are welcome to redistribute it
under certain conditions; type 'show c' for details.
```

The hypothetical commands 'show w' and 'show c' should show the appropriate parts of the General Public License. Of course, your program's commands might be different; for a GUI interface, you would use an "about box".

You should also get your employer (if you work as a programmer) or school, if any, to sign a "copyright disclaimer" for the program, if necessary. For more information on this, and how to apply and follow the GNU GPL, see http://www.gnu.org/licenses/.

The GNU General Public License does not permit incorporating your program into proprietary programs. If your program is a subroutine library, you may consider it more useful to permit linking proprietary applications with the library. If this is what you want to do, use the GNU Lesser General Public License instead of this License. But first, please read http://www.gnu.org/philosophy/why-not-lgpl.html.

GNU Free Documentation License

Version 1.3, 3 November 2008

Copyright © 2000, 2001, 2002, 2007, 2008 Free Software Foundation, Inc.
http://fsf.org/

Everyone is permitted to copy and distribute verbatim copies
of this license document, but changing it is not allowed.

0. PREAMBLE

   The purpose of this License is to make a manual, textbook, or other functional and useful document *free* in the sense of freedom: to assure everyone the effective freedom to copy and redistribute it, with or without modifying it, either commercially or noncommercially. Secondarily, this License preserves for the author and publisher a way to get credit for their work, while not being considered responsible for modifications made by others.

   This License is a kind of "copyleft", which means that derivative works of the document must themselves be free in the same sense. It complements the GNU General Public License, which is a copyleft license designed for free software.

   We have designed this License in order to use it for manuals for free software, because free software needs free documentation: a free program should come with manuals providing the same freedoms that the software does. But this License is not limited to software manuals; it can be used for any textual work, regardless of subject matter or whether it is published as a printed book. We recommend this License principally for works whose purpose is instruction or reference.

1. APPLICABILITY AND DEFINITIONS

   This License applies to any manual or other work, in any medium, that contains a notice placed by the copyright holder saying it can be distributed under the terms of this License. Such a notice grants a world-wide, royalty-free license, unlimited in duration, to use that work under the conditions stated herein. The "Document", below, refers to any such manual or work. Any member of the public is a licensee, and is addressed as "you". You accept the license if you copy, modify or distribute the work in a way requiring permission under copyright law.

   A "Modified Version" of the Document means any work containing the Document or a portion of it, either copied verbatim, or with modifications and/or translated into another language.

   A "Secondary Section" is a named appendix or a front-matter section of the Document that deals exclusively with the relationship of the publishers or authors of the Document to the Document's overall subject (or to related matters) and contains nothing that could fall directly within that overall subject. (Thus, if the Document is in part a textbook of mathematics, a Secondary Section may not explain any mathematics.) The relationship could be a matter of historical connection with the subject or with related matters, or of legal, commercial, philosophical, ethical or political position regarding them.

   The "Invariant Sections" are certain Secondary Sections whose titles are designated, as being those of Invariant Sections, in the notice that says that the Document is released under this License. If a section does not fit the above definition of Secondary then it is not allowed to be designated as Invariant. The Document may contain zero Invariant Sections. If the Document does not identify any Invariant Sections then there are none.

The "Cover Texts" are certain short passages of text that are listed, as Front-Cover Texts or Back-Cover Texts, in the notice that says that the Document is released under this License. A Front-Cover Text may be at most 5 words, and a Back-Cover Text may be at most 25 words.

A "Transparent" copy of the Document means a machine-readable copy, represented in a format whose specification is available to the general public, that is suitable for revising the document straightforwardly with generic text editors or (for images composed of pixels) generic paint programs or (for drawings) some widely available drawing editor, and that is suitable for input to text formatters or for automatic translation to a variety of formats suitable for input to text formatters. A copy made in an otherwise Transparent file format whose markup, or absence of markup, has been arranged to thwart or discourage subsequent modification by readers is not Transparent. An image format is not Transparent if used for any substantial amount of text. A copy that is not "Transparent" is called "Opaque".

Examples of suitable formats for Transparent copies include plain ASCII without markup, Texinfo input format, LaTeX input format, SGML or XML using a publicly available DTD, and standard-conforming simple HTML, PostScript or PDF designed for human modification. Examples of transparent image formats include PNG, XCF and JPG. Opaque formats include proprietary formats that can be read and edited only by proprietary word processors, SGML or XML for which the DTD and/or processing tools are not generally available, and the machine-generated HTML, PostScript or PDF produced by some word processors for output purposes only.

The "Title Page" means, for a printed book, the title page itself, plus such following pages as are needed to hold, legibly, the material this License requires to appear in the title page. For works in formats which do not have any title page as such, "Title Page" means the text near the most prominent appearance of the work's title, preceding the beginning of the body of the text.

The "publisher" means any person or entity that distributes copies of the Document to the public.

A section "Entitled XYZ" means a named subunit of the Document whose title either is precisely XYZ or contains XYZ in parentheses following text that translates XYZ in another language. (Here XYZ stands for a specific section name mentioned below, such as "Acknowledgements", "Dedications", "Endorsements", or "History".) To "Preserve the Title" of such a section when you modify the Document means that it remains a section "Entitled XYZ" according to this definition.

The Document may include Warranty Disclaimers next to the notice which states that this License applies to the Document. These Warranty Disclaimers are considered to be included by reference in this License, but only as regards disclaiming warranties: any other implication that these Warranty Disclaimers may have is void and has no effect on the meaning of this License.

2. VERBATIM COPYING

You may copy and distribute the Document in any medium, either commercially or noncommercially, provided that this License, the copyright notices, and the license notice saying this License applies to the Document are reproduced in all copies, and that you add no other conditions whatsoever to those of this License. You may not use technical measures to obstruct or control the reading or further copying of the copies you make or distribute. However, you may accept compensation in exchange for copies. If you distribute a large enough number of copies you must also follow the conditions in section 3.

You may also lend copies, under the same conditions stated above, and you may publicly display copies.

3. COPYING IN QUANTITY

    If you publish printed copies (or copies in media that commonly have printed covers) of the Document, numbering more than 100, and the Document's license notice requires Cover Texts, you must enclose the copies in covers that carry, clearly and legibly, all these Cover Texts: Front-Cover Texts on the front cover, and Back-Cover Texts on the back cover. Both covers must also clearly and legibly identify you as the publisher of these copies. The front cover must present the full title with all words of the title equally prominent and visible. You may add other material on the covers in addition. Copying with changes limited to the covers, as long as they preserve the title of the Document and satisfy these conditions, can be treated as verbatim copying in other respects.

    If the required texts for either cover are too voluminous to fit legibly, you should put the first ones listed (as many as fit reasonably) on the actual cover, and continue the rest onto adjacent pages.

    If you publish or distribute Opaque copies of the Document numbering more than 100, you must either include a machine-readable Transparent copy along with each Opaque copy, or state in or with each Opaque copy a computer-network location from which the general network-using public has access to download using public-standard network protocols a complete Transparent copy of the Document, free of added material. If you use the latter option, you must take reasonably prudent steps, when you begin distribution of Opaque copies in quantity, to ensure that this Transparent copy will remain thus accessible at the stated location until at least one year after the last time you distribute an Opaque copy (directly or through your agents or retailers) of that edition to the public.

    It is requested, but not required, that you contact the authors of the Document well before redistributing any large number of copies, to give them a chance to provide you with an updated version of the Document.

4. MODIFICATIONS

    You may copy and distribute a Modified Version of the Document under the conditions of sections 2 and 3 above, provided that you release the Modified Version under precisely this License, with the Modified Version filling the role of the Document, thus licensing distribution and modification of the Modified Version to whoever possesses a copy of it. In addition, you must do these things in the Modified Version:

    A. Use in the Title Page (and on the covers, if any) a title distinct from that of the Document, and from those of previous versions (which should, if there were any,

be listed in the History section of the Document). You may use the same title as
a previous version if the original publisher of that version gives permission.

B. List on the Title Page, as authors, one or more persons or entities responsible for
authorship of the modifications in the Modified Version, together with at least five
of the principal authors of the Document (all of its principal authors, if it has fewer
than five), unless they release you from this requirement.

C. State on the Title page the name of the publisher of the Modified Version, as the
publisher.

D. Preserve all the copyright notices of the Document.

E. Add an appropriate copyright notice for your modifications adjacent to the other
copyright notices.

F. Include, immediately after the copyright notices, a license notice giving the public
permission to use the Modified Version under the terms of this License, in the form
shown in the Addendum below.

G. Preserve in that license notice the full lists of Invariant Sections and required Cover
Texts given in the Document's license notice.

H. Include an unaltered copy of this License.

I. Preserve the section Entitled "History", Preserve its Title, and add to it an item
stating at least the title, year, new authors, and publisher of the Modified Version
as given on the Title Page. If there is no section Entitled "History" in the Document, create one stating the title, year, authors, and publisher of the Document
as given on its Title Page, then add an item describing the Modified Version as
stated in the previous sentence.

J. Preserve the network location, if any, given in the Document for public access to
a Transparent copy of the Document, and likewise the network locations given in
the Document for previous versions it was based on. These may be placed in the
"History" section. You may omit a network location for a work that was published
at least four years before the Document itself, or if the original publisher of the
version it refers to gives permission.

K. For any section Entitled "Acknowledgements" or "Dedications", Preserve the Title
of the section, and preserve in the section all the substance and tone of each of the
contributor acknowledgements and/or dedications given therein.

L. Preserve all the Invariant Sections of the Document, unaltered in their text and
in their titles. Section numbers or the equivalent are not considered part of the
section titles.

M. Delete any section Entitled "Endorsements". Such a section may not be included
in the Modified Version.

N. Do not retitle any existing section to be Entitled "Endorsements" or to conflict in
title with any Invariant Section.

O. Preserve any Warranty Disclaimers.

If the Modified Version includes new front-matter sections or appendices that qualify
as Secondary Sections and contain no material copied from the Document, you may at
your option designate some or all of these sections as invariant. To do this, add their

titles to the list of Invariant Sections in the Modified Version's license notice. These titles must be distinct from any other section titles.

You may add a section Entitled "Endorsements", provided it contains nothing but endorsements of your Modified Version by various parties—for example, statements of peer review or that the text has been approved by an organization as the authoritative definition of a standard.

You may add a passage of up to five words as a Front-Cover Text, and a passage of up to 25 words as a Back-Cover Text, to the end of the list of Cover Texts in the Modified Version. Only one passage of Front-Cover Text and one of Back-Cover Text may be added by (or through arrangements made by) any one entity. If the Document already includes a cover text for the same cover, previously added by you or by arrangement made by the same entity you are acting on behalf of, you may not add another; but you may replace the old one, on explicit permission from the previous publisher that added the old one.

The author(s) and publisher(s) of the Document do not by this License give permission to use their names for publicity for or to assert or imply endorsement of any Modified Version.

5. COMBINING DOCUMENTS

    You may combine the Document with other documents released under this License, under the terms defined in section 4 above for modified versions, provided that you include in the combination all of the Invariant Sections of all of the original documents, unmodified, and list them all as Invariant Sections of your combined work in its license notice, and that you preserve all their Warranty Disclaimers.

    The combined work need only contain one copy of this License, and multiple identical Invariant Sections may be replaced with a single copy. If there are multiple Invariant Sections with the same name but different contents, make the title of each such section unique by adding at the end of it, in parentheses, the name of the original author or publisher of that section if known, or else a unique number. Make the same adjustment to the section titles in the list of Invariant Sections in the license notice of the combined work.

    In the combination, you must combine any sections Entitled "History" in the various original documents, forming one section Entitled "History"; likewise combine any sections Entitled "Acknowledgements", and any sections Entitled "Dedications". You must delete all sections Entitled "Endorsements."

6. COLLECTIONS OF DOCUMENTS

    You may make a collection consisting of the Document and other documents released under this License, and replace the individual copies of this License in the various documents with a single copy that is included in the collection, provided that you follow the rules of this License for verbatim copying of each of the documents in all other respects.

    You may extract a single document from such a collection, and distribute it individually under this License, provided you insert a copy of this License into the extracted document, and follow this License in all other respects regarding verbatim copying of that document.

7. AGGREGATION WITH INDEPENDENT WORKS

   A compilation of the Document or its derivatives with other separate and independent documents or works, in or on a volume of a storage or distribution medium, is called an "aggregate" if the copyright resulting from the compilation is not used to limit the legal rights of the compilation's users beyond what the individual works permit. When the Document is included in an aggregate, this License does not apply to the other works in the aggregate which are not themselves derivative works of the Document.

   If the Cover Text requirement of section 3 is applicable to these copies of the Document, then if the Document is less than one half of the entire aggregate, the Document's Cover Texts may be placed on covers that bracket the Document within the aggregate, or the electronic equivalent of covers if the Document is in electronic form. Otherwise they must appear on printed covers that bracket the whole aggregate.

8. TRANSLATION

   Translation is considered a kind of modification, so you may distribute translations of the Document under the terms of section 4. Replacing Invariant Sections with translations requires special permission from their copyright holders, but you may include translations of some or all Invariant Sections in addition to the original versions of these Invariant Sections. You may include a translation of this License, and all the license notices in the Document, and any Warranty Disclaimers, provided that you also include the original English version of this License and the original versions of those notices and disclaimers. In case of a disagreement between the translation and the original version of this License or a notice or disclaimer, the original version will prevail.

   If a section in the Document is Entitled "Acknowledgements", "Dedications", or "History", the requirement (section 4) to Preserve its Title (section 1) will typically require changing the actual title.

9. TERMINATION

   You may not copy, modify, sublicense, or distribute the Document except as expressly provided under this License. Any attempt otherwise to copy, modify, sublicense, or distribute it is void, and will automatically terminate your rights under this License.

   However, if you cease all violation of this License, then your license from a particular copyright holder is reinstated (a) provisionally, unless and until the copyright holder explicitly and finally terminates your license, and (b) permanently, if the copyright holder fails to notify you of the violation by some reasonable means prior to 60 days after the cessation.

   Moreover, your license from a particular copyright holder is reinstated permanently if the copyright holder notifies you of the violation by some reasonable means, this is the first time you have received notice of violation of this License (for any work) from that copyright holder, and you cure the violation prior to 30 days after your receipt of the notice.

   Termination of your rights under this section does not terminate the licenses of parties who have received copies or rights from you under this License. If your rights have been terminated and not permanently reinstated, receipt of a copy of some or all of the same material does not give you any rights to use it.

10. FUTURE REVISIONS OF THIS LICENSE

    The Free Software Foundation may publish new, revised versions of the GNU Free Documentation License from time to time. Such new versions will be similar in spirit to the present version, but may differ in detail to address new problems or concerns. See http://www.gnu.org/copyleft/.

    Each version of the License is given a distinguishing version number. If the Document specifies that a particular numbered version of this License "or any later version" applies to it, you have the option of following the terms and conditions either of that specified version or of any later version that has been published (not as a draft) by the Free Software Foundation. If the Document does not specify a version number of this License, you may choose any version ever published (not as a draft) by the Free Software Foundation. If the Document specifies that a proxy can decide which future versions of this License can be used, that proxy's public statement of acceptance of a version permanently authorizes you to choose that version for the Document.

11. RELICENSING

    "Massive Multiauthor Collaboration Site" (or "MMC Site") means any World Wide Web server that publishes copyrightable works and also provides prominent facilities for anybody to edit those works. A public wiki that anybody can edit is an example of such a server. A "Massive Multiauthor Collaboration" (or "MMC") contained in the site means any set of copyrightable works thus published on the MMC site.

    "CC-BY-SA" means the Creative Commons Attribution-Share Alike 3.0 license published by Creative Commons Corporation, a not-for-profit corporation with a principal place of business in San Francisco, California, as well as future copyleft versions of that license published by that same organization.

    "Incorporate" means to publish or republish a Document, in whole or in part, as part of another Document.

    An MMC is "eligible for relicensing" if it is licensed under this License, and if all works that were first published under this License somewhere other than this MMC, and subsequently incorporated in whole or in part into the MMC, (1) had no cover texts or invariant sections, and (2) were thus incorporated prior to November 1, 2008.

    The operator of an MMC Site may republish an MMC contained in the site under CC-BY-SA on the same site at any time before August 1, 2009, provided the MMC is eligible for relicensing.

ADDENDUM: How to use this License for your documents

To use this License in a document you have written, include a copy of the License in the document and put the following copyright and license notices just after the title page:

```
Copyright (C)  year  your name.
Permission is granted to copy, distribute and/or modify this document
under the terms of the GNU Free Documentation License, Version 1.3
or any later version published by the Free Software Foundation;
with no Invariant Sections, no Front-Cover Texts, and no Back-Cover
Texts.  A copy of the license is included in the section entitled ``GNU
Free Documentation License''.
```

If you have Invariant Sections, Front-Cover Texts and Back-Cover Texts, replace the "with...Texts." line with this:

```
with the Invariant Sections being list their titles, with
the Front-Cover Texts being list, and with the Back-Cover Texts
being list.
```

If you have Invariant Sections without Cover Texts, or some other combination of the three, merge those two alternatives to suit the situation.

If your document contains nontrivial examples of program code, we recommend releasing these examples in parallel under your choice of free software license, such as the GNU General Public License, to permit their use in free software.

Contributors to GCC

The GCC project would like to thank its many contributors. Without them the project would not have been nearly as successful as it has been. Any omissions in this list are accidental. Feel free to contact law@redhat.com or gerald@pfeifer.com if you have been left out or some of your contributions are not listed. Please keep this list in alphabetical order.

- Analog Devices helped implement the support for complex data types and iterators.
- John David Anglin for threading-related fixes and improvements to libstdc++-v3, and the HP-UX port.
- James van Artsdalen wrote the code that makes efficient use of the Intel 80387 register stack.
- Abramo and Roberto Bagnara for the SysV68 Motorola 3300 Delta Series port.
- Alasdair Baird for various bug fixes.
- Giovanni Bajo for analyzing lots of complicated C++ problem reports.
- Peter Barada for his work to improve code generation for new ColdFire cores.
- Gerald Baumgartner added the signature extension to the C++ front end.
- Godmar Back for his Java improvements and encouragement.
- Scott Bambrough for help porting the Java compiler.
- Wolfgang Bangerth for processing tons of bug reports.
- Jon Beniston for his Microsoft Windows port of Java and port to Lattice Mico32.
- Daniel Berlin for better DWARF 2 support, faster/better optimizations, improved alias analysis, plus migrating GCC to Bugzilla.
- Geoff Berry for his Java object serialization work and various patches.
- David Binderman tests weekly snapshots of GCC trunk against Fedora Rawhide for several architectures.
- Laurynas Biveinis for memory management work and DJGPP port fixes.
- Uros Bizjak for the implementation of x87 math built-in functions and for various middle end and i386 back end improvements and bug fixes.
- Eric Blake for helping to make GCJ and libgcj conform to the specifications.
- Janne Blomqvist for contributions to GNU Fortran.
- Hans-J. Boehm for his garbage collector, IA-64 libffi port, and other Java work.
- Segher Boessenkool for helping maintain the PowerPC port and the instruction combiner plus various contributions to the middle end.
- Neil Booth for work on cpplib, lang hooks, debug hooks and other miscellaneous cleanups.
- Steven Bosscher for integrating the GNU Fortran front end into GCC and for contributing to the tree-ssa branch.
- Eric Botcazou for fixing middle- and backend bugs left and right.
- Per Bothner for his direction via the steering committee and various improvements to the infrastructure for supporting new languages. Chill front end implementation.

Initial implementations of cpplib, fix-header, config.guess, libio, and past C++ library (libg++) maintainer. Dreaming up, designing and implementing much of GCJ.

- Devon Bowen helped port GCC to the Tahoe.
- Don Bowman for mips-vxworks contributions.
- James Bowman for the FT32 port.
- Dave Brolley for work on cpplib and Chill.
- Paul Brook for work on the ARM architecture and maintaining GNU Fortran.
- Robert Brown implemented the support for Encore 32000 systems.
- Christian Bruel for improvements to local store elimination.
- Herman A.J. ten Brugge for various fixes.
- Joerg Brunsmann for Java compiler hacking and help with the GCJ FAQ.
- Joe Buck for his direction via the steering committee from its creation to 2013.
- Craig Burley for leadership of the G77 Fortran effort.
- Tobias Burnus for contributions to GNU Fortran.
- Stephan Buys for contributing Doxygen notes for libstdc++.
- Paolo Carlini for libstdc++ work: lots of efficiency improvements to the C++ strings, streambufs and formatted I/O, hard detective work on the frustrating localization issues, and keeping up with the problem reports.
- John Carr for his alias work, SPARC hacking, infrastructure improvements, previous contributions to the steering committee, loop optimizations, etc.
- Stephane Carrez for 68HC11 and 68HC12 ports.
- Steve Chamberlain for support for the Renesas SH and H8 processors and the PicoJava processor, and for GCJ config fixes.
- Glenn Chambers for help with the GCJ FAQ.
- John-Marc Chandonia for various libgcj patches.
- Denis Chertykov for contributing and maintaining the AVR port, the first GCC port for an 8-bit architecture.
- Kito Cheng for his work on the RISC-V port, including bringing up the test suite and maintenance.
- Scott Christley for his Objective-C contributions.
- Eric Christopher for his Java porting help and clean-ups.
- Branko Cibej for more warning contributions.
- The GNU Classpath project for all of their merged runtime code.
- Nick Clifton for arm, mcore, fr30, v850, m32r, msp430 rx work, '`--help`', and other random hacking.
- Michael Cook for libstdc++ cleanup patches to reduce warnings.
- R. Kelley Cook for making GCC buildable from a read-only directory as well as other miscellaneous build process and documentation clean-ups.
- Ralf Corsepius for SH testing and minor bug fixing.
- François-Xavier Coudert for contributions to GNU Fortran.

Contributors to GCC

- Stan Cox for care and feeding of the x86 port and lots of behind the scenes hacking.
- Alex Crain provided changes for the 3b1.
- Ian Dall for major improvements to the NS32k port.
- Paul Dale for his work to add uClinux platform support to the m68k backend.
- Palmer Dabbelt for his work maintaining the RISC-V port.
- Dario Dariol contributed the four varieties of sample programs that print a copy of their source.
- Russell Davidson for fstream and stringstream fixes in libstdc++.
- Bud Davis for work on the G77 and GNU Fortran compilers.
- Mo DeJong for GCJ and libgcj bug fixes.
- Jerry DeLisle for contributions to GNU Fortran.
- DJ Delorie for the DJGPP port, build and libiberty maintenance, various bug fixes, and the M32C, MeP, MSP430, and RL78 ports.
- Arnaud Desitter for helping to debug GNU Fortran.
- Gabriel Dos Reis for contributions to G++, contributions and maintenance of GCC diagnostics infrastructure, libstdc++-v3, including `valarray<>`, `complex<>`, maintaining the numerics library (including that pesky `<limits>` :-) and keeping up-to-date anything to do with numbers.
- Ulrich Drepper for his work on glibc, testing of GCC using glibc, ISO C99 support, CFG dumping support, etc., plus support of the C++ runtime libraries including for all kinds of C interface issues, contributing and maintaining `complex<>`, sanity checking and disbursement, configuration architecture, libio maintenance, and early math work.
- François Dumont for his work on libstdc++-v3, especially maintaining and improving `debug-mode` and associative and unordered containers.
- Zdenek Dvorak for a new loop unroller and various fixes.
- Michael Eager for his work on the Xilinx MicroBlaze port.
- Richard Earnshaw for his ongoing work with the ARM.
- David Edelsohn for his direction via the steering committee, ongoing work with the RS6000/PowerPC port, help cleaning up Haifa loop changes, doing the entire AIX port of libstdc++ with his bare hands, and for ensuring GCC properly keeps working on AIX.
- Kevin Ediger for the floating point formatting of num_put::do_put in libstdc++.
- Phil Edwards for libstdc++ work including configuration hackery, documentation maintainer, chief breaker of the web pages, the occasional iostream bug fix, and work on shared library symbol versioning.
- Paul Eggert for random hacking all over GCC.
- Mark Elbrecht for various DJGPP improvements, and for libstdc++ configuration support for locales and fstream-related fixes.
- Vadim Egorov for libstdc++ fixes in strings, streambufs, and iostreams.
- Christian Ehrhardt for dealing with bug reports.
- Ben Elliston for his work to move the Objective-C runtime into its own subdirectory and for his work on autoconf.

- Revital Eres for work on the PowerPC 750CL port.
- Marc Espie for OpenBSD support.
- Doug Evans for much of the global optimization framework, arc, m32r, and SPARC work.
- Christopher Faylor for his work on the Cygwin port and for caring and feeding the gcc.gnu.org box and saving its users tons of spam.
- Fred Fish for BeOS support and Ada fixes.
- Ivan Fontes Garcia for the Portuguese translation of the GCJ FAQ.
- Peter Gerwinski for various bug fixes and the Pascal front end.
- Kaveh R. Ghazi for his direction via the steering committee, amazing work to make '-W -Wall -W* -Werror' useful, and testing GCC on a plethora of platforms. Kaveh extends his gratitude to the CAIP Center at Rutgers University for providing him with computing resources to work on Free Software from the late 1980s to 2010.
- John Gilmore for a donation to the FSF earmarked improving GNU Java.
- Judy Goldberg for c++ contributions.
- Torbjorn Granlund for various fixes and the c-torture testsuite, multiply- and divide-by-constant optimization, improved long long support, improved leaf function register allocation, and his direction via the steering committee.
- Jonny Grant for improvements to collect2's '--help' documentation.
- Anthony Green for his '-Os' contributions, the moxie port, and Java front end work.
- Stu Grossman for gdb hacking, allowing GCJ developers to debug Java code.
- Michael K. Gschwind contributed the port to the PDP-11.
- Richard Biener for his ongoing middle-end contributions and bug fixes and for release management.
- Ron Guilmette implemented the protoize and unprotoize tools, the support for DWARF 1 symbolic debugging information, and much of the support for System V Release 4. He has also worked heavily on the Intel 386 and 860 support.
- Sumanth Gundapaneni for contributing the CR16 port.
- Mostafa Hagog for Swing Modulo Scheduling (SMS) and post reload GCSE.
- Bruno Haible for improvements in the runtime overhead for EH, new warnings and assorted bug fixes.
- Andrew Haley for his amazing Java compiler and library efforts.
- Chris Hanson assisted in making GCC work on HP-UX for the 9000 series 300.
- Michael Hayes for various thankless work he's done trying to get the c30/c40 ports functional. Lots of loop and unroll improvements and fixes.
- Dara Hazeghi for wading through myriads of target-specific bug reports.
- Kate Hedstrom for staking the G77 folks with an initial testsuite.
- Richard Henderson for his ongoing SPARC, alpha, ia32, and ia64 work, loop opts, and generally fixing lots of old problems we've ignored for years, flow rewrite and lots of further stuff, including reviewing tons of patches.
- Aldy Hernandez for working on the PowerPC port, SIMD support, and various fixes.

Contributors to GCC 715

- Nobuyuki Hikichi of Software Research Associates, Tokyo, contributed the support for the Sony NEWS machine.
- Kazu Hirata for caring and feeding the Renesas H8/300 port and various fixes.
- Katherine Holcomb for work on GNU Fortran.
- Manfred Hollstein for his ongoing work to keep the m88k alive, lots of testing and bug fixing, particularly of GCC configury code.
- Steve Holmgren for MachTen patches.
- Mat Hostetter for work on the TILE-Gx and TILEPro ports.
- Jan Hubicka for his x86 port improvements.
- Falk Hueffner for working on C and optimization bug reports.
- Bernardo Innocenti for his m68k work, including merging of ColdFire improvements and uClinux support.
- Christian Iseli for various bug fixes.
- Kamil Iskra for general m68k hacking.
- Lee Iverson for random fixes and MIPS testing.
- Balaji V. Iyer for Cilk+ development and merging.
- Andreas Jaeger for testing and benchmarking of GCC and various bug fixes.
- Martin Jambor for his work on inter-procedural optimizations, the switch conversion pass, and scalar replacement of aggregates.
- Jakub Jelinek for his SPARC work and sibling call optimizations as well as lots of bug fixes and test cases, and for improving the Java build system.
- Janis Johnson for ia64 testing and fixes, her quality improvement sidetracks, and web page maintenance.
- Kean Johnston for SCO OpenServer support and various fixes.
- Tim Josling for the sample language treelang based originally on Richard Kenner's "toy" language.
- Nicolai Josuttis for additional libstdc++ documentation.
- Klaus Kaempf for his ongoing work to make alpha-vms a viable target.
- Steven G. Kargl for work on GNU Fortran.
- David Kashtan of SRI adapted GCC to VMS.
- Ryszard Kabatek for many, many libstdc++ bug fixes and optimizations of strings, especially member functions, and for auto_ptr fixes.
- Geoffrey Keating for his ongoing work to make the PPC work for GNU/Linux and his automatic regression tester.
- Brendan Kehoe for his ongoing work with G++ and for a lot of early work in just about every part of libstdc++.
- Oliver M. Kellogg of Deutsche Aerospace contributed the port to the MIL-STD-1750A.
- Richard Kenner of the New York University Ultracomputer Research Laboratory wrote the machine descriptions for the AMD 29000, the DEC Alpha, the IBM RT PC, and the IBM RS/6000 as well as the support for instruction attributes. He also made changes to better support RISC processors including changes to common subexpression

elimination, strength reduction, function calling sequence handling, and condition code support, in addition to generalizing the code for frame pointer elimination and delay slot scheduling. Richard Kenner was also the head maintainer of GCC for several years.

- Mumit Khan for various contributions to the Cygwin and Mingw32 ports and maintaining binary releases for Microsoft Windows hosts, and for massive libstdc++ porting work to Cygwin/Mingw32.
- Robin Kirkham for cpu32 support.
- Mark Klein for PA improvements.
- Thomas Koenig for various bug fixes.
- Bruce Korb for the new and improved fixincludes code.
- Benjamin Kosnik for his G++ work and for leading the libstdc++-v3 effort.
- Maxim Kuvyrkov for contributions to the instruction scheduler, the Android and m68k/Coldfire ports, and optimizations.
- Charles LaBrec contributed the support for the Integrated Solutions 68020 system.
- Asher Langton and Mike Kumbera for contributing Cray pointer support to GNU Fortran, and for other GNU Fortran improvements.
- Jeff Law for his direction via the steering committee, coordinating the entire egcs project and GCC 2.95, rolling out snapshots and releases, handling merges from GCC2, reviewing tons of patches that might have fallen through the cracks else, and random but extensive hacking.
- Walter Lee for work on the TILE-Gx and TILEPro ports.
- Marc Lehmann for his direction via the steering committee and helping with analysis and improvements of x86 performance.
- Victor Leikehman for work on GNU Fortran.
- Ted Lemon wrote parts of the RTL reader and printer.
- Kriang Lerdsuwanakij for C++ improvements including template as template parameter support, and many C++ fixes.
- Warren Levy for tremendous work on libgcj (Java Runtime Library) and random work on the Java front end.
- Alain Lichnewsky ported GCC to the MIPS CPU.
- Oskar Liljeblad for hacking on AWT and his many Java bug reports and patches.
- Robert Lipe for OpenServer support, new testsuites, testing, etc.
- Chen Liqin for various S+core related fixes/improvement, and for maintaining the S+core port.
- Weiwen Liu for testing and various bug fixes.
- Manuel López-Ibáñez for improving '-Wconversion' and many other diagnostics fixes and improvements.
- Dave Love for his ongoing work with the Fortran front end and runtime libraries.
- Martin von Löwis for internal consistency checking infrastructure, various C++ improvements including namespace support, and tons of assistance with libstdc++/compiler merges.

- H.J. Lu for his previous contributions to the steering committee, many x86 bug reports, prototype patches, and keeping the GNU/Linux ports working.
- Greg McGary for random fixes and (someday) bounded pointers.
- Andrew MacLeod for his ongoing work in building a real EH system, various code generation improvements, work on the global optimizer, etc.
- Vladimir Makarov for hacking some ugly i960 problems, PowerPC hacking improvements to compile-time performance, overall knowledge and direction in the area of instruction scheduling, and design and implementation of the automaton based instruction scheduler.
- Bob Manson for his behind the scenes work on dejagnu.
- John Marino for contributing the DragonFly BSD port.
- Philip Martin for lots of libstdc++ string and vector iterator fixes and improvements, and string clean up and testsuites.
- Michael Matz for his work on dominance tree discovery, the x86-64 port, link-time optimization framework and general optimization improvements.
- All of the Mauve project contributors for Java test code.
- Bryce McKinlay for numerous GCJ and libgcj fixes and improvements.
- Adam Megacz for his work on the Microsoft Windows port of GCJ.
- Michael Meissner for LRS framework, ia32, m32r, v850, m88k, MIPS, powerpc, haifa, ECOFF debug support, and other assorted hacking.
- Jason Merrill for his direction via the steering committee and leading the G++ effort.
- Martin Michlmayr for testing GCC on several architectures using the entire Debian archive.
- David Miller for his direction via the steering committee, lots of SPARC work, improvements in jump.c and interfacing with the Linux kernel developers.
- Gary Miller ported GCC to Charles River Data Systems machines.
- Alfred Minarik for libstdc++ string and ios bug fixes, and turning the entire libstdc++ testsuite namespace-compatible.
- Mark Mitchell for his direction via the steering committee, mountains of C++ work, load/store hoisting out of loops, alias analysis improvements, ISO C `restrict` support, and serving as release manager from 2000 to 2011.
- Alan Modra for various GNU/Linux bits and testing.
- Toon Moene for his direction via the steering committee, Fortran maintenance, and his ongoing work to make us make Fortran run fast.
- Jason Molenda for major help in the care and feeding of all the services on the gcc.gnu.org (formerly egcs.cygnus.com) machine—mail, web services, ftp services, etc etc. Doing all this work on scrap paper and the backs of envelopes would have been... difficult.
- Catherine Moore for fixing various ugly problems we have sent her way, including the haifa bug which was killing the Alpha & PowerPC Linux kernels.
- Mike Moreton for his various Java patches.
- David Mosberger-Tang for various Alpha improvements, and for the initial IA-64 port.

- Stephen Moshier contributed the floating point emulator that assists in cross-compilation and permits support for floating point numbers wider than 64 bits and for ISO C99 support.
- Bill Moyer for his behind the scenes work on various issues.
- Philippe De Muyter for his work on the m68k port.
- Joseph S. Myers for his work on the PDP-11 port, format checking and ISO C99 support, and continuous emphasis on (and contributions to) documentation.
- Nathan Myers for his work on libstdc++-v3: architecture and authorship through the first three snapshots, including implementation of locale infrastructure, string, shadow C headers, and the initial project documentation (DESIGN, CHECKLIST, and so forth). Later, more work on MT-safe string and shadow headers.
- Felix Natter for documentation on porting libstdc++.
- Nathanael Nerode for cleaning up the configuration/build process.
- NeXT, Inc. donated the front end that supports the Objective-C language.
- Hans-Peter Nilsson for the CRIS and MMIX ports, improvements to the search engine setup, various documentation fixes and other small fixes.
- Geoff Noer for his work on getting cygwin native builds working.
- Diego Novillo for his work on Tree SSA, OpenMP, SPEC performance tracking web pages, GIMPLE tuples, and assorted fixes.
- David O'Brien for the FreeBSD/alpha, FreeBSD/AMD x86-64, FreeBSD/ARM, FreeBSD/PowerPC, and FreeBSD/SPARC64 ports and related infrastructure improvements.
- Alexandre Oliva for various build infrastructure improvements, scripts and amazing testing work, including keeping libtool issues sane and happy.
- Stefan Olsson for work on mt_alloc.
- Melissa O'Neill for various NeXT fixes.
- Rainer Orth for random MIPS work, including improvements to GCC's o32 ABI support, improvements to dejagnu's MIPS support, Java configuration clean-ups and porting work, and maintaining the IRIX, Solaris 2, and Tru64 UNIX ports.
- Steven Pemberton for his contribution of 'enquire' which allowed GCC to determine various properties of the floating point unit and generate 'float.h' in older versions of GCC.
- Hartmut Penner for work on the s390 port.
- Paul Petersen wrote the machine description for the Alliant FX/8.
- Alexandre Petit-Bianco for implementing much of the Java compiler and continued Java maintainership.
- Matthias Pfaller for major improvements to the NS32k port.
- Gerald Pfeifer for his direction via the steering committee, pointing out lots of problems we need to solve, maintenance of the web pages, and taking care of documentation maintenance in general.
- Andrew Pinski for processing bug reports by the dozen.
- Ovidiu Predescu for his work on the Objective-C front end and runtime libraries.

- Jerry Quinn for major performance improvements in C++ formatted I/O.
- Ken Raeburn for various improvements to checker, MIPS ports and various cleanups in the compiler.
- Rolf W. Rasmussen for hacking on AWT.
- David Reese of Sun Microsystems contributed to the Solaris on PowerPC port.
- Volker Reichelt for keeping up with the problem reports.
- Joern Rennecke for maintaining the sh port, loop, regmove & reload hacking and developing and maintaining the Epiphany port.
- Loren J. Rittle for improvements to libstdc++-v3 including the FreeBSD port, threading fixes, thread-related configury changes, critical threading documentation, and solutions to really tricky I/O problems, as well as keeping GCC properly working on FreeBSD and continuous testing.
- Craig Rodrigues for processing tons of bug reports.
- Ola Rönnerup for work on mt_alloc.
- Gavin Romig-Koch for lots of behind the scenes MIPS work.
- David Ronis inspired and encouraged Craig to rewrite the G77 documentation in texinfo format by contributing a first pass at a translation of the old 'g77-0.5.16/f/DOC' file.
- Ken Rose for fixes to GCC's delay slot filling code.
- Ira Rosen for her contributions to the auto-vectorizer.
- Paul Rubin wrote most of the preprocessor.
- Pétur Runólfsson for major performance improvements in C++ formatted I/O and large file support in C++ filebuf.
- Chip Salzenberg for libstdc++ patches and improvements to locales, traits, Makefiles, libio, libtool hackery, and "long long" support.
- Juha Sarlin for improvements to the H8 code generator.
- Greg Satz assisted in making GCC work on HP-UX for the 9000 series 300.
- Roger Sayle for improvements to constant folding and GCC's RTL optimizers as well as for fixing numerous bugs.
- Bradley Schatz for his work on the GCJ FAQ.
- Peter Schauer wrote the code to allow debugging to work on the Alpha.
- William Schelter did most of the work on the Intel 80386 support.
- Tobias Schlüter for work on GNU Fortran.
- Bernd Schmidt for various code generation improvements and major work in the reload pass, serving as release manager for GCC 2.95.3, and work on the Blackfin and C6X ports.
- Peter Schmid for constant testing of libstdc++—especially application testing, going above and beyond what was requested for the release criteria—and libstdc++ header file tweaks.
- Jason Schroeder for jcf-dump patches.
- Andreas Schwab for his work on the m68k port.
- Lars Segerlund for work on GNU Fortran.

- Dodji Seketeli for numerous C++ bug fixes and debug info improvements.
- Tim Shen for major work on <regex>.
- Joel Sherrill for his direction via the steering committee, RTEMS contributions and RTEMS testing.
- Nathan Sidwell for many C++ fixes/improvements.
- Jeffrey Siegal for helping RMS with the original design of GCC, some code which handles the parse tree and RTL data structures, constant folding and help with the original VAX & m68k ports.
- Kenny Simpson for prompting libstdc++ fixes due to defect reports from the LWG (thereby keeping GCC in line with updates from the ISO).
- Franz Sirl for his ongoing work with making the PPC port stable for GNU/Linux.
- Andrey Slepuhin for assorted AIX hacking.
- Trevor Smigiel for contributing the SPU port.
- Christopher Smith did the port for Convex machines.
- Danny Smith for his major efforts on the Mingw (and Cygwin) ports. Retired from GCC maintainership August 2010, having mentored two new maintainers into the role.
- Randy Smith finished the Sun FPA support.
- Ed Smith-Rowland for his continuous work on libstdc++-v3, special functions, <random>, and various improvements to C++11 features.
- Scott Snyder for queue, iterator, istream, and string fixes and libstdc++ testsuite entries. Also for providing the patch to G77 to add rudimentary support for INTEGER*1, INTEGER*2, and LOGICAL*1.
- Zdenek Sojka for running automated regression testing of GCC and reporting numerous bugs.
- Jayant Sonar for contributing the CR16 port.
- Brad Spencer for contributions to the GLIBCPP_FORCE_NEW technique.
- Richard Stallman, for writing the original GCC and launching the GNU project.
- Jan Stein of the Chalmers Computer Society provided support for Genix, as well as part of the 32000 machine description.
- Nigel Stephens for various mips16 related fixes/improvements.
- Jonathan Stone wrote the machine description for the Pyramid computer.
- Graham Stott for various infrastructure improvements.
- John Stracke for his Java HTTP protocol fixes.
- Mike Stump for his Elxsi port, G++ contributions over the years and more recently his vxworks contributions
- Jeff Sturm for Java porting help, bug fixes, and encouragement.
- Shigeya Suzuki for this fixes for the bsdi platforms.
- Ian Lance Taylor for the Go frontend, the initial mips16 and mips64 support, general configury hacking, fixincludes, etc.
- Holger Teutsch provided the support for the Clipper CPU.
- Gary Thomas for his ongoing work to make the PPC work for GNU/Linux.

- Paul Thomas for contributions to GNU Fortran.
- Philipp Thomas for random bug fixes throughout the compiler
- Jason Thorpe for thread support in libstdc++ on NetBSD.
- Kresten Krab Thorup wrote the run time support for the Objective-C language and the fantastic Java bytecode interpreter.
- Michael Tiemann for random bug fixes, the first instruction scheduler, initial C++ support, function integration, NS32k, SPARC and M88k machine description work, delay slot scheduling.
- Andreas Tobler for his work porting libgcj to Darwin.
- Teemu Torma for thread safe exception handling support.
- Leonard Tower wrote parts of the parser, RTL generator, and RTL definitions, and of the VAX machine description.
- Daniel Towner and Hariharan Sandanagobalane contributed and maintain the picoChip port.
- Tom Tromey for internationalization support and for his many Java contributions and libgcj maintainership.
- Lassi Tuura for improvements to config.guess to determine HP processor types.
- Petter Urkedal for libstdc++ CXXFLAGS, math, and algorithms fixes.
- Andy Vaught for the design and initial implementation of the GNU Fortran front end.
- Brent Verner for work with the libstdc++ cshadow files and their associated configure steps.
- Todd Vierling for contributions for NetBSD ports.
- Andrew Waterman for contributing the RISC-V port, as well as maintaining it.
- Jonathan Wakely for contributing libstdc++ Doxygen notes and XHTML guidance.
- Dean Wakerley for converting the install documentation from HTML to texinfo in time for GCC 3.0.
- Krister Walfridsson for random bug fixes.
- Feng Wang for contributions to GNU Fortran.
- Stephen M. Webb for time and effort on making libstdc++ shadow files work with the tricky Solaris 8+ headers, and for pushing the build-time header tree. Also, for starting and driving the `<regex>` effort.
- John Wehle for various improvements for the x86 code generator, related infrastructure improvements to help x86 code generation, value range propagation and other work, WE32k port.
- Ulrich Weigand for work on the s390 port.
- Janus Weil for contributions to GNU Fortran.
- Zack Weinberg for major work on cpplib and various other bug fixes.
- Matt Welsh for help with Linux Threads support in GCJ.
- Urban Widmark for help fixing java.io.
- Mark Wielaard for new Java library code and his work integrating with Classpath.
- Dale Wiles helped port GCC to the Tahoe.

- Bob Wilson from Tensilica, Inc. for the Xtensa port.
- Jim Wilson for his direction via the steering committee, tackling hard problems in various places that nobody else wanted to work on, strength reduction and other loop optimizations.
- Paul Woegerer and Tal Agmon for the CRX port.
- Carlo Wood for various fixes.
- Tom Wood for work on the m88k port.
- Chung-Ju Wu for his work on the Andes NDS32 port.
- Canqun Yang for work on GNU Fortran.
- Masanobu Yuhara of Fujitsu Laboratories implemented the machine description for the Tron architecture (specifically, the Gmicro).
- Kevin Zachmann helped port GCC to the Tahoe.
- Ayal Zaks for Swing Modulo Scheduling (SMS).
- Xiaoqiang Zhang for work on GNU Fortran.
- Gilles Zunino for help porting Java to Irix.

The following people are recognized for their contributions to GNAT, the Ada front end of GCC:

- Bernard Banner
- Romain Berrendonner
- Geert Bosch
- Emmanuel Briot
- Joel Brobecker
- Ben Brosgol
- Vincent Celier
- Arnaud Charlet
- Chien Chieng
- Cyrille Comar
- Cyrille Crozes
- Robert Dewar
- Gary Dismukes
- Robert Duff
- Ed Falis
- Ramon Fernandez
- Sam Figueroa
- Vasiliy Fofanov
- Michael Friess
- Franco Gasperoni
- Ted Giering
- Matthew Gingell

- Laurent Guerby
- Jerome Guitton
- Olivier Hainque
- Jerome Hugues
- Hristian Kirtchev
- Jerome Lambourg
- Bruno Leclerc
- Albert Lee
- Sean McNeil
- Javier Miranda
- Laurent Nana
- Pascal Obry
- Dong-Ik Oh
- Laurent Pautet
- Brett Porter
- Thomas Quinot
- Nicolas Roche
- Pat Rogers
- Jose Ruiz
- Douglas Rupp
- Sergey Rybin
- Gail Schenker
- Ed Schonberg
- Nicolas Setton
- Samuel Tardieu

The following people are recognized for their contributions of new features, bug reports, testing and integration of classpath/libgcj for GCC version 4.1:

- Lillian Angel for `JTree` implementation and lots Free Swing additions and bug fixes.
- Wolfgang Baer for `GapContent` bug fixes.
- Anthony Balkissoon for `JList`, Free Swing 1.5 updates and mouse event fixes, lots of Free Swing work including `JTable` editing.
- Stuart Ballard for RMI constant fixes.
- Goffredo Baroncelli for `HTTPURLConnection` fixes.
- Gary Benson for `MessageFormat` fixes.
- Daniel Bonniot for `Serialization` fixes.
- Chris Burdess for lots of gnu.xml and http protocol fixes, `StAX` and `DOM` `xml:id` support.
- Ka-Hing Cheung for `TreePath` and `TreeSelection` fixes.
- Archie Cobbs for build fixes, VM interface updates, `URLClassLoader` updates.
- Kelley Cook for build fixes.

- Martin Cordova for Suggestions for better `SocketTimeoutException`.
- David Daney for `BitSet` bug fixes, `HttpURLConnection` rewrite and improvements.
- Thomas Fitzsimmons for lots of upgrades to the gtk+ AWT and Cairo 2D support. Lots of imageio framework additions, lots of AWT and Free Swing bug fixes.
- Jeroen Frijters for `ClassLoader` and nio cleanups, serialization fixes, better `Proxy` support, bug fixes and IKVM integration.
- Santiago Gala for `AccessControlContext` fixes.
- Nicolas Geoffray for `VMClassLoader` and `AccessController` improvements.
- David Gilbert for `basic` and `metal` icon and plaf support and lots of documenting, Lots of Free Swing and metal theme additions. `MetalIconFactory` implementation.
- Anthony Green for `MIDI` framework, `ALSA` and `DSSI` providers.
- Andrew Haley for `Serialization` and `URLClassLoader` fixes, gcj build speedups.
- Kim Ho for `JFileChooser` implementation.
- Andrew John Hughes for `Locale` and net fixes, URI RFC2986 updates, `Serialization` fixes, `Properties` XML support and generic branch work, VMIntegration guide update.
- Bastiaan Huisman for `TimeZone` bug fixing.
- Andreas Jaeger for mprec updates.
- Paul Jenner for better '`-Werror`' support.
- Ito Kazumitsu for `NetworkInterface` implementation and updates.
- Roman Kennke for `BoxLayout`, `GrayFilter` and `SplitPane`, plus bug fixes all over. Lots of Free Swing work including styled text.
- Simon Kitching for `String` cleanups and optimization suggestions.
- Michael Koch for configuration fixes, `Locale` updates, bug and build fixes.
- Guilhem Lavaux for configuration, thread and channel fixes and Kaffe integration. JCL native `Pointer` updates. Logger bug fixes.
- David Lichteblau for JCL support library global/local reference cleanups.
- Aaron Luchko for JDWP updates and documentation fixes.
- Ziga Mahkovec for `Graphics2D` upgraded to Cairo 0.5 and new regex features.
- Sven de Marothy for BMP imageio support, CSS and `TextLayout` fixes. `GtkImage` rewrite, 2D, awt, free swing and date/time fixes and implementing the Qt4 peers.
- Casey Marshall for crypto algorithm fixes, `FileChannel` lock, `SystemLogger` and `FileHandler` rotate implementations, NIO `FileChannel.map` support, security and policy updates.
- Bryce McKinlay for RMI work.
- Audrius Meskauskas for lots of Free Corba, RMI and HTML work plus testing and documenting.
- Kalle Olavi Niemitalo for build fixes.
- Rainer Orth for build fixes.
- Andrew Overholt for `File` locking fixes.
- Ingo Proetel for `Image`, `Logger` and `URLClassLoader` updates.

- Olga Rodimina for `MenuSelectionManager` implementation.
- Jan Roehrich for `BasicTreeUI` and `JTree` fixes.
- Julian Scheid for documentation updates and gjdoc support.
- Christian Schlichtherle for zip fixes and cleanups.
- Robert Schuster for documentation updates and beans fixes, `TreeNode` enumerations and `ActionCommand` and various fixes, XML and URL, AWT and Free Swing bug fixes.
- Keith Seitz for lots of JDWP work.
- Christian Thalinger for 64-bit cleanups, Configuration and VM interface fixes and `CACAO` integration, `fdlibm` updates.
- Gael Thomas for `VMClassLoader` boot packages support suggestions.
- Andreas Tobler for Darwin and Solaris testing and fixing, `Qt4` support for Darwin/OS X, `Graphics2D` support, `gtk+` updates.
- Dalibor Topic for better `DEBUG` support, build cleanups and Kaffe integration. `Qt4` build infrastructure, `SHA1PRNG` and `GdkPixbugDecoder` updates.
- Tom Tromey for Eclipse integration, generics work, lots of bug fixes and gcj integration including coordinating The Big Merge.
- Mark Wielaard for bug fixes, packaging and release management, `Clipboard` implementation, system call interrupts and network timeouts and `GdkPixpufDecoder` fixes.

In addition to the above, all of which also contributed time and energy in testing GCC, we would like to thank the following for their contributions to testing:

- Michael Abd-El-Malek
- Thomas Arend
- Bonzo Armstrong
- Steven Ashe
- Chris Baldwin
- David Billinghurst
- Jim Blandy
- Stephane Bortzmeyer
- Horst von Brand
- Frank Braun
- Rodney Brown
- Sidney Cadot
- Bradford Castalia
- Robert Clark
- Jonathan Corbet
- Ralph Doncaster
- Richard Emberson
- Levente Farkas
- Graham Fawcett
- Mark Fernyhough

- Robert A. French
- Jörgen Freyh
- Mark K. Gardner
- Charles-Antoine Gauthier
- Yung Shing Gene
- David Gilbert
- Simon Gornall
- Fred Gray
- John Griffin
- Patrik Hagglund
- Phil Hargett
- Amancio Hasty
- Takafumi Hayashi
- Bryan W. Headley
- Kevin B. Hendricks
- Joep Jansen
- Christian Joensson
- Michel Kern
- David Kidd
- Tobias Kuipers
- Anand Krishnaswamy
- A. O. V. Le Blanc
- llewelly
- Damon Love
- Brad Lucier
- Matthias Klose
- Martin Knoblauch
- Rick Lutowski
- Jesse Macnish
- Stefan Morrell
- Anon A. Mous
- Matthias Mueller
- Pekka Nikander
- Rick Niles
- Jon Olson
- Magnus Persson
- Chris Pollard
- Richard Polton
- Derk Reefman

- David Rees
- Paul Reilly
- Tom Reilly
- Torsten Rueger
- Danny Sadinoff
- Marc Schifer
- Erik Schnetter
- Wayne K. Schroll
- David Schuler
- Vin Shelton
- Tim Souder
- Adam Sulmicki
- Bill Thorson
- George Talbot
- Pedro A. M. Vazquez
- Gregory Warnes
- Ian Watson
- David E. Young
- And many others

And finally we'd like to thank everyone who uses the compiler, provides feedback and generally reminds us why we're doing this work in the first place.

Option Index

GCC's command line options are indexed here without any initial '-' or '--'. Where an option has both positive and negative forms (such as '-foption' and '-fno-option'), relevant entries in the manual are indexed under the most appropriate form; it may sometimes be useful to look up both forms.

F

`fltrans` 680
`fltrans-output-list` 680
`fresolution` 680

`fwpa` 680

M

`msoft-float` 12

Concept Index

!
'!' in constraint 345

#
'#' in constraint 347
in template 334
`#pragma` 628

$
'$' in constraint 345

%
'%' in constraint 346
% in GTY option 656
'%' in template 333

&
'&' in constraint 346

(
(gimple 210
(gimple_stmt_iterator 681
(nil) 250

*
'*' in constraint 347
* in template 334
*gimple_build_asm_vec 213
*gimple_build_assign 214
*gimple_build_bind 215
*gimple_build_call 216
*gimple_build_call_from_tree 216
*gimple_build_call_vec 216
*gimple_build_catch 217
*gimple_build_cond 218
*gimple_build_cond_from_tree 218
*gimple_build_debug_bind 219
*gimple_build_eh_filter 220
*gimple_build_goto 221
*gimple_build_label 221
*gimple_build_omp_atomic_load 221
*gimple_build_omp_atomic_store 222
*gimple_build_omp_continue 222
*gimple_build_omp_critical 223
*gimple_build_omp_for 223
*gimple_build_omp_parallel 225
*gimple_build_omp_sections 226
*gimple_build_omp_single 227
*gimple_build_resx 228
*gimple_build_return 228
*gimple_build_switch 228
*gimple_build_try 229

+
'+' in constraint 346

-
'-fsection-anchors' 255, 551

/
'/c' in RTL dump 259
'/f' in RTL dump 259
'/i' in RTL dump 260
'/j' in RTL dump 260
'/s' in RTL dump 259
'/u' in RTL dump 260
'/v' in RTL dump 261

<
'<' in constraint 341

=
'=' in constraint 346

>
'>' in constraint 341

?
'?' in constraint 345

^
'^' in constraint 345

_
__absvdi2 11
__absvsi2 11
__addda3 22
__adddf3 12
__adddq3 22
__addha3 22
__addhq3 22
__addqq3 22

__addsa3	22
__addsf3	12
__addsq3	22
__addta3	22
__addtf3	12
__adduda3	23
__addudq3	22
__adduha3	22
__adduhq3	22
__adduqq3	22
__addusa3	23
__addusq3	22
__adduta3	23
__addvdi3	11
__addvsi3	11
__addxf3	12
__ashlda3	28
__ashldi3	9
__ashldq3	28
__ashlha3	28
__ashlhq3	28
__ashlqq3	28
__ashlsa3	28
__ashlsi3	9
__ashlsq3	28
__ashlta3	28
__ashlti3	9
__ashluda3	28
__ashludq3	28
__ashluha3	28
__ashluhq3	28
__ashluqq3	28
__ashlusa3	28
__ashlusq3	28
__ashluta3	28
__ashrda3	29
__ashrdi3	9
__ashrdq3	29
__ashrha3	29
__ashrhq3	29
__ashrqq3	29
__ashrsa3	29
__ashrsi3	9
__ashrsq3	29
__ashrta3	29
__ashrti3	9
__bid_adddd3	17
__bid_addsd3	17
__bid_addtd3	17
__bid_divdd3	17
__bid_divsd3	17
__bid_divtd3	17
__bid_eqdd2	21
__bid_eqsd2	21
__bid_eqtd2	21
__bid_extendddtd2	18
__bid_extendddtf	18
__bid_extendddxf	18
__bid_extenddfdd	19
__bid_extenddftd	18
__bid_extendsddd2	17
__bid_extendsddf	18
__bid_extendsdtd2	17
__bid_extendsdtf	18
__bid_extendsdxf	18
__bid_extendsfdd	18
__bid_extendsfsd	19
__bid_extendsftd	18
__bid_extendtftd	19
__bid_extendxftd	18
__bid_fixdddi	19
__bid_fixddsi	19
__bid_fixsddi	19
__bid_fixsdsi	19
__bid_fixtddi	19
__bid_fixtdsi	19
__bid_fixunsdddi	19
__bid_fixunsddsi	19
__bid_fixunssddi	19
__bid_fixunssdsi	19
__bid_fixunstddi	19
__bid_fixunstdsi	19
__bid_floatdidd	20
__bid_floatdisd	20
__bid_floatditd	20
__bid_floatsidd	20
__bid_floatsisd	20
__bid_floatsitd	20
__bid_floatunsdidd	20
__bid_floatunsdisd	20
__bid_floatunsditd	20
__bid_floatunssidd	20
__bid_floatunssisd	20
__bid_floatunssitd	20
__bid_gedd2	21
__bid_gesd2	21
__bid_getd2	21
__bid_gtdd2	22
__bid_gtsd2	22
__bid_gttd2	22
__bid_ledd2	21
__bid_lesd2	21
__bid_letd2	21
__bid_ltdd2	21
__bid_ltsd2	21
__bid_lttd2	21
__bid_muldd3	17
__bid_mulsd3	17
__bid_multd3	17
__bid_nedd2	21
__bid_negdd2	17
__bid_negsd2	17
__bid_negtd2	17
__bid_nesd2	21
__bid_netd2	21
__bid_subdd3	17

Concept Index

__bid_subsd3 17
__bid_subtd3 17
__bid_truncdddf 19
__bid_truncddsd2 18
__bid_truncddsf 18
__bid_truncdfsd 18
__bid_truncsdsf 19
__bid_trunctddd2 18
__bid_trunctddf 18
__bid_trunctdsd2 18
__bid_trunctdsf 18
__bid_trunctdtf 19
__bid_trunctdxf 18
__bid_trunctfdd 18
__bid_trunctfsd 18
__bid_truncxfdd 18
__bid_truncxfsd 18
__bid_unorddd2 20
__bid_unordsd2 20
__bid_unordtd2 20
__bswapdi2 12
__bswapsi2 12
__builtin_classify_type 536
__builtin_next_arg 536
__builtin_saveregs 536
__chkp_bndcl 632
__chkp_bndcu 632
__chkp_bndldx 632
__chkp_bndmk 632
__chkp_bndret 632
__chkp_bndstx 632
__chkp_intersect 632
__chkp_narrow 632
__chkp_sizeof 632
__clear_cache 57
__clzdi2 11
__clzsi2 11
__clzti2 11
__cmpda2 30
__cmpdf2 15
__cmpdi2 10
__cmpdq2 30
__cmpha2 30
__cmphq2 30
__cmpqq2 30
__cmpsa2 30
__cmpsf2 15
__cmpsq2 30
__cmpta2 30
__cmptf2 15
__cmpti2 10
__cmpuda2 30
__cmpudq2 30
__cmpuha2 30
__cmpuhq2 30
__cmpuqq2 30
__cmpusa2 30
__cmpusq2 30
__cmputa2 30
__CTOR_LIST__ 592
__ctzdi2 11
__ctzsi2 11
__ctzti2 11
__divda3 26
__divdc3 16
__divdf3 12
__divdi3 9
__divdq3 26
__divha3 26
__divhq3 26
__divqq3 26
__divsa3 26
__divsc3 16
__divsf3 12
__divsi3 9
__divsq3 26
__divta3 26
__divtc3 16
__divtf3 12
__divti3 9
__divxc3 16
__divxf3 12
__dpd_addddd3 17
__dpd_addsd3 17
__dpd_addtd3 17
__dpd_divdd3 17
__dpd_divsd3 17
__dpd_divtd3 17
__dpd_eqdd2 21
__dpd_eqsd2 21
__dpd_eqtd2 21
__dpd_extendddtd2 17
__dpd_extendddtf 18
__dpd_extendddxf 18
__dpd_extenddfdd 19
__dpd_extenddftd 18
__dpd_extendsddd2 17
__dpd_extendsddf 18
__dpd_extendsdtd2 17
__dpd_extendsdtf 18
__dpd_extendsdxf 18
__dpd_extendsfdd 18
__dpd_extendsfsd 19
__dpd_extendsftd 18
__dpd_extendtftd 19
__dpd_extendxftd 18
__dpd_fixdddi 19
__dpd_fixddsi 19
__dpd_fixsddi 19
__dpd_fixsdsi 19
__dpd_fixtddi 19
__dpd_fixtdsi 19
__dpd_fixunsdddi 19
__dpd_fixunsddsi 19
__dpd_fixunssddi 19
__dpd_fixunssdsi 19

__dpd_fixunstddi	19	__eqsf2	15
__dpd_fixunstdsi	19	__eqtf2	15
__dpd_floatdidd	20	__extenddftf2	13
__dpd_floatdisd	20	__extenddfxf2	13
__dpd_floatditd	20	__extendsfdf2	13
__dpd_floatsidd	20	__extendsftf2	13
__dpd_floatsisd	20	__extendsfxf2	13
__dpd_floatsitd	20	__ffsdi2	11
__dpd_floatunsdidd	20	__ffsti2	11
__dpd_floatunsdisd	20	__fixdfdi	13
__dpd_floatunsditd	20	__fixdfsi	13
__dpd_floatunssidd	20	__fixdfti	13
__dpd_floatunssisd	20	__fixsfdi	13
__dpd_floatunssitd	20	__fixsfsi	13
__dpd_gedd2	21	__fixsfti	13
__dpd_gesd2	21	__fixtfdi	13
__dpd_getd2	21	__fixtfsi	13
__dpd_gtdd2	22	__fixtfti	13
__dpd_gtsd2	22	__fixunsdfdi	13
__dpd_gttd2	22	__fixunsdfsi	13
__dpd_ledd2	21	__fixunsdfti	14
__dpd_lesd2	21	__fixunssfdi	13
__dpd_letd2	21	__fixunssfsi	13
__dpd_ltdd2	21	__fixunssfti	14
__dpd_ltsd2	21	__fixunstfdi	13
__dpd_lttd2	21	__fixunstfsi	13
__dpd_muldd3	17	__fixunstfti	14
__dpd_mulsd3	17	__fixunsxfdi	13
__dpd_multd3	17	__fixunsxfsi	13
__dpd_nedd2	21	__fixunsxfti	14
__dpd_negdd2	17	__fixxfdi	13
__dpd_negsd2	17	__fixxfsi	13
__dpd_negtd2	17	__fixxfti	13
__dpd_nesd2	21	__floatdidf	14
__dpd_netd2	21	__floatdisf	14
__dpd_subdd3	17	__floatditf	14
__dpd_subsd3	17	__floatdixf	14
__dpd_subtd3	17	__floatsidf	14
__dpd_truncdddf	19	__floatsisf	14
__dpd_truncddsd2	18	__floatsitf	14
__dpd_truncddsf	18	__floatsixf	14
__dpd_truncdfsd	18	__floattidf	14
__dpd_truncsdsf	19	__floattisf	14
__dpd_trunctddd2	18	__floattitf	14
__dpd_trunctddf	18	__floattixf	14
__dpd_trunctdsd2	18	__floatundidf	14
__dpd_trunctdsf	18	__floatundisf	14
__dpd_trunctdtf	19	__floatunditf	14
__dpd_trunctdxf	18	__floatundixf	14
__dpd_trunctfdd	18	__floatunsidf	14
__dpd_trunctfsd	18	__floatunsisf	14
__dpd_truncxfdd	18	__floatunsitf	14
__dpd_truncxfsd	18	__floatunsixf	14
__dpd_unorddd2	20	__floatuntidf	14
__dpd_unordsd2	20	__floatuntisf	14
__dpd_unordtd2	20	__floatuntitf	14
__DTOR_LIST__	592	__floatuntixf	14
__eqdf2	15	__fractdadf	34

Concept Index

__fractdadi 34
__fractdadq 33
__fractdaha2 33
__fractdahi 33
__fractdahq 33
__fractdaqi 33
__fractdaqq 33
__fractdasa2 33
__fractdasf 34
__fractdasi 34
__fractdasq 33
__fractdata2 33
__fractdati 34
__fractdauda 33
__fractdaudq 33
__fractdauha 33
__fractdauhq 33
__fractdauqq 33
__fractdausa 33
__fractdausq 33
__fractdauta 33
__fractdfda 41
__fractdfdq 41
__fractdfha 41
__fractdfhq 41
__fractdfqq 41
__fractdfsa 41
__fractdfsq 41
__fractdfta 41
__fractdfuda 41
__fractdfudq 41
__fractdfuha 41
__fractdfuhq 41
__fractdfuqq 41
__fractdfusa 41
__fractdfusq 41
__fractdfuta 41
__fractdida 40
__fractdidq 40
__fractdiha 40
__fractdihq 40
__fractdiqq 40
__fractdisa 40
__fractdisq 40
__fractdita 40
__fractdiuda 40
__fractdiudq 40
__fractdiuha 40
__fractdiuhq 40
__fractdiuqq 40
__fractdiusa 40
__fractdiusq 40
__fractdiuta 40
__fractdqda 32
__fractdqdf 32
__fractdqdi 32
__fractdqha 32
__fractdqhi 32
__fractdqhq2 32
__fractdqqi 32
__fractdqqq2 32
__fractdqsa 32
__fractdqsf 32
__fractdqsi 32
__fractdqsq2 32
__fractdqta 32
__fractdqti 32
__fractdquda 32
__fractdqudq 32
__fractdquha 32
__fractdquhq 32
__fractdquqq 32
__fractdqusa 32
__fractdqusq 32
__fractdquta 32
__fracthada2 32
__fracthadf 33
__fracthadi 33
__fracthadq 32
__fracthahi 33
__fracthahq 32
__fracthaqi 33
__fracthaqq 32
__fracthasa2 32
__fracthasf 33
__fracthasi 33
__fracthasq 32
__fracthata2 32
__fracthati 33
__fracthauda 32
__fracthaudq 32
__fracthauha 32
__fracthauhq 32
__fracthauqq 32
__fracthausa 32
__fracthausq 32
__fracthauta 33
__fracthida 39
__fracthidq 39
__fracthiha 39
__fracthihq 39
__fracthiqq 39
__fracthisa 39
__fracthisq 39
__fracthita 39
__fracthiuda 39
__fracthiudq 39
__fracthiuha 39
__fracthiuhq 39
__fracthiuqq 39
__fracthiusa 39
__fracthiusq 39
__fracthiuta 39
__fracthqda 31
__fracthqdf 31
__fracthqdi 31

__fracthqdq2	31	__fractsadf	33
__fracthqha	31	__fractsadi	33
__fracthqhi	31	__fractsadq	33
__fracthqqi	31	__fractsaha2	33
__fracthqqq2	31	__fractsahi	33
__fracthqsa	31	__fractsahq	33
__fracthqsf	31	__fractsaqi	33
__fracthqsi	31	__fractsaqq	33
__fracthqsq2	31	__fractsasf	33
__fracthqta	31	__fractsasi	33
__fracthqti	31	__fractsasq	33
__fracthquda	31	__fractsata2	33
__fracthqudq	31	__fractsati	33
__fracthquha	31	__fractsauda	33
__fracthquhq	31	__fractsaudq	33
__fracthquqq	31	__fractsauha	33
__fracthqusa	31	__fractsauhq	33
__fracthqusq	31	__fractsauqq	33
__fracthquta	31	__fractsausa	33
__fractqida	39	__fractsausq	33
__fractqidq	39	__fractsauta	33
__fractqiha	39	__fractsfda	40
__fractqihq	39	__fractsfdq	40
__fractqiqq	39	__fractsfha	40
__fractqisa	39	__fractsfhq	40
__fractqisq	39	__fractsfqq	40
__fractqita	39	__fractsfsa	40
__fractqiuda	39	__fractsfsq	40
__fractqiudq	39	__fractsfta	40
__fractqiuha	39	__fractsfuda	41
__fractqiuhq	39	__fractsfudq	41
__fractqiuqq	39	__fractsfuha	41
__fractqiusa	39	__fractsfuhq	41
__fractqiusq	39	__fractsfuqq	41
__fractqiuta	39	__fractsfusa	41
__fractqqda	30	__fractsfusq	41
__fractqqdf	31	__fractsfuta	41
__fractqqdi	31	__fractsida	39
__fractqqdq2	30	__fractsidq	39
__fractqqha	30	__fractsiha	39
__fractqqhi	31	__fractsihq	39
__fractqqhq2	30	__fractsiqq	39
__fractqqqi	31	__fractsisa	39
__fractqqsa	30	__fractsisq	39
__fractqqsf	31	__fractsita	39
__fractqqsi	31	__fractsiuda	40
__fractqqsq2	30	__fractsiudq	40
__fractqqta	30	__fractsiuha	40
__fractqqti	31	__fractsiuhq	40
__fractqquda	31	__fractsiuqq	39
__fractqqudq	31	__fractsiusa	40
__fractqquha	31	__fractsiusq	40
__fractqquhq	30	__fractsiuta	40
__fractqquqq	30	__fractsqda	31
__fractqqusa	31	__fractsqdf	32
__fractqqusq	30	__fractsqdi	32
__fractqquta	31	__fractsqdq2	31
__fractsada2	33	__fractsqha	31

Concept Index

```
__fractsqhi ..................... 32
__fractsqhq2 .................... 31
__fractsqqi ..................... 32
__fractsqqq2 .................... 31
__fractsqsa ..................... 31
__fractsqsf ..................... 32
__fractsqsi ..................... 32
__fractsqta ..................... 31
__fractsqti ..................... 32
__fractsquda .................... 32
__fractsqudq .................... 31
__fractsquha .................... 31
__fractsquhq .................... 31
__fractsquqq .................... 31
__fractsqusa .................... 31
__fractsqusq .................... 31
__fractsquta .................... 32
__fracttada2 .................... 34
__fracttadf ..................... 34
__fracttadi ..................... 34
__fracttadq ..................... 34
__fracttaha2 .................... 34
__fracttahi ..................... 34
__fracttahq ..................... 34
__fracttaqi ..................... 34
__fracttaqq ..................... 34
__fracttasa2 .................... 34
__fracttasf ..................... 34
__fracttasi ..................... 34
__fracttasq ..................... 34
__fracttati ..................... 34
__fracttauda .................... 34
__fracttaudq .................... 34
__fracttauha .................... 34
__fracttauhq .................... 34
__fracttauqq .................... 34
__fracttausa .................... 34
__fracttausq .................... 34
__fracttauta .................... 34
__fracttida ..................... 40
__fracttidq ..................... 40
__fracttiha ..................... 40
__fracttihq ..................... 40
__fracttiqq ..................... 40
__fracttisa ..................... 40
__fracttisq ..................... 40
__fracttita ..................... 40
__fracttiuda .................... 40
__fracttiudq .................... 40
__fracttiuha .................... 40
__fracttiuhq .................... 40
__fracttiuqq .................... 40
__fracttiusa .................... 40
__fracttiusq .................... 40
__fracttiuta .................... 40
__fractudada .................... 38
__fractudadf .................... 38
__fractudadi .................... 38
__fractudadq .................... 38
__fractudaha .................... 38
__fractudahi .................... 38
__fractudahq .................... 37
__fractudaqi .................... 38
__fractudaqq .................... 37
__fractudasa .................... 38
__fractudasf .................... 38
__fractudasi .................... 38
__fractudasq .................... 38
__fractudata .................... 38
__fractudati .................... 38
__fractudaudq ................... 38
__fractudauha2 .................. 38
__fractudauhq ................... 38
__fractudauqq ................... 38
__fractudausa2 .................. 38
__fractudausq ................... 38
__fractudauta2 .................. 38
__fractudqda .................... 36
__fractudqdf .................... 36
__fractudqdi .................... 36
__fractudqdq .................... 36
__fractudqha .................... 36
__fractudqhi .................... 36
__fractudqhq .................... 36
__fractudqqi .................... 36
__fractudqqq .................... 36
__fractudqsa .................... 36
__fractudqsf .................... 36
__fractudqsi .................... 36
__fractudqsq .................... 36
__fractudqta .................... 36
__fractudqti .................... 36
__fractudquda ................... 36
__fractudquha ................... 36
__fractudquhq2 .................. 36
__fractudquqq2 .................. 36
__fractudqusa ................... 36
__fractudqusq2 .................. 36
__fractudquta ................... 36
__fractuhada .................... 37
__fractuhadf .................... 37
__fractuhadi .................... 37
__fractuhadq .................... 36
__fractuhaha .................... 36
__fractuhahi .................... 37
__fractuhahq .................... 36
__fractuhaqi .................... 37
__fractuhaqq .................... 36
__fractuhasa .................... 36
__fractuhasf .................... 37
__fractuhasi .................... 37
__fractuhasq .................... 36
__fractuhata .................... 37
__fractuhati .................... 37
__fractuhauda2 .................. 37
__fractuhaudq ................... 37
```

__fractuhauhq	37
__fractuhauqq	37
__fractuhausa2	37
__fractuhausq	37
__fractuhauta2	37
__fractuhqda	35
__fractuhqdf	35
__fractuhqdi	35
__fractuhqdq	35
__fractuhqha	35
__fractuhqhi	35
__fractuhqhq	35
__fractuhqqi	35
__fractuhqqq	35
__fractuhqsa	35
__fractuhqsf	35
__fractuhqsi	35
__fractuhqsq	35
__fractuhqta	35
__fractuhqti	35
__fractuhquda	35
__fractuhqudq2	35
__fractuhquha	35
__fractuhquqq2	35
__fractuhqusa	35
__fractuhqusq2	35
__fractuhquta	35
__fractunsdadi	51
__fractunsdahi	51
__fractunsdaqi	51
__fractunsdasi	51
__fractunsdati	51
__fractunsdida	53
__fractunsdidq	53
__fractunsdiha	53
__fractunsdihq	53
__fractunsdiqq	53
__fractunsdisa	53
__fractunsdisq	53
__fractunsdita	53
__fractunsdiuda	53
__fractunsdiudq	53
__fractunsdiuha	53
__fractunsdiuhq	53
__fractunsdiuqq	53
__fractunsdiusa	53
__fractunsdiusq	53
__fractunsdiuta	53
__fractunsdqdi	50
__fractunsdqhi	50
__fractunsdqqi	50
__fractunsdqsi	50
__fractunsdqti	50
__fractunshadi	51
__fractunshahi	51
__fractunshaqi	50
__fractunshasi	51
__fractunshati	51
__fractunshida	52
__fractunshidq	52
__fractunshiha	52
__fractunshihq	52
__fractunshiqq	52
__fractunshisa	52
__fractunshisq	52
__fractunshita	53
__fractunshiuda	53
__fractunshiudq	53
__fractunshiuha	53
__fractunshiuhq	53
__fractunshiuqq	53
__fractunshiusa	53
__fractunshiusq	53
__fractunshiuta	53
__fractunshqdi	50
__fractunshqhi	50
__fractunshqqi	50
__fractunshqsi	50
__fractunshqti	50
__fractunsqida	52
__fractunsqidq	52
__fractunsqiha	52
__fractunsqihq	52
__fractunsqiqq	52
__fractunsqisa	52
__fractunsqisq	52
__fractunsqita	52
__fractunsqiuda	52
__fractunsqiudq	52
__fractunsqiuha	52
__fractunsqiuhq	52
__fractunsqiuqq	52
__fractunsqiusa	52
__fractunsqiusq	52
__fractunsqiuta	52
__fractunsqqdi	50
__fractunsqqhi	50
__fractunsqqqi	50
__fractunsqqsi	50
__fractunsqqti	50
__fractunssadi	51
__fractunssahi	51
__fractunssaqi	51
__fractunssasi	51
__fractunssati	51
__fractunssida	53
__fractunssidq	53
__fractunssiha	53
__fractunssihq	53
__fractunssiqq	53
__fractunssisa	53
__fractunssisq	53
__fractunssita	53
__fractunssiuda	53
__fractunssiudq	53
__fractunssiuha	53

Concept Index

__fractunssiuhq............................. 53
__fractunssiuqq............................. 53
__fractunssiusa............................. 53
__fractunssiusq............................. 53
__fractunssiuta............................. 53
__fractunssqdi............................. 50
__fractunssqhi............................. 50
__fractunssqqi............................. 50
__fractunssqsi............................. 50
__fractunssqti............................. 50
__fractunstadi............................. 51
__fractunstahi............................. 51
__fractunstaqi............................. 51
__fractunstasi............................. 51
__fractunstati............................. 51
__fractunstida............................. 54
__fractunstidq............................. 54
__fractunstiha............................. 54
__fractunstihq............................. 54
__fractunstiqq............................. 54
__fractunstisa............................. 54
__fractunstisq............................. 54
__fractunstita............................. 54
__fractunstiuda............................. 54
__fractunstiudq............................. 54
__fractunstiuha............................. 54
__fractunstiuhq............................. 54
__fractunstiuqq............................. 54
__fractunstiusa............................. 54
__fractunstiusq............................. 54
__fractunstiuta............................. 54
__fractunsudadi............................. 52
__fractunsudahi............................. 52
__fractunsudaqi............................. 52
__fractunsudasi............................. 52
__fractunsudati............................. 52
__fractunsudqdi............................. 51
__fractunsudqhi............................. 51
__fractunsudqqi............................. 51
__fractunsudqsi............................. 51
__fractunsudqti............................. 51
__fractunsuhadi............................. 51
__fractunsuhahi............................. 51
__fractunsuhaqi............................. 51
__fractunsuhasi............................. 51
__fractunsuhati............................. 52
__fractunsuhqdi............................. 51
__fractunsuhqhi............................. 51
__fractunsuhqqi............................. 51
__fractunsuhqsi............................. 51
__fractunsuhqti............................. 51
__fractunsuqqdi............................. 51
__fractunsuqqhi............................. 51
__fractunsuqqqi............................. 51
__fractunsuqqsi............................. 51
__fractunsuqqti............................. 51
__fractunsusadi............................. 52
__fractunsusahi............................. 52

__fractunsusaqi............................. 52
__fractunsusasi............................. 52
__fractunsusati............................. 52
__fractunsusqdi............................. 51
__fractunsusqhi............................. 51
__fractunsusqqi............................. 51
__fractunsusqsi............................. 51
__fractunsusqti............................. 51
__fractunsutadi............................. 52
__fractunsutahi............................. 52
__fractunsutaqi............................. 52
__fractunsutasi............................. 52
__fractunsutati............................. 52
__fractuqqda............................. 34
__fractuqqdf............................. 35
__fractuqqdi............................. 35
__fractuqqdq............................. 34
__fractuqqha............................. 34
__fractuqqhi............................. 35
__fractuqqhq............................. 34
__fractuqqqi............................. 35
__fractuqqqq............................. 34
__fractuqqsa............................. 34
__fractuqqsf............................. 35
__fractuqqsi............................. 35
__fractuqqsq............................. 34
__fractuqqta............................. 34
__fractuqqti............................. 35
__fractuqquda............................. 34
__fractuqqudq2............................. 34
__fractuqquha............................. 34
__fractuqquhq2............................. 34
__fractuqqusa............................. 34
__fractuqqusq2............................. 34
__fractuqquta............................. 35
__fractusada............................. 37
__fractusadf............................. 37
__fractusadi............................. 37
__fractusadq............................. 37
__fractusaha............................. 37
__fractusahi............................. 37
__fractusahq............................. 37
__fractusaqi............................. 37
__fractusaqq............................. 37
__fractusasa............................. 37
__fractusasf............................. 37
__fractusasi............................. 37
__fractusasq............................. 37
__fractusata............................. 37
__fractusati............................. 37
__fractusauda2............................. 37
__fractusaudq............................. 37
__fractusauha2............................. 37
__fractusauhq............................. 37
__fractusauqq............................. 37
__fractusausq............................. 37
__fractusauta2............................. 37
__fractusqda............................. 35

__fractusqdf	36
__fractusqdi	36
__fractusqdq	35
__fractusqha	35
__fractusqhi	36
__fractusqhq	35
__fractusqqi	36
__fractusqqq	35
__fractusqsa	35
__fractusqsf	36
__fractusqsi	36
__fractusqsq	35
__fractusqta	35
__fractusqti	36
__fractusquda	36
__fractusqudq2	35
__fractusquha	36
__fractusquhq2	35
__fractusquqq2	35
__fractusqusa	36
__fractusquta	36
__fractutada	38
__fractutadf	39
__fractutadi	39
__fractutadq	38
__fractutaha	38
__fractutahi	39
__fractutahq	38
__fractutaqi	38
__fractutaqq	38
__fractutasa	38
__fractutasf	39
__fractutasi	39
__fractutasq	38
__fractutata	38
__fractutati	39
__fractutauda2	38
__fractutaudq	38
__fractutauha2	38
__fractutauhq	38
__fractutauqq	38
__fractutausa2	38
__fractutausq	38
__gedf2	15
__gesf2	15
__getf2	15
__gtdf2	16
__gtsf2	16
__gttf2	16
__ledf2	16
__lesf2	16
__letf2	16
__lshrdi3	9
__lshrsi3	9
__lshrti3	9
__lshruda3	29
__lshrudq3	29
__lshruha3	29

__lshruhq3	29
__lshruqq3	29
__lshrusa3	29
__lshrusq3	29
__lshruta3	29
__ltdf2	15
__ltsf2	15
__lttf2	15
__main	651
__moddi3	10
__modsi3	10
__modti3	10
__morestack_current_segment	58
__morestack_initial_sp	58
__morestack_segments	58
__mulda3	25
__muldc3	16
__muldf3	12
__muldi3	10
__muldq3	25
__mulha3	25
__mulhq3	25
__mulqq3	25
__mulsa3	25
__mulsc3	16
__mulsf3	12
__mulsi3	10
__mulsq3	25
__multa3	25
__multc3	16
__multf3	12
__multi3	10
__muluda3	25
__muludq3	25
__muluha3	25
__muluhq3	25
__muluqq3	25
__mulusa3	25
__mulusq3	25
__muluta3	25
__mulvdi3	11
__mulvsi3	11
__mulxc3	16
__mulxf3	12
__nedf2	15
__negda2	27
__negdf2	12
__negdi2	10
__negdq2	27
__negha2	27
__neghq2	27
__negqq2	27
__negsa2	27
__negsf2	12
__negsq2	27
__negta2	27
__negtf2	12
__negti2	10

Concept Index

__neguda2................................. 27
__negudq2................................. 27
__neguha2................................. 27
__neguhq2................................. 27
__neguqq2................................. 27
__negusa2................................. 27
__negusq2................................. 27
__neguta2................................. 27
__negvdi2................................. 11
__negvsi2................................. 11
__negxf2.................................. 12
__nesf2................................... 15
__netf2................................... 15
__paritydi2............................... 11
__paritysi2............................... 11
__parityti2............................... 11
__popcountdi2............................. 12
__popcountsi2............................. 12
__popcountti2............................. 12
__powidf2................................. 16
__powisf2................................. 16
__powitf2................................. 16
__powixf2................................. 16
__satfractdadq............................ 43
__satfractdaha2........................... 43
__satfractdahq............................ 43
__satfractdaqq............................ 43
__satfractdasa2........................... 43
__satfractdasq............................ 43
__satfractdata2........................... 43
__satfractdauda........................... 43
__satfractdaudq........................... 43
__satfractdauha........................... 43
__satfractdauhq........................... 43
__satfractdauqq........................... 43
__satfractdausa........................... 43
__satfractdausq........................... 43
__satfractdauta........................... 43
__satfractdfda............................ 50
__satfractdfdq............................ 50
__satfractdfha............................ 50
__satfractdfhq............................ 50
__satfractdfqq............................ 50
__satfractdfsa............................ 50
__satfractdfsq............................ 50
__satfractdfta............................ 50
__satfractdfuda........................... 50
__satfractdfudq........................... 50
__satfractdfuha........................... 50
__satfractdfuhq........................... 50
__satfractdfuqq........................... 50
__satfractdfusa........................... 50
__satfractdfusq........................... 50
__satfractdfuta........................... 50
__satfractdida............................ 49
__satfractdidq............................ 49
__satfractdiha............................ 49
__satfractdihq............................ 49

__satfractdiqq............................ 49
__satfractdisa............................ 49
__satfractdisq............................ 49
__satfractdita............................ 49
__satfractdiuda........................... 49
__satfractdiudq........................... 49
__satfractdiuha........................... 49
__satfractdiuhq........................... 49
__satfractdiuqq........................... 49
__satfractdiusa........................... 49
__satfractdiusq........................... 49
__satfractdiuta........................... 49
__satfractdqda............................ 42
__satfractdqha............................ 42
__satfractdqhq2........................... 42
__satfractdqqq2........................... 42
__satfractdqsa............................ 42
__satfractdqsq2........................... 42
__satfractdqta............................ 42
__satfractdquda........................... 42
__satfractdqudq........................... 42
__satfractdquha........................... 42
__satfractdquhq........................... 42
__satfractdquqq........................... 42
__satfractdqusa........................... 42
__satfractdqusq........................... 42
__satfractdquta........................... 42
__satfracthada2........................... 43
__satfracthadq............................ 43
__satfracthahq............................ 42
__satfracthaqq............................ 42
__satfracthasa2........................... 43
__satfracthasq............................ 42
__satfracthata2........................... 43
__satfracthauda........................... 43
__satfracthaudq........................... 43
__satfracthauha........................... 43
__satfracthauhq........................... 43
__satfracthauqq........................... 43
__satfracthausa........................... 43
__satfracthausq........................... 43
__satfracthauta........................... 43
__satfracthida............................ 48
__satfracthidq............................ 48
__satfracthiha............................ 48
__satfracthihq............................ 48
__satfracthiqq............................ 48
__satfracthisa............................ 48
__satfracthisq............................ 48
__satfracthita............................ 48
__satfracthiuda........................... 48
__satfracthiudq........................... 48
__satfracthiuha........................... 48
__satfracthiuhq........................... 48
__satfracthiuqq........................... 48
__satfracthiusa........................... 48
__satfracthiusq........................... 48
__satfracthiuta........................... 48

__satfracthqda............................. 42
__satfracthqdq2............................ 41
__satfracthqha............................. 42
__satfracthqqq2............................ 41
__satfracthqsa............................. 42
__satfracthqsq2............................ 41
__satfracthqta............................. 42
__satfracthquda............................ 42
__satfracthqudq............................ 42
__satfracthquha............................ 42
__satfracthquhq............................ 42
__satfracthquqq............................ 42
__satfracthqusa............................ 42
__satfracthqusq............................ 42
__satfracthquta............................ 42
__satfractqida............................. 48
__satfractqidq............................. 48
__satfractqiha............................. 48
__satfractqihq............................. 48
__satfractqiqq............................. 48
__satfractqisa............................. 48
__satfractqisq............................. 48
__satfractqita............................. 48
__satfractqiuda............................ 48
__satfractqiudq............................ 48
__satfractqiuha............................ 48
__satfractqiuhq............................ 48
__satfractqiuqq............................ 48
__satfractqiusa............................ 48
__satfractqiusq............................ 48
__satfractqiuta............................ 48
__satfractqqda............................. 41
__satfractqqdq2............................ 41
__satfractqqha............................. 41
__satfractqqhq2............................ 41
__satfractqqsa............................. 41
__satfractqqsq2............................ 41
__satfractqqta............................. 41
__satfractqquda............................ 41
__satfractqqudq............................ 41
__satfractqquha............................ 41
__satfractqquhq............................ 41
__satfractqquqq............................ 41
__satfractqqusa............................ 41
__satfractqqusq............................ 41
__satfractqquta............................ 41
__satfractsada2............................ 43
__satfractsadq............................. 43
__satfractsaha2............................ 43
__satfractsahq............................. 43
__satfractsaqq............................. 43
__satfractsasq............................. 43
__satfractsata2............................ 43
__satfractsauda............................ 43
__satfractsaudq............................ 43
__satfractsauha............................ 43
__satfractsauhq............................ 43
__satfractsauqq............................ 43

__satfractsausa............................ 43
__satfractsausq............................ 43
__satfractsauta............................ 43
__satfractsfda............................. 49
__satfractsfdq............................. 49
__satfractsfha............................. 49
__satfractsfhq............................. 49
__satfractsfqq............................. 49
__satfractsfsa............................. 49
__satfractsfsq............................. 49
__satfractsfta............................. 49
__satfractsfuda............................ 50
__satfractsfudq............................ 50
__satfractsfuha............................ 50
__satfractsfuhq............................ 50
__satfractsfuqq............................ 49
__satfractsfusa............................ 50
__satfractsfusq............................ 50
__satfractsfuta............................ 50
__satfractsida............................. 48
__satfractsidq............................. 48
__satfractsiha............................. 48
__satfractsihq............................. 48
__satfractsiqq............................. 48
__satfractsisa............................. 48
__satfractsisq............................. 48
__satfractsita............................. 48
__satfractsiuda............................ 49
__satfractsiudq............................ 49
__satfractsiuha............................ 49
__satfractsiuhq............................ 48
__satfractsiuqq............................ 48
__satfractsiusa............................ 49
__satfractsiusq............................ 49
__satfractsiuta............................ 49
__satfractsqda............................. 42
__satfractsqdq2............................ 42
__satfractsqha............................. 42
__satfractsqhq2............................ 42
__satfractsqqq2............................ 42
__satfractsqsa............................. 42
__satfractsqta............................. 42
__satfractsquda............................ 42
__satfractsqudq............................ 42
__satfractsquha............................ 42
__satfractsquhq............................ 42
__satfractsquqq............................ 42
__satfractsqusa............................ 42
__satfractsqusq............................ 42
__satfractsquta............................ 42
__satfracttada2............................ 44
__satfracttadq............................. 44
__satfracttaha2............................ 44
__satfracttahq............................. 44
__satfracttaqq............................. 43
__satfracttasa2............................ 44
__satfracttasq............................. 44
__satfracttauda............................ 44

Concept Index

__satfracttaudq................................44
__satfracttauha................................44
__satfracttauhq................................44
__satfracttauqq................................44
__satfracttausa................................44
__satfracttausq................................44
__satfracttauta................................44
__satfracttida.................................49
__satfracttidq.................................49
__satfracttiha.................................49
__satfracttihq.................................49
__satfracttiqq.................................49
__satfracttisa.................................49
__satfracttisq.................................49
__satfracttita.................................49
__satfracttiuda................................49
__satfracttiudq................................49
__satfracttiuha................................49
__satfracttiuhq................................49
__satfracttiuqq................................49
__satfracttiusa................................49
__satfracttiusq................................49
__satfracttiuta................................49
__satfractudada................................47
__satfractudadq................................47
__satfractudaha................................47
__satfractudahq................................47
__satfractudaqq................................47
__satfractudasa................................47
__satfractudasq................................47
__satfractudata................................47
__satfractudaudq...............................47
__satfractudauha2..............................47
__satfractudauhq...............................47
__satfractudauqq...............................47
__satfractudausa2..............................47
__satfractudausq...............................47
__satfractudauta2..............................47
__satfractudqda................................45
__satfractudqdq................................45
__satfractudqha................................45
__satfractudqhq................................45
__satfractudqqq................................45
__satfractudqsa................................45
__satfractudqsq................................45
__satfractudqta................................45
__satfractudquda...............................46
__satfractudquha...............................46
__satfractudquhq2..............................45
__satfractudquqq2..............................45
__satfractudqusa...............................46
__satfractudqusq2..............................45
__satfractudquta...............................46
__satfractuhada................................46
__satfractuhadq................................46
__satfractuhaha................................46
__satfractuhahq................................46
__satfractuhaqq................................46

__satfractuhasa................................46
__satfractuhasq................................46
__satfractuhata................................46
__satfractuhauda2..............................46
__satfractuhaudq...............................46
__satfractuhauhq...............................46
__satfractuhauqq...............................46
__satfractuhausa2..............................46
__satfractuhausq...............................46
__satfractuhauta2..............................46
__satfractuhqda................................44
__satfractuhqdq................................44
__satfractuhqha................................44
__satfractuhqhq................................44
__satfractuhqqq................................44
__satfractuhqsa................................44
__satfractuhqsq................................44
__satfractuhqta................................44
__satfractuhquda...............................45
__satfractuhqudq2..............................45
__satfractuhquha...............................45
__satfractuhquqq2..............................44
__satfractuhqusa...............................45
__satfractuhqusq2..............................45
__satfractuhquta...............................45
__satfractunsdida..............................56
__satfractunsdidq..............................55
__satfractunsdiha..............................56
__satfractunsdihq..............................55
__satfractunsdiqq..............................55
__satfractunsdisa..............................56
__satfractunsdisq..............................55
__satfractunsdita..............................56
__satfractunsdiuda.............................56
__satfractunsdiudq.............................56
__satfractunsdiuha.............................56
__satfractunsdiuhq.............................56
__satfractunsdiuqq.............................56
__satfractunsdiusa.............................56
__satfractunsdiusq.............................56
__satfractunsdiuta.............................56
__satfractunshida..............................55
__satfractunshidq..............................55
__satfractunshiha..............................55
__satfractunshihq..............................55
__satfractunshiqq..............................55
__satfractunshisa..............................55
__satfractunshisq..............................55
__satfractunshita..............................55
__satfractunshiuda.............................55
__satfractunshiudq.............................55
__satfractunshiuha.............................55
__satfractunshiuhq.............................55
__satfractunshiuqq.............................55
__satfractunshiusa.............................55
__satfractunshiusq.............................55
__satfractunshiuta.............................55
__satfractunsqida..............................54

__satfractunsqidq	54	__satfractuqquhq2	44
__satfractunsqiha	54	__satfractuqqusa	44
__satfractunsqihq	54	__satfractuqqusq2	44
__satfractunsqiqq	54	__satfractuqquta	44
__satfractunsqisa	54	__satfractusada	46
__satfractunsqisq	54	__satfractusadq	46
__satfractunsqita	54	__satfractusaha	46
__satfractunsqiuda	54	__satfractusahq	46
__satfractunsqiudq	54	__satfractusaqq	46
__satfractunsqiuha	54	__satfractusasa	46
__satfractunsqiuhq	54	__satfractusasq	46
__satfractunsqiuqq	54	__satfractusata	46
__satfractunsqiusa	54	__satfractusauda2	47
__satfractunsqiusq	54	__satfractusaudq	46
__satfractunsqiuta	54	__satfractusauha2	46
__satfractunssida	55	__satfractusauhq	46
__satfractunssidq	55	__satfractusauqq	46
__satfractunssiha	55	__satfractusausq	46
__satfractunssihq	55	__satfractusauta2	47
__satfractunssiqq	55	__satfractusqda	45
__satfractunssisa	55	__satfractusqdq	45
__satfractunssisq	55	__satfractusqha	45
__satfractunssita	55	__satfractusqhq	45
__satfractunssiuda	55	__satfractusqqq	45
__satfractunssiudq	55	__satfractusqsa	45
__satfractunssiuha	55	__satfractusqsq	45
__satfractunssiuhq	55	__satfractusqta	45
__satfractunssiuqq	55	__satfractusquda	45
__satfractunssiusa	55	__satfractusqudq2	45
__satfractunssiusq	55	__satfractusquha	45
__satfractunssiuta	55	__satfractusquhq2	45
__satfractunstida	56	__satfractusquqq2	45
__satfractunstidq	56	__satfractusqusa	45
__satfractunstiha	56	__satfractusquta	45
__satfractunstihq	56	__satfractutada	47
__satfractunstiqq	56	__satfractutadq	47
__satfractunstisa	56	__satfractutaha	47
__satfractunstisq	56	__satfractutahq	47
__satfractunstita	56	__satfractutaqq	47
__satfractunstiuda	56	__satfractutasa	47
__satfractunstiudq	56	__satfractutasq	47
__satfractunstiuha	56	__satfractutata	47
__satfractunstiuhq	56	__satfractutauda2	48
__satfractunstiuqq	56	__satfractutaudq	47
__satfractunstiusa	56	__satfractutauha2	47
__satfractunstiusq	56	__satfractutauhq	47
__satfractunstiuta	56	__satfractutauqq	47
__satfractuqqda	44	__satfractutausa2	47
__satfractuqqdq	44	__satfractutausq	47
__satfractuqqha	44	__splitstack_find	57
__satfractuqqhq	44	__ssaddda3	23
__satfractuqqqq	44	__ssadddq3	23
__satfractuqqsa	44	__ssaddha3	23
__satfractuqqsq	44	__ssaddhq3	23
__satfractuqqta	44	__ssaddqq3	23
__satfractuqquda	44	__ssaddsa3	23
__satfractuqqudq2	44	__ssaddsq3	23
__satfractuqquha	44	__ssaddta3	23

Concept Index

`__ssashlda3` 29
`__ssashldq3` 29
`__ssashlha3` 29
`__ssashlhq3` 29
`__ssashlsa3` 29
`__ssashlsq3` 29
`__ssashlta3` 29
`__ssdivda3` 27
`__ssdivdq3` 27
`__ssdivha3` 27
`__ssdivhq3` 27
`__ssdivqq3` 27
`__ssdivsa3` 27
`__ssdivsq3` 27
`__ssdivta3` 27
`__ssmulda3` 25
`__ssmuldq3` 25
`__ssmulha3` 25
`__ssmulhq3` 25
`__ssmulqq3` 25
`__ssmulsa3` 25
`__ssmulsq3` 25
`__ssmulta3` 25
`__ssnegda2` 28
`__ssnegdq2` 28
`__ssnegha2` 28
`__ssneghq2` 28
`__ssnegqq2` 28
`__ssnegsa2` 28
`__ssnegsq2` 28
`__ssnegta2` 28
`__sssubda3` 24
`__sssubdq3` 24
`__sssubha3` 24
`__sssubhq3` 24
`__sssubqq3` 24
`__sssubsa3` 24
`__sssubsq3` 24
`__sssubta3` 24
`__subda3` 24
`__subdf3` 12
`__subdq3` 23
`__subha3` 24
`__subhq3` 23
`__subqq3` 23
`__subsa3` 24
`__subsf3` 12
`__subsq3` 23
`__subta3` 24
`__subtf3` 12
`__subuda3` 24
`__subudq3` 24
`__subuha3` 24
`__subuhq3` 23
`__subuqq3` 23
`__subusa3` 24
`__subusq3` 24
`__subuta3` 24
`__subvdi3` 11
`__subvsi3` 11
`__subxf3` 12
`__truncdfsf2` 13
`__trunctfdf2` 13
`__trunctfsf2` 13
`__truncxfdf2` 13
`__truncxfsf2` 13
`__ucmpdi2` 10
`__ucmpti2` 10
`__udivdi3` 10
`__udivmoddi4` 10
`__udivmodti4` 10
`__udivsi3` 10
`__udivti3` 10
`__udivuda3` 26
`__udivudq3` 26
`__udivuha3` 26
`__udivuhq3` 26
`__udivuqq3` 26
`__udivusa3` 26
`__udivusq3` 26
`__udivuta3` 26
`__umoddi3` 10
`__umodsi3` 10
`__umodti3` 10
`__unorddf2` 15
`__unordsf2` 15
`__unordtf2` 15
`__usadduda3` 23
`__usaddudq3` 23
`__usadduha3` 23
`__usadduhq3` 23
`__usadduqq3` 23
`__usaddusa3` 23
`__usaddusq3` 23
`__usadduta3` 23
`__usashluda3` 30
`__usashludq3` 29
`__usashluha3` 29
`__usashluhq3` 29
`__usashluqq3` 29
`__usashlusa3` 29
`__usashlusq3` 29
`__usashluta3` 30
`__usdivuda3` 27
`__usdivudq3` 27
`__usdivuha3` 27
`__usdivuhq3` 27
`__usdivuqq3` 27
`__usdivusa3` 27
`__usdivusq3` 27
`__usdivuta3` 27
`__usmuluda3` 26
`__usmuludq3` 26
`__usmuluha3` 26
`__usmuluhq3` 26
`__usmuluqq3` 26

`__usmulusa3` 26
`__usmulusq3` 26
`__usmuluta3` 26
`__usneguda2` 28
`__usnegudq2` 28
`__usneguha2` 28
`__usneguhq2` 28
`__usneguqq2` 28
`__usnegusa2` 28
`__usnegusq2` 28
`__usneguta2` 28
`__ussubuda3` 24
`__ussubudq3` 24
`__ussubuha3` 24
`__ussubuhq3` 24
`__ussubuqq3` 24
`__ussubusa3` 24
`__ussubusq3` 24
`__ussubuta3` 24

\

\ 333

0

'0' in constraint 342

A

abort 5
abs 281
abs and attributes 437
`ABS_EXPR` 169
`absence_set` 447
abs*m*2 instruction pattern 394
absolute value 281
access to operands 252
access to special operands 253
accessors 252
`ACCUM_TYPE_SIZE` 483
`ACCUMULATE_OUTGOING_ARGS` 516
`ACCUMULATE_OUTGOING_ARGS` and stack frames
 531
acos*m*2 instruction pattern 395
`ADA_LONG_TYPE_SIZE` 482
Adding a new GIMPLE statement code 234
`ADDITIONAL_REGISTER_NAMES` 595
add*m*3 instruction pattern 388
add*mode*cc instruction pattern 404
addptr*m*3 instruction pattern 389
`addr_diff_vec` 292
`addr_diff_vec`, length of 441
`addr_vec` 291
`addr_vec`, length of 441
`ADDR_EXPR` 167
address constraints 343
`address_operand` 337, 343

addressing modes 542
add*vm*4 instruction pattern 389
`ADJUST_FIELD_ALIGN` 476
`ADJUST_INSN_LENGTH` 441
`ADJUST_REG_ALLOC_ORDER` 489
aggregates as return values 527
alias 246
`ALL_REGS` 493
`allocate_stack` instruction pattern 410
alternate entry points 296
anchored addresses 551
and 281
and and attributes 436
and, canonicalization of 422
and*m*3 instruction pattern 388
`ANNOTATE_EXPR` 169
annotations 237
`APPLY_RESULT_SIZE` 527
`arg_pointer_rtx` 513
`ARG_POINTER_CFA_OFFSET` 507
`ARG_POINTER_REGNUM` 512
`ARG_POINTER_REGNUM` and virtual registers 273
`ARGS_GROW_DOWNWARD` 504
argument passing 7
arguments in registers 518
arguments on stack 516
arithmetic library 12
arithmetic shift 281
arithmetic shift with signed saturation 281
arithmetic shift with unsigned saturation 281
arithmetic, in RTL 278
`ARITHMETIC_TYPE_P` 188
array 155
`ARRAY_RANGE_REF` 167
`ARRAY_REF` 167
`ARRAY_TYPE` 155
`AS_NEEDS_DASH_FOR_PIPED_INPUT` 463
ashift 281
ashift and attributes 437
ashiftrt 281
ashiftrt and attributes 437
ashl*m*3 instruction pattern 394
ashr*m*3 instruction pattern 394
asin*m*2 instruction pattern 395
`asm_fprintf` 597
`asm_input` 291
`asm_input` and '/v' 256
`asm_noperands` 299
`asm_operands` and '/v' 256
`asm_operands`, RTL sharing 305
`asm_operands`, usage 293
`ASM_APP_OFF` 577
`ASM_APP_ON` 577
`ASM_COMMENT_START` 577
`ASM_DECLARE_COLD_FUNCTION_NAME` 586
`ASM_DECLARE_COLD_FUNCTION_SIZE` 586
`ASM_DECLARE_FUNCTION_NAME` 585
`ASM_DECLARE_FUNCTION_SIZE` 585

Concept Index

ASM_DECLARE_OBJECT_NAME 586
ASM_DECLARE_REGISTER_GLOBAL 586
ASM_FINAL_SPEC 463
ASM_FINISH_DECLARE_OBJECT 586
ASM_FORMAT_PRIVATE_NAME 590
ASM_FPRINTF_EXTENSIONS 598
ASM_GENERATE_INTERNAL_LABEL 590
ASM_MAYBE_OUTPUT_ENCODED_ADDR_RTX 509
ASM_NO_SKIP_IN_TEXT 604
ASM_OUTPUT_ADDR_DIFF_ELT 599
ASM_OUTPUT_ADDR_VEC_ELT 599
ASM_OUTPUT_ALIGN 604
ASM_OUTPUT_ALIGN_WITH_NOP 604
ASM_OUTPUT_ALIGNED_BSS 583
ASM_OUTPUT_ALIGNED_COMMON 582
ASM_OUTPUT_ALIGNED_DECL_COMMON 582
ASM_OUTPUT_ALIGNED_DECL_LOCAL 583
ASM_OUTPUT_ALIGNED_LOCAL 583
ASM_OUTPUT_ASCII 580
ASM_OUTPUT_CASE_END 599
ASM_OUTPUT_CASE_LABEL 599
ASM_OUTPUT_COMMON 582
ASM_OUTPUT_DEBUG_LABEL 590
ASM_OUTPUT_DEF 590
ASM_OUTPUT_DEF_FROM_DECLS 590
ASM_OUTPUT_DWARF_DATAREL 610
ASM_OUTPUT_DWARF_DELTA 610
ASM_OUTPUT_DWARF_OFFSET 610
ASM_OUTPUT_DWARF_PCREL 610
ASM_OUTPUT_DWARF_TABLE_REF 610
ASM_OUTPUT_DWARF_VMS_DELTA 610
ASM_OUTPUT_EXTERNAL 588
ASM_OUTPUT_FDESC 580
ASM_OUTPUT_FUNCTION_LABEL 584
ASM_OUTPUT_INTERNAL_LABEL 584
ASM_OUTPUT_LABEL 583
ASM_OUTPUT_LABEL_REF 589
ASM_OUTPUT_LABELREF 589
ASM_OUTPUT_LOCAL 583
ASM_OUTPUT_MAX_SKIP_ALIGN 604
ASM_OUTPUT_MEASURED_SIZE 584
ASM_OUTPUT_OPCODE 596
ASM_OUTPUT_POOL_EPILOGUE 581
ASM_OUTPUT_POOL_PROLOGUE 580
ASM_OUTPUT_REG_POP 599
ASM_OUTPUT_REG_PUSH 598
ASM_OUTPUT_SIZE_DIRECTIVE 581
ASM_OUTPUT_SKIP 603
ASM_OUTPUT_SOURCE_FILENAME 577
ASM_OUTPUT_SPECIAL_POOL_ENTRY 581
ASM_OUTPUT_SYMBOL_REF 589
ASM_OUTPUT_TYPE_DIRECTIVE 585
ASM_OUTPUT_WEAK_ALIAS 591
ASM_OUTPUT_WEAKREF 587
ASM_PREFERRED_EH_DATA_FORMAT 509
ASM_SPEC 463
ASM_STABD_OP 605
ASM_STABN_OP 606
ASM_STABS_OP 605
ASM_WEAKEN_DECL 587
ASM_WEAKEN_LABEL 587
assemble_name 583
assemble_name_raw 584
assembler format 576
assembler instructions in RTL 293
ASSEMBLER_DIALECT 598
assigning attribute values to insns 438
ASSUME_EXTENDED_UNWIND_CONTEXT 514
asterisk in template 334
atan2m3 instruction pattern 396
atan$m$2 instruction pattern 395
atomic 659
atomic_add_fetch$mode$ instruction pattern 417
atomic_add$mode$ instruction pattern 416
atomic_and_fetch$mode$ instruction pattern 417
atomic_and$mode$ instruction pattern 416
atomic_bit_test_and_complement$mode$ instruction
   pattern 417
atomic_bit_test_and_reset$mode$ instruction
   pattern 417
atomic_bit_test_and_set$mode$ instruction pattern
   417
atomic_compare_and_swap$mode$ instruction pattern
   415
atomic_exchange$mode$ instruction pattern 416
atomic_fetch_add$mode$ instruction pattern 416
atomic_fetch_and$mode$ instruction pattern 416
atomic_fetch_nand$mode$ instruction pattern .. 416
atomic_fetch_or$mode$ instruction pattern 416
atomic_fetch_sub$mode$ instruction pattern 416
atomic_fetch_xor$mode$ instruction pattern 416
atomic_load$mode$ instruction pattern 416
atomic_nand_fetch$mode$ instruction pattern .. 417
atomic_nand$mode$ instruction pattern 416
atomic_or_fetch$mode$ instruction pattern 417
atomic_or$mode$ instruction pattern 416
atomic_store$mode$ instruction pattern 416
atomic_sub_fetch$mode$ instruction pattern 417
atomic_sub$mode$ instruction pattern 416
atomic_test_and_set instruction pattern 417
atomic_xor_fetch$mode$ instruction pattern 417
atomic_xor$mode$ instruction pattern 416
attr 438, 439
attr_flag 438
attribute expressions 436
attribute specifications 440
attribute specifications example 440
ATTRIBUTE_ALIGNED_VALUE 475
attributes 164
attributes, defining 434
attributes, target-specific 613
autoincrement addressing, availability 5
autoincrement/decrement addressing 341
automata_option 448
automaton based pipeline description 444
automaton based scheduler 444

AVOID_CCMODE_COPIES 492

B

backslash 333
barrier 297
barrier and '/f' 258
barrier and '/v' 256
BASE_REG_CLASS 495
basic block 307
Basic Statements 178
basic-block.h 307
basic_block 307
BASIC_BLOCK 307
bb_seq 231
BB_HEAD, BB_END 314
BIGGEST_ALIGNMENT 475
BIGGEST_FIELD_ALIGNMENT 475
BImode 261
BIND_EXPR 169
BINFO_TYPE 191
bit-fields 284
BIT_AND_EXPR 169
BIT_IOR_EXPR 169
BIT_NOT_EXPR 169
BIT_XOR_EXPR 169
BITFIELD_NBYTES_LIMITED 479
BITS_BIG_ENDIAN 472
BITS_BIG_ENDIAN, effect on sign_extract 284
BITS_PER_UNIT 268
BITS_PER_WORD 473
bitwise complement 280
bitwise exclusive-or 281
bitwise inclusive-or 281
bitwise logical-and 281
BLKmode 263
BLKmode, and function return values 303
BLOCK_FOR_INSN, gimple_bb 313
BLOCK_REG_PADDING 522
blockage instruction pattern 413
Blocks 180
BND32mode 264
BND64mode 264
bool 638
BOOL_TYPE_SIZE 482
BOOLEAN_TYPE 155
branch prediction 312
BRANCH_COST 557
break_out_memory_refs 544
BREAK_STMT 195
BSS_SECTION_ASM_OP 571
bswap 282
bswap*m*2 instruction pattern 394
btrunc*m*2 instruction pattern 397
build0 154
build1 154
build2 154
build3 154
build4 154
build5 154
build6 154
builtin_longjmp instruction pattern 411
builtin_setjmp_receiver instruction pattern
  411
builtin_setjmp_setup instruction pattern 411
byte_mode 268
BYTES_BIG_ENDIAN 472
BYTES_BIG_ENDIAN, effect on subreg 275

C

c_register_pragma 628
c_register_pragma_with_expansion 628
C statements for assembler output 334
C_COMMON_OVERRIDE_OPTIONS 470
cache 657
call 259, 288
call instruction pattern 405
call usage 303
call, in call_insn 257
call, in mem 257
call-clobbered register 487, 488
call-saved register 487, 488
call-used register 487, 488
call_insn 296
call_insn and '/c' 257
call_insn and '/f' 258
call_insn and '/i' 257
call_insn and '/j' 258
call_insn and '/s' 256, 258
call_insn and '/u' 256, 257
call_insn and '/u' or '/i' 257
call_insn and '/v' 256
call_pop instruction pattern 406
call_used_regs 488
call_value instruction pattern 406
call_value_pop instruction pattern 406
CALL_EXPR 169
CALL_INSN_FUNCTION_USAGE 296
CALL_POPS_ARGS 518
CALL_REALLY_USED_REGISTERS 488
CALL_USED_REGISTERS 487
calling conventions 504
calling functions in RTL 303
can_create_pseudo_p 383
can_fallthru 308
canadian 61
canonicalization of instructions 422
canonicalize_funcptr_for_compare instruction
  pattern 408
caret 345
CASE_VECTOR_MODE 622
CASE_VECTOR_PC_RELATIVE 622
CASE_VECTOR_SHORTEN_MODE 622
casesi instruction pattern 407
cbranch*mode*4 instruction pattern 405

Concept Index

cc_status 552
cc0 .... 277, 552
cc0, RTL sharing 304
cc0_rtx 277
CC_STATUS_MDEP 553
CC_STATUS_MDEP_INIT 553
CC1_SPEC 462
CC1PLUS_SPEC 463
CCmode 263, 553
CDImode 264
CEIL_DIV_EXPR 169
CEIL_MOD_EXPR 169
ceil*m*2 instruction pattern 397
CFA_FRAME_BASE_OFFSET 508
CFG verification 315
CFG, Control Flow Graph 307
cfghooks.h 313
cgraph_finalize_function 123
chain_circular 658
chain_next 658
chain_prev 658
change_address 383
CHAR_TYPE_SIZE 482
check_stack instruction pattern 410
CHImode 264
class definitions, register 493
class preference constraints 346
class, scope 191
CLASS_MAX_NREGS 502
CLASS_TYPE_P 188
classes of RTX codes 250
CLASSTYPE_DECLARED_CLASS 191
CLASSTYPE_HAS_MUTABLE 192
CLASSTYPE_NON_POD_P 192
CLEANUP_DECL 195
CLEANUP_EXPR 195
CLEANUP_POINT_EXPR 169
CLEANUP_STMT 195
Cleanups 181
clear_cache instruction pattern 418
CLEAR_INSN_CACHE 540
CLEAR_RATIO 559
clobber 288
clrsb 281
clrsb*m*2 instruction pattern 398
clz 282
CLZ_DEFINED_VALUE_AT_ZERO 626
clz*m*2 instruction pattern 398
cmpmem*m* instruction pattern 401
cmpstr*m* instruction pattern 400
cmpstrn*m* instruction pattern 400
code generation RTL sequences 423
code iterators in '.md' files 458
code_label 296
code_label and '/i' 256
code_label and '/v' 256
CODE_LABEL 308
CODE_LABEL_NUMBER 296

codes, RTL expression 249
COImode 264
COLLECT_EXPORT_LIST 635
COLLECT_SHARED_FINI_FUNC 594
COLLECT_SHARED_INIT_FUNC 593
COLLECT2_HOST_INITIALIZATION 645
commit_edge_insertions 314
compare 279
compare, canonicalization of 422
COMPARE_MAX_PIECES 559
comparison_operator 338
compiler passes and files 123
complement, bitwise 280
complex_mode 265
COMPLEX_CST 165
COMPLEX_EXPR 169
COMPLEX_TYPE 155
COMPONENT_REF 167
Compound Expressions 207
Compound Lvalues 207
COMPOUND_EXPR 169
COMPOUND_LITERAL_EXPR 169
COMPOUND_LITERAL_EXPR_DECL 175
COMPOUND_LITERAL_EXPR_DECL_EXPR 175
computed jump 310
computing the length of an insn 441
concat 278
concatn 278
cond 283
cond and attributes 436
cond_add*mode* instruction pattern 404
cond_and*mode* instruction pattern 404
cond_exec 291
cond_ior*mode* instruction pattern 404
cond_smax*mode* instruction pattern 404
cond_smin*mode* instruction pattern 404
cond_sub*mode* instruction pattern 404
cond_umax*mode* instruction pattern 404
cond_umin*mode* instruction pattern 404
cond_xor*mode* instruction pattern 404
COND_EXPR 169
condition code register 277
condition code status 552
condition codes 282
conditional execution 450
Conditional Expressions 207
conditions, in patterns 328
configuration file 644, 645
configure terms 61
CONJ_EXPR 169
const 271
const_double 268
const_double, RTL sharing 304
const_double_operand 337
const_fixed 269
const_int 268
const_int and attribute tests 436
const_int and attributes 436

const_int, RTL sharing 304
const_int_operand 336
const_poly_int 270
const_poly_int, RTL sharing 304
const_string 271
const_string and attributes 436
const_true_rtx 268
const_vector 270
const_vector, RTL sharing 304
const0_rtx 268
const1_rtx 268
const2_rtx 268
CONST_DECL 160
CONST_DOUBLE_LOW 269
CONST_WIDE_INT 269
CONST_WIDE_INT_ELT 269
CONST_WIDE_INT_NUNITS 269
CONST_WIDE_INT_VEC 269
CONST0_RTX 272
CONST1_RTX 272
CONST2_RTX 272
constant attributes 442
constant definitions 453
CONSTANT_ADDRESS_P 543
CONSTANT_P 543
CONSTANT_POOL_ADDRESS_P 256
CONSTANT_POOL_BEFORE_FUNCTION 580
constants in constraints 341
constm1_rtx 268
constraint modifier characters 346
constraint, matching 342
constraint_num 381
constraint_satisfied_p 381
constraints 340
constraints, defining 378
constraints, machine specific 347
constraints, testing 381
constructors, automatic calls 651
constructors, output of 591
CONSTRUCTOR 169
container 155
CONTINUE_STMT 195
contributors 711
controlling register usage 488
controlling the compilation driver 462
conventions, run-time 7
conversions 285
CONVERT_EXPR 169
copy_rtx 545
copy_rtx_if_shared 305
copysign*m*3 instruction pattern 398
cos*m*2 instruction pattern 395
costs of instructions 556
cp_namespace_decls 190
cp_type_quals 187, 188
CP_INTEGRAL_TYPE 188
CP_TYPE_CONST_NON_VOLATILE_P 188
CP_TYPE_CONST_P 188

CP_TYPE_RESTRICT_P 188
CP_TYPE_VOLATILE_P 188
CPLUSPLUS_CPP_SPEC 462
CPP_SPEC 462
CPSImode 264
CQImode 264
cross compilation and floating point 611
CROSSING_JUMP_P 256
CRT_CALL_STATIC_FUNCTION 572
crtl->args.pops_args 531
crtl->args.pretend_args_size 531
crtl->outgoing_args_size 516
CRTSTUFF_T_CFLAGS 647
CRTSTUFF_T_CFLAGS_S 647
CSImode 264
cstore*mode*4 instruction pattern 405
CTImode 264
ctrap*MM*4 instruction pattern 412
ctz 282
CTZ_DEFINED_VALUE_AT_ZERO 626
ctz*m*2 instruction pattern 398
CUMULATIVE_ARGS 520
current_function_is_leaf 493
current_function_uses_only_leaf_regs 493
current_insn_predicate 450

D

DAmode 263
data bypass 445, 446
data dependence delays 444
Data Dependency Analysis 324
data structures 471
DATA_ABI_ALIGNMENT 476
DATA_ALIGNMENT 476
DATA_SECTION_ASM_OP 571
dbr_sequence_length 597
DBR_OUTPUT_SEQEND 597
DBX_BLOCKS_FUNCTION_RELATIVE 607
DBX_CONTIN_CHAR 606
DBX_CONTIN_LENGTH 606
DBX_DEBUGGING_INFO 605
DBX_FUNCTION_FIRST 607
DBX_LINES_FUNCTION_RELATIVE 607
DBX_NO_XREFS 606
DBX_OUTPUT_MAIN_SOURCE_FILE_END 608
DBX_OUTPUT_MAIN_SOURCE_FILENAME 608
DBX_OUTPUT_NULL_N_SO_AT_MAIN_SOURCE_FILE_
    END 608
DBX_OUTPUT_SOURCE_LINE 607
DBX_REGISTER_NUMBER 604
DBX_REGPARM_STABS_CODE 606
DBX_REGPARM_STABS_LETTER 606
DBX_STATIC_CONST_VAR_CODE 606
DBX_STATIC_STAB_DATA_SECTION 606
DBX_TYPE_DECL_STABS_CODE 606
DBX_USE_BINCL 607
DCmode 264

Concept Index

DDmode 262
De Morgan's law 422
dead_or_set_p 431
debug_expr 294
debug_implicit_ptr 294
debug_insn 298
debug_marker 294
debug_parameter_ref 294
DEBUG_EXPR_DECL 160
DEBUG_SYMS_TEXT 605
DEBUGGER_ARG_OFFSET 605
DEBUGGER_AUTO_OFFSET 604
decimal float library 16
DECL_ALIGN 160
DECL_ANTICIPATED 193
DECL_ARGUMENTS 185
DECL_ARRAY_DELETE_OPERATOR_P 195
DECL_ARTIFICIAL 160, 184, 186
DECL_ASSEMBLER_NAME 184
DECL_ATTRIBUTES 165
DECL_BASE_CONSTRUCTOR_P 194
DECL_COMPLETE_CONSTRUCTOR_P 193
DECL_COMPLETE_DESTRUCTOR_P 194
DECL_CONST_MEMFUNC_P 193
DECL_CONSTRUCTOR_P 193
DECL_CONTEXT 190
DECL_CONV_FN_P 194
DECL_COPY_CONSTRUCTOR_P 194
DECL_DESTRUCTOR_P 194
DECL_EXTERN_C_FUNCTION_P 193
DECL_EXTERNAL 160, 186
DECL_FUNCTION_MEMBER_P 193
DECL_FUNCTION_SPECIFIC_OPTIMIZATION 184, 186
DECL_FUNCTION_SPECIFIC_TARGET 184, 186
DECL_GLOBAL_CTOR_P 194
DECL_GLOBAL_DTOR_P 194
DECL_INITIAL 160, 185
DECL_LINKONCE_P 193
DECL_LOCAL_FUNCTION_P 193
DECL_MAIN_P 193
DECL_NAME 160, 184, 190
DECL_NAMESPACE_ALIAS 190
DECL_NAMESPACE_STD_P 190
DECL_NON_THUNK_FUNCTION_P 194
DECL_NONCONVERTING_P 193
DECL_NONSTATIC_MEMBER_FUNCTION_P 193
DECL_OVERLOADED_OPERATOR_P 194
DECL_PURE_P 186
DECL_RESULT 185
DECL_SAVED_TREE 185
DECL_SIZE 160
DECL_STATIC_FUNCTION_P 193
DECL_STMT 195
DECL_STMT_DECL 195
DECL_THUNK_P 194
DECL_VIRTUAL_P 186
DECL_VOLATILE_MEMFUNC_P 193

declaration 160
declarations, RTL 287
DECLARE_LIBRARY_RENAMES 541
decrement_and_branch_until_zero instruction pattern 408
default 657
default_file_start 576
DEFAULT_GDB_EXTENSIONS 605
DEFAULT_INCOMING_FRAME_SP_OFFSET 507
DEFAULT_PCC_STRUCT_RETURN 528
DEFAULT_SIGNED_CHAR 484
define_address_constraint 380
define_asm_attributes 440
define_attr 434
define_automaton 444
define_bypass 446
define_c_enum 454
define_code_attr 458
define_code_iterator 458
define_cond_exec 450
define_constants 453
define_constraint 379
define_cpu_unit 445
define_delay 443
define_enum 455
define_enum_attr 435, 455
define_expand 423
define_insn 327
define_insn example 329
define_insn_and_split 429
define_insn_reservation 445
define_int_attr 459
define_int_iterator 459
define_memory_constraint 380
define_mode_attr 456
define_mode_iterator 456
define_peephole 431
define_peephole2 433
define_predicate 338
define_query_cpu_unit 445
define_register_constraint 379
define_reservation 446
define_special_memory_constraint 380
define_special_predicate 338
define_split 426
define_subst 451, 453, 460
define_subst_attr 460
defining attributes and their values 434
defining constraints 378
defining jump instruction patterns 419
defining looping instruction patterns 420
defining peephole optimizers 430
defining predicates 338
defining RTL sequences for code generation ... 423
delay slots, defining 443
deletable 658
DELETE_IF_ORDINARY 645
Dependent Patterns 419

desc	657
destructors, output of	591
deterministic finite state automaton	444, 448
DFmode	262
digits in constraint	342
DImode	262
DIR_SEPARATOR	644
DIR_SEPARATOR_2	644
directory options .md	430
disabling certain registers	488
dispatch table	599
div	280
div and attributes	437
division	280
divm3 instruction pattern	388
divmodm4 instruction pattern	393
DO_BODY	195
DO_COND	195
DO_STMT	195
dollar sign	345
DOLLARS_IN_IDENTIFIERS	629
doloop_begin instruction pattern	408
doloop_end instruction pattern	408
DONE	424
DONT_USE_BUILTIN_SETJMP	601
DOUBLE_TYPE_SIZE	483
DQmode	262
driver	462
DRIVER_SELF_SPECS	462
dump examples	137
dump setup	135
dump types	137
dump verbosity	136
dump_basic_block	137
dump_generic_expr	137
dump_gimple_stmt	137
dump_printf	137
DUMPFILE_FORMAT	645
DWARF_ALT_FRAME_RETURN_COLUMN	506
DWARF_CIE_DATA_ALIGNMENT	602
DWARF_FRAME_REGISTERS	513
DWARF_FRAME_REGNUM	514
DWARF_LAZY_REGISTER_VALUE	514
DWARF_REG_TO_UNWIND_COLUMN	514
DWARF_ZERO_REG	506
DWARF2_ASM_LINE_DEBUG_INFO	609
DWARF2_ASM_VIEW_DEBUG_INFO	609
DWARF2_DEBUGGING_INFO	608
DWARF2_FRAME_INFO	609
DWARF2_FRAME_REG_OUT	514
DWARF2_UNWIND_INFO	601
DYNAMIC_CHAIN_ADDRESS	505

E

'E' in constraint	342
earlyclobber operand	346
edge	309
edge in the flow graph	309
edge iterators	309
edge splitting	314
EDGE_ABNORMAL	310
EDGE_ABNORMAL, EDGE_ABNORMAL_CALL	311
EDGE_ABNORMAL, EDGE_EH	310
EDGE_ABNORMAL, EDGE_SIBCALL	310
EDGE_FALLTHRU, force_nonfallthru	310
EDOM, implicit usage	542
eh_return instruction pattern	411
EH_FRAME_SECTION_NAME	600
EH_FRAME_THROUGH_COLLECT2	600
EH_RETURN_DATA_REGNO	508
EH_RETURN_HANDLER_RTX	508
EH_RETURN_STACKADJ_RTX	508
EH_TABLES_CAN_BE_READ_ONLY	601
EH_USES	531
ei_edge	309
ei_end_p	309
ei_last	309
ei_next	309
ei_one_before_end_p	309
ei_prev	309
ei_safe_safe	309
ei_start	309
ELIMINABLE_REGS	515
ELSE_CLAUSE	195
Embedded C	22
Empty Statements	180
EMPTY_CLASS_EXPR	195
EMPTY_FIELD_BOUNDARY	478
Emulated TLS	616
enabled	377
ENDFILE_SPEC	464
endianness	5
entry_value	294
ENTRY_BLOCK_PTR, EXIT_BLOCK_PTR	307
enum reg_class	494
ENUMERAL_TYPE	155
enumerations	454
epilogue	529
epilogue instruction pattern	412
EPILOGUE_USES	531
eq	283
eq and attributes	437
eq_attr	437
EQ_EXPR	169
equal	283
errno, implicit usage	542
EXACT_DIV_EXPR	169
examining SSA_NAMEs	245
exception handling	310, 508
exception_receiver instruction pattern	411
exclamation point	345
exclusion_set	447
exclusive-or, bitwise	281
EXIT_EXPR	169
EXIT_IGNORE_STACK	531

Concept Index

exp10*m*2 instruction pattern 396
exp2*m*2 instruction pattern 396
expander definitions 423
expm1*m*2 instruction pattern 396
exp*m*2 instruction pattern 395
expr_list 303
EXPR_FILENAME 160
EXPR_LINENO 160
EXPR_STMT 195
EXPR_STMT_EXPR 195
expression 165
expression codes 249
extend*mn*2 instruction pattern 402
extensible constraints 343
EXTRA_SPECS 465
extract_last_*m* instruction pattern 390
extv instruction pattern 403
extv*m* instruction pattern 402
extv*m*isalign*m* instruction pattern 402
extzv instruction pattern 403
extzv*m* instruction pattern 403
extzv*m*isalign*m* instruction pattern 403

F

'F' in constraint 342
FAIL 424
fall-thru 309
FATAL_EXIT_CODE 645
FDL, GNU Free Documentation License 703
features, optional, in system conventions 469
ffs 281
ffs*m*2 instruction pattern 398
FIELD_DECL 160
file_end_indicate_exec_stack 576
files and passes of the compiler 123
files, generated 662
final_absence_set 447
final_presence_set 447
final_sequence 597
FINAL_PRESCAN_INSN 596
FIND_BASE_TERM 544
FINI_ARRAY_SECTION_ASM_OP 572
FINI_SECTION_ASM_OP 571
finite state automaton minimization 448
FIRST_PARM_OFFSET 505
FIRST_PARM_OFFSET and virtual registers 273
FIRST_PSEUDO_REGISTER 487
FIRST_STACK_REG 493
FIRST_VIRTUAL_REGISTER 272
fix 286
fix_trunc*mn*2 instruction pattern 401
FIX_TRUNC_EXPR 169
fixed register 487
fixed-point fractional library 22
fixed_regs 488
fixed_size_mode 265
FIXED_CONVERT_EXPR 169
FIXED_CST 165
FIXED_POINT_TYPE 155
FIXED_REGISTERS 487
fix*mn*2 instruction pattern 401
fixuns_trunc*mn*2 instruction pattern 402
fixuns*mn*2 instruction pattern 401
flags in RTL expression 256
float 286
float_extend 285
float_truncate 286
FLOAT_EXPR 169
FLOAT_LIB_COMPARE_RETURNS_BOOL 541
FLOAT_STORE_FLAG_VALUE 626
FLOAT_TYPE_SIZE 482
FLOAT_WORDS_BIG_ENDIAN 473
FLOAT_WORDS_BIG_ENDIAN, (lack of) effect on subreg 275
floating point and cross compilation 611
float*mn*2 instruction pattern 401
floatuns*mn*2 instruction pattern 401
FLOOR_DIV_EXPR 169
FLOOR_MOD_EXPR 169
floor*m*2 instruction pattern 397
flow-insensitive alias analysis 246
flow-sensitive alias analysis 246
fma 280
fma*m*4 instruction pattern 389
fmax*m*3 instruction pattern 389
fmin*m*3 instruction pattern 389
fmod*m*3 instruction pattern 394
fms*m*4 instruction pattern 389
fnma*m*4 instruction pattern 389
fnms*m*4 instruction pattern 389
fold_extract_last_*m* instruction pattern 390
fold_left_plus_*m* instruction pattern 390
for_user 657
FOR_BODY 195
FOR_COND 195
FOR_EXPR 195
FOR_INIT_STMT 195
FOR_STMT 195
force_reg 382
FORCE_CODE_SECTION_ALIGN 572
fract_convert 286
FRACT_TYPE_SIZE 483
fractional types 22
fract*mn*2 instruction pattern 402
fractuns*mn*2 instruction pattern 402
frame layout 504
frame_pointer_needed 529
frame_pointer_rtx 513
frame_related 259
frame_related, in insn, call_insn, jump_insn, barrier, and set 258
frame_related, in mem 257
frame_related, in reg 257
frame_related, in symbol_ref 258
FRAME_ADDR_RTX 506

FRAME_GROWS_DOWNWARD 504
FRAME_GROWS_DOWNWARD and virtual registers .. 273
FRAME_POINTER_CFA_OFFSET 507
FRAME_POINTER_REGNUM 512
FRAME_POINTER_REGNUM and virtual registers .. 273
frequency, count, BB_FREQ_BASE 312
ftruncm2 instruction pattern 401
function 184, 192
function call conventions 7
function entry and exit 529
function entry point, alternate function entry point
 311
function properties 186
function-call insns 303
FUNCTION_ARG_REGNO_P 522
FUNCTION_BOUNDARY 475
FUNCTION_DECL 184, 192
FUNCTION_MODE 627
FUNCTION_PROFILER 532
FUNCTION_TYPE 155
FUNCTION_VALUE 526
FUNCTION_VALUE_REGNO_P 526
functions, leaf 492
fundamental type 155

G

'g' in constraint 342
'G' in constraint 342
garbage collector, invocation 663
garbage collector, troubleshooting 664
gather_loadm instruction pattern 386
GCC and portability 5
GCC_DRIVER_HOST_INITIALIZATION 645
gcov_type 312
ge 283
ge and attributes 437
GE_EXPR 169
GEN_ERRNO_RTX 542
gencodes 132
general_operand 338
GENERAL_REGS 493
generated files 662
generating assembler output 334
generating insns 329
generic predicates 336
GENERIC 123, 153
genflags 132
get_attr 437
get_attr_length 441
get_insns 295
get_last_insn 295
get_thread_pointermode instruction pattern
 418
GET_CLASS_NARROWEST_MODE 267
GET_CODE 249
GET_MODE 267
GET_MODE_ALIGNMENT 267
GET_MODE_BITSIZE 267
GET_MODE_CLASS 267
GET_MODE_FBIT 267
GET_MODE_IBIT 267
GET_MODE_MASK 267
GET_MODE_NAME 267
GET_MODE_NUNITS 267
GET_MODE_SIZE 267
GET_MODE_UNIT_SIZE 267
GET_MODE_WIDER_MODE 267
GET_RTX_CLASS 250
GET_RTX_FORMAT 252
GET_RTX_LENGTH 252
geu 283
geu and attributes 437
ggc_collect 663
GGC 655
gimple 200
gimple_addresses_taken 211
gimple_asm_clobber_op 213
gimple_asm_input_op 213
gimple_asm_nclobbers 213
gimple_asm_ninputs 213
gimple_asm_noutputs 213
gimple_asm_output_op 213
gimple_asm_set_clobber_op 213
gimple_asm_set_input_op 213
gimple_asm_set_output_op 213
gimple_asm_set_volatile 213
gimple_asm_string 213
gimple_asm_volatile_p 213
gimple_assign_cast_p 209, 215
gimple_assign_lhs 214
gimple_assign_lhs_ptr 215
gimple_assign_rhs_class 214
gimple_assign_rhs_code 214
gimple_assign_rhs1 215
gimple_assign_rhs1_ptr 215
gimple_assign_rhs2 215
gimple_assign_rhs2_ptr 215
gimple_assign_rhs3 215
gimple_assign_rhs3_ptr 215
gimple_assign_set_lhs 215
gimple_assign_set_rhs1 215
gimple_assign_set_rhs2 215
gimple_assign_set_rhs3 215
gimple_bb 210
gimple_bind_add_seq 216
gimple_bind_add_stmt 216
gimple_bind_append_vars 215
gimple_bind_block 216
gimple_bind_body 215
gimple_bind_set_block 216
gimple_bind_set_body 216
gimple_bind_set_vars 215
gimple_bind_vars 215
gimple_block 210
gimple_build 681, 682

Concept Index

gimple_build_debug_begin_stmt............. 220
gimple_build_debug_inline_entry.......... 220
gimple_build_nop........................... 221
gimple_build_omp_master 224
gimple_build_omp_ordered 225
gimple_build_omp_return 226
gimple_build_omp_section 226
gimple_build_omp_sections_switch 226
gimple_build_wce........................... 230
gimple_call_arg............................ 217
gimple_call_arg_ptr........................ 217
gimple_call_chain.......................... 217
gimple_call_copy_skip_args 217
gimple_call_fn............................. 216
gimple_call_fndecl......................... 217
gimple_call_lhs............................ 216
gimple_call_lhs_ptr........................ 216
gimple_call_noreturn_p..................... 217
gimple_call_num_args....................... 217
gimple_call_return_type 217
gimple_call_set_arg........................ 217
gimple_call_set_chain...................... 217
gimple_call_set_fn......................... 216
gimple_call_set_fndecl..................... 217
gimple_call_set_lhs........................ 216
gimple_call_set_tail....................... 217
gimple_call_tail_p......................... 217
gimple_catch_handler....................... 218
gimple_catch_set_handler 218
gimple_catch_set_types..................... 218
gimple_catch_types......................... 217
gimple_catch_types_ptr..................... 218
gimple_code................................ 210
gimple_cond_code........................... 218
gimple_cond_false_label 219
gimple_cond_lhs............................ 218
gimple_cond_make_false..................... 219
gimple_cond_make_true...................... 219
gimple_cond_rhs............................ 218
gimple_cond_set_code....................... 218
gimple_cond_set_false_label 219
gimple_cond_set_lhs........................ 218
gimple_cond_set_rhs........................ 218
gimple_cond_set_true_label 218
gimple_cond_true_label..................... 218
gimple_convert............................. 682
gimple_copy................................ 212
gimple_debug_bind_get_value 219
gimple_debug_bind_get_value_ptr 220
gimple_debug_bind_get_var 219
gimple_debug_bind_has_value_p............. 220
gimple_debug_bind_p........................ 210
gimple_debug_bind_reset_value............. 220
gimple_debug_bind_set_value 220
gimple_debug_bind_set_var 220
gimple_def_ops............................. 211
gimple_eh_filter_failure 220
gimple_eh_filter_set_failure 221

gimple_eh_filter_set_types 221
gimple_eh_filter_types..................... 220
gimple_eh_filter_types_ptr 220
gimple_eh_must_not_throw_fndecl 221
gimple_eh_must_not_throw_set_fndecl...... 221
gimple_expr_code........................... 210
gimple_expr_type........................... 210
gimple_goto_dest........................... 221
gimple_goto_set_dest....................... 221
gimple_has_mem_ops......................... 211
gimple_has_ops............................. 211
gimple_has_volatile_ops 212
gimple_label_label......................... 221
gimple_label_set_label..................... 221
gimple_loaded_syms 212
gimple_locus 210
gimple_locus_empty_p 211
gimple_modified_p.......................... 212
gimple_no_warning_p........................ 211
gimple_nop_p............................... 221
gimple_num_ops 208, 211
gimple_omp_atomic_load_lhs 222
gimple_omp_atomic_load_rhs 222
gimple_omp_atomic_load_set_lhs 222
gimple_omp_atomic_load_set_rhs 222
gimple_omp_atomic_store_set_val 222
gimple_omp_atomic_store_val 222
gimple_omp_body............................ 225
gimple_omp_continue_control_def 222
gimple_omp_continue_control_def_ptr...... 222
gimple_omp_continue_control_use 222
gimple_omp_continue_control_use_ptr...... 223
gimple_omp_continue_set_control_def 222
gimple_omp_continue_set_control_use 223
gimple_omp_critical_name 223
gimple_omp_critical_name_ptr 223
gimple_omp_critical_set_name 223
gimple_omp_for_clauses..................... 223
gimple_omp_for_clauses_ptr 223
gimple_omp_for_cond 224
gimple_omp_for_final 224
gimple_omp_for_final_ptr 224
gimple_omp_for_incr 224
gimple_omp_for_incr_ptr 224
gimple_omp_for_index 223
gimple_omp_for_index_ptr 223
gimple_omp_for_initial 224
gimple_omp_for_initial_ptr 224
gimple_omp_for_pre_body 224
gimple_omp_for_set_clauses 223
gimple_omp_for_set_cond 224
gimple_omp_for_set_final 224
gimple_omp_for_set_incr 224
gimple_omp_for_set_index 224
gimple_omp_for_set_initial 224
gimple_omp_for_set_pre_body 224
gimple_omp_parallel_child_fn.............. 225
gimple_omp_parallel_child_fn_ptr 225

gimple_omp_parallel_clauses	225
gimple_omp_parallel_clauses_ptr	225
gimple_omp_parallel_combined_p	225
gimple_omp_parallel_data_arg	226
gimple_omp_parallel_data_arg_ptr	226
gimple_omp_parallel_set_child_fn	225
gimple_omp_parallel_set_clauses	225
gimple_omp_parallel_set_combined_p	225
gimple_omp_parallel_set_data_arg	226
gimple_omp_return_nowait_p	226
gimple_omp_return_set_nowait	226
gimple_omp_section_last_p	226
gimple_omp_section_set_last	226
gimple_omp_sections_clauses	227
gimple_omp_sections_clauses_ptr	227
gimple_omp_sections_control	226
gimple_omp_sections_control_ptr	227
gimple_omp_sections_set_clauses	227
gimple_omp_sections_set_control	227
gimple_omp_set_body	225
gimple_omp_single_clauses	227
gimple_omp_single_clauses_ptr	227
gimple_omp_single_set_clauses	227
gimple_op	208, 211
gimple_op_ptr	211
gimple_ops	208, 211
gimple_phi_arg	228, 243
gimple_phi_arg_def	243
gimple_phi_arg_edge	243
gimple_phi_capacity	227
gimple_phi_num_args	227, 243
gimple_phi_result	227, 243
gimple_phi_result_ptr	227
gimple_phi_set_arg	228
gimple_phi_set_result	227
gimple_plf	211
gimple_resx_region	228
gimple_resx_set_region	228
gimple_return_retval	228
gimple_return_set_retval	228
gimple_seq_add_seq	230
gimple_seq_add_stmt	230
gimple_seq_alloc	231
gimple_seq_copy	231
gimple_seq_deep_copy	230
gimple_seq_empty_p	231
gimple_seq_first	230
gimple_seq_init	231
gimple_seq_last	231
gimple_seq_reverse	230
gimple_seq_set_first	231
gimple_seq_set_last	231
gimple_seq_singleton_p	231
gimple_set_block	210
gimple_set_def_ops	211
gimple_set_has_volatile_ops	212
gimple_set_locus	211
gimple_set_op	211
gimple_set_plf	211
gimple_set_use_ops	212
gimple_set_vdef_ops	212
gimple_set_visited	211
gimple_set_vuse_ops	212
gimple_simplify	681
gimple_statement_with_ops	201
gimple_stored_syms	212
gimple_switch_default_label	229
gimple_switch_index	228
gimple_switch_label	229
gimple_switch_num_labels	228
gimple_switch_set_default_label	229
gimple_switch_set_index	229
gimple_switch_set_label	229
gimple_switch_set_num_labels	228
gimple_try_catch_is_cleanup	229
gimple_try_cleanup	229
gimple_try_eval	229
gimple_try_kind	229
gimple_try_set_catch_is_cleanup	229
gimple_try_set_cleanup	229
gimple_try_set_eval	229
gimple_use_ops	212
gimple_vdef_ops	212
gimple_visited_p	211
gimple_vuse_ops	212
gimple_wce_cleanup	230
gimple_wce_cleanup_eh_only	230
gimple_wce_set_cleanup	230
gimple_wce_set_cleanup_eh_only	230
GIMPLE	123, 124, 199
GIMPLE API	681
GIMPLE class hierarchy	202
GIMPLE Exception Handling	205
GIMPLE instruction set	205
GIMPLE sequences	230
GIMPLE statement iterators	308, 313
GIMPLE_ASM	213
GIMPLE_ASSIGN	214
GIMPLE_BIND	215
GIMPLE_CALL	216
GIMPLE_CATCH	217
GIMPLE_COND	218
GIMPLE_DEBUG	219
GIMPLE_DEBUG_BEGIN_STMT	219
GIMPLE_DEBUG_BIND	219
GIMPLE_DEBUG_INLINE_ENTRY	219
GIMPLE_EH_FILTER	220
GIMPLE_GOTO	221
GIMPLE_LABEL	221
GIMPLE_NOP	221
GIMPLE_OMP_ATOMIC_LOAD	221
GIMPLE_OMP_ATOMIC_STORE	222
GIMPLE_OMP_CONTINUE	222
GIMPLE_OMP_CRITICAL	223
GIMPLE_OMP_FOR	223
GIMPLE_OMP_MASTER	224

Concept Index

GIMPLE_OMP_ORDERED 225
GIMPLE_OMP_PARALLEL 225
GIMPLE_OMP_RETURN 226
GIMPLE_OMP_SECTION 226
GIMPLE_OMP_SECTIONS 226
GIMPLE_OMP_SINGLE 227
GIMPLE_PHI 227
GIMPLE_RESX 228
GIMPLE_RETURN 228
GIMPLE_SWITCH 228
GIMPLE_TRY 229
GIMPLE_WITH_CLEANUP_EXPR 230
gimplification 123, 124
gimplifier 123
gimplify_assign 214
gimplify_expr 124
gimplify_function_tree 124
global_regs 488
GLOBAL_INIT_PRIORITY 194
GO_IF_LEGITIMATE_ADDRESS 544
greater than 283
gsi_after_labels 232
gsi_bb 232
gsi_commit_edge_inserts 234, 314
gsi_commit_one_edge_insert 234
gsi_end_p 232, 314
gsi_for_stmt 234
gsi_insert_after 233, 314
gsi_insert_before 233, 314
gsi_insert_on_edge 234, 314
gsi_insert_on_edge_immediate 234
gsi_insert_seq_after 234
gsi_insert_seq_before 233
gsi_insert_seq_on_edge 234
gsi_last 232, 314
gsi_last_bb 232
gsi_link_after 233
gsi_link_before 233
gsi_link_seq_after 233
gsi_link_seq_before 233
gsi_move_after 234
gsi_move_before 234
gsi_move_to_bb_end 234
gsi_next 232, 314
gsi_one_before_end_p 232
gsi_prev 232, 314
gsi_remove 232, 314
gsi_replace 233
gsi_seq 232
gsi_split_seq_after 233
gsi_split_seq_before 233
gsi_start 232, 313
gsi_start_bb 232
gsi_stmt 232
gsi_stmt_ptr 232
gt 283
gt and attributes 437
GT_EXPR 169
gtu 283
gtu and attributes 437
GTY 655

H

'H' in constraint 342
HAmode 263
HANDLE_PRAGMA_PACK_WITH_EXPANSION 628
HANDLER 195
HANDLER_BODY 195
HANDLER_PARMS 195
hard registers 272
HARD_FRAME_POINTER_IS_ARG_POINTER 512
HARD_FRAME_POINTER_IS_FRAME_POINTER 512
HARD_FRAME_POINTER_REGNUM 512
HARD_REGNO_CALLER_SAVE_MODE 529
HARD_REGNO_NREGS_HAS_PADDING 490
HARD_REGNO_NREGS_WITH_PADDING 490
HARD_REGNO_RENAME_OK 491
HAS_INIT_SECTION 593
HAS_LONG_COND_BRANCH 621
HAS_LONG_UNCOND_BRANCH 622
HAVE_DOS_BASED_FILE_SYSTEM 644
HAVE_POST_DECREMENT 542
HAVE_POST_INCREMENT 542
HAVE_POST_MODIFY_DISP 543
HAVE_POST_MODIFY_REG 543
HAVE_PRE_DECREMENT 542
HAVE_PRE_INCREMENT 542
HAVE_PRE_MODIFY_DISP 543
HAVE_PRE_MODIFY_REG 543
HCmode 264
HFmode 262
high 271
HImode 261
HImode, in insn 299
HONOR_REG_ALLOC_ORDER 489
host configuration 643
host functions 643
host hooks 643
host makefile fragment 650
HOST_BIT_BUCKET 644
HOST_EXECUTABLE_SUFFIX 644
HOST_HOOKS_EXTRA_SIGNALS 643
HOST_HOOKS_GT_PCH_ALLOC_GRANULARITY 643
HOST_HOOKS_GT_PCH_GET_ADDRESS 643
HOST_HOOKS_GT_PCH_USE_ADDRESS 643
HOST_LACKS_INODE_NUMBERS 645
HOST_LONG_FORMAT 646
HOST_LONG_LONG_FORMAT 646
HOST_OBJECT_SUFFIX 644
HOST_PTR_PRINTF 646
HOT_TEXT_SECTION_NAME 570
HQmode 262

I

'i' in constraint	341
'I' in constraint	341
identifier	155
IDENTIFIER_LENGTH	155
IDENTIFIER_NODE	155
IDENTIFIER_OPNAME_P	155
IDENTIFIER_POINTER	155
IDENTIFIER_TYPENAME_P	155
IEEE 754-2008	16
if_then_else	283
if_then_else and attributes	436
if_then_else usage	288
IF_COND	195
IF_STMT	195
IFCVT_MACHDEP_INIT	630
IFCVT_MODIFY_CANCEL	630
IFCVT_MODIFY_FINAL	630
IFCVT_MODIFY_INSN	630
IFCVT_MODIFY_MULTIPLE_TESTS	630
IFCVT_MODIFY_TESTS	630
IMAGPART_EXPR	169
Immediate Uses	241
immediate_operand	336
IMMEDIATE_PREFIX	598
in_struct	259
in_struct, in code_label and note	256
in_struct, in insn and jump_insn and call_insn	256
in_struct, in insn, call_insn, jump_insn and jump_table_data	258
in_struct, in subreg	259
include	429
INCLUDE_DEFAULTS	467
inclusive-or, bitwise	281
INCOMING_FRAME_SP_OFFSET	507
INCOMING_REG_PARM_STACK_SPACE	517
INCOMING_REGNO	488
INCOMING_RETURN_ADDR_RTX	506
INCOMING_STACK_BOUNDARY	475
INDEX_REG_CLASS	495
indirect_jump instruction pattern	407
indirect_operand	337
INDIRECT_REF	167
init_machine_status	472
init_one_libfunc	541
INIT_ARRAY_SECTION_ASM_OP	572
INIT_CUMULATIVE_ARGS	520
INIT_CUMULATIVE_INCOMING_ARGS	521
INIT_CUMULATIVE_LIBCALL_ARGS	521
INIT_ENVIRONMENT	467
INIT_EXPANDERS	472
INIT_EXPR	169
INIT_SECTION_ASM_OP	571, 593
INITIAL_ELIMINATION_OFFSET	515
INITIAL_FRAME_ADDRESS_RTX	505
initialization routines	591
inlining	614
insert_insn_on_edge	314
insn	295
insn and '/f'	258
insn and '/j'	258
insn and '/s'	256, 258
insn and '/u'	256
insn and '/v'	256
insn attributes	434
insn canonicalization	422
insn includes	429
insn lengths, computing	441
insn notes, notes	308
insn splitting	426
insn-attr.h	435
insn_list	303
INSN_ANNULLED_BRANCH_P	256
INSN_CODE	299
INSN_DELETED_P	256
INSN_FROM_TARGET_P	256
INSN_REFERENCES_ARE_DELAYED	629
INSN_SETS_ARE_DELAYED	629
INSN_UID	294
INSN_VAR_LOCATION	298
insns	294
insns, generating	329
insns, recognizing	329
instruction attributes	434
instruction latency time	444, 445, 446
instruction patterns	327
instruction splitting	426
insv instruction pattern	403
insvm instruction pattern	403
insvmisalignm instruction pattern	403
int iterators in '.md' files	459
INT_FAST16_TYPE	485
INT_FAST32_TYPE	485
INT_FAST64_TYPE	485
INT_FAST8_TYPE	485
INT_LEAST16_TYPE	485
INT_LEAST32_TYPE	485
INT_LEAST64_TYPE	485
INT_LEAST8_TYPE	485
INT_TYPE_SIZE	482
INT16_TYPE	485
INT32_TYPE	485
INT64_TYPE	485
INT8_TYPE	485
INTEGER_CST	165
INTEGER_TYPE	155
Interdependence of Patterns	419
interfacing to GCC output	7
interlock delays	444
intermediate representation lowering	123
INTMAX_TYPE	485
INTPTR_TYPE	485
introduction	1
INVOKE__main	594
ior	281

Concept Index

ior and attributes........................... 436
ior, canonicalization of...................... 422
ior*m*3 instruction pattern.................... 388
IRA_HARD_REGNO_ADD_COST_MULTIPLIER....... 489
is_a... 266
is_gimple_addressable..................... 209
is_gimple_asm_val......................... 209
is_gimple_assign.......................... 209
is_gimple_call............................ 209
is_gimple_call_addr....................... 209
is_gimple_constant........................ 209
is_gimple_debug........................... 209
is_gimple_ip_invariant.................... 209
is_gimple_ip_invariant_address........... 209
is_gimple_mem_ref_addr.................... 209
is_gimple_min_invariant................... 209
is_gimple_omp............................. 210
is_gimple_val............................. 209
IS_ASM_LOGICAL_LINE_SEPARATOR............. 581
iterators in '.md' files...................... 455
IV analysis on GIMPLE..................... 321
IV analysis on RTL........................ 322

J

JMP_BUF_SIZE............................... 601
jump... 260
jump instruction pattern..................... 405
jump instruction patterns.................... 419
jump instructions and set................... 288
jump, in call_insn......................... 258
jump, in insn.............................. 258
jump, in mem............................... 256
jump_insn.................................. 295
jump_insn and '/f'......................... 258
jump_insn and '/j'......................... 256
jump_insn and '/s'..................... 256, 258
jump_insn and '/u'......................... 256
jump_insn and '/v'......................... 256
jump_table_data............................ 297
jump_table_data and '/s'................... 258
jump_table_data and '/v'................... 256
JUMP_ALIGN................................. 602
JUMP_LABEL................................. 295
JUMP_TABLES_IN_TEXT_SECTION............... 572
Jumps.. 180

L

label_ref.................................... 271
label_ref and '/v'......................... 256
label_ref, RTL sharing..................... 304
LABEL_ALIGN................................ 603
LABEL_ALIGN_AFTER_BARRIER................. 603
LABEL_ALT_ENTRY_P......................... 296
LABEL_ALTERNATE_NAME...................... 311
LABEL_DECL................................. 160
LABEL_KIND................................. 296

LABEL_NUSES................................ 296
LABEL_PRESERVE_P........................... 256
LABEL_REF_NONLOCAL_P...................... 256
lang_hooks.gimplify_expr.................. 124
lang_hooks.parse_file..................... 123
language-dependent trees...................... 187
language-independent intermediate representation
    123
large return values........................... 527
LAST_STACK_REG............................. 493
LAST_VIRTUAL_REGISTER..................... 272
lceil*mn*2.................................... 398
LCSSA.. 320
LD_FINI_SWITCH............................. 593
LD_INIT_SWITCH............................. 593
LDD_SUFFIX................................. 595
ldexp*m*3 instruction pattern.................. 395
le... 283
le and attributes............................ 437
LE_EXPR..................................... 169
leaf functions............................... 492
leaf_function_p............................ 407
LEAF_REG_REMAP............................. 492
LEAF_REGISTERS............................. 492
left rotate................................... 281
left shift................................... 281
LEGITIMATE_PIC_OPERAND_P.................. 575
LEGITIMIZE_RELOAD_ADDRESS................. 545
length....................................... 656
less than.................................... 283
less than or equal........................... 283
leu.. 283
leu and attributes........................... 437
lfloor*mn*2................................... 398
LIB_SPEC.................................... 463
LIB2FUNCS_EXTRA............................ 647
LIBCALL_VALUE.............................. 526
'libgcc.a'................................... 541
LIBGCC_SPEC................................ 463
LIBGCC2_CFLAGS............................. 647
LIBGCC2_GNU_PREFIX......................... 483
LIBGCC2_UNWIND_ATTRIBUTE.................. 639
library subroutine names..................... 541
LIBRARY_PATH_ENV........................... 630
LIMIT_RELOAD_CLASS......................... 498
LINK_COMMAND_SPEC.......................... 465
LINK_EH_SPEC............................... 464
LINK_GCC_C_SEQUENCE_SPEC.................. 465
LINK_LIBGCC_SPECIAL_1...................... 465
LINK_SPEC.................................. 463
list... 155
Liveness representation....................... 315
lo_sum....................................... 278
load address instruction..................... 343
load_multiple instruction pattern............ 384
LOAD_EXTEND_OP............................. 623
Local Register Allocator (LRA)............... 134
LOCAL_ALIGNMENT............................ 477

LOCAL_CLASS_P 192
LOCAL_DECL_ALIGNMENT 477
LOCAL_INCLUDE_DIR 467
LOCAL_LABEL_PREFIX 598
LOCAL_REGNO 489
log10*m*2 instruction pattern 396
log1p*m*2 instruction pattern 396
log2*m*2 instruction pattern 396
LOG_LINKS 299
logb*m*2 instruction pattern 396
Logical Operators 207
logical-and, bitwise 281
LOGICAL_OP_NON_SHORT_CIRCUIT 560
log*m*2 instruction pattern 396
LONG_ACCUM_TYPE_SIZE 483
LONG_DOUBLE_TYPE_SIZE 483
LONG_FRACT_TYPE_SIZE 483
LONG_LONG_ACCUM_TYPE_SIZE 483
LONG_LONG_FRACT_TYPE_SIZE 483
LONG_LONG_TYPE_SIZE 482
LONG_TYPE_SIZE 482
longjmp and automatic variables 7
Loop analysis 317
Loop manipulation 320
Loop querying 319
Loop representation 317
Loop-closed SSA form 320
LOOP_ALIGN 603
LOOP_EXPR 169
looping instruction patterns 420
lowering, language-dependent intermediate
    representation 123
lrint*mn*2 397
lround*mn*2 397
LSHIFT_EXPR 169
lshiftrt 281
lshiftrt and attributes 437
lshr*m*3 instruction pattern 394
lt 283
lt and attributes 437
LT_EXPR 169
LTGT_EXPR 169
lto 673
ltrans 673
ltu 283

M

'm' in constraint 341
MACH_DEP_SECTION_ASM_FLAG 572
machine attributes 613
machine description macros 461
machine descriptions 327
machine mode conversions 285
machine mode wrapper classes 265
machine modes 261
machine specific constraints 347
machine-independent predicates 336

machine_mode 261
macros, target description 461
madd*mn*4 instruction pattern 393
make_safe_from 426
MAKE_DECL_ONE_ONLY 588
makefile fragment 647
makefile targets 66
MALLOC_ABI_ALIGNMENT 475
Manipulating GIMPLE statements 210
marking roots 662
mask_gather_load*m* instruction pattern 386
mask_scatter_store*m* instruction pattern 386
MASK_RETURN_ADDR 601
maskload*mn* instruction pattern 388
maskstore*mn* instruction pattern 388
Match and Simplify 681
match_dup 330, 433
match_dup and attributes 441
match_op_dup 332
match_operand 329
match_operand and attributes 437
match_operator 331
match_par_dup 333
match_parallel 332
match_scratch 330, 433
match_test and attributes 437
matching constraint 342
matching operands 333
math library 12
math, in RTL 278
MATH_LIBRARY 629
matherr 542
MAX_BITS_PER_WORD 473
MAX_BITSIZE_MODE_ANY_INT 268
MAX_BITSIZE_MODE_ANY_MODE 268
MAX_CONDITIONAL_EXECUTE 630
MAX_FIXED_MODE_SIZE 480
MAX_MOVE_MAX 623
MAX_OFILE_ALIGNMENT 476
MAX_REGS_PER_ADDRESS 543
MAX_STACK_ALIGNMENT 476
max*m*3 instruction pattern 389
may_trap_p, tree_could_trap_p 310
maybe_undef 658
mcount 532
MD_EXEC_PREFIX 466
MD_FALLBACK_FRAME_STATE_FOR 509
MD_HANDLE_UNWABI 510
MD_STARTFILE_PREFIX 466
MD_STARTFILE_PREFIX_1 467
mem 278
mem and '/c' 257
mem and '/f' 257
mem and '/j' 256
mem and '/u' 257
mem and '/v' 256
mem, RTL sharing 305
mem_thread_fence instruction pattern 418

Concept Index

MEM_ADDR_SPACE 254
MEM_ALIAS_SET 253
MEM_ALIGN 254
MEM_EXPR 253
MEM_KEEP_ALIAS_SET_P 256
MEM_NOTRAP_P 257
MEM_OFFSET 253
MEM_OFFSET_KNOWN_P 253
MEM_POINTER 257
MEM_READONLY_P 257
MEM_REF 167
MEM_SIZE 254
MEM_SIZE_KNOWN_P 254
MEM_VOLATILE_P 256
memory model 247
memory reference, nonoffsettable 344
memory references in constraints.............. 341
memory_barrier instruction pattern 413
memory_blockage instruction pattern 413
memory_operand 337
MEMORY_MOVE_COST 556
METHOD_TYPE 155
MIN_UNITS_PER_WORD 473
MINIMUM_ALIGNMENT 478
MINIMUM_ATOMIC_ALIGNMENT 475
min*m*3 instruction pattern 389
minus 279
minus and attributes 437
minus, canonicalization of 422
MINUS_EXPR 169
MIPS coprocessor-definition macros............ 617
miscellaneous register hooks 535
mnemonic attribute 442
mod 280
mod and attributes 437
mode classes 264
mode iterators in '.md' files................. 456
mode switching 612
MODE_ACCUM 264
MODE_BASE_REG_CLASS 495
MODE_BASE_REG_REG_CLASS 495
MODE_CC 265, 553
MODE_CODE_BASE_REG_CLASS 495
MODE_COMPLEX_FLOAT 265
MODE_COMPLEX_INT 265
MODE_DECIMAL_FLOAT 264
MODE_FLOAT 264
MODE_FRACT 264
MODE_FUNCTION 265
MODE_INT 264
MODE_PARTIAL_INT 264
MODE_POINTER_BOUNDS 265
MODE_RANDOM 265
MODE_UACCUM 265
MODE_UFRACT 264
modifiers in constraints 346
MODIFY_EXPR 169
MODIFY_JNI_METHOD_CALL 636

mod*m*3 instruction pattern 388
modulo scheduling 133
MOVE_MAX 623
MOVE_MAX_PIECES 559
MOVE_RATIO 558
mov*m* instruction pattern 382
movmem*m* instruction pattern 399
movmisalign*m* instruction pattern 384
mov*mode*cc instruction pattern 404
movstr instruction pattern.................... 400
movstrict*m* instruction pattern 384
msub*mn*4 instruction pattern 393
mulhisi3 instruction pattern 392
mul*m*3 instruction pattern 388
mulqihi3 instruction pattern 392
mulsidi3 instruction pattern 392
mult 280
mult and attributes 437
mult, canonicalization of 422, 423
MULT_EXPR 169
MULT_HIGHPART_EXPR 169
MULTIARCH_DIRNAME 650
MULTILIB_DEFAULTS 466
MULTILIB_DIRNAMES 648
MULTILIB_EXCEPTIONS 648
MULTILIB_EXTRA_OPTS 649
MULTILIB_MATCHES 648
MULTILIB_OPTIONS 647
MULTILIB_OSDIRNAMES 649
MULTILIB_REQUIRED 648
MULTILIB_REUSE 649
multiple alternative constraints 345
MULTIPLE_SYMBOL_SPACES 629
multiplication 280
multiplication with signed saturation 280
multiplication with unsigned saturation 280
mulv*m*4 instruction pattern 389

N

'n' in constraint 341
N_REG_CLASSES 494
name 155
named address spaces 619
named patterns and conditions 328
names, pattern 382
namespace, scope.............................. 189
NAMESPACE_DECL 160, 189
NATIVE_SYSTEM_HEADER_COMPONENT 467
ne 283
ne and attributes 437
NE_EXPR 169
nearbyint*m*2 instruction pattern 397
neg 279
neg and attributes 437
neg, canonicalization of 422
NEGATE_EXPR 169
negation 279

negation with signed saturation	279
negation with unsigned saturation	279
`neg`*m*`2` instruction pattern	394
`neg`*mode*`cc` instruction pattern	404
`negv`*m*`3` instruction pattern	394
nested functions, trampolines for	539
`nested_ptr`	658
`next_bb, prev_bb, FOR_EACH_BB, FOR_ALL_BB`	307
`NEXT_INSN`	295
`NEXT_OBJC_RUNTIME`	542
nil	250
`NM_FLAGS`	595
`NO_DBX_BNSYM_ENSYM`	607
`NO_DBX_FUNCTION_END`	607
`NO_DBX_GCC_MARKER`	608
`NO_DBX_MAIN_SOURCE_DIRECTORY`	608
`NO_DOLLAR_IN_LABEL`	584
`NO_DOT_IN_LABEL`	585
`NO_FUNCTION_CSE`	560
`NO_IMPLICIT_EXTERN_C`	627
`NO_PROFILE_COUNTERS`	533
`NO_REGS`	493
`NON_LVALUE_EXPR`	169
nondeterministic finite state automaton	448
`nonimmediate_operand`	338
nonlocal goto handler	311
`nonlocal_goto` instruction pattern	410
`nonlocal_goto_receiver` instruction pattern	411
`nonmemory_operand`	338
nonoffsettable memory reference	344
`nop` instruction pattern	407
`NOP_EXPR`	169
normal predicates	336
`not`	280
`not` and attributes	436
not equal	283
`not`, canonicalization of	422
`note`	297
`note` and '/i'	256
`note` and '/v'	256
`NOTE_INSN_BASIC_BLOCK`	308
`NOTE_INSN_BEGIN_STMT`	298
`NOTE_INSN_BLOCK_BEG`	297
`NOTE_INSN_BLOCK_END`	297
`NOTE_INSN_DELETED`	297
`NOTE_INSN_DELETED_LABEL`	297
`NOTE_INSN_EH_REGION_BEG`	297
`NOTE_INSN_EH_REGION_END`	297
`NOTE_INSN_FUNCTION_BEG`	297
`NOTE_INSN_INLINE_ENTRY`	298
`NOTE_INSN_VAR_LOCATION`	298
`NOTE_LINE_NUMBER`	297
`NOTE_SOURCE_FILE`	297
`NOTE_VAR_LOCATION`	298
`NOTICE_UPDATE_CC`	553
`not`*mode*`cc` instruction pattern	404
`NUM_MACHINE_MODES`	267
`NUM_MODES_FOR_MODE_SWITCHING`	612
`NUM_POLY_INT_COEFFS`	139
Number of iterations analysis	322

O

'o' in constraint	341
`OACC_CACHE`	183
`OACC_DATA`	183
`OACC_DECLARE`	183
`OACC_ENTER_DATA`	183
`OACC_EXIT_DATA`	183
`OACC_HOST_DATA`	183
`OACC_KERNELS`	183
`OACC_LOOP`	183
`OACC_PARALLEL`	183
`OACC_UPDATE`	183
`OBJC_GEN_METHOD_LABEL`	591
`OBJC_JBLEN`	639
`OBJECT_FORMAT_COFF`	594
`OFFSET_TYPE`	155
offsettable address	341
`OImode`	262
`OMP_ATOMIC`	181
`OMP_CLAUSE`	181
`OMP_CONTINUE`	181
`OMP_CRITICAL`	181
`OMP_FOR`	181
`OMP_MASTER`	181
`OMP_ORDERED`	181
`OMP_PARALLEL`	181
`OMP_RETURN`	181
`OMP_SECTION`	181
`OMP_SECTIONS`	181
`OMP_SINGLE`	181
`one_cmpl`*m*`2` instruction pattern	399
operand access	252
Operand Access Routines	239
operand constraints	340
Operand Iterators	239
operand predicates	336
operand substitution	333
Operands	206
operands	237, 328
operator predicates	336
`opt_mode`	266
'optc-gen.awk'	115
`OPTGROUP_ALL`	136
`OPTGROUP_INLINE`	136
`OPTGROUP_IPA`	136
`OPTGROUP_LOOP`	136
`OPTGROUP_OMP`	136
`OPTGROUP_OTHER`	136
`OPTGROUP_VEC`	136
optimization dumps	135
optimization groups	135
optimization info file names	136

Concept Index

Optimization infrastructure for GIMPLE 237
OPTIMIZE_MODE_SWITCHING 612
option specification files 115
OPTION_DEFAULT_SPECS 462
optional hardware or system features 469
options, directory search 430
order of register allocation 489
ordered_comparison_operator 338
ORDERED_EXPR 169
Ordering of Patterns 419
ORIGINAL_REGNO 254
other register constraints 343
outgoing_args_size 516
OUTGOING_REG_PARM_STACK_SPACE 517
OUTGOING_REGNO 488
output of assembler code 576
output statements 334
output templates 333
output_asm_insn 335
OUTPUT_QUOTED_STRING 577
OVERLAPPING_REGISTER_NAMES 595
OVERLOAD 192
OVERRIDE_ABI_FORMAT 520
OVL_CURRENT 192
OVL_NEXT 192

P

'p' in constraint 343
PAD_VARARGS_DOWN 522
parallel 290
parameters, c++ abi 618
parameters, miscellaneous 621
parameters, precompiled headers 617
parity 282
paritym2 instruction pattern 399
PARM_BOUNDARY 475
PARM_DECL 160
PARSE_LDD_OUTPUT 595
pass dumps 123
pass_duplicate_computed_gotos 311
passes and files of the compiler 123
passing arguments 7
PATH_SEPARATOR 644
pattern conditions 328
pattern names 382
Pattern Ordering 419
patterns 327
PATTERN 299
pc 278
pc and attributes 441
pc, RTL sharing 304
pc_rtx 278
PC_REGNUM 489
PCC_BITFIELD_TYPE_MATTERS 478
PCC_STATIC_STRUCT_RETURN 528
PDImode 261
peephole optimization, RTL representation 290

peephole optimizer definitions 430
per-function data 471
percent sign 333
PHI nodes 243
PIC 575
PIC_OFFSET_TABLE_REG_CALL_CLOBBERED 575
PIC_OFFSET_TABLE_REGNUM 575
pipeline hazard recognizer 444
Plugins 665
plus 278
plus and attributes 437
plus, canonicalization of 422
PLUS_EXPR 169
Pmode 627
pmode_register_operand 337
pointer 155
POINTER_DIFF_EXPR 169
POINTER_PLUS_EXPR 169
POINTER_SIZE 473
POINTER_TYPE 155
POINTERS_EXTEND_UNSIGNED 473
poly_int 139
poly_int, invariant range 139
poly_int, main typedefs 139
poly_int, runtime value 139
poly_int, template parameters 139
poly_int, use in target-independent code 140
poly_int, use in target-specific code 140
POLY_INT_CST 165
polynomial integers 139
pop_operand 338
popcount 282
popcountm2 instruction pattern 399
pops_args 531
portability 5
position independent code 575
post_dec 292
post_inc 292
post_modify 292
post_order_compute,
    inverted_post_order_compute,
    walk_dominator_tree 307
POST_LINK_SPEC 465
POSTDECREMENT_EXPR 169
POSTINCREMENT_EXPR 169
POWI_MAX_MULTS 637
powm3 instruction pattern 306
pragma 628
pre_dec 292
pre_inc 292
pre_modify 293
PRE_GCC3_DWARF_FRAME_REGISTERS 514
PREDECREMENT_EXPR 169
predefined macros 468
predicates 336
predicates and machine modes 336
predication 450
predict.def 312

PREFERRED_DEBUGGING_TYPE 605
PREFERRED_RELOAD_CLASS..................... 497
PREFERRED_STACK_BOUNDARY 475
prefetch 292
prefetch and '/v'.......................... 257
prefetch instruction pattern 412
PREFETCH_SCHEDULE_BARRIER_P 257
PREINCREMENT_EXPR 169
presence_set 447
preserving SSA form........................ 243
pretend_args_size 531
prev_active_insn........................... 431
PREV_INSN................................... 294
PRINT_OPERAND 597
PRINT_OPERAND_ADDRESS..................... 597
PRINT_OPERAND_PUNCT_VALID_P 597
probe_stack instruction pattern 410
probe_stack_address instruction pattern..... 410
processor functional units 444, 445
processor pipeline description 444
product 280
profile feedback............................ 312
profile representation 312
PROFILE_BEFORE_PROLOGUE 533
PROFILE_HOOK 533
profiling, code generation 532
program counter............................ 278
prologue.................................... 529
prologue instruction pattern 412
PROMOTE_MODE............................... 474
pseudo registers 272
PSImode..................................... 261
PTRDIFF_TYPE............................... 484
purge_dead_edges...................... 310, 314
push address instruction 343
push_operand 338
push_reload 545
PUSH_ARGS................................... 516
PUSH_ARGS_REVERSED 516
PUSH_ROUNDING.............................. 516
push$m$1 instruction pattern................ 388
PUT_CODE.................................... 249
PUT_MODE.................................... 267
PUT_REG_NOTE_KIND 300

Q

QCmode...................................... 264
QFmode...................................... 262
QImode...................................... 261
QImode, in insn 299
QQmode...................................... 262
qualified type........................... 155, 187
querying function unit reservations............ 445
question mark............................... 345
quotient.................................... 280

R

'r' in constraint 341
RDIV_EXPR................................... 169
READONLY_DATA_SECTION_ASM_OP............. 571
real operands............................... 237
REAL_CST.................................... 165
REAL_LIBGCC_SPEC............................ 464
REAL_NM_FILE_NAME 595
REAL_TYPE................................... 155
REAL_VALUE_ABS.............................. 611
REAL_VALUE_ATOF............................ 611
REAL_VALUE_FIX.............................. 611
REAL_VALUE_ISINF............................ 611
REAL_VALUE_ISNAN........................... 611
REAL_VALUE_NEGATE 611
REAL_VALUE_NEGATIVE 611
REAL_VALUE_TO_TARGET_DECIMAL128 582
REAL_VALUE_TO_TARGET_DECIMAL32 582
REAL_VALUE_TO_TARGET_DECIMAL64 582
REAL_VALUE_TO_TARGET_DOUBLE............... 581
REAL_VALUE_TO_TARGET_LONG_DOUBLE......... 581
REAL_VALUE_TO_TARGET_SINGLE............... 581
REAL_VALUE_TYPE 611
REAL_VALUE_UNSIGNED_FIX 611
REALPART_EXPR............................... 169
recog_data.operand 596
recognizing insns 329
RECORD_TYPE.......................... 155, 191
redirect_edge_and_branch 313
redirect_edge_and_branch, redirect_jump
    314
reduc_and_scal_m instruction pattern 390
reduc_ior_scal_m instruction pattern 390
reduc_plus_scal_m instruction pattern 390
reduc_smax_scal_m instruction pattern 390
reduc_smin_scal_m instruction pattern 390
reduc_umax_scal_m instruction pattern 390
reduc_umin_scal_m instruction pattern 390
reduc_xor_scal_m instruction pattern 390
reference 155
REFERENCE_TYPE.............................. 155
reg 272
reg and '/f'............................... 257
reg and '/i'............................... 257
reg and '/v'............................... 257
reg, RTL sharing............................ 304
reg_class_contents 488
reg_class_for_constraint 382
reg_label and '/v'......................... 256
reg_names............................. 488, 597
REG_ALLOC_ORDER............................ 489
REG_BR_PRED 303
REG_BR_PROB 303
REG_BR_PROB_BASE, BB_FREQ_BASE, count 313
REG_BR_PROB_BASE, EDGE_FREQUENCY.......... 312
REG_CALL_NOCF_CHECK 303
REG_CC_SETTER.............................. 302
REG_CC_USER 302

Concept Index

REG_CLASS_CONTENTS 495
REG_CLASS_NAMES 494
REG_DEAD 300
REG_DEAD, REG_UNUSED 315
REG_DEP_ANTI 302
REG_DEP_OUTPUT 302
REG_DEP_TRUE 302
REG_EH_REGION, EDGE_ABNORMAL_CALL 310
REG_EQUAL 301
REG_EQUIV 301
REG_EXPR 254
REG_FRAME_RELATED_EXPR 303
REG_FUNCTION_VALUE_P 257
REG_INC 300
REG_LABEL_OPERAND 300
REG_LABEL_TARGET 301
REG_NONNEG 300
REG_NOTE_KIND 300
REG_NOTES 299
REG_OFFSET 254
REG_OK_STRICT 544
REG_PARM_STACK_SPACE 516
REG_PARM_STACK_SPACE, and TARGET_FUNCTION_ARG
 518
REG_POINTER 257
REG_SETJMP 301
REG_UNUSED 300
REG_USERVAR_P 257
REG_VALUE_IN_UNWIND_CONTEXT 514
REG_WORDS_BIG_ENDIAN 473
register allocation order 489
register class definitions 493
register class preference constraints 346
register pairs 490
Register Transfer Language (RTL) 249
register usage 487
register_operand 337
REGISTER_MOVE_COST 556
REGISTER_NAMES 595
REGISTER_PREFIX 598
REGISTER_TARGET_PRAGMAS 628
registers arguments 518
registers in constraints 341
REGMODE_NATURAL_SIZE 275, 276, 490
REGNO_MODE_CODE_OK_FOR_BASE_P 496
REGNO_MODE_OK_FOR_BASE_P 496
REGNO_MODE_OK_FOR_REG_BASE_P 496
REGNO_OK_FOR_BASE_P 495
REGNO_OK_FOR_INDEX_P 496
REGNO_REG_CLASS 495
regs_ever_live 529
regular expressions 444, 445
relative costs 556
RELATIVE_PREFIX_NOT_LINKDIR 466
reload_completed 407
reload_in instruction pattern 383
reload_in_progress 383
reload_out instruction pattern 383

reloading 134
remainder 280
remainder$m$3 instruction pattern 395
reorder 658
representation of RTL 249
reservation delays 444
rest_of_decl_compilation 123
rest_of_type_compilation 123
restore_stack_block instruction pattern 409
restore_stack_function instruction pattern
 409
restore_stack_nonlocal instruction pattern
 409
RESULT_DECL 160
return 288
return instruction pattern 406
return values in registers 525
return_val 260
return_val, in call_insn 257
return_val, in reg 257
return_val, in symbol_ref 259
RETURN_ADDR_IN_PREVIOUS_FRAME 506
RETURN_ADDR_OFFSET 509
RETURN_ADDR_RTX 506
RETURN_ADDRESS_POINTER_REGNUM 513
RETURN_EXPR 195
RETURN_STMT 195
returning aggregate values 527
returning structures and unions 7
reverse probability 313
REVERSE_CONDITION 555
REVERSIBLE_CC_MODE 555
right rotate 281
right shift 281
rint$m$2 instruction pattern 397
RISC 444, 447
roots, marking 662
rotate 281
rotatert 281
rotl$m$3 instruction pattern 394
rotr$m$3 instruction pattern 394
ROUND_DIV_EXPR 169
ROUND_MOD_EXPR 169
ROUND_TYPE_ALIGN 480
round$m$2 instruction pattern 397
RSHIFT_EXPR 169
rsqrt$m$2 instruction pattern 394
RTL addition 278
RTL addition with signed saturation 278
RTL addition with unsigned saturation 278
RTL classes 250
RTL comparison 279
RTL comparison operations 282
RTL constant expression types 268
RTL constants 268
RTL declarations 287
RTL difference 279
RTL expression 249

RTL expressions for arithmetic 278
RTL format 251
RTL format characters 251
RTL function-call insns 303
RTL insn template 329
RTL integers 249
RTL memory expressions 272
RTL object types 249
RTL postdecrement 292
RTL postincrement 292
RTL predecrement 292
RTL preincrement 292
RTL register expressions 272
RTL representation 249
RTL side effect expressions 287
RTL strings 249
RTL structure sharing assumptions 304
RTL subtraction 279
RTL subtraction with signed saturation 279
RTL subtraction with unsigned saturation ... 279
RTL sum 278
RTL vectors 249
RTL_CONST_CALL_P 257
RTL_CONST_OR_PURE_CALL_P 257
RTL_LOOPING_CONST_OR_PURE_CALL_P 257
RTL_PURE_CALL_P 257
RTX (See RTL) 249
RTX codes, classes of 250
RTX_FRAME_RELATED_P 258
run-time conventions 7
run-time target specification 468

S

's' in constraint 342
SAD_EXPR 176
same_type_p 157
SAmode 263
sat_fract 286
satfract*mn*2 instruction pattern 402
satfractuns*mn*2 instruction pattern 402
satisfies_constraint_*m* 381
save_stack_block instruction pattern 409
save_stack_function instruction pattern 409
save_stack_nonlocal instruction pattern 409
SAVE_EXPR 169
SBSS_SECTION_ASM_OP 571
Scalar evolutions 321
scalar_float_mode 265
scalar_int_mode 265
scalar_mode 265
scalars, returned as values 525
scalb*m*3 instruction pattern 395
scatter_store*m* instruction pattern 386
SCHED_GROUP_P 258
SCmode 264
scratch 277
scratch operands 277
scratch, RTL sharing 304
scratch_operand 337
SDATA_SECTION_ASM_OP 571
SDmode 262
sdot_prod*m* instruction pattern 390
search options 430
SECONDARY_INPUT_RELOAD_CLASS 499
SECONDARY_MEMORY_NEEDED_RTX 500
SECONDARY_OUTPUT_RELOAD_CLASS 499
SECONDARY_RELOAD_CLASS 499
SELECT_CC_MODE 553
sequence 291
Sequence iterators 231
set 287
set and '/f' 258
set_attr 439
set_attr_alternative 439
set_bb_seq 231
set_optab_libfunc 541
set_thread_pointer*mode* instruction pattern
    418
SET_ASM_OP 590
SET_DEST 288
SET_IS_RETURN_P 258
SET_LABEL_KIND 296
SET_RATIO 559
SET_SRC 288
SET_TYPE_STRUCTURAL_EQUALITY 155, 157
setmem*m* instruction pattern 400
SETUP_FRAME_ADDRESSES 505
SFmode 262
sharing of RTL components 304
shift 281
SHIFT_COUNT_TRUNCATED 623
SHLIB_SUFFIX 595
SHORT_ACCUM_TYPE_SIZE 483
SHORT_FRACT_TYPE_SIZE 483
SHORT_IMMEDIATES_SIGN_EXTEND 623
SHORT_TYPE_SIZE 482
shrink-wrapping separate components 534
sibcall_epilogue instruction pattern 412
sibling call 310
SIBLING_CALL_P 258
SIG_ATOMIC_TYPE 485
sign_extend 285
sign_extract 284
sign_extract, canonicalization of 423
signed division 280
signed division with signed saturation 280
signed maximum 280
signed minimum 280
significand*m*2 instruction pattern 396
SImode 261
simple constraints 340
simple_return 288
simple_return instruction pattern 406
sincos*m*3 instruction pattern 395
sin*m*2 instruction pattern 395

Concept Index

SIZE_ASM_OP 584
SIZE_TYPE 484
SIZETYPE 484
skip 657
SLOW_BYTE_ACCESS 557
smax 280
smin 280
sms, swing, software pipelining 133
smul*m*3_highpart instruction pattern 392
soft float library 12
special 659
special predicates 336
SPECS 650
speed of instructions 556
split_block 314
splitting instructions 426
SQmode 262
sqrt 281
sqrt*m*2 instruction pattern 394
square root 281
ss_abs 281
ss_ashift 281
ss_div 280
ss_minus 279
ss_mult 280
ss_neg 279
ss_plus 278
ss_truncate 285
SSA_NAME_DEF_STMT 245
SSA_NAME_VERSION 245
ssadd*m*3 instruction pattern 388
ssad*m* instruction pattern 391
ssashl*m*3 instruction pattern 394
SSA 242
ssdiv*m*3 instruction pattern 388
ssmadd*mn*4 instruction pattern 393
ssmsub*mn*4 instruction pattern 393
ssmul*m*3 instruction pattern 388
ssneg*m*2 instruction pattern 394
sssub*m*3 instruction pattern 388
stack arguments 516
stack frame layout 504
stack smashing protection 535
stack_pointer_rtx 513
stack_protect_set instruction pattern 418
stack_protect_test instruction pattern 418
STACK_ALIGNMENT_NEEDED 504
STACK_BOUNDARY 475
STACK_CHECK_BUILTIN 510
STACK_CHECK_FIXED_FRAME_SIZE 511
STACK_CHECK_MAX_FRAME_SIZE 511
STACK_CHECK_MAX_VAR_SIZE 511
STACK_CHECK_MOVING_SP 511
STACK_CHECK_PROBE_INTERVAL_EXP 510
STACK_CHECK_PROTECT 511
STACK_CHECK_STATIC_BUILTIN 510
STACK_DYNAMIC_OFFSET 505
STACK_DYNAMIC_OFFSET and virtual registers 273

STACK_GROWS_DOWNWARD 504
STACK_PARMS_IN_REG_PARM_AREA 517
STACK_POINTER_OFFSET 505
STACK_POINTER_OFFSET and virtual registers 273
STACK_POINTER_REGNUM 512
STACK_POINTER_REGNUM and virtual registers 273
STACK_PUSH_CODE 504
STACK_REG_COVER_CLASS 493
STACK_REGS 493
STACK_SAVEAREA_MODE 480
STACK_SIZE_MODE 480
STACK_SLOT_ALIGNMENT 477
standard pattern names 382
STANDARD_STARTFILE_PREFIX 466
STANDARD_STARTFILE_PREFIX_1 466
STANDARD_STARTFILE_PREFIX_2 466
STARTFILE_SPEC 464
Statement and operand traversals 235
Statement Sequences 180
statements 186, 195
Statements 178
Static profile estimation 312
static single assignment 242
STATIC_CHAIN_INCOMING_REGNUM 513
STATIC_CHAIN_REGNUM 513
'stdarg.h' and register arguments 518
STDC_0_IN_SYSTEM_HEADERS 627
STMT_EXPR 169
STMT_IS_FULL_EXPR_P 195
storage layout 472
'store_multiple' instruction pattern 384
STORE_FLAG_VALUE 625
STORE_MAX_PIECES 559
strcpy 476
strict_low_part 287
strict_memory_address_p 545
STRICT_ALIGNMENT 478
STRING_CST 165
STRING_POOL_ADDRESS_P 258
strlen*m* instruction pattern 401
structure value address 527
STRUCTURE_SIZE_BOUNDARY 478
structures, returning 7
sub*m*3 instruction pattern 388
SUBOBJECT 195
SUBOBJECT_CLEANUP 195
subreg 273
subreg and '/s' 259
subreg and '/u' 259
subreg and '/u' and '/v' 258
subreg, in strict_low_part 287
SUBREG_BYTE 276
SUBREG_PROMOTED_UNSIGNED_P 258
SUBREG_PROMOTED_UNSIGNED_SET 259
SUBREG_PROMOTED_VAR_P 259
SUBREG_REG 276
subst iterators in '.md' files 460
subv*m*4 instruction pattern 389

SUCCESS_EXIT_CODE	645
SUPPORTS_INIT_PRIORITY	594
SUPPORTS_ONE_ONLY	588
SUPPORTS_WEAK	587
SWITCH_BODY	195
SWITCH_COND	195
SWITCH_STMT	195
SWITCHABLE_TARGET	471
symbol_ref	271
symbol_ref and '/f'	258
symbol_ref and '/i'	259
symbol_ref and '/u'	256
symbol_ref and '/v'	259
symbol_ref, RTL sharing	304
SYMBOL_FLAG_ANCHOR	255
SYMBOL_FLAG_EXTERNAL	255
SYMBOL_FLAG_FUNCTION	255
SYMBOL_FLAG_HAS_BLOCK_INFO	255
SYMBOL_FLAG_LOCAL	255
SYMBOL_FLAG_SMALL	255
SYMBOL_FLAG_TLS_SHIFT	255
SYMBOL_REF_ANCHOR_P	255
SYMBOL_REF_BLOCK	255
SYMBOL_REF_BLOCK_OFFSET	255
SYMBOL_REF_CONSTANT	254
SYMBOL_REF_DATA	254
SYMBOL_REF_DECL	254
SYMBOL_REF_EXTERNAL_P	255
SYMBOL_REF_FLAG	259
SYMBOL_REF_FLAG, in TARGET_ENCODE_SECTION_INFO	574
SYMBOL_REF_FLAGS	254
SYMBOL_REF_FUNCTION_P	255
SYMBOL_REF_HAS_BLOCK_INFO_P	255
SYMBOL_REF_LOCAL_P	255
SYMBOL_REF_SMALL_P	255
SYMBOL_REF_TLS_MODEL	255
SYMBOL_REF_USED	259
SYMBOL_REF_WEAK	259
symbolic label	304
sync_add*mode* instruction pattern	414
sync_and*mode* instruction pattern	414
sync_compare_and_swap*mode* instruction pattern	413
sync_ior*mode* instruction pattern	414
sync_lock_release*mode* instruction pattern	415
sync_lock_test_and_set*mode* instruction pattern	414
sync_nand*mode* instruction pattern	414
sync_new_add*mode* instruction pattern	414
sync_new_and*mode* instruction pattern	414
sync_new_ior*mode* instruction pattern	414
sync_new_nand*mode* instruction pattern	414
sync_new_sub*mode* instruction pattern	414
sync_new_xor*mode* instruction pattern	414
sync_old_add*mode* instruction pattern	414
sync_old_and*mode* instruction pattern	414
sync_old_ior*mode* instruction pattern	414
sync_old_nand*mode* instruction pattern	414
sync_old_sub*mode* instruction pattern	414
sync_old_xor*mode* instruction pattern	414
sync_sub*mode* instruction pattern	414
sync_xor*mode* instruction pattern	414
SYSROOT_HEADERS_SUFFIX_SPEC	464
SYSROOT_SUFFIX_SPEC	464

T

't-*target*'	647
table jump	308
tablejump instruction pattern	408
tag	657
tagging insns	438
tail calls	533
TAmode	263
tan$m$2 instruction pattern	395
target attributes	613
target description macros	461
target functions	461
target hooks	461
target makefile fragment	647
target specifications	468
target_flags	469
TARGET_ABSOLUTE_BIGGEST_ALIGNMENT	475
TARGET_ADDITIONAL_ALLOCNO_CLASS_P	503
TARGET_ADDR_SPACE_ADDRESS_MODE	620
TARGET_ADDR_SPACE_CONVERT	621
TARGET_ADDR_SPACE_DEBUG	621
TARGET_ADDR_SPACE_DIAGNOSE_USAGE	621
TARGET_ADDR_SPACE_LEGITIMATE_ADDRESS_P	620
TARGET_ADDR_SPACE_LEGITIMIZE_ADDRESS	621
TARGET_ADDR_SPACE_POINTER_MODE	620
TARGET_ADDR_SPACE_SUBSET_P	621
TARGET_ADDR_SPACE_VALID_POINTER_MODE	620
TARGET_ADDR_SPACE_ZERO_ADDRESS_VALID	621
TARGET_ADDRESS_COST	561
TARGET_ALIGN_ANON_BITFIELD	479
TARGET_ALLOCATE_INITIAL_VALUE	635
TARGET_ALLOCATE_STACK_SLOTS_FOR_ARGS	639
TARGET_ALWAYS_STRIP_DOTDOT	466
TARGET_ARG_PARTIAL_BYTES	519
TARGET_ARM_EABI_UNWINDER	602
TARGET_ARRAY_MODE	523
TARGET_ARRAY_MODE_SUPPORTED_P	524
TARGET_ASAN_SHADOW_OFFSET	640
TARGET_ASM_ALIGNED_DI_OP	579
TARGET_ASM_ALIGNED_HI_OP	579
TARGET_ASM_ALIGNED_SI_OP	579
TARGET_ASM_ALIGNED_TI_OP	579
TARGET_ASM_ASSEMBLE_UNDEFINED_DECL	587
TARGET_ASM_ASSEMBLE_VISIBILITY	588
TARGET_ASM_BYTE_OP	579
TARGET_ASM_CAN_OUTPUT_MI_THUNK	532
TARGET_ASM_CLOSE_PAREN	581
TARGET_ASM_CODE_END	577
TARGET_ASM_CONSTRUCTOR	594

Concept Index

TARGET_ASM_DECL_END 580
TARGET_ASM_DECLARE_CONSTANT_NAME 586
TARGET_ASM_DESTRUCTOR 594
TARGET_ASM_ELF_FLAGS_NUMERIC 578
TARGET_ASM_EMIT_EXCEPT_PERSONALITY 600
TARGET_ASM_EMIT_EXCEPT_TABLE_LABEL 600
TARGET_ASM_EMIT_UNWIND_LABEL 600
TARGET_ASM_EXTERNAL_LIBCALL 589
TARGET_ASM_FILE_END 576
TARGET_ASM_FILE_START 576
TARGET_ASM_FILE_START_APP_OFF 576
TARGET_ASM_FILE_START_FILE_DIRECTIVE 576
TARGET_ASM_FINAL_POSTSCAN_INSN 596
TARGET_ASM_FUNCTION_BEGIN_EPILOGUE 530
TARGET_ASM_FUNCTION_END_PROLOGUE 530
TARGET_ASM_FUNCTION_EPILOGUE 530
TARGET_ASM_FUNCTION_PROLOGUE 529
TARGET_ASM_FUNCTION_RODATA_SECTION 573
TARGET_ASM_FUNCTION_SECTION 578
TARGET_ASM_FUNCTION_SWITCHED_TEXT_SECTIONS
    578
TARGET_ASM_GLOBALIZE_DECL_NAME 587
TARGET_ASM_GLOBALIZE_LABEL 587
TARGET_ASM_INIT_SECTIONS 572
TARGET_ASM_INTEGER 580
TARGET_ASM_INTERNAL_LABEL 589
TARGET_ASM_JUMP_ALIGN_MAX_SKIP 603
TARGET_ASM_LABEL_ALIGN_AFTER_BARRIER_MAX_
    SKIP 603
TARGET_ASM_LABEL_ALIGN_MAX_SKIP 603
TARGET_ASM_LOOP_ALIGN_MAX_SKIP 603
TARGET_ASM_LTO_END 576
TARGET_ASM_LTO_START 576
TARGET_ASM_MARK_DECL_PRESERVED 589
TARGET_ASM_MERGEABLE_RODATA_PREFIX 573
TARGET_ASM_NAMED_SECTION 577
TARGET_ASM_OPEN_PAREN 581
TARGET_ASM_OUTPUT_ADDR_CONST_EXTRA 580
TARGET_ASM_OUTPUT_ANCHOR 551
TARGET_ASM_OUTPUT_DWARF_DTPREL 610
TARGET_ASM_OUTPUT_IDENT 577
TARGET_ASM_OUTPUT_MI_THUNK 532
TARGET_ASM_OUTPUT_SOURCE_FILENAME 577
TARGET_ASM_PRINT_PATCHABLE_FUNCTION_ENTRY
    529
TARGET_ASM_RECORD_GCC_SWITCHES 578
TARGET_ASM_RECORD_GCC_SWITCHES_SECTION .. 579
TARGET_ASM_RELOC_RW_MASK 573
TARGET_ASM_SELECT_RTX_SECTION 574
TARGET_ASM_SELECT_SECTION 573
TARGET_ASM_TM_CLONE_TABLE_SECTION 574
TARGET_ASM_TRAMPOLINE_TEMPLATE 539
TARGET_ASM_TTYPE 602
TARGET_ASM_UNALIGNED_DI_OP 579
TARGET_ASM_UNALIGNED_HI_OP 579
TARGET_ASM_UNALIGNED_SI_OP 579
TARGET_ASM_UNALIGNED_TI_OP 579
TARGET_ASM_UNIQUE_SECTION 573
TARGET_ASM_UNWIND_EMIT 600
TARGET_ASM_UNWIND_EMIT_BEFORE_INSN 600
TARGET_ATOMIC_ALIGN_FOR_MODE 640
TARGET_ATOMIC_ASSIGN_EXPAND_FENV 640
TARGET_ATOMIC_TEST_AND_SET_TRUEVAL 640
TARGET_ATTRIBUTE_TABLE 613
TARGET_ATTRIBUTE_TAKES_IDENTIFIER_P 613
TARGET_BINDS_LOCAL_P 575
TARGET_BRANCH_TARGET_REGISTER_CALLEE_SAVED
    636
TARGET_BRANCH_TARGET_REGISTER_CLASS 636
TARGET_BUILD_BUILTIN_VA_LIST 522
TARGET_BUILTIN_CHKP_FUNCTION 631
TARGET_BUILTIN_DECL 631
TARGET_BUILTIN_RECIPROCAL 546
TARGET_BUILTIN_SETJMP_FRAME_VALUE 505
TARGET_C_EXCESS_PRECISION 474
TARGET_C_PREINCLUDE 627
TARGET_CALL_ARGS 537
TARGET_CALL_FUSAGE_CONTAINS_NON_CALLEE_
    CLOBBERS 535
TARGET_CALLEE_COPIES 520
TARGET_CAN_CHANGE_MODE_CLASS 502
TARGET_CAN_CHANGE_MODE_CLASS and subreg
    semantics 276
TARGET_CAN_ELIMINATE 515
TARGET_CAN_FOLLOW_JUMP 634
TARGET_CAN_INLINE_P 616
TARGET_CAN_USE_DOLOOP_P 634
TARGET_CANNOT_FORCE_CONST_MEM 546
TARGET_CANNOT_MODIFY_JUMPS_P 636
TARGET_CANNOT_SUBSTITUTE_MEM_EQUIV_P 503
TARGET_CANONICAL_VA_LIST_TYPE 523
TARGET_CANONICALIZE_COMPARISON 554
TARGET_CASE_VALUES_THRESHOLD 622
TARGET_CC_MODES_COMPATIBLE 555
TARGET_CHECK_PCH_TARGET_FLAGS 618
TARGET_CHECK_STRING_OBJECT_FORMAT_ARG ... 470
TARGET_CHKP_BOUND_MODE 633
TARGET_CHKP_BOUND_TYPE 633
TARGET_CHKP_FUNCTION_VALUE_BOUNDS 538
TARGET_CHKP_INITIALIZE_BOUNDS 633
TARGET_CHKP_MAKE_BOUNDS_CONSTANT 633
TARGET_CLASS_LIKELY_SPILLED_P 501
TARGET_CLASS_MAX_NREGS 501
TARGET_COMMUTATIVE_P 634
TARGET_COMP_TYPE_ATTRIBUTES 613
TARGET_COMPARE_BY_PIECES_BRANCH_RATIO ... 559
TARGET_COMPARE_VERSION_PRIORITY 633
TARGET_COMPUTE_FRAME_LAYOUT 515
TARGET_COMPUTE_PRESSURE_CLASSES 504
TARGET_CONDITIONAL_REGISTER_USAGE 488
TARGET_CONST_ANCHOR 639
TARGET_CONST_NOT_OK_FOR_DEBUG_P 546
TARGET_CONSTANT_ALIGNMENT 477
TARGET_CONVERT_TO_TYPE 639
TARGET_CPU_CPP_BUILTINS 468
TARGET_CSTORE_MODE 503

TARGET_CUSTOM_FUNCTION_DESCRIPTORS 540
TARGET_CXX_ADJUST_CLASS_AT_DEFINITION ... 619
TARGET_CXX_CDTOR_RETURNS_THIS 618
TARGET_CXX_CLASS_DATA_ALWAYS_COMDAT 619
TARGET_CXX_COOKIE_HAS_SIZE 618
TARGET_CXX_DECL_MANGLING_CONTEXT 619
TARGET_CXX_DETERMINE_CLASS_DATA_VISIBILITY
    619
TARGET_CXX_GET_COOKIE_SIZE 618
TARGET_CXX_GUARD_MASK_BIT 618
TARGET_CXX_GUARD_TYPE 618
TARGET_CXX_IMPLICIT_EXTERN_C 627
TARGET_CXX_IMPORT_EXPORT_CLASS 618
TARGET_CXX_KEY_METHOD_MAY_BE_INLINE 618
TARGET_CXX_LIBRARY_RTTI_COMDAT 619
TARGET_CXX_USE_AEABI_ATEXIT 619
TARGET_CXX_USE_ATEXIT_FOR_CXA_ATEXIT 619
TARGET_DEBUG_UNWIND_INFO 609
TARGET_DECIMAL_FLOAT_SUPPORTED_P 481
TARGET_DECLSPEC 614
TARGET_DEFAULT_PACK_STRUCT 628
TARGET_DEFAULT_SHORT_ENUMS 484
TARGET_DEFAULT_TARGET_FLAGS 469
TARGET_DEFERRED_OUTPUT_DEFS 591
TARGET_DELAY_SCHED2 609
TARGET_DELAY_VARTRACK 609
TARGET_DELEGITIMIZE_ADDRESS 546
TARGET_DIFFERENT_ADDR_DISPLACEMENT_P 503
TARGET_DLLIMPORT_DECL_ATTRIBUTES 614
TARGET_DWARF_CALLING_CONVENTION 608
TARGET_DWARF_FRAME_REG_MODE 602
TARGET_DWARF_HANDLE_FRAME_UNSPEC 506
TARGET_DWARF_POLY_INDETERMINATE_VALUE ... 507
TARGET_DWARF_REGISTER_SPAN 602
TARGET_EDOM 542
TARGET_EMPTY_RECORD_P 528
TARGET_EMUTLS_DEBUG_FORM_TLS_ADDRESS 617
TARGET_EMUTLS_GET_ADDRESS 616
TARGET_EMUTLS_REGISTER_COMMON 616
TARGET_EMUTLS_TMPL_PREFIX 616
TARGET_EMUTLS_TMPL_SECTION 616
TARGET_EMUTLS_VAR_ALIGN_FIXED 617
TARGET_EMUTLS_VAR_FIELDS 616
TARGET_EMUTLS_VAR_INIT 617
TARGET_EMUTLS_VAR_PREFIX 616
TARGET_EMUTLS_VAR_SECTION 616
TARGET_ENCODE_SECTION_INFO 574
TARGET_ENCODE_SECTION_INFO and address
    validation 544
TARGET_ENCODE_SECTION_INFO usage 597
TARGET_END_CALL_ARGS 538
TARGET_ENUM_VA_LIST_P 523
TARGET_ESTIMATED_POLY_VALUE 562
TARGET_EXCEPT_UNWIND_INFO 601
TARGET_EXECUTABLE_SUFFIX 635
TARGET_EXPAND_BUILTIN 631
TARGET_EXPAND_BUILTIN_SAVEREGS 536
TARGET_EXPAND_DIVMOD_LIBFUNC 570

TARGET_EXPAND_TO_RTL_HOOK 481
TARGET_EXPR 169
TARGET_EXTRA_INCLUDES 637
TARGET_EXTRA_LIVE_ON_ENTRY 533
TARGET_EXTRA_PRE_INCLUDES 637
TARGET_FIXED_CONDITION_CODE_REGS 555
TARGET_FIXED_POINT_SUPPORTED_P 481
TARGET_FLAGS_REGNUM 555
TARGET_FLOAT_EXCEPTIONS_ROUNDING_SUPPORTED_
    P 471
TARGET_FLOATN_BUILTIN_P 524
TARGET_FLOATN_MODE 524
TARGET_FN_ABI_VA_LIST 523
TARGET_FOLD_BUILTIN 633
TARGET_FORMAT_TYPES 638
TARGET_FRAME_POINTER_REQUIRED 514
TARGET_FUNCTION_ARG 518
TARGET_FUNCTION_ARG_ADVANCE 521
TARGET_FUNCTION_ARG_BOUNDARY 522
TARGET_FUNCTION_ARG_OFFSET 521
TARGET_FUNCTION_ARG_PADDING 521
TARGET_FUNCTION_ARG_ROUND_BOUNDARY 522
TARGET_FUNCTION_ATTRIBUTE_INLINABLE_P ... 614
TARGET_FUNCTION_INCOMING_ARG 519
TARGET_FUNCTION_OK_FOR_SIBCALL 533
TARGET_FUNCTION_VALUE 525
TARGET_FUNCTION_VALUE_REGNO_P 527
TARGET_GEN_CCMP_FIRST 636
TARGET_GEN_CCMP_NEXT 637
TARGET_GENERATE_VERSION_DISPATCHER_BODY
    634
TARGET_GET_DRAP_RTX 639
TARGET_GET_FUNCTION_VERSIONS_DISPATCHER
    634
TARGET_GET_PCH_VALIDITY 617
TARGET_GET_RAW_ARG_MODE 528
TARGET_GET_RAW_RESULT_MODE 528
TARGET_GIMPLE_FOLD_BUILTIN 633
TARGET_GIMPLIFY_VA_ARG_EXPR 523
TARGET_GOACC_DIM_LIMIT 550
TARGET_GOACC_FORK_JOIN 551
TARGET_GOACC_REDUCTION 551
TARGET_GOACC_VALIDATE_DIMS 550
TARGET_HANDLE_C_OPTION 469
TARGET_HANDLE_OPTION 469
TARGET_HARD_REGNO_CALL_PART_CLOBBERED ... 488
TARGET_HARD_REGNO_MODE_OK 490
TARGET_HARD_REGNO_NREGS 490
TARGET_HARD_REGNO_SCRATCH_OK 492
TARGET_HAS_IFUNC_P 640
TARGET_HAS_NO_HW_DIVIDE 542
TARGET_HAVE_CONDITIONAL_EXECUTION 636
TARGET_HAVE_CTORS_DTORS 594
TARGET_HAVE_NAMED_SECTIONS 578
TARGET_HAVE_SRODATA_SECTION 575
TARGET_HAVE_SWITCHABLE_BSS_SECTIONS 578
TARGET_HAVE_TLS 575
TARGET_IN_SMALL_DATA_P 575

TARGET_INIT_BUILTINS	631
TARGET_INIT_DWARF_REG_SIZES_EXTRA	602
TARGET_INIT_LIBFUNCS	541
TARGET_INIT_PIC_REG	519
TARGET_INSERT_ATTRIBUTES	614
TARGET_INSN_COST	562
TARGET_INSTANTIATE_DECLS	481
TARGET_INVALID_ARG_FOR_UNPROTOTYPED_FN	638
TARGET_INVALID_BINARY_OP	638
TARGET_INVALID_CONVERSION	638
TARGET_INVALID_UNARY_OP	638
TARGET_INVALID_WITHIN_DOLOOP	634
TARGET_IRA_CHANGE_PSEUDO_ALLOCNO_CLASS	502
TARGET_KEEP_LEAF_WHEN_PROFILED	533
TARGET_LEGITIMATE_ADDRESS_P	543
TARGET_LEGITIMATE_COMBINED_INSN	634
TARGET_LEGITIMATE_CONSTANT_P	546
TARGET_LEGITIMIZE_ADDRESS	544
TARGET_LEGITIMIZE_ADDRESS_DISPLACEMENT	503
TARGET_LIB_INT_CMP_BIASED	541
TARGET_LIBC_HAS_FUNCTION	542
TARGET_LIBCALL_VALUE	526
TARGET_LIBFUNC_GNU_PREFIX	541
TARGET_LIBGCC_CMP_RETURN_MODE	480
TARGET_LIBGCC_FLOATING_MODE_SUPPORTED_P	524
TARGET_LIBGCC_SDATA_SECTION	572
TARGET_LIBGCC_SHIFT_COUNT_MODE	480
TARGET_LOAD_BOUNDS_FOR_ARG	538
TARGET_LOAD_RETURNED_BOUNDS	538
TARGET_LOOP_UNROLL_ADJUST	637
TARGET_LRA_P	502
TARGET_MACHINE_DEPENDENT_REORG	631
TARGET_MANGLE_ASSEMBLER_NAME	589
TARGET_MANGLE_DECL_ASSEMBLER_NAME	574
TARGET_MANGLE_TYPE	481
TARGET_MAX_ANCHOR_OFFSET	551
TARGET_MAX_NOCE_IFCVT_SEQ_COST	562
TARGET_MD_ASM_ADJUST	629
TARGET_MEM_CONSTRAINT	544
TARGET_MEM_REF	167
TARGET_MEMBER_TYPE_FORCES_BLK	479
TARGET_MEMMODEL_CHECK	640
TARGET_MEMORY_MOVE_COST	557
TARGET_MERGE_DECL_ATTRIBUTES	614
TARGET_MERGE_TYPE_ATTRIBUTES	613
TARGET_MIN_ANCHOR_OFFSET	551
TARGET_MIN_ARITHMETIC_PRECISION	622
TARGET_MIN_DIVISIONS_FOR_RECIP_MUL	623
TARGET_MODE_AFTER	612
TARGET_MODE_DEPENDENT_ADDRESS_P	545
TARGET_MODE_EMIT	612
TARGET_MODE_ENTRY	613
TARGET_MODE_EXIT	613
TARGET_MODE_NEEDED	612
TARGET_MODE_PRIORITY	613
TARGET_MODE_REP_EXTENDED	624
TARGET_MODES_TIEABLE_P	491
TARGET_MS_BITFIELD_LAYOUT_P	480
TARGET_MUST_PASS_IN_STACK	519
TARGET_MUST_PASS_IN_STACK, and TARGET_FUNCTION_ARG	518
TARGET_N_FORMAT_TYPES	638
TARGET_NARROW_VOLATILE_BITFIELD	479
TARGET_NO_REGISTER_ALLOCATION	610
TARGET_NO_SPECULATION_IN_DELAY_SLOTS_P	562
TARGET_NOCE_CONVERSION_PROFITABLE_P	562
TARGET_OBJC_CONSTRUCT_STRING_OBJECT	470
TARGET_OBJC_DECLARE_CLASS_DEFINITION	470
TARGET_OBJC_DECLARE_UNRESOLVED_CLASS_REFERENCE	470
TARGET_OBJECT_SUFFIX	635
TARGET_OBJFMT_CPP_BUILTINS	469
TARGET_OFFLOAD_OPTIONS	641
TARGET_OMIT_STRUCT_RETURN_REG	527
TARGET_OPTAB_SUPPORTED_P	560
TARGET_OPTF	637
TARGET_OPTION_DEFAULT_PARAMS	471
TARGET_OPTION_FUNCTION_VERSIONS	615
TARGET_OPTION_INIT_STRUCT	471
TARGET_OPTION_OPTIMIZATION_TABLE	471
TARGET_OPTION_OVERRIDE	615
TARGET_OPTION_POST_STREAM_IN	615
TARGET_OPTION_PRAGMA_PARSE	615
TARGET_OPTION_PRINT	615
TARGET_OPTION_RESTORE	615
TARGET_OPTION_SAVE	615
TARGET_OPTION_VALID_ATTRIBUTE_P	614
TARGET_OS_CPP_BUILTINS	469
TARGET_OVERRIDE_OPTIONS_AFTER_CHANGE	470
TARGET_OVERRIDES_FORMAT_ATTRIBUTES	638
TARGET_OVERRIDES_FORMAT_ATTRIBUTES_COUNT	638
TARGET_OVERRIDES_FORMAT_INIT	638
TARGET_PASS_BY_REFERENCE	520
TARGET_PCH_VALID_P	617
TARGET_POSIX_IO	630
TARGET_PREFERRED_OUTPUT_RELOAD_CLASS	498
TARGET_PREFERRED_RELOAD_CLASS	497
TARGET_PREFERRED_RENAME_CLASS	496
TARGET_PREPARE_PCH_SAVE	618
TARGET_PRETEND_OUTGOING_VARARGS_NAMED	538
TARGET_PROFILE_BEFORE_PROLOGUE	575
TARGET_PROMOTE_FUNCTION_MODE	474
TARGET_PROMOTE_PROTOTYPES	516
TARGET_PROMOTED_TYPE	639
TARGET_PTRMEMFUNC_VBIT_LOCATION	486
TARGET_RECORD_OFFLOAD_SYMBOL	640
TARGET_REF_MAY_ALIAS_ERRNO	523
TARGET_REGISTER_MOVE_COST	556
TARGET_REGISTER_PRIORITY	502
TARGET_REGISTER_USAGE_LEVELING_P	503
TARGET_RELAYOUT_FUNCTION	616
TARGET_RESET_LOCATION_VIEW	609
TARGET_RESOLVE_OVERLOADED_BUILTIN	633
TARGET_RETURN_IN_MEMORY	527

TARGET_RETURN_IN_MSB 527
TARGET_RETURN_POPS_ARGS 517
TARGET_RTX_COSTS 560
TARGET_RUN_TARGET_SELFTESTS 641
TARGET_SCALAR_MODE_SUPPORTED_P 523
TARGET_SCHED_ADJUST_COST 563
TARGET_SCHED_ADJUST_PRIORITY.............. 563
TARGET_SCHED_ALLOC_SCHED_CONTEXT 567
TARGET_SCHED_CAN_SPECULATE_INSN 568
TARGET_SCHED_CLEAR_SCHED_CONTEXT 567
TARGET_SCHED_DEPENDENCIES_EVALUATION_HOOK
  564
TARGET_SCHED_DFA_NEW_CYCLE 566
TARGET_SCHED_DFA_POST_ADVANCE_CYCLE 565
TARGET_SCHED_DFA_POST_CYCLE_INSN 565
TARGET_SCHED_DFA_PRE_ADVANCE_CYCLE 565
TARGET_SCHED_DFA_PRE_CYCLE_INSN 565
TARGET_SCHED_DISPATCH 568
TARGET_SCHED_DISPATCH_DO 568
TARGET_SCHED_EXPOSED_PIPELINE............. 568
TARGET_SCHED_FINISH 564
TARGET_SCHED_FINISH_GLOBAL 565
TARGET_SCHED_FIRST_CYCLE_MULTIPASS_
  BACKTRACK 566
TARGET_SCHED_FIRST_CYCLE_MULTIPASS_BEGIN
  566
TARGET_SCHED_FIRST_CYCLE_MULTIPASS_DFA_
  LOOKAHEAD 565
TARGET_SCHED_FIRST_CYCLE_MULTIPASS_DFA_
  LOOKAHEAD_GUARD 566
TARGET_SCHED_FIRST_CYCLE_MULTIPASS_END .. 566
TARGET_SCHED_FIRST_CYCLE_MULTIPASS_FINI
  566
TARGET_SCHED_FIRST_CYCLE_MULTIPASS_INIT
  566
TARGET_SCHED_FIRST_CYCLE_MULTIPASS_ISSUE
  566
TARGET_SCHED_FREE_SCHED_CONTEXT 567
TARGET_SCHED_FUSION_PRIORITY 569
TARGET_SCHED_GEN_SPEC_CHECK 568
TARGET_SCHED_H_I_D_EXTENDED 567
TARGET_SCHED_INIT 564
TARGET_SCHED_INIT_DFA_POST_CYCLE_INSN ... 565
TARGET_SCHED_INIT_DFA_PRE_CYCLE_INSN 565
TARGET_SCHED_INIT_GLOBAL 564
TARGET_SCHED_INIT_SCHED_CONTEXT 567
TARGET_SCHED_IS_COSTLY_DEPENDENCE 567
TARGET_SCHED_ISSUE_RATE 562
TARGET_SCHED_MACRO_FUSION_P 564
TARGET_SCHED_MACRO_FUSION_PAIR_P 564
TARGET_SCHED_NEEDS_BLOCK_P 568
TARGET_SCHED_REASSOCIATION_WIDTH 569
TARGET_SCHED_REORDER 563
TARGET_SCHED_REORDER2 564
TARGET_SCHED_SET_SCHED_CONTEXT 567
TARGET_SCHED_SET_SCHED_FLAGS 568
TARGET_SCHED_SMS_RES_MII 568
TARGET_SCHED_SPECULATE_INSN 567

TARGET_SCHED_VARIABLE_ISSUE 563
TARGET_SECONDARY_MEMORY_NEEDED 500
TARGET_SECONDARY_MEMORY_NEEDED_MODE 501
TARGET_SECONDARY_RELOAD 498
TARGET_SECTION_TYPE_FLAGS 578
TARGET_SELECT_EARLY_REMAT_MODES 501
TARGET_SET_CURRENT_FUNCTION 635
TARGET_SET_DEFAULT_TYPE_ATTRIBUTES 613
TARGET_SET_UP_BY_PROLOGUE 533
TARGET_SETUP_INCOMING_VARARG_BOUNDS 538
TARGET_SETUP_INCOMING_VARARGS 537
TARGET_SHIFT_TRUNCATION_MASK 624
TARGET_SHRINK_WRAP_COMPONENTS_FOR_BB 534
TARGET_SHRINK_WRAP_DISQUALIFY_COMPONENTS
  534
TARGET_SHRINK_WRAP_EMIT_EPILOGUE_COMPONENTS
  534
TARGET_SHRINK_WRAP_EMIT_PROLOGUE_COMPONENTS
  534
TARGET_SHRINK_WRAP_GET_SEPARATE_COMPONENTS
  534
TARGET_SHRINK_WRAP_SET_HANDLED_COMPONENTS
  535
TARGET_SIMD_CLONE_ADJUST 550
TARGET_SIMD_CLONE_COMPUTE_VECSIZE_AND_
  SIMDLEN 550
TARGET_SIMD_CLONE_USABLE 550
TARGET_SIMT_VF 550
TARGET_SLOW_UNALIGNED_ACCESS 558
TARGET_SMALL_REGISTER_CLASSES_FOR_MODE_P
  525
TARGET_SPILL_CLASS 503
TARGET_SPLIT_COMPLEX_ARG 522
TARGET_STACK_CLASH_PROTECTION_FINAL_
  DYNAMIC_PROBE 511
TARGET_STACK_PROTECT_FAIL 535
TARGET_STACK_PROTECT_GUARD 535
TARGET_STACK_PROTECT_RUNTIME_ENABLED_P .. 535
TARGET_STARTING_FRAME_OFFSET 504
TARGET_STARTING_FRAME_OFFSET and virtual
  registers 273
TARGET_STATIC_CHAIN 513
TARGET_STATIC_RTX_ALIGNMENT 476
TARGET_STORE_BOUNDS_FOR_ARG 538
TARGET_STORE_RETURNED_BOUNDS 538
TARGET_STRICT_ARGUMENT_NAMING............. 537
TARGET_STRING_OBJECT_REF_TYPE_P 470
TARGET_STRIP_NAME_ENCODING 574
TARGET_STRUCT_VALUE_RTX 528
TARGET_SUPPORTS_SPLIT_STACK 535
TARGET_SUPPORTS_WEAK 588
TARGET_SUPPORTS_WIDE_INT 641
TARGET_TERMINATE_DW2_EH_FRAME_INFO 602
TARGET_TRAMPOLINE_ADJUST_ADDRESS 540
TARGET_TRAMPOLINE_INIT 539
TARGET_TRULY_NOOP_TRUNCATION 624
TARGET_UNSPEC_MAY_TRAP_P 635
TARGET_UNWIND_TABLES_DEFAULT 601

Concept Index

TARGET_UNWIND_WORD_MODE 480
TARGET_UPDATE_STACK_BOUNDARY 639
TARGET_USE_ANCHORS_FOR_SYMBOL_P 552
TARGET_USE_BLOCKS_FOR_CONSTANT_P 546
TARGET_USE_BLOCKS_FOR_DECL_P 546
TARGET_USE_BY_PIECES_INFRASTRUCTURE_P ... 558
TARGET_USE_PSEUDO_PIC_REG 519
TARGET_USES_WEAK_UNWIND_INFO 510
TARGET_VALID_DLLIMPORT_ATTRIBUTE_P 614
TARGET_VALID_POINTER_MODE 523
TARGET_VECTOR_ALIGNMENT 477
TARGET_VECTOR_MODE_SUPPORTED_P 523
TARGET_VECTORIZE_ADD_STMT_COST 549
TARGET_VECTORIZE_AUTOVECTORIZE_VECTOR_SIZES
   549
TARGET_VECTORIZE_BUILTIN_CONVERSION 548
TARGET_VECTORIZE_BUILTIN_GATHER 550
TARGET_VECTORIZE_BUILTIN_MASK_FOR_LOAD .. 547
TARGET_VECTORIZE_BUILTIN_MD_VECTORIZED_
   FUNCTION 548
TARGET_VECTORIZE_BUILTIN_SCATTER 550
TARGET_VECTORIZE_BUILTIN_VECTORIZATION_COST
   547
TARGET_VECTORIZE_BUILTIN_VECTORIZED_
   FUNCTION 548
TARGET_VECTORIZE_DESTROY_COST_DATA 550
TARGET_VECTORIZE_EMPTY_MASK_IS_EXPENSIVE
   549
TARGET_VECTORIZE_FINISH_COST 549
TARGET_VECTORIZE_GET_MASK_MODE 549
TARGET_VECTORIZE_INIT_COST 549
TARGET_VECTORIZE_PREFERRED_SIMD_MODE 548
TARGET_VECTORIZE_PREFERRED_VECTOR_ALIGNMENT
   547
TARGET_VECTORIZE_SPLIT_REDUCTION 548
TARGET_VECTORIZE_SUPPORT_VECTOR_
   MISALIGNMENT 548
TARGET_VECTORIZE_VEC_PERM_CONST 547
TARGET_VECTORIZE_VECTOR_ALIGNMENT_REACHABLE
   547
TARGET_VTABLE_DATA_ENTRY_DISTANCE 487
TARGET_VTABLE_ENTRY_ALIGN 486
TARGET_VTABLE_USES_DESCRIPTORS 486
TARGET_WANT_DEBUG_PUB_SECTIONS 609
TARGET_WARN_FUNC_RETURN 534
TARGET_WARN_PARAMETER_PASSING_ABI 529
TARGET_WEAK_NOT_IN_ARCHIVE_TOC 588
targetm 461
targets, makefile 66
TCmode 264
TDmode 262
TEMPLATE_DECL 160
Temporaries 206
termination routines 591
testing constraints 381
TEXT_SECTION_ASM_OP 570
TFmode 262
The Language 682

THEN_CLAUSE 195
THREAD_MODEL_SPEC 464
THROW_EXPR 169
THUNK_DECL 160
THUNK_DELTA 160
TImode 262
TImode, in insn 299
TLS_COMMON_ASM_OP 571
TLS_SECTION_ASM_FLAG 571
'tm.h' macros 461
TQFmode 262
TQmode 263
TRAMPOLINE_ALIGNMENT 539
TRAMPOLINE_SECTION 539
TRAMPOLINE_SIZE 539
trampolines for nested functions 539
TRANSFER_FROM_TRAMPOLINE 541
trap instruction pattern 412
tree 153, 154
Tree SSA 237
tree_fits_shwi_p 165
tree_fits_uhwi_p 165
tree_int_cst_equal 165
tree_int_cst_lt 165
tree_size 154
tree_to_shwi 165
tree_to_uhwi 165
TREE_CHAIN 154
TREE_CODE 153
TREE_INT_CST_ELT 165
TREE_INT_CST_LOW 165
TREE_INT_CST_NUNITS 165
TREE_LIST 155
TREE_OPERAND 165
TREE_PUBLIC 184, 186
TREE_PURPOSE 155
TREE_READONLY 186
TREE_STATIC 186
TREE_STRING_LENGTH 165
TREE_STRING_POINTER 165
TREE_THIS_VOLATILE 186
TREE_TYPE 154, 155, 160, 165, 185, 187
TREE_VALUE 155
TREE_VEC 155
TREE_VEC_ELT 155
TREE_VEC_LENGTH 155
TRUNC_DIV_EXPR 169
TRUNC_MOD_EXPR 169
truncate 285
trunc$mn2$ instruction pattern 402
TRUTH_AND_EXPR 169
TRUTH_ANDIF_EXPR 169
TRUTH_NOT_EXPR 169
TRUTH_OR_EXPR 169
TRUTH_ORIF_EXPR 169
TRUTH_XOR_EXPR 169
TRY_BLOCK 195
TRY_HANDLERS 195

TRY_STMTS 195
Tuple specific accessors 213
tuples 200
type 155
type declaration 160
TYPE_ALIGN 155, 156, 187, 188
TYPE_ARG_TYPES 155, 187
TYPE_ASM_OP 585
TYPE_ATTRIBUTES 165
TYPE_BINFO 191
TYPE_BUILT_IN 188
TYPE_CANONICAL 155, 156
TYPE_CONTEXT 155, 187
TYPE_DECL 160
TYPE_FIELDS 155, 187, 191
TYPE_HAS_ARRAY_NEW_OPERATOR 192
TYPE_HAS_DEFAULT_CONSTRUCTOR 192
TYPE_HAS_MUTABLE_P 192
TYPE_HAS_NEW_OPERATOR 192
TYPE_MAIN_VARIANT 155, 156, 187
TYPE_MAX_VALUE 155
TYPE_METHOD_BASETYPE 155, 187
TYPE_MIN_VALUE 155
TYPE_NAME 155, 156, 187, 188
TYPE_NOTHROW_P 195
TYPE_OFFSET_BASETYPE 155, 187
TYPE_OPERAND_FMT 585
TYPE_OVERLOADS_ARRAY_REF 192
TYPE_OVERLOADS_ARROW 192
TYPE_OVERLOADS_CALL_EXPR 192
TYPE_POLYMORPHIC_P 192
TYPE_PRECISION 155, 187
TYPE_PTR_P 189
TYPE_PTRDATAMEM_P 187, 189
TYPE_PTRFN_P 189
TYPE_PTROB_P 189
TYPE_PTROBV_P 187
TYPE_QUAL_CONST 155, 187
TYPE_QUAL_RESTRICT 155, 187
TYPE_QUAL_VOLATILE 155, 187
TYPE_RAISES_EXCEPTIONS 195
TYPE_SIZE 155, 156, 187, 188
TYPE_STRUCTURAL_EQUALITY_P 155, 157
TYPE_UNQUALIFIED 155, 187
TYPE_VFIELD 191
TYPENAME_TYPE 187
TYPENAME_TYPE_FULLNAME 155, 187
TYPEOF_TYPE 187

U

uadd*vm*4 instruction pattern 389
UDAmode 263
udiv 280
udiv*m*3 instruction pattern 388
udivmod*m*4 instruction pattern 394
udot_prod*m* instruction pattern 391
UDQmode 263

UHAmode 263
UHQmode 263
UINT_FAST16_TYPE 485
UINT_FAST32_TYPE 485
UINT_FAST64_TYPE 485
UINT_FAST8_TYPE 485
UINT_LEAST16_TYPE 485
UINT_LEAST32_TYPE 485
UINT_LEAST64_TYPE 485
UINT_LEAST8_TYPE 485
UINT16_TYPE 485
UINT32_TYPE 485
UINT64_TYPE 485
UINT8_TYPE 485
UINTMAX_TYPE 485
UINTPTR_TYPE 485
umadd*mn*4 instruction pattern 393
umax 280
umax*m*3 instruction pattern 388
umin 280
umin*m*3 instruction pattern 388
umod 280
umod*m*3 instruction pattern 388
umsub*mn*4 instruction pattern 393
umulhisi3 instruction pattern 392
umul*m*3_highpart instruction pattern 393
umulqihi3 instruction pattern 392
umulsidi3 instruction pattern 392
umulv*m*4 instruction pattern 389
unchanging 260
unchanging, in call_insn 257
unchanging, in jump_insn, call_insn and insn
   256
unchanging, in mem 257
unchanging, in subreg 258, 259
unchanging, in symbol_ref 256
UNEQ_EXPR 169
UNGE_EXPR 169
UNGT_EXPR 169
UNION_TYPE 155, 191
unions, returning 7
UNITS_PER_WORD 473
UNKNOWN_TYPE 155, 187
UNLE_EXPR 169
UNLIKELY_EXECUTED_TEXT_SECTION_NAME 571
UNLT_EXPR 169
UNORDERED_EXPR 169
unshare_all_rtl 305
unsigned division 280
unsigned division with unsigned saturation .. 280
unsigned greater than 283
unsigned less than 283
unsigned minimum and maximum 280
unsigned_fix 286
unsigned_float 286
unsigned_fract_convert 286
unsigned_sat_fract 286
unspec 291, 455

Concept Index

unspec_volatile 291, 455
untyped_call instruction pattern 406
untyped_return instruction pattern 407
update_ssa 243
update_stmt 212, 237
update_stmt_if_modified 212
UPDATE_PATH_HOST_CANONICALIZE (path) 644
UQQmode 263
us_ashift 281
us_minus 279
us_mult 280
us_neg 279
us_plus 278
us_truncate 285
usadd*m*3 instruction pattern 388
usad*m* instruction pattern 391
USAmode 263
usashl*m*3 instruction pattern 394
usdiv*m*3 instruction pattern 388
use 289
USE_C_ALLOCA 645
USE_LD_AS_NEEDED 464
USE_LOAD_POST_DECREMENT 560
USE_LOAD_POST_INCREMENT 559
USE_LOAD_PRE_DECREMENT 560
USE_LOAD_PRE_INCREMENT 560
USE_SELECT_SECTION_FOR_FUNCTIONS 573
USE_STORE_POST_DECREMENT 560
USE_STORE_POST_INCREMENT 560
USE_STORE_PRE_DECREMENT 560
USE_STORE_PRE_INCREMENT 560
used 260
used, in symbol_ref 259
user 659
user gc 660
USER_LABEL_PREFIX 598
USING_STMT 195
usmadd*mn*4 instruction pattern 393
usmsub*mn*4 instruction pattern 393
usmulhisi3 instruction pattern 392
usmul*m*3 instruction pattern 388
usmulqihi3 instruction pattern 392
usmulsidi3 instruction pattern 392
usneg*m*2 instruction pattern 394
USQmode 263
ussub*m*3 instruction pattern 388
usubv*m*4 instruction pattern 389
UTAmode 263
UTQmode 263

V

'V' in constraint 341
VA_ARG_EXPR 169
values, returned by functions 525
var_location 294
VAR_DECL 160
varargs implementation 535

variable 160
Variable Location Debug Information in RTL
.... 294
vashl*m*3 instruction pattern 394
vashr*m*3 instruction pattern 394
vcond_mask_*mn* instruction pattern 388
vcondeq*mn* instruction pattern 388
vcond*mn* instruction pattern 387
vcondu*mn* instruction pattern 388
vec_cmpeq*mn* instruction pattern 387
vec_cmp*mn* instruction pattern 387
vec_cmpu*mn* instruction pattern 387
vec_concat 284
vec_duplicate 285
vec_duplicate*m* instruction pattern 387
vec_extract*mn* instruction pattern 386
vec_init*mn* instruction pattern 386
vec_load_lanes*mn* instruction pattern 384
vec_mask_load_lanes*mn* instruction pattern .. 385
vec_mask_store_lanes*mn* instruction pattern
.... 385
vec_merge 284
vec_pack_sfix_trunc_*m* instruction pattern .. 391
vec_pack_ssat_*m* instruction pattern 391
vec_pack_trunc_*m* instruction pattern 391
vec_pack_ufix_trunc_*m* instruction pattern .. 391
vec_pack_usat_*m* instruction pattern 391
vec_perm*m* instruction pattern 388, 547
vec_select 284
vec_series 285
vec_series*m* instruction pattern 387
vec_set*m* instruction pattern 386
vec_shl_insert_*m* instruction pattern 391
vec_shr_*m* instruction pattern 391
vec_store_lanes*mn* instruction pattern 385
vec_unpacks_float_hi_*m* instruction pattern
.... 392
vec_unpacks_float_lo_*m* instruction pattern
.... 392
vec_unpacks_hi_*m* instruction pattern 391
vec_unpacks_lo_*m* instruction pattern 391
vec_unpacku_float_hi_*m* instruction pattern
.... 392
vec_unpacku_float_lo_*m* instruction pattern
.... 392
vec_unpacku_hi_*m* instruction pattern 392
vec_unpacku_lo_*m* instruction pattern 392
vec_widen_smult_even_*m* instruction pattern
.... 392
vec_widen_smult_hi_*m* instruction pattern 392
vec_widen_smult_lo_*m* instruction pattern 392
vec_widen_smult_odd_*m* instruction pattern .. 392
vec_widen_sshiftl_hi_*m* instruction pattern
.... 392
vec_widen_sshiftl_lo_*m* instruction pattern
.... 392
vec_widen_umult_even_*m* instruction pattern
.... 392

vec_widen_umult_hi_*m* instruction pattern.... 392
vec_widen_umult_lo_*m* instruction pattern.... 392
vec_widen_umult_odd_*m* instruction pattern .. 392
vec_widen_ushiftl_hi_*m* instruction pattern
.... 392
vec_widen_ushiftl_lo_*m* instruction pattern
.... 392
VEC_COND_EXPR.............................. 176
VEC_DUPLICATE_EXPR.......................... 176
VEC_LSHIFT_EXPR............................. 176
VEC_PACK_FIX_TRUNC_EXPR..................... 176
VEC_PACK_SAT_EXPR........................... 176
VEC_PACK_TRUNC_EXPR......................... 176
VEC_RSHIFT_EXPR............................. 176
VEC_SERIES_EXPR............................. 176
VEC_UNPACK_FLOAT_HI_EXPR.................... 176
VEC_UNPACK_FLOAT_LO_EXPR.................... 176
VEC_UNPACK_HI_EXPR.......................... 176
VEC_UNPACK_LO_EXPR.......................... 176
VEC_WIDEN_MULT_HI_EXPR...................... 176
VEC_WIDEN_MULT_LO_EXPR...................... 176
vector...................................... 155
vector operations........................... 284
VECTOR_CST.................................. 165
VECTOR_STORE_FLAG_VALUE..................... 626
verify_flow_info............................ 315
virtual operands............................ 237
VIRTUAL_INCOMING_ARGS_REGNUM................ 273
VIRTUAL_OUTGOING_ARGS_REGNUM................ 273
VIRTUAL_STACK_DYNAMIC_REGNUM................ 273
VIRTUAL_STACK_VARS_REGNUM................... 273
VLIW.................................. 444, 447
vlshr*m*3 instruction pattern 394
VMS... 644
VMS_DEBUGGING_INFO.......................... 610
void................................... 632, 633
VOID_TYPE................................... 155
VOIDmode.................................... 263
volatil..................................... 261
volatil, in insn, call_insn, jump_insn,
    code_label, jump_table_data, barrier, and
    note.................................... 256
volatil, in label_ref and reg_label......... 256
volatil, in mem, asm_operands, and asm_input
.... 256
volatil, in reg............................. 257
volatil, in subreg..................... 258, 259
volatil, in symbol_ref...................... 259
volatile memory references.................. 261
volatile, in prefetch....................... 257
voting between constraint alternatives 346
vrotl*m*3 instruction pattern................... 394
vrotr*m*3 instruction pattern................... 394

W

walk_dominator_tree......................... 245
walk_gimple_op.............................. 235
walk_gimple_seq............................. 235
walk_gimple_stmt............................ 235
WCHAR_TYPE.................................. 484
WCHAR_TYPE_SIZE............................. 484
which_alternative........................... 335
while_ult*mn* instruction pattern............... 387
WHILE_BODY.................................. 195
WHILE_COND.................................. 195
WHILE_STMT.................................. 195
whopr....................................... 673
widen_ssum*m*3 instruction pattern.............. 391
widen_usum*m*3 instruction pattern.............. 391
WIDEST_HARDWARE_FP_SIZE..................... 483
window_save instruction pattern............. 412
WINT_TYPE................................... 484
word_mode................................... 268
WORD_REGISTER_OPERATIONS.................... 622
WORDS_BIG_ENDIAN............................ 473
WORDS_BIG_ENDIAN, effect on subreg.......... 275
wpa... 673

X

'x-*host*'................................... 650
'X' in constraint........................... 342
XCmode...................................... 264
XCOFF_DEBUGGING_INFO........................ 605
XEXP.. 252
XFmode...................................... 262
XImode...................................... 262
XINT.. 252
'xm-*machine*.h'....................... 644, 645
xor... 281
xor, canonicalization of.................... 423
xor*m*3 instruction pattern..................... 388
XSTR.. 252
XVEC.. 253
XVECEXP..................................... 253
XVECLEN..................................... 253
XWINT....................................... 252

Z

zero_extend................................. 285
zero_extend*mn*2 instruction pattern............ 402
zero_extract................................ 284
zero_extract, canonicalization of........... 423

Lightning Source UK Ltd.
Milton Keynes UK
UKHW030756071020
371169UK00010B/537